ADVANCED SOCIAL PSYCHOLOGY

ADVANCED SOCIAL PSYCHOLOGY

THE STATE OF THE SCIENCE

Second Edition

Edited by

Eli J. Finkel

and

Roy F. Baumeister

OXFORD
UNIVERSITY PRESS

OXFORD
UNIVERSITY PRESS

Oxford University Press is a department of the University of Oxford. It furthers
the University's objective of excellence in research, scholarship, and education
by publishing worldwide. Oxford is a registered trade mark of Oxford University
Press in the UK and certain other countries.

Published in the United States of America by Oxford University Press
198 Madison Avenue, New York, NY 10016, United States of America.

CIP data is on file at the Library of Congress
ISBN 978–0–19–063559–6

9 8 7 6 5 4 3

Printed by Sheridan Books, Inc., United States of America

To our mentors, Caryl Rusbult and Ned Jones.

CONTENTS

PREFACE

Every year, hundreds of students, perhaps even a thousand or more, enter graduate school at one of the hundreds of institutions offering advanced degrees in social psychology. Although most of these students take a general survey course covering the discipline as a whole, the field long lacked any sort of core social psychology training across graduate programs. Instructors sought to cover the major topics by assigning a blend of empirical and review articles, but the authors of such articles generally wrote them for a narrower and more advanced audience, not for a survey course. Readings tailored to first-year graduate students seeking general overviews were largely nonexistent. As a result, new social psychology doctoral students experienced wildly different introductions to the discipline depending upon which instructor happened to teach their course. Many students completed their degrees while still possessing near-complete ignorance of some of the major topics in the field.

In 2010, we published the first edition of *Advanced Social Psychology* to fill this gap. Finally, the field had a coherent set of broad, integrative, cutting-edge topical overviews that were relatively brief and accessible to new scholars. The chapter authors were leading experts on their respective topics, whom we selected because their writing skills match their scholarly eminence. We asked them to provide an engaging introduction to their topic suitable for students taking a graduate-level (or an advanced undergraduate-level) survey course in social psychology. These authors didn't disappoint. In addition to providing terrific overviews of the most important ideas, research methods, and findings encompassed by their topic, these chapters offered snapshots of thriving research areas that conveyed the excitement of social-psychological research.

Of course, 2010 was a long time ago, which means that those chapters are a bit outdated. In addition, the 2010s saw a major surge in research on certain topics, including morality and computational psychology, that had not garnered their own chapters in the first edition of this book. This second addition updates the coverage of the discipline, and it offers new chapters on freshly prominent topics in the field.

Speaking of freshly prominent topics, the 2010s also witnessed major upheaval within the field, as concerns about replicability became increasingly pervasive. The field adopted major changes oriented toward bolstering the replicability of its research findings and the transparency of its research process. The introductory chapter of this revised edition provides a brief summary of the major developments, and the third chapter—another new one for this edition—discusses the major methodological developments from the past decade. For the more topical chapters in this edition, we encouraged authors to address replication-related issues in the manner that, in their estimation, most appropriately fits the state of the research literature they are reviewing.

The 21 chapters are self-contained rather than cumulative. Although working through them in order works well, instructors may wish to cover them in a different sequence. Instructors can also omit a few of the chapters without impairing their students' ability to comprehend the assigned ones. Indeed, we deliberately designed the book to have more chapters than there are weeks in the typical graduate seminar so instructors can tailor the course to their own preferences and their particular students' needs. Should the student later wish to have had an introduction to one of the skipped topics, that chapter will be ready and waiting.

Most graduate students will ultimately become experts on a small subset (perhaps just one) of the topics reviewed in the present volume. The textbook is not intended to make anyone an expert. Rather, it is intended to familiarize readers with much of what is happening across the field. Students who have read this book will glean the sort of familiarity required to converse intelligently with visiting speakers and fellow conference attendees, to understand the issues relevant to articles or presentations outside of their primary research area, and to make a good impression when interviewing for faculty positions. The broad, integrative nature of these chapters also makes them useful as reference pieces for students whose research interests take them in new directions, which can happen at any point in graduate school (or even after graduate school).

This is a textbook, not a handbook, so the chapters can't cover everything. The page limits required that the authors omit many fascinating findings. We encourage students to view this book as a valuable resource and introductory overview but, ultimately, as only a first step toward mastering the field.

It is a big step. While underscoring the vigilance required to generate a replicable science, these chapters also convey some of the excitement and the fun of social psychology. We can't imagine any field of study that is more interesting than the study of people. Being a social psychologist is a wonderful vocation, in part because it enables scholars to spend their life asking and occasionally answering some of the most fundamental questions about the human experience.

Eli J. Finkel
Evanston, IL, USA

Roy F. Baumeister
Brisbane, QLD, Australia
June, 2018

ABOUT THE EDITORS

Eli J. Finkel, whom the *Economist* has identified as "one of the leading lights in the realm of relationship psychology," is a professor at Northwestern University, where he holds appointments in the psychology department and the Kellogg School of Management. He earned his BA in 1997 from Northwestern and his PhD in 2001 from the University of North Carolina at Chapel Hill. He has published 140+ academic papers, is a frequent contributor to the Op-Ed page of the *New York Times*, and is the author of the bestselling book *The All-Or-Nothing Marriage: How the Best Marriages Work* (2017). He lives in Evanston, IL, with his wife, children, and stepcat.

Roy F. Baumeister is professor of psychology at the University of Queensland, in Australia, as well as professor emeritus at Florida State. He received his PhD in social psychology from Princeton University in 1978, having worked with the great Edward E. Jones as his mentor. Alongside social psychology, his education emphasized philosophy and sociology. Sometimes regarded as a renegade contrarian, Baumeister is a suburban intellectual with promiscuous intellectual interests, combining a relentless open-mindedness with a deep restless curiosity about the human condition. He has published hundreds of articles and a couple dozen books on a broad range of topics, including self and identity, interpersonal belongingness and rejection, sexuality, evil and violence, emotion, self-regulation, free will, decision-making, consciousness, and the meaning of life. He has received several lifetime achievement awards, including the William James Fellow award, which is the highest honor given by the Association for Psychological Science. As of 2018, his publications have been cited in the scientific journals over 150,000 times. Writing for publication and mentoring graduate students are his favorite parts of the job. In his free time, he plays a bit of jazz guitar, composes music, and occasionally enjoys windsurfing and skiing.

CONTRIBUTORS

Roy F. Baumeister
University of Queensland
Brisbane, Australia
and
Department of Psychology
Florida State University
Tallahassee, Florida, USA

Wendy Berry Mendes
Department of Psychiatry
University of California,
San Francisco
San Francisco, California, USA

Marilynn B. Brewer
Department of Psychology
The Ohio State University
Columbus, Ohio, USA

Pablo Briñol
Department of Social Psychology
Universidad Autonoma
de Madrid
Madrid, Spain

Brad J. Bushman
College of Arts and Sciences
The Ohio State University
Columbus, Ohio, USA

Charles S. Carver
Department of Psychology
University of Miami
Coral Gables, Florida, USA

Robert B. Cialdini
Arizona State University
Phoenix, Arizona, USA

Paul Conway
Department of Psychology
Florida State University
Tallahassee, Florida, USA

John F. Dovidio
Department of Psychology
Yale University
New Haven, Connecticut, USA

Leandre R. Fabrigar
Department of Psychology
Queen's University
Kingston, Ontario, CA

Eli J. Finkel
Department of Psychology and the Kellogg
School of Management
Northwestern University
Evanston, Illinois, USA

Susan T. Fiske
Department of Psychology
Princeton University
Princeton, New Jersey, USA

Mary Frances Luce
The Fuqua School of Business
Duke University
Durham, North Carolina, USA

SHELLY L. GABLE
Department of Psychological and Brain Sciences
University of California, Santa Barbara
Santa Barbara, California, USA

VLADAS GRISKEVICIUS
Carlson School of Management
University of Minnesota
Minneapolis, Minnesota, USA

STEVEN J. HEINE
Department of Psychology
University of British Columbia
Vancouver, British Columbia, CA

JAMES M. JONES
Department of Psychological and Brain Sciences
University of Delaware
Newark, Delaware, USA

DOUGLAS T. KENRICK
Department of Psychology
Arizona State University
Tempe, Arizona, USA

MICHAL KOSINSKI
Stanford Graduate School of Business
Stanford University
Stanford, California, USA

ALISON LEDGERWOOD
Department of Psychology
University of California, Davis
Davis, California, USA

JON K. MANER
Department of Management and Organizations
Kellogg School of Management
Northwestern University
Evanston, Illinois, USA

RICHARD E. PETTY
Department of Psychology
The Ohio State University
Columbus, Ohio, USA

HARRY T. REIS
Department of Clinical and Social Sciences
in Psychology
University of Rochester
Rochester, New York, USA

THEODORE F. ROBLES
Department of Psychology
University of California, Los Angeles
Los Angeles, California, USA

LINDA J. SKITKA
Department of Psychology
University of Illinois at Chicago
Chicago, Illinois, USA

KATHLEEN D. VOHS
Carlson School of Management
University of Minnesota
Minneapolis, Minnesota, USA

DUANE T. WEGENER
Department of Psychology
The Ohio State University
Columbus, Ohio, USA

THALIA WHEATLEY
Department of Psychological and
Brain Sciences
Dartmouth College
Hanover, New Hampshire, USA

ADVANCED SOCIAL PSYCHOLOGY

Chapter 1

Social Psychology: Crisis and Renaissance

Eli J. Finkel and Roy F. Baumeister

The first edition of this book was published in 2010, which, in retrospect, were halcyon days for social psychology. The discipline retained its long-standing strengths—including an emphasis on exciting and important research questions, a seemingly endless fount of innovative research paradigms, and a dedication to unpacking the mechanism driving key effects—while also enjoying a surge of influence within and beyond the ivory tower. Psychology was firmly established as one of a handful of hub sciences (Cacioppo, 2007), and social psychology was, in many respects, the scientific hub of psychology. Meanwhile, the most prestigious and influential media outlets regularly reported social-psychological findings, and new media channels, including TED talks, had helped to turn some of the more charismatic members of our community into major public intellectuals. Despite some significant challenges, including a weak funding climate in the wake of the worldwide recession of 2007–2008, the foundation of social psychology felt strong, the forecast sunny.

Then, suddenly, a crisis hit. More and more social psychologists came to doubt the replicability of social-psychological findings. This crisis resulted not from concerns about the behavior of a few bad actors (although a few high-profile fraud cases broke in 2011 and 2012) but rather from concerns about systemic problems embedded within our normative research practices. These concerns emerged from the intersection of two aspects of our publication process. First, researchers had strong incentives to find statistically significant results in their data. Virtually all professional rewards—landing a faculty position, getting tenure, procuring grant funding, garnering respect from one's peers, and so forth—depended on publishing articles, and journals strongly favored statistically significant results. Second, researchers possessed substantial flexibility in analyzing and reporting on their data. These two factors produced a situation in which researchers' careers benefited from analyzing their data in many ways and then (a) reporting only those data-analytic procedures that yielded statistically significant support for their hypothesis or (b) adapting their hypothesis in light of what the data showed (and thereby violating the logic underlying hypothesis testing).

Such tactics increased the likelihood that researchers would find statistically significant results, but they obviously did not increase the likelihood that the hypothesis in question is actually correct. Although the field nominally accepted a *false-positive* rate of 5% ($\alpha = .05$)—a rate of concluding from a study that an effect exists in the population when it actually does not—the actual rate was substantially higher than that. Precisely how much higher is impossible to discern, but the existence of these excess false-positive findings meant that too many findings in the published literature were nonreplicable.

These problems were not unique to social psychology. Indeed, the seminal article that launched the replication crisis focused on the biomedical sciences (Ioannidis, 2005), and few of the empirical sciences are immune. But social psychology has been ground zero for the most important conversations about how to strengthen scientific practice, and our discipline has taken the lead in developing new norms and tools for doing so. Consequently, at the end of a grueling decade, we are enjoying something of a renaissance.

The 2010s: A Glance Back on a Turbulent Decade

In 2011, the *Journal of Personality and Social Psychology* (*JPSP*), our field's flagship empirical outlet, published an article on *psi*—a type of extrasensory perception (ESP) characterized by "anomalous retroactive influence of some future event on an individual's current responses"—from the eminent social psychologist Daryl Bem (2011, p. 407). The article reported nine studies, eight of which yielded statistically significant support for psi. Bem acknowledged (p. 407) that psi-related phenomena "are currently unexplained in terms of known physical or biological mechanisms" and, indeed, many readers found the idea inherently implausible on its face. In this way, Bem's paper provided a smoking-gun example for people seeking to argue that the standard approach to scientific discovery in social psychology—a process to which the Bem paper apparently hewed closely—was fundamentally flawed. After all, if the standard data-analytic and reporting procedures could reveal consistent evidence of a phenomenon that (in the view of the many skeptics) cannot be real, the headline was less about psi than about those standard procedures.

Shortly thereafter, researchers published major articles seeking to identify how such procedures can produce false-positive results at significantly inflated rates. The journal *Psychological Science* published an article by Joseph Simmons, Leif Nelson, and Uri Simonsohn (2011) called "False-Positive Psychology: Undisclosed Flexibility in Data Collection and Analysis Allows Presenting Anything as Significant." This article introduced the term *researcher degrees of freedom* to refer to data-analytic procedures designed to get a key *p*-value below .05, such as selectively reporting one of two possible dependent variables, repeatedly rerunning hypothesis tests after collecting data on a small number of additional participants ("data snooping"), and statistically controlling for participants' gender. Simmons et al. reported simulations suggesting that such researcher degrees of freedom dramatically increase the false-positive rate. Shortly thereafter, *Perspectives on Psychological Science* published an article by Leslie John, George Loewenstein, and Drazen Prelec (2012) reporting that a large proportion of the 2,000 psychological scientists who responded to their survey had engaged in behaviors that could be used to get *p*-values below .05, which they called *questionable research practices*. In 2015, *Science* published an article from Brian Nosek and 269 collaborators (Open Science Collaboration, 2015) that replicated 100 studies published in major psychology journals, including *JPSP*, revealing that only 35% to 40% of the statistically significant results achieved statistical significance in the replication attempt.

None of these studies is perfect, and all have been critiqued. For example, Eli Finkel (2016) argued that although the Simmons et al. (2011) paper served as a devastating proof of concept, it is unlikely that many researchers had ever *p*-hacked their data like an algorithm would (e.g., with complete indifference to the truth). Klaus Fiedler and Norbert Schwarz (2016) argued that the meaning of many of the John et al. (2012) survey items was ambiguous, raising questions about whether engaging in such research practices is, in fact, "questionable." For example, "failing to report all of a study's dependent measures" could result from the motivation to dupe readers into believing an effect is robust when it is not, but it could also result from an array of benign motivations; perhaps the researchers included a number of dependent variables that were always intended as subsidiary and exploratory, and they never analyzed the results for those variables. Daniel Gilbert, Gary King, Stephen Pettigrew, and Timothy Wilson (2016) reanalyzed data from the 100-replication study (Open Science Collaboration, 2015)— seeking to account for issues like statistical power, possible bias in study selection, and ways in which the replications might have deviated methodologically from the original studies—and concluded that "the data are consistent with [the conclusion] that the reproducibility of psychological science is quite high" (p. 1037). Although debate about such issues is ongoing, there is little doubt that, on balance, the 2010s witnessed a major surge in social psychologists' concerns regarding the replicability of the field's published results, which in turn has produced concomitant changes in our normative research and publication practices.

The 2020s: A Glance Forward to a Stronger Discipline

When the first edition of this book was released, there was minimal infrastructure for promoting transparency regarding the collection, analysis, and reporting of data, and it was virtually impossible to publish direct replications in top journals. In pursuit of a more replicable discipline, (social) psychology made wholesale changes on these fronts over the past decade. For example, in 2013, Brian Nosek and Jeffrey Spies launched the Center for Open Science, a nonprofit tech startup with the mission to "increase the openness, integrity, and reproducibility of scientific research" (Center for Open Science, n.d.). The center provides a suite of Internet-based tools for (a) preregistering hypotheses and data-analytic plans and (b) sharing research materials and data.

Meanwhile, most major empirical journals revised their editorial policies to encourage direct replications, and many new options have emerged for the publication of such studies. For example, *Comprehensive Results in Social Psychology*, which launched in 2016, is

> devoted to publishing social psychological research using the registered report format where a plan for the research is submitted for initial review. . . . If the plan for research is accepted as being methodologically sound and theoretically important, authors are guaranteed publication of the manuscript irrespective of the outcome of data analysis." ("Aim and Scope," 2018)

Advances in Methods and Practices in Psychological Science, which launched in 2018, dedicates a section to "Registered Replication Reports," which serves to bolster "the foundation of psychological science by publishing collections of replications based on a shared and vetted protocol." To publish Registered Replication Reports, which had been housed at *Perspectives on Psychological Science* from 2014 until 2017, "authors submit a detailed description of the method and analysis plan" which is then "sent to the author(s) of the replicated study for review" ("Mission Statement," n.d.). Once the plan has been vetted, a public announcement is made, and many labs—perhaps 20 or 25—run the study following the standard protocol. The primary goals are to discern the robustness of a high-profile effect from the published literature and to estimate its magnitude.

Riding sidecar with the emergence of a robust technological infrastructure for promoting open practices and the surging priority afforded to direct replications is a third major development oriented toward bolstering the replicability and information value of the field's findings: a sharply increased emphasis on statistical power. Social psychologists had long appreciated that low statistical power placed studies at risk for producing *false negatives*—concluding from a study that an effect does not exist in the population when it actually does exist—but few of us sufficiently appreciated that it also placed studies at risk for producing false positives. Low power can produce false positives in part because parameter estimates tend to be bouncy when statistical power is low (Schönbrodt & Perugini, 2013). For example, in a two-cell between-participants design, the p-value testing for a mean difference is likely to change much more when increasing the sample from 15 to 20 participants per condition than when changing from 215 to 220 per condition. If the researchers in the small-sample case are snooping on their data and stopping if the p-value falls below .05—or are, for example, tinkering with the inclusion or exclusion of participants with a mean score greater than 2.5 standard deviations from the mean to get the effect below .05—the actual false-positive rate will be higher than 5%, perhaps much higher.

The extensive discussion surrounding replicability triggered a more wide-ranging dialogue regarding the characteristics of a healthy scientific discipline. Indeed, as the field converges on the conclusion that, under most circumstances, sample sizes should be orders of magnitude larger than what was normative in the past, some scholars have also expressed concerns that certain valuable research methods will become vanishingly rare. The sort of labor-intensive, small-sample studies that put social psychology on the intellectual map in the 1950s and 1960s—consider Solomon Asch's (1956) conformity studies, Stanley Milgram's (1963) obedience studies, and John Darley's and Bibb Latané (1968) bystander intervention studies—would be especially difficult to publish today, even setting aside challenges associated with running such studies in a fully ethical manner. Psychology's claim to be a science once rested on emphasizing direct observation of objective behavior, but these observations have been getting rarer as such labor-intensive methods have been increasingly eclipsed by cheaper and easier methods, typically involving individuals sitting alone at computer terminals (Baumeister, Vohs, & Funder, 2007). This trend is likely to accelerate in the new era of large samples.

Eli Finkel, Paul Eastwick, and Harry Reis (2015, 2017) observed that efforts to optimize the use of the field's finite resources—money, time, research participants, and so forth—require the simultaneous consideration of multiple scientific desiderata, including others that (like replicability) have long received insufficient attention in our discipline. This discussion began by considering the optimal balance between discovery (Do the findings document support for novel hypotheses?) and replicability (Do the findings emerge in other samples using a design that retains the key features of the original design?), but it quickly expanded to include desiderata like internal validity (Do the findings permit inferences about causal relationships?), external validity (Do the findings generalize across populations of persons, settings, and times?), construct validity (Do the findings enable researchers to correctly link theoretical constructs to operationalizations?), consequentiality (Do the findings have implications or consequences for other sciences and the real world?), and cumulativeness (Do the findings cohere in a manner that affords conceptual integration across studies?). For social psychology to flourish, it must achieve at least moderate success on all such desiderata, an undertaking that requires a broad range of different types of studies. But as we narrow the focus to any given study, it becomes impossible (or at least impractical) to optimize all of them at once. Given the state of the relevant research literature, should the study seek to rule out alternative explanations for an established effect (to bolster internal validity)? Should it investigate whether the effect emerges in other contexts (to bolster external validity)? Should it assess whether procedures that are virtually identical to those from an earlier study produce similar results (to bolster replicability)? Should it prioritize one of the other desiderata or perhaps seek to bolster more than one of them?

Scholars are continuing to discuss the best strategies for allocating resources across the various desiderata. Indeed, even the two editors of this volume are not entirely aligned: One of us is more convinced that the benefits of the recent methodological changes significantly outweigh the costs, whereas the other is less sure. Overall, however, there appears to be widespread agreement among social psychologists (a) that bolstering replicability is essential and (b) that we must do so in a way that also attends to the other desiderata. As illustrated in Chapter 3 of this volume—"New Developments in Research Methods" (Ledgerwood, 2019)—social psychologists have much better conceptual, methodological, and statistical tools for meeting these goals today than we did a decade ago.

Overview of This Book

This new research methods chapter points to one of the major ways in which the second edition of *Advanced Social Psychology* differs from the first: The revised edition deals directly with issues surrounding replicability. Indeed, we asked the authors of all other chapters to at least consider incorporating a discussion of replicability "in whatever manner seems appropriate in light of where issues currently stand in the literature."

A second major change from the first edition is the inclusion of two new content chapters, each covering research domains that enjoyed a major surge of interest in the 2010s. First, Linda Skitka and Paul Conway have contributed a chapter on morality (Chapter 13), offering an even-handed overview of the rapidly expanding, and sometimes contentious, social-psychological literature on moral judgment and behavior. Second, Michal Kosinski has contributed a chapter on computational psychology (Chapter 21), offering a tutorial on the latest developments in the world of "big data" and computational analytic methods, along with a compelling discussion of how social psychology and big data can make for compatible bedfellows.

Alongside these various updates, the second edition continues to underscore the strengths of social psychology, especially by illustrating how exciting the research questions are, highlighting the remarkable creativity behind the field's research paradigms, and emphasizing the importance of psychological mechanisms underlying key findings. As a group, the chapter authors are not only eminent scholars but also terrific writers. They serve as deep-thinking, engaging tour guides through their area of primary expertise. Table 1.1 demonstrates this point by providing an illustrative research question from each chapter.

Onward and Upward

As we look back at social psychology circa 2010, the images betray a sepia-toned innocence. This was a simpler discipline, one unaware of its replication problems and unprepared for the turbulence ahead. But it was also a field with many strengths. As social psychologists continue to make the changes required to bolster the replicability of our published findings, we can double down even more forcefully on those longstanding strengths. In this sense, the 2020s hold promise as social psychology's best thus far.

TABLE 1.1   Illustrating the Sorts of Research Questions Addressed in the Chapters

Number	Title	Authors	Illustrative Research Question
1	Social Psychology: Crisis and Renaissance	Eli J. Finkel and Roy F. Baumeister	How did a study of extrasensory perception (ESP) help to launch a revolution in how social psychologists collect, analyze, and report their data?
2	A Brief History of Social Psychology	Harry T. Reis	How did Adolph Hitler alter the intellectual course of social psychology?
3	New Developments in Research Methods	Alison Ledgerwood	Why is preregistration so valuable, and what does a convincing preregistration plan look like?
4	Social Cognition	Susan T. Fiske	Why do we pay so much more attention to high-power people than they pay to us?
5	The Self	Roy F. Baumeister	If humans evolved from great apes, why are human selves so much more elaborate?
6	Attitude Structure and Change	Richard E. Petty, Pablo Briñol, Leandre R. Fabrigar, and Duane T. Wegener	Why are some persuasive appeals so much more convincing than others?
7	Social Influence	Robert B. Cialdini and Vladas Griskevicius	Is Leonardo da Vinci correct that "it is easier to resist at the beginning than at the end"—and, if so, why?
8	Aggression	Brad J. Bushman	How can social psychology contribute to a more peaceful world?
9	Attraction and Rejection	Eli J. Finkel and Roy F. Baumeister	Are heterosexual women attracted to different sorts of men during the fertile (vs. nonfertile) phase of their ovulatory cycle?
10	Close Relationships	Shelly L. Gable	How does our attachment to our parents when we are infants influence the success or failure of our romantic relationships when we are adults?
11	Intergroup Relations	Marilynn B. Brewer	Does the tendency to divide the world into "us" and "them" influence our thoughts, feelings, and behaviors even when the social groupings are entirely arbitrary?
12	Prejudice, Stereotyping, and Discrimination	John F. Dovidio and James M. Jones	What social-psychological interventions have been developed to reduce prejudice, stereotyping, and discrimination, and are they effective?
13	Psychological Perspectives on Morality	Linda J. Skitka and Paul Conway	Can behaving morally "license" us to behave immorally shortly afterward?
14	Emotion	Wendy Berry Mendes	How did Charles Darwin ultimately jump-start social-psychological research on emotion?
15	Social Neuroscience	Thalia Wheatley	What characteristics do our brains possess that allow us to be social in uniquely human ways?
16	Evolutionary Social Psychology	Jon K. Maner and Douglas T. Kenrick	How has the evolutionary imperative of reproduction influenced the psychology underlying our pursuit and maintenance of romantic relationships?
17	Cultural Psychology	Steven J. Heine	How does our cultural context influence the conclusions we draw about why a stranger enacted a certain behavior?
18	Health, Stress, and Coping	Theodore F. Robles	What are the psychological and biological processes through which social relationships make us more versus less prone toward physical illness?
19	Judgment and Decision-Making	Kathleen D. Vohs and Mary Frances Luce	Why is a system as sophisticated as the human mind so prone toward making a systematic set of errors in judgment and decision-making?
20	Personality	Charles S. Carver	Why must any comprehensive theory of social behavior dedicate substantial attention individual differences?
21	Computational Psychology	Michal Kosinski	How can scholars leverage the vast data people leave behind every day—for example, through behavior on smartphones or on social media—to develop novel insights into human nature?

References

Aim and scope. (2018). Taylor and Francis Online: *Comprehensive Results in Social Psychology*. Retrieved from https://www.tandfonline.com/action/journalInformation?show=aimsScope&journalCode=rrsp20&

Asch, S. E. (1956). Studies of independence and conformity: I. A minority of one against a unanimous majority. *Psychological Monographs: General and Applied, 70*, 1–70.

Baumeister, R. F., Vohs, K. D., & Funder, D. C. (2007). Psychology as the science of self-reports and finger movements: Whatever happened to actual behavior? *Perspectives on Psychological Science, 2*, 396–403.

Bem, D. J. (2011). Feeling the future: Experimental evidence for anomalous retroactive influences on cognition and affect. *Journal of Personality and Social Psychology, 100*, 407–425.

Cacioppo, J. T. (2007, September). Psychology is a hub science. *APS Observer, 20*, 5, 42.

Center for Open Science. (n.d.). [Homepage]. Retrieved from https://cos.io/about/mission/

Darley, J. M., & Latané, B. (1968). Bystander intervention in emergencies: Diffusion of responsibility. *Journal of Personality and Social Psychology, 8*, 377–383.

Fiedler, K., & Schwarz, N. (2016). Questionable research practices revisited. *Social Psychological and Personality Science, 7*, 45–52.

Finkel, E. J. (2016). *Taking stock of the evidentiary value movement* [Video File]. Talk presented at the annual meeting of the Society of Personality and Social Psychology. Retrieved from https://youtu.be/IguSyHhYU3A?list=PLtAL5tCifMi5iq9dnkcC9XWocMjq12jgZ

Finkel, E. J., Eastwick, P. W., & Reis, H. T. (2015). Best research practices in psychology: Illustrating epistemological and pragmatic considerations with the case of relationship science. *Journal of Personality and Social Psychology, 108*, 275–297.

Finkel, E. J., Eastwick, P. E., & Reis, H. T. (2017). Replicability and other features of a high-quality science: Toward a balanced and empirical approach. *Journal of Personality and Social Psychology, 113*, 244–253.

Gilbert, D. T., King, G., Pettigrew, S., & Wilson, T. D. (2016). Comment on "Estimating the reproducibility of psychological science." *Science, 351*, 1037–1037.

Ioannidis, J. P. (2005). Why most published research findings are false. *PLoS Medicine, 2*, e124. http://dx.doi.org/10.1371/journal.pmed.0020124

John, L. K., Loewenstein, G., & Prelec, D. (2012). Measuring the prevalence of questionable research practices with incentives for truth telling. *Psychological Science, 23*, 524–532.

Milgram, S. (1963). Behavioral study of obedience. *Journal of Abnormal and Social Psychology, 67*, 371–378.

Mission statement. (n.d.). Association for Psychological Science: *Registered Replication Reports*. Retrieved from https://www.psychologicalscience.org/publications/replication

Open Science Collaboration. (2015). Estimating the reproducibility of psychological science. *Science, 349*, aac4716.

Schönbrodt, F. D., & Perugini, M. (2013). At what sample size do correlations stabilize? *Journal of Research in Personality, 47*, 609–612.

Simmons, J. P., Nelson, L. D., & Simonsohn, U. (2011). False-positive psychology: Undisclosed flexibility in data collection and analysis allows presenting anything as significant. *Psychological Science, 22*, 1359–1366.

Chapter 2

A Brief History of Social Psychology

Harry T. Reis

> She that from whom
>   We all were sea-swallow'd, though some cast again
>   (And by that destiny) to perform an act
>   Whereof what's past is prologue; what to come,
>   In yours and my discharge.

William Shakespeare, The Tempest

One of the first lessons I learned teaching introductory Social Psychology was, never start with history. History, I quickly realized, is more compelling to those who have lived with its consequences than those who are approaching the field for the first time. In other words, it is easier to appreciate the role of history in shaping a field when we know and appreciate its dominant traditions and themes than when we have no general sense of what the field is all about. In writing this chapter for an advanced social psychology textbook, I assume that the reader already has some reasonable conception of the field and its subject matter. My further hope is that the reader has some longer-term interest in social psychology. That way, she or he can take advantage of the goals of this chapter: to reveal how our past is prologue to the field's current character and, at the same time, to help set the stage for where the next generation of young social psychologists will take it.

Social psychologists sometimes find ideas in the field's history (e.g., see Jones, 1985). Contemporary trends, both in science and in the culture at large, are also influential. The social and political zeitgeist has often inspired the field's research and theory, as is evident in the emergence of broad themes across our history: individualism in the early part of the 20th century; group influence and obedience in the aftermath of World War II; and social inequality, stereotyping, and prejudice in the 1960s and 1970s and then again in the 2010s. Moreover, social psychologists are opportunistic, quickly taking advantage of new scientific approaches and tools, as seen, for example, in the rise of cognitive perspectives in the 1970s, biological approaches at the beginning of the 21st century, and, more recently, Internet-based methods of data collection (Maniaci & Rogge, 2014b). In these and other instances, the field's deep-seated interest in understanding fundamental principles of human social behavior was galvanized by emerging theoretical perspectives, new methods, or dramatic events (e.g., the 1964 murder of Kitty Genovese, which spawned research on bystander intervention; Latané & Darley, 1970), and sometimes all three. It is impossible, in other words, to separate historical trends in social psychology from parallel developments in science and culture.

This tendency of social psychological research to be linked to the cultural, political, and scientific zeitgeist has led some commentators to conclude that social psychology is faddish and noncumulative, in the sense that certain topics or approaches become fashionable and active for a time and then dissipate, not so much because a comprehensive, accurate, and well-documented understanding has been achieved but rather because researchers simply tire of the subject. That interest in one or another research topic waxes and wanes seems indisputable. Jones (1998) wrote,

> Many social psychologists feel that their field is uniquely or especially vulnerable to faddism. . . . Surely there are bandwagons upon which graduate students and more established scholars climb in all research fields. However, it may be that such labels as "fad" or "fashion" are more easily applied to the social sciences than to the natural sciences because developments in the social sciences tend to be less cumulative and each research concern is therefore more limited by time. In any event, any student of social psychology knows that particular theories or methods or paradigms gain favor, dominate segments of the literature for a period of time, and then recede from view. (p. 9)

Jones went on to attribute this waxing and waning to several factors. Among the former are the timely interests of innovating researchers, the explanatory power and potential for novel findings provided by new theories or tools, the leadership of prestigious researchers, and (as seems even more true today than in Jones's era) the priorities of funding agencies. Factors responsible for the waning of research interests include progress in understanding a phenomenon, so that remaining questions provide incrementally smaller yields and are therefore less attractive to young scholars; theoretical or empirical "dead ends" (i.e., once-promising ideas or findings turn out to be mundane, untenable, or artifactual); and what might be called "benign neglect"—diminished interest in the familiar (for an intriguing collection in this regard, see Arkin, 2011).

If research interests wax and wane, what is the purpose of studying the history of social psychology? Several reasons stand out. First, although fads exist, certain topics do endure. For example, few researchers today study the authoritarian personality, the risky shift, or ingratiation, but bias in perceiving others, persuasion, and social self-regulation have remained persistently popular topics for more than a half-century. Better appreciation of why research and theory on certain ideas continue to evolve while others fade away may provide signposts for researchers considering what to study and how to study it. Also, highlighting broad themes and trends in social-psychological research is a useful way of identifying the contribution of social psychology to knowledge relative to other sciences and disciplines (Hinde, 1997).

Second, knowledge in any discipline grows both horizontally and vertically. That is, some advances occur when researchers build on earlier work, whereas other advances arise from entirely new directions (McGuire, 1973). Building, or what Mischel (2006) called becoming a more cumulative science, depends on knowing the history of a phenomenon or theory; new findings deepen, elaborate, or add complexity to what is already known. Discovering new directions also benefits from an awareness of history, because a direction is new only if it is not "old wine in a new bottle."

Third, in social psychology, unlike many more technical fields, new scholars begin with "entry biases"—preconceived notions, based on "a lifetime of experience in observing and hypothesizing about human behavior" (Cacioppo, 2004, p. 115), and grounded in common sense, intuition, and personal theories.

Formal theorizing is one means of minimizing the harmful effects of these biases, while capitalizing on whatever novel insights they might suggest (Cacioppo, 2004; McGuire, 1997). A good sense of the field's history is also helpful here.

For these reasons, this chapter subscribes to a remark widely attributed to Winston Churchill: "The farther backward you look, the farther forward you are likely to see." I propose that future research is likely to be better informed if planned with an awareness of what came before and is also more likely to fill a useful niche within the broad network of theories that define social psychology. Research conducted without such awareness is more likely to yield isolated results, with ambiguous or even inconsistent links to other principles and theories.

An historical perspective is also conducive to interdisciplinary research, or what Van Lange (2006) described as building bridges between social psychology and other disciplines. Social psychologists have not always taken advantage of links to other disciplines, and scholars in other disciplines are sometimes unaware of social-psychological research that bears directly on their interests. If transdisciplinary research is the future of science, as most science administrators argue, then the long-term outlook for social psychology depends on our ability to make such bridges explicit and generative. Many such bridges already exist, as Van Lange (2006) illustrates. Awareness of historical trends in theories and research may help illuminate how and why some bridges led to sparsely inhabited territory while others opened the door to progress.

This chapter[1] is organized around seven historical periods, catalogued imprecisely according to major research trends and professional issues that defined the era and distinguished it from preceding periods. These developments reflect far more research and many more contributors than can be mentioned in a brief chapter such as this. For that reason, I emphasize contributions that played pivotal roles in the evolution of social-psychological research and theory. Readers interested in more detailed accounts will find Allport (1954), Goethals (2003), Jahoda (2007), Jones (1985), Kruglanski and Stroebe (2012), and Ross, Ward, and Lepper (2009) particularly informative.

Classical Roots

1908 is often cited as the starting line of social psychology because the first two textbooks bearing that name, one by the psychologist William McDougall and the other by the sociologist Edward Alsworth Ross, appeared in that year. This designation is misleading. McDougall and Ross had direct intellectual predecessors in the 18th and 19th centuries, and their writing featured concepts similar in scope, ideology, and method to the earlier work. Moreover, if social psychology is defined as "an attempt to understand and explain how the thought, feeling, and behavior of individuals are influenced by the actual, imagined, or implied presence of other human beings" (Allport, 1954, p. 5), then it is no overstatement to say that social-psychological theorizing dates back to at least the origins of recorded history. This is because *Homo sapiens* have tried to articulate systematic principles for understanding, predicting and controlling the ways in which people influence one another ever since cognitive evolution gave us the capacities for self-awareness, symbolic thought, and theory of mind.

For example, one of the oldest known legal codes, the ancient Babylonian Codex Hammurabi (*ca.* 1760 BCE), contains 282 laws defining properties of interdependence for living in social groups, how responsibilities and rights are linked to social positions, rules for distributive and procedural justice, and attributions for misdeeds. The principle of "an eye for an eye" (known today as the norm of reciprocity) first appears here. The Sanskrit Bhagavad Gita, considered the sacred scripture of Hinduism, offers numerous allegorical teachings describing the association between motivation and action, the self, and social and divine influence. In the 6th century, Benedict of Nursia, the founder of western Christian monasticism, compiled 73 "rules" describing how a monastery ought to be run and how a spiritual life ought to be lived. The so-called Rule of Benedict includes many social-psychological ideas, for example, about regulating individual responsibility and interdependence in the monks' activities. Innumerable social-psychological principles can be found in the Judeo-Christian Bible, encompassing issues such as free will, prosocial and antisocial behavior, self-centered and other-centered motives, the self in relation to others, causal attributions, the nature of human needs and motives (and how to deal with them in social living), forgiveness and guilt, self-regulation, social cognition, and justice motives. Several social-psychological effects are even named after biblical passages (e.g., the Good Samaritan experiment).

Some have argued that Aristotle was the first social psychologist (e.g., Taylor, 1998). Aristotle maintained that because humans are inherently social, it is necessary to understand how the social environment affects the individual. This general principle led him to numerous specific ideas, such as the role of goals in construing situations, rationality in social judgment and action, and reciprocity of affection as a basis for love and friendship. Nevertheless, Aristotle's predecessors Plato and Socrates also established important wellsprings for the waters of later social-psychological thinking. For example, Plato described the utilitarian functions of groups, introducing constructs later to reemerge as the social contract, the group mind, obedience, conformity, social facilitation, and social loafing. Plato's *Symposium* provides a seminal description of the varieties of love. As for Socrates, the conflict between Socratic rationality and Sophist rhetoric might be considered the first dual process model of persuasion. In short, it seems safe to conclude that there are ample examples of social-psychological theorizing, in character if not in name, throughout antiquity to the present day.

There is little doubt that the social philosophers and early scientists of the Age of Enlightenment set the stage for modern social psychology (Jahoda, 2007). Many ideas introduced during this period (broadly construed here to start in the latter part of the 17th century and end early in the 19th century) were instrumental in the later appearance of social psychological thinking during the latter half of the 19th century. Particularly influential examples include the following:

- Thomas Hobbes's (1588–1679) account of power-seeking as a basic human motive;
- Rene Descartes's (1596–1650) ideas about cognition and the mind/body problem;
- John Locke's (1632–1704) insistence on observation as the basis of both personal and scientific knowledge;
- David Hume's (1711–1776) attention to reason, as well as his suggestion that sympathy for others provides a foundation for social relations;
- Jean Jacques Rousseau's (1712–1778) social contract, which explained how people cede certain rights to authorities to maintain well-functioning groups;
- Adam Smith (1723–1790), whose *Wealth of Nations* celebrated self-interest as a moral good and who proposed a theory of sympathy, in which the act of observing others fosters awareness of one's own behavior and moral motives;
- Immanuel Kant's (1724–1804) *Critique of Pure Reason*, which suggested that the properties of objects and the way that humans perceive those objects were not one and the same;
- Jeremy Bentham's (1748–1832) *hedonic calculus*, which argued that humans act to obtain pleasure and avoid pain;
- Georg Hegel's (1770–1831) account of the social (group) mind as an entity unto itself, which subsumes individual minds; and
- Charles Darwin (1809–1882), whose theory of evolution prominently features the role of social relations in reproduction and survival.

None of these scholars used the term *social psychology*, but their influence on what came later is clear. Insofar as their thinking contributed to a systematic understanding of how individuals function within social groups and society, with some even using scientific methods in that quest, they sowed the intellectual seeds that flowered into modern social psychology.

The Emergence of a Discipline: 1850–1930

As previously explained, assigning a start date to social psychology is an ambiguous enterprise. One reasonable line of demarcation is the first appearance of the term *social psychology* to denote a field of inquiry. Jahoda (2007) credits an obscure Italian philosopher, Carlo Cattaneo, with coining the term *psicologia sociale* in 1864, to describe the psychology of "associated minds"—how new ideas emerge from the interaction of individual minds. A more influential early user of the term was Gustav Lindner, an Austrian/Czech psychologist whose 1871 textbook discussed many matters of "deriving from the mutual effects . . . of individuals in society the phenomena and laws of social life" (Jahoda, 2007, p. 59). Lindner's book included a section entitled "Fundamentals of Social Psychology," and because the book was widely read, it is more likely to be the source of what followed than Cattaneo's article.

Wilhelm Wundt was a substantial intellectual force in the early development of the field. Wundt's 10-volume *Völkerpsychologie* (often loosely translated into English as social psychology, a translation to which Wundt objected because the term *social* at that time connoted culture, whereas Wundt had a more comprehensive intent; Greenwood, 2004), published between 1900 and 1920, was a tour de force of ideas about "those mental products which are created by a community of human life and are, therefore, inexplicable in terms merely of individual consciousness since they presuppose the reciprocal action of many" (Wundt, 1916, p. 2). Wundt is widely considered to be the father of modern experimental psychology, but perhaps curiously, he felt that the experimental approach was not conducive to his *Völkerpsychologie*, which may help explain why Wundtian concepts have not endured in contemporary experimental social psychology (e.g., he believed that measurement and statistics were useful only for studying elementary conscious processes; Fahrenberg, 2015). Nevertheless, because Wundt's laboratory in Leipzig was one of the most influential hubs in early psychology, and because Wundt himself was not to be ignored, his writings undoubtedly popularized the study of the individual within group contexts.

Another early landmark was the first social-psychological laboratory experiment, conducted by Norman Triplett at Indiana University in 1897. Stimulated by his observation that bicycle racers rode faster when paced by another rider, Triplett reported results from a study of 40 children asked to wind silk cord onto fishing reels, alternately doing so alone and together (Triplett, 1898). Others picked up on Triplett's use of experimentation to study social-psychological questions, but the experimental method did not become popular until the 1920s, when it was championed by Floyd Allport at Syracuse University. (Indeed, experimentation did not become the predominant method of research in social psychology until the 1950s and 1960s, following Kurt Lewin's influence; McMartin & Winston, 2000.) Allport made two important contributions to the early development of social psychology. The first, already noted, was his conviction that controlled laboratory experimentation would provide the necessary rigor for advancing (social) psychology as a science. The second was his insistence that group phenomena had to be studied in individualist terms: "There is no psychology of groups which is not essentially and entirely a psychology of individuals. Social psychology . . . *is a part of the psychology of the individual*, whose behavior it studies in relation to that sector of his environment composed by his fellows" (F. Allport, 1924, p. 4; italics in the original). To the extent that social psychology in the 1980s was "largely a North American phenomenon," as E. E. Jones (1985, p. 47) asserted, it was because of Allport's legacy.

As Jahoda (2007) points out, contemporary social psychology more nearly resembles Allport's 1924 textbook than its 1908 predecessors, previously mentioned. Nevertheless, the two 1908 textbooks were influential in putting the term *social psychology* on the scholarly map and in introducing certain key concepts to the field. In one, Ross (1908) defined social psychology as being concerned with "uniformities due to *social* causes, i.e., to *mental contacts* or *mental interactions*. . . . It is *social* only insofar as it arises out of the interplay of minds" (1908, p. 3; italics in the original). What Ross called "uniformities" attributable to the "conditions of life"—features of the environment not subject to mental interplay between persons, such as the physical setting, visual cues, culture, or race—were explicitly excluded. Ross had been influenced by earlier sociologists such as Gustave Le Bon and Gabriel Tarde, who popularized concepts such as crowd psychology and the group mind, using suggestion and imitation as mechanisms. Ross sought to explain social influence and control and thus may be considered a bridge between early sociologists and later group-process researchers.

McDougall (1908) was somewhat less explicit in his charge, designating social psychology with the task of showing "how, given the native propensities and capacities of the individual human mind, all the complex mental life of societies is shaped by them and in turn reacts upon the course of their development and operation in the individual" (p. 18). As Allport later did, McDougall emphasized the individual, having been influenced by Darwin. He assigned a prominent role to instincts, which he believed underlie human sociality and more complex forms of social organization. In this emphasis, McDougall faced considerable opposition from followers of then-emerging behaviorism.

Two additional trends during this period played significant roles in social psychology, although these would not be evident until later. The first, psychoanalytic theory, was not particularly influential in early social psychology (with the possible exception of the idea of instincts; G. Allport, 1954). Nonetheless, constructs introduced by psychoanalytic theorists such as Sigmund Freud, Carl Jung, Alfred Adler, and Karen Horney are relevant to contemporary social psychology, not necessarily in their original forms but rather as they have been modernized. For example, ideas such as motivation outside of awareness, chronic accessibility, subliminal perception, the effects of ego defense on self-regulation, repression, the functional basis of attitudes, the importance of early-life relationships with caregivers, relational conceptions of self, terror management, transference, compensatory behaviors associated with low self-esteem, and the ideal self can all be traced, at least in rudimentary form, to psychoanalytic writings. (See, for example, the December 1994 special issue of the *Journal of Personality* on social cognition and psychoanalysis.) Erdelyi (1990) suggests that these concepts took hold in social psychology only after having been recast as processes and mechanisms amenable to modern cognitive theories and methods.

A second development that later bore fruit is the work of William James. James, ever the philosopher-psychologist, had a long and productive career at Harvard University, beginning in 1873 and ending with his death in 1910. James's influence, not particularly visible during this early period of social psychology, became influential later, when topics such as the self, emotion, and theory of mind became central to the discipline. In particular, James first proposed the "motivated tactician" model of social cognition—that thinking is for doing (Fiske, 1992)—and that the self could vary in response to social context (an idea elaborated by James Mark Baldwin and George Herbert Mead). In one sense, it is striking testimony to James's vision and generativity that although his work was somewhat tangential to social psychology during his time, the field eventually came to him.

To summarize, during the period from 1850 to 1930, social psychology was transformed from a relatively informal conglomeration of ideas about the relationship of individuals to the groups and societies in which they lived to a viable, self-identified discipline. One sign that the field had come of age was the decision by Morton Prince, then editor of the *Journal of Abnormal Psychology*, to rename that journal as

The Journal of Abnormal Psychology and Social Psychology, designating Floyd Allport as a co-editor. Their editorial statement nicely summarizes the field's progress:

> At its inception, less than two decades ago, social psychology was variously defined according to different opinions as to its subject matter. The following classes of data were among those stressed in the various definitions: crowd action, the social bases of human nature, the psychological aspects of social formations and movements, and "planes and currents" of thought and action which arise by virtue of the association of human beings. Through the enterprise of the pioneers these formulations, supplemented by many incidental contributions from others, have grown into a science having as its field a unique set of natural phenomena, and a wide range of practical application. A distinct method also is emerging, though progress here is necessarily slow owing to the large scale and the intangibility of much of the data. Interest in the subject is rapidly growing, and there are many courses given in it in colleges throughout the country. . . . In view therefore both of the present need of an organ for social psychology and of the mutually helpful contacts between that science and abnormal psychology, The Journal is pleased to announce the extension of its scope to include the former, and cordially invites those who are interested in the advancement of social psychology to join the ranks of its readers and contributors. (Prince & Allport, 1921, pp. 1–5)

Maturation and Migration: 1930–1945

By 1930, social psychology had established itself as an important psychological subdiscipline. As the 1930s began, American social psychology was dominated by the Floyd Allport–inspired individualist emphasis whereas European social psychology still reflected earlier notions of a group mind (Franzoi, 2007). All this was to change shortly, for both intellectual and geopolitical reasons.

Notable landmarks in American social psychology in the 1930s included the following: (a) the frustration-aggression hypothesis (Dollard, Doob, Miller, Mowrer, & Sears, 1939), which, derived from stimulus–response concepts, remains social psychology's primary legacy from the behaviorist tradition, along with the later-appearing social learning theory (Bandura & Walters, 1963); (b) interest in the structure and function of attitude, following the growing importance of public opinion research in American society, Gordon Allport's (1935) seminal chapter in the *Handbook of Social Psychology*, Newcomb's (1943) longitudinal study of attitude change among Bennington College students (conducted from 1935 to 1939), and LaPiere's (1934) classic study demonstrating noncorrespondence between attitudes and action toward outgroup members; (c) Katz and Braley's (1933) study of ethnic stereotypes among Princeton University students, which opened the door to the abiding interest in prejudice and stereotyping in social psychology; and (d) Mead's (1934) theorizing about the role of internalized social experience in the self.

It also seems appropriate to cite Henry Murray's (1938) personality theory. Primarily a personality theorist, Murray presaged much of what was to follow by proposing that both situations (press) and dispositions (needs) influenced behavior. By allowing for the existence of numerous needs, in contrast to the more structured conceptions of earlier models, Murray's flexible approach became popular among social psychologists who wanted to study how one or another predisposition (broadly construed to include needs, goals, and motives) affected behavior in social situations. Murray, along with Lewin (see the following discussion), set the stage for contemporary interactionist approaches, which advocate for simultaneous consideration of the *interactive* effects of dispositional and situational influences. As Funder (2006) put it, "nowadays, everybody is an interactionist" (p. 22; see also Mischel & Shoda, 1995).

Significant as these advances were, they pale in comparison to other developments, born in Europe but coming of age in America. Kurt Lewin was a German social psychologist who, alarmed by the rise of Nazism in his native country, emigrated to the United States in 1933. Lewin formulated field theory (1951)[2] with the intent of describing the social environment in terms of relations between individuals who "'locomoted' through a field of bounded 'regions' impelled by 'forces' or drawn by 'valences' along power 'vectors'" (Jones, 1985, p. 21). These forces were both interpersonal and intrapersonal, leading Lewin to propose that behavior was a function of the person and the environment, represented in his now-famous dictum, $B = f(P, E)$. Even if this dictum is often misconstrued—Lewin (1951) did not intend P and E to be separable, additive factors but rather "*one* constellation of interdependent factors" (p. 240; italics in the original; for elaboration of this point, see Reis, 2008)—it set the stage for examining social behavior in terms of motivational dynamics arising both within and outside the person. In this sense, Lewin's approach may be seen as a hybrid of the American individualist and European group mind traditions that were popular at the time. Lewin's goal plainly was to develop a set of quantifiable constructs, using the mathematics of topology, that could be used to formally test propositions about human social relations. Despite the fact these efforts were unsuccessful, Lewin's general approach turned out to be extraordinarily influential.

Lewin's lasting influence on social psychology went well beyond his theoretical vision. In 1945, he founded the Research Center for Group Dynamics (RCGD) at the Massachusetts Institute of Technology. Although Lewin died prematurely just two years later (in the midst of the RCGD's move to the University of Michigan), the group of social psychologists who worked or trained there under Lewin's far-sighted and inspiring spell were central players in the field's rapid postwar expansion. These included Leon Festinger, Stanley Schachter, Kurt Back, Morton Deutsch, Dorwin Cartwright, Murray Horwitz, Albert Pepitone, John French, Ronald Lippitt, Alvin Zander, John Thibaut, and Harold Kelley. Almost all current social psychologists will find one or more of these figures in their scholarly genogram.

Another enduring impact was Lewin's resolute belief in the value of applied research. In 1943, he asserted that "there is nothing so practical as a good theory" (Lewin, 1951, p. 169), and he backed this up with the conviction that social psychologists should test their theories in applied settings. Lewin was known for conducting bold "action-oriented" experiments in field settings (e.g., his studies during World War II using group pressure to induce American housewives to prepare family meals with more plentiful organ meats, because better quality meat was being used for the troops; Lewin, 1943). Lewin was instrumental in founding the Society for the Psychological Study of Social Issues, in 1936, an organization that continues to be a hub for social psychologists committed to social action.

Lewin's decision to emigrate to the United States, then, turns out to be one of the most important milestones in the history of social psychology. Many other significant European scholars also emigrated to the United States in that era, including Muzafer Sherif (whose pioneering work on social norm development led to Asch's famous conformity experiments involving the estimation of the length of lines) and Fritz Heider, which led Cartwright (1979) to name Adolf Hitler as the person who most influenced the development of social psychology. World War II had a further influence on the field's progress in that many leading researchers of that or the next generation worked for US government research agencies involved in the war effort, including Lewin himself, Rensis Likert (who advanced survey research methods for the Department of Agriculture), Samuel Stouffer (whose army experience led to the concept of relative deprivation and its extension in social justice research), Murray (who conducted personality assessments for the Office of Special Services), and Carl Hovland (whose evaluations of military training films for the United States Army led to the Yale tradition of persuasion research). Thus, the impact of the zeitgeist on the development of social psychology is not solely a matter of stimulating research topics; it also involves the movement and activities of the people who do social psychology.

Full Steam Ahead! 1946–1969

The post–World War II era was a heady time for social psychology. The field was expanding rapidly, fueled by the growth of universities and research. The GI Bill, which funded undergraduate and graduate education for soldiers returning from the war effort, created an immediate need for faculty and facilities. Research funding also increased exponentially, particularly in psychology, reflecting greater government investment in science and the mental health needs of returning veterans and others affected by the war. Opportunities were therefore great for European émigrés and young American social psychologists alike. Social psychology was a relatively new science whose potential resonated with the national mood, and universities were quick to add programs and positions. It was not uncommon in the early postwar era for positions to be offered on the basis of a telephone conversation. Tenure could be achieved in a year or two, and research grants were plentiful.

All these opportunities fed on the ideas and enthusiasms of social psychologists, especially young social psychologists, and their accomplishments largely fulfilled their expectations. The theoretical and empirical achievements of this period were considerable. Researchers expanded on the grand theories of prior eras, adding and fleshing out theoretical models, extending the field's reach to new phenomena, and building an empirical knowledge base to support theory. The laboratory experiment entered its golden age, as researchers found ways to manipulate complex concepts in clever, well-controlled, and highly involving scenarios (e.g., Asch's [1956] conformity experiments or Latané and Darley's [1970] bystander intervention experiments). It was a good time to be a social psychologist.

Early in this interval, the dominant theme was group dynamics, reflecting the influence of Lewin's students and contemporaries, who fanned out across the country following his death. Much of this research used field-theory concepts and language, although this was usually more an approach than a set of theory-derived propositions. The Lewinian tradition was plainly evident in graduate curricula, embodied in a popular textbook of readings, *Group Dynamics: Theory and Research* (Cartwright & Zander, 1953, 1960, 1968). Among the more influential programs of group dynamics research among Lewin's disciples were Festinger's (1950) *Theory of Informal Social Communication,* which identified and described three sources of communication ("pressures toward uniformity") within groups (to establish social reality through consensus, to move toward a goal, and to express emotional states), and Deutsch's (1949) studies of cooperation and competition. Another example (albeit one that did not directly use field theory terminology) was Thibaut and Kelley's *Interdependence Theory* (1959; Kelley & Thibaut, 1978), which provided an elegant theoretical model for explaining how interdependence with respect to outcomes influences individuals' behavior.

By no means was the study of group processes limited to the Lewinians, however. As noted previously, Asch (1956) was busily conducting experiments on conformity. He had been struck by Sherif's (1936) experiments showing the effects of social influence when subjects were confronted with ambiguous stimuli. Asch removed the ambiguity, by asking naïve subjects to judge which line among a set of lines was longest. Despite the fact that the correct answer was plainly visible, confederates would give the wrong response, creating a dilemma for subjects: Accept the group consensus or go it alone. Asch's work is often cited for showing "blind conformity," but this is a substantial misrepresentation of his thinking. Asch (1954) believed that disagreement in a group of your peers, each of whom has as much legitimacy as yourself in making a perceptual judgment, required considering the possibility that your own judgment might somehow be erroneous: "Not to take it [the group] into account, not to allow one's self to be in any way affected by it, would be willful" (p. 484). This important point led to a distinction between private acceptance (informational conformity) and public compliance (normative conformity) as bases for conformity, which was to fuel subsequent research and theory (Deutsch & Gerard, 1955). Research identifying situational and dispositional bases for nonconformity also became important during this period (e.g., Allen, 1965).

Nevertheless, by the mid-1960s, American social psychologists were losing interest in group process research (Wittenbaum & Moreland, 2008). In part, this waning may have reflected the emphasis in American social psychology on the individual. European social psychology had been decimated by the war's destruction and the emigration of many important scholars to America. American social psychologists, including the European-trained scholars and their students who were interested in groups, moved away from studies of within-group processes and instead focused in a more conceptually limited way on how groups influence the individual, a topic that acquired the label "social influence." For example, research on the "risky shift"—the tendency of individuals to take more risk in group decisions than when deciding alone (Wallach, Kogan, & Bem, 1962)—was popular for a time.

Another such example was Stanley Milgram's (1963, 1965) obedience studies. Arguably, nothing has defined social psychology more sharply in the public mind, for better and for worse, than Milgram's research. Milgram's thinking derived from his penetrating synthesis of the group process and social influence studies that preceded him, as well as on his personal observations about the Holocaust (Milgram, 1974). In a series of dramatic experiments that remain controversial to this day (Burger, 2009), Milgram demonstrated how, under certain circumstances, ordinary adults could be induced to deliver lethal electric shocks. Identifying those circumstances, as well as the dispositional factors that interacted with them, became the centerpiece of his programmatic research and the research of others. In contrast, public and scholarly attention outside the field largely ignored these moderators, focusing instead on the striking and, to some, morally repugnant behaviors that Milgram's paradigm had elicited.

Social influence processes were pivotal in other phenomena that became central to the field in the late 1950s and 1960s. For example, at Yale University, Carl Hovland and his colleagues and students began the Yale Communication and Attitude Change Program, which blended Hovland's experience with propaganda during World War II, Hullian learning theory, and group dynamics. The basic premise of the Yale approach to persuasion was to ask, in a somewhat mechanistic way, "Who said what to whom?" This led to numerous studies concerning the factors that predict attitude change, many of which are still cited and applied today. Festinger's interests evolved in a similarly individual-centered direction, as reflected in his social comparison theory (Festinger, 1954). Social comparison theory argued that people develop a sense of social reality—that is, their beliefs about the world and where they stand in it—by comparing their personal abilities and opinions with the abilities and opinions of similar others. In this theory, we can clearly see the field's move from a discipline concerned with group dynamics to one examining the influence of others on the individual.

Social psychology's bandwidth was also widening during this expansionary era. Social psychological theorizing and methods were being applied to an ever-increasing range of phenomena. Person perception became a major topic, following two important developments: (a) Asch's (1946) work on trait-based impressions, in which he showed that a list of traits such as industrious, skillful, and practical would lead to a very different overall impression if paired with the adjective "warm" than if paired with the adjective "cold," and (b) the then-innovative "New Look" approach to perception research, which proposed that the act of perception (e.g., what we see) was influenced by motives and expectancies. These models fostered growing interest in understanding the relative contribution of perceivers and percepts in the act of person perception, including enduring questions about bias. Hastorf and Cantril's (1954) classic "They Saw a Game," in which Princeton and Dartmouth students provided strikingly different accounts of rough play in a football game between their two schools, dramatically illustrated principles being studied in several laboratories (Bruner & Tagiuri, 1954). Another, although very different, influence was Cronbach's (1955) seminal critique of simple trait ratings, in which he demonstrated that a single rating—for example, choosing a value of 5 to describe a friend's intellect on a 1–7 rating scale—was actually composed of several distinct components, which had to be sorted out statistically to make sense of the processes that contribute to trait ratings. The complexities that he introduced to the study of accuracy in person perception remain vital today (Funder, 1987; Kenny, 1994; Wood & Furr, 2016).

In 1957, Festinger introduced the theory of cognitive fissonance, which some believe to be the single-most influential theory in the history of social psychology (Cooper, 2007). The basic premise of this theory exemplified Festinger's talent for simple yet elegant and generative theorizing: When two cognitions do not fit together, there is pressure to make them fit, which can be resolved through various cognitive or behavioral changes. In its emphasis on cognitive consistency, dissonance theory was not unlike other models popular at the time (e.g., balance theory; for a collection of theories and approaches, see Abelson et al., 1968), but dissonance theory took a more dynamic, self-regulatory approach. The original theory and experiments led to enthusiastic acceptance on some sides and extensive criticism on other sides, particularly among behaviorists (e.g., Rosenberg, 1965), whose reinforcement principles made very different predictions. It seems safe to say that over time, the cognitive dissonance position won out, but more important are the changes the theory went through and the various new theories it inspired. Over time, Festinger's propositions were transformed into a theory of behavior justification, postulating that behaviors inadequately explained by external rewards or constraints would engender a need for self-justifying attitude change. Other important work stimulated by the cognitive dissonance tradition includes Bem's model of self-perception (Bem, 1972), reactance theory (Brehm, 1966), self-affirmation theory (Steele, 1988), and cognitive evaluation theory (Deci, 1975).

Still other enduring theories and phenomena introduced during this fertile period include Schachter and Singer's (1962) two-factor theory of emotion, which popularized emotion as a topic for social-psychological inquiry and introduced influential ideas about the attribution and misattribution of arousal (Gendron & Barrett, 2009). Interest in interpersonal attraction and friendship formation grew, spurred by Newcomb's (1961) detailed study of the acquaintance process among new students at the University of Michigan, Byrne's (1971) studies of similarity and attraction, Altman and Taylor's (1973) studies of self-disclosure and social penetration, and, slightly later, Berscheid and Walster's (1974) physical attractiveness research (for a comprehensive review, see Reis, 2012). Also, George Homans (1950) proposed social exchange theory, which influenced interdependence theory (Thibaut & Kelley, 1959), equity theory (Adams, 1965), and later, social justice research.

Finally, 1968 was the year in which Walter Mischel proposed that the then-dominant stable-trait models of personality, which sought to identify cross-situational and cross-temporal consistencies in behavior, be replaced by contextually varying "if–then" models that sought to identify distinctive yet stable patterns of response to particular situations. Mischel's work was an influential reminder of Lewin's famous dictum, and was instrumental to the subsequent popularity of Person × Situation interaction research. Moreover, Mischel's influence reminded the field that personality psychology and social psychology were most effective as a single discipline (a reminder still heeded more in principle than in practice).

Zeitgeist continued to play a significant role in the field's evolution, as social psychologists pursued research addressing important events of the day. One of the most compelling examples began in 1964, when Kitty Genovese was brutally stabbed to death outside her Kew Gardens (New York) apartment while 38 witnesses reportedly did nothing to intervene or call the police. Public outrage about urban apathy and callousness was intense. Bibb Latané and John Darley, two young social psychologists residing in the New York City area, proposed and began what became an extensive research program testing a more social-psychological interpretation of factors that determine bystander intervention and nonintervention. Two principles were key: diffusion of responsibility—–that bystanders feel less personal responsibility to act when others are present—–and situational ambiguity—that bystanders use situational cues, such as the nonresponse of others, to determine whether or not the event is truly an emergency. Even though later reports have questioned key details about this crime (Rasenberger, 2004), Latané and Darley's (1970) research made bystander intervention an important part of the field's legacy. Perhaps more important, media coverage of their studies demonstrated to the public the value of social-psychological research.

Another historical event of the era, the civil rights movement, also dramatically affected the field's research agenda. Research on the causes and consequences of prejudice and discrimination grew in popularity, serving as a theoretical foundation for later interventions (e.g., the jigsaw classroom, first used in 1971; Aronson & Patnoe, 1997). *Brown vs. Board of Education of Topeka, Kansas,* the landmark 1954 decision in which the US Supreme Court ruled that racially segregated schools should not and could not be considered equal in their educational value also energized the field, largely because social science research, as summarized in Kenneth B. Clark's testimony, was cited as particularly influential in the court's decision. Student antiwar protests in the late 1960s also found a receptive audience in social psychology (e.g., Block, Haan, & Smith, 1969), perhaps because social psychologists were at least sympathetic to and often active in the cause.

As the presence of social psychology on American university campuses grew, so did the field's infrastructure. Division 8 (Social and Personality Psychology) of the American Psychological Association was formed in 1947, with Gordon Allport as the first chair. (In 1974, the independent Society for Personality and Social Psychology [SPSP] replaced Division 8 as the field's leading professional organization.) Table 2.1 presents a list of the presidents of Division 8 and SPSP since then. The Society of Experimental Social Psychology was founded in 1965, because, in the words of its first president, Edwin Hollander (1968), Division 8 had reached "intimidating dimensions" that made "personal contact and communication unwieldy" (p. 280). Hollander envisioned slow growth "to perhaps 100" members[3] (p. 281). European social psychology began to rebuild, with significant input from the American-sponsored Committee on Transnational Social Psychology, leading to the formation in 1966 of the European Association of Experimental Social Psychology, with Serge Moscovici as President.[4]

Journals also expanded, reflecting the need to disseminate the new research generated by the growing field. The renamed *Journal of Abnormal and Social Psychology* split into two journals in 1965. Daniel Katz (1965), editor of the new *Journal of Personality and Social Psychology* (*JPSP*) remarked:

> It is appropriate with the launching of a new journal to hail the dawn of a new day and to sound a call for revolutionary departures from traditions of the past. . . . Now that the field of social psychology and its sister discipline of personality have a journal all their own, we should take advantage of the fact by . . . dealing more adequately with variables appropriate to our own subject matter. . . . It is our conviction that social psychology is no longer divorced from the other behavioral sciences and that in the long run a journal of personality and social psychology can profitably take account of this rapprochement. (pp. 1–2)

Another primary journal formed during this expansionary period was the *Journal of Experimental Social Psychology*, founded in 1965. John Thibaut was the inaugural editor.

As the 1960s came to a close, two trends were apparent. The first concerned personnel. It is sometimes said that "social psychology is what social psychologists do," and to this point, the social psychologists were, with very few exceptions, white males. Academic institutions were starting to admit more women at all levels, and social psychology was no exception. Looking back on the period 1967 to 1992, Berscheid (1992) speculated that "the proportional increase of women into research positions in social psychology was greater than in any other subarea of psychology" (p. 527). Arguably more important than personnel statistics was the way in which the influx of women intrinsically changed the field, by creating "a single social psychology that has integrated, and has been enriched by, the different experiences and views that female social psychologists have brought to their work" (p. 527). Progress in integrating the perspectives of nonwhite individuals has been much slower.

TABLE 2.1 Past Presidents of Division 8 (American Psychological Association) and the Society for Personality and Social Psychology

Division 8, American Psychological Association (Social and Social Psychology)		Society for Personality Personality Psychology	
1947	Gordon Allport	1974	Urie Bronfenbrenner
1948	Gardner Murphy	1975	Paul Secord
1949	Theodore Newcomb	1976	Marcia Guttentag
1950	Otto Klineberg	1977	Harry Triandis
1951	J. McVicker Hunt	1978	Bibb Latané
1952	Donald MacKinnon	1979	Irwin Altman
1953	O. Hobart Mowrer	1980	Lawrence Wrightsman
1954	Richard Crutchfield	1981	Alice Eagly
1955	Nevitt Sanford	1982	Jerome Singer
1956	Abraham Maslow	1983	Ellen Berscheid
1957	Solomon Asch	1984	Albert Pepitone
1958	Else Frenkel-Brunswik	1985	Walter Mischel
1959	Jerome Bruner	1986	Ladd Wheeler
1960	Ross Stagner	1987	Elliot Aronson
1961	Robert Sears	1988	Edward Jones
1962	Henry Murray	1989	John Darley
1963	Leon Festinger	1990	Marilynn Brewer
1964	Garnder Lindzey	1991	Kay Deaux
1965	Morton Deutsch	1992	Mark Snyder
1966	Roger Brown	1993	Nancy Cantor
1967	Harold Kelley	1994	Susan Fiske
1968	Silvan Tompkins	1995	John Cacioppo
1969	Donald Campbell	1996	Robert Cialdini
1970	Julian Rotter	1997	Mark Zanna
1971	Herbert Kelman	1998	Gifford Weary
1972	Leonard Berkowitz	1999	Shelley Taylor
1973	William McGuire	2000	Abraham Tesser
		2001	Ed Diener
		2002	Claude Steele
		2003	James Blascovich
		2004	Hazel Markus
		2005	Margaret Clark
		2006	Brenda Major
		2007	Harry Reis
		2008	John Dovidio
		2009	Richard Petty
		2010	Jennifer Crocker
		2011	Todd Heatherton
		2012	Patricia Devine
		2013	David Funder
		2014	Jamie Pennebaker
		2015	Mark Leary
		2016	Wendy Wood
		2017	Diane Mackie
		2018	M. Lynne Cooper

The second indisputable trend was that the pace of the field's growth was slowing. Social psychology was young no more. Faculties and enrollments were no longer expanding at a rapid pace, and grant funding would become increasingly competitive. An impressive literature of theory and empirical findings had been established, but future advances would be more challenging.

The Ascent of Social Cognition: 1970–1990

With the benefit of hindsight, it seems only natural that the rapid expansion of social psychology after World War II would inevitably lead to soul-searching about the value of the field's work. In part, this may reflect the prevailing "question authority" attitude of the late 1960s. Perhaps more strikingly, as the growth in resources slowed, and as the field matured from vibrant adolescence into early adulthood, doubts were voiced about its accomplishments and goals, so much so that the early 1970s became the occasion of a "crisis of confidence" that was unmistakably visible in journals and at meetings. Many critiques appeared, ranging from concerns about methodology and the ethics of experimental manipulation (especially involving deception) to more fundamental questions about the value of social-psychological findings and theories.

Two critiques were particularly prominent. In one, Gergen (1973, 2001) argued that social psychology should be considered an historical rather than a scientific discipline, because the principles underlying social behavior vary as a function of time and culture. Gergen's position, which dovetailed with growing reservations (previously noted) about the dominance of North American white males in social psychology, led many to question the experimental methods and theoretical assumptions that were foundational at the time. The other critique, more evolutionary and ultimately more influential[5] than Gergen's revolutionary charge, was offered by William McGuire. In "The Yin and Yang of Progress in Social Psychology: Seven Koan," McGuire (1973) proposed:

> [T]he paradigm that has recently guided experimental social psychology—testing of theory driven hypotheses by means of laboratory manipulated experiments [is dissatisfying] . . . an adequate new paradigm will . . . [involve], on the creative side, deriving hypotheses from a systems theory of social and cognitive structures that takes into account multiple and bidirectional causality among social variables. (p. 446)

In other words, McGuire felt that social-psychological theorizing and research needed to become more elaborate, moving away from single-variable models to models of complex systems of variables, each of which influences, and is influenced by, the other variables in the system. Although his forecast has yet to be realized, it clearly did usher in a new generation of studies emphasizing process models and their basic mechanisms, as well as heightened interest in methodological diversity (addressed in the following discussion). More generally, as the crisis of confidence faded, researchers in the late 1970s and 1980s era redirected their energy from self-criticism to improved research.

McGuire's critique was prescient in calling attention to the cognitive structures underlying social behavior. The 1970s heralded the arrival of social cognition as a dominant area of social-psychological research. In large part, this movement reflected the so-called cognitive revolution, as psychology distanced itself from the antimentalist behaviorist tradition (which had only an irregular influence within social psychology) and instead whole-heartedly embraced the study of cognitive processes and their impact on behavior. To be sure, there had been earlier examples of social cognition within social psychology (e.g., person perception, attitude structure), but the new-found legitimacy of studying cognitive processes opened the door to a different level of analysis and to the discovery of many new phenomena.

The first of these new social-cognitive phenomena was causal attribution. Seminal groundwork had been laid in three earlier theoretical models. These were Heider's (1958) "common sense psychology," which examined how people make ordinary judgments about causation, in particular describing the constellation of factors that fosters environmental or personal causation; Jones and Davis's (1965) theory of correspondent inferences, which proposed that lay persons ascribe intentionality (and hence dispositional causation) to the extent that actions deviate from what the average person would and could do; and Kelley's (1967) covariation model, which proposed that causal inferences were based on comparative judgments about whether a given action was consistent over time, distinctive among related entities, and consensual across persons. Attribution research prospered for a time, and although interest subsequently waned, it set the stage for what followed.

In a broad perspective, the primary contribution of the new emphasis on social cognition was to situate the major mechanisms for social-psychological explanations of behavior squarely within the mind of the individual. Contemporary social psychology thus moved away from the interpersonal and group process models favored in earlier approaches, notably those popular in Europe and in sociological social psychology, and doubled down on the more individualistic approach introduced by Floyd Allport (which was also characteristic of the increasingly popular field of cognitive psychology). Social psychological phenomena were seen as being caused proximately by "what the individual makes of the situation" (Kelley et al., 2003, pp. 5–6) more so than by its distal causes, namely the situation itself. This idea was expressed famously in Ross and Nisbett's (1991) principle of construal: that causal analysis should focus on the personal and subjective meaning of the situation to the individual actor.

Between 1970 and 1990, social cognition research flourished. Some of the more influential and enduring work of this era includes research on judgment and decision-making (which contributed to the development of behavioral economics, now a thriving discipline in its own right), such as Nisbett and Ross's (1980) classic book on strategies and shortcomings in human inference and Kahneman and Tversky's (1973) research on heuristics; early studies of automaticity (e.g., Winter & Uleman, 1984); formal theories of attitude change, such as the elaboration likelihood model (Petty & Cacioppo, 1986; see Chapter 6), and of the attitude–behavior association, such as the theory of reasoned action (Ajzen & Fishbein, 1974); various models of social categorization and schema use, including models of person memory (Ostrom, 1989); dual-process models, such as those differentiating deliberative and implemental mind-sets (Gollwitzer & Kinney, 1989) or systematic and heuristic processing (e.g., Chaiken, Liberman, & Eagly, 1989); and models differentiating automatic and controlled processes in stereotyping, prejudice, and discrimination (e.g., Devine, 1989). Many other examples might be cited (for a review, see North & Fiske, 2012). The enthusiasm for social cognition was such that Ostrom (1984) could proclaim, not without ample credibility, that "social cognition reigns sovereign" (p. 29) over other approaches to understanding social behavior.

This is not to say that other topics were dormant, however. Motivation was becoming more important in social psychology, as exemplified by growing attention to self-regulation. Several major models were formulated during this period, among them Carver and Scheier's (1981) control theory, Deci and Ryan's (1985) self-determination theory, Higgins's (1987) self-discrepancy theory, and Greenberg, Pyszczynski, and Solomon's (1986) terror management theory (for a review, see Higgins, 2012). More broadly, self-related research expanded from viewing the self as the object of knowledge (i.e., self-esteem, contents of the self-concept) to also considering the self as a causal agent motivated to pursue personal and psychological goals (see Chapter 5). Numerous "self-"related processes became popular, such as self-evaluation maintenance, self-enhancement, self-verification, and self-assessment (Sedikides & Strube, 1997; Taylor, 1998). Some of this work, under the heading of motivated social cognition, provided a much needed "hot" dynamic contrast to then prevailing "cool" information-processing approaches to social cognition. It was not until the 1990s, however, that these approaches became widely adopted.

Social psychology's net was also widening during this period. Emotion and emotion regulation were becoming increasingly popular topics (Manstead, 2012; Zajonc, 1998), coincident with the founding of the International Society for Research on Emotions in 1984. Research on interpersonal attraction gradually slowed but was supplanted beginning in the 1980s by research on social psychological processes affecting the development, maintenance, and termination of close relationships (for a review, see Reis, 2012). This vigorous extension was facilitated by a key pair of conferences held in Madison, Wisconsin, in 1982 and 1984, which led to the founding of a new professional organization (now called the International Association for Relationship Research) and two specialty journals. And what about social psychology's original research interest—groups? It became less central than in earlier periods, although groups research was still being conducted, somewhat more in a renaissance of European social psychology than in North America, led by scholars such as Serge Moscovici and Henri Tajfel (for a review, see Levine & Moreland, 2012). Nevertheless, even here the limits of models based in the mind of the individual were plain. As Moreland, Hogg, and Hains (1994) document, research on traditional topics such as group structure, performance, and influence ebbed whereas intergroup relations research (social identity, stereotyping, and prejudice) thrived (see Chapter 12).

Perhaps more significant than all of these changes in content were changes in the way that research was conducted. Research ethics boards became standard (and, some would say, overzealous), requiring more thorough attention to the protection of research participants' welfare and raising questions about procedures such as deception and informed consent (McGaha & Korn, 1995). A more substantive change involved the introduction of microprocessors, which made available sophisticated tools for conducting research and analyzing data. For example, computerized technology allowed researchers to measure reaction times within milliseconds or to present stimuli at exposure lengths that could be carefully controlled to be subliminal or supraliminal (Bargh & Chartrand, 2014; Gawronski & de Houwer, 2014). These tools afforded unprecedented opportunities to ask questions (e.g., about automaticity or implicit processes) that earlier researchers could barely imagine.

Yet more widespread were changes in data analysis. In 1970, most analyses were conducted using large, cumbersome, malfunction-prone manual calculators. Nearly all published studies presented very simple statistics, largely because analyses involving more than three variables required matrix algebra (which most social psychologists eschewed). By 1990, sophisticated statistical software on mainframe or personal computers was ubiquitous, making complex multivariate procedures routine. Invention thus spawned necessity, in the sense that social psychologists began to rely extensively, and often insist, on research and statistical methods that took advantage of this new-found computing power. For example, diary methods such as experience sampling first appeared in the 1970s (for a history, see Wheeler & Reis, 1991), structural equation models became known and useful (Reis, 1982), and Kenny's social relations model transformed studies of person perception (Kenny, 1994). Baron and Kenny's (1986) paper on mediation, the most-cited article in the history of JPSP, also changed the way that research is done. Methods for assessing mediation were not just a new tool for social psychologists; they altered the research agenda and broadly helped advance theory by making routine the pursuit of evidence for mediating processes.

Journals were changing, too. In April, 1980, JPSP split into its current three independent sections under a single cover. Nominally designed to contend with the distinct expertise that the three areas were presumed to require, as well as the workload created by ever-increasing submissions, the split was a sign of growing specialization and complexity. For similar reasons, in this era several other new journals were founded, including the *Personality and Social Psychology Bulletin* in 1975, and the *European Journal of Social Psychology* and the *Journal of Applied Social Psychology* in 1971. Reis and Stiller (1992) documented the field's increasing complexity. Comparing articles published in JPSP in 1968, 1978, and 1988, they found that, over time, articles had become longer, had more citations, and reported more studies with more subjects per study, more detailed methods, and more complex statistical analyses.

All these activities suggest that although McGuire (1973) seems to have missed the mark in predicting the demise of the laboratory experiment, he was spot-on about much of the rest of it: "deriving hypotheses from a systems theory of social and cognitive structures that takes into account multiple and bidirectional causality among social variables" (p. 446). By 1990, social psychologists were asking multifaceted questions about more intricate concepts, they were using more sophisticated methods to collect and analyze their data, and their publications were growing in length, detail, and complexity. Even if bidirectionality had not yet become common—for example, experiments with single-direction causality continued to dominate over correlational approaches—researchers were thinking in terms of and beginning to test mediational models. All of these signs indicated that social psychology had progressed along the path of becoming an established science (Kuhn, 1962).

Spreading Tentacles, Deeper Roots, and a Move toward Biology: 1990–2010

As 1990 arrived, SPSP had about 2,800 postgraduate and student members. By the end of 2008, membership had doubled, to over 5,600. Although some of this increase may reflect growth in mainstream academic psychology departments, a larger portion likely reflects the spread of social psychology into related disciplines and applied positions. Several such expansions are apparent. Social psychological research is increasingly represented in law (e.g., eyewitness testimony, jury decision-making), business and economics (e.g., judgment and decision-making, behavioral economics), medicine (e.g., motivational processes in health-related behavior, social influences on health and well-being), family studies (e.g., interpersonal processes in family relationships), education (e.g., achievement motivation, student–teacher interaction), and politics (e.g., voting behavior). This scholarly diaspora may be seen as a sign of the field's health. The domain of social psychology is the study of how the social context affects behavior, an expertise increasingly sought by basic scientists and applied practitioners in other disciplines. Social psychologists also tend to have excellent skills conceptualizing and conducting research on the effects of social context, which is also valued in various academic and applied settings.

There is no irony in the fact that the influence of social psychology has grown steadily by exporting its theories, methods, and talent to other fields. Taylor (2004) noted, "Whereas social psychology used to be a relatively small field of scholars talking primarily to each other, now we have unprecedented opportunities to collaborate with the other sciences in ways that we would have never imagined even a few years ago" (p. 139). Such outreach is an essential part of scientific relevance in the contemporary world. It has often been argued that the future of science rests in interdisciplinary research programs involving multiple investigators with specialized expertise (sometimes called "big science") to address important problems, and this is no less true in designing interventions and applied programs that build on basic science. The spreading tentacles of social psychology, a trend that, if anything, appears to be accelerating (though it is far from an accomplished fact), thus augurs the field's continued participation in the most important science and applications of the day.

Social psychology's dispersion did not occasion neglect of the field's core. Topics popular or emerging at the beginning of this period, discussed earlier in this chapter, experienced theoretical advances, partly due to the accumulation of research and partly due to the availability of yet more sophisticated methods and tools. For example, programming packages such as E-Prime®, MediaLab®, and DirectRT® enabled most researchers with access to a desktop computer to run complex, precisely timed experiments. Relatively sophisticated social-cognitive protocols, such as lexical decision tasks, subliminal and supraliminal priming, and implicit assessment, became standard, and topics amenable to study by these and similar methods, such as automaticity, dual-process models, the impact of nonconscious goals, motivated social cognition, emotion, and affective influences on judgment and decision-making, prospered. To be sure, social psychologists had long been interested in nonconscious processes, but they lacked the tools to study them and the data to theorize in a knowledgeable way about them. The availability of such methods, and the resultant impact on research and (especially) theory, might be considered a hallmark of this period.

Similarly, in the 2000s, the Internet grew in reach and bandwidth, making large, international, specialized, and diverse samples accessible for surveys and experiments to any and all researchers (a trend that accelerated post-2010, as will be discussed). Newer Internet-based tools, such as social networking sites and immersive virtual worlds, and other microprocessor-based technologies (e.g., ambulatory assessment, virtual reality) are poised to further expand the possibilities (Reis & Gosling, 2009). If the most influential figure in the social psychology of the middle 20th century was Hitler, arguably the most influential figures since 1980 were the inventors of microprocessors.[6]

Indispensable as these new tools may be, Baumeister, Vohs, and Funder (2007) noted a downside: Direct observation of behavior has been increasingly supplanted by the study of "self-reports and finger movements"—that is, by data provided through hand-written self-reports or keystrokes on a computer keyboard. By their tally, only about 15% of the articles published in *JPSP* in 2006 included behavioral measures (compared to about 80% in 1976). Many social psychologists trace their interest in the field to the "golden era" of laboratory experiments, when experimental realism was high and research participants were fully engrossed in experimentally created circumstances. (Think, for example, about Milgram's obedience experiment, Latané and Darley's bystander intervention studies, or Asch's conformity research.) Vivid laboratory experiments of this sort are rare these days, because, as Baumeister et al. (2007) suggest, they may be impractical or unethical for certain topics (e.g., sexual behavior), they are difficult, time-consuming, and labor-intensive to conduct, and it is unclear that journals value them any more than they do studies of self-reports and finger movements. Given that the correspondence between self-reports, implicit associations, and reaction times on the one hand and actual behavior on the other hand is imperfect, the paucity of actual behavioral studies raises questions for some about the relevance of contemporary research (Baumeister et al., 2007).

Although many of the substantive advances in social psychology after 1990 represent a deepening of what is understood about established theories and phenomena, two novel trends have also been influential. One of these is greater attention to biology, both in developing new methods (e.g., functional magnetic resonance imaging [fMRI]) and theoretically, in particular the biological functions, consequences, and mechanisms of social behavior. For example, because social psychologists were interested in situational causes of behavior, they historically tended to avoid evolutionary accounts. Nevertheless, as evolutionary psychology moved away from models featuring inherited, relatively immutable dispositions and toward concepts that asked about flexible behavioral adaptations designed to solve problems of survival and reproduction (see Chapter 16), social psychologists became more intrigued. This interest was emphasized in a seminal review by Buss and Kenrick (1998), who noted:

> [E]volutionary psychology places social interaction and social relationships squarely within the center of the action. In particular, social interactions and relationships surrounding mating, kinship, reciprocal alliances, coalitions, and hierarchies are especially critical, because all appear to have strong consequences for successful survival and reproduction. From an evolutionary perspective, the functions served by social relationships have been central to the design of the human mind. (p. 994).

Since then, concepts in evolutionary psychology have appeared regularly in social psychology texts (albeit not without controversy; e.g., see Park, 2007) and are an increasingly valuable source of research hypotheses about, for example, attraction, close relationships, prosocial behavior, aggression, social identity, group identity and formation, leadership, social cognition, and emotion.

Another sign of the influence of biological approaches in social psychology is the birth and exceptional growth of social neuroscience, which seeks to identify and understand neural processes underlying social behavior (see Chapter 15). To be sure, psychophysiological studies of social behavior, including psychophysiological processes occurring primarily in the brain, are not new (Cacioppo & Petty, 1983). But the rapid advance of cognitive neuroscience in the past two decades has had a profoundly energizing effect. The key in this regard is the development of fMRI for noninvasively capturing patterns of brain activation associated with psychological processes. Social neuroscientists use neuroscientific methods to test hypotheses about the neural processes responsible for the phenomena that social psychologists traditionally study at a behavioral level. For example, Beer (2007) examined evidence about activity in the medial prefrontal cortex to determine whether chronic self-evaluation is best represented by accurate self-assessment or self-enhancement; Aron et al. (2005) used fMRI to support their model of intense romantic love as a motivational state rather than as an emotion; and Decety and Jackson (2006) have used fMRI to better understand the neural and cognitive foundations of empathy. Social neuroscience is misconstrued when it is described as "finding social behavior in the brain." Rather, the goal is to inform social-psychological theory according to what is known about neural function and architecture (i.e., how the brain works and does not work) and, simultaneously, to better understand how the brain enacts the psychological and social processes that characterize everyday life (Blascovich, 2014; Cacioppo et al., 2003). Though social neuroscience is still very young, there is reason to believe that over time it will do much to better ground social-psychological theories in a biologically plausible reality.

The second trend that became prominent during the 1990s was culture. Although culture was surely a part of social psychology in the early days (e.g., in Wundt's folk psychology), over the years interest in culture waned, probably because of the field's quest for invariant basic processes of social behavior. Nonetheless, as social psychologists reconsidered the impact of culture, partly stimulated by the growth of social psychology outside of North America, research began to accumulate showing that many social psychological processes once thought to be "basic" or "universal" did in fact vary from one culture to another (Fiske, Kitayama, Markus, & Nisbett, 1998). Nowhere was this more evident than in studies of social cognition comparing individualist cultures (North America, Western Europe) with communal cultures (East Asia). In one compelling instance, the so-called fundamental attribution error was shown to be characteristic of European Americans but not of Asians (e.g., Miller, 1984). By now there is sufficient evidence to indicate that cultural influences are relevant to most domains of social psychology, as reflected in a special section of the journal *Perspectives on Psychological Science* that addressed many such examples (Sternberg, 2017).

It is too soon to know which of these trends will continue, which may turn out to be dead ends, and where they will lead social psychology. But if nothing else, they demonstrate that the relentless curiosity of social psychologists has few boundaries.

Change Is Here—The Rise of Big Data and the Reproducibility Crisis:

2010–The Present Day

Since the publication of the first edition of this textbook, social psychologists have continued their vigorous pursuit of any and all topics within the field's purview. Indeed, judging by journal publications and conference presentations, it seems clear that activity in the field has grown, perhaps even exponentially. At the same time, two important new developments have initiated major changes in how social psychologists go about their business.

The first of these developments concerns large, Internet-based samples, either through web-hosted data collection sites (e.g., mTurk, ResearchMatch, Qualtrics Online Sample) or "big data"—extremely large and potentially complex data sets compiled from social media (e.g., Facebook, online dating sites) or other pre-existing data sources (e.g., cell phone records, archived longitudinal panel studies such as Midlife in the United States, MIDUS). Both of these data sources allowed researchers to generate, sometimes with relatively little effort, extremely large samples with several important benefits (aside from the obvious benefit of statistical power): the possibility of efficiently conducting multiple direct and conceptual replications; the ability to test hypotheses with naturalistic field data; the statistical power to examine multiple-variable or complex patterns of moderation; and the capacity to examine longitudinal trends without waiting for time to pass. These data sources have unquestionably changed the landscape of social psychological research for the better (see Chapter 21).

Aside from the ease of conducting research, studies conducted on web-hosted data collection sites have proliferated for another reason: the claim that they offer more diverse and representative samples than the typical pool of freshmen and sophomores enrolled in psychology courses (Gosling, Vazire, Srivastava, & John, 2004). On its face, there seems little reason to doubt this claim, but other concerns have been raised about these samples—for example, that participants are prone to be inattentive to instructions or materials (Maniaci & Rogge, 2014a), that the same individuals participate multiple times in a single study, that worker communities communicate about studies before participating, or that participants have a potentially problematic degree of insight into the content or methods of a study, owing to past participation in similar, perhaps numerous, studies (Chandler, Mueller, & Paolacci, 2014). These concerns have not diminished the appeal of web-hosted data collection, but they have given rise to the development of procedures intended to minimize their impact (Chandler et al., 2014; Maniaci & Rogge, 2014a). Optimizing the manner in which data can be collected via the Internet is very much a "work in progress" for social psychology.

Trouble in Paradise? The Reproducibility Crisis

As the discipline of social psychology prospered, questions began to appear about its substantive core. Seminal in this challenge were two articles that confronted what their authors felt were serious empirical shortcomings. The first, by Simmons, Nelson, and Simonsohn (2011), argued that flexible and often undisclosed research practices were likely to have created a literature with an abundance of published "false positives"—that is, findings that yielded nominally significant results for a false hypothesis. In the second article, John, Loewenstein, and Prelec (2012) anonymously surveyed a large sample of academic psychologists, identifying what they labeled as a "surprisingly high" rate of questionable research practices (QRPs). Both of these reports focused on psychological science in general and not on social psychology in particular; in fact, they may be seen as part of a much broader challenge to the validity of scientific research, occasioned by a controversial and much debated article by Ioannidis (2005), provocatively entitled "Why Most Published Research Findings Are False." Nevertheless, despite the wide disciplinary reach of the concerns raised in these and other articles, the response of social psychology has been particularly and perhaps uniquely robust and self-critical.

Fuel was added to this fire by the apparent low rate of replication found in several large-scale multisite replications.[7] For example, in one replication of 100 experimental and correlational studies published in three psychology journals, depending on the criterion used, only 36% to 47% of the replications yielded significant results (Open Science Collaboration, 2015). Other similar replication projects have yielded mixed results; in one case, replications supported 11 of the 13 classic and contemporary effects that were tested (Klein et al., 2014), whereas in another example, a 23-lab replication failed to support the well-known ego depletion effect (Hagger et al., 2016). The interpretation of such results remains contentious. For example, Gilbert, King, Pettigrew, and Wilson (2016) noted that when the Open Science Collaboration's replications are corrected for error, power, and bias, "the data are consistent with the opposite conclusion, namely, that the reproducibility of psychological science is quite high" (p. 1037). In another case, Baumeister and Vohs (2016) pointed out that all of Hagger et al.'s (2016) replications were conducted with a method that had never been used in the original research establishing the ego depletion effect. All social psychologists agree about the importance of reproducibility, but the degree to which a problem exists remains an open question (Motyl et al., 2017).

Advocates of the "reproducibility is a problem" position usually cite QRPs as a major reason for what they see as a prevalence of false positives in the published literature. To be sure, critics have identified methodological issues in the John et al. (2012) research, arguing that when these issues are corrected, QRPs appear to be much less common than the original authors claimed (e.g., Fiedler & Schwarz, 2016). Nevertheless, at least some of the concerns raised in this debate have a long-standing history that predates the current controversy: for example, low statistical power (Cohen, 1962), publication bias (Greenwald, 1976; Rosenthal, 1979), selective reporting of results and hypothesizing after results are known (Kerr, 1998), incentive systems that reward novelty and positive results over replications and failures (Nosek, Spies, & Motyl, 2012), and limitations of significance testing (Kline, 2004). As a result, there currently exists a discipline-wide endeavor to address at least some of these issues. For example, in the mid-2010s, virtually all major journals in social psychology began attending much more closely to issues surrounding sample sizes and statistical power. They also began to endorse greater transparency about methods and data management, such as by providing online access to additional documentation for published articles through supplemental online material. Other less widely adopted but still increasingly common changes included preregistration of hypotheses and the provision of archival access to materials and data (e.g., through the Center for Open Science).

Although the debate over these and related concerns sometimes produces more heat than light, especially in the occasional blog post, most social psychologists see empirically informed and temperate discussion about questionable practices and their potential remedies as a healthy sign of progress in the field, or, as Motyl et al. (2017) assessed it, evidence that "the field is evolving in a positive direction" (p. 34). As of this writing, it seems clear that the field has agreed on greater statistical power, greater transparency, and replication as essential practices. There is less consensus about other changes (e.g., preregistration, fully open-to-all data, and replications in independent labs prior to publication).

For some commentators, confidence in the reproducibility of one's findings trumps other criteria, leading them to prioritize practices such as high levels of statistical power, replication, preregistration, and/or open access to one's data (e.g., LeBel, Berger, Campbell, & Loving, 2017; LeBel, Campbell, & Loving, 2017; Munafò et al., 2017; Zwaan, Etz, Lucas, & Donnellan, 2017). In one case, Benjamin et al. (2017) proposed adoption of $p < 0.005$ as a criterion for all new discoveries. Other commentators have underscored trade-offs among several criteria of high-quality, high-impact science, including discovery, internal and external validity, consequentiality, and cumulativeness along with reproducibility, thus encouraging flexibility in the application of rules and guidelines (e.g., Fiedler, Kutzner, & Krueger, 2012; Finkel, Eastwick, & Reis, 2015, 2017; McGrath, 1981; Reis & Lee, 2016; Stroebe, 2016). What is clear is that the general turmoil in the field stimulated by the aforementioned challenges has galvanized attention to questions about how to make social psychological research maximally meaningful, informative, influential, and cumulative.

Conclusion

Past is prologue, Shakespeare wrote, but the future is ours to create. What can the history of social psychology reveal that might usefully guide new investigators preparing to create the field's future? Our progress as a discipline suggests several trends. Social psychologists have always been interested in the same core phenomena—how behavior is affected by the social world in which our lives are embedded—but, as we have seen, the ways in which that interest is explored and expressed have varied markedly. Part of this variability reflects the intellectual, social, and political context of the world in which we live and work. Social psychologists by custom and by inclination tend to rely on the best available conceptual and methodological tools available to them. To be sure, social psychologists are not mere followers of contemporary trends—through research, teaching, and writing, social psychologists contribute to scholarly and popular movements. We might reasonably expect, then, that future social psychologists will continue to explore important questions about timely topics, using state-of-the-art tools.

These trends notwithstanding, the processes and phenomena most central to social psychology have a certain timelessness to them, in the sense that the best principles and theories are general enough to apply to whatever particulars are most prominent at the moment. Whether the principle is Hammurabi's assertion that taking "an eye for an eye" will result in a well-functioning social group, Festinger's theory of cognitive dissonance, or automaticity in social evaluation, the goal is to provide an abstract account of behavior that transcends specific circumstances. For example, good theories of social influence ought to include principles that help us explain social interaction, regardless of whether it occurs face to face, over the telephone, on Facebook, with robots, or by some medium not yet invented.

Of course this does not mean that established theories will not be displaced by better ones. A clear sense of history allows scholars to propose and test better (more accurate, more comprehensive, or more deeply detailed) theories. Isaac Newton (1676) famously remarked, "If I have seen a little further it is by standing on the shoulders of giants." One way in which history informs current progress is by providing a ladder up to the giant's shoulders: identifying what has been determined and dispensing important clues about what needs to be understood better and what novel research directions might be most informative. In this regard, then, I disagree with one distinguished social psychologist's recommendation that new students *not* read the literature, because it would constrain their imagination (for additional information, see Jost, 2004).

An indisputable prediction is that technological and statistical advances will provide innovative methods that allow social psychologists to ask and answer more probing and, in some instances, entirely new types of questions. As the complexity of these tools grows, so too will specialization, increasing the necessity for collaboration with scholars who possess different expertise. I expect, then, that the trend toward "big science" will continue—multidisciplinary collaborations among researchers with diverse training and proficiency. Social psychologists have often been reluctant to initiate such collaborations, but there is little doubt that such participation is needed for the field to thrive (Taylor, 2004). Even more important, social psychologists must make their expertise visible so that researchers from other disciplines will invite their contributions (Reis, 2008). A similar conclusion applies to becoming more involved in the translation and application of our theories and research to improve people's lives.

The history of social psychology is the history of people trying to better understand the intrinsically social world in which they live. Studying the field's history represents one step in creating not just the future of a field of scholarship but all of our futures.

Notes

1. For helpful suggestions and comments on an earlier version of this chapter, I thank David Buss, David Funder, Bill Graziano, Mike Maniaci, and the editors of this volume.
2. Field theory is actually more a perspective and method than a formal theory, as Lewin himself acknowledged.
3. Current membership in Society of Experimental Social Psychology is 1,115. By contrast, SPSP had almost 4,000 nonstudent members in July of 2017. The European Association for Social Psychology had 1,042 post-PhD members at roughly the same time.
4. Another change that took place during this period was the split of psychological social psychology and sociological social psychology. Earlier, these two approaches to social behavior had been at least partially aligned, reflected, for example, in the University of Michigan's Institute for Social Research, which expressly incorporated both approaches. By the mid-1970s, these two fields with the same subdisciplinary names had become essentially independent, each with its own traditions, literature, journals, and meetings.
5. Within social psychology, that is. Gergen's writing has had more influence in fields where textual analysis is more important, such as discourse analysis and communications.
6. Just who deserves this credit remains a matter of considerable debate, in both historical accounts and the US patent office.
7. A few highly publicized instances of outright fraud also upped the ante in this furor, notably the case of Diederik Stapel, to that point an eminent researcher who admits to having fabricated the results of dozens of studies (Enserink, 2012).

References

Abelson, R. P., Aronson, E., McGuire, W. J., Newcomb, T. M., Rosenberg, M. J., & Tannenbaum, P. H. (Eds.). (1968). *Theories of cognitive consistency: A sourcebook.* Chicago, IL: Rand McNally.

Adams, J. S. (1965). Inequity in social exchange. In L. Berkowitz (Ed.), *Advances in experimental social psychology* (Vol. 2, pp. 267–300). New York, NY: Academic Press.

Ajzen, I., & Fishbein, M. (1974). Factors influencing intentions and the intention–behavior relation. *Human Relations, 27,* 1–15.

Allen, V. L. (1965). Situational factors in conformity. In L. Berkowitz (Ed.), *Advances in experimental social psychology* (Vol. 2, pp. 133–175). New York, NY: Academic Press.

Allport, F. H. (1924). *Social psychology.* Boston: Houghton Mifflin.

Allport, G. W. (1935). Attitudes. In C. Murchison (Ed.), *A handbook of social psychology.* Worcester, MA: Clark University Press.

Allport, G. W. (1954). The historical background on modern social psychology. In G. Lindzey (Ed.), *Handbook of social psychology* (2nd ed., Vol. 1, pp. 1–80). Reading, MA: Addison-Wesley.

Altman, I, & Taylor, D. A. (1973). *Social penetration: The development of interpersonal relationships.* New York, NY: Holt, Rinehart & Winston.

Arkin, R. (Ed.). (2011). *Most underappreciated: 50 prominent social psychologists talk about hidden gems.* New York, NY: Oxford University Press.

Aron, A., Fisher, H., Mashek, D., Strong, G., Li, H., & Brown, L. (2005). Reward, motivation and emotion systems associated with early-stage intense romantic love. *Journal of Neurophysiology, 93,* 327–337.

Aronson, E., & Patnoe, S. (1997). The jigsaw classroom: Building cooperation in the classroom (2nd ed.). New York, NY: Addison Wesley Longman.

Asch, S. E. (1946). Forming impressions of personality. *Journal of Abnormal and Social Psychology, 41,* 258–290.

Asch, S. E. (1952). *Social Psychology.* New York, NY: Prentice Hall, Inc.

Asch, S. E. (1956). Studies of independence and conformity: A minority of one against a unanimous majority. *Psychological Monographs, 70*(9), 1–70.

Bandura, A., & Walters, R. H. (1963). *Social learning and personality development.* New York, NY: Holt, Rinehart, and Winston.

Bargh, J. A., & Chartrand, T. L. (2014). The mind in the middle: A practical guide to priming and automaticity research. In H. T. Reis & C. Judd (Eds.), *Handbook of research methods in social psychology* (pp. 311–344). New York, NY: Cambridge University Press.

Baron, R. M., & Kenny, D. A. (1986). The moderator-mediator variable distinction in social psychological research: Conceptual, strategic, and statistical considerations. *Journal of Personality and Social Psychology, 51,* 1173–1182.

Baumeister, R. F., & Vohs, K. D. (2016). Misguided effort with elusive implications. *Perspectives on Psychological Science, 11,* 574–575.

Baumeister, R. F., Vohs, K. D., & Funder, D. C. (2007). Psychology as the science of self-reports and finger movements: Whatever happened to actual behavior? *Perspectives on Psychological Science, 2,* 396–403.

Beer, J. S. (2007). The default self: Feeling good or being right? *Trends in Cognitive Sciences, 11,* 187–189.

Bem, D. (1972). Self-perception theory. In L. Berkowitz (Ed.), *Advances in Experimental Social Psychology* (Vol. 6, pp. 2–62). New York, NY: Academic Press.

Benjamin, D. J., Berger, J. O., Johannesson, M., Nosek, B. A., Wagenmakers, E.-J., Berk, R., . . . Johnson, V. E. (2017). Redefine statistical significance. *Nature Human Behaviour, 1,* 1–5.

Berscheid, E. (1992). A glance back at a quarter century of social psychology. *Journal of Personality and Social Psychology, 63,* 525–533.

Berscheid, E., & Walster, E. (1974). Physical attractiveness. *Advances in Experimental Social Psychology, 7,* 157–215.

Blascovich, J. (2014). Psychophysiological methods. In H. T. Reis & C. M. Judd (Eds.), *Handbook of research methods in social psychology* (pp. 101–122). New York, NY: Cambridge University Press.

Block, J. H., Haan, N., & Smith, M. B. (1969). Socialization correlates of student activism. *Journal of Social Issues, 25,* 143–177.

Brehm, J. W. (1966). *A theory of psychological reactance.* New York, NY: Academic Press.

Bruner, J., & Tagiuri, R. (1954). The perception of people. In G. Lindzey (Ed.) *The handbook of social psychology* (Vol. 2, pp. 634–654). Cambridge, MA: Addison-Wesley.

Burger, J. M. (2009). Replicating Milgram: Would people still obey today? *American Psychologist, 64,* 1–11.

Buss, D. M., & Kenrick, D. T. (1998). Evolutionary social psychology. In D. Gilbert & S. Fiske (Eds.), *The Handbook of Social Psychology* (4th ed., Vol. 2, pp. 982–1026). Boston, MA: McGraw-Hill.

Byrne, D. (1971). *The attraction paradigm.* New York, NY: Academic Press.

Cacioppo, J. T. (2004). Common sense, intuition, and theory in personality and social psychology. *Personality and Social Psychology Review, 8,* 114–122.

Cacioppo, J. T., Berntson, G. G., Lorig, T. S., Norris, C. J., Rickett, E., & Nusbaum, H. (2003). Just because you're imaging the brain doesn't mean you can stop using your head: A primer and set of first principles. *Journal of Personality and Social Psychology, 85,* 650–661.

Cacioppo, J. T., & Petty, R. E. (1983). *Social psychophysiology: A sourcebook.* New York, NY: Guilford.

Cartwright, D. (1979). Contemporary social psychology in historical perspective. *Social Psychology Quarterly, 42,* 82–93.

Cartwright, D., & Zander, A. (1953). *Group dynamics: Theory and research.* New York, NY: Harper & Row.

Cartwright, D., & Zander, A. (1960). *Group dynamics: Theory and research* (2nd ed.). New York, NY: Harper & Row.

Cartwright, D., & Zander, A. (1968). *Group dynamics: Theory and research* (3rd ed.). New York, NY: Harper & Row.

Carver, C. S., & Scheier, M. F. (1981). *Attention and self-regulation: A control-theory approach to human behavior.* New York, NY: Springer.

Chaiken, S., Liberman, A., & Eagly, A. H. (1989). Heuristic and systematic information processing within and beyond the persuasion context. In J. S. Uleman & J. A. Bargh (Eds.), *Unintended thought* (pp. 212–252). New York, NY. Guilford.

Chandler, J., Mueller, P., & Paolacci, G. (2014). Nonnaïveté among Amazon mechanical Turk workers: Consequences and solutions for behavioral researchers. *Behavior Research Methods, 46,* 112–130.

Cohen, J. (1962). The statistical power of abnormal-social psychological research: A review. *Journal of Abnormal and Social Psychology, 65,* 145–153.

Cooper, J. M. (2007). *Cognitive dissonance: Fifty years of a classic theory.* Thousand Oaks, CA: SAGE.

Cronbach, L. J. (1955). Processes affecting scores on "understanding of others" and "assumed similarity." *Psychological Bulletin, 52,* 177–193.

Decety, J., & Jackson, P. L. (2006). A social-neuroscience perspective on empathy. *Current Directions in Psychological Science, 15,* 54–58.

Deci, E. L. (1975). *Intrinsic motivation.* New York, NY: Plenum.

Deutsch, M. (1949). A theory of cooperation and competition. *Human Relations, 2,* 129–152.

Deutsch, M., & Gerard, H. G. (1955). A study of normative and informational social influence upon individual judgment. *Journal of Abnormal and Social Psychology, 51,* 629–636.

Devine, P. G. (1989). Stereotypes and prejudice: Their automatic and controlled components. *Journal of Personality and Social Psychology, 56,* 5–18.

Dollard, J., Doob, L. W., Miller, N. E., Mowrer, O. H., & Sears, R. R. (1939). *Frustration and aggression.* New Haven, CT: Yale University Press.

Enserink, M. (2012). Final report on Stapel also blames field as a whole. *Science, 338,* 1270–1271.

Erdelyi, M. H. (1990). Repression, reconstruction, and defense: History and integration of the psychoanalytic and experimental frameworks. In J. L. Singer (Ed.), *Repression and dissociation: Implications for personality theory, psychopathology, and health* (pp. 1–31). Chicago, IL: University of Chicago Press.

Fahrenberg, J. (2015). *Theoretische psychologie* [Theoretical psychology]. Lengerich, Germany: Pabst Scientific.

Festinger, L. (1950). Informal social communication. *Psychological Review, 57,* 271–282.

Festinger, L. (1954). A theory of social comparison processes. *Human Relations, 7,* 117–140.

Festinger, L. (1957). *A theory of cognitive dissonance.* Evanston, IL: Row, Peterson.

Fiedler, K., Kutzner, F., & Krueger, J. I. (2012). The long way from α-error control to validity proper problems with a short-sighted false-positive debate. *Perspectives on Psychological Science, 7,* 661–669.

Fiedler, K., & Schwarz, N. (2016). Questionable research practices revisited. *Social Psychological and Personality Science, 7,* 45–52.

Finkel, E. J., Eastwick, P. W., & Reis, H. T. (2015). Best research practices in psychology: Illustrating epistemological and pragmatic considerations with the case of relationship science. *Journal of Personality and Social Psychology, 108,* 275–297.

Finkel, E. J., Eastwick, P. W., & Reis, H. T. (2017). Replicability and other features of a high-quality science: Toward a balanced and empirical approach. *Journal of Personality and Social Psychology, 113,* 244–253.

Fiske, A. P., Kitayama, S., Markus, H. R., & Nisbett, R. E. (1998). The cultural matrix of social psychology. In D. T. Gilbert, S. T. Fiske, & G. Lindzey (Eds.), *The handbook of social psychology,* (4th ed., Vol. 2, pp. 915–981). New York, NY: McGraw-Hill.

Fiske, S. T. (1992). Thinking is for doing: Portraits of social cognition from Daguerreotype to laserphoto. *Journal of Personality and Social Psychology, 63,* 877–889.

Franzoi, S. L. (2007). History of social psychology. In R. F. Baumeister & K. D. Vohs (Eds.), *Encyclopedia of social psychology* (Vol. 1, pp. 431–439). Thousand Oaks, CA: SAGE.

Funder, D. C. (1987). Errors and mistakes: Evaluating the accuracy of social judgment. *Psychological Bulletin, 101,* 75–90.

Funder, D. C. (2006). Towards a resolution of the personality triad: Persons, situations and behaviors. *Journal of Research in Personality, 40,* 21–34.

Gawronski, B., & De Houwer, J. (2014). Implicit measures in personality and social psychology. In H. T. Reis & C. Judd (Eds.) Handbook of research methods in social psychology (pp. 283–310). New York, NY: Cambridge University Press.

Gendron, M., & Barrett, L. F. (2009). Reconstructing the past: A century of ideas about emotion in psychology. *Emotion Review, 1,* 316–339.

Gergen, K. J. (1973). Social psychology as history. *Journal of Personality and Social Psychology, 26,* 309–320.

Gergen, K. J. (2001). Psychological science in a postmodern context. *American Psychologist, 56,* 803–813.

Gilbert, D. T., King, G., Pettigrew, S., & Wilson, T. D. (2016). Comment on "Estimating the reproducibility of psychological science." *Science, 351,* 1037–1037.

Goethals, G. R. (2003). A century of social psychology: Individuals, ideas, and investigations. In M. A. Hogg & J. Cooper (Eds.), *The SAGE handbook of social psychology* (pp. 3–23). Thousand Oaks, CA: SAGE.

Gollwitzer, P. M., & Kinney, R. F. (1989). Effects of deliberative and implemental mind-sets on illusion of control. *Journal of Personality and Social Psychology, 56,* 531–542.

Gosling, S. D., Vazire, S., Srivastava, S., & John, O. P. (2004). Should we trust web-based studies? A comparative analysis of six preconceptions about Internet questionnaires. *American Psychologist, 59,* 93–104.

Greenberg, J., Pyszczynski, T., & Solomon, S. (1986). The causes and consequences of a need for self-esteem: A terror management theory. In R. F. Baumeister (Ed.), *Public self and private self* (pp. 189–212). New York, NY: Springer-Verlag.

Greenwald, A. G. (1976). An editorial. *Journal of Personality and Social Psychology, 33,* 1–7.

Greenwood, J. D. (2004). *The disappearance of the social in American social psychology.* New York, NY: Cambridge University Press.

Hagger, M. S., Chatzisarantis, N. L., Alberts, H., Anggono, C. O., Batailler, C., Birt, A. R., . . . & Calvillo, D. P. (2016). A multilab preregistered replication of the ego-depletion effect. *Perspectives on Psychological Science, 11,* 546–573.

Hastorf, A., & Cantril, H. (1954). They saw a game: A case study. *Journal of Abnormal and Social Psychology, 49,* 129–134.

Heider, F. (1958). *The psychology of interpersonal relations.* New York, NY: Wiley.

Higgins, E. T. (1987). Self-discrepancy: A theory relating self and affect. *Psychological Review, 94,* 319–340.

Higgins, E. T. (2012). Motivation science in social psychology: A tale of two histories. In A. W. Kruglanski & W. Stroebe (Eds.), *Handbook of the history of social psychology* (pp. 199–218). New York, NY: Psychology Press.

Hinde, R. A. (1997). *Relationships: A dialectical perspective.* East Sussex, England: Psychology Press.

Hollander, E. P. (1968). The society of experimental social psychology: An historical note. *Journal of Personality and Social Psychology, 9,* 280–282.

Homans, G. C. (1950). *The human group.* New York, NY: Harcourt, Brace.

Ioannidis, J. P. (2005). Why most published research findings are false. *PLoS Medicine, 2*(8), e124.

Jahoda, G. (2007). *A history of social psychology: From the eighteenth-century Enlightenment to the Second World War.* New York, NY: Cambridge University Press.

John, L. K., Loewenstein, G., & Prelec, D. (2012). Measuring the prevalence of questionable research practices with incentives for truth telling. *Psychological Science, 23,* 524–532.

Jones, E. E. (1985). Major developments in social psychology during the past five decades. In G. Lindzey & E. Aronson (Eds.), *The handbook of social psychology,* (3rd ed., Vol. 1, pp. 47–107). New York, NY: Random House.

Jones, E. E. (1998). Major developments in social psychology during the past five decades. In G. Lindzey & E. Aronson (Eds.), *The handbook of social psychology,* (4th ed., Vol. 1, pp. 3–57). New York, NY: Random House.

Jones, E. E., & Davis, K. E. (1965). From acts to dispositions: The attribution process in person perception. In L. Berkowitz (Ed.), *Advances in experimental social psychology* (Vol. 2, pp. 219–266). New York, NY: Academic Press.

Jost, J. T. (2004). A perspectivist looks at the past, present and (perhaps) the future of intergroup relations: A quixotic defense of system justification theory. In J. T. Jost, M. R. Banaji, & D. Prentice (Eds.), *Perspectivism in social psychology: The yin and yang of scientific progress* (pp. 215–230). Washington, DC: APA.

Kahneman, D., & Tversky, A. (1973). On the psychology of prediction. *Psychological Review, 80,* 237–251.

Katz, D. (1965). Editorial. *Journal of Personality and Social Psychology, 1,* 1–2.

Katz, D., & Braley, K. W. (1933). Racial stereotypes of 100 college students. *Journal of Abnormal and Social Psychology, 28,* 280–290.

Kelley, H. H. (1967). Attribution theory in social psychology. In D. Levine (Ed.), *Nebraska Symposium on Motivation* (Vol. 15, pp. 192–238). Lincoln, NE: University of Nebraska Press.

Kelley, H. H., Holmes, J. G., Kerr, N. L., Reis, H. T., Rusbult, C. E., & Van Lange, P. A. M. (2003). *An atlas of interpersonal situations.* New York, NY: Cambridge University Press.

Kelley, H. H., & Thibaut, J. W. (1978). *Interpersonal relations: A theory of interdependence.* New York, NY: Wiley.

Kenny, D. A. (1994). *Interpersonal perception: A social relations analysis.* New York, NY: Guilford.

Kerr, N. L. (1998). HARKing: Hypothesizing after the results are known. *Personality and Social Psychology Review, 2,* 196–217.

Klein, R. A., Ratliff, K. A., Vianello, M., Adams, R. B., Jr., Bahník, S., Bernstein, M. J., . . . Nosek, B. A. (2014). Investigating variation in replicability. *Social Psychology, 45,* 142–152.

Kline, R. B. (2004). *Beyond significance testing: Reforming data analysis methods in behavioral research.* Washington, DC: APA.

Kruglanski, A. W., & Stroebe, W. (Eds.) (2012). *Handbook of the history of social psychology.* New York, NY: Psychology Press.

Kuhn, T. S. (1962). *The structure of scientific revolutions.* Chicago, IL: University of Chicago Press.

LaPiere, R. T. (1934). Attitudes versus actions. *Social Forces, 13,* 230–237.

Latané, B., & Darley, J. (1970). *The unresponsive bystander: Why doesn't he help?* New York, NY: Appleton-Century-Crofts.

LeBel, E. P., Berger, D., Campbell, L., & Loving, T. J. (2017). Falsifiability is not optional. *Journal of Personality and Social Psychology, 113,* 254–261.

LeBel, E. P., Campbell, L., & Loving, T. J. (2017). Benefits of open and high-powered research outweigh costs. *Journal of Personality and Social Psychology, 117,* 230–243.

Levine, J. M., & Moreland, R. L. (2012). A history of small group research. In A. W. Kruglanski & W. Stroebe (Eds.), *Handbook of the history of social psychology* (pp. 383–405). New York, NY: Psychology Press.

Lewin, K. (1943). Forces behind food habits and methods of change. *Bulletin of the National Research Council and National Academy of Sciences, 108,* 35–65.

Lewin, K. (1951). *Field theory in social science.* New York, NY: Harper.

Maniaci, M. R., & Rogge, R. D. (2014a). Caring about carelessness: Participant inattention and its effects on research. *Journal of Research in Personality, 48,* 61–83.

Maniaci, M. R. & Rogge, R. D. (2014b). Conducting research on the Internet. In H. T. Reis & C. M. Judd (Eds.), *Handbook of research methods in social psychology* (2nd ed., pp. 443–470). New York, NY: Cambridge University Press.

Manstead, A. S. R. (2012). A history of affect and emotion research in social psychology. In A. W. Kruglanski & W. Stroebe (Eds.), *Handbook of the history of social psychology* (pp. 177–198). New York, NY: Psychology Press.

McDougall, W. (1908). *Introduction to social psychology.* Boston, MA: Luce.

McGaha, A., & Korn, J. H. (1995). The emergence of interest in the ethics of psychological research with humans. *Ethics and Behavior, 5,* 147–159.

McGrath, J. E. (1981). Dilemmatics: The study of research choices and dilemmas. *American Behavioral Scientist, 25,* 179–210.

McGuire, W. J. (1973). The yin and yang of progress in social psychology: Seven koan. *Journal of Personality and Social Psychology, 26,* 446–456.

McGuire, W. J. (1997). Creative hypothesis generating in psychology: Some useful heuristics. *Annual Review of Psychology, 48,* 1–30.

McMartin, C., & Winston, A. S. (2000). The rhetoric of experimental social psychology, 1930–1960: From caution to enthusiasm. *Journal of the History of the Behavioral Sciences, 36,* 349–364.

Mead G. H. (1934). *Mind, self, and society.* Chicago, IL: University of Chicago Press.

Milgram, S. (1963). Behavioral study of obedience. *Journal of Abnormal and Social Psychology, 67,* 371–378.

Milgram, S. (1965). Some conditions of obedience and disobedience to authority. *Human Relations, 18,* 57–76.

Milgram, S. (1974). *Obedience to authority.* New York, NY: Harper & Row.

Miller, J. G. (1984). Culture and the development of everyday social explanation. *Journal of Personality and Social Psychology, 46,* 961–978

Mischel, W. (1968). *Personality and assessment.* New York, NY: Wiley.

Mischel, W. (2006). Bridges toward a cumulative psychological science. In P. A. M. Van Lange (Ed.), *Bridging social psychology* (pp. 437–446). Mahwah, NJ: Erlbaum.

Mischel, W., & Shoda, Y. (1995). A cognitive-affective system theory of personality: reconceptualizing situations, dispositions, dynamics, and invariance in personality structure. *Psychological Review, 102,* 246–268.

Moreland, R. L., Hogg. M. A., & Hains, S. C. (1994). Back to the future: Social psychological research on groups. *Journal of Experimental Social Psychology, 30,* 527–555.

Motyl, M., Demos, A. P., Carsel, T. S., Hanson, B. E., Melton, Z. J., Mueller, A. B., . . . Skitka, L. J. (2017). The state of social and personality science: Rotten to the core, not so bad, getting better, or getting worse? *Journal of Personality and Social Psychology, 113,* 34–58.

Munafò, M. R., Nosek, B. A., Bishop, D. V. M., Button, K. S., Chambers, C. D., Percie du Sert, N., . . . Ioannidis, J. P. A. (2017). A manifesto for reproducible science. *Nature Human Behaviour, 1,* 0021.

Murray, H. A. (1938). *Explorations in personality.* New York, NY: Oxford University Press.

Newcomb, T. M. (1943). *Personality and social change: Attitude formation in a student community.* New York, NY: Holt, Rinehart and Winston.

Newcomb, T. M. (1961). *The acquaintance process.* New York, NY: Holt, Rinehart, and Winston.

Newton, I. (1676). Letter to Robert Hooke. Retrieved from http://en.wikiquote.org/wiki/Isaac_Newton

Nisbett, R. E., & Ross, L. (1980). *Human inference: Strategies and shortcomings of social judgment.* Englewood Cliffs, NJ: Prentice-Hall.

North, M. S., & Fiske, S. T. (2012). A history of social cognition. In A. W. Kruglanski & W. Stroebe (Eds.), *Handbook of the history of social psychology* (pp. 81–99). New York, NY: Psychology Press.

Nosek, B. A., Spies, J. R., & Motyl, M. (2012). Scientific utopia: II. Restructuring incentives and practices to promote truth over publishability. *Perspectives on Psychological Science, 7,* 615–631.

Open Science Collaboration. (2015). Estimating the reproducibility of psychological science. *Science, 349*(6251), aac4716.

Ostrom, T. M. (1984). The sovereignty of social cognition. In R. S. Wyer Jr. & T. K. Srull (Eds.), *Handbook of social cognition* (Vol. 1, pp. 1–38). Hillsdale, NJ: Erlbaum.

Ostrom, T. M. (1989). Three catechisms for social memory. In P. R. Solomon, G. R. Goethals, C. M. Kelley, & B. R. Stephens (Eds.), *Memory: Interdisciplinary approaches* (pp. 201–210). New York, NY: Springer-Verlag.

Park, J. H. (2007). Persistent misunderstandings of inclusive fitness and kin selection: Their ubiquitous appearance in social psychology textbooks. *Evolutionary Psychology, 5,* 860–873.

Petty, R. E., & Cacioppo, J. T. (1986). The elaboration likelihood model of persuasion. In L. Berkowitz (Ed.), *Advances in experimental social psychology* (Vol. 19, pp. 123–205). New York, NY: Academic Press.

Prince, M., & Allport, F. H. (1921). Editorial announcement. *Journal of Abnormal Psychology and Social Psychology, 16,* 1–5.

Rasenberger, J. (2004, February 8). Kitty, 40 years later. *New York Times* (Final ed.), Sect. 14, p. 1, col. 2.

Reis, H. T. (1982). An introduction to the use of structural equations: Prospects and problems. In L. Wheeler (Ed.), *Review of Personality and Social Psychology* (Vol. 3, pp. 255–287). Thousand Oaks, CA: SAGE.

Reis, H. T. (2008). Reinvigorating the concept of situation in social psychology. *Personality and Social Psychology Review, 12,* 311–329.

Reis, H. T. (2012). A brief history of relationship research in social psychology. In A. W. Kruglanski & W. Stroebe (Eds.), *Handbook of the history of social psychology* (pp. 363–382). New York, NY: Psychology Press.

Reis, H. T., & Gosling, S. D. (2009). Social psychological methods outside the laboratory. In D. Gilbert, S. Fiske, & G. Lindzey (Eds.), *Handbook of social psychology* (5th ed., pp. 82–114). New York: Oxford University Press.

Reis, H. T., & Lee, K. Y. (2016). Promise, peril, and perspective: Addressing concerns about reproducibility in social-personality psychology. *Journal of Experimental Social Psychology, 66,* 148–152.

Reis, H. T., & Stiller, J. (1992). Publication Trends in JPSP: A three-decade review. *Personality and Social Psychology Bulletin, 18,* 465–472.

Rosenberg, M. J. (1965). When dissonance fails: On eliminating evaluation apprehension from attitude measurement. *Journal of Personality and Social Psychology, 1,* 28–43.

Rosenthal, R. (1979). The file drawer problem and tolerance for null results. *Psychological Bulletin, 86,* 638–641.

Ross, E. A. (1908). *Social psychology.* New York, NY: McMillan.

Ross, L., & Nisbett, R. E. (1991). *The person and the situation: Perspectives of social psychology.* Philadelphia, PA: Temple University Press.

Ross, L., Ward, A., & Lepper, M. R. (2009). A history of social psychology. In D. Gilbert, S. Fiske, & G. Lindzey (Eds.), *Handbook of social psychology* (5th ed., Vol. 1, pp. 3–50). New York, NY: Oxford University Press.

Schachter, S., & Singer, J. (1962). Cognitive, social, and physiological determinants of emotional state. *Psychological Review, 69,* 379–399.

Sedikides, C., & Strube, M. J. (1997). Self-evaluation: To thine own self be good, to thine own self be sure, to thine own self be true, and to thine own self be better. In M. P. Zanna (Ed.), *Advances in experimental social psychology* (Vol. 29, pp. 209–269). New York, NY: Academic Press.

Sherif, M. (1936). *The psychology of social norms.* New York, NY: Harper Bros.

Simmons, J. P., Nelson, L. D., & Simonsohn, U. (2011). False–positive psychology: Undisclosed flexibility in data collection and analysis allows presenting anything as significant. *Psychological Science, 22,* 1359–1366.

Steele, C. M. (1988). The psychology of self-affirmation: Sustaining the integrity of the self. In L. Berkowitz (Ed.), *Advances in experimental social psychology.* Vol. 21, *Social psychological studies of the self: Perspectives and programs* (pp. 261–302). San Diego, CA: Academic Press.

Sternberg, R. J. (2017). Types of generalization: Introduction to the special section of *Perspectives on Psychological Science* on cultural psychology. *Perspectives on Psychological Science, 12,* 757–761.

Stroebe, W. (2016). Are most published social psychological findings false? *Journal of Experimental Social Psychology, 66,* 134–144.

Taylor, S. E. (1998). The social being in social psychology. In D. T. Gilbert, S. T. Fiske, & G. Lindzey (Eds.), *The handbook of social psychology,* (4th ed., Vol. 1, pp. 58–95). New York, NY: McGraw-Hill.

Taylor, S. E. (2004). Preparing for social psychology's future. *Journal of Experimental Social Psychology, 40,* 139–141.

Thibaut, J. W., & Kelley, H. H. (1959). *The social psychology of groups.* New York, NY: Wiley.

Triplett, N. (1898). The dynamogenic factors in pacemaking and competition. *American Journal of Psychology, 9,* 507–533.

Van Lange, P. A. M. (Ed.). (2006). *Bridging social psychology.* Mahwah, NJ: Erlbaum.

Wallach, M. A., Kogan, N., & Bem, D. J. (1962). Group influence on individual risk taking. *Journal of Abnormal and Social Psychology, 65,* 75–86.

Wheeler, L., & Reis, H. T. (1991). Self-recording of everyday life events: Origins, types, and uses. *Journal of Personality, 59,* 339–354.

Winter, L., & Uleman, J. S. (1984). When are social judgments made? Evidence for the spontaneousness of trait inferences. *Journal of Personality and Social Psychology, 47,* 237–252.

Wittenbaum, G. M., & Moreland, R. L. (2008). Small-group research in social psychology: Topics and trends over time. *Social and Personality Psychology Compass, 2,* 187–203.

Wood, D., & Furr, R. M. (2016). The correlates of similarity estimates are often misleadingly positive: The nature and scope of the problem, and some solutions. *Personality and Social Psychology Review, 20,* 79–99.

Wundt, W. (1916). *Elements of folk psychology: Outlines of a psychological history of the development of mankind.* London, England: Allan & Unwin.

Zajonc, R. B. (1998). Emotions. In D. T. Gilbert, S. T. Fiske, & G. Lindzey (Eds.), *The handbook of social psychology,* (4th ed., Vol. 2, pp. 591–632). New York, NY: McGraw-Hill.

Zwaan, R. A., Etz, A., Lucas, R. E., & Donnellan, M. B. (2017). Making replication mainstream. *Brain and Behavioral Sciences, 41,* e120.

Chapter 3

New Developments in Research Methods

Alison Ledgerwood

Our field has witnessed a recent surge of attention to questions about how researchers can maximize the knowledge they get from the research they do (see Chapter 2). This new emphasis has placed psychological science at the forefront of a broad movement to improve methods and practices across scientific disciplines (Begley & Ellis, 2012; Button et al., 2013; Ledgerwood, 2016; McNutt, 2014; Nosek, Spies, & Motyl, 2012; Nyhan, 2015; Vazire, 2017).

In many ways, it makes sense that psychology would spearhead these new meta-scientific and quantitative developments. After all, many of the recently voiced concerns about methods and practices in psychology have been raised before, and repeatedly: Our field has a long and rich history of noting the challenges posed by publication bias, low statistical power, and the failure to distinguish clearly between exploratory and confirmatory analyses (Cohen 1962; de Groot, 2014; Greenwald 1975; Kerr, 1998; Maxwell, 2004; Rosenthal 1979). Until recently, however, although many scholars tended to nod along when such concerns were raised, attempts to address them were somewhat isolated and sporadic. Meanwhile, entrenched reviewer expectations and traditional publishing models created an inertia that limited change.

Yet something new happened over the last decade: The audience interested in listening to and acting on methodological concerns suddenly mushroomed (Simons, 2018). This surge of interest arose partly in response to a confluence of specific papers and events within the field (e.g., Bem, 2011; Simmons, Nelson, & Simohnson, 2011; Tilburg University, 2011; Vul, Harris, Winkielman, & Pashler, 2009). These developments within the field were situated within the broader context of replicability concerns emerging across disciplines ranging from cancer research to neuroscience, and they were galvanized by new communication technologies that kept conversations about methods and practices front and center (Fanelli, 2018; Ledgerwood, 2014; Spellman, 2015). The resulting widespread interest in understanding and leveraging ideas for improving methods and practices has created a new and exciting opportunity for advancing the rigor and quality of our science.

Many of the methodological and statistical tools and recommendations that have emerged within this new context have focused on two core aims. The first aim is to maximize what researchers can learn from each individual study they conduct. If each study is a brick, then the goal here is to ensure that each brick is solid—a useful and reliable building block (Forscher, 1963; Poincaré, 1902). This chapter will survey several tools that promote this first aim, including distinguishing between exploratory and confirmatory hypotheses and analyses, planning for unexpected results, boosting statistical power, and conducting direct, systematic, and conceptual replications.

The second aim is to maximize what researchers can learn from synthesizing across multiple studies. The goal in this case is to improve the soundness of the structures built from the individual bricks. This chapter will survey new advancements in meta-analytic techniques that promote this second aim, including within-paper meta-analysis and methods for adjusting for publication bias.

Making Good Bricks: How to Maximize What We Learn from Individual Studies

Numerous considerations go into designing an informative study, from thinking broadly about how to balance different scientific goals (Brewer & Crano, 2014; Finkel, Eastwick, & Reis, 2017) to making careful decisions about how to write effective questionnaire items (Bandalos, 2018; Schwarz, 1999) or whether to use an online sample (Ledgerwood, Soderberg, & Sparks, 2017). This chapter focuses on reviewing a subset of these tools that have recently received considerable attention in the field as part of the push to improve methods and practices in psychological science.

Exploratory and Confirmatory Predictions and Analyses

One set of issues that has received considerable attention in recent years revolves around the importance of clearly and transparently distinguishing between exploratory and confirmatory aspects of a study. One of these issues stems from the goal of properly testing theories: If you want to *test* a theoretical prediction (e.g., "Downward social comparison improves affect"), the prediction must be constructed independently from data that will be used to test that prediction (Mayo, 1991). When researchers portray a post-hoc *explanation* for a study's results as a theoretical *prediction* that they made before seeing those results (often called "HARKing," or Hypothesizing After Results are Known), it leads readers to mistakenly infer that data used to inform a theory were actually used to test the theory, when no such test has yet occurred (Kerr, 1998; Rubin, 2007).[1] Blurring the distinction between exploration and confirmation with respect to theory testing hinders scientific progress because it undermines our ability to accurately assess the extent to which various theories have been tested.

Another of these issues stems from the goal of controlling Type I error (i.e., the likelihood that you see a significant result in your data when in fact it is just chance fluctuation). If you want to conduct an analysis with a specific Type I error rate (most commonly, 0.05), decisions about how to construct the data set and analyze the data must be made independently from the data themselves (Gelman & Loken, 2014). When researchers do not clearly and transparently label which of these decisions were made before versus after knowing something about the data in question, it can lead to an unknown (and sometimes very high) degree of Type I error inflation (Mills, 1993; Simmons, Nelson, & Simonsohn, 2011). Blurring the distinction between exploration and confirmation with respect to data analytic decisions hinders scientific progress because it undermines our ability to accurately calibrate our confidence in a particular study's results.

Thus, when planning a new study, it is important to make a conscious choice about whether you want it to be exploratory or confirmatory in terms of its (a) predictions and/or (b) analyses (see Box 3.1). First, you must ask yourself: Is my goal in conducting this study to test a theoretical prediction? If so, then the data cannot influence the theoretical prediction that you choose to make. Second, you must ask yourself: Do

BOX 3.1 A Study Can Be Exploratory or Confirmatory in Terms of Its Predictions as well as in Terms of Its Analyses.

	Exploratory research question (Information gathering, theory building)	Confirmatory hypothesis (theory testing; involves a directional, a priori prediction)
Exploratory analyses (data-dependent researcher decisions)	Question: Does X affect Y? Approach: Explore results using data-dependent analyses.	Prediction(s): Theory 1 predicts that X will increase Y, whereas Theory 2 predicts that X will decrease Y. Approach: Explore results using data-dependent analyses.
Confirmatory analyses (data-independent researcher decisions)	Question: Does X affect Y? Approach: Preanalysis plan that specifies the exact manipulation, measure construction, and analysis.	Prediction(s): Theory 1 predicts that X will increase Y, whereas Theory 2 predicts that X will decrease Y. Approach: Preanalysis plan that specifies the exact manipulation, measure construction, and analysis.

I want to know my precise Type I error rate (which can enable greater confidence in a study's results)? If so, then the data cannot influence the decisions you make about data set construction and analysis. Note that there are good reasons to answer "no" as well as "yes" to either or both of these questions, and many studies have a combination of exploratory and confirmatory elements.

For example, imagine a researcher who wants to conduct a study on framing. One goal of her study might be to test a theory-derived prediction that a particular framing manipulation will influence participants' attitudes. If she is also able to foresee the decisions she will have to make about data analysis, she may want to plan these analytic decisions ahead of time (so that the results of these data-independent analyses can provide stronger evidence testing the prediction). This part of her study would be captured by the bottom right quadrant of Box 3.1 (directional predictions, data-independent analyses). Meanwhile, the researcher might have an additional, exploratory question she wants to ask in this study that isn't based on theory or existing literature—perhaps she wonders whether her framing effect would generalize to a sample of participants with relatively low socioeconomic status (SES). She could plan ahead of time her analytic decisions for testing this research question—a "confirmatory" analysis of an "exploratory" research question (bottom left quadrant of Box 3.1). Alternatively, she might prefer to approach analyses of the low SES sample in a data-dependent manner, given that this new sample might respond to the paradigm or manipulation in unexpected ways (top left quadrant of Box 3.1).

Exploratory Research Questions versus Confirmatory Hypotheses

The first way in which a study can be exploratory or confirmatory is in terms of its predictions. Many research questions—especially those asked early on in a topic area, during the theory generation phase—are exploratory vis-à-vis theory. You might have an intuition or a question about how two variables are related, but there is no strong theory clearly articulating that they should be related in a particular way. In these cases, the results of your study might give you good ideas for building toward a future theory, but they will not provide clear evidence for or against an existing theory or claim.

Once theories are developed and refined, they make specific, testable hypotheses that can be supported or refuted. You might be interested in testing a theory that makes a clear prediction about the relationship between two or more variables. In these cases, the results of your study may support the hypothesis, thereby providing a data point that helps corroborate the theory, or refute the hypothesis, thereby providing a data point that helps falsify the theory. Preregistering a hypothesis is crucial for theory testing because it circumvents the natural human tendency to misremember past events in line with current knowledge and goals (Ross & Wilson, 2000): For example, a researcher who finds an initially unexpected result may easily convince herself that the result actually fits the theory she was trying to test. Such motivated remembering hampers theory testing because it can lead theories to be unfalsifiable to the extent that any result can be reinterpreted as providing evidence in favor of the theory.

How to Preregister a Theoretical Prediction

If you want your study to provide a confirmatory test of a theoretical prediction, it is useful to specify and record that hypothesis ahead of time, before conducting the study (or at least before looking at the data). A *test* of a prediction should be a fair test; that is, it should be possible to specify a set of results that would support the claim being tested as well as a set of results that would refute that claim. For example, the prediction that downward social comparison will enhance perceived ability (derived from social comparison theory; Gerber, Wheeler, & Suls, 2017) would be supported by results showing that perceived ability is higher following a downward (vs. upward) social comparison manipulation and refuted by results showing the opposite. Preregistration provides a useful tool for ensuring that a study provides a fair test of a theoretical claim, enabling researchers to assess whether the theory can predict something new as well as explaining something already known.

Directional hypotheses can be recorded privately (e.g., stored on a shared lab drive) or publicly (e.g., a preregistration uploaded to an online repository or stated in a published theoretical article). Public preregistrations of theoretical predictions may be particularly useful and compelling insofar as accountability to a public audience can (under the right circumstances) help researchers think more carefully and evenhandedly (Lerner & Tetlock, 1999). When *preregistering a theoretical prediction*, it is important to specify clearly the theory or model you are using to derive the prediction. You should also describe the prediction not only in terms of the relevant conceptual variables (e.g., "Psychological distance will increase abstraction") but also in terms of the specific manipulations and measures you will use in this particular study (e.g., "Asking participants to imagine their life in one year vs. one week will increase their scores on the Behavioral Identification Form, a common measure of abstraction"). Note that you can preregister multiple competing predictions to test two or more theories against each other (e.g., "Whereas construal level theory would predict that distance will increase the value placed on abstract features of a product, models of temporal discounting would predict the reverse").

When writing up the results of a study whose results bear on a theory of interest, you should transparently state whether you set and recorded your predictions ahead of time. For example, you might clarify that the results of your study helped you refine a theory (i.e., that you were theory building, not theory testing), or that you preregistered your theoretical hypotheses (i.e., that you were theory testing), or that you did not predict a result but think it seems consistent with a particular theory (i.e., that you are connecting to a theory without seeking to refine or test it). Such clarity and transparency is critical for enabling readers to understand whether to interpret your results as *informing* versus *testing* versus *connecting to* the theory or theories that you discuss in your paper.

Exploratory versus Confirmatory Analyses

The second way in which a study can be exploratory or confirmatory is in terms of its data set construction and analysis decisions. Exploratory in this sense means that your decisions about your data (e.g., when to stop collecting data, how to construct your measures, and how to analyze your results) are to some degree data-dependent—tailored to the particular nuances of your data to help capture potentially interesting patterns. For example, you might run a study, find an ambiguous result (e.g., two condition means differ in a potentially interesting way but $p = 0.11$) and decide to collect another 100 participants to see if the difference disappears (suggesting that it was noise) or becomes clearer (suggesting that it's probably worth following up; Sagarin, Ambler, & Lee, 2014). Or, you might explore a correlation table and notice that one variable positively (and perhaps nonsignificantly) predicts several items that could potentially tap a common construct; you might then collapse those related items together in a single measure and find a stronger relation between the predictor and the new aggregate measure, suggesting a fruitful direction for further research (Ghiselli, Campbell, & Zedeck, 1981). Or, you might explore the effect of a failed manipulation on a number of auxiliary measures to try to gain insight into what went wrong and how you could design a better manipulation in the future (e.g., if telling student participants that a policy will affect their classmates failed to influence the perceived relevance of the policy, you might explore whether participants reported liking and caring about their classmates).

In exploratory analyses, then, the point is to learn from suggestive patterns in the data rather than to use inferential statistics for the purpose of drawing strong conclusions based on p-values. Purely exploratory research can be enormously generative, especially in the first phases of a research program when venturing into new scientific territory.

In contrast, confirmatory analyses are data-independent—planned ahead of time, before knowing anything about how the variables in your data set are related to each other. If you are interested in being able to attach a high level of confidence to a particular statistical result (e.g., you want to be able to conclude that your experimental manipulation influenced your key dependent measure of interest or that two groups differ in their level of a particular individual difference measure), it is important to set and record the analysis plan that you will use to test this particular finding ahead of time. There are two simple reasons for this.

First, your Type I error rate increases to the extent that you look for a given result in a variety of different ways. For instance, if you test one correlation and set your alpha at 0.05, you have a 5% chance of incorrectly concluding that there is an association between those two variables in the population when in fact none exists. But of course, if you test 10 different correlations, your chance of erroneously detecting an association when none exists between at least one pair of variables increases substantially. There are many other forms of flexible testing that can increase Type I error as well—for example, testing an effect before and after excluding a subset of participants from the analysis, testing an effect with and without a variety of covariates included in the model, or testing an effect on several different outcome measures (Gelman & Loken, 2014; Kaplan & Irvin, 2015; MacCallum, Roznowski, & Necowitz, 1992; Sagarin et al., 2014; Simmons et al., 2011). In reality, knowing anything about your data can produce flexible testing by subtly influencing the kinds of tests you think to run (e.g., noticing that one condition mean is higher than three others might lead you to think to run a complex contrast; knowing that two variables are correlated in a large dataset might lead you to think of testing the correlation between a pair of related variables). If you want to be able to interpret a small p-value (e.g., $p = 0.02$) as relatively strong evidence for your effect, you need to know that you have not unintentionally inflated your Type I error rate by testing your effect in multiple ways or by tailoring the test you choose to run to what the data happen to look like (de Groot, 2014). In some cases, you can account for data-dependent flexibility (often called "researcher degrees of freedom"; Simmons et al., 2011) by adjusting your p-value, as in the case of optional stopping (Sagarin et al., 2014) or post-hoc adjustments for multiple comparisons (Welkowitz, Cohen, & Lea, 2012); of course, such adjustments require that you know exactly which analyses were data-dependent. In many contexts, then, setting an analysis plan can be a useful tool: It enables researchers to take a statistical result at face value in terms of the strength of evidence it provides for a particular finding (Nosek, Ebersole, DeHaven, & Mellor, 2018).

Second, analysis plans enable scientists to circumvent human biases that can otherwise creep into the data analysis and inference process. As noted earlier, the human mind tends to be biased in how it processes and remembers information, especially when a person is motivated to reach a particular conclusion (Chaiken & Ledgerwood, 2011; Kunda, 1990; Nosek, Spies, & Motyl, 2012). Thus, once you notice that an effect is significant when you analyze the data one way but not another way, your own mind can easily convince you that whichever test "worked" was the most appropriate test—perhaps even the test you intended to run all along. Recording a plan ahead of time allows you to clearly demarcate for yourself which analyses you planned and which were data-dependent, thus enabling you to accurately distinguish between findings that came from confirmatory versus exploratory analyses.

How to Preregister a Preanalysis Plan

There is no single correct way to record a preanalysis plan, but a preanalysis plan can only help you meet the goals described in the previous section if you specify your data-analytic choices (a) in enough detail that they effectively constrain any foreseeable researcher degrees of freedom available in your study and (b) with enough clarity that a reviewer or reader can easily compare what you planned to do (as recorded in your preanalysis plan) with what you actually did (as described in your paper). It is therefore crucial to think carefully about your options and to select one that works well for your research context.

Preanalysis plans can be private or public and range from very basic to very detailed. For instance, one research team might decide to use an independent registry (e.g., AsPredicted.org, opensscienceframework. org, socialscienceregistry.org) to publicly preregister a detailed preanalysis plan for each study they conduct.[2] Another team might develop an internal lab workflow in which they always record certain core elements of a study ahead of time (e.g., planned total sample size, planned exclusion criteria, and any planned confirmatory statistical tests) so that they can easily distinguish for themselves between exploratory and confirmatory findings. The most useful format and content of a preanalysis plan will vary across research teams and projects, depending on the type of research, the complexity of the analyses, and the norms of a given field (Casey, Glennester, & Miguel., 2011). Note that if you want to maximize transparency, it will be useful to (a) post your preanalysis plan in a public repository (as opposed to keeping it private) and (b) make sure that it is easy for others to compare what you planned to do with what you actually did. Note too that a preanalysis plan does not automatically prevent Type I error inflation: For example, one could record ahead of time a plan to examine all main effects and interactions in a three-way analysis of variance (ANOVA), but without a plan to adjust for multiple comparisons, the Type I error rate for this preregistered ANOVA would be quite high (Cramer et al., 2016).

The first time you create a preanalysis plan, consider starting with something basic that you feel comfortable with and build from there. Your main goals are to ensure that you will be able to accurately distinguish between exploratory and confirmatory analyses and that any decisions you make for your confirmatory analyses are independent of the data themselves. Box 3.2 lists common examples of content that a researcher might specify in a preanalysis plan. Labs may also find it helpful to register their "standard operating procedures" for common decisions that are relevant across many of the studies that the lab tends to run (e.g., standard procedures for using attention checks on Amazon Mechanical Turk [MTurk] or for handling outliers in reaction time data; see Lin & Green, 2016).

Gray Areas in Distinguishing between Exploratory and Confirmatory Analyses

The distinction between exploratory and confirmatory analyses is simple in the abstract (i.e., are all researcher decisions data-independent?) but often complex and nuanced in practice. Most research involves a combination of planned and exploratory analyses; you might record a preanalysis plan for a primary analysis and then also conduct a number of unplanned analyses to explore what else you can learn from

---

BOX 3.2 Common Content for a Preanalysis Plan

Consider Specifying	Example
Planned sample size and stopping rule	Target total $N = 100$. We will collect data until MTurk indicates that we have completed surveys from 100 participants.
Inclusion criteria	MTurkers aged 18 and up will be allowed to participate.
Exclusion criteria	Participants will be excluded if they respond incorrectly to the attention check at the beginning of the study (i.e., if they do not select "Blue" when asked what color appears in the blue square). Updated 10/20/2017 after downloading the data but before running any analyses: We noticed that three participants completed the study in under 3 minutes whereas the average participant took 18 minutes, so we decided to exclude these three participants.
Manipulation(s) and conditions	Group identity symbol (two within-subjects conditions): Control (pictures of alien creatures grouped around a palm tree) vs. symbol (pictures of alien creatures grouped around a flag)
Predictor(s) and how they will be constructed	N/A
Dependent measure(s) and how they will be constructed	Primary/Focal DV: Perceived group entitativity (average of the six-item scale for each picture of alien creatures) Additional DV: Perceived threat (average of the two-item scale for each picture of alien creatures)
Any planned covariates	N/A
Planned statistical tests involving specific operational variables	Primary/Focal analysis: Paired t-test (two-tailed) examining the effect of condition on average perceived entitativity for control pictures vs. symbol pictures. Additional analysis: Paired t-test (two-tailed) examining the effect of condition on average perceived threat for control pictures vs. symbol pictures.
Any planned follow-up or subgroup analyses	No
Any plan for Type I error control (e.g., for multiple comparisons)	No

Notes. Notice that preanalysis plans must be specific to be useful: They must clearly constrain potential researcher degrees of freedom. For example, writing "participants have to be paying attention" does not clearly constrain flexibility in data analysis because there are multiple ways to decide whether participants were paying attention (e.g., passing a particular attention check vs. how long participants spent completing the survey vs. whether a participant clicked the same number for every item on a survey). DV = dependent variable.

---

your data set. Exploratory analyses can range from highly principled and still fairly constrained (e.g., deciding to include a single, carefully chosen covariate in one's analysis to boost power after finding a nonsignificant key result; see Wang, Sparks, Gonzales, Hess, & Ledgerwood, 2017) to completely unconstrained (e.g., examining a giant correlation table looking for any potentially interesting correlations pop out). And, planned analyses can turn out to be inappropriate once you fully examine (and explore!) your actual data; for instance, you might plan to run a t-test on the amount participants choose to donate to charity only to find that the actual distribution of this variable is binary rather than continuous. Always check the assumptions underlying your statistical tests and always graph your data (preferably in a way that allows you to see the distribution of the actual data points): You should never blindly follow a preanalysis plan or let it prevent you from also exploring what your actual data look like. Instead, use preanalysis plans to help you (a) think carefully about various data collection and analysis decisions and (b) accurately distinguish and transparently report which of your analyses are data-independent.

Planning for Unexpected Results

Regardless of whether the study you are designing is exploratory or confirmatory in its predictions and its analyses, it is worth thinking carefully about how to maximize what you will learn from any possible pattern of results. For example, you may be designing a study to test the prediction that Manipulation X will increase Measure Y. But what will you learn if you find an unexpected effect in the opposite direction, or no effect at all?

Often, it is possible to design a study so that it pits two interesting predictions against each other—perhaps Theory 1 predicts that X will increase Y, whereas Theory 2 predict the opposite. Such an approach ensures that a difference in either direction will be interesting and informative. It can be helpful to graph or think through the various possible patterns of results you might see in a given study and ask what you would learn from each one. If most patterns of results would not be informative—if they would not lead you to update your beliefs in some way and/or point the way to the next study idea—then you may want to rethink your study design or the way that your variables are operationalized (i.e., manipulated or measured).

It can be more difficult—but just as important—to think about how to make a potential null result informative. One important tool is to maximize the statistical power of your study (see next section), so that a null result is less likely to reflect a Type II error (i.e., a false negative, or failing to detect an effect that is in fact there). Another useful tool is to assess the validity of the manipulation by including a manipulation check, either as the dependent measure in a pilot study or as an additional measure in the main study (van't Veer & Giner-Sorolla, 2016). If Manipulation X affects the manipulation check but not the dependent variable Y, you could reasonably infer that X does not affect Y. If, on the other hand, Manipulation X affects neither the manipulation check nor the dependent variable Y, you could instead infer that you were not successful at manipulating your construct of interest. The inclusion of a manipulation check allows you to pull apart these two possible explanations for a null effect of X on Y (Finkel, 2016). It can also be useful to think about why a particular manipulation might not work in a given sample (e.g., a well-established manipulation of cognitive load in the lab might not work for an online sample if online participants simply write down the long digit string they are asked to remember in the high load condition or if online participants are highly distracted in all conditions; see also Zhou & Fishbach, 2016) and to include exploratory questions that could help assess that potential explanation.

In general, null results are more informative when the manipulations and measures used in a study have been carefully validated. Researches often think about the importance of using well validated measures in their research (although perhaps not as much as they should; for recommendations on best practices for validating measures, see Flake, Pek, & Hehmann, 2017). Ideally, researchers would also attend carefully to the construct validity of their manipulations, either by using previously validated manipulations in their studies or by conducting validation work themselves to ensure that a particular manipulation is successfully influencing only the intended construct of interest. Papers conducting such careful validation work for manipulations of common research constructs will hopefully become more prevalent in the future; arguably, they should be just as highly prized and cited as papers validating widely used measures.

Finally, whereas traditional statistical analyses using the most typical form of null hypothesis significance testing (NHST) make it notoriously difficult for researchers to draw strong inferences from null results, other analytic approaches provide possible solutions. For instance, *equivalence testing* allows researchers to conclude that two group means or two correlations are not meaningfully different from each other (Rogers, Howard, & Vessey, 1993; for concrete instructions, see Lakens, 2017). Meanwhile, Bayesian statistics allow researchers to test carefully specified null and alternative hypotheses (e.g., that a given effect size is $d = 0.00$ vs. $d = 0.30$) and to assess the extent to which the evidence favors one versus the other (Etz, Haaf, Rouder, & Vandekerckhove, 2018).

Maximizing Statistical Power

Although statisticians have long emphasized the importance of power (e.g., Cohen, 1962; Maxwell, 2004; Rossi, 1997), many researchers only recently began appreciating how crucial it is to think about power in a careful way. Boosting statistical power helps to increase the informational value of an individual study, for reasons relating to both the likelihood of a Type II error (i.e., failing to detect a true effect) and the false-positive rate (i.e., the proportion of effects in a set of significant findings that reflect spurious results rather than true effects). Furthermore, thinking carefully about the statistical power of a study—regardless of whether it is low or high—helps you draw better inferences from the results.

Many researchers think about power as being important for avoiding Type II errors: High power makes it more likely that an effect will be detected if it is there. This conceptualization of power can lead researchers to assume that although high power is desirable, low power is problematic only if you *fail* to see an effect. A researcher thinking about power in this way might conclude—understandably, but incorrectly—that if he runs an underpowered study and detects an effect, it represents especially trust-worthy evidence for that effect ("I found it even with low power working against me!").

However, low statistical power also undermines researchers' ability to trust effects when they *do* see them. It turns out that reducing power also reduces the *positive predictive value* (PPV) of a significant finding (Button et al., 2013). PPV is the probability that a statistically significant result reflects a true posi-tive (i.e., a real effect in the population). In other words, the PPV of all of your own findings in a given year would be the likelihood that any given significant effect that you detect in that year is real (i.e., the pro-portion of all of your significant results in that year that are true positives). As the average power of your studies decreases, the number of true positives in your personal pool of significant results also decreases. The dwindling number of true positives means that the probability of any one of your significant results being true goes down.

Another way to think about underpowered studies is that they tend to produce "bouncy" results—effect size estimates will fluctuate more from one study to the next, and p-values will "dance" more dramatically (Cumming, 2009). That is, compared to the more precise and stable estimates provided by highly powered studies (see Ioannidis, 2008; Schönbrodt & Perugini, 2013), the estimates produced by underpowered research will tend to bounce more wildly from one study to the next. They will also tend to bounce more wildly from one subjective researcher decision to the next (e.g., decisions about which items to include in a scale or whether to exclude outliers). Low power therefore reduces the informational value of your results, and it can lead to problems later on when you or other researchers try to replicate your findings (Maxwell, 2004). In fact, when power drops below 50%, the average effect size estimate from significant studies starts to become dramatically inflated (because only the highly overestimated effect sizes will manage to hit sig-nificance), and when power drops below 10%, effect size estimates can actually be in the wrong direction (leading a researcher to conclude, for example, that an intervention manipulation decreased a problem when in fact the opposite is true; see Gelman & Carlin, 2014). Thus, low power reduces your ability to trust your results not only when you fail to see a significant effect but also when you do see one.

Taken together, these issues point to the crucial importance of estimating power when planning a study, so that you can (a) try to boost power when necessary and (b) acknowledge the uncertainty inherent in underpowered studies when achieving high power is not possible.

Estimating Power

To calculate the approximate power of a planned study, you first have to estimate the effect size of interest. That might sound easy in theory, but there are a number of issues that can make it challenging in practice. First, if you are conducting the first study in a brand new line of basic research, you may have no idea what effect size to expect. Second, even if previous studies exist, they may not provide you with a good estimate. Unless sample sizes are very large, effect size estimates tend to fluctuate quite widely from one study to the next—which means that the correlation or mean difference observed in a single previous study or pilot study may be quite far away from the true population effect size. A useful heuristic for social-personality psychologists is that a total sample size of at least $N = 240$ provides a fairly stable estimate of a bivariate correlation or two-group mean difference that approximates the average effect size of $r = 0.21$ observed in social and personality psychology research (see Schönbrodt & Perugini, 2013). That means that the effect size point estimate from a Study 1 with $N = 100$ is probably not a good number to use when calculating power for Study 2 (instead, researchers should use the power-calibrated effect size approach; for a discussion and easy-to-use resources, see McShane & Bockenholt, 2016). Moreover, when combined with publication bias, this fluctuation of estimates from one study to the next means that published studies are likely to overestimate the size of an effect. If each study provides a guess about the true population effect size, then some guesses are too high while some are too low; publication bias effectively truncates that distribution at the low end such that overestimated effect sizes are published while the underestimates that would have balanced them out end up in a file drawer.

Third and relatedly, although meta-analytic estimates of effect sizes can provide much more precise effect size estimates by aggregating across many individual studies, they can also be highly inflated due to publication bias. Such inflation is likely to occur when publication decisions were based on the presence or size of the effect of interest (e.g., in cases where publication decisions are determined by the presence of a single significant effect). Because it is extremely difficult to adjust for publication bias in meta-analysis once the bias has occurred (see later section Building Good Buildings), it is important to think carefully about whether a set of meta-analyzed effects was likely to be influenced by publication bias before assuming the resulting estimate is accurate. If publication bias is likely to be present, researchers may want to use methods for power analysis that help guard against the problem of overestimated effect sizes leading to underpowered subsequent studies; Anderson, Kelley, & Maxwell, 2017; Perugini, Gallucci, & Costantini, 2014). For example, Anderson et al. (2017) provide an R package and simple-to-use Shiny Web applications that help researchers easily calculate sample sizes for planned studies that account for both uncertainty and publication bias in published effect size estimates (see https://designingexperiments.com/shiny-r-web-apps).

Another option in such cases is to identify the smallest effect size of interest (sometimes abbreviated SESOI) and use that effect size in your power calculations—to say, in essence, that you only care about the effect if it is larger than size X. Indeed, this practice of defining a smallest effect size of interest is what researchers do implicitly when they decide to run a study with a particular sample size without conducting a power analysis. For instance, if you decide that a given research question is worth the resources it would take to conduct a two-condition experiment with a total N of 80 participants, you effectively are deciding that you are only interested in the effect if it is at least $d = 0.63$ (the effect size that can be detected with 80% power in a sample this size). It is worth developing an intuition about effect sizes—a Cohen's d of 0.63 is about the size of the difference between men and women in sprinting speed (Thomas & French, 1985), and it is bigger than about 70% of the effects studied in social psychology (based on effect size estimates found in meta-analyses; Lovakov & Agadullina, 2017). If you conduct a power analysis, you can make this kind

---

BOX 3.3 Rules of Thumb for Estimating the Sample Size Needed to Examine a 2×2 Between-Subjects Interaction in Study 2 That Qualifies a Between-Subjects Main Effect Observed in Study 1

Expected interaction type	Required cell size (n) to have same power as Study 1	Required total sample size (N) to have same power as Study 1
Reversal of main effect	Same as n in Study 1	$2 \times N$ in Study 1
Elimination of main effect	$2 \times n$ in Study 1	$4 \times N$ in Study 1
50% attenuation of main effect	$7 \times n$ in Study 1	$14 \times N$ in Study 1

Note. In this example, Study 1 tested a main effect (a two-group experiment) and planned Study 2 will test a potential moderator of this main effect (a 2×2 between-subjects factorial design).

---

of implicit decision process an explicit one, allowing you to consider whether it is worth running the study (maybe not, if you suspect the effect you are interested in may be more subtle than an easy-to-casually-observe effect such as sex differences in sprinting speed), whether you want to spend more resources, and how confident you can be in your conclusions. Alternatively, if you can identify the smallest effect size that would be theoretically or practically meaningful, powering your study to detect such a SESOI increases the ultimate informational value of a null result.

Another important consideration when estimating power is to recognize that the sample size necessary to conduct a well powered test of an interaction is often dramatically larger than the sample size necessary to detect a main effect. G*Power, a commonly used software for power computations, can produce misleading estimates for powering interactions when researchers rely on the kinds of effect size estimates that are typical for main effects (e.g., conventions for "small" and "medium" effect sizes like $d = 0.2$ and $d = 0.5$, or the effect size estimate from a main effect observed in Study 1). Instead, try using the rules of thumb summarized in Box 3.3 (for a full discussion, see Giner-Sorolla, 2018).

Sequential Analysis

Because it is often difficult to estimate accurately the size of an expected effect (especially when conducting initial studies in new lines of research) and because even relatively small variations in expected effect sizes can lead to dramatically different answers about the sample size needed to achieve adequate power, it can be challenging to decide on a target sample size for a new study. Your study could be woefully underpowered if you guess an effect size that is too high, but you would waste substantial resources if you guess too low. In such cases, sequential analyses are a valuable tool that enables you to adequately power your study to detect a potentially small effect size but stop early and conserve resources if the effect turns out to be larger than anticipated (Lakens & Evers, 2014; Proschan, Lan, & Wittes, 2006).

For instance, you might decide that it is worth spending the resources to power your study to detect an effect as small as $d = 0.18$ (the effect size that captures the average tendency for women to be higher in conscientiousness than men [Feingold, 1994]; you would need $n = 486$ men and $n = 486$ women to have 80% power to detect this effect), but that you would rather stop early if at all possible so that you have resources left to run Study 2. Sequential analysis allows you to do this by choosing ahead of time a planned total sample size as well as specific interim analysis points (for a step-by-step guide, see Open Science Network, 2014; for an illustrative example and additional discussion, see https://osf.io/qtufw/ and Lakens, 2014).[3] Whereas unplanned optional stopping inflates Type I error (Sagarin, Ambler, & Lee, 2014), planned optional stopping in a sequential analysis controls Type I error by portioning out the total desired alpha level (often 0.05) across interim and final analyses.

Beyond Sample Size: Other Tools for Boosting Power

Large samples are one route to high power, but they are not the only one, nor necessarily the most efficient in some contexts. Understanding the other factors that affect power can provide you with a toolbox of different strategies for conducting well-powered research. For instance, when they are feasible, within-subjects designs can dramatically boost the power of an experiment, relative to between-subjects designs (Greenwald, 1976; Rivers & Sherman, 2018). Also, when conducting basic research, it may be possible to increase the size of the effect that you are studying (e.g., by using extreme groups or developing a stronger manipulation). Likewise, reducing measurement error by finding or creating more reliable measures of your constructs can substantially boost power, particularly in studies that examine small effects (Ledgerwood & Shrout, 2011; Stanley & Spence, 2014). Furthermore, when designing an experiment, it is worth thinking carefully about a potential covariate that could correlate strongly with the dependent variable. Such a covariate can boost power by soaking up noise in your dependent measure (Wang et al., 2017). For example, a researcher interested in a manipulation that could influence participants' nationalism might decide to include a measure of social dominance orientation at the beginning of her experiment as a preregistered covariate, given that social dominance orientation and nationalism show strong correlations in large samples (Pratto, Sidanius, Stallworth, & Malle, 1994).

Aggregating across small studies can provide another useful tool for boosting statistical power. Researchers limited in the number of participants they can recruit in a particular time frame (e.g., an academic term) or setting (e.g., a public event) might choose to run two or more separate, small studies testing the same effect that, when aggregated, achieve adequate power. Likewise, researchers interested in conducting systematic replications to test the generalizability of an effect across various samples and/or stimuli might wish to conduct a series of smaller studies that vary these elements (rather than a single large study with only one sample and stimulus set) and then meta-analyze the studies to provide a better powered test (and more precise estimate) of the effect. Similarly, researchers who are constrained in their access to participants or research funds can conduct a multilab collaboration in which two or more research teams conduct a study using identical protocols and then meta-analyze the results. Importantly, because each individual study will be underpowered in such cases, researchers should plan to conduct and interpret analyses only at the meta-analytic level.

Discussing Power in a Manuscript

If you conduct a power analysis to determine the target sample size for your study, make sure to record the software you used, the specific effect size you estimated and where the estimate came from, and any other information that you will want to eventually report when writing up the study methods. If you do not conduct a power analysis, you should still consider discussing power in the study manuscript to help readers calibrate their conclusions appropriately (e.g., a null result is not very informative if a study is likely to be underpowered). In such cases, it may be helpful to conduct and report a *sensitivity power analysis*, which calculates the minimum effect size that you were powered to detect given your sample size and a particular level of power (e.g., 80%). It can also be useful to graph the relation between effect size and power given your actual sample size. The goal is to give readers (and yourself!) an intuitive sense of the size of the effect that you could reasonably expect to detect in your study (see Box 3.4 for examples).[4]

BOX 3.4 Examples of How to Discuss Power in the Method Section of a Manuscript

Example 1: A priori power analysis An a priori power analysis in R using the meta-analytic effect size estimate for the correlation between X and Y across all 10 previous studies conducted by our lab ($r = 0.3$) indicated we would need a total sample size of $N = 82$ to achieve 80% power in our new study. Given that we had the resources to collect a larger sample and that we expected we would have to drop a few participants based on our a priori exclusion criteria, we decided to recruit at least 100 participants.

Example 2: Sensitivity analysis We decided to collect data until the end of the semester, which resulted in a total sample size of $N = 140$ ($n = 70$ per condition). A sensitivity power analysis in G*Power indicated that a sample of this size would provide 80% power to detect an effect of Cohen's $d = 0.42$ and 60% power to detect an effect of Cohen's $d = 0.32$. For reference, the estimated median effect size in social psychological research is about $d = 0.38$ (Lovakov & Agadullina, 2017).

Example 3: Estimated power for a range of effect size estimates We set an a priori target sample size of $N = 200$ ($n = 100$ per condition). A recent meta-analysis suggests that the effect of X on Y is in the range of $d = 0.27$ to $d = 0.38$ (Someone & Whosit, 2018, Table 3). Power analyses in G*Power indicated that a sample of $N = 200$ provided 48% power to detect an effect as small as $d = 0.27$ and 76% power to detect an effect as large as $d = 0.38$.

Conducting Programmatic Research: Direct, Systematic, and Conceptual Replications

Increasing the power of a study helps make the results more informative, but at the end of the day, it is still a single study. It can be useful to think of a single study as a data point that can contribute to a cumulative understanding of a phenomenon, to the extent that it is well designed and adequately powered, rather than something that can provide a definitive conclusion in isolation (Braver, Thoemmes, & Rosenthal, 2014; Ledgerwood & Sherman, 2012; Soderberg & Errington, 2018). Obviously, you want each study or data point to be as informative as possible, but you may also want to accumulate multiple data points that can together provide a more substantial contribution to a given research question. When thinking about the best way to construct a package of studies, it is useful to consider how direct, systematic, and conceptual replication could each contribute to your cumulative understanding of a research topic.

Direct replications (sometimes called "close" or "exact" replications) aim to repeat as closely as possible the procedures used in a prior study (Fabrigar & Wegener, 2016; Schmidt, 2009). Direct replications serve to increase confidence in an observed relationship between two or more operationalizations (i.e., the specific manipulations and/or measures used in a previous study). For instance, if exploratory analyses in a first study provide suggestive evidence for a particular pattern of results (e.g., you observed an interesting effect of your manipulation on your dependent measure, but only after an unanticipated change to your preanalysis plan), conducting a direct replication would provide an opportunity to corroborate that pattern in an independent dataset. Suppose that in Study 1, a research team tests whether MTurk participants judge an ambiguous face as more threatening after seeing black versus white faces (Kreiglmeyer & Sherman, 2012). A direct replication would involve the same operationalizations of race (black faces vs. white faces) and threat judgments (responses to an ambiguous face), as well as the same stimuli and population, to assess the robustness of the relation between operationalizations observed in Study 1. In sum, if you wish to increase your confidence in a particular result, direct replication is often a useful next step.

Systematic replications aim to vary presumably incidental aspects of the context in which a result was initially obtained to test the critical assumption that those details are in fact irrelevant to the result (Kantowitz, Roediger, & Elmes, 2014). Systematic replications serve to increase confidence in the generalizability of an observed relation between particular operationalizations. For instance, if a research team found an interesting effect of showing participants black versus white faces on threat judgments in Study 1, they might want to conduct a systematic replication using different stimuli in Study 2, which would allow them to test whether Study 1's results were specific to a particular stimulus set (e.g., the particular black and white faces used in Study 1; Roediger, 2012; Westfall, Judd, & Kenny, 2015). Or, the research team might want to conduct a systematic replication that uses a different cover story and experimenter, allowing them to test the generalizability of the results across different contextual details. If they observe an interesting effect in a sample of students at their own university, they might want to use StudySwap (2018) to systematically replicate the study at a different university or with older participants. An especially useful tool for thinking about and fostering systematic replications is to write a "Constraints on Generality" statement that explicitly articulates the extent to which you expect a set of finding to generalize across different stimuli, samples, and situations (Simons, Shoda, & Lindsay, 2017). Importantly, systematic replications help researchers combat confirmation bias in their research process by pushing them to explicitly consider and test whether variables presumed irrelevant for producing an effect might in fact be relevant. They encourage the question "What shouldn't be important for producing this effect?" rather than only "What should be important?" Systematic replication is therefore often a useful intermediate step between direct and conceptual replication.

Conceptual replications aim to vary the particular operationalizations of a given theoretical construct (i.e., the manipulations and/or measures employed in a particular study) to test whether different operationalizations of the same theoretical construct will produce the same effect. Conceptual replications serve to increase confidence in the meaning of a particular result. If multiple possible operationalizations of the same theoretical variable produce similar patterns of findings, a researcher can be more confident that the results reflect something about the theoretical construct rather than the particular operationalization used to manipulate or assess it (Brewer & Crano, 2014; Cook & Campbell, 1979). For example, if our research team wanted to conduct a conceptual replication of their Study 1 finding that participants judge ambiguous faces as more threatening after seeing black (vs. white) faces, they might change the operationalizations of their conceptual independent and dependent variables by examining whether participants sit further away from a black (vs. white) confederate when waiting late at night in a waiting room. Conceptual replications are therefore useful when researchers are (a) confident about the presence of a particular pattern of results between operational variables but (b) unsure whether those operational variables are really tapping the theoretical constructs of interest. If the theoretical predictions hold up across a range of operationalizations, then researchers can be more confident that they are learning about the underlying concepts and theory rather than a specific instance of an effect (Crandall & Sherman, 2016; Fabrigar & Wegener, 2016).

Regardless of which type of replication you are conducting, it is important to appreciate how widely results can fluctuate from one study to the next due to chance, especially with imperfect measures and small samples (for useful illustrations, see Cumming, 2009; Stanley & Spence, 2014). When conducting a series of studies on a given research question, it is often best to take a cumulative approach that aggregates across studies rather than bean-counting each one in isolation as a "success" or "failure" (Braver et al., 2014; Fabrigar & Wegener, 2016). For instance, suppose you are embarking on a new line of basic research. You conduct a confirmatory (planned) analysis of a particular effect in three independent data sets and find a significant result in one dataset and a nonsignificant result in the other two. The best approach to understanding these data will often be a meta-analytic one that aggregates across the three findings to provide a cumulative understanding of the effect, rather than concluding that one study "succeeded" and the other two "failed." It can be tempting to think that some aspect of the method or sample of the significant study must have led it to "work" better than the other two, but unless the studies are very highly powered, a likely explanation for variability across study results is often chance fluctuation (see also Gelman & Stern, 2006).

It is also important to recognize that the goals served by conducting an independent direct, systematic, or conceptual replication can be served in other ways as well, and the best tool for pursuing a given goal is likely to vary across different research contexts. For instance, the goal to attain high confidence in a given relation between operational variables can be served by conducting a series of smaller, tightly controlled experiments or by conducting one very large and well-powered study in the first place. The goal to increase confidence in the generalizability of a given relation between operational variables can be served by conducting a series of systematic replication studies that use different sets of stimuli, or by including a larger set of stimuli in the original study and treating stimuli as a random factor in the design (Judd, Westfall, & Kenny, 2012). And the goal to increase confidence in the meaning of a particular result can be served by conducting conceptual replications, or by conducting additional analyses in a large data set that help provide converging evidence for an effect across a range of measures, boosting confidence in convergent and divergent validity (Finkel et al., 2015). Choose the tools that work best for addressing your particular goals in your own particular research context.

Open and Transparent Science: Sharing Materials, Data, and Code

Another useful tool for improving the informational value of your research is to make your materials, data, and syntax as easily findable and understandable as possible. Doing so improves the study's informational value in a number of ways, including enabling other researchers to easily use (and cite!) your materials in their own research, enabling readers of your manuscript to better understand the details of your study and the data behind your conclusions, and enabling scholars to find and include your data in a meta-analysis.

When seeking to enhance the openness and transparency of your research, several considerations merit careful attention (for particularly helpful resources, see Levenstein & Lyle, 2018; Meyer, 2018). For example, many kinds of data can in principle be shared with the public, but ethical and legal constraints can arise either due to unintended stumbling blocks (e.g., not using the right language in your consent form and institutional review board application; for how to avoid this problem, see Meyer, 2018) or due to the sensitive or confidential nature of some data (e.g., dyadic data where one person could identify the other based on the partner's responses, identifiable video recordings, etc.; for helpful resources, see Gilmore, Kennedy, & Adolph, 2017; Joel, Eastwick, & Finkel, 2018; Levenstein & Lyle, 2018). Researchers must also decide where to share study information among various options, including personal or institutional websites, in supplementary materials linked to a particular article, in a data repository such as Dryad (https://datadryad.org), or using an open-science service like Open Science Foundation (OSF; https://osf.io/). These options vary in their ability to address different goals you may have, such as maximizing accessibility for various audiences, protecting the privacy of your participants when working with sensitive data, maximizing the likelihood that future meta-analysts or researchers in this topic area will find your study information, and/or streamlining efficiency within your lab.

One especially important issue to consider is whether the information you are sharing will be easily understandable by someone other than you. Uploading a set of files to an online site is easy, but it may not actually be transparent: The information you are trying to share needs to be findable, accessible, interoperable, and reusable by other people (Wilkinson et al., 2016). Are your materials in a file format that can be opened easily by other researchers, or are they saved in a program that few other scholars would have? Are the variables in your data file carefully labeled? Have you included a codebook that clearly explains any information secondary users will need to understand and use the data file? Is your syntax clearly annotated? Levenstein and Lyle (2018) review resources for data management practices that you can incorporate as a standard part of your workflow to enable transparent sharing.

Building Good Buildings: How to Maximize What
We Learn from Research Synthesis

Ultimately, no matter how carefully a study is designed, it is only one study—one data point. In isolation, a single study always has limitations—for instance, it often contains only one possible set of operationalizations, in one particular kind of sample, in one particular kind of context. Research is cumulative; it involves incrementally adding individual studies together to build an increasingly clear picture of a given phenomenon or process. We want each individual study or data point to be as solid as possible, but we need multiple data points (including direct, systematic, and conceptual replications) to start to shed light on a research question.

Integrating or aggregating across findings is therefore an essential part of the research process. To integrate well, we need (a) solid individual data points (b) an unbiased set of data points, and (c) a good way of synthesizing the data points.

The second of these elements may in fact be the most challenging: One of the biggest threats to cumulative research is arguably publication bias (Dickersin, 1990; Fanelli, 2011; Ferguson & Heene, 2012; Sterling, 1959). There is considerable pressure throughout the scientific system (including authors, reviewers, and journal editors) to publish positive results while relegating negative results to a file drawer. Some of this pressure comes from the fact that a null finding is often difficult to interpret—does it reflect a Type II error, a failure of the manipulation to influence the construct of interest, a true null effect (or an effect too small to matter), or something else? Thus, one important strategy for combating publication bias is to design studies that are informative regardless of how the results turn out (see the previous section on planning for unexpected results). But much of the pressure to publish only positive results comes from entrenched biases in the scientific publication system and incentive structure (Fanelli, 2010; Song, Eastwood, Gilbody, Duley, & Sutton, 2000). Moreover, bias against null findings can affect the research and publication process at multiple stages and in different ways (Greenwald, 1975).

Publication bias is therefore extremely difficult to model accurately (McShane, Bockenholt, & Hansen, 2016). Perhaps at a given time point in the field's history, a researcher would be twice as likely to write up a finding if the p-value is significant rather than "marginal," and 10 times as likely to write it up if the finding is "marginal" than if $p > 0.10$. But those values might change depending on whether this is a first study or a third study in a line of work and depending on whether there are other results in the same study that support a given conclusion. Furthermore, the values might change as prevailing norms about research practices change across time. Estimating these relative likelihoods of publication (rather than guessing at them) in any given research area would require a very large number of studies.

The prevalence and complexity of publication bias poses a challenge for cumulative science for two reasons (McShane et al., 2016). First, once publication bias contaminates a literature, it is extraordinarily difficult to figure out (and then to model accurately) how exactly the bias has operated. Second, meta-analytic techniques are very sensitive to the assumptions made by a given model of publication bias. In other words, if a meta-analyst does not use a model of publication bias that accurately captures the way publication bias actually operated on a given set of results, the meta-analytic estimates will often do a poor job of recovering the true population parameters of interest.

There are many things that researchers can do to mitigate the problem of publication bias. For example, meta-analysts can avoid drawing strong conclusions about an overall average effect size, focusing instead on moderator analyses that are less likely to be affected by publication bias in a particular area (e.g., study-level moderators that would not have been considered in publication decisions about individual papers). Likewise, meta-analyses that aggregate ancillary findings (rather than primary findings that would have provided the basis for a decision about whether to publish a given paper) are less likely to be plagued by the problems of publication bias. The remainder of this chapter reviews additional tools that have featured prominently in recent discussions about improving research synthesis.

Within-Paper Meta-Analysis

One way to avoid the problem of publication bias is to meta-analyze all of the studies you have conducted in a given line of research. For example, if you conduct six studies testing a particular effect and find a significant result in four out of the six studies, you could report all of the studies in a manuscript along with a within-paper meta-analysis that aggregates across the individual studies to provide the best estimate of the effect(s) of interest. Such within-paper meta-analyses can help researchers, reviewers, and editors move away from thinking about each individual study in isolation (e.g., "This study worked, but that study didn't") and toward focusing on cumulative, meta-analytic estimates that provide more stable, precise, and useful information about a research question. Increasingly, resources are available that enable researchers to easily conduct within-paper meta-analyses for a range of research designs (including an on-line application that allows researchers to synthesize data across studies with different designs; McShane & Bockenholt, 2017; see also Braver, Thoemmes, & Rosenthal, 2014).[5] When you report a within-paper meta-analysis, you should transparently disclose whether you included all of the studies you conducted to test the research question (and if not, why not), since the informational value of such an approach depends on your ability to fully "empty the file drawer" and include all relevant studies.

Adjusting for Publication Bias in Meta-Analysis: Using Selection Methods to Generate a Range of Plausible Estimates

When you do not have full access to the file drawer (either because you are meta-analyzing other researchers' results or because you do not necessarily remember and have not systematically archived all the studies you have conducted on a given research question), you have to guess how publication bias may have operated on the set of studies you want to meta-analyze. This guess is captured by how you choose to model publication bias. (Note that "publication bias" in the context of meta-analysis means any bias in the set of studies that are *available for and included in* the meta-analysis; this set of studies may include some unpublished studies as well as the published ones.) For example, a classic fixed-effect or random-effects meta-analysis assumes no publication bias has occurred (and therefore gives upwardly biased effect size estimates in the common situation when publication bias does in fact characterize a given set of studies).[6] Hedges (1984) selection method, *p*-curve (Simonsohn, Nelson, & Simmons, 2014), and *p*-uniform (van Assen, van Aert, & Wicherts, 2016) all model a very simple form of publication bias: They assume that all statistically significant results are published (i.e., available for and included in the meta-analysis) and that no statistically nonsignificant results are published (i.e., available for and included in the meta-analysis).[7] Other selection methods model more complex forms of publication bias by assuming that both significant and nonsignificant results are published but with different likelihoods (e.g., Iyengar & Greenhouse, 1988; Vevea & Hedges, 1995)—for example, one might imagine that the likelihood that a statistically nonsignificant result is published would increase as the *p*-value approaches significance (think, for example, of the common terms "marginally significant," "approaching significance," or "trending in the expected direction").

Again, because many factors can influence whether a given result makes it into the published literature and/or the set of unpublished studies to which you have access, any one model of publication bias is unlikely to be accurate; moreover, even small variations in the choice of how to model publication bias can lead a meta-analysis to produce remarkably different estimates of an effect. Thus, if it is likely that a given set of results has been filtered by some form of publication bias, the most fruitful approach to meta-analysis may be to use a variety of selection methods—that is, to model a range of plausible forms of publication bias in order to generate a range of estimates that are consistent with the data under different reasonable assumptions (e.g., Inzlicht, Gervais, & Berkman, 2015; for concrete resources, see McShane et al., 2016). If these estimates vary considerably, it suggests that the results are telling you more about the assumptions of publication bias made by each model than about a true underlying effect. If the estimates tend to be consistent, you can be more confident that the different models are converging on useful information about the true underlying effect.

Conclusion

Over the last decade, psychological science has emerged as a leader in the push to improve research methods and practices across scientific disciplines. Researchers are increasingly implementing the cutting edge methodological and statistical approaches outlined above. Meanwhile, the field continues to identify and hone additional tools for improving scientific methods and practices. By understanding the basic concepts underlying these tools and applying them to your own research, you can both maximize the informational value of each study you conduct as well as the picture that emerges from synthesizing across multiple findings, thereby helping to improve the quality of our cumulative and collaborative science.

Notes

1. Think of it this way: To provide a fair test of a theoretical prediction, a study must be able to either corroborate or falsify the prediction. Once you use a study's results to inform a theoretical prediction, you cannot test that prediction using those same results.
2. Note that public preregistration can have the added benefit of helping address publication bias, or the "file-drawer problem" in which nonsignificant results are never shared with the scientific community (Rosenthal, 1979; Simes, 1986), but only to the extent that (a) the preregistration can be easily found and understood by other researchers and (b) your results and/or data can be easily found as understood as well.
3. Note that because sequential analyses can lead to overestimated effect sizes (Zhang et al., 2012), they are best suited for studies in which researchers are primarily interested in testing whether an effect exists rather than determining a precise estimate of the effect size itself (Lakens, 2014).
4. Do not calculate or report post-hoc (sometimes called "achieved" or "observed") power in a study using the effect size estimate from that same study; it is redundant with the p-value and can be extremely misleading (Hoenig & Heisey, 2001).
5. Online app, example, and tutorials available at https://blakemcshane.shinyapps.io/spmeta
6. When publication bias is present, regular meta-analysis also gives a false impression of effect size homogeneity, leading researchers to incorrectly conclude that effect size heterogeneity is not an issue when in fact it is.
7. These methods also either ignore effect size heterogeneity or assume that the researcher is not interested in generalizing beyond a specific set of studies to make inferences about a larger population (the goal of a

random-effects meta-analysis); when these assumptions are violated, they perform poorly (McShane et al., 2016; van Aert, Wicherts, & van Assen, 2016).

References

Anderson, S. F., Kelley, K., & Maxwell, S. E. (2017). Sample-size planning for more accurate statistical power: A method adjusting sample effect sizes for publication bias and uncertainty. *Psychological Science, 28*, 1547–1562.

Bandalos, D. L. (2018). *Measurement Theory and Applications for the Social Sciences*. New York, NY: Guilford.

Begley, C. G., & Ellis, L. M. (2012). Drug development: Raise standards for preclinical cancer research. *Nature, 483*, 531–533.

Bem, D. J. (2011). Feeling the future: experimental evidence for anomalous retroactive influences on cognition and affect. *Journal of Personality and Social Psychology, 100*, 407–425.

Braver, S. L., Thoemmes, F. J., & Rosenthal, R. (2014). Continuously cumulating meta-analysis and replicability. *Perspectives on Psychological Science, 9*, 333–342.

Brewer, M. B., & Crano, W. D. (2014). Research design and issues of validity. In H. T. Reis & C. Judd (Eds.) *Handbook of research methods in social and personality psychology* (2nd ed., pp. 11–26). New York, NY: Cambridge University Press.

Button, K. S., Ioannidis, J. P., Mokrysz, C., Nosek, B. A., Flint, J., Robinson, E. S., & Munafò, M. R. (2013). Power failure: Why small sample size undermines the reliability of neuroscience. *Nature Reviews Neuroscience, 14*, 365–376.

Casey, K., Glennerster, R., & Miguel, E. (2011). *Reshaping institutions: Evidence on aid impacts using a pre-analysis plan* (No. w17012). Washington, DC: National Bureau of Economic Research.

Chaiken, S., & Ledgerwood, A. (2011). A theory of heuristic and systematic information processing. In Paul A.M. Van Lange, Arie W. Kruglanski, & E. Tory Higgins (Eds.), *Handbook of theories of social psychology* (Vol. 1, pp. 246–166). Los Angeles, CA: SAGE.

Cohen J. (1962). The statistical power of abnormal-social psychological research: A review. *Journal of Abnormal and Social Psychology, 65*, 145–153.

Cook, T. D., & Campbell, D. T. (1979). *Quasi-experimentation: Design and analysis for field settings*. Chicago, IL: Rand McNally.

Cramer, A. O., van Ravenzwaaij, D., Matzke, D., Steingroever, H., Wetzels, R., Grasman, R. P., . . . Wagenmakers, E. J. (2016). Hidden multiplicity in exploratory multiway ANOVA: Prevalence and remedies. *Psychonomic Bulletin & Review, 23*, 640–647.

Crandall, C. S., & Sherman, J. W. (2016). On the scientific superiority of conceptual replications for scientific progress. *Journal of Experimental Social Psychology, 66*, 93–99.

Cumming, G. (2009). Dance of the *p* values. Retrieved from https://www.youtube.com/watch?v=ez4DgdurRPg

de Groot, A. D. (2014). The meaning of "significance" for different types of research (E.-J. Wagenmakers, D. Borsboom, J. Verhagen, R. Kievit, M. Bakker, A. Cramer, . . . H. L. J. Van der Maas, Trans. & Ann.). *Acta Psychologica, 148*, 188–194.

Dickersin, K. (1990). The existence of publication bias and risk factors for its occurrence. *JAMA, 263*, 1385–1389.

Etz, A., Haaf, J. M., Rouder, J. N., & Vandekerckhove, J. (2018). Bayesian inference and testing any hypothesis you can specify. *Advances in Methods and Practices in Psychological Science, 1*, 281–295.

Fabrigar, L. R., & Wegener, D. T. (2016). Conceptualizing and evaluating the replication of research results. *Journal of Experimental Social Psychology, 66*, 68–80.

Fanelli, D. (2010). Do pressures to publish increase scientists' bias? An empirical support from US States Data. *PloS One, 5*, e10271.

Fanelli, D. (2011). Negative results are disappearing from most disciplines and countries. *Scientometrics, 90*, 891–904.

Fanelli, D. (2018). Opinion: Is science really facing a reproducibility crisis, and do we need it to? *Proceedings of the National Academy of Sciences, 115,* 2628–2631.

Feingold, A. (1994). Gender differences in personality: A meta-analysis. *Psychological Bulletin, 116,* 429–456.

Ferguson, C. J., & Heene, M. (2012). A vast graveyard of undead theories: Publication bias and psychological science's aversion to the null. *Perspectives on Psychological Science, 7,* 555–561.

Finkel, E. J. (2016). Reflections on the commitment-forgiveness registered replication report. *Perspectives on Psychological Science, 11,* 765–767.

Finkel, E. J., Eastwick, P. W., & Reis, H. T. (2015). Best research practices in psychology: Illustrating epistemological and pragmatic considerations with the case of relationship science. *Journal of Personality and Social Psychology, 108,* 275–297.

Finkel, E. J., Eastwick, P. W., & Reis, H. T. (2017). Replicability and other features of a high-quality science: Toward a balanced and empirical approach. *Journal of Personality and Social Psychology, 113,* 244–253.

Flake, J. K., Pek, J., & Hehman, E. (2017). Construct validation in social and personality research: Current practice and recommendations. *Social Psychological and Personality Science, 8,* 370–378.

Forscher, B. K. (1963). Chaos in the brickyard. *Science, 142,* 339.

Gelman, A., & Carlin, J. (2014). Beyond power calculations: assessing type S (sign) and type M (magnitude) errors. *Perspectives on Psychological Science, 9,* 641–651.

Gelman, A., & Loken, E. (2014). The statistical crisis in science. *American Scientist, 102,* 460–465.

Gelman, A., & Stern, H. (2006). The difference between "significant" and "not significant" is not itself statistically significant. *American Statistician, 60,* 328–331.

Gerber, J. P., Wheeler, L., & Suls, J. (2017, November 16). A social comparison theory meta-analysis 60+ years on. *Psychological Bulletin, 144,* 177–197.

Ghiselli, E. E., Campbell, J. P., & Zedeck, S. (1981). *Measurement theory for the behavioral sciences: Origin and evolution.* San Francisco, CA: W. H, Freeman.

Gilmore, R. O., Kennedy, J. L., & Adolph, K. E. (2017). Practical solutions for sharing data and materials from psychological research. *Advances in Methods and Practices in Psychological Science, 1,* 121–130.

Giner-Sorolla, 2018. Announcement of new policies for 2018 at JESP. Retrieved from https://www.journals.elsevier.com/journal-of-experimental-social-psychology/news/announcement-of-new-policies-for-2018-at-jesp

Greenwald, A. G. (1975). Consequences of prejudice against the null hypothesis. *Psychological Bulletin, 82,* 1–20.

Greenwald, A. G. (1976). Within-subjects designs: To use or not to use? *Psychological Bulletin, 83,* 314–320.

Hedges, L. V. (1984). Estimation of effect size under nonrandom sampling: The effects of censoring studies yielding statistically insignificant mean differences. *Journal of Educational Statistics, 9,* 61–85.

Hoenig, J. M., & Heisey, D. M. (2001). The abuse of power: The pervasive fallacy of power calculations for data analysis. *American Statistician, 55,* 19–24.

Inzlicht, M., Gervais, W., & Berkman, E. (2015). *Bias-correction techniques alone cannot determine whether ego depletion is different from zero: Commentary on Carter, Kofler, Forster, & McCullough.* Unpublished manuscript.

Ioannidis, J. P. (2008). Why most discovered true associations are inflated. *Epidemiology, 19,* 640–648.

Iyengar, S., & Greenhouse, J. B. (1988). Selection models and the file drawer problem. *Statistical Science, 3,* 109–117.

Joel, S., Eastwick, P. W., & Finkel, E. J. (2018). Open sharing of data on close relationships and other sensitive social psychological topics: Challenges, tools, and future directions. *Advances in Methods and Practices in Psychological Science, 1,* 86–94.

Judd, C. M., Westfall, J., & Kenny, D. A. (2012). Treating stimuli as a random factor in social psychology: A new and comprehensive solution to a pervasive but largely ignored problem. *Journal of Personality and Social Psychology, 103,* 54–69.

Kantowitz, B., Roediger III, H., & Elmes, D. (2014). *Experimental psychology.* Stamford, CT: Cengage Learning.

Kaplan, R. M., & Irvin, V. L. (2015). Likelihood of null effects of large NHLBI clinical trials has increased over time. *PLoS One, 10,* e0132382.

Kerr, N. L. (1998). HARKing: Hypothesizing after the results are known. *Personality and Social Psychology Review, 2,* 196–217.

Krieglmeyer, R., & Sherman, J. W. (2012). Disentangling stereotype activation and stereotype application in the stereotype misperception task. *Journal of Personality and Social Psychology, 103,* 205.

Kunda, Z. (1990). The case for motivated reasoning. *Psychological Bulletin, 108,* 480–498.

Lakens, D. (2014). Performing high-powered studies efficiently with sequential analyses. *European Journal of Social Psychology, 44,* 701–710.

Lakens, D. (2017). Equivalence tests: A practical primer for *t* tests, correlations, and meta-analyses. *Social Psychological and Personality Science, 8,* 355–362.

Lakens, D., & Evers, E. R. (2014). Sailing from the seas of chaos into the corridor of stability: Practical recommendations to increase the informational value of studies. *Perspectives on Psychological Science, 9,* 278–292.

Ledgerwood, A. (2014). Introduction to the special section on advancing our methods and practices. *Perspectives on Psychological Science, 9,* 275–277.

Ledgerwood, A. (2016). Introduction to the special section on improving research practices: Thinking deeply across the research cycle. *Perspectives on Psychological Science, 11,* 661–663.

Ledgerwood, A., & Sherman, J. W. (2012). Short, sweet, and problematic? The rise of the short report in psychological science. *Perspectives on Psychological Science, 7,* 60–66.

Ledgerwood, A., & Shrout, P. E. (2011). The trade-off between accuracy and precision in latent variable models of mediation processes. *Journal of Personality and Social Psychology, 101,* 1174–1188.

Ledgerwood, A., Soderberg, C. K., & Sparks, J. (2017). Designing a study to maximize informational value. In M. C. Makel & J. A. Plucker (Eds.), *Toward a more perfect psychology: Improving trust, accuracy, and transparency in research* (pp. 33–58). Washington, DC: American Psychological Association.

Lerner, J. S., & Tetlock, P. E. (1999). Accounting for the effects of accountability. *Psychological Bulletin, 125,* 255–275.

Levenstein, M. C., & Lyle, J. A. (2018). Data: Sharing is caring. *Advances in Methods and Practices in Psychological Science, 1,* 95–103.

Lin, W., & Green, D. P. (2016). Standard operating procedures: A safety net for pre-analysis plans. *PS: Political Science & Politics, 49,* 495–500.

Lovakov, A., & Agadullina, E. (2017). Empirically derived guidelines for interpreting effect size in social psychology. Unpublished manuscript. https://doi.org/10.31234/osf.io/2epc4

MacCallum, R. C., Roznowski, M., & Necowitz, L. B. (1992). Model modifications in covariance structure analysis: The problem of capitalization on chance. *Psychological Bulletin, 111,* 490–504.

Maxwell, J. A. (2004). Causal explanation, qualitative research, and scientific inquiry in education. *Educational Researcher, 33,* 3–11.

Mayo, D. G. (1991). Novel evidence and severe tests. *Philosophy of Science, 58,* 523–552.

McNutt, M. (2014). Journals unite for reproducibility. *Science, 346,* 679.

McShane, B. B., & Böckenholt, U. (2016). Planning sample sizes when effect sizes are uncertain: The power-calibrated effect size approach. *Psychological Methods, 21,* 47.

McShane, B. B., & Böckenholt, U. (2017). Single-paper meta-analysis: Benefits for study summary, theory testing, and replicability. *Journal of Consumer Research, 43,* 1048–1063.

McShane, B. B., Böckenholt, U., & Hansen, K. T. (2016). Adjusting for publication bias in meta-analysis: An evaluation of selection methods and some cautionary notes. *Perspectives on Psychological Science, 11,* 730–749.

Meyer, M. N. (2018). Practical tips for ethical data sharing. *Advances in Methods and Practices in Psychological Science, 1,* 131–141.

Mills, J. L. (1993). Data torturing. *New England Journal of Medicine, 329,* 1196–1199.

Nosek, B. A., Ebersole, C. R., DeHaven, A. C., & Mellor, D. T. (2018). The preregistration revolution. *Proceedings of the National Academy of Sciences.* https://doi.org/10.1073/pnas.1708274114

Nosek, B. A., Spies, J. R., & Motyl, M. (2012). Scientific utopia: II. Restructuring incentives and practices to promote truth over publishability. *Perspectives on Psychological Science, 7,* 615–631.

Nyhan, B. (2015). Increasing the credibility of political science research: A proposal for journal reforms. *PS: Political Science & Politics, 48*(Suppl 1), 78–83.

Open Science Foundation. (2014, February). Sequential analyses step by step guide using R (Version: 1). Retrieved from https://osf.io/qtufw/

Perugini, M., Gallucci, M., & Costantini, G. (2014). Safeguard power as a protection against imprecise power estimates. *Perspectives on Psychological Science, 9,* 319–332.

Poincaré, H. (1902). *La science et l'hypothese.* Paris, France: Ernest Flammarion.

Pratto, F., Sidanius, J., Stallworth, L. M., & Malle, B. F. (1994). Social dominance orientation: A personality variable predicting social and political attitudes. *Journal of Personality and Social Psychology, 67,* 741–763.

Proschan, M. A., Lan, K. G., & Wittes, J. T. (2006). *Statistical monitoring of clinical trials: A unified approach.* New York, NY: Springer.

Rivers, A. M., & Sherman, J. (2018, January 19). Experimental design and the reliability of priming effects: Reconsidering the "train wreck." Unpublished manuscript. Retrieved from https://osf.io/kpqv8/

Roediger, H. L. (2012). Psychology's woes and a partial cure: The value of replication. *APS Observer, 25*(2). https://www.psychologicalscience.org/observer/psychologys-woes-and-a-partial-cure-the-value-of-replication

Rogers, J. L., Howard, K. I., & Vessey, J. T. (1993). Using significance tests to evaluate equivalence between two experimental groups. *Psychological Bulletin, 113,* 553–565.

Rosenthal R. (1979). The "file drawer problem" and tolerance for null results. *Psychological Bulletin, 86,* 638–641.

Ross, M., & Wilson, A. E. (2000). Constructing and appraising past selves. In D. L. Schacter & E. Scarry (Eds.), *Memory, Brain, and Belief* (pp. 231–258). Cambridge, MA: Harvard University Press.

Rossi, J. S. (1997). A case study in the failure of psychology as a cumulative science: The spontaneous recovery of verbal learning. In L. L. Harlow, S. A. Mulaik, & J. H. Steiger (Eds.), *What if there were no significance tests?* (pp. 175–197). Mahwah, NJ: Erlbaum.

Rubin, M. (2017). When does HARKing hurt? Identifying when different types of undisclosed post hoc hypothesizing harm scientific progress. *Review of General Psychology, 21,* 308–320.

Sagarin, B. J., Ambler, J. K., & Lee, E. M. (2014). An ethical approach to peeking at data. *Perspectives on Psychological Science, 9,* 293–304.

Sagarin, B. J., West, S. G., Ratnikov, A., Homan, W. K., Ritchie, T. D., & Hansen, E. J. (2014). Treatment noncompliance in randomized experiments: Statistical approaches and design issues. *Psychological Methods, 19,* 317–333.

Schönbrodt, F. D., & Perugini, M. (2013). At what sample size do correlations stabilize? *Journal of Research in Personality, 47,* 609–612.

Schwarz, N. (1999). Self-reports: How the questions shape the answers. *American Psychologist, 54,* 93–105.

Schmidt, S. (2009). Shall we really do it again? The powerful concept of replication is neglected in the social sciences. *Review of General Psychology, 13,* 90–100.

Simes, R. J. (1986). Publication bias: The case for an international registry of clinical trials. *Journal of Clinical Oncology, 4,* 1529–1541.

Simmons, J. P., Nelson, L. D., & Simonsohn, U. (2011). False-positive psychology: Undisclosed flexibility in data collection and analysis allows presenting anything as significant. *Psychological Science, 22,* 1359–1366.

Simons, D. J. (2018). AMPPS makes its entrance. *APS Observer 31*(2). https://www.psychologicalscience.org/observer/ampps-makes-its-entrance

Simons, D. J., Shoda, Y., & Lindsay, D. S. (2017). Constraints on generality (COG): A proposed addition to all empirical papers. *Perspectives on Psychological Science, 12,* 1123–1128.

Simonsohn, U., Nelson, L. D., & Simmons, J. P. (2014). *p*-curve and effect size: Correcting for publication bias using only significant results. *Perspectives on Psychological Science, 9,* 666–681.

Soderberg, C. K., & Errington, T. M. (in press). Replications and the social sciences. In J. Edlund & A. L. Nichols (Eds.), *Advanced Research Methods and Statistics for the Behavioral and Social Sciences.* Cambridge, England: Cambridge University Press.

Song, F., Eastwood, A., Gilbody, S., Duley, L., & Sutton, A. (2000). Publication and related biases: A review. *Health Technology Assessment, 4*(10), 1–115.

Spellman, B. A. (2015). A short (personal) future history of revolution 2.0. *Perspectives on Psychological Science, 10,* 886–899.

Stanley, D. J., & Spence, J. R. (2014). Expectations for replications: Are yours realistic? *Perspectives on Psychological Science, 9,* 305–318.

Sterling, T. D. (1959). Publication decisions and their possible effects on inferences drawn from tests of significance— or vice versa. *Journal of the American Statistical Association, 54,* 30–34.

StudySwap: A platform for interlab replication, collaboration, and research resource exchange. (2018, February 25). Retrieved from https://osf.io/view/studyswap/

Thomas, J. R., & French, K. E. (1985). Gender differences across age in motor performance: A meta-analysis. *Psychological Bulletin, 98,* 260–282.

Tilburg University (2011). *Interim report regarding the breach of scientific integrity committed by prof. D. A. Stapel.* Tilburg, The Netherlands: Author.

van Aert, R. C., Wicherts, J. M., & van Assen, M. A. (2016). Conducting meta-analyses based on *p* values: Reservations and recommendations for applying p-uniform and p-curve. *Perspectives on Psychological Science, 11,* 713–729.

van't Veer, A. E., & Giner-Sorolla, R. (2016). Pre-registration in social psychology: A discussion and suggested template. *Journal of Experimental Social Psychology, 67,* 2–12.

Vazire, S. (2017). Quality uncertainty erodes trust in science. *Collabra: Psychology, 3*(1). http://doi.org/10.1525/collabra.74

Vevea, J. L., & Hedges, L. V. (1995). A general linear model for estimating effect size in the presence of publication bias. *Psychometrika, 60,* 419–435.

Vul, E., Harris, C., Winkielman, P., & Pashler, H. (2009). Puzzlingly high correlations in fMRI studies of emotion, personality, and social cognition. *Perspectives on Psychological Science, 4,* 274–290.

Wang, Y. A., Sparks, J., Gonzales, J. E., Hess, Y. D., & Ledgerwood, A. (2017). Using independent covariates in experimental designs: Quantifying the trade-off between power boost and Type I error inflation. *Journal of Experimental Social Psychology, 72,* 118–124.

Welkowitz, J., Cohen, B. H., & Lea, R. B. (2012). *Introductory statistics for the behavioral sciences.* Hoboken, NJ: Wiley.

Westfall, J., Judd, C. M., & Kenny, D. A. (2015). Replicating studies in which samples of participants respond to samples of stimuli. *Perspectives on Psychological Science, 10,* 390–399.

Wilkinson M. D., Dumontier M., Aalbersberg IJ. J., Appleton G., Axton M., Baak A. . . . Mons B. (2016). The FAIR guiding principles for scientific data management and stewardship. *Scientific Data, 3,* art. 160018. http://doi.org/10.1038/sdata.2016.18

Zhang, J. J., Blumenthal, G. M., He, K., Tang, S., Cortazar, P., & Sridhara, R. (2012). Overestimation of the effect size in group sequential trials. *Clinical Cancer Research, 18,* 4872–4876.

Zhou, H., & Fishbach, A. (2016). The pitfall of experimenting on the web: How unattended selective attrition leads to surprising (yet false) research conclusions. *Journal of Personality and Social Psychology, 111,* 493–504.

Chapter 4

Social Cognition

Susan T. Fiske

How much do you think about that special someone—compared to your letter carrier? How much do you think about your advisor or your boss, compared to how much they think about you? The more we need other people, the more we need to make sense of them. This helps us to figure out how to relate to them. Social cognition describes this understanding process that allows us to act in our social world. Formally, social cognition is people making sense of other people and themselves (Fiske & Taylor, 2017).

Social cognition is at the micro end of social psychology. This book's chapters ascend from the individual lost in thought, to that person relating to one other person, to people relating with others in progressively larger groups. In this way, social cognition is a foundation of sociality. That is, our core social motive is a desire for belonging with others (Baumeister & Leary, 1995). The reason you obsess about your boss and your crush is that you want to belong with them (in different ways, of course). Belonging requires, first, that you try to engage in social cognition: understanding them, in the hope of predicting and maybe controlling what happens. Social cognition also has a more affective side, as it aims to help people feel better about themselves (or at least to find ways to improve) and to feel trust in others (if they deserve it). That is, you are likely to keep your self-esteem intact by being optimistic about your chances at work and at romance, as well as trusting the boss and the crush both to be basically good people (until proven otherwise). These core social motives (belonging, understanding, controlling, enhancing self, and trusting others; Fiske, 2014) drive social cognition and, with it, the rest of our sociality.

Our business here is describing how individuals understand their social world in order to navigate it. We start by identifying some principles of social cognition. People make sense of bosses and crushes (and everyone else) by following these general principles:

1. flexibly using both *automatic and deliberate* processes,
2. pragmatically *attending* to cues that seem diagnostic, and
3. representing apparently useful information in *memory*.

Then, three processes exemplify social cognition:

1. how people get inside the heads of other people, via amateur *mind-reading* (often called attribution theory or theory of mind);
2. how people *categorize* each other, often triggering stereotypes; and
3. how cognition generates *feelings and behavior*.

Along the way, we'll see how well you understand your crush or your boss—and how they most likely understand you.

Keep in mind that another human offers an incredibly challenging stimulus for forming a coherent impression. Other people are way more complex than objects. For example, people are autonomous agents with predispositions that are only indirectly observable: That is, they have intentions, other internal states (e.g., emotions), and enduring traits (e.g., personalities)—more than most furniture does. What's more, while you are perceiving other people, they are perceiving you back, and they may adjust accordingly, so they often are more variable and certainly more strategic than objects are (except for my laptop, who regularly conspires to manipulate me). We can know others with only indeterminate accuracy, given their intrinsic complexity. When thinking about your crush—or your boss—you want to know what they intend, how they feel, as well as what kind of person they are. This becomes more difficult if they know you are trying to figure them out, leading to some potentially awkward moments as you each try to manage each other's impressions. All this makes it amazing that we ever manage to form good-enough, clear-enough impressions of each other. But people matter to us—or at least some do—so they require explanation.

People Flexibly Use Both Automatic and Deliberate Processes

Perceivers are no fools. We know we cannot devote our full cognitive resources to each passerby, each complicated human, in the midst of our busy lives. Fortunately, people practice person perception, early and often, from infancy onward, so much of it becomes automatic. This automaticity saves time and effort in everyday encounters. Yet, we are flexible, so when the situation demands it, we can think more slowly and deliberately about someone puzzling or particularly important (e.g., the boss, the crush).

Automatic processing reflects people's shortcut strategies. People as *cognitive misers* (Fiske & Taylor, 2017) prioritize cognitive efficiency over accuracy, using effort-saving devices such as well-practiced procedures and familiar categories. Bur people also know when to change gears and devote more cognitive capacity. Thus, a more complete picture views people as *motivated tacticians* who know when to think hard and when to punt. At least three dozen theories of dual processes reflect this automatic-controlled distinction, especially in social cognition and attitude change (Chaiken & Trope, 1999) but also in popular culture as thinking fast and slow (Kahneman, 2011). We describe them here as a continuum, not a dichotomy (see Figure 4.1).

Operating on Automatic

Fully *automatic* processes are unintentional, uncontrollable, efficient, autonomous, unconscious, goal-independent, purely stimulus-driven, and fast (Bargh, 1997; Moors & De Houwer, 2006). Nonsocial examples include startling to a loud noise or dropping a hot object. Everyday social examples might include noticing when someone special or simply peculiar walks into class; a glance seems obligatory. Research illustrates a continuum from the fully automatic (most of the defining characteristics), to more conditionally automatic (only a few), to various controlled processes.

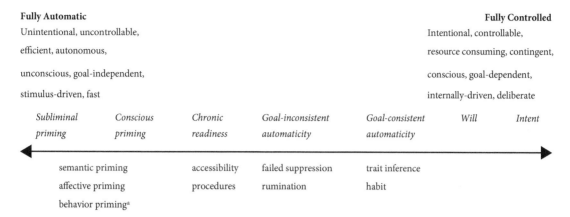

FIGURE 4.1. The motivated tactician's continuum: from automatic to controlled processes.
aThese three types of priming can operate either more subliminally or more consciously; semantic and affective priming are more reliably established than is behavioral priming.

Subliminal Priming

Long a debated topic, unconsciously cued associations comprise three types, only one of which is controversial. Unconscious cognitive and affective priming are fundamental processes; behavioral priming is under debate. Almost no one doubts semantic (cognitive) priming at an unconscious level: Present a word rapidly, followed by a mask (e.g., scrambled letters), so that participants cannot report seeing it. Then observe speeded response to identify a related word (Nosek, Hawkins, & Frazzier, 2012; Payne, 2012). Likewise, an affect-laden stimulus (e.g., smiley face)—even presented subliminally—can prime compatible evaluations of an ambiguous subsequent stimulus (e.g., a foreign word). In a more social vein, one study suggests that subliminally priming the department chair's scowling face (i.e., their boss) caused graduate students to devalue their research ideas (Baldwin, Carrell, & Lopez, 1990).

More complicated are subliminal words or images priming behavior (for a popular-press summary, see Bargh, 2017; for commentary, see Cesario, 2014; Doyen et al., 2012). For example, priming White students with pictures of African American men made them respond more hostilely when provoked (Bargh, Chen, & Burrows, 1996), but the effect is delicate and difficult to replicate. Although the jury may still be out on behavioral priming, the evidence is clearer on subliminal semantic and affective priming.

Conscious Priming

One of the bedrock results in cognitive psychology, conscious priming of related semantic content is well established and replicates with social concepts. For instance, many intergroup bias studies show that group labels prime stereotypic associations (see categorization section in this chapter and Chapter 12). Several attitude measures also rely on conscious evaluative priming (see Chapter 6). Deliberately thinking of good experiences with previous bosses might prime optimistic expectations about a current one.

Chronic Readiness

Priming depends on situations that activate a concept. Another source of activation is habitual; chronic activation depends on individual people's distinctive experiences. Moving from contextual primes (experimental manipulations) to personal predispositions (individual differences in readiness), two examples illustrate. First, people tend to have different social concepts chronically primed (Higgins, 1996). Suppose you often have love on your mind, because you have always been an incurable romantic. Also, it's been a while since your last relationship, and you are ready for a new one. Meanwhile, from another perspective, your crush might always have trustworthiness on the mind, because of a series of unfortunate earlier experiences. When each of you interpret the same chance encounter, you personally might see it as fate bringing you together, but your crush might worry about being stalked. At the same time, your middle-aged boss has no patience for any of this nonsense because she has deadlines on her mind. Each might inadvertently apply these concepts to you in the current situation. You could be viewed as a stalker or a slacker, instead of the irresistible romantic prospect you imagine. Accessible concepts appear quickly and early in people's descriptions of self and others; they are the lens a particular perceiver uses to filter impressions (Higgins, 1996).

Concepts become chronically accessible through practice, a process termed proceduralization (Smith, 1994). For example, beleaguered bosses judge employee ability every day, so it likely becomes routinized. Each person's own habitual dimensions of judgment proceed faster, with higher priority, more consistency, and greater efficiency. People may or may not be aware that they overuse certain dimensions, but once set in motion, a procedure has several characteristics of automaticity. Nevertheless, because perceivers could with effort employ a different dimension—you could judge trustworthiness or ability—procedural processes are not fully automatic; they border on controlled ones (see Figure 4.1).

Operating under Control

Moving toward the other end of the continuum (Figure 4.1): Controlled processes come in degrees, just as automatic ones do. A fully controlled process would have all characteristics opposite to fully automatic ones; complete control includes being intentional, controllable, resource consuming, contingent, conscious, goal-dependent, internally driven, and deliberate. But let's start with the hybrid cases in the middle of the automatic-to-controlled continuum and work our way to the purely controlled endpoint.

Goal-Inconsistent Automaticity

In the middle of the continuum, automaticity may beat control. Control fails when, despite the best goals, automatic thought patterns persist. One example is failed thought suppression. Trying not to think about an unrequited crush may work briefly while you monitor your thoughts, but as soon as you relax, your mind automatically wanders back to the one you love in vain. After attempted suppression, the forbidden thoughts surge in frequency: a rebound effect (Wegner, 1994). Ironically, monitoring to check whether one is having the banned thoughts instead keeps them active.

Persistent unwanted thoughts often take the form of rumination—repetitive, counterproductive thinking (Martin & Tesser, 1989)—as in obsession with a special someone who is not reciprocally obsessed with you. Or an unpredictable boss may provoke subordinates to unconstructive speculation about what the boss might do next. Simply having a goal (predict the crush's or the boss's next move) can backfire, leaving the perceiver in the grip of automaticity (in this case, being cognitively stuck in repetitious thinking).

Goal-Driven Automaticity

Relatively controlled processes tend to involve a goal, which mentally represents a desired end state (Aarts, 2012). Conscious choice frequently sets in motion simple automatic processes. Suppose you have lost track of the time over coffee with your crush, and you must contact your boss (goal). On deliberating, you decide to text instead of phoning, typing the text (process) is then automatic. In social cognition, goals often trigger more complex automatic processes. For example, the deliberate goal of forming an impression encourages (relatively automatic) spontaneous trait inferences from the person's behavior (your crush buying coffee for you implies generosity; Uleman, 1999). Instant trait judgments are useful deductions from evidence to general patterns that predict the other person; automatic predictions may allow control over one's outcomes in the interactions.

Not just cognition varies in automaticity. Clearly behavior can be relatively automatic: Sometimes people allow habit to guide their actions. Habits—frequently repeated behavior (Wood, Quinn, & Kashy, 2002)—can help or hinder one's conscious goals. Letting automatic processes dominate controlled ones is an advantage only when the automatic behaviors are consistent with conscious goals (e.g., commuting to work in the usual way; Aarts & Dijksterhuis, 2000). But habits may undermine goals when they are inconsistent (e.g., reflexively biking toward work when you intended to meet your crush for lunch).

Intent

If people only sometimes follow their intent, how do the cognitive features of intent explain when might they succeed or fail? Intent matters because it predicts behavior and holds people responsible. Social psychologists, lawyers, and lay people agree on intent's essentials: choice, attention, and effort (Fiske, 1989). When your crush (or your boss) misses a lunch date, their intent matters. Intent presupposes the person has a choice (e.g., no transportation breakdowns). If they had a choice to show up or not, you then want to know whether they paid attention to try to make the meet-up happen (e.g., forgetting is not a good sign). Suppose also that your lunch date made the hard choice to stand you up, by overriding their normal lunch routine; that suggests even more clearly an intent to avoid you. So you consider your lunch date's degree of choice, attention, and effort in trying to meet up, to decide whether they no-showed intentionally or not.

The intended harm would hurt more than an accidental or uncontrollable one. More broadly, observers use intent to judge not only responsibility but also the degree of damage. Suppose your friend is interning at a nursing home. If he mixed-up the medications by accident, that could cause considerable harm. But if he did it on purpose, as a misguided prank, you and other observers would estimate the objective medical costs as higher. Various scenarios, all with intentional and unintentional harms replicate: Observers asked to judge actual damages inflated their estimates when a person did it on purpose, even if the victims don't know this. Intentional harms seem worse, even when they are not (Ames & Fiske, 2013a). The point is that intent matters so much to perceivers that we see the harms as intrinsically worse when intended.

Will

Relatively controlled processes tend to involve a goal, which mentally represents a desired end state (Aarts, 2012). As part of enacting a goal, conscious will—a thought that precedes, fits, and explains an action—would seem a prime example of intent and, in the default case, will likely does reflect intent. Nevertheless, two contrarian views challenge this common-sense assumption.

First, people may exercise their will less often than they think because many goals arise automatically. When situations trigger goals—a dark, plush restaurant makes a working dinner seem romantic—"automotives" may kick in (Bargh, 1999). The conscious will (working over dinner) may sometimes be less relevant than stimulus–response processes (romantic associations). Many a tragic misunderstanding has resulted this way.

Another contrarian view likewise argues that conscious will can be illusory (Wegner, 2003). If people thought about an action before acting, they infer that the thought caused the action. But what if both resulted from the same random cause? In that case, the thought did not actually cause the action. For example, an experiment first induced participants to think ill of a confederate. Then they were made to stick pins in a doll supposedly representing the obnoxious confederate; later, they felt they had magically caused the confederate's headache (Pronin, Wegner, McCarthy, & Rodriguez, 2006). With equally illusory control, how many of us have "willed" our team to win?

Consciousness

Regarding what might seem the most deliberate of mental processes, consciousness entails being awake and aware, subjectively describing one's surroundings and experiences, as well as meta-cognition, such as noticing that one is daydreaming—but not necessarily controlling it (Winkielman & Schooler, 2012). Researchers document the contents of people's consciousness in daily life by experience-sampling methods that send queries at random moments or in the lab by requesting them to think aloud as they perform a task. Spontaneous thoughts often describe the current surroundings, drift toward dilemmas (unfinished business, current concerns), and frequently reflect one's social relationships.

A further clue to what consciously preoccupies us: Activations in the brain's default (resting) network overlap with its social-cognition network (Lieberman, 2013), suggesting the priority of thinking about other people, arguably preparing to interact with them. In our running example, your conscious mind is preoccupied with current concerns about your crush, more than unfinished business at work, as you wait to meet up.

Motives Control Dual-Mode Processes

To some extent, the motivated tactician chooses along this continuum of more automatic or controlled processes, as if they serve as social cognitive tactics, depending on current motives. Motivations shape people's tendency either to rely on automatic processes to make sense of each other efficiently or to engage more deeply in controlled processes. Most of these core social motives cut both ways, encouraging automatic or controlled processes under different circumstances.

For example, the need to belong (introduced earlier; Baumeister & Leary, 1995) can make people think deeply about their own ingroup and superficially about the outgroup. Because you want to belong with the ingroup (and not the outgroup), ingroupers are more motivationally relevant. That outcome dependence drives your attention to them. Wanting to belong with a particular person or group may motivate much thinking but also bias that thinking in wishful, optimistic directions (see Fiske & Taylor, 2017, Ch. 2, for references). For example, participants hoping to meet dating partners evaluated two videos of eligible peers making a pitch for an ideal restaurant. One pitch was good; the other was not. And one peer was available to meet-up; the other was not. Participants could distinguish the unavailable peer's good performance from the bad one. Objectivity went out the window for the available peer's video: Participants thought the inferior performance was just fine (Goodwin, Fiske, Rosen, & Rosenthal, 2002). Thinking more deliberately about your crush will not necessarily make you more accurate because your cognition is motivated toward affiliation (belonging).

Motives to understand and to control one's outcomes can make people want to reach a decision, any decision. These knowledge-oriented motives make people want to feel a sense of accuracy, so they may think harder but not necessarily better. In a series of studies, participants' outcomes (a cash prize) either depended on teamwork with a partner or was independent of the partner. This task-oriented outcome dependency motivated participants' cognitive processes aimed at understanding (attention to the most informative, surprising information about the partner; Erber & Fiske, 1984). They also made dispositional inferences, which would increase their sense of being able to predict the partner; they even used the mind-reading regions of the brain (Ames & Fiske, 2013b). But their impressions were not necessarily accurate;

everyone drew their own conclusions (Ruscher & Fiske, 1990). Interpreting your boss's behavior may provide a sense of prediction and control without being accurate. Knowledge-oriented motives also cut both ways.

Affect-driven motives to feel better about self and others particularly put accuracy at risk. But this may not be a bad thing (Taylor, 1989). Positive illusions about how much others like and respect you may ensure a degree of self-esteem, and positive illusions about close others' good qualities may build trust. Being optimistic about yourself and your crush may (within limits) facilitate the relationship. A bit of benign bias can grease the social wheels more than brutal accuracy.

Section Summary

People use a variety of more automatic and more controlled processes to form impressions, depending on the situation and on their motives. The motivated tactician must balance costly deliberations that offer a sense of accuracy against the efficiency of shortcuts that often yield good-enough impressions for everyday use. People think harder mainly when the stakes are raised, as when thinking about the crush or the boss.

People Pragmatically Attend to Cues that Seem Diagnostic

Social attention is a precious cognitive resource. In the midst of an ongoing interaction, the motivated tactician must choose whom to notice, where to fix attention, and what to consider. To learn more about your crush over lunch, you certainly should pay attention to not only that person's conversation but also nonverbal behavior (gaze, facial expression, seating distance).

Choosing to attend to your crush's face instead of your phone is selective attention; it allows you to take in (encode) information. As the next sections show, research on social attention has documented some principles of selectivity: the intrinsic attentional appeal of faces (mutual crushes gaze into each other's eyes), attention to cues that are salient by virtue of being informative in context (your crush is the only one who laughs at your jokes), and attention to cues that are accessible by virtue of being useful in the past (your crush visibly enjoys the same music as you).

When you relive the encounter later, you replay some parts more than others. Even the isolated social cognizer lost in thought about another person devotes attention to some knowledge more than others. Attention reflects the two processes, selective encoding in real time and internal activation in consciousness (Chun, Golumb, & Turk-Browne, 2011). Consciousness is often occupied by unfinished business, whether from romance or work, thoughts activated in the hope of knowing what to do.

In reaction to the seeming power of consciousness (thinking is for doing) is a contrarian view: Maybe conscious attention is irrelevant, and maybe social perception is direct from environment to action, without cognitive mediation. But first, let's look at some noncontroversial principles.

Faces Capture Attention

People attend to each other's faces to extract information about the other's gaze (indicating focus of attention), configuration of features (facilitating recognition), and apparent traits (assembling an impression).

Gaze

Attention indicates intention, as noted earlier. Perceivers rightly discern another's gaze—attentional focus—as a clue to what the other might do next. People look where others look because their attention suggests their intention. Gaze-following occurs even when humans look where a cartoon animal is looking (Quadflieg, Mason, & Macrae, 2004). Joint attention reflects sociality (Happé, Cook, & Bird, 2017). People direct attention to coordinate joint activities (both looking into the camera for a selfie) and to bond over their joint focus (as when both check the result).

Eye contact often initiates interaction. Social gaze is especially informative when it concerns us personally. If another face is gazing at you, then presumably you are the target of their attention and perhaps intention. This is so ingrained that it generalizes to still photos. All else equal, people prefer photos with a direct gaze (Mason, Tatkow, & Macrae, 2005). A direct gaze is not only appealing but it also speeds categorization of the face (e.g., by gender), eases associated inferences (e.g., stereotypes), and facilitates memory (Hood, Macrae, Cole-Davies, & Dias, 2003; Macrae, Hood, Hill, Rowe, & Mason, 2002).

Features

Suppose you are unabashedly looking at your crush. Face perception encodes both fixed features and changeable expressions, as well as prior knowledge about the person, implicating distinct brain areas (Haxby, Hoffman, & Gobbini, 2000). People are experts at recognizing another's face, and the process is global and holistic, not piecemeal, feature-by-feature (Macrae & Lewis, 2002). People rapidly encode, first, that the stimulus is a face, then its category (gender, age, race), then individual identity, and finally attractiveness or other inferences.

Sometimes one face will present a visual configuration that resembles other naturally occurring face configurations. For example, people infer that a baby-faced adult is innocent and trustworthy, like a baby (Zebrowitz et al., 2012). The baby-faced adult seems to afford (offer opportunities for) caretaking. Similarly, masculine faces look more dominant to people than submissive faces do, as we shall see next. Such fixed features trigger instant impressions.

Trait Inferences

People infer people's personalities from their facial structure (Todorov, 2012), a strategy shown to be unreliable more than a century ago. Nevertheless, people do it. The fastest trait that judges infer is trustworthiness: Happy-looking faces seem trustworthy, and angry-looking faces seem untrustworthy. For example, furrowed brows make anyone look angry, but as a fixed facial feature, they make a person look untrustworthy (Todorov, Said, Engell, & Oosterhof, 2008).

The second fastest dimension overgeneralizes features of age/gender/strength to imply competence (dominance/maturity). Both gender and racially fixed facial features that resemble emotions overgeneralize to personality traits (female faces looked surprised and therefore open; Zebrowitz, Kikuchi, & Fellous, 2010). Face-based inferences of competence predict which politicians get elected (Todorov, Mandisodza, Goren, & Hall, 2005), and face-based inferences of criminality predict which people get incarcerated or executed (Blair, Judd, & Chapleau, 2004; Eberhardt, Davies, Purdie-Vaughns, & Johnson, 2006). Faces can launch a thousand slip-ups.

Salience in the Environment

Few stimuli are as socially attention-grabbing as faces. However, almost any stimulus can be salient in context (see Fiske & Taylor, 2017, Chapter 3). The sheer juxtaposition of a stimulus to context—an immediate situation, long-term expectations, or instructions—easily directs attention. For example, in the immediate context, visual novelty attracts attention (e.g., the only older person in a roomful of young people or someone wearing a black sweater among orange ones; McArthur & Post, 1977). Being perceptually figural does too: Bright, moving, and complex stimuli are salient relative to duller, stiller, simpler ones. One can also be figural by physical location, being front-and-center, dominating the perceiver's visual field (Taylor & Fiske, 1975). Students know this, sometimes choosing their classroom seats to attract or avoid faculty attention.

Long-term context likewise determines salience over time: as novelty, relative to expectations, general or specific. A person can be or behave in ways unusual (unexpected) for people in general. For example, being an outlier on height or helpfulness attracts attention. So too does negative behavior, because (all else equal) people expect moderately positive behavior from others, so negative behavior attracts attention. A person can also behave in ways unusual for that person's social group; counter-stereotypic information captures attention. Moreover, one can behave in ways unusual for oneself, which leaves friends and colleagues puzzling.

Finally, people can be salient by virtue of being goal-relevant. That special someone attracts attention because of one's desire to affiliate. The boss attracts attention because one hopes to advance on the job. Eager employees make sure their bosses notice them in return. Outcome dependency attracts attention to the people who control our fate. Simple instructions also can direct attention in more mundane ways, as when one watches the safety video because of the boss's instructions.

Whatever its origin, salience affects judgments in various ways that make little logical sense (Taylor & Fiske, 1975). Visual salience makes people loom larger: Salient people seem to cause events (even when they don't). So the solo older student in a roomful of younger students seems more impactful than everyone else (the same would be true for the only youth in a roomful of elders). By seeming more influential, salient people also garner more polarized evaluations; praiseworthy behavior seems especially laudable, and blameworthy behavior seems especially egregious. Salience exaggerates judgments in whatever direction they would otherwise tend.

Part of the process involved is this: Attracting attention makes perceivers think about a target person. All else being equal, this scrutiny makes the overall impression more coherent than it would be otherwise, as thinking makes all the pieces fit; people expect another person's personality to be coherent. Remember that the cognitive miser defaults to the simplest impression that will do for present purposes. Waiting in the wings, however, the motivated tactician may decide that more thought is needed, for example, under outcome dependency. Then, scrutiny reveals inconsistencies that need to be resolved if one aims to predict and control one's outcomes—say, with a boss.

In the default case of no outcome dependency, the superficial coherence doubtless encourages more extreme, confident judgments and attributed influence. Arguably, perceivers are not wrong to notice and consider people who are unusual—because novelty may be diagnostic—as when that older student wants to mix outside their own age-mates. But novelty could also be random: Salience is not necessarily logically relevant, in proportion to its social cognitive consequences. Should you strive to capture your boss's or crush's attention? It depends on what kind of first impression you can produce, because salience will exaggerate it, in either direction.

Accessibility in the Mind

As just described, external salience captures attention; salience affects the selective part of attention, noted earlier. The other part of attention is what is currently activated in mind; accessibility is internal attention. Accessibility describes the ease with which stored knowledge comes to mind. Recall that earlier sections introduced two fixedly automatic forms of mental accessibility: In one, the environment determines relatively automatic subliminal priming, outside the perceiver's control (a movie primes snacks without thinking because of relentless advertising). In the other fixed form, chronic accessibility is based on individually well-practiced judgments, which become an individual difference in automaticity (some people learn the snacks' calorie counts). Here, we consider a third form, a more changeable conscious accessibility; this is a short-term function of the frequency and recency of a concept's activation (someone nags you often or nagged you just now about healthy eating). Other conscious, short-term situational primes illustrate accessibility.

At one extreme are rich primes, such as asking participants to write about a time they felt powerful (e.g., Galinsky, Magee, Inesi, & Gruenfeld, 2006). This manipulation primes power and makes people act that way. At the simpler extreme are bare-bones primes, such as when experimental participants read a series of positive or negative trait adjectives. For example, priming "adventurous" suggests a daring interpretation of solo-sailing across the Atlantic but priming "reckless" suggests it might be foolish (Higgins, Rholes, & Jones, 1977). Notice that the primes shape not just a positive–negative evaluation but also a specific meaning, so the priming effects are likely to be stronger than simply positive ("good") or negative ("bad") primes. Regardless, to prime meaning as well as valence has the most effect on subsequent judgment. Other frequent primes include social group labels ("Black," "White") or pronouns for "us" and "them" (Devine, 1989; Dovidio, Evans, & Tyler, 1986; Gaertner & McLaughlin, 1983). These too can prime meaning as well as valence.

Primes are more powerful under specific conditions, which explain how they work (e.g., Srull & Wyer, 1979): Primes are stronger when they can affect encoding, that is, by shaping the initial interpretation of behavior (e.g., as adventurous instead of reckless). Therefore, primes are strong also when the prime precedes the stimulus, rather than vice versa; if the prime is already in mind, the prime can shape the meaning of the stimulus more easily than if it has to do so after the stimulus is already encoded. Likewise, when the prime and stimulus are contiguous, rather than farther apart, the prime has more influence. Finally, when the rating is delayed, this allows the primed interpretation to beat memory for the original stimulus. So, if you want your boss (or your crush, for that matter) to interpret your long silences as deep thinking instead of mind-wandering, it's best to plant the "wisdom" idea immediately before any potential lapses ("My family always weighed their words and wasted none").

Not only traits can prime selective accessibility of relevant meanings: Accessibility research has primed social categories, such as race. Police and probation officers, first primed below awareness (subliminally) with "Black," then go on to rate a race-unspecified teenager as having more guilt, a worse personality, and more likelihood to reoffend, thereby justifying harsher punishment (Graham & Lowery, 2004). Just about any concept can prime interpretations of a relevant stimulus (for a stunning array, see research reviewed in Fiske & Taylor, 2017, Chapter 3). Because priming represents one interpretation of a stimulus, which then goes into memory, priming effects can be long-lived.

Yet, priming effects are not so simple. Described so far are accessibility effects reflecting assimilation—using the prime ("adventurous") to construct a compatible interpretation (skydiving is a thrill). Sometimes, the prime is so far-fetched that participants react to the misfit between prime ("safe") and stimulus ("skydiving"), so they judge by contrast (skydiving is dumb). Priming your boss with the name of your brilliant young advisor should more effectively assimilate that positive image to seeing you also as intelligent.

Priming your field's Nobel Awardees would probably make you look unimpressive because of the far-fetched comparison.

In conclusion, primes aid a lazy mind that's operating on automatic, in a default mode: When unmotivated perceivers notice similarities between a preconscious and abstract prime ("us"), that greatly overlaps with an ambiguous stimulus (your latest presentation on behalf of the team; Mussweiler, 2003). Contrast results in the opposite circumstances (when motivated perceivers, testing for differences, consciously encounter specific primes that overlap very little with an unambiguous stimulus—comparing the class valedictorian's record and your own transcript would create contrast, making you look bad). Whether assimilation or contrast, the plausible cognitive processes supports priming both relevant meaning and evaluations.

Direct Perception: What the Environment Affords

So far, this chapter on social cognition has presumed that cognition plays a leading role in automatic and controlled processes and in attentional processes such as priming. A contrarian perspective on attention rejects the role of cognition. In this view, thinking is irrelevant. Instead, proponents argue that the environment directly "affords" certain responses: Perception is direct and unmediated by the mind.

One strand of evidence is the already-described finding that people react to baby-faced adults as if they seem to afford caretaking. Actual babies do afford cuddling—more than an elephant or a porcupine does. The perceiver's body allows some responses to objects and beings in the environment. Watching a practiced and well-conditioned rock-climber gauge what to grab and where to step shows the fit between one body and one ecology, responses that would not be available to all of us.

Another illustration of direct perception emerges in current approaches to embodied cognition, sometimes called situated cognition (Semin, Garrido, & Palma, 2012). Gesture, posture, facial expressions, and other experiences of self in space can affect cognition. For example, it's hard to dislike someone if you are nodding, smiling, leaning forward, and looking into each other's eyes. Akin to direct-perception approaches, embodied cognition emphasizes both bottom--up perceptions and top–down frames (expectations). The experience of self-in-setting prepares for action afforded by the setting. Social interaction is crucially driven by the body-in-context. For two people, relative size, reciprocal posture, nonverbal imitation, and other enacted coordination reflect embodied cognition (Semin et al., 2012). Your crush's nonverbal reciprocity (e.g., leaning forward and smiling when you do) affords further interaction.

Finally, observers often agree in apparently direct perceptions of other people. Another line of work examines natural breakpoints in action sequences. Much like scenes in a video drama, spontaneous interactions naturally segment into scenes that observers reliably identify (Newtson, Hairfield, Bloomingdale, & Cutino, 1987). For example, if you watch your crush talking to an eligible stranger in a bar, it matters who spoke first. If it's your crush, you might reconsider their exclusive interest in you. The person initiating the conversation affords a causal perception—speaker and responder. Let's hope that it ends with one unit, but, if not, the give-and-take of ordinary interaction has recognizable units. Finer units emerge for unexpected activity, reflecting more information gain. As you notice the stranger point your crush toward the facilities, your interpretation adjusts accordingly, but only if you watched closely enough to notice.

All the direct-perception approaches usefully spotlight what a stimulus configuration can provide the adapted social animal. We now return to more conventional social cognition approaches.

People Represent Apparently Useful Information in Memory

Social memory research tracks theories in cognitive psychology and cognitive neuroscience, with a lag of several years. The borrowing systematically follows the original work, but with a twist: The resulting social cognitive models sometimes reveal what is distinctive about social memory. But, first, let's briefly overview the range of ideas about how people remember things about other people.

Associative Networks: Organizing Declarative Memory

Suppose you are trying to remember the name of your boss's partner or your crush's roommate, whom you've met only once, at a crowded party. "Skyler and . . . Skyler and . . . ," you rehearse mentally, hoping to spring the association. Or you link the elusive person to the one conversation you all had: "I remember Skyler said they both love biking: I know Skyler's athletic." Yes, but what was that name of Skyler's associate?

Early views of social memory usually posited each target person as a node linked to traits, each in turn linked to relevant behaviors (e.g., Hastie, 1988; Srull & Wyer, 1989). Initial social memory models organized person memory into these node-link networks. Retrieving information required activation spreading along retrieval pathways. The more often the particular link is activated, the more likely it is to be activated again; the nodes' joint activation strengthens the pathway that determines retrieval. ("Skyler and . . . Skyler and . . .")

Let's rewind to when you met that one time and decided that Skyler's associate is friendly. Impressions can form online, as a perceiver encounters behavioral information and infers a personality trait from a consistent pattern of behavior (greeting with a smile, "I've heard so much about you," asking questions, joking). This behavior gets encoded as information residing in short-term memory (current attention); there, the incoming information links to memories about related information and the individual.

Suddenly, Skyler's pal makes a harsh judgment about another guest across the room. Whoa! If the information is inconsistent with a developing impression of friendliness, it stays longer, as the perceiver attempts to make sense of it (friendly and harsh?!). This may result in a memory advantage for inconsistent information, under some circumstances. Either way, the resulting associations enter long-term memory. (Except that darned name . . .)

Sometimes, impressions can form on the basis of information retrieved from memory, as you review your impression after the party. Memory-based impressions correlate with whatever is memorable (kind greeting but harsh judgment). But suppose you had already formed an impression: Your memory for the data might not match the impression. Online impressions do not correlate so much with memory because what determines impression weight (e.g., extraordinary friendliness) differs from what determines memorability (e.g., that inconsistent harshness, which, in the end, you dismissed as uncharacteristic).

This approximation of several person-memory network models (see Fiske & Taylor, 2017, Chapter 4) illustrates the flexibility of efficiently learning about someone, a process that requires short-term memory capacity to store content (declarative memory), establishing shared pathways between nodes, retrievable through automatic or controlled processes. ("Skyler and Chris!!")

Procedural Memory: Memory in Action

Declarative memory models, just illustrated, describe rapid encoding of content, such as other people's names, traits, and interests. Procedural memory focuses instead on learned sequences, such as repeating a warm-up series before a workout. This slower-learning memory process requires practice on specific, focused routines, resulting in durable memory traces that eventually execute quickly and automatically. If certain conditions apply (workout clothes, warm-up mat, a free hour), then the procedure executes (child pose, then downward dog . . .). Current stimuli and goals trigger procedures through matching and selecting processes. As described earlier (Smith, 1998), procedural memory nicely explains the facilitation of routinized judgments (detecting your boss's moods).

Parallel Processes: Coordinating Memory

Our running illustration has the perceiver first gathering information and then storing it away, both in the service of thinking for doing. Generally viewing declarative memory as a serial process entails forming a sequence: encoding, memory, and response. Subsequent work developed simultaneous parallel process models of encoding and retrieval. Gone were the node-link networks of spreading activation (admittedly itself a parallel process). Broadly, parallel distributed processing models view encoding and responding both as emerging from the activated configuration. Smartphone photos of your crush might activate pixels variously representing different images by patterns of information (parallel, distributed, procedural processing). In contrast would be a series of sketches on paper, each representing only one image (serial, declarative memory).

The parallel distributed processing, applied to social encoding and memory, provides a useful way to represent simultaneous encoding of new information, balanced with prior knowledge, each reciprocally constraining interpretation of the other (e.g., Kunda & Thagard, 1996).

Social Memory Structures: Why Social Memory Matters

Some memory models more readily focus on abstract generalizations (e.g., expectations), while others emphasize specific inputs (e.g., nonverbals). Social cognition research has gravitated more toward the top–down representations, focusing on categories, concepts, and expectations—prior knowledge sometimes called schemas (Macrae & Bodenhausen, 2000). These theory-driven cognitive structures hypothetically represent knowledge about a concept's attributes and the relationships among them. Commonly studied categories include race, gender, occupation, and traits, on the assumption that people use these as shortcuts to make sense of each other. These categories certainly guide the getting-acquainted process.

To be sure, just because perceivers use generic representations, this does not mean that they never engage bottom–up, data-driven processes. For example, you may know that your boss belongs to a book club (category: bibliophile), but unless you learn of some specific titles (data), conversation will stall.

Categories often appear as fuzzy sets, a collection of exemplars loosely unified by family resemblance, centered around a prototype. Social category inclusion does not operate by rigid rules, but rather by overlapping attributes. That is, a bibliophile might read e-books or physical ones, literary fiction or modern history, and one book a month or 20. Loving books might prime a prototype of the ideal bibliophile: wearing glasses, tweed, comfortable shoes, and disheveled hair. Categories guide encoding, inference, and memory; they organize social knowledge but sometimes distort it to fit. For example, you may misremember the bibliophile as carrying a backpack because book-lovers often need a place to stow all those printed pages. Categories provide abstract, typical knowledge, automatically accessible and often stable.

People also store specific instances, which might embellish some aspects (tweed jacket with jeans) and omit others (no glasses). Exemplars besides your boss might include the school librarian, the owner of a local bookstore, and your friend the English Lit major. Such collections of exemplars allow perceivers to answer novel questions (do bibliophiles mark up library books?), estimate variability of category members (what range of books per month?), and report feature correlations (are fiction readers more often female?). Both prototypes and exemplars help the social perceiver to navigate the buzzing, blooming social world.

Interim Summary of Principles

Motivated tacticians use either relatively automatic or more controlled processes to make sense of each other, depending on motives to belong, understand and control, enhance self-esteem or build trust. Perceivers attend not only to apparently diagnostic cues, especially faces, but also cues salient in context or accessible because of recent or frequent activation. Perception that reflects the situated person may link directly to action without substantial cognitive mediation. Memory too may be embodied, but more commonly studied memory processes involve associate networks of declarative knowledge and if–then procedures perhaps represented in parallel distributed processes. Social categories play a critical role in social cognition; the next sections describe categories for dispositions such as traits, categories for stereotyped social groups, and categories of social emotions and behavior.

Mind-Reading: Attribution and Theory of Mind

It's a miracle that people make sense of each other at all, for all the reasons mentioned earlier: People, compared with furniture, have intrinsic complexity, with hidden but crucial features that guide their action. To cope, social perceivers rely on generic prior knowledge about kinds of people in kinds of situations, though research has focused most on perceiving kinds of people. Thinking is for doing. To predict another's behavior, people often try to figure out the other person's underlying predispositions, such as personality traits and intentions. In the process, perceivers explain others' behavior in causal terms (seeking to know why they do what they do). This is what can keep you up at night, wondering about your unpredictable boss or your mysterious crush.

Enthusiastic Social Explanation

Attribution is the term for inferring a causal explanation for someone's actions. Just as psychological scientists try to explain behavior, so do regular people, making them common-sense psychologists (Heider, 1958). People believe some basic rules of causality in everyday settings (Taylor, 1982): Causes precede effects, close in time and place; causes seem plausible if they are salient, comparable in magnitude, and resemble the effect. In trying to explain your unexpectedly small bonus at work, plausible causes might involve an unfortunate just-prior incident (recent, prominent, significant) but not your history of forgetting to close your office door or clean-up your social media record (which seems habitual, trivial, background). Causal analysis often explores the other person's mind: knowledge, beliefs, mental state, attitudes, personality, desires, and intent (Ames & Mason, 2012). We take for granted this often-effortless mind-reading.

People's ability to imagine other minds is arguably how we manage to adapt as social beings (Hare, 2017). Theory of mind emerges when children realize that someone might act on beliefs that differ from their own. For example, in the false-belief paradigm, a child observes a story in which one character hides candy while another character is out of the room. The child might know where candy is hidden but comes to realize that another child does not. Toddlers expect the other child to search what the perceiver knows to be the candy's actual location, but kindergarteners know that the other child will search where they believe it to be (e.g., Saxe, Carey, & Kanwisher, 2004). Becoming able to guess what's in someone else's mind is a learned ability.

Sometimes mind-readers are overenthusiastic; people perceive intent and feelings in objects, animals, and deities. Consider how often people talk to their cars, pets, and computers as if they were human. People anthropomorphize (treat nonhumans as if they were human) particularly when they have unmet needs for affiliation (everyone else has weekend plans; Epley, Waytz, & Cacioppo, 2007). People who have a big need to belong are especially sensitive to social cues (Pickett, Gardner, & Knowles, 2004). People also overattribute minds when they need to feel more socially effective (friends aren't responding to your messages). Anthropomorphism works best when plausible human-like cues are available (the cat is gazing at you).

Attributing mental states requires a fraction of a second (e.g., Willis & Todorov, 2006). Several stage models explain why, namely, that initially identifying, categorizing, and characterizing behavior intrinsically entails relating it to traits ("Paying for breakfast was a nice thing to do; she's generous"; Gilbert, 1998). Only afterwards, as a second step, do perceivers correct for situational influences ("It's going on a work account"). The dispositional attribution is relatively automatic and spontaneous, whereas the adjustment for context requires controlled deliberation.

Rational Attribution Ideals

One view of attribution portrays the ideal reasoning that a rational thinker would use to weight the evidence and deliberately choose an explanation. These deliberative models provide standards to evaluate the spontaneous attributions just described. In assessing the ideal case, they reveal how we fall short, the systematic errors and biases that emerge, by comparison.

Heider's Common-Sense Psychology

Heider listened to lay people explaining why other people do what they do, which provided insights into their amateur mind-reading processes. People demonstrably search for patterns of invariances, stability, and change. Understanding your boss's competence and plans requires that you notice patterns: If the boss consistently fires people just before the end of the fiscal year, inferring the boss's cost-cutting priorities is not hard. Chief among the useful patterns to watch are ones that reveal, first, the person's ability (capacity compared to environmental forces); that is, does the boss have authority to act on this priority, despite social pressures? Does the boss consistently show the ability to bring about this goal? Second, even if the boss has the ability to fire people, to balance the budget, does the boss have the motivation (intention and effort) to bring about the outcome? Is the boss seriously motivated (perhaps for fear of keeping the job)? Mind-reading depends on observing patterns of what people can do and try to do. Heider's original, rich, and nuanced writings inspired the next theories.

Jones's Correspondent Inference Theory

Building on Heider, this theory assumes the target person has both ability and knowledge about their behavior and its consequences; the boss can fire people, knowing the consequences for the individual and for the bottom line. Correspondent inference then describes how people extract dispositional evidence from behavior (Jones & Davis, 1965): In short, does that action reflect a corresponding intention (and therefore a relevant attitude or trait). If external pressures can sufficiently explain the action, then perceivers should resist a dispositional inference. For instance, socially desirable behavior has a sufficient external explanation, so an internal one is unnecessary: A person who tells the truth is not necessarily of exceptional honesty. But lying is more informative because it runs against social norms. Likewise, a person who does what their role demands—a professor who professes—does not reveal any disposition distinct from external pressures. But a train conductor who professes must be distinctively knowledgeable.

Attributing intent follows from what is distinctive about the outcomes of an actor's behavior. Jones identified effects that are unique ("noncommon") as diagnostic of underlying intent: Choosing a series of jobs that differ in many respects but always involve living near trains suggests trains reflect the chooser's main intent. Heider's search for invariance (constants) emerges here. Knowing your boss's patterns (senior staff always go first) suggest that either cost-cutting or ageism is the primary intent, but retaining experience is not. This is a logical view.

However, humans are not so tidy. Despite emphasizing rational attribution processes, correspondent inference research soon revealed one minor bias and one robust bias. First, people make more dispositional inferences when the actor's behavior bears on the perceiver's own interests, especially if apparently directed on purpose. Your boss's behavior toward you ("didn't say hello") seems more informative ("uh oh!") than the same behavior toward someone else ("get over it").

Second, in a bigger and more persistent bias, perceivers overemphasize dispositional causes and underemphasize situational ones. For example, even when behavior is situationally constrained, observers show a correspondence bias (Gilbert & Malone, 1995). A student assigned to defend a controversial viewpoint for a class essay should not be inferred to have the corresponding attitude; the student had no choice. Perhaps the boss has no choice, either; the boss's own job may depend on eliminating other people's jobs. But we still attribute at least some intent toward the unpopular behavior in both cases. This dispositional bias (even constrained behavior corresponds to intent) foreshadows the lay perceiver's other departures from rational models.

Kelley's Covariation Model

Overlapping with correspondent inference theory, but more comprehensive and formal, Kelley (1972) posited that three sources of information determine the ideal analysis of causality. Suppose your boss critiques your suggestions in a meeting. How you interpret this depends on three answers: First, does this behavior target only you as the receiving entity, or does the boss do this to everyone? The object of the action, unique versus widespread, is its distinctiveness. Second, does everyone think your suggestions are hogwash, or just the boss does? The subject or origin of the action, individual versus general, shows its consensus. Third, does the boss inflict this criticism on you in this meeting and other venues, or just this one meeting? The stability of this behavior (in effect, its adverb) is its consistency.

The combination of low distinctiveness (the boss critiqued everyone that day), low consensus (no one else critiqued you), and high consistency (the boss is always doing this) suggests an abusive boss. On the other hand, critiques that are distinctive to you, a shared consensus, and delivered consistently across venues, suggests your work needs to improve. Either way, you might look for another job. Other combinations of cues would be less clear on causality.

Experimental manipulations of the three dimensions independently support the model (McArthur, 1972). However, evidence soon accumulated that consensus did not work as expected. Like Jones's correspondence bias, finding that anyone would do it (under similar circumstances) does not prevent perceivers from attributing action to the actor's distinct personality. Rational, ideal-thinker models begin to unravel at the edges.

Biases

As normative (idealized) models frayed, more descriptive approaches identified patterns of perceiver bias. First, the correspondence bias expanded into the fundamental attribution error (Ross, 1977), also observing that people exaggerate dispositional causes and underestimate situational ones. What's more, although observers do this, actors explaining their own behavior do the opposite, exaggerating situational causes (Jones & Nisbett, 1972) especially for negative events (Malle, 2006; "The dog ate my homework"). The dispositional bias holds more for Western cultures, who emphasize individual agency, but not always for Eastern cultures, who emphasize collective and contextual causes (e.g., Morris & Peng, 1994).

Second, perceivers fail to correct for their own perspectives in three ways: In a self-serving bias (Miller & Ross, 1975), people take credit for success more than failure (Arkin, Cooper, & Kolditz, 1980). In a self-centered bias, people each take more credit for their own contributions to joint work than the other person would assign (Ross & Sicoly, 1979). Ironically, people believe that they alone see reality as it is, while viewing most others as biased, a phenomenon termed naïve realism (Pronin, Gilovich, & Ross, 2004).

Third, people especially attribute blame for negative events (Shaver, 1985), and the worse the event, the more a specific person seems responsible (Burger, 1981). People do not like randomness. Instead, people prefer to believe that people get what they deserve. In a just world, victims who can't be helped are seen as deserving their hopeless fate—more than victims whose problems can be solved by charity (Lerner & Miller, 1978). People prefer not to think that bad things can happen to good people.

Section Summary

Attribution processes are a form of mind-reading, imagining another's mental state. People explain each other's behavior by attributing it to personal predispositions or situational factors, with marked dispositional biases (at least, in the West). The process is not fully rational; instead it is prone to systematic errors and biases.

Stereotyping: How People Categorize by Social Groups

Attributions essentially categorize people by personality traits, based on their behavior. As noted, in addition, people rapidly categorize faces by gender, race, and age—and infer dispositions accordingly. Categorization goes beyond specific behavior and facial cues to the whole person. And that's not all. Categorization reflects a host of other social distinctions: social class, sexual orientation, occupation, and religion. A later chapter addresses intergroup relations more thoroughly; here we address some cognitive features of group categorization, namely, its automaticity, ambiguity, and ambivalence. Together, these features explain why category-based stereotypes often go unexamined, under the mind's radar.

Automatic Categories

Lay people underestimate how difficult it is to be color-blind. People cannot help noticing each other's social categories, especially visual ones such as gender, ethnicity, age, and perhaps class. Besides evidence from instantaneous face perception, neural indicators show immediate electro-cortical responses to gender and race (e.g., Ito & Urland, 2003). Social groups even act as positive and negative primes to identify subsequent words (Fazio & Olson, 2003). That is, recall how positive and negative adjectives (adventurous, reckless) shape interpretations of relevant behavior (skydiving) because they make its positive or negative aspects salient. In the same way, minority group labels can prime negative stereotypic interpretations of ambiguous behavior because the culture associates, for example, being Black with being criminal (Devine, 1989). Implicit associations spontaneously link between group labels and stereotypes (Banaji & Greenwald, 2016). Social group primes facilitate stereotype-relevant lexical decisions (word/nonword perceptions). Showing White participants photographs of Black faces and White faces speeds up their recognition of (even irrelevant) negative and positive words, respectively, because the category makes its valence (positivity/negativity) more accessible (Fazio, Jackson, Dunton, & Williams, 1995).

Categorization has immediate behavioral effects (Fazio & Olson, 2003). Unacknowledged outgroup stereotypes spill over to more distant, less friendly nonverbal cues that can poison an interaction (Dovidio, Kawakami, & Gaertner, 2002; Word, Zanna, & Cooper, 1974). People combine cues, encoding an actor's social category along with behavior: In the who-said-what paradigm, people misremember by group; they confuse speakers' statements within category more than between categories (a woman said it, but which one? Taylor, Fiske, Etcoff, & Ruderman, 1978; see Chapter 12 for a thorough review). The point here is simply that social categories have immediate cognitive and behavioral effects that are more automatic than most people realize.

To be sure, category activation is conditionally automatic, depending on cognitive factors: overload (Gilbert & Hixon, 1991), categorizing instructions (Wheeler & Fiske, 2005), practice (Kawakami et al., 2000), category relevance (Quinn & Macrae, 2005), and category accessibility (Castelli, Macrae, Zogmaister, & Arcuri, 2004). Motivational factors also matter: Perspective-taking (Galinsky & Moskowitz, 2000), motivation (Blair & Banaji, 1996), and guilt (Hing, Li, & Zanna, 2002) can reduce spontaneous stereotyping. Social categorization is less automatic than researchers first thought. But categorization by social group is more automatic than lay people think: integral to social cognition, yet often unexamined.

Ambiguous Categories

Social categorization also goes unremarked because of its ambiguity in two respects. First, people categorizing people are self-categorizing, differentiating ingroup from outgroup. And they favor the ingroup at least as much as disfavoring the outgroup (Brewer, 2007). Being comfortable with people like yourself is only human; the fit feels right. However, in a zero-sum world, this tendency denies access to those in the outgroup, perpetuating segregated settings. Ingroup positivity makes bias ambiguous because people think of bias as being anti-them, no so much pro-us. Nevertheless, both are biases that disadvantage some categories of people.

Second, categories are not only ambiguous in their effects but also in their origins. People belong to multiple categories (Bodenhausen, Kang, & Peery, 2012), categories' boundaries overlap (Freeman & Ambady, 2009), and mash-ups combine categories (Nicolas, de la Fuente, & Fiske, 2017), all in unexpected ways that disguise the influence of categories.

Ambivalent Categories

Social categorization is often unexamined, too, because it is often ambivalent, mixing positive and negative attributions (Fiske, Cuddy, Glick, & Xu, 2002). Groups are not only viewed as admirable and praiseworthy (us, the middle class, our citizens) versus stereotyped as contemptible and disgusting (the homeless, drug addicts, undocumented immigrants), though this certainly represents the worst case. But there's more. Groups categorized as pitiful (old people, disabled people) are trusted but disrespected. Groups categorized as enviable (rich people, business people) are respected but not trusted. Perceivers can cite their liking for elders and their respect for CEOs as evidence of being unbiased, but the positive in the one dimension implies the negative on the other dimension, in stereotyping by omission (Bergsieker, Leslie, Constantine, & Fiske, 2012).

How Cognition Generates Affect and Behavior

Social cognition certainly guides affective and behavioral responses to other people, but research has been slow to establish the links (Macrae & Miles, 2012). Almost certainly, affect and motivation play decisive roles in linking social cognition to social behavior.

Cognition and Affect: Mutual Influence

Cognition influences affect, and vice versa (Fiske & Taylor, 2017, Chapters 13 and 14). To illustrate the first, cognition–affect, attributional analyses guide emotions (Weiner, 1987): A person with bad outcomes (your crush has a broken leg) will elicit pity if blameless (an uncontrollable accident) but will elicit anger if responsible (poor choice of substance use). The cognitively driven causal analysis results in emotions. Similarly, people appraise events and situations for pleasantness, responsibility, certainty, attention, effort, and control, with these various cognitive appraisals leading to various emotions (Smith & Ellsworth, 1985). Not all emotions result from such deliberate analysis, but some from more automatic cognitive processes: Sometimes spontaneously categorizing someone as resembling an old flame will trigger emotions accordingly (Andersen, Saribay, & Przybylinski, 2012). All these cognition–affect linkages also facilitate associated behavior.

Conversely, affect influences cognition, as shown by evaluative priming research reviewed earlier. Transitory mood also shapes cognition: Memory, judgment, decision-making style, persuasion, and well-being all respond to feeling state. Most often, good moods prime relatively superficial and optimistic responses, compared with neutral moods. Negative mood are more variable effects because people actively try to escape them (for details, see Fiske & Taylor, Chapter 14). Moods and their effects in turn may guide behavior.

When Do Cognitions Predict Behavior?

Mostly, cognitions predict behavior when they are strong, relevant, and accessible; when the situation and the person encourage acting on one's own interpretation; and when they are measured at comparable levels of generality. The attitude–behavior literature teaches this (see Fiske & Taylor, 2017, Chapter 15; also see Chapter 12).

Distinctive to social cognition are impression management and other social goals. Typically, people try to make a positive impression, for example, by ingratiating to seem likable or self-promoting to see competent (Jones & Pittman, 1982; also see Chapter 12). When they cannot avoid a negative impression, they may self-handicap, making excuses.

Impression managers also use behavior to test hypotheses about others, but they may easily behave in ways that confirm their hypotheses: They ask leading questions, selectively interpret answers, nonverbally communicate expectations, and reinforce confirmatory responses (Darley & Fazio, 1980). Self-confident targets and self-doubting perceivers can prevent behavioral confirmation.

Conclusion

Social perceivers engage in thinking for doing, so many social cognition strategies are functional much of the time (Fiske, 1992). Motivated tacticians balance automatic and controlled processes, allocate attention and dedicate memory to diagnostic information. Mind-reading attributes traits and intentions, categorization by social group attributes stereotypes, and attributions and appraisals elicit emotions.

Together, these processes produce social behavior. Social cognition shapes the social interactions that the rest of the book describes; in that sense, social cognition is foundational. But the influence goes both ways, as social cognition results from social interaction. For both reasons, it is emphatically *social* cognition, as you'll soon see.

References

Aarts, H. (2012). Goals, motivated social cognition and behavior. In S. T. Fiske & C. N. Macrae (Eds.), *Sage handbook of social cognition* (pp. 75–95). Thousand Oaks, CA: SAGE.

Aarts, H., & Dijksterhuis, A. (2000). Habits as knowledge structures: Automaticity in goal-directed behavior. *Journal of Personality and Social Psychology, 78,* 53–63.

Ames, D. L., & Fiske, S. T. (2013a). Intentional harms are worse, even when they're not. *Psychological Science, 24,* 1755–1762.

Ames, D. L., & Fiske, S. T. (2013b). Outcome dependency alters the neural substrates of impression formation. *NeuroImage, 83,* 599–608.

Ames, D. R., & Mason, M. F. (2012). Mind perception. In S. T. Fiske & C. N. Macrae (Eds.), *Sage handbook of social cognition* (pp. 115–137). Thousand Oaks, CA: SAGE.

Andersen, S. M., Saribay, S. A., & Przybylinski, E. (2012). Social cognition in close relationships. In S. T. Fiske & C. N. Macrae (Eds.), *Sage handbook of social cognition* (pp. 350–371). Thousand Oaks, CA: SAGE.

Arkin, R. M., Cooper, H. M., & Kolditz, T. A. (1980). A statistical review of the literature concerning the self-serving attribution bias in interpersonal influence situations. *Journal of Personality, 48,* 435–448.

Baldwin, M. W., Carrell, S. E., & Lopez, D. F. (1990). Priming relationship schemas: My advisor and the Pope are watching me from the back of my mind. *Journal of Experimental Social Psychology, 26,* 435–454.

Banaji, M. R., & Greenwald, A. G. (2016). *Blindspot: Hidden biases of good people.* New York, NY: Bantam.

Bargh, J. A. (1997). The automaticity of everyday life. In R. S. Wyer Jr. (Ed.), *The automaticity of everyday life* (pp. 1–62). Mahwah, NJ: Erlbaum.

Bargh, J. A. (1999). The cognitive monster: The case against the controllability of automatic stereotype effects. In S. Chaiken & Y. Trope (Eds.), *Dual-process theories in social psychology* (pp. 361–382). New York: Guilford Press.

Bargh, J. A. (2017). *Before you know it: The unconscious reasons we do what we do.* New York, NY: Simon & Schuster.

Bargh, J. A., Chen, M., & Burrows, L. (1996). Automaticity of social behavior: Direct effects of trait construct and stereotype activation on action. *Journal of Personality and Social Psychology, 71,* 230–244.

Baumeister, R. F., & Leary, M. R. (1995). The need to belong: Desire for interpersonal attachments as a fundamental human motivation. *Psychological Bulletin, 117,* 497–529.

Bergsieker, H. B., Leslie, L. M., Constantine, V. S., & Fiske, S. T. (2012). Stereotyping by omission: Eliminate the negative, accentuate the positive. *Journal of Personality and Social Psychology, 102,* 1214–1238.

Blair, I. V., & Banaji, M. R. (1996). Automatic and controlled processes in stereotype priming. *Journal of Personality and Social Psychology, 70,* 1142–1163.

Blair, I. V., Judd, C. M., & Chapleau, K. M. (2004). The influence of Afrocentric facial features in criminal sentencing. *Psychological Science, 15,* 674–679.

Bodenhausen, G. V., Kang, S. K., & Peery, D. (2012). Social categorization and the perception of social groups. In S. T. Fiske & C. N. Macrae (Eds.), *Sage handbook of social cognition* (pp. 311–329). Thousand Oaks, CA: SAGE.

Brewer, M. B. (2007). The importance of being we: Human nature and intergroup relations. *American Psychologist, 62,* 728–738.

Burger, J. M. (1981). Motivational biases in the attribution of responsibility for an accident: A meta-analysis of the defensive-attribution hypothesis. *Psychological Bulletin, 90,* 496–512.

Castelli, L., Macrae, C. N., Zogmaister, C., & Arcuri, L. (2004). A tale of two primes: Contextual limits on stereotype activation. *Social Cognition, 22,* 233–247.

Cesario, J. (2014). Priming, replication, and the hardest science. *Perspectives on Psychological Science, 9,* 40–48.

Chaiken, S., & Trope, Y. (Eds.). (1999). *Dual-process theories in social psychology.* New York, NY: Guilford.

Chun, M. M., Golomb, J. D., & Turk-Browne, N. B. (2011). A taxonomy of external and internal attention. *Annual Review of Psychology, 62,* 73–101.

Darley, J. M., & Fazio, R. H. (1980). Expectancy confirmation processes arising in the social interaction sequence. *American Psychologist, 35,* 867–881.

Devine, P. G. (1989). Stereotypes and prejudice: Their automatic and controlled components. *Journal of Personality and Social Psychology, 56,* 5–18.

Dovidio, J. F., Evans, N., & Tyler, R. B. (1986). Racial stereotypes: The contents of their cognitive representations. *Journal of Experimental Social Psychology, 22,* 22–37.

Dovidio, J. F., Kawakami, K., & Gaertner, S. L. (2002). Implicit and explicit prejudice and interracial interaction. *Journal of Personality and Social Psychology, 82,* 62–68.

Doyen, S., Klein, O., Pichon, C. L., & Cleeremans, A. (2012). Behavioral priming: It's all in the mind, but whose mind? *PloS One, 7,* e29081.

Eberhardt, J. L., Davies, P. G., Purdie-Vaughns, V. J., & Johnson, S. L. (2006). Looking deathworthy: Perceived stereotypically of Black defendants predicts capital sentencing outcomes. *Psychological Science, 17,* 383–386.

Epley, N., Waytz, A., & Cacioppo, J. T. (2007). On seeing human: A three-factor theory of anthropomorphism. *Psychological Review, 114,* 864–886.

Erber, R., & Fiske, S. T. (1984). Outcome dependency and attention to inconsistent information. *Journal of Personality and Social Psychology, 47,* 709–726.

Fazio, R. H., Jackson, J. R., Dunton, B. C., & Williams, C. J. (1995). Variability in automatic activation as an unobtrusive measure of racial attitudes: A bona fide pipeline? *Journal of Personality and Social Psychology, 69*(6), 1013–1027.

Fazio, R. H., & Olson, M. A. (2003). Implicit measures in social cognition research: Their meaning and use. *Annual Review of Psychology, 54,* 297–327.

Fiske, S. T. (1989). Examining the role of intent: Toward understanding its role in stereotyping and prejudice. In J. S. Uleman & J. A. Bargh (Eds.), *Unintended thought* (pp. 253–283). New York, NY: Guilford.

Fiske, S. T. (1992). Thinking is for doing: Portraits of social cognition from daguerreotype to laserphoto. *Journal of Personality and Social Psychology, 63,* 877–889.

Fiske, S. T. (2014). *Social beings* (4th ed). New York, NY: Wiley.

Fiske, S. T., Cuddy, A. J., Glick, P., & Xu, J. (2002). A model of (often mixed) stereotype content: Competence and warmth respectively follow from perceived status and competition. *Journal of Personality and Social Psychology, 82*, 878–902.

Fiske, S. T., & Taylor, S. E. (2017). *Social cognition: From brains to culture* (3rd ed.). London, England: SAGE.

Freeman, J. B., & Ambady, N. (2009). Motions of the hand expose the partial and parallel activation of stereotypes. *Psychological Science, 20,* 1183–1188.

Gaertner, S. L., & McLaughlin, J. P. (1983). Racial stereotypes: Associations and ascriptions of positive and negative characteristics. *Social Psychology Quarterly, 46,* 23–40.

Galinsky, A. D., Magee, J. C., Inesi, M. E., & Gruenfeld, D. H. (2006). Power and perspectives not taken. *Psychological Science, 17,* 1068–1074.

Galinsky, A. D., & Moskowitz, G. B. (2000). Perspective-taking: Decreasing stereotype expression, stereotype accessibility, and in-group favoritism. *Journal of Personality and Social Psychology, 78,* 708–724.

Gilbert, D. T. (1998). Ordinary personology. In D. T. Gilbert, S. T. Fiske, & G. Lindzey (Eds.), *The handbook of social psychology* (4th ed., Vol. 2, pp. 89–150). New York, NY: McGraw-Hill.

Gilbert, D. T., & Hixon, J. G. (1991). The trouble of thinking: Activation and application of stereotypic beliefs. *Journal of Personality and Social Psychology, 60,* 509–517.

Gilbert, D. T., & Malone, P. S. (1995). The correspondence bias. *Psychological Bulletin, 117,* 21–38.

Goodwin, S. A., Fiske, S. T., Rosen, L. D., & Rosenthal, A. M. (2002). The eye of the beholder: Romantic goals and impression biases. *Journal of Experimental Social Psychology, 38,* 232–241.

Graham, S., & Lowery, B. S. (2004). Priming unconscious racial stereotypes about adolescent offenders. *Law and Human Behavior, 28,* 483–504.

Happé, F., Cook, J., & Bird, G. (2017). Exploring the structure of social cognition. *Annual Review of Psychology, 68,* 243–267.

Hare, B. (2017). Survival of the friendliest: Homo sapiens evolved via selection for prosociality. *Annual Review of Psychology, 68,* 155–186.

Hastie, R. (1988). A computer simulation model of person memory. *Journal of Experimental Social Psychology, 24,* 423–447.

Haxby, J. V., Hoffman, E. A., & Gobbini, M. I. (2000). The distributed human neural system for face perception. *Trends in Cognitive Science, 4,* 223–233.

Heider, F. (1958). *The psychology of interpersonal relations.* New York, NY: Wiley.

Higgins, E. T. (1996). Knowledge activation: Accessibility, applicability, and salience. In E. T. Higgins & A. W. Kruglanski (Eds.), *Social psychology: Handbook of basic principles* (pp. 133–168). New York, NY: Guilford.

Higgins, E. T., Rholes, W. S., & Jones, C. R. (1977). Category accessibility and impression formation. *Journal of Experimental Social Psychology, 13,* 141–154.

Hing, L. S., Li, W., & Zanna, M. P. (2002). Inducing hypocrisy to reduce prejudicial responses among aversive racists. *Journal of Experimental Social Psychology, 38,* 71–78.

Hood, B. M., Macrae, C. N., Cole-Davies, V., & Dias, M. (2003). Eye remember you: The effects of gaze direction on face recognition in children and adults. *Developmental Science, 6,* 67–71.

Ito, T. A., & Urland, G. R. (2003). Race and gender on the brain: Electrocortical measures of attention to the race and gender of multiple categorizable individuals. *Journal of Personality and Social Psychology, 85,* 616–626.

Jones, E. E., & Davis, K. E. (1965). From acts to dispositions: The attribution process in person perception. In L. Berkowitz (Ed.), *Advances in experimental social psychology* (Vol. 2, pp. 220–266). New York, NY: Academic Press.

Jones, E. E., & Nisbett, R. E. (1972). The actor and the observer: Divergent perceptions of the causes of behavior. In E. E. Jones, D. E. Kanouse, H. H. Kelley, R. E. Nisbett, S. Valins, & B. Weiner (Eds.), *Attribution: Perceiving the causes of behavior* (pp. 79–94). Morristown, NJ: General Learning.

Jones, E. E., & Pittman, T. S. (1982). Toward a general theory of strategic self-presentation. In J. Suls (Ed.), *Psychological perspectives on the self* (pp. 231–262). Hillsdale, NJ: Erlbaum.

Kahneman, D. (2011). *Thinking, fast and slow.* New York, NY: Farrar, Straus & Giroux.

Kawakami, K., Dovidio, J. F., Moll, J., Hermsen, S., & Russin, A. (2000). Just say no (to stereotyping): Effects of training in the negation of stereotypic associations on stereotype activation. *Journal of Personality and Social Psychology, 78,* 871–888.

Kelley, H. H. (1972). Attribution in social interaction. In E. E. Jones, D. E. Kanouse, H. H. Kelley, R. E. Nisbett, S. Valins, & B. Weiner (Eds.), *Attribution: Perceiving the causes of behavior* (pp. 1–26). Morristown, NJ: General Learning.

Kunda, Z., & Thagard, P. (1996). Forming impressions from stereotypes, traits, and behaviors: A parallel-constraint-satisfaction theory. *Psychological Review, 103,* 284–308.

Lerner, M. J., & Miller, D. T. (1978). Just world research and the attribution process: Looking back and ahead. *Psychological Bulletin, 85,* 1030–1051.

Lieberman, M. D. (2013). *Social: Why our brains are wired to connect.* New York, NY: Crown.

Macrae, C. N., & Bodenhausen, G. V. (2000). Social cognition: Thinking categorically about others. *Annual Review of Psychology, 51,* 93–120.

Macrae, C. N., Hood, B. M., Milne, A. B., Rowe, A. C., & Mason, M. F. (2002). Are you looking at me? Eye gaze and person perception. *Psychological Science, 13,* 460–464.

Macrae, C. N., & Lewis, H. L. (2002). Do I know you? Processing orientation and face recognition. *Psychological Science, 13,* 194–196.

Macrae, C. N., & Miles, L. K. (2012). Revisiting the sovereignty of social cognition: Finally some action. In S. T. Fiske & C. N. Macrae (Eds.), *Sage handbook of social cognition* (pp. 1–11). Thousand Oaks, CA: SAGE.

Malle, B. F. (2006). The actor–observer asymmetry in attribution: A (surprising) meta-analysis. *Psychological Bulletin, 132,* 895–919.

Martin, L. L., & Tesser, A. (1989). Toward a motivational and structural theory of ruminative thought. In J. S. Uleman & J. A. Bargh (Eds.), *Unintended thought* (pp. 306–326). New York, NY: Guilford.

Mason, M. F., Tatkow, E. P., & Macrae, C. N. (2005). The look of love: Gaze shifts and person perception. *Psychological Science, 16,* 236–239.

McArthur, L. Z. (1972). The how and what of why: Some determinants and consequences of causal attribution. *Journal of Personality and Social Psychology, 22,* 171–193.

McArthur, L. Z., & Post, D. L. (1977). Figural emphasis and person perception. *Journal of Experimental Social Psychology, 13,* 520–535.

Miller, D. T., & Ross, M. (1975). Self-serving biases in the attribution of causality: Fact or fiction? *Psychological Bulletin, 82,* 213–225.

Moors, A., & De Houwer, J. (2006). Automaticity: A theoretical and conceptual analysis. *Psychological Bulletin, 132*(2), 297–326.

Morris, M. W., & Peng, K. (1994). Culture and cause: American and Chinese attributions for social and physical events. *Journal of Personality and Social psychology, 67,* 949–971.

Mussweiler, T. (2003). Comparison processes in social judgment: Mechanisms and consequences. *Psychological Review, 110,* 472–489.

Newtson, D., Hairfield, J., Bloomingdale, J., & Cutino, S. (1987). The structure of action and interaction. *Social Cognition, 5,* 191–237.

Nicolas, G., de la Fuente, M., & Fiske, S. T. (2017). Mind the overlap in categorization: A review of crossed-categorization, intersectionality, and multiracial perception. *Group Processes and Intergroup Relations, 20,* 621–631.

Nosek, B. A., Hawkins, C. B., & Frazier, R. S. (2012). Implicit social cognition. In S. T. Fiske & C. N. Macrae (Eds.), *Sage handbook of social cognition* (pp. 31–53). Thousand Oaks, CA: SAGE.

Payne, B. K. (2012). Control, awareness, and other things we might learn to live without. In S. T. Fiske & C. N. Macrae (Eds.) *Sage handbook of social cognition* (pp. 12–30). Thousand Oaks, CA: SAGE.

Pickett, C. L., Gardner, W. L., & Knowles, M. (2004). Getting a cue: The need to belong and enhanced sensitivity to social cues. *Personality and Social Psychology Bulletin, 30,* 1095–1107.

Pronin, E., Gilovich, T., & Ross, L. D. (2004). Objectivity in the eye of the beholder: Divergent perceptions of self versus others. *Psychological Review, 111,* 781–799.

Pronin, E., Wegner, D. M., McCarthy, K., & Rodriguez, S. (2006). Everyday magical powers: The role of apparent mental causation in the overestimation of personal influence. *Journal of Personality and Social Psychology, 91,* 218–231.

Quadflieg, S., Mason, M. F., & Macrae, C. N. (2004). The owl and the pussycat: Gaze cues and visuospatial orienting. *Psychonomic Bulletin and Review, 22,* 826–831.

Quinn, K. A., & Macrae, C. N. (2005). Categorizing others: The dynamics of person construal. *Journal of Personality and Social Psychology, 88,* 467–479.

Ross, L. D. (1977). The intuitive psychologist and his shortcomings: Distortions in the attribution process. In L. Berkowitz (Ed.), *Advances in experimental social psychology* (Vol. 10, pp. 174–221). New York, NY: Academic Press.

Ross, M., & Sicoly, F. (1979). Egocentric biases in availability and attribution. *Journal of Personality and Social Psychology, 37,* 322–337.

Ruscher, J. B., & Fiske, S. T. (1990). Interpersonal competition can cause individuating processes. *Journal of Personality and Social Psychology, 58,* 832–843.

Saxe, R., Carey, S., & Kanwisher, N. (2004). Understanding other minds: Linking developmental psychology and functional neuroimaging. *Annual Review of Psychology, 55,* 87–124.

Semin, G. R., Garrido, M. V., & Palma, T. A. (2012). Socially situated cognition: Recasting social cognition as an emergent phenomenon. In S. T. Fiske & C. N. Macrae (Eds.), *Sage handbook of social cognition* (pp. 138–164). Thousand Oaks, CA: SAGE.

Shaver, K. G. (1985). *The attribution of blame: Causality, responsibility, and blameworthiness.* New York, NY: Springer-Verlag.

Smith, C. A., & Ellsworth, P. C. (1985). Patterns of cognitive appraisal in emotion. *Journal of Personality and Social Psychology, 48,* 813–838.

Smith, E. R. (1994). Procedural knowledge and processing strategies in social cognition. In R. S. Wyer & T. K. Srull (Eds.), *Handbook of social cognition* (Vol. 1, pp. 99–151). Mahwah NJ: Erlbaum.

Smith, E. R. (1998). Mental representation and memory. In D. T. Gilbert, S. T. Fiske, & G. Lindzey (Eds.), *The handbook of social psychology* (4th ed., Vol. 1, pp. 391–445). New York, NY: McGraw-Hill.

Srull, T. K., & Wyer, R. S., Jr. (1979). The role of category accessibility in the interpretation of information about persons: Some determinants and implications. *Journal of Personality and Social Psychology, 37,* 1660–1672.

Srull, T. K., & Wyer, R. S., Jr. (1989). Person memory and judgment. *Psychological Review, 96,* 58–83.

Taylor, S. E. (1982). The availability bias in social psychology. In D. Kahneman & A. Tversky (Eds.). *Judgment under uncertainty: Heuristics and biases.* New York NY: Cambridge University Press.

Taylor, S. E. (1989). *Positive illusions: Creative self-deception and the healthy mind.* New York: Basic Books.

Taylor, S. E., & Fiske, S. T. (1975). Point of view and perceptions of causality. *Journal of Personality and Social Psychology, 32,* 439–445.

Taylor, S. E., Fiske, S. T., Etcoff, N. L., & Ruderman, A. J. (1978). Categorical and contextual bases of person memory and stereotyping. *Journal of Personality and Social Psychology, 36,* 778–793.

Todorov, A. (2012). The social perception of faces. In S. T. Fiske & C. N. Macrae (Eds.), *Sage handbook of social cognition* (pp. 96–114). Thousand Oaks, CA: SAGE.

Todorov, A., Mandisodza, A. N., Goren, A., & Hall, C. (2005). Inferences of competence from faces predict election outcomes. *Science, 308,* 1623–1626.

Todorov, A., Said, C. P., Engel, A. D., & Oosterhof, N. N. (2008). Understanding evaluation of faces on social dimensions. *Trends in Cognitive Sciences, 12,* 455–460.

Uleman, J. S. (1999). Spontaneous versus intentional inferences in impression formation. In S. Chaiken & Y. Trope (Eds.), *Dual-process theories in social psychology* (pp. 141–160). New York, NY: Guilford.

Wegner, D. M. (1994). Ironic processes of mental control. *Psychological Review, 101,* 34–52.

Wegner, D. M. (2003). The mind's best trick: How we experience conscious will. *Trends in Cognitive Sciences, 7,* 65–69.

Weiner, B. (1987). The social psychology of emotion: Applications of a naive psychology. *Journal of Social and Clinical Psychology, 5,* 405–419.

Wheeler, M. E., & Fiske, S. T. (2005). Controlling racial prejudice and stereotyping: Social cognitive goals affect amygdala and stereotype activation. *Psychological Science, 16,* 56–63.

Willis, J., & Todorov, A. (2006). First impressions: Making up your mind after 100 ms exposure to a face. *Psychological Science, 17,* 592–598.

Winkielman, P., & Schooler, J. W. (2012). Consciousness, metacognition and the unconscious. In S. T. Fiske & C. N. Macrae (Eds.), *Sage handbook of social cognition* (pp. 54–74). Thousand Oaks, CA: SAGE.

Wood, W., Quinn, J., & Kashy, D. (2002). Habits in everyday life: Thought, emotion, and action. *Journal of Personality and Social Psychology, 83,* 1281–1297.

Word, C. O., Zanna, M. P., & Cooper, J. (1974). The nonverbal mediation of self-fulfilling prophecies in interracial interaction. *Journal of Experimental Social Psychology, 10,* 109–120.

Zebrowitz, L. A., Kikuchi, M., & Fellous, J.-M. (2010). Facial resemblance to emotions: Group differences, impression effects, and race stereotypes. *Journal of Personality and Social Psychology, 98,* 175–189.

Chapter 5

The Self

Roy F. Baumeister

If humans evolved from great apes, why are human selves so much more elaborate than those of apes? To answer this question is to address the question of what the self essentially is. The self is not a part of the brain, nor is it an illusion, nor is there a "true self" hidden in some magical realm.

Rather, the self is an essential part of the interface between the animal body and the social system. Human social systems—including culture and civilization—are vastly more complex than the social systems of other great apes. They present more opportunities and more challenges. The human self has to have capabilities and properties that enable it to deal with these.

As a simple example, consider your name. Your name is not a part of your brain, though your brain has to be able to know and use the name. The name is given to you by others. It locates you in the social system: Imagine trying to live in your town without a name! Your name refers to your body but evokes much more, such as group memberships, bank accounts, transcripts, and resumes. It links you to a family, and some people even change their names when they change families (by marrying). Your name tells people how to treat you. (In modern China, which has an acute shortage of names, there are reports of surgery being performed on the wrong person because several hospital patients have identical names. Police work is likewise easily confused by duplicate names.)

Most animals get what they need (food, shelter, and the like) from the physical environment. Humans get it from each other, that is, from their social system. The functions of the self thus include helping the animal self negotiate the social world to get what it needs. Social needs are also prominent in human behavior, and the self is, if anything, more important for satisfying them than for satisfying physical needs. The first job of the self is thus to garner social acceptance. Beyond that, the self works to secure and improve its position in the social group. It keeps track of information about itself, works to improve how it is regarded by others, identifies itself with important relationships and roles, and makes choices (most of which are social).

If the self exists at the animal/culture interface, then vastly different cultures would likely produce different versions of selfhood. There is some evidence that this is true. The most studied cultural difference in selfhood describes modern Western selves as emphasizing independence, whereas East Asian selfhood features interdependence (Markus & Kitayama, 1991). That is, Asians base their self-understanding on things that connect them to other people, including family, groups, country, and other relationships. Americans and Western Europeans, in contrast, think of themselves as unique and self-creating. Related to this is a greater emphasis on self-promotion and personal superiority in the West, as compared to more pervasive humility in Asian selves (Heine, Lehmann, Markus, & Kitayama, 1999). For more on this, see Chapter 17.

Even within Western culture, there are ample variations. American women are more similar to Asians than American men are, often building interdependent self-concepts (Cross & Madsen, 1997), though it is a mistake to see this as indicating that women are more social than men (Baumeister & Sommer, 1997). The independent thrust of modern Western selfhood probably originated in the political and economic changes that occurred starting in the Renaissance, such as the sharp rise in social mobility (Baumeister, 1987). Medieval Western selfhood, as far as can be reconstructed from the literature and historical evidence, lacked many of the problems and motivations of modern Western selfhood, including concern with self-deception, identity crises, and even the belief in an extensive inner, hidden selfhood. Obviously, the human body did not change greatly from the Middle Ages to modern times, so these extensive historical changes in selfhood almost certainly reflect a response to the changing demands of the social system.

History

Social psychology's interest in self had an odd history with unpromising beginnings. As Chapter 2 indicates, modern social psychology began to take shape in the 1950s. At that time, psychology was dominated by two wildly different paradigms. One was behaviorism, which took a dim view of selfhood. Behavior in that view was a product of reinforcement histories and situational contingencies. There was little room for self-esteem, identity crises, or "black box" invisible entities like the self.

The other dominant view was Freudian psychoanalysis. It did not quite talk about the self but did find it useful to talk about the "ego," which was seen in classic Freudian theory as the relatively weak servant of two powerhouse masters, namely, the instinctual drives in the id and the socialized guilt-mongering agent called the superego, which internalized society's rules. The ego, which can be seen as an early theory of self, was a rather pathetic creature trying to carry out the often contradictory demands of these two masters amid the further and often severe constraints of the external world. To be sure, after Freud died there was a movement to revise his theory to give more respect and assign more autonomous power to the ego. Across the Atlantic, in the United States, Gordon Allport (1943) predicted that psychology would devote increasing research attention to the study of ego, and although the term self gradually supplanted the Freudian term ego, he was quite right.

Interest in the self escalated rapidly in the 1960s and 1970s. Quite likely this was fueled by the zeitgeist, which was dominated by youthful rebellion against the Establishment and its rules for who to be and how to act and by the quest to explore and understand inner selves as a crucial pathway to fulfillment and as a vital basis for making life's difficult decisions. By the late 1970s, social psychologists had begun to study many phenomena loosely associated with the self. Incorporating ideas and methods pertinent to the self proved useful in research, and so the evidence accumulated. In the 1980s, before email was available, Anthony Greenwald began distributing an informal newsletter with abstracts of new research findings on the self. His list of addresses on the so-called Self Interest Group rapidly expanded to include hundreds of researchers who wanted to be kept abreast of the latest work.

Since then, the interest in self has remained a strong theme of social psychology, though the continuity is misleading. The study of self is a big tent containing many other areas of study, and these have waxed and waned over the years. As an incomplete list, consider these terms: self-affirmation, self-appraisal, self-awareness, self-concept, self-construal, self-deception, self-defeating behavior, self-enhancement, self-esteem, self-evaluation maintenance, self-interest, self-monitoring, self-perception, self-presentation, self-reference, self-regulation, self-serving bias, and self-verification.

What Is the Self?

In the middle 1990s, faced with the task of producing an integrative overview of research on the self, I searched long and hard for a single core phenomenon or basic root of selfhood, one that could serve as a useful framework for discussing all the work social psychologists had done. I failed. Instead, I reluctantly concluded that at least three important types of phenomena provided three basic roots of selfhood (Baumeister, 1998). This conceptual structure seems still viable and will be the organizational basis for this chapter.

The first basis for selfhood is consciousness turning around toward itself, which is sometimes called "reflexive consciousness." You can be aware of yourself and know things about yourself. For example, you might think about a recent success or failure experience you have had, including its implications for what possibilities the future may hold for you. You might seek to learn more about yourself by reading your horoscope, by weighing yourself, by timing yourself running a mile, or by taking a magazine quiz. After an accident, you might check your body systematically for injuries. You might read about something that someone did and wonder whether you yourself could do such a thing, whether it be climbing a mountain, learning to paint, shooting someone to death, or winning a Pulitzer prize. All these processes involve how the self is aware of itself and builds a stock of knowledge about itself.

The second basis of selfhood is in interpersonal relations. The self does not emerge from inside the person but rather is formed in interactions and relationships with other people. Moreover, the self functions to create and sustain relationships, to fulfill important roles, and to keep a favored position in the social system. Examples of the interpersonal aspect of self would include getting dressed up for an interview or date or ceremony, changing your behavior to live up to someone else's expectations, and competing against a rival. You might feel embarrassed upon finding that someone has been watching you. You may tell private, personal stories to help a new romantic partner get to know you. You may take on a new identity by joining a group or getting a job. All these involve the self being defined by how it is connected to others and to its efforts to make those relationships strong and satisfying.

The third and final basis of selfhood is making choices and exerting control. You may make yourself keep trying to achieve something despite failure, frustration, and discouragement. You may resist temptation to be true to your diet, your wedding vows, or your religious beliefs. You decide what to major in or where to live. You choose your goals and then work toward them even when you might not feel like doing so. You vote, you borrow money and pay it back, you make a promise to a friend and then keep it, and so forth. All these show the self at work, facing and making decisions, following through on previous commitments, and exerting control over itself.

Reflexive Consciousness: Building Self-Knowledge

One important part of the self exists mainly inside the individual's own mind. It consists of information. It starts as people pay attention to themselves, and it grows as they develop concepts and ideas about themselves. Self-knowledge has been extensively studied by social psychologists.

Self-Awareness

Self-knowledge would be impossible without self-awareness, which is the basic process by which attention turns around toward its source. An influential early theory by Duval and Wicklund (1972) proposed that awareness could be directed either inward or outward and that inward, self-directed attention would have various motivating effects on behavior. They came up with a startlingly simple way to induce high levels of self-awareness: seating the research participant in front of a mirror. Later refinements included inducing self-awareness with a video camera or with a real or imagined audience (see Carver & Scheier, 1981).

A trait scale that sorted people according to their habitual levels of high or low self-consciousness also proved to be a reliable source of significant differences (Fenigstein, Scheier, & Buss, 1975). Many articles (for reviews, see Carver & Scheier, 1981, 1982) contained one study that used a mirror or camera and a second study that relied on trait differences. The trait scale also promoted a useful conceptual distinction. It measured private self-consciousness, which referred to people's tendency to reflect on their inner selves and be aware of inner states and processes. It also measured public self-consciousness, which meant attunement to how oneself was regarded by others.

Being aware of oneself has many benefits. It improves introspection and awareness of inner states. Attitude self-reports filled out in front of a mirror are more accurate (in the sense that they predict subsequent behavior better) than those filled out with no mirror present, presumably because of the boost in self-awareness (Pryor, Gibbons, Wicklund, Fazio, & Hood, 1977). Self-awareness likewise seems to intensify awareness of one's emotional reactions and may intensify the emotions themselves (e.g., Scheier & Carver, 1977). As we shall see later, it improves self-regulation.

Many aspects of the original self-awareness theory gradually faded from use, but one that has gained in importance over the years was comparison to standards (Duval & Wicklund, 1972). Self-awareness is more than just noticing yourself or thinking about yourself: It usually involves an evaluative comparison to a standard. Standards are ideas about how things might or ought to be: ideals, goals, expectations (held by self or others), norms, laws, averages, past or present levels, and more. Even the simplest acts of self-awareness, such as a glance in the mirror, are more than "Hey, there I am!" Instead, they include comparisons to standard: My hair is a mess, that shirt looks better on me than I thought, am I gaining weight?

Comparison to standards motivates people to try to fit the standard (even combing one's hair). Hence, people often behave better when they are self-aware than when they are not. Increasing self-awareness improves performance and increases socially desirable behavior (Diener & Wallbom, 1976; Scheier, Fenigstein, & Buss, 1974; Wicklund & Duval, 1971).

The other side of the coin is that when behavior or outcomes are bad, people wish to avoid self-awareness. Counterattitudinal behavior, such as was induced in countless studies of cognitive dissonance, made participants avoid mirrors, presumably because they did not want to be aware of themselves when acting contrary to their beliefs (Greenberg & Musham, 1981).

Many behavioral patterns are associated with efforts to avoid self-awareness, including, though not limited to, wishes to stop being aware of self in connection with unpleasant things such as failures or misdeeds. Hull (1981) proposed that alcohol use reduces self-awareness and that people often drink alcohol precisely for that effect, either to forget their troubles or to reduce inhibitions and celebrate. (Inhibitions often center around self-awareness, because they invoke a particular standard of behavior and censure the self for violating it.) Thus, alcohol does not actually increase desires to misbehave but rather removes the inner restraints against them (Steele & Southwick, 1985; see also Steele & Josephs, 1990).

Binge eating is also associated with loss of self-awareness and may reflect an active attempt to lose awareness of self by submerging attention in low-level sensory experiences (Heatherton & Baumeister, 1991). Suicidal behavior likewise can be essentially a flight from painful self-awareness (Baumeister, 1991).

Escape from self-awareness may also be central to a variety of more unusual behaviors, such as sexual masochism, spiritual meditation, and spurious memories of being abducted by UFOs (Baumeister, 1991; Newman & Baumeister, 1996). The variety of such acts suggests that people have many reasons for wanting to escape the self, possibly because the modern human self is sometimes experienced as burdensome and stressful (Baumeister, 1991; Leary, 2004).

Greenberg and Pyszczynski (1986) proposed that depression is sometimes marked by getting stuck in a state of self-awareness, especially when that state is unpleasant. Even more broadly, Ingram (1990) found that many pathological symptoms are associated with high self-awareness. In general, one must assume that the capacity for self-awareness is a positive contribution to many uniquely human psychological achievements and capabilities, but it carries significant costs and drawbacks.

Self-Concepts, Schemas, and Beyond

The traditional term *self-concept* suggests that a person has a single, coherent, integrated idea (concept) that integrates self-knowledge. Although the term is still used sometimes, the assumption of coherent unity has proven untenable. Instead, people have plenty of specific ideas about themselves, and these may be only loosely related and sometimes contradictory. Markus (1977) proposed using the term *self-schema* to refer to each specific idea or piece of information about the self (e.g., "I am shy"). The self-schema term has the added benefit that a person can be aschematic on some dimension, which means not having a specific or clear idea about the self. Thus, someone may have a self-schema as talkative, quiet, or in between—or the person may be aschematic, which means not having any opinion as to how talkative versus quiet he or she is.

The multiplicity of self-schemas, as well as multiple social identifications, led many researchers for a while to speak of multiple selves, as if each person had many selves. The idea appealed as counterintuitive but presented all sorts of mischief. For example, if you and each of your roommates all have multiple selves, how could you possibly know which shoes to put on in the morning? Mercifully, the talk of multiple of multiple selves has largely subsided. Each person may have ideas of different versions of self (e.g., possible future selves; Markus & Nurius, 1986), but these are different versions of the same self. It is no accident that everywhere people refer to themselves with the singular "I" rather than the plural "we" (occasional kings and editors excepted—and even they know themselves as singular beings).

The diversity of self-knowledge makes people pliable in their self-views. Meehl (1956) coined the term the "Barnum effect" to refer to people's willingness to accept random feedback from ostensible experts as an accurate characterization of their personalities. Laboratory participants can be induced to regard themselves in many different ways with bogus feedback (e.g., Aronson & Mettee, 1968). Most social psychologists believe that horoscopes have no scientific validity, and so something like the Barnum effect is necessary to explain their appeal: If we tell you that you sometimes struggle to meet deadlines or are sometimes overly critical of partners, you may be willing to think this is correct.

The emerging picture is that a person has a vast store of beliefs about the self, only a few of which are active in focal awareness at any given time. The term "the phenomenal self" refers to this small portion of self-knowledge that is the current focus of awareness (Jones & Gerard, 1967), though other terms such as working self-concept and spontaneous self-concept have also been used (Markus & Kunda, 1986; McGuire, McGuire, Child, & Fujioka, 1978).

This view provides several useful implications. First, different situations can activate different self-schemas, and this produces different versions of self. McGuire et al. (1978; see also McGuire, McGuire, Child, & Winton, 1979) showed that things like race and gender stand out in one's self-concept precisely when they stand out in the immediate social context by virtue of being unusual. For example, a boy in a room full of girls is more aware of being a boy than is a boy in a crowd of boys.

Second, people can be manipulated by having them comb through their stock of self-views in a biased manner. Asking people to recall extraverted versus introverted tendencies—because almost everyone has some memories of both kinds—can get them to think of themselves as relatively extraverted or introverted, and their behavior is likely to be altered to be more consistent with those induced views of self (Fazio, Effrein, & Falendar, 1981; Jones, Rhodewalt, Berglas, & Skelton, 1981). These studies provide important basic clues as to how the self-concept can be changed.

Third, this view calls into question the sometimes popular notions of one "true" self that differs from other ideas of self. For centuries, writers have romanticized the notion that each person has a single true version of self that is buried inside and can be discovered or realized or, alternatively, can be lost and betrayed by inauthentic or other false behavior. Although people may be wrong about themselves in various particulars, the notion of an inner true self that is discovered by some kind of treasure hunt is probably best regarded as a troublesome myth. Ideas of self come in multiple, sometimes conflicting versions, and the reality of selfhood is likely an emerging project rather than a fixed entity.

Recent work has nevertheless confirmed that most people believe they have a true self. They consider this a proper guide to decision-making, and so when they are satisfied with their decisions, they think this indicates that their true self was guiding the choice (Schlegel, Hicks, Davis, Hirsch, & Smith, 2013). They distinguish their true self from self in general (and certainly from false self), and they regard the true self as generally positive and in particular highly moral (Strohminger, Knobe, & Newman, 2017).

Cognitive Roots of Self-Knowledge

Social psychologists have identified several ways that people acquire self-knowledge and self-schemas, though there does not seem to be any grand or integrative theory about this. It is helpful for new generations of researchers to know these classic contributions, however.

The self-reference effect refers to the tendency for information pertaining to the self to be processed more thoroughly than other information. In the original studies, Rogers, Kuiper, and Kirker (1977) presented participants with various adjectives and asked them a question about each one. Later they were given a surprise recall test. If the question had been "Does this word describe you?" the word was remembered better than if a different question had been used (e.g., "Do you know what this word means?" or "Is this a short word?"). Thus, thinking about the word in relation to the self created a stronger memory trace. This was true even if the person's answer had been no. Later work confirmed that the self is a particularly potent hook on which memory can hang information, though it is by no means unique (Greenwald & Banaji, 1989; Higgins & Bargh, 1987).

The self-reference effect is understood as a cognitive process, but it works with affect as well. The self appears to transfer its generally positive tone to information connected with it. People like things that are associated with the self. For example, people like the letters in their names better than other letters in the alphabet (Nuttin, 1985, 1987). Some researchers have begun using preference for the letters in one's name as a subtle measure of implicit (unconscious) self-esteem.

Items seem to gain in value by virtue of being associated with the self. People place a higher cash value on lottery tickets they chose than on ones given to them, even though all tickets have the same objective value (Langer, 1975). People like things more when they own them than when not, even though ownership stemmed from a random gift and they had not used them yet (Beggan, 1992; in this case, the items were insulator sleeves for cold drinks—hardly a major symbol of personal identity!). Thus, things that are mentally associated with the self acquire emotional overtones from that association.

Self-perception theory was proposed by Bem (1965, 1972) to explain one process of acquiring self-knowledge. The gist was that people learn about themselves much as they learn about others, namely, by observing behaviors and making inferences. The core idea is that people learn about themselves the same way they learn about others: They see what the person (in this case, the self) does and draw conclusions about traits that produce such acts. Such processes may be especially relevant when other sources of self-knowledge, such as direct awareness of one's feelings, are not strong or clear.

The most famous application of self-perception theory is the *overjustification effect*. It can be summarized by the expression that "rewards turn play into work." That is, when people perform an activity both because they enjoy doing it (intrinsic motivation) and because they are getting paid or otherwise rewarded (extrinsic motivation), the action is overly justified in the sense that there are multiple reasons for doing it. In such cases, the extrinsic rewards tend to take over and predominate, so that the person gradually comes to feel that he or she is mainly doing it for the sake of the extrinsic rewards. As a result, the person loses the desire or interest in doing it for its own sake.

This effect was first demonstrated by Deci (1971), who showed that students who were paid for doing puzzles subsequently (i.e., after the pay stopped coming) showed less interest in doing them than other students who had done the same tasks without pay. The self-perception aspect became more salient in studies by Lepper, Greene, and Nisbett (1973). In their work, getting rewards reduced children's intrinsic motivation to draw pictures with markers—but only if they knew in advance that they would get a reward. Surprise rewards had no such effect. If you saw someone else painting a picture and getting a surprise reward for it afterward, you would not conclude that the person painted for the sake of the reward, because the person did not know the reward was coming. In contrast, if the person knew about the reward before starting to paint, you might well infer that the person was painting to get the reward. Apparently, people sometimes apply the same logic in learning about themselves.

Motivational Influences on Self-Knowledge

The importance of the self and the diversity of potential information about the self create ample scope for motivations. Self-knowledge does not just happen. Rather, people seek out self-knowledge generally, and they often have highly selective preferences for some kinds of information over others.

Over the years, social psychologists have converged on three main motives that influence self-knowledge, corresponding to three types of preferences. One is a simple desire to learn the truth about the self, whatever it may be. This motive has been called diagnosticity, in that it produces a preference to find out whatever information can provide the clearest, most unambiguous information about the self (Trope, 1983, 1986). For example, taking a valid test under optimal conditions has high diagnosticity because it provides good evidence about one's knowledge and abilities. Taking an invalid test under adverse conditions, such as distracting noise or while intoxicated, has much less diagnosticity.

A second motive is called self-enhancement. It refers to a preference for favorable information about the self (for reviews, see Alicke & Sedikides, 2009; Sedikides & Gregg, 2008). Sometimes the term is used narrowly to refer to desiring information that will actually entail a favorable upward revision of beliefs about the self. Other usages are broader and include self-protection, that is, preference for avoiding information that would entail a downward revision of beliefs about the self. The idea that people like to hear good things about themselves and prefer to avoid being criticized is consistent with a broad range of findings.

The third motive emphasizes consistency. Consistency motives have a long and influential history in social psychology, such as in research on cognitive dissonance (Festinger, 1957). Applied to the self, the consistency motive has been dubbed self-verification, and in the sense that people seek to verify (confirm) whatever they already believe about themselves (see Swann, 1987), even if that information is unflattering. The underlying assumption is that revising one's views is effortful and aversive, so people prefer to stick with what they already think.

Much has been written about what happens when the consistency and enhancement motives clash. If a man believes he is incompetent at golf, does he prefer to hear further evidence of that incompetence, or would he like to be told his golf is pretty good after all? One resolution has been that emotionally he favors praise but cognitively he may be skeptical of it and hence more apt to believe confirmation (Swann, 1987).

A systematic effort to compare the relative power and appeal of the three motives was undertaken by Sedikides (1993). He concluded that all three motives are genuine and exert influence over self-knowledge. In general, though, he found that the self-enhancement motive was the strongest and the diagnosticity motive the weakest. In other words, people's appetite to learn the unvarnished truth about themselves is genuine, but it is outshone by their appetite for flattery and to a lesser extent by their wish to have their preconceptions confirmed.

One area of convergence between the two strongest motives (enhancement and verification) is the resistance to downward change. That is, both motives would make people reluctant to entertain new information that casts the self in a less favorable light than what they already think. Defensive processes should thus be very strong. This brings up self-deception.

Self-Deception

The very possibility of self-deception presents a philosophical quandary, insofar as the same person must seemingly be both the deceiver and the deceived. That seemingly implies that that person must both know something and not know it at the same time. Not much research has convincingly demonstrated effects that meet those criteria (Gur & Sackeim, 1979; Sackeim & Gur, 1979).

In contrast, self-deception becomes much more common and recognizable if it is understood more as a kind of wishful thinking, by which a person manages to end up believing what he or she wants to believe without the most rigorous justifications. An often-cited early survey by Svenson (1981) yielded the rather implausible result that 90% of people claimed to be above-average drivers. Many subsequent studies have yielded similar (and similarly implausible) statistics (see Gilovich, 1991). Because in principle only about half the population can truly be above average on any normally distributed trait, the surplus of self-rated excellence is generally ascribed to self-deception. In general, self-concepts are more favorable than the objective facts would warrant.

The widespread tendencies for self-deception led Greenwald (1980) to compare the self to a totalitarian regime (the "totalitarian ego") in its willingness to rewrite history and distort the facts to portray itself as benevolent and successful. A highly influential review by Taylor and Brown (1988) listed three main positive illusions. First, people overestimate their successes and good traits (and, in a related manner, undercount and downplay their failures and bad traits). Second, they overestimate how much control they have over their lives and their fate. Third, they are unrealistically optimistic, believing that they are more likely than other people to experience good outcomes and less likely to experience bad ones. Taylor and Brown went on to suggest that these distorted perceptions are part and parcel of good mental health and psychological adjustment and that people who see themselves in a more balanced, realistic manner are vulnerable to unhappiness and mental illness.

Self-deception has been analyzed in evolutionary terms by von Hippel and Trivers (2011). They pointed out that deceiving yourself has little benefit for survival and reproduction—but deceiving others can often be very helpful, such as when you persuade them to share their food or bed with you. Because people become sensitive to the fact that others sometimes lie, however, people become alert to subtle signs of deception. Hence, the deceiver faces a problem of how to deceive without revealing that he or she is deceiving. A solution is to deceive oneself first. Your statements will be more persuasive if you sincerely believe them yourself than if you are aware you are lying. Note that this explains why people want to believe favorable things about themselves: That will enable them to present themselves favorably to others in a credible manner.

How do people manage to deceive themselves? A wide assortment of strategies and tricks has been documented. Here are some. The self-serving bias is a widely replicated pattern by which people assign more responsibility to external causes for failures than for successes (Zuckerman, 1979). People are selectively critical of evidence that depicts them badly while being uncritical of more agreeable feedback (Pyszczynski, Greenberg, & Holt, 1985; Wyer & Frey, 1983). People pay more attention to good than to bad feedback, allowing for better encoding into memory (Baumeister & Cairns, 1992), so they selectively forget failures more than successes (Crary, 1966; Mischel, Ebbesen, & Zeiss, 1976). People compare themselves against targets that make them look good rather than against other, more intimidating targets (Crocker & Major, 1989; Wills, 1981). They also persuade themselves that their good traits are unusual while their bad traits are widely shared (Campbell, 1986; Marks, 1984; Suls & Wan, 1987).

Another group of strategies involves distorting the meaning of ambiguous traits (Dunning, 2005; Dunning, Meyerowitz, & Holzberg, 1989). Everyone wants to be smart, but there are book smarts, street smarts, emotional intelligence, and other forms, so most everyone can find some basis for thinking themselves smart.

The downside of self-deception would seemingly be an increased risk of failures and other misfortunes stemming from making poor choices. For example, people routinely overestimate how fast they can get things done, with the result that many projects take longer and cost more than originally budgeted (Buehler, Griffin, & Ross, 1994). Sometimes people procrastinate based on an overconfident expectation about how fast they can get a project done, with the result that last-minute delays or problems force them either to miss the deadline or to turn in subpar work (Ferrari, Johnson, & McCown, 1995; Tice & Baumeister, 1997).

One remarkable way that people seem to reduce the risks and costs of self-deception is to turn positive illusions on and off. Normally they maintain pleasantly inflated views of their capabilities, but when they face a difficult decision involving making a commitment, they seem to suspend these illusions and temporarily become quite realistic about what they can and cannot accomplish. Once the decision is made, they blithely resume their optimistic, self-flattering stance (Gollwitzer & Kinney, 1989; Gollwitzer & Taylor, 1995). The full implications of these findings—that apparently people maintain parallel but different views of self and can switch back and forth among them as is useful for the situation—have yet to be fully explored and integrated into theory of self.

Self-Esteem and Narcissism

The motivation to protect and enhance self-esteem has figured prominently in social psychology, but self-esteem has also been studied as a trait dimension along which people differ. Over the years, a great many studies have examined how people with high self-esteem differ from those with low self-esteem, typically using the Rosenberg (1965) scale to distinguish the two. Interest has been sustained by belief in practical applications, such as the notion that raising self-esteem among schoolchildren will facilitate learning and good citizenship while reducing drug abuse and problem pregnancies (California Task Force, 1990).

Unfortunately, the fond hopes that boosting self-esteem would make people wiser, kinder, and healthier have been largely disappointed. There are in fact replicable positive correlations between self-esteem and school performance, but high self-esteem appears to be the result rather than the cause of good grades (e.g., Bachman & O'Malley, 1977). If anything, experimental evidence suggests that boosting self-esteem causes students to perform worse subsequently (Forsyth et al., 2007). The long-standing belief that low self-esteem causes violence has likewise been shown to depend mainly on overinterpreted correlations and self-reports. Seriously violent persons, ranging from the Nazi "Master Race" killers and despotic tyrants to wife-beaters, murderers, rapists, and bullies, tend to think very favorably of themselves (Baumeister, Smart, & Boden, 1996).

There does remain some controversy on the latter score. A New Zealand sample studied by Donnellan et al. (2005) provided comfort to those who believe that low self-esteem contributes to violence, insofar as their survey found that children scoring low in self-esteem were later rated by teachers as more likely to get into fights. However, that sample may be unusual because of its high representation of native Maoris, a downtrodden culture with low self-esteem that romanticizes its violent warrior traditions. Controlled laboratory experiments with ethnically homogeneous, Western samples have consistently failed to find any sign of elevated aggression among people with low self-esteem. On the contrary, high narcissism and high self-esteem contribute most directly to aggression (Bushman & Baumeister, 1998; Bushman et al., 2009; Menon et al., 2007).

One fairly thorough literature review concluded that two benefits of high self-esteem are well established (Baumeister, Campbell, Krueger, & Vohs, 2003). High self-esteem supports initiative, possibly because it lends confidence to act on one's beliefs and assumptions and a willingness to go against the crowd. It also contributes to feeling good and happy. These two benefits take multiple forms, such as promoting persistence in the face of failure and a resilience under stress and adversity. (The dynamics of self-esteem in close relationships are covered in Chapter 10.)

Many contributions to understanding self-esteem do not depend on searching for benefits of high self-esteem. Campbell (1990) showed that self-esteem levels are associated with differential self-concept clarity. People with high self-esteem have clear and consistent beliefs about themselves, whereas the beliefs of people with low self-esteem are often confused, contradictory, and fluctuating. The lack of a stable image of self also may contribute to the greater emotional lability of people low in self-esteem (Campbell, Chew, & Scratchley, 1991).

Self-esteem can be based on different things. Crocker and Wolfe's (2001) research on contingencies of self-worth has found that identical outcomes may affect people differently depending on whether the underlying dimension is an important basis of each person's self-esteem. For example, academic success will boost self-esteem among some students more than others, insofar as some base their self-esteem on school success and achievement more than others.

Although self-esteem tends to be fairly stable over time, it fluctuates more among some people than others. Kernis and his colleagues have studied this by administering a self-esteem scale repeatedly and determining how much each individual changes. Higher instability of self-esteem (i.e., more change) has been linked to multiple outcomes, including aggression and emotional reactions (Kernis, 1993; Kernis, Cornell, Sun, Berry, & Harlow, 1993; Kernis, Granneman, & Barclay, 1989).

Different levels of self-esteem are associated with different social motivations. People with high self-esteem are attracted to new challenges and opportunities for success. People with low self-esteem favor a cautious, self-protective orientation that seeks to minimize risks, resolve problems, and avoid failures (Baumeister, Tice, & Hutton, 1989; Wood, Heimpel, & Michela, 2003; Wood, Heimbel, Newby-Clark, & Ross, 2005; Wood, Michela, & Giordano, 2000).

Given how few direct benefits flow from high self-esteem, why do people care so much about sustaining and even increasing their favorable views of self? The widespread concern is even more surprising given the remarkable range of evidence, reviewed by Crocker and Park (2004), that the pursuit of high self-esteem is often costly and destructive to the individual as well as to other people. The pursuit of high self-esteem can reduce learning, empathy, and prosocial behavior, while increasing aggression and rule-breaking.

One promising answer, proposed by Leary and his colleagues, depicts self-esteem as a sociometer, that is, an internal measure of how much one is likely to be accepted by others (e.g., Leary, Tambor, Terdal, & Downs, 1995). Self-esteem is typically based on the attributes that make one desirable as a group member or relationship partner: competence, attractiveness, likeability, social skills, trustworthiness, reliability, and more. Although having a favorable opinion of oneself may have relatively little benefit, being accepted by others is highly important, and indeed belonging to social groups is central to the biological strategies by which human beings survive and reproduce (Baumeister, 2005; Baumeister & Leary, 1995). Thus, ultimately, concern with self-esteem is nature's way of making people want to be accepted by others. When people cultivate self-esteem by deceiving themselves and overestimating their good traits, rather than by actually trying to be a good person, they are in effect misusing the system for emotional satisfactions and thwarting its purpose.

Recent work has begun to suggest that the sociometer theory focuses too much on being liked and accepted. In this view, self-esteem is much more about succeeding in the social realm, such as rising in the status hierarchy. Some scholars propose that the term *sociometer* be replaced, or at least augmented with the idea of a "hierometer," that is, a measure of how well regarded one is within the group's status hierarchy (Mahadevan, Gregg, Sedikides, & deWall-Andrews, 2016; see also Gebauer et al., 2015). While it is tempting to pit the two theories against each other, it may ultimately turn out that both being liked/accepted and gaining status are important contributors to self-esteem.

Viewing self-esteem as a sociometer and/or a hierometer brings us to the interpersonal aspect of self. Essentially, sociometer theory proposes that self-esteem serves interpersonal functions, and the reasons people care about self-esteem are based on the fundamental importance of being accepted by other people (Leary & Baumeister, 2000). This approach reverses one simple and common approach to understanding psychological phenomena, which is to assume that what happens between people is a result of what is inside them (in this case, that interpersonal behavior is a result of self-esteem). Instead, it contends that the inner processes such as self-esteem emerged or evolved to facilitate social interaction.

In recent years, some interest has shifted from self-esteem to narcissism, which can be understood as a relatively obnoxious form of high self-esteem (though there are a few puzzling individuals who score high in narcissism but low in self-esteem). Narcissism is not just having a favorable view of self as superior to others but also reflects a motivational concern with thinking well of oneself and with getting other people to admire the self (Morf & Rhodewalt, 2001).

Interpersonal Self

The interpersonal aspects of self have received only intermittent attention from social psychologists, though by now most would acknowledge their importance. Indeed, in recent decades, some of the most creative of these contributions have come not from the self researchers themselves but from the relationships experts. In particular, the blurring of self-concept boundaries has shown in a program indicating that people incorporate attributes of close relationship partners in to their own self-concepts, known as "including others in the self" (e.g., Aron et al., 2004). Extending this approach from self-concept to self-regulation, Fitzsimons, Finkel, and vanDellen (2015) explained that partners not only regulate themselves within relationships, but they also regulate each other and regulate on behalf of the relationship, as well as (sometimes) supporting each other's self-regulatory efforts. This develops to the point at which it ceases to be helpful or meaningful to think only in terms of one person self-regulating. Instead, partners in a close relationship form a system that self-regulates via each person. How well they self-regulate together predicts how long the relationship lasts, as well as predicting success at pursuing their goals.

Self-presentation was perhaps the first interpersonal aspect of self that had a major impact on how researchers think about selfhood. Research on self-presentation spread widely during the 1980s but has tapered off considerably in recent years, partly because many of the basic questions were answered.

Self-Presentation

Self-presentation, also sometimes called impression management, refers to people's efforts to portray themselves in particular ways to others (Schlenker, 1975, 1980). That is, it indicates how people try to make others view them as having certain traits and properties. Most commonly, people seek to make a good impression, but there can be other intended impressions. For example, a violent criminal may seek to convince others that he is dangerous and unpredictable, so that they will do what he says without fighting back or resisting.

Self-presentation first began to influence social psychology when it was put forward as an alternative explanation for research findings that emphasized inner processes. In particular, studies of attitude change and cognitive dissonance had proposed that when people act in ways contrary to their beliefs, they experience an inner state of unpleasant inconsistency, which they resolve by changing their inner attitude to conform to what they have done. Tedeschi, Schlenker, and Bonoma (1971) proposed instead that people merely want to appear consistent, so they might report attitudes consistent with their behavior, even if they did not actually change their attitude. That is, instead of seeking to rationalize their behavior to themselves, they were simply trying to make a good impression on the experimenters. As evidence, self-presentation researchers pointed out that people showed attitude change when their behavior had been viewed by others but not when it was secret or anonymous (Carlsmith, Collins, & Helmreich, 1966; Helmreich & Collins, 1968). The inconsistency and hence the need to rationalize should have been the same regardless of whether others were watching, but the concern with making a good impression would only arise if other people were paying attention.

The controversy over dissonance raged for years. Eventually the conclusion was that people do change attitudes more under public than private conditions, but this involved a genuine inner change rather than just saying something to look good to the experimenter (e.g., Baumeister & Tice, 1984; Cooper & Fazio, 1984; Schlenker, 1980; Tetlock & Manstead, 1985). Dissonance is not our concern here but that resolution is quite important for the development of self-presentation theory. Self-presentation came to mean more than just saying things that one does not really mean to make a good impression. Rather, inner processes are strongly affected by the interpersonal context. Over the years, researchers continued to show that a great deal of inner cognitive and emotional work is done to project the desired image of self (e.g., Schlenker & Leary, 1982; Vohs, Baumeister, & Ciarocco, 2005).

Methodologically, self-presentation research came to rely heavily on comparing behavior in public versus private conditions (Schlenker, 1980). The assumption was that if people behaved differently in public, the difference reflected their concern with how others perceived them and hence showed that they were motivated to send a particular message about themselves. Over the years, a wide variety of phenomena had been shown to change as a function of whether the behavior was public or private, and so the implications were far wider than cognitive dissonance and attitude change. Aggression, helping, reactance, attributions, self-handicapping, prejudice, and many other behaviors showed these differences, indicating that often such behaviors were guided by interpersonal motivations (Baumeister, 1982). Taken together, these shifts pushed social psychology to become more interpersonal, because many of these phenomena had hitherto been discussed and explained purely in terms of what happens inside the individual mind, but now they had to be acknowledged as influenced by the interpersonal context.

Crucially, though, evidence of self-presentational and interpersonal motives could not be interpreted as denying that genuine inner processes were at work also (such as with cognitive dissonance; e.g., Tetlock & Manstead, 1985). Instead, it became necessary to understand the inner and the interpersonal as linked. Ultimately, these findings pointed toward the general conclusion that *inner processes serve interpersonal functions.* This is possibly one of the most important general principles in social psychology.

Self-presentation was widely studied in the 1980s, but then the basic points had been made, and work showing that people seek to manage the impressions they make on others has subsided. Recently, however, there is renewed interest in reputation, particularly in connection with the rise in study of morality (see Chapter 13). A remarkable study by Engelmann, Herrmann, and Tomasello (2012) investigated whether participants would perform an immoral act (stealing) to benefit the self, as a function of whether others were present. The participants were either human children or adult chimpanzees. The chimps (humankind's closest biological relatives) were indifferent to the presence of others, whereas human five-year-olds stole much less when someone else was present. Thus, concern with moral reputation starts early in (human) life but does not seem to be present in chimpanzees.

One of the more creative extensions of self-presentation theory in recent decades was a review by Leary, Tchividjian, and Kraxberger (1994) showing that self-presentation can be hazardous to one's health. That is, people do things to make a good impression even though they know these things may be harmful. Interest in this work was sparked by Mark Leary's conversation with a friend who continued to sunbathe despite having had skin cancer (which is often caused by high exposure to the sun). Leary discovered that his friend was far from unique, and in fact many people sunbathe even after they have had skin cancer, because they believe that a suntan makes them attractive to others. (A tan itself has a mixed history as a self-presentational tool. In the 1800s, sun-darkened skin was taken as a sign of being from a low or working class, because it meant that the person worked out in the sun. The term "redneck" today still conveys this link between sun exposure and low socioeconomic class. However, in the early 1920s, rich people began to play tennis, thereby getting suntans, and the tanned look became fashionable.)

Moving on beyond sunbathing, Leary et al. (1994) identified a host of things people do that are bad for their health but presumably useful for self-presentation. They ride motorcycles without helmets. They smoke cigarettes, to look cool or to stay thin (nicotine suppresses appetite). They fail to use condoms, in case partners might suspect them of being overly concerned or of having a sexual disease. They balk at going to the gym for exercise in case others might see them as fat or unfit. They have cosmetic surgery simply to improve their looks, despite cost, pain, and risk of complications.

The implications of this work are thought-provoking. Indeed, one influential theory in social psychology has held that people are mainly motivated by fear of death and that everything people do is aimed toward the overarching goal of prolonging life and even of avoiding the very thought of death (Pyszczynski, Greenberg, & Solomon, 1997). (In fact, the original statement of this theory was in an edited book about self-presentation; see Greenberg, Pyszczynski, & Solomon, 1986.) Yet the review by Leary et al. (1994) showed, over and over, that many people do things that endanger their lives, when those actions help to make a good impression on others. Hence, making a good impression can sometimes be a stronger motivation than avoiding death. To be sure, making a good impression is probably an important part of maintaining social acceptance, which itself generally serves the goal of protecting and prolonging life, even if sometimes the goals conflict.

Self-Concept Change and Stability

Can the self-concept change? Of course it can, and does. But demonstrating self-concept change in the laboratory has proven difficult.

Interpersonal context and processes appear to be important in self-concept change. Harter (1993) has found that children's self-esteem is most likely to change when the child's social network changes, such as when the child enters a different school or when the family moves. This finding suggests that one source of stability of self-concept is interacting with people who know you and have a stable impression of you.

Laboratory studies have sought to show change in self-concept stemming from interpersonal behavior. When people present themselves in a particular way to strangers, they sometimes internalize how they acted, leading them to view themselves as being the sort of person they presented themselves as being (Jones, Rhodewalt, Berglas, & Skelton, 1991). There are competing views as to how this occurs. One is that to present themselves as being ambitious, for example, people must retrieve evidence from memory that would depict them as ambitious and then when asked to describe themselves, that information has more weight than it would otherwise.

It seems essential, however, that another person hear and believe the self-presentation. When people present themselves in one way but privately scan their memories for evidence of the opposite trait, the memory scans have little effect on self-concept whereas the self-concept shifts to resemble the version that the other person saw (Schlenker, Dlugolecki, & Doherty, 1994). The decisiveness of the interpersonal context was shown by Tice (1992), who showed that essentially identical behaviors led to self-concept change when witnessed by others but not when they were private or confidential.

Receiving feedback from others may or may not bring about self-concept change. People accept favorable feedback more readily than critical feedback (Taylor & Brown, 1988). Apart from favorability, another factor is whether people receive the evaluations passively or can assert themselves interpersonally by disputing the feedback. They are less affected if they can dispute it interpersonally than if they receive it without the opportunity to respond (Swann & Hill, 1982).

One of the most elegant theories linking self-concept stability to interpersonal processes is Tesser's (1988) self-evaluation maintenance theory. Two different processes govern how a person's self-esteem is affected by relationship partners. The first is reflection, which means that the partner's achievements and attributes reflect on the self in a consistent manner. That is, your partner's good works reflect well on you, and your partner's misdeeds reflect badly on you. The other process is comparison, which reverses the valence: Your partner's successes make you look worse by comparison. Which process predominates depends on several factors. If the partner's attribute is highly relevant to your own career or self-concept, comparison is more important, whereas your partner's successes and failures on things irrelevant to your own work foster reflection. The closeness of the relationship intensifies both outcomes. Thus, you are more affected by the successes and failures of your romantic partner than by those of a distant cousin or casual acquaintance.

Executive Function: Self as Agent

The third aspect of self involves what it does, in the sense of how the self acts on the world (and acts on itself). This area of study was slower to develop, as compared with self-knowledge and interpersonal dynamics. Self-regulation, however, has become a major theme of research. It began to increase in the late 1980s and by 2000 had become an ongoing focus of many laboratories. Other aspects of the self as executive function, such as the self as decision maker or as the controller of controlled processes, seem promising areas for further work.

Dual process theories that distinguish between automatic and controlled processes have become widely influential in social psychology. The self is essentially the controller of controlled processes (if not the self, then who else?), and so it plays an important role in such theories. How the self exerts such control is not well understood, and researchers have developed elaborate theories of automatic response processes but fewer and vaguer ones about controlled processes but illuminating the processes of control promise to shed considerable light on this important function of the self. Decision-making also involves the self, but that work will be covered in Chapter 19 rather than here.

Self-Regulation

Self-regulation refers to the self's capacity to alter and change itself and its states, particularly to bring them into line with standards such as norms, goals, ideals, or rules. Self-regulation includes such diverse areas as controlling one's thoughts, controlling one's emotions, impulse control and the restraint of problem behavior, and optimizing performance. The everyday term *self-control* is quite similar to *self-regulation* and sometimes the terms are used interchangeably, though some researchers make a slight distinction on the basis that self-control refers exclusively to conscious, effortful processes whereas self-regulation also includes nonconscious or automatic regulatory processes, even such as the bodily processes that keep the temperature constant and regulate the speed of the heartbeat.

A landmark step in the development of self-regulation theory was Carver and Scheier's (1981, 1982) assertion that self-awareness is essentially for the sake of self-regulation. As you recall, the earlier section on self-awareness pointed out that humans are almost always self-aware in relation to some standard, so that the current state of the self is compared to how it might be. This fact fits well with the idea that self-regulation is the purpose of self-awareness.

Building on that insight, Carver and Scheier (1981, 1982, 1998) imported the concept of the feedback loop from cybernetic theory (e.g., Powers, 1973). The feedback loop is best remembered with its acronym TOTE, which stands for test, operate, test, and exit. Such loops supervise effective self-regulation. Test involves comparing the current state of the self to the goal or standard. If the test produces an unsatisfactory result, so that the self is not as it should be, then an operate phase is commenced to fix the problem. From time to time, there is another test phase, to ensure that progress is being made toward the goal. Eventually one of these tests indicates that the self now meets the standard, and the loop is exited.

The feedback loop incorporates the three essential ingredients of self-regulation. Let us consider each in turn.

Standards

The term *regulate* means not just to change but rather to change based on some concept of what ought (or ought not) to be. These concepts are standards. Without standards, self-regulation would have no meaning. Standards can come from external sources such as laws, norms, and expectations, but the self-regulating person internalizes the standard to some degree. The standards are not simply ideas or rules but rather incorporate the motivational aspect of self-regulation. The amount of effort devoted to self-regulation—and, therefore to some degree, the success or failure of self-regulation—depends on the extent to which the person embraces the standard and desires to regulate behavior to match it.

Standards can be sorted into two main types according to whether the person wants to move toward or away from them (Carver & Scheier, 1998). Positive standards are ones the person wants to approach, and so the purpose of the feedback loop is to reduce the discrepancy between how you are and the standard. For example, a dieter may have a specific target weight (the standard) and strives to lose pounds to match that weight. In contrast, negative standards are ones that the person seeks to avoid matching, such as being a liar, a loser, or a drug addict. In these cases, the goal of the feedback loop is to maximize the difference between the actual self and the standard.

An important implication is that the negative standards are more difficult to implement (Carver, & Scheier, 1998). It is harder to regulate yourself to not be something than to become something, because there is no obvious direction or goal of change. This can be illustrated by the analogy to a spatial goal. If your goal is to go to Pittsburgh, then you know where you want to be, you can work on changing your location to get closer, and you know when you have successfully arrived there. In contrast, if your goal is to be far away from Pittsburgh, you do not know exactly where to go, and there is no point at which your regulatory task can be pronounced to have reached success. Thus, common self-regulatory tasks such as quitting smoking are by their very nature problematic, because one is never sure one has quit once and for all, and the steps along the way do not prescribe doing any specific thing.

The difference between positive and negative standards has also been the focus of research by E. T. Higgins. In an influential 1987 article, he proposed that standards could be sorted into ideals (how one wanted to be) and oughts (how one is expected to be, which often involves specifics about what not to do and how not to be) and argued, more provocatively, that different emotional reactions were associated with these two types of standards. Specifically, he contended that failure to reach ideals led to low-energy emotions such as sadness and depression, whereas failure to do as one ought to do produced high-energy emotions such as guilt and anxiety (Higgins, 1987). However, the considerable amount of research aimed at pursuing this intriguing theory of emotion produced results that were mixed at best (Tangney, Niedenthal, Covert, & Barlow, 1998).

The impasse prompted Higgins to revise his approach and emphasize a basic distinction between promotion (standards oriented toward approaching gains) and prevention (standards oriented toward avoiding losses; Higgins, 1997). Higgins has also proposed that one can approach or avoid in either a promotion-oriented or prevention-oriented way, which creates a 2×2 motivational space. According to his regulatory focus theory, individuals self-regulate differently when they are pursuing promotion-focused versus prevention-focused goals (Higgins, 1997; Higgins & Spiegel, 2004; Molden, Lee, & Higgins, 2008). Promotion-focused goals emphasize advancement, aspiration, and accomplishment, whereas prevention-focused goals emphasize safety, security, and protection. Individuals in a promotion focus experience self-regulatory success as achieving a positive outcome (a gain) and unsuccessful self-regulation as a missed opportunity for a positive outcome (a nongain), whereas individuals in a prevention focus experience self-regulatory success as protecting against a negative outcome (a nonloss) and unsuccessful self-regulation as incurring a negative outcome (a loss). Furthermore, individuals tend to pursue promotion-focused goals with *eager* self-regulatory strategies and prevention-focused goals with *vigilant* self-regulatory strategies.

One application of regulatory focus theory to self-regulation research involves the tradeoff between speed and accuracy in goal pursuit, with the eagerness of promotion-focused goal pursuit predicting greater speed and diminished accuracy relative to the vigilance of prevention goal pursuit (Förster, Higgins, & Bianco, 2003). In an illustrative study, relative to individuals primed with a prevention focus, those primed with a promotion focus were faster at a proofreading task (indicating eagerness) but less accurate at finding complex grammatical errors (indicating lower vigilance).

Regulatory focus also influences whether individuals tend to view goals as luxuries or necessities. A promotion focus facilitates viewing an adopted goal as one of many opportunities for advancement (i.e., as a luxury), whereas a prevention focus facilitates viewing an adopted goal as the essential means for achieving the goal (i.e., as a necessity). As a result, individuals in a prevention focus tend to initiate goal pursuit faster than do those in a promotion focus (Freitas, Liberman, Salovey, & Higgins, 2002).

Monitoring

Monitoring refers to paying attention to and keeping track of the behavior that is to be changed. Just as it is difficult to shoot at a target you cannot see, it is difficult to regulate a behavior that you do not monitor. When people want to improve their self-control, the most effective first steps usually involve improved monitoring: Write down what you spend, weigh yourself daily, count the laps you run, and so forth. Failures of self-control often begin with ceasing to monitor. For example, when dieters go on an eating binge, they lose track of how much they eat, much more than other people (Polivy, 1976).

The feedback loop theory by Carver and Scheier (1981) is essentially a theory of monitoring. As we noted, it made the crucial link between self-awareness and self-regulation. Monitoring thus depends on self-awareness. It is no mere coincidence that loss of self-awareness contributes to poor self-regulation. For example, alcohol reduces self-awareness (Hull, 1981), and alcohol intoxication contributes to almost all known manner of self-control problems. Intoxicated persons spend more money, gamble more, eat more, behave more aggressively, engage in inappropriate sexual activities, and so forth (Baumeister, Heatherton, & Tice, 1994).

Willpower

The third ingredient is the capacity to change the self. The folk notion of willpower appears to have some psychological validity, in the sense that the self consists partly of an energy resource that is expended during acts of self-control. Following an initial act of self-control, performance on a second, unrelated self-control task is often impaired, suggesting that some energy was expended during the first task and hence was not available to help with the second task (e.g., Baumeister, Bratslavsky, Muraven, & Tice, 1998). The stated of reduced resources has been dubbed *ego depletion*, because it suggests that some of the self's (ego's) resources have been depleted.

Is the self made partly from energy? For several decades, self theories were mainly cognitive. They focused on self-knowledge and self-awareness and how these influenced information processing. The first ego depletion findings were thus something of an oddity, because the very idea of self as energy was foreign to prevailing views. However, the influx of biological concepts into psychological theory made energy more plausible, insofar as life itself is an energy process and all biological activities depend on energy.

Depleted willpower does not doom the person to poor self-control. People can overcome depletion and perform effectively. Motivational incentives can encourage people to do this (Muraven & Slessareva, 2003), as can positive emotion (Tice, Baumeister, Shmueli, & Muraven, 2007). Thinking at a highly meaningful, abstract level that incorporates long-range perspectives can also improve self-control, even despite depletion (Fujita, Trope, Liberman, & Levin-Sagi, 2006). Having faith in one's unlimited willpower can help as well (Job et al., 2010, 2013). However, these things mainly work when one is only slightly depleted, just as it is easy to overcome slight tiredness of physical muscles. With more extensive depletion, they lose effectiveness and even backfire (Vohs et al., 2013).

The theories of limited self-regulatory strength and ego depletion have led to much research, including some criticism (see Baumeister, Tice, & Vohs, 2018; Baumeister & Vohs, 2016). Two main lines of criticism are presently being debated. As they contradict each other, one of them at least has to be false, but if you wish to understand the current research issues, it is important to know them both. First, some researchers argue that although depletion effects are robust, they are driven not by a basic motivation resource, but by beliefs, motivations, attentional processes, or cost–benefit analyses (Inzlicht, Schmeichel, & Macrae, 2014;

Kurzban, Duckworth, Kable, & Myers, 2013). Second, some researchers have questioned whether the entire literature on depletion adds up to a massive false positive—that there is no effect in the first place (e.g., Carter, Kofler, Forster, & McCullough, 2015; Hagger et al., 2016). My sense is that this second objection is wildly implausible in view of the hundreds of significant findings, but the first objection is an intriguing challenge worth further study.

Beyond Self-regulation: Executive Function

The idea that the self consists partly of energy, rather than merely concepts, offers a basis for thinking about some of the self's activities beyond self-regulation. The category of executive function (also called agency, as in being an agent) invokes several other things the self does, including making choices, exerting control over the physical and social environment, and taking initiative. In philosophy, questions of agency invoke debates about free will and freedom of action.

There is some evidence that the same energy used for self-control is used for these other activities. After people make choices, their self-control is impaired, which suggests that the same energy is used for both decision-making and self-regulation (Vohs et al., 2008). Conversely, after exerting self-control, decision processes are changed and seemingly impaired (Pocheptsova et al., 2009). There is even some evidence that glucose depletion contributes to irrational decision-making (Masicampo & Baumeister, 2008).

The study of executive function is a promising area for advances in the next decade (see Miyake et al., 2000; Suchy, 2009). Planning, decision-making, task-switching and resumption, goal maintenance and change, information updating and monitoring, and other supervisory processes fall into this category, which is of interest not only to social psychology's self theorists but also to brain researchers, cognitive scientists, and others. A full accounting of how these processes operate and interact will contribute greatly to the understanding of this important aspect of the self.

Self-Determination Theory

Social psychology has a long tradition of studying behavior by assuming that the individual responds to causes that lie outside, in the situation. Rebelling against this view, Deci and Ryan (1995; also see Ryan & Deci, 2017) have advocated Self-Determination Theory, which depicts the self as an active agent and emphasizes causes that lie inside the self. In their view, human behavior produces much more beneficial outcomes when people act from internal causes than when they allow themselves to be pushed by external factors. Of course, the simple dichotomy of internal versus external causes is not rigid, and there are many intermediate causes, such as when people internalize and accept influences from their social worlds, but these are seen as in between. The more internal the cause, the better.

Self-Determination Theory grew out of Deci's (1971) research on intrinsic motivation, which was defined as the desire to do something for the sake of enjoyment of the activity itself. It was contrasted with extrinsic motivation, which meant a desire to do something based on the results or outcomes it would bring. This distinction led to the discovery of the overjustification effect (see the previous section on the cognitive roots of self-knowledge).

Self-Determination Theory was developed to respond to the complications surrounding the simple distinction between intrinsic and extrinsic motivation. The core emphasis on the importance of agentic action based on inner values and causes remained central, however. Deci and Ryan (1991, 1995) proposed that people have a fundamental need for autonomy, which can only be satisfied by acting in ways that bring the feeling that one's acts originate from within the self, as opposed to being controlled or directed by outside forces. It is not enough to contemplate an external reason to do something and then deliberately decide to go along with it. Instead, it is essential that the very reasons for the action be seen as originating within the self.

Not all researchers accept that autonomy is truly a need, in the sense that people will suffer pathological outcomes if they mainly do what they are told or what the situation requires instead of following their inner promptings. Nonetheless, this controversial position represents an important perspective on human behavior and likely points the way toward the most satisfying and fulfilling ways to live. Ryan and Deci (2017) review ample evidence that autonomy is a need, such as findings that evidence for it is found from diverse cultures and individuals and that failing to achieve autonomy (i.e., satisfy the need) impairs motivation, well-being, and health.

What is autonomy? The literal meaning is self-government, that is, initiating behavior and exerting control over oneself. It does not mean that the person is immune to external causes but rather that the person acts with the whole self. That is, the person considers the possible action and decides to do it on the basis of the person's values and preferences. It is the opposite of being controlled by external forces.

Another notable assertion of Self-Determination Theory is that people have a need for competence. This means learning to control events and to experience oneself as capable and effective. The notion that there is a natural drive to achieve mastery and control is well rooted in psychological theory and implicit in many phenomena, such as findings about learned helplessness (Seligman, 1975) and stress (Brady, 1958). The novel point in Self-Determination Theory is that it is not just control but specifically an awareness of the self as capably exerting control that is central to human motivation. People are motivated to believe that they can effectively exert control.

Managing Multiple Goals

Much of self-regulation involves keeping one's behavior on track toward goals. Yet people have more than one goal at a time, and so part of managing oneself effectively is juggling the different goals. In recent years, researchers have begun to look at how people manage multiple goals.

Several relevant processes and strategies have been identified. *Goal shielding* refers to the process of protecting one's pursuit of one goal from the distracting thoughts and feelings associated with other goals (Shah, Friedman, & Kruglanski, 2002). When people are shielding their pursuit of one goal, they are less prone to think of other goals and less effective at coming up with means of reaching these alternative goals.

Another set of processes involves managing limited amounts of time and effort to allocate them where they are most needed. People appraise progress toward various goals. If they think they are ahead of schedule on pursuing one goal, they may cut back effort on it, a response known as *coasting* (Carver & Scheier, 2009). This allows them to focus effort on other goals, for which progress may be more urgent. Notably this is not the same as reducing effort when one actually reaches or fulfills a goal, because it may happen anywhere along the way, as long as one feels one has made good progress.

Work by Fishbach (2009; see also Fishbach & Dhar, 2005; Fishbach & Zhang, 2009) has focused on the tension between juggling multiple goals (which she calls balancing) and featuring a single primary goal (which she calls *highlighting*). The greater the commitment to one goal, the more likely it is to be highlighted, which is to say pursued even at the possible cost of neglecting other goals. Meanwhile, when balancing multiple goals, an important factor is how much progress one has made toward each. Focusing on how much is left to do makes you want to zero in on that goal; focusing on how much you have already achieved can make you temporarily satisfied so you can shift efforts elsewhere (as in the concept of coasting).

Conclusion: Looking Ahead

It is safe to say that the self will remain an important focus of theorizing and research in social psychology. Within the broad topic of self, however, the so-called hot areas of study continue to change. Cultural differences in self-construal have continued to provide new research findings. Self-esteem continues to attract interest, most recently in terms of questions about how much it contributes to positive, desirable outcomes and whether it has a downside. Self-regulation remains a thriving focus of research, possibly because it is one of the central activities of the self and therefore is involved at some level in most of the other processes of self. Other aspects of executive function, such as how the self is involved in decision-making and initiative, have only begun to be studied, and these seem likely to attract more attention in coming years.

The rise of interest in brain processes has not been kind to self research, however. There has not been great success at finding a particular part of the brain that corresponds to self. Quite possibly the brain operates as many distributed, independent processes, whereas the self is a unity constructed for purposes of social action. Reconciling the reality of self in social life with its elusiveness to cognitive neuroscientists will be a fascinating chapter in the history of self theory.

Other puzzles remain. Self-affirmation, which refers to acting or thinking in ways that bolster the self's main values, continues to have an assortment of intriguing effects, but people are not sure just what the process is that produces those effects (e.g., Schmeichel & Vohs, 2009; Steele, 1988). Self-concept change and self change remain important but understudied phenomena. It is clear that self researchers will not run out of questions in the foreseeable future.

References

Alicke, M., & Sedikides, C. (2009). Self-enhancement and self-protection: What they are and what they do. *European Review of Social Psychology, 20,* 1–48.

Allport, G. W. (1943). The ego in contemporary psychology. *Psychological Review, 50,* 451–478.

Aron, A., McLaughlin-Volpe, T., Mashek, D., Lewandowski, G., Wright, S. C., & Aron, E. N. (2004). Including others in the self. *European Review of Social Psychology, 15,* 101–132.

Aronson, E., & Mettee, D. (1968). Dishonest behavior as a function of differential levels of induced self-esteem. *Journal of Personality and Social Psychology, 9,* 121–127.

Bachman, J. G., & O' Malley, P. M. (1977). Self-esteem in young men: A longitudinal analysis of the impact of educational and occupational attainment. *Journal of Personality and Social Psychology, 35,* 365–380.

Baumeister, R. F. (1982). A self-presentational view of social phenomena. *Psychological Bulletin, 91,* 3–26.

Baumeister, R. F. (1987). How the self became a problem: A psychological review of historical research. *Journal of Personality and Social Psychology, 52,* 163–176.

Baumeister, R. F. (1991). *Escaping the self: Alcoholism, spirituality, masochism, and other flights from the burden of selfhood.* New York, NY: Basic Books.

Baumeister, R. F. (1998). The self. In D. T. Gilbert, S. T. Fiske, & G. Lindzey (Eds.), *Handbook of social psychology* (4th ed.; pp. 680–740). New York, NY: McGraw-Hill.

Baumeister, R. F. (2005). *The cultural animal: Human nature, meaning, and social life.* New York, NY: Oxford University Press.

Baumeister, R. F., Bratslavsky, E., Muraven, M., & Tice, D. M. (1998). Ego depletion: Is the active self a limited resource? *Journal of Personality and Social Psychology, 74,* 1252–1265.

Baumeister, R. F., & Cairns, K. J. (1992). Repression and self-presentation: When audiences interfere with self-deceptive strategies. *Journal of Personality and Social Psychology, 62,* 851–862.

Baumeister, R. F., Campbell, J. D., Krueger, J. I., & Vohs, K. D. (2003). Does high self-esteem cause better performance interpersonal success, happiness, or healthier lifestyles? *Psychological Science in the Public Interest, 4,* 1–44.

Baumeister, R. F., Heatherton, T. F., & Tice, D. M. (1994). *Losing control: How and why people fail at self-regulation.* San Diego, CA: Academic Press.

Baumeister, R. F., & Leary, M. R. (1995). The need to belong: Desire for interpersonal attachments as a fundamental human motivation. *Psychological Bulletin, 117,* 497–529.

Baumeister, R. F., Smart, L., & Boden, J. M. (1996). Relation of threatened egotism to violence and aggression: The dark side of high self-esteem. *Psychological Review, 103,* 5–33.

Baumeister, R. F., & Sommer, K. L. (1997). What do men want? Gender differences and two spheres of belongingness: Comment on Cross and Madson (1997). *Psychological Bulletin, 122,* 38–44.

Baumeister, R. F., & Tice, D. M. (1984). Role of self-presentation and choice in cognitive dissonance under forced compliance: Necessary or sufficient causes? *Journal of Personality and Social Psychology, 46,* 5–13.

Baumeister, R. F., Tice, D. M., & Hutton, D. G. (1989). Self-presentational motivations and personality differences in self-esteem. *Journal of Personality, 57,* 547–579.

Baumeister, R. F., Tice, D. M., & Vohs, K. D. (2018). The strength model of self-regulation: Conclusions from the second decade of willpower research. *Perspectives on Psychological Science, 13,* 141–145.

Baumeister, R. F., & Vohs, K. D. (2016). Strength model of self-regulation as limited resource: Assessment, controversies, update. *Advances in Experimental Social Psychology, 54,* 67–127.

Beggan, J. K. (1992). On the social nature of nonsocial perception: The mere ownership effect. *Journal of Personality and Social Psychology, 62,* 229–237.

Bem, D. J. (1965). An experimental analysis of self-persuasion. *Journal of Experimental Social Psychology, 1,* 199–218.

Bem, D. J. (1972). Self-perception theory. In. L Berkowitz (Ed.), *Advances in experimental social psychology* (Vol. 6, pp. 1–62). New York, NY: Academic Press.

Brady, J. V. (1958). Ulcers in "executive" monkeys. *Scientific American, 199,* 95–100.

Buehler, R., Griffin, D., & Ross, M. (1994). Exploring the "planning fallacy": Why people underestimate their task completion times. *Journal of Personality and Social Psychology, 67,* 366–381.

Bushman, B. J., & Baumeister, R. F. (1998). Threatened egotism, narcissism, self-esteem, and direct and displaced aggression: Does self-love or self-hate lead to violence? *Journal of Personality and Social Psychology, 75,* 219–229.

Bushman, B. J., Baumeister, R. F., Thomaes, S., Ryu, E., Begeer, S., & West, S. G. (2009). Looking again, and harder, for a link between low self-esteem and aggression. *Journal of Personality, 77,* 427–446.

California Task Force to Promote Self-Esteem and Personal and Social Responsibility. (1990). *Toward a state of self-esteem.* Sacramento, CA: California State Department of Education.

Campbell, J. D. (1986). Similarity and uniqueness: The effects of attribute type, relevance, and individual differences in self-esteem and depression. *Journal of Personality and Social Psychology, 50,* 281–294.

Campbell, J. D. (1990). Self-esteem and clarity of the self-concept. *Journal of Personality and Social Psychology, 59,* 538–549.

Campbell, J. D., Chew, B., & Scratchley, L. S. (1991). Cognitive and emotional reactions to daily events: The effects of self-esteem and self-complexity. *Journal of Personality, 59,* 473–505.

Carlsmith, J. M., Collins, B. E., & Helmreich, R. L. (1966). Studies in forced compliance: 1. The effect of pressure for compliance on attitude change produced by face-to-face role playing and anonymous essay writing. *Journal of Personality and Social Psychology, 4,* 1–13.

Carter, E. C., Kofler, L. M., Forster, D. E., & McCullough, M. E. (2015). A series of meta-analytic tests of the depletion effect: Self-control does not seem to rely on a limited resource. *Journal of Experimental Psychology: General, 144,* 796–815.

Carver, C. S., & Scheier, M. F. (1981). *Attention and self-regulation: A control theory approach to human behavior*. New York, NY: Springer-Verlag.

Carver, C. S., & Scheier, M. F. (1982). Control theory: A useful conceptual framework for personality-social, clinical and health psychology. *Psychological Bulletin, 92,* 111–135.

Carver, C. S., & Scheier, M. F. (1998). *On the self-regulation of behavior*. New York, NY: Cambridge University Press.

Carver, C. S., & Scheier, M. F. (2009). Action, affect, multitasking, and layers of control. In J. Forgas, R. Baumeister, & D. Tice (Eds.), *Psychology of self-regulation* (pp. 109–126). New York, NY: Psychology Press.

Cooper, J., & Fazio, R. H. (1984). A new look at dissonance theory. In L. Berkowitz (Ed.), *Advances in experimental social psychology* (Vol. 17, pp. 229–266). New York, NY: Academic Press.

Crary, W. G. (1966). Reactions to incongruent self-experiences. *Journal of Consulting Psychology, 30,* 246–252.

Crocker, J., & Major, B. (1989). Social stigma and self-esteem: The self-protective properties of stigma. *Psychological Review, 96,* 608–630.

Crocker, J., & Park, L. E. (2004). The costly pursuit of self-esteem. *Psychological Bulletin, 130,* 392–414.

Crocker, J., & Wolfe, C. T. (2001). Contingencies of self-worth. *Psychological Review, 108,* 593–623.

Cross, S. E., & Madson, L. (1997). Models of the self: Self-construals and gender. *Psychological Bulletin, 122,* 5–37.

Deci, E. L. (1971). Effects of externally mediated rewards on intrinsic motivation. *Journal of Personality and Social Psychology, 18,* 105–115.

Deci, E. L., & Ryan, R. M. (1991). A motivational approach to self: Integration in personality. In R. Dienstbier (Ed.), *Nebraska symposium on motivation* (Vol. 38, pp. 237–288). Lincoln, NE: University of Nebraska Press.

Deci, E. L., & Ryan, R. M. (1995). Human autonomy: The basis for true self-esteem. In M. Kernis (Ed.), *Efficacy, agency, and self-esteem* (pp. 31–49). New York, NY: Plenum.

Diener, E., & Wallbom, M. (1976). Effects of self-awareness on antinormative behavior. *Journal of Research in Personality, 10,* 107–111.

Donnellan, M. B., Trzesniewski, K. H., Robins, R. W., Moffitt, T. E., & Caspi, A. (2005). Low self-esteem is related to aggression, antisocial behavior, and delinquency. *Psychological Science, 16,* 328–335.

Dunning, D. (2005). *Self-insight: Roadblocks and detours on the path to knowing thyself*. New York, NY: Psychology Press.

Dunning, D., Meyerowitz, J. A., & Holzberg, A. (1989). Ambiguity and self-evaluation: The role of idiosyncratic trait definitions in self-serving assessments of ability. *Journal of Personality and Social Psychology, 57,* 1082–1090.

Duval, S., & Wicklund, R. A. (1972). *A theory of objective self-awareness*. New York, NY: Academic Press.

Engelmann, J. M., Herrmann, E., & Tomasello, M. (2012). Five-year-olds, but not chimpanzees, attempt to manage their reputations. *PLoS One, 7,* e48433.

Fazio, R. H., Effrein, E. A., & Falender, V. J. (1981). Self-perceptions following social interactions. *Journal of Personality and Social Psychology, 41,* 232–242.

Fenigstein, A., Scheier, M. F., & Buss, A. H. (1975). Public and private self-consciousness: Assessment and theory. *Journal of Consulting and Clinical Psychology, 43,* 522–527.

Ferrari, J. R., Johnson, J. L., & McCown, W. G. (1995). *Procrastination and task avoidance: Theory, research, and treatment*. New York, NY: Plenum.

Festinger, L. (1957). *A theory of cognitive dissonance*. Stanford, CA: Stanford University Press.

Fishbach, A. (2009). The dynamics of self-regulation. In J. Forgas, R. Baumeister, & D. Tice (Eds.), *Psychology of self-regulation* (pp. 163–181). New York, NY: Psychology Press.

Fishbach, A., & Dhar, R. (2005). Goals as excuses or guides: The liberating effect of perceived goal progress on choice. *Journal of Consumer Research, 32,* 370–377.

Fishbach, A., & Zhang, Y. (2008). Together or apart: When goals and temptations complement versus compete. *Journal of Personality and Social Psychology, 94,* 547–559.

Fitzsimons, G. M., Finkel, E. J., & vanDellen, M. R. (2015). Transactive goal dynamics. *Psychological Review, 122,* 648–673.

Förster, J., Higgins, E. T., & Bianco, A. T. (2003). Speed/accuracy decisions in task performance: Built-in trade-offs or separate strategic concerns? *Organization Behavior and Human Decision Processes, 90,* 148–164.

Forsyth, D. R., Kerr, N. A., Burnette, J. L., & Baumeister, R. F. (2007). Attempting to improve the academic performance of struggling college students by bolstering their self-esteem: An intervention that backfired. *Journal of Social and Clinical Psychology, 26,* 447–459.

Freitas, A. L., Liberman, N., Salovey, P., & Higgins, E. T. (2002). When to begin? Regulatory focus and initiating goal pursuit. *Personality and Social Psychology Bulletin, 28,* 121–130.

Fujita, K., Trope, Y., Liberman, N., & Levin-Sagi, M. (2006). Construal levels and self-control. *Journal of Personality and Social Psychology, 90,* 351–367.

Gebauer, J. E., Wagner, J., Sedikides, C., Bleidorn, W., Rentfrow, P. J., Potter, J., & Gosling, S. D. (2015). Cultural norm fulfillment, interpersonal belonging, or getting-ahead? A large-scale cross-cultural test of three perspectives on the function of self-esteem. *Journal of Perosnality and Social Psychology, 109,* 526–648.

Gilovich, T. (1991). *How we know what isn't so.* New York, NY: Free Press.

Gollwitzer, P. M., & Kinney, R. F. (1989). Effects of deliberative and implemental mind-sets on illusion of control. *Journal of Personality and Social Psychology, 56,* 531–542.

Gollwitzer, P. M., & Taylor, S. E. (1995). Effects of mindset on positive illusions. *Journal of Personality and Social Psychology, 669,* 213–226.

Greenberg, J., & Musham, C. (1981). Avoiding and seeking self-focused attention. *Journal of Research in Personality, 15,* 191–200.

Greenberg, J., & Pyszczynski, J. (1986). Persistent high self-focus after failure and low self-focus after success: The depressive self-focusing style. *Journal of Personality and Social Psychology, 50,* 1039–1044.

Greenberg, J., Pyszczynski, T., & Solomon, S. (1986). The causes and consequences of self-esteem: A terror management theory. In R. Baumeister (Ed.), *Public self and private self* (pp. 189–212). New York, NY: Springer-Verlag.

Greenwald, A. G. (1980). The totalitarian ego: Fabrication and revision of personal history. *American Psychologist, 35,* 603–618.

Greenwald, A. G., & Banaji, M. R. (1989). The self as a memory system: Powerful, but ordinary. *Journal of Personality and Social Psychology, 57,* 41–54.

Gur, R. C., & Sackeim, H. A. (1979). Self-deception: A concept in search of a phenomenon. *Journal of Personality and Social Psychology, 37,* 147–169.

Hagger, M. S., Chatzisarantis, N. L., Alberts, H., Anggono, C. O., Batailler, C., Birt, A. R., . . . Calvillo, D. P. (2016). A multilab preregistered replication of the ego-depletion effect. *Perspectives on Psychological Science, 11,* 546–573.

Harter, S. (1993). Causes and consequences of low self-esteem in children and adolescents. In R. Baumeister (Ed.), *Self-esteem: The puzzle of low self-regard* (pp. 87–116). New York, NY: Plenum.

Heatherton, T. F., & Baumeister, R. F. (1991). Binge eating as escape from self-awareness. *Psychological Bulletin, 110,* 86–108.

Heine, S. J., Lehman, D. R., Markus, H. R., & Kitayama, S. (1999). Is there a universal need for positive self-regard? *Psychological Review, 106,* 766–794.

Helmreich, R., & Collins, B. E. (1968). Studies in forced compliance: Commitment and magnitude of inducement to comply as determinants of opinion change. *Journal of Personality and Social Psychology, 10,* 75–81.

Higgins, E. T. (1987). Self-discrepancy: A theory relating self and affect. *Psychological Review, 94,* 319–340.

Higgins, E. T. (1997). Beyond pleasure and pain. *American Psychologist, 52,* 1280–1300.

Higgins, E. T., & Bargh, J. A. (1987). Social cognition and social perception. *Annual Review of Psychology, 38,* 369–425.

Higgins, E. T., & Spiegel, S. (2004). Promotion and prevention strategies for self-regulation: A motivated cognition perspective. In R. F. Baumeister & K. D. Vohs (Eds.), *Handbook of self-regulation: Research, theory, and applications* (pp. 171–187). New York, NY: Guilford.

Hull, J. G. (1981). A self-awareness model of the causes and effects of alcohol consumption. *Journal of Abnormal Psychology, 90,* 586–600.

Ingram, R. E. (1990). Self-focused attention in clinical disorders: Review and a conceptual model. *Psychological Bulletin, 107*, 156–176.

Inzlicht, M., Schmeichel, B. J., & Macrae, C. N. (2014). Why self-control seems (but may not be) limited. *Trends in cognitive sciences, 18*, 127–133.

Job, V., Dweck, C. S., & Walton, G. M. (2010). Ego depletion—Is it all in your head? Implicit theories about willpower affect self-regulation. *Psychological Science, 21*, 1686–1693.

Job, V., Walton, G. M., Bernecker, K., & Dweck, C. S. (2013). Beliefs about willpower determine the impact of glucose on self-control. *Proceedings of the National Academy of Sciences, 110*, 14837–14842.

Jones, E. E., Rhodewalt, F., Berglas, S. C., & Skelton, A. (1981). Effects of strategic self-presentation on subsequent self-esteem. *Journal of Personality and Social Psychology, 41*, 407–421.

Kernis, M. H. (1993). The roles of stability and level of self-esteem in psychological functioning. In R. Baumeister (Ed.), *Self-esteem: The puzzle of low self-regard* (pp. 167–182). New York, NY: Plenum.

Kernis, M. H., Cornell, D. P., Sun, C. R., Berry, A., & Harlow, T. (1993). There's more to self-esteem than whether it's high or low: The importance of stability of self-esteem. *Journal of Personality and Social Psychology, 65*, 1190–1204.

Kernis, M. H., Granneman, B. D., & Barclay, L. C. (1989). Stability and level of self-esteem as predictors of anger arousal and hostility. *Journal of Personality and Social Psychology, 56*, 1013–1022.

Kurzban, R., Duckworth, A., Kable, J. W., & Myers, J. (2013). An opportunity cost model of subjective effort and task performance. *Behavioral and Brain Sciences, 36*, 661–679.

Langer, E. (1975). The illusion of control. *Journal of Personality and Social Psychology, 32*, 311–328.

Leary, M. R. (2004). *The curse of the self*. New York, NY: Oxford University Press.

Leary, M. R., & Baumeister, R. F. (2000). The nature and function of self-esteem: Sociometer theory. In M. Zanna (Ed.), *Advances in experimental social psychology* (Vol. 32, pp. 1–62). San Diego, CA: Academic Press.

Leary, M. R., Tambor, E. S., Terdal, S. K., & Downs, D. L. (1995). Self-esteem as an interpersonal monitor: The sociometer hypothesis. *Journal of Personality and Social Psychology, 68*, 518–530.

Leary, M. R., Tchividjian, L. R., & Kraxberger, B. E. (1994). Self-presentation can be hazardous to your health: Impression management and health risk. *Health Psychology, 13*, 461–470.

Lepper, M. R., Greene, D., & Nisbett, R. E. (1973). Undermining children's intrinsic interest with extrinsic reward: A test of the "overjustification" hypothesis. *Journal of Personality and Social Psychology, 28*, 129–137.

Mahadevan, N., Gregg, A. P., Sedikides, C., & de Wall-Andrews, W. G. (2016). Winners, losers, insiders, and outsiders: Comparing hierometer and sociometer theories of self-regard. *Frontiers in Psychology, 7*, art. 334.

Marks, G. (1984). Thinking one's abilities are unique and one's opinions are common. *Personality and Social Psychology Bulletin, 10*, 203–208.

Markus, H. R. (1977). Self-schemata and processing information about the self. *Journal of Personality and Social Psychology, 35*, 63–78.

Markus, H. R., & Kitayama, S. (1991). Culture and the self: Implications for cognition, emotion, and motivation. *Psychological Review, 98*, 224–253.

Markus, H. R., & Kunda, Z. (1986). Stability and malleability of the self-concept. *Journal of Personality and Social Psychology, 51*, 858–866.

Markus, H., & Nurius, P. S. (1986). Possible selves. *American Psychologist, 41*, 954–969.

Masicampo, E. J., & Baumeister, R. F. (2008). Toward a physiology of dual-process reasoning and judgment: Lemonade, willpower, and expensive rule-based analysis. *Psychological Science, 19*, 255–260.

McGuire, W. J., McGuire, C. V., Child, P., & Fujioka, T. (1978). Salience of ethnicity in the spontaneous self-concept as a function of one's ethnic distinctiveness in the social environment. *Journal of Personality and Social Psychology, 36*, 511–520.

McGuire, W. J., McGuire, C. V., Child, P., & Winton, W. (1979). Effects of household gender composition on the salience of one's gender in the spontaneous self-concept. *Journal of Experimental Social Psychology, 15*, 77–90.

Meehl, P. E. (1956). Wanted—a good cookbook. *American Psychologist, 11*, 263–272.

Menon, M., Tobin, D. D., Corby, B. C., Menon, M., Hodges, E. V., & Perry, D. G. (2007). The developmental costs of high self-esteem for antisocial children. *Child Development, 78,* 1627–1639.

Mischel, W., Ebbesen, E. B., & Zeiss, A. R. (1976). Determinants of selective memory about the self. *Journal of Consulting and Clinical Psychology, 44,* 92–103.

Miyake, A., Friedman, N. P., Emerson, M. J., Witzki, A. H., Howerter, A., & Wager, T. D. (2000). Contributions to complex "frontal lobe" tasks: A latent variable analysis. *Cognitive Psychology, 41,* 49–100.

Molden, D. C., Lee, A. Y., & Higgins, E. T. (2008). Motivations for promotion and prevention. In J. Shah & W. Gardner (Eds.), *Handbook of motivation science* (pp.169–187). New York, NY: Guilford.

Morf, C. C., & Rhodewalt, F. (2001). Unraveling the paradoxes of narcissism: A dynamic self-regulatory processing model. *Psychological Inquiry, 12,* 177–196.

Muraven, M., & Slessareva, E. (2003). Mechanism of self-control failure: Motivation and limited resources. *Personality and Social Psychology Bulletin, 29,* 894–906.

Newman, L. S., & Baumeister, R. F. (1996). Toward an elaboration of the UFO abduction phenomenon: Hypnotic elaboration, extraterrestrial sadomasochism, and spurious memories. *Psychological Inquiry, 7,* 99–126.

Nuttin, J. M. (1985). Narcissism beyond Gestalt and awareness: The name letter effect. *European Journal of Social Psychology, 15,* 353–361.

Nuttin, J. M. (1987). Affective consequences of mere ownership: The name letter effect in twelve European languages. *European Journal of Social Psychology, 17,* 381–402.

Pelham, B. W., Mirenberg, M. C., & Jones, J. T. (2002). Why Susie sells seashells by the seashore: Implicit egoism and major life decisions. *Journal of Personality and Social Psychology, 82,* 469–487.

Pocheptsova, A., Amir, O., Dhar, R., & Baumeister, R. F. (2009). Deciding without resources: Resource depletion and choice in context. *Journal of Marketing Research, 46,* 344–355.

Polivy, J. (1976). Perception of calories and regulation of intake in restrained and unrestrained subjects. *Addictive Behaviors, 1,* 237–243.

Powers, W. T. (1973). *Behavior: The control of perception.* Chicago, IL: Aldine.

Pryor, J. B., Gibbons, F. X., Wicklund, R. A., Fazio, R. H., & Hood, R. (1977). Self-focused attention and self-report validity. *Journal of Personality, 45,* 514–527.

Pyszczynski, T., Greenberg, J., & Holt, K. (1985). Maintaining consistency between self-serving beliefs and available data: A bias in information processing. *Personality and Social Psychology Bulletin, 11,* 179–190.

Pyszczynski, T., Greenberg, J., & Solomon, S. (1997). Why do we need what we need? A terror management perspective on the roots of human social motivation. *Psychological Inquiry, 8,* 1–20.

Rogers, T. B., Kuiper, N. A., & Kirker, W. S. (1977). Self-reference and the encoding of personal information. *Journal of Personality and Social Psychology, 35,* 677–688.

Rosenberg, M. (1965). *Society and the adolescent self-image.* Princeton, NJ: Princeton University Press.

Ryan, R., & Deci, E. (2017). *Self-determination theory.* New York, NY: Guilford.

Sackeim, H. A., & Gur, R. C. (1979). Self-deception, other-deception, and self-reported psychopathology. *Journal of Consulting and Clinical Psychology, 47,* 213–215.

Scheier, M. F., & Carver, C. S. (1977). Self-focused attention and the experience of emotion: Attraction, repulsion, elation, and depression. *Journal of Personality and Social Psychology, 35,* 625–636.

Scheier, M. F., Fenigstein, A., & Buss, A. H. (1974). Self-awareness and physical aggression. *Journal of Experimental Social Psychology, 10,* 264–273.

Schlegel, R. J., Hicks, J. A., Davis, W. E., Hirsch, K. A., & Smith, C. M. (2013). The dynamic interplay between perceived true self-knowledge and decision satisfaction. *Journal of Personality and Social Psychology, 104,* 542–558.

Schlenker, B. R. (1975). Self-presentation: Managing the impression of consistency when reality interferes with self-enhancement. *Journal of Personality and Social Psychology, 32,* 1030–1037.

Schlenker, B. R. (1980). *Impression management: The self-concept, social identity, and interpersonal relations.* Monterey, CA: Brooks/Cole.

Schlenker, B. R., Dlugolecki, D. W., & Doherty, K. (1994). The impact of self-presentations on self-appraisals and behavior: The roles of commitment and biased scanning. *Personality and Social Psychology Bulletin, 20,* 20–33.

Schlenker, B. R., & Leary, M. R. (1982). Social anxiety and self-presentation: A conceptualization and model. *Psychological Bulletin, 92,* 641–669.

Schmeichel, B. J., & Vohs, K. D. (2009). Self-affirmation and self-control: Affirming core values counteracts ego depletion. *Journal of Personality and Social Psychology, 96,* 770–782.

Sedikides, C. (1993). Assessment, enhancement, and verification determinants of the self-evaluation process. *Journal of Personality and Social Psychology, 65,* 317–338.

Sedikides, C., & Gregg, A. P. (2008). Self-enhancement: Food for thought. *Perspectives on Psychological Science, 3,* 102–116.

Seligman, M. E. P. (1975). *Helplessness: On depression, development, and death.* San Francisco, CA: Freeman.

Shah, J. Y., Friedman, R., & Kruglanski, A. W. (2002). Forgetting all else: On the antecedents and consequences of goal shielding. *Journal of Personality and Social Psychology, 83,* 1261–1280.

Steele, C. M. (1988). The psychology of self-affirmation: Sustaining the integrity of the self. In L. Berkowitz (Ed.), *Advances in experimental social psychology* (Vol. 21, pp. 261–302). New York, NY: Academic Press.

Steele, C. M., & Josephs, R. A. (1990). Alcohol myopia: Its prized and dangerous effects. *American Psychologist, 45,* 921–933.

Steele, C. M., & Southwick, L. (1985). Alcohol and social behavior I: The mediating role of inhibitory conflict. *Journal of Personality and Social Psychology, 48,* 18–34.

Strohminger, N., Knobe, J., & Newman, G. (2017). The true self: A psychological concept distinct from the self. *Perspectives in Psychological Science, 12,* 551–560.

Suchy, Y. (2009). Executive functioning: Overview, assessment, and research issues for non-neuropsychologists. *Annals of Behavioral Medicine, 37,* 106–116.

Suls, J., & Wan, C. K. (1987). In search of the false-uniqueness phenomenon: Fear and estimates of social consensus. *Journal of Personality and Social Psychology, 52,* 211–217.

Svenson, O. (1981). Are we all less risky and more skillful than our fellow drivers? *Acta Psychologica, 47,* 143–148.

Swann, W. B. (1987). Identity negotiation: Where two roads meet. *Journal of Personality and Social Psychology, 53,* 1038–1051.

Swann, W. B., & Hill, C. A. (1982). When our identities are mistaken: Reaffirming self-conceptions through social interaction. *Journal of Personality and Social Psychology, 43,* 59–66.

Tangney, J. P., Niedenthal, P. M., Covert, M. V., & Barlow, D. H. (1998). Are shame and guilt related to distinct self-discrepancies? A test of Higgins's (1987) hypothesis. *Journal of Personality and Social Psychology, 75,* 256–268.

Taylor, S. E., & Brown, J. D. (1988). Illusion and well-being: A social psychological perspective on mental health. *Psychological Bulletin, 103,* 193–210.

Tedeschi, J. T., Schlenker, B. R., & Bonoma, T. V. (1971). Cognitive dissonance: Private ratiocination or public spectacle? *American Psychologist, 26,* 685–695.

Tesser, A. (1988). Toward a self-evaluation maintenance model of social behavior. In L. Berkowitz (Ed.), *Advances in experimental social psychology* (Vol. 21, pp. 181–227). San Diego, CA: Academic Press.

Tetlock, P. E., & Manstead, A. S. (1985). Impression management versus intrapsychic explanations in social psychology: A useful dichotomy? *Psychological Review, 92,* 59–77.

Tice, D. M. (1992). Self-presentation and self-concept change: The looking glass self as magnifying glass. *Journal of Personality and Social Psychology, 63,* 435–451.

Tice, D. M., & Baumeister, R. F. (1997). Longitudinal study of procrastination, performance, stress, and health: The costs and benefits of dawdling. *Psychological Science, 8,* 454–458.

Tice, D. M., Baumeister, R. F., Shmueli, D., & Muraven, M. (2007). Restoring the self: Positive affect helps improve self-regulation following ego depletion. *Journal of Experimental Social Psychology, 43,* 379–384.

Trope, Y. (1983). Self-assessment in achievement behavior: In J. Suls & A. Greenwald (Eds.), *Psychological perspectives on the self* (Vol. 2, pp. 93–121). Hillsdale, NJ: Erlbaum.

Trope, Y. (1986). Self-enhancement and self-assessment in achievement behavior. In R. Sorrentino & E. T. Higgins (Eds.), *Handbook of motivation and cognition* (Vol. 2, pp. 350–378). New York, NY: Guilford.

Vohs, K. D., Baumeister, R. F., & Ciarocco, N. (2005). Self-regulation and self-presentation: Regulatory resource depletion impairs impression management and effortful self-presentation depletes regulatory resources. *Journal of Personality and Social Psychology, 88,* 632–657.

Vohs, K. D., Baumeister, R. F., & Schmeichel, B. J. (2013). Motivation, personal beliefs, and limited resources all contribute to self-control. *Journal of Experimental Social Psychology, 49,* 184–188.

Vohs, K. D., Baumeister, R. F., Schmeichel, B. J., Twenge, J. M., Nelson, N. M., & Tice, D. M. (2008). Making choices impairs subsequent self-control: A limited resource account of decision making, self-regulation, and active initiative. *Journal of Personality and Social Psychology, 94,* 883–898.

Von Hippel, W., & Trivers, R. (2011). The evolution and psychology of self-deception. *Behavioral and Brain Sciences, 34,* 1–16.

Wicklund, R. A., & Duval, S. (1971). Opinion change and performance facilitation as a result of objective self-awareness. *Journal of Experimental Social Psychology, 7,* 319–342.

Wills, T. A. (1981). Downward comparison principles in social psychology. *Psychological Bulletin, 90,* 245–271.

Wood, J. V., Heimpel, S. A., & Michela, J. L. (2003). Savoring versus dampening: Self-esteem differences in regulating positive affect. *Journal of Personality and Social Psychology, 85,* 566–580.

Wood, J. V., Heimpel, S. A., Newby-Clark, I. R., & Ross, M. (2005). Snatching defeat from the jaws of victory: Self-esteem differences in the experience and anticipation of success. *Journal of Personality and Social Psychology, 89,* 764–780.

Wood, J. V., Michela, J. L., & Giordano, C. (2000). Downward comparison in everyday life: Reconciling self-enhancement models with the mood-cognition priming model. *Journal of Personality and Social Psychology, 79,* 563–579.

Wyer, R. S., & Frey, D. (1983). The effects of feedback about self and others on the recall and judgments of feedback-relevant information. *Journal of Experimental Social Psychology, 19,* 540–559.

Zuckerman, M. (1979). Attribution of success and failure revisited, or: The motivational bias is alive and well in attribution theory. *Journal of Personality, 47,* 245–287.

Chapter 6

Attitude Structure and Change

Richard E. Petty, Pablo Briñol, Leandre R. Fabrigar, and Duane T. Wegener

Attitudes refer to general evaluations people have regarding people (including oneself), places, objects, and issues (e.g., "Ice-cream is good"; "I favor capital punishment"). Attitudes are accorded special status in social psychology because of their influence on people's choices and actions. In particular, modifying attitudes is one way to influence people's behavior. That is, all else equal, people will decide to buy the brand they like the most, attend the university they evaluate most favorably, and vote for the candidate they approve of most strongly, though as we will see, some attitudes are better at predicting behavior than others. Our review of basic social psychological approaches to attitudes is divided into four main sections.

We begin by focusing on definitional issues regarding attitudes and the properties of attitudes that are particularly relevant for making them consequential. In this section, we describe the functions of attitudes (i.e., what purpose they serve) as well as their common bases and structure. One important point we emphasize is that the various functions, origins, and structural variables can be assessed in a relatively objective way or in a more subjective way, and this has implications for various attitude-relevant outcomes.

The second section turns to some of the most popular approaches to understanding attitude change. We begin with some of the early persuasion theories, which tended to focus on single processes by which variables could produce attitude change such as proposing that getting people to learn your message was the key to effective influence. We then move to more contemporary multiprocess perspectives. We describe the fundamental psychological processes by which any variable relevant to persuasion can exert its effects on attitudes and attitude change. We see that although changing attitudes is complex, it can be understood by breaking the underlying psychological processes responsible for influence into a finite set and specifying the circumstances under which these processes are more versus less likely to operate.

The third section describes research on attitude change organized around the key variables that determine the extent of influence—the source, the message, and the recipient of influence. We describe how many seemingly different variables (e.g., an attractive message source, a message recipient in a good mood) can each affect attitudes by the same fundamental processes. We explain how these variables can not only have direct effects on attitudes but also interact with each other in affecting persuasion processes and outcomes.

In our fourth section, we turn to the issue of why we should care about the underlying processes of persuasion. Of most importance, knowing something about the particular process behind an attitude change can tell us whether the change is likely to be consequential (i.e., whether the attitude change lasts over time, resists counterpersuasion, and predicts behavior). In this final section, we examine implications of the extent of thinking involved in attitude change for both explicit and implicit measures of attitudes.

Part I: Attitude Function, Strength and Structure

Definition of Attitudes and Attitude Strength

Although attitudes refer to the general and relatively enduring evaluations people have of other people, objects, or ideas (Petty, Briñol, & DeMarree, 2007), attitudes can vary in a number of important ways. Most obviously, attitudes can vary in *valence*. Some attitudes are positive, some are negative, and others are relatively neutral. Moreover, attitudes can differ in their *extremity*, or the extent to which they deviate from neutrality (i.e., just how positive or negative they are). In addition to these, attitudes can differ in other ways such as their underlying *bases* (i.e., what serves as input to the attitude such as whether the attitude is based more on emotion or cognition), and attitudes can also differ in their *strength*—the extent to which attitudes are durable and impactful (Petty & Krosnick, 1995).

The durability of an attitude refers to its ability to persist over time and resist attacks. Impact refers to the attitude's influence over thoughts, feelings, and behavior. In general, strong attitudes exert greater influence (e.g., produce more attitude-consistent thinking) and behavior (e.g., produce more attitude-consistent behavior) than do their weaker counterparts. Attitude strength can also be a crucial moderator of persuasion effects—making it harder to change attitudes in some cases than in others (e.g., it is more difficult to change attitudes of which people are certain). Thus, one might aim to reduce an attitude's strength before attacking it (e.g., instilling doubt in the attitude before it is challenged).

Research has identified a number of indicators of whether a given attitude is relatively strong or weak. Some indicators of strength relate to the underlying structural properties of the attitude such as how quickly the attitude comes to mind (i.e., accessibility; see Fazio, 1995) or the extent to which the attitude contains mostly one-sided information (e.g., all positive) or is linked to mixed information (i.e., both positive and negative; Kaplan, 1972). Attitudes that are based on both positive and negative information are ambivalent, and people experience conflict in the presence of objects for which they hold ambivalent attitudes (Priester & Petty, 1996). Low-accessibility and high-ambivalence attitudes tend to be weak rather than strong.

In addition to structural indicators of strength, perceptions of one's attitudes can also index strength. For example, when people see an attitude as important (e.g., Boninger, Krosnick, Berent, & Fabrigar, 1995), or the attitude is believed to be based on considerable knowledge (Davidson, Yantis, Norwood, & Montano, 1985), or a person has high confidence in the validity of the attitude (Rucker, Tormala, Petty, & Briñol, 2014), the attitude is stronger (more consequential) than when the attitude is seen as unimportant or believed to be based on little information or when the attitude is held with doubt.

Many of the structural indicators of attitude strength are based on relatively objective measures. For instance, a reaction-time measure of attitude accessibility (Fazio, 1995) does not require people to introspect and report their perception of how quickly and easily the attitude comes to mind. Similarly, inferring amount of elaboration based on effects of argument quality on evaluative judgments (e.g., Petty, Wells, & Brock, 1976) does not require research participants to introspect about how much they elaborated (Blankenship & Wegener, 2008). However, these same attitude strength constructs could be assessed in a more subjective way such as by simply asking people how quickly the attitude comes to mind or how much they thought about the issue.

In contrast to the fact that most structural features of attitudes such as accessibility have been assessed with both objective and subjective measures, for some of the most commonly employed subjective strength indicators (e.g., importance, certainty), there is no widely accepted objective indicator. Nonetheless, regardless of whether the attitude strength dimension is assessed in a relatively objective or subjective manner, the dominant perspective in the field is that each dimension of strength is somewhat independent of the others and that each dimension of strength matters because it helps to shape the attitude's durability and impact (Krosnick & Petty, 1995). Furthermore, as explained shortly, objective and subjective assessments of the same attitude strength construct can predict different outcomes (e.g., See, Fabrigar, & Petty, 2013).

Understanding how to change attitudes is important because attitude change increases the likelihood that behavior will change as well, especially if the new attitudes produced are strong ones (e.g., based on extensive knowledge, held with certainty, highly accessible, etc.). Later in this review, we discuss when changes in attitudes are more or less likely to spread to related thinking, judgment, and behavior.

Functions of Attitudes

Attitudes not only can guide behavior and influence thoughts and feelings, but they can also serve to define and express who we are (give us identity), providing people with a sense of consistency, self-worth, belonging, and acceptance. When an attitude is self-defining, people are more likely to advocate it spontaneously to others (Zunick, Teeny, & Fazio, 2017). Attitudes can also serve other needs that people have—such as understanding the world, fitting in with others, expressing important values, and so forth (for a review, see Maio & Olson, 2000). For example, Katz (1960) proposed that attitudes can serve a knowledge function, helping to organize and structure a person's environment and provide consistency in one's frame of reference. Attitudes can also help to maximize the rewards and minimize the punishments obtained from objects in the environment. Furthermore, attitudes guide attention, especially when they are strong (Fazio, 1995), and they can serve to build and maintain self-esteem in a variety of ways. For example, a person might develop a prejudice toward a minority group because this negative evaluation of the outgroup makes the person feel better about the ingroup and himself or herself.

In addition to different attitudes serving different functions for the same person, some attitudes toward might serve a common function for most people. For example, attitudes toward aspirin might be based primary on utilitarian or practical concerns such as how well aspirin works to alleviate pain (e.g., Abelson & Prentice, 1989; Shavitt, 1989). Similarly, some situations might invoke the same attitude function for most people. For example, when at a party, the social-adjustive function of attitudes (i.e., how well the attitude helps one fit in socially with other people) might dominate. Finally, attitudes might chronically serve different functions for different people. For example, for some people, most of their attitudes might serve a value-expressive function, but for others, most attitudes might serve a social-adjustive function (Snyder & DeBono, 1985).

Considering attitude functions is important because persuasive messages that appeal to or match the function served by an attitude can be more persuasive than messages that are irrelevant to or mismatch the function served by that attitude (see Briñol & Petty, 2018; Petty, Wheeler, & Bizer, 2000; Salovey & Wegener, 2003). For example, people who score highly on the self-monitoring scale (Snyder, 1974) are oriented toward social approval whereas low self-monitors are more motivated to be consistent with their internal beliefs and values. Messages can often be made more effective by matching the message to a person's self-monitoring status. For example, in one early study, Snyder and DeBono (1985) exposed high and low self-monitors to advertisements for a variety of products that contained arguments appealing either to the social adjustment function (i.e., describing the social image that consumers could gain from the use of the product) or to the value-expressive function (i.e., presenting content regarding the intrinsic quality of the product). High self-monitors were more influenced by ads with image content than ads with quality content. In contrast, low self-monitors were more vulnerable to messages that made appeals to values or quality. As we explain shortly, there are multiple processes by which this matching effect can come about.

Basis of Attitudes

People's attitudes can be based on a number of underlying factors. For example, attitudes can be based on behavioral information, as illustrated by research on *embodiment* (Briñol & Petty, 2008; Briñol, Petty, Santos, & Mello, 2017). Embodiment or *embodied cognition* refers to situations in which one's posture or movement of one's body affects one's judgments (Shapiro, 2011). For example, placing your face in a smiling expression can produce more positive attitudes (Noah, Schul, & Mayo, 2018; Strack, Martin, & Stepper, 1988) as can nodding your head while listening to a message (Tom et al., 1991; Wells & Petty, 1980). Beyond behavioral components, one important and classic distinction is whether attitudes are based more on emotion (affect) or cognition (Zanna & Rempel, 1988).

A number of studies have shown that it is possible to determine whether a given attitude is based on emotion, cognition, or a combination of the two. This can be done, for example, by seeing whether a global measure of people's attitudes (e.g., to what extent the attitude object is rated as good versus bad) is more congruent with their ratings of various emotion-relevant qualities (e.g., to what extent the attitude object is rated as producing happiness vs. sadness) or cognition-relevant qualities (e.g., to what extent the attitude object is rated as useful vs. useless; see Crites, Fabrigar, & Petty, 1994). Another possibility is to examine the words people use to describe their attitudes and see whether they contain emotional content or not (e.g., Rocklage & Fazio, 2015).

Differences in the cognitive versus affective structural basis of attitudes have important consequences. For example, persuasive messages with emotional content tend to be more successful in changing emotion-based attitudes than cognition-based attitudes, with the reverse tending to hold for cognitive persuasive appeals (Fabrigar & Petty, 1999). This matching effect is amplified when people have high certainty in their attitudes (Clarkson, Tormala, & Rucker, 2011). Just as individual attitudes can be based more on affect or cognition, so too some people tend to base most of their attitudes primarily on affect or cognition (e.g., Aquino, Haddock, Maio, Wolf, & Alparone, 2016; Haddock, Maio, Arnold, & Huskinson, 2008; Huskinson & Haddock, 2004; for a review, see Maio & Haddock, 2015). Research suggests that attitudes based on emotion tend to be stronger than those based on cognition in that they are more accessible in memory (Giner-Sorolla, 2004; Rocklage & Fazio, 2018) and tend to predict behavior better (Lavine et al., 1998).

Independent of the extent to which attitudes actually are based on affect or cognition, people also differ in their *perceptions* of the basis of their attitudes (See, Petty, & Fabrigar, 2008). These self-perceptions of attitude bases (called meta-bases) tend to be uncorrelated with structural bases and predict advocacy and persuasion independent of the assessed structural basis. For example, in a series of studies on advocacy (Teeny & Petty, 2018), the more people's attitudes were perceived to be based on affect versus cognition, the more they expressed interest in spontaneously advocating their views to others. However, the more people's attitudes were perceived to be based on cognition versus affect, the more willing they were to advocate when requested.

With respect to persuasion, structural and meta-bases predict some different outcomes. For example, in one study (See, Fabrigar, & Petty, 2013), more affective structural bases of attitudes predicted faster reading time for affective than cognitive information whereas more cognitive structural bases predicted faster reading time for cognitive than affective information. This was presumed to reflect the greater processing efficiency that is possible when information is matched to one's structural basis. This same study showed that when people simply perceived their attitudes to be based primarily on emotion (high affective meta-basis) regardless of whether or not they objectively were, they showed a slower reading time for affective than cognitive information. The opposite was true when people rated their attitudes as being based primarily on cognition (high cognitive meta-basis). These individuals showed a slower reading time for cognitive than affective information. Slower reading times were presumed to reflect the greater interest in processing that occurs when information is matched to one's meta-basis.

With respect to the affective versus cognitive bases of people's attitudes, research suggests that when people are asked to consider why they hold the attitudes they do, what comes to mind may not be representative of the actual structural content of their attitudes. For instance, in one study (Wilson, Dunn, Bybee, Hyman, & Rotondo, 1984), when participants were asked to examine why they liked or disliked an attitude object, they were able to do so, but attitudes assessed shortly after this were largely unpredictive of behavior. Wilson et al. (1984) suggested that this was because the reasons people listed as supporting their attitudes were not complete. In particular, people often underestimated the role of affect in determining attitudes. Moreover, even if people could identify a representative sample of the bases of their attitudes (both affective and cognitive), they would also have to be able to gauge the unique contribution of each basis to their global evaluation to have an accurate assessment. This is likely to be difficult, particularly when affect and cognition are evaluatively consistent. Thus, true insight into the actual affective versus cognitive basis of many attitudes is likely to be rare.

In sum, attitudes can vary in their underlying structure or bases, with some attitudes being based relatively more on behavior, affect, or cognition. Furthermore, perceptions of one's attitude basis can differ from reality. Other variations are also important with regard to the basis of attitudes. For instance, some attitudes are based on direct experience whereas others are based on semantic information from other people (i.e., indirect experience; Fazio & Zanna, 1978). Attitudes are sometimes based on issue-relevant ambivalent (evaluatively mixed; Kaplan, 1972) or univalent (one-sided) information (DeMotta, Chao, & Kramer, 2016; Haddock, Foad, Windsor-Shellard, Dummel, & Adarves-Yorno, 2017; Reich & Wheeler, 2016), whereas at other times attitudes are based on largely irrelevant information and transitory states (e.g., feelings of power; Briñol et al., 2017). Some people may hold attitudes that are linked to moral principles (Day, Fiske, Downing, & Trail, 2014; Feinberg & Willer, 2015; Skitka, Morgan, & Sargis, 2005) and general values (Blankenship, Wegener, & Murray, 2015; Maio, Rakizeh, Cheung, & Rees, 2009) whereas others do not link attitudes to values. Some of these differences are important with regard to attitude change, and we will refer to them where relevant later in this review.

Explicit versus Implicit Measures of Attitudes

After a long tradition of assessing attitudes using people's responses to self-report measures (e.g., "Is soup good or bad?"), more recent work has also assessed attitudes with measures intended to focus on people's automatic evaluations. Techniques that assess automatically activated evaluations without directly asking people to report their attitudes are often referred to as *implicit measures*, and assessments that tap more deliberative and acknowledged evaluations are referred to as *explicit measures* (Gawronski & Payne, 2010; Petty, Fazio, & Briñol, 2009a; Wittenbrink & Schwarz, 2007). Implicit measures aim to assess whether positivity or negatively comes to mind spontaneously when the attitude object is presented and are akin to "gut reactions" to objects. Common explicit measures include the semantic differential (Osgood, 1964) and Likert (1932) scales, whereas common implicit measures include the Implicit Association Test

(Greenwald, McGhee, & Schwarz, 1998), the evaluative priming measure (Fazio, Sanbonmatsu, Powell, & Kardes, 1986), and the Affect Misattribution Procedure (Payne & Lundberg, 2014).

Because implicit and explicit measures of attitudes are useful in predicting behavior separately (e.g., Greenwald, Banaji, & Nosek, 2015; Greenwald, Poehlman, Uhmann, & Banaji, 2009) and in combination (e.g., Briñol, Petty, & Wheeler, 2006), it is useful to understand how each is modified by various persuasion techniques. Before turning to research on persuasion, we provide a brief discussion of attitude structure because it is important for understanding some of the consequences of attitude change described throughout this chapter (for a more extended discussion of attitude structure, see Fabrigar & Wegener, 2010).

Attitude Structure: How Attitudes Are Represented in Memory

Some theorists have argued that all attitudes are constructed anew each time an evaluation is needed (e.g., Schwarz, 2007). One well-developed example of this approach is the associative propositional evaluation (APE) model (Gawronski & Bodenhausen, 2006, 2007). This theory holds that people respond positively or negatively to attitude objects based on the affect (feelings) or the propositions that come to mind when confronted with the object. These reactions are then evaluated for their validity by examining whether the reactions are consistent with other knowledge. In this model, global attitudes need not be stored in memory but only affect and beliefs associated with objects that serve as input to an expressed attitude.

Although some models do not rely on stored attitudes, most scholars in the field believe that many attitudes are represented in some form in memory (Eagly & Chaiken, 1993; Fazio, 2007; Petty & Cacioppo, 1981). An attitude strength approach (Petty & Krosnick, 1995) helps to resolve the dichotomy between a purely constructivist perspective and a stored representation view by proposing that it is mostly strong attitudes (e.g., those that are highly accessible, held with high certainty) that are stored in memory and come to mind spontaneously when the attitude object is encountered. In contrast, some attitudes may exist in a weaker form (e.g., low in accessibility or certainty) and require some (or a complete) online construction process (Nayakankuppam, Priester, Kwon, Donovan, & Petty, 2018).

There has been much speculation about how attitudes that are stored in memory are structured. Perhaps the most basic approach for understanding the structure of attitudes is represented by the motivation and opportunity as determinants of attitude to behavior processes (MODE) model. This theory holds that attitude objects are linked in memory to an overall evaluation (e.g., candy—good; see Fazio, Towles-Schwen, 1999). The MODE model is the most well-known example of what has been called the *single attitude* approach because people are presumed to hold just one true attitude in memory toward any given object (Petty et al., 2007). However, retrieval of this evaluation can vary in its speed (accessibility) and what is reported on an explicit measure can be modified by what a person considers after their initial evaluation is activated. The MODE model holds that a person's attitude can guide behavior either spontaneously, without conscious reflection, when motivation and opportunity to think are low, or more deliberatively when a person is motivated and able to carefully consider their attitudes toward all behavioral options and then decide upon a behavioral plan (cf. Ajzen & Fishbein, 2005).

A second approach, called a *dual attitudes* perspective, assumes that people can hold separate deliberative and automatic attitudes in memory that can take on different values (e.g., Wilson, Lindsey, & Schooler, 2000). Although there are several versions of the dual attitudes perspective, in the most extreme renditions it is assumed that the two attitudes have separate representations and may be stored in different areas of the brain (e.g., DeCoster, Banner, Smith, & Semin, 2006). It is also sometimes assumed that the different attitudes stem from different psychological processes, with automatic attitudes deriving from simple associative processes such as classical conditioning and deliberative attitudes deriving from propositional reasoning (e.g., Rydell, McConnel, Mackie, & Strain, 2006). Finally, automatic attitudes are typically assumed to govern automatic behavior whereas deliberative attitudes are assumed to guide deliberative behavior (e.g., Dovidio, Kawakami, Johnson, & Howard, 1997).

A third view draws on features of each of the prior approaches and is called the *meta-cognitive model* (MCM) of attitude structure (Petty & Briñol, 2006a; Petty et al., 2007). In contrast to *primary cognition,* which refers to people's initial thoughts about an object (e.g., "Candy is sweet"), *meta-cognition* refers to peoples' thoughts about their thoughts (e.g., "I am sure that candy is sweet"; Jost, Kruglanski, & Nelson, 1988). The MCM holds that in addition to associating attitude objects with general evaluative summaries (e.g., good/bad), people sometimes develop an attitude structure in which attitude objects are linked to both positivity and negativity separately (see also Cacioppo, Gardner, & Berntsen, 1997). Furthermore, the MCM assumes that people can have meta-cognitive validity tags for these evaluations that indicate whether they believe the evaluation is relatively valid or invalid. Thus, in contrast to the exclusively online validation process in the APE, in the MCM, people can store and later retrieve the perceived validity of their positive and/or negative reactions to an object. For many attitude objects, one evaluation is dominant and is seen as valid (the default; see Gilbert, 1991). In such cases, the MCM is similar to the MODE (Fazio et al., 1986).

The MCM postulates that evaluative associations in memory (positive or negative) only determine explicit attitude measures to the extent that people endorse them or perceive them as valid. On the other hand, evaluative associations whether endorsed or not can affect automatic attitude measures (see also Gawronski & Bodenhausen, 2006). That is, the perceived validity tags tend not to influence implicit measures until these tags become so well learned that that are automatically activated (Maddux, Barden, Brewer, & Petty, 2005). One of the more interesting and useful aspects of the MCM is that it points to a difference between explicit versus implicit attitudinal ambivalence. Specifically, *explicit ambivalence* occurs when people have an attitude object linked in memory to both positivity and negativity and they further believe that both of these reactions are valid (e.g., "Candy tastes good, but it is also bad for you"). In *implicit ambivalence,* however, a person also has an attitude object linked to both positivity and negativity in memory, but one of these reactions is tagged as invalid. This person does not report being ambivalent because the person does not consider both reactions to be valid. A person's evaluative reaction to an attitude object might be seen as invalid for a number of reasons including that (a) the person believes the reaction is a mere cultural association (e.g., from the media) and does not represent what he or she truly believes (e.g., "I have a negative reaction to Hispanics because they are portrayed as criminals on TV, but I know that is not true") and (b) the reaction represents a prior attitude (e.g., "I used to like cigarettes, but now I no longer do"; Petty, Tormala, Briñol, & Jarvis, 2006; see also Wilson et al., 2000).

When people endorse both positive and negative reactions to an attitude object, they report feeling conflicted, confused, and mixed about the object (e.g., Priester & Petty, 1996; Thompson, Zanna, & Griffin, 1995). This conflict is especially apparent when people are about to make an attitude-relevant decision (van Harreveld et al., 2009). Other causes of explicit feelings of ambivalence include holding attitudes that differ from one's friends (Priester & Petty, 2001) and having attitudes that are different from those one wants to have (e.g., wanting to be less positive about ice cream; DeMarree, Wheeler, Briñol, & Petty, 2014). In contrast, in cases of implicit ambivalence, the person does not report being conflicted or mixed about the object, but he or she can nevertheless feel generally uncomfortable when considering the object because unendorsed gut feelings conflict with endorsed evaluations (see Epstein, 2003; Petty & Briñol, 2009; Rydell, McConnell, & Mackie, 2008). Both explicit and implicit ambivalence can lead to enhanced information processing about the attitude object (Briñol et al., 2006, Johnson, Petty, Briñol, & See, 2017; Maio, Bell, & Esses, 1996).

Part II: Processes of Persuasion

Traditional Psychological Approaches

We now turn to some of the classic approaches to understanding attitude change. The earliest studies were guided by relatively simple questions such as: Is an appeal to the emotions more effective than an appeal to reason? When the science of persuasion began a century ago, researchers tended to focus on just one outcome for any variable (e.g., positive emotions should always increase persuasion) and only one process by which any variable had its effect (e.g., positive feelings became classically conditioned to the target; for discussion, see Petty, 1997). As data accumulated, however, researchers began to recognize that any one variable did not always have the same effect on persuasion, and each variable could affect attitudes by more than one process.

Furthermore, the fact that some attitude changes tended to be relatively durable and impactful (e.g., guiding behavior) but other attitude changes were rather transitory and inconsequential was puzzling. Contemporary theories of persuasion, such as the elaboration likelihood model (ELM; Petty & Cacioppo, 1986), the heuristic-systematic model (HSM; Chaiken, Liberman, & Eagly, 1989), and the unimodel (Kruglanski & Thompson, 1999) were generated to articulate multiple ways in which variables could affect attitudes in different situations and produce divergent outcomes (for an historical overview, see Petty & Briñol, 2008). Before turning to these more contemporary theories, we briefly review some approaches that highlight a single mechanism of influence.

Message Learning and Reception Approaches

A prominent early approach to persuasion stemmed from Carl Hovland's attempt to apply verbal learning principles to persuasion during World War II (Hovland, Janis, & Kelley, 1953). The core assumption of this approach was that effective influence required a sequence of steps leading to absorption of the content of a message (e.g., exposure, attention, comprehension, learning, retention; see McGuire, 1985). Once the relevant information was learned, people were assumed to yield to it. Thus, the core aspect of persuasion was providing incentives (e.g., an attractive source) to get people to learn the material in a communication so that they would be persuaded by it. In one important variation of this approach proposed by McGuire (1968), the reception phase (e.g., attention, learning) was separated from the yielding phase because several variables could have opposite effects on each. For example, the intelligence of the message recipient is related positively to learning processes (more intelligence makes it easier to learn) but negatively to yielding (more intelligence makes it less likely to yield to what is learned). The joint action of reception and yielding processes implies that people of moderate intelligence should often be easier to persuade than people at the extremes because moderate intelligence maximizes the impact of reception and yielding on persuasion (for evidence and a review, see Rhodes & Wood, 1992).

One enduring contribution of the learning approach was identification of a *sleeper effect* in persuasion (i.e., when an initially ineffective source of low credibility becomes more effective over time; Hovland & Weiss, 1951; Kelman & Hovland, 1953). This unusual effect was later shown to be most likely to occur when the low credible source followed presentation of a strong message (Pratkanis et al., 1988), and the initial message was processed carefully (Priester, Wegener, Petty, & Fabrigar, 1999). Under these conditions, the message is initially discounted because of the low credible source, but because of the high processing of the message, it recovers once the source is forgotten (for a review, see Kumkale & Albarracín, 2004).

Self-Persuasion Approaches

Despite how sensible the message learning approach seemed, the accumulated evidence showed that message learning could occur in the absence of attitude change and that attitudes could change without learning the specific information in the communication (Petty & Cacioppo, 1981). The *cognitive response approach* (Greenwald, 1968; Petty, Ostrom, & Brock, 1981) proposed that persuasion depended on the thoughts people generated to messages rather than learning the message per se. Thus, appeals that elicited primarily favorable thoughts toward a particular recommendation (e.g., "If that new laundry detergent makes my clothes smell fresh, I'll be more popular") produced more persuasion than appeals that elicited mostly unfavorable thoughts toward the recommendation—regardless of the amount of message learning.

A person's thoughts in the absence of any explicit message can also produce attitude change. The persuasive effect of self-generated messages was shown in early research on *role-playing*. For example, individuals who actively generated arguments through playing a role (e.g., convincing a friend to quit smoking) were more turned off to cigarettes than those who passively received the same information (Elms, 1966; see also Greenwald & Albert, 1968; Janis & King, 1954; Watts, 1967). Although most work on self-persuasion focused on incidental persuasion when one attempted to persuade another person, more recent work has compared the effectiveness of intended self-persuasion versus other persuasion. In general, the outcome appears to depend on whether the topic is pro- or counterattitudinal. For a counterattitudinal issue, people are more effective in convincing themselves when they rather than a friend are the presumed target of the message, but the opposite occurs when the topic is proattitudinal (Briñol, McCaslin, & Petty, 2012). The explanation is that people work harder at the persuasion task when they try to convince themselves of a counterattitudinal position, but when it is proattitudinal, they work harder at convincing others than themselves.

People can also be persuaded when they try to remember past behaviors, imagine future behaviors, explain some behavior, or merely think about an event. For example, people who are asked to imagine hypothetical events come to believe that these events have a higher likelihood of occurring than before they thought about them (e.g., Anderson, 1983; Sherman, Cialdini, Schwartzman, & Reynolds, 1985). Similarly, Tesser and his colleagues showed that merely asking people to think about an attitude object can lead to attitude change. In one study, thinking about a person who did something nice led that person to be evaluated more favorably than when distracted from thinking, whereas thinking about a person who was insulting led to more negative evaluations than when distracted (see Tesser, Martin, & Mendolia, 1995). Similar effects have been observed in studies of self-presentation where people generate information about themselves (e.g., Baumeister, 1982; Tice, 1992; Wicklund & Gollwitzer, 1982).

Meta-Cognitive Approaches

The self-persuasion approaches focus on the (primary) thoughts individuals have about the attitude object. Recent research suggests that people can also have thoughts about their thoughts (i.e., *meta-cognitions*; Petty, Briñol, Tormala, & Wegener, 2007). One feature of thoughts that has proven to be useful is the perceived validity of those thoughts, or the confidence with which people hold their thoughts. That is, two people can have the same favorable thought about the message (e.g., "The proposed tax increase should help our schools"), but one person can have considerably more confidence in the validity of that thought than another person. According to *self-validation theory* (Petty, Briñol, & Tormala, 2002), people should rely on their thoughts more when they have confidence rather than doubt in those thoughts. In support of this idea, Petty et al. (2002) found that when the thoughts in response to a message were primarily favorable, increasing confidence in their validity increased persuasion, but increasing doubt in their validity decreased persuasion. When the thoughts to a message were mostly unfavorable, the reverse occurred.

An early demonstration of the importance of meta-cognition for persuasion came from research on what is called the *ease of retrieval* effect. In a classic study, Schwarz et al. (1991) asked participants to rate their own assertiveness after recalling 6 versus 12 examples of their own assertive behavior. They found that people viewed themselves as more assertive after retrieving just 6 rather than 12 examples. This result was initially surprising because a straightforward application of the self-persuasion approach would have suggested that people generating 12 instances of assertiveness would have judged themselves to be more assertive than those generating 6 instances. So, something other than the mere content of the thoughts must have played a role. Schwarz et al. reasoned that people also considered the ease with which the thoughts could be retrieved from memory.

Why would ease matter? One possibility suggested by Schwarz et al. (1991) is based on the *availability heuristic* (Tversky & Kahneman, 1974). That is, the easier it is to generate information in favor of something (e.g., your own assertiveness), the more supportive information people assume there must be. Although this heuristic explanation makes sense when people have limited ability to think, more recent work has suggested that when people are engaged in thoughtful judgments, ease affects attitudes by affecting thought confidence. Thus, when people have an easy time generating thoughts, they are more confident in them and use them more than when they have a difficult time generating them (Tormala, Falces, Briñol, & Petty, 2007; Tormala, Petty, & Briñol, 2002).

To date, numerous studies have appeared showing that not only feelings of ease (for reviews, see Schwarz, 1998, 2004), but many other variables can influence attitudes by affecting thought confidence. For example, if people feel happy following a message it can increase confidence in one's thoughts to a message thereby making people rely more on their thoughts, whether positive or negative (Briñol, Petty, & Barden, 2007). Simply writing one's thoughts on a piece of paper and placing that paper in one's pocket (to protect it) can lead to more use of those thoughts than throwing the paper in the trash (Briñol, Gascó, Petty, & Horcajo, 2013). Thought confidence also plays a role in the mere thought polarization effect mentioned earlier. With more time to think (up to a point) people not only generate more attitude consistent thoughts, but they also become more confident in them (Clarkson, Tormala, & Leone, 2011). Although as a single process, self-validation can account for the results of numerous studies (for a review, see Briñol & Petty, 2009a), as we explain shortly, multiprocess theories of persuasion specify the conditions under which this process of thought validation is mostly likely to occur.

Motivational Approaches

The previous approaches tend to treat each attitude object as associated with salient information that people either add up (Fishbein & Ajzen, 1981) or average (Anderson, 1981), either deliberatively or automatically (see Betsch, Plessner, & Schallies, 2004), to arrive at their attitudes (sometimes weighting their mental content by its perceived validity). People are sometimes rather impartial in their information-processing activity, carefully assessing whatever is presented for its merits or attempting to generate information on both sides of an issue. At other times, however, people are rather biased in their assessment. Persuasion theorists have examined a number of motives that bias people toward a particular conclusion rather than objectively weighing all possibilities (Kruglanski & Webster, 1996).

Perhaps the most studied biasing motive is based on the need for cognitive consistency as evident in Festinger's (1957) theory of *cognitive dissonance*. However, other motives can also bias information processing such as a desire to be free and independent (*reactance* motive; Brehm, 1966; Wicklulnd, 1974) or to belong to a group (for a discussion, see Briñol & Petty, 2005). When particular motives bias thinking (sometimes called *motivated reasoning*; Kunda, 1990), people actively try to generate favorable or unfavorable thoughts consistent with their desired conclusion. Biased thinking does not require a specific motive, however, as some variables can bias thinking outside of conscious intentions such as when a good mood simply makes positive thoughts more accessible in memory (Forgas, 1995; Petty, Schumann, Richman, & Strathman, 1993).

The Elaboration Likelihood Model (ELM) of Persuasion

To organize and understand the fundamental processes underlying persuasion, we rely on a key notion of the ELM (Petty & Cacioppo, 1986). This theory holds that the core processes of persuasion fall along an elaboration continuum. That is, sometimes attitudes are changed by relatively low thought mechanisms (e.g., as in mere association of emotion to an object), but at other times considerable thinking is involved (e.g., such as when people generate their own arguments). Furthermore, sometimes the thinking is relatively objective, and sometimes it is biased by various motives or abilities that are present.

The ELM (Petty & Cacioppo, 1981, 1986) was developed in an attempt to integrate the literature on persuasion by proposing that there was a limited set of core processes by which variables could affect attitudes and that these processes required different amounts of thought. Thoughtful persuasion was referred to as following the *central route* (the high end of the elaboration continuum) whereas low thought persuasion was said to follow the *peripheral route* (the low end of the elaboration continuum). A common finding in ELM research is that the attitudes of people who are motivated and able to think about a message are influenced by their own thoughts following an assessment of the merits of the appeal, but when they are relatively unmotivated to think, attitudes are influenced by their reactions to variables in the persuasion setting serving as simple cues such as the attractiveness of the message source (for reviews, see Petty & Briñol, 2012; Petty & Wegener, 1998a).

The ELM is an early example of what became an explosion of dual process and dual system theories that distinguished thoughtful (deliberative) from nonthoughtful (gut, experiential, snap) judgments (Petty & Briñol, 2006b; for reviews, see Chaiken & Trope, 1999; Sherman, Gawronski, & Trope, 2014). Acrding to the ELM, the extent of thinking is important not only because it can determine the process by which a variable affects attitudes but also because more thoughtful persuasion is postulated to be more consequential than is persuasion produced by lower thought processes (Petty et al., 1995).

In the next section, we review each of the five roles that variables can serve in producing persuasion according to the ELM. Variables in persuasion settings can be part of the communication source (e.g., credibility), the message itself (e.g., complexity), or the recipient of influence (e.g., one's mood). In the ELM, these variables can affect (a) the amount of thinking that takes place, (b) the direction (favorable or unfavorable) of the thinking, (c) the structural properties of the thoughts generated (e.g., thought confidence), or can serve as (d) persuasive arguments for the merits of a proposal, or (e) as simple cues to the desirability of the proposal. We rely on the ELM primarily because it has guided numerous studies in persuasion, and it is comprehensive in outlining the multiple processes by which variables can impact attitudes depending on a person's extent of thinking.

Variables Can Affect the Amount of Thinking

One of the most important and fundamental ways in which variables can influence attitudes is by affecting the amount of thinking in which people engage when making an evaluation. This effect is most likely to occur when thinking is not already constrained to be high or low by other variables.

Motivation to think. Perhaps the most important determinant of a person's motivation to process a message is its perceived *personal relevance*. Whenever the message can be linked to some aspect of the message recipient's "self," it becomes more personally relevant and more likely to be processed. Linking the message to almost any aspect of the self, such as a person's values, goals, outcomes, and identities, can enhance involvement in the issue and processing of related messages (Blankenship & Wegener, 2008; Fleming & Petty, 2000; Petty & Cacioppo, 1990). In one of the earliest demonstrations, Petty and Cacioppo (1979b) told undergraduates that their university was considering a proposal for comprehensive examinations in their major area as a requirement for graduation. The proposal was said to be under consideration for the participants' own university (high relevance) or for a distant university (low relevance). The students then received a message on the topic containing either strong (cogent) or weak (specious) arguments. The key result was that enhancing the relevance of the issue led the students to think more about the arguments that were presented. When the arguments were strong, increasing relevance led to more persuasion, but when the arguments were weak, increasing relevance led to less persuasion.

Beyond perceived *personal relevance*, variables that increase motivation to think include making people individually accountable for message evaluation (Petty, Harkins, & Williams, 1980), summarizing the key arguments as *questions* rather than as *assertions* (Petty, Cacioppo, & Heesacker, 1981), introducing interruptions to the message (Kupor & Tormala, 2015), and having the message presented by multiple people rather than just one (Harkins & Petty, 1981). In addition, any combination of variables that produces a sense of surprise, uncertainty, or incongruity also tends to increase information processing such as when the message source has both positive and negative traits (e.g., is likable but not expert or expert but not likable; Ziegler, Diehl, & Ruther, 2002) or when an expert source expresses uncertainty or a nonexpert expresses certainty (Karmarkar & Tormala, 2010; see also Smith & Petty, 1996). In each case, motivating more thinking led attitudes to be more affected by the quality of the arguments in the message (for a review of many motivational variables that interact with argument quality to influence attitudes, see Carpenter, 2015).

In addition to these situational factors, there are also individual differences in people's motivation to think about persuasive communications. Some people like to engage in thoughtful cognitive activities, but others do not. The former are described as being high in *need for cognition* whereas the latter are low in this trait (Cacioppo & Petty, 1982). Individuals high in need for cognition tend to form attitudes on the basis of an effortful analysis of relevant object-relevant information, whereas people low in need for cognition tend to be more reliant on simple cues. However, this pattern can be reversed in some circumstances such as when people think the message will be very easy to process and thus unchallenging for those high in need for cognition (See, Petty, & Evans, 2009; for a review, see Petty, Briñol, Loersch, & McCaslin, 2009).

One interesting discovery is that the impact of some variables on the motivation to think changes when the message advocacy becomes proattitudinal rather than counterattitudinal. For example, Baker and Petty (1994) found that endorsement from a small minority rather than a majority led to more message processing when a message took a proattitudinal position but majority endorsement led to more processing than minority endorsement when the message was counterattitudinal. As another example, when a message is proattitudinal, people with ambivalent attitudes tend to process it more than people who are univalent, whereas the opposite is the case when the message is counterattitudinal (Clark, Wegener, & Fabrigar, 2008b). Similarly, when a message is proattitudinal, people whose attitudes are low in accessibility tend to process it more than those whose attitudes are high in accessibility, whereas the opposite is the case when the message is counterattitudinal (Clark, Wegener, & Fabrigar, 2008a).

Integrating these seemingly diverse findings, the *discrepancy-motives model* (Clark & Wegener, 2013) holds that a proattitudinal message serves recipients' goals to bolster their current views and this bolstering is more necessary when one's attitudes are weak (e.g., ambivalent, inaccessible) or there is little other support for one's view (e.g., endorsed by a minority rather than a majority). In contrast, a counterattitudinal message threatens one's attitude, and people respond with attempts to defend against this threat more when one's attitudes are strong (e.g., univalent, accessible) and when there is a lot rather than a little support for the contrary view (e.g., endorsed by a majority rather than a minority).

Ability to think. Having the necessary motivation to process a message is not sufficient for high levels of processing. People must also be able to think. For example, a complex or long message might require more than one exposure for maximal processing, even if the recipient was highly motivated to think about it (Cacioppo & Petty, 1989; Ratneshwar & Chaiken, 1991). Of course, repetition is just one variable that can exert an impact on a person's ability to think. For example, if a message is accompanied by distraction (Petty, Wells, & Brock, 1976) or if the speaker talks too fast (Briñol & Petty, 2003; Smith & Shaffer, 1995), thinking about the message will be disrupted, leading people to fail to distinguish strong from weak arguments. Just as there are individual differences in motivation to think about messages, there are also individual differences in ability to think. For instance, as general working knowledge about a topic increases, people become more able to think about issue-relevant information (Wood, Rhodes, & Biek, 1995).

Variables Can Affect the Direction of Thinking

A second mechanism by which variables can influence attitudes is by affecting not the amount, but the valence (favorability) of the thinking. This mechanism is most likely when thinking is already set to be high by other situational and dispositional variables. In such cases, the cogency of the information presented will be an important determinant of the valence of the thoughts generated (with greater cogency leading to more favorable thoughts). However, thoughts can be biased by factors outside of the message itself. Some factors in the persuasion setting, such as being in a positive mood or having the message presented by an expert source, can increase the likelihood that positive thoughts in response to the message are generated (e.g., DeSteno, Petty, Wegener, & Rucker, 2000; Petty et al., 1993). Other factors, such as being the target of an explicit persuasion attempt, can increase the likelihood that counterarguing occurs (Petty & Cacioppo, 1979a). In general, biasing influences tend to be more impactful when the message itself is somewhat ambiguous in its quality and thus more open to biased interpretation (Chaiken & Maheswaran, 1994).

Any time a message contradicts an existing attitude, people are likely to be biased against it. And when a message supports one's attitude, people likely will be biased in favor of it. Similarly, if a message is perceived as counter to one's outcomes, values, or identities, people will be biased against it, but if it is perceived to be supportive, people will be biased in favor of it (Petty, Cacioppo, & Haugtvedt, 1992). As noted earlier, when a message is framed as simply relevant to the self, the *amount* of information processing is affected. But when a message takes a particular position (pro or con) with respect to the self, the *valence* of the processing can be affected (Petty & Cacioppo, 1990).

Individual differences can also motivate or enable people to either increase the likelihood of generating favorable thoughts or unfavorable thoughts. For example, optimists are more likely to generate favorable thoughts to a message whereas pessimists are more likely to do the opposite (Geers, Handley, & McLarney, 2003; Geers, Wellman, & Fowler, 2013). The distinction between amount and direction of thinking suggests that some individual differences are more likely to be associated with enhancing relatively objective (undirected) thinking whereas others are more likely to enhance biased (directed) thinking. For example, with respect to motives, the need to know is likely to be associated with extensive and largely objective elaboration since the motive to understand is relatively independent of the content. In contrast, the need for self-worth could focus information processing activity in a particular direction if one side or the other reflected more favorably on the self.

Motivational biases. As noted earlier, the most studied biasing motive in the persuasion literature is the need to maintain cognitive consistency (e.g., Heider, 1958; Kiesler, 1971; Rosenberg, 1960), and the most prominent consistency theory is the theory of *cognitive dissonance*. In Festinger's (1957) original formulation of dissonance theory, two elements in a cognitive system (e.g., a belief and an attitude; an attitude and a behavior) are consonant if one follows from the other (e.g., "I voted for Candidate X. She has the same positions that I do on the major issues") and dissonant if one belief implies the opposite of the other (e.g., "I voted for Candidate X. His political party is opposed to mine"). Festinger proposed that the psychological state of dissonance was aversive and that people would be motivated to reduce it.

One interesting dissonance situation occurs when a person's behavior contradicts his or her attitudes. For example, one common laboratory procedure for producing dissonance is inducing a person to write an attitude-inconsistent essay under high choice conditions and with little incentive (e.g., Zanna & Cooper, 1974). Because behavior is usually difficult to undo, dissonance can be reduced by changing attitudes to be consistent with the behavior. Dissonance can result in a reanalysis of the reasons why a person engaged in a particular behavior and cause a person to rethink (rationalize) the merits of an attitude object. The end result of this effortful but biased cognitive activity can be a change in attitude toward the object (Cooper, 2007).

In perhaps the most famous dissonance experiment, undergraduates were induced to engage in a boring task (Festinger & Carlsmith, 1959). Following this, some of the students were told that the experimenter's assistant was absent today and they were asked to take his place and try to convince a waiting participant that the task was actually quite interesting. Some of these students were informed that they would be paid $1 for assuming this role and others were told that the pay was $20. After talking to the waiting student, all participants completed an ostensibly standard department survey that asked how interesting they found the experimental task to be. As expected by dissonance theory, the participants who received $1 rated the task as more interesting than those who received $20. This result was predicted from dissonance theory because the $1 participants had insufficient justification for their behavior, whereas the $20 participants had sufficient justification. Thus, the former participants experienced cognitive dissonance and felt a need to justify their actions by convincing themselves that the task was interesting.

The focus of subsequent dissonance research has been on understanding the precise cause of the tension that sometimes accompanies counterattitudinal action. Various theorists have questioned that inconsistency per se produces tension in people or that inconsistency reduction is the motive behind attitude change. For example, the *new look approach* argues that dissonance requires that people believe that they have freely chosen to bring about some foreseeable and unwanted negative consequence for themselves or others (e.g., Cooper & Fazio, 1984; Scher & Cooper, 1989). The *action-based model* (Harmon-Jones & Harmon-Jones, 2008; Harmon-Jones & Mills, 1999) contends that discomfort results from inconsistent beliefs especially when the conflict has the potential to immobilize people and prevent action. For example, if an attitude object had both positive and negative qualities, either choosing it or rejecting it could cause dissonance. Thus, focusing on either the positive or negative features (making one's attitude more positive or negative) would lead to a more clear choice and thus reduce the discomfort (see also van Harreveld, van der Pligt, & De Liver, 2009).

Still other theorists argue that the inconsistency must involve a critical aspect of the self or a threat to one's positive self-concept for dissonance to occur (e.g., Aronson, 1968; Greenwald & Ronis, 1978; Steele, 1988; Tesser, 1988). Of course, bringing about negative consequences for others is inconsistent with most people's views of themselves as caring individuals. If people are provided with social support for their actions (Stroebe & Diehl, 1988) or are given an opportunity to restore or bolster their self-esteem in some other manner (Tesser, 2001), dissonance-reducing attitude change is less likely (for a review, see Sherman & Cohen, 2006).

In fact, bolstering the esteem of the persuasion target can serve as a general avenue to undermine resistance to persuasion (Knowles & Linn, 2004). That is, one proposed method of decreasing a person's resistance to attitude change is to provide some self-affirmation prior to an attacking message. *Self-affirmation theory* (Steele, 1988) holds that affirming an important aspect of the self (e.g., thinking about one's cherished values) prior to receipt of a counterattitudinal message can buffer the self against the threat imposed by the message and thereby increase the likelihood that participants will respond to the message favorably (e.g., Cohen, Aronson, & Steele, 2000).

Although different conceptual approaches to dissonance phenomena have emerged in contemporary research, there have been attempts to integrate these varying perspectives. Most notably, the *self-standards model* (Stone & Cooper, 2001, 2003) postulates that when inconsistent behavior is judged against a personal standard (i.e., one's own idiosyncratic expectancies for behavior), self-driven processes (e.g., Aronson, 1968; Steele, 1988) are responsible for dissonance effects. However, when behavior is judged against a normative standard (i.e., the expectancies of most people in a given culture), the self is not implicated in dissonance effects, and dissonance is instead caused by perceptions of the negative consequences of one's behavior (Cooper & Fazio, 1984).

Ability biases. Although most studies of bias in persuasion explore motivational processes, ability factors can also produce bias. For example, people who possess accessible attitudes bolstered by considerable attitude-congruent knowledge are better *able* to defend their attitudes than those who have inaccessible attitudes or attitudes with a minimal underlying foundation (Fazio & Williams, 1986; Wood 1982). For some variables, a combination of motivational and ability factors could be at work. For example, being in a positive mood might make it easier for positive thoughts to come to mind (an ability bias; Bower, 1981) but might also motivate people to want to stay in that positive state by generating positive thoughts (e.g., Wegener & Petty, 1994).

Variables Can Affect Meta-Cognitive Processes

A third way in which variables can influence attitudes is via meta-cognitive processes. This occurs when variables affect what people think about their own thoughts. That is, in addition to affecting the number of thoughts (amount of thinking) and the valence of the thoughts (whether they are positive or negative), variables can also affect meta-cognitive features of the thoughts such as how much confidence people have in them, how much they like them, or how desirable and biasing they are perceived to be.

Expectancy–value model. Two key aspects of thoughts are the expectancy (i.e., likelihood) and value (i.e., desirability) of consequences considered in a thought. In Fishbein and Ajzen's (1975, 1981) *expectancy-value* formulation that is part of their *theory of reasoned action*, if a person has a thought in response to an advertisement such as "Using this new detergent will make my clothes smell fresh," the key aspects of the thought relevant for attitude change are the desirability of smelling fresh and the likelihood that the new detergent will produce this outcome. Thus, messages are effective to the extent that they produce changes in either the likelihood or the desirability component of a consequence that is linked to the attitude object (e.g., making smelling fresh seem more desirable and/or likely; Johnson, Smith-McLallen, Killeya, & Levin, 2004).

Emotions have been shown to affect the perceived likelihood of the outcomes in a persuasive message. For example, DeSteno, Petty, Rucker, Wegener, and Braverman (2004) induced sadness or anger in participants before exposing them to arguments that articulated the sad or angering consequences for failure to enact a policy. When the emotion was matched to the type of argument, persuasion was higher than when it was not. Importantly, these effects were mediated by the perceived likelihoods that the angering and sad events included in the message would happen (e.g., when angry, participants saw the angering but not the sad events as more likely to occur, but when sad, the opposite was true). When the events were seen as more likely to occur, they led to more persuasion (for additional examples, see Petty & Briñol, 2015; Petty, Fabrigar, & Wegener, 2003).

The self-validation hypothesis. Whatever the likelihood or desirability of a given consequence, the thoughts themselves can vary in the confidence with which they are held (i.e., the extent to which the thought is seen as valid). Confidence in thoughts is important because the greater the confidence in a given thought, the more likely it will be used in forming judgments. The notion that thought confidence determines thought usage is referred to as the *self-validation hypothesis* (Petty, Briñol, & Tormala, 2002).

As described earlier in our discussion of meta-cognitive approaches to persuasion, many variables have been shown to affect perceptions of thought validity and thereby influence attitudes (see Briñol & Petty, 2009a). In general, variables that enhance confidence after thought generation (e.g., feelings of power) produce greater reliance on thoughts such that when thoughts are primarily positive, these variables are associated with more persuasion, but when thoughts are primarily negative, variables increasing confidence are associated with less persuasion.

Flexible correction processes. Just as enhanced confidence in thoughts leads to greater reliance on them, increased doubt leads people to discard their thoughts. Sometimes, people might be so doubtful of their thoughts that they think the opposite is true. In such cases, doubt can lead to reversed effects with positive thoughts leading to less positive attitudes than negative thoughts (e.g., Briñol, Petty, & Barden, 2007). If people have doubt in their thoughts because they fear that their thoughts stemmed from some source of bias (e.g., an attractive source), they could attempt to correct for their biased thoughts in a manner specified by the *flexible correction model* (FCM; for a review, see Wegener & Petty, 1997). According to the FCM, people estimate the magnitude and direction of the perceived biasing effect on their judgment and attempt to adjust for this bias. If they correct too much, reverse effects of variables can be obtained (Petty & Wegener, 1993; Wegener & Petty, 1995; Wilson & Brekke, 1994). For example, in one study (Petty, Wegener, & White, 1998), when people became aware that a likable source might be biasing their attitudes, they became more favorable toward the proposal when it was endorsed by a dislikable source. Such explicit corrections typically require relatively high degrees of thinking. However, if certain corrections are practiced repeatedly, they can become less effortful and even automatic (e.g., Glaser & Banaji, 1999; Maddux et al., 2005).

Variables Can Be Evaluated as Persuasive Arguments

Another way that variables can affect attitudes is by serving as persuasive arguments for a proposal. When thinking is high, people assess the relevance of *all* of the information in the context and that comes to mind to determine the merits of the attitude object under consideration. That is, people examine source, message, recipient, and contextual information as possible arguments or reasons for favoring or disfavoring the attitude object. Here, the same variable (e.g., one's mood) that served in other roles in other circumstances (e.g., biasing thinking when motivation and ability to think are high) can itself be scrutinized as to whether it provides a meaningful reason for adopting the advocated position. For example, whereas an attractive source might affect the amount of thinking about a message when thinking is unconstrained by other variables (e.g., people might be interested in what an attractive person has to say), under high elaboration conditions, people scrutinize whether the attractiveness of the source is relevant to the advocacy and provides evidence for it.

Thus, under high thinking conditions, an attractive source will exert little impact as an argument when people view the attractiveness as irrelevant to the merits of the advocacy. However, when attractiveness is relevant (e.g., the source is advertising a beauty product), then physically attractive sources could be more persuasive than unattractive sources by serving as a cogent argument (i.e., providing visual evidence; Kruglanski et al., 2005; Miniard, Bhatla, Lord, Dickson, & Unnava, 1991; Petty & Cacioppo, 1984b). Importantly, individuals can vary in what type of information is viewed as relevant persuasive evidence. For example, attractiveness is more likely to serve as a relevant argument for individuals high in self-monitoring than those low in this trait because the former individuals care more about image than the latter (DeBono & Harnish, 1988).

Variables Can Operate as Simple Cues

The final role for variables is the most basic—serving as a simple cue. When variables serve as cues, they influence attitudes in accord with their valence. For example, under low thinking conditions or for people who don't like to think, source attractiveness is likely to increase persuasion regardless of its relevance to the advocacy because people are not carefully assessing all information for its merits (i.e., source attractiveness would work as well in an advertisement for a bank as a beauty product; Haugtvedt, Petty, & Cacioppo, 1992). Thus, attitude change does not always require effortful evaluation of the information presented. Next, we briefly describe some specific attitude change processes that involve relatively little (if any) effortful thinking.

Attribution theory. According to *self-perception theory* (Bem, 1965), people have no special knowledge of their own internal states. Instead, they simply infer their attitudes in a manner similar to how they infer the attitudes of others (e.g., "If I [she] walked a mile to Target, I [she] must like that store"). During much of the 1970s, self-perception theory was thought to provide an alternative account of dissonance effects (Bem, 1972). However, research indicates that both dissonance and self-perception processes can operate, but in different domains. In particular, dissonance processes operate when a person engages in attitude-discrepant action that is unacceptable to a person whereas self-perception processes are more likely when a person engages in attitude-discrepant but more agreeable behavior (Fazio, Zanna, & Cooper, 1977). Self-perception theory also accounts for some unique attitudinal phenomena. For example, the *overjustification effect* occurs when people come to dislike a previously liked behavior when they are provided with more than sufficient reward for engaging in it. For example, if someone paid you to eat your favorite food, you might reason that you are only eating it for the money, and liking for the food would decrease (e.g., Lepper, Greene, & Nisbett, 1973; also see Deci, 1995).

Use of persuasion heuristics. The term *heuristics* refers to simple rules or shortcuts used to simplify decision-making (Shah & Oppenheimer, 2008). A number of simple heuristics that can be processed very quickly have featured prominently in the literature on social influence (Cialdini, 2008). That is, under low thinking conditions, appeals tend to be more effective when they are merely associated with scarcity, authoritative or likable sources, and consensus from others (see also Chapter 7).

The *heuristic/systematic model* of persuasion (HSM) represents an explicit attempt to use heuristics to explain why certain variables such as source expertise or message length have their impact (Chaiken, 1987; Chaiken et al., 1989). That is, the HSM proposes that in contrast to "systematic" (central route) processes, many source, message, and other cues are evaluated by means of simple schemas or cognitive heuristics that people have learned on the basis of past experience and observation. According to the HSM, the likelihood of careful processing increases whenever confidence in one's attitude drops below the desired level (the *sufficiency threshold*). Whenever actual and desired confidence are equal, heuristic processing is more likely. For example, because of prior personal experience, people could base their acceptance of a message on the mere number of arguments it contains by invoking the heuristic "The more arguments, the better" (Petty & Cacioppo, 1984a; Wood, Kallgren, & Preisler, 1985). Generally, the HSM makes predictions that are similar to the ELM, though the language and specific mechanisms of each theory are a bit different (for further discussion, see Eagly & Chaiken, 1993; Petty & Briñol, 2012; Petty & Wegener, 1998).

Conditioning processes. The attribution and heuristic models focus on simple cognitive inferences that can modify attitudes. Other approaches, such as *classical conditioning*, emphasize the role of relatively simple association processes. In brief, conditioning occurs when an initially neutral stimulus such as an unfamiliar shape (the conditioned stimulus; CS) is associated with another stimulus such as electric shock (the unconditioned stimulus; UCS) that is connected directly or through prior learning to some response such as feeling bad (the unconditioned response; UCR). By pairing the UCS with the CS many times, the CS becomes able to elicit a conditioned response (CR) that is similar to the UCR. Thus, pairing an unfamiliar shape with electric shock many times will cause you to dislike that shape. Over the past several decades, a wide variety of conditioning stimuli have been used to create positive or negative attitudes (e.g., see Gouaux, 1971; Staats, Staats, & Crawford, 1962; Stuart, Shimp, & Engle, 1987). People are especially susceptible to conditioning effects when the likelihood of thinking is rather low (Cacioppo, Marshall-Goodell, Tassinary, & Petty, 1992; see also Shimp, Stuart, & Engle, 1991).

Theorists have suggested that classical conditioning applied to attitudes might be a somewhat different phenomenon more appropriately called *evaluative conditioning* (Martin & Levey, 1978). This is because the conditioned attitudes do not follow the same properties as do the behaviors examined in typical classical conditioning paradigms (e.g., the conditioning of a salivary response in dogs). In classical conditioning, the phenomenon works best when there is some awareness of the pairing of the CS and UCS so that the UCS comes to signal the appearance of the CS. In evaluative conditioning, contingency awareness is not necessary, though it can aid conditioning (e.g., Schmidt & de Houwer, 2012). Perhaps because contingency awareness is not necessary, evaluative conditioning is somewhat resistant to extinction when the UCS is no longer presented, unlike classical conditioning (for a review, see Hofmann, De Houwer, Perugini, Baeyens, & Crombez, 2010).

If the mechanism of attitude change is not classical conditioning, then what is it? Jones, Fazio, and Olson (2009) suggested evaluative conditioning occurs because of misattribution of the feelings elicited by the UCS to the CS. In a series of studies in which the UCS and CS were presented simultaneously over many trials, Jones et al. (2009) showed that the easier it was to confuse the source of one's feelings, the greater the conditioning effect. For example, when the UCS and CS were presented spatially close together, conditioning was greater than when the stimuli were further apart. This research suggests that evaluative conditioning might be reliant on relatively simple misattribution inferences similar to self-perception and heuristic inferences.

Mere exposure. The mere exposure effect occurs when attitudes toward stimuli become more favorable as a consequence of their mere repeated presentation without any need to pair the stimuli with other positive stimuli as in evaluative conditioning (Zajonc, 1968). Mere exposure effects have been found even when the stimuli could not be consciously recognized (e.g., Kunst-Wilson & Zajonc, 1980). Moreover, it has been shown that mere exposure can affect mood and that this mood can spread to other, related stimuli that were not even presented (Monahan, Murphy, & Zajonc, 2000).

Perhaps the most accepted explanation of the mere exposure effect relies on the notion of *perceptual fluency.* Repeated exposure to stimuli can make those stimuli easier to process, and this fluency enhances subsequent liking. Specifically, the feeling of ease of processing is thought to be misattributed to a positive evaluation of the stimulus (Bornstein, 1989; Bornstein & D'Agostino, 1992; Jacoby, Kelley, Brown, & Jasechko, 1989), at least when people perceive fluency as something good (Briñol, Petty, & Tormala, 2006). The fluency process is most likely to occur when the repeated stimuli are not thought about much (Bornstein, 1989). When the repeated stimuli already have some dominant meaning, repeated exposure can accentuate that dominant response (Brickman, Redfield, Harrison, & Crandall, 1972; see also Cacioppo & Petty, 1989; Grush, 1976). One explanation for these polarization effects is that people's positive assessments of positive information might seem more valid or plausible as exposure increases, as do their negative assessments of negative information (Kruglanski, Freund, & Bar-Tal, 1996).

Attitude change on implicit measures of attitudes. Although the research just described on simple (relatively low thought) mechanisms of attitude change has assessed change using explicit attitude measures, these same mechanisms are capable of affecting implicit measures of attitudes. For example, Dijksterhuis (2004) found that automatic evaluations of the self were affected by subliminal evaluative conditioning trials in which the word *I* was repeatedly associated with positive or negative trait terms (see also Baccus, Baldwin, & Packer, 2004; Olson & Fazio, 2001; Petty et al., 2006; Walther, 2002).

Perhaps the area in which researchers have examined changes on implicit measures from seemingly simple processes the most is in the domain of prejudice (see Chapter 12). For example, automatic evaluations of Blacks have been shown to be affected by exposure to various exemplars of admired Black individuals (e.g., Dasgupta & Greenwald, 2001; Dasgupta & Rivera, 2008; Rudman, Ashmore, & Gary,

2001; for a review, see Gawronski & Payne, 2010). In general, research suggests that automatic measures of attitudes can be affected by relatively low thought attitude change processes. In fact, implicit measures of attitudes have sometimes been assumed to change only (cf. Smith & DeCoster, 1999) or to a greater extent (Gawronski, Strack, & Bodenhausen, 2009; Rydell & McConnell, 2006) as a result of low rather than high thought processes.

However, other work contradicts the general idea that automatic attitude measures respond mostly to simple persuasion techniques via relatively low thinking processes. For example, recent research has shown that automatic evaluations can be affected by thoughtful processing of persuasive messages, advertisements, marketing campaigns, and other treatments involving effortful processing of verbal information (e.g., Horcajo, Briñol, & Petty, 2010; Mann & Ferguson, 2015, 2017; Smith & de Houwer, 2014; Wyer, 2010, 2016; for reviews, see Gawronski & Bodenhausen, 2006; Gawronski & Sritharan, 2010; Maio, Haddock, Watt, & Hewstone, 2009, Petty & Briñol, 2010). Thus, the most accurate conclusion is that, like explicit measures, implicit measures can be affected by both automatic and deliberative processes.

A final point worth mentioning is that research has shown that changes on implicit measures of attitudes are sometimes related to change on explicit measures, but sometimes they are independent of each other (e.g., Gregg, Seibt, & Banaji, 2006; Petty et al., 2006). In general, deliberative measures are more likely to correspond with automatic measures when participants complete the automatic measures after being told to "trust their intuition" (Jordan, Whitfield, & Ziegler-Hill, 2007) or "go with their gut" before responding (Ranganath, Smith, & Nosek, 2008). Such instructions apparently free participants to report evaluative stirrings of which they are aware but may not report spontaneously due to uncertainty regarding their origins or appropriateness (Loersch, McCaslin, & Petty, 2011).

Part III: The Impact of Key Variables in Persuasion

In addition to specifying the general mechanisms of persuasion, the ELM postulates that any communication variable (i.e., whether part of the source, message, or recipient) can influence attitudes via one or more of the key processes just outlined. Because the number of documented persuasion variables is vast, our review of variables is meant to be illustrative of how understanding the basic mechanisms of persuasion can be useful for analyzing any possible variable of interest, even if it has never been studied previously.

Source Factors

From the earliest days of persuasion research, scholars have divided the variables central to persuasion into aspects of the *source* of the persuasive proposal, the *message* that the source provides, and the *recipient* of the communication (cf. Hovland, Janis, & Kelley, 1953). Source factors refer to aspects of the person or group that is delivering the message. Commonly studied source factors include credibility (e.g., having extensive knowledge, expertise, and/or honesty), attractiveness (e.g., physical attractiveness of a source, perceived similarity, and general likability), whether the advocacy comes from a person in a numerical majority or minority, and whether the source has power—real or perceived—over the message recipient. Other source factors frequently studied in persuasion include race and gender and even whether or not the self is a source (Briñol, McCaslin, & Petty, 2012; Maio & Thomas, 2007).

When the likelihood of thinking about the advocacy is low (e.g., low personal relevance topic, high distraction), source factors influence attitudes by serving as simple peripheral cues, affecting implicit (Forehand & Perkins, 2005; McConnell, Rydell, Strain, & Mackie, 2008) as well as explicit attitudes

(Chaiken, 1980; Petty, Cacioppo, & Goldman, 1981) in the same direction as their valence. That is, any positive features of the source (e.g., higher credibility) tend to produce more persuasion. Some research suggests that this simple cue effect of sources is especially likely when people do not already have an attitude on the issue (Kumkale, Albarracín, & Seignourel, 2010).

When the likelihood of thinking is very high (e.g., high personal relevance, low distraction), source factors function in other roles. For example, as previously discussed, if a source factor is relevant to the merits of a proposal, it can serve as a persuasive argument. Thus, an attractive endorser can provide persuasive visual evidence for the effectiveness of a beauty product (Petty & Cacioppo, 1984b). Also, under high thinking conditions sources can bias information processing. Chaiken and Maheswaran (1994) found that when recipients under high thinking conditions received a message of ambiguous quality, expert sources led to more favorable thoughts about the message and thus more favorable attitudes than low expertise sources. This did not occur when the arguments were clearly strong or weak. Under high elaboration conditions, source factors can also influence persuasion by affecting the confidence people have in the validity of their thoughts. This effect is most likely to occur when the source information follows rather than precedes the persuasive message (Tormala, Briñol, & Petty, 2007).

If the likelihood of thinking is not set to be very high or low by other variables then source factors can affect how much thinking people do (e.g., Moore, Hausknecht, & Thamodaran, 1986; Puckett, Petty, Cacioppo, & Fisher, 1983). For example, Priester and Petty (1995) demonstrated that if source expertise is high, people process messages more carefully when they came from a source whose trustworthiness is in doubt than from a clearly trustworthy source. If trustworthiness is high, however, then people are more likely to process a message from an expert source than from a source who lacks expertise (Heesacker, Petty, & Cacioppo, 1983). As also noted earlier, incongruent message sources (e.g., attractive but not credible) tend to enhance information processing (Ziegler et al., 2002; for a review of source factors, see Briñol & Petty, 2009b).

Message Factors

Message factors involve any aspect of the persuasive communication itself. For example, does the message present strong or weak arguments (Petty, Wells, & Brock, 1976) or does it emphasize primarily affect or cognition (Haddock et al., 2008)? Other message features that have been studied include its perceived complexity (See, Petty, & Evans, 2009), abstractness (Fujita, Eyal, Chaiken, Trope, & Liberman, 2008), use of imagery (Petrova & Cialdini, 2008), whether it relies on anecdotes and stories versus facts (Green & Brock, 2004), presents one or both sides of the issue (Rucker, Petty, & Briñol, 2008), (mis)matches the recipients' characteristics in some way (Petty & Wegener, 1998), argues in favor of or against the recipient's own view (Clark & Wegener, 2013), and many others.

As was the case with source factors, message variables can also affect attitudes via different processes in different situations. Consider the number of arguments that a message contains. This variable serves as a simple cue when people are unmotivated or unable to think about the information (Petty & Cacioppo, 1984a). People can simply count the arguments in a message and agree with it more as more information is presented, regardless of the cogency of that information. When processing is high, however, the informational items in a message are not simply counted, but instead processed for their quality. Thus, under low thinking conditions, adding weak reasons in support of a position enhances persuasion, but when the items in a message are processed carefully, adding weak reasons reduces persuasion (Alba & Marmorstein, 1987; Friedrich, Fetherstonhaugh, Casey, & Gallagher, 1996; Petty & Cacioppo, 1984a). Additionally, the number of arguments has the potential to validate thoughts. Imagine if a person had already processed a message and generated either largely favorable or unfavorable thoughts. If the recipient subsequently learns that there are many more arguments similar to the one's already processed, this would likely validate one's thoughts to the initial message producing a more polarized attitude.

Recipient Factors

Recipient factors refer to any aspect of the person. This includes chronic states such as one's level of intelligence (e.g., Rhodes & Wood, 1992) and one's personality such as indicated by scores on self-monitoring (e.g., Snyder & DeBono, 1985) or need for cognition (Cacioppo, Petty, & Morris, 1983) scales (for a detailed review of chronic individual differences in persuasion, see Briñol & Petty, 2018). Recipient factors also refer to more transitory states such as whether the recipient is feeling powerful or powerless at the moment (Briñol, Petty, Valle, Rucker, & Becerra, 2007) and whether the recipient is experiencing ease or difficulty in processing the message (Tormala et al., 2002).

One extensively studied recipient factor in persuasion concerns the incidental emotions the recipient is experiencing at the time of persuasion. Research has shown that emotions can serve in all of the roles for variables that we have summarized (see Petty & Briñol, 2015; Petty et al., 2003). That is, when thinking is constrained to be low, emotions tend to serve as simple associative cues and produce evaluations consistent with their valence via either conditioning or as input to a heuristic (e.g., "I feel good so I must like it"; Petty et al., 1993). When thinking is high, emotions can be evaluated as evidence. For example, negative emotions such as sadness or fear can lead to positive evaluations of a movie if these are the intended states (e.g., see Martin, 2000). In addition, under high thinking, emotions can bias the ongoing thoughts such as when positive consequences seem more likely when people are in a happy than sad state (e.g., DeSteno et al., 2000). If an emotion is induced after thinking about the message, then emotions can affect confidence in thoughts. For example, people feel more confident in their thoughts and rely on them more if made to feel happy rather than sad following message processing (Briñol, Petty, & Barden, 2007).

Finally, when the likelihood of thinking is not constrained to be high or low, emotions can affect the extent of thinking. For example, people might think about messages more when in a sad than happy state because sadness signals a problem to be solved (Schwarz, Bless, & Bohner, 1991) or when the message conveys a sense of uncertainty (Tiedens & Linton, 2001) or invokes a motive to maintain one's happiness (Wegener & Petty, 1994). Other transitory recipient factors that similarly have been shown to serve in these multiple roles include feelings of power (Briñol, Petty, Durso, & Rucker, 2017) and one's bodily movements (Briñol, Petty, & Wagner, 2012).

Matching Variables

Although we have focused on source, message, and recipient factors taken in isolation, these variables are often considered jointly such as when the source of a message matches the recipient (e.g., a male source speaking to a male audience) or the message matches the recipient in some way (e.g., a message focusing on image presented to a high self-monitor). Such matches can affect persuasion by invoking the same core processes that we have already articulated for the variables in isolation. For example, when matching the gender of the source to the recipient or matching an image message to a high self-monitor enhances persuasion, it could be for one of the following reasons: The match serves as a simple acceptance cue (DeBono, 1987), it biases thinking in a positive way (Lavine & Snyder, 1996), it increases elaboration of the strong arguments (Petty & Wegener, 1998b), or it validates the positive thoughts people had to the message (Evans & Clark, 2012). Importantly, consideration of the multiple roles for matching also suggests that matching can reduce persuasion such as when a match increases elaboration of weak arguments (Petty & Wegener, 1998b; Wheeler, Petty, & Bizer, 2005).

Part IV: Consequences of Attitude Change

Consequences of Different Persuasion Processes for Explicit Measures

We have already seen that knowing about the process by which a variable impacts attitudes can aid in prediction of whether that variable will enhance or undermine persuasion. We now focus on a second important benefit of understanding the underlying process of persuasion—whether or not the attitude change produced will be consequential. Sometimes a high and a low thought process can result in the same attitude. However, according to the ELM (Petty & Cacioppo, 1986), attitudes formed or changed through high thinking processes should be more persistent over time, resistant to change, and predictive of behavior than attitudes formed or changed via low thinking processes. There are both structural and meta-cognitive reasons for this. First, as thinking increases during attitude change, people should acquire more support for their attitudes and their attitudes should become more accessible (Bizer & Krosnick, 2001). Furthermore, people should become more confident in their views (Barden & Petty, 2008). Each of these factors would increase the likelihood that attitudes would be consequential (for a review, see Petty et al., 1995).

Attitude Persistence and Resistance

When attitude changes are based on extensive issue-relevant thinking, they tend to *persist* (endure) over time. For example, research has shown that encouraging self-generation of arguments (e.g., Elms, 1966; Watts, 1967), using interesting or involving communication topics (Ronis et al., 1977), leading recipients to believe that they might have to explain or justify their attitudes to other people (e.g., Boninger et al., 1990; Chaiken, 1980), and having them evaluate a message during its receipt rather than afterward (Mackie, 1987) are all associated with increased persistence of attitude change. Also, people who characteristically enjoy thinking (high need for cognition) show greater persistence of attitude change than people who do not (e.g., Cárdaba, Briñol, Horcajo, & Petty, 2013; Haugtvedt & Petty, 1992; Wegener, Clark, & Petty, 2006).

Resistance refers to the extent to which an attitude is capable of surviving an attack from contrary information. Although persistence and resistance tend to co-occur, their potential independence is shown in McGuire's (1964) classic work on cultural truisms. Truisms such as "You should brush your teeth after every meal" tend to last forever if not challenged but are susceptible to influence when attacked because people have no practice in defending them. In his work on *inoculation theory*, McGuire demonstrated that two kinds of bolstering can be effective in facilitating resistance. One relies on providing individuals with a supportive defense of their attitudes (Ross, McFarland, Conway, & Zanna, 1983), and a second provides a mild attack and refutation of it (the inoculation). Just as people can be made more resistant to a disease by giving them a mild form of it, people can be made more resistant to discrepant messages by inoculating their initial attitudes (see Petty, Tormala, & Rucker, 2004). The separation of persistence and resistance also suggests that some low effort persuasion strategies such as classical conditioning might be effective in producing relatively persistent attitudes, but these attitudes would have difficulty surviving a substantive attack since they do not have a well elaborated informational basis.

Prediction of Behavior

Once an attitude has changed, behavior change requires that the new attitude rather than the old attitude or previous habits guide action (Petty, Gleicher, & Jarvis, 1993). If a new attitude is based on high thought, it is likely to be highly accessible and come to mind automatically in the presence of the attitude object. Therefore, it will be available to guide behavior even if people do not think much before acting (see Fazio, 1990, 1995). However, even if people do engage in some thought, attitudes based on high thinking are still more likely to guide behavior because these attitudes are held with more certainty and people are more willing to act on attitudes of which they are certain (e.g., Barden & Petty, 2008; Brown, 1974).

Of course, behavior is determined by more than individuals' attitudes even if those attitudes are based on high thought. The *theory of reasoned action* (Fishbein & Ajzen, 1975) mentioned earlier highlights *social norms* (what others think you should do) as an important determinant of behavior in addition to one's own attitudes toward the behavior (which are determined by the perceived desirability and likelihood of consequences of the behavior). Building on this framework, the *theory of planned behavior* (Ajzen, 1991) points to a person's sense of self-efficacy or competence to perform the behavior in addition to one's personal attitudes and social norms (see Ajzen & Fishbein, 2005). Finally, prior behavioral *habits* also play an important role in current behavior as people tend to do what they have done in the past, and it is sometimes difficult for a new attitude to overcome this (Itzchakov, Uziel, & Wood, 2018; for a review, see Wood, 2017). Thus, it is clear that although attitude change can be an important first step, it might still be insufficient to produce the desired behavioral responses even if appropriate new attitudes are formed by the central route.

Certainty as a Source of Attitude Strength

We noted earlier that when attitudes change as a result of high thinking processes, they are likely to be held with greater certainty than when they are changed to the same extent by low thinking processes. Certainty refers to a sense of validity concerning one's attitudes (Gross, Holtz, & Miller, 1995) and magnifies attitude effects (Petty et al., 2007). For example, when attitudes are consistent and largely univalent, increasing certainty in them enhances attitude stability and resistance to change, but if an attitude is mixed (ambivalent), increasing certainty is associated with less stability and resistance (Clarkson, Tormala, & Rucker, 2008; Luttrell, Petty, & Briñol, 2016). Coherent attitudes held with certainty also tend to be more predictive of behavior (Fazio & Zanna, 1978; for a review of attitude certainty, see Rucker, Tormala, Petty, & Brinol, 2014). Gross et al. (1995) suggest that it is useful to distinguish "true confidence" in one's attitude from "compensatory confidence." The former is based on the extent of one's knowledge or social support whereas the latter actually reflects an absence of confidence (for a discussion of compensatory attitude confidence, see Briñol, DeMarree, & Petty, 2009).

Initial conceptualizations of attitude certainty tended to assume that certainty sprang solely from structural features of attitudes such as how much knowledge or experience one has about the issue (e.g., Fazio & Zanna, 1981). However, people sometimes infer greater certainty in the absence of any structural differences (Petty, Tormala, & Rucker, 2004). Notably, people can even come to infer greater certainty in their attitudes if they merely believe that they have done much thinking about the attitude object even if they have not (Barden & Petty, 2008). And, certainty that comes from simple inferences rather than structural differences can also cause the attitudes to be more consequential (Rucker, Petty, & Briñol, 2008; Tormala & Petty, 2002).

Morality as a Source of Attitude Strength

Studies have suggested that having a moral basis to one's attitude is a strength indicator akin to having more knowledge, accessibility, or certainty. For example, Skitka, Morgan, and Sargis (2005) have shown that moral conviction is associated with strength outcomes such as resistance to influence and attitude-behavior correspondence. Most of the literature has been oriented to answering why would having a moral basis for one's attitude be associated with making an attitude stronger? One possibility is that morally based attitudes are stronger because they are different in some fundamental way from nonmorally based attitudes (e.g., greater basis in affect). Some have suggested that morally based attitudes develop from stable, internal influences (Rozin, 1999) including being partially inherited (Brandt & Wetherell, 2011; Tesser, 1993). Additionally, moral attitudes could be more heavily based on ideology, rendering them more impactful (Skitka, Morgan, & Wisneski, 2015).

In contrast to the proposition that there must be some necessary substantive difference between morally and non-morally based attitudes, Luttrell, Petty, Briñol, and Wagner (2016) have suggested that the mere perception that attitudes have a moral basis is sufficient to render them more consequential. By manipulating perceived moral bases independent of actual bases, Luttrell et al. demonstrated that a perceived moral basis can serve as an attitude strength heuristic independent of actual differences in the basis of one's attitude. That is, leading people to believe their attitudes were based in morality rather than practicality through false feedback made the attitudes more resistant to change. This outcome contributes to an emerging body of work highlighting the importance of perceived attitude qualities irrespective of their objectively measured counterparts in producing durable and impactful attitudes (cf. Smith, Fabrigar, MacDougall, & Wiesenthal, 2008).

Consequences of Different Persuasion Processes for Implicit Measures

When considering the consequences of attitude change, it is important to note that just as high thinking can strengthen attitudes at the explicit level by increasing attitude confidence, high thinking can also enhance strength at the automatic level by making attitudes more accessible. Thoughtful attitude change processes are likely to result in attitude representations that are well integrated and connected to other relevant material in memory (e.g., McGuire, 1981; Tesser, 1978), enhancing access to the attitudes (Bizer & Krosnick, 2001).

Additionally, high thought attitudes should also be more likely to spill over and influence the attitude-relevant material to which they are linked in memory (e.g., Crano & Chen, 1998). For example, in one study (Horcajo et al., 2010), students were randomly assigned to receive a persuasive message containing strong arguments in favor of using green as the institutional color for their university. Control group participants received an irrelevant message (also containing the word "green," but not advocating it). Participants' need for cognition (Cacioppo & Petty, 1982; Petty et al., 2009) was measured to assess the participants' motivation to process the information carefully. Instead of assessing the impact of this persuasive induction directly on automatic evaluations of the color green, the impact of the treatment was assessed on an automatic measure that was for an attitude object only indirectly related to the color—the beer brand, *Heineken* (whose packaging prominently features the color green). The results showed that an implicit measure of attitudes toward Heineken (using the Implicit Association Test; Greenwald et al., 1998) was affected by the message advocating green but only for participants high in need for cognition.

It is plausible that the generation of thoughts allowed high need for cognition participants to rehearse their evaluative links to green repeatedly, leading to changes in evaluation of this color that spread to related constructs such as Heineken. In contrast, the automatic evaluations of participants low in need for cognition did not reveal any impact of the manipulation on evaluations of Heineken. This finding suggests that participants engaging in little elaboration did not think about the merits of the arguments in the message (i.e., did not generate thoughts that allowed them to rehearse their attitudes) and thus did not show indirect automatic changes. These findings indicate that automatic changes that result from deliberative thinking can be consequential in terms of spreading activation, at least when thinking is high (for another example, see Ye & Gawronski, 2016).

Attitude Research Today

In this review we have argued that persuasion can be understood by breaking the processes responsible for attitude change into a finite set. These processes relate to many of the classic topics of persuasion (e.g., source credibility, recipient emotion) and explain how any one variable can produce opposite outcomes and how the same outcome can be produced by different processes. Our review emphasized that understanding the underlying mechanisms of persuasion is important because different processes are associated with different consequences. In particular, greater thinking underlying persuasion tends to result in stronger, more consequential attitudes.

Attitude research remains a dynamic area of inquiry today. In addition to continued exploration of many of the classic topics we have covered here, there also is considerable work exploring various novel domains. One promising new area of inquiry that we have already mentioned briefly concerns the moral foundations of attitudes (e.g., Skitka et al., 2005; see also Chapter 13), with special attention focused on the different foundations of beliefs for individuals with liberal versus conservative ideologies (e.g., Feinberg & Willer, 2013; Haidt, 2012). A second exploding new area involves understanding how attitudes and persuasion are represented in the brain (Cacioppo, Cacioppo, & Petty, 2018; Falk & Scholz, 2018; Huskey, Mangus, Turner, & Weber, 2017; see also Chapter 13). There is now some intriguing initial evidence that activation in particular brain regions can foreshadow and predict long-term persuasive influence (e.g., Falk, Berkman, Mann, Harrison, & Lieberman, 2010; Vezich, Katzman, Ames, Falk, & Lieberman, 2017). Brain studies are also beginning to examine attitude strength constructs such as ambivalence and certainty (Luttrell, Briñol, Petty, Cunningham, & Diaz, 2013; Luttrell, Stillman, Hasinski, & Cunningham, 2016). Finally, the application of persuasion work is thriving in many applied areas (Albarracín & Johnson, 2019). These include marketing (e.g., Teeny et al., 2017), health communication (Jones & Albarracín, 2016; Sheeran et al., 2016), and educational interventions to help underrepresented individuals succeed and stay in school (e.g., Walton, Logel, Peach, Spencer, & Zanna, 2015). Thus, attitude research has long been and continues to be one of social psychology's most successful exports to the broader social science community.

References

Abelson, R. P., & Prentice, D. A. (1989). Beliefs as possessions: A functional perspective. In A. R. Pratkanis, S. J. Breckler, & A. G. Greenwald (Eds.), *Attitude structure and function* (pp. 361–381). Hillsdale, NJ: Lawrence.

Ajzen, I. (1991). The theory of planned behavior. *Organizational Behavior and Human Decision Processes, 50,* 179–211.

Ajzen, I., & Fishbein, M. (2005). The influence of attitudes on behavior. In D. Albarracín, B. T. Johnson & M. P. Zanna (Eds.), *The handbook of attitudes* (pp. 173–221). Mahwah, NJ: Erlbaum.

Alba, J. W., & Marmorstein, H. (1987). The effects of frequency knowledge on consumer decision making. *Journal of Consumer Research, 13,* 411–454.

Albarracín, D., & Johnson, B. T. (Eds.) (2019). *The handbook of attitudes* (Volume 2: Applications). New York: Routledge.

Anderson, C. A. (1983). Imagination and expectation: The effect of imagining behavioral scripts on personal intentions. *Psychological Bulletin, 93,* 30–56.

Anderson, N. (1981). Integration theory applied to cognitive responses and attitudes. In R. E. Petty, T. Ostrom, & T. Brock (Eds.), *Cognitive responses in persuasion* (pp. 361–397). Hillsdale, NJ: Erlbaum.

Aquino, A., Haddock, G., Maio, G. R., Wolf, L. J., & Alparone, F. R. (2016). The role of affective and cognitive individual differences in social perception. *Personality and Social Psychology Bulletin, 42,* 798–810.

Aronson, E. (1968). Dissonance theory: Progress and problems. In R. P. Abelson, E. Aronson, W. J. McGuire, T. M. Newcomb, M. J. Rosenberg, & P. H. Tannenbaum (Eds.), *Theories of cognitive consistency: A sourcebook* (pp. 5–27). Chicago, IL: Rand McNally.

Baccus, J. R., Baldwin, M. W., & Packer, D. J. (2004). Increasing implicit self-esteem through classical conditioning. *Psychological Science, 15,* 498–502.

Baker, S. M., & Petty, R. E. (1994). Majority and minority influence: Source-position imbalance as a determinant of message scrutiny. *Journal of Personality and Social Psychology, 67,* 5–19.

Barden, J., & Petty, R. E. (2008). The mere perception of elaboration creates attitude certainty: Exploring the thoughtfulness heuristic. *Journal of Personality and Social Psychology, 95,* 489–509.

Baumeister, R. F. (1982). A self-presentational view of social phenomena. *Psychological Bulletin, 91,* 3–26.

Bem, D. J. (1965). An experimental analysis of self-persuasion. *Journal of Experimental Social Psychology, 1,* 199–218.

Bem, D. J. (1972). Self-perception theory. In L. Berkowitz (Ed.), *Advances in experimental social psychology* (Vol. 6, pp. 1–62). New York, NY: Academic Press.

Betsch, T., Plessner, H., & Schallies, E. (2004). The value-account model of attitude formation. In G. R. Maio & G. Haddock (Eds.), *Contemporary perspectives on the psychology of attitudes* (pp. 252–273). Hove, England: Psychology Press.

Bizer, G. Y., & Krosnick, J. A. (2001). Exploring the structure of strength-related attitude features: The relation between attitude importance and attitude accessibility. *Journal of Personality and Social Psychology, 81,* 566–586.

Blankenship, K. L., & Wegener, D. T. (2008). Opening the mind to close it: Considering a message in light of important values increases message processing and later resistance to change. *Journal of Personality and Social Psychology, 94,* 196–213.

Blankenship, K. L., Wegener, D. T., & Murray, R. A. (2015). Values, inter-attitudinal structure, and attitude change: Value accessibility can increase a related attitude's resistance to change. *Personality and Social Psychology Bulletin, 41,* 1739–1750.

Boninger, D. S., Brock, T. C., Cook, T. D., Gruder, C. L., & Romer, D. (1990). Discovery of reliable attitude change persistence resulting from a transmitter turning set. *Psychological Science, 1,* 268–271.

Boninger, D. S., Krosnick, J. A., Berent, M. K., & Fabrigar, L. R. (1995). The causes and consequences of attitude importance. In R. E. Petty & J. A. Krosnick (Eds.), *Attitude strength: Antecedents and consequences* (pp. 159–190). Mahwah, NJ: Erlbaum.

Bornstein, R. F. (1989). Exposure and affect: Overview and meta-analysis of research, 1968–1987. *Psychological Bulletin, 106,* 265–289.

Bornstein, R. F., & D'Agostino, P. R. (1992). Stimulus recognition and the mere exposure effect. *Journal of Personality and Social Psychology, 63,* 545–552.

Bower, G. H. (1981). Mood and memory. *American Psychologist, 36,* 129–148.

Brandt, M. J., & Wetherell, G. A. (2011). What attitudes are moral attitudes? The case of attitude heritability. *Social Psychological and Personality Science, 3,* 172–179.

Brehm, J. W. (1966). *A theory of psychological reactance.* New York, NY: Academic Press.

Brickman, P., Redfield, J., Harrison, A. A., & Crandall, R. (1972). Drive and pre-disposition as factors in the attitudinal effects of mere exposure. *Journal of Experimental Social Psychology, 8,* 31–44.

Briñol, P., DeMarree, K. G., & Petty, R. E. (2010). Processes by which confidence (vs. doubt) influences the self. In R. Arkin, K. Oleson, & P. Carroll (Eds.), *Handbook of the uncertain self* (pp. 13–35). New York: Psychology Press.

Briñol, P., Gascó, M., Petty, R. E., & Horcajo, J. (2013). Treating thoughts as material objects can increase or decrease their impact on evaluation. *Psychological Science, 24,* 41–47.

Briñol, P., McCaslin, M. J., & Petty, R. E. (2012). Self-generated persuasion: Effects of the target and direction of arguments. *Journal of Personality and Social Psychology, 102,* 925–940.

Briñol, P., & Petty, R. E. (2003). Overt head movements and persuasion: A self-validation analysis. *Journal of Personality and Social Psychology, 84,* 1123–1139.

Briñol, P., & Petty, R. E. (2005). Individual differences in attitude change. In D. Albarracín, B. T. Johnson, & M. P. Zanna (Eds.), *The handbook of attitudes and attitude change* (pp. 575–616). Hillsdale, NJ: Erlbaum.

Briñol, P., & Petty, R. E. (2008). Embodied persuasion: Fundamental processes by which bodily responses can impact attitudes. In G. R. Semin & E. R. Smith (Eds.), *Embodiment grounding: Social, cognitive, affective, and neuroscientific approaches* (pp. 184–207). Cambridge, England: Cambridge University Press.

Briñol, P., & Petty, R. E. (2009a). Persuasion: Insights from the self-validation hypothesis. In M. P. Zanna (Ed.), *Advances in experimental social psychology* (Vol. 41, pp. 69–118). New York, NY: Elsevier.

Briñol, P., & Petty, R. E. (2009b). Source factors in persuasion: A self-validation approach. *European Review of Social Psychology, 20,* 49–96.

Briñol, P., & Petty, R. E. (2018). The impact of individual differences on attitudes and attitude change. In D. Albarracín, & B. T. Johnson (Eds.), *Handbook of attitudes* (2nd ed., Vol. 1, pp. 520–556). New York, NY: Routledge.

Briñol, P., Petty, R. E., & Barden, J. (2007). Happiness versus sadness as a determinant of thought confidence in persuasion: A self-validation analysis. *Journal of Personality and Social Psychology, 93,* 711–727.

Briñol, P., Petty, R. E., Durso, G. R. O., & Rucker, D. D. (2017). Power and persuasion: Processes by which perceived power can influence evaluative judgments. *Review of General Psychology, 21,* 223–241.

Briñol, P., Petty, R. E., & Tormala, Z. L. (2006). The malleable meaning of subjective ease. *Psychological Science, 17,* 200–206.

Brinol, P., Petty, R. E., Valle, C., Rucker, D. D., & Becerra, A. (2007). The effects of message recipients' power before and after persuasion: a self-validation analysis. *Journal of Personality and Social Psychology, 93,* 1040–1053.

Briñol, P., Petty, R. E., & Wagner, B. C. (2012). Embodied validation: Our body can change and also validate our thoughts. In P. Briñol, & K. G. DeMarree (Eds.), *Social metacognition* (pp. 219–242). New York, NY: Psychology Press.

Brown, D. (1974). Adolescent attitudes and lawful behavior. *Public Opinion Quarterly, 38,* 98–106.

Cacioppo, J. T., Cacioppo, S., & Petty, R. E. (2018). The neuroscience of persuasion: A review with emphasis on issues and opportunities. *Social Neuroscience, 13,* 129–172.

Cacioppo, J. T., Gardner, W. L., & Berntson, G. G. (1997). Beyond bipolar conceptualizations and measures: The case of attitudes and evaluative space. *Personality and Social Psychology Review, 1,* 3–25.

Cacioppo, J. T., Marshall-Goodell, B. S., Tassinary, L. G., & Petty, R. E. (1992). Rudimentary determinants of attitudes: Classical conditioning is more effective when prior knowledge about the attitude stimulus is low than high. *Journal of Experimental Social Psychology, 28,* 207–233.

Cacioppo, J. T., & Petty, R. E. (1982). The need for cognition. *Journal of Personality and Social Psychology, 42,* 116–131.

Cacioppo, J. T., & Petty, R. E. (1989). Effects of message repetition on argument processing, recall, and persuasion. *Basic and Applied Social Psychology, 10,* 3–12.

Cacioppo, J. T., Petty, R. E., & Morris, K. J. (1983). Effects of need for cognition on message evaluation, recall, and persuasion. *Journal of Personality and Social Psychology, 45*(4), 805–818.

Cárdaba, M. M. A., Briñol, P., Horcajo, J., & Petty, R. E. (2013). The effect of need for cognition on the stability of prejudiced attitudes toward South American immigrants. *Psicothema, 25,* 73–78.

Carpenter, C. J. (2015). A meta-analysis of the ELM's argument quality × processing type predictions. *Human Communication Research, 41,* 501–534.

Chaiken, S. (1980). Heuristic versus systematic information processing in the use of source versus message quest in persuasion. *Journal of Personality and Social Psychology, 39,* 752–766.

Chaiken, S. (1987). The heuristic model of persuasion. In M. P. Zanna, J. Olson, & C. P. Herman (Eds.), *Social influence: The Ontario symposium* (Vol. 5, pp. 3–39). Hillsdale, NJ: Erlbaum.

Chaiken, S., Liberman, A., & Eagly, A. H. (1989). Heuristic and systematic processing within and beyond the persuasion context. In J. S. Uleman & J. A. Bargh (Eds.), *Unintended thought* (pp. 212–252). New York, NY: Guilford.

Chaiken, S., & Maheswaran, D. (1994). Heuristic processing can bias systematic processing: Effects of source credibility, argument ambiguity, and task importance on attitude judgment. *Journal of Personality and Social Psychology, 66,* 460–473.

Chaiken, S., & Trope, Y. (Eds.) (1999). *Dual process theories in social psychology.* New York, NY: Guilford.

Cialdini, R. B. (2008). *Influence: Science and practice* (5th ed.). Boston, MA: Allyn and Bacon.

Clark, J. K., & Wegener, D. T. (2013). Message position, information processing, and persuasion: The discrepancy motives model. In P. Devine & A. Plant (Eds.), *Advances in Experimental Social Psychology* (Vol. 47, pp. 189–232). San Diego, CA: Academic Press.

Clark, J. K., Wegener, D. T., & Fabrigar, L. R. (2008a). Attitude accessibility and message processing: The moderating role of message position. *Journal of Experimental Social Psychology, 44,* 354–361.

Clark, J. K., Wegener, D. T., & Fabrigar, L. R. (2008b). Attitudinal ambivalence and message-based persuasion: Motivated processing of pro-attitudinal information and avoidance of counter-attitudinal information. *Personality and Social Psychology Bulletin, 34,* 565–577.

Clarkson, J. J., Tormala, Z. L., & Leone, C. (2011). A self-validation perspective on the mere thought effect. *Journal of Experimental Social Psychology, 47,* 449–454.

Clarkson, J. J., Tormala, Z. L., & Rucker, D. D. (2008). A new look at the consequences of attitude certainty: The amplification hypothesis. *Journal of Personality and Social Psychology, 95,* 810–825.

Clarkson, J. J., Tormala, Z. L., & Rucker, D. (2011). Cognitive and affective matching effects in persuasion: An amplification perspective. *Personality and Social Psychology Bulletin, 37,* 1415–1427.

Cohen, G., Aronson, J., & Steele, C. (2000). When beliefs yield to evidence: Reducing biased evaluation by affirming the self. *Personality and Social Psychology Bulletin, 26,* 1151–1164.

Cooper, J. (2007). *Cognitive dissonance: 50 years of a classic theory.* London, England: SAGE.

Cooper, J., & Fazio, R. H. (1984). A new look at dissonance theory. In L. Berkowitz (Ed.), *Advances in experimental social psychology* (Vol. 17, pp. 229–266). New York, NY: Academic Press.

Crano, W. D., & Chen, X. (1998). The leniency contract and persistence of majority and minority influence. *Journal of Personality and Social Psychology, 6,* 1437–1450.

Crites, S., Fabrigar, L., & Petty, R. E. (1994). Measuring the affective and cognitive properties of attitudes: Conceptual and methodological issues. *Personality and Social Psychology Bulletin, 20,* 619–634.

Dasgupta, N., & Greenwald, A. G. (2001). On the malleability of automatic attitudes: Combating automatic prejudice with images of admired and disliked individuals. *Journal of Personality and Social Psychology, 81,* 800–814.

Dasgupta, N., & Rivera, L. M. (2008). When social context matters: The influence of long-term contact and short-term exposure to admired outgroup members on implicit attitudes and behavioral intentions. *Social Cognition, 26,* 112–123.

Davidson, A. R., Yantis, S., Norwood, M., & Montano, D. E. (1985). Amount of information about the attitude object and attitude-behavior consistency. *Journal of Personality and Social Psychology, 49,* 1184–1198.

Day, M. V., Fiske, S. T., Downing, E. L., & Trail, T. E. (2014). Shifting liberal and conservative attitudes using moral foundations theory. *Personality and Social Psychology Bulletin, 40,* 1559–1573.

DeBono, K. G. (1987). Investigating the social adjustive and value expressive functions of attitudes: Implications for persuasion processes. *Journal of Personality and Social Psychology, 52,* 279–287.

DeBono, K. G., & Harnish, R. J. (1988). Source expertise, source attractiveness, and processing or persuasive information: A functional approach. *Journal of Personality and Social Psychology, 55,* 541–546.

Deci, E. L. (1995). *Why we do what we do.* New York, NY: Putnam.

DeCoster, J., Banner, M. J., Smith, E. R., Semin, G. R. (2006). On the inexplicability of the implicit: Differences in the information provided by implicit and explicit tests. *Social Cognition, 24,* 5–21.

DeMotta, Y., Chao, M. C., & Kramer, T. (2016). The effect of dialectical thinking on the integration of contradictory information. *Journal of Consumer Psychology, 26,* 40–52.

DeSteno, D., Petty, R. E., Rucker, D. D., Wegener, D. T., & Braverman, J. (2004). Discrete emotions and persuasion: The role of emotion-induced expectancies. *Journal of Personality and Social Psychology, 86,* 43–56.

DeSteno, D., Petty, R. E., Wegener, D. T., & Rucker, D. D. (2000). Beyond valence in the perception of likelihood: The role of emotion specificity. *Journal of Personality and Social Psychology, 78,* 397–416.

Dijksterhuis, A. (2004). I like myself but I don't know why: Enhancing implicit self- esteem by subliminal evaluative conditioning. *Journal of Personality and Social Psychology, 86,* 345–355.

Dovidio, J., Kawakami, K., Johnson, C., Johnson, B., & Howard, A. (1997). The nature of prejudice: Automatic and controlled processes. *Journal of Experimental Social Psychology, 33,* 510–540.

Eagly A. H., & Chaiken, S. (1993). *The psychology of attitudes.* Fort Worth, TX: Harcourt, Brace, Jovanovich.

Elms, A. C. (1966). Influence of fantasy ability on attitude change through role playing. *Journal of Personality and Social Psychology, 4,* 36–43.

Epstein, S. (2003). Cognitive-experiential self-theory of personality. In T. Millon & M. Lerner (Eds.). *Handbook of psychology: Personality and social psychology* (Vol. 5, pp. 59–184). Hoboken, NJ: Wiley.

Evans, A. T., & Clark, J. K., (2012). Source characteristics and persuasion: The role of self-monitoring in self-validation. *Journal of Experimental Social Psychology, 48,* 383–386.

Fabrigar, L. R., & Petty, R. E. (1999). The role of the affective and cognitive bases of attitudes in susceptibility to affectively and cognitively based persuasion. *Personality and Social Psychology Bulletin, 25,* 363–381.

Fabrigar, L. R., & Wegener, D. T. (2010). Attitude structure. In R. F. Baumeister & E. J. Finkel (Eds.), *Advanced social psychology: The state of the science* (pp. 177–216). New York, NY: Oxford University Press.

Falk, E. B., Berkman, E. T., Mann, T., Harrison, B., & Lieberman, M. D. (2010). Predicting persuasion-induced behavior change from the brain. *Journal of Neuroscience, 30,* 8421–8424.

Falk, E. B., & Scholz, C. (2018). Persuasion, influence, and value: Perspectives from communication and social neuroscience. *Annual Review of Psychology, 69,* 329–356.

Fazio, R. H. (1990). Multiple processes by which attitudes guide behavior: The MODE model as an integrative framework. In M. P. Zanna (Ed.), *Advances in experimental social psychology* (Vol. 23, pp. 75–109). New York: Academic Press.

Fazio, R. H. (1995). Attitudes as object-evaluation associations: Determinants, consequences, and correlates of attitude accessibility. In R. E. Petty & J. A. Krosnick (Eds.), *Attitude strength: Antecedents and consequences* (pp. 247–283). Hillsdale, NJ: Erlbaum.

Fazio, R. H. (2007). Attitudes as object-evaluation associations of varying strength. *Social Cognition, 25,* 603–637.

Fazio, R. H., Sanbonmatsu, D. M., Powell, M. C., & Kardes, F. R. (1986). On the automatic activation of attitudes. *Journal of Personality and Social Psychology, 50,* 229–238.

Fazio, R. H., & Towles-Schwen, T. (1999). The MODE model of attitude-behavior processes. In S. Chaiken & Y. Trope (Eds.), *Dual process theories in social psychology* (pp. 97–116). New York, NY: Guilford.

Fazio, R. H., & Williams, C. J. (1986). Attitude accessibility as a moderator of the attitude-perception and attitude-behavior relations: An investigation of the 1984 presidential election. *Journal of Personality and Social Psychology, 51,* 505–514.

Fazio, R. H., & Zanna, M. P. (1978). Attitudinal qualities relating to the strength of the attitude–behavior relationship. *Journal of Experimental Social Psychology, 14,* 398–408.

Fazio, R. H., & Zanna, M. P. (1981). Direct experience and attitude-behavior consistency. *Advances in Experimental Social Psychology, 14,* 161–202.

Fazio, R. H., Zanna, M. P., & Cooper, J. (1977). Dissonance and self-perception: An integrative view of each theory's proper domain of application. *Journal of Experimental Social Psychology, 13,* 464–479.

Feinberg, M., & Willer, R. (2013). The moral roots of environmental attitudes. *Psychological Science, 24,* 56–62.

Feinberg, M., & Willer, R. (2015). From gulf to bridge: When do moral arguments facilitate political influence? *Personality and Social Psychology Bulletin, 41,* 1665–1681.

Festinger, L. (1957). *A theory of cognitive dissonance.* Stanford, CA: Stanford University Press.

Festinger, L., & Carlsmith, J. M. (1959). Cognitive consequences of forced compliance. *Journal of Abnormal and Social Psychology, 58,* 203–210.

Fishbein, M., & Ajzen, I. (1975). *Belief, attitude, intention, and behavior.* Reading, MA: Addison-Wesley.

Fishbein, M., & Ajzen, I. (1981). Acceptance, yielding and impact: Cognitive processes in persuasion. In R. E. Petty, T. M. Ostrom, & T. C. Brock (Eds.), *Cognitive responses in persuasion* (pp. 339–359). Hillsdale, NJ: Erlbaum.

Fleming, M. A., & Petty, R. E. (2000). Identity and persuasion: An elaboration likelihood approach. In D. J. Terry & M. A. Hogg (Eds.), *Attitudes, behavior, and social context: The role of norms and group membership* (pp. 171–199). Mahwah, NJ: Erlbaum.

Forehand, M. R., & Perkins, A. (2005). Implicit assimilation and explicit contrast: A set/reset model of response to celebrity voiceovers. *Journal of Consumer Research, 32,* 435–441.

Forgas, J. P. (1995). Mood and judgment: The affect infusion model (AIM). *Psychological Bulletin, 117,* 39–66.

Friedrich, J., Fetherstonhaugh, D., Casey, S., & Gallagher, D. (1996). Argument integration and attitude change: Suppression effects in the integration of one-sided arguments that vary in persuasiveness. *Personality and Social Psychology Bulletin, 22,* 179–191.

Fujita, K., Eyal, T., Chaiken, S., Trope, Y., & Liberman, N. (2008). Influencing attitudes toward near and distant objects. *Journal of Experimental Social Psychology, 44,* 562–572.

Gawronski, B., & Bodenhausen, V. (2006). Associative and propositional processes in evaluation: An integrative review of implicit and explicit attitude change. *Psychological Bulletin, 132,* 692–731.

Gawronski, B., & Bodenhausen, G. V. (2007). Unraveling the processes underlying evaluation: Attitudes from the perspective of the APE model, *Social Cognition, 25,* 687–717.

Gawronski, B., & Payne, B. K. (Eds.). (2010). *Handbook of implicit social cognition: Measurement, theory, and applications.* New York, NY: Guilford.

Gawronski, B., & Sritharan, R. (2010). Formation, change, and contextualization of mental associations: Determinants and principles of variations in implicit measures. In B. Gawronski, & B. K. Payne (Eds.), *Handbook of implicit social cognition: Measurement, theory, and applications* (pp. 216–240). New York, NY: Guilford Press.

Gawronski, B., Strack, F., & Bodenhausen, G. V. (2009). Attitudes and cognitive consistency: The role of associative and propositional processes. In R. E. Petty, R. H. Fazio, & P. Briñol (Eds.), *Attitudes: Insights from the new implicit measures* (pp. 85–117). New York, NY: Psychology Press.

Geers, A. L., Handley, I. M., & McLarney, A. R. (2003). Discerning the role of optimism in persuasion: The valence-enhancement hypothesis. *Journal of Personality and Social Psychology, 85,* 554–565.

Geers, A. L., Wellman, J. A., & Fowler, S. L. (2013). Unique and interactive effects of comparative and dispositional optimism. *Psychology and Health, 28,* 30–48.

Gilbert, D. T. (1991). How mental systems believe. *American Psychologist, 46,* 107–119.

Giner-Sorolla, R. (2004). Is affective material in attitudes more accessible than cognitive material? The moderating role of attitude basis. *European Journal of Social Psychology, 34,* 761–780.

Glaser, J., & Banaji, M. R. (1999). When fair is foul and foul is fair: Reverse priming in automatic evaluation. *Journal of Personality and Social Psychology, 77,* 669–687.

Gouaux, C. (1971). Induced affective states and interpersonal attraction. *Journal of Personality and Social Psychology, 29,* 37–43.

Green, M. C., & Brock, T. C. (2000). The role of transportation in the persuasiveness of public narratives. *Journal of Personality and Social Psychology, 79,* 701–721.

Greenwald, A. G. (1968). Cognitive learning, cognitive response to persuasion, and attitude change. In A. Greenwald, T. Brock, & T. Ostrom (Eds.), *Psychological foundations of attitudes.* New York, NY: Academic Press.

Greenwald, A. G., & Albert, R. D. (1968). Acceptance and recall of improvised arguments. *Journal of Personality and Social Psychology, 8,* 31–34.

Greenwald, A. G., Banaji, M. R., & Nosek, B. A. (2015). Statistically small effects of the Implicit Association Test can have societally large effects. *Journal of Personality and Social Psychology, 4,* 553–561.

Greenwald, A. G., McGhee, D. E., & Schwartz, J. L. K. (1998). Measuring individual differences in implicit cognition: The Implicit Association Task. *Journal of Personality and Social Psychology, 74,* 1464–1480.

Greenwald, A. G., Poehlman, T. A., Uhlmann, E. L., & Banaji, M. R. (2009). Understanding and using the Implicit Association Test: III. Meta-analysis of predictive validity. *Journal of Personality and Social Psychology, 97,* 17–41.

Greenwald, A. G., & Ronis, D. L. (1978). Twenty years of cognitive dissonance: Case study of the evolution of a theory. *Psychological Review, 85,* 53–57.

Gregg, A. P., Seibt, B., & Banaji, M. R. (2006). Easier done than undone: asymmetry in the malleability of implicit preferences. *Journal of Personality and Social Psychology, 9,* 1–20.

Gross, S. R., Holtz, R., & Miller, N. (1995). Attitude certainty. In R. E. Petty & J. A. Krosnick (Eds.), *Attitude strength: Antecedents and consequences* (pp. 215–245). Hillsdale, NJ: Erlbaum.

Grush, J. E. (1976). Attitude formation and mere exposure phenomena: A non-artificial explanation of empirical findings. *Journal of Personality and Social Psychology, 33,* 281–290.

Haddock, G., Foad, C., Windsor-Shellard, B., Dummel, S., & Adarves-Yorno, I. (2017). On the attitudinal consequences of being mindful: Links between mindfulness and attitudinal ambivalence. *Personality and Social Psychology Bulletin, 43,* 439–452.

Haddock, G., Maio, G. R., Arnold, K, & Huskinson, T. (2008). Should persuasion be affective or cognitive? The moderating effects of need for affect and need for cognition. *Personality and Social Psychology Bulletin, 34,* 769–778.

Haidt, J. (2012). *The righteous mind: Why good people are divided by politics and religion.* New York, NY: Random House.

Harkins, S. G., & Petty, R. E. (1981). The effects of source magnification of cognitive effort on attitudes: An information processing view. *Journal of Personality and Social Psychology, 40,* 401–413.

Harmon-Jones, E., & Harmon-Jones, C. (2008). Action-based model of dissonance: A review of behavioral, anterior cingulate and prefrontal cortical mechanisms. *Social and Personality Psychology Compass, 2–3,* 1518–1538.

Harmon-Jones, E., & Mills, J. S. (Eds.) (1999). *Cognitive dissonance: Progress on a pivotal theory in social psychology.* Washington, DC: American Psychological Association.

Haugtvedt, C. P., & Petty, R. E. (1992). Personality and persuasion: Need for cognition moderates the persistence and resistance of attitude changes. *Journal of Personality and Social Psychology, 63,* 308–319.

Haugtvedt, C. P., Petty, R. E., & Cacioppo, J. T. (1992). Need for cognition and advertising: Understanding the role of personality variables in consumer behavior. *Journal of Consumer Psychology, 1*(3), 239–260.

Heesacker, M. H., Petty, R. E., & Cacioppo, J. T. (1983). Field dependence and attitude change: Source credibility can alter persuasion by affecting message-relevant thinking. *Journal of Personality, 51,* 653–666.

Heider, F. (1958). *The psychology of interpersonal relations.* New York, NY: Wiley.

Hofmann, W., De Houwer, J., Perugini, M., Baeyens, F., & Crombez, G. (2010). Evaluative conditioning in humans: A meta-analysis. *Psychological Bulletin, 136,* 390–421.

Horcajo, J., Briñol, P., & Petty, R. E. (2010). Consumer persuasion: Indirect change and implicit balance. *Psychology and Marketing, 27,* 938–963.

Hovland, C. I., Janis, I. L., & Kelley, H. H. (1953). *Communication and persuasion: Psychological studies of opinion change.* New Haven, CT: Yale University Press.

Hovland, C. I., & Weiss, W. (1951). The influence of source credibility on communication effectiveness. *Public Opinion Quarterly, 15,* 635–650.

Huskey, R. Mangus, J. M., Turner, B.O., & Weber, R. (2017). The persuasion network is modulated by drug use risk and predicts anti-drug message effectiveness. *Social Cognitive and Affective Neuroscience, 12,* 1902–1915.

Huskinson, T. L., & Haddock, G. (2004). Individual differences in attitude structure: Variance in the chronic reliance on affective and cognitive information. *Journal of Experimental Social Psychology, 40,* 82–90.

Itzhakov, G., Uziel, L., & Wood, W. (2018). When attitudes and habits don't correspond: Self-control depletion increases persuasion but not behavior. *Journal of Experimental Social Psychology, 75,* 1–10.

Jacoby, L. L., Kelley, C. M., Brown, J., & Jasechko, J. (1989). Becoming famous overnight: Limits on the ability to avoid unconscious influences of the past. *Journal of Personality and Social Psychology, 56,* 326–338.

Janis, I. L., & King, B. T. (1954). The influence of role-playing on opinion change. *Journal of Abnormal and Social Psychology, 49,* 211–218.

Johnson, B. T., Smith-McLallen, A., Killeya, L. A., & Levin, K. D. (2004). Truth or consequences: Overcoming resistance to persuasion with positive thinking. In E. S. Knowles & J. A. Linn (Eds.), *Resistance and persuasion.* Mahwah, NJ: Erlbaum.

Johnson, I., Petty, R. E., Briñol, P., & See, Y. H. M. (2017). Persuasive message scrutiny as a function of implicit-explicit discrepancies in racial attitudes. *Journal of Experimental Social Psychology, 70,* 222–234.

Jones, C. R., & Albarracín, D. (2016). Public communication for drug abuse prevention: A synthesis of current meta-analytic evidence of message efficacy. In E. C. Kopetz, & C. W. Lejuez (Eds.), *Addictions: A social psychological perspective* (pp. 257–280). New York, NY: Routledge.

Jones, C. R., Fazio, R. H., & Olson, M. A. (2009). Implicit misattribution as a mechanism underlying evaluative conditioning. *Journal of Personality and Social Psychology, 96,* 933–948.

Jordan, C. H., Whitfield, M., & Zeigler-Hill, V. (2007). Intuition and the correspondence between implicit and explicit self-esteem. *Journal of Personality and Social Psychology, 93,* 1067–1079.

Jost, J. T., Kruglanski, A. W., & Nelson, T. O. (1998). Social metacognition: An expansionist review. *Personality and Social Psychology Review, 2,* 137–154.

Kaplan, K. J. (1972). On the ambivalence-indifference problem in attitude theory and measurement: A suggested modification of the semantic differential technique. *Psychological Bulletin, 77,* 361–372.

Karmarkar, U. R., & Tormala, Z. L. (2010). Believe me, I have no idea what I'm talking about: The effects of source certainty on consumer involvement and persuasion. *Journal of Consumer Research, 36,* 1033–1049.

Katz, D. (1960). The functional study of attitudes. *Public Opinion Quarterly, 24,* 163–204.

Kelman, H. C., & Hovland, C. I. (1953). "Reinstatement" of the communicator in delayed measurement of opinion change. *Journal of Abnormal and Social Psychology, 48,* 327–335.

Kiesler, C.A. (1971). *The psychology of commitment: Experiments linking behavior to beliefs.* New York, NY: Academic Press.

Knowles, E. S., & Linn, J. A. (Eds.) (2004). *Resistance and persuasion.* Mahwah, NJ: Erlbaum.

Krosnick, J. A., & Petty, R. E. (1995). Attitude strength: An overview. In R. E. Petty & J. A. Krosnick (Eds.), *Attitude strength: Antecedents and consequences* (pp. 1–24). Mahwah, NJ: Erlbaum.

Kruglanski, A. W., Freund, T., & Bar-tal, D. (1996). Motivational effects in the mere-exposure paradigm. *European Journal of Social Psychology, 26*(3), 479–499.

Kruglanski, A. W., Raviv, A., Bar-Tal, D., Raviv, A., Sharvit, K., Ellis, S., . . . Mannetti, L. (2005). Says who? Epistemic authority effects in social judgment. In M. P. Zanna (Ed.), *Advances in experimental social psychology* (Vol. 37, pp. 346–392). San Diego, CA: Academic Press.

Kruglanski, A. W., & Thompson, E. P. (1999). Persuasion by a single route: A view from the unimodel. *Psychological Inquiry, 10,* 83–110.

Kruglanski, A. W., & Webster, D. M., (1996). Motivated closing of the mind: Seizing and Freezing. *Psychological Review, 103,* 263–283.

Kumkale, G. T., & Albarracín, D. (2004). The sleeper effect in persuasion: A meta-analytic review. *Psychological Bulletin, 130,* 143–172.

Kumkale, G. T., Albarracín, D., & Seignourel, P. J. (2010). The effects of source credibility in the presence or absence of prior attitudes: Implications for the design of persuasive communication campaigns. *Journal of Applied Social Psychology, 40,* 1325–1356.

Kunda, Z. (1990). The case for motivated reasoning. *Psychological Bulletin, 108,* 480–498.

Kunst-Wilson, W. R., & Zajonc, R. B. (1980). Affective discrimination of stimuli that cannot be recognized. *Science, 207,* 557–558.

Kupor, D. M., & Tormala, Z. L. (2015). Persuasion, interrupted: The effect of momentary interruptions on message processing and persuasion. *Journal of Consumer Research, 42*(2), 300–315.

Lavine, H., & Snyder, M. (1996). Cognitive processing and the functional matching effect in persuasion: The mediating role of subjective perceptions of message quality. *Journal of Experimental Social Psychology, 32,* 580–604.

Lavine, H., Thomsen, C. J., Zanna, M. P., & Borgida, E. (1998). On the primacy of affect in the determination of attitudes and behavior: The moderating role of affective-cognitive ambivalence. *Journal of Experimental Social Psychology, 34,* 398–421.

Lepper, M. R., Greene, D., & Nisbett, R. E. (1973). Undermining children's intrinsic interest with extrinsic reward: A test of the "over justification" hypothesis. *Journal of Experimental Social Psychology, 28,* 129–137.

Likert, R. (1932). A technique for the measurement of attitudes. *Archives of Psychology, 140,* 1–55.

Loersch, C., McCaslin, M. J., & Petty, R. E. (2011). Exploring the impact of social judgeability concerns on the interplay of associative and deliberative attitude processes. *Journal of Experimental Social Psychology, 47,* 1029–1032.

Luttrell, A., Briñol, P., Petty, R. E., Cunningham, W., & Diaz, D. (2013). Metacognitive confidence: A neuroscience approach. *Revista de Psicologia Social, 28,* 317–332.

Luttrell, A., Petty, R. E., & Briñol, P. (2016). Ambivalence and certainty can interact to predict attitude stability over time. *Journal of Experimental Social Psychology, 63,* 56–68.

Luttrell, A., Petty, R. E., Briñol, P., & Wagner, B. C. (2016). Making it moral: Merely labelling an attitude as moral increases its strength. *Journal of Experimental Social Psychology, 65,* 82–93.

Luttrell, A., Stillman, P. E., Hasinski, A., & Cunningham, W. A. (2016). Neural dissociations in attitude strength: Distinct regions of cingulate cortex track ambivalence and certainty. *Journal of Experimental Psychology: General, 145,* 419–433.

Mackie, D. M. (1987). Systematic and nonsystematic processing of majority and minority persuasive communications. *Journal of Personality and Social Psychology, 53,* 41–52.

Maddux, W. W., Barden, J., Brewer, M. B., & Petty, R. E. (2005). Saying no to negativity: The effects of context and motivation to control prejudice on automatic evaluative responses. *Journal of Experimental Social Psychology, 41,* 19–35.

Maio, G. R., Bell, D. E., & Esses, V. M. (1996). Ambivalence and persuasion: The processing of messages about immigrant groups. *Journal of Experimental Social Psychology, 32,* 513–536.

Maio, G. R., & Haddock, G. (2015). *The psychology of attitudes and attitude change* (2nd ed.). Thousand Oaks, CA: SAGE.

Maio, G. R., Haddock, G., Watt, S. E., & Hewstone, M. (2009). Implicit measures in applied contexts: An illustrative examination of antiracism advertising. In R. E. Petty, R. H. Fazio, & P. Brinol (Eds.), *Attitudes: Insights from the new implicit measures* (pp. 327–360). New York: Psychology Press.

Maio, G. R., & Olson, J. (Eds.). (2000). *Why we evaluate: Functions of attitudes.* Mahwah, NJ: Erlbaum.

Maio, G. R., Pakizeh, A., Cheung, W., & Rees, K. J. (2009). Changing, priming, and acting on values: Effects via motivational relations in a circular model. *Journal of Personality and Social Psychology, 97,* 699–715.

Maio, G. R., & Thomas, G. (2007). The epistemic-teleologic model of deliberate self-persuasion. *Personality and Social Psychology Review, 11*(1), 46–67.

Mann, T. C., & Ferguson, M. (2015). Can we undo our first impressions? The role of reinterpretation in reversing implicit evaluations. *Journal of Personality and Social Psychology, 108,* 823–849.

Mann, T. C., Ferguson, M. (2017). Reversing implicit first impressions through reinterpretation after a two day delay. *Journal of Experimental Social Psychology, 68,* 122–127.

Martin, D. G., & Levey, A. B. (1978). Evaluative conditioning. *Advances in Behavior Research and Therapy, 1,* 57–102.

Martin, L. L. (2000). Moods do not convey information: Moods in context do. In J. P. Forgas (Ed.), *Feeling and thinking: The role of affect in social cognition* (pp. 153–177). Cambridge, England: Cambridge University Press.

McConnell, A. R., Rydell, R. J., Strain, L. M., & Mackie, D. M. (2008). Forming implicit and explicit attitudes toward individuals: Social group association cues. *Journal of Personality and Social Psychology, 94,* 792–807.

McGuire, W. J. (1964). Inducing resistance to persuasion: Some contemporary approaches. In L. Berkowitz (Ed.), *Advances in experimental social psychology* (Vol. 1, pp. 191–229). New York, NY: Academic Press.

McGuire, W. J. (1968). Personality and attitude change: An information-processing theory. In A. G. Greenwald, T. C. Brock, & T. M. Ostrom (Eds.), *Psychological foundations of attitudes* (pp. 171–196). New York, NY: Academic Press.

McGuire, W. J. (1981). The probabilogical model of cognitive structure and attitude change. In R. E. Petty, T. M. Ostrom, & T. C. Brock (Eds.), *Cognitive responses in persuasion* (pp. 291–307). Hillsdale, NJ: Erlbaum.

McGuire, W. J. (1985). Attitudes and attitude change. In G. Lindzey & E. Aronson (Eds.), *Handbook of social psychology* (3rd ed., Vol. 2, pp. 233–346). New York, NY: Random House.

Miniard, P. W., Bhatla, S., Lord, K. R., Dickson, P. R., & Unnava, H. R. (1991). Picture-based persuasion processes and the moderating role of involvement. *Journal of Consumer Research, 18*(1), 92–107.

Monahan, J. L., Murphy, S. T., & Zajonc, R. B. (2000). Subliminal mere exposure: Specific, general, and diffuse effects. *Psychological Science, 11,* 462–466.

Moore, D. L., Hausknecht, D., & Thamodaran, K. (1986). Time pressure, response opportunity, and persuasion. *Journal of Consumer Research, 13,* 85–99.

Nayakankuppam, D. J., Priester, J. R., Kwon, J. H., Donovan, L. A., & Petty, R. E. (2018). Construction and retrieval of evaluative judgments: The attitude strength moderation model. *Journal of Experimental Social Psychology, 76,* 54–66.

Noah, T., Schul, Y., & Mayo, R. (2018). When both the original study and its failed replication are correct: Feeling observed eliminates the facial-feedback effect. *Journal of Personality and Social Psychology, 114,* 657–664.

Olson, M. A., Fazio, R. H. (2001). Implicit attitude formation through classical conditioning. *Psychological Science, 12,* 413–417.

Osgood, C. E. (1964). Semantic differential technique in the comparative study of cultures. *American Anthropologist, 66,* 171–200.

Payne, B. K., & Lundberg, K. B. (2014). The Affect Misattribution Procedure: Ten years of evidence on reliability, validity, and mechanisms. *Social and Personality Psychology Compass, 8,* 672–686.

Petrova, P. K., & Cialdini, R. B. (2008). Evoking the imagination as a strategy of influence. In C. P. Haugtvedt, P. M. Herr, & F. R. Kardes (Eds.), *Marketing and consumer psychology series: Vol. 4. Handbook of consumer psychology* (pp. 505–524. New York, NY: Taylor & Francis.

Petty, R. E. (1997). The evolution of theory and research in social psychology: From single to multiple effect and process models. In C. McGarty & S. A. Haslam (Eds.), *The message of social psychology: Perspectives on mind in society* (pp. 268–290). Oxford, England: Blackwell.

Petty, R. E., & Briñol, P. (2006a). A meta-cognitive approach to "implicit" and "explicit" evaluations: Comment on Gawronski and Bodenhausen (2006). *Psychological Bulletin, 132,* 740–744.

Petty, R. E., & Briñol, P. (2006b). Understanding social judgment: Multiple systems and processes. *Psychological Inquiry, 17,* 217–223.

Petty, R. E., & Briñol, P. (2008). Persuasion: From single to multiple to meta-cognitive processes. *Perspectives on Psychological Science, 3,* 137–147.

Petty, R. E., & Briñol, P. (2009). Implicit ambivalence: A meta-cognitive approach. In R. E. Petty, R. H. Fazio, & P. Briñol (Eds.), *Attitudes: Insights from the new implicit measures* (pp. 119–161). New York, NY: Psychology Press.

Petty, R. E., & Briñol, P. (2010). Attitude structure and change: Implications for implicit measures. In B. Gawronski & B. K. Payne (Eds.), *Handbook of implicit social cognition: Measurement, theory, and applications* (pp.335–352). New York: Guilford Press.

Petty, R. E. & Briñol, P. (2012). The elaboration likelihood model. In P. A. M. Van Lange, A. Kruglanski, & E. T. Higgins (Eds.), *Handbook of theories of social psychology* (Vol. 1, pp. 224–245). London, England: SAGE.

Petty, R. E., & Briñol, P. (2015). Emotion and persuasion: Cognitive and meta-cognitive processes impact attitudes. *Cognition and Emotion, 29,* 1–26.

Petty, R. E., Briñol, P., & DeMarree, K. G. (2007). The meta-cognitive model (MCM) of attitudes: Implications for attitude measurement, change, and strength. *Social Cognition, 25,* 657–686.

Petty, R. E., Briñol, P., Loersch, C., & McCaslin, M. J. (2009). The need for cognition. In M. R. Leary & R. H. Hoyle (Eds.), *Handbook of individual differences in social behavior* (pp. 318–329). New York, NY: Guilford.

Petty, R. E., Briñol, P., & Tormala, Z. L. (2002). Thought confidence as a determinant of persuasion: The self-validation hypothesis. *Journal of Personality and Social Psychology, 82,* 722–741.

Petty, R. E., Briñol, P., Tormala, Z. L., & Wegener, D. T. (2007). The role of meta-cognition in social judgment. In E. T. Higgins & A. W. Kruglanski (Eds.), *Social psychology: A handbook of basic principles* (2nd ed., pp. 254–284). New York, NY: Guilford.

Petty, R. E., & Cacioppo, J. T. (1979a). Effects of forewarning of persuasive intent on cognitive responses and persuasion. *Personality and Social Psychology Bulletin, 5,* 173–176.

Petty, R. E., & Cacioppo, J. T. (1979b). Issue-involvement can increase or decrease persuasion by enhancing message-relevant cognitive responses. *Journal of Personality and Social Psychology, 37,* 1915–1926.

Petty, R. E., & Cacioppo, J. T. (1981). *Attitudes and persuasion: Classics and contemporary approaches.* Dubuque, IA: Win C. Brown.

Petty, R. E., & Cacioppo, J. T. (1984a). The effects of involvement on responses to argument quantity and quality: Central and peripheral routes to persuasion. *Journal of Personality and Social Psychology, 46,* 69–81.

Petty, R. E., & Cacioppo, J. T. (1984b). Source factors and the elaboration likelihood model of persuasion. *Advances in Consumer Research, 11,* 668–672.

Petty, R. E., & Cacioppo, J. T. (1986). *Communication and persuasion: Central and peripheral routes to attitude change.* New York, NY: Springer-Verlag.

Petty, R. E., & Cacioppo, J. T. (1990). Involvement and persuasion: Tradition versus integration. *Psychological Bulletin, 107,* 367–374.

Petty, R. E., Cacioppo, J. T., & Goldman, R. (1981). Personal involvement as a determinant of argument-based persuasion. *Journal of Personality and Social Psychology, 41,* 847–855.

Petty, R. E., Cacioppo, J. T., & Haugtvedt, C. (1992). Involvement and persuasion: An appreciative look at the Sherifs' contribution to the study of self-relevance and attitude change. In D. Granberg & G. Sarup (Eds.), *Social judgment and intergroup relations: Essays in honor of Muzafer Sherif* (pp. 147–174). New York, NY: Springer/Verlag.

Petty, R. E., Cacioppo, J. T., & Heesacker, M. (1981). The use of rhetorical questions in persuasion: A cognitive response analysis. *Journal of Personality and Social Psychology, 40,* 432–440.

Petty, R. E., & Fabrigar, L. R. (2008). Affective and cognitive meta-bases of attitudes: Unique effects on information interest and persuasion. *Journal of Personality and Social Psychology, 94,* 938–955.

Petty, R. E., Fabrigar, L. R., & Wegener, D. T. (2003). Emotional factors in attitudes and persuasion. In R. J. Davidson, K. R. Scherer, & H. H. Goldsmith (Eds.), *Handbook of affective sciences* (pp. 752–772). Oxford, England: Oxford University Press.

Petty, R. E., Fazio, R. H., & Briñol, P. (Eds.). (2009a). *Attitudes: Insights from the new implicit measures.* New York, NY: Psychology Press.

Petty, R. E., Fazio, R. H., & Briñol, P., (2009b). The new implicit measures: An overview. In R. E. Petty, R. H. Fazio, & P. Briñol (Eds.), *Attitudes: Insights from the new implicit measures* (pp. 3–18). New York, NY: Psychology Press.

Petty, R. E., Gleicher, F. H., & Jarvis, B. (1993). Persuasion theory and AIDS prevention. In J. B. Pryor & G. Reeder (Eds.), *The social psychology of HIV infection* (pp. 155–182). Hillsdale, NJ: Erlbaum.

Petty, R. E., Harkins, S. G., & Williams, K. D. (1980). The effects of group diffusion of cognitive effort on attitudes: An information processing view. *Journal of Personality and Social Psychology, 38,* 81–92.

Petty, R. E., Haugtvedt, C., & Smith, S. M. (1995). Elaboration as a determinant of attitude strength: Creating attitudes that are persistent, resistant, and predictive of behavior. In R. E. Petty & J. A. Krosnick (Eds.), *Attitude strength: Antecedents and consequences* (pp. 93–130). Mahwah, NJ: Erlbaum.

Petty, R. E., & Krosnick, J. A. (Eds.). (1995). *Attitude strength: Antecedents and consequences.* Mahwah, NJ: Erlbaum.

Petty, R. E., Ostrom, T. M., & Brock, T. C. (1981). *Cognitive responses in persuasion.* Hillsdale, NJ: Erlbaum.

Petty, R. E., Schumann, D. W., Richman, S. A., & Strathman, A. J. (1993). Positive mood and persuasion: Different roles for affect under high and low elaboration conditions. *Journal of Personality and Social Psychology, 64,* 5–20.

Petty, R. E., Tormala, Z. L., Briñol, P., & Jarvis, W. B. G. (2006). Implicit ambivalence from attitude change: An exploration of the PAST model. *Journal of Personality and Social Psychology, 90,* 21–41.

Petty, R. E., Tormala, Z. L., & Rucker, D. D. (2004). Resisting persuasion by counterarguing: An attitude strength perspective. In J. T. Jost, M. R. Banaji, & D. A. Prentice (Eds.), *Perspectivism in social psychology: The yin and yang of scientific progress* (pp. 37–51). Washington, DC: American Psychological Association.

Petty, R. E., & Wegener, D. T. (1993). Flexible correction processes in social judgment: Correcting for context-induced contrast. *Journal of Experimental Social Psychology, 29,* 137–165.

Petty, R. E., & Wegener, D. T. (1998a). Attitude change: Multiple roles for persuasion variables. In D. Gilbert, S. Fiske, & G. Lindzey (Eds.), *The handbook of social psychology* (4th ed., Vol. 1, pp. 323–390). New York, NY: McGraw-Hill.

Petty, R. E., & Wegener, D. T. (1998b). Matching versus mismatching attitude functions: Implications for scrutiny of persuasive messages. *Personality and Social Psychology Bulletin, 24,* 227–240.

Petty, R. E., Wegener, D. T., & White, P. (1998). Flexible correction processes in social judgment: Implications for persuasion. *Social Cognition, 16,* 93–113.

Petty, R. E., Wells, G. L., & Brock, T. C. (1976). Distraction can enhance or reduce yielding to propaganda: Thought disruption versus effort justification. *Journal of Personality and Social Psychology, 34,* 874–884.

Petty, R. E., Wheeler, S. C., & Bizer, G. (2000). Matching effects in persuasion: An elaboration likelihood analysis (pp. 133–162). In G. Maio & J. Olson (Eds.), *Why we evaluate: Functions of attitudes.* Mahwah, NJ: Erlbaum.

Powers, J. T., Cook, J. E.; Purdie-Vaughns, V., Garcia, J., Apfel, N. & Cohen, G. L. (2016). Changing environments by changing individuals: The emergent effects of psychological intervention. *Psychological Science, 27,* 150–160.

Pratkanis, A. R., Greenwald, A. G., Leippe, M. R., & Baumgardner, M. H. (1988). In search of reliable persuasion effects: III. The sleeper effect is dead: Long live the sleeper effect. *Journal of Personality and Social Psychology, 54*(2), 203–218.

Priester, J. M., & Petty, R. E. (1995). Source attributions and persuasion: Perceived honesty as a determinant of message scrutiny. *Personality and Social Psychology Bulletin, 21,* 637–654.

Priester, J. M. & Petty, R. E. (1996). The gradual threshold model of ambivalence: Relating the positive and negative bases of attitudes to subjective ambivalence. *Journal of Personality and Social Psychology, 71,* 431–449.

Priester, J. R., & Petty, R. E. (2001). Extending the bases of subjective attitudinal ambivalence: Interpersonal and intrapersonal antecedents of evaluative tension. *Journal of Personality and Social Psychology, 80,* 19–34.

Priester, J. M., Wegener, D., Petty, R. E., & Fabrigar, L. (1999). Examining the psychological processess underlying the sleeper effect: The elaboration likelihood model explanation. *Media Psychology, 1,* 27–48.

Puckett, J. M., Petty, R. E., Cacioppo, J. T., & Fisher, D. L. (1983). The relative impact of age and attractiveness stereotypes on persuasion. *Journal of Gerontology, 38,* 340–343.

Ranganath, K. A., Smith, C. T., & Nosek, B. A. (2008). Distinguishing automatic and controlled components of attitudes from direct and indirect measurement methods. *Journal of Experimental Social Psychology, 44,* 386–396.

Ratneshwar, S., & Chaiken, S. (1991). Comprehension's role in persuasion: The case of its moderating effect on the persuasive impact of source cues. *Journal of Consumer Psychology, 18,* 52–62.

Reich, T., & Wheeler, S. C. (2016). The good and bad of ambivalence: Desiring ambivalence under outcome uncertainty. *Journal of Personality and Social Psychology, 110,* 493–508.

Rhodes, N., & Wood, W. (1992). Self-esteem and intelligence affect influenciability: The mediating role of message reception. *Psychological Bulletin, 111,* 156–171.

Rocklage, M. D., & Fazio, R. H. (2015). The evaluative lexicon: Adjective use as a means of assessing and distinguishing atitude valence, extremity, and emotionality. *Journal of Experimental Social Psychology, 56,* 214–227.

Rocklage, M. D., & Fazio, R. H. (2018). Attitude accessibility as a function of emotionality. *Personality and Social Psychology Bulletin, 44,* 508–520.

Ronis, D. L., Baumgardner, M. H., Leippe, M. R., Cacioppo, J. T., & Greenwald, A. G. (1977). In search of reliable persuasion effects: I. A computer-controlled procedure for studding persuasion. *Journal of Personality and Social Psychology, 35,* 548–569.

Rosenberg, M. J. (1960). An analysis of affective-cognitive consistency. In C. I. Hovland, & M. J. Rosenberg (Eds.), *Attitude organization and change: An analysis of consistency among attitude components* (pp. 15–64). New Haven, CT: Yale University Press.

Ross, M., McFarland, C., Conway, M., & Zanna, M. P. (1983). Reciprocal relation between attitudes and behavior recall: Committing people to newly formed attitudes. *Journal of Personality and Social Psychology, 45,* 257–267.

Rozin, P. (1999). The process of moralization. *Psychological Science, 10,* 218–221.

Rucker, D. D., Petty, R. E., & Briñol, P. (2008). What's in a frame anyway? A meta-cognitive analysis of the impact of one versus two sided message framing on attitude certainty. *Journal of Consumer Psychology, 18,* 137–149.

Rucker, D. D., Tormala, Z. L., Petty, R. E., & Briñol, P. (2014). Consumer conviction and commitment: An appraisal-based framework for attitude certainty. *Journal of Consumer Psychology, 24,* 119–136.

Rudman, L. A., Ashmore, R. D., & Gary, M. L. (2001). "Unlearning" automatic biases: The malleability of implicit prejudice and stereotypes. *Journal of Personality and Social Psychology, 81,* 856–868.

Rydell, R. J. & McConnell, A. R. (2006). Understanding implicit and explicit attitude change: A systems of reasoning analysis. *Journal of Personality and Social Psychology, 91,* 995–1008.

Rydell, R. J., McConnell, A. R., & Mackie, D. M. (2008). Consequences of discrepant explicit and implicit attitudes: Cognitive dissonance and increased information processing. *Journal of Experimental Social Psychology, 44,* 1526–1532.

Rydell, R. J., McConnell, A. R., Mackie, D. M., & Strain, L. M. (2006). Of two minds: Forming and changing valence-inconsistent implicit and explicit attitudes. *Psychological Science, 17,* 954–958.

Salovey, P., & Wegener, D. T. (2003). Communicating about health: Message framing, persuasion, and health behavior. In J. Suls & K. Wallston (Eds.), *Social psychological foundations of health and illness* (pp. 54–81). Oxford, England: Blackwell.

Santos, D., Briñol, P., Mello, J., & Petty, R. E. (2017). Meaning moderates the persuasive effect of physical actions: Buying, selling, touching, carrying, and cleaning thoughts as if they were commercial products. *Journal of the Association for Consumer Research, 2,* 460–471.

Scher, S. J., & Cooper, J. (1989). Motivational basis of dissonance: The singular role of behavioural consequences. *Journal of Personality and Social Psychology, 56,* 899–906.

Schmidt, J., & De Houwer, J. (2012). Learning, awareness, and instruction: Subjective contingency awareness does matter in the colour-word contingency learning paradigm. *Consciousness and Cognition, 21,* 1754–1768.

Schwarz, N. (1998). Accessible content and accessibility experiences: The interplay of declarative and experiential information in judgment. *Personality and Social Psychology Review, 2*(2), 87–99.

Schwarz, N. (2004). Metacognitive experiences in consumer judgment and decision making. *Journal of Consumer Psychology, 14*(4), 332–348.

Schwarz, N. (2007). Attitude construction: Evaluation in context. *Social Cognition, 25,* 638–656.

Schwarz, N., Bless, H., & Bohner, G. (1991). Mood and persuasion: Affective states influence the processing of persuasive communications. *Advances in Experimental Social Psychology, 24,* 161–199.

Schwarz, N., Bless, H., Strack, F., Klumpp, G., Rittenauer-Schatka, H., & Simons, A. (1991). Ease of retrieval as information: Another look at the availability heuristic. *Journal of Personality and Social Psychology, 61,* 195–202.

See, Y. H. M., Fabrigar, L. R., & Petty, R. E. (2013). Affective-cognitive meta-bases versus structural bases of attitudes predict processing interest versus efficiency. *Personality and Social Psychology Bulletin, 39,* 1111–1123.

See, Y. H. M., Petty, R. E., & Evans, L. M. (2009). The impact of perceived message complexity and need for cognition on information processing and attitudes. *Journal of Research in Personality, 43,* 880–889.

See, Y. H. M., Petty, R. E., & Fabrigar, L. R. (2008). Affective and cognitive meta-bases of attitudes: Unique effects on information interest and persuasion. *Journal of Personality and Social Psychology, 94,* 938–955.

Shah, A. K., & Oppenheimer, D. M. (2008). Heuristics made easy: An effort reduction framework. *Psychological Bulletin, 134,* 207–222.

Shapiro, L. (2011). *Embodied cognition.* Abingdon, England: Routeledge.

Shavitt, S. (1989). Operationalizing functional theories of attitude. In A. R. Pratkanis, S. J. Vreckler, and A. G. Greenwald (Eds.), *Attitude structure and function* (pp. 311–338). Hillsdale, NJ: Erlbaum.

Sherman, D. K., & Cohen, G. L. (2006). The psychology of self-defense: Self-affirmation theory. In L. M. P. Zanna (Ed.), *Advances in experimental social psychology* (Vol. 38, pp. 183–242). San Diego, CA: Academic Press.

Sherman, J., Gawronski, B., & Trope, Y. (Eds.) (2014). *Dual-process theories of the social mind*. New York, NY: Guildford.

Sherman, S. J., Cialdini, R. B., Schwartzman, D. F., & Reynolds, K. D. (1985). Imagining can heighten or lower the perceived likelihood of contracting a disease: The mediating effect of ease of imagery. *Personality and Social Psychology Bulletin, 16,* 405–418.

Sheeran, P., Maki, A., Montanaro, E., Avishai-Yitshak, A., Bryan, A., Klein, W., & Rothman, A. (2016). The impact of changing attitudes, norms, and self-efficacy on health-related intentions and behavior: A meta-analysis. *Health Psychology, 35,* 1178–1188.

Shimp, T. A., Stuart, W. W., & Engle, R. W. (1991). A program of classical conditioning experiments testing variations in the conditioned stimulus and context. *Journal of Consumer Research, 18,* 1–12.

Skitka, L. J., Bauman, C. W., & Sargis, E. G. (2005). Moral conviction: Another contributor to attitude strength or something more? *Journal of Personality and Social Psychology, 88,* 895–917.

Skitka, L. J., Morgan, G. S., & Wisneski, D. C. (2015). Political orientation and moral conviction: A conservative advantage or an equal opportunity motivator of political engagement? In J. Forgas, W. Crano, & K. Fiedler (Eds.) *Social psychology and politics*. New York, NY: Psychology Press.

Smith, C. T., & De Houwer, J. (2014). The impact of persuasive messages on IAT performance is moderated by source attractiveness and likeability. *Social Psychology, 45,* 437–448.

Smith, E. R., & DeCoster, J. (1999). Associative and rule-based processing: A connectionist interpretation of dual-process models. In S. Chaiken & Y. Trope (Eds.), *Dual-process theories in social psychology*. New York, NY: Guilford.

Smith, S. M., Fabrigar, L. R., MacDougall, B. L., & Wiesenthal, N. L. (2008). The role of amount, cognitive elaboration, and structural consistency of attitude-relevant knowledge in the formation of attitude certainty. *European Journal of Social Psychology, 38,* 280–295.

*Smith, S. M., & Petty, R. E. (1996). Message framing and persuasion: A message processing analysis. *Personality and Social Psychology Bulletin, 22*(3), 257–268.

Smith, S. M., & Shaffer, D. R. (1995). Speed of speech and persuasion: Evidence for multiple effects. *Personality and Social Psychology Bulletin, 21,* 1051–1060.

Snyder, M. (1974). Self-monitoring of expressive behavior. *Journal of Personality and Social Psychology, 30,* 526–537.

Snyder, M., & DeBono, K. G. (1985). Appeals to image and claims about quality: Understanding the psychology of advertising. *Journal of Personality and Social Psychology, 49,* 586–597.

Staats, A. W., Staats, A. W., Crawford, H. L. (1962). First-order conditioning. *Journal of Abnormal and Social Psychology, 57,* 37–40.

Steele, C. M. (1988). The psychology of self-affirmation: Sustaining the integrity of the self. In L. Berkowitz (Ed.), *Advances in experimental social psychology* (Vol. 21, pp. 261–302). New York, NY: Academic Press.

Stone, J., & Cooper, J. (2001). A self-standards model of cognitive dissonance. *Journal of Experimental Social Psychology, 37,* 228–243.

Stone, J., & Cooper, J. (2003). The effect of self-attribute relevance on how self-esteem moderates attitude change in dissonance processes. *Journal of Experimental Social Psychology, 39*(5), 508–515.

Strack, F., Martin, L. L., & Stepper, S. (1988). Inhibiting and facilitating conditions of the human smile: A non-obtrusive test of the facial feedback hypothesis. *Journal of Personality and Social Psychology, 54,* 768–777.

Stroebe, W., & Diehl, M. (1988). When social support fails: Supporter characteristics in compliance-induced attitude change. *Personality and Social Psychology Bulletin, 14,* 136–144.

Stuart, E. W., Shimp, T. A., & Engle, R. W. (1987). Classical conditioning of consumer attitudes: Four experiments in an advertising context. *Journal of Consumer Research, 14,* 334–349.

Teeny, J., Briñol, P., & Petty, R. E. (2017). The elaboration likelihood model: Understanding consumer attitude change. In C. V. Jansson-Boyd & M. J. Zawisza (Eds.). *Routeledge international handbook of consumer psychology* (pp. 390–410). Abingdon, England: Routledge.

Teeny, J., & Petty, R.E. (2018). The role of perceived attitudinal bases on spontaneous and requested advocacy. *Journal of Experimental Social Psychology, 76*, 175–185.

Tesser, A. (1978). Self-generated attitude change. In L. Berkowitz (Ed.), *Advances in experimental social psychology* (Vol. 11, pp. 289–338). New York, NY: Academic Press.

Tesser, A. (1988). Toward a self-evaluation maintenance model of social behavior. In L. Berkowitz (Ed.), *Advances in experimental social psychology* (Vol. 21, pp. 181–227). New York, NY: Academic Press.

Tesser, A. (1993). The importance of heritability in psychological research: The case of attitudes. *Psychological Review, 100*, 129–142.

Tesser, A. (2001). On the plasticity of self-defense. *Current Directions in Psychological Science, 10*, 66–69.

Tesser, A., Martin, L., & Mendolia, M. (1995). The impact of thought on attitude extremity and attitude-behavior consistency. (pp. 73–92). In R. E. Petty & J. A. Krosnick (Eds.), *Attitude strength: Antecedents and consequences.* Mahwah, NJ: Erlbaum.

Thompson, M. M., Zanna, M. P., & Griffin, D. W. (1995). Let's not be indifferent about (attitudinal) ambivalence. In R. E. Petty & J. A. Korsnick (Eds.). *Attitude strength: Antecedents and consequences* (pp. 361–386). Mahwah, NJ: Erlbaum.

Tice, D. M. (1992). Self-concept change and self-presentation: The looking glass self is also a magnifying glass. *Journal of Personality and Social Psychology, 63*, 435–451.

Tiedens, L. Z., & Linton, S. (2001). Judgment under emotional certainty and uncertainty: The effects of specific emotions on information processing. *Journal of Personality and Social Psychology, 81*, 973–988.

Tom, G., Pettersen, P., Lau, T., Burton, T., & Cook, J. (1991). The role of overt head movement in the formation of affect. *Basic and Applied Social Psychology, 12*, 281–289.

Tormala, Z. L., Briñol, P., & Petty, R. E. (2007). Multiple roles for source credibility under high elaboration: It's all in the timing. *Social Cognition, 25*, 536–552.

Tormala, Z. L., Falces, C., Briñol, P., & Petty, R. E. (2007). Ease of retrieval effects in social judgment: The role of unrequested cognitions. *Journal of Personality and Social Psychology, 93*, 143–157.

Tormala, Z. L., & Petty, R. E. (2002). What doesn't kill me makes me stronger: The effects of resisting persuasion on attitude certainty. *Journal of Personality and Social Psychology, 83*, 1298–1313.

Tormala, Z. L., Petty, R. E., & Briñol, P. (2002). Ease of retrieval effects in persuasion: A self-validation analysis. *Personality and Social Psychology Bulletin, 28*, 1700–1712.

Tversky, A., & Kahneman, D. (1974). Judgment under uncertainty: Heuristics and biases. *Science, 185*, 1124–1130.

van Harreveld, F., van der Pligt, J., & de Liver, Y. N. (2009). The agony of ambivalence and ways to resolve it: Introducing the MAID model. *Personality and Social Psychology Review, 13*, 45–61.

Vezich, S. I., Katzman, P. L, Ames, D. L., Falk, E. B., & Lieberman, M. D. (2017). Modulating the neural bases of persuasion: Why/how, gain/loss, users/non-users. *Social Cognitive and Affective Neuroscience, 12*, 283–297.

Walther, E. (2002). Guilty by mere association: Evaluative conditioning and the spreading attitude effect. *Journal of Personality and Social Psychology, 82,* 919–934.

Walton, G. M., Logel, C., Peach, J.M., Spencer, S.J., & Zanna, M. P. (2015). Two brief interventions to mitigate a chilly climate transform women's experience, relationships, and achievement in engineering. *Journal of Educational Psychology, 107*, 468–485.

Watts, W. A. (1967). Relative persistence of opinion change induced by active compared to passive participation. *Journal of Personality and Social Psychology, 5*, 4–15.

Wegener, D. T., Clark, J. K., & Petty, R. E. (2006). Not all stereotyping is created equal. Differential consequences of thoughtful versus non-thoughtful stereotyping. *Journal of Personality and Social Psychology, 90*, 42–59.

Wegener, D. T., & Petty, R. E. (1994). Mood management across affective states: The hedonic contingency hypothesis. *Journal of Personality and Social Psychology, 66,* 1034–1048.

Wegener, D. T., & Petty, R. E. (1995). Flexible correction processes in social judgment: The role of naive theories in corrections for perceived bias. *Journal of Personality and Social Psychology, 68,* 36–51.

Wegener, D. T., & Petty, R. E. (1997). The flexible correction model: The role of naive theories of bias in bias correction. In M. P. Zanna (Ed.), *Advances in experimental social psychology* (Vol. 29, pp. 141–208). Mahwah, NJ: Erlbaum.

Wells, G. L., & Petty, R. E. (1980). The effects of overt head movements on persuasion: Compatibility and incompatibility of responses. *Basic and Applied Social Psychology, 1,* 219–230.

Wheeler, S. C., Petty, R. E., & Bizer, G. Y. (2005). Self-schema matching and attitude change: Situational and dispositional determinants of message elaboration. *Journal of Consumer Research, 31,* 787–797.

Wicklund, R. A. (1974). *Freedom and reactance.* Hillsdale, NJ: Erlbaum.

Wicklund, R. A., & Gollwitzer, P. M. (1982). *Symbolic self-completion.* Hillsdale, NJ: Erlbaum.

Wilson, T. D., & Brekke, N. (1994). Mental contamination and mental correction: Unwanted influences on judgments and evaluations. *Psychological Bulletin, 116,* 117–142.

Wilson, T. D., Dunn, D. S., Bybee, J. A., Hyman, D. B., & Rotondo, J. A. (1984). Effects of analyzing reasons on attitude-behavior consistency. *Journal of Personality and Social Psychology, 47,* 5–16.

Wilson, T. D., Lindsey, S., & Schooler, T. Y. (2000). A model of dual attitudes. *Psychological Review, 107,* 101–126.

Wittenbrink, B., & Schwarz, N. (Eds.). (2007). *Implicit measures of attitudes.* New York, NY: Guilford.

Wood, W. (1982). Retrieval of attitude relevant information from memory: Effects on susceptibility to persuasion and on intrinsic motivation. *Journal of Personality and Social Psychology, 42,* 798–810.

Wood, W. (2017). Habit in personality and social psychology. *Personality and Social Psychology Review, 21,* 389–403.

Wood, W. W., Kallgren, C. A., & Preisler, R. M. (1985). Access to attitude relevant information in memory as a determinant of persuasion: The role of message attributes. *Journal of Personality and Social Psychology, 21,* 73–85

Wood, W., Rhodes, N., & Biek, M. (1995). Working knowledge and attitude strength: An information processing analysis. In R. E. Petty & J. A. Krosnick (Eds.), *Attitude strength: Antecedents and consequences.* Hillsdale, NJ: Erlbaum.

Wyer, N. A. (2010). You never get a second chance to make a first (implicit) impression: The role of elaboration in the formation and revision of implicit impressions. *Social Cognition, 28,* 1–19.

Wyer, N. A. (2016). Easier done than undone . . . by some of the people some of the time: The role of elaboration in explicit and implicit group preferences. *Journal of Experimental Social Psychology, 63,* 77–85.

Ye, Y., & Gawronski, B. (2016). When possessions become part of the self: Ownership and implicit self-object linking. *Journal of Experimental Social Psychology, 64,* 72–87.

Zajonc, R. B. (1968). Attitudinal effects of mere exposure. *Journal of Personality and Social Psychology, 9,* 1–27.

Zanna, M. P., & Cooper, J. (1974). Dissonance and the pill: An attribution approach to studying the arousal properties of dissonance. *Journal of Personality and Social Psychology, 29,* 703–709.

Zanna, M. P., & Rempel, J. K. (1988). Attitudes: A new look at an old concept. In D. Bar-Tal & A. Kruglanski (Eds.), *The social psychology of knowledge.* New York, NY: Cambridge University Press.

Ziegler, R., Diehl, M., & Ruther, A. (2002). Multiple source characteristics and persuasion: Source inconsistency as a determinant of message scrutiny. *Personality and Social Psychology Bulletin, 28,* 496–580.

Zunick, P. V., Teeny, J. D., & Fazio, R. H. (2017). Are some attitudes more self-defining than others? Assessing self-related attitude functions and their consequences. *Personality and Social Psychology Bulletin, 43,* 1136–1149.

Chapter 7

Social Influence

Robert B. Cialdini and Vladas Griskevicius

Blandishing persuasion steals the mind even of the wise.

—Homer

For nearly a century, social psychologists have been investigating the process of social influence, wherein one person's attitudes, cognitions, or behaviors are changed through the deeds of another. Because other authors within this volume have addressed social influences on attitudes and cognitions (see Chapter 6), our focus will be on the realm of behavior change and on the factors that cause one individual to comply with another's request for action of some sort. In the process, we will consider a set of seven psychological principles that appear to influence behavioral compliance decisions most powerfully. Briefly, these principles involve pressures to comply because of human tendencies to (a) return a gift, favor, or service; (b) be consistent with prior commitments; (c) follow the lead of multiple similar others; (d) accommodate the requests of those we like; (e) conform to the directives of legitimate authority; (f) seize opportunities that are scarce or dwindling in availability; and (g) assist those with whom we share a group identity.

A proper understanding of social influence is of vast consequence, as the process appears to be an elemental feature of human functioning. It is inescapable that those individuals able to influence, artfully and usefully, the responding of those around them gain an enormous competitive advantage from it. As a result, their capacity for survival will almost certainly be enhanced and social influence-related traits, abilities, and processes are likely to have evolved to be fundamental to human nature. Indeed, two of the most universal features of human interaction, language and facial expression, have recently been reinterpreted in terms of social influence motives. As regards the first of these universals, consider the conclusion from a research program (led by the psycholinguist Gün Semin) designed to resolve the question, "What is language principally for?" The emergent answer seems groundbreaking: No longer should we think of language as primarily a mechanism of conveyance, as a means for delivering to recipients a communicator's conception of reality. Instead, we should think of language as primarily a mechanism of influence, as a means for *inducing* recipients to share that conception of reality and to act in accord with it (Cavicchio, Melcher, & Poesio, 2014; Semin, 2012; Semin & Fiedler, 1988). A similar paradigm shift is occurring in the domain of facial displays, where the long-standing "basic theory of emotions"—that conceptualizes facial expressions as primarily operating to mirror and reveal one or another of a set of primitive human emotions (Ekman, 1972, 2017)—is being upset by a view of those expressions as functioning principally to influence others to act (Crivelli & Fridlund, 2018). According to this conception, facial displays should no longer be interpreted as "the royal road to emotions" but, instead, as a common road to influence. In both cases, the basic human operations of language and facial expression are being redefined in terms of what appears to be the even more basic operation of producing advantageous change in others.

Social Influences on Compliance

Focusing on Powerful Effects

Within academic social psychology, research into the behavioral compliance process has emphasized two questions: "Which principles and techniques reliably affect compliance?" and "How do these principles and techniques work to affect compliance as they do?" The first of these questions is concerned with the identification of real effects, whereas the second is concerned with their theoretical/conceptual bases. Almost without exception, the vehicle that has been used to answer these two questions has been the controlled experiment. And this is understandable, as controlled experimentation provides an excellent context for addressing issues such as whether an effect is real (i.e., reliable) and which theoretical account best explains its occurrence.

Regrettably, when the question of primary interest includes a determination of the *power* of possible influences on ordinary compliance behavior, the controlled experiment becomes less suited to the job. The high levels of experimental rigor and precision that allow us to determine that an effect is genuine and theoretically interpretable simultaneously decrease our ability to assess the potency of that effect. That is, because the best-designed experiments (a) eliminate or control all sources of influence except the one under study and (b) possess highly sensitive measurements techniques that may register whisper-like effects so small as to never make a difference when other (extraneous) factors are allowed to vary naturally, as they typically do in the social environment.

Thus, rigorous experimentation should not be used as the primary device for deciding which compliance-related influences are powerful enough to be submitted to rigorous experimentation for further study. Some other *starting point* should be found to identify the most potent influences on the compliance process. Otherwise, valuable time could well be spent seeking to investigate and to apply effects that are only epiphenomena of the controlled experimental setting.

The Development of Powerful Compliance Inducers

A crucial question thus becomes, "How are the most *powerful* compliance principles and tactics determined?" One answer involves the systematic observation of the behaviors of commercial compliance professionals.

Who are the commercial compliance professionals, and why should their actions be especially informative as to the identification of powerful influences on everyday compliance decisions? They can be defined as those individuals whose business or financial well-being is dependent on their ability to induce compliance (e.g., salespeople, fundraisers, advertisers, lobbyists, cult recruiters, negotiators, con artists, etc.). With this definition in place, it becomes possible to recognize why the regular and widespread practices of these professionals would be noteworthy indicators of the powerful influences on the compliance process: Because the livelihoods of commercial compliance professionals depend on the effectiveness of their procedures, those professionals who use procedures that work well to elicit compliance responses will survive and flourish. In addition, they will pass these successful procedures on to the succeeding generations (trainees). However, those practitioners who use unsuccessful compliance procedures will either drop them or quickly go out of business; in either case, the procedures themselves will not be passed on to newer generations.

Accordingly, these procedures will point a careful observer toward the major principles that people use to decide when to comply. Several years ago, one of the authors of this chapter resolved to become such an observer. What emerged from this period of systematic observation was a list of six principles on which compliance professionals appeared to base most of their psychological attempts: (a) reciprocity, (b) consistency, (c) social proof, (d) liking, (e) authority, and (f) scarcity. A full account of the origins, workings, and prevalence of these six principles is available elsewhere (Cialdini, 2008; see also Goldstein, Martin, & Cialdini, 2008). More recently, a seventh principle, unity, has been added to the list (Cialdini, 2016). The remainder of this chapter offers a summary description of these principles and of the social scientific theory and evidence regarding when, how, and why each principle functions to motivate compliance.

The Principles of Influence

Goal-Directed Nature of Behavior

Before discussing each principle in detail, it is useful to consider why these principles are so powerful at influencing human behavior. An important thread that links all of the principles is related to the goal-directed character of human behavior. Our actions are aimed at achieving goals on several levels (Kenrick, Griskevicius, Neuberg, & Schaller, 2010; also see Chapter 16). At a surface level, for instance, people behave so as to attain a variety of moment-to-moment or day-to-day goals: A person might want to make a good impression on a teacher or save enough money to buy a car. At a deeper level, behavior promotes ultimate or evolutionary motives, including survival and reproduction. Indeed, part of the reason why the principles discussed in this chapter are effective at influencing behavior is because they promote adaptive behavior. That is, the sense of obligation to reciprocate a gift, the tendency to value scarce items, the inclination to turn to similar others or to experts in times of uncertainty, and the desire to say "yes" to people we like all have likely evolutionary bases (Sundie, Cialdini, Griskevicius, & Kenrick, 2006).

Let's consider how the seven principles of influence help achieve at least three human goals: affiliation, accuracy, and consistency (Cialdini & Goldstein, 2004). Humans are fundamentally motivated to affiliate, creating and maintaining meaningful social relationships with others (Baumeister & Leary, 1995). Reciprocating favors and saying "yes" to those we like and those with whom we share a group identity are adaptive strategies for affiliation. Humans are similarly motivated to make accurate decisions that will help further their other goals in the most effective manner. When the best course of action is unclear, it is adaptive to follow the advice of authority or the behavior of similar others. People also have a strong need to behave in a manner that is consistent with their actions, statements, commitments, and beliefs.

Reciprocity

Pay every debt as if God wrote the bill.

—Ralph Waldo Emerson

One of the most powerful norms in all human cultures is that for reciprocity (Cialdini, 2008), which obligates individuals to return the form of behavior they have received from another. As a result, people say "yes" to those they owe. Not always, of course—nothing in human social interaction works like that—but often enough that behavioral scientists have labeled this tendency the *rule for reciprocation*. Not only does the rule apply to all cultures, but it also applies broadly to various behaviors within those cultures (Gintis et al., 2003; Gouldner, 1960). Indeed, children respond to the rule before they are two years old (Dunfield & Kuhlmeier, 2010). By the time they are adults, its power influences all aspects of their lives, including their buying patterns. For example, visitors to a candy store became 42% more likely to make a purchase if they'd received a gift piece of chocolate upon entry (Lammers, 1991). Much more worrisome is the impact of the rule on the voting actions of legislators. In the United States, companies that make sizable campaign contributions to lawmakers who sit on tax policymaking committees experience significant reductions in their tax rates (Brown, Drake, & Wellman, 2015). The legislators will deny any quid pro quo, but, manifestly, the companies know better. Although the rule tends to operate most reliably in public domains, it is so deeply ingrained in most individuals that it also directs behavior in private settings (Burger, Sanchez, Imberi, & Grande, 2009; Whatley et al., 1999) and virtual environments (Eastwick & Gardner, 2009).

A *reciprocation rule* for compliance can be worded as follows: *One should be more willing to comply with a request from someone who has previously provided a favor or concession.* Under this general rule, people will feel obligated to provide gifts, favors, services, and aid to those who have given them such things first (Goldstein, Griskevicius, & Cialdini, 2011; Singer, Van Holwyk, & Maher, 2000), sometimes even returning larger favors than those they have received. For example, restaurant servers who gave two candies to guests along with the check increased their tips by 14.1% (Strohmetz et al., 2002). A number of sales and fundraising tactics also use this factor to advantage: The compliance professional initially gives something to the target person, thereby causing the target to be more likely to give something in return. Often, this "something in return" is the target's compliance with a substantial request.

The unsolicited gift, accompanied by a request for a donation, is a commonly used technique that employs the norm for reciprocity. One example is organizations sending free gifts through the mail. Such groups count on the fact that most people will not go to the trouble of returning the gift and will feel uncomfortable about keeping it without reciprocating in some way. For instance, the Disabled American Veterans organization reports that its simple mail appeal for donations produces a response rate of about 18%. But when the mailings also includes an unsolicited gift (gummed, individualized address labels), the success rate nearly doubles to 35% (Smolowe, 1990).

A crucial aspect of successful reciprocity-based influence techniques involves activating the sense of obligation. The creation of obligation necessitates that the individual who desires to influence another needs to be the first to provide a gift. It is noteworthy that this important aspect of reciprocity-based influence techniques is often misemployed. For example, numerous commercial organizations offer donations to charity in return for the purchase of products or services—a general strategy falling under the rubric of "cause-related marketing." Yet such tit-for-tat appeals often fail to engage reciprocity properly because influence agents do not provide benefits first and then allow recipients to return the favor. The suboptimal nature of such messages can be clearly seen in a field experiment in hotels, in which our research team varied messages that urged guests to reuse their towels. Messages that promised a donation in guests' name to an environmental cause if guests first reused their towels were no more effective than standard pro-environmental messages (Goldstein et al., 2011). Consistent with the obligating force of reciprocity, however, a message informing guests that the hotel had already made a donation in the guests' name increased towel reuse by 26%.

Reciprocal Concessions

A variation of the norm for reciprocation of favors is that for reciprocation of concessions. A reciprocal concessions procedure (or *door-in-the-face technique*) for inducing compliance has been documented repeatedly (e.g., Cialdini, Vincent, Lewis, Catalan, Wheeler, & Darby, 1975; for meta-analyses, see O'Keefe & Hale, 1998, 2001). A requester uses this procedure by beginning with an extreme request that is usually rejected and then retreating to a more moderate favor—the one the requester had in mind from the outset. In doing so, the requester hopes that the retreat from an extreme to a moderate request will spur the target person to make a reciprocal concession by moving from initial rejection of the larger favor to acceptance of the smaller one. This reciprocal concessions strategy has been successfully used in fundraising contexts where, after refusing a larger request for donations, people become substantially more likely than before to give a moderately sized contribution (e.g., Reingen, 1978). Cialdini and Ascani (1976) also used this technique in soliciting blood donors. They first requested a person's involvement in a long-term donor program. When that request was refused, the solicitor made a smaller request for a one-time donation. This pattern of a large request (that is refused) followed by a smaller request significantly increased compliance with the smaller request, as compared to a control condition of people who were asked only to perform the smaller one-time favor (a 50% vs. a 32% compliance rate).

Of special interest to university students is evidence that the door-in-the-face technique can greatly increase a professor's willingness to spend time helping a student (Harari, Mohr, & Hosey, 1980). In that study, only 59% of faculty members were willing to spend 15 to 20 minutes to meet with a student on an issue of interest to the student—when that was the only request the student made. However, significantly more faculty members (78%) were willing to agree to that same request if they had first refused the student's request to meet for two hours a week for the rest of the semester.

Social Proof

> *If you can keep your head when people all around you are losing theirs, you probably haven't grasped the situation.*
>
> —Jean Kerr

People frequently use the beliefs, attitudes, and actions of others, particularly similar others, as a standard of comparison against which to evaluate the correctness of their own beliefs, attitudes, and actions. Thus, it is common for individuals to decide on appropriate behaviors for themselves in a given situation by searching for information as to how similar others have behaved or are behaving in that situation—a phenomenon social psychologists have long recognized (e.g., Asch, 1956; Bandura & Menlove, 1968; Darley & Latane, 1970). This simple principle of behavior accounts for an amazingly varied army of human responses. For instance, research has shown that hotel guests use it when deciding whether to reuse their towels (Goldstein, Cialdini, & Griskevicius, 2008), amusement park visitors use it to decide whether to litter in a public place (Cialdini, Reno, & Kallgren, 1990), audience members use it in deciding whether a joke is funny (Provine, 2000), National Park visitors use it when deciding whether to commit theft (Cialdini, 2003), pedestrians use it in deciding whether to stop and stare at an empty spot in the sky (Milgram, Bickman, & Berkowitz, 1969), alarmingly, college students use it to judge that torture is proper in military interrogations (Aramovich, Lytle, & Sitka, 2012), and, even more alarmingly, troubled individuals use it in deciding whether to commit suicide (Phillips & Carstensen, 1988).

Much of this evidence can be understood in terms of Festinger's (1954) *social comparison theory,* which states that (a) people have a constant drive to evaluate themselves (i.e., the appropriateness of their abilities, beliefs, feelings, and behaviors); (b) if available, people will prefer to use objective cues to make these evaluations; (c) if objective evidence is not available, people will rely on social comparison evidence instead; and (d) when seeking social comparison evidence for self-evaluations, people will look to similar others as the preferred basis for comparison.

When the goal is to evaluate the correctness of an opinion or action, research has generally supported the theory. Social comparison is most likely to occur in situations that are objectively unclear (Higgs, 2015; Zitek & Hebl, 2007) and is most likely to involve similar others (Cruwys, Bevelander, & Hermans, 2015; Platow et al., 2005). For example, people are strongly influenced by the behavior of others when deciding whether to conserve energy in their homes (Schultz, Nolan, Cialdini, Goldstein, & Griskevicius, 2007). However, the influence of others' conservation behaviors increased as those others became more similar to the actual home resident: Whereas other citizens of the state had an effect on conservation, behavior was more strongly influenced by the residents of the same city and even more strongly influenced by the residents of their own neighborhood (Nolan, Schultz, Cialdini, Goldstein, & Griskevicius, 2008).

The *social proof rule* for compliance can be stated as follows: *One should be more willing to comply with a request for behavior if the action fits with what similar others are thinking or doing.* Our tendency to assume that an action is more correct if others are performing it is employed in a variety of commercial settings. Bartenders often "salt" their tip jars with a few dollar bills at the beginning of the evening to simulate tips left by prior customers and, thereby, to give the impression that tipping with folded money is proper barroom behavior (Griskevicius, Cialdini, & Goldstein, 2008). Restaurant managers identify the most popular items on their menus, with a positive effect on proceeds (Cai, Chen, & Feng, 2009). Advertisers love to inform us when a product is the "fastest growing" or "largest selling" because they do not have to convince us directly that the product is good; they need only say that many others think so, which seems proof enough (Griskevicius et al., 2009). The producers of charity telethons devote inordinate amounts of time to the incessant listing of viewers who have already pledged contributions. The message being communicated to the holdouts is clear: "Look at all the people who have decided to give; it *must* be the correct thing to do" (see Surowiecki, 2005).

Another tactic that compliance professionals use to engage the principle of social proof has been put to scientific test. Called the *list technique,* it involves asking for a request only after the target person has been shown a list of similar others who have already complied. Reingen (1982) conducted several experiments in which college students or homeowners were asked to donate money or blood to a charitable cause. Those individuals who were initially shown a list of similar others who had already complied were significantly more likely to comply themselves. What's more, the longer the list, the greater was the effect. In sum, when it comes to social proof, the more you see, the more there will be.

Consistency

It is easier to resist at the beginning than at the end.

—Leonardo da Vinci

Social psychologists have long understood the strength of the consistency principle to direct human action. Prominent early theorists such as Theodore Newcomb (1953), Leon Festinger (1957), and Fritz

Heider (1958) viewed the desire for consistency as a prime motivator of behavior. Other theorists (e.g., Baumeister, 1982) recognized that the desire to *appear* consistent exerts considerable influence over our behavior as well. If we grant that the power of consistency is formidable in directing human action, an important practical question immediately arises: How is that force engaged? Social psychologists think they know the answer—through commitment. If a person can get you to make a commitment (i.e., to take action, to go on record), that person will have set the stage for your consistency with the earlier commitment. Once a stand is taken, there is a natural tendency to behave in ways that are stubbornly consistent with the stand (Burger & Caldwell, 2003; Clifford & Jerit, 2016).

A *consistency rule* for compliance can be worded as follows: *After committing themselves to a position, people become more willing to comply with requests for behaviors that are congruent with that position.* Any of a variety of strategies may be used to generate the crucial instigating commitment. One such strategy is the *foot-in-the-door technique* (Freedman & Fraser, 1966). A solicitor using this procedure will first ask for a small favor that is almost certain to be granted. The initial compliance is then followed by a request for a larger, *related* favor. Research has repeatedly shown that people who have agreed to the initial small favor become more willing to do the larger one, seemingly to be consistent with the implication of the initial action (for reviews, see Burger, 1999; Pascual & Gueguen, 2005).

Freedman and Fraser (1966) have argued that the foot-in-the-door technique is successful because performance of the initially requested action causes individuals to see themselves as possessing certain traits (e.g., "I am the sort of person who helps others" or "I am the sort of person who says yes to legitimate requests."). This explanation has received good support (e.g., Burger & Caldwell, 2003; Burger & Guadagno, 2003; Dolinski, 2000). For example, children are not influenced by the foot-in-the-door technique until they are old enough to understand the idea of a stable personality trait (around six to seven years); moreover, once children are old enough to understand the meaning of a stable trait, the foot-in-the-door tactic becomes especially effective among those children who prefer consistency in behavior (Eisenberg, Cialdini, McCreath, & Shell, 1987).

Other, more unsavory techniques induce a commitment to an item and then remove the inducements that generated the commitment. Remarkably, the commitment frequently remains. For example, the *bait-and-switch procedure* is used by some retailers who may advertise certain merchandise (e.g., a room of furniture) at a special low price. When customers arrive to take advantage of the special, they find the merchandise of low quality or sold out. However, because they have by now made an active commitment to getting new furniture at that particular store, they are more willing to agree to examine and, consequently, buy alternative merchandise there (Joule, Gouilloux, & Weber, 1989).

A similar strategy is often employed by car dealers in the *low-ball technique*, which proceeds by obtaining a commitment to a specified action and then increasing the costs of performing the action (Cialdini, Cacioppo, Bassett, & Miller, 1978). The automobile salesperson who "throws the low ball" induces the customer to decide to buy a particular model car by offering a low price on the car or an inflated one on the customer's trade-in. After the decision has been made (and, at times, after the commitment is enhanced by allowing the customer to arrange financing, take the car home overnight, etc.), something happens to remove the reason the customer decided to buy. Perhaps a price calculation error is found, or the used car assessor disallows the inflated trade-in figure. By this time, though, many customers have experienced an internal commitment to that specific automobile and proceed with the purchase. Experimental research has documented the effectiveness of this tactic in settings beyond automobile sales (e.g., Gueguen. Pascual, & Dagot, 2002; for a review, see Burger & Caputo, 2015).

One thing that these procedures (and others like them) have in common is the establishment of an earlier commitment that is consistent with a later action desired by the compliance professional. The need for consistency then takes over to compel performance of the desired behavior, often for considerable lengths of time (Lokhorst, Werner, Staats, van Dijk, & Gale, 2013; Sharot, Fleming, Yu, Koster, & Dolan,

2012). Even mere reminders of past commitments can spur individuals to act in accord with those earlier positions (Grant & Dutton, 2012; van der Werff, Steg, & Keizer, 2014).

A more manipulative tactic than merely focusing people on their existing values is to put them in a situation in which to refuse a specific request would be inconsistent with a value that people wish to be known as possessing. One such tactic is the *legitimization-of-paltry favors* (or even-a-penny-would-help) *technique* (Cialdini & Schroeder, 1976). Most people prefer to behave in ways that are consistent with a public (and private) image as helpful, charitable individuals. Consequently, a fund-\raiser who makes a request that legitimizes a paltry amount of aid ("Could you give a contribution, even a penny would help") makes it difficult for a target to refuse to give at all; to do so risks appearing to be a very unhelpful person. Notice that this procedure does not specifically request a trivial sum; that would probably lead to a profusion of pennies and a small total take. Instead, the request simply makes a minuscule form of aid acceptable, thereby reducing the target's ability to give nothing and still remain consistent with the desirable image of a helpful individual. After all, how could a person retain a helpful image after refusing to contribute when "even a penny would help"? Experimental research done to validate the effectiveness of the technique has shown it to be successful in increasing the percentage of charity contributors and total monetary contributions (for a review, see Lee, Moon, & Feeley, 2016).

Liking

The main work of a trial attorney is to make the jury like his client.

—Clarence Darrow

A fact of social interaction to which each of us can attest is that people are more favorably inclined toward the needs of those they know and like. Consequently, a *friendship/liking rule* for compliance can be worded as follows: *We should be more willing to comply with the requests of friends or other liked individuals.* Could there be any doubt that this is the case after examining the remarkable success of the Tupperware Corporation and their "home party" demonstration concept (Frenzen & Davis, 1990)? The demonstration party for Tupperware products is hosted by an individual, usually a woman, who invites to her home an array of friends, neighbors, and relatives, all of whom know that their hostess receives a percentage of the profits from every piece sold by the Tupperware representative, who is also there. In this way, the Tupperware Corporation arranges for its customers to buy from and *for* a friend rather than from an unknown salesperson. So favorable has been the effect on proceeds ($3 million in sales per day!) that the Tupperware Corporation has wholly abandoned its early retail outlets, and a Tupperware party begins somewhere every 2.7 seconds (Cialdini, 2008). Indeed, the success of this strategy has inspired many companies to use parties to sell their products, including cosmetics, arts and crafts, and even video games.

Most influence agents, however, attempt to engage the friendship/liking principle in a different way: Before making a request, they get their targets to like *them*. Studies show that a surprisingly underestimated component of liking stems from one's grooming and physical attractiveness, with good-looking people being more influential (e.g., Chaiken, 1979; Lynn & Simons, 2000; McCall, 1997). But two other approaches have been shown to be particularly effective at increasing liking: similarity and compliments.

We like people who are similar to us (Burger et al., 2004; Carli, Ganley, & Pierce-Otay, 1991). This fact seems to hold true whether the similarity occurs in the area of opinions, personality traits, background, or lifestyle. Not only has research demonstrated that even trivial similarities can increase liking and have profound effects on important decisions such as careers and marriage partners (e.g., Garner, 2005; Jones, Pelham, Carvallo, & Mirenberg, 2004; Pelham, Mirenberg, & Jones, 2002), but perceived attitude similarity between yourself and a stranger can automatically activate kinship cognitions, inducing a person to be-have prosocially toward that similar other (Park & Schaller, 2005). Consequently, those who wish to be liked to increase our compliance can accomplish that purpose by appearing similar to us in any of a wide variety of ways. For that reason, it would be wise to be careful around salespeople who *seem* to be just like us. Many sales training programs urge trainees to "mirror and match" the customer's body posture, mood, and verbal style, as similarities along each of these dimensions have been shown to lead to positive results (Maddux, Mullen, & Galinski, 2008; van Baaren, Holland, Steenaert, & van Knippenberg, 2003). Similarity in dress provides still another example. Several studies have demonstrated that we are more likely to help those who dress like us. In one study, done in the early 1970s when young people tended to dress either in "hippie" or "straight" fashion, experimenters donned hippie or straight attire and asked college students on campus for money to make a phone call. When the experimenter was dressed in the same way as the stu-dent, the request was granted in over two thirds of the instances, but when the student and requester were dissimilarly dressed, money was provided less than half of the time (Emswiller, Deaux, & Willits, 1971).

Praise, compliments, and other forms of positive estimation also stimulate liking (e.g., Gordon, 1996; Howard et al., 1995, 1997; Vonk, 2002). The actor Maclain Stevenson once described how his wife tricked him into marriage: "She said she liked me." Although designed for a laugh, the remark is as much instruc-tive as humorous. The simple information that someone fancies us can be a bewitchingly effective device for producing return liking and willing compliance. Although there are limits to our gullibility—especially when we can be sure that the flatterer's intent is manipulative (Jones & Wortman, 1973)—we tend as a rule to believe praise and to like those who provide it. Evidence for the power of praise on liking comes from a study (Drachman, deCarufel, & Insko, 1978) in which men received personal comments from someone who needed a favor from them. Some of the men got only positive comments, some only negative comments, and some got a mixture of good and bad. There were three interesting findings. First, the eval-uator who offered only praise was liked best. Second, this was so even though the men fully realized that the flatterer stood to gain from their liking of him. Finally, unlike the other types of comments, pure praise did not have to be accurate to work. Compliments produced just as much liking for the flatterer when they were untrue as when they were true. Because of this, salespeople are educated in the art of praise. A poten-tial customer's home, clothes, car, taste, etc. are all frequent targets for compliments.

Scarcity

The way to love anything is to realize that it might be lost.

—Gilbert Keith Chesterton

Opportunities seem more valuable to us when they are less available (Lynn, 1991; McKensie & Chase, 2010). Interestingly, this is often true even when the opportunity holds little attraction for us on its own merits. Take, as evidence, the experience of Florida State University students who, like most undergraduates, rated themselves as dissatisfied with the quality of their cafeteria's food. Nine days later, they had changed their minds, rating that food significantly better than they had before. It is instructive that no actual improvement in food service had occurred between the two ratings. Instead, earlier in the day of the second rating students had learned that because of a fire, they could not eat at the cafeteria for two weeks (West, 1975).

There appear to be two major sources of the power of scarcity. First, because we know that the things that are difficult to possess are typically better than those that are easy to possess, we can often use an item's availability to help us quickly and correctly decide on its quality (Lynn, 1992). Thus, one reason for the po-tency of scarcity is that, by assessing it, we can obtain a quick indication of an item's value.

In addition, there is a unique, secondary source of power within scarcity: As the things we can have become less available, we lose freedoms, and we *hate* to lose the freedoms we already have. This desire to preserve our established prerogatives is the centerpiece of *psychological reactance theory* (Brehm, 1981; Burgoon, Alvaro, Grandpre, & Voulodakis, 2002) developed to explain the human response to diminishing personal control. According to the theory, whenever our freedoms are limited or threatened, the need to retain those freedoms makes us want them (as well as the goods and services associated with them) significantly more than we previously did. So, when increasing scarcity—or anything else—interferes with our prior access to some item, we will *react against* the interference by wanting and trying to possess the item more than before. For example, individuals typically respond to censorship by wanting to receive the banned information to a greater extent and by becoming more favorable to it than before the ban (e.g., Brown, 2008; Worchel, 1992). Especially interesting is the finding that people will come to believe in banned information more even though they have not received it (Worchel, Arnold, & Baker, 1975).

A *scarcity rule* for compliance can be worded as follows: *One should try to secure those opportunities that are scarce or dwindling.* With scarcity operating powerfully on the worth assigned to things, it is not surprising that compliance professionals have a variety of techniques designed to convert this power to compliance. Probably the most frequently used technique is the "limited number" tactic in which the customer is informed that membership opportunities, products, or services exist in a limited supply that cannot be guaranteed to last for long. For example, at one large grocery chain, brand promotions that included a purchase limit ("Only X per customer") more than doubled sales for seven different types of products compared to promotions for the same products that didn't include a purchase limit (Inman, Peter, & Raghubir, 1997). Other research has suggested that, in addition to commodities, limited access to information makes the information more desirable and more influential (Brock, 1968; Brock & Bannon, 1992). For instance, wholesale beef buyers who were told of an impending imported beef shortage purchased significantly more beef when they were informed that the shortage information came from certain "exclusive" contacts that the importer had (Knishinsky, 1982). Apparently, the fact that the scarcity news was itself scarce made it more valued and persuasive.

Related to the limited number tactic is the "deadline" technique in which an official time limit is placed on the customer's opportunity to get what is being offered. Newspaper ads abound with admonitions to the customer regarding the folly of delay: "Last three days." "Limited time offer." "One week only sale." The purest form of a decision deadline—right now—occurs in a variant of the deadline technique in which customers are told that unless they make an immediate purchase decision, they will have to buy the item at a higher price, or they will not be able to purchase it at all.

The idea of potential loss plays a large role in human decision-making (see Chapter 19). In fact, people seem to be more motivated by the thought of losing something than by the thought of gaining something of equal value (Hobofoll, 2001; Tversky & Kahneman, 1981). For instance, homeowners told about how much money they could lose from inadequate insulation are more likely to insulate their homes than those told about how much money they could save (Gonzales, Aronson, & Costanzo, 1988). Similar results have been obtained on college campuses where students experienced much stronger emotions when asked to imagine losses rather than gains in their romantic relationships or grade point averages (Ketelaar, 1995).

Authority

Follow an expert.

—Virgil

Legitimately constituted authorities are extremely influential persons (e.g., Aronson, Turner, & Carlsmith, 1963; Blass, 2004; Burger, 2009; Milgram, 1974). Whether they have acquired their positions through knowledge, talent, or fortune, their positions bespeak of superior information and power. For each of us, this has always been the case. Early on, these people (e.g., parents, teachers) knew more than us, and we found that taking their advice proved beneficial—partly because of their greater wisdom and partly because they controlled our rewards and punishments. As adults, the authority figures have changed to employers, judges, police officers, and the like, but the benefits associated with doing as they say have not. For most people, then, conforming to the dictates of authority figures produces genuine practical advantages. Consequently, it makes great sense to comply with the wishes of properly constituted authorities. It makes so much sense, in fact, that people often do so when it makes no sense at all.

The most dramatic research evidence for the power of legitimate authority comes from the famous Milgram experiment in which 65% of the subjects were willing to deliver continued, intense, and dangerous levels of electric shock to a kicking, screeching, pleading other subject simply because an authority figure—in this case a scientist—directed them to do so. Although almost everyone who has ever taken a psychology course has learned about this experiment, Milgram (1974) conducted a series of variations on his basic procedure that are less well known but equally compelling in making the point about the powerful role that authority played in causing subjects to behave so cruelly. For instance, in one variation, Milgram had the scientist and the victim switch scripts so that the scientist told the subject to stop delivering shock to the victim, while the victim insisted bravely that the subject continue for the good of the experiment. The results couldn't have been clearer: Not a single subject gave even one additional shock when it was a nonauthority who demanded it. Even more than 30 years later, replications of Milgram's classic studies continue to demonstrate the power of authority (Burger, 2009; Dolinski et al., 2015).

An *authority rule* for compliance can be worded as follows: *One should be more willing to follow the suggestions of someone who is a legitimate authority.* Authorities may be seen as falling into two categories: authorities with regard to the specific situation and more general authorities. Compliance practitioners employ techniques that seek to benefit from the power invested in authority figures of both types. In the case of authority relevant to a specific situation, we can note how often advertisers inform their audiences of the level of expertise of product manufacturers (e.g., "Fashionable men's clothiers since 1841"; "Babies are our business, our only business").

At times, the expertise associated with a product has been more symbolic than substantive, for instance, when actors in television commercials wear physicians' white coats to recommend a product. In one famous coffee commercial, the actor involved, Robert Young, did not need a white coat, as his prior identity as TV doctor Marcus Welby, M.D., provided the medical connection. It is instructive that the mere symbols of a physician's expertise and authority are enough to trip the mechanism that governs authority influence. One of the most prominent of these symbols, the bare title "Dr.," has been shown to be devastatingly effective as a compliance device among trained hospital personnel. In what may be the most frightening study we know, a group of physicians and nurses conducted an experiment that documented the dangerous degree of blind obedience that hospital nurses accorded to an individual whom they had never met, but who claimed in a phone call to be a doctor (Hofling, Brotzman, Dalrymple, Graves, & Pierce, 1966). Ninety-five percent of those nurses were willing to administer an unsafe level of a drug merely because a caller they thought was a doctor requested it.

In the case of influence that generalizes outside of relevant expertise, the impact of authority (real and symbolic) appears equally impressive. For instance, researchers have found that when wearing a security guard's uniform, a requester could produce more compliance with requests (e.g., to pick up a paper bag in the street, to stand on the other side of a bus stop sign) that were irrelevant to a security guard's domain of authority (Bickman, 1974; Bushman, 1988). Less blatant in its connotation than a uniform, but nonetheless effective, is another kind of attire that has traditionally bespoken of authority status in our culture—the well-tailored business suit. Take as evidence the results of a study by Lefkowitz, Blake, and Mouton (1955), who found that three and a half times as many people were willing to follow a jaywalker into traffic when he wore a suit and tie versus a work shirt and trousers.

Unity

We is the shared me.

—Robert B. Cialdini

Automatically and incessantly, observers divide people into those to whom the pronoun "we" does and does not apply. The implications for compliance are great because, inside the former category, everything influence-related is easier to achieve. Ingroup members get more agreement (Stallen, Smidts, & Sanfey, 2013), trust (Foddy, Platow, & Yamagishi, 2009), help (Greenwald & Pettigrew, 2014), liking (Cialdini et al., 1997), cooperation (Balliet, Wu, & De Dreu, 2014), emotional support (Westmaas & Silver, 2006), forgiveness (Karremans & Aarts, 2007), and even more judged creativity (Adarves-Yorno, Haslam, & Postmes, 2008), morality (Gino & Galinsky, 2012), and humanity (Brant & Reyna, 2011). This favoritism seems not only far-ranging in its impact on human action but also primal, as it appears in other primates and spontaneously in human children as young as infants (Buttleman & Bohm, 2014; Mahajan et al., 2011). Thus, social influence is often and importantly grounded in personal relationships.

Still, a crucial question remains: What kind of relationships maximize the favorable treatment of fellow members? The answer requires a subtle but crucial distinction. The relationships that most effectively lead people to favor another are not those that allow them to say, "Oh, that person is like us." They are the ones that allow people to say, "Oh, that person is *of* us." The experience of *unity* is not about simple similarities (although those can work, too, but to a lesser degree, via the liking principle). It's about identities, shared identities. It's about the categories that individuals use to define themselves and their groups such as race, ethnicity, nationality, and family, as well as political and religious affiliations. A key characteristic of these categories is that their members feel at one with, merged with, the others. A *unity rule* for compliance can be worded as: *We are inclined to say "yes" to someone we consider one of us.*

Social scientists have uncovered two categories of factors that lead to a sense of we-ness or shared identity—those involving particular ways of being together and particular ways of acting together. Each deserves our examination.

Being together. From a genetic point of view, *kinship*—being in the same family, the same bloodline—is the ultimate form of self-other unity. Indeed, the widely accepted concept of "inclusive fitness" within evolutionary biology specifically undermines the distinction between self and genetically close others, asserting that individuals do not so much attempt to ensure their own survival as the survival of copies of their genes. The crucial implication is that the *self* in self-interest can lie outside of one's body and inside the skin of another who shares a goodly amount of genetic material. For this reason, people are particularly willing to help genetically close relatives (Curry, Roberts, & Dunbar, 2013). Brain-imaging research has identified a proximate cause: People experience unusually high stimulation in the reward centers of their brains after aiding a family member; it's as if, by doing so, they are aiding themselves (Telzer et al., 2010).

Besides family ties, there is another usually reliable cue of heightened genetic commonality. It is the perception of *being of the same place* as another. Because we evolved from small but stable groupings of genetically related individuals, we have also evolved a tendency to feel *of* the people who exist in close proximity to us. Sports team championships stimulate feelings of personal pride in residents of the team's surrounding zones—as if the *residents* had won (Cialdini et al., 1976; Kwon, Trail, & Lee, 2008). In addition, we favor those in our locales. In one study, citizens agreed to participate in a survey to a greater extent if it emanated from a home-state university (Edwards, Dillman, & Smyth, 2014); in another study, readers of a news story about a military fatality in Afghanistan became more opposed to the war there upon learning that the fallen soldier was from their own state (Kriner & Shen, 2012).

People also succumb to a "local dominance effect," in which they are especially moved by the urgings of local voices (Zell & Alike, 2010). During the 2008 presidential election campaign, Obama officials made strategic use of this effect by encouraging pro-Obama door-to-door and phone volunteers to employ scripts describing their local credentials (Masket, 2009).

Acting together. All human societies have developed ways to respond together, in unison or synchrony, inside songs, marches, rituals, chants, prayers, and dances. What's more, they've been doing so since prehistoric times. The behavioral science record is clear as to why. When people act in unitary ways, they become unit*ized* (Paladino et al., 2010). The effects are similar to those encountered in our coverage of common kinship and place—feelings of self-other merger (we-ness), and consequent supportiveness (Wheatley et al., 2012).

The feeling of becoming merged with others through coordinated activity can be produced easily. In one set of studies, participants played a game in which to win money they were required to make either the same choice as their partner or a different choice. Compared to the participants who had to win by mismatching choices, those who had to win by matching choices with their partner came to see that individual as significantly more comparable to them. There was something about performing in exactly the same way as another person that led to greater perceived alikeness (Able & Stasser, 2008). Moreover, when people act in unison, they not only see themselves as more alike, they also evaluate one another more positively afterward; their elevated lik*eness* turns into elevated lik*ing*, which turns into elevated cooperation and support (Wheatley et al., 2012; Wiltermuth & Heath, 2009).

There's another form of collaborative action that leads to unitization—*co-creation*. Companies often try to get consumers bonded with their brands by inviting them to co-create novel or updated products and services, most often by providing ongoing feedback to the company. But there is a specific form that consumers' input must take to produce optimal bonding to the brand: It must be offered as *advice* regarding the company's offerings, not as *opinions* about its offerings. Why? Because providing advice puts a person in a merging state of mind, which stimulates a linking of one's own identity with another party's. Providing an opinion, on the other hand, puts a person in a self-focused, introspective state of mind that is less likely to produce bonding.

That's what happened to online survey-takers from around the U.S. who were shown a description of the business plan for a new restaurant. All survey participants were asked for their feedback—but some for any "advice" they might have, whereas others for any "opinions" they might have regarding the restaurant. Finally, they indicated how likely they'd be to patronize the restaurant. Those participants who provided advice reported wanting to visit the restaurant significantly more than participants who provided opinions. And, just as would be expected if giving advice is indeed a mechanism of unitization, the increased desire to support the restaurant came from feeling more personally linked to the brand (Liu & Gal, 2011).

Social Influence Today

Whereas influencing behavior through social factors—social influence—is distinctly different from influencing behavior through economic factors, social influence today is increasingly characterized by approaches that use combinations of social and economic factors. For example, a recent study found that providing small financial incentives was more effective than using social factors (providing information pertaining to social proof) at motivating customers to write an online review after purchasing a product (Burtch, Hong, Bapna, & Griskevicius, 2017). However, the reviews stimulated by financial incentives tended to be brief and not very useful. Instead, providing social proof information motivated customers to write longer and more informative reviews compared to when they were provided only with financial incentives. While using either social proof or small financial incentives proved to be suboptimal for different reasons, the approach that yielded the greatest overall benefit was using a *combination* of social proof and small financial incentives, which produced the largest number and the greatest length of reviews. Future research is poised to examine how social influence can work in concert with other types of incentives to influence behavior in optimal ways.

Also, although much research has documented *which* social influences are most effective, much less attention has been paid to *when* those influences are most effective. We expect future research to demonstrate the importance of timing within the influence process. For example, because the previously described seven principles of influence often operate as behavioral heuristics—single-factor rules of thumb that typically inform individuals of when to act correctly—we believe the principles will be most often followed under circumstances that favor heuristic rather than fully considered decision-making (Chaiken, 1987; Kahneman, 2011; also see Chapter 6). That is, people will most likely respond to these principles when they have first come to feel unable or unmotivated to perform a deliberative analysis of all relevant factors and will rely on a normally reliable single factor (Petty & Cacioppo, 1986). Owing to the accelerating pace and complexity of today's world, we anticipate progressively more such heuristic responding as people increasingly feel unsure, rushed, overloaded, preoccupied, indifferent, stressed, or distracted whenever encountering an influence attempt.

Finally, besides the impact of such naturally existing prior life conditions on the influence process, we think researchers are also likely to document the impact of situationally placed prior conditions on the process. There is growing evidence that savvy communicators can greatly affect their success not just by what they put into their messages but, as well, by what they put into the moment just before they send those messages—an approach called *pre-suasion* (Cialdini, 2016). The claim is: To change recipients' minds optimally, one should first change their states of mind. This is accomplished by using devices (cognitive sets, primes, frames, or anchors) to *ready* recipients for an influence attempt and, thereby, to make them sympathetic to a message before they experience it.

Support for the contentions comes from both influence scientists and influence practitioners. In the first case, consider the results of studies showing that the effect a social proof message for a museum ("Visited by over a Million People Each Year") was significantly enhanced by initially showing recipients a scary movie. Why? Because when people are in a frightened state of mind, they are particularly likely to seek the safety provided by the crowd (Griskevicius et al., 2009). In the domain of marketing practice, consider what happened in 2016 when Royal Caribbean International Cruise Lines offered a scarcity-based promotion to its customers—a deal that had a dwindling, limited time character. Half of the customers learned of the offer in an email that had a pair of ticking clock emojis in the subject line; the other half received the same scarcity-based offer but without the emojis. Remarkably, although only 3% more customers who saw the emojis opened the email, 15% more of those who did then clicked through the message to be able to purchase the deal. Why? Because, according to the marketers, the scarcity-based emojis put customers in mind of the principle of scarcity, which primed them for the scarcity appeal before they experienced it. As a result, the pre-suasive approach "created a several hundred percent increase in revenue" (BEHAVE, 2016). Outcomes such as these suggest a worthwhile direction for future investigation.

Summary

At the outset of this chapter, it was suggested that an important question for anyone interested in understanding, resisting, or harnessing the process of interpersonal influence is, "Which are the most powerful principles that motivate us to comply with another's request?" It was also suggested that one way to assess such power would be to examine the practices of commercial compliance professionals for their pervasiveness. That is, if compliance practitioners made widespread use of certain principles, this would be evidence for the natural power of these principles to affect everyday compliance. Seven psychological principles emerged as the most popular in the repertoires of the compliance pros: reciprocity, social proof, consistency, liking, scarcity, authority, and unity. Close examination of the principles revealed broad professional usage that could be validated and explained by controlled experimental research. As with most research perspectives, additional work needs to be done before we can have high levels of confidence in the conclusions. However, there is considerable evidence at this juncture to indicate that these principles engage central features of the human condition in the process of motivating compliance.

Suggestions for Further Reading

Burger, J. M. (2009). Replicating Milgram: Would people still obey today? *American Psychologist, 64,* 1–11.

Cialdini, R. B. (2008). *Influence: Science and practice* (5th ed.). Boston, MA: Allyn & Bacon.

Cialdini, R. B. (2016). *Pre-suasion: A revolutionary way to influence and persuade.* New York, NY: Simon & Schuster.

Cialdini, R. B., & Goldstein, N. J. (2004). Social influence: Compliance and conformity. *Annual Review of Psychology, 55,* 591–621.

Garner, R. (2005). Post-It Note persuasion: A sticky influence. *Journal of Consumer Psychology, 15,* 230–237.

Goldstein, N. J., Cialdini, R. B., & Griskevicius, V. (2008). A room with a viewpoint: Using social norms to motivate environmental conservation in hotels. *Journal of Consumer Research, 35,* 472–482.

Goldstein, N. J., Martin, S., & Cialdini, R. B. (2008). *Yes! 50 scientifically proven ways to be persuasive.* New York, NY: Free Press.

Griskevicius, V., Cialdini, R. B., & Goldstein, N. J. (2008). Applying (and resisting) peer influence. *MIT/Sloan Management Review, 49,* 84–88.

Griskevicius, V., Goldstein, N. J., Mortensen, C. R., Sundie, J. M., Cialdini, R. B., & Kenrick, D. T. (2009). Fear and loving in Las Vegas: Evolution, emotion, and persuasion. *Journal of Marketing Research, 46,* 384–395.

Oriña, M. M., Wood, W., & Simpson, J. A. (2002). Strategies of influence in close relationships. *Journal of Experimental Social Psychology, 38,* 459–472.

References

Able, S., & Stasser, G. (2008). Coordination success and interpersonal perceptions: Matching versus mismatching. *Journal of Personality and Social Psychology, 95,* 576–592.

Adarves-Yorno, I., Haslam, S. A., & Postmes, T. (2008). And now for something completely different? The impact of group membership on perceptions of creativity. *Social Influence, 3,* 248–266.

Aramovich, N. P., Lytle, B. L., & Skitka, L. J. (2012). Opposing torture: Moral conviction and resistance to majority influence. *Social Influence, 7,* 21–34.

Aronson, E., Turner, J. A., & Carlsmith, J. M. (1963). Communicator credibility and communication discrepancy as a determinant of opinion change. *Journal of Abnormal and Social Psychology, 67*, 31–36.

Asch, S. E. (1956). Studies of independence and conformity: I. A minority of one against a unanimous majority. *Psychological Monographs, 70*(9), 1–70.

Balliet, D., Wu, J., & De Dreu, C. K. W. (2014). Ingroup favoritism in cooperation: A meta-analysis. *Psychological Bulletin, 140*, 1556–1581.

Bandura, A., & Menlove, F. L. (1968). Factors determining vicarious extinction of avoidance behavior through symbolic modeling. *Journal of Personality and Social Psychology, 8*, 99–108.

Baumeister, R. F. (1982). A self-presentational view of social phenomena. *Psychological Bulletin, 91*, 3–26.

Baumeister, R. F., & Leary, M. R. (1995). The need to belong: Desire for interpersonal attachments as a fundamental human motivation. *Psychological Bulletin, 177*, 497–529.

BEHAVE (2016). Which subject line drove increased engagement? Retrieved from https://www.behave.org/case-study/subject-line-drove-increased-engagement/

Bickman, L. (1974). The social power of a uniform. *Journal of Applied Social Psychology, 4*, 47–61.

Blass, T. (2004). The man who shocked the world: The life and legacy of Stanley Milgram. New York, NY: Basic Books.

Brandt, M. J., & Reyna, C. (2011). The chain of being: A hierarchy of morality. *Perspectives on Psychological Science, 6*, 428–446.

Brehm, S. S. (1981). Psychological reactance and the attractiveness of unattainable objects: Sex differences in children's responses to an elimination of freedom. *Sex Roles, 7*, 937–949.

Brock, T. C. (1968). Implications of commodity theory for value change. In A. G. Greenwald, T. C. Brock, & T. M. Ostrom (Eds.), *Psychological foundations of attitudes*. New York, NY: Academic Press.

Brock, T. C., & Bannon, L. A. (1992). Liberalization of commodity theory. *Basic and Applied Social Psychology, 13*, 135–143.

Brown, J. L., Drake, K. D., & Wellman, L. (2015). The benefits of a relational approach to corporate political activity: Evidence from political contributions to tax policymakers. *Journal of the American Taxation Association, 37*, 69–102.

Brown, M. (2008, January 17). Montana high school cancels climate speech. *MiamiHerald.com*. Retrieved from http://www.miamiherald.com/news/nation/AP/story/383710.

Burger, J. M. (1999). The foot-in-the-door compliance procedure: A multiple-process analysis and review. *Personality and Social Psychology Review, 3*, 303–325.

Burger, J. M. (2009). Replicating Milgram: Would people still obey today? *American Psychologist, 64*, 1–11.

Burger, J. M., & Caldwell, D. C. (2003). The effects of monetary incentives and labeling on the foot-in-the-door effect: Evidence for a self-perception process. *Basic and Applied Social Psychology, 25*, 235–241.

Burger, J. M., & Caputo, D. (2015). The low-ball compliance procedure: A meta-analysis. *Social Influence, 10*, 1–7.

Burger, J. M., & Guadagno, R. E. (2003). Self-concept clarity and the foot-in-the-door procedure. *Basic and Applied Social Psychology, 25*, 79–86.

Burger, J. M., Messian, N., Patel, S., del Prado, A., & Anderson, C. (2004). What a coincidence! The effects of incidental similarity on compliance. *Personality and Social Psychology Bulletin, 30*, 35–43.

Burger, J. M., Sanchez, J., Imberi, J. E., & Grande, L. R. (2009). The norm of reciprocity as an internalized social norm: Returning favors even when no one finds out. *Social Influence, 4*, 11–17.

Burgoon, M., Alvaro, E., Grandpre, J., & Voulodakis, M. (2002). Revisiting the theory of psychological reactance. In J. P. Dillard and M. Pfau (Eds.), *The persuasion handbook: Theory and practice* (pp. 213–232). Thousand Oaks, CA: SAGE.

Burtch, G., Hong, Y., Bapna, R., & Griskevicius, V. (2017). Stimulating online reviews by combining financial incentives and social norms. *Management Science, 64*, 1975–2471.

Bushman, B. A. (1988). The effects of apparel on compliance. *Personality and Social Psychology Bulletin, 14*, 459–467.

Buttleman, D., & Bohm, R. (2014). The ontogeny of the motivation that underlies in-group bias. *Psychological Science, 25*, 921–927.

Cai, H., Chen, Y., & Fang, H. (2009). Observational learning: Evidence from a randomized natural field experiment. *American Economic Review, 99,* 864–882.

Carli, L. L., Ganley, R., & Pierce-Otay, A. (1991). Similarity and satisfaction in roommate relationships. *Personality and Social Psychology Bulletin, 17,* 419–426.

Cavicchio, F., Melcher, D., & Poesio, M. (2014). The effect of linguistic and visual salience in visual world studies. *Frontiers in Psychology, 5,* art. 176. http://www.doi.org/10.3389/fpsyg.2014.00176

Chaiken, S. (1979). Communicator physical attractiveness and persuasion. *Journal of Personality and Social Psychology, 37,* 1387–1397.

Chaiken, S. (1987). The heuristic model of persuasion. In M. P. Zanna, J. Olson, & C. P. Herman (Eds.), *Social influence: The Ontario symposium* (Vol. 5, pp. 3–39). Hillsdale, NJ: Erlbaum.

Cialdini, R. B. (2003). Crafting normative messages to protect the environment. *Current Directions in Psychological Science, 12,* 105–109.

Cialdini, R. B. (2008). *Influence: Science and practice* (5th ed.). Boston, MA: Allyn & Bacon.

Cialdini, R. B. (2016). *Pre-suasion: A revolutionary way to influence and persuade.* New York, NY: Simon & Schuster.

Cialdini, R. B., & Ascani, K. (1976). Test of a concession procedure for inducing verbal, behavioral, and further compliance with a request to give blood. *Journal of Applied Psychology, 61,* 295–300.

Cialdini, R. B., Borden, R. J., Thorne, A., Walker, M., Freeman, S., & Sloan, L. (1976). Basking in reflected glory: Three (football) field studies. *Journal of Personality and Social Psychology, 34,* 366–375.

Cialdini, R.B., Brown, S.L., Lewis, B.P., Luce, C., & Neuberg, S.L. (1997). Reinterpreting the empathy-altruism relationship: When one into one equals oneness. *Journal of Personality and Social Psychology, 73,* 481–494.

Cialdini, R. B., Cacioppo, J. T., Bassett, R., & Miller, J. A. (1978). Low-ball procedure for producing compliance: Commitment then cost. *Journal of Personality and Social Psychology, 36,* 463–476.

Cialdini, R. B., & Goldstein, N. J. (2004). Social influence: Compliance and conformity. *Annual Review of Psychology, 55,* 591–621.

Cialdini, R. B., Reno, R. R., & Kallgren, C. A. (1990). A focus theory of normative conduct: Recycling the concept of norms to reduce littering in public places. *Journal of Personality and Social Psychology, 58,* 1015–1026.

Cialdini, R. B., & Schroeder, D. A. (1976). Increasing compliance by legitimizing paltry contributions: When even a penny helps. *Journal of Personality and Social Psychology, 34,* 599–604.

Cialdini, R. B., Vincent, J. E., Lewis, S. K., Catalan, J., Wheeler, D., & Darby, B. L. (1975). Reciprocal concessions procedure for inducing compliance: The door-in-the-face technique. *Journal of Personality and Social Psychology, 31,* 206–215.

Clifford, S., & Jerit, J. (2016). Cheating on political knowledge questions in online surveys. *Public Opinion Quarterly, 80,* 858–887.

Crivelli, C., & Fridlund, A. J. (2018). Facial displays are tools for social influence. *Trends in Cognitive Sciences, 22,* 388–399.

Cruwys, T., Bevelander, K. E., & Hermans, R. C. J. (2015). Social modeling of eating: When and why social influence affects food intake and choice. *Appetite, 86,* 3–18.

Curry, O., Roberts, S. G., & Dunbar, R. I. M. (2013). Altruism in social networks: Evidence for a "kinship premium." *British Journal of Psychology, 104,* 283–295.

Darley, J. M., & Latane, B. (1970). Norms and normative behavior: Field studies of social interdependence. In J. Macaulay & L. Berkowitz (Eds.), *Altruism and helping behavior* (pp. 83–102). New York, NY: Academic Press.

Dolinski, D. (2000). On inferring one's beliefs from one's attempt and consequences for subsequent compliance. *Journal of Personality and Social Psychology, 78,* 260–272.

Dolinski, D., Grzyb, T., Folwarczny, M., Grzybala, P., Krzyszycha, K, Martynowska, K., & Trojanowski, J. (2015). Would you deliver an electric shock in 2015? Obedience in the experimental paradigm developed by Stanley Milgram in the 50 years following the original studies. *Social Psychological and Personality Science, 8,* 927–933.

Drachman, D., DeCarufel, A., & Insko, C. (1978). The extra credit effect in interpersonal attraction. *Journal of Experimental Social Psychology 14*, 458–469.

Dunfield, K. A., & Kuhlmeier, V. A. (2010). Intention-mediated selective helping in infancy. *Psychological Science, 21*, 523–527.

Eastwick, P. W., & Gardner, W. I. (2009). Is it just a game? Evidence for social influence in the virtual world. *Social Influence, 4*, 18–32.

Edwards, M. L., Dillman, D. A., & Smyth, J. D. (2014). An experimental test of the effects of survey sponsorship on Internet and mail survey response. *Public Opinion Quarterly, 78*, 734–750.

Eisenberg, N. E., Cialdini, R. B., McCreath, H., & Shell, R. (1987). Consistency-based compliance: When and why do children become vulnerable? *Journal of Personality and Social Psychology, 52*, 1174–1181.

Ekman, P. (1972). Universal and cultural differences in facial expressions of emotion. In J. R. Cole (Ed.), *Nebraska Symposium on Motivation* (Vol. 19, pp. 207–283). Lincoln, NE: Nebraska University Press.

Ekman, P. (2017). Facial expressions. In J. M. Fernandez-Dols & J. A. Russell (Eds.), *The Science of Facial Expression* (pp. 39–56). Oxford, England: Oxford University Press.

Emswiller, T., Deaux, K., & Willits, J. E. (1971). Similarity, sex, and requests for small favors. *Journal of Applied Social Psychology, 1*, 284–291.

Festinger, L. (1954). A theory of social comparison processes. *Human Relations, 7*, 117–140.

Festinger, L. (1957). *A theory of cognitive dissonance*. Stanford, CA: Stanford University Press.

Foddy, M., Platow, M. J., & Yamagishi, T. (2009). Group-based trust in strangers. *Psychological Science, 20*, 419–422.

Freedman, J. L., & Fraser, S. C. (1966). Compliance without pressure: The foot-in-the-door technique. *Journal of Personality and Social Psychology, 4*, 195–203.

Frenzen, J. R., & Davis, H. L. (1990). Purchasing behavior in embedded markets. *Journal of Consumer Research, 17*, 1–12.

Gino, F., & Galinsky, A. D. (2012). Vicarious dishonesty: When psychological closeness creates distance from one's moral compass. *Organizational Behavior and Human Decision Processes, 119*, 15–26.

Gintis, H., Bowles, S., Boyd, R., & Fehr, E. (2003). Explaining altruistic behavior in humans. *Evolution and Human Behavior, 24*, 153–172.

Goldstein, N. J., Cialdini, R. B., & Griskevicius, V. (2008). A room with a viewpoint: Using social norms to motivate environmental conservation in hotels. *Journal of Consumer Research, 35*, 472–482.

Goldstein, N. J., Griskevicius, V., & Cialdini, R. B. (2011). Reciprocity by proxy: Harnessing the power of obligation to foster cooperation. *Administrative Science Quarterly, 56*, 441–473.

Goldstein, N. J., Martin, S., & Cialdini, R. B. (2008). *Yes! 50 scientifically proven ways to be persuasive*. New York: Free Press.

Gonzales, M. H., Aronson, E., & Costanzo, M. (1988). Increasing the effectiveness of energy auditors: A field experiment. *Journal of Applied Social Psychology, 18*, 1046–1066.

Gordon, R. A. (1996). Impact of ingratiation on judgments and evaluations: a meta-analytic investigation. *Journal of Personality and Social Psychology, 71*, 54–70.

Gouldner, A. W. (1960). The norm of reciprocity: A preliminary statement. *American Sociological Review, 25*, 161–178.

Grant, A., & Dutton, J. (2012). Beneficiary or benefactor: Are people more prosocial when they reflect on receiving or giving? *Psychological Science, 23*, 1033–1039.

Greenwald, A. G., & Pettigrew, T. F. (2014). With malice toward none and charity for some. *American Psychologist, 69*, 669–684.

Griskevicius, V., Cialdini, R. B., & Goldstein, N. J. (2008). Applying (and resisting) peer influence. *MIT/Sloan Management Review, 49*, 84–88.

Griskevicius, V., Goldstein, N. J., Mortensen, C. R., Sundie, J. M., Cialdini, R. B., & Kenrick, D. T. (2009). Fear and loving in Las Vegas: Evolution, emotion, and persuasion. *Journal of Marketing Research, 46*, 384–395.

Gueguen, N., Pascual, A., & Dagot, L. (2002). Lowball and compliance to a request: An application in a field setting. *Psychological Reports, 91*, 81–84.

Harari, H., Mohdr, D., & Hosey, K. (1980). Faculty helpfulness to students: A comparison of compliance techniques. *Personality and Social Psychology Bulletin, 6,* 373–377.

Heider, F. (1958). *The psychology of interpersonal relations.* New York, NY: Wiley.

Higgs, S. (2015). Social norms and their influence on eating behaviours. *Appetite, 86,* 38–44.

Hobofoll, S. E. (2001). The influence of culture, community, and the nested-self in the stress process. *Applied Psychology, 50,* 337–421.

Hofling, C. K., Brotzman, E., Dalrymple, S., Graves, N., & Pierce, C. M. (1966). An experimental study of nurse-physician relationships. *Journal of Nervous and Mental Disease, 143,* 171–180.

Howard, D. J., Gengler, C. E., & Jain, A. (1995). What's in a name? A complimentary means of persuasion. *Journal of Consumer Research, 22,* 200–211.

Howard, D. J., Gengler, C. E., & Jain, A. (1997). The name remembrance effect: A test of alternative explanations. *Journal of Social Behavior and Personality, 12,* 801–810.

Inman, J. J., Peter, A. C., & Raghubir, P. (1997). Framing the deal: The role of restrictions in accentuating deal value. *Journal of Consumer Research, 24,* 68–79.

Jones, E. E., & Wortman, C. (1973). *Ingratiation: An attributional approach.* Morristown, NJ: General Learning.

Jones, J. T., Pelham, B. W., Carvallo, M., & Mirenberg, M. C. (2004). How do I love three? Let me count the Js: Implicit egoism and interpersonal attraction. *Journal of Personality and Social Psychology, 87,* 665–683.

Joule, R. V., Gouilloux, F., & Weber, F. (1989). The lure: A new compliance procedure. *Journal of Social Psychology, 129,* 741–749.

Kahneman, D. (2011). *Thinking, fast and slow.* New York, NY: Farrar, Straus, and Giroux.

Karremans, J. C., & Aarts, H. (2007). The role of automaticity in determining the inclination to forgive close others. *Journal of Experimental Social Psychology, 43,* 902–917.

Kenrick, D. T., Griskevicius, V., Neuberg, S. L., & Schaller, M. (2010). Renovating the pyramid of needs: Contemporary extensions built upon ancient foundations. *Perspectives on Psychological Science, 5,* 292–314.

Ketelaar, T. (1995). *Emotions as mental representations of gains and losses: Translating prospect theory into positive and negative affect.* Paper presented at the meeting of the American Psychological Society, New York.

Knishinsky, A. (1982). *The effects of scarcity of material and exclusivity of information on industrial buyer perceived risk in provoking a purchase decision.* Unpublished doctoral dissertation. Arizona State University, Tempe.

Kriner, D. L., & Shen, F. X. (2012). How citizens respond to combat casualties: The differential impact of local casualties on support for the war in Afghanistan. *Public Opinion Quarterly, 76,* 761–770.

Kwon, H. H., Trail, G. T., & Lee, D. H. (2008). The effects of vicarious achievement and team identification on BIRGing and CORFing. *Sport Marketing Quarterly, 17,* 209–217.

Lammers, H. B. (1991). The effect of free samples on immediate consumer purchase. *Journal of Consumer Marketing, 8,* 31–37.

Lee, S., Moon, S-I., & Feeley, T. H. (2016). A meta-analytic review of the legitimation of paltry favors compliance strategy. *Psychological Reports, 118,* 748–771.

Lefkowitz, M., Blake, R. R., & Mouton, J. S. (1955). Status factors in pedestrian violation of traffic signals. *Journal of Abnormal and Social Psychology, 51,* 704–706.

Liu, W., & Gal, D. (2011). Bringing us together or driving us apart: The effect of soliciting consumer input on consumers' propensity to transact with an organization. *Journal of Consumer Research, 38,* 242–259.

Lokhorst, A. M., Werner, C., Staats, H., van Dijk, & Gale, J. L. (2013). Commitment and behavior change: A meta-analysis and critical review or commitment-making strategies in environmental research. *Environment and Behavior, 45,* 3–34.

Lynn, M. (1991). Scarcity effects on value. *Psychology and Marketing, 8,* 43–57.

Lynn, M. (1992). Scarcity's enhancement of desirability. *Basic and Applied Social Psychology, 13,* 67–78.

Lynn, M., & Simons, T. (2000). Predictors of male and female servers' average tip earnings. *Journal of Applied Social Psychology, 30,* 241–252

Maddux, W. W., Mullen, E., & Galinsky, A. D. (2008). Chameleons bake bigger pies and take bigger pieces: Strategic behavioral mimicry facilitates negotiation outcomes. *Journal of Experimental Social Psychology, 44,* 461–468.

Mahajan, N., Martinez, M. A., Gutierrez, N. L., Diesendruck, G., Banaji, M. R., & Santos, L. R. (2011). The evolution of intergroup bias: Perceptions and attitudes in Rhesus Macaques. *Journal of Personality and Social Psychology, 100,* 387–405.

Masket, S. E. (2009). Did Obama's ground game matter? The influence of local field offices during the 2008 presidential election. *Public Opinion Quarterly, 73,* 1023–1039.

McCall, M. (1997). Physical attractiveness and access to alcohol: What is beautiful does not get carded. *Journal of Applied Social Psychology, 27,* 453–462.

McKensie, C. R. M., & Chase, V. M. (2010). Why rare things are precious: The importance of rarity in lay inference. In P. M. Todd, G. Gigerenzer, & the ABC Research Group (Eds.), *Ecological rationality: Intelligence in the world.* Oxford, England: Oxford University Press.

Milgram, S. (1974). *Obedience to authority.* New York, NY: Harper & Row.

Milgram, S., Bickman, L., & Berkowitz, L. (1969). Note on the drawing power of crowds of different size. *Journal of Personality and Social Psychology, 13,* 79–82.

Newcomb, T. (1953). An approach to the study of communicative acts. *Psychological Review, 60,* 393–404.

Nolan, J. P., Schultz, P. W., Cialdini, R. B., Goldstein, N. J., & Griskevicius, V. (2008). Normative social influence is underdetected. *Personality and Social Psychology Bulletin, 34,* 913–923.

O'Keefe, D. J., & Hale, S. L. (1998). The door-in-the-face influence strategy: A random-effects meta-analytic review. In M. E. Roloff (Ed.), *Communication yearbook* (pp. 1–33). Thousand Oaks, CA: SAGE.

O'Keefe, D. J., & Hale, S. L. (2001). An odds-ratio-based meta-analysis of research on the door-in-the-face influence strategy. *Communication Reports,14,* 31–38.

Palidino, M-P, Mazzurega, M., Pavani, F., & Schubert, T. W. (2010). Synchronous multisensory stimulation blurs self-other boundaries. *Psychological Science, 21,* 1202–1207.

Park, J. H., & Schaller, M. (2005). Does attitude similarity serve as a heuristic cue for kinship? Evidence of an implicit cognitive association. *Evolution and Human Behavior, 26,* 158–170.

Pascual, A., & Guegen, N. (2005). Foot-in-the-door and door-in-the-face: A comparative meta-analytic study. *Psychological Reports, 91,* 122–128.

Pelham, B. W., Mirenberg, M. C., & Jones, J. T. (2002). Why Susie sells seashells by the seashore: Implicit egoism and major life decisions. *Journal of Personality and Social Psychology, 82,* 469–487.

Petty, R. E., & Cacioppo, J. T. (1986). *Communication and persuasion: Central and peripheral routes to attitude change.* New York, NY: Springer-Verlag.

Phillips, D. P., & Carstensen, L. L. (1988). The effect of suicide stories on various demographic groups, 1968–1985. *Suicide and Life-Threatening Behavior, 18,* 100–114.

Platow, M. J., Haslam, S. A., Both, B., Chew, I., Cuddon, M., Goharpey, N., . . . Grace, D. M. (2005). "It's not funny if *they're* laughing": Self-categorization, social influence, and responses to canned laughter. *Journal of Experimental Social Psychology, 41,* 542–550.

Provine, R. (2000). *Laughter: A scientific investigation.* New York, NY: Viking.

Reingen, P. H. (1978). On inducing compliance with requests. *Journal of Consumer Research, 5,* 96–102.

Reingen, P. H. (1982). Test of a list procedure for inducing compliance with a request to donate money. *Journal of Applied Psychology, 67,* 110–118.

Schultz, P. W., Nolan, J. P., Cialdini, R. B., Goldstein, N. J., & Griskevicius, V. (2007). The constructive, destructive, and reconstructive power of social norms. *Psychological Science, 18,* 429–434.

Semin, G. R. (2012). The linguistic category model. In P. A. M. Van Lange, A. Kruglanski, & E. T. Higgins (Eds.), *Handbook of theories of social psychology.* (Vol. 1, pp. 309–326) London, England: SAGE.

Semin, G. R., & Fiedler, K. (1988). The cognitive functions of linguistic categories in describing persons: Social cognition and language. *Journal of Personality and Social Psychology, 54,* 558–568.

Sharot, T., Fleming, S. M., Yu, X., Koster, R., & Dolan, R. J. (2012). Is choice-induced preference change long lasting? *Psychological Science, 23,* 1123–1129.

Singer, E., Van Hoewyk, J., & Maher, M. P. (2000). Experiments with incentives in telephone surveys. *Public Opinion Quarterly, 64,* 171–188.

Smolowe, J. (1990, November 26). Contents require immediate attention. *Time,* p. 64.

Stallen, M., Smidts, A., & Sanfey, A. G. (2013). Peer influence: neural mechanisms underlying in-group conformity. *Frontiers in Human Neuroscience, 7,* art. 50. http://www.doi.org/10.3389/fnhum.2013.00050

Strohmetz, D. B., Rind, B., Fisher, R., & Lynn, M. (2002). Sweetening the till: The use of candy to increase restaurant tipping. *Journal of Applied Social Psychology, 32,* 300–309.

Sundie, J. M., Cialdini, R. B., Griskevicius, V., & Kenrick, D. T. (2006). In M. Schaller, J. A. Simpson, & D. T. Kenrick (Eds.), *Evolutionary social influence* (pp. 287–316). New York, NY: Psychology Press.

Surowiecki, J. (2005). *The wisdom of crowds.* New York, NY: Doubleday Press.

Telzer, E. H., Masten, C. L., Berkman, E. T., Lieberman, M. D., & Fuligni, A. J. (2010). Gaining while giving: An fMRI study of the rewards of family assistance among White and Latino youth. *Social Neuroscience, 5,* 508–518.

Tversky, A. & Kahneman, D. (1981). The framing of decisions and psychology of choice. *Science, 211,* 453–458.

van Baaren, R. B., Holland, R. W., Steenaert, B., & van Knippenberg, A. (2003). Mimicry for money: Behavioral consequences of imitation. *Journal of Experimental Social Psychology, 39,* 393–398.

van der Werff, E., Steg, L., & Keizer, K. (2014). Follow the signal: When past pro-environmental actions signal who you are. *Journal of Environmental Psychology, 40,* 273–282.

Vonk, R. (2002). Self-serving interpretations of flattery: Why ingratiation works. *Journal of Personality and Social Psychology, 82,* 515–526.

West, S. G., (1975). Increasing the attractiveness of college cafeteria food. *Journal of Applied Psychology, 10,* 656–658.

Westmaas, J. L., & Silver, R. C. (2006). The role of perceived similarity in supportive responses to victims of negative life events. *Personality and Social Psychology Bulletin, 32,* 1537–1546.

Whatley, M. A., Webster, M. J., Smith, R. H., & Rhodes, A. (1999). The effect of a favor on public and private compliance: How internalized is the norm of reciprocity? *Basic and Applied Social Psychology, 21,* 251–259.

Wheatley, T., Kang, O., Parkinson, C., & Looser, C. E. (2012). From mind perception to mental connection: Synchrony as a mechanism for social understanding. *Social and Personality Compass, 68,* 589–606.

Wiltermuth, S. S., & Heath, C. (2009). Synchrony and cooperation. *Psychological Science, 20,* 1–5.

Worchel, S. (1992). Beyond a commodity theory analysis of censorship: When abundance and personalism enhance scarcity effects. *Basic and Applied Social Psychology, 13,* 79–93.

Worchel, S., Arnold, S. E., & Baker, M. (1975). The effect of censorship on attitude change: The influence of censor and communicator characteristics. *Journal of Applied Social Psychology, 5,* 222–239.

Zell, E., & Alicke, M. D. (2010). The local dominance effect in self-evaluations: Evidence and explanations. *Personality and Social Psychology Bulletin, 14,* 368–384.

Zitek, E. M., & Hebl, M. R. (2007). The role of social norm clarity in the influenced expression of prejudice over time. *Journal of Experimental Social Psychology, 43,* 867–876.

Chapter 8

Aggression

Brad J. Bushman

The human failing I would most like to correct is aggression. It may have had survival advantage in caveman days, to get more food, territory or a partner with whom to reproduce, but now it threatens to destroy us all.

—Stephen Hawking (cited in Clark, 2015)

In the world today, aggression and violence seem far too normal and common place. Globally, almost half a million people are murdered each year, and millions more suffer violence-related injuries (World Health Organization, 2017). Violence has been compared to a contagious disease that spreads from person to person (Patel, Simon, & Taylor, 2013).

American actor and director Edward James Olmos noted, "Education is the vaccine for violence." In this chapter, I will attempt to educate readers about aggression and violence and how to reduce it. First, I define the terms *aggression* and *violence*. Second, I describe different theoretical explanations for aggression. Third, I describe several individual risk factors for aggression and violence. Fourth, I describe several contextual risk factors for aggression and violence. Fifth, I describe internal states related to aggression. Sixth, I discuss biases related to hostile appraisals. Finally, I discuss different approaches for reducing aggression and violence.

Aggression and Violence Defined

In sports and in business, the term *aggressive* is frequently used when the terms *assertive, enthusiastic,* or *confident* would be more accurate. For example, an aggressive salesperson is one who tries really hard to sell you something. However, the salesperson is not trying to harm you. In social psychology, the term *aggression* is generally defined as any behavior that is intended to harm another person who does not want to be harmed (e.g., Baron & Richardson, 1994). This definition contains four important features. First, aggression is an external behavior that you can see. For example, you can see a person hit someone, curse someone, or try to destroy someone's reputation by spreading gossip. (These behaviors represent different forms of aggression, which I discuss in the next section.) Aggression is not an emotion that occurs inside a person, such as an angry feeling. Aggression is not a thought that occurs inside someone's brain, such as mentally rehearsing a murder one would like to commit. Second, aggression is a social behavior because it involves at least two people. Third, aggression is intentional, not accidental. However, not all intentional behaviors that hurt others are aggressive behaviors. For example, a dentist might intentionally give a patient a shot of Novocain (and the shot hurts!), but the goal is to help rather than hurt the patient. Fourth, the victim wants to avoid the harm. Thus, again, the dental patient is excluded, because he or she is not seeking to avoid the harm (in fact, the patient probably booked the appointment weeks in advance and paid to have it done!). Suicide would also be excluded, because the person who commits suicide does not want to avoid the harm. Sado-masochism would likewise be excluded, because the masochist enjoy being harmed by the sadist.

Social psychologists and laypeople also differ in their use of the term *violence*. A meteorologist might call a storm "violent" if it has intense winds, rain, thunder, and lightning. In social psychology, *violence* is aggression that has extreme physical harm, such as injury or death, as its goal (Bushman & Huesmann, 2010). For example, intentionally hitting, kicking, shooting, or stabbing another person is an act of violence. Violence is a subset of aggression. All violent acts are aggressive, but not all aggressive acts are violent. The US Federal Bureau of Investigation (FBI) classifies four crimes as violent: murder, assault, rape, and robbery. Social psychologists would also classify other physically aggressive acts as violent even if they do not meet the FBI definition of a violent crime, such as getting in a fist fight with someone. But a husband who screams and swears at his wife would not be committing an act of violence by this definition.

Forms and Functions of Aggression

Different Forms of Aggression: Physical/Verbal, Direct/Indirect, Passive/Active, Relational, and Displaced Aggression

It is useful to distinguish between forms and functions of aggression. By *forms*, I mean how the aggressive behavior is expressed. Some common forms of aggression are physical versus verbal, direct versus indirect, and active versus passive (Buss, 1961). *Physical aggression* involves harming others with body parts or weapons (e.g., hitting, kicking, stabbing, or shooting). *Verbal aggression* involves harming others with words (e.g., yelling, screaming, swearing, name-calling).

The different forms of aggression can be expressed directly or indirectly. With *direct aggression*, the victim is physically present. With *indirect aggression*, the victim is physically absent. For example, physical aggression can be direct (e.g., choking a person) or indirect (e.g., puncturing the tires of a person's car when he or she isn't looking). Similarly, verbal aggression can be direct (e.g., cursing a person face to face) or indirect (e.g., spreading rumors about a person who is not present).

The form of aggression may be active or passive. With *active aggression*, the aggressor responds in a harmful manner (e.g., hitting, cursing). With *passive aggression*, the aggressor fails to respond in a helpful manner. For example, the aggressor might "forget" to deliver an important message to the person. It is more difficult to establish blame with passive aggression than with active aggression, which is a desirable feature from the aggressor's perspective.

Direct and active forms of aggression can be quite risky, leading to injury or even death. Thus, most people would rather use indirect and passive forms of aggression.

Other scholars have proposed other forms of aggression, namely, relational aggression and displaced aggression. *Relational aggression* (also called *social aggression*) is defined as intentionally harming another person's social relationships, feelings of acceptance by others, or inclusion within a group (e.g., Crick & Grotpeter, 1995). Some examples of relational aggression include saying bad things about people behind their backs, withdrawing affection to get what you want, excluding others from your circle of friends, and giving someone the "silent treatment." Relational aggression is similar to the concept of ostracism. *Ostracism* refers to being excluded, rejected, and ignored by others (Williams, 2001). Note that the different forms of aggression can overlap. For example, spreading rumors about a person behind his or her back is an example of relational aggression as well as indirect verbal aggression.

Sometimes aggression is *displaced* against an innocent, substitute aggression (e.g., Marcus-Newhall, Pedersen, Carlson, & Miller, 2000). The substitute target has not done anything to provoke an aggressive response but just happens to be in wrong place at the wrong time. For example, a man is berated by his boss at work and "suffers in silence" rather than retaliating against his boss. When he gets home, however, the man yells at his kids instead. Sometimes the substitute target is not entirely innocent but has committed a minor or trivial offense—called *triggered displaced aggression* (Pedersen, Gonzales, & Miller, 2000). For example, perhaps the man's kids left toys in the family room rather than putting them away like he asked them to. People displace aggression for two main reasons. First, directly aggressing against the initial provoker may not be possible because the source is unavailable (e.g., the provoker has left the area) or because the source is an intangible entity (e.g., hot temperature). Second, fear of retaliation or punishment from the provoker may inhibit direct aggression. For example, the employee who was reprimanded by his boss may be reluctant to retaliate because he does not want to lose his job.

Different Functions of Aggression: Reactive and Proactive Aggression

Aggressive acts may also differ in their function. Consider two hypothetical examples. In the first example, a husband finds his wife and her secret lover together in bed. He takes his rifle from the closet and shoots and kills them both. In the second example, a "hitman" uses a rifle to kill someone for money. The form of aggression is the same in both examples—physical aggression (violence) caused by shooting and killing victims with a rifle. However, the motives appear quite different. In the first example, the husband appears to be motivated by anger. He is enraged when he finds his wife making love to another man, so he shoots them both. In the second example, the "hitman" appears to be motivated by money. The "hitman" probably does not hate his victim and probably is not angry with him. He might not even know his victim, but he kills the person anyway because he wants the money. To capture different functions or motives for aggression, researchers have distinguished between reactive aggression (also called hostile, affective, angry, impulsive, or retaliatory aggression) and proactive aggression (also called instrumental aggression; e.g., Buss, 1961; Dodge & Coie, 1987; Feshbach, 1964). *Reactive aggression* is "hot," impulsive, angry behavior that is motivated by a desire to harm someone. Harming the person is the end goal. *Proactive aggression* is "cold," premeditated, calculated behavior that is motivated by some other goal (obtaining money, restoring one's image, restoring justice). Harming the other person is a means to some other end goal. Some researchers have argued that it is difficult to distinguish between reactive and proactive aggression because they are highly correlated and because motives are often mixed (Bushman & Anderson, 2001). For example, what if the husband who finds his wife making love to another man hires a hitman to kill them both? Would this be reactive or proactive aggression?

Theoretical Approaches to the Study of Aggression

As Stephen Hawking noted at the beginning of this chapter, although aggression was adaptive for our ancient ancestors, it seems maladaptive today. Aggression breeds more aggression, and "violence begets violence" as noted by Martin Luther King Jr. This can create a destructive "downward spiral" (Slater, Henry, Swaim, & Anderson, 2003). We might therefore ask: Why do humans behave aggressively? Is it because our brains are old and the aggressive tendencies that were so useful for our ancient ancestors are difficult to override now? Is it because of biological abnormalities or poor upbringing? Is it because of frustration? In this section, we review the major psychological theories that have been proposed to understand human aggression.

Instinctive/Psychoanalytic Theories

First given scientific prominence by Darwin (1871), the instinct theory of aggression viewed aggressive behavior as motivated neither by the seeking of pleasure nor the avoidance of pain, but rather as an evolutionary adaptation that had enabled our ancient ancestors to survive better. According to this view, aggression is instinctive in humans just as it is in many other animals. Aggression has several adaptive functions, from an evolutionary perspective. Aggression helps to disperse populations over a wide area, thereby ensuring maximum use of available natural resources. Aggression helps animals to successfully compete for limited resources in their environment and, consequently, can be beneficial to their individual survival and ability to reproduce. Male animals also fight for the ability to mate with females. Thus, aggression also helps ensure that only the strongest individuals will pass their genes on to the next generation. The existence of innate, relatively automatic, aggressive responses has been demonstrated for many species (e.g., Lorenz, 1966). For example, for the male Stickleback fish, a red object triggers attack 100% of the time (Timbergen, 1952). However, no parallel innate aggressive response has been demonstrated for humans (Hinde, 1970).

Sigmund Freud (1930) wrote, "The tendency to aggression is an innate, independent, instinctual disposition in man" (p. 77). In his early writings, Sigmund Freud proposed that all human behavior stems from a life or self-preservation instinct, which he called *eros*. Freud did not acknowledge the presence of an independent instinct to explain the darker side of human nature. He wrote: "I cannot bring myself to assume the existence of a special aggressive instinct alongside the familiar instincts of self-preservation and of sex, on an equal footing with them" (Freud, 1909/1961, p. 140). The atrocities of World War I changed his mind. By 1920, Freud had proposed the existence of an independent death or self-destruction instinct, which he called *thanatos*. The life instinct supposedly counteracts the death instinct and preserves life by diverting destructive urges outward toward others in the form of aggressive acts (Freud, 1933/1950).

Frustration-Aggression Theory

In 1939, psychologists from Yale University published a seminal book titled *Frustration and Aggression* (Dollard, Doob, Miller, Mowrer, & Sears, 1939). In this book, the authors proposed that aggression results from frustration rather than from an aggressive instinct, as Freud had proposed. Frustration is an unpleasant emotion that arises when a person is being blocked from achieving a goal. The Yale scholars' theory was summarized in two bold statements: (a) "The occurrence of aggressive behavior always presupposes the existence of frustration" (p. 1), and (b) "the existence of frustration always leads to some form of aggression" (p. 1). In their view, frustration depended on an "expected" or "hoped for" goal being denied and was not simply absence of achieving a goal.

Although frustration-aggression theory seemed to explain a large amount of everyday occurrences of aggression, it soon became apparent to the authors that not every frustration led to observable aggression. Rather than discard the theory, Leonard Berkowitz (1989) revised it by proposing that all unpleasant events—instead of only frustration—deserve to be recognized as important causes of aggression. The idea is that unpleasant events (including frustrations) automatically produce a primitive fight-or-flight response. This fight-or-flight response is an adaptive stress-reducing response that occurs in humans and other animals (Cannon, 1915). Thus, anything that makes us feel bad automatically produces aggressive tendencies. Whether or not aggression occurs depends on how the unpleasant event is interpreted and on the presence of aggressive cues. For example, if a person has just seen a violent movie—and, consequently, has aggression on his or her mind—the person might respond to being pushed from behind while exiting the theater in an aggressive manner rather than by trying to flee.

Learning Theories

The earliest learning theory explanations for individual differences in aggressiveness focused on operant and classical conditioning processes. *Operant conditioning theory* proposed that people are more likely to repeat behaviors that have been rewarded and are less likely to repeat behaviors that have been punished (e.g., Ferster & Skinner, 1957; Thorndike, 1901). *Classical conditioning theory* proposed that through repeated pairing of an unconditioned stimulus with a conditioned stimulus, the unconditioned stimulus eventually elicits a response similar to the one elicited by the conditioned stimulus (e.g., Pavlov, 1927). Dogs that heard a bell (conditioned stimulus) every time they received food (unconditioned stimulus) eventually salivated when they heard the bell alone (conditioned response). Research showed that children who are reinforced for behaving aggressively learn to behave aggressively (e.g., Eron, Walder, & Lefkowitz, 1971).

By the early 1960s, however, it became clear that operant and classical conditioning processes could not fully explain individual differences in aggression. Albert Bandura theorized that people learn to behave aggressively by observing and imitating others (e.g., Bandura, 1973, 1977; Bandura, Ross, & Ross, 1961, 1963). In several classic experiments, Bandura tested his *observational learning theory* (also called *social learning theory*) by showing that young children imitated specific aggressive acts they observed in aggressive models. Bandura also developed the concept of *vicarious learning* of aggression by showing that children were especially likely to imitate models who had been rewarded for behaving aggressively (Bandura, 1965; Bandura et al., 1963). Bandura argued that the imitation was the key to social learning. The child doesn't just imitate whatever behaviors he or she observes. What is important is how the child interprets the observed behavior and how competent the child feels in carrying out the behavior (Bandura, 1986). These cognitions provide a basis for stability of behavior tendencies across a variety of situations. Watching one parent hit the other parent may not only increase a child's likelihood of hitting but may also increase the child's belief that hitting is okay when someone makes you angry.

More recent research helps us better understand observational learning processes. Human and primate young have an innate tendency to imitate what they observe (Meltzoff, 2005; Meltzoff & Moore, 1977). They imitate expressions in early infancy, and they imitate behaviors by the time they can walk. Thus, the hitting, grabbing, pushing behaviors that young children see around them or in the mass media are generally immediately mimicked unless the child has been taught not to mimic them (Bandura, 1977; Bandura et al., 1961, 1963). Furthermore, automatic imitation of expressions on others' faces can lead to the automatic activation of the emotion that the other was experiencing. For example, observing angry expressions can stimulate angry emotions in viewers (Prinz, 2005; Zajonc, Murphy, & Inglehart, 1989).

Theories Based on Physiological Arousal

Many stimuli that increase aggression (e.g., provocation, heat, media violence) also increase physiological arousal levels (e.g., heart rate, blood pressure), suggesting that arousal may have a role in stimulating aggression. But why would arousal increase aggression? There are at least four possible reasons. First, high levels of arousal may be experienced as aversive (e.g., Mendelson, Thurston, & Kubzansky, 2008) and may therefore stimulate aggression in the same way as other aversive stimuli (Berkowitz, 1989). Second, arousal narrows our span of attention (Easterbrook, 1959). If aggressive cues are salient in the situation, then people will focus most of their attention on the aggressive cues, which will facilitate aggression. Third, arousal increases the dominant response, which is defined as the most common response in that situation (Zajonc, 1965). If people are inclined to behave aggressively, they will be even more inclined to behave aggressively when aroused. Fourth, arousal may be mislabeled as anger in situations involving provocation, thus producing anger-motivated aggressive behavior. This mislabeling of arousal forms the basis of excitation-transfer theory (Zillmann, 1979, 1988). Excitation-transfer theory assumes that physiological arousal, however it is produced, dissipates slowly. If two arousing events are separated by a short amount of time, some of the arousal caused by the first event may transfer to the second event. In other words, arousal from the first event may be misattributed to the second event. If the second event increases anger, then the additional arousal should make the person even angrier. Excitation-transfer theory also suggests that anger may be extended over long periods of time, if the person attributes his or her heightened arousal to anger and ruminates about it. Thus, even after the arousal has dissipated the person may remain ready to aggress for as long as the self-generated label of "anger" persists.

Social-Cognitive, Information-Processing Models of Aggression

Two important cognitive information-processing models were proposed in the 1980s. One model focuses primarily on scripts (Huesmann, 1988, 1998; Huesmann & Eron, 1984). Scripts can be learned by direct experience or by observing others (e.g., parents, siblings, peers, mass media characters). In a play or movie, a script tells the actor what to say and do. In memory, a *script* also tells the person what to say and do. The person first searches his or her memory for a script to guide behavior in the current situation and then assumes a role in the retrieved script. For example, most people know what to do when they enter a restaurant because they have learned a restaurant script by observing how others behave in a restaurant (i.e., enter restaurant, go to table, look at menu, order food, eat food, pay for food, leave tip, exit restaurant; see Abelson, 1981). As another example, children can learn scripts for aggression by observing violence in the mass media.

What determines which of the many scripts in a person's memory will be retrieved on a given occasion? One factor involves the principle of encoding specificity. According to this principle, the recall of information depends in large part on the similarity of the recall situation to the situation in which encoding occurred (Tulving & Thomson, 1973). As a child develops, he or she may observe cases in which aggression is used to solve interpersonal conflicts. The observed information is then stored in memory, possibly to be retrieved later when the child is involved in a conflict situation. Whether the script is retrieved will depend partly on the similarity between cues present at the time of encoding and those present at the time of retrieval. If the cues are similar, the child may retrieve the script and use it as a guide for behavior.

The other model focuses primarily on attributions (Dodge, 1980, 1993; Dodge & Frame, 1982). *Attributions* are the explanations people give about why others behave the way they do. Aggressive people have a *hostile attribution bias*—they tend to perceive ambiguous actions by others as hostile, which can lead them to respond in hostile ways themselves (Orobrio de Castro, Veerman, Koops, Bosch, & Monshouwer, 2002). For example, if someone bumps into them, they might infer that the person did it intentionally to harm or annoy them and might therefore respond aggressively.

Although these two models differ in their details, both view aggression as the outcome of a social problem-solving process in which situational factors are evaluated, social scripts are retrieved or attributions are made, and these scripts or attributions are evaluated (often nonconsciously) until one is selected to guide behavior.

Meta-Aggression Theories

Two important meta-theories have also been proposed to explain aggression—the I³ (I-cubed) model (Finkel & Hall, 2018) and the general aggression model (Anderson & Bushman, 2002). Meta-theories are broad theories that encompass other theories.

The three Is in the I³ model (Finkel & Hall, 2018) are instigation, impellance, and inhibition. *Instigation* encompasses immediate environmental stimuli (e.g., provocation) that normatively afford an aggressive response. *Impellance* encompasses situational or dispositional stimuli (e.g., trait aggressiveness) that influence how strongly the instigator produces an urge or proclivity to aggress. *Inhibition* encompasses situational or dispositional stimuli (e.g., alcohol intoxication) that influence how strongly the urge or proclivity is overridden rather than producing an aggressive behavior. An aggressive behavior is especially likely, and especially intense, to the extent that instigation and impellance are strong and inhibition is weak—called a *perfect storm*.

In the general aggression model (e.g., Anderson & Bushman, 2002; see Figure 8.1), certain person and situation *inputs* are risk factors for aggression. Person inputs include anything the person brings to the situation (e.g., gender, age, genetic predispositions, IQ, brain functions, hormones, neurotransmitters,

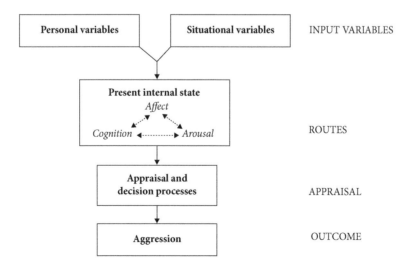

FIGURE 8.1. General aggression model. Adapted from "Human Aggression," by C. A. Anderson and B. J. Bushman, 2002, *Annual Review of Psychology, 53,* 27–51.

personality traits, attitudes, values, beliefs). Situation inputs include all external factors that can influence aggression (e.g., provocation, frustration, social rejection, hot temperatures, crowding, family influences, aggressive peers, alcohol intoxication, exposure to violent media, and availability of guns, external motives for aggression). These personal and situational factors influence the person's internal state, which includes affect, cognition, and arousal (e.g., skin conductance, heart rate, blood pressure). Thus, there are three possible routes to aggression—through angry feelings, aggressive thoughts, and physiological arousal. However, these internal states are not mutually exclusive or even independent, as indicated by the dashed lines with double-headed arrows shown in Figure 8.1. For example, someone who feels angry might also have aggressive thoughts and have elevated blood pressure. The internal states influence the decisions the person makes. These decisions influence whether the person will behave aggressively.

The general aggression model provides a meta-theoretical model for discussing the personal and risk factors related to aggressive behavior, as well as the underlying processes of internal states and hostile appraisals. I briefly discuss these risk factors and processes next.

Personal Variables

Personal variables include all the characteristics that the person brings to the situation that can influence aggression. Due to space limitations, I cannot discuss all personal variables that can influence aggression, so I will briefly mention a few—gender, age, cognitive executive brain functions, the neurotransmitter serotonin, and the dark tetrad of personality (i.e., narcissism, psychopathy, Machiavellianism, and sadism).

Age

In all cultures, aggressive behavior appears very early in childhood (e.g., Caplan, Vespo, Pedersen, & Hay, 1991), although it is difficult to be certain about "intent" to harm. These findings cast doubt on learning theory as an explanation of aggressive behavior in young children. It is more likely that aggressive proclivities are inborn. Most children don't have to learn how to behave aggressively—it comes quite naturally. What children have to learn is how to inhibit their aggressive impulses.

In terms of age differences, physical aggression levels peak between the ages of 1 and 3. In daycare settings, about 25% of interactions among toddlers involve some kind of physical aggression (Tremblay, 2000). No other group resorts to physical aggression 25% of the time, not even hardened criminals. Fortunately, most toddler aggression isn't serious enough to qualify as violence.

Exact developmental trends in general aggression are difficult to measure because aggressiveness manifests itself in different ways at different ages (e.g., physical aggression at ages 1–3, fighting at age 8, telling lies about others at age 12, vandalism at age 16, murder at ages 20–24). Although most people become less aggressive after age 3, a subset of people become *more* aggressive over time. The most dangerous years for this subset of individuals (and for their targets) are late adolescence and early adulthood. This is because aggressive acts become more extreme (e.g., weapons are used more frequently), and the consequences become more severe (Cairns & Cairns, 1994). Official records show that on average violent criminal offending is highest between ages 17 and 34 and declines significantly after that (FBI, 2017).

Aggressiveness is almost as stable over time as intelligence (Olweus, 1979). For example, one study reported 22-year continuity correlations of .50 for males and .35 for females (Huesmann, Eron, Lefkowitz, & Walder, 1984). The more aggressive child grows up to be the more aggressive adult, whereas the less aggressive child grows up to be the less aggressive adult (Hartup, 2005). There are two types of people tend to commit serious aggressive acts: (a) those for whom aggression is stable and persistent—called *life-course-persistent*—and (b) those for whom aggression is temporary and situational—called *adolescent-limited* (Moffitt, 1993). The results from longitudinal studies have found that aggressive behaviors are more serious in life-course-persistent individuals than in adolescent-limited individuals (e.g., Huesmann, Dubow, & Boxer, 2009; Moffitt, 2007).

Gender

There are gender differences in aggression, but the main difference is in the form of aggression (Björkqvist, 2018). Physical aggression is greater for males than females, whereas indirect and relational aggression is greater for females than males. The most dramatic gender differences are in physically violent behavior in young adulthood, where men commit most of the violent crimes (FBI, 2017). There is no known society in which women commit most of the violent crimes (Steffensmeier & Allan, 1996).

However, it would be wrong to think that females are never physically aggressive. Gender differences in physical aggression shrink under conditions of provocation (Bettencourt & Miller, 1996). Females are especially likely to respond with aggression when provoked by other females (Collins, Quigley, & Leonard, 2007). When it comes to heterosexual domestic partners, women are slightly *more* likely than men to use physical aggression against their partners (Archer, 2000). However, men are more likely than women to inflict serious injuries and death on their partners.

Cognitive Executive Brain Functions

Executive functions are the cognitive abilities that help us control our behavior, including aggressive behavior. The primary source of executive functioning appears to be the frontal lobes and, in particular, the prefrontal cortex, which is the part of the brain located just behind the forehead (Roberts, Robbins, & Weiskrantz, 1998). Generally speaking, frontal lobe function is negatively related to aggression and violence (Bartholow, 2018).

Serotonin

Serotonin is a naturally occurring chemical in the brain that is known to influence aggression, particularly impulsive aggression. Serotonin is called a "feel good" neurotransmitter. If people don't have enough of it, they feel bad and may therefore behave more aggressively. Although serotonin can act in other parts of the body (e.g., the digestive system), in the brain serotonin is important in modulating a number of emotional and behavioral responses, including anger, mood, and aggression. Research has shown a consistent link between low levels of serotonin and reactive aggression, but not for proactive aggression (for a review, see Bartholow, 2018).

Dark Personalities

Some scholars have challenged the notion that aggressiveness is a unitary trait and have proposed instead that it consists of four dark traits: narcissism, psychopathy, Machiavellianism, and sadism (Paulhus, Curtis, & Jones, 2018).

The term *narcissism* comes from the Greek myth about a handsome young man named Narcissus who fell in love with his own image reflected in the still water. Narcissus said, "I burn with love for me!" Narcissists have grandiose self-views, a selfish orientation, and a lack of empathy for others. Narcissists think they are special people who deserve special treatment. When they do not get the respect they think they are entitled to, they can lash out at others in an aggressive and violent manner. Psychopaths are callous and unemotional individuals who mainly focus on obtaining their own goals, regardless of whether they hurt others in the process. The term *Machiavellianism* comes from the Italian philosopher and writer Niccolò Machiavelli, who advocated using any means necessary to gain raw political power, including aggression and violence. Most people experience distress after hurting an innocent person, but for sadists it produces pleasure, excitement, and perhaps even sexual arousal. Although the four dark traits are theoretically distinct, they share common features (e.g., lack of empathy, callous manipulation of others). Although all four dark personalities are related to aggression and violence, the strongest relations appear be with psychopathy (for a review, see Paulhus et al., 2018).

Situational Variables

Situational variables include all the factors external to the person that can influence aggression. I cannot discuss all situational variables that can influence aggression, so I will briefly mention three—alcohol intoxication, violent media exposure, and the availability of guns. I previously discussed briefly the role of unpleasant external events (e.g., frustration, provocation, hot temperatures, social rejection) on aggression in the section on frustration-aggression theory. Unpleasant events are very strong predictors of aggression and violence (for a review, Groves & Anderson, 2018). Of course, family members (e.g., Labella & Masten, 2018) and peers (e.g., Bond & Bushman, 2017) can also have a significant influence on aggression and violence. However, I do not discuss these risk factors in this chapter because they are typically the domain of developmental psychologists rather than social psychologists.

Alcohol Intoxication

It is well-known that alcohol intoxication is associated with aggressive and violent behavior (for a review, see Parrott & Eckhardt, 2018). In fact, sometimes alcohol is deliberately used to promote aggression. For example, it has been standard practice for many centuries to issue soldiers some alcohol before they went into battle, both to reduce fear and to increase aggression (Keegan, 1993).

Several theories have been proposed to explain alcohol's aggression-enhancing effects, most of which emphasize effects of alcohol on disrupting cognitive processing. One explanation is that alcohol reduces the cognitive inhibitions against behaving aggressively (Graham, 1980). To use a car analogy, alcohol increases aggression by cutting the brake line rather than by stepping on the gas. Another explanation is that alcohol has a myopic (near-sighted) or narrowing effect on attention (Steele & Josephs, 1990), which causes people to focus attention on the most salient features of a situation and to ignore more subtle features. For example, after a few drinks, a bar patron might be especially likely to focus attention on a highly salient, apparent provocation (e.g., being pushed from behind) and to ignore peripheral cues that might inhibit an aggressive response (e.g., the push was accidental, the provocateur is much larger and stronger). A third explanation is that alcohol increases aggression by decreasing self-awareness (Hull, 1981). When people become self-aware, they focus attention on their internal standards. Most people have internal standards against behaving aggressively, but alcohol reduces people's ability to focus on these internal standards. A fourth explanation is that alcohol disrupts executive functions (Giancola, 2000), which allow people to control their aggressive impulses. A fifth explanation is that alcohol increases aggression because people expect it to. In many cultures, drinking occasions are culturally agreed-on "time-out" periods when people are not held responsible for their actions (MacAndrew & Edgerton, 1969). People who behave aggressively while intoxicated can therefore "blame the bottle" for their actions. A sixth explanation is that alcohol decreases serotonin levels (Badawy, 2003). Recall that low serotonin levels are related to reactive aggression.

Does all of this mean that aggression is somehow contained in alcohol? No. Alcohol disinhibits rather than causes aggressive tendencies. Factors that normally increase aggression have a stronger effect on intoxicated people than on sober people (Bushman, 1997). Put another way, alcohol mainly seems to increase aggression in combination with other factors. If someone insults or attacks you, your response will be more aggressive if you are drunk than sober. When there is no provocation, however, the effect of alcohol on aggression may be negligible.

Violent Media Exposure

Public debate on violent media effects can become especially contentious in the wake of a shooting rampage, after it is revealed that the shooter frequently played violent video games (Bushman et al., 2016). However, it is impossible to make causal inferences about what caused a shooting rampage. Violent behavior is complex and is caused by multiple factors, often acting together. The rarer the violent behavior (e.g., from hitting, to shooting, to rampage shooting), the more complex the causality may be. Exposure to violent media is just one of many possible risk factors for violence. Exposure to violent media is correlated with violent criminal behavior (Bushman & Anderson, 2015), but correlation does not necessarily imply causation. One can, however, draw causal inferences about the link between exposure to violent media and aggressive behavior from the results of experimental studies. Hundreds of experiments have shown that exposure to violent media *causes* an increase in aggressive behavior (Bushman & Anderson, 2015). Longitudinal studies also are useful in establishing cause, because they help establish the direction of the relationship and often control for several possible confounding variables. Longitudinal studies have shown that violent media effects persist over time. For example, a 15-year longitudinal study involving 329 participants found that heavy viewers of violent TV shows in first and third grade were three times more likely to be convicted of criminal behavior by the time they were in their 20s (Huesmann, Moise, Podolski, & Eron, 2003). They were also more likely to abuse their spouses and assault other people. Exposure to violent media appears to increase aggression through all three routes to aggression—by increasing angry feelings, aggressive thoughts, and physiological arousal (e.g., Anderson et al., 2010). Exposure to violent media also increases hostile appraisals (Bushman, 2016). Some scholars have questioned how robust the meta-analytic results are for violent video game effects, due to possible publication bias (see Hilgard, Engelhardt & Rouder, 2017; for a response to Hilgard et al., see Kepes, Bushman, & Anderson, 2017).

Availability of Guns

Around the world, guns may be hazardous to your health. In the United States, gun violence has been described as a "public health crisis" (Bauchner et al., 2017). More Americans have died from gun violence than from all the wars combined since 1775 (Bailey, 2017). In 2015, more Americans died from guns than from motor vehicles (36,252 vs. 36,161 deaths, respectively; Centers for Disease Control, 2017). Contrary to popular opinion, guns do not make individuals, their families, or their homes safer. For every person killed by a gun in self-defense in the United States each year, there are 34 homicides, 78 suicides, and 2 accidental gun deaths (Ingraham, 2015). Ample research from around the world suggests the availability of guns increases the risk of lethal violence (Cukier & Eagen, 2018).

Indeed, research shows that just seeing a gun can also increase aggression. Leonard Berkowitz (1968) noted, "Guns not only permit violence, they can stimulate it as well. The finger pulls the trigger, but the trigger may also be pulling the finger" (p. 22). This finding, called the "weapons effect," was first demonstrated by Berkowitz and LePage in 1967. Since then, the weapons effect has been replicated many times, both inside and outside the lab (for a recent meta-analytic review, see Benjamin, Kepes, & Bushman, 2018).

Present Internal State

The general aggression model posits three routes to aggression—through aggressive thoughts, angry feelings, and physiological arousal. However, these routes are not mutually exclusive or even independent, as indicated by the dashed lines with double-headed arrows shown in Figure 8.1. For example, someone who has aggressive ideas might also feel angry and have elevated blood pressure. Someone who has aggressive thoughts, who feels angry inside, and who is physiologically aroused should be more likely to lash out at others aggressively than someone who has no aggressive thoughts, who does not feel angry, and who is not physiologically aroused. I considered physiological arousal previously (in the section on theories based on physiological arousal); I consider aggressive thoughts and angry feelings here.

The link between cognition and behavior follows from social priming theory (e.g., Strack & Schwarz, 2016). Semantic memory can be represented as an associative network consisting of nodes and links (Collins & Loftus, 1975). The nodes represent concepts, and the links represent associations among concepts. When a concept is primed or activated in memory, other related concepts become activated as well. Once a concept has been activated, it is more accessible in memory. The more accessible a concept, the more likely it is to be used to process and interpret social information (e.g., Bruner, 1957).

Anger is the primary emotional response linked to aggression. That is why aggressive people are sometimes ordered by courts to take an anger-management course. Recall that reactive aggression is motivated by anger. Why is anger likely to increase aggression? One possible reason is that angry people aggress in the hope that doing so will help them to feel better. Research has consistently shown that people who feel bad often try to remedy or repair their moods (Morris & Reilly, 1987). Because many people believe that venting is a healthy way to reduce anger and aggression (see Bushman, Baumeister, & Phillips, 2001), they might vent by lashing out at others to improve their mood. One series of studies replicated the standard finding that anger increases aggression but also found an interesting (and revealing) exception: When participants believed that their angry mood would not change for the next hour no matter what they did (ostensibly because of side effects of a pill they had taken), anger did not lead to aggression (Bushman et al., 2001). The implication of this finding is that anger does not *directly* or *inevitably* cause aggression. Rather, angry people attack others because they believe that lashing out will help get rid of their anger and enable them to feel better.

Appraisal and Decision Processes

In the general aggression model, internal states can influence appraisal and decision processes. These are the explanations people give for their own and others' behaviors, which can have a strong influence on their behavior, including aggressive behavior. When others behave in an ambiguous manner, do people give them the benefit of the doubt, or do they assume others are out to get them? People are more likely to behave aggressively when they perceive ambiguous behaviors from others as stemming from hostile intentions than when they perceive the same behaviors as coming from benign intentions.

Research has shown that hostile biases can influence appraisal and decision processes. Some examples of hostile biases include the hostile attribution bias, the hostile expectation bias, and the hostile perception bias (Dill, Anderson, Anderson, & Deuser, 1997). The *hostile attribution bias* was described previously. The *hostile expectation bias* is the tendency to expect others to react to potential conflicts with aggression. For example, if you bump into another person, a hostile expectation would be that the person will assume that you did it on purpose and will attack you in return. The *hostile perception bias* is the tendency to perceive social interactions in general as being aggressive. For example, if you see two people having a conversation, a hostile perception would be that they are arguing. All of these biases are linked to aggression. The world would be a more peaceful place if more people could give each other the benefit of the doubt. Fortunately, hostile biases can be changed. In one study (Penton-Voak, Thomas, Gage, McMurran, McDonald, & Munafò, 2013), for example, participants were teens considered high risk for committing a crime (70% already had a criminal record). Teens saw 15 faces on a continuum that ranged from clearly happy to clearly angry, with several ambiguous faces in between. First, they indicated the point in the continuum when the faces changed from happy to angry. Next, teens were randomly assigned to treatment or control groups. The treatment consisted of telling the teens that two of the faces they thought were angry were in fact happy. They were told this each day for four days, just to make sure they got it. To measure the effect of the treatment, staff members recorded incidents of aggressive behavior the week prior to the experiment and two weeks after the experiment. The results showed that teens in the treatment group were significantly less aggressive than those in the control group.

What Can be Done to Reduce Aggression?

Even though one can kill a lot more people with modern weapons (e.g., bombs, missiles, tanks) than with ancient weapons (e.g., sticks, stones, spears), quantitative studies have shown that violence levels around the world are actually decreasing over time—by millennia, century, and even decade (Pinker, 2011). A primary factor in curbing aggression and violence around the world is culture (Baumeister, 2005). People don't have to learn how to behave aggressively—it comes quite naturally. What people have to learn is how to inhibit and control their aggressive tendencies.

The fact that there is no single cause for aggression makes it difficult to design effective interventions. An intervention that works for one person may not work for another person. There are two important general points to emphasize about interventions (Bushman & Huesmann, 2010). First, successful interventions target as many causes of aggression as possible and attempt to tackle them collectively. Interventions that are narrowly focused at removing a single cause of aggression, however well conducted, are likely to fail. Second, aggressive behavior problems are best treated in childhood, when they are still malleable. It is much more difficult to alter aggressive behaviors when they are part of an adult personality than when they are still in development. Thus, interventions should target aggressive children before they grow up to become aggressive adults. In this section, I discuss some interventions that have been used to reduce aggression. Before I discuss the effective interventions, I first debunk two ineffective ones—catharsis and punishment.

Ineffective Methods

Catharsis

The term *catharsis* dates back to Aristotle, who taught in *Poetics* that viewing tragic plays gave people emotional release from negative emotions such as pity and fear. In Greek drama, the heroes didn't just grow old and die of natural causes—they were often murdered. In modern times, Sigmund Freud revived the ancient concept of catharsis. Freud believed that if people repressed their negative emotions, psychological symptoms such as hysteria and neuroses could surface (e.g., Breuer & Freud, 1893–1895). Freud's ideas are the foundation of the hydraulic model of anger, which suggests that frustrations lead to anger. Anger, in turn, builds up inside an individual like hydraulic pressure inside a closed circuit until it is vented. If the anger is not vented, the build-up of anger will presumably cause the individual to explode in an aggressive rage. People can supposedly vent their anger by engaging in aggressive activities (e.g., yelling, screaming, swearing, punching a pillow, throwing objects, tearing phone books, kicking trash cans, slamming doors), or even by watching others engage in aggressive activities in the real world or in the virtual world (e.g., watching violent TV programs or films, playing violent video games).

Almost as soon as researchers started testing catharsis theory, it ran into trouble. In one early experiment (Hornberger, 1959), for example, participants who had been insulted by an actor either pounded nails with a hammer for 10 minutes or did nothing. Next, all participants had a chance to criticize the actor who had insulted them. According to catharsis theory, the act of pounding nails should reduce anger and subsequent aggression. However, the opposite was true: Participants who pounded nails were *more* hostile toward the actor afterward than were the participants who did nothing. Subsequent research has found similar results (e.g., Geen & Quanty, 1977). Other research has shown that venting anger by pounding on a punching bag doesn't reduce aggression even among people who believe in the value of venting and even among people who report feeling better after venting (Bushman, Baumeister, & Stack, 1999). Indeed, it increases aggression, even against innocent bystanders (Bushman et al., 1999).

One variation of venting anger is physical exercise. Although physical exercise is good for your heart, research has shown that physical exercise does not reduce aggression (Bushman, 2002). Angry people are physiologically aroused, and physical exercise just keeps the arousal level high. To reduce anger, people should try to reduce their arousal level rather than increase it by exercising.

Punishment

Most cultures assume that punishment is an effective way to reduce aggression. *Punishment* is defined as inflicting pain (*positive punishment*) or removing pleasure (*negative punishment*) for a misdeed to reduce the likelihood that the punished individual will repeat the misdeed (or related misdeeds) in the future. Parents use it, organizations use it, and governments use it. But does it work? Today, aggression researchers think punishment does more harm than good (Grogan-Kaylor, Ma, & Graham-Bermann, 2018). This is because punishment only temporarily suppresses aggression, and it has several undesirable side effects (Baron & Richardson, 1994; Berkowitz, 1993; Eron et al., 1971). Punishment models the behavior it seeks to prevent. For example, suppose a father with two sons sees the older one beating up the younger one. The father starts spanking the older boy while proclaiming, "I'll teach you not to hit your little brother!" The father is teaching the older boy something—that it is okay to behave aggressively as long as you are an authority figure. In addition, because punishment is aversive, it can classically condition children to avoid their parents and, in the short run, can instigate retaliatory aggression. Longitudinal studies have shown that children who are physically punished by their parents at home are more aggressive outside the home, such as at school (e.g., Lefkowitz. Huesmann, & Eron, 1978).

Developing Nonaggressive Ways of Behaving

Most aggression treatment programs can be divided into one of two broad categories, depending upon whether aggression is viewed as proactive or reactive (Berkowitz, 1993, pp. 358–370). Recall that proactive aggression is cold-blooded and is a means to some other end, whereas reactive aggression is hot-blooded and is an end in itself.

Approaches to Reducing Proactive Aggression

People often resort to aggression because they think it is the easiest and fastest way to achieve their goals. Psychologists who view aggression as proactive behavior use *behavior modification* learning principles to teach aggressive people to use nonaggressive behaviors to achieve their goals, and it works (e.g., Patterson, Reid, Jones, & Conger, 1975). A major problem with punishment is that it does not teach the aggressor new, nonaggressive forms of behavior. One way to get rid of an undesirable behavior is to replace it with a desirable behavior (called *differential reinforcement of alternative behavior*). The idea is that by reinforcing nonaggressive behavior, aggressive behavior should decrease. Other effective programs include social skills training, where people are taught how to better read verbal and nonverbal behaviors in social interactions (e.g., Pepler, King, Craig, Byrd, & Bream, 1995). Exposure to prosocial role models also reduces aggression and increases helping (e.g., Spivey & Prentice-Dunn, 1990), even if the models are media characters (e.g., Greitemeyer & Mügge, 2014; Mares & Woodward, 2005).

Approaches to Reducing Reactive Aggression

Other approaches to reducing aggression focus on lessening emotional reactivity using relaxation and cognitive-behavioral techniques (for a meta-analytic review, see Lee & DiGuiseppe, 2018). Most relaxation-based techniques involve deep breathing, visualizing peaceful images, or tightening and loosening muscle groups in succession. People practice relaxing after imaging or experiencing a provocative event. In this way, they learn to calm down after they have been provoked. Cognitive-based techniques focus on how a potentially provocative event is interpreted and how to respond to such events. For example, people rehearse statements in their mind such as "Stay calm. Just continue to relax" and "You don't need to prove yourself." It is especially effective to combine relaxation and cognitive techniques (e.g., Novaco, 1975). Another effective technique involves taking a more distant perspective, like a "fly on the wall" (Mischkowski, Kross, & Bushman, 2012). In people who are characteristically angry, avoidance cues such as leaning backward (instead of forward) or pushing away (instead of pulling toward) can reduce anger and aggression (Veenstra, Bushman, & Koole, 2018).

Future Research

I don't have a crystal ball, and predictions of the future can be hazardous, to say the least. Indeed, in Dante's Inferno, futurists and fortune-tellers are consigned to the eighth circle of hell. Despite Dante's warning, I will make four speculations about promising areas for future research on aggression. The first is social neuroscience, which is a hot topic today (see Chapter 15) and will probably become even hotter in the future. The link between brain activity and human aggression is a promising area of current and future research (e.g., Bartholow, 2018). The second area is the impact of guns, in both the virtual world and the real world. The third area is the impact of climate. When people think about the consequences of global warming, they generally focus on such things as weather, crops, islands sinking, glaciers melting, and polar bears losing their habitat. People rarely think about how global warming influences aggression and violence levels, but it does (Anderson, Bushman, & Groom 1997). New theoretical models have focused on explaining the link between climate and aggression and violence levels, such as the climate, aggression, and self-control in humans model (CLASH; Van Lange, Rinderu, & Bushman, 2017). CLASH might also shed light on intergroup conflict (Van Lange, Rinderu, & Bushman, in press). The fourth area is self-control. Aggression often starts when self-control stops (e.g., DeWall, Baumeister, Stillman, & Gailliot, 2007). Hopefully social psychologists will be at the forefront of conducting research on these and other important topics, which ultimately have the potential to make a society a more peaceful place to live. If anything can correct the "human failing" of aggression that Stephen Hawking bemoaned, it is scientific research.

References

Abelson, R. P. (1981). Psychological status of the script concept. *American Psychologist, 36,* 715–729.

Anderson, C. A., & Bushman, B. J. (2002). Human aggression. *Annual Review of Psychology, 53,* 27–51.

Anderson, C. A., Bushman, B. J., & Groom, R. W. (1997). Hot years and serious and deadly assault: Empirical tests of the heat hypothesis. *Journal of Personality and Social Psychology, 73,* 1213–1223.

Anderson, C. A., Shibuya, A., Ihori, N., Swing, E. L., Bushman, B. J., Sakamoto, A., . . . Saleem, M. (2010). Violent video game effects on aggression, empathy, and prosocial behavior in Eastern and Western countries: A meta-analytic review. *Psychological Bulletin, 136,* 151–173.

Archer, J. (2000). Sex differences in aggression between heterosexual partners: A meta-analytic review. *Psychological Bulletin, 126,* 697–702.

Badawy, A. A.-B. (2003). Alcohol and violence and the possible role of serotonin. *Criminal Behaviour and Mental Health, 13,* 31–44.

Bailey C. (2017, October 4). More Americans killed by guns since 1968 than in all U.S. wars-combined. *NBC News.* Retrieved from https://www.nbcnews.com/storyline/las-vegas-shooting/more-americans-killed-guns-1968-all-u-s-wars-combined-n807156

Bandura, A. (1965). Influence of models' reinforcement contingencies on the acquisition of imitative responses. *Journal of Abnormal and Social Psychology, 66,* 575–582.

Bandura, A. (1973). *Aggression: A social learning theory analysis.* Englewood Cliffs, NJ: Prentice-Hall.

Bandura, A. (1977). *Social learning theory.* Englewood Cliffs, NJ: Prentice Hall.

Bandura, A. (1986). *Social foundations of thought and action: A social-cognitive theory.* Englewood Cliffs, NJ: Prentice-Hall.

Bandura, A., Ross, D., & Ross, S.A. (1961). Transmission of aggression through imitation of aggressive models. *Journal of Abnormal and Social Psychology, 63,* 575–582.

Bandura, A., Ross, D., & Ross, S.A. (1963). Vicarious reinforcement and imitative learning. *Journal of Abnormal and Social Psychology, 67,* 601–607.

Baron, R. A., & Richardson, D. R. (1994). *Human aggression* (2nd ed.). New York, NY: Plenum.

Bartholow, B. D. (2018). The aggressive brain: Insights from neuroscience. *Current Opinion in Psychology, 19,* 60–64.

Bauchner, H., Rivara, F. P., Bonow, R. O., Bressler, N. M., Disis, M. L. N., Heckers, S. . . . Robinson, J. K. (2017). Death by gun violence—A public health crisis. *JAMA, 38,* 1763–1764.

Baumeister, R. F. (2005). *The cultural animal: Human nature, meaning, and social life.* New York, NY: Oxford University Press.

Benjamin, A. J., Jr., Kepes, S., & Bushman, B. J. (2018). Effects of weapons on aggressive thoughts, angry feelings, hostile appraisals, and aggressive behavior: A meta-analytic review of the weapons effect literature. *Personality and Social Psychology Review, 22,* 347–377.

Berkowitz, L. (1968, September). Impulse, aggression and the gun. *Psychology Today*, 18–22.

Berkowitz, L. (1989). Frustration-aggression hypothesis: Examination and reformulation. *Psychological Bulletin, 106*, 59–73.

Berkowitz, L. (1993). *Aggression: Its causes, consequences, and control.* New York, NY: McGraw- Hill.

Berkowitz L., LePage A. (1967). Weapons as aggression-eliciting stimuli. *Journal of Personality and Social Psychology, 7,* 202–207.

Bettencourt, B. A., & Miller, N. (1996). Gender differences in aggression as a function of provocation: A meta-analysis. *Psychological Bulletin, 119,* 422–447.

Björkqvist, K. (2018). Gender differences in aggression. *Current Opinion in Psychology, 19,* 39–42.

Bond, R. M., & Bushman, B. J. (2017). The contagious spread of violence through social networks in U.S. adolescents. *American Journal of Public Health, 107,* 288–294.

Breuer, J., & Freud, S. (1893–1895/1955). *Studies on hysteria* (Standard ed., Vol. 2). London, England: Hogarth.

Bruner, J. S. (1957). On perceptual readiness. *Psychological Review, 64,* 123–152.

Bushman, B. J. (1997). Effects of alcohol on human aggression: Validity of proposed explanations. In D. Fuller, R. Dietrich, & E. Gottheil (Eds.), *Recent developments in alcoholism: Alcohol and violence* (Vol. 13, pp. 227–243). New York, NY: Plenum.

Bushman, B. J. (2002). Does venting anger feed or extinguish the flame? Catharsis, rumination, distraction, anger, and aggressive responding. *Personality and Social Psychology Bulletin, 28,* 724–731.

Bushman, B. J. (2016). Violent media exposure and hostile appraisals: A meta-analytic review. *Aggressive Behavior, 42,* 605–613.

Bushman, B. J., & Anderson, C. A. (2001). Is it time to pull the plug on the hostile versus instrumental aggression dichotomy? *Psychological Review, 108,* 273–279.

Bushman, B. J., & Anderson, C. A. (2015). Understanding causality in the effects of media violence. *American Behavioral Scientist, 59,* 1807–1821.

Bushman, B. J., Baumeister, R. F., & Phillips, C. M. (2001). Do people aggress to improve their mood? Catharsis beliefs, affect regulation opportunity, and aggressive responding. *Journal of Personality and Social Psychology, 81,* 17–32.

Bushman, B. J., Baumeister, R. F., & Stack, A. D. (1999). Catharsis, aggression, and persuasive influence: Self-fulfilling or self-defeating prophecies? *Journal of Personality and Social Psychology, 76,* 367–376.

Bushman, B. J., & Huesmann, L. R. (2010). Aggression. In S. T. Fiske, D. T. Gilbert, & G. Lindzey (Eds.), *Handbook of social psychology* (5th ed., pp. 833–863). New York, NY: Wiley.

Bushman, B. J., Jamieson, P. E., Weitz, I., & Romer, D. (2013). Gun violence trends in movies. *Pediatrics, 132,* 1014–1018.

Bushman, B. J., Newman, K., Calvert, S. L., Downey, G., Dredze, M., Gottfredson, M., . . . Webster, D. (2016). Youth violence: What we know and what we need to know. *American Psychologist, 71,* 17–39.

Buss, A. H. (1961). *The psychology of aggression.* New York, NY: Wiley.

Cairns, R. B., & Cairns, B. D. (1994). *Lifelines and risks: Pathways of youth in our time.* New York, NY: Cambridge University Press

Cannon, W. B. (1915). *Bodily changes in pain, hunger, fear and rage: An account of recent researches into the function of emotional excitement.* New York, NY: Appleton.

Caplan, M., Vespo, J., Pedersen, J., & Hay, D. F. (1991). Conflict over resources in small groups of one-and two-year-olds. *Child Development, 62,* 1513–1524.

Centers for Disease Control (2017). Web-based injury statistics query and reporting system (WISQARS). Retrieved from http://www.cdc.gov/injury/wisqars

Clark, N. (2015, February19). Stephen Hawking: Aggression could destroy us. *Independent.* Retrieved from http://www.independent.co.uk/news/science/stephen-hawking-aggression-could-destroy-us-10057658.html

Collins, A. M., & Loftus, E. F. (1975). A spreading-activation theory of semantic processing. *Psychological Review, 82,* 407–428.

Collins, R. L., Quigley, B., & Leonard, K. (2007). Women's physical aggression in bars: An event-based examination of precipitants and predictors of severity. *Aggressive Behavior, 33,* 304–313.

Crick, N. R., & Grotpeter, J. K. (1995). Relational aggression, gender, and social-psychological adjustment. *Child Development, 66,* 710–722.

Cukier, W., & Eagen, S. A. (2018). Gun violence. *Current Opinion in Psychology, 19,* 109–112.

Darwin, C. (1948). *Origin of species.* New York, NY: Modern Library. (Original work published 1871)

DeWall, C. N., Baumeister, R. F., Stillman, T. F., & Gailliot, M. T. (2007). Violence restrained: Effects of self-regulation and its depletion on aggression. *Journal of Experimental Social Psychology, 43,* 62–76.

Dill, K. E., Anderson, C. A., Anderson, K. B., & Deuser, W. E. (1997). Effects of aggressive personality on social expectations and social perceptions. *Journal of Research in Personality, 31,* 272–292.

Dillon, K. P., & Bushman, B. J. (2017). Effects of exposure to gun violence in movies on children's interest in real guns. *JAMA Pediatrics, 171,* 1057–1062.

Dodge, K. A. (1980). Social cognition and children's aggressive behavior. *Child Development, 51,* 620–635.

Dodge, K. A. (1993). Social-cognitive mechanisms in the development of conduct disorder and depression. *Annual Review of Psychology, 44,* 559–584.

Dodge, K. A., & Coie, J. D. (1987). Social-information-processing factors in reactive and proactive aggression in children's peer groups. *Journal of Personality and Social Psychology, 53,* 1146–1158.

Dodge, K. A., & Frame, C. L. (1982). Social cognitive biases and deficits in aggressive boys. *Child Development, 53,* 620–635.

Dollard, J., Doob, L. W., Miller, N. E., Mower, O. H., & Sears, R. R. (1939). *Frustration and aggression.* New Haven, CT: Yale University Press.

Easterbrook, J. A. (1959). The effect of emotion on the utilization and the organization of behavior. *Psychological Review, 66,* 183–201.

Eron, L. D., Walder, L. O., & Lefkowitz, M. M. (1971). *The learning of aggression in children.* Boston, MA: Little Brown.

Feshbach, S. (1964). The function of aggression and the regulation of aggressive drive. *Psychological Review, 71,* 257–272.

Ferster, C. B., & Skinner, B. F. (1957). *Schedules of reinforcement.* New York, NY: Appleton-Century-Crofts.

Finkel, E. J., & Hall, A. N. (2018). The I³ model: A metatheoretical framework for understanding aggression. *Current Opinion in Psychology, 19,* 125–130.

Freud, S. (1930). *Civilization and its discontents.* London, England: Penguin.

Freud, S. (1950). Why war? In *Collected Works of Sigmund Freud* (Vol. 16). London, England: Imagio. (Original work published 1933)

Freud, S. (1961). *Analysis of a phobia in a five-year-old boy* (Standard ed.). London, England: Norton. (Original work published 1909)

Geen, R. G., & Quanty M. B. (1977). The catharsis of aggression: An evaluation of a hypothesis. In L. Berkowitz (Ed.), *Advances in experimental social psychology* (Vol. 10., pp. 1–37) New York, NY: Academic Press.

Giancola, P.R. (2000). Executive functioning: A conceptual framework for alcohol-related aggression. *Experimental and Clinical Psychopharmacology, 8,* 576–597.

Grogan-Kaylor, A., Ma, J., & Graham-Bermann, S. A. (2018). The case against physical punishment. *Current Opinion in Psychology, 19,* 144–148.

Groves, C. L., & Anderson, C. A. (2018). Aversive events and aggression. *Current Opinion in Psychology, 19,* 144–148.

Graham, K. (1980). Theories of intoxicated aggression. *Canadian Journal of Behavioral Science, 12,* 141–158.

Greitemeyer, T., & Mügge, D. O. (2014). Video games do affect social outcomes: A meta-analytic review of the effects of violent and prosocial video game play. *Personality and Social Psychology Bulletin, 40,* 578–589.

Hartup, W. W. (2005). The development of aggression: Where do we stand? In R. E. Tremblay, W. W. Hartup, & J. Archer (Eds.), *Developmental origins of aggression* (pp. 3–24), New York, NY: Guilford.

Heatherton, T. & Wheatley, T. (2019). Social neuroscience. In R. F. Baumeister and E. J. Finkel (Eds.), *Advanced social psychology* (2nd ed.). New York: Oxford University Press.

Hilgard, J., Engelhardt C. R., & Rouder J. N. (2017). Overstated evidence for short-term effects of violent games on affect and behavior: A reanalysis of Anderson et al. (2010). *Psychological Bulletin, 143,* 757–774.

Hinde, R. A. (1970). *Animal behavior.* New York, NY: McGraw-Hill.

Hornberger, R. H. (1959). The differential reduction of aggressive responses as a function of interpolated activities. *American Psychologist, 14,* 354.

Huesmann, L. R. (1988). An information processing model for the development of aggression. *Aggressive Behavior, 14,* 13–24.

Huesmann, L. R. (1998). The role of social information processing and cognitive schemas in the acquisition and maintenance of habitual aggressive behavior. In R. G. Geen & E. Donnerstein (Eds.), *Human aggression: Theories, research, and implications for policy* (73–109). New York, NY: Academic Press.

Huesmann, L. R., Dubow, E. F., & Boxer, P. (2009). Continuity of childhood, adolescent, and early adulthood aggression as predictors of adult criminality and life outcomes: Implications for the adolescent-limited and life-course-persistent models. *Aggressive Behavior, 35,* 136–149.

Huesmann, L. R., & Eron, L. D. (1984). Cognitive processes and the persistence of aggressive behavior. *Aggressive Behavior, 10,* 243–251.

Huesmann, L. R., Eron, L. D, Lefkowitz, M. M., & Walder, L. O. (1984). Stability of aggression over time and generations. *Developmental Psychology, 20,* 1120–1134.

Huesmann, L. R., Moise, J., Podolski, C. P., & Eron, L. D. (2003). Longitudinal relations between childhood exposure to media violence and adult aggression and violence: 1977–1992. *Developmental Psychology, 39,* 201–221.

Hull, J. G. (1981). A self-awareness model of the causes and effects of alcohol consumption. *Journal of Abnormal Psychology, 90,* 586–600.

Ingraham, C. (2015, June 19). Guns in America: For every criminal killed in self-defense, 34 innocent people die. *Washington Post.* Retrieved from https://www.washingtonpost.com/news/wonk/wp/2015/06/19/guns-in-america-for-every-criminal-killed-in-self-defense-34-innocent-people-die/

Keegan, J. (1993). *A history of warfare.* New York, NY: Knopf.

Kepes, S., Bushman, B. J., & Anderson, C. A. (2017). Violent video game effects remain a societal concern: Comment on Hilgard, Engelhardt, and Rouder (2017). *Psychological Bulletin, 143,* 775–782.

Labella, M. H., & Masten, A. (2018). Family influences on the development of aggression and violence. *Current Opinion in Psychology, 19,* 11–16.

Lee, A. H., & DiGiuseppe, R. (2018). Anger and aggression treatments: A review of meta-analyses. *Current Opinion in Psychology, 19,* 65–74.

Lefkowitz, M. M., Huesmann, L. R., & Eron, L. D. (1978). Parental punishment: A longitudinal analysis of effects. *Archives of General Psychiatry, 35,* 186–191.

Lorenz, K. (1966). *On aggression* (M. K. Wilson, Trans.). New York, NY: Harcourt, Brace.

MacAndrew, C., & Edgerton, R. (1969). *Drunken comportment: A social explanation.* Chicago, IL: Aldine.

Marcus-Newhall, A., Pedersen, W. C., Carlson, M., & Miller, N. (2000). Displaced aggression is alive and well: A meta-analytic review. *Journal of Personality and Social Psychology, 78,* 670–689.

Mares, M. L., & Woodard, E. (2005). Positive effects of television on children's social. interactions: A meta-analysis. *Media Psychology, 7,* 301–322.

Meltzoff, A. N. (2005). Imitation and other minds: The "Like Me" hypothesis. In S. Hurley & N. Chater (Eds.), *Perspectives on imitation: From mirror neurons to memes* (Vol. 2, pp. 55–78). Cambridge, MA: MIT Press.

Meltzoff, A. N., & Moore, K. M. (1977). Imitation of facial and manual gestures by human neonates. *Science, 109,* 77–78.

Mendelson, T., Thurston, R. C., & Kubzansky, L. D. (2008). Arousal and stress: Affective and cardiovascular effects of experimentally-induced social status. *Health Psychology, 27,* 482–489.

Mischkowski, D., Kross, E., & Bushman, B. J. (2012). Flies on the wall are less aggressive: Self-distanced reflection reduces angry feelings, aggressive thoughts, and aggressive behaviors. *Journal of Experimental Social Psychology, 48,* 1187–1191.

Moffitt, T. E. (1993). Adolescence-limited and life-course-persistent antisocial behavior: A developmental taxonomy. *Psychological Review, 100,* 674–701.

Moffitt, T. E. (2007). A review of research on the taxonomy of life-course-persistent versus adolescence-limited antisocial behaviour. In D. J. Flannery, A. T. Vaxsonyi, & I. D. Waldman (Eds.), *The Cambridge handbook of violent behavior and aggression* (pp. 545–570). Cambridge, England: Cambridge University Press.

Morris, W. N., & Reilly, N. P. (1987). Toward the self-regulation of mood: Theory and research. *Motivation and Emotion, 11,* 215–249.

Novaco, R. W. (1975). *Anger control: The development and evaluation of an experimental treatment.* Lexington, MA: Lexington.

Orobio de Castro, B., Veerman, J. W., Koops, W., Bosch, J. D., & Monshouwer, H. J. (2002). Hostile attribution of intent and aggressive behavior: A meta-analysis. *Child Development, 73,* 916–934.

Olweus, D. (1979). The stability of aggressive reaction patterns in males: A review. *Psychological Bulletin, 86,* 852–875.

Parrott, D. J. & Eckhardt, C. I. (2018). Effects of alcohol on human aggression. *Current Opinion in Psychology, 19,* 1–5.

Patel, D. M., Simon, M. A., & Taylor, R. M. (2013). *Contagion of violence: Workshop summary.* Washington, DC: National Academies Press.

Patterson, G. R., Reid, J. B., Jones, R. R., & Conger, R. E. (1975). *A social learning approach to family intervention. Vol. 1: Families with aggressive children.* Eugene, OR: Castalia.

Paulhus, D. L., Curtis, S. R., & Jones, D. N. (2018). Aggression as a trait: the Dark Tetrad alternative. *Current Opinion in Psychology, 19,* 88–92.

Pavlov, I. P. (1927). *Conditioned reflexes: An investigation of the physiological activity of the cerebral cortex* (G. V. Anrep, Ed. & Trans.). London, England: Oxford University Press.

Pedersen, W. C., Gonzales, C., & Miller, N. (2000). The moderating effect of trivial triggering provocation on displaced aggression. *Journal of Personality and Social Psychology, 78,* 913–927.

Penton-Voak I. S., Thomas, J., Gage, S. H., McMurran, M., McDonald, S., & Munafò M. R. (2013). Increasing recognition of happiness in ambiguous facial expressions reduces anger and aggressive behavior. *Psychological Science, 24,* 688–697.

Pepler, D., King, G., Craig, W., Byrd, B., & Bream, L. (1995). The development and evaluation of a multisystem social skills group training program for aggressive children. *Child & Youth Care Forum, 24,* 297–313.

Pinker, S. (2011). *The better angels of our nature.* New York, NY: Viking.

Prinz, J. J. (2005). Imitation and moral development. In S. Hurley & N. Chater (Eds.), *Perspectives on imitation: From mirror neurons to memes* (Vol. 2, pp. 267–282). Cambridge, MA: MIT Press.

Roberts, A. C., Robbins, T. W., & Weiskrantz, L. (Eds.) (1998). *The prefrontal cortex: Executive and cognitive functions.* New York, NY: Oxford University Press.

Sears, R. R., Whiting, J. W., Nowlis, V., & Sears, P. S. (1953). Some child-rearing antecedents of aggression and dependency in young children. *Genetic Psychology Monographs, 47,* 135–236.

Slater, M. D., Henry, K. L., Swaim, R. C., & Anderson, L. L. (2003). Violent media content and aggressiveness in adolescents: A downward spiral model. *Communication Research, 30,* 713–736.

Slutkin, G. (2013). Violence is a contagious disease. In D. M. Patel, M. A. Simon, & R. M. Taylor (Eds.), *Contagion of violence: Workshop summary* (pp. 94–111). Washington, DC: National Academies Press.

Spivey, C. B., & Prentice-Dunn S. (1990). Assessing the directionality of deindividuated behavior: Effects of deindividuation, modeling, and private self-consciousness on aggressive and prosocial responses. *Basic and Applied Social Psychology, 11,* 387–403.

Steele, C. M., & Josephs, R. A. (1990). Alcohol myopia: Its prized and dangerous effects. *American Psychologist, 45,* 921–933.

Steffensmeier, D., & Allan, E. (1996). Gender and crime: Toward a gendered theory of female offending. *Annual Review of Sociology, 22,* 459–487.

Strack, F., & Schwarz, N. (2016). Editorial overview: Social priming: Information accessibility and its consequences. *Current Opinion in Psychology, 12,* iv–vii.

Thorndike, E. L. (1901). Animal intelligence: An experimental study of the associative processes in animals. *Psychological Review Monograph Supplement, 2,* 1–109.

Timbergen, N. (1952). The curious behavior of the Stickleback. *Scientific American, 187,* 22–26.

Tremblay, R. E. (2000). The development of aggressive behavior during childhood: What have we learned in the past century? *International Journal of Behavioral Development, 24,* 129–141.

Tulving, E., & Thomson, D.M. (1973). Encoding specificity and retrieval processes in episodic memory. *Psychological Review, 80,* 352–373.

US Federal Bureau of Investigation. (2017). *Uniform crime reports.* Washington, DC: US Government Printing Office.

van Lange, P. A. M., Rinderu, M. I., & Bushman, B. J. (2017). Aggression and violence around the world: A model of climate, aggression, and self-control in humans (CLASH). *Behavioral and Brain Sciences, 40,* e75.

van Lange, P. A. M., Rinderu, M. I., & Bushman, B. J. (2018). CLASH: Climate (change) and cultural evolution of intergroup conflict. *Group Processes & Intergroup Relations, 21,* 457–471.

Veenstra, L., Bushman, B. J., & Koole, S. L. (2018). The facts on the furious: A brief review of the psychology of trait anger. *Current Opinion in Psychology, 19,* 98–103.

Williams, K. D. (2001). *Ostracism: The power of silence.* New York, NY: Guilford.

World Health Organization. (2017). Violence and injury prevention. Retrieved from http://www.who.int/violence_injury_prevention/violence/en/

Zajonc, R. B. (1965). Social facilitation *Science, 149,* 269–274.

Zajonc, R. B., Murphy, S. T., & Inglehart, M. (1989). Feeling and facial efference: Implications of vascular theory of emotions. *Psychological Review, 96,* 395–416.

Zillmann, D. (1979). *Hostility and aggression.* Hillsdale, NJ: Erlbaum.

Zillmann, D. (1988). Cognitive-excitation interdependencies in aggressive behavior. *Aggressive Behavior, 14,* 51–64.

Chapter 9

Attraction and Rejection

Eli J. Finkel and Roy F. Baumeister

Human beings are social animals, and being social requires having relationships with others. We seek people to bond with, and we try to avoid rejection. But humans are more than just social—we are also cultural. Indeed, although other creatures, like ants and bees, are more social than humans, no other species is more cultural, nor even nearly as cultural, as we are (Baumeister, 2005).

How do we, as social animals, leverage the opportunities afforded by our culture to help us meet our needs? We evolve and fine-tune sophisticated psychological machinery, including mind-reading skills and self-awareness, to determine with whom we would like to pursue a relationship (attraction) and to reduce the odds of exclusion from our primary social groups (rejection). This chapter considers both of these social-psychological phenomena, starting with attraction.

Attraction

Historical Perspective

Although theorizing on *interpersonal attraction*—the tendency to evaluate positively, and seek closeness with, a target person to whom we are not (yet) close—is millennia old, only a smattering of empirical investigations existed before the 1960s. Notable among them were studies on assortative mating (Harris, 1912), popularity (Moreno, 1934), power (Waller, 1938), mate preferences (Hill, 1945), sexuality (Kinsey, Pomeroy, & Martin, 1948), and physical proximity (Festinger, Schachter, & Back, 1950). Such studies set the stage for the development of an organized subdiscipline of interpersonal attraction within social psychology.

This subdiscipline coalesced in the 1960s and 1970s. Newcomb (1961) and Byrne (1961) launched it with landmark publications investigating whether similarity predicts attraction. Shortly thereafter, scholars began investigating a broad range of attraction-relevant topics, including the effects of a target's physical attractiveness (Huston, 1973; Walster, Aronson, Abrahams, & Rottman, 1966), the effects of a perceiver's physiological arousal (Berscheid & Walster, 1974; Dutton & Aron, 1974), whether a target reciprocates liking from a perceiver (Walster, Walster, Piliavin, & Schmidt, 1973), whether a target who is "too perfect" is less likeable than an otherwise-identical target who has benign imperfections (Aronson, Willerman, & Floyd, 1966), and whether perceivers tend to be more attracted to a target who grows to like them over time than to a target who has liked them from the beginning (Aronson & Linder, 1965). Indeed, the empirical yield of attraction research was substantial enough to warrant a book, *Interpersonal Attraction*, which Ellen Berscheid and Elaine Walster published in 1969 and revised in 1978.

Meanwhile, in the United States and other Western nations, the countercultural revolution was shattering long-held assumptions about gender roles and relationship dynamics, yielding skyrocketing divorce rates and widespread hand-wringing about the breakdown of traditional family life (Finkel, 2017). As a response, researchers across the social sciences redoubled their efforts to understand the contours of marriage and other long-term relationships, unearthing alarming findings regarding important topics like the rate of physical aggression within marriage (Straus, Gelles, & Steinmetz, 1980). Such developments altered social psychologists' research priorities, strengthening their desire to understand what makes established relationships satisfying versus dissatisfying, stable versus unstable (see Chapter 10). As a result, starting in the 1980s, "the field of interpersonal attraction, as an organized literature, largely faded into the background, supplanted but not replaced by a field called 'close relationships'" (Graziano & Bruce, 2008, p. 272; also see Berscheid, 1985; Reis, 2007).

In the late 1980s and 1990s, a new, more evolutionarily grounded approach to understanding interpersonal attraction emerged and gained prominence (Buss, 1989), filling the void left when the field of attraction research largely abdicated its perch within social psychology in favor of close relationships research. The evolutionary approach leverages Darwin's principles of natural and sexual selection (see Chapter 16) to derive novel hypotheses regarding when and how individuals experience attraction to a given target.

In the 21st century, the broader field of interpersonal attraction has enjoyed a renaissance, surging alongside the still-robust field of evolutionary psychology. A major impetus behind this resurgence was the advent of technological and methodological developments in dating practices and social networking in the real world, including online dating, speed-dating, and social networking (Boyd & Ellison, 2007; Finkel & Eastwick, 2008; Finkel, Eastwick, Karney, Reis, & Sprecher, 2012). These technological developments have converged with the growth of evolutionary models to influence the types of attraction social psychologists study. In particular, although scholars have long investigated both romantic and nonromantic forms of attraction, the influence of online dating, speed-dating, and evolutionary perspectives have tilted the field increasingly toward romantic attraction in recent decades. The present chapter reflects that shift.

Attraction Research Methods

Social-psychological studies of close relationships typically involve the recruitment of research participants who are already involved in a close relationship—frequently a serious romantic relationship—and the studies address topics like how satisfying the relationship is and how likely it is to dissolve within a given follow-up period. Social-psychological studies of attraction, in contrast, typically involve the recruitment of research participants who report on a stranger.

Most such studies assess participants' attraction to targets they have never met or have just met for the first time. Some ask participants to report on a hypothetical partner, as when they express how important it is that a potential partner has a good sense of humor. Some ask participants to report on a specific target (or more than one), perhaps by showing them a photograph or profile of him or her. Although such studies enjoy high levels of experimental control, the extent to which the attraction-related processes they identify generalize to situations in which people actually meet a potential partner is often unknown.

To address such concerns about generalizability while maintaining strong experimental control, scholars sometimes invest the resources required to introduce strangers to each other in a psychology laboratory or in another structured context. They might, for example, have participants interact with a research confederate. One method that seeks to maximize both external and internal validity is speed-dating (Finkel & Eastwick, 2008). In speed-dating studies, participants volunteer for an actual speed-dating event in which they meet around a dozen preferred-sex partners for interactions of, say, four minutes in duration. The value of speed-dating methods has come into sharper focus as concerns about replicability within social psychology have grown, because speed-dating events provide an efficient means of collecting high-impact data characterized by strong statistical power. For example, one study included eight heterosexual speed-dating events conducted over a three-day period, running 187 participants through a procedure that yielded more than 1,100 videorecorded speed-dates and 2,200 interaction-record questionnaires. Such data enable researchers to answer questions that are unanswerable with most methods, such as the extent to which David's attraction to Kyoko is due to something about David (he's generally to the women at the event), something about Kyoko (all men at the event are generally attracted to her), or something about their unique chemistry (even after control for David's general attraction to the women and the men's general attraction to Kyoko, he is uniquely attraction to her; Joel, Eastwick, & Finkel, 2017; also see Kenny and La Voie, 1984).

When evaluating research methods, the most important consideration is the extent to which the methods are aligned with the research question. If a researcher wants to know what qualities people think they want in a hypothetical partner, simply asking participants what they want is sufficient. But if the researcher wants to know whether people exhibit greater attraction to partners who possess more of a given quality, the researcher is better served by observing how much attraction participants experience toward a real-life potential partner who possesses more versus less of that quality (Eastwick, Finkel, & Simpson, 2018).

Theory and Research on Attraction

Recent methodological advances have emerged alongside notable, and desperately needed, theoretical advances. According to the original, 2010 version of this chapter, research on attraction is "a theoretical morass. Dozens of theories have guided research, and scholars have devoted little effort toward linking these far-flung theories into an integrated framework" (Finkel & Baumeister, 2010, pp. 421–422). This conclusion echoed that of Ellen Berscheid (1985), who observed a quarter-century earlier that the field " 'just grew', proceeding without the advantage of a master plan" (p. 417)—and that of Theodore Newcomb (1956), who observed a half-century earlier that "there exists no very adequate theory of interpersonal attraction" (p. 575).

Instrumentality: The Foundation of Attraction

In the 2010s, two research teams, working independently, took some initial steps to impose theoretical coherence on this unruly literature, offering compatible perspectives on how attraction works. Montoya and Horton (2014) argued that we tend to be especially attracted to targets who are both willing and able to meet our needs or goals. Finkel and Eastwick (2015) argued that the essence of interpersonal attraction is *instrumentality*: "People become attracted to others who help them achieve needs or goals that are currently high in motivational priority" (p. 180). These ideas built on research on close relationships, where Fitzsimons and Shah (2008) had demonstrated that people tend to draw closer to significant others who are instrumental for such goals.

Two Metatheoretical Frameworks

In addition to functioning as the basis of attraction, instrumentality also serves as the (frequently implicit) foundation for the major theoretical frameworks for understanding how attraction works (Finkel & Eastwick, 2015). The two most influential frameworks are domain-general reward models and domain-specific evolutionary models. *Domain-general reward models* conceptualize needs or goals as general motivations that can be fulfilled through diverse routes, as when a man looks to various relationship partners (e.g., romantic partner, sibling, friend, coworker), or even to himself, to meet his need to feel competent. *Domain-specific evolutionary models*, in contrast, conceptualize needs or goals as adaptations oriented toward solving specific problems in our evolutionary past—as when a woman finds a particular man attractive because her same-sex ancestors were able to procure good genes through sexual encounters with men who, like this man, were socially dominant. Such needs and goals can be fulfilled only by a particular type of relationship partner; in our example, neither a less dominant man nor the woman's sister could not substitute for the dominant man.[1]

Domain-General Reward Models

In the 1950s, Newcomb (1956) asserted that "[w]e acquire favorable or unfavorable attitudes toward persons as we are rewarded or punished by them" (p. 577). This observation, which forms the foundation of domain-general reward models and remains influential today, builds on classic reinforcement ideas initially developed by Thorndike (1898) and Skinner (1938).

Physical attractiveness. All else equal, we tend to be more attracted to a given target insofar as he or she is physically attractive, at least in part because it is pleasurable to look at, and perhaps touch, people who are hot. Indeed, neuroscience research suggests that merely looking at photos of attractive people activates reward circuitry in the brain (Aharon et al., 2001; Cloutier, Heatherton, Whalen, & Kelley, 2008; O'Doherty et al., 2003). In a seminal study, college students who attended an evening-long dance party experienced greater attraction to their randomly assigned partner (a stranger) to the extent that objective coders rated him or her higher in physical attractiveness (Walster et al., 1966). Decades of subsequent research have done little to temper the conclusion that we tend to be especially attracted to physically attractive targets (Eastwick et al., 2014). Indeed, the effect emerges even in platonic contexts (Feingold, 1990; Langlois et al., 2000) and even when the perceivers are young children (Langlois et al., 1987; Slater et al., 1998), findings that speak to the domain-generality of the effect.

What characteristics make a target physically attractive? We perceive targets as warm and friendly when they exhibit a large smile, dilated pupils, highly set eyebrows, full lips, and a confident posture (Cunningham & Barbee, 2008). Men tend to be attracted to women with sexually mature features like prominent cheekbones, whereas women tend to be attracted to men with sexually mature features like a broad jaw (Cunningham, Barbee, & Philhower, 2002; Rhodes, 2006). As depicted in Figure 9.1, a clever line of research employs computer morphing procedures to produce composite versions of human faces, demonstrating that composites become more attractive when they consist of a larger number of human faces, perhaps because such composites are easy to process due to their "average" features or their symmetry (Langlois, Roggman, & Musselman, 1994; Rhodes, Harwood, Yoshikawa, Nishitani, & MacLean, 2002; Rubenstein, Langlois, & Roggman, 2002).

FIGURE 9.1. Composite male and female faces (on left of figure), along with photographs of the 16 individual faces incorporated into each composite. We thank FaceResearch.org for supplying the composites and the photographs.

Self-enhancement. We also tend to be attracted to others who make us feel good about ourselves. For example, we like people who ingratiate themselves to us but not people who ingratiate themselves to somebody else (Gordon, 1996; Vonk, 2002). We like people who like us (Backman & Secord, 1959; Curtis & Miller, 1986), especially if they like us more than they like others (Eastwick, Finkel, Mochon, & Ariely, 2007; Walster et al., 1973). We experience greater attraction to more competent people, especially if they also have some minor imperfection that makes them less threatening to our sense of self-worth (Aronson et al., 1966; Deaux, 1972; Herbst, Gaertner, & Insko, 2003). We like people whom we perceive to have attitudes and values that are similar to our own (Montoya et al., 2008; Tidwell, Eastwick, & Finkel, 2013), in part because we experience such similarity as validation for our own views (Thibaut & Kelley, 1959, p. 43).[2]

Belonging. In addition, we tend to be attracted to strangers whom we perceive as having the potential to help us fulfill our need to belong—our need for "for frequent, nonaversive interactions within an ongoing relational bond" (Baumeister & Leary, 1995, p. 497). The human psyche is built to bond with others (Hazan & Diamond, 2000; Hazan & Zeifman, 1994), and, indeed, we experience greater attraction to a stranger when we have gazed into his or her eyes for two minutes than if the two of us have gazed at each other's hands or had asymmetric eye contact (Kellerman, Lewis, & Laird, 1989). We are especially attracted to people who disclose intimate information to us, or to whom we have disclosed intimate information, even if the impetus to disclose results from random assignment to a high-disclosure experimental condition rather than from some more endogenous motivation (Collins & Miller, 1994). Similarly, we are especially attracted to people who ask us lots of questions—especially follow-up questions—in part because such questions make us feel like they care about our needs (Huang, Yeomans, Brooks, Minson, & Gino, 2017). We tend to become more attracted to people if we have been randomly assigned to have many rather than few brief instant-messaging chats with them (say, eight instead of one), another effect that is mediated by the perception that he or she cares about our needs (Reis et al., 2011). If we are open to the possibility of forming a close relationship with a stranger, we experience greater attraction if he or she responds to our generosity with a simple thank-you rather than if he or she offers to pay us back, presumably because we perceive the thank-you response, relative to the payback response, as indicating greater potential interest in forming a relationship with us (Clark & Mills, 1979).

Domain-general reward models: Conclusion. These findings—regarding a target's physical attractiveness or how he or she influences our self-esteem or our sense of belonging—speak to a broader truth. We tend to be attracted to others who are, in a domain-general way, rewarding for us.

Domain-Specific Evolutionary Models

In contrast to domain-general reward models, domain-specific evolutionary models suggest that we are attracted to people who can help us meet specific needs or goals that evolution bequeathed to us because the need or goal inspired actions that yielded successful solutions to particular adaptive challenges in our ancestral past. The intellectual foundation supporting the evolutionary psychology of interpersonal attraction, which gained widespread prominence in the work of David Buss (Buss, 1989; Buss & Barnes, 1986), consists of three major developments. The first was Robert Trivers's theory of differential parental investment, which argues that whichever sex invests more resources in gestating and rearing offspring should be more cautious about mating decisions (Trivers, 1972). Among mammals, females tend to invest more than males, which has led them to be more selective and has led males to compete more vigorously for sexual access to them. The second development was E. O. Wilson's analysis applying the concept of adaptation to the domain of human behavior (Wilson, 1975). Just as long necks became prevalent among giraffes because long-necked giraffes were more likely to survive and reproduce than their short-necked counterparts, certain forms of human behavior—in domains like helping, aggression, and mating—have become increasingly prevalent among *Homo sapiens* because such behaviors, too, bolstered ancestral survival and reproduction. The third development was Leda Cosmides's theory of the modular mind (Cosmides, 1989; Tooby & Cosmides, 1992), which argues that the brain consists of a large number of distinct computational systems that evolved to regulate physiology and behavior in ways that, among our hunter-gatherer ancestors, promoted survival and reproduction in response to specific adaptive challenges.

The ideas emerging from evolutionary perspectives on attraction have proven to be innovative and generative. They also have the benefit of linking the attraction literature to the most influential theory in the life sciences. At the same time, many of these ideas are scientifically controversial. One issue is that some of the ideas paint an image of human sociality that is at odds with other major perspectives in the social sciences, including those attributing primary causality to socialization pressures. A second issue is that certain seminal ideas in evolutionary tradition fare poorly when confronted with relevant data, at least in the judgment of some scholars. Because so much of the recent research on attraction resides at the intersection of these various perspectives, the ensuing discussion focuses on both the central evolutionary ideas in this research space and the debates surrounding them.

Mate preferences. In 1989, Buss published a study that examined people's mate preferences in a sample of over 10,000 participants from 37 cultures, which were spread across 33 countries located on 6 continents and 5 islands. Although scholars had asked people to report on the qualities they find appealing in a mate for decades (Hill, 1945), Buss's approach was new in its attempt to link such preferences to specific adaptive problems confronted by our hunter-gatherer ancestors. In particular, Buss built on Trivers's (1972) idea of differential parental investment to advance hypotheses surrounding sex differences in mate preferences. Because our female ancestors were likely to be dependent on others for resource acquisition when gestating and rearing their offspring, Buss hypothesized, women today should show stronger preferences for mates with qualities linked to resource acquisition, such as good earning prospects. In contrast, because our male ancestors' reproductive success depended on garnering sexual access to fertile women, men today should show stronger preferences for qualities in a mate that are linked to fertility, such as physical attractiveness. Results from Buss's (1989) study yielded strong cross-cultural support for these hypotheses. These effects have been replicated many times, including in a self-report study using a national representative sample of Americans (Sprecher, Sullivan, & Hatfield, 1994) and in a study investigating whom online daters contact after viewing profiles of potential partners (Hitsch, Hotaçsu, & Ariely, 2010).

Although the robustness of such sex differences has not been questioned, these findings have been the target of two major critiques. The first, from Alice Eagly and Wendy Wood (Eagly & Wood, 1999; Wood & Eagly, 2002), is that they are caused not by domain-specific mating adaptations but rather by socialization pressures that sort men and women into particular roles—pressures that owe more to evolved differences in the body than to evolved differences in the brain. Women lactate and have a uterus, which has increased their likelihood of occupying caretaker roles. Men have greater upper-body strength, which has increased their likelihood of occupying resource-provider roles, like agricultural or construction laborer, that require bursts of strength (and, frequently, extended time away from home). Because an individual (of whatever sex or gender) in a caretaker role is likely to require some other means of procuring resources, whereas an individual (of whatever sex or gender) in a resource-provider role is likely to require some other means of procuring caretaking, men and women come to develop the sorts of sex-differentiated preferences demonstrated in Buss's data. Consistent with this possibility, a reanalysis of those data revealed that the sex differences get much smaller as the nation's gender equality increases; that is, as the roles occupied by men and women become more similar, so do their mate preferences (Eagly & Wood, 1999).

The second critique, from Paul Eastwick and his collaborators (Eastwick, Luchies, Finkel, & Hunt, 2014), focuses less on explanations for the sex differences than on their relevance to actual mating encounters. The sex differences are robust in research paradigms in which participants have never met the target—for example, those in which people report on a hypothetical ideal partner or on a target presented in static content on a piece of paper or a computer monitor. But they tend to be nonexistent in studies in which participants have actually met the target. In one study (Eastwick & Finkel, 2008), which was closely replicated with virtually identical results (Selterman, Chagnon, & Mackinnon, 2015) as part of the famous 100-study replication effort undertaken by the Open Science Collaboration (2015), heterosexual participants reported their mate preferences 10 days before attending a speed-dating event where they met 12 potential partners. Immediately following each speed-date, they evaluated that partner in terms of mate-preference dimensions like physical attractiveness and earning prospects. Although these participants exhibited the standard sex differences on the pre-event questionnaire—men expressed a stronger preference than women for physical attractiveness and women expressed a stronger preference than men for earning prospects—these effects essentially disappeared when participants reported on the flesh-and-blood partners they met at the speed-dating event. The extent to which participants evaluated a particular partner as physically attractive or as having strong earning prospects predicted their level of romantic desire for him or her, but the magnitude of these effects was virtually identical for men and women.

This conclusion is not limited to speed-dating methods. Indeed, a meta-analysis of all existing studies in which participants had, at minimum, met the target face-to-face—including paradigms ranging from speed-dating and confederate studies to studies of dating or married couples—revealed no evidence for sex differences in the association of either physical attractiveness (N = 29,414) or earning prospects (N = 50,113) with romantic outcomes like attraction or relationship satisfaction (Eastwick et al., 2014). Debate surrounding the circumstances under which sex-differentiated mate preferences emerge is on-going, as is a broader discussion about the extent to which, regardless of gender, people's self-reported mate preferences matter in predicting how much attraction they experience when meeting real people (for a comprehensive list of studies relevant to this latter issue, see Eastwick et al., 2018, Tables 3 and 4).

Short-term vs. long-term mating strategies. Shortly after publishing his 37-cultures study, Buss joined forces with David Schmitt to develop sexual strategies theory, the first full-fledged evolutionary theory of human mating (Buss & Schmitt, 1993). A central element of this theory is the distinction between short-term and long-term mating strategies, with *strategies* defined as "evolved solutions to adaptive problems, with no consciousness or awareness on the part of the strategist implied" (p. 206). Short-term mating strategies are characterized by the pursuit of casual and time-limited liaisons such as a brief fling or a one-night stand. Long-term mating strategies, in contrast, are characterized by the pursuit of serious and extended liaisons such as a steady dating relationship or a marriage. Buss and Schmitt observe that, throughout evolutionary history, both our male and our female ancestors have pursued both short-term and long-term matings, with the adoption of a particular strategy determined by contextual conditions that made its reproductive benefits outweigh the costs. That said, because the minimum parental investment has been so much larger for our female than our male ancestors, evolution bequeathed greater interest in short-term mating to men than to women. Consistent with this hypothesis, although men in one set of studies (Clark, 1990; Clark & Hatfield, 1989) were slightly more likely than women to accept a date from an opposite-sex research confederate who approached them on campus (58% vs. 48%), they were much more likely to accept an offer to go home with (63% vs. 7%) or to "go to bed with" (71% vs. 0%) the confederate. These studies have been critiqued, including on domain-general grounds by Conley (2011), who presents evidence that the large sex difference in the latter two conditions disappears once researchers control for (a) how physically safe it is to accept the invitation and (b) how enjoyable participants believe the casual sex is likely to be.

Nonetheless, the short-term/long-term distinction remains influential in evolutionary models. In developing strategic pluralism theory, for example, Gangestad and Simpson (2000) adopt the short-term/long-term distinction while also emphasizing how people allocate their mating-relevant resources through strategic tradeoffs. Although a select few of our male ancestors probably achieved reproductive success through short-term matings with many partners, most would have been unable to pull off such a strategy. Not only were most of them insufficiently appealing to entice lots of partners to have uncommitted sex with them, but such a loose strategy involved other perils, including the risk of being killed by a female's kin following a one-time sexual encounter. As a result, our male ancestors were probably more likely to achieve reproductive success through long-term matings with few partners, perhaps just one. Similarly, although some of our female ancestors achieved reproductive success through short-term matings oriented toward procuring good genes for their offspring, such a strategy involved a great deal of risk, including the risk of being deserted with insufficient resources to gestate and rear the child. As a result, our female ancestors, too, were probably more likely to achieve reproductive success through long-term matings with few partners, perhaps just one.

One critique of this line of research, also from Eastwick and his collaborators (Eastwick, Keneski, Morgan, McDonald, & Huang, 2018), surrounds the extent to which real-life short-term and long-term romantic relationships are distinguishable as people initially pursue them. Consider studies that plot the trajectories of participants' real-life short-term and long-term relationships using particular relationship milestones, such as first meeting, first flirtation, first kiss, first saying "I love you," first sexual intercourse, and first meeting each other's parents. Adopting standard language from the literature investigating short-term and long-term relationships, participants reported their level of romantic interest at the time each event occurred—if it occurred—within both a short-term romantic relationship (e.g., a fling, one-night stand, or brief affair) and a long-term, committed romantic relationship. If they were currently involved in a short-term and/or a long-term relationship, they responded regarding that relationship; if not, they responded regarding a previous relationship of the relevant type.

As illustrated in Figure 9.2, the level of romantic interest participants experienced at the time of a given relationship event was, early on, identical for short-term and long-term relationships (and among men and women). Indeed, the tendency for long-term relationships to be characterized by greater romantic interest did not emerge until the advent of sexuality-linked behaviors like kissing and oral sex; there had been no detectable differences when the nascent relationship was at the level of flirting or initially spending time together. As a result, although there is no doubt that the short-term and long-term relationships end up being quite different—especially in that long-term relationships last longer and are characterized by higher peak levels of romantic interest—there is little evidence that people tend to approach a potential relationship with either a long-term or a short-term *strategy*. Instead, despite the existence of individual differences and fluctuations over time, it seems that the dominant mentality when approaching a new relationship is closer to "let's see how it goes," an open-minded orientation toward updating compatibility assessments over time.

Ovulatory cycle effects. Evolutionary psychologists have also generated an array of intriguing hypotheses about how hormonal shifts linked to women's ovulatory cycle influence attraction-related outcomes. Such research, which was launched by Steven Gangestad and his collaborators (Gangestad & Thornhill, 1998), begins with the observation that heterosexual intercourse is especially likely to result in a pregnancy when it occurs shortly before the woman ovulates. Consequently, women's sexual preferences and decisions during that interval should be especially influenced by the genetic material offered by the man, particularly if they are considering him for a short-term sexual relationship. They should prioritize indicators of "good genes" in the man, such as symmetrical features, masculine facial and vocal qualities, creativity, and socially dominant behavior (Gangestad, Thornhill, & Garver-Apgar, 2005). Analogously, women who are already involved in a serious romantic relationship should report greater attraction to, and flirt more with, other men during the fertile phase of their ovulatory cycle, particularly if their current partner is not physically attractive (Haselton & Gangestad, 2006).

Two meta-analyses of this research space were published in 2014, yielding starkly different conclusions. The first, from Gildersleeve, Haselton, and Fales (2014), concluded that ovulatory cycle shifts are robust—and that, consistent with long-standing evolutionary theorizing, the effects are limited to qualities linked to (ancestral) genetic quality and to contexts in which women are considering men for a short-term relationship. The second, from Wood, Kressel, Joshi, and Louie (2014), concluded that ovulatory cycle shift

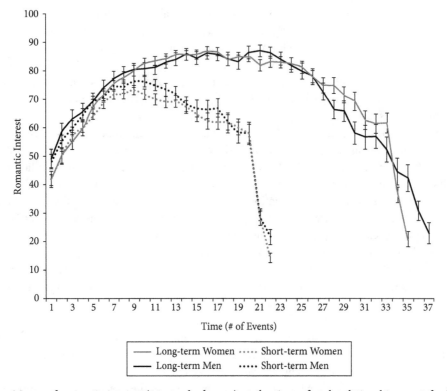

FIGURE 9.2. Means of romantic interest (±1 standard error) at the time of each relationship event for long-term relationships (solid lines) and short-term relationships (dotted lines), plotted separately for women (gray lines) and men (black lines). For example, Event 5 is "First went on a long date (e.g., dinner, dancing, movie)," Event 10 is "First make-out," and Event 20 is "I first said 'I love you.'" For ease of presentation, this graph includes the most recent relationship of each type, although the conclusions are identical for current relationships. Figure reproduced from "What Do Short-Term and Long-Term Relationships Look Like? Building the Relationship Coordination and Strategic Timing (ReCAST) model," by P. W. Eastwick, E. Keneski, T. A. Morgan, M. A. McDonald, & S. A. Huang, 2018, *Journal of Experimental Psychology: General, 147*, 747–781, with permission from the American Psychological Association.

effects are not robust. The two research teams subsequently published back-and-forth critiques defending their positions, but there has been little progress toward an integration or a resolution. It is likely that the next major salvos in this debate will involve large-sample preregistered studies using direct hormonal tests of ovulatory status (as assessed in urine, for example).

Domain-specific evolutionary models: Conclusion. Domain-specific evolutionary perspectives breathed new life into attraction research at a time when the field was waning. In developing a novel approach to hypothesis generation, it introduced an array of important new research questions. Given the prominence and influence of this work, it is not surprising that it has also been the target of major critiques. But even some of the major critiques (e.g., Eastwick, 2009) are, at root, evolutionary in ways that would have been difficult to imagine before Buss and others began developing this approach to understanding how attraction works.

Attraction Research Today

Recognition of the fundamental role that instrumentality plays in interpersonal attraction can help to generate a new research agenda for this literature (Finkel & Eastwick, 2015). In particular, attraction research can benefit from closer ties to the self-regulation literature, especially in terms of the conceptualization of goal-related dynamics. Researchers could fruitfully investigate goal properties like importance (how essential a given goal currently is for us), chronicity (how frequently a goal is activated for us), and multifinality (the extent to which a given target can help us meet many vs. few of our goals) in determining how attracted we are to a target. Researchers could also explore, for example, how we evaluate the likelihood that a given target will help us fulfill a given goal, or the circumstances under which attraction manifests itself as a warm feeling of liking versus a hot feeling of passion.

Perhaps the most radical implication of the emphasis on instrumentality is its suggestion that our experience of attraction can fluctuate markedly throughout the day, often in surprisingly ways, as our goals shift in motivational priority. Consider an example from Finkel and Eastwick (2015), who argue that instrumentality perspective "implies that Jason should be more attracted to Scott, the telephone-based tech-support representative who is currently helping him fix a problem with his computer, than to Rachel, his wife of 20 years" (p. 198). Such a result would be unlikely to emerge on research surveys, of course, which rely more on cognitive abstraction than on immediate experience, but surveys are not the only means of assessing attraction. Consider a scenario in which (a) Jason's computer issue is urgent (he has to give a major presentation in an hour), and (b) Rachel, unaware of this urgency, starts to seduce him. Jason may well rebuff her advances in favor of focusing all of his attention on Scott, behavior that could certainly count as a reasonable operationalization of attraction.

This scenario points to a broader truth: The lack of an overarching theoretical framework has stunted research on attraction, but we appear to be arriving at a moment when such a framework is coming into focus. On first blush, it looks like the low-hanging fruit is plentiful.

Rejection

We turn now to other side of the coin, from attraction to rejection. The shift in content is accompanied by a shift in the design variable. Attraction is typically studied as a dependent variable, whereas rejection is most commonly studied an independent variable—that is, researchers mostly explore the *causes* of attraction but the *consequences* of rejection. We discuss rejection research methods and theoretical perspectives before reviewing the consequences of being rejected. We then discuss loneliness and explore why people get rejected.

Rejection research emerged in a rather brief time, as several different strands converged to stimulate research. Baumeister and Leary's (1995) paper on the need to belong led them to begin to explore the consequences of having that need thwarted (which is what rejection does). Around the same time, Kipling Williams had begun to reflect on ostracism and to conduct some initial studies, later summarized in his 2002 book. Loneliness research had been going on for some time, but it also received a new boost around this time, especially in connection with work by John Cacioppo and colleagues, later summarized in his 2008 book (Cacioppo & Patrick, 2008).

Rejection Research Methods

As with almost any research topic, progress depends on having good methods. Multiple procedures have assisted researchers in exploring the effects of rejection, although most of them use stranger interactions and rejections (so one should be cautious in generalizing to cases of rejection by important, long-term relationship partners). In one method, a group of strangers engages in a get-acquainted conversation and then is told that they will pair off for the next part (e.g., Leary, Tambor, Terdal, & Downs, 1995; Nezlek, Kowalski, Leary, Blevins, & Holgate, 1997; Twenge, Baumeister, Tice, & Stucke, 2001). Each is asked to list two desired partners, and then everyone goes to a separate room. The experimenter visits each room and gives bogus feedback that everyone, or no one, has selected you as a desirable partner. Thus, rejection means being chosen by no one as a desirable partner. In another procedure, people take a personality test by questionnaire and are given feedback that includes the ostensible prediction that you will end up alone in life (e.g., Twenge et al., 2001). In a third procedure, two participants exchange get-acquainted videos, and then the experimenter tells the participant that after seeing your video, the other person does not want to meet with you—as opposed to saying the other person had to leave because of a dentist appointment (e.g., DeWall, Baumeister, & Vohs, 2008). A fourth procedure asks people to recall or imagine experiences of rejection (e.g., DeWall & Baumeister, 2006).

The first study on ostracism sent the participant into a room with two confederates posing as participants (Williams & Sommer, 1997). All were instructed to remain silent. One confederate pretended to discover a ball and started tossing it to the others. In the control condition, all three threw the ball back and forth for several minutes. In the ostracism condition, the confederates briefly included the participant in the game and then gradually stopped throwing the ball to him or her. Later, a computerized version of this game called "Cyberball" was developed, and it has proven very popular as a convenient and inexpensive substitute for using live confederates (e.g., Eisenberger, Lieberman, & Williams, 2003; see also Van Beest & Williams, 2006).

Ostracism procedures may manipulate more than rejection. Williams (2002) argues that ostracism thwarts not just the need to belong but also other needs, including desires for control and understanding (meaning). If so, ostracism procedures cannot be considered pure manipulations of social rejection, and their effects may or may not stem from the interpersonal rejection aspect. However, a meta-analysis found that at least some effects of ostracism were indistinguishable from those of other rejection manipulations (Blackhart, Knowles, Nelson, & Baumeister, 2009).

Loneliness is mostly studied as an individual difference measure, assessed by questionnaire. Several scales are available for measuring loneliness per se, including the UCLA Loneliness Scale (Russell, Peplau, & Cutrona, 1980). There are also scales to measure degree of perceived social support.

General Theory

Approaches to rejection have generally been based on the assumption that people have a strong, basic drive to form and maintain social bonds. Most theories of personality and human nature have recognized this to some degree (e.g., Freud, 1930; Maslow, 1968). Recent assertions of the need to belong, such as Baumeister and Leary's (1995), have not really discovered or posited a new motivation but rather given it more prominence and primacy among motivations. Regardless, given that rejection thwarts this pervasive and powerful drive, it should be upsetting and disturbing to people, and it should set in motion other behaviors aimed at forming other bonds or strengthening the remaining ones.

A link to self-esteem has been proposed by Leary and colleagues (e.g., Leary et al., 1995; also Leary & Baumeister, 2000). Self-esteem presents a puzzle because people seem highly motivated to maintain and enhance it, yet high self-esteem has relatively few palpable advantages. It is puzzling why people would care so much about something that has so little apparent benefit. Leary's solution is to say that self-esteem, albeit perhaps not important in and of itself, is closely tied to something that is important, namely, belongingness. In his term, self-esteem functions as a sociometer—an inner gauge of one's likelihood of having sufficient social ties. High self-esteem is generally associated with believing oneself to have traits that bring social acceptance, including likability, competence, attractiveness, and moral goodness. Hence, rejection tends to reduce self-esteem, whereas acceptance increases it.

Thus, people seem designed by nature, in a rather general way, to want to connect with others. Some people may seem to like to be alone but usually still desire to have at least a few friends and close relationships. Even religious hermits typically maintain a close bond with at least one person who visits regularly and provides some companionship. In prison, solitary confinement may seem a more attractive alternative than being with the other prisoners and suffering the associated risks of assault and rape, but in fact solitary confinement is highly stressful and damaging (Rebman, 1999), and most prisoners seek to avoid it if they can.

People who are rejected or otherwise alone suffer more mental and physical health problems than other people (Baumeister & Leary, 1995). In some cases, one could argue that the problems led to the rejection, but other cases (e.g., heart attacks, decreased immune function) make that seem implausible. Being alone is bad for the person. Indeed, mortality from all causes of death is significantly higher among people who are relatively alone in the world than among people with strong social ties (House, Landis, & Umberson, 1988). A meta-analysis of 148 studies and over 300,000 people found that risk of dying increased substantially as a function of having fewer social relationships, and this was true regardless of age, gender, cause of death, and initial health status (Holt-Lunstad, Smith, &Layton, 2010). Lonely people take longer than others to recover from stress, illness, and injuries (Cacioppo & Hawkley, 2005). Even a cut on the finger, administered in a carefully controlled manner in a laboratory study, heals more slowly than normal in a lonely person.

Consequences of Rejection

What happens to people who are rejected? We divide this exploration into sections on (a) behavioral consequences; (b) cognitive, motivational, and self-regulatory consequences; and (c) emotional consequences.

Behavioral Consequences

Rejection produces robust effects on behavior. The potential link between feeling rejected and turning violent gained national prominence from widely publicized episodes in which high school students in the United States brought guns to school and fired upon classmates and teachers. A compilation and analysis of the first 15 of these school shootings indicated that most of the shooters had felt rejected by their peers, and the feelings of rejection had fueled their violent tendencies (Leary, Kowalski, Smith, & Phillips, 2003). Laboratory experiments confirmed that participants who were randomly assigned to experience rejection by other participants became highly aggressive toward other participants, even toward innocent third parties who had not provoked them in any other way (Twenge et al., 2001). Only new persons who praised the rejected person were exempted from the aggressive treatment.

Parallel to the increase in aggression, rejected people show a broad decrease in prosocial behavior. In multiple studies, rejected people were less generous in donating money to worthy causes, less willing to do a favor that was asked of them, less likely to bend over and pick up spilled pencils, and less likely to cooperate with others on a laboratory game (the Prisoner's Dilemma; Twenge, Baumeister, DeWall, Ciarocco, & Bartels, 2007).

Ostracized people, too, seem quite positively responsive to friendly gestures and overtures by others (e.g., Williams & Zadro, 2005). For example, on a Solomon Asch-style conformity task, ostracized people conformed more than other participants—they were more likely to give the obviously wrong answer endorsed by other group members (Williams, Cheung, & Choi, 2000). Such behavior could indicate that they hope to win friends by going along with the group.

Cognitive, Motivational, and Self-Regulatory Consequences

The behavioral effects of rejection were puzzling in some ways. The underlying theory, after all, was that people are driven by a need to belong, and rejection thwarts that need, so rejected people should be trying extra hard to find new ways of connecting with others. Instead, they seemed to become unfriendly, aggressive, and uncooperative. Why?

Alongside the antisocial behaviors noted in the preceding section, some researchers have found signs that rejected people may become interested in forming new social bonds. They show heightened interest in other people's interpersonal activities. For example, Gardner, Pickett, and Brewer (2000) administered a laboratory rejection intervention and then let participants read other people's diaries. The rejected persons showed relatively high interest in the diary writers' social lives, such as going on a date or playing tennis with someone. Another investigation found that rejected persons were especially likely to search for and notice smiling faces (DeWall, Maner, & Rouby, 2009). For example, they were quicker than others to spot a smiling face in a crowd of faces, and they tended to look longer at smiling faces than neutral faces, relative to other participants.

Some actual signs of trying to form a new social connection were found by Maner, DeWall, Baumeister, and Schaller (2007). In these studies, rejected persons were more interested than others in joining a campus service to facilitate meeting people. They also bestowed more rewards on future interaction partners than other people did, possibly to get the person in a good mood.

None of these findings indicates that rejected persons rush off to make new friends. Rather, the findings suggest that they are cautiously interested in finding people who seem likely to accept them. Perhaps the best integration is to suggest that rejected people want to be accepted but also want to avoid being rejected again. They may want the other person to make the first move, and then they may respond positively. If social overtures may not bring acceptance, the rejected persons may be especially antisocial. Consistent with this view, some evidence indicates that rejected people adopt a broad motivational orientation toward minimizing dangers and risks—what Higgins (1997) calls a prevention focus, as opposed to a promotion focus that seeks to cultivate positive outcomes (Park & Baumeister, 2015).

Rejection appears to affect cognitive processes other than attention to the likelihood of others' acceptance. Rejection seems to have a strong, though presumably temporary, effect on one's intelligence. One series of studies found substantial drops in IQ scores among rejected persons (Baumeister, Twenge, & Nuss, 2002). Perhaps surprisingly, rejected people were quite capable when performing simple intellectual tasks, even able to concentrate well enough to read a passage and answer questions about it correctly. But performance on more complicated mental tasks, such as logical reasoning and extrapolation, was seriously impaired. The implication is that rejection undermines controlled but not automatic processes.

However, an alternative explanation for a number of these findings is that rejected and ostracized people simply do not want to exert themselves. They may become passive, exhibiting a lack of desire to put forth the effort to think for themselves. Consistent with this possibility is research linking rejection to impaired self-regulation. This line of work was stimulated in part by Cacioppo's observation that lonely people often have poor attention control (see Cacioppo & Patrick, 2008), as indicated by poor performance on dichotic listening. In a dichotic listening task, participants wear headphones, and different voices are piped into each ear, so that the person must screen out one voice and focus attention on what the other one is saying. Rejected persons show similar deficits, and they also self-regulate poorly on other tests of self-control (Baumeister, DeWall, Ciarocco, & Twenge, 2005). However, they remain capable of performing perfectly well when external incentives are present, such as if a cash incentive is available for good performance.

One way of integrating these findings is to suggest that humans desire to be accepted but recognize that they have to pay a price for belongingness, such as by exerting themselves to self-regulate and behave properly. If they perceive themselves to be rejected, they lose their willingness to pay that price and make those efforts. Hence they become passive, lazy, and uncooperative. But if they see a chance to be accepted again, or if another motivation comes to the fore, they are quite capable of pulling themselves together and making the right efforts.

Emotional Consequences

It is hardly controversial to suggest that rejection makes people feel bad. A literature review on anxiety concluded that the most common and widespread cause is fear of being rejected or otherwise excluded from groups or relationships (Baumeister & Tice, 1990). Baumeister and Leary (1995) went so far as to suggest that a basic function of emotions is to promote interpersonal connection, insofar as most negative emotions have some link to threat or damage to relationships (think of grief, jealousy, anger, sadness, anxiety, etc.), whereas any event that conveys social acceptance, such as forming or solidifying social bonds, typically brings positive emotion.

The link between rejection and emotion seemed like one of the easier tasks for psychological theory to handle. As sometimes happens, however, the data did not cooperate. Some early studies of interpersonal rejection found no sign of changes in mood or emotion (e.g., Twenge et al., 2001). Even when emotional differences were found, they often failed to mediate the behavioral effects (e.g., Buckley, Winkel, & Leary, 2004; Williams et al., 2000). At first it was assumed that researchers had used the wrong scale or that participants simply refused to acknowledge their distress, but evidence with multiple measures continued to produce the same pattern.

At the same time, links to physical pain were emerging. An investigation to what people mean when they say their "feelings were hurt" found that hurt feelings essentially signify the feeling of being rejected or excluded, or at least a step in that direction (Leary, Springer, Negel, Ansell, & Evans, 1998). In this case, it may not even matter whether the person intended to hurt you. Rather, your hurt feelings depend on how much you value the relationship and how strongly you got the impression that the other person did not value it as much as you do (Leary, 2005). Brain scans indicated that similar brain sites were activated when people were rejected during the Cyberball game as were activated when people suffered physical pain (Eisenberger et al., 2003).

Perhaps most remarkably, a review by MacDonald and Leary (2005) showed that being rejected often causes a feeling of numbness. The review mainly emphasized research with animals. For example, when rat pups are excluded from the litter, they develop some loss of sensitivity to physical pain (Kehoe & Blass, 1986; Naranjo & Fuentes, 1985; Spear, Enters, Aswad, & Louzan, 1985). This research pointed to something Jaak Panksepp had theorized decades earlier (Herman & Panksepp, 1978; Panksepp, Herman, Conner, Bishop, & Scott, 1978; Panksepp, Vilberg, Bean, Coy, & Kastin, 1978). When animals evolved to become social, they needed biological systems to respond to social events, and rather than developing entirely new systems in the body to deal with the social world, evolution piggybacked the social responses onto the already-existing systems. Hence, social rejection activated some of the same physiological responses as physical injury, just as Eisenberger et al. (2003) later showed.

Physical injury does not always cause maximum pain right away. A shock reaction often numbs the pain for a brief period. Possibly this was something that developed to enable an injured animal to make its way to safety without being distracted by intense pain. Regardless, the shock or numbness reaction offered a possible explanation for the lack of immediate emotion reported by many studies of rejection.

The links between rejection, emotion, and physical pain were explored most directly in a series of experiments by DeWall and Baumeister (2006). Consistent with the ideas of MacDonald and Leary (2005) and Panksepp, Herman, Conner, Bishop, and Scott (1978), rejected participants in those studies showed low sensitivity to pain: Rejected participants were slower than others to report that something hurt and slower to complain that it became intolerable. Moreover, the lack of pain sensitivity correlated closely with a lack of report of emotional reaction to pain. This generalized even to other emotional phenomena, such as feeling sympathy with someone else's misfortune or predicting how one would feel depending on the outcome of the university's much-anticipated football game next month.

A comprehensive review of the effects of rejection was provided in a meta-analysis by Blackhart et al. (2009). Their results showed that rejection does indeed produce significant changes in emotion. The reason many researchers had failed to report significant results was that the effect was rather weak, and so the small to medium samples used in most studies lacked the statistical power to detect them. But when results from many studies were combined, it was clear that rejected people did feel worse than accepted ones—and even, though just barely, worse than neutral controls. Accepted people felt better than controls, though this effect, too, was weak.

Yet feeling worse does not necessarily mean feeling bad. When Blackhart et al. (2009) compiled the data about just how bad people felt, it emerged that rejected people typically reported emotional states that were near the neutral point on the scale and, if anything, slightly on the positive side.

Does that mean rejection is not upsetting? Hardly. The lab studies examine one-time, immediate reactions to rejection experiences that mainly involve strangers. Being rejected repeatedly and by people you love may be more immediately upsetting.

All of this has made for an intriguing mixture. It appears that being rejected produces an immediate reaction that is not quite what anyone expected. There is a shift away from positive mood and happy emotions toward a neutral state, but it is not entirely the same as the numbness of shock, either. Impaired emotional responsiveness appears to be one way of characterizing it. Most researchers assume that genuine distress does come along at some point, but it has been surprisingly hard to get rejected people to say that they feel bad right now. Meanwhile, the impairment of emotional responsiveness may prove a useful tool for researchers who wish to study the effects of emotion on other factors, such as judgment and cognition.

Loneliness

The laboratory studies of immediate reactions to carefully controlled rejection experiences can be augmented by studying people who feel rejected and socially excluded over a long period of time. The largest body of work on such effects concerns loneliness. Being left out of social relationships makes people lonely.

Research has largely discredited the stereotype of lonely persons as social misfits or unattractive, socially inept losers. Lonely and nonlonely people are quite similar in most respects, including attractiveness, intelligence, and social skills. In fact, lonely people even spend about the same amount of time as other people in social interaction (Cacioppo & Patrick, 2008). In general, then, loneliness is not a lack of contact with other people (Wheeler, Reis, & Nezlek, 1983). Rather, it seems to reflect a dissatisfaction with the quality of interaction. Lonely people come away social interactions feeling that something important was lacking (Cacioppo & Hawkley, 2005).

If there is one core problem that seems to produce loneliness, it is that lonely people are worse than normal at emotional empathy—at understanding other people's emotional states (Pickett & Gardner, 2005). Even with this finding, however, it is not yet fully clear what is cause and what is effect. Conceivably, the difficulty of empathic connection with another person's emotions is a result of loneliness rather than its cause.

Once we understand loneliness as a lack of certain kinds of satisfying relationships, we can begin to ask what those are. Marriage and family are obviously important bonds to many people. Although simply being married is no guarantee against loneliness, married people are somewhat less likely than single people to be lonely (Peplau & Perlman, 1982; Russell et al., 1980). The new mobility of modern life also takes its toll in terms of loneliness, because people will move far from home for college or work, and the farther someone lives from home, the more likely he or she is to be lonely.

If one does not have close ties to romantic partners or best friends, what other sorts of bonds can reduce loneliness? For men but not women, feeling connected to a large organization reduces loneliness (Gardner, Pickett, & Knowles, 2005). For example, men can feel a bond with their university, their employer, or even a sports team, and this helps prevent loneliness, but it does not work for women. The reason, very likely, is that the social inclinations of women tend to focus very heavily on close, intimate social connections. Men like those intimate relationships also, but men are also oriented toward large groups and organizations (Baumeister & Sommer, 1997).

Some people even form pseudo-relationships with celebrities or fictional characters such as people on television shows. Women who watch many situation comedies feel less lonely than other women, even when both have the same quantity of real friends and lovers (Kanazawa, 2002). Other people are able to reduce loneliness by feeling connected to nonhuman living things, such as a dog or even a plant. These diverse strands have been pulled together into a provocative theory of "social surrogates" by Gabriel, Valenti, and Young (2015). These scholars noted three main classes of things people do to keep loneliness at bay when they do not have enough actual relationships with close others. First, they immerse themselves in alternative social worlds, such as books and television shows. These often simulate social interaction, and one can feel one is learning about how to get along with people. Second, they collect nonhuman reminders of real social relationships, such as pictures or keepsakes from loved ones who are far away. Some people develop eating habits associated with so-called comfort foods, which might be what their mother or another loving person fed them. Third, they form one-sided "parasocial" relationships with media figures, such as favorite celebrities or even fictional characters.

If the causes of loneliness are only slowly becoming clear, its consequences seem better known, and they are not good (see Cacioppo & Patrick, 2008). By middle age, lonely people drink more alcohol than other people, exercise less, and eat less healthy food. They sleep as much as others but not as well. Their lives are no more stressful than other people's lives in any objective sense, but subjectively they feel more stress. They enjoy the good things in life less than other people do, and they suffer more from the bad things.

Why Rejection Occurs

Why do people reject each other? There are many answers. Studies of rejection among children focus on three main things that lead to rejection (e.g., Juvonen & Gross, 2005). The first is being aggressive. Probably because children do not want to risk getting hurt, they avoid other children who are aggressive. This seems ironic in the context of what we noted previously, namely, that being rejected causes people to become more aggressive. One way to put this together is that aggression is seen as incompatible with human social life, and so aggressive people are rejected, just as rejection fosters aggression.

A second reason is that isolation seems to breed more isolation. That is, some children tend to withdraw from others and keep to themselves, and other children respond to this by avoiding them all the more. This can create an unfortunate spiral leading to loneliness and many of the problems that go with it. Possibly children view the loner as someone who is rejecting them, and so they respond by rejecting the person in return.

The third reason is deviance. Children who are different in any respect are prone to be rejected by others. Regardless of whether they look different, talk differently, have an unusual family, or act in unusual ways, differentness invites rejection. Children at both extremes of intellectual ability are rejected, which again suggests that merely being different from the average or typical is enough to cause rejection.

What about romantic rejection? An early study on romantic rejection by Folkes (1982) explored women's reasons for refusing a date with a man. The reasons the women told the researchers were not, however, the reasons they reported telling the men. They differed along all three of the major dimensions of attribution theory (Kelley, 1967). The reasons they gave to the man who asked them out tended to be unstable, external (to the man), and specific, whereas their actual reasons tended to be stable, internal, and global. For example, she might say she was busy that particular night. Such an excuse is unstable (it applies to only that night; tomorrow might be different), external (it has nothing to do with him), and specific (it's one narrow issue). In reality, she might be declining the invitation because she finds him unattractive (which is a permanent, general aspect of him).

Romantic rejection sometimes is more than declining a date. Sometimes one person has developed strong romantic feelings toward the other, who does not feel the same way. This is called *unrequited love*. Studies indicate that the two roles have very different experiences (e.g., Baumeister, Wotman, & Stillwell, 1993; Hill, Blakemore, & Drumm, 1997). Rejecters often have a difficult time refusing love even if they do not really want it. They feel guilty, which is one reason they may make excuses or avoid the other person rather than clearly stating the reasons for refusing the other's advances. They do not want to hurt the other person's feelings—and as we saw earlier, hurt feelings are precisely a response to discovering that the other person does not desire or value a connection with you to the extent that you want that connection. Sure enough, unrequited love often precipitates feelings of low self-esteem and other self-doubts among the rejected persons.

Returning to why rejection occurs, the fact is that it can serve important social goals. Like children, adults reject people who are different from them (Wright, Giammarino, & Parad, 1986). They have a more negative reaction to deviance among members of their group than among outsiders (Hogg, 2005). Indeed, given exactly the same amount of deviance, groups reject insiders more than outsiders (Marques & Yzerbyt, 1988). Even just performing badly at a task is more troubling and, hence, more likely to cause rejection when it is by a member of the group than by someone outside the group (Marques & Paez, 1994; Marques, Abrams, Paez, & Hogg, 2001). To be sure, it works both ways: Good performance by ingroup members is appreciated and rewarded more than equally good performance by someone outside the group.

Thus, rejection can serve a valuable function for solidifying the group in two ways. It gets rid of people who do not fit in or who otherwise detract from the group. And it motivates the people in the group to behave properly, cooperate with others, and contribute to the group, so that they will not be rejected.

Rejection Research Today

Research on rejection boomed from about 2000 until recently, and some researchers are still doing excellent work on the topic. Loneliness remains a major social problem and is likely to increase as people become more fragmented, partly because more and more people live alone. The rise of the Internet and social media has seemed to promise new forms of belonging, but recent data suggest that online interactions by social media do not really satisfy the need to belong. If anything, high use of social media seems to intensify loneliness rather than solve it. At best, online interactions can strengthen weak offline social relationships into more satisfying ones, rather than substituting for offline live human interaction (for reviews, see Liu, Ainsworth, & Baumeister, 2016; Liu & Baumeister, 2016).

Social psychology's new emphasis on large samples has made it difficult to conduct the sorts of labor-intensive rejection studies that many researchers were running a decade ago, in which people endured a rejection experience during live interaction in the laboratory. Online rejection manipulations sacrifice some scientific precision but may be the main way ahead. The Cyberball and its variants are convenient because they are readily scalable for online data collection, but they are limited insofar as they deprive the person both of social participation and control (consistent with Williams's [2002] theory that ostracism involves both control and belongingness). Having people recall a personal experience of rejection and briefly describe it can evoke the memories, but distant memories tend to have been already understood and interpreted, unlike the often baffling and disorienting effects of immediate rejection.

Conclusion

Because functioning within cultural systems is complex, so are interpersonal attraction and rejection. Although this chapter has reviewed many of the most promising social-psychological ideas and findings on these topics, a primary conclusion is that there is so much left to learn. Given how central the experiences of attraction and rejection are to achieving a high-quality life, developing a more complete understanding of how these processes work represents an essential goal for social psychology in the coming decade.

Notes

1. These two metatheoretical frameworks do not encompass all research on attraction. Indeed, Finkel and Eastwick (2015) also discussed a third framework—attachment-based models—but we set such research aside for the present review because few attraction studies to date have drawn from it. Still, the two meta-theoretical frameworks can speak to vast swaths of the literature and can facilitate the development of a common lexicon for attraction research.
2. Although the effect of *perceived* (psychological) similarity on attraction is robust, evidence that *actual* similarity predicts attraction has been oddly elusive (Finkel et al., 2012; Luo & Zhang, 2009; Tidwell et al., 2013).

References

Aharon, I., Etcoff, N., Ariely, D., Chabris, C. F., O'Connor, E., & Breiter, H. C. (2001). Beautiful faces have variable reward value: fMRI and behavioral evidence. *Neuron, 32,* 537–551.

Aronson, E., & Linder, D. (1965). Gain and loss of esteem as determinants of interpersonal attractiveness. *Journal of Experimental Social Psychology, 1,* 156–172.

Aronson, E., Willerman, B., & Floyd, J. (1966). The effect of a pratfall on increasing interpersonal attractiveness. *Psychonomic Science, 4,* 227–228.

Backman, C. W., & Secord, P. F. (1959). The effect of perceived liking on interpersonal attraction. *Human Relations, 12,* 379–384.

Baumeister, R. F. (2005). *The cultural animal: Human nature, meaning, and social life.* New York: Oxford University Press.

Baumeister, R. F., DeWall, C. N., Ciarocco, N. J., & Twenge, J. M. (2005). Social exclusion impairs self-regulation. *Journal of Personality and Social Psychology, 88,* 589–604.

Baumeister, R. F., & Leary, M. R. (1995). The need to belong: Desire for interpersonal attachments as a fundamental human motivation. *Psychological Bulletin, 117,* 497–529.

Baumeister, R. F., & Sommer, K. L. (1997). What do men want? Gender differences and two spheres of belongingness: Comment on Cross and Madson (1997). *Psychological Bulletin, 122,* 38–44.

Baumeister, R. F., & Tice, D. M. (1990). Anxiety and social exclusion. *Journal of Social and Clinical Psychology, 9,* 165–195.

Baumeister, R. F., Twenge, J. M., & Nuss, C. (2002). Effects of social exclusion on cognitive processes: Anticipated aloneness reduces intelligent thought. *Journal of Personality and Social Psychology, 83,* 817–827.

Baumeister, R. F., Wotman, S. R., & Stillwell, A. M. (1993). Unrequited love: On heartbreak, anger, guilt, scriptlessness, and humiliation. *Journal of Personality and Social Psychology, 64,* 377–394.

Berscheid, E. (1985). Interpersonal attraction. In G. Lindzey & E. Aronson (Eds.), *The handbook of social psychology* (3rd ed., Vol. 2, pp. 413–484). New York, NY: Random House.

Berscheid, E., & Walster, E. (1974). A little bit about love. In T. Huston (Ed.), *Foundations of interpersonal attraction* (pp. 355–381). New York, NY: Academic Press.

Berscheid, E., & Walster, E. (1978). *Interpersonal attraction* (2nd ed.). Reading, MA: Addison-Wesley.

Blackhart, G. C., Nelson, B. C., Knowles, M. L., & Baumeister, R. F. (2009). Rejection elicits emotional reactions but neither causes immediate distress nor lowers self-esteem: A meta-analytic review of 192 studies on social exclusion. *Personality and Social Psychology Review, 13,* 269–309

Boyd, D. M., & Ellison, N. B. (2007). Social network sites: Definition, history, and scholarship. *Journal of Computer-Mediated Communication, 13,* 210–230.

Buckley, K. E., Winkel, R. E., & Leary, M. R. (2004) Emotional and behavioral responses to interpersonal rejection: Anger, sadness, hurt, and aggression. *Journal of Experimental Social Psychology, 40,* 14–28.

Buss, D. M. (1989). Sex differences in human mate preferences: Evolutionary hypotheses tested in 37 cultures. *Behavioral and Brain Sciences, 12,* 1–49.

Buss, D. M., & Barnes, M. L. (1986). Preferences in human mate selection. *Journal of Personality and Social Psychology, 50,* 559–570.

Buss, D. M., & Schmitt, D. P. (1993). Sexual strategies theory: An evolutionary perspective on human mating. *Psychological Review, 100,* 204–232.

Byrne, D. (1961). Interpersonal attraction and attitude similarity. *Journal of Abnormal and Social Psychology, 62,* 713–715.

Cacioppo, J. T., & Hawkley, L. C. (2005). People thinking about people: The vicious cycle of being a social outcast in one's own mind. In K. D. Williams, J. P. Forgas, & W. von Hippel (Eds.), *The social outcast: Ostracism, social exclusion, rejection, and bullying* (pp. 91–108). New York, NY: Psychology Press.

Cacioppo, J. T., & Patrick, W. (2008). *Loneliness: Human nature and the need for social connection.* New York, NY: Norton.

Clark, R. D. III. (1990). The impact of AIDS on gender differences in the willingness to engage in casual sex. *Journal of Applied Social Psychology, 20,* 771–782.

Clark, R. D. III, & Hatfield, E. (1989). Gender differences in receptivity to sexual offers. *Journal of Psychology and Human Sexuality, 2,* 39–55.

Clark, M. S., & Mills, J. (1979). Interpersonal attraction in exchange and communal relationships. *Journal of Personality and Social Psychology, 37,* 12–24.

Cloutier, J., Heatherton, T. F., Whalen, P. J., & Kelley, W. M. (2008). Are attractive people rewarding? Sex differences in the neural substrates of facial attractiveness. *Journal of Cognitive Neuroscience, 20,* 941–951.

Collins, N. L., & Miller, L. C. (1994). Self-disclosure and liking: A meta-analytic review. *Psychological Bulletin, 116,* 457–575.

Conley, T. D. (2011). Perceived proposer personality characteristics and gender differences in acceptance of casual sex offers. *Journal of Personality and Social Psychology, 100,* 309–329.

Cosmides, L. (1989). The logic of social exchange: Has natural selection shaped how humans reason? Studies with the Wason selection task. *Cognition, 31,* 187–276.

Cunningham, M. R., & Barbee, A. P. (2008). Prelude to a kiss: Nonverbal flirting, opening gambits, and other communication dynamics in the initiation of romantic relationships. In S. Sprecher, A. Wenzel, & J. Harvey (Eds.), *Handbook of relationship initiation* (pp. 97–120). New York, NY: Guilford.

Cunningham, M. R., & Barbee, A. P., & Philhower, C. L. (2002). Dimensions of facial physical attractiveness: The intersection of biology and culture. In G. Rhodes & L. A. Zebrowitz (Eds.), *Facial attractiveness: Evolutionary, cognitive, and social perspectives* (pp. 193–238). Westport, CT: Ablex.

Curtis, R. C., & Miller, K. (1986). Believing another likes or dislikes you: Behaviors making the beliefs come true. *Journal of Personality and Social Psychology, 51,* 284–290.

Deaux, K. (1972). To err is humanizing: But sex makes a difference. *Representative Research in Social Psychology, 3,* 20–28.

DeWall C. N., & Baumeister, R. F. (2006). Alone but feeling no pain: Effects of social exclusion on physical pain tolerance and pain threshold, affective forecasting, and interpersonal empathy. *Journal of Personality and Social Psychology, 91,* 1–15.

DeWall, C. N., Baumeister, R. F., & Vohs, K. D. (2008). Satiated with belongingness? Effects of acceptance, rejection, and task framing on self-regulatory performance. *Journal of Personality and Social Psychology, 95,* 1367–1382.

DeWall C. N., Maner, J. K., & Rouby, D. A. (2009). Social exclusion and early-stage interpersonal perception: Selective attention to signs of acceptance. *Journal of Personality and Social Psychology, 96,* 729–741.

Dutton, D. G., & Aron, A. P. (1974). Some evidence for heightened sexual attraction under conditions of high anxiety. *Journal of Personality and Social Psychology, 30,* 510–517.

Eagly, A. H., & Wood, W. (1999). The origins of sex differences in human behavior. *American Psychologist, 54,* 408–423.

Eastwick, P. W. (2009). Beyond the Pleistocene: using phylogeny and constraint to inform the evolutionary psychology of human mating. *Psychological Bulletin, 135,* 794–821.

Eastwick, P. W., & Finkel, E. J. (2008). Sex differences in mate preferences revisited: Do people know what they initially desire in a romantic partner? *Journal of Personality and Social Psychology, 94,* 245–264.

Eastwick, P. W., Finkel, E. J., Mochon, D., & Ariely, D. (2007). Selective versus unselective romantic desire: Not all reciprocity is created equal. *Psychological Science, 18,* 317–319.

Eastwick, P. W., Finkel, E. J., & Simpson, J. A. (2018). Best practices for testing the predictive validity of ideal partner preference-matching. *Personality and Social Psychology Bulletin.* https://doi.org/10.1177/0146167218780689

Eastwick, P. W., Keneski, E., Morgan, T. A., McDonald, M. A., & Huang, S. A. (2018). What do short-term and long-term relationships look like? Building the relationship coordination and strategic timing (ReCAST) model. *Journal of Experimental Psychology: General, 147,* 747–781.

Eastwick, P. W., Luchies, L. B., Finkel, E. J., & Hunt, L. L. (2014). The predictive validity of ideal partner preferences: A review and meta-analysis. *Psychological Bulletin, 140,* 623–665.

Eisenberger, N. I., Lieberman, M. D., & Williams, K. D. (2003). Does rejection hurt? An fMRI study of social exclusion. *Science, 302,* 290–292.

Feingold, A. (1990). Gender differences in effects of physical attractiveness on romantic attraction: A comparison across five research paradigms. *Journal of Personality and Social Psychology, 59,* 981–993.

Festinger, L., Schachter, S., & Back, K. (1950). *Social pressures in informal groups: A study of human factors in housing.* Stanford, CA: Stanford University Press.

Finkel, E. J. (2017). *The all-or-nothing marriage: How the best marriages work.* New York, NY: Dutton.

Finkel, E. J., & Baumeister, R. F. (2010). Attraction and rejection. In R. F. Baumeister, and E. J. Finkel (Eds.), *Advanced social psychology: The state of the science* (pp. 419–459). New York, NY: Oxford University Press.

Finkel, E. J., & Eastwick, P. W. (2008). Speed-dating. *Current Directions in Psychological Science, 17,* 193–197.

Finkel, E. J., & Eastwick, P. W. (2015). Interpersonal attraction: In search of a theoretical Rosetta stone. In J. A. Simpson & J. F. Dovidio (Eds.), *APA Handbook of personality and social psychology. Vol. 3: Interpersonal relations* (pp. 179–210). Washington, DC: American Psychological Association.

Finkel, E. J., Eastwick, P. W., Karney, B. R., Reis, H. T., & Sprecher, S. (2012). Online dating: A critical analysis from the perspective of psychological science. *Psychology Science in the Public Interest, 13,* 3–66.

Fitzsimons, G. M., & Shah, J. Y. (2008). How instrumentality shapes relationship evaluations. *Journal of Personality and Social Psychology, 95,* 319–337.

Folkes, V. S. (1982). Communicating the reasons for social rejection. *Journal of Experimental Social Psychology, 18,* 235–252.

Freud, S. (1930). *Civilization and its discontents.* (J. Riviere, Trans.). London, England: Hogarth.

Gabriel, S., Valenti, J., & Young, A.F. (2016). Social surrogates, social motivations, and everyday activities: The case for a strong, subtle, and sneaky social self. In M. Zanna & J. Olson (Eds.), *Advances in experimental social psychology* (Vol. 53, pp. 189–243). Cambridge, MA: Academic Press.

Gangestad, S. W., & Simpson, J. A. (2000). The evolution of human mating: Trade-offs and strategic pluralism. *Behavioral and Brain Sciences, 23,* 573–644.

Gangestad, S. W., & Thornhill, R. (1998). Menstrual cycle variation in women's preferences for the scent of symmetrical men. *Proceedings of the Royal Society of London B: Biological Sciences, 265,* 927–933.

Gangestad, S. W., Thornhill, R., & Garver-Apgar, C. E. (2005). Adaptations to ovulation: Implications for sexual and social behavior. *Current Directions in Psychological Science, 14,* 312–316.

Gardner, W. L., Pickett, C. L., & Brewer, M. B. (2000). Social exclusion and selective memory: How the need to belong influences memory for social events. *Personality and Social Psychology Bulletin, 26,* 486–496.

Gardner, W. L., Pickett, C. L., & Knowles, M. (2005). Social snacking and shielding Using social symbols, selves, and surrogates in the service of belonging needs. In K. D. Williams, J. P. Forgas, & W. von Hippel (Eds.), *The social outcast: Ostracism, social exclusion, rejection, and bullying* (pp. 227–242). New York, NY: Psychology Press.

Gildersleeve, K., Haselton, M. G., & Fales, M. R. (2014). Do women's mate preferences change across the ovulatory cycle? A meta-analytic review. *Psychological Bulletin, 140,* 1205–1259.

Gordon, R. A. (1996). Impact of ingratiation on judgments and evaluations: A meta-analytic investigation. *Journal of Personality and Social Psychology, 71,* 54–70.

Graziano, W. G., & Bruce, J. W. (2008). Attraction and the initiation of relationships: A review of the empirical literature. In S. Sprecher, A. Wenzel, & J. Harvey (Eds.), *Handbook of relationship initiation* (pp. 269–295). New York, NY: Guilford.

Harris, J. A. (1912). Assortive mating in man. *Popular Science Monthly, 80,* 476–492.

Haselton, M. G., & Gangestad. S. W. (2006). Conditional expression of women's desires and men's mate guarding across the ovulatory cycle. *Hormones and Behavior, 49,* 509–518.

Hazan, C., & Diamond, L. M. (2000). The place of attachment in human mating. *Review of General Psychology, 4,* 186–204.

Hazan, C., & Zeifman, D. (1994). Sex and the psychological tether. *Advances in Personal Relationships, 5,* 151–177.

Herbst, K. C., Gaertner, L., & Insko, C. A. (2003). My head says yes but my heart says no: Cognitive and affective attraction as a function of similarity to the ideal self. *Journal of Personality and Social Psychology, 84,* 1206–1219.

Herman, B. H., & Panksepp, J. (1978). Effects of morphine and naloxone on separation distress and approach attachment: Evidence for opiate mediation of social affect. *Pharmacology, Biochemistry & Behavior, 9,* 213–220.

Higgins, E. T. (1997). Beyond pleasure and pain. *American Psychologist, 52,* 1280–1300.

Hill, C. A., Blakemore, J., & Drumm, P. (1997). Mutual and unrequited love in adolescence and adulthood. *Personal Relationships, 4,* 15–23.

Hill, R. (1945). Campus values in mate-selection. *Journal of Home Economics, 37,* 554–558.

Hitsch, G. J., Hotaçsu, A., & Ariely, D. (2010). What makes you click? Mate preferences in online dating. *Quantitative Marketing and Economics, 8,* 393–427.

Hogg, M. A. (2005). All animals are equal but some animals are more equal than others: Social identity and marginal membership. In K. D. Williams, J. P. Forgas, & W. von Hippel (Eds.), *The social outcast: Ostracism, social exclusion, rejection, and bullying* (pp. 243–262). New York, NY: Psychology Press.

Holt-Lunstad, J., Smith, T. B., & Layton, J. B. (2010). Social relationships and mortality risk: A meta-analytic review. *PLoS Medicine, 7,* e1000316.

House, J. S., Landis, K. R., & Umberson, D. (1988). Social relationships and health. *Science, 241,* 540–545.

Huang, K., Yeomans, M., Brooks, A. W., Minson, J., & Gino, F. (2017). It doesn't hurt to ask: Question-asking increases liking. *Journal of Personality and Social Psychology, 113,* 430–452.

Huston, T. L. (1973). Ambiguity of acceptance, social desirability, and dating choice. *Journal of Experimental Social Psychology, 9,* 32–42.

Joel, S., Eastwick, P. W., & Finkel, E. J. (2017). Is romantic desire predictable? Machine learning applied to initial romantic attraction. *Psychological Science, 28,* 1478–1489.

Juvonen, J., & Gross, E. F. (2005). The rejected and the bullied: Lessons about social misfits from developmental psychology. In K. D. Williams, J. P. Forgas, & W. von Hippel (Eds.), *The social outcast: Ostracism, social exclusion, rejection, and bullying* (pp. 155–170). New York: Psychology Press.

Kanazawa, S. (2002). Bowling with our imaginary friends. *Evolution and Human Behavior, 23,* 167–171.

Kehoe, P., & Blass, E. M. (1986). Behaviorally functional opioid systems in infant rats: II. Evidence for pharmacological, physiological, and psychological mediation of pain and stress. *Behavioral neuroscience, 100,* 624–630.

Kellerman, J., Lewis, J., & Laird, J. D. (1989). Looking and loving: The effects of mutual gaze on feelings of romantic love. *Journal of Research in Personality, 23,* 145–161.

Kelley, H. H. (1967). Attribution theory in social psychology. In D. Levine (Ed.), *Nebraska Symposium on Motivation* (Volume 15, pp. 192–238). Lincoln, NE: University of Nebraska Press.

Kenny, D. A., & La Voie, L. (1984). The social relations model. In L. Berkowitz (Ed.), *Advances in experimental social psychology* (Vol. 18, pp. 141–182). New York, NY: Academic Press.

Kinsey, A. C., Pomeroy, W. B., & Martin, C. E. (1948). *Sexual behavior in the human male.* Philadelphia, PA: Saunders.

Langlois, J. H., Kalakanis, L., Rubenstein, A. J., Larson A., Hallam, M., & Smoot, M. (2000). Maxims or myths of beauty? A meta-analytic and theoretical review. *Psychological Bulletin, 126,* 390–423.

Langlois, J. H., Roggman, L. A., Casey, R. J., Ritter, J. M., Rieser-Danner, L. A., & Jenkins. V. Y. (1987). Infant preferences for attractive faces: Rudiments of a stereotype? *Developmental Psychology, 23,* 363–369.

Langlois, J. H., Roggman, L. A., & Musselman, L. (1994). What is average and what is not average about attractive faces. *Psychological Science, 5,* 214–220.

Leary, M. R. (2005). Varieties of interpersonal rejection. In K. D. Williams, J. P. Forgas, & W. von Hippel (Eds.), *The social outcast: Ostracism, social exclusion, rejection, and bullying* (pp. 35–52). New York, NY: Psychology Press.

Leary, M. R., & Baumeister, R. F. (2000). The nature and function of self-esteem: Sociometer theory. In M. Zanna (Ed.), *Advances in experimental social psychology* (Vol. 32, pp. 1–62). San Diego, CA: Academic Press.

Leary, M. R., Kowalski, R. M., Smith, L., & Phillips, S. (2003). Teasing, rejection, and violence: Case studies of the school shootings. *Aggressive Behavior, 29,* 202–214.

Leary, M. R., Springer, C., Negel, L., Ansell, E., & Evans, K. (1998). The causes, phenomenology, and consequences of hurt feelings. *Journal of Personality and Social Psychology, 74,* 1225–1237.

Leary, M. R., Tambor, E. S., Terdal, S. K., & Downs, D. L. (1995). Self-esteem as an interpersonal monitor: The sociometer hypothesis. *Journal of Personality and Social Psychology, 68,* 518–530.

Liu, D., Ainsworth, S. E., & Baumeister, R.F. (2016). A meta-analysis of social networking online and social capital. *Review of General Psychology, 20,* 363–391.

Liu, D., & Baumeister, R.F. (2016). Social networking online and personality of self-worth: A meta-analysis. *Journal of Research in Personality, 64,* 79–89.

MacDonald, G., & Leary, M. R. (2005). Why does social exclusion hurt? The relationship between social and physical pain. *Psychological Bulletin, 131,* 202–223.

Maner, J. K., DeWall, C. N., Baumeister, R. F., & Schaller, M. (2007). Does social exclusion motivate interpersonal reconnection? Resolving the "porcupine problem." *Journal of Personality and Social Psychology, 92,* 42–55.

Marques, J. M., Abrams, D., Paez, D., & Hogg, M. A. (2001). Social categorization, social identification, and rejection of deviant group members. In G. Fletcher & M. Clark (Eds.), *Blackwell handbook of social psychology: Group processes* (pp. 400–424). New York, NY: Wiley.

Marques, J. M., & Paez, D. (1994). The 'black sheep effect': Social categorization, rejection of ingroup deviates, and perception of group variability. *European Review of Social Psychology, 5*(1), 37–68.

Marques, J. M., & Yzerbyt, V. Y. (1988). The black sheep effect: Judgmental extremity in inter- and intra-group situations. *European Journal of Social Psychology, 18,* 287–292.

Maslow, A. H. (1968). *Toward a psychology of being.* New York, NY: Wiley.

Montoya, R. M., & Horton, R. S. (2014). A two-dimensional model for the study of interpersonal attraction. *Personality and Social Psychology Review, 18,* 59–86.

Montoya, R. M., Horton, R. S., & Kirchner, J. (2008). Is actual similarity necessary for attraction? A meta-analysis of actual and perceived similarity. *Journal of Social and Personal Relationships, 25,* 889–922.

Moreno, J. L. (1934). *Who shall survive? A new approach to the problem of human interrelationships.* Washington, DC: Nervous and Mental Disease Publishing.

Naranjo, J. R., & Fuentes, J. A. (1985). Association between hypoalgesia and hypertension in rats after short-term isolation. *Neuropharmacology, 24,* 167–171.

Newcomb, T. M. (1956). The prediction of interpersonal attraction. *American Psychologist, 11,* 575–586.

Newcomb, T. M. (1961). *The acquaintance process.* New York, NY: Holt, Rinehart, and Winston.

Nezlek, J. B., Kowalski, R. M., Leary, M. R., Blevins, T., & Holgate, S. (1997). Personality moderators of reactions to interpersonal rejection: Depression and trait self-esteem. *Personality and Social Psychology Bulletin, 23,* 1235–1244.

O'Doherty, J., Winston, J., Critchley, H., Perrett, D., Burt, D. M., & Dolan, R. J. (2003). Beauty in a smile: the role of medial orbitofrontal cortex in facial attractiveness. *Neuropsychologia, 41,* 147–155.

Open Science Collaboration. (2015). Estimating the reproducibility of psychological science. *Science, 349,* aac4716. http://science.sciencemag.org/content/349/6251/aac4716

Panksepp, J., Herman, B., Conner, R., Bishop, P., & Scott, J. P. (1978). The biology of social attachments: Opiates alleviate separation distress. *Biological Psychiatry, 13,* 607–618.

Panksepp, J., Vilberg, T., Bean, N. J., Coy, D. H., & Kastin, A. J. (1978). Reduction of distress vocalization in chicks by opiate-like peptides. *Brain Research Bulletin, 3,* 663–667.

Park, J., & Baumeister, R. F. (2015). Social exclusion causes a shift toward prevention motivation. *Journal of Experimental Social Psychology, 56,* 153–159.

Peplau, L. A., & Perlman, D. (Eds.). (1982). *Loneliness: A sourcebook of current theory, research, and therapy.* New York, NY: Wiley.

Pickett, C. L., & Gardner, W. L. (2005). The social monitoring system: Enhanced sensitivity to social cues and information as an adaptive response to social exclusion and belonging need. In K. D. Williams, J. P. Forgas, & W. von Hippel (Eds.), *The social outcast: Ostracism, social exclusion, rejection, and bullying* (pp. 213–226). New York, NY: Psychology Press.

Rebman, C. (1999). Eighth amendment and solitary confinement: The gap in protection from psychological consequences. *DePaul Law Review, 49,* 567–620.

Reis, H. T. (2007). Steps toward the ripening of relationship science. *Personal Relationships, 14,* 1–23.

Reis, H. T., Maniaci, M. R., Caprariello, P. A., Eastwick, P. W., & Finkel, E. J. (2011). Familiarity does indeed lead to attraction in live interaction. *Journal of Personality and Social Psychology,* 557–570.

Rhodes, G. (2006). The evolutionary psychology of facial beauty. *Annual Review of Psychology, 57,* 199–226.

Rhodes, G., Harwood, K., Yoshikawa, S., Nishitani, M., & MacLean, I. (2002). The attractiveness of average faces: Cross-cultural evidence and possible biological basis. In G. Rhodes & L. A. Zebrowitz (Eds.), *Facial attractiveness: Evolutionary, cognitive and social perspectives* (pp. 35–58). Westport, CT: Ablex.

Rubenstein, A. J., Langlois, J. H., & Roggman, L. A. (2002). What makes a face attractive and why: The role of averageness in defining facial beauty. In G. Rhodes & L. A. Zebrowitz (Eds.), *Facial attractiveness: Evolutionary, cognitive and social perspectives* (pp. 1–33). Westport, CT: Ablex.

Russell, D., Peplau, L. A., & Cutrona, C. E. (1980). The revised UCLA Loneliness Scale: Concurrent and discriminant validity evidence. *Journal of Personality and Social Psychology, 39*, 472–480.

Selterman, D. F., Chagnon, E., & Mackinnon, S. P. (2015). Do men and women exhibit different preferences for mates? A replication of Eastwick and Finkel (2008). *SAGE Open.* https://doi.org/10.1177/2158244015605160

Skinner, B. F. (1938). *The behavior of organisms: An experimental analysis.* New York, NY: Appleton-Century.

Slater, A., Von der Schulenburg, C., Brown, E., Badenoch, M., Butterworth, G., Parsons, S., & Samuels, C. (1998). Newborn infants prefer attractive faces. *Infant Behavior and Development, 21*, 345–354.

Spear, L. P., Enters, E. K., Aswad, M. A., & Louzan, M. (1985). Drug and environmentally induced manipulations of the opiate and serotonergic systems alter nociception in neonatal rat pups. *Behavioral and Neural Biology, 44*, 1–22.

Sprecher, S., Sullivan, Q., & Hatfield, E. (1994). Mate selection preferences: Gender differences examined in a national sample. *Journal of Personality and Social Psychology, 66*, 1074–1080.

Straus, M. A., Gelles, R. J., & Steinmetz, S. K. (1980). *Behind closed doors: Physical violence in the American family.* New York, NY: Doubleday/Anchor.

Thibaut, J. W., & Kelley, H. H. (1959). *The social psychology of groups.* New York, NY: Wiley.

Thorndike, E. L. (1898). Animal intelligence: An experimental study of the associative processes in animals. *Psychological Review: Monograph Supplements, 2*(4).

Tidwell, N. D., Eastwick, P. W., & Finkel, E. J. (2013). Perceived, not actual, similarity predicts initial attraction in a live romantic context: Evidence from the speed-dating paradigm. *Personal Relationships, 20*, 199–215.

Tooby, J., & Cosmides, L. (1992). The psychological foundations of culture. In J. H. Barkow, L. Cosmides & J. Tooby (Eds.), *The adapted mind: Evolutionary psychology and the generation of culture* (pp. 19–136). New York, NY: Oxford University Press.

Trivers, R. L. (1972). Parental investment and sexual selection. In B. G. Campbell (Ed.), *Sexual selection and the descent of man, 1871–1971* (pp. 136–179). Chicago, IL: Aldine.

Twenge, J. M., Baumeister, R. F., DeWall, C. N., Ciarocco, N. J., & Bartels, J. M. (2007). Social exclusion decreases prosocial behavior. *Journal of Personality and Social Psychology, 92*, 56–66.

Twenge, J. M., Baumeister, R. F., Tice, D. M., & Stucke, T.S. (2001). If you can't join them, beat them: Effects of social exclusion on aggressive behavior. *Journal of Personality and Social Psychology, 81*, 1058–1069.

Van Beest, I., & Williams, K. (2006). When inclusion costs and ostracism pays, ostracism still hurts. *Journal of Personality and Social Psychology, 91*, 918–928.

Vonk, R. (2002). Self-serving interpretations of flattery: Why ingratiation works. *Journal of Personality and Social Psychology, 82*, 515–526.

Waller, W. (1938). *The family: A dynamic interpretation.* New York, NY: Gordon.

Walster, E., Aronson, V., Abrahams, D., & Rottman, L. (1966). Importance of physical attractiveness in dating behavior. *Journal of Personality and Social Psychology, 4*, 508–516.

Walster, E., Walster, G. W., Piliavin, J., & Schmidt, L. (1973). "Playing hard to get": Understanding an elusive phenomenon. *Journal of Personality and Social Psychology, 26*, 113–121.

Wheeler, L., Reis, H. T., & Nezlek, J. (1983). Loneliness, social interaction, and sex roles. *Journal of Personality and Social Psychology, 45*, 943–953.

Williams, K. D. (2002). *Ostracism: The power of silence.* New York, NY: Guilford.

Williams, K. D., Cheung, C. K. T., & Choi, W. (2000). CyberOstracism: Effects of being ignored over the Internet. *Journal of Personality and Social Psychology, 79*, 748–762.

Williams, K. D., & Sommer, K. L. (1997). Social ostracism by coworkers: Does rejection lead to loafing or compensation? *Personality and Social Psychology Bulletin, 23,* 693–706.

Williams, K. D., & Zadro, L. (2005). Ostracism: The indiscriminate early detection system. In K. D. Williams, J. P. Forgas, & W. von Hippel (Eds.), *The social outcast: Ostracism, social exclusion, rejection, and bullying* (pp. 19–34). New York, NY: Psychology Press.

Wilson, E. O. (1975). *Sociobiology: The new synthesis.* Cambridge, MA: Harvard University Press.

Wood, W., & Eagly, A. H. (2002). A cross-cultural analysis of the behavior of women and men: Implications for the origins of sex differences. *Psychological Bulletin, 128,* 699–727.

Wood, W., Kressel, L., Joshi, P. D., & Louie, B. (2014). Meta-analysis of menstrual cycle effects on women's mate preferences. *Emotion Review, 6,* 229–249.

Wright, J. C., Giammarino, M., & Parad, H. W. (1986). Social status in small groups: Individual-group similarity and the social "misfit." *Journal of Personality and Social Psychology, 50,* 523–536.

Chapter 10

Close Relationships

Shelly L. Gable

Think about the close relationships you have had in your life. Chances are you thought of your relationships with family members, friends, roommates, and romantic partners. Although these relationships are unique, they all have somethings in common—characteristics that made you label these relationships "close" but label your relationships with your barber, office mate, and doctor as something else. What is it about connections that make them qualify as *close*? Social psychologists have come up with different definitions for close relationships but they converge on several features. First, close relationships have *interdependence*. Interdependent partners influence one another's thoughts, feelings, and behaviors, and this influence is strong and pervasive across contexts and time. So, even though you and your co-worker might influence one another's thoughts and behaviors related to your jobs while at work, when your work day is over you both go your separate ways until your shifts begin again. Your relationship with your co-worker in this case would not be a close relationship because the mutual influence is confined to a particular context (the office) and time (the workday).

Another feature of close relationships is that the two partners know things about one another that nonclose others do not necessarily know—intimate things such as their backgrounds, likes and dislikes, attitudes, and future goals. Typically, this *intimate knowledge* is relatively balanced, such that each one has knowledge of the other that goes beyond the superficial. As the president of the local Justin Bieber fan club, you might know everything there is to know about his background and his latest tweet, but the fact that Mr. Bieber has no intimate knowledge of you means that (sadly) your relationship is not close. Finally, close relationships don't have a predetermined expiration date. Close relationship partners have some degree of *commitment* to maintaining their relationship. This does doesn't mean that all close relationships last forever; family members stop speaking to each other, friends drift apart, and spouses divorce. However, close relationship partners typically assume the relationship will last into the future, and friends and spouses do not form relationships while anticipating their eventual demise. The features of interdependence, intimacy, and commitment are central to close relationships and have long been the topic of songs, novels, gossip, and, yes, scientific inquiry.

Relationship Science: A Brief Trip Down Memory Lane

Given how much time we spend thinking about relationships with others in our own lives, it is probably not surprising that close relationships are also of interest to social psychologists. However, the scientific study of relationships is a relative newcomer to the field of behavioral science. Historically, people relied on the poets and playwrights for the business of understanding relationships. There was also active opposition to the formal study of close relationships. Some people believed that relationships were too complex to lend themselves to the scientific method or that understanding the underpinnings of things such as love would somehow cause them to lose their appeal or magic. Still others thought that topics such as friendship, family, and attraction were not important enough to put resources toward understanding them.

Nevertheless, there were pioneering empirical inquiries into relationship topics beginning in the late 19th century and first half of the 20th century. Emile Durkheim, a founding figure in modern sociology published the book *Suicide* in 1897 (Durkheim, 1951). In this work, Durkheim gathered information from public records and church archives to support his hypothesis that individuals with few close social ties (e.g., marriage, church ties) had higher incidents of suicide than those with more social connections. In the 1930s, Alfred Kinsey began his systematic study of human sexual behavior. Kinsey, trained as a biologist,[1] was well versed in scientific methods. He and his colleagues interviewed more than 18,000 individuals about their sexual histories. Although Kinsey and his work were the source of public and scientific controversy, the books detailing his findings, *Sexual Behavior of the Human Male*, published in 1948, and *Sexual Behavior of Human Female*, published in 1953, were bestsellers and made Kinsey a celebrity.

Prior to the mid-1960s, there was a smattering of studies published on relationship topics, but relationship science in psychology really came into its own in the late 1960s and early 1970s as studies on topics such as affiliation, love, attraction, and interdependence began to emerge. Still, public reaction to scientific studies of relationships was mixed. In 1976, William Proxmire, a senator from Wisconsin, started handing out the *Golden Fleece* award to projects he deemed to be a waste of taxpayer money. The first "award" was given to the National Science Foundation for funding a study on attraction and romantic love. This award led to a great deal of media attention and public speculation on the feasibility and moral implications of a scientific approach to relationships, especially romantic relationships. In the midst of this controversy, a tabloid publication polled its readers about whether romantic love could be understood scientifically, and only 12.5% of readers thought so (Hatfield, 2006)![2]

Today, the landscape is different. Despite the occasional grandstanding of a politician, relationships research has thrived in the last 30 years. Fueled by the growing realization that close relationships are deeply entwined with human and societal health and well-being (more on this in the next section), and the public's appetite for information that might help them understand their own relationships, the scientific study of relationships has flourished. Today, academic journals and societies are devoted to publishing the best research on the topic, and books based on scientific findings in relationships but written for a general audience are avidly consumed by the public. Researchers are busy replicating important findings as well as testing theories and hypotheses in different populations and circumstances. Social psychologists are currently using both traditional methods and the latest tools to help them understand relationships. In addition to investigating many novel questions, they have also sought scientific, evidence-based answers to many of the questions that have long been on everyone's mind. Questions include: What is love? How do people maintain their relationships? What makes relationships good or bad? Is conflict the beginning of the end for a relationship? Which relationships last? Social psychologists have asked these and many other questions using the tools of science. Perhaps the question to consider first is: Why should anyone care about relationships in the first place?

Are Close Relationships Important?

Some topics in social psychology are intuitively important to study because they have an obvious impact on people's lives. Prejudice and discrimination have detrimental effects on a vast swath of people, so understanding stereotypes from which they spring is critical (e.g., Williams, Neighbors, & Jackson, 2003). The ubiquity of first-person shooter games demands research on whether playing violent video games causes people to be more aggressive in real life (e.g., Anderson et al., 2010). However, just because close relationships are intrinsically fascinating and are the topic of many discussions and forms of art doesn't necessarily mean they are associated with important outcomes such as happiness and health. After all, cat videos on YouTube are very popular, but few would argue that watching them is associated one way or other with public health.[3] To assess whether close relationships have any implications for important outcomes, we can turn to studies examining the role that relationships play in health, happiness, and having a meaningful life.

Physical Health

Epidemiologists study health patterns in the population; they typically collect data from a large sample and follow them over time to find out the risk factors associated with later disease onset and death. In addition to risk factors such as living a sedentary life, epidemiology studies have consistently found another, not so obvious risk factor for disease and early death: the lack of close relationships (e.g., House, Landis, & Umberson, 1988). Based on a recent meta-analysis of these types of studies (over 150 longitudinal studies), researchers concluded that having high-quality supportive relationships was as strong or stronger a predictor of death as other well-known mortality risks like smoking, excessive alcohol use, and obesity (Holt-Lunstad, Smith, & Layton, 2010). To get concrete, people who reported having low-quality social connections had a 40% higher mortality rate (during the follow-up interval of the relevant study) than those who reported having positive and supportive relationships with others.

Relationships that have a lot of conflict, and ones in which the relationship partners are cold and uncaring to one another are quite literally bad for your health (e.g., Miller, Rohleder, & Cole, 2009). On the other hand, warm and supportive ties can buffer people from a variety of other stresses and strains in life that otherwise take a toll on health (e.g., Farrell et al., 2017). It also should be noted that there is a direct pathway linking close relationships to health; violence committed by intimate partners, especially against women, is a world-wide health crisis (e.g., Ellsberg et al., 2008). Overall the data are clear and convincing: Warm, caring, and supportive ties are associated with better health, enhanced recovery from disease, and lower mortality. In contrast, a lack of close relationships or hostile, cold, and distant relationships are associated with worse health, poorer recovery from disease, and increased mortality.

Happiness and Meaning in Life

Close relationships and happiness are also tightly linked. Studies consistently find that people who have rewarding social and family relationships have higher overall happiness and satisfaction with life than those with less rewarding social and family ties (e.g., Helliwell & Putman, 2004). In fact, in one study, researchers compared the happiest people in a sample (those who scored in the top 10% on a combination of several happiness measures) to the least happy people in the sample (those who scored in the bottom 10% on the same measures) to try to determine what differentiated these two groups of people. The characteristic that uniformly separated these two groups was the quality of their close relationships; all those in the happiest group reported having higher quality relationships with their family, close friends, and romantic partners that those in the least happy group did not (Diener & Seligman, 2002).

Happiness is important, but many philosophers and psychologists have argued convincingly that having a sense of purpose and meaning in life is also a critical component of well-being. Here again, research suggests that high-quality close relationships predict whether one reports experiencing meaning in life (Hicks & King, 2009; Krause, 2007; Steger, Kashdan, Sullivan, & Lorentz, 2008). People regularly answer the question "What gives your life purpose and meaning?" with variations of "my close relationships." In short, studies consistently find that relationship quality is a better predictor of happiness and life satisfaction than many of the other things long assumed to underpin happiness, such as having a prestigious occupation or making a ton of money (e.g., Campbell, Converse, & Rodgers, 1976).

In summary it is clear that close relationships play an important role in both psychological well-being and physical health. They *are* important to understand. As noted in the opening section, social bonds that share the features of interdependence, intimacy, and commitment are considered close relationships. However, the majority of research on adult relationships has focused on romantic relationships; there are fewer studies on friendships and family relationships. The remainder of this chapter provides an overview of some of the areas of interest and representative findings from the social psychology of close relationships in adults, and the theories and studies covered reflect the emphasis in the literature on romantic relationships.

Attachment

Bowlby (1969) argued that humans are born with the architecture for forming strong attachments to primary caregivers. The blueprints for forming bonds are like hardware in the sense that they function basically the same for everyone. These basic functions are referred to as the *normative functions*. However, these blueprints can also be tweaked in response to the environment and experiences with those with whom we form attachment bonds. Thus, one can also think of individuals as having different software running within the design of the underlying hardware. These variations in the software are known as *individual differences* in attachment. Although Bowlby first proposed attachment theory to explain the relationship between infants and primary caregivers, both the normative functions and individual difference components are critical for understanding adult relationships as well.

Normative Functions

Human babies are extremely cute but in the grand scheme of things they are also rather useless. They cannot keep themselves warm; they cannot feed or defend themselves; they can't even hide from predators very well (try playing hide and seek with a one-year-old; you will win *every* time). Moreover, compared to most other mammals, this helpless state lasts a really long time. How does the human infant survive its prolonged period of development to become a relatively self-sufficient person? The attachment behavioral system, selected through evolution, relies on the social nature of humans to increase the likelihood that the infant survives. Through the process of natural selection, we are left with a hardwired *behavioral system* that functions to get someone, known as the attachment figure, to take care of us and meet our many needs.

A behavioral system is a suite of goals, cognitions, and behavioral options that are activated under certain cues in the environment. The attachment behavioral system has several elements that function to increase the likelihood of survival and eventual reproduction, which are the only things that really count in terms of evolution (e.g., Bowlby, 1969; Hazan & Zeifman, 1994; Mikulincer & Shaver, 2003). The first element is *proximity seeking* and functions to keep us close to attachment figures by approaching them and keeping them near. Related to the desire for proximity is the experience of distress when separated from attachment figures and resisting sudden or prolonged separations, known as *separation protest*. The second element is *safe haven:* We turn to attachment figures for comfort and protection when we feel threatened, sad, or otherwise distressed. The final function of an attachment figure is to serve as *secure base* from which to take risks and explore new environments and opportunities.

Mary Ainsworth and her colleagues developed a procedure to assess attachment behavior in the lab, known as the *strange situation* (Ainsworth & Bell, 1970). In a strange situation test 12- to 18-month-old babies are put in a room with their primary caregiver and some toys. Then over several steps a stranger enters the room, and the primary caregiver leaves and then returns. Throughout the session observers note what the child does—how she interacts with the caregiver and stranger: how she explores the room when the caregiver is there and how she reacts when the caregiver leaves and then returns. In general, this provides evidence that children prefer being close to their primary givers over other adults (e.g., the stranger) and become distressed when separated from them. They also seek out the attachment figure when scared but explore new environments when the attachment figure is nearby (e.g., Ainsworth, Blehar, Waters, & Wall, 1978).

Parents or other primary caregivers serve as attachment figures for infants and children. As children grow into adolescents and then adults, they increasingly report that their attachment bonds are with a larger network of relationship partners, including friends, other family members, and romantic partners (Hazan & Zeifman, 1994; Mikulincer & Shaver, 2003). Although as adults we may have several attachment bonds, the relationship that has been studied the most as the primary attachment bond is the romantic relationship. Indeed, most people who have been in a romantic relationship two years or more report that their partner serves as their primary attachment figure—at least in Western nations where this topic has been studied most extensively. However, you may wonder whether the normative functions of attachment that serve to enhance the survival of babies and children continue to play out in adults who presumably can fend for themselves (and even play hide and seek fairly well). That is, is there any evidence that many of the same goals, cognitions, and behavioral tendencies involved in the attachment normative functions (e.g., safe haven) are alive and well in adults?

Obviously, it would be quite useless (but possibly quite amusing) to put adults through Ainsworth's strange situation laboratory paradigm to answer this question. Researchers, however, have used a variety of other methods to assess whether and, if so, how the attachment system works in adults. In a series of studies, Mario Mikulincer and his colleagues harnessed the power of classic social cognition techniques to address this broad question. For example, in set of studies participants were first subliminally primed with either threatening words (e.g., *failure*) or neutral words (e.g., *hat*; Mikulincer, Gillath, & Shaver, 2002). In this type of priming paradigm stimuli are presented so quickly that participants were not even aware a word had been presented (20 milliseconds) and can only report seeing a flash. Immediately after each of these quick presentations they completed a lexical decision task, which consists of a string of letters that are presented on the computer screen. Sometimes these letters spell a word and sometimes they are just a series of letters (nonwords); participants are asked to determine, as quickly as possible, whether the string of letters is a word or a nonword. The idea here is that certain primes, even when presented outside of people's awareness, should facilitate their ability to process certain words. For example, Americans who are subliminally primed with *peanut butter* likely would be faster to subsequently recognize the word *jelly* in the lexical decision task than other words or a nonword or than if they had been primed with something else, like *starfish*.

In these studies, the researchers hypothesized that if the attachment system is still active in adults then they should be faster at identifying words related to their attachment figures after threat primes than after neutral primes. This would happen because threats should make the attachment figures more cognitively accessible due to the secure base function. That's exactly what they found. Participants were faster to recognize their attachment figures (but not other familiar people or nonwords) following a threat prime compared to a neutral prime (Mikulincer et al., 2002). Other studies using similar logic and methods showed that priming threat (compared to nonthreatening primes) made words related to proximity such as *closeness* and *hug* more cognitively accessible than neutral words such as *office* and *boat* (Mikulincer, Birnbaum, Woddis, & Nachmias, 2000).

Research has also found that feelings of security in adult relationships are related to exploration and motivation in the achievement domain (Elliot & Reis, 2003). Other work has targeted the brain regions possibly associated with attachment related function. In one study, participants viewed photos of their romantic partner or a stranger while they were scanned in an functional magnetic resonance imaging machine during trials in which a painful heat stimulation was administered (Eisenberger et al., 2011). The results showed that the stimuli were rated as less painful during trials in which the attachment figure was viewed, and the brain scans showed increased neural activity in regions of the brain associated with signals of safety. Other studies have similarly shown that proximity, in the form of holding a loved one's hand reduces reports of painful shock, but only for those who report high-quality bonds with their attachment figure (Coan, Schaefer, & Davidson, 2006).

Although attachment behavior observed in infants is not the same as we see in adults, adults have parallel and developmentally appropriate cognitions, goals, and behavior that maintain the same basic functions of attachment. For example, we might text our partners during the day to maintain a sense of proximity or call them for some reassurance when we are feeling stressed. In short, the findings from the previously described studies and other similar studies are consistent with the notion that the proximity seeking, safe haven, and secure base functions of attachment are alive and well in adults. Understanding the underlying hardware governing the attachment system helps put the formation and maintenance of adult close relationships in context.

Individual Differences in Attachment

Although the basic architecture of attachment is thought to be endowed by evolution and universal across humans, there is also plenty of room for variations in attachment processes. These variations are thought to result from a combination of temperamental differences and responses to experiences with caregivers. Some caregivers are responsive to a child's needs, attending to them when the child is hungry, tired, or otherwise uncomfortable. These responsive caregivers encourage exploration and some risk-taking but also are quick to offer support if the child becomes distressed. Other caregivers may not be as optimally responsive; the caregiver may have difficulty himself or herself being responsive or the child may be temperamentally difficult to parent. Caregivers in these situations can be distant and neglecting of a child's needs, or they can be inconsistently responsive or provide care that is not contingent on the child's needs (sometimes not responding to a need or interjecting care when it is not needed). Based on these experiences, Bowlby (1973) hypothesized that children learn what to expect from their caregivers and develop patterns of interactions with others accordingly.

Indeed, Mary Ainsworth's studies (Ainsworth & Bell, 1970; Ainsworth et al., 1978) using the strange situation paradigm showed that not all infants react the same. Consistent with Bowlby's (1969) original theory, Ainsworth identified three different patterns of behavior in infants, which she called *attachment types*. One pattern was called the *secure* pattern. Infants of this type maintained proximity to the caregiver but explored the laboratory environment. They were upset when the caregiver left but easily comforted when she returned (the caregivers in this early research were typically mothers). Roughly 60% of infants fall into this category. A second pattern of behavior was called the *anxious-ambivalent* style. These infants

TABLE 10.1   Hazan and Shaver's (1987) Self-Report Measure Assessing Secure, Avoidant, and Anxious-Ambivalent Attachment Tendencies in Adulthood

Which one of the following describes your feelings?

A. I find it relatively easy to get close to others and am comfortable depending on them and having them depend on me. I don't often worry about being abandoned or about someone getting too close to me.

B. I am somewhat uncomfortable being close to others; I find it difficult to trust them completely, difficult to allow myself to depend on them. I am nervous when anyone gets too close, and often, love partners want me to be more intimate than I feel comfortable being.

C. I find that others are reluctant to get as close as I would like. I often worry that my partner doesn't really love me or won't want to stay with me. I want to merge completely with another person, and this desire sometimes scares people away

Note: A = secure; B = avoidant; C = anxious-ambivalent. From "Romantic Love Conceptualized as an Attachment Process, by C. Hazan and P. Shaver, 1987. *Journal of Personality and Social Psychology, 52,* 511–524, Study 1.

maintained close proximity to the caregivers, minimally exploring the laboratory environment. They exhibit extreme distress in response to the caregiver's absence and are difficult to soothe when she returns, simultaneously clinging to the caregiver and pushing her away. Roughly 20% of infants fall into this category. A third category is called the *avoidant* style. These children make little distinction between caregiver and stranger. They show little signs of protest when the caregiver leaves, or interest in reestablishing contact when she returns. They explore the environment regardless of whether the caregiver is there. Roughly 20% of children fall into this category.

Given the evidence that the basic architecture of the attachment system plays out in adult close relationships, could it also be that the individual differences observed in infants distinguish adult relationships? Hazan and Shaver (1987) asked this exact question in a study on adult romantic relationships. They created three descriptions (see Table 10.1) of adult relationships that corresponded roughly to the three different styles of attachment observed by Ainsworth in infants. They asked people to choose which one of the descriptions best described them. The majority of people, about 56% described themselves as secure, being comfortable and relaxed about closeness and intimacy. The remaining people described themselves as either being worried their partners didn't love them and would leave them (25%; anxious-ambivalent) or just not being comfortable getting close to others and relying on them in any meaningful way (19%; avoidant). They say Helen of Troy's face launched a thousand ships; although by no means definitive, Hazan and Shaver's paper launched a thousand studies. Building on their findings, researchers began examining individual differences in attachment styles and how these variations were related to a variety of behaviors and experiences in close relationships.

Bartholomew (1990) maintained that three categories were not sufficient to described adult attachment. Specifically, one can avoid closeness for two different reasons: Avoidance can be based on a fear of being hurt and abandoned (fearful) or on a preference for independence and self-sufficiency (dismissing). Within this system, people can describe themselves as characterized by one of four different attachment styles: secure, preoccupied (formerly knowns as anxious-ambivalent), fearful, or dismissing (see the descriptions of each style in Figure 10.1). As Bowlby (1973) originally proposed, underlying these categories were two independent working models—a *model of self* and a *model of other.* The model of self concerns an internalized a sense of self-worth. Those who have a positive model of self think of themselves as worthy of others' esteem and expect others to respond positively, whereas those who have a negative model of self view themselves as unworthy of regard and are anxious about how others will respond to them. The model of other reflects whether other people in general are available and supportive. People who hold a positive model of other see people as capable of being depended upon, whereas a negative model of other is predicated on the expectation the other people are not dependable or supportive. People with secure attachment styles have positive models of both self and other whereas people with one of the three

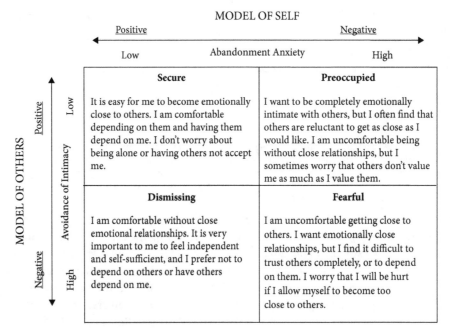

FIGURE 10.1. Attachment categories, working models of self and other, and the two-dimensional model of attachment. Adapted from "Avoidance of Intimacy: An Attachment Perspective," by K. Bartholomew, 1990, *Journal of Social and Personal Relationships, 7,* 147–178; "Are Adult Attachment Styles Categorical or Dimensional? A Taxometric Analysis of General and Relationship-Specific Attachment Orientations," by R. C. Fraley, N. W. Hudson, M. E. Heffernan, & N. Segal, 2015, *Journal of Personality and Social Psychology, 109,* 354–368; and "Models of the Self and Other: Fundamental Dimensions Underlying Measures of Adult Attachment, by D. W. Griffin & K. Bartholomew, 1994, *Journal of Personality and Social Psychology, 67,* 430–445.

insecure styles have a negative model of self, other, or both. In Figure 10.1 the model of self and the model of other are overlaid on the four category system.

If you think that you do not fit neatly into one of the four categories of attachment, there is a good reason. The most up-to-date research on attachment jettisons the categories and instead measures two *continuous* and independent dimensions of individual differences in attachment (Mikulincer & Shaver, 2003). Continuous dimensions are those in which people can score high, low, or somewhere in the middle, and there are no cut-offs indicating different categories or types. The two dimensions are *avoidance of intimacy*, representing the degree of comfort people have in being close to an intimate with others, and *abandonment anxiety*, representing the degree people worry that others will find them worthless and leave. These two underlying dimensions, often referred to simply as avoidance and anxiety, are also depicted in Figure 10.1 so you can see how they correspond to the four categories and the working models of self and other. Contemporary research has shown that these two largely uncorrelated dimensions better represent individual differences in attachment related experiences and behaviors than a categorical system (Fraley, Hudson, Heffernan, & Segal, 2015).

Research also suggests that experiences with caregivers in childhood are associated with individual differences in later attachment (e.g., Fraley, 2002). The evidence suggests that the working models, or relationship schemas, that infants learned early in life are filters through which they view new relationships when they are older. For example, those with a secure attachment may enter a new relationship expecting others to be caring and responsive and thus interpret behavior and events in a manner consistent with those expectations. On the other hand, those with insecure models have less optimistic expectations about how relationships unfold and may interpret the same behaviors and events in a new relationship as threatening. Moreover, early-established working models can lead people to seek out situations (and partners) that confirm their working models (Fraley, 2002). However, changes to working models also occur with experience when people repeatedly encounter information that is inconsistent with their expectations. Thus, people can become more or less secure on either dimension (e.g., Fraley et al., 2011). In short, there is evidence for both long-term stability and change in attachment from childhood to adulthood.

Not surprisingly, individual differences in abandonment anxiety and avoidance of closeness can have a large impact on relationship experiences and behaviors. For example, compared to those low on the anxiety dimension, those high on anxiety tend to be oversensitive to negative emotion in partners during conflict, see their partners as less supportive, and are more prone to jealousy, even on Facebook (e.g., Collins & Feeney, 2004; Marshall et al., 2013; Overall et al., 2015). Compared to those low on the avoidance dimension, those high on avoidance tend to seek out others less for support, have more casual sex, and are less forgiving of their partners (e.g., Chung, 2014; Collins & Feeney, 2004; Gentzler & Kerns, 2004). Finally, people who are insecure (high on either dimension) *and* those who are partnered with them tend to report lower relationship satisfaction and lower sexual satisfaction (e.g., Butzer & Campbell, 2008; Chung, 2014).

Relationships and Accounting 101

Close relationships have both rewards and costs. *Rewards* are anything valuable gained from being in the relationship. *Costs* are anything undesirable coming from the being in the relationship or anything of value given up as part of the relationship. Perhaps your romantic partner is the source of benefits such as companionship, opportunities for growth, and access to a wider social network. The same person may also be the source of costs such as being frustrating sometimes, hurting your feelings, and taking time that you could be spending on other activities outside of the relationship, such as indulging in your Dungeons and Dragons obsession (Gable, 2015). Benefits and costs can be social, emotional, or tangible. How do people decide whether the benefits of relationships outweigh the costs?

Social Exchange Theory

George Homans (1958) proposed an economic theory of human behavior in which people try to maximize their profits and minimize their losses in social interactions. He called this *social exchange theory* and reasoned that people keep track of rewards and costs and maintain relationships that provide the most benefits for the least cost. However, relationships are also governed by a norm of reciprocity such that we expect to give as well as receive, and we are uncomfortable with what might be seen as extreme overbenefits from someone else. According to exchange theory, we all engage in a little simple math and tally up our outcomes by subtracting our costs from our rewards. Thus, the manner in which value is assigned to those rewards and costs is critical in this equation.

In general, the value put on rewards and costs are governed by some of the same principles that govern basic economic behavior. A reward may be more or less valuable according to how scarce it is—the lone eligible man in a retirement home filled with women may be more popular than in other situations. Value judgments are also affected by people's recent experiences with the reward or cost. That is, the exact same reward (or cost) may be more or less valuable (or costly) to a person depending on his or her recent exposure. The first love letter may be a heart stopper, but the hundredth love letter in month may barely raise the recipient's pulse. Going up a flight of stairs once to retrieve a partner's car keys is a cost, but going up the same flight of stairs a second time to retrieve his wallet may be psychologically more costly than that first trip.

People also differ in their sensitivities to rewards and costs, which is referred to as individual differences in approach and avoidance motivation, respectively (Gable, 2006, 2015). These individual differences influence experiences and behavior in close relationships in a variety of ways including how much value is placed on rewards and costs in relationships. In one study, participants first completed measures of their approach and avoidance orientations to gauge their reward and cost sensitivity, respectively. Over the next week, they received a signal from a handheld device at several random intervals throughout the day in what is known as a signal-contingent daily experience study (Gable & Poore, 2008). At each signal, they reported their positive thoughts and feelings about their partner and their negative thoughts and feelings about their partners. The positive thoughts and feelings are rewarding, but the negative thoughts and worries about partners are costs in relationships. They also reported once at the end of the day how satisfied they felt with their relationship overall.

On average, and not surprisingly, on days that people reported more rewards and fewer costs they were more satisfied than on days that they reported fewer rewards and more costs. However, individual differences moderated this pattern; people who were more approach-oriented showed big increases in satisfaction on days they reported more rewards and big decreases in satisfaction on days they reported fewer rewards. However, those who were low on approach-orientation were not sensitive to rewards; their satisfaction levels did not vary in accordance with how many or few rewards they experienced. A similar pattern was seen for avoidance-orientation such that the satisfaction of those high on avoidance-orientation varied depending on whether they had incurred bigger or smaller costs throughout the day; however, the relationship satisfaction reported by those low on avoidance orientation was independent of the costs they incurred during the day.

Interdependence Theory

A classic pair of books by John Thibaut and Harold Kelley (Kelley & Thibaut, 1978; Thibaut & Kelly, 1959) outlined a type of exchange theory called *interdependence theory* in which additional concepts to the exchange theory notions of outcomes, costs, and rewards were introduced. The first important addition is the comparison level (CL), which is the level of outcomes people think they deserve. Each person has his or her own CL based on learning, prior relationships, and personality. The CL is an expectation for what you *should* get from relationships. Some people may think their rewards minus costs should leave them with a relatively high positive amount (a high CL) while others may be just fine if that hypothetical equation leaves them with a number just above zero (a low CL). A person, such as one with poor self-worth, might even expect that others will or should treat them poorly such that their costs will *outweigh* rewards, leaving them with a hypothetical negative number for a CL. Interdependence theory argues that satisfaction with a relationship is a function of the outcomes (rewards – costs) minus the CL: the more outcomes *exceed* CL, the greater the satisfaction and happiness is experienced in the relationship, and the more outcomes fall *below* CL, the greater the dissatisfaction and unhappiness.

Another critical component of interdependence theory is CL for alternatives (CL_{ALT}). The CL_{ALT} is the perceived value of outcomes available if one left his or her current relationship. The CL_{ALT} is what is expected to be obtained in another relationship or situation (e.g., being single). Some people might think there are lots of potential good relationship partners out there (a high CL_{ALT}) while others are convinced that there are very few proverbial fish in the sea (a low CL_{ALT}). The CL_{ALT} is critical for another important dimension of a relationship—its stability. Stability is a function of how dependent the partners are on the relationship and is determined by comparing outcomes to the CL_{ALT}. If outcomes exceed the available alternatives, one is dependent on the relationship. On the other hand, if the available alternatives are better than the current outcomes, then one is not dependent on that relationship.

Thus, to understand both a person's satisfaction with and stability of their relationship one needs to know his or her outcomes, CL and CL_{ALT}. Outcomes and CL contribute to the happiness (satisfaction) of a relationship while outcomes and the CL_{ALT} contribute to the stability (dependence) of a relationship. If outcomes in a relationship exceed both the CL and CL_{ALT}, then the relationship is both happy and stable. If outcomes exceed the CL but not the CL_{ALT}, then the relationship is happy but unstable (the person is happy, but there are also lots of alternatives so who knows when something better might come along). If outcomes fall short of the CL but exceed the CL_{ALT}, the relationship is unhappy but stable (the person is not satisfied, but the other options to the relationship are worse). Finally, if outcomes do not reach either the CL or CL_{ALT}, then the relationship is both unhappy and unstable (the person is not satisfied and is likely actively looking at all those wonderful opportunities out there).

Keeping track of outcomes and making ongoing comparisons seems a bit calculating and cold. Are we really engaged in a constant arithmetic exercise in our closest relationships? Clark and Mills (1979) suggest not; they argue that it is important to distinguish two different kinds of relationships. In some relationships, we keep a careful ledger and have expectations that favors will be returned in kind and within a relatively brief period of time. When we hand over cash to a salesperson, we expect the items to be handed over to us right way. When we do a favor for someone, we expect immediate return of something similar for us. These are called *exchange relationships,* and the rules that govern them center on expectations regarding the mutual exchange of benefits and keeping the ledger book even. On the other hand, we have relationships in which we actually don't expect immediate repayment of benefits. It would feel strange if your child wrote you a check because you gave her a ride home from basketball practice. Instead these relationships are based on the expectation that you will each respond to one another's needs, and if benefits are given based on this premise, in the long run there is no need for a ledger book. These are called *communal relationships.*

Commitment

Rob Reiner directed a movie called *The Story of Us* about a married couple played by Bruce Willis and Michelle Pfeiffer. Their two children head off to camp for the summer and Willis's and Pfeiffer's characters take this opportunity to evaluate their struggling marriage, deciding whether to divorce. The movie is chock-full of flashback scenes (using weird hairstyles to signify the passage of time) of the ups and downs of their relationship over the years. And, the characters try living apart for the summer, realizing they are capable of being on their own. In the end, Pfeiffer's character wants a divorce, but (spoiler alert) in the final scene as they pick up the kids from camp and prepare to tell them the news, Pfeiffer's character has a revelation that abruptly changes her decision. Her revelation is in the form of a montage of flashbacks focused on everything that *would be lost* if they divorce—things such as mutual memories, their shared knowledge, the household, and the experience of raising children together. They are lost in the sense that were forged in what her character describes as a "dance that can only be perfected over time." In a scene, her commitment to her marriage shifts, and she vows to work on making their outcomes better and more satisfying.

Rusbult (1980) extended interdependence theory to focused on this critical variable of commitment. Commitment is the intention to continue in a relationship, including a long-term orientation and a sense of psychological attachment and predicts the behavior of staying or leaving an established relationship. In Rusbult's *investment model*, depicted in Figure 10.2, she theorized that commitment stems not only from satisfaction (determined from outcomes and CL) and quality of alternatives (CL_{ALT}) but also from the size of the *investments* made in the relationship. Investments are the things, both tangible and intangible,

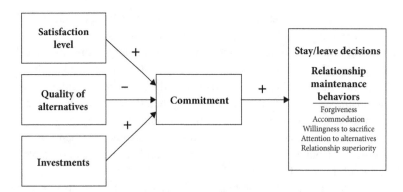

FIGURE 10.2. The investment model. Adapted from "Commitment and Satisfaction in Romantic Associations: A Test of the Investment Model," by C. E. Rusbult, 1980, *Journal of Experimental Social Psychology, 16,* 172–186, and "Commitment Processes in Close Relationships: An Interdependence Analysis, by C. E. Rusbult & B. P. Buunk, 1993," *Journal of Social and Personal Relationships, 10,* 175–204.

that would be lost if the relationship ended; they are what Pfeiffer's character sees in the final scene of the movie. It is the sum of the efforts already put forth in the relationship, as well as the results of those efforts (children, the house, shared friends, etc.). While some investments might be replaced eventually in other relationships, the effort put into those particular investments is already expended. Higher satisfaction, lower quality of alternatives, and more investments predict greater commitment.

Commitment predicts the decision to stay in a relationship or dissolve that relationship. There is a great deal of evidence supporting the investment model; people who are more satisfied, have fewer alternatives, and have more invested in the relationship tend to stay in relationship more than people who are less satisfied, have more alternatives, or have less invested in that relationship (Le & Agnew, 2003). Importantly, investments and alternatives help us understand why people stay committed to seemingly unsatisfying relationships, such as those that are abusive; people often stay because their investments are high and their alternatives are poor (e.g., Rusbult & Martz, 1995). In addition to predicting stay or leave behaviors, commitment predicts a broad array of behaviors that act to keep the relationship going, referred to as *relationship maintenance behaviors* (Rusbult & Buunk, 1993).

Relationship maintenance behaviors are enacted to protect the relationship, especially when confronted with information from inside or outside of the relationship that might threaten its stability. When a relationship partner does something hurtful, such as saying something critical or doing something thoughtless, an automatic response may be to return the hurtful behavior in kind. However, when people resist the urge to react in kind and instead do something constructive such as calmly discuss the problem or quietly wait for the situation to resolve, it is called *accommodation* (Rusbult, Verette, Whitney, Slovik, & Lipkus, 1991). People who are more committed accommodate more and accommodation is associated with better relationship quality. Another reaction to a partner's bad behavior is *forgiveness* (Finkel, Rusbult, Kumashiro, & Hannon, 2002). Degree of commitment also predicts how willing people are to forgive when they feel betrayed by the partner. People who are committed shift their motivations from one that is focused on the self to one that more focused on the relationship.

Another type of compromise that happens in relationships is *sacrificing* for a partner. Sacrificing can take the form of small everyday sacrifices, such as seeing a movie you have little interest in because it stars your partner's favorite actor, or they take the form of big sacrifices, such as quitting your job to move across the country with a partner. People who have higher levels of commitment are more willing to sacrifice for their partners (Van Lange et al., 1997). However, it should also be noted that not all sacrifice is created equal. Research has also shown that when people make sacrifices with the intention of making positive things happen (e.g., making the partner happy or improving the relationship), they are happier about their sacrifice and more satisfied with the relationship. However, when people engage in the very same sacrifice for reasons that are aimed at avoiding negative outcomes (e.g., disappointing a partner or avoiding an argument), they are not as happy with the sacrifice and less satisfied with their relationship. Most interestingly, if people believe that their partner made a sacrifice to avoid negative outcomes (as opposed to create positive outcomes), they too are less satisfied with the relationship (Impett, Gable, & Peplau, 2005).

Finally, commitment also predicts the interpretation of and attention to information outside of the relationship in ways that help to maintain it. Commitment leads people to pay less attention to attractive alternatives, even *derogating* the positivity of those alternatives. In addition, people who are committed also tend to see their relationship as better than other relationships in a phenomenon called the *relationship superiority effect* (Rusbult & Buunk, 1993). All of these maintenance behaviors serve to keep the relationship intact and stable.

The Head in the Heart

The environment bombards us with a constant stream of stimuli of which we need to make sense. One of the most important insights gained in early social psychology studies is that the objective properties of a stimuli are only part of the story; how a person construes that stimuli can be equally important. In bottom–up processing, features of the stimuli guide how it is processed. In top–down processing, features of the perceiver and/or the broader context in which she finds herself guide how the stimuli is understood. For example, although on the surface the question "How are you doing today?" can be processed a simple inquiry from another human being (bottom–up), it can also be processed differently depending on whether it was said by a car salesman as one walked into a showroom or by a good friend who knows you were sick yesterday. Although humans are ruthlessly efficient information-processing machines, there are shortcuts and ways of seeing the world that guide our thinking in certain directions. In close relationships, these processes are often in the service of interpreting information in a manner that is consistent with our expectations about the relationship. These cognitive processes help people figure out what to pay attention to, discern which information from the past to recall, evaluate whether something is good or bad for them, interpret ambiguous information, and make judgments and decisions. In this section, some of the cognitive processes that govern understanding relationship-relevant information are outlined.

Stress and Sadness

Feelings can influence how information is processed, and this is certainly the case in close relationships. In research that spans decades, scholars have documented the effects that feelings, especially negative mood states, have on relationship judgments. One set of studies showed that temporarily and randomly inducing a happy, sad, or neutral mood state in people led to differences in people's ratings of how satisfied and positively they viewed both their relationship and the qualities of their relationship partner (Forgas, Levinger, & Moylan, 1994). Sad participants rated their relationships and partners less positively and also blamed themselves more for conflict than happy participants or participants in a neutral mood.

In a related line of work focused on stress, researchers have found evidence for what is called the *stress spillover effect*. Specifically, there is good evidence that stress experienced at work is brought home (by both men and women) and has a negative impact on close relationships (Bolger, DeLongis, Kessler, & Wethington, 1989). In particular, researchers have found that stress interferes with the ability or motivation to engage in adaptive cognitions. One such adaptive cognition noted by research is separating *global* evaluations from *specific* evaluations. One can have the global evaluation that the partner is dependable. However, if the partner fails to show up for a dinner date, one can make a specific evaluation that the partner tends to lose track of time at the end of the day and thus still maintain the overall evaluation that the partner is dependable. That is, one can compartmentalize a shortcoming to a particular domain (e.g., an inability to keep track of time) without letting it effect an overall perception of the person's qualities. People who are better able to separate global and specific evaluations tend to be more satisfied in their relationships (Neff & Karney, 2005).

Attributions

Why did he forgot to pick up my dry cleaning order? Why did she buy me flowers? Why is he talking to that other girl? These are some of the many questions one might ask to understand other people's behavior. Attributions are attempts to assess the causes of other people's behavior. They are important because the reasons assigned to people's behavior determine our feelings, attitudes, and behaviors toward that person in the future. Making an attribution involves judgements on three dimensions: locus (internal or external), stability (stable or temporary), and generalizability (global or specific). Locus refers to whether the behavior was the result of something internal or within the person (e.g., personality, mood, attitude) or something external or outside of the person (e.g., the situation, another person). Stability is the judgment as to whether the behavior has been seen often in the past and likely to be seen in the future (stable) or not seen in the past or not likely to repeated in the future (temporary). Generalizability refers to whether we think the behavior is likely to occur in similar contexts (global) or only in this particular context (specific).

In a series of studies, researchers have found that these judgments are tied closely to relationship quality (Bradbury & Fincham, 1990) People in dissatisfying relationships make maladaptive attributions. They attribute their partner's positive behavior (bringing home a surprise gift) to external, unstable and specific causal factors ("It was on sale"; "He was in a rare generous mood"; "He isn't thoughtful about anything else"). Dissatisfied couples attribute their partners' negative behavior (forgetting to pick up the dry cleaning) to internal, stable, and global causal reasons ("He is self-centered"; "He always was self-centered"; "He thinks about himself in all situations").

On the other hand, satisfied couples engage in adaptive causal reasoning. They attribute their partner's positive behaviors to internal, stable, and global reasons ("He bought the gift because he was thinking about me"; "He often thinks of me first, in many situations"). They attribute their partner's negative behavior to external, unstable, and specific reasons ("He forgot the dry cleaning because his boss kept him late at work"; "He usually remembers that stuff"; "It's just small household chores he forgets, not the important stuff"). Adaptive patterns of attribution predict increased relationship satisfaction and maladaptive pattern predict decreases in satisfaction. In addition, couples who are dissatisfied adopt more maladaptive attribution patterns to justify their dissatisfaction.

Positive Illusions

Murray and Holmes (1997) hypothesized that some degree of positive distortion and idealization is good for relationships. In particular, they argued that the degree to which people hold views of their partners that are more positive than the views that the partners hold of themselves—a discrepancy that they refer to as a *positive illusion*—are likely to be associated with higher-quality relationships. A series of studies showed that positive illusions regarding a partner predicted more satisfaction, love, and trust, and less conflict in both dating and marital relationships. Positive illusions also predicted relationship persistence and stability. The researchers reasoned that positive illusions help ward off insecurity and doubts that people have in relationships by overemphasizing one's partner positive qualities.

What's Love Got to Do with It?

So far this chapter has covered evolutionary imperatives, economic approaches, and cognitive biases. Where are the juicy emotions like love? Psychologists' early views of love were strongly influenced by behaviorism. The predominant view was that love was the result of secondary reinforcement; a positive association formed over time by the pairing of certain people with primary reinforcements. Babies love their mothers because they associate them with food and the satisfaction of other needs. Romantic partners feel love for each other because the partners are paired with attraction and sexual excitement. Then along came Harry Harlow and his rhesus monkeys.[4] Harlow separated baby monkeys from their mothers shortly after birth and provided them with one model "monkey" made of wire that had a bottle that the babies could feed from and one cloth-covered model "monkey" that did not provide any food. He found that the baby monkeys preferred to spend their time with the soft cloth covered "monkey" over the cold, hard wire monkey even though the cloth monkey did not provide food or water (Harlow, 1958). There was something more to this thing called love than secondary reinforcement and researchers began to examine it more closely.

Certainly an emotion-filled experience, most scholars do not consider love an emotion per se. It is more accurately described as a subjective experience that involves particular motives and thoughts (Diamond, 2014). Love does come in different flavors. The love felt for one's new boyfriend or girlfriend is different than the love felt for one's best friend since second grade. Researchers such as Robert Sternberg have theorized that different types of love are characterized by the relative degree that they entail feelings of physiological arousal (high arousal vs. low/no arousal), intimacy/warmth (a lot vs. a little) and long-term orientation (high commitment vs. little commitment; Sternberg, 1986). The two types of love that have received, by far, the most attention in romantic relationships are *passionate love* and *companionate love* (Berscheid & Walster, 1978).

Passionate love is the intense excitement about, preoccupation with, and attraction to another person. People who are passionately in love tend to agree with statements such as "I want my partner—physically, emotionally, mentally" and "I would feel deep despair if my partner left me" (Hatfield & Sprecher, 1986). Passionate love tends to be high at the beginning stages of romantic relationships. Starting a new relationship involves disrupting ongoing activities, forgoing alternatives, and directing energy to build the new relationship. Evolutionary theorists argue that feeling passionate love and intense desire facilitates relationship formation by focusing attention on the potential mate. Research has shown that feelings of love are associated with the ability and willingness to suppress thoughts of attractive alternatives to one's mate (e.g., Gonzaga, Haselton, Smurda, sian Davies, & Poore, 2008). Also consistent with the idea of solidifying relationships, intense passionate love is associated with changes in the self-concept and self-esteem (Aron, Paris, & Aron, 1995). In what Aron et al. have described as self-expansion, passionate love is associated with incorporating characteristics of the other into one's own sense of self—blurring the boundaries between "me" and "you," forming an "us."

Companionate love is the deep sense of warmth, affection, and liking we feel for another person. People who feel companionate love agree to statements like "My partner is one of the most likeable people

I know" and "My love for my partner involves solid, deep affection" (Grote & Frieze, 1994; Rubin, 1973). Companionate love is associated with bonding and intimacy and is a defining feature of communal relationships (Reis & Aron, 2008). Companionate love is also the best predictor of long-term stability in marriages. In particular, Huston (2009) has been carefully following a set of newlywed couples, and after 13 years, he found that the best predictor of later divorce was low warmth and affection (i.e., low levels of companionate love) at the beginning of the marriage. Levels of passionate love at the beginning of a marriage, on the other hand, did not predict later divorce. In fact, one particularly bad combination at the beginning of marriage was high passionate love that was not accompanied by strong feelings of companionate love. Individuals experiencing that combination felt the sting of disappointment when feelings of passionate love inevitably faded in the early years of marriage and had little to fall back on to maintain satisfying marriages.

Who's Got Your Back?

As noted at the beginning of this chapter, close relationships influence one's health and well-being. One reason that relationships affect individuals is that friends, romantic partners, and family members can be there for one another (or not) across a variety of situations that life throws at us. Relationship partners can try to make things better or worse when bad things happen; they can help or hinder people's pursuit of personal goals, and they can help to maximize or minimize the good things that happen in life. Relationship researchers have studied all three of these circumstances.

When Times Are Tough

Unfortunately, bad things happen, and people cope with them in a variety of ways including turning to close others for support. There have been numerous studies examining what researchers call *social support*. In short, research has shown that the simple *belief* that social partners would be available to help *if* help was needed is associated with individual well-being as well as relationship quality (e.g., Kaul & Lakey, 2003). The *perceived availability of support* has been associated with positive outcomes when highly stressful and thankfully infrequent events occur, such as natural and manmade disasters (Fleming, Baum, Gisriel, & Gatchel, 1982) as well as when the more mundane and common everyday hassles that people encounter occur (e.g., Delongis et al., 1988). Perceptions of the availability of support are also closely linked with relationship satisfaction; people who don't believe their partners will be there for them if things go wrong report more dissatisfaction with that relationship (e.g., Lakey & Orehek, 2011). Moreover, people who feel insecure in their relationship, such as those who are anxiously attached, also perceive that others will not be available to them in times of need (e.g., Ognibene & Collins, 1998). In summary, expectations about the availability of social support if needed are closely tied to personal outcomes and relationship functioning.

However, expectations of support availability may or may not be accurate reflections of real support transactions. Researchers have also examined the support that is provided when bad things actually happen, and this *support provision* can come in the form of emotional or tangible support. Again, high-quality close relationships are characterized by partners who effectively offer one another support and are responsive to each other's needs. In particular, support that conveys an understanding of the situation, validation of the other's point of view, and caring for his or her welfare is associated with better outcomes for the recipient and increased relationship quality (e.g., Maisel & Gable, 2009). The feature of being understanding, validating, and caring is central to high-quality close relationships and is called *responsiveness*

(Reis & Shaver, 1988). Responsiveness can potentially be communicated in any type of interaction between relationship partners but is critical in social support situations.

Conveying responsiveness when a partner is feeling bad can be difficult; knowing exactly what to say or do to help someone in distress, even someone with whom we are intimately involved, is challenging. Even if the support is responsive, there still may be unintended consequences. Receiving support may make the distressed person feel incompetent for not coping on his or her own, they may feel indebted to the person who gave them support, or the act of support can be a blow to self-esteem because a vulnerability has been made salient (for a review of these issues, see Rafaeli & Gleason, 2009). In sum, while receiving support may be helpful for reducing the distress associated with negative events, that support from a relationship partner can create other problems for both the individual and the relationship. In a series of studies, researchers (Bolger, DeLongis, Kessler, & Wethington, 2000) suggested that the best type of support is that which is provided *without the recipient even noticing*, known as *invisible support*. That is, when one partner says he or she is providing support, but the other person doesn't recognize that behavior as support seems to avoid the unintended consequences of receiving support while maximizing the benefits.

During Goal Pursuit

Close relationship partners also play a role in the pursuit of personal goals and shaping of the self-concept (Fitzsimons, Finkel, & vanDellen, 2015). Specifically, research has found the degree to which relationship partners support personal growth, exploration, and goal pursuit also has an impact on individual well-being and overall relationship quality (e.g., Feeney & Collins, 2015). For example, the results of one recent study showed that greater support from romantic partners led to more self-improvement and relationship satisfaction over the course of a year, whereas less support from romantic partners was associated with less self-improvement and relationship satisfaction (Overall, Fletcher, & Simpson, 2010). Another study found that perceptions that one's personal goals are supported by a romantic partner predicted subjective well-being and relationship quality (Molden, Lucas, Finkel, Kumashiro, & Rusbult, 2009).

In a separate line of research studying the poetically named *Michelangelo phenomenon*,[5] researchers found that partners are also active participants in each other's personal development in general (Rusbult et al., 2009). Close relationship partners can promote (or hinder) pursuit of one's ideal self. The ideal self can be an explicit, clearly defined set of goals or a more vague and nebulous set of aspirations. One way partners help (or hinder) growth toward the ideal self is through something called *partner affirmation*. That is, those who see their partners as already possessing the attributes of their ideal self and treat their partners as if they are (already) that ideal self, actually can elicit aspects of the ideal self from the partner through these interactions (Rusbult, Finkel, & Kumashiro, 2009). Partner affirmations are associated with the partner feeling more similar to his or her ideal self and higher personal well-being and great relationship quality (Drigotas et al., 1999; Rusbult, et al., 2009).

When Times Are Good

What may not be obvious is that people often turn to others when good things happen. Sharing positive events with others, a process called *capitalization*, can lead to benefits beyond those that come from the original positive event being shared; benefits such as increased positive affect and well-being (Gable et al., 2004). And, just as with social support processes, how the close other reacts when a positive event is shared has an impact on well-being and relationship quality. Reactions that are responsive (understanding, validating, and caring) are associated with better outcomes for the individual and higher relationship quality while reactions that are not responsive are associated with worse outcomes and lower relationship quality. Moreover, when individuals are perceived to be typically responsive to their partner's capitalization attempts, the relationship is of higher quality (more satisfaction, trust, and commitment) than when partner are seen as typically unresponsive to capitalization attempts.

There are four prototypical reactions when good events are shared: active-constructive responses, passive-constructive responses, active-destructive responses, and passive-destructive responses (Gable et al., 2004, 2006). Active-constructive responses convey excitement and enthusiasm for event and interest in the interaction ("That is wonderful! Tell me more, I want to hear every detail"). Passive-constructive responses are pleasant but restrained in nature ("That's nice, dear"). Active-destructive responses convey interest in the interaction but do so by diminishing the positive event or focusing on potential negative outcomes ("Does that new promotion mean longer hours? You hate working late."). Passive-destructive responses fail to acknowledge the positive event being disclosed, perhaps by changing the subject ("Wait until I tell you happened to *me* today!"). Active-constructive responses signal understanding, validation, and caring and are associated with higher relationship quality and well-being (e.g., Maisel & Gable, 2009). Passive or destructive responses, on the other hand, are associated with reduced relationship quality and lower well-being.

Summary

Humans are a species born to form relationships, and those relationships can be the source of wonderful rewards as well the source of great pain. We take great care in assessing how those relationships are working out, engaging in a variety of behaviors and thought processes that are geared toward maintaining relationships that are worthwhile and dissolving those are not. One reason that relationship quality is so important is that relationship partners also determine, in part, how we navigate the ups and downs of life. In short, relationships are sewn into the very fabric of the human experience.

Notes

1. Prior to becoming interested in human sexual behavior, Kinsey's research focused on the gall wasp.
2. Senator Proxmire later apologized for some of his Golden Fleece Awards, including the one that tagged the Search for Extraterrestrial Intelligence project but never for the one he gave to Hatfield and her colleagues.
3. No offense is intended toward funny cat videos. Who doesn't love a video of kitten chasing a laser pointer?
4. In case it comes up on Jeopardy!, Harlow was Mary Ainsworth's academic advisor.
5. The Michelangelo reference is to the great Renaissance artist's view that sculpting is less a process of creating a sculptor than of *revealing* it; from Michelangelo's perspective, the beautiful form was resting within the rock before the artist started sculpting it.

References

Ainsworth, M. D. S., & Bell, S. M. (1970). Attachment, exploration, and separation: Illustrated by the behavior of one-year-olds in a strange situation. *Child Development, 41,* 49–67.

Ainsworth, M. D. S., Blehar, M. C., Waters, E., & Wall, S. N. (1978). *Patterns of attachment: A psychological study of the strange situation*. Hillsdale, NJ: Ellsworth.

Anderson, C. A., Shibuya, A., Ihori, N., Swing, E. L., Bushman, B. J., Sakamoto, A., . . . Saleem, M. (2010). Violent video game effects on aggression, empathy, and prosocial behavior in Eastern and Western countries: A meta-analytic review. *Psychological Bulletin, 136,* 151–173.

Aron, A., Paris, M., & Aron, E. N. (1995). Falling in love: Prospective studies of self-concept change. *Journal of Personality and Social Psychology, 69,* 1102–1112.

Bartholomew, K. (1990). Avoidance of intimacy: An attachment perspective. *Journal of Social and Personal Relationships, 7,* 147–178.

Berscheid, E., & Walster, E. (1978). *Interpersonal attraction* (2nd ed.). Reading, MA: Addison-Wesley.

Bolger, N., DeLongis, A., Kessler, R. C., & Wethington, E. (1989). The contagion of stress across multiple roles. *Journal of Marriage and the Family, 51,* 175–183.

Bowlby, J. (1969). *Attachment and loss: Vol. 1. Loss.* New York, NY: Basic Books.

Bowlby, J. (1973). *Attachment and loss: Vol. 2. Separation.* London, England: Hogarth.

Bradbury, T. N., & Fincham, F. D. (1990). Attributions in marriage: Review and critique. *Psychological Bulletin, 107,* 3–33.

Butzer, B., & Campbell, L. (2008). Adult attachment, sexual satisfaction, and relationship satisfaction: A study of married couples. *Personal Relationships, 15,* 141–154.

Campbell, A., Converse, P. E., & Rodgers, W. L. (1976). *The quality of American life: Perceptions, evaluations, and satisfactions.* New York: Russell Sage Foundation.

Chung, M. S. (2014). Pathways between attachment and marital satisfaction: The mediating roles of rumination, empathy, and forgiveness. *Personality and Individual Differences, 70,* 246–251.

Clark, M. S., & Mills, J. (1979). Interpersonal attraction in exchange and communal relationships. *Journal of Personality and Social Psychology, 37,* 12–24.

Coan, J. A., Schaefer, H. S., & Davidson, R. J. (2006). Lending a hand: Social regulation of the neural response to threat. *Psychological Science, 17,* 1032–1039.

Collins, N. L., & Feeney, B. C. (2004). Working models of attachment shape perceptions of social support: evidence from experimental and observational studies. *Journal of Personality and Social Psychology, 87*(3), 363–383.

DeLongis, A., Folkman, S., & Lazarus, R. S. (1988). The impact of daily stress on health and mood: Psychological and social resources as mediators. *Journal of Personality and Social Psychology, 54,* 486–495.

Diamond, L. M. (2004). Emerging perspectives on distinctions between romantic love and sexual desire. *Current Directions in Psychological Science, 13,* 116–119.

Diener, E., & Seligman, M. E. P. (2002). Very happy people. *Psychological Science, 13,* 81–84.

Drigotas, S. M., Rusbult, C. E., Wieselquist, J., & Whitton, S. (1999). Close partner as sculptor of the ideal self: Behavioral affirmation and the Michelangelo phenomenon. *Journal of Personality and Social Psychology, 77,* 293–323.

Durkheim, E. (1951). *Suicide: A study in sociology* (G. Simpson, Ed., J. A. Spaulding & G. Simpson, Trans.). New York, NY: Free Press. (Original work published 1897).

Eisenberger, N. I., Master, S. L., Inagaki, T. K., Taylor, S. E., Shirinyan, D., Lieberman, M. D., & Naliboff, B. D. (2011). Attachment figures activate a safety signal-related neural region and reduce pain experience. *Proceedings of the National Academy of Sciences, 108,* 11721–11726.

Elliot, A. J., & Reis, H. T. (2003). Attachment and exploration in adulthood. *Journal of Personality and Social Psychology, 85,* 317–331.

Ellsberg, M., Jansen, H. A., Heise, L., Watts, C. H., & Garcia-Moreno, C. (2008). Intimate partner violence and women's physical and mental health in the WHO multi-country study on women's health and domestic violence: An observational study. *Lancet, 371,* 1165–1172.

Farrell, A. K., Simpson, J. A., Carlson, E. A., Englund, M. M., & Sung, S. (2017). The impact of stress at different life stages on physical health and the buffering effects of maternal sensitivity. *Health Psychology, 36,* 35–44.

Feeney, B. C., & Collins, N. L. (2015). A new look at social support: A theoretical perspective on thriving through relationships. *Personality and Social Psychology Review, 19*, 113–147.

Finkel, E. J., Rusbult, C. E., Kumashiro, M., & Hannon, P. A. (2002). Dealing with betrayal in close relationships: Does commitment promote forgiveness? *Journal of Personality and Social Psychology, 82*, 956–974.

Fitzsimons, G. M., Finkel, E. J., & vanDellen, M. R. (2015). Transactive goal dynamics. *Psychological Review, 122*, 648–673.

Fleming, R., Baum, A., Gisriel, M. M., & Gatchel, R. J. (1982). Mediating influences of social support on stress at Three Mile Island. *Journal of Human Stress, 8*(3), 14–23.

Forgas, J. P., Levinger, G., & Moylan, S. J. (1994). Feeling good and feeling close: Affective influences on the perception of intimate relationships. *Personal Relationships, 1,* 165–184.

Fraley, R. C. (2002). Attachment stability from infancy to adulthood: Meta-analysis and dynamic modeling of developmental mechanisms. *Personality and Social Psychology Review, 6,* 123–151.

Fraley, R. C., Hudson, N. W., Heffernan, M. E., & Segal, N. (2015). Are adult attachment styles categorical or dimensional? A taxometric analysis of general and relationship-specific attachment orientations. *Journal of Personality and Social Psychology, 109,* 354–368.

Fraley, R. C., Vicary, A. M., Brumbaugh, C. C., & Roisman, G. I. (2011). Patterns of stability in adult attachment: An empirical test of two models of continuity and change. *Journal of Personality and Social Psychology, 101,* 974–992.

Gable, S. L. (2006). Approach and avoidance social motives and goals. *Journal of Personality, 74*(1), 175–222.

Gable, S. L. (2015). Balancing rewards and cost in relationships: An approach–avoidance motivational perspective. In A. J. Elliot (Ed.), *Advances in motivation science* (Vol. 2, pp. 1–31). Amsterdam, The Netherlands: Elsevier.

Gable, S. L., Gonzaga, G. C., & Strachman, A. (2006). Will you be there for me when things go right? Supportive responses to positive event disclosures. *Journal of Personality and Social Psychology, 91*(5), 904–917.

Gable, S. L., & Poore, J. (2008). Which thoughts count? Algorithms for evaluating satisfaction in relationships. *Psychological Science, 19*(10), 1030–1036.

Gable, Shelly L., et al. (2004). What do you do when things go right? The intrapersonal and interpersonal benefits of sharing positive events. *Journal of Personality and Social Psychology, 87*(2), 228–245.

Gentzler, A. L., & Kerns, K. A. (2004). Associations between insecure attachment and sexual experiences. *Personal Relationships, 11,* 249–265.

Gonzaga, G. C., Haselton, M. G., Smurda, J., sian Davies, M., & Poore, J. C. (2008). Love, desire, and the suppression of thoughts of romantic alternatives. *Evolution and Human Behavior, 29,* 119–126.

Griffin, D. W., & Bartholomew, K. (1994). Models of the self and other: Fundamental dimensions underlying measures of adult attachment. *Journal of Personality and Social Psychology, 67,* 430–445.

Grote, N. K., & Frieze, I. H. (1994). The measurement of Friendship-based Love in intimate relationships. *Personal Relationships, 1*(3), 275–300.

Harlow, H. F. (1958). The nature of love. *American Psychologist, 13,* 19–31.

Hatfield, E. (2006, June 1). The Golden Fleece Award: Loves labors almost lost. *Observer,* p. 19.

Hatfield, E., & Sprecher, S. (1986). Measuring passionate love in intimate relationships. *Journal of Adolescence, 9,* 383–410.

Hazan, C., & Shaver, P. (1987). Romantic love conceptualized as an attachment process. *Journal of Personality and Social Psychology, 52,* 511–524.

Hazan, C., & Zeifman, D. (1994). Sex and the psychological tether. In K. Bartholomew & D. Perlman (Eds.), *Advances in personal relationships, Vol. 5. Attachment processes in adulthood* (pp. 151–178). London, England: Kingsley.

Helliwell, J. F., & Putnam, R. D. (2004). The social context of well-being. *Philosophical Transactions of the Royal Society of London Series B: Biological Sciences, 359,* 1435–1446.

Hicks, J. A., & King, L. A. (2009). Positive mood and social relatedness as information about meaning in life. *Journal of Positive Psychology, 4,* 471–482.

Holt-Lunstad, J., Smith, T. B., & Layton, J. B. (2010) Social relationships and mortality risk: A meta-analytic review. *PLoS Med 7*(7), e1000316.

Homans, G. C. (1958). Social behavior as exchange. *American Journal of Sociology, 63*, 597–606.

House, J. S., Landis, K. R., & Umberson, D. (1988). Social relationships and health. *Science, 241*, 540–545.

Huston, T. L. (2009). What's love got to do with it? Why some marriages succeed and others fail. *Personal Relationships, 16*, 301–327.

Impett, E. A., Gable, S. L., & Peplau, L. A. (2005). Giving up and giving in: The costs and benefits of daily sacrifice in intimate relationships. *Journal of Personality and Social Psychology, 89*, 327–344.

Kaul, M., & Lakey, B. (2003). Where is the support in perceived support? The role of generic relationship satisfaction and enacted support in perceived support's relation to low distress. *Journal of Social and Clinical Psychology, 22*, 59–78.

Kelley, H. H., & Thibaut, J. W. (1978) Interpersonal relations: A theory of interdependence. New York, NY: Wiley.

Krause, N. (2007). Longitudinal study of social support and meaning in life. *Psychology and Aging, 22*, 456–469.

Lakey, B., & Orehek, E. (2011). Relational regulation theory: A new approach to explain the link between perceived social support and mental health. *Psychological Review, 118*, 482–495.

Le, B., & Agnew, C. R. (2003). Commitment and its theorized determinants: A meta–analysis of the investment model. *Personal Relationships, 10*, 37–57.

Maisel, N. C., & Gable, S. L. (2009). The paradox of received social support: The importance of responsiveness. *Psychological Science, 20*, 928–932.

Marshall, T. C., Bejanyan, K., Di Castro, G., & Lee, R. A. (2013). Attachment styles as predictors of Facebook-related jealousy and surveillance in romantic relationships. *Personal Relationships, 20*, 1–22.

Mikulincer, M., Birnbaum, G., Woddis, D., & Nachmias, O. (2000). Stress and accessibility of proximity-related thoughts: Exploring the normative and intraindividual components of attachment theory. *Journal of Personality and Social Psychology, 78*, 509–523.

Mikulincer, M., Gillath, O., & Shaver, P. R. (2002). Activation of the attachment system in adulthood: Threat-related primes increase the accessibility of mental representations of attachment figures. *Journal of Personality and Social Psychology, 83*, 881–895.

Mikulincer, M., & Shaver, P. R. (2003). The attachment behavioral system in adulthood: Activation, psychodynamics, and interpersonal processes. *Advances in Experimental Social Psychology, 35*, 56–152.

Miller, G., Rohleder, N., & Cole, S. W. (2009). Chronic interpersonal stress predicts activation of pro-and anti-inflammatory signaling pathways six months later. *Psychosomatic Medicine, 71*, 57–62.

Molden, D. C., Lucas, G. M., Finkel, E. J., Kumashiro, M., & Rusbult, C. (2009). Perceived support for promotion-focused and prevention-focused goals: Associations with well-being in unmarried and married couples. *Psychological Science, 20*, 787–793.

Murray, S. L., & Holmes, J. G. (1997). A leap of faith? Positive illusions in romantic relationships. *Personality and Social Psychology Bulletin, 23*, 586–604.

Neff, L. A., & Karney, B. R. (2005). To know you is to love you: The implications of global adoration and specific accuracy for marital relationships. *Journal of Personality and Social Psychology, 88*, 480–497.

Ognibene, T. C., & Collins, N. L. (1998). Adult attachment styles, perceived social support and coping strategies. *Journal of Social and Personal Relationships, 15*(3), 323–345.

Overall, N. C., Fletcher, G. J., Simpson, J. A., & Fillo, J. (2015). Attachment insecurity, biased perceptions of romantic partners' negative emotions, and hostile relationship behavior. *Journal of Personality and Social Psychology, 108*, 730–749.

Rafaeli, E., & Gleason, M. E. (2009). Skilled support within intimate relationships. *Journal of Family Theory & Review, 1*, 20–37.

Reis, H. T., & Aron, A. (2008). Love: What is it, why does it matter, and how does it operate? *Perspectives on Psychological Science, 3*, 80–86.

Reis, H. T., & Shaver, P. (1988). Intimacy as an interpersonal process. In S. Duck (Ed.), *Handbook of personal relationships* (pp. 367–389). Chichester, England: Wiley.

Rubin, Z. (1973). *Liking and loving: An invitation to social psychology*. Holt, Rinehart & Winston.

Rusbult, C. E. (1980). Commitment and satisfaction in romantic associations: A test of the investment model. *Journal of Experimental Social Psychology, 16,* 172–186.

Rusbult, C. E., & Buunk, B. P. (1993). Commitment processes in close relationships: An interdependence analysis. *Journal of Social and Personal Relationships, 10,* 175–204.

Rusbult, C. E., Finkel, E. J., & Kumashiro, M. (2009). The Michelangelo phenomenon. *Current Directions in Psychological Science, 18,* 305–309.

Rusbult, C. E., & Martz, J. M. (1995). Remaining in an abusive relationship: An investment model analysis of nonvoluntary dependence. *Personality and Social Psychology Bulletin, 21,* 558–571.

Rusbult, C. E., Verette, J., Whitney, G. A., Slovik, L. F., & Lipkus, I. (1991). Accommodation processes in close relationships: Theory and preliminary empirical evidence. *Journal of Personality and Social Psychology, 60,* 53–78.

Steger, M. F., Kashdan, T. B., Sullivan, B. A., & Lorentz, D. (2008). Understanding the search for meaning in life: Personality, cognitive style, and the dynamic between seeking and experiencing meaning. *Journal of Personality, 76,* 199–228.

Sternberg, R. J. (1986). A triangular theory of love. *Psychological Review, 93,* 119–135.

Van Lange, P. A., Rusbult, C. E., Drigotas, S. M., Arriaga, X. B., Witcher, B. S., & Cox, C. L. (1997). Willingness to sacrifice in close relationships. *Journal of Personality and Social Psychology, 72,* 1373–1394.

Williams, D. R., Neighbors, H. W., & Jackson, J. S. (2003). Racial/ethnic discrimination and health: Findings from community studies. *American Journal of Public Health, 93,* 200–208.

Chapter 11

Intergroup Relations

Marilynn B. Brewer

In the 1990s, the demise of the Soviet Union brought an end to the Cold War era with its focus on relations between two political superpowers. In its aftermath, an apparent resurgence of ethnic conflict throughout the world gave rise to the idea that local group loyalties and intergroup hostilities were never far below the surface. The media began talking about the "new tribalism" that seemed to be emerging everywhere. As public interest in these issues grew, so did the resurgence of interest in theory and research on intergroup relations within social psychology in Europe and in the United States. By the turn of the millennium, concern about issues of intergroup relations had become even more intense for social scientists and laypersons alike. In addition to organized conflict carried on by nations against nations, states against subgroups within their own populations, and ethnic and religious conflicts within nations, acts of international terrorism by small groups of extremists have riveted attention and concern across the globe. It is more clear than ever that group identities play a major role in human behavior—impelling heroic action on behalf of *ingroups*, as well as horrific atrocities against designated *outgroups*. Social-psychological understanding of these processes has also grown as the study of intergroup relations took center stage within the discipline.

The salience and extremity of intergroup hostility and violence lead to the impression that the study of intergroup relations is equivalent to the study of intergroup conflict. However, although escalation of conflict and hostility between groups is the form of intergroup relationships of most concern in the real world, social-psychological research on intergroup behavior starts with other, more subtle forms of responding that reflect differences in disposition toward others as a function of their group membership. Understanding intergroup relations invokes most areas of social-psychological inquiry—from the study of person perception, social attitudes, aggression, self-esteem, social comparison, equity, cooperation, and competition to conformity and compliance. From research in all of these areas, we have a wealth of information about the cognitive and motivational foundations of intergroup behavior.

Defining Intergroup Relations

It is a basic fact of human existence that people are organized into social groups. We are all members of many different types of groups, ranging from small, face-to-face groupings of family and friends to large social categories such as gender, religion, and nationality. As a consequence, much of our interaction with others takes place in a group setting, where we are not only individual persons but representatives of our respective social groups. For social psychologists, the classic definition of intergroup situations is that provided by Sherif (1966): "Whenever individuals belonging to one group interact, collectively or individually, with another group or its members in terms of their group identification, we have an instance of intergroup behavior" (p. 12). What this definition implies is that intergroup relations can occur at the level of two persons interacting (the dyadic level) as well as the level of exchanges between groups as a whole (the intergroup level).

The essence of the social-psychological approach to the study of intergroup relations is to understand the causes and consequences of the distinction between ingroups (those groups to which an individual belongs) and outgroups (social groups that do not include the individual as a member)— the apparently universal propensity to differentiate the social world into "us" and "them." In general, feelings, beliefs, and interpersonal behaviors tend to be more positive when they involve members of the same group (ingroup behavior) than when they occur between groups. An intergroup orientation arises when ingroup–outgroup differentiation is engaged in connection with particular social categorizations. Attitudes and behavior toward members of the ingroup and outgroup then follow from the level of the individual's attachment to the ingroup and his or her assessment of the nature of the outgroup *in relation to* the ingroup.

It is this relational aspect of intergroup behavior that distinguishes the study of intergroup relations from the study of prejudice as an individual attitude toward specific groups or social categories (cf. John F. Dovidio & James M. Jones, Chapter 12, this volume). Ingroup–outgroup differentiation involves thinking of social groups or categories in us–them terms. Category membership alone is not sufficient to engage this intergroup orientation. Ingroup activation involves an additional process of *self*-categorization (Turner, Hogg, Oakes, Reicher, & Wetherell, 1987) or social identification whereby the sense of self is extended to the group as a whole. Similarly, a social category becomes an outgroup only when the self is actively disassociated from the group, in a "not-me" sense. Thus, to understand intergroup relations, we first need to understand the processes and motivations underlying an individual's attachment to his or her social groups and the conditions under which ingroup–outgroup differentiation becomes engaged.

Social Identity and Ingroup Bias

Social identity is defined as "that part of an individual's self-concept which derives from his knowledge of his membership of a social group . . . together with the value and emotional significance attached to that membership" (Tajfel, 1981, p. 255). Social identity theory, as articulated by Tajfel (1978) and Turner (1975), represents the convergence of two traditions in the study of intergroup attitudes and behavior— social categorization (as represented by Doise, 1978; Tajfel, 1969; Wilder, 1986) and social comparison (as exemplified by Lemaine, 1974; Vanneman & Pettigrew, 1972). The theoretical perspective rests on two basic premises:

1. Individuals organize their understanding of the social world on the basis of categorical distinctions that transform continuous variables into discrete classes; categorization has the effect of minimizing perceived differences *within* categories and accentuating intercategory differences.
2. Because individuals are members of some social categories and not others, social categorization carries with it implicit *ingroup–outgroup* (we–they) distinctions; because of the self-relevance of

social categories, the ingroup–outgroup classification is a superimposed category distinction with affective and emotional significance.

These two premises provide a framework for conceptualizing any social situation in which a particular ingroup–outgroup categorization is made salient. In effect, the theory posits a basic *intergroup schema* with the following characteristic features (Turner, 1975):

1. Assimilation within category boundaries and contrast between categories such that all members of the ingroup are perceived to be more similar to the self than members of the outgroup (the *intergroup accentuation* principle).
2. Positive affect (trust, liking) selectively generalized to fellow ingroup members but not outgroup members (the *ingroup favoritism* principle).
3. Intergroup social comparison and perceived competition between ingroup and outgroup for positive value (the *social competition* principle).

Social identity theory in conjunction with self-categorization theory (Turner et al., 1987) provides a comprehensive view of group behavior and the cognitive processes that underlie a range of intergroup and group phenomena. The basic tenet of these theories is that group behaviors derive from cognitive representations of the self in terms of a shared social category membership, in which there is effectively no psychological separation between the self and the group as a whole. This phenomenon is referred to as *depersonalization of self-representation*, whereby the cognitive representation of the self shifts from *personal self* to *collective self* (Hogg & Abrams, 1988; Hogg & Turner, 1987). In self-categorization terms, social identity entails "a shift towards the perception of self as an interchangeable exemplar of some social category and away from the perception of self as a unique person" (Turner et al., 1987, p. 50). As a consequence of this shift in level of self-categorization, self-interest becomes equated with ingroup interests, and the welfare and status of the ingroup become primary motivations.

Mere Categorization and Intergroup Behavior

In a laboratory setting in Bristol, England, Henri Tajfel and his colleagues undertook initial experiments with the so-called minimal intergroup situation (Tajfel, 1970; Tajfel, Billig, Bundy, & Flament, 1971) in which individuals are assigned to arbitrary social categories. In these experiments, participants chose to allocate higher rewards to members of their own category relative to members of the outgroup category, even in the absence of any personal identification of group members, any past history, or any direct benefit to the self. The results provided a powerful demonstration that merely classifying individuals into arbitrary distinct social categories was sufficient to produce ingroup–outgroup discrimination and bias, even in the absence of any interactions with fellow group members or any history of competition or conflict between the groups.

Since the initial minimal group experiments, hundreds of studies in the laboratory and the field have documented ingroup favoritism in myriad forms (Brewer, 1979; Brewer & Campbell, 1976; Diehl, 1990; Mullen, Brown, & Smith, 1992). In addition to the allocation bias demonstrated by Tajfel, preferential treatment and evaluation of ingroups relative to outgroups appear in evaluations of group products (e.g., Gerard & Hoyt, 1974), application of rules of fairness (Ancok & Chertkoff, 1983; Ng, 1984; Platow, McClintock, & Liebrand, 1990), attributions for positive and negative behavior (Hewstone, 1990; Weber, 1994), and willingness to trust and cooperate (Brewer & Kramer, 1986; Miller, Downs, & Prentice, 1998; Wit & Kerr, 2002; Yuki, Maddux, Brewer, & Takemura, 2005). There is considerable evidence that such ingroup favoritism is considered normative in its own right (Blanz, Mummendey, & Otten, 1997; Platow, O'Connell, Shave, & Hanning, 1995) and that it is activated automatically when a group identity is salient (Otten & Moskowitz, 2000; Otten & Wentura, 1999).

These studies succeeded in confirming the power of we–they distinctions to produce differential evaluation, liking, and treatment of other persons depending on whether or not they are identified as members of the ingroup category. The laboratory experiments with the minimal intergroup situation demonstrated that ethnocentric loyalty and bias clearly do not depend on kinship or an extensive history of interpersonal relationships among group members but can apparently be engaged readily by symbolic manipulations that imply shared attributes or a common fate. What appears to be critical for ingroup attachment is a distinctive identification of who is "us" and who is "them"—a rule of exclusion as well as inclusion.

Ethnocentrism and Ingroup Positivity

The hallmark of ingroup identification is ingroup positivity, or positive feelings about the ingroup and fellow ingroup members. There is even ample evidence that positive affect and positive evaluation are activated automatically by an ingroup label or whenever a group (even a minimal group) is associated with the self (Farnham, Greenwald, & Banaji, 1999; Otten, 2002; Perdue, Dovidio, Gurtman, & Tyler, 1990; Rudman, Greenwald, & McGhee, 2001).

This idea that ingroups are inevitably positively regarded accords with the concept of "ethnocentrism" as introduced by Sumner (1906) several decades earlier. Ethnocentrism was described by Sumner as a universal characteristic of human social groups whereby

> a differentiation arises between ourselves, the we-group, or ingroup, and everybody else, or
> the others-group, outgroups. The insiders in a we-group are in a relation of peace, order, law,
> government, and industry, to each other. . . . Ethnocentrism is the technical name for this view
> of things in which one's own group is the center of everything, and all others are scaled and rated
> with reference to it. . . . Each group nourishes its own pride and vanity, boasts itself superior,
> exalts its own divinities, and looks with contempt on outsiders. . . . (Sumner, 1906, pp. 12–13)

This does not mean, however, that ingroup evaluations are indiscriminantly positive on all dimensions of assessment. When there is objective evidence of outgroup achievement or a consensual status hierarchy in which the outgroup is recognized to be of higher status than the ingroup, then some degree of outgroup positivity (relative to the ingroup) is frequently obtained (Jost, 2001). However, ingroup positivity is consistently found on traits or attributes that are self-defining or self-relevant (Otten, 2002) and on traits reflecting basic moral values (e.g., warmth, trustworthiness, cooperativeness) (Leach, Ellemers, & Barreto, 2007). On these basic value dimensions, ingroup positivity appears to be essentially universal (Brewer, 2001; LeVine & Campbell, 1972).

Motives Underlying Ingroup Attachment and Positivity

Self-Esteem

The motivational concept most associated with social identity theory is that of self-esteem enhancement. To the extent that individuals identify with a social group, they derive benefit from their group's successes and achievements, even when the individual has not contributed directly to the group's accomplishment.

Thus, ingroup status and achievements become a source of self-esteem that goes beyond what can be achieved by the individual alone. This is the basis for the social identity theory idea that group members are motivated to seek *positive distinctiveness* in comparing their ingroups to outgroups (Turner, 1975). However, it is not clear from the social identity literature whether positive self-esteem was being invoked as a motive for social identity itself or as a motive for ingroup favoritism *given that* social identity had been engaged. Whatever the original intent, subsequent research on the role of self-esteem in ingroup bias has generally supported the idea that enhanced self-esteem may be a *consequence* of achieving a positively distinct social identity, but there is little evidence that the need to increase self-esteem motivates social identification in the first place (Rubin & Hewstone, 1998). To the contrary, there is considerable evidence that individuals often identify strongly with groups that are disadvantaged, stigmatized, or otherwise suffer from negative intergroup comparison (e.g., Branscombe, Ellemers, Spears, & Doosje, 1999; Crocker, Luhtanen, Blaine, & Broadnax, 1994; Jetten, Branscombe, Schmitt, & Spears, 2001; Turner, Hogg, Turner, & Smith, 1984). Some experimental research indicates that social identification with a group may actually be increased when the group is threatened or stigmatized (Jetten, Branscombe, Schmitt, & Spears, 2001; Turner et al., 1984).

Cognitive Motives: Uncertainty Reduction

Given the inadequacy of self-esteem as an explanation for why social identity is engaged, other motives have been proposed that do not require positive ingroup status as a basis for attachment to groups and self-definition as a group member. One proposal is that group identity meets fundamental needs for reducing uncertainty and achieving meaning and clarity in social contexts (Hogg & Abrams, 1993; Hogg & Mullin, 1999). In support of this hypothesis, Hogg and his colleagues (Grieve & Hogg, 1999; Mullin & Hogg, 1998) have generated compelling evidence that identification and ingroup bias are increased under conditions of high cognitive uncertainty and reduced or eliminated when uncertainty is low. And it is undoubtedly true that one function that group memberships and identities serve for individuals is that of providing self-definition and guidance for behavior in otherwise ambiguous social situations (Deaux, Reid, Mizrahi, & Cotting, 1999; Vignoles, Chryssochoou, & Breakwell, 2000). However, group identity is only one of many possible modes of reducing social uncertainty. Roles, values, laws, etc. serve a similar function without necessitating social identification processes. Thus, uncertainty reduction alone cannot account for the pervasiveness of group identification as a fundamental aspect of human life.

Security and Belonging

Uncertainty reduction as a theory of social identity places the explanation for group identification in a system of cognitive motives that includes needs for meaning, certainty, and structure. An alternative perspective is that the motivation for social identification arises from even more fundamental needs for security and safety. Consistent with this idea, Baumeister and Leary (1995) postulate a universal need for *belonging* as an aspect of human nature derived from our vulnerability as lone individuals who require connection with others to survive. But belonging alone cannot account for the selectivity of social identification, as any and all group memberships should satisfy the belonging motive. The theory of optimal distinctiveness (Brewer, 1991) thus postulates that the need for belonging and inclusion is paired with an opposing motive—the need for differentiation—that together regulate the individual's social identity and attachment to social groups.

The basic premise of the optimal distinctiveness model is that the two identity needs (inclusion/assimilation and differentiation/distinctiveness) are independent and work in opposition to motivate group identification. Optimal identities are those that satisfy the need for inclusion *within* the ingroup and simultaneously serve the need for differentiation through distinctions *between* the ingroup and outgroups.

In effect, optimal social identities involve *shared distinctiveness* (Stapel & Marx, 2007). Individuals will resist being identified with social categorizations that are either too inclusive or too differentiating but will define themselves in terms of social identities that are optimally distinctive. Equilibrium is maintained by correcting for deviations from optimality. A situation in which a person is overly individuated will excite the need for assimilation, motivating the person to adopt a more inclusive social identity. Conversely, situations that arouse feelings of overinclusion will activate the need for differentiation, resulting in a search for more exclusive or distinct identities.

Evidence for competing social motives comes from empirical demonstrations of efforts to achieve or restore group identification when these needs are not met. Results of experimental studies have shown that activation of the need for assimilation or the need for differentiation increases the importance of distinctive group memberships (Pickett, Silver, & Brewer, 2002), and any threat to inclusion enhances self-stereotyping on group-characteristic traits (Brewer & Pickett, 1999; Pickett, Bonner, & Coleman, 2002; Spears, Doosje, & Ellemers, 1997). Furthermore, assignment to distinctive minority group categories engages greater group identification and self-stereotyping than does membership in large, inclusive majority groups (Brewer & Weber, 1994; Leonardelli & Brewer, 2001; Simon & Hamilton, 1994). Thus, there is converging evidence that group attachment is regulated by motives for both inclusion and distinctiveness.

Also consistent with optimal distinctiveness theory, threats to group distinctiveness (e.g., too much similarity to outgroups or ambiguity of group boundaries) arouse concern about restoring ingroup boundaries and intergroup differentiation (Hornsey & Hogg, 1999; Jetten, Spears, & Manstead, 1998; Jetten, Spears, & Postmes, 2004; Roccas & Schwartz, 1993). Research on the ingroup overexclusion effect (Castano, Yzerbyt, Bourguignon, & Seron, 2002; Leyens & Yzerbyt, 1992; Yzerbyt, Leyens, & Bellour, 1995) demonstrates that group members tend to take more time and employ more stringent criteria when deciding whether someone is a potential ingroup member than when deciding whether the person is a potential outgroup member. This overexclusion effect is enhanced when distinctiveness motives have been aroused (Brewer & Pickett, 2002).

Ingroup Positivity and Outgroup Derogation

There is a widespread assumption in the social-psychological literature that high levels of social identification and ingroup positivity are associated with derogation and hostility toward outgroups. However, despite a common belief that ingroup positivity and outgroup derogation are reciprocally related, empirical research demonstrates little consistent relation between the two. Indeed, results from both laboratory experiments and field studies indicate that variations in ingroup positivity and social identification do not systematically correlate with degree of bias or negativity toward outgroups (Brewer, 1979; Hinkle & Brown, 1990; Kosterman & Feshbach, 1989; Struch & Schwartz, 1989).

Experiments with the minimal intergroup situation also provided additional evidence that ingroup favoritism is prior to, and not necessarily associated with, outgroup negativity or hostility. Brewer (1979) reported that most minimal group studies that assessed ratings of the ingroup and outgroup separately found that categorization into groups leads to enhanced ingroup ratings in the absence of decreased outgroup ratings. Furthermore, the ingroup favoritism that is exhibited in the allocation of positive resources in the minimal intergroup situation (Tajfel et al., 1971) is essentially eliminated when allocation decisions involve the distribution of negative outcomes or costs (e.g., Mummendey et al., 1992), suggesting that individuals are willing to differentially benefit the ingroup compared to outgroups but are reluctant to harm outgroups more directly.

Subsequent research in both laboratory and field settings has come to acknowledge the important distinction between ingroup bias that reflects beneficence and positive sentiments toward the ingroup that are withheld from outgroups (subtle prejudice) and discrimination that reflects hostility, derogation, and intent to harm the outgroup (blatant prejudice; Pettigrew & Meertens, 1995). This is not to say that ingroup-based discrimination is benign or inconsequential. Indeed, many forms of institutional racism and sexism are probably attributable to discrimination based on ingroup preference rather than prejudice against outgroups (Brewer, 1996). Nonetheless, the absence of positive regard and the lack of trust for outgroups that are characteristic of most ingroup–outgroup differentiation can be conceptually and empirically distinguished from the presence of active hostility, distrust, and hate for outgroups that characterize virulent prejudice. Thus, ingroup identity alone is not sufficient to predict attitudes and behavior toward outgroups, and we must look beyond social identity theory to account for intergroup hostility and conflict.

Theories of Intergroup Conflict

Traditional Theories: Realistic Group Conflict and Relative Deprivation

Traditional theories of intergroup relations trace hostility and conflict with outgroups to the nature of the structural relations between group interests. Realistic group conflict theory (LeVine & Campbell, 1972, Chapter 3) posits that conflict derives from competition between groups for material resources and power. Within social psychology one of the most influential proponents of realistic group conflict theory was Sherif (e.g., Sherif, 1966). In a famous series of field experiments conducted in the context of a boys' summer camp (known as the Robber's Cave experiments), he and his colleagues showed how the behavior of a group of strangers could be predictably transformed by first dividing them into groups and then arranging for those groups to compete with one another for valued resources (Sherif, Harvey, White, Hood, & Sherif, 1961). During and after competition, the boys exhibited hostile intergroup behavior and showed marked ingroup favoritism in friendship choices and judgments. Consistent with the conflict of interests approach, when the researchers changed the structural arrangements so that the groups were placed in a series of cooperative encounters (in which group interests were compatible and interdependent), the intergroup behavior became more amicable and the favoritism declined.

Subsequent research largely confirmed these basic findings. In laboratory studies when the interdependence between groups is experimentally controlled to be either negative, neutral, or positive, the results are quite consistent: There is usually more ingroup bias, less intergroup liking, and greater intergroup discrimination when groups are objectively in competition than when they are independent or must cooperate over some common goal (e.g. Kahn & Ryen, 1972; Rabbie & Wilkins, 1971; Rabbie, Benoist, Oosterbaan, & Visser, 1974; Worchel, Andreoli, & Folger, 1977). In field settings, a similar correspondence between objective or perceived goal relationships linking groups and intergroup attitudes has been observed. Evaluative or affective judgments of outgroups are generally correlated with perceptions of groups being positively or negatively interdependent (Brown & Abrams, 1986; Esses, Jackson, & Armstrong, 1998; Struch & Schwartz, 1989).

Realistic group conflict theory provides a powerful explanation for many instances of intergroup discrimination and conflict. Moreover, it has the advantage of being able to account for changes in levels of prejudice over time or across different social contexts reflecting changing economic and political relations between the groups concerned. Nevertheless, there are, as Turner (1981) has noted, a number of empirical and theoretical difficulties with the perspective. First, functional interdependence per se may not be sufficient to determine intergroup behavior unless some degree of ingroup identification is also present. Consistent with this conclusion, Struch and Schwartz (1989) found that the correlation between perceived conflicts of interests among religious groups in Israel and levels of intergroup hostility were higher for those respondents who identified strongly with their religious ingroup than it was for those who identified less strongly.

A more serious issue in realistic group conflict theory concerns whether the negative interdependence that it assumes to underlie hostilities need always be based on real conflicts over concrete things such as land, money, or political power. It could derive from perceived conflicts or competition over some rather less tangible assets such as prestige or "to be the winner." Sherif (1966) was deliberately vague on this point, defining group interests as "a real or imagined threat to the safety of the group, an economic interest, a political advantage, a military consideration, prestige, or a number of others" (p. 15). Allowing perceived conflicts to have causal status similar to actual conflicts poses a theoretical problem. If perceptions of competing goals can underlie intergroup hostility and if such perceptions are not always correlated with the groups' actual material interests, where do they come from? Apart from actual structural relations between groups, there may be additional social-psychological origins for subjective competitive orientations and perceived threats from outgroups.

Realistic Conflict Updated: Integrated Threat Theory

A more recent approach to conceptualizing how perceptions of ingroup–outgroup relations may lead to outgroup negativity is integrated threat theory (Stephan & Stephan, 2000). This model distinguishes four different sources of experienced threat from a specific outgroup: *realistic threats* (threats to the existence, power, or material well-being of the ingroup or ingroup members), *symbolic threats* (threats to the ingroup world view arising from perceived group differences in morals, values, and standards), *intergroup anxiety* (personal fear or discomfort experienced in connection with actual or anticipated interactions with members of the outgroup), and *negative stereotypes* (beliefs about outgroup characteristics that imply unpleasant or conflictual interactions and negative consequences for the self or the ingroup). Field tests of this model have found that ratings of realistic threat, symbolic threat, and intergroup anxiety are significant predictors of negative interracial attitudes and that these threat perceptions mediate the effects of other predictor variables such as ingroup identification, intergroup contact, and status differences (Riek, Mania, & Gaertner, 2006; Stephan et al., 2002).

The nature of symbolic threat is of particular interest because of the role that symbolic threats to group identity apparently play in many intractable intergroup conflicts (Bar-Tal, 2007; Rouhana & Bar-Tal, 1998). Concerns for symbolic threats to group values and icons or lack of respect and recognition are often conceptualized as the subjective, "irrational" bases of intergroup hostility and fear, posed in opposition to concerns for objective, "realistic" threats to material welfare and group existence. But objective assessments of conflict of interest and subjective perceptions of identity threat are inextricably intertwined. Especially in the modern world, competition over resources (e.g., land, power) has as much to do with the identity meaning of those resources as it does actual group survival (e.g., Ledgerwood, Liviatan, & Carnevale, 2007). Many intractable conflicts are characterized by conceptualizations of group identity in which the identities of the groups involved become oppositional, such that a key component of each group's identity is based on negation of the other (Kelman, 1999). The role of such symbolic identity concerns in sustaining intractable conflicts is of particular importance because the costs of extensive and protracted conflict in terms of material resources and human lives defy rational choice theories of group behavior. Members of both groups generally recognize that they would be collectively better off if the conflicts were resolved. Yet deeply held identity concerns stand as a barrier to negotiated resolution (Kelman, 1999, 2001).

Intergroup Comparison, Relative Deprivation, and Social Change

The social identity theory approach to understanding intergroup relations places particular attention on comparisons between the status and outcomes of the ingroup and those of relevant outgroups. Considerable research on social justice supports the idea that individuals' feelings of being deprived or disadvantaged are based on the comparisons they make rather than the absolute value of their own condition. Feelings of resentment and the sense of injustice that arises from perceiving that you have less than what you deserve compared to others are called *relative deprivation.*

The concept of relative deprivation was developed by social scientists during World War II to explain some paradoxic findings that emerged in the study of morale among American soldiers (Stouffer, Suchman, DeVinney, Stat, & Williams, 1949). Researchers found, for instance, that soldiers in air force units, in which rates of promotion were quite high, had more complaints about the promotion system than did soldiers in the military police, where promotions were few and far between. Equally surprising, they found that black soldiers who were stationed in southern states in the United States (where overt discrimination based on race was very visible) had higher morale than black soldiers stationed in the less racist northern states. Stouffer and his colleagues explained these anomalous results in terms of different standards of comparison being used by soldiers in different units. Compared to peers who were advancing at a rapid rate, air force soldiers who had not yet been promoted felt deprived, even though their objective chances of promotion were higher than those of soldiers in other units. Similarly, the high morale of black soldiers stationed in the South may have derived from comparisons with black civilians who fared very poorly; black soldiers in the North, on the other hand, may have felt deprived relative to civilian blacks in that region who were earning higher wages in war-related factory jobs.

Parallel to relative deprivation at the personal level is what Runciman (1966) called *fraternal deprivation.* Fraternal deprivation arises from comparisons between the outcomes of your ingroup as a whole and those of more advantaged groups. Whereas personal deprivation depends on interpersonal comparisons with similar others, fraternal deprivation involves intergroup comparisons between dissimilar groups and becomes a source of resentment and potential conflict with groups perceived as being unjustly more advantaged than the ingroup.

Relative deprivation may be experienced even by those who are objectively advantaged but feel they are losing by comparison to previous expectations. This principle was dramatically illustrated by behavior of young members of the upper castes of India in a series of incidents in 1990. During one period that year, scores of middle-class youths (members of the Brahmin, Kshatriya, and Vaishya castes) committed suicide in protest against government policies that open more jobs to the poor. By any objective standards, the upper castes were doing quite well, even in the presence of government economic reforms designed to benefit the disadvantaged castes. Yet the perception that their own caste was losing position relative to the lower castes created a sense of comparative disadvantage that was sufficient to motivate dramatic protest against the reforms.

Perceptions of unjust ingroup deprivation can spur collective action on the part of disadvantaged group members to improve the status and outcomes of the ingroup. Theories of social identity, social comparison, and relative deprivation all suggest that members of lower-status groups will be discontented with the resources and valuation attached to their collective identity and will be motivated toward social change. Yet it seems to take a great deal more than perceived discrepancies and status differentials to mobilize collective action.

In reviewing the options available to members of low-status social categories to achieve positive distinctiveness, Tajfel and Turner (1986) distinguished three different avenues of responding to negative social identity, each with different implications for collective movements:

1. *Individual mobility.* With this option, individuals dissociate themselves from the lower-status ingroup and seek identification with the higher-status outgroup. This route to achieving positive social identity is most likely in social systems characterized by permeability of group boundaries and high opportunity for upward social mobility.

2. *Social creativity.* Group members may achieve positive distinctiveness by redefining the bases of intergroup comparison, choosing new dimensions on which the ingroup can be assigned higher values than relevant outgroups or changing the valuation attached to existing comparisons. The "Black is beautiful" movement in the United States is an example of this latter strategy. This option essentially leaves the social relationships between groups unchanged but alters the implications for group self-esteem.

3. *Social competition.* Finally, low-status group members may seek to change the structure of intergroup dominance and status differentials by engaging in direct competition with higher-status outgroups. It is only under this condition that perceptions of relative deprivation will lead to intergroup conflict.

Tajfel and Turner (1986) distinguish three different aspects of the status relationships among groups that determine what mode of adaptation disadvantaged group members are likely to pursue. These are the perceived *permeability* of group boundaries and the perceived stability and *legitimacy* of the status differences between groups. Permeability refers to the extent to which group members can expect to be able to move from one group to another, or shift their social identity, on an individual basis. According to social identity theory, under conditions of high permeability, members of lower-status groups will tend to prefer membership in the higher-status outgroup and seek social mobility as a strategy for improving positive social identity (van Knippenberg & Ellemers, 1990). Experimental studies have confirmed that manipulations of perceived permeability interact with group status to affect ingroup identification. Members of low-status groups express more dissatisfaction with their group membership and less ingroup preference when group boundaries are permeable rather than impermeable (Ellemers, van Knippenberg, de Vries, & Wilke, 1988). However, when individuals could potentially change their group affiliation (high permeability), members of high-status groups increase their commitment to their current group membership. Under the risk of losing their attractive group membership, members of permeable high-status groups express significantly stronger ingroup identification than when group membership is fixed (Ellemers, Doosje, van Knippenberg, & Wilke, 1992).

Permeability creates instability of group membership but does not necessarily alter the status relationships between the groups as a whole. More important for social identity is the perceived stability or security of the status or dominance hierarchy itself (Sidanius, 1993; Sidanius & Pratto, 1999; Tajfel & Turner, 1986; van Knippenberg & Ellemers, 1993). When status differentials are perceived to be unstable or illegitimate, members of lower status groups exhibit significantly stronger ingroup identification than when status relationships are stable (Caddick, 1982; Ellemers, van Knippenberg, & Wilke, 1990). Although perceived injustice at the personal level often motivates individuals to dissociate from low-status ingroups, perceived collective injustice enhances group identification and efforts to improve the status position of the group as a whole (Ellemers, Wilke, & van Knippenberg, 1993; Taylor, Moghaddam, Gamble, & Zellerer, 1987; Wright, Taylor, & Moghaddam, 1990).

At the same time, perceived instability of the status hierarchy threatens the positive distinctiveness of high-status groups. In experiments manipulating both group size and group status, discrimination in intergroup allocations is particularly high for minority high-status groups (Mullen, Brown, & Smith, 1992). Sachdev and Bourhis (1991) argue that this is because when the dominant group is in the minority, the status structure is inherently more unstable than when the majority is dominant. Secure status differentials may reduce the salience of intergroup comparisons and discrimination, but insecurity heightens the motivation to maintain status distinctions on the part of high-status group members. Thus, conditions of social change increase the motivation for intergroup conflict, distrust, and heightened discrimination for groups in all positions of the status hierarchy.

Intergroup Emotions Theory

The general idea that intergroup attitudes are shaped by the perceived relationship between the ingroup and outgroup (in particular, whether the existence of the outgroup poses a threat to the ingroup) is consistent with recent theories of prejudice as intergroup emotion (Smith, 1993). Emotional reactions to a particular outgroup can include positive emotions (e.g., admiration, respect) as well as a range of negative emotions (e.g., fear, disgust, anxiety, and hate). In Dijker's (1987) examination of the relation between emotions and attitudes toward two minority groups in the Netherlands, although both types of emotion predicted evaluation of the outgroups, positive emotions were more predictive of attitudes toward one group and negative emotions were more predictive of attitudes toward the other. Similarly, in an investigation of the relationship between positive and negative emotional responses toward seven minority groups in the United States, both types of emotion predicted prejudice toward these groups (Stangor, Sullivan, & Ford, 1991, Study 1).

In addition to distinguishing between positive and negative emotions as components of intergroup attitudes, researchers have begun to recognize the importance of distinguishing among different types of negative emotions in intergroup contexts. Distinct emotions reflect different underlying causes and lead to different types of behavior. Smith (1993) has suggested that five specific emotions are most likely to be aroused in intergroup situations: fear, disgust, contempt, anger, and jealousy. Of these, fear and disgust can be distinguished as emotions that imply avoidance or movement away from the outgroup, whereas contempt and anger imply movement against the outgroup (although fear can also elicit the attack response if the perceiver feels trapped or cornered and unable to effectively flee the source of fear). Attitudes that are driven by the former emotional states are likely to have different cognitive contents and behavioral implications than attitudes that are associated with the latter forms of emotion.

Mackie, Devos, and Smith (2000) demonstrated, across three empirical studies, that (a) for groups that are defined by a basic value conflict, anger and fear can be differentiated as distinct negative emotional responses to the outgroup; (b) appraisals of relative ingroup strength determine the degree of reported anger toward the outgroup; and (c) the level of felt anger mediates the relationship between strength appraisals and participants' desire to confront, oppose, or attack members of the outgroup. Based on these findings, Mackie et al. concluded that intergroup attitudes and behavior are channeled by the specific emotions that are elicited in response to appraisals of a particular outgroup in relation to the ingroup.

According to appraisal theories of emotion, the type of emotion directed toward outgroups may be a function of the degree of conflict of interest that is perceived to exist between the outgroup and the ingroup. When the perceived conflict or threat is relatively low, negative emotions toward outgroups are likely to be associated with appraisals of status and legitimacy. The perception that the outgroup is different from the ingroup in ways that are devalued or illegitimate gives rise to feelings of moral superiority, intolerance, and concomitant emotions of contempt and disgust toward relevant outgroups. The emotions associated with moral superiority may justify some negative discrimination against outgroups but do not necessarily lead directly to hostility or conflict. The emotions of contempt and disgust are associated with avoidance rather than attack, so intergroup peace may be maintained through segregation and mutual avoidance. As perceived conflict increases, avoidant emotions such as anxiety and disgust may be replaced by emotions such as anger, which instigate active hostility and aggression. Thus, the nature of the appraisal of the intergroup situation and the specific emotion that is engaged determine whether outgroup negativity gives rise to intergroup conflict.

Changing Intergroup Relations: Cooperative Contact

Whether realistic or perceived, the idea that an outgroup constitutes a threat to the welfare, values, or position of the ingroup is the primary basis of intergroup negativity and hostility. From that perspective, the route to improved intergroup relations lies in changing the perception of the outgroup vis-à-vis the ingroup. Ever since Sherif's classic Robber's Cave experiments, social psychologists have advocated cooperative intergroup contact as an effective strategy for improving intergroup relations. The key idea behind the "contact hypothesis" (Allport, 1954) is that isolation and segregation perpetuate intergroup hostility and negative attitudes. Interpersonal contact with members of the outgroup provides an opportunity for disconfirming negative expectations and building positive relations that can influence attitudes toward the outgroup as a whole.

Of course, mere contact between members of hostile groups does not always have such benign or positive outcomes. For contact to be an effective means of improving intergroup relations, at least two requirements have to be met. First, the contact must occur under conditions that reduce intergroup anxiety and promote positive interpersonal experiences (Voci & Hewstone, 2003). Second, group membership must be sufficiently salient in the contact situation so that the positive experience generalizes to the group as a whole (Brown, Vivian, & Hewstone, 1999; Ensari & Miller, 2002; Hewstone & Brown, 1986).

To meet the first requirement, the original contact hypothesis was qualified to include a number of preconditions for positive contact. According to Allport (1954), the four most important of these qualifying conditions were (a) integration has the support of authority, fostering *social norms* that favor intergroup acceptance; (b) the situation has high "acquaintance potential," promoting *intimate contact* among members of both groups; (c) the contact situation promotes *equal status* interactions among members of the social groups; and (d) the situation creates conditions of *cooperative interdependence* among members of both groups. Of these qualifiers, personalized contact and cooperation have received the most attention in both field and laboratory research (Pettigrew, 1998).

From Robbers Cave onward, many field studies of intergroup contact have confirmed that intergroup cooperation leads to more friendliness and less ingroup bias than situations that do not promote or require cooperative interaction. Probably the most extensive application of the contact hypothesis has been the implementation of cooperative learning programs in desegregated school classrooms. There is a sizable body of evidence that demonstrates the effectiveness of cooperative learning groups for increasing attraction and interaction between members of different social categories (Aronson et al., 1978; Johnson & Johnson, 1981; Slavin, 1985). Meta-analyses of studies in ethnically mixed classrooms confirm the superiority of cooperative learning methods over individualistic or competitive learning in promoting cross-ethnic friendships and reduced prejudice (Johnson, Johnson, & Maruyama, 1984).

Issues of Generalization

One concern about the validity of the contact hypothesis is whether findings obtained under relatively benign conditions can be generalized to real-world social groups with a history of conflict and hostility, inequalities of status and power, and political struggle. With established groups, resistance to contact and cooperative interdependence may be strong enough to make questions of the conditions of contact moot, and the history of outcomes of forced desegregation and contact is mixed at best (e.g., Cook, 1985; Gerard, 1983; Gerard & Miller, 1975; Stephan, 1986).

Another issue is whether any positive effects of contact, when they do occur, are generalized from the immediate contact experience to attitudes toward the outgroup as a whole. Many laboratory experiments on contact effects are limited in that they assess only attitudes toward ingroup and outgroup participants within the contact setting. Presumably, however, the ultimate goal of contact interventions is reduction of prejudice toward whole social groups, not simply creation of positive attitudes toward specific group members, so promoting generalization may be as important as conditions of the contact itself.

In what is probably the most comprehensive laboratory test of interracial contact effects, Cook (1971, 1984) conducted a series of experiments in which highly prejudiced White subjects worked with a Black confederate in an ideal contact situation (equal status, cooperative interdependence, with high acquaintance potential and equalitarian social norms) over an extended period of time. Perceptions of the Black co-worker were measured at the completion of the contact experience, and general racial attitudes were assessed before, immediately after, and up to three years following the experimental sessions. Across all variations of this experiment, White participants displayed predominantly positive behaviors toward their Black co-worker and expressed highly favorable evaluations in the postexperimental questionnaires. Whether liking for this individual member of the outgroup resulted in changed attitudes toward Blacks and race-related issues, however, varied across the experiments and for different attitude measures.

One major reason why generalization fails is that the newly positively valued outgroup member is regarded as an exception and not as typical or representative of the outgroup in general (Allport, 1954; Rothbart & John, 1985; Wilder, 1984). In Cook's (1971, 1984) studies, significant differences in postcontact attitude change among those who participated in the contact experience compared to control subjects were obtained only in an initial experiment in which what Cook (1984) referred to as a "cognitive booster" was introduced during the course of the experiment. This added element was a guided conversation (led by a research confederate) in which the negative effects of discriminatory policies and practices were directly connected to the now-liked Black co-worker. This booster served to make salient the co-worker's category membership and to establish a link between feelings toward this individual and members of the group as a whole. In a later, conceptually related experiment, van Oudenhoven, Groenewoud, and Hewstone (1996) found that Dutch students' evaluations of Turkish people in general were more positive after an episode of cooperative interaction with an individual Turkish person when his ethnicity was explicitly mentioned during the cooperative session than when ethnicity remained implicit only. Again, the explicit linkage appears to be a necessary mechanism for generalized contact effects.

Results from a recent meta-analysis of data from years of contact research suggests that, overall, positive contact experiences do generalize to intergroup attitudes (Pettigrew & Tropp, 2006). Collapsing findings across a wide range of field and laboratory studies with different types of groups, the average effect of contact on measures of prejudice toward the outgroup proved to be significant—more contact and less prejudice. Furthermore, consistent with the tenets of the qualified contact hypothesis, contact in the form of interpersonal friendships proved to have a greater effect on average than contact in less personalized contexts (Pettigrew & Tropp, 2006). Thus, contact does seem to have a robust prejudice-reducing effect overall, despite considerable variation in its effects under specific circumstances.

Theoretical Underpinnings of Contact Effects

Although it is encouraging to learn that the effects of contact on intergroup attitudes are more likely to be positive than negative, this result does not indicate how to manage contact situations to ensure such beneficial outcomes. In his review of the current status of contact research, Pettigrew (1998) suggested that the challenge is to distinguish between factors that are *essential* to the processes underlying positive contact experiences and their generalization and those that merely *facilitate* (or inhibit) the operation of these processes. To make this distinction, contact researchers needed a more elaborate theory of what the underlying processes are and how they mediate the effects of intergroup contact under different conditions. One advance toward a more integrative theory of intergroup relations was achieved when contact research was combined with concepts of social categorization and social identity theory to provide a theoretical framework for understanding the cognitive mechanisms by which cooperative contact is presumed to work (see Brewer & Miller, 1984; Brown & Hewstone, 2005; Gaertner, Mann, Murrell, & Dovidio, 1989; Hewstone, 1996; Hewstone & Brown, 1986; Wilder, 1986).

Based on the premises of social identity theory, three alternative models for contact effects have been developed and tested in experimental and field settings, namely, decategorization, recategorization, and mutual differentiation. The first two models seek to change attitudes and perceptions by altering the salience of ingroup–outgroup social categorization in the contact situation. The third model addresses how intergroup attitudes can be changed while ingroup–outgroup differentiation remains salient.

Decategorization: The Personalization Model

The first model is essentially a formalization and elaboration of the assumptions implicit in the contact hypothesis itself (Brewer & Miller, 1984; Miller 2002). A primary consequence of salient ingroup–outgroup categorization is the deindividuation of members of the outgroup. The personalization perspective on the contact situation implies that intergroup interactions should be structured so as to reduce the salience of category distinctions and promote opportunities to get to know outgroup members as individual persons. Attending to personal characteristics of group members not only provides the opportunity to disconfirm category stereotypes, it also breaks down the monolithic perception of the outgroup as a homogeneous unit (Wilder, 1978). In this scheme, the contact situation encourages attention to information at the individual level that replaces category identity as the most useful basis for classifying participants.

Repeated personalized contacts with a variety of outgroup members should, over time, undermine the value and meaningfulness of the social category stereotype as a source of information about members of that group. This is the process by which contact experiences are expected to generalize—via reducing the salience and meaning of social categorization in the long run (Brewer & Miller, 1988).

A number of experimental studies provide evidence supporting this perspective on contact effects (Bettencourt, Brewer, Croak, & Miller, 1992; Marcus-Newhall, Miller, Holtz, & Brewer, 1993). Miller, Brewer, and Edwards (1985), for instance, demonstrated that a cooperative task that required personalized interaction with members of the outgroup resulted not only in more positive attitudes toward outgroup members in the cooperative setting but also toward other outgroup members shown on a videotape, compared to task-focused rather than person-focused cooperative contact.

The personalization model is also supported by early empirical evidence for the effects of extended, intimate contact on racial attitudes. More recently, extensive data on effects of intergroup friendships have been derived from surveys in Western Europe regarding attitudes toward minority immigrant groups (Hamberger & Hewstone, 1997; Pettigrew, 1997; Pettigrew & Meertens, 1995). Across samples in France, Great Britain, the Netherlands, and Germany, Europeans with outgroup friends scored significantly lower on measures of prejudice, particularly affective prejudice (Pettigrew, 1998). This positive relationship did not hold for other types of contact (work or residential) that did not involve formation of close personal relationships with members of the outgroup. Although there is clearly a bidirectional relationship between positive attitudes and extent of personal contact, path analyses indicate that the path from friendship to reduction in prejudice is stronger than the other way around (Pettigrew, 1998).

Recategorization: The Common Ingroup Identity Model

The second social categorization model of intergroup contact and prejudice reduction is also based on the premise that reducing the salience of ingroup–outgroup category distinctions is the key to positive effects. In contrast to the decategorization approaches previously described, recategorization is not designed to reduce or eliminate categorization but rather to create group categorization at a higher level of category inclusiveness. Specifically, the "common ingroup identity model" (Gaertner & Dovidio, 2000; Gaertner, Dovidio, Anastasio, Bachman, & Rust, 1993) proposes that intergroup bias and conflict can be reduced by factors that transform participants' representations of memberships from two groups to one more inclusive group. With common ingroup identity, the cognitive and motivational processes that initially produced ingroup favoritism are redirected to benefit the former outgroup members.

Among the antecedent factors proposed by the common ingroup identity model are the features of contact situations (Allport, 1954) that are necessary for intergroup contact to be successful (e.g., interdependence between groups, equal status, equalitarian norms). From this perspective, cooperative interaction, for example, enhances positive evaluations of outgroup members, at least in part, because cooperation transforms members' representations of the memberships from "us" and "them" to a more inclusive "we." To test this hypothesis directly, Gaertner, Mann, Dovidio, Murrell, and Pomare (1990) conducted a laboratory experiment that brought two 3-person laboratory groups together under conditions designed to vary independently the members' representations of the aggregate as one group or two groups (by varying factors such as seating arrangement) and the presence or absence of intergroup cooperative interaction. Supportive of the hypothesis, the introduction of cooperative interaction increased participants' perceptions of one group and also reduced their bias in evaluative ratings relative to those who did not cooperate during the contact period. In further support for the common ingroup identity model, this effect of cooperation was mediated by the extent to which members of both groups perceived themselves as one group.

Outside of the laboratory, survey studies conducted in natural settings across very different intergroup contexts offered converging support for the proposal that the features specified by the contact hypothesis can increase intergroup harmony in part by transforming members' representations of the memberships from separate groups to one more inclusive group (Gaertner, Dovidio, & Bachman, 1996; Gaertner, Rust, Dovidio, Bachman, & Anastasio, 1994; Gaertner et al., 2000).

Challenges to the Decategorization/Recategorization Models

Although the structural representations of the contact situation advocated by the decategorization (personalization) and recategorization (common ingroup identity) models are different, the two approaches share common assumptions about the need to reduce category differentiation and associated processes. Because both models rely on reducing or eliminating the salience of intergroup differentiation, they involve structuring contact in a way that will challenge or threaten existing social identities. Both cognitive and motivational factors conspire to create resistance to the dissolution of category boundaries or to reestablish category distinctions across time. Although the salience of a common superordinate identity or personalized representations may be enhanced in the short run, these may be difficult to maintain across time and social situations.

Pre-existing social-structural relationships between groups may also create strong forces of resistance to changes in category boundaries. Cognitive restructuring may be close to impossible (at least as a first step) for groups already engaged in deadly hostilities. Even in the absence of overt conflict, asymmetries between social groups in size, power, or status create additional sources of resistance. When one group is substantially numerically smaller than the other in the contact situation, the minority category is especially salient, and minority group members may be particularly reluctant to accept a superordinate category identity that is dominated by the other group. Another major challenge is created by preexisting status differences between groups, in which members of both high- and low-status groups may be threatened by contact and assimilation (Hornsey & Hogg, 2000a; Riek, Mania, & Gaertner, 2006).

The Mutual Differentiation Model

These challenges to processes of decategorization and recategorization led Hewstone and Brown (1986; Brown & Hewstone, 2005) to recommend an alternative approach to intergroup contact wherein cooperative interactions between groups are introduced without degrading the original ingroup–outgroup categorization. To promote positive intergroup experience, Hewstone and Brown recommended that the contact situation be structured so that members of the respective groups have distinct but complementary roles to contribute toward common goals. In this way, both groups can maintain positive distinctiveness within a cooperative framework. This strategy allows group members to maintain their social identities and positive distinctiveness while avoiding insidious intergroup comparisons. Thus, the intergroup contact model does not seek to change the basic category structure of the intergroup contact situation but to change the intergroup affect from negative to positive interdependence and evaluation.

Evidence in support of this approach comes from the results of an experiment by Brown and Wade (1987) in which work teams composed of students from two different faculties engaged in a cooperative effort to produce a two-page magazine article. When the representatives of the two groups were assigned separate roles in the team task (one group working on figures and layout and the other group working on text), the contact experience had a more positive effect on intergroup attitudes than when the two groups were not provided with distinctive roles (see also Deschamps & Brown, 1983; Dovidio, Gaertner, & Validzic, 1998).

Hewstone and Brown (1986) argued that generalization of positive contact experiences is more likely when the contact situation is defined as an *intergroup* situation rather than an interpersonal interaction. Generalization in this case is direct rather than requiring additional cognitive links between positive affect toward individuals and representations of the group as a whole. This position is supported by evidence that cooperative contact with a member of an outgroup leads to more favorable generalized attitudes toward the group as a whole when category membership is made salient during contact (e.g., Brown, Vivian, & Hewstone, 1999; Hewstone et al., 2005; van Oudenhoven, Groenewoud, & Hewstone, 1996).

Although ingroup–outgroup category salience is usually associated with ingroup bias and the negative side of intergroup attitudes, cooperative interdependence is assumed to override the negative intergroup schema, particularly if the two groups have differentiated, complementary roles to play. The affective component of the model, however, is potentially unstable. Salient intergroup boundaries are associated with mutual distrust (Insko & Schopler, 1987) and intergroup anxiety (Greenland & Brown, 1999; Islam & Hewstone, 1993), which undermine the potential for cooperative interdependence and mutual liking over any length of time. By reinforcing perceptions of group differences, the differentiation model risks reinforcing negative beliefs about the outgroup, and the potential for fission and conflict along group lines remains high.

Hybrid Models: An Integration of Approaches

As reviewed, each of the cognitive–structural models of intergroup contact and prejudice reduction has its weaknesses and limitations, particularly when we seek to generalize beyond small group interactions in laboratory settings. These criticisms have led a number of writers to suggest that some combination of all three models may be necessary to create conditions for long-term attitude change (e.g., Brewer & Gaertner,

2001; Brown & Hewstone, 2005; Gaertner et al., 2000; Hewstone, 1996; Pettigrew, 1998). More integrative models of intergroup contact take advantage of the fact that individuals are members of multiple social groups, which implies different social identities and ingroup loyalties.

Nested Dual Identities

In recent work regarding the development of a common ingroup identity, it has been proposed that embracing a more inclusive superordinate identity does not necessarily require each group to forsake its original group identity completely (Gaertner, Rust, Dovidio, Bachman, & Anastasio, 1994). Instead, group members may simultaneously perceive themselves as members of different groups but also as part of the same team or superordinate entity. For example, in a multiethnic high school, minority students who identified themselves in terms of both their ethnic group and their American identity (e.g., Korean American) had lower intergroup affective bias than minority students who identified themselves only in terms of their ethnicity. Dual identified students were also more likely to endorse the statement "Although there are different groups at school, it feels like we are playing on the same team" (Gaertner et al., 1994).

Other studies indicate that the intergroup benefits of a strong superordinate identity remain relatively stable even when the strength of the subordinate identity is equivalently high (Huo, Smith, Tyler, & Lind, 1996; Smith & Tyler, 1996). This suggests that identification with a more inclusive social group does not require individuals to deny their ethnic identity. In addition, a dual identity can also lead to even more positive outgroup attitudes than those associated with a superordinate identity alone (Hornsey & Hogg, 2000b). In terms of promoting more harmonious intergroup interactions, a dual identity capitalizes on the benefits of common ingroup membership as well those accrued from mutual differentiation between the groups.

On the other hand, dual identities are not always associated with positive relations between subgroups within the superordinate category. Mummendey and Wenzel (1999) make a convincing case that under some circumstances, making a shared superordinate category salient can lead to enhanced derogation of other subgroups when both subgroup and superordinate group identities are strong. This can happen if the values and attributes of the ingroup are projected onto the superordinate group, in which case subgroups that differ from these attributes come to be seen as *deviant* (rather than just "different") and a potential source of symbolic threat to the ingroup and the superordinate group. In studies of national groups in the European Union, Mummendey and Waldzus (2004) demonstrated that individuals who profess dual identification (strong national identity and European identity) also exhibit higher ingroup projection, which in turn is associated with negative attitudes toward other subgroup nations. Thus, ironically, nested dual identities may enhance rather than reduce ingroup bias and discrimination against other subgroups.

Cross-Cutting Identities

Nested categories at different levels of inclusiveness represent only one form of multiple ingroup identities. Individuals may also be members of social categories that overlap only partially, if at all. Many bases of social category differentiation—gender, age, religion, ethnicity, and occupation—represent cross-cutting cleavages. From the standpoint of a particular person, other individuals may be fellow ingroup members on one dimension of category differentiation but outgroup members on another. (For instance, for a woman business executive, a male colleague is an ingroup member with respect to occupation but an outgrouper with respect to her gender identification.) It is possible that such orthogonal social identities are kept isolated from each other so that only one ingroup–outgroup distinction is activated in a particular social context. But there are reasons to expect that simultaneous activation of multiple ingroup identities is possible and has the potential to reduce prejudice and discrimination based on any one category distinction.

Evidence from both anthropology (e.g., Gluckman, 1955) and political sociology (e.g., Coser, 1956) has long suggested that societies characterized by cross-cutting loyalty structures are less prone to schism and internal intergroup conflict than societies characterized by a single hierarchical loyalty structure. More recently, social psychologists have also begun to consider the implications of such multiple cross-cutting social identities for reduction of ingroup bias at the individual level (Brown & Turner, 1979; Deschamps & Doise, 1978; 1979; Marcus-Newhall et al., 1993; Roccas & Brewer, 2002; Vanbeselaere, 1991).

Experimental studies with both natural and artificial categories have demonstrated that adding a cross-cutting category distinction reduces ingroup bias and increases positive attitudes toward crossed category members compared to simple ingroup–outgroup differentiation (Vanbeselaere, 1991) or compared to situations in which category distinctions are convergent or superimposed (Bettencourt & Dorr, 1998; Marcus-Newhall et al., 1993; Rust, 1996). In these studies, cooperative interaction in the context of cross-cutting social identities and roles increases intracategory differentiation and reduces perceived intercategory differences, resulting in less category-based evaluations of individual group members. Furthermore, the benefits of cross-categorization may be enhanced when both category distinctions are embedded in a common superordinate group identity (Gaertner et al., 1999; Rust, 1996). Thus, crossed categorization and recategorization may work together to produce enhanced inclusiveness and reduced intergroup discrimination.

Intergroup Relations Today: Implications for Pluralistic Societies

The principles of social categorization, ingroup favoritism, and outgroup prejudice discussed in this chapter have important implications for promoting positive intergroup relations within a context in which groups must live together interdependently. The same basic principles apply whether we are considering departments or companies combined within an organization, diverse ethnic or religious groups within a nation, or nation-states within an international community. In any of these contexts, the goals of contact and cooperation compete with natural tendencies toward ingroup–outgroup differentiation, separation, and exclusion. Processes that reduce the social meaning of category boundaries and associated us–them distinctions are in tension with pluralistic values that seek to maintain cultural variation and distinct social identities. The tension between differentiation and integration must be recognized and acknowledged in any complex social system. Exclusive focus on either assimilation or separation as the solution to intergroup discrimination and conflict is neither desirable nor realistic (Verkuyten, 2006). New directions in the social psychology of intergroup relations involve putting the study of intergroup processes back into the context of the social and political systems within which they are embedded and the multiple social identities that characterize our complex social world.

References

Allport, G. (1954). *The nature of prejudice*. Cambridge, MA: Addison-Wesley.

Ancok, D., & Chertkoff, J. M. (1983). Effects of group membership, relative performance, and self-interest on the division of outcomes. *Journal of Personality and Social Psychology, 45,* 1256–1262.

Aronson, E., Blaney, N., Stephan, C., Sikes, J., & Snapp, M. (1978). *The jigsaw classroom*. Beverly Hills: Sage.

Bar-Tal, D. (2007). Sociopsychological foundations of intractable conflicts. *American Behavioral Scientist, 50,* 1430–1453.

Baumeister, R. F., & Leary, M. R. (1995). The need to belong: Desire for interpersonal attachments as a fundamental human motivation. *Psychological Bulletin, 117*, 497–529.

Bettencourt, B. A., Brewer, M. B., Croak, M. R., & Miller, N. (1992). Cooperation and the reduction of intergroup bias: The role of reward structure and social orientation. *Journal of Experimental Social Psychology, 28*, 301–319.

Bettencourt, B. A., & Dorr, N. (1998). Cooperative interaction and intergroup bias: Effects of numerical representation and cross-cut role assignment. *Personality and Social Psychology, 24*, 1276–1293

Blanz, M., Mummendey, A., & Otten, S. (1997). Normative evaluations and frequency expectations regarding positive and negative outcome allocations between groups. *European Journal of Social Psychology, 27*, 165–176.

Branscombe, N. R., Ellemers, N., Spears, R., & Doosje, B. (1999). The context and content of social identity threat. In N. Ellemers, R. Spears, & B. Doosje (Eds.), *Social identity: Context, commitment, content* (pp. 35–58). Oxford, England: Blackwell.

Brewer, M. B. (1979). Ingroup bias in the minimal intergroup situation: A cognitive-motivational analysis. *Psychological Bulletin, 86*, 307–324.

Brewer, M. B. (1991). The social self: On being the same and different at the same time. *Personality and Social Psychology Bulletin, 17*, 475–482.

Brewer, M. B. (1996). In-group favoritism: The subtle side of intergroup discrimination. In D. Messick & A. Tenbrunsel (Eds.), *Codes of conduct: Behavioral research into business ethics* (pp. 160–170). New York, NY: SAGE.

Brewer, M. B. (2001). Ingroup identification and intergroup conflict: When does ingroup love become outgroup hate? In R. Ashmore, L. Jussim, & D. Wilder (Eds.), *Social identity, intergroup conflict, and conflict reduction* (pp. 17–41). New York, NY: Oxford University Press.

Brewer, M. B., & Campbell, D. T. (1976). *Ethnocentrism and intergroup attitudes: East African evidence.* New York, NY: Halsted.

Brewer, M. B., & Gaertner, S. L. (2001). Toward reduction of prejudice: Intergroup contact and social categorization. In R. Brown & S. Gaertner (Eds.), *Blackwell handbook of social psychology: Intergroup processes* (pp. 451–472). Oxford, England: Blackwell.

Brewer, M. B., & Kramer, R. M. (1986). Choice behavior in social dilemmas: Effects of social identity, group size, and decision framing. *Journal of Personality and Social Psychology, 50*, 543–549.

Brewer, M., & Miller, N. (1984). Beyond the contact hypothesis: Theoretical perspectives on desegregation. In N. Miller & M. Brewer (Eds.), *Groups in contact: The psychology of desegregation* (pp. 281–302). New York, NY: Academic Press.

Brewer, M. B., & Miller, N. (1988). Contact and cooperation: When do they work? In P. Katz & D. Taylor (Eds.), *Eliminating racism: Means and controversies* (pp. 315–326). New York, NY: Plenum Press.

Brewer, M. B., & Pickett, C. A. (1999). Distinctiveness motives as a source of the social self. In T. Tyler, R. Kramer, & O. John (Eds.), *The psychology of the social self* (pp. 71–87). Mahwah, NJ: Erlbaum.

Brewer, M. B., & Pickett, C. L. (2002). The social self and group identification: Inclusion and distinctiveness motives in interpersonal and collective identities. In J. Forgas & K. Williams (Eds.), *The social self: Cognitive, interpersonal, and intergroup perspectives* (pp. 255–271). Philadelphia, PA: Psychology Press.

Brewer, M. B., & Weber, J. G. (1994). Self-evaluation effects of interpersonal versus intergroup social comparison. *Journal of Personality and Social Psychology, 66*, 268–275.

Brown, R. J., & Abrams, D. (1986). The effects of intergroup similarity and goal interdependence on intergroup attitudes and task performance. *Journal of Experimental Social Psychology, 22*, 78–92.

Brown, R. J., & Hewstone, M. (2005). An integrative theory of intergroup contact. In M. Zanna (Ed.), *Advances in experimental social psychology* (Vol. 37, pp. 256–343). New York, NY: Elsevier.

Brown, R. J., & Turner, J. C. (1979). The criss-cross categorization effect in intergroup discrimination. *British Journal of Social and Clinical Psychology, 18*, 371–383.

Brown, R. J., Vivian, J., & Hewstone, M. (1999). Changing attitudes through intergroup contact: The effects of group membership salience. *European Journal of Social Psychology, 29*, 741–764.

Brown, R. J., & Wade, G. (1987). Superordinate goals and intergroup behaviour: The effect of role ambiguity and status on intergroup attitudes and task performance. *European Journal of Social Psychology, 17,* 131–142.

Caddick, B. (1982). Perceived illegitimacy and intergroup relations. In H. Tajfel (Ed.), *Social identity and intergroup relations* (pp. 137–154). Cambridge, England: Cambridge University Press.

Castano, E., Yzerbyt, V. Y., Bourguignon, D., & Seron, E. (2002). Who may come in? The impact of ingroup identification on ingroup-outgroup categorization. *Journal of Experimental Social Psychology, 38,* 315–322.

Cook, S. W. (1971). *The effect of unintended interracial contact upon racial interaction and attitude change* (Final report, Project no. 5-1320). Washington, DC: US Department of Health, Education, and Welfare.

Cook, S. W. (1984). Cooperative interaction in multiethnic contexts. In N. Miller & M. Brewer (Eds.), *Groups in contact: The psychology of desegregation* (pp. 155–185). New York: Academic Press.

Cook, S. W. (1985). Experimenting on social issues: The case of school desegregation. *American Psychologist, 40,* 452–460.

Coser, L. A. (1956). *The functions of social conflict.* New York, NY: Free Press.

Crocker, J., Luhtanen, R., Blaine, B., & Broadnax, S. (1994). Collective self-esteem and psychological well-being among White, Black, and Asian college students. *Personality and Social Psychology Bulletin, 20,* 503–513.

Deaux, K., Reid, A., Mizrahi, K., & Cotting, D. (1999). Connecting the person to the social: The functions of social identification. In T. Tyler, R. Kramer, & O. John (Eds.), *The psychology of the social self* (pp. 91–113). Mahwah, NJ: Erlbaum.

Deschamps, J.-C., & Brown, R. J. (1983). Superordinate goals and intergoup conflict. *British Journal of Social Psychology, 22,* 189–195.

Deschamps, J-C., & Doise, W. (1978). Crossed category memberships in intergroup relations. In H. Tajfel (Ed.), *Differentiation between social groups* (pp. 141–158). Cambridge, England: Cambridge University Press.

Diehl, M. (1990). The minimal group paradigm: Theoretical explanations and empirical findings. *European Review of Social Psychology, 1,* 263–292.

Dijker, A. J. M. (1987). Emotional reaction to ethnic minorities. *European Journal of Social Psychology, 17,* 305–325.

Doise, W. (1978). *Groups and individuals: Explanations in social psychology.* Cambridge, England: Cambridge University Press.

Dovidio, J. F., Gaertner, S. L., & Validzic, A. (1998). Intergroup bias: Status differentiation and a common ingroup identity. *Journal of Personality and Social Psychology, 75,* 109–120.

Ellemers, N., Doosje, B., van Knippenberg, A., & Wilke, H. (1992). Status protection in high status minority groups. *European Journal of Social Psychology, 22,* 123–140.

Ellemers, N., van Knippenberg, A., de Vries, N., & Wilke, H. (1988). Social identification and permeability of group boundaries. *European Journal of Social Psychology, 18,* 497–513.

Ellemers, N., van Knippenberg, A., & Wilke, H. (1990). The influence of permeability of group boundaries and stability of group status on strategies of individual mobility and social change. *British Journal of Social Psychology, 29,* 233–246.

Ellemers, N., Wilke, H., & van Knippenberg, A. (1993). Effects of the legitimacy of low group or individual status on individual and collective identity enhancement strategies. *Journal of Personality and Social Psychology, 64,* 766–778.

Ensari, N., & Miller, N. (2002). The out-group must not be so bad after all: The effects of disclosure, typicality, and salience on intergroup bias. *Journal of Personality and Social Psychology, 83,* 313–329.

Esses, V. M., Jackson, L. M., & Armstrong, T. L. (1998). Intergroup competition and attitudes toward immigrants and immigration: An instrumental model of group conflict. *Journal of Social Issues, 54,* 699–724.

Farnham, S. D., Greenwald, A. G., & Banaji, M. R. (1999). Implicit self-esteem. In D. Abrams & M. Hogg (Eds.), *Social identity and social cognition* (pp. 230–248). Oxford, England: Blackwell.

Gaertner, S. L., & Dovidio, J. F. (2000). *Reducing intergroup bias: The common ingroup identity model.* Philadelphia, PA: Psychology Press.

Gaertner, S. L., Dovidio, J. F., Anastasio, P. A., Bachman, B. A., & Rust, M. C. (1993). The Common Ingroup Identity Model: Recategorization and the reduction of intergroup bias. *European Review of Social Psychology, 4,* 1–26.

Gaertner, S. L., Dovidio, J. F., & Bachman, B. A. (1996). Revisiting the contact hypothesis: The induction of a common ingroup identity. *International Journal of Intercultural Relations, 20,* 271–290.

Gaertner, S. L., Dovidio, J. F., Banker, B., Houlette, M., Johnson, K., & McGlynn, E. (2000). Reducing intergroup conflict: From superordinate goals to decategorization, recategorization, and mutual differentiation. *Group Dynamics, 4,* 98–114.

Gaertner, S. L., Dovidio, J. F., Nier, J. A., Ward, C. M., & Banker, B. S. (1999). Across cultural divides: The value of a superordinate identity. In D. Prentice & D. Miller (Eds.), *Cultural divides: Understanding and overcoming group conflict* (pp. 173–212). New York, NY: SAGE.

Gaertner, S. L., Mann, J. A., Dovidio, J. F., Murrell, A. J., & Pomare, M. (1990). How does cooperation reduce intergroup bias? *Journal of Personality and Social Psychology, 59,* 692–704.

Gaertner, S. L., Mann, J. A., Murrell, A. J., & Dovidio, J. F. (1989). Reduction of intergroup bias: The benefits of recategorization. *Journal of Personality and Social Psychology, 57,* 239–249.

Gaertner, S. L., Rust, M. C., Dovidio, J. F., Bachman, B. A., & Anastasio, A. (1994). The contact hypothesis: The role of a common ingroup identity on reducing intergroup bias. *Small Groups Research, 25,* 224–290.

Gerard, H. B. (1983). School desegregation: The social science role. *American Psychologist, 38,* 869–887.

Gerard, H. B., & Hoyt, M. (1974). Distinctiveness of social categorization and attitude toward in-group members. *Journal of Personality and Social Psychology, 29,* 836–842.

Gerard, H. B., & Miller, N. (1975). *School desegregation: A long-term study.* New York, NY: Plenum.

Gluckman, M. (1955). *Customs and conflict in Africa.* London, England: Blackwell.

Greenland, K., & Brown, R. J. (1999). Categorization and intergroup anxiety in contact between British and Japanese nationals. *European Journal of Social Psychology, 29,* 503–521.

Grieve, P. G., & Hogg, M. A. (1999). Subjective uncertainty and intergroup discrimination in the minimal group situation. *Personality and Social Psychology Bulletin, 25,* 926–940.

Hamberger, J., & Hewstone, M. (1997). Inter-ethnic contact as a predictor of prejudice: Tests of a model in four West European nations. *British Journal of Social Psychology, 36,* 173–190.

Hewstone, M. (1990). The "ultimate attribution error"? A review of the literature on intergroup causal attribution. *European Journal of Social Psychology, 20,* 311–335.

Hewstone, M. (1996). Contact and categorization: Social psychology interventions to change intergroup relations. In C. N. Macrae, C. Stangor, & M. Hewstone (Eds.), *Stereotypes and stereotyping* (pp. 323–368). New York, NY: Guilford.

Hewstone, M., & Brown, R. J. (1986). Contact is not enough: An intergroup perspective on the "contact hypothesis." In M. Hewstone & R. Brown (Eds.), *Contact and conflict in intergroup encounters* (pp. 1–44). Oxford, England: Basil Blackwell.

Hewstone, M., Cairns, Voci, A., Paolini, S., McLernon, F., Crisp, R., . . . Craig, J. (2005). Intergroup contact in a divided society: Challenging segregation in Northern Ireland. In D. Abrams, J. M. Marques, & M. A. Hogg (Eds.), *The social psychology of inclusion and exclusion* (pp. 265–292). Philadelphia, PA: Psychology Press.

Hinkle, S., & Brown, R. (1990). Intergroup comparisons and social identity: Some links and lacunae. In D. Abrams & M. Hogg (Eds.), *Social identity theory: Construction and critical advances* (pp. 48–70). London, England: Harvester Wheatsheaf.

Hogg, M. A., & Abrams, D. (1988). *Social identifications.* London, England: Routledge.

Hogg, M. A., & Abrams, D. (1993). Towards a single-process uncertainty-reduction model of social motivation in groups. In M. Hogg & D. Abrams (Eds.), *Group motivation: Social psychological perspectives* (pp. 173–190). New York, NY: Harvester Wheatsheaf.

Hogg, M. A., & Mullin, B-A. (1999). Joining groups to reduce uncertainty: Subjective uncertainty reduction and group identification. In D. Abrams & M. A. Hogg (Eds.), *Social identity and social cognition* (pp. 249–279). Oxford, England: Blackwell.

Hogg, M. A., & Turner, J. C. (1987). Intergroup behaviour, self-stereotyping, and the salience of social categories. *British Journal of Social Psychology, 26,* 325–340.

Hornsey, M. J., & Hogg, M. A. (1999). Subgroup differentiation as a response to an overly-inclusive group: A test of optimal distinctiveness theory. *European Journal of Social Psychology, 29,* 543–550.

Hornsey, M. J., & Hogg, M. A. (2000a) Assimilation and diversity: An integrative model of subgroup relations. *Personality and Social Psychology Review, 4,* 143–156.

Hornsey, M. J., & Hogg, M. A. (2000b). Subgroup relations: A comparison of mutual intergroup differentiation and common ingroup identity models of prejudice reduction. *Personality and Social Psychology Bulletin, 26,* 242–256.

Huo, Y., Smith, H., Tyler, T. R., & Lind, E. A. (1996). Superordinate identification, subgroup identification, and justice concerns: Is separatism the problem; is assimilation the answer? *Psychological Science, 7,* 40–45.

Insko, C. A., & Schopler, J. (1987). Categorization, competition, and collectivity. In C. Hendrick (Ed.), *Group processes. Review of personality and social psychology* (Vol. 8, pp. 213–251). Beverly Hills, CA: SAGE.

Islam, M. R., & Hewstone, M. (1993). Dimensions of contact as predictors of intergroup anxiety, perceived outgroup variability and outgroup attitude: An integrative account. *Personality and Social Psychology Bulletin, 19,* 700–710.

Jetten, J., Branscombe, N. R., Schmitt, M. T., & Spears, R. (2001). Rebels with a cause: Group identification as a response to perceived discrimination from the mainstream. *Personality and Social Psychology Bulletin, 27,* 1204–1213.

Jetten, J., Spears, R., & Manstead, A. S. R. (1998). Intergroup similarity and group variability: The effects of group distinctiveness on the expression of in-group bias. *Journal of Personality and Social Psychology, 74,* 1481–1492.

Jetten, J., Spears, R., & Postmes, T. (2004). Intergroup distinctiveness and differentiation: A meta-analytic integration. *Journal of Personality and Social Psychology, 86,* 862–879.

Johnson, D. W., & Johnson, R. T. (1981). Effects of cooperative and individualistic learning experiences on interethnic interaction. *Journal of Educational Psychology, 73,* 444–449.

Johnson, D. W., Johnson, R., & Maruyama, G. (1984). Goal interdependence and interpersonal attraction in heterogeneous classrooms: A metaanalysis. In N. Miller & M. Brewer (Eds.), *Groups in contact: The psychology of desegregation* (pp. 187–212). New York, NY: Academic Press.

Jost, J. T. (2001). Outgroup favoritism and the theory of system justification: An experimental paradigm for investigating the effects of socio-economic success on stereotype content. In G. Moskowitz (Ed.), *Cognitive social psychology: The Princeton symposium on the legacy and future of social cognition* (pp. 89–102). Hillsdale, NJ: Erlbaum.

Kahn, A., & Ryen, A. (1972). Factors influencing the bias towards one's own group. *International Journal of Group Tensions, 2,* 33–50.

Kelman, H. C. (1999). The interdependence of Israeli and Palestinian national identities: The role of the other in existential conflicts. *Journal of Social Issues, 55,* 581–600.

Kelman, H. C. (2001). The role of national identity in conflict resolution. In R. D. Ashmore, L. Jussim, & D. Wilder (Eds.), *Social identity, intergroup conflict, and conflict reduction* (pp. 187–212). New York, NY: Oxford University Press.

Kosterman, R., & Feshbach, S. (1989). Toward a measure of patriotic and nationalistic attitudes. *Political Psychology, 10,* 257–274.

Leach, C. W., Ellemers, N., & Barreto, M. (2007). Group virtue: The importance of morality (vs. competence and sociability) in the positive evaluation of in-groups. *Journal of Personality and Social Psychology, 93,* 234–249.

Ledgerwood, A., Liviatan, I., & Carnevale, P. (2007). Group-identity completion and the symbolic value of property. *Psychological Science, 18,* 873–878.

Lemaine, G. (1974). Social differentiation and social originality. *European Journal of Social Psychology, 4,* 17–52.

Leonardelli, G., & Brewer, M. B. (2001). Minority and majority discrimination: When and why. *Journal of Experimental Social Psychology, 37,* 468–485.

LeVine, R. A., & Campbell, D. T. (1972). *Ethnocentrism: Theories of conflict, ethnic attitudes and group behavior.* New York, NY: Wiley.

Leyens, J-P., & Yzerbyt, V. (1992). The ingroup overexclusion effect: Impact of valence and confirmation on stereotypical information search. *European Journal of Social Psychology, 22,* 549–569.

Mackie, D. M., Devos, T., & Smith, E. R. (2000). Intergroup emotions: Explaining offensive action tendencies in an intergroup context. *Journal of Personality and Social Psychology, 79,* 602–616.

Marcus-Newhall, A., Miller, N., Holtz, R., & Brewer, M. B. (1993). Crosscutting category membership with role assignment: A means of reducing intergroup bias. *British Journal of Social Psychology, 32,* 125–146.

Miller, D. T., Downs, J. S., & Prentice, D. A. (1998). Minimal conditions for the creation of a unit relationship: The social bond between birthday mates. *European Journal of Social Psychology, 28,* 475–481.

Miller, N. (2002). Personalization and the promise of contact theory. *Journal of Social Issues, 58,* 387–410.

Miller, N., Brewer, M. B., & Edwards, K. (1985). Cooperative interaction in desegregated settings: A laboratory analogue. *Journal of Social Issues, 41*(3), 63–79.

Mullen, B., Brown, R., & Smith, C. (1992). In-group bias as a function of salience, relevance, and status: An integration. *European Journal of Social Psychology, 22,* 103–122.

Mullin, B-A., & Hogg, M. A. (1998). Dimensions of subjective uncertainty in social identification and minimal intergroup discrimination. *British Journal of Social Psychology, 37,* 345–365.

Mummendey, A., Simon, B., Dietze, C., Grunert., M., Haeger, G., Kessler, S., . . . Schäferhoff, S. (1992). Categorization is not enough: Intergroup discrimination in negative outcome allocations. *Journal of Experimental Social Psychology, 28,* 125–144.

Mummendey, A., & Waldzus, S. (2004). National differences and European plurality: Discrimination or tolerance between European countries. In R. Herrmann, T. Risse, & M. Brewer (Eds.), *Transnational identities: Becoming European in the EU* (pp. 59–72). Lanham, MD: Rowman & Littlefield.

Mummendey, A., & Wenzel, M. (1999). Social discrimination and tolerance in intergroup relations. *Personality and Social Psychology Review, 3,* 158–174.

Ng, S. H. (1984). Equity and social categorization effects on intergroup allocation of rewards. *British Journal of Social Psychology, 23,* 165–172.

Otten, S. (2002). I am positive and so are we: The self as determinant of favoritism toward novel ingroups. In J. Forgas & K. Williams (Eds.), *The social self: Cognitive, interpersonal, and intergroup processes* (pp. 273–291). New York, NY: Psychology Press.

Otten, S., & Moskowitz, G. B. (2000). Evidence for implicit evaluative in-group bias: Affect-biased spontaneous trait inference in a minimal group paradigm. *Journal of Experimental Social Psychology, 36,* 77–89.

Otten, S., & Wentura, D. (1999). About the impact of automaticity in the minimal group paradigm: Evidence from affective priming tasks. *European Journal of Social Psychology, 29,* 1049–1071.

Perdue, C., Dovidio, J., Gurtman, M., & Tyler, R. (1990). Us and them: Social categorization and the process of ingroup bias. *Journal of Personality and Social Psychology, 59,* 475–486.

Pettigrew, T. F. (1997). Generalized intergroup contact effects on prejudice. *Personality and Social Psychology Bulletin, 23,* 173–185.

Pettigrew, T. F. (1998). Intergroup contact theory. *Annual Review of Psychology, 49,* 65–85.

Pettigrew, T. F., & Meertens, R. W. (1995). Subtle and blatant prejudice in Western Europe. *European Journal of Social Psychology, 25,* 57–75.

Pettigrew, T. F., & Tropp, L. R. (2006). A meta-analytic test of intergroup contact theory. *Journal of Personality and Social Psychology, 90,* 751–783.

Pickett, C. L., Bonner, B. L., & Coleman, J. M. (2002). Motivated self-stereotyping: Heightened assimilation and differentiation needs result in increased levels of positive and negative self-stereotyping. *Journal of Personality and Social Psychology, 82,* 543–562.

Pickett, C. L., Silver, M. D., & Brewer, M. B. (2002). The impact of assimilation and differentiation needs on perceived group importance and judgments of group size. *Personality and Social Psychology Bulletin, 28,* 546–558.

Platow, M. J., McClintock, C. G., & Liebrand, W. G. (1990). Predicting intergroup fairness and in-group bias in the minimal group paradigm. *European Journal of Social Psychology, 20,* 221–239.

Platow, M. J., O'Connell, A., Shave, R., & Hanning, P. (1995). Social evaluations of fair and unfair allocations in interpersonal and intergroup situations. *British Journal of Social Psychology, 34,* 363–381.

Rabbie, J. M., Benoist, F., Oosterbaan, H., & Visser, L. (1974). Differential power and effects of expected competitive and cooperative intergroup interaction on intragroup and outgroup attitudes. *Journal of Personality and Social Psychology, 30,* 46–56.

Rabbie, J. M., & Wilkins, G. (1971). Intergroup competition and its effect on intragroup and intergroup relations. *European Journal of Social Psychology, 1,* 215–234.

Riek, B. M., Mania, E. W., & Gaertner, S. L. (2006). Intergroup threat and outgroup attitudes: A meta-analytic review. *Personality and Social Psychology Review, 10,* 336–353.

Roccas, S., & Brewer, M. B. (2002). Social identity complexity. *Personality and Social Psychology Review, 6,* 88–106.

Roccas, S., & Schwartz, S. (1993). Effects of intergroup similarity on intergroup relations. *European Journal of Social Psychology, 23,* 581–595.

Rothbart, M., & John, O. P. (1985). Social categorization and behavioral episodes: A cognitive analysis of the effects of intergroup contact. *Journal of Social Issues, 41*(3), 81–104.

Rouhana, N. N., & Bar-Tal, D. (1998). Psychological dynamics of intractable ethnonational conflicts: The Israeli-Palestinian case. *American Psychologist, 53,* 761–770.

Rubin, M., & Hewstone, M. (1998). Social identity theory's self-esteem hypothesis: A review and some suggestions for clarification. *Personality and Social Psychology Review, 2,* 40–62.

Rudman, L. A., Greenwald, A. G., & McGhee, D. E. (2001). Implicit self-concept and evaluative implicit gender stereotypes: Self and ingroup share desirable traits. *Personality and Social Psychology Bulletin, 27,* 1164–1178.

Runciman, W. C. (1966). *Relative deprivation and social justice: A study of attitudes to social inequality in twentieth century England.* Berkeley, CA: University of California Press.

Rust, M. C. (1996). *Social identity and social categorization.* Unpublished doctoral dissertation. University of Delaware, Newark, DE.

Sachdev, I., & Bourhis, R. (1991). Power and status differentials in minority and majority group relations. *European Journal of Social Psychology, 21,* 1–24.

Sherif, M. (1966). *In common predicament: Social psychology of intergroup conflict and cooperation.* New York, NY: Houghton Mifflin.

Sherif, M., Harvey, O. J., White, B. J., Hood, W. R., & Sherif, C. W. (1961). *Intergroup conflict and cooperation: The Robbers Cave experiment.* Norman, OK: University of Oklahoma Book Exchange.

Sidanius, J. (1993). The psychology of group conflict and the dynamics of oppression: A social dominance perspective. In S. Iyengar & W. McGuire (Eds.), *Explorations in political psychology* (pp. 183–219). Durham, NC: Duke University Press.

Sidanius, J., & Pratto, F. (1999). *Social dominance: An intergroup theory of social hierarchy and oppression.* New York, NY: Cambridge University Press.

Simon, B., & Hamilton, D. H. (1994). Social identity and self-stereotyping: The effects of relative group size and group status. *Journal of Personality and Social Psychology, 66,* 699–711.

Slavin, R. E. (1985). Cooperative learning: Applying contact theory in desegregated schools. *Journal of Social Issues, 41*(3), 45–62.

Smith, E. R. (1993). Social identity and social emotions: Toward new conceptualizations of prejudice. In D. Mackie & D. Hamilton (Eds.), *Affect, cognition, and stereotyping* (pp. 297–315). San Diego, CA: Academic Press.

Smith, H. J., & Tyler, T. R. (1996). Justice and power: When will justice concerns encourage the advantaged to support policies which redistribute economic resources and the disadvantaged to willingly obey the law? *European Journal of Social Psychology, 26,* 171–200.

Spears, R., Doosje, B., & Ellemers, N. (1997). Self-stereotyping in the face of threats to group status and distinctiveness: The role of group identification. *Personality and Social Psychology Bulletin, 23,* 538–553.

Stangor, C., Sullivan, M. W., & Ford (1991). Affective and cognitive determinants of prejudice. *Social Cognition, 9,* 359–380.

Stapel, D. A., & Marx, D. M. (2007). Distinctiveness is key: How different types of self-other similarity moderate social comparison effects. *Personality and Social Psychology Bulletin, 33,* 439–448.

Stephan, W. G. (1986). The effects of school desegregation: An evaluation 30 years after *Brown.* In M. Saks & L. Saxe (Eds.), *Advances in applied social psychology* (Vol. 3, pp. 181–206). Hillsdale, NJ: Erlbaum.

Stephan, W. G., Boniecki, K. A., Ybarra, O., Bettencourt, A., Ervin, K. S., Jackson, L. A., . . . Renfro, C. L. (2002). The role of threats in the racial attitudes of Blacks and Whites. *Personality and Social Psychology Bulletin, 28,* 1242–1254.

Stephan, W. G., & Stephan, C. W. (2000). An integrated threat theory of prejudice. In S. Oskamp (Ed.), *Reducing prejudice and discrimination* (pp. 23–45). Mahwah, NJ: Erlbaum.

Stouffer, S., Suchman, E., DeVinney, L., Stat, S., & Williams, R. (1949). *The American soldier: Adjustments during Army life* (Vol. 1). Princeton, NJ: Princeton University Press.

Struch, N., & Schwartz, S. H. (1989). Intergroup aggression: Its predictors and distinctness from in-group bias. *Journal of Personality and Social Psychology, 56,* 364–373.

Sumner, W. G. (1906). *Folkways.* New York, NY: Ginn.

Tajfel, H. (1969). Cognitive aspects of prejudice. *Journal of Social Issues, 25,* 79–97.

Tajfel, H. (1970). Experiments in intergroup discrimination. *Scientific American, 223,* 96–102.

Tajfel, H. (1978). *Differentiation between social groups: Studies in the social psychology of intergroup relations.* London, England: Academic Press.

Tajfel, H. (1981). *Human groups and social categories.* Cambridge, England: Cambridge University Press.

Tajfel, H., Billig, M., Bundy, R., & Flament, C. (1971). Social categorization and intergroup behaviour. *European Journal of Social Psychology, 1,* 149–178.

Tajfel, H., & Turner, J. C. (1986). The social identity theory of intergroup behavior. In S. Worchel & W. Austin (Eds.), *Psychology of intergroup relations* (pp. 7–24). Chicago, IL: Nelson-Hall.

Taylor, D. M., Moghaddam, F. M., Gamble, I., & Zellerer, E. (1987). Disadvantaged group responses to perceived inequality: From passive acceptance to collective action. *Journal of Social Psychology, 127,* 259–272.

Turner, J. C. (1975). Social comparison and social identity: Some prospects for intergroup behaviour. *European Journal of Social Psychology, 5,* 5–34.

Turner, J. C . (1981). The experimental social psychology of intergroup behaviour. In J. Turner & H. Giles (Eds.), *Intergroup behaviour* (pp. 66–101). Oxford, England: Blackwell.

Turner, J. C., Hogg, M., Oakes, P., Reicher, S., & Wetherell, M. (1987). *Rediscovering the social group: A self-categorization theory.* Oxford, England: Basil Blackwell.

Turner, J. C., Hogg, M., Turner, P., & Smith, P. (1984). Failure and defeat as determinants of group cohesiveness. *British Journal of Social Psychology, 23,* 97–111.

Vanbeselaere, N. (1991). The different effects of simple and crossed categorizations: A result of the category differentiation process or of differential category salience? *European Review of Social Psychology, 2,* 247–278.

van Knippenberg, A., & Ellemers, N. (1990). Social identity and intergroup differentiation processes. *European Review of Social Psychology, 1,* 137–169.

van Oudenhoven, J. P., Groenewoud, J. T., & Hewstone, M. (1996). Cooperation, ethnic salience and generalisation of interethnic attitudes. *European Journal of Social Psychology, 26,* 649–661.

Vanneman, R. D., & Pettigrew, T. F. (1972). Race and relative deprivation in the urban United States. *Race, 13,* 461–486.

Verkuyten, M. (2006). Multicultural recognition and ethnic minority rights: A social identity perspective. *European Review of Social Psychology, 17,* 148–184.

Vignoles, V. L., Chryssochoou, Z., & Breakwell, G. M. (2000). The distinctiveness principle: Identity, meaning, and the bounds of cultural relativity. *Personality and Social Psychology Review, 4,* 337–354.

Voci, A., & Hewstone, M. (2003). Intergroup contact and prejudice toward immigrants in Italy: The mediational role of anxiety and the moderation role of group salience. *Group Processes and Intergroup Relations, 6*, 37–54.

Weber, J. G. (1994). The nature of ethnocentric attribution bias: In-group protection or enhancement? *Journal of Experimental Social Psychology, 30*, 482–504.

Wilder, D. A. (1978). Reduction of intergroup discrimination through individuation of the outgroup. *Journal of Personality and Social Psychology, 36*, 1361–1374.

Wilder, D. A. (1984). Intergroup contact: The typical member and the exception to the rule. *Journal of Experimental Social Psychology, 20*, 177–194.

Wilder, D. A. (1986). Social categorization: Implications for creation and reduction of intergroup bias. In L. Berkowitz (Ed.), *Advances in experimental social psychology* (Vol. 19, pp. 291–355). New York, NY: Academic Press.

Wit, A. P., & Kerr, N. L. (2002). "Me versus just us versus us all": Categorization and cooperation in nested social dilemmas. *Journal of Personality and Social Psychology, 83*, 616–637.

Worchel, S., Andreoli, V., & Folger, R. (1977). Intergroup cooperation and intergroup attraction: The effect of previous interaction and outcome of combined effort. *Journal of Experimental Social Psychology, 13*, 131–140.

Wright, S. C., Taylor, D. M., & Moghaddam, F. M. (1990). Responding to membership in a disadvantaged group: From acceptance to collective protest. *Journal of Personality and Social Psychology, 58*, 994–1003.

Yuki, M., Maddux, W. W., Brewer, M. B., & Takemura, K. (2005). Cross-cultural differences in relationship- and group-based trust. *Personality and Social Psychology Bulletin, 31*, 48–62.

Yzerbyt, V. Y., Leyens, J-P., & Bellour, F. (1995). The ingroup overexclusion effect: Identity concerns in decisions about group membership. *European Journal of Social Psychology, 25*, 1–16.

Chapter 12

Prejudice, Stereotyping, and Discrimination

John F. Dovidio and James M. Jones

The assassination in 1968 of Martin Luther King Jr., who was one of the most important and influential leaders of the civil rights movement in the United States, profoundly affected people of all ages across the country. King spoke eloquently about the evils of prejudice, stereotyping, and discrimination, and he strongly advocated for racial equality and integration. Shortly after King's death, Jane Elliot, a third-grade teacher, wanted to teach her students in Riceville, Iowa—a virtually all-White community—a lesson about discrimination. In a classic demonstration, captured on film as *The Eye of the Storm*, she divided her class into two groups: those with blue eyes and those with brown eyes. Mrs. Elliot told the class that the blue-eyed children were superior, gave them the best seats in the room and often cited examples of famous people who had blue eyes ("George Washington had blue eyes"). By contrast, she described brown-eyed children as inferior, and when one child with brown eyes forgot his lunch, Mrs. Elliott rebuked him and attributed his forgetfulness to his brown-eyed status. Soon the blue-eyed children became suspicious of the brown-eyed children. They wanted the cafeteria workers to limit how much food the brown-eyed students could have and asked Jane Elliot to keep a yardstick close by in case the brown-eyed kids "got out of hand." They teased the brown-eyed children until a fight broke out at recess.

The next day, Jane Elliot resumed the exercise but explained that she made a mistake: It was the brown-eyed children that were superior! The second day was a mirror image of the first, with the brown-eyed children acting superior to the blue-eyed children. On the second day, the brown-eyed children's school performance improved, while the blue-eyed children did worse. Even the meaning of being "blue-eyed" changed in students' minds. At recess, a brown-eyed child taunted another student in the class with the chant, "blue-eyes, blue-eyes" until a fight broke out. Over the next two decades, Jane Elliot repeated this exercise for a range of audiences. She demonstrated time and time again how easy it is to get people—adults as well as children—to discriminate on the basis of a superficial distinction.

In this chapter we explain, from a social psychological perspective, that the behavior of children in Jane Elliot's class, as well as biases in the attitudes, beliefs, and behavior toward members of different groups more generally, are grounded in fundamental and in some ways adaptive psychological processes.

People are, by nature, social animals. Evolutionarily, being part of a group not only offered greater physical protection but also enabled us, through systems of trust and reciprocity, to achieve and prosper through coordinated action substantially more than we could alone. Identifying other individuals as members of one's group (the ingroup) was thus of primary importance, but knowing who is a member of a different, potentially competitive group was also valuable. Because of the central importance of distinguishing whether another person is an ingroup or outgroup member, we automatically think differently about someone we see as an ingroup as opposed to an outgroup member. Moreover, as social neuroscience has revealed, our thoughts about these individuals originate in different areas of the brain: Information about ingroup members often activates the brain in ways similar to the activation that occurs when we think about ourselves. However, despite the enormous benefits of these ways of thinking and the architecture in our brains that support it, distinguishing between ingroup and outgroup members lays the foundation for the occurrence and pervasive influence of prejudice, stereotyping, and discrimination in social life today.

In this chapter, we first define and distinguish prejudice, stereotypes, and discrimination. We then consider the bases of these forms of bias, both in terms of the dimensions on which we differ (e.g., personality) and those inclinations that we have in common (e.g., social categorization). After that, we review the empirical relationship of prejudice and stereotyping with discrimination. We specifically examine how the complex and often subtle ways people express their bias and how institutional and cultural influences operate to produce disparate outcomes. These multilevel effects go beyond the direct effects of personal prejudice or stereotypes. The effects of these forces on the targets of discrimination are also briefly considered. In our last substantive section, we consider the most established and promising interventions for reducing prejudice, stereotyping, and discrimination.

Definitions and Measurement of Prejudice, Stereotyping, and Discrimination

Prejudice, stereotypes, and discrimination are the three major elements of intergroup bias. However, they differ in important ways.

Prejudice

Broadly considered, prejudice is an attitude that represents generalized feelings toward and evaluation of a group or its members and can result in discriminatory behavior or behavioral intentions. However, conceptualizations of prejudice have evolved over time. In his seminal volume, *The Nature of Prejudice,* Allport (1954) defined *prejudice* as "an antipathy based on faulty and inflexible generalization. It may be felt or expressed. It may be directed toward a group as a whole, or toward an individual because he [sic] is a member of that group" (p. 9). The current, more expansive view defines prejudice as "an individual-level attitude (subjectively positive *or* negative) toward groups and their members that creates or maintains hierarchical status relations between groups" (Dovidio, Hewstone, Glick, & Esses, 2010, p. 7).

Consistent with this definition, prejudice can involve both positive and negative responses that can vary in response to group members' observed conformity or nonconformity to social roles (Eagly & Diekman, 2005). People who deviate from their group's traditional role typically arouse negative reactions, whereas those who exhibit behaviors that reinforce the status quo elicit positive responses. Related research on ambivalent sexism (Glick & Fiske, 2001) suggests that prejudice toward women can have a "hostile" component, which punishes women who deviate from a traditional subordinate role, as well as a "benevolent" component that celebrates women's supportive, but subordinate, position. Thus, prejudice need not always reflect negative attitudes toward a target group but can also consist of seemingly positive attitudes toward an outgroup that may nevertheless relate to discriminatory behavior (e.g., patronizing responses toward women).

Stereotypes

By most historical accounts, the term *stereotype* was coined in 1922 to refer to the typical picture that comes to mind when thinking about a particular social group (Lippmann, 1922). Current definitions are similar, describing stereotypes as qualities associated with particular groups of people. Katz and Braly (1933) conducted some of the classic work on stereotypes by asking Princeton University undergraduates to select from a list of traits those that seem "most typical of" several groups. The responses were telling in both their content and the degree of consensus. The most frequent traits selected for Blacks (referred to as Negroes in the study) were superstitious (by 84% of the participants) and lazy (75%). Americans were characterized as industrious (49%) and intelligent (48%). These were not the only groups included: Jewish people were most frequently described as shrewd (79%), Japanese as intelligent (48%), Italians as artistic (53%), Irish as pugnacious (45%), and Germans as scientifically minded (78%).

Several researchers, using the same materials, have repeated the study with new cohorts of Princeton students, over time. By the end of the 1960s, a decade in which the civil rights movement was prominent, the dominant stereotypical traits—at least as publicly expressed—had changed dramatically (Karlins, Coffman & Walters, 1969). For example, by 1967, the percentage of Princeton men who selected superstitious as a stereotype of Blacks declined from 84% to 13% and was replaced at the top of the list of traits by musical, which increased from 26% to 47%. Similarly, Jewish people were less frequently characterized as shrewd (79% to 30%) but more frequently described as ambitious (21% to 48%), Irish people were less frequently represented as pugnacious (45% to 13%) but more somewhat frequently described as quick-tempered (39% to 43%) and nationalistic (21% to 41%), and Japanese people were less frequently characterized by intelligence (45% to 20%) but more often by industriousness (43% to 57%). Germans continued to be stereotyped as scientifically minded and industrious, but those percentages dropped by 31% (78% to 47%), and 6% (65% to 59%), respectively. Moreover, the results using this adjective checklist methodology tend to reflect more what people believe are the stereotypes that other people hold rather than what they personally believe: Personal endorsement of social stereotypes tends to be weaker, particularly among people low in prejudice (Devine & Elliot, 1995).

Whereas early research generally conceived of stereotyping as a faulty thought process, more recent research has focused on the functional aspects of stereotypes in simplifying a complex environment. They are now considered to be cognitive schemas, often rooted in culturally held beliefs that are used by social perceivers to process information about others. Stereotypes not only reflect beliefs about the traits characterizing typical group members but also contain information about other qualities, such as expected social roles and characteristics of the group (e.g., within-group homogeneity). Although stereotypes can contain evaluative content and are often congruent with prejudice, they (a) need not be evaluative, (b) can include different types of content (e.g., conceptual associations with a target group), and (c) may rely on different neural pathways than does prejudice (Amodio & Lieberman, 2009).

Explicit and Implicit Measures of Prejudice and Stereotypes

The ways both attitudes and stereotypes are measured have also changed dramatically. Traditionally, prejudice and stereotyping have been measured in direct, explicit ways, using self-reports. One widely recognized problem with explicit measures is that they allow people to control their responses to appear in socially desirable ways. Thus, it would be difficult to determine whether the negative stereotypes observed by Katz and Braly (1933) had actually faded or whether people have learned that it would be socially inappropriate to admit to such beliefs. With respect to the assessment of racial attitudes, for example, among the most commonly used measures of Whites' attitudes toward Blacks are currently Symbolic Racism Scale (Sears & Henry, 2005) and the Modern Racism Scale (McConahay, 1986). Both measures are indirect assessments of attitudes in that they do not ask directly about negative qualities of Blacks but instead about responses to a number of political or social opinions in which a pattern of responses implicates underlying racial prejudice. For example, people who indicate greater opposition to programs (e.g., affirmative action) perceived to be especially beneficial for Blacks and who believe more strongly that discrimination is no longer a problem for Blacks would score higher in modern racism.

Moreover, in a highly influential article, Devine (1989) argued that explicit bias is not the whole story. In contrast, *implicit attitudes and stereotypes* are unconscious thoughts, feelings, and beliefs that are automatically activated when we are exposed to a member of a social group unlike ours and for which we have developed a bias. Implicit attitudes and stereotypes represent well-learned and habitual cultural associations of which people may not be fully aware. Whereas explicit attitudes and stereotypes are typically measured with self-reports, implicit attitudes and stereotypes are typically gauged with response latency procedures, memory tasks, physiological measures (e.g., heart rate and galvanic skin response), and indirect self-report measures (e.g., biases in behavioral and trait attributions).

The basic principle behind most of the response latency techniques is that a person will respond more quickly to ideas or concepts that are associated in the mind than to those that are not. For example, is each of the following strings of letters made up of two words: table–chair, doctor–nurse, chair–nurse? The answer is yes in all three cases, but it takes people a split-second longer to say yes to chair–nurse because those two words are not as strongly associated in your mind as doctor–nurse or table–chair. How about Blacks–good, Blacks–bad, Whites–good, Whites–bad? Notice that you are not asked directly about whether you believe that there is an association between the pairs of words.

The most commonly used method of this type is the Implicit Association Test (IAT; Greenwald, Poehlman, Uhlmann, & Banaji, 2009). In the IAT, people have to make decisions, by pressing a response key on a computer keyboard, about different groups (such as Anglos and Latinos or Whites and Blacks) in conjunction with positive and negative words (https://implicit.harvard.edu/). Because these responses occur in a split second, they are very difficult to control.

Although the issue remains controversial and unresolved, many psychologists consider implicit and explicit attitudes and stereotypes to reflect different components of a system of dual attitudes. In this view, implicit responses are rooted in a slow-learning, associative system while explicit responses are tied to fast-learning systems in the brain. Implicit responses represent older attitudes and stereotypes that have been overwritten by newer, explicit attitudes, either completely or in part (Wilson, Lindsey, & Schooler, 2000). Whereas implicit responses often have a strong emotional component, cognition and deliberative thought play a strong role in explicit attitudes and stereotypes.

One of the provocative implications of the distinction between implicit and explicit attitudes is that we live in societies that strongly endorse the principle of equality but, at the same time, have racist, sexist, and ethnically discriminatory traditions and well-established racial and ethnic disparities in wealth, health, and residence. Repeated exposure to these pervasive disparities and repeated media portrayals of members of various groups in stereotype-consistent ways produces systemic differences in implicit attitudes and stereotypes. Hundreds of thousands of people have taken the IAT, and a large body of research demonstrates systematic biases—of a magnitude much greater than what explicit, self-report measures reveal—against Latinos (mainly by Anglos), Blacks (mainly by non-Blacks), LGBT persons, overweight people, women, and people with disabilities. These biases, at least in US culture, are similar across levels of socio-economic status, educational achievement, and region of the country.

Although research using the IAT has produced a large body of empirical evidence indicating widespread implicit biases toward members of particular groups, scholars in this area debate the meaning of these differences. Some have criticized the IAT based on its psychometric properties or questioned the degree to which it actually measures automatically activated associations. Others have expressed concerns about whether IAT responses represent general cultural associations rather than a particular individual's implicit stereotypes or attitudes, as well as about how well the IAT predicts subsequent discriminatory behavior (Oswald, Mitchell, Blanton, Jaccard, & Tetlock, 2013). Despite, and perhaps in part because of, these controversial issues surrounding the IAT, work on implicit bias is one of the most active areas of research on prejudice and stereotyping and a topic that has attracted substantial interest in the media.

Discrimination

Whereas prejudice represents and attitude and stereotypes reflect beliefs, discrimination is a behavior. *Discrimination* refers to an act that creates, maintains, or reinforces an advantage for some groups and their members over other groups and their members (Dovidio et al., 2010). Discrimination is often represented in terms of the behavior of individuals directed toward members, but these acts are not necessarily consciously motivated. Moreover, individual bias expressed by individuals is not necessary for discrimination to be experienced by members of some groups. Instead, discrimination may be enacted broadly through institutional structures and policies or embedded in cultural beliefs and representations that value various groups differently. Thus, individual-, institutional-, and cultural-level processes may operate in concert to provide some groups systematic advantages and/or to impose disadvantages on other groups (Jones, 1997). These multilevel processes are related, such that biases at the individual level of analysis, whether regarding explicit or implicit processes, necessarily implicate higher-order institutional and cultural influences and biases. Often these influences are cloaked in justifications or ideologies that obscure the biases and thus allow the discriminatory nature of the treatment to go undetected and unaddressed.

Although prejudice, stereotyping, and discrimination are distinct concepts, important to understand in their own right, much of the work in psychology has examined their common roots. In the next section, we consider the role that personality and individual differences play in creating and perpetuating intergroup bias.

Bases of Bias: Personality and Individual Differences

The study of how personality and other stable personal orientations relate to prejudice, stereotyping, and discrimination has been highly influential in understanding intergroup biases. The historic trends on this topic also illustrate the shift in the field from characterizing bias as a form of psychopathology to understanding it as a consequence of the way people try to adapt to everyday situations.

The Authoritarian Personality (and Its Legacy)

Early work on personality and individual differences related to discrimination, inspired by Sigmund Freud's psychodynamic theory, viewed discrimination as stemming from displaced hostility and aggression. In this tradition, Adorno, Frenkel-Brunswik, Levinson, and Sanford (1950) in their classic volume, *The Authoritarian Personality,* identified a unique pattern of family experiences that made people susceptible to developing a personality profile that predisposed them to extreme bias. These individuals, "high authoritarians," tended to submit to authority, adhere to conventional values, and think in rigid ways. People who scored higher on a measure of authoritarianism were more likely to exhibit prejudice toward, endorse negative stereotypes of, and discriminate against a broad range of marginalized groups.

The classic work on the authoritarian personality was subsequently critiqued heavily on both methodological and theoretical grounds, and the theory fell into disrepute. Yet, aspects of its legacy are currently evident. For example, there is evidence that individuals commonly harbor "generalized prejudice": People who tend to discriminate against one group also tend to be biased against a wide range of other groups (Bergh, Akrami, Sidanius, & Sibley 2016). In addition, many of these measures—such as need for structure, need for closure, intolerance of ambiguity, and being low on a fundamental personality dimension of openness to new experiences—are characteristics resembling those associated with the authoritarian personality (Hodson & Dhont, 2015). People who have a greater need for structure are particularly prone to stereotyping, over and above their tendency to be prejudiced (Newheiser & Dovidio, 2012). In addition, people who are more religious (regardless of their religion) and more conservative tend to show greater prejudice, stereotyping, and discrimination.

However, the assertion that political conservatives are necessarily more prone to exhibit biased attitudes toward other groups than political liberals has been challenged in recent studies. For instance, more politically conservative people display more negative attitudes toward Blacks and homosexuals, but they report that the basis of this attitude is they perceive these groups as politically liberal and as violating conservative moral values (Chambers, Schlenker, & Collisson, 2013). By contrast, more politically liberal people exhibit more negative attitudes toward business people and Christian fundamentalists, again in large part, because they view these as groups in conflict with liberal values. Thus, both liberals and conservatives tend to be biased toward groups perceived to be on the opposite end of the political spectrum. These mirror-image biases play a substantial role in the "political divide."

Two of the most prominent individual difference measures relating to the tendency to discriminate against members of different groups are the Right-Wing Authoritarianism (RWA) Scale and the Social Dominance Orientation (SDO) Scale.

Right-Wing Authoritarianism

The RWA Scale (Altemeyer, 1996) was derived from the classic work on authoritarianism but is currently characterized as an ideological dimension that is related to social and cultural conservatism and conventionalism (Duckitt & Sibley, 2017). Individuals who score higher on RWA tend to endorse more strongly statements such as, "What our country needs is a strong, determined leader who will crush evil and take us back to our true path" and "The established authorities generally turn out to be right about things, whereas the radicals and the protestors are usually just 'loud mouths' showing off their ignorance." As indicated in meta-analysis, RWA robustly predicts bias toward a range of different social groups, including ethnic minorities, women, disabled people, and sexual minorities (Sibley & Duckitt, 2008).

Social Dominance Orientation

The SDO Scale measures an individual's preference for systems of group-based dominance and for ideologies that support this hierarchy (Ho et al., 2015). The net result of these preferences is support for policies and practices that permit the oppression of low-status groups. For example, people higher in SDO tend to be more sexist, racist, and biased toward immigrants, lesbians, gay men, feminists, and physically disabled people (Sibley & Duckitt, 2008). The scale has been recently updated to highlight the two dimensions of this orientation: *SDO-Dominance*, which represents a preference for systems of group-based dominance ("An ideal society requires some groups to be on top and others to be on the bottom") and *SDO-Anti-egalitarianism*, which represents a preference for social ideologies and policies that normalize inequalities ("We shouldn't guarantee that every group has the same quality of life"). SDO-Dominance correlates more strongly with prejudice than SDO-Anti-egalitarianism.

Although both SDO and RWA are robust predictors of prejudice, they are only moderately correlated with each other. One reason for their relatively weak relationship is that they reflect different worldviews: People higher in SDO are more likely to see the world as a "competitive jungle" in which the tough-minded prevail, whereas those higher in RWA tend to see the world as a "dangerous place" that needs to be managed through strict order (Duckitt & Sibley, 2017). SDO primarily reflects beliefs about how groups should relate to one another and perceptions of group hierarchies, whereas RWA reflects submission to those higher in authority, with an emphasis on conformity and punishing deviants. As a consequence, although both scales predict prejudice toward a range of groups, each has unique predictive utility: SDO is a stronger predictor of prejudice toward low-status groups and attitudes toward economic issues, whereas RWA more strongly predicts prejudice toward unconventional groups and attitudes toward social issues.

Bases of Bias: Social Psychological Factors

Whereas the personality and individual difference perspective focuses on the meaning of the ways we are different, social psychological approaches emphasize the influences that we experience in common that affect prejudice, stereotyping, and discrimination. Many of these processes relate to basic principles that shape intergroup relations, as discussed in Chapter 11.

Social Categorization

Social categorization is a fundamental building block of social life that is based on the general tendency to classify people into groups (Kawakami, Amodio, & Hugenberg, 2017). Social categorization processes occur for the same reasons that guide social cognition processes: We are "cognitive misers"—an adaptive mechanism that enables us to simplify the world to understand and function when we are confronted by the vast amount of information that exceeds our capacity to process and comprehend at any one time. Thinking about people as individuals rather than in terms of their group membership requires much more cognitive effort and resources so, as a result, social categorization is the cognitive default (Fiske, 2012). We think about others based on their group membership and switch to more personalized processing only when we believe that there is a particular reason to do so (e.g., when motivated to form a relationship with them).

In general, viewing others in terms of their group membership makes us *feel* that we understand the world better. Once we categorize a person into a group (e.g., Italian, Latino, Red Sox fan), we see that person as similar to other members of the same group whom we know, ascribe the characteristics that we believe members of that group share to that person, and thus feel that we can understand and can predict that person's behavior better. Seeing a person as a member of a social category allows top–down perceptions: We fill in gaps in the available information about the particular person with information about what people in that group are generally like. Groups do not have to be meaningful for people to think and feel positively about members of their own group and become wary of others.

The effects of social categorization are profound and highly replicable: Psychologists worldwide have documented what occurs when people perceive, think about or interact with others on the basis of whether they belong to their ingroup or an outgroup (Dovidio & Gaertner, 2010). People tend to:

- see members of the other group as very similar to each other (outgroup homogeneity);
- exaggerate differences between ingroup and outgroup members;
- feel closer to ingroup members;
- perceive outgroup members as less human;
- value the lives of ingroup members more than those of outgroup members;
- think more deeply and in a more detailed fashion about ingroup members;
- believe that ingroup members share their attitudes while outgroup members have contrasting attitudes;
- want to approach ingroup members but avoid outgroup members;
- anticipate outgroup members to be biased against them and value ingroup members more when they are biased against the outgroup; and
- be more helpful, cooperative and generous with ingroup members.

It is important to note, as Brewer discusses in Chapter 11, that two biasing processes occur: (a) favoritism toward the ingroup and (b) avoidance or hostility toward the outgroup.

Social Identity

Categorizing the social world into ingroups and outgroups also activates basic motivational processes that ultimately lead to prejudice, stereotyping, and discrimination. As initially explained by social identity theory (Tajfel & Turner, 1979; see also Hogg, Abrams, & Brewer, 2017) and discussed in some detail by Brewer in Chapter 11 on intergroup relations, people are motivated to be perceived favorably by themselves and others. This desire for positive self-regard may be satisfied by their own accomplishments (associated with their personal identity), as well as by membership in prestigious social groups (reflecting their social identity). This need for positive distinctiveness motivates social comparisons that favorably differentiate the ingroup from the outgroup and, consequently, the self from others. Think for a minute about students at another university. Almost immediately, ideas about how your school or program is different and better than the other school will pop into your mind!

This basic and spontaneous motivation has important consequences for how we treat members of other groups and how we connect to members of our own group (see Chapter 11). In general, people who are more highly identified with a group work harder for the group, adhere more strongly to group norms and values, and are more affected by the successes or failure of the group. Becoming identified with a social group also helps to alleviate an uncertainty about who we are and anxiety about our self-worth, but this process can also have it dire consequences. It can lead be people to be attracted to extremist groups. These groups are tightly organized, with clear and rigid rules, homogeneous memberships, a strong sense of mission, and strong and often charismatic leadership—all characteristics that can reduce uncertainly and make people feel secure (Hogg, 2012).

The more strongly we identify with a group, the more likely we are to see ourselves as a typical member of the group. As explained by *self-categorization theory* (Turner, Hogg, Oakes, Reicher, & Wetherell, 1987; see also Hogg et al., 2017)—a derivative of social identity theory—this typically includes ways of thinking and behaving that are specific to and characteristic of the group. We think, feel, and act like members of that group *should*. We are not simply conforming to what people around us do; we actually take on the character of what we imagine the typical member of group (the "prototype") is like. We also tend to see others in ways prototypic of their group membership, and, as a consequence, when our social identity is activated, stereotypes of their group become a potent guide to behavior toward members of that group.

Strong social identity can come entirely at the expense of personal identity—people can "lose" themselves in the group or become "fused" with a group. *Identity fusion* (Swann & Buhrmester, 2015) describes an extreme, visceral sense of oneness with an ingroup in which the self and the group are indistinguishable. Identity fusion occurs when individuals fully incorporate their group's values into their understanding of who they are, leading to fusion of aspects of the personal and social self. The profound feeling of connection with fellow ingroup members that can give rise to identity fusion often results from sharing intense bonding experiences and can produce extreme group-serving behaviors, such as people sacrificing their lives for the ingroup. "Being part of a collectivist cause," Arie Kruglanski, co-director of the National Consortium for the Study of Terrorism and Responses to Terrorism, observed, "has always been a hallmark of people willing to undergo personal sacrifices" (DeAngelis, 2009, p. 60).

Functional Relations between Groups

Social categorization and social identity not only create a foundation for the development and operation of prejudice, stereotyping, and discrimination but also predispose people to be competitive and to see other groups as aggressive competitors. When people interact as representatives of different groups, rather than as individuals, they behave in a greedier and less trustworthy manner (Wildschut & Insko, 2007). Actual competition, in turn, often readily stimulates overt and sometimes extreme forms of bias against members of outgroups.

A classic field study by Sherif, Harvey, White, Hood, and Sherif (1961) vividly illustrates this effect. In a series of studies known as the Robber's Cave studies (Robber's Cave is a state park in Oklahoma), Sherif and his colleagues randomly assigned twenty-two 12-year-old boys attending summer camp to two groups (who subsequently named themselves Eagles and Rattlers). When the groups engaged in a series of competitive activities (a tug-of-war and baseball and touch football games), intergroup bias and conflict quickly developed. Group members regularly exchanged verbal insults (e.g., "sissies," "stinkers," "pigs," "bums," "cheaters"), and each group conducted raids on the other's cabins that resulted in the destruction and theft of property. Later, Sherif and his colleagues arranged intergroup contact under neutral, noncompetitive conditions. These interventions did not calm the ferocity of the exchanges, however. Only by altering the functional relations between the groups by introducing a series of superordinate goals—ones that could not be achieved without the full cooperation of both groups—such as pulling a stalled truck back to camp—were the experimenters able to reduce prejudice, stereotyping, and discrimination between the groups.

The Robbers Cave research showed how easy it is to arouse prejudice, stereotyping, and discrimination between groups. Moreover, as Brewer (see Chapter 11) discusses, the conflict that produces these biases may not only be about material resources (realistic threat) but also about how another group threatens core ideas and beliefs (symbolic threat; see Stephan, Ybarra, & Morrison, 2016). Greater endorsement of the statement "Blacks have too many positions of power and responsibility in this country" indicates greater realistic threat among Whites, whereas greater agreement with the statement "Whites and Blacks have differing conceptions of what American culture should be" reflects greater symbolic racial threat.

Although you might think that physical threats would produce greater bias and ignite conflict more readily than symbolic threat, each type of threat contributes to bias, and both predict bias to about the same degree (Riek, Mania, & Gaertner, 2006). Moreover, conflict over symbolic issues may be more likely to escalate and more difficult to resolve than conflict over material possessions. It might be possible, for example, to reach a political compromise between Israeli Jews and Palestinians over statehood and physical boundaries. However, there is no compromise when the discussions about territories involve "holy lands." When two opposing principles are involved, people typically stand on one side or the other; there is little compromise in principles.

To summarize to this point, a substantial body of psychological evidence has identified a number of common factors that facilitate and support the development of prejudice, stereotyping, and discrimination and has illuminated how these phenomena operate individually and in concert to perpetuate inequality. However, somewhat surprisingly, given this empirical evidence and the general belief that both prejudice and stereotyping are precursors to discrimination, the actual interrelationships among prejudice, stereotyping, and discrimination are significant but not especially strong. We explore this issue in the next section.

Empirical Relationships among Prejudice, Stereotyping, and Discrimination

One main reason we study prejudice and stereotyping is the belief that they predict behavior that has important consequences for others, our group, and our society. Fortunately, this assumption has been empirically substantiated, but the picture is not a simple one. In this section, we discuss how prejudice and stereotyping predict discrimination.

Prejudice and Discrimination

Using different measures of prejudice and assessing various types of behavior, research results converge on the conclusion that prejudice does systematically predict behavior. However, the magnitude of that effect (a meta-analytic r between 0.26 and 0.36; Greenwald et al., 2009; Talaska, Fiske, & Chaiken, 2008) is lower than the general attitude–behavior relationship observed in other domains. Moreover, the relationship between explicit prejudice and discrimination was weaker in various important intergroup domains, including Whites' attitudes and behavior toward Blacks ($r = 0.12$), and attitudes and behavior in the domain of gender/sexual orientation ($r = 0.22$; Greenwald et al., 2009; cf. Oswald et al., 2013).

One possible reason why the relationship between explicit prejudice and discrimination tends to be weaker than the general attitude–behavior relationship is that, as we mentioned earlier, expressions of intergroup attitudes are susceptible to pressures to appear in a socially desirable way. Thus, one might expect that implicit measures of prejudice, which are less susceptible to social desirability effects, would be a better predictor of discrimination than explicit attitudes. The evidence in support of this conjecture is suggestive but controversial (Gawronski & Bodenhausen, 2014). In their meta-analysis, Greenwald et al. (2009) found—for example, with respect to orientations of Whites toward Blacks—that the relationship implicit attitudes, measured using the IAT, and behavior was twice as strong as the explicit attitude–behavior relationship reported in the same meta-analysis. However, Oswald et al. (2013), using the same studies but applying different criteria in their analysis, concluded that the effects of implicit bias on discrimination were much weaker than those presented by Greenwald et al. Although evidence that responses on the IAT reliably predict discriminatory behavior continues to accumulate, the strength of the relationships are generally modest. Perhaps because of this, reducing implicit bias does not necessarily lead to reductions in discriminatory behavior (for a meta-analytic review, see Forscher et al., 2017).

Stereotypes and Behavior

The relationship between the degree to which individuals hold stereotypes of a group and discrimination against that group is, overall, similarly modest, although that relationship holds more strongly when the behavior (e.g., hiring someone for a specific job) relates more directly to the central aspects of the group stereotype (e.g., leadership ability or intelligence).

However, work by Fiske and her colleagues on the stereotype content model (Fiske, Cuddy, Glick, & Xu, 2002; see also Fiske, 2012) has shown how a fuller understanding of the principles underlying stereotyping can lead to more accurate and sophisticated understanding of its behavioral consequences. According to the stereotype content model, a stereotype is a function of how a group is perceived on two dimensions: warmth and competence. When we have to think or interact with a group from which we are different, we process what we know about their competence or ability to perform and how we feel about them. Although groups do indeed have unique characteristics related to history and to the specific intergroup context (e.g., the history of slavery and discrimination against persons described often as "Black" in the United States), there appear to be systematic principles that shape the content of stereotypes in all cultures.

Groups high in warmth and high in competence (e.g., the ingroup, close allies) elicit pride and admiration; groups high in warmth but low in competence (e.g., housewives, the elderly) produce pity and sympathy; those low in warmth but high in competence (e.g., Asians, Jews) elicit envy and jealousy; and groups low on both warmth and competence (e.g., welfare recipients, poor people) are associated with feelings of disgust, anger, and resentment. These emotional responses, in turn, shape how a person responds to a group: Admiration promotes active facilitation or support for the group, contempt relates to active harm, envy predicts passive support, and pity leads to passive harm. The stereotype content model encompasses the way people classify, characterize, and respond to a broad range of social groups across different countries and time periods.

Taken together, there is evidence that both prejudice (measured either explicitly or implicitly) and stereotyping do predict discriminatory behavior. However, there is considerable heterogeneity in these relationships, with effects varying across different forms of intergroup behavior and ranging from strongly positive to weak or even negligible effects. Rather than viewing the modest magnitude and variability of the results in this area as a failure of science, they represent opportunities to appreciate the complexities of bias in a contemporary world. In the remainder of this section, we discuss some insights that can help illuminate the ways prejudice and stereotyping influence discrimination.

Correspondence between Predictors and Outcomes

One key factor affecting the relative predictive strength of implicit and explicit measures is the type of behavior being examined and the context in which the behavior occurs. For example, whereas implicit measures may better predict spontaneous behaviors, explicit measures may better predict deliberative behaviors, including those in situations in which social desirability factors are salient (Fazio & Olson, 2014). Consistent with this argument, explicit anti-immigrant prejudice has recently been shown to predict deliberate action against immigrants among White British and Italian participants (Shepherd, Fasoli, Pereira, & Branscombe, 2018). By contrast, implicit intergroup attitudes are better predictors of nonverbal behavior in intergroup interactions (McConnell & Leibold, 2001). These effects of implicit bias also help to explain why doctors with more negative implicit racial attitudes are perceived by Black patients as less friendly and less patient-centered in their interactions (Penner, Phelan, Earnshaw, Albrecht, & Dovidio, 2018).

Prediction at an Aggregated Level

Social psychology has typically examined intergroup relations through the lens of individuals and their intrapsychic processes, including prejudice and stereotypes. As the previous sections reveal, when measured at the individual level, the relationship between explicit and implicit prejudice and discrimination is systematic and statistically significant but generally only modest in magnitude. However, the cumulative effects of individuals' prejudices can considerably limit opportunities for members of traditionally disadvantaged groups, and even small individual biases, when aggregated, can produce substantial social inequities over time (Greenwald, Banaji, & Nosek, 2015).

In contrast to social psychology's traditional focus on individual-level processes, contextual factors, such as geography and social setting, are critical when examining the effects of prejudice and stereotyping in the aggregate. In the United States, for example, there are systematic differences in racial prejudice by geographic area, and these regional differences in prejudice (i.e., individual prejudice aggregated by region) profoundly shape the social environment and, subsequently, the experiences and well-being of minority groups. In a recent study, for instance, Leitner, Hehman, Ayduk, and Mendoza-Denton (2016) integrated explicit and implicit measures of White Americans' prejudice ($N > 1$ million) with health-related measures from the US Centers for Disease Control, including access to healthcare and circulatory disease risk. In counties in which Whites expressed less favorable explicit attitudes toward Blacks, Blacks had lower access to affordable healthcare and greater mortality from circulatory disease, compared to Whites. These findings demonstrate that aggregated by geographical location or social setting, both explicit and implicit prejudice can be associated with a number of highly consequential outcomes, at times literally involving matters of life and death (Payne, Vuletich, & Lundberg, 2017).

Subtle Discrimination

Prejudice, stereotyping, and discrimination are pervasive yet, as forms of unfair bias, they seem to stand in contrast to prevailing principles of justice and norms of fairness. These principles and norms not only limit the extent to which individuals discriminate against others but also shape the way bias is justified and expressed when it does occur, producing subtle patterns of bias.

System-Justifying Ideology

Cross-cultural evidence suggests that societies in which groups are hierarchically organized function efficiently, but hierarchies differ with regard to power and control. As a result, these power disparities provide advantages and privileges enjoyed by members of some groups and promote the disadvantages experienced by members of other groups. Social dominance theory (Sidanius, Cotterill, Sheehy-Skeffington, Kteily, & Cavarch, 2017) proposes that the development of group-based hierarchies is motivated by ideologies that reinforce social and structural inequality and views racism, sexism, and other forms of discrimination as special cases of a general tendency for people to form, maintain, and enhance group-based hierarchies. Social dominance theory highlights that prejudice, stereotyping, and discrimination are key mechanisms that members of high-status groups use to create and sustain group hierarchy.

System Justification

System justification theory (Jost, Gaucher, & Stern, 2015) further emphasizes processes that maintain and exacerbate inequality between groups. According to the theory, people are not simply motivated to promote the interests of their immediate group but are also motivated to defend, justify, and bolster existing social, economic, and political systems, institutions, and arrangements. This framework focuses on the social and psychological process by which people—as individuals and as members of groups—legitimize the institutions and arrangements in society, thereby coming to see social inequality (and associated discriminatory practices) as not only legitimate but also natural and necessary.

If, as system justification theory suggests, people try to see the social system as fair and just, then they should see the way society *is* as the way it *should be*. This effect should be particularly strong for people who feel dependent on the current system. In one study (Kay et al., 2009), for instance, experimenters tried to increase female Canadian students' feelings of dependency by having them read a newspaper article, supposedly from the *Toronto Star*, indicating that the government's actions and the quality of services it provides has a profound influence on Canadian citizen's lives. Students in a low-dependency condition read a similar article, but it emphasized that the policies of the government had negligible effects on what people do on a daily basis. Participants next read a brief description of the responsibilities of Canadian members of Parliament, accompanied by a graph showing that currently only 20% of the members of Parliament were women. Consistent with system justification theory, women who were led to believe that they were highly dependent on the government were more likely to defend the status quo. These women were less likely to endorse statements that there should be more women in politics and in Parliament than those who believed that they were low in dependency. From their perspective, having only 20% female members of Parliament was just fine. System justification theory thus accounts for the fact that low-status group members often support the status quo, often at a cost to themselves and fellow group members.

Benevolent Bias

The tension between the psychological forces that promote prejudice, stereotyping, and discrimination and the desire to appear in socially desirable ways, or to genuinely desire to be fair and unbiased, have also created other subtle forms of bias in the way individuals behave toward others. Whereas overtly negative actions by an individual toward a member of another group may readily be recognized as unfair discrimination, unmerited positive behavior toward one's own group (e.g., nepotism) is less generally recognized as discrimination but still puts members of other groups at a disadvantage (Greenwald & Pettigrew, 2014; see also Chapter 11).

In her classic book, *The Velvet Glove*, Jackman (1994) describes how paternalism represents another subtle form of discrimination perpetuated by ostensibly positive actions. Glick and Fiske (2001) further show that benevolent sexism, the seemingly positive view that women are "pure creators who ought to be protected, supported, and adored" (p. 109), carries with it the idea that women are weak. This system-justifying view legitimates the status inequality between men and women and promotes acceptance of inequality. Research guided by Nadler's (2002) intergroup helping as status relations model illuminates how subtle bias also operates through prosocial behavior. When intergroup relations are perceived as insecure, members of high-status groups are more likely to offer dependency-oriented help (e.g., offering a full solution to a problem, which reinforces the group's superior status) than autonomy-oriented help (e.g., showing how a solution can be reached, which promotes independence in the future) to members of low-status groups.

Personal Justification and Rationalization

Subtle discrimination can also involve negative behaviors toward members of another group, as noted by Crandall and Eshleman (2003), but mainly when the act can be justified in some way. According to the aversive racism framework (Dovidio, Gaertner, & Pearson, 2017), this process of rationalization of discrimination occurs even among people who consciously endorse egalitarian principles but who may unconsciously (implicitly) harbor negative attitudes. These individuals—aversive racists—generally do not discriminate when appropriate behavior is clearly defined, but they do systematically discriminate when such norms are unclear or they can justify their behavior on the basis of some element of the situation (e.g., a candidate's lack of "fit" for a job) that is ostensibly unrelated to group membership. Like other forms of subtle bias, the unfair nature of this act may not be easily recognizable as discrimination, but, like blatant bias, these acts systematically disadvantage members of certain groups.

Institutional and Cultural Bias

Recent work in psychology that draws on more macro-level perspectives in sociology and public health illuminates the role of structural stigma (e.g., Bonilla-Silva, 2014). This perspective recognizes that historical, economic, ideological, and institutional factors can perpetuate racial inequality in the absence of personal intentions to discriminate. Rather than focusing on the role of individual prejudice or stereotypes, it views intergroup bias (e.g., in the form of racism, sexism, heterosexism) as embedded in social structures, which leads members of socially disadvantaged groups to view inequality as normative and legitimate (Jones, 1997). The perspective presents a provocative analysis of inequality and illuminates how and why both members of dominant and dominated groups may be unaware of the unfair influences that affect their lives. Structural stigma, which includes both institutional and cultural discrimination (Jones, Dovidio, & Vietze, 2014), relies on processes beyond individual and interpersonal acts such as "societal-level conditions, cultural norms, and institutional policies that constrain the opportunities, resources, and wellbeing of the stigmatized" (Hatzenbueher & Link, 2014, p. 2). Institutional biases, unlike individual bias, magnify the adverse effects over thousands of instances and many decades (Jones, 1997). The cumulative effect is systemic bias that transcends individual prejudice, stereotyping, and discrimination.

Institutional Discrimination

Institutional discrimination refers to institutional policies (e.g., voting laws, immigration policies) that may unfairly restrict the opportunities of particular groups of people. Although institutional racism can develop originally from intentional biases, it does not require individuals' intention to discriminate, the active support of individuals, or even the awareness of discrimination to operate. Institutional racism becomes "ritualized" in ways that minimize the effort and energy individuals and groups need to expend to support it. Because institutional discrimination is not necessarily intentional or dependent on the overt efforts of individuals, it often must be inferred from disparate outcomes between groups traced back to differential policies (e.g., particular forms of identification required to vote).

Cultural Discrimination

Whereas institutional discrimination is associated with formal laws and policies, cultural discrimination is deeply embedded in the fiber of a culture's history, standards, and normative ways of behaving. Cultural discrimination represents beliefs about the superiority of a dominant group's cultural heritage over those of other groups and the expression of such beliefs in individual actions or institutional policies. It occurs when one group exerts the power to define values for a society. Cultural discrimination involves not only privileging the culture, heritage, and values of the dominant group but also imposing this culture on other groups. As a consequence, everyday activities implicitly communicate group-based bias, passing it to new generations. Culturally transmitted values, beliefs, goals, and standards are primary influences on the structure and function of institutions. Thus, cultural, institutional, and individual biases are intimately intertwined (Jones, 1997). These interconnections create the conditions that give rise to the implicit biases we discussed earlier.

Impact of Bias on Targets of Bias

Being the target of discrimination not only has significant material consequences, such as the restriction of employment opportunities, but also profound psychological and social consequences. Historically, Goffman's (1963) book, *Stigma: Notes on the Management of a Spoiled Identity*, represents seminal work on this topic. Although identifying strongly with one's group may buffer, to some extent, the worst effects of being stigmatized, being victimized by prejudice, stereotyping, and discrimination still has substantial adverse effects, including poorer mental and physical health (Richman, Pascoe, & Lattenner, 2018; Schmitt, Branscombe, Postmes, & Garcia 2014). Individuals higher in an individual difference measure of rejection sensitivity—the tendency to anxiously expect being rejected because of their group membership—are particularly susceptible to these adverse effects (Page-Gould, Mendoza-Denton, & Mendes, 2014).

Anticipated and Internalized Stigma

People who are frequently the targets of discrimination often chronically anticipate bias and, with repeated experiences with discrimination, may internalize stigma. Both have negative psychological consequences. Anticipating discrimination heightens vigilance toward others who are perceived as potential sources of unfair actions and enhances sensitivity to subtle forms of discrimination (Carter & Murphy, 2015). These reactions, however, also increase stress. Both anticipated and internalized stigma can thus create psychological barriers to behaviors, such as applying for a job, that ultimately disadvantage the person.

In part, because of perceptions of discrimination toward their group, people may experience stereotype threat—concerns about being judged or treated negatively because of negative cultural views of their group—in situations in which their social identity is salient. As first demonstrated in classic work by Steele and Aronson (1995; see also Schmader, Johns, & Forbes 2008), experiencing stereotype threat negatively influences performance on tasks that people believe are relevant and important, and when it is experienced regularly, it leads to decreased identification with the related domain.

Although current research on this topic has identified factors that affect the influence the degree to which stereotype threat has detrimental effects (e.g., assessing performance with cognitive tasks and placing the test closer in time to the manipulation), there is general meta-analytic evidence that this phenomena has systematic negative effects for a range of groups. For example, in addition to the well-documented impact on racial and ethnic minority group members, experiencing stereotype threat leads to poorer performance by older individuals (Lamont, Swift, & Abrams, 2015), by girls (younger than 18; see Flore & Wicherts, 2015) as well as women in areas of science and technology, and among White participants playing golf when performance was described as reflecting "natural athletic ability" (Stone, Lynch, Sjomeling, & Darley, 1999).

Individual and Collective Action

People also often actively resist being discriminated against. However, individuals typically overestimate the degree to which they will directly confront discrimination. For example, in one study (Woodzicka & LaFrance, 2001), women were presented with an imaginary scenario in which they were being asked questions by a male interviewer for a position as a research assistant. A number of these questions qualify as sexual harassment in an interview context. The interviewer asked: "Do you have a boyfriend?" "Do people find you desirable?" "Do you think it is important for women to wear bras to work?" The majority of participants said they would confront the man; 62% reported that they would tell him that the questions were inappropriate or at least ask him why he posed the question, and over one fourth (28%) of the women said that they would take stronger action by either rudely confronting the man or walking out of the interview. But how did women who directly encountered a situation like this actually respond? The majority (52%) ignored the harassment and responded directly to the question! A sizable portion (36%) did express their concerns about being asked the questions but mainly by politely asking the interviewer why he posed that question and mostly only after the interview was completed.

This and many other studies in which people experience discrimination consistently show that, because such encounters with discrimination based on gender, race, ethnicity, or other dimensions are unexpected and arouse complex emotional responses, targets of discrimination often respond much less forcefully than they anticipate they would. However, when they recognize such actions as a threat to their group, not just a personal affront, they are not only more likely to respond to the discrimination but to do so in coordination with other members of their group—that is, engage in *collective* action (Van Zomeren, Postmes, & Spears, 2008).

Reducing Prejudice, Stereotyping, and Discrimination and Their Adverse Effects

A vast body of intergroup research has theorized and tested interventions aimed at improving intergroup relations through changing intergroup attitudes (Paluck & Green, 2009). Many of the approaches Brewer (see Chapter 11) discusses are designed to improve intergroup relations by reducing prejudice and stereotyping. In this section, we highlight examples of four general approaches: (a) intergroup contact, (b) recategorization, (c) intervention to reduce the adverse impact of implicit prejudice and stereotyping, and (d) interventions aimed at inhibiting discrimination directly. These are not competitive positions; these various interventions can be combined to have greater impact on reducing discrimination than any one approach alone (Devine, Forscher, Austin, & Cox, 2012).

Intergroup Contact

Intergroup contact has enormous potential for reducing prejudice and intergroup bias generally. There is robust evidence that more frequent and more positive intergroup contact produces lower levels of prejudice, (Pettigrew & Tropp, 2006, 2011; Tausch & Hewstone, 2010). Frequent positive intergroup contact can also lead to lower levels of implicit prejudice and stereotyping over time. The impact of this work on intergroup contact is substantial, practically as well as theoretically: This work has guided legal interventions, such as school, residential, and employment integration laws and policies.

Nevertheless, classic views of contact have some limitations. One limitation is that the original version of the hypothesis stated that personal, first-hand contact is required. This implies that we can only improve intergroup relations one or two people at a time. However, some of the most exciting new extensions of contact theory involve *indirect* forms of contact. For instance, bias can be reduced by mentally simulating having positive contact with a member of another group (imagined contact), by witnessing another member of your group interacting successfully with a member of another group or by interacting in favorable ways with members of other groups over the Internet (Dovidio, Love, Schellhaas, & Hewstone, 2017). These indirect forms of contact are particularly pertinent because of new developments in communication technology that allow us to interact instantaneously and regularly with others across group lines.

Recategorization

Recategorization is an alternative bias-reduction strategy, one also discussed by Brewer (see Chapter 11) with respect to improving intergroup relations, rooted in research on how people socially categorize others as ingroup or outgroup members. Imagine you are walking down a busy street. As people approach you, you automatically notice their race, and you think about them in terms of their racial group membership. However, as a person from another race approaches you, you notice that he is wearing a sweatshirt from your college. Will you feel differently about him now? According to one theory of recategorization, you will.

This is the key idea of the common ingroup identity model (Gaertner & Dovidio, 2000; Gaertner et al., 2016)—that it is possible to change the ways we think about others by changing the way we think about their group membership. Emphasizing a common group membership can change the way we typically think of others from an "us" versus "them" to a more inclusive, superordinate "we" connection. This approach builds upon the principles of social categorization and social identity theory discussed earlier in this chapter. Once you categorize me as an ingroup member (a "we") rather than an outgroup member (a "they"), I will benefit from all of the pro-ingroup biases that will make you like me more, discount my flaws, and want to work with me to promote "our" group.

These more positive reactions occur spontaneously and without much thought. Consider a variation of the example that began this section. Suppose you are a White college student walking around the football stadium before a game against a rival team. A White or Black person approaches you and asks for your help by answering a few questions about your food preferences for a survey he or she is doing. Would you help? And would it matter whether the person had on the colors and insignia of your school or the other school? Nier Gaertner, Dovidio, Banker, and Ward (2001) actually conducted this study and found that White participants did not help a White confederate more when he or she was wearing the home team's signature clothing than when he or she was wearing the other team's insignia; they were already part of the same (racial) ingroup. However, when White participants were asked for help by Black confederates, they were almost twice as likely to help (59% vs. 36% of the time) when the confederates wore the same team (university ingroup) insignia than when they wore the rival team's signature clothing. The home-team clothing represented a common ingroup identity between White and Black students at the game. But what if the person in need was physically injured and in real trouble? Are you the type of person whose decision about whether to help would be determined by something so superficial as whether he or she was wearing a soccer shirt of your team or an opposing team? The research shows that, no matter what you think now, the answer is probably "yes" (Levine, Prosser, Evans & Reicher, 2005).

Reducing the Influence Implicit Prejudice and Stereotyping

Whereas intergroup contact and recategorization are broad strategies that can reduce prejudice, stereotyping, and discrimination and improve intergroup relations through multiple mechanisms, other approaches are more focused in their objectives. One of the main problems with implicit forms of prejudice and stereotyping is that many people—including those who genuinely believe that they are unbiased—are unaware that they possess these negative orientations. In addition, because we are typically motivated to see ourselves as good and fair people, we have well-practiced mechanisms for denying or explaining away discrimination. Thus, one key step in helping people behave in a more unbiased fashion is to make them aware of implicit bias.

One way to begin this process is by having people discover that they might be unintentionally biased. When people who score low on prejudice acknowledge discrepancies between their behavior toward minorities (what they *would* do) and their personal standards (what they *should* do), they feel guilt and compunction (Burns, Monteith, & Parker, 2017). Guilt and compunction are unpleasant psychological states that motivate people to respond without prejudice in the future. With practice, these individuals learn to reduce biased responses, including implicit prejudice and stereotypes, and respond in ways that are consistent with their nonprejudiced personal standards.

A related strategy is to promote the development of positive thoughts that are unconsciously activated more strongly than are prejudice or negative stereotypes. For example, some people have been socialized to hold *chronic egalitarian goals*—habitual ways of thinking that, when activated, inhibit even implicit biases that are normally automatically activated. For these people, seeing a Black person more strongly activates egalitarian thoughts than bias. They are faster to respond to egalitarian-relevant words (e.g., "equality") when primed with Black faces compared to White faces (Moskowitz & Ignarri, 2009). And, how can we acquire chronic egalitarian goals? The answer is simple to state but difficult to accomplish: Practice, practice, practice. For example, extended practice in responding "no" to stereotypic group members and saying "yes" to affirm culturally nonstereotypic positive qualities (e.g., "intelligent" with minorities) inhibits the activation of spontaneous racial stereotypes (Kawakami, Dovidio, Moll, Hermsen, & Russin, 2000). Practice makes perfect.

Reducing Discriminatory Behavior Directly

Other strategies focus directly on controlling discriminatory behavior, rather than on inhibiting the attitudes or stereotypes, either implicit or explicit, that underlie that behavior. One promising intervention relies on *implementation intentions*, a method derived from research on goal pursuit whereby explicitly formulating if–then plans—if this happens, what I will do is . . .—to create reflexive response patterns (Gollwitzer & Oettengen, 2011). In the domain of intergroup bias, when people deliberately prepare and establish a nondiscriminatory response for an anticipated intergroup encounter, prejudice and stereotyping cues are less likely to translate into discriminatory behavior and more likely to promote interest in engaging in activities—such intergroup contact—that can reduce prejudice in the longer term (Stern & West, 2014).

Besides personal efforts to control discriminatory responses, other, social forces may be invoked. The influence of norms on behavior has been studied extensively in social psychology, and intergroup norms have been identified as significant drivers of prejudice and discrimination (Crandall & Stangor, 2005). As such, targeting perceptions of social norms may provide a more efficient way to promote positive relations between groups than targeting individual attitudes, which may be deeply anchored in personal experiences and long-term socialization. Indeed, perceptions of social norms can shift relatively rapidly in response to significant new information, such as the US Supreme Court ruling in favor of same-sex marriage (Tankard & Paluck, 2017).

New norms can also be communicated through mass media. For instance, one intervention to promote reconciliation after the 1994 genocide in Rwanda was a radio soap opera (Paluck, 2009). The soap opera portrayed the rise of tensions between Tutsis and Hutus over a land shortage and—in a situation resembling the events leading up to the 1994 genocide—the more prosperous community is attacked. However, unlike what actually happened earlier, a number of characters in the soap opera banded together across group lines to support one another and spoke out against those who advocated violence. The objective was to depict how the people of Rwanda currently *should* behave under these circumstances. Although personal attitudes about the other group did not change, listeners' perceptions of social norms and anticipated behaviors toward members of the other group changed (compared a control condition) with respect to intermarriage, trust, empathy, and cooperation. This normative approach thus holds considerable promise for improving intergroup relations even in the absence of changes in personal attitudes or stereotypes.

Conclusion

Prejudice, stereotyping, and discrimination are rooted in many of the same basic psychological processes, individual differences in personality and ideology, intergroup relations, and structural factors in society. However, they are also distinct aspects of intergroup bias conceptually and empirically. Because of the multiple forces that shape prejudice, stereotyping, and discrimination and their functional natures, these biases are difficult to change. However, both explicit and implicit prejudice may be reduced through intergroup contact and recategorization, as well as interventions developed specifically to reduce implicit prejudice toward outgroups and to reduce the extent to which intergroup bias translates into discrimination. The study of prejudice, stereotyping, and discrimination remains an active field of research, with important theoretical and practical implications.

References

Adorno, T. W., Frenkel-Brunswik, E., Levinson, D. J., & Sanford, R. N. (1950). *The authoritarian personality*. New York, NY: Harper.

Allport, G.W. (1954). *The nature of prejudice*. Cambridge, MA: Addison-Wesley.

Altemeyer, B. (1996). *The authoritarian specter*. Cambridge, MA: Harvard University Press.

Amodio, D. M., & Lieberman, M. D. (2009). Pictures in our heads: Contributions of fMRI to the study of prejudice and stereotyping. In T. D. Nelson (Ed.), *Handbook of prejudice, stereotyping, and discrimination* (pp. 347–366). New York, NY: Psychology Press.

Bergh, R., & Akrami, N. (2017). Generalized prejudice: Old wisdom and new perspectives. In C. G. Sibley & F. K. Barlow (Eds.), *The Cambridge handbook of the psychology of prejudice* (pp. 438–460). Cambridge, England: Cambridge University Press.

Bergh, R., Akrami, N., Sidanius, J., & Sibley, C. G. (2016). Is group membership necessary for understanding generalized prejudice? A re-evaluation of why prejudices are interrelated. *Journal of Personality and Social Psychology, 111,* 367–395.

Bonilla-Silva, E. (2014). *Racism without racists. Color-blind racism and the persistence of racial inequality in America* (4th ed.) Lanham, MD: Rowman & Littlefield.

Brown, R., & Hewstone, M. (2005). An integrative theory of intergroup contact. In M. P. Zanna (Ed.), *Advances in experimental social psychology* (Vol. 37, pp. 255–343). San Diego, CA: Academic Press.

Burns, M.D., Parker, L. R., & Monteith, M. J. (2017). Self-regulation strategies for combatting prejudice. In C. G. Sibley & F. K. Barlow (Eds.), *The Cambridge handbook of the psychology of prejudice* (pp. 500–518). Cambridge, England: Cambridge University Press.

Carter, E. R., & Murphy, M. C. (2015). Group-based differences in perceptions of racism: What counts, to whom, and why? *Social and Personality Psychology Compass, 9,* 269–280.

Chambers, J. R., Schlenker, B. R., & Collisson, B. (2013). Ideology and prejudice: The role of value conflicts. *Psychological Science, 24,* 140–149.

Crandall, C. S., & Eshleman, A. (2003). A justification-suppression model of the expression and experience of prejudice. *Psychological Bulletin, 129,* 414–446.

Crandall, C. S., & Stangor, C. (2005). Conformity and prejudice. In J. F. Dovidio, P. Glick, & L. A. Rudman (Eds.), *On the nature of prejudice: Fifty years after Allport* (pp. 295–309). Malden, MA: Blackwell.

DeAngelis, T. (2009). Understanding terrorism. *Monitor on Psychology, 40,* 60.

Devine, P. G. (1989). Stereotypes and prejudice: Their automatic and controlled components. *Journal of Personality and Social Psychology, 56,* 5–18.

Devine, P. G., & Elliot, A. J. (1995) Are racial stereotypes really fading? The Princeton trilogy revisited. *Personality and Social Psychology Bulletin, 21,* 1139–1150.

Devine, P. G., Forscher, P. S., Austin, A. J., & Cox, W. T. L. (2012). Long-term reduction in implicit racial prejudice: A prejudice habit-breaking intervention. *Journal of Experimental Social Psychology, 48,* 1267–1278.

Dovidio, J. F., & Gaertner, S. L. (2010). Intergroup bias. In S. T. Fiske, D. Gilbert, & G. Lindzey (Eds.), *Handbook of social psychology* (Vol. 2, 5th ed., pp. 1084–1121). New York, NY: Wiley.

Dovidio, J. F., Gaertner, S. L., & Pearson, A. R. (2017). Aversive racism and contemporary bias. In C. G. Sibley & F. K. Barlow (Eds.), *The Cambridge handbook of the psychology of prejudice* (pp. 267–294). Cambridge, England: Cambridge University Press.

Dovidio, J. F., Hewstone, M., Glick, P., & Esses, V. M. (2010). Prejudice, stereotyping, and discrimination: Theoretical and empirical overview. In J. F. Dovidio, M. Hewstone, P. Glick, & V. M. Esses (Eds.), *SAGE handbook of prejudice, stereotyping, and discrimination* (pp. 3–28). London, England: SAGE.

Dovidio, J. F., Love, A., Schellhaas, F. M. H., & Hewstone, M. (2017). Reducing intergroup bias through intergroup contact: Twenty years of progress and future directions. *Group Processes & Intergroup Behavior, 20,* 606–620.

Duckitt, J., & Sibley, C. G. (2017). The dual process motivational model of ideology and prejudice. In F. K. Barlow & C. G. Sibley (Eds.), *The Cambridge handbook of the psychology of prejudice* (pp. 188–221). Cambridge, England: Cambridge University Press.

Eagly, A. H., & Diekman, A. B. (2005). What is the problem? Prejudice as an attitude-in-context. In J. F. Dovidio, P. Glick, & L. A. Rudman (Eds.), *On the nature of prejudice: Fifty years after Allport* (pp. 19–35). Malden, MA: Blackwell.

Fazio, R.H., & Olson, M. A. (2014). The MODE model: Attitude-behavior processes as a function of motivation and opportunity. In J. W. Sherman, B. Gawronski, & Y. Trope (Eds.), *Dual process theories of mind* (pp. 155–171). New York, NY: Guilford.

Fiske, S. T. (2012). The continuum model and the stereotype content model. In P. A. M. Van Lange, A. W. Kruglanski, & E. Tory Higgins (Eds.), *Handbook of theories of social psychology* (Vol. 1, pp. 267–288). London, England: SAGE.

Fiske, S. T., Cuddy, A. J. C., Glick, P., & Xu, J. (2002). A model of (often mixed) stereotype content: Competence and warmth respectively follow from perceived status and competition. *Journal of Personality and Social Psychology, 82,* 878–902.

Flore, P. C., & Wicherts, J. M. (2015). Does stereotype threat influence performance of girls in stereotyped domains? A meta-analysis. *Journal of School Psychology, 53,* 25–44.

Forscher, P. S., Lai, C. K., Axt, J. R., Ebersole, C. R., Herman, M., Devine, P. G., & Nosek, B. A. (2017). *A meta-analysis of change in implicit bias.* Unpublished manuscript, Department of Psychology, University of Wisconsin–Madison. Retrieved from https://osf.io/awz2p/

Gaertner, S. L., & Dovidio, J. F. (2000). *Reducing intergroup bias: The common ingroup identity model.* Philadelphia, PA: Psychology Press.

Gaertner, S. L., Dovidio, J. F., Guerra, R., Hehman, E., & Saguy, T. (2016). A common in-group identity: A categorization-based approach for reducing intergroup bias. In T. Nelson (Ed.), *Handbook of prejudice, discrimination, and stereotyping* (2nd ed., pp. 433–454). New York, NY: Psychology Press.

Gawronski, B., & Bodenhausen, G. V. (2014). Implicit and explicit evaluation: A brief model of the associative-propositional evaluation model. *Social and Personality Compass, 8,* 448–462.

Glick, P., & Fiske, S.T. (2001). An ambivalent alliance: Hostile and benevolent sexism as complementary justifications for gender inequality. *American Psychologist, 56,* 109–118.

Goffman, I. (1963). *Stigma: Notes on the management of a spoiled identity.* New York, NY: Simon & Schuster.

Gollwitzer, P. M., Oettingen, G. (2011). Planning promotes goal striving. In K. D. Vohs & R. F. Baumeister (Eds.), *Self-regulation: Research, theory, and applications* (2nd ed., pp. 162–185). New York, NY: Guilford.

Greenwald, A. G., Banaji, M. R., & Nosek, B. A. (2015). Statistically small effects of the implicit Association Test can have societally large effects. *Journal of Personality and Social Psychology, 108,* 553–561.

Greenwald, A. G., & Pettigrew, T. F. (2014). With malice toward none: Ingroup favoritism enables discrimination. *American Psychologist, 69,* 669–684.

Greenwald, A. G., Poehlman, T. A., Uhlmann, E. L., & Banaji, M. R. (2009). Understanding and using the Implicit Association Test: III. Meta-analysis of predictive validity. *Journal of Personality and Social Psychology, 97,* 17–41.

Hatzenbuehler, M. L., & Link, B. G. (2014). Introduction to the special issue on structural stigma and health. *Social Science & Medicine (1982), 103,* 1–6.

Ho, A. K., Sidanius, J., Kteily, N., Sheehy-Skeffington, J., Pratto, F., Henkel, K. E., . . . Stewart, A. L. (2015). The nature of social dominance orientation: Theorizing and measuring preferences for intergroup inequality using the new SDO_7 scale. *Journal of Personality and Social Psychology, 109,* 1003–1028.

Hodson, G., & Dhont, K. (2015). The person-based nature of prejudice: Individual difference predictors of intergroup negativity. *European Review of Social Psychology, 26,* 1–42.

Hogg, M. A. (2012). Self-uncertainty, social identity, and the solace of extremism. In M. A. Hogg & D. Blaylock (Eds.), *Extremism and the psychology of uncertainty* (pp. 19–35). Malden, MA: Wiley-Blackwell.

Hogg, M. A., Abrams, D., & Brewer, M. B. (2017). Social identity: The role of self in group processes and intergroup relations. *Group Processes & Intergroup Relations, 20,* 570–581.

Jackman, M. R. (1994). *The velvet glove: Paternalism and conflict in gender, class, and race relations.* Berkeley, CA: University of California Press.

Jones, J. M. (1997). *Prejudice and racism* (2nd ed.). New York, NY: McGraw Hill.

Jones, J. M., Dovidio, J. F., & Vietze, D. L. (2014). *The psychology of diversity: Beyond prejudice and racism*. Malden, MA: Wiley-Blackwell.

Jost, J. T., Gaucher, D., & Stern, D. (2015). "The world isn't fair": A system justification perspective on social stratification and inequality. In M. Mikulincer, P. R. Shaver, J. F. Dovidio, & J. A. Simpson (Eds.), *APA handbook of personality and social psychology, Vol. 2: Group processes* (pp. 317–340). Washington, DC: American Psychological Association.

Karlins, M., Coffman, T. L. & Walters, G. (1969). On the fading of stereotypes: Studies in three generations of college students. *Journal of Personality and Social Psychology, 13*, 1–16.

Katz, D., & Braly, K. (1933). Racial stereotypes in one hundred college students. *Journal of Abnormal and Social Psychology, 28*, 280–290.

Kawakami, K., Amodio, D. M., & Hugenberg, K. (2017). Intergroup perception and cognition: An integrative framework, for understanding the causes and consequences of social categorization. *Advances in Experimental Social Psychology, 55*, 1–80.

Kawakami, K., Dovidio, J. F., Moll, J., Hermsen, S., & Russin, A. (2000). Just say no (to stereotyping: Effects of training in the negation of stereotypic associations on stereotype activation. *Journal of Personality and Social Psychology, 78*, 871–888.

Kay, A. C., Gaucher, D., Peach, J. M., Laurin, K., Friesen, J., Zanna, M. P., & Spencer, S. J. (2009). Inequality, discrimination, and the power of the status quo: Direct evidence for a motivation to see the way things are as the way they should be. *Journal of Personality and Social Psychology, 97*, 421–434.

Lamont, R. A., Swift, H. J., & Abrams, D. (2015). A review and meta-analysis of age-based stereotype threat: Negative stereotypes, not facts, do the damage. *Psychology and Aging, 30*, 180–193.

Leitner, J. B., Hehman, E., Ayduk, O., & Mendoza-Denton, R. (2016). Blacks' death rate due to circulatory diseases is positively related to Whites' explicit racial bias: A nationwide investigation using Project Implicit. *Psychological Science, 27*, 1299–1311.

Levine, M., Prosser, A. Evans, D., & Reicher, S. (2005). Identity and emergency intervention: How social group membership and inclusiveness of group boundaries shape helping behavior. *Personality and Social Psychology Bulletin, 31*, 443–453.

Lippmann, W. (1922). *Public opinion*. New York, NY: Harcourt, Brace.

McConahay, J.B. (1986). Modern racism, ambivalence, and the Modern Racism Scale. In J. F. Dovidio & S. L. Gaertner (Eds.), *Prejudice, discrimination, and racism* (pp. 99–125). Orlando, FL: Academic Press.

McConnell, A. R., & Leibold, J. M. (2001). Relations among the Implicit Association Test, discriminatory behavior, and explicit measures of racial attitudes. *Journal of Experimental Social Psychology, 37*, 435–442.

Moskowitz, G. B., & Ignarri, C. (2009). Implicit volition and stereotype control. *European Review of Social Psychology, 20*, 97–145.

Nadler, A. (2002). Inter-group helping relations as power relations: Maintaining or challenging social dominance between groups through helping. *Journal of Social Issues, 58*, 487–502.

Newheiser, A-K., & Dovidio, J. F. (2012). Individual differences and intergroup bias: Divergent dynamics associated with prejudice and stereotyping. *Personality and Individual Differences, 53*, 70–74.

Nier, J. A., Gaertner, S. L., Dovidio, J. F., Banker, B. S., & Ward, C. M. (2001). Changing interracial evaluations and behavior: The effects of a common group identity. *Group Processes and Intergroup Relations, 4*, 299–316.

Oswald, F. L., Mitchell, G., Blanton, H., Jaccard, J., & Tetlock, P. E. (2013). Predicting ethnic and racial discrimination: A meta-analysis of IAT criterion studies. *Journal of Personality and Social Psychology, 105*, 171–192.

Page-Gould, E., Mendoza-Denton, R., & Mendes, W. B. (2014). Stress and coping in interracial contexts: The influence of race-based rejection sensitivity and cross-group friendship in daily experiences of health. *Journal of Social Issues, 70*, 256–278.

Paluck, E. L. (2009). Reducing intergroup prejudice and conflict using the media: A field experiment in Rwanda. *Journal of Personality and Social Psychology, 96*, 574–587.

Paluck, E. L., & Green, D. P. (2009). Prejudice reduction: What works? A review and assessment of research and practice. *Annual Review of Psychology, 60,* 339–367.

Payne, B. K., Vuletich, H. A., & Lundberg, K. B. (2017). The bias of crowds: How implicit bias bridges personal and systemic prejudice. *Psychological Inquiry, 28,* 233–248.

Penner, L. A., Phelan, S. M., Earnshaw, V., Albrecht, T. L., & Dovidio, J. F. (2018). Patient stigma, medical interactions, and healthcare disparities: A selective review. In B. Major, J. F. Dovidio, & B. G. Link (Eds.), *The Oxford handbook of stigma and health* (pp. 183–201). New York, NY: Oxford University Press.

Pettigrew, T. F. & Tropp, L. R. (2006). A meta-analytic test of intergroup contact theory. *Journal of Personality and Social Psychology, 90,* 751–783.

Pettigrew, T. F., & Tropp, L. R. (2011). *When groups meet: The dynamics of intergroup contact.* New York, NY: Psychology Press.

Richman, L. S., Pascoe, E., & Lattanner, M. (2018). Interpersonal discrimination and physical health. In B. Major, J. F. Dovidio, & B. G. Link (Eds.), *The Oxford handbook of stigma, discrimination, and health* (pp. 203–218). New York, NY: Oxford University Press.

Riek, B. M., Mania, E. W., & Gaertner, S. L. (2006). Intergroup threat and outgroup attitudes: A meta-analytic review. *Personality and Social Psychology Review, 10,* 336–353.

Schmader, T., Johns, M., & Forbes, C. (2008). An integrated process model of stereotype threat effects on performance. *Psychological Review, 115,* 336–356.

Schmitt, M. T., Branscombe, N. R., Postmes, T., & Garcia, A. (2014). The consequences of perceived discrimination for psychological well-being: A meta-analytic review. *Psychological Bulletin, 140,* 921–948.

Sears, D. O., & Henry, P. J. (2005). Over thirty years later: A contemporary look at symbolic racism. In M. P. Zanna (Ed.), *Advances in experimental social psychology* (Vol. 37, pp. 95–150). San Diego, CA: Academic Press.

Shepherd, L., Fasoli, F., Pereira, A., & Branscombe, N. R. (2018). The role of threat, emotions, and prejudice in promoting collective action against immigrant groups. *European Journal of Social Psychology, 48,* 447–459.

Sherif, M., Harvey, O. J., White, B. J., Hood, W. R., & Sherif, C. W. (1961). *Intergroup conflict and cooperation: The Robbers Cave experiment* (Vol. 10). Norman, OK: University Book Exchange.

Sibley, C. G., & Duckitt, J. (2008). Personality and prejudice: A meta-analysis and theoretical review. *Personality and Social Psychology Review, 12,* 248–279.

Sidanius, J., Cotterill, S., Sheehy-Skeffington, J., Kteily, N., & Cavarch, H. (2017). Social dominance theory: Explorations in the psychology of oppression. In C. G. Sibley & F. K. Barlow (Eds.), *The Cambridge handbook of the psychology of prejudice* (pp. 149–187). Cambridge, UK: Cambridge University Press.

Steele, C. M. & Aronson, J. (1995). Stereotype threat and the intellectual test performance of African Americans. *Journal of Personality and Social Psychology, 69,* 797–811.

Stephan, W. G., Ybarra, O., & Morrison, K. R. (2016). Intergroup threat theory. In T. D. Nelson (Ed.), *Handbook of prejudice, stereotyping, and discrimination* (2nd ed., pp. 43–60). New York, NY: Psychology Press.

Stern, C., & West, T. V. (2014). Circumventing anxiety during interpersonal encounters to promote interest in contact: An implementation intention approach. *Journal of Experimental Social Psychology, 50,* 82–93.

Stone, J., Lynch, C. I., Sjomeling, M., & Darley, J. M. (1999). Stereotype threat effects on Black and White athletic performance. *Journal of Personality and Social Psychology, 77,* 1213–1227.

Swann, W. B., Jr., & Buhrmester, M. D. (2015). Identity fusion. *Current Directions in Psychological Science, 24,* 52–57.

Tajfel, H., & Turner, J. C. (1979). An integrative theory of intergroup conflict. In W. G. Austin & S. Worchel (Eds.), *The social psychology of intergroup relations* (pp. 33–48). Monterey, CA: Brooks/Cole.

Talaska, C. A., Fiske, S. T., & Chaiken, S. (2008). Legitimating racial discrimination: Emotions, not beliefs, best predict discrimination in a meta-analysis. *Social Justice Research, 21,* 263–296.

Tankard, M., & Paluck, E. L. (2017). The effect of a Supreme Court decision regarding gay marriage on social norms and personal attitudes. *Psychological Science, 28,* 1334–1344.

Tausch, N., & Hewstone, M. (2010). Intergroup contact. In J. F. Dovidio, M. Hewstone, P. Glick, & V. M. Esses (Eds.), *SAGE handbook of prejudice, stereotyping, and discrimination* (pp. 544–560). London, England: SAGE.

Turner, J. C., Hogg, M. A., Oakes, P. J., Reicher, S. D., & Wetherell, M. S. (1987). *Rediscovering the social group: A self-categorization theory*. Oxford, England: Blackwell.

Van Zomeren, M., Postmes, T., & Spears, R. (2008). Toward an integrative social identity model of collective action: A quantitative research synthesis of three socio-psychological perspectives. *Psychological Bulletin, 134*, 504–535.

Wildschut, T., & Insko, C. A. (2007). Explanations of interindividual-intergroup discontinuity: A review of the evidence. *European Review of Social Psychology, 18*, 175–211.

Wilson, T. D., Lindsey, S., & Schooler, T. Y. (2000). A model of dual attitudes. *Psychological Review, 107*, 101–126.

Woodzicka, J. A., & LaFrance, M. (2001). Real versus imagined gender harassment. *Journal of Social Issues, 57*, 15–30.

Chapter 13

Morality

Linda J. Skitka and Paul Conway

US Supreme Court Justice Potter Stewart famously argued that he did not need to provide a formal definition of what counts as "hard-core pornography" because "I know it when I see it." People (including scholars) seem to have the same sense about morality: They simply know what morality is, often without being able to concretely define what exactly what it means to label something as a moral kind. Some aspects of morality are seemingly universal and necessary for social functioning. People feel they have the right to tend to their own welfare in socially acceptable ways and, at the same time, a duty to fulfil their social obligations (Berkowitz, 1972), to reciprocate kindnesses and favors (Gouldner, 1960), to support their ingroups (Sober & Wilson, 1998), and to refrain from needlessly harming others (Turiel, 2002). People in all cultures seem to endorse some version of the Golden Rule (Hauser, 2006), even if people individually or within cultures might prioritize some beliefs, rules, and values differently (e.g., Buchtel et al., 2015; Vasquez, Keltner, Ebenbach, & Banazynski, 2001). It is when one tries to more precisely and scientifically define what morality is, however, that things become much less clear. Our goal with this chapter is to try to map how psychologists have tried to grapple with the challenge of studying what turns out to be a surprisingly fuzzy construct: morality.

The study of morality has historically been the special province of philosophy and moral development. Social psychological interest in the topic intensified around the turn of the millennium. To provide a sense of the field and developments in it over time, we first provide a review the lessons learned from theory and research in moral development from approximately 1930 to 2000. We then review major developments in social psychological approaches to questions of morality from 2000 to the present. As the reader will soon learn, the field is animated by questions about the relative roles of reason and emotion in moral phenomena, often takes its lead from moral philosophy (sometimes blurring the lines between normative and descriptive claims), and is characterized more by competing theories and perspectives than by theoretical or scientific consensus.

Moral Psychology ~1930–2000

Moral psychology from approximately 1930 until 2000 was primarily studied from a developmental perspective. The focus was largely on character development, something people were deeply concerned about as society became increasingly secularized. This period of theory and research focused primarily on how people make moral judgments and on moral reasoning, particularly in response to various moral dilemmas that required people to grapple with difficult choices between competing values (e.g., do not harm, maximize the collective good). Because of its focus on character and character education, this period of theory and research tended to have a prescriptive spin, by implicitly or explicitly positing that some kinds of moral reasoning are superior to others.

Probably the earliest scientific study of moral psychology was Jean Piaget's focus on the moral lives of children as revealed through games and play. Piaget (1932/1997) observed that children's games tended to be dominated by concerns about fairness. Young children focus on rigidly following rules imposed by outside authorities, but eventually most children learn that fair rules can be negotiated by taking others' perspectives into account. Over time, coordinating play becomes more important than the rules themselves. From these observations, Piaget described moral development as arising through interpersonal interactions whereby people find solutions that everyone will accept as fair.

Kohlberg (1969) embraced Piaget's conclusion that morality centers around fairness and justice and elaborated his developmental model into six stages (a theoretical approach that would dominate psychological discourse about morality for several decades). At Stages 1 and 2, people's conception of justice is defined primarily by self-interest: They do little more than try to minimize punishments and maximize rewards. At Stages 3 and 4, people begin to consider others' expectations for their behavior and the implications of their behavior for group functioning. They show concern for others' feelings, strive to appear as good people, and feel obligated to contribute to larger groups (e.g., their school or society). At Stage 5, people define justice in terms of basic human rights and values. People at this stage conceptualize life as a social contract where they agree to abide by rules that foster the common good by protecting individuals and society and challenge rules that do not (such as slavery). Finally, at Stage 6, people believe that rules, laws, and other social agreements are valid only if they are based on universal ethical principles derived from logic; someone at this stage, for example, might object to abortion even though it is legally allowed.[1] People at Stage 6 are motivated to personally live up to such standards regardless of social approbation.

Kolhberg and his colleagues and students generally studied the stages of moral reasoning by analyzing the justifications people provided for their responses to moral dilemmas to glean whether their moral reasoning was more consistent with one another stage of moral development. One of the classic examples of one of the dilemmas used in this research was the Heinz dilemma (Kohlberg, 1981, p. 186):

A woman was near death from a special kind of cancer. There was one drug that the doctors thought might save her. It was a form of radium that a druggist in the same town had recently discovered. The drug was expensive to make, but the druggist was charging 10X what the drug cost him to make. He paid $400 for the radium, and charged $4K for a small dose of the drug. The sick woman's husband, Heinz, went to everyone he knew to borrow the money and tried every legal means, but could only get $2K, which is half of what it cost. He told the druggist that his wife was dying, and asked him to sell it cheaper or let him pay later. But the druggist said, "No, I discovered the drug and I'm going to make money from it." So, having tried every legal means, Heinz gets desperate and considers breaking into the store to steal the drug for his wife.

Should Heinz still the drug? Why or why not?

Although Kohlberg's theory was very generative and influential, overtime research revealed serious limitations. Most problematic, people seldom give responses that fall neatly into any single Kohlbergian stage; evidence for stage regression abounds (e.g., Simpson, 1974; Sullivan, 1977). In addition to this core problem, critics increasingly accused the theory of cultural insensitivity and championing a Western worldview (e.g., Simpson, 1974; Sullivan, 1977), and for sexism in its construction and interpretation of morality because it does not make any reference to an ethic of care, a moral principle traditionally ascribed more to women than men (Gilligan, 1982). Perhaps most important, the theory at its heart is more normative than descriptive—that is, it prescribes what kind of moral reasoning is more "mature" or one should aspire to achieve (e.g., Stage 5 or 6), without any scientific basis for establishing what makes for better or worse forms of moral reasoning.

More contemporary versions of the theory have adapted some components of Kohlberg's ideas, and some of his methodological choices. A considerable amount of modern moral psychology continues to rely on people's reactions to hypothetical dilemmas that pit one moral concern against another (e.g., whether to steal to save a life, whether to sacrifice one to save several others) to gain insight into how people morally juggle competing concerns. More contemporary theories in both moral development and social psychology, however, have dropped the most controversial aspects of Kohlberg's theorizing, including the notion of ordered developmental stages and the idea that some ways of thinking about morality are normatively better or more mature than others. We briefly review two neo-Kohlbergian moral theories (moral schema theory and domain theory) before turning to the renaissance of interest in morality that began to emerge in social psychology at the turn of the millennium.

Moral Schema Theory

Moral schema theory recast the Kolhberg's stages of moral reasoning as three cognitive schemas instead (Rest, Narvaez, Bebeau, & Thoma, 1999). According to this theoretical update, socio-moral judgments arise from three kinds of schemas: (a) personal interests (much like Kohlberg's Stages 1 and 2), (b) norm maintenance (much like Kohlberg's Stages 3 and 4), and (c) postconventional (much like Kohlberg's Stages 5 and 6). Rest et al. (1999) theorized that, once formed in childhood and early development, people may use any of these schemas to guide judgments and behavior and move fluidly between them depending on how features of situations and social relationships activate or map onto one or another. Yet, Rest et al. continued to emphasize rationality and justice: "We still agree with Kohlberg that the aim of the developmental analysis of moral judgment is the *rational* reconstruction of the ontogenesis of *justice* operations" (p. 56; emphasis added).

Moral Domain Theory

As criticism of Kolhberg's theory continued to mount, domain theory also emerged as a reformulation and extension. Domain theory grew out of the key empirical observation that people—including very young children—differentiate actions that harm innocent people from actions that break rules but harm no one (e.g., Nucci & Turiel, 1978; Smetana, 1981; Turiel, 1983). This observation led domain theorists to surmise that two distinct systems underlie people's judgments of social events: a system focused on morality and another system focused on social convention.

The moral domain is defined as people's conceptions of rights, fairness, and human welfare that depend on inherent features of actions (Turiel, 1983). From the domain theory perspective, harming someone for no reason is wrong because it hurts them—not because doing so violates a law, rule, or custom (i.e., the act itself is wrong). Social conventions, in contrast, are rules that a particular group has developed to create and maintain order and cooperation within the group. Unlike moral standards, conventional standards are arbitrary in the sense that they depend on group norms and practices rather than the actions they govern. Greeting someone by shaking hands rather than raising your middle finger is only meaningful in societies that have norms about what those actions mean. Other societies establish different greetings that similarly regulate social interactions (e.g., kisses on the cheek, placing palms together with a slight bow). Importantly, there is nothing inherent about these actions that make them right or wrong outside of group norms. In domain theory, morality is something that psychologically generalizes to members of other groups and cultures: If something is morally wrong, it is perceived as morally wrong for all groups, not just one's own group.

Consistent with domain theory predictions, people judge and punish moral transgressors more severely than those who transgress social conventions (for reviews, see Smetana, 2006; Turiel, 2006). Moreover, people believe that moral rules do not depend on authorities. Children say that hitting and stealing are wrong, for example, even if an authority figure like a teacher tells them it is okay (Nucci & Turiel, 1978; Smetana, 1981, 1984). Similarly, children obey moral requests (e.g., to stop fighting) made by any person, including other children, but they only endorse obedience to social norms (such as seat assignments) from legitimate authorities (Laupa, 1994). Children and adults reliably treat moral transgressions involving harm as more wrong, punishable, independent of structures of authority, and more universally wrong than transgressions against social conventions, and these findings replicate well across cultures (e.g., Hollos et al., 1986; Huebner, Lee, & Hauser, 2010).[2]

Social conventions stretch across a continuum from arbitrary personal preferences (e.g., flavor preferences, getting a tattoo) to important and widely shared social standards subject to legitimate sanction (e.g., driving on the correct side of the street; Huebner et al., 2010). The boundaries between the moral and conventional domains may not always be perfectly sharp (e.g., Haidt, Koller, & Dias, 1993; cf. Gray & Keeney, 2015) but are sharp enough that even very young children (e.g., 39 months) recognize and reliably distinguish between moral and conventional notions of right and wrong (Smetana & Braeges, 1990). Although the distinction between moral and conventional concerns is for the most part settled science in moral development, this distinction has been relatively glossed over in contemporary social psychological theories of morality, something we will also bring up later in this chapter.

Developmental theories and research dominated moral psychology for most of the 20th century, and there continues to be interest in moral development—for example, the study of moral awareness of preverbal infants (e.g., Bloom, 2013; Van de Vondermoot & Hamlin, 2016). The turn of the millennium witnessed a new surge of interest in moral psychology outside developmental psychology. This new wave of theory and research adopts a more descriptive than prescriptive approach and revitalized debates between the role of emotion and reason in people's moral judgment. The turn of the millennium seemed to be a watershed moment with the introduction of two new theories: the social intuitionist model (SIM; Haidt, 2001) and a dual process model (Greene, Summerville, Nystrom, Darley, & Cohen, 2001) that independently and jointly ignited a huge interest in questions of morality seemingly overnight; the field is still experiencing the ripple effects of this new focused attention on moral psychology nearly 20 years later. We first review the SIM and the dual process model and then turn to a review of subsequent theories that have been proposed as alternatives to them.

The Social Intuitionist Model

Haidt (2001) proposed a social intuitionist account of morality as a distinct counterpoint to the Kolhbergian focus on rationalism. He took seriously Hume's (1888/1978) claim that "morals excite passions, and produce or prevent actions. Reason of itself is utterly impotent in this particular way. The rules of morality, therefore are not conclusions of our reason" (p. 325). Haidt proposed that moral judgments rarely if ever stem from conscious reasoning about moral concerns. Instead, moral judgments stem from intuition: "the sudden appearance in consciousness of a moral judgment, including an affective valence (good–bad, like–dislike) without any conscious awareness of having gone through the steps of searching, weighing evidence, or inferring conclusion" (p. 818). Moral intuitions are thought to be innate cognitive adaptions that evolutionarily developed to allow people to respond rapidly and effectively to challenges and opportunities faced by humans over long periods of time. After flashes of moral intuition cause judgments, reasoning nearly always operates as a post hoc justification to provide additional support.

Even though the SIM of moral judgment places intuition (a form of cognition) as the central causal variable that leads people to recognize that something is moral or immoral, nearly all tests of the SIM have manipulated emotional cues (and, in particular, disgust) because emotions are thought to trigger intuition (e.g., Wheatley & Haidt, 2005). For example, some researchers have focused on the emotion of disgust as a possible trigger for moral intuitions. Some theorists conceptualize disgust as an evolutionarily adaptive response that allowed humans as an omnivorous species to decide what they could eat while avoiding parasites and illnesses that can be spread by physical contact (Rozin & Fallon, 1987). Disgust is thought to be an aversive cue that functionally generalized to facilitate rejection of socially non-adaptive or dangerous people or behaviors, such as cannibalism, incest, and betrayal (Haidt, Rozin, McCauley, & Imada, 1997). Therefore, Haidt (2001) reasoned that people respond aversively to transgressions largely because they experience a strong visceral sense of disgust when encountering one.

If the SIM is true, people should make moral judgments even when they are consciously unaware of what led them to make that judgment and make harsher moral judgments of others' actions when they experience a moralized emotion, such as disgust. To test this idea, Wheatley and Haidt (2005) gave research participants posthypnotic suggestions to feel disgust whenever they read an arbitrary word and then judge the morality of harmless transgressions that either did or did not include the disgust-inducing word. People hypnotically induced to feel disgusted rated these transgressions as more wrong than those not induced to feel disgust. In other studies, disgust was induced with bad smells, working in a filthy room, or by recalling a physically disgusting experience (e.g., Schnall, Haidt, Clore, & Jordan, 2008). Although some studies (like the previously mentioned studies) support the SIM hypothesis that people's moral judgments become amplified when participants are induced to feel disgust, a recent meta-analysis of 50 studies designed to test this hypothesis indicated that if moral amplification effects of disgust exist, the effect size is very small, it is limited only to some modes of induction (olfactory and gustatory and not manipulations like cleanliness), and even in these modes, the effects are not robust to corrections for publication bias (Landy & Goodwin, 2015). Taken together, these findings suggest that the SIM implication that incidental disgust is sufficient to lead to moral amplification effects has not received strong support.

The SIM also predicts that people should be able to make moral judgments and see the moral significance of something even in the absence of having reasons for claiming that it is wrong, such as when there is an absence of harm. In other words, people should not have clear access to why they make judgments that something is wrong, because they are making these judgments based on visceral and negative intuitions or feelings, rather than reasoning or conscious recognition of harm. To demonstrate the possibility of making moral judgments in the absence of reasons or harm, Haidt, Bjorklund, and Murphy (2000)[3] asked a small sample of participants to react to hypothetical situations such as the following:

Julie and Mark are brother and sister. They are traveling together in France on summer vacation from college. One night they are staying alone in a cabin near the beach. They decide that it would be interesting and fun if they tried making love. At the very least, it would be a new experience for each of them. Julie was already taking birth control pills, but Mark uses a condom too, just to be safe. They both enjoy making love, but they decide never to do it again. They keep that night as a special secret, which makes them feel even closer to each other. What do you think about that? Was it ok for them to make love? (p. 18)

Because the scenario is carefully crafted to thwart the usual reasons one might avoid incest (e.g., the dangers of inbreeding), Haidt et al. reasoned that objections to it must therefore be due to something other than reasoning or reasons.

Many participants do find the Mark and Julie situation wrong and persist in insisting it is wrong even in the absence of being able to provide evidence for its wrongness when challenged to do so by the experimenter (i.e., they are "morally dumbfounded"; Haidt et al., 2000). Other researchers, however, have found that participants do not believe that the protagonists' actions in these "harmless" scenarios are, in fact, harmless. Rather, participants are responding to these and other taboo-defying scenarios as wrong jointly because they do not accept the experimenter's insistence of no harm and because the behaviors are excessively nonnormative or weird (e.g., Gray & Keeney, 2015; Royzman, Kim, & Leeman, 2015). To a considerable degree, however, interpretation of what the results of moral dumbfounding demonstrations mean and whether those results support the SIM's moral intuition hypothesis hinges on philosophical (and not scientific) debates about what kinds of reasons should count as legitimate, rational, or real reasons for calling a behavior wrong (for more details, see Jacobson, 2012; Royzman et al., 2015).

Dual Process Theory

At approximately the same time that Haidt's (2001) SIM challenged older rationalist models, another model suggested that both affective and cognitive processes causally contribute to moral judgments—but *different kinds* of judgments. Greene et al. (2001) presented a dual process model to "steer a middle course between traditional rationalism and more recent emotivism that [has] dominated moral psychology" (p. 2107) based on responses to philosophical dilemmas where causing harm maximizes overall outcomes (Foot, 1967). The most famous example involves a certain errant rail car:

> A runaway trolley is headed for five people who will be killed if it proceeds on its present course. The only way to save them is to hit a switch that will turn the trolley onto an alternate set of tracks where it will kill one person instead of five. Ought you to turn the trolley in order to save five people at the expense of one? (Greene et al., 2001, p. 2105).

The original, "hard" version of dual process theory suggests that when people encounter a moral dilemma, they immediately and involuntarily experience a negative, affect-laden reaction to the prospect of causing harm, leading them to reject harmful actions (consistent with deontological ethics).[4] Given sufficient time, motivation, and resources, they may follow up with deliberative cognitive processing focused on weighing options to determine which action leads to better outcomes overall (consistent with utilitarian ethics; Greene et al., 2001).[5] Ordinarily, these processes align because causing harm makes the world worse, but moral dilemmas present a rare case where maximizing the good requires harming someone. How people approach this dilemma provides a unique window into moral processing (Paxton & Greene, 2010). Although there are serious doubts about the temporal order of processes (i.e., whether affect precedes cognitive processing, or vice versa) and the validity of a hard version of dual process theory (e.g., Baron, Gürçay, Moore, & Starcke, 2012), there is considerable support for a "softer" dual process model. The soft version of the dual process model jettisons hypotheses about temporal order and retains only the claim that deontological judgments primarily reflect affective processing focused on performing harmful actions, whereas utilitarian judgments primarily reflect cognitive processing focused on achieving positive outcomes (Crockett, 2013; Cushman 2013).

The dual process model generated a dramatic rise in research that examined the contributions of affect and cognitive processing to moral dilemma responses. Early work noted that people typically accept causing harm in *impersonal* dilemmas such as the classic trolley dilemma where causing harm involves merely pressing a button. Conversely, people typically reject causing harm on *personal* dilemmas like the footbridge dilemma where harm requires pushing someone off a footbridge to save five others using the personal force of one's own hands (Greene et al., 2009, cf. Mikhail, 2007).[6]

Participants who consider personal dilemmas or reject harm show greater activation in brain regions linked to social emotion processing, whereas participants considering impersonal dilemmas or who accept harm show greater activation in regions associated abstract reasoning (Greene et al., 2004). Likewise, individual differences in processing related to affective concerns about harm (e.g., empathic concern) predict increased harm rejection judgments (e.g., Gleichgerrcht & Young, 2013), whereas individual differences in processing related to deliberation over outcomes predict harm acceptance judgments (e.g., Moore, Clark, & Kane, 2008). Manipulations inducing or suppressing emotion, as well as those that promote or undermine deliberative processing, tend to have corresponding impacts on dilemma judgments in line with dual process claims (e.g. Amit & Greene, 2012). In short, whether reasoning or emotion dominates people's moral reasoning depends on both individual differences in cognitive and affective processing tendencies, as well as circumstances that promote or suppress cognitive and affective processing.

One challenge in dilemma research is that researchers treat dilemma decisions as dichotomous—participants must either accept or reject outcome-maximizing harm—or else assess responses along a continuum from one answer to the other. Thus, accepting the deontological answer entails rejecting the utilitarian answer and vice versa. Yet, researchers conceptualize the impact of affective and cognitive processes as independent and not opposing or hydraulic forces, whereby if one increases the other decreases. Rather, some people may experience more of both—they want both to avoid causing harm and to maximize outcomes, or little of either. If so, these competing motivations would largely cancel out, becoming invisible in the usual way dilemmas are analyzed or understood. Moreover, because researchers essentially measure the impact of affective and cognitive processing using a single dependent measure, they typically conflate the two, which leads to theoretical confusion.

Many researchers have reported that people make "more utilitarian" dilemma decisions when their emotional concern for others is impaired, for example, whether via psychopathy, low empathic concern, or brain lesions (e.g., Bartels & Pizarro, 2011; Gleichgerrcht & Young, 2013; Koenigs et al., 2007). Some theorists describe results like these (i.e., that psychopaths are utilitarians) as threats to the validity of dilemma research, because utilitarian decisions should reflect prosocial rather than antisocial motivations (something psychopaths are not thought to have). What these interpretations often fail to consider, however, is that perhaps utilitarian judgments in these cases reflect psychopaths' and selected others' mere willingness to sacrifice others rather than any desire to proactively and impartially help (e.g., Kahane et al., 2015, 2018). In other words, these findings may not reflect increased concern for utilitarian outcomes but decreased concern about causing harm instead. But how to tell?

A recent solution to this challenge is to measure responses to different kinds of dilemmas, including dilemmas that do not pit affective and cognitive processing against each other, using techniques such as process dissociation (Conway & Gawronski, 2013) or multilevel modeling (Gawronski, Conway, Armstrong, Friesdorf, & Hütter, 2015). The bulk of this research corroborates the basic affective–cognitive dual process distinction: The deontological tendency to reject causing harm regardless of outcomes seems to reflect primarily affective processes and the utilitarian tendency to maximize outcomes regardless of whether doing so causes harm seems to reflect primarily cognitive processes. This technique clarifies previous work. For example, process dissociation reveals that psychopathy correlates negatively with deontological responding (harm rejection) but either fails to correlate or correlates negatively with genuine utilitarian responding (Conway, Goldstein-Greenwood, Polacek, & Greene, 2018). Hence, psychopaths are not really "more utilitarian"; they are "less deontological," corroborating the dual process model.[7]

This new strain of research corroborates the claim that dilemma responses reflect genuinely moral rocessing—tendencies invisible to conventional methods. For example, aversion to witnessing harm predicts both deontological and utilitarian responses tendencies (Reynolds & Conway, 2018), as does moral identity internalization (Aquino & Reed, 2002). These dual positive relationships, however, cancel out in analyses that treat deontology and utilitarianism as opposites (measured on a single measure) rather than disassociating them instead. Hence, researchers should be careful when interpreting correlations and null effects in studies that do not disassociate deontological from utilitarian responses.

Taken together, research that disassociates how people make dilemma decisions rarely *contradict* the dual process claim that affective reactions to harm and cognitive evaluations of outcomes independently contribute to moral judgments. That said, this research nonetheless suggests the dual process model is too simplistic because we now know that some cognitive processes contribute to deontological responding (e.g., Gamez-Djokic & Molden, 2016), and some affective processes may contribute to utilitarian responding (e.g., Reynolds & Conway, 2018). In addition, whereas many theorists have theorized deontological dilemma judgments as driven by intuitive, emotional responses to harm (Miller, Hannikainen, & Cushman, 2014), others have argued that deontological judgments entail adherence to moral rules, such as "do not harm" (e.g., Baron 1994; Sunstein, 2005) or a combination of emotional response and rule-based thinking (Nichols & Mallon, 2006). Research using dissociation methodology confirm that adherence to moral rules is another important contributor to dilemma judgments (Gawronski et al., 2017), in addition to the independent effects of affect (Conway, Velasquez, Reynolds, Forstmann, & Love, 2018). Finally, researchers are beginning to identify a multitude of new processes that impact dilemma judgments, such as strategic self-presentation (e.g., Rom & Conway, 2018). Taken together, it is clear that more than two processes explain how people react to moral dilemmas.

Research on moral dilemmas has provided insight into how people deal with difficult trade-offs between being a good person (e.g., don't harm anyone) and doing good (e.g., saving lives). Examining difficult cases like these can advance our knowledge of the limits of both people's commitment to being good and doing good. That said, some critics argue that hypothetical dilemmas are uninformative because they lack mundane realism (few people face such life-and death decisions in their everyday lives, and even if they did, they would seldom encounter anything like the trolley problem).[8] Participants also report difficulty buying some assumptions such as the idea that pushing a human into the path of a trolley could effectively stop it, chafe at the limited options they are provided for responding to the situation, or find some dilemmas more amusing than alarming (Bauman, McGraw, Bartels, & Warren, 2014; Bennis, Medin, & Bartels, 2010), all of which could threaten the validity of findings using this research method.

Moral Psychology 2002–Present

Interest in moral psychology continued to grow after the watershed publications of the SIM and the dual process theories. In addition to continuing to examine the relative roles of emotion and reason in people's moral judgments, theorists also began to debate the essence of what moral concerns really are by testing ideas about underlying features that lead people to see something in moral terms (e.g., moral foundations theory, the dyadic model of morality). These programs of research continued to focus primarily on moral judgments, that is, factors that lead people to make attributions of blame (and to a lesser degree, moral praise). Other researchers branched out to study aspects of the moral self, or moral identity. Most theory and research since 2000 have worked deductively, starting with theorists' definitions of moral foundations (for example) to generate hypotheses. However, other research has taken a more inductive approach, and started with lay people's perceptions of morality instead. We devote the remainder of this chapter to reviewing these different strains of contemporary moral psychology.

Moral Foundations Theory

Moral foundations theory (MFT) was proposed later than either the SIM or the dual process theories but to some degree is built on the SIM by attempting to articulate the specific kinds of moral intuitions people might have. Building largely on insights from cultural anthropology, MFT was designed to describe broad cultural (and very soon after, ideological) differences in what people consider as moral. Based on their reading of cultural anthropology, moral foundational theorists proposed that there are five core moral concerns, or "modules," each with positive and negative valences: harm/care, fairness/cheating, loyalty/betrayal, authority/subversion, and sanctity/degradation (Haidt & Graham, 2007; Haidt & Joseph, 2004; for a review, see Graham et al., 2013; cf. Rozin, Lowery, Imada, & Haidt, 1999).[9] Modules are thought to be evolutionarily adapted response tendencies, or "little bits of input–output programming, ways of enabling fast and automatic responses to specific emotional triggers" that behave much like cognitive heuristics (Haidt & Joseph, 2004, p. 60). Moreover, "when a module takes the conduct or character of another person as its input and emits a sense of approval or disapproval, that output is a moral intuition" (p. 60), which, in turn, has a unique emotional signature. Suffering triggers compassion, corrupt behavior triggers contempt, cannibalism triggers disgust, and so on. Although the intuitive triggers themselves are thought to be universal, how people respond to them can be molded by culture or group specific norms as part of socialization (Graham, Haidt, & Nosek, 2009).

Most research inspired by MFT so far has not focused as much on testing its key premises (e.g., whether the foundations are modular or operate intuitively) but, instead, has been inspired by the early finding that liberals and conservatives endorse each of these foundations as morally relevant to different degrees. Liberals perceive harm and fairness as more important than authority, loyalty, and purity in their moral thinking. Conservatives, in contrast, view all five moral foundations as approximately equally important moral concerns (Graham et al., 2009).

Although MFT has generated a lot of research in the short time since its original formulation (for a thorough review, see Graham et al., 2013), it has also been subject to considerable criticism. Among other things, critics are concerned that the theory lacks conceptual clarity on what constitutes a foundation, about the lack of evidence to support the notion that morality is modular or innate, and even some evidence that can be marshalled to suggest they are not, in fact, modular (e.g., Suhler & Churchland, 2011). Some scholars reject the MFT's pluralist perspective and argue that all morality comes down to the dimension of harm (Gray, Young & Waytz, 2012). From a domain theory perspective, one can also argue that only the harm and fairness dimensions are truly moral, and the other foundations represent conventional beliefs instead and would fail key definitional tests of the constitutional properties of morality (e.g., authority independence, perceived universal applicability; e.g., Jost, 2009).

Still others criticize MFT for missing other vital elements of morality (e.g., Janoff-Bulman & Carnes, 2013) or have found evidence of other key moral concerns when working inductively from people's moral concerns (e.g., honesty/dishonesty, self-discipline; Hofmann, Wisneski, Brandt & Skitka, 2014). Finally, some argue that MFT does not pay enough attention to the relational context in which concerns about morality arise and play themselves out (Rai & Fiske, 2011). Progress on resolving most of these issues has been hampered by psychometric problems with the different versions of the measures developed to try to measure the moral foundations, which have weak scale reliabilities, and frequently cluster into two rather than five factors. The authors of MFT acknowledge these criticisms and discuss ways that future research can address these concerns (see Graham et al., 2013).

Despite its detractors, MFT has been incredibly generative of research, some of it yielding important new insights, such as how to more successfully frame persuasive appeals for different audiences. Liberals are more persuaded, for example, by messages framed in terms of the individuating foundations, whereas conservatives are more persuaded by messages framed in terms of the binding foundations (e.g., Day, Fiske, Downing, & Trail, 2014).

The Dyadic Model of Morality

The dyadic model of morality was proposed as an alternative to MFT. According to this theoretical perspective, mind perception is the essence of morality (Gray et al., 2012; Schein & Gray, 2018). Morality arises as a function of an awareness that there are two kinds of minds: an intending mind that belongs to moral agents and an experiencing mind that belongs to moral patients. Moral agents' minds are focused on intention, knowledge, and belief, whereas patients' minds are focused on emotions. A prototypical immoral act is one in which an agent intentionally causes harm to a patient who therefore suffers. When acts conform to this prototype, people can easily make judgments of blame. Dyadic theorists argue that because all morality can be reduced to intention and suffering, it logically follows that there is really only a single moral essence: harm. Dyadic moral theory is therefore diametrically opposed to pluralistic moral theories, such as MFT, that posit that concerns about morality can be based on other considerations absent any recognition of harm, such as purity or loyalty.

Consistent with the idea that mind perception is closely tied to perceptions of morality/immorality, people find great harm, including genocide, as more morally acceptable when they ascribe a weakened capacity of the targeted group to experience uniquely human emotions (i.e., when they infrahumanize the victims; Castano & Giner-Sorolla 2006). Conversely, people can see harm in apparently victimless acts by ascribing more mind to animals (Bastian, Costello, Loughnan, & Hodson, 2012), fetuses (Gray, Gray, & Wegner, 2007), vegetative patients (Gray, Knickman, & Wegner, 2011), and robots (Gray & Wegner, 2012; Ward, Olsen, & Wegner, 2013). In short, the perception of harm and suffering minds appears to be implicated in people's willingness to recognize moral wrongs.

An implication of the dyadic theory of morality is that whenever people make a judgment that something is morally wrong, they will also perceive an agent intentionally inflicting harm and a patient who suffers. To explicitly test this idea, Gray, Schein, and Ward (2014) examined people's reactions to four presumably victimless but impure scenarios (e.g., masturbating to a picture of one's dead sister, covering a bible with feces), four harmful transgressions (e.g., insulting a colleague's obesity, kicking a dog hard), and four neutral scenarios (e.g., eating toast). Participants were asked to judge how wrong these actions were and whether they perceived a victim under conditions of time pressure or no time pressure. Although participants did not make as strong of wrongness/victim judgments of the impure as they did the harm scenarios, they nonetheless inferred more wrongness and victims than they did in the control condition (especially under time pressure). Ostensibly harmless wrongs also activate concepts of harm and increase perceptions of suffering relative to controls (Gray et al., 2014). Results like these are argued by Gray et al. as presenting a major challenge to MFT: Rather than there being several moral foundations (not only harm, but also fairness, loyalty, authority, and impurity), Gray et al. argue that the essence of morality reduces to a core psychological perception of harm inflicted by an intentional agent on a suffering patient because even in the absence of an objective victim or clear harm, people mentally insert these aspects to facilitate dyadic completion.

Whereas MFT originated from insights from cultural anthropology, the dyadic approach to morality is more distinctively psychological. It provides an overarching framework geared toward describing the cognitive and emotional mechanisms that give rise to people's experiences with morality, and therefore connects research on morality with mainstream theories about basic cognitive and emotional processes. This approach also highlights the idea that morality is fundamentally relational, a view consistent with functionalist perspectives that view morality as a system that facilitates social interaction (e.g., Krebs, 2008; Rai & Fiske, 2011). That said, it remains unclear just how much some aspects of the theory move the field as a whole forward, given there already were very well-established programs of research that emphasize the role of personal causality and attributions in the way people assign blame (e.g., Alicke, 2000; Shaver, 1985; Weiner, 1995) and connections other theorists have already noted (e.g., Cushman, 2008; Guglielmo & Malle, 2010; Pizarro & Tannenbaum, 2011). Moral agency appears to be a catch-all label for these well-understood attributional processes.

The dyadic model's focus on moral patiency in addition to agency, however, is a more novel contribution; previous theory and research have tended to almost exclusively consider actors. Unlike actor-only models, a model that explicitly incorporates moral patiency provides a way to understand how and when people differentiate between moral versus amoral situations. Morality is relevant, for example, when someone kicks another person but not when a person kicks a bicycle tire because the former situation involves a suffering mind, and the other does not (Bauman, Wisneski, & Skitka, 2012).

The dyadic theory has been critiqued, however, on a number of grounds. One challenge is how to account for the perceived immorality of self-harm. Although dyadic theorists argue that the self serves as both the agent and patient in these situations, the critique nonetheless remains that the situation is not dyadic (see Alicke, 2012). Other issues involve how to interpret people's reactions to presumably harmless moral dilemmas. Although there is some evidence that people have implicit associations and insert the missing victim or harm into the scenarios in a form of dyadic completion (e.g., Gray et al., 2014), not everyone is persuaded by the logic or evidence offered to date (e.g., Alicke, 2012; Pizarro, Tannebaum, & Uhlmann, 2012).

A narrow emphasis on harm also ignores a host of other variables known to affect moral judgments about transgressions (e.g., outcome bias; e.g., Mazzocco, Alicke, & Davis, 2004) and does not do a good job explaining people's concerns about the broader social good, which are often expressed in moral terms (e.g., Janoff-Bulman & Carnes, 2013). Describing issues people often see in a moral light—such as same-sex marriage or immigration—in dyadic terms, for example, would require attributing minds to a nation or the body politic, something that many see as a stretch (e.g., Bauman et al., 2012; Carnes & Janoff-Bulman, 2012; Rai & Fiske, 2012).

Recent research also poses some challenges for the dyadic model. For example, a comparison of Chinese and Western samples revealed that when asked to generate examples of immorality, Westerners more frequently generated examples of harm (e.g., killing), whereas the Chinese generated examples of incivility (e.g., spitting in the street; Buchtel et al., 2015). Another more open-ended examination of the kinds of things people see in a moral light similarly found many examples that cannot be easily understood as harms and also found that people reported many more examples of beneficence than harm when asked about their everyday moral and immoral experiences (Hofmann et al., 2014). The model also does not account for people's moral strivings, or desires to both do good and be good, or the kind of morality people attach to altruism and heroism (e.g., Monroe, 2002; Walker & Frimer, 2007). For these and a variety of other reasons, the strong claim that morality is only about agents harming patients seems to be an incomplete account of the role morality plays in people's lives and moral motivations (see also Dillon & Cushman, 2012; Koleva & Haidt, 2012; Monroe, Guglielmo, & Malle, 2012; Sinnott-Armstrong, 2012).

Moral Motives Theory

Like the dyadic theory of morality, the moral motives model (MMM) was proposed as an alternative to MFT. The MMM builds on dual process theories of motivation and self-regulation to argue that people's moral motivations are fundamentally approach or avoidance oriented (Janoff-Bulman & Carnes, 2013). Proscriptive morality (rooted in avoidance motivations) is focused on what people should not do and on protecting against harms. Prescriptive morality (rooted in approach motivations), in contrast, focuses on what people should do and on providing for people's well-being and the social good. Janoff-Bulman and Carnes (2013) further argue that moral motives operate at three different regulatory levels: self-regulation, interpersonal regulation, and social or collective regulation (see Table 13.1).

This model explicitly tries to lay out the different ways morality plays out in social life. Sometimes morality is focused on self-regulation, such as restraint and industriousness. Other times, morality is focused on how we interact with individual others, such as avoiding telling falsehoods and helping others. Morality, however, also plays out on a broader societal level. At the macro level, proscriptive concerns about social order are responsive to dangers and threats to the group and oriented toward shoring up the moral perimeter. Similarly, macro-level prescriptive concerns about social justice refer to communal responsibility to advance the group's welfare (Janoff-Bulman & Carnes, 2013, 2016).

In addition to proposing that moral motives come in approach and avoidance forms, another key proposition of the MMM is that people on the political left and right are likely to be attracted to or governed more by one set of motives than another, especially at the societal level. Specifically, the MMM predicts that liberals' societal level sense of morality is likely to be more approach oriented (i.e., social justice), whereas conservatives' societal level moral motives are more likely to be avoidance oriented (i.e., social order).

There are several points of contrast between the MMM and other contemporary models of morality. First, the MMM can be contrasted with most other theories of morality by the degree to which it places theoretical weight on approach and not only avoidance moral motives. Most other contemporary theorists tend to describe morality in terms of suppression of immorality or judgments of third party transgressions and avoidance and not in terms of people's desire to approach ideals or moral goods. The MMM, in contrast, focuses as much on people's striving for the good and not only their avoidance of the bad. In addition, the MMM takes issue with one implication of MFT, specifically, that by implication, liberals do not have a morality focused on the greater group because they do not endorse the binding foundations as strongly as conservatives do. MMM argues instead that MFT overlooked a prescriptive form of group morality (i.e., a concern for social justice) in large part because MFT is generally more oriented toward describing avoidance to the relative neglect of approach moral motives.

Consistent with the idea that morality comes in both approach and avoidance forms (rather than being primarily or only about the latter), people believe that others should be equally motivated to engage in moral actions as they are to avoid engaging in immoral actions (Janoff-Bulman, Sheikh, & Hepp, 2009). Other research finds that people's morally motivated political engagement is better explained by people's hopes about the benefits of their preferred policy outcomes than by their fears about the harms of

TABLE 13.1   The Moral Motives Model

	Self (Personal)	Other (Interpersonal)	Group (Collective)
Proscriptive morality (avoidance)	Self-restraint	Not harming	Social order
Prescriptive morality (approach)	Industriousness	Helping/fairness	Social justice

their nonpreferred policy outcomes (Skitka et al., 2017). Taken together, the MMM emphasis on the idea that people are not only morally motivated by suppression or avoidance but are motivated by approach considerations with respect to themselves, their interpersonal relationships, and the common good has been a useful addition to our understanding of moral psychology.

The Moral Self and Moral Identity

Although most of the theory and research we have reviewed in this chapter so far has focused on moral judgments, another stream of inquiry has focused more on moral motivations and behavior. To a considerable degree, this branch of moral psychology began as a reaction to some of the limitations of Kolhberg's stage theory (Bergman, 2002). Damon (1984) argued, "A person's level of moral judgment does not determine the person's views on morality's place in one's life. To know how an individual deals with the latter issue, we must know about not only the person's moral beliefs but also the person's understanding of the self in relation to those beliefs" (p. 110). This line of inquiry led to the discovery that in most cases, the answer to the question of "Why be moral?" is because "that is who I am." In other words, people behave morally because they strive for self-consistency with their views of themselves as moral beings (Blasi, 1980, 1984). Consistent with this idea, people's ability to live up to internalized notions of "ought" and "should" has an important impact on their sense of personal identity (Bandura, 1986; Higgins, 1987; Steele, 1988, 1999), and individual differences in moral desires, rather than moral capacity (i.e., moral reasoning ability), account for individual differences in prosocial and moral behavior (for a review, see Hardy & Carlo, 2005).

Aquino and Reed (2002) refined the concept of moral identity into a social cognitive model of the moral self. They argued that the cognitive accessibility of people's sense of moral identity is a potent regulator of behavior (Aquino & Reed, 2002; see also Lapsley & Lasky, 2001; Narvaez, Lapsley, Hagele, & Lasky, 2006). Unlike character approaches to moral identity, social-cognitive conceptualizations of moral identity posit that situational cues can affect the relative accessibility of people's sense of moral identity and, therefore, whether they will behave morally in any given situation. Because people must balance multiple and competing identities, the regulatory influence of people's moral identities depend on whether this particular identity is currently part of their working self-concept (Markus & Kunda, 1986; Skitka, 2003). Consistent with these ideas, the relative accessibility of moral identity motivates increased prosocial and reduced antisocial behavior (for a review, see Shao, Aquino, & Freeman, 2008) and, in particular, motivates prosociality with respect to outgroup members (Reed & Aquino, 2003).

Moral Licensing and Credentials

More recent research has built on the idea that people might be motivated to engage in *moral balancing* or *moral licensing* with respect to both themselves and others. When people feel that they have been or are especially moral, they may feel a psychological license to reduce subsequent moral strivings (Miller & Effron, 2010). For example, people who reject sexist or racist statements at one time sometimes go on to subsequently endorse sexist or racist decisions shortly thereafter (Effron, Cameron, & Monin, 2009). Similarly, people who donate to one charity are more likely to spurn a request to give to second charity (Sachdeva, Iliev, & Medin, 2009), and people who reduce consumption in one domain for pro-environmental reasons sometimes offset this behavior by increasing consumption in another (Mazar & Zhong, 2010; for reviews, see Effron & Conway, 2015).

One explanation for why moral licensing occurs is that people experience momentary fluctuations their moral self-perceptions around a personalized equilibrium (Monin & Jordan, 2009; Mullen & Monin,

2016). Doing something morally good boosts the moral self-concept above equilibrium, and a subsequent transgression restores people's equilibrium. According to this view, people strive to maintain a balance of credits and debits to a psychological "bank account" (Miller & Effron, 2010; Nisan & Kurtines, 1991).

Other accounts for moral licensing effects posit that it is more a matter of self-construal than it is psychological balance. For example, one study found that reminding people that they voted for Barack Obama just before the 2008 election led them to be more willing to make racist judgments later, something that did not occur when they expressed support for a White presidential candidate or when they identified Obama as the younger of two presidential candidates without an opportunity to endorse him (Effron, Cameron, & Monin, 2009). A moral credits or balancing interpretation of this finding is that people were more comfortable expressing racist attitudes because they had been reminded that they previously had done something nonracist (i.e., they supported Obama).

A licensing via construal interpretation, however, is that people did not perceive their subsequent behavior as racist at all; after all, they couldn't be racist because (as they had just been reminded), they had supported Obama (Merritt, Effron, & Monin, 2010; Monin & Miller, 2001). It seems likely that credentials and credits models each apply in different circumstances. When behavior is clear and easily interpreted as morally positive or negative (e.g., donating money to charity), the credits account likely best explains findings, because people must balance morally questionable deeds with laudatory ones over time to feel good about themselves. Conversely, when behavior is ambiguous and open to interpretation (e.g., was that comment due to racism or other factors?), then the credentials model likely best explains findings, because people seek to establish credentials to clarify the ostensible meaning behind their ambiguous actions (Miller & Effron, 2010).

Whereas classic moral self and moral identity theory suggests that moral self-perceptions motivate moral striving (Hardy & Carlo, 2005), moral licensing work conceptualizes the moral self as a self-regulatory mechanism that helps people balance self-interest with societal interest. Researchers have identified a number of moderating factors that may influence whether moral self-perceptions increase or reduce moral strivings (e.g., Conway & Peetz, 2012), but more work remains to be done to tease out when one or the other effect is most likely to emerge (see Blanken, van de Ven, & Zeelenberg, 2015; Mullen & Monin, 2016; Simbrunner, & Schlegelmilch, 2017).

Inductive Approaches to Moral Psychology

One way to start thinking about moral psychology is to turn to philosophy or cultural anthropology for ideas to inform theory. Another approach is to start from the bottom up or inductively. An example of this approach is Buchtel et al.'s (2015) research that asked people from different cultural backgrounds to provide examples of immoral acts and to examine their similarities and differences. Unlike Westerners, Butchtel et al.'s Chinese sample did not generate examples of mostly harmful acts; they generated examples of incivility instead (e.g., littering). We briefly review two other examples of inductive approaches to studying morality and what they can tell us about the feasibility of existing theoretical accounts of moral psychology.

Everyday Morality

Almost all research examining morality has drawn heavily on well-controlled but artificial laboratory settings and a heavy reliance on hypothetical dilemmas. In response to this fact, Hofmann, Wisneski, Brandt, and Skitka (2014) embarked on a large-scale effort to use ecological momentary assessment to explore how morality plays out in people's everyday lives. The goal of the project was to explore how often people commit, witness, or learn about moral and immoral acts in their daily lives; what kinds of experiences they label as moral and immoral; how well existing taxonomies (e.g., MFT) can account for these experiences; and a variety of other questions, such as whether committing a moral act boosts people's momentary sense of happiness and sense of purpose. A large ($N = 1,252$) demographically and geographically diverse Western sample was randomly signaled five times daily on their smartphones for three days between 9 AM and 9 PM. At each assessment, participants indicated whether they committed, were the target of, witnessed, or learned about a moral or immoral act within the last hour (they could also respond "none of the above"). For each moral or immoral event, they described via text entry what the event was about and provided contextual information (e.g., location, relationship) and rated a number of emotions, happiness, and sense of moral purpose, yielding 13,240 reports. Participants were most likely to report committing moral acts and learning about immoral acts. The reported acts were more likely to be moral than immoral, and the majority emphasized acts of caring, followed by harm and unfairness. Although most events could be classified in terms of moral foundations, this research also found reliably high mentions of events that could not be easily understood in the original MFT terms, including examples of liberty/oppression,[10] honesty/dishonesty, and self-discipline or the lack of it.[11]

Political orientation was associated with the examples of immorality/morality people reported, but these differences were more a matter of nuance than stark contrast. Religious and nonreligious participants did not differ in the likelihood or kind of committed moral and immoral acts, contrary to stereotypes of religious people as morally superior. Finally, being the target of moral or immoral actions had the strongest impact on people's sense of happiness, whereas committing moral or immoral acts had the strongest impact on people's sense of purpose.

Taken together, this research seems to support the idea that morality comes in more than one basic form (consistent with the basic premise of MFT and in contrast to the dyadic model), even if harm and beneficence are the dominant components of everyday morality. Moreover, people's everyday experiences of morality/immorality are equally if not more likely to be positively valenced as they are negatively valenced (consistent with the emphasis of MMM on approach and not only avoidance moral orientations).

Moral Conviction

Another inductive approach to the study of morality has examined the antecedents and consequences of the perception that an attitude is a reflection of one's moral beliefs. People vary in the degree to which they report that their attitudes reflect moral convictions, something even true of issues we tend to think of as normatively moral, such as abortion (for a review, see Skitka, 2014). Someone might have a prochoice position on abortion, for example, simply because she prefers to have a backup form of birth control and not because of any moral attachment to the issue. Someone else, however, may see her position on this issue as a reflection of her core moral beliefs. This variation in the moral significance people attach to certain issues has a number of social and political consequences. People higher in moral conviction about a given issue are more intolerant of those who do not share their position on the issue, are unwilling to compromise or accept procedural solutions about the issue, are inoculated against the normal pressures to either conform or obey authorities (including the law) with respect to this issue, and are more willing to accept violence if it serves the perceivers' moralized end. Consistent with domain theory predictions, attitudes that are experienced as moral convictions are perceived as more universally and objectively true than attitudes that are weak moral convictions (for reviews, see Skitka, 2010, Skitka & Morgan, 2014).

Recent research has attempted to begin to understand how attitudes become moralized. Targeted emotional cues experienced at conscious levels of awareness (e.g., exposure to photos of aborted fetuses), but not incidental emotional cues (e.g., exposure to photos of mutilated animals or people, or toilets overflowing feces) or cues presented at subliminal levels of awareness, led to increased moralization of abortion attitudes (Wisneski & Skitka, 2017). Other research that examined attitudes toward candidates over the 2012 presidential election cycle found that emotions (enthusiasm and hostility) predicted increased moralization of preferred and nonpreferred candidates, respectively. Perceived harms and benefits associated with electing each candidate, however, were only consequences of increased moralization, rather than antecedents of it (Brandt, Wisneski, & Skitka, 2015). Taken together, these results challenge the idea that morality is necessarily intuitive (as predicted by the SIM and MFT) or exclusively rooted in perceptions of harm (as predicted by the dyadic model; see also Skitka, Wisneski, & Brandt, 2018).

Issues of Replicability

Finally, let us briefly consider issues of replicability in moral psychology. Like work in the rest of the field, some (particularly older) research in moral psychology has suffered from relatively slim samples, incomplete reporting, lack of preregistration, and other features that increase the likelihood of introducing erroneous findings into the published literature. In a few high-profile cases, ostensibly well-established effects (e.g., Sachdeva, Iliev, & Medin, 2009; Schnall, Benton, & Harvey, 2008) have been challenged by null findings in replication studies (e.g., Blanken, van de Ven, Zeelenberg, & Meijers, 2014; Johnson, Cheung, & Donnellan, 2014). However, such cases have typically been followed up with meta-analytic investigations that clarify effect sizes and the conditions or domains where effects appear stronger or weaker (e.g., Blanken, van de Ven, & Zeelenberg, 2015; Landy & Goodwin, 2015). Moreover, it seems the majority of work in moral psychology does not suffer from considerable replication issues, because many independent laboratories document similar findings. The basic pattern of responding to trolley and footbridge moral dilemmas, for example, has been replicated dozens (if not hundreds) of times and emerges for children as young as three (Pellizzoni et al., 2010).

One possibility for why much of the work in moral psychology seems replicable might relate to the fact that moral concerns appear inherently interesting and tend to matter a great deal to lay people. Research on moral topics, therefore, may benefit from increased attention to the focal information and reduced extraneous factors than obscure effects in research on other issues. Consistent with this possibility, a number of findings suggest that moral information carries a powerful influence over judgments and behavior that often trumps nonmoral information (e.g., Goodwin, Piazza, & Rozin, 2014; Skitka, Bauman, & Sargis, 2005). Certainly, there is always room to improve the quality of science, and all claims should be approached with a degree of skepticism. That said, the primary challenges in moral psychology are disagreements over theoretical and conceptual issues rather than disagreements about methodological decisions or the reliability of results.

Discussion and Conclusion

Our goal in this chapter was to provide readers with a broad overview of theory and research in moral psychology. There is almost an embarrassment of empirical and theoretical riches in moral psychology, including much more than we could adequately cover in the page limits here. One thing that is clear from this review is how incredibly active and dynamic the field currently is; new theories, approaches, and findings emerge almost daily, especially since the turn of the millennium. It is a very exciting time to study moral psychology, and each new contribution reveals new factors and considerations that need further study.

As we noted at the outset of this chapter, moral psychology is currently better characterized as a field with competing perspectives rather than theoretical or empirical consensus. The lack of consensus and the speed with which new theoretical perspectives have emerged in the field presents both advantages and disadvantages. On the one hand, the field can feel fragmented and difficult to synthesize into a coherent whole. What, for example, do moral licensing effects have in common with moral judgments or moral convictions? How does what we know about the psychology of moral dilemmas inform or have in common with MFT or the MMM?

On the other hand, each new theoretical perspective emphasizes slightly different aspects and elements that generally turn out to be important. The idea that morality might not only be about deliberative reasoning, for example, has led to a much richer and nuanced understanding of the independent and intersecting roles of reason, intuition, and emotion in moral judgment. The idea that mind perception is intimately involved in moral judgment led to taking into account the perspective of not only the agent of harm but also the target of it in the dyadic model of morality. The emphasis on harm in the dyadic model and on social order in MFT, however, led others to posit that theory and research might be neglecting the prescriptive and approach side of morality and people's striving to be good, which was subsequently incorporated into the MMM. Even if this period of theory and research might be characterized as reactionary or fragmented, it has nonetheless been incredibly generative—the field as a whole is perhaps only beginning the grasp the full complexity of what it is attempting to describe. After all, humans attach moral significance to behavior, decisions, aspects of character, emotions, and more. Humans both reason about and intuit morality. Morality is perceived by many to have universal elements but nonetheless varies in form across cultures. Morality involves minds, emotions, convictions, and values and is something we use to regulate ourselves, our interpersonal conduct, and how we define the collective good.

In other words, the task of moral psychology is *big*. One could say it is as big as the elephant encountered in John Godfrey Saxe's parable of the blind men of Indostan. Each man was asked to approach and describe an elephant. Because each examined a different part of the elephant they came to very different conclusions about the fundamental character of "elephantness" ("It is very like a tree," "a wall," or "a snake"). The tree, wall, and snake descriptions were each accurate but limited perspectives on the elephant; one man accurately describes the elephant's leg, another its body, and yet another, its trunk. We suspect morality researchers are at a similar stage as the men from Indostan in getting a sense of what, exactly, we are studying: As a field, we are still in the process of assembling descriptions of a very big and complex animal. Only with time will we be able to bring these descriptions together into a broader theoretical whole.

Acknowledgements

We would like to thank Brittany Hanson, Allison Mueller, Dan Wisneski, and Bilge Yalçindağ for their helpful comments on an earlier draft of this manuscript.

Notes

1. The reasons people provide for their moral judgments determines their stage, not the content of their moral judgment (i.e., their specific position on something like abortion is irrelevant).

2. When authorities condone instrumental harm, such as interrogating terrorist suspects, such harm can seem more permissible (Kelly, Stich, Haley, Eng, & Fessler, 2007), but not when such harm also involves perceived rights violations (Sousa, Holbrook, & Piazza, 2009).

3. Haidt, Bjorklund, and Murphy (2000) has never been published, despite the paper being widely cited as evidence in support of moral intuitionism, largely because the research is more of a demonstration than an actual study or experiment: Variables were not manipulated, and hypotheses were not tested.

4. According *deontological ethics*, the morality of an action is determined by its intrinsic nature; harming one person to benefit others treats is fundamentally degrading and must be avoided at all costs (Kant, 1785/1959). Hence, decisions to reject causing harm on moral dilemmas are frequently referred to as deontological judgments. According utilitarian ethics (a variant of consequentialism), the morality of an action depends on the consequences (utility) it produces (Mill, 1861/1998). Actions that produce net positive outcomes are morally acceptable, even if they entail causing harm. Hence, decisions to accept causing harm to maximize outcomes on moral dilemmas are frequently referred to as utilitarian judgments.

5. One challenge in this area of research is the tendency not to conceptually distinguish between (a) the actual judgments people make, (b) the psychological processes theorized to drive judgments, and (c) the philosophical concepts those judgments are said to align with. Rejecting harm may be consistent with deontological ethics, for example, but this does not mean it was caused by philosophical considerations. Psychological processes that have nothing to do with rational adherence to deontological moral rules may lead to harm rejection judgments. Likewise, accepting outcome-maximizing harm is consistent with utilitarian ethics, but such judgments may not be caused by an impartial focus on overall utility (e.g., Kahane, 2015).

6. Other examples of impersonal dilemmas include the *fumes* dilemma (Should one redirect deadly fumes to a room with one person instead of five?) and the *submarine* dilemma (Should the captain of a damaged submarine lock a crewmember out of the oxygenated compartment to save enough oxygen for the rest of the crew?) whereas other personal dilemmas include the *crying baby* dilemma (Should one smoother an infant to prevent its cries from summoning murderous soldiers?) and the *vitamins* dilemma (Should one kill and harvest the kidneys of one jungle adventurer to save five others from a rare disease?).

7. Recently, Gawronski et al. (2015, 2017) noted that deontological judgments in both conventional and process dissociation dilemmas always require avoiding causing harm. Hence, some participants currently classified as making deontological decisions may have simply wished to avoid personal involvement. Hence, they expanded upon the process dissociation framework to develop a CNI model that distinguishes between decisions that maximize Consequences, follow deontological Norms, of result from general Inaction. This model is useful for disentangling different processes that the process dissociation deontological parameter cannot distinguish. Yet, it is not directly comparable to previous dilemma research, which focuses on decisions to cause outcome-maximizing harm. The CNI model combines norms to refrain from causing harm with norms to save someone from harm, even though Kant (1785/1959) and laypeople view these norms as qualitatively distinct (Janoff-Bulman, Sheikh, & Hepp, 2009).

8. However, when people in history have faced such dilemmas, the consequences have been enormous, such as when Truman deliberated the decision to use atomic weapons to prevent further war casualties (Gosnell, 1980).

9. Haidt et al. have been open to expanding the number of foundations to other possibilities including liberty/oppression, efficiency/waste, and ownership/theft. Criteria for foundationhood are that the premise has to be observed in many cultures, and there has to be a Darwinian explanation for why humans may have developed these concerns (Graham et al., 2013).

10. Later versions of MFT have included liberty as a candidate foundation (Haidt, 2012).

11. Especially given the emphasis on studying reactions to moral dilemmas to understand moral psychology, it may be somewhat surprising that not one participant in this study brought up a run away trolley, incest, or chicken carcasses ☺.

References

Alicke, M. D. (2000). Culpable control and the psychology of blame. *Psychological Bulletin, 126,* 556–574.

Alicke, M. D. (2012). Self-injuries, harmless wrongdoing, and morality. *Psychological Inquiry, 23,* 125–128.

Amit, E., & Greene, J. D. (2012). You see, the ends don't justify the means: Visual imagery and moral judgment. *Psychological Science, 23,* 861–868.

Aquino, K., & Reed, A., II. (2002). The self-importance of moral identity. *Journal of Personality and Social Psychology, 83,* 1423–1440.

Bandura, A. (1986). *Social foundations of thought and action: A social cognitive view.* Englewood Cliffs, NJ: Prentice-Hall.

Baron, J. (1994). Nonconsequentialist decisions. *Behavioral and Brain Sciences, 17,* 1–10.

Bartels, D. M., & Pizarro, D. A. (2011). The mismeasure of morals: Antisocial personality traits predict utilitarian responses to moral dilemmas. *Cognition, 121,* 154–161.

Baron, J., Gürçay, B., Moore, A. B., & Starcke, K. (2012). Use of a Rasch model to predict response times to utilitarian moral dilemmas. *Synthese, 189,* 107–117.

Bastian, B., Costello, K., Loughnan, S., & Hodson, G. (2012). When closing the human-animal divide expands moral concern: The importance of framing. *Social Psychological and Personality Science, 3,* 421–429.

Bauman, C. W., McGraw, A. P., Bartels, D. M., & Warren, C. (2014). Revisiting external validity: Concerns about trolley problems and other sacrificial dilemmas in moral psychology. *Social and Personality Compass, 8–9,* 536–554.

Bauman, C. W., Wisneski, D. C., & Skitka, L. J. (2012). Cubist consequentialism: The pros and cons of an agent-patient template for morality. *Psychological Inquiry, 23,* 129–133.

Bennis, W. M., Medin, D. L., & Bartels, D. M. (2010). The costs and benefits of calculation and moral rules. *Perspectives on Psychological Science, 5,* 187–202.

Bergman, R. (2002). Why be moral? A conceptual model from developmental psychology. *Human development, 45,* 104–124.

Berkowitz, L. (1972). Social norms, feelings, and other factors affecting helping behavior and altruism. In L. Berkowitz (Ed.), *Advances in experimental social psychology* (Vol. 6, pp. 62–106). New York, NY: Academic Press.

Blanken, I., van de Ven, N., & Zeelenberg, M. (2015). A meta-analytic review of moral licensing. *Personality and Social Psychology Bulletin, 41,* 540–558.

Blanken, I., van de Ven, N., Zeelenberg, M., & Meijers, M. H. (2014). Three attempts to replicate the moral licensing effect. *Social Psychology, 45,* 232–238.

Blasi, A. (1980). Bridging moral cognition and moral action: A critical review of the literature. *Psychological Bulletin, 88,* 1–45.

Blasi, A. (1984). Moral identity: Its role in moral functioning. In W. M. Kurtines & J. L. Gewirtz (Eds.), *Morality, moral behavior, and moral development* (pp. 128–139). New York, NY: Wiley.

Bloom, P. (2013). *Just babies: The origins of good and evil.* New York, NY: Crown.

Brandt, M. J., Wisneski, D. C., & Skitka, L. J. (2015). Moralization and the 2012 US presidential election campaign. *Journal of Social and Political Psychology, 3,* 211–237.

Buchtel, E. E., Guan, Y., Peng, Q., Su, Y., Sang, B., Chen, S. X., & Bond, M. H. (2015). Immorality east and west: Are immoral behaviors especially harmful, or especially uncivilized? *Personality and Social Psychology Bulletin, 41,* 1382–1394.

Carnes, N., & Janoff-Bulman, R. (2012). Harm, help, and the nature of (im) moral (in) action. *Psychological Inquiry, 23,* 137–142.

Castano, E., & Giner-Sorolla, R. (2006). Not quite human: Infrahumanization in response to collective responsibility for intergroup killing. *Journal of Personality and Social Psychology, 90,* 804–818.

Conway, P., & Gawronski, B. (2013). Deontological and utilitarian inclinations in moral decision-making: A process dissociation approach. *Journal of Personality and Social Psychology, 104,* 216–235.

Conway, P., Goldstein-Greenwood, J., Polacek, D., & Greene, J. D. (2018). Sacrificial utilitarian judgments do reflect concern for the greater good: Conceptual clarification and empirical evidence concerns from via process dissociation and the judgments of philosophers. *Cognition, 179*, 241–265.

Conway, P., & Peetz, J. (2012). When does feeling moral actually make you a better person? Conceptual abstraction moderates whether past moral deeds motivate consistency or compensatory behavior. *Personality and Social Psychology Bulletin, 38*(7), 907–919.

Conway, P., Velasquez, K., Reynolds, C., Forstmann, M., & Love, E. (2018). *Affect, deliberation, rules, and sentiment: Clarifying different orientations towards moral dilemma decision-making.* Unpublished manuscript.

Crockett, M. J. (2013). Models of morality. *Trends in Cognitive Sciences, 17*, 363–366.

Cushman, F. (2008). Crime and punishment: Distinguishing the roles of causal and intentional analyses in moral judgment. *Cognition, 108*, 353–380

Cushman, F. (2013). Action, outcome, and value a dual-system framework for morality. *Personality and Social Psychology Review, 17*, 273–292.

Damon, W. (1984). Self-understanding and moral development from childhood to adolescence. In W. M. Kurtines & J. L. Gerwitz (Eds.), *Morality, moral behavior, and moral development* (pp. 109–127). New York, NY: Wiley.

Day, M. V., Fiske, S. T., Downing, E. L., & Trail, T. E. (2014). Shifting liberal and conservative attitudes using moral foundations theory. *Personality and Social Psychology Bulletin, 40*, 1559–1573.

Dillon, K. D., & Cushman, F. (2012). Agent, Patient . . . ACTION! What the dyadic model misses. *Psychological Inquiry, 23*, 150–154.

Effron, D. A., Cameron, J. S., & Monin, B. (2009). Endorsing Obama licenses favoring Whites. *Journal of Experimental Social Psychology, 45*, 590–593.

Effron, D. A., & Conway, P. (2015). When virtue leads to villainy: Advances in research on moral self-licensing. *Current Opinion in Psychology, 6*, 32–35.

Foot, P. (1967). The problem of abortion and the doctrine of double effect. *Oxford Review, 5*, 5–15.

Gamez-Djokic, M., & Molden, D. (2016). Beyond affective influences on deontological moral judgment: The role of motivations for prevention in the moral condemnation of harm. *Personality and Social Psychology Bulletin, 42*, 1522–1537.

Gawronski, B., Conway, P., Armstrong, J., Friesdorf, R., & Hütter, M. (2015). Moral dilemma judgments: Disentangling deontological inclinations, utilitarian inclinations, and general action tendencies. In J. P. Forgas, P. A. M. Van Lange, & L. Jussim (Eds.), *Social psychology of morality*. New York, NY: Psychology Press.

Gawronski, B., Conway, P., Armstrong, J., Friesdorf, R., & Hütter, M. (2017). Consequences, norms, and generalized inaction in moral dilemmas: The CNI model of moral decision-making. *Journal of Personality and Social Psychology, 113*, 343–376.

Gilligan, C. (1982). *In a different voice*. Boston, MA: Harvard University Press.

Gleichgerrcht, E., & Young, L. (2013). Low levels of empathic concern predict utilitarian moral judgment. *PLoS One, 8*, e60418.

Goodwin, G. P., Piazza, J., & Rozin, P. (2014). Moral character predominates in person perception and evaluation. *Journal of Personality and Social Psychology, 106*, 148–168.

Gosnell, H. F. (1980). *Truman's crises: A political biography of Harry S. Truman*. Westport, CT: Greenwood.

Gouldner, A. W. (1960). The norm of reciprocity: A preliminary statement. *American Sociological Review, 25*, 161–178.

Graham, J., Haidt, J., Koleva, S., Motyl, M., Iyer, R., Wojcik, S. P., & Ditto, P. H. (2013). Moral foundations theory: The pragmatic validity of moral pluralism. In *Advances in experimental social psychology* (Vol. 47, pp. 55–130). Academic Press.

Graham, J., Haidt, J., & Nosek, B. A. (2009). Liberals and conservatives rely on different sets of moral foundations. *Journal of Personality and Social Psychology, 96*, 1029–1046.

Gray, H. M., Gray, K., & Wegner, D. M. (2007). Dimensions of mind perception. *Science, 315*, 619–619.

Gray, K., & Keeney, J. E. (2015). Impure or just weird? Scenario sampling bias raises questions about the foundation of morality. *Social Psychological and Personality Science, 6,* 859–868.

Gray, K., Knickman, T. A., & Wegner, D. M. (2011). More dead than dead: Perceptions of persons in the persistent vegetative state. *Cognition, 121,* 275–280.

Gray, K., Schein, C., & Ward, A. F. (2014). The myth of harmless wrongs in moral cognition: Automatic dyadic completion from sin to suffering. *Journal of Experimental Psychology: General, 143,* 1600–1615.

Gray, K., & Wegner, D. M. (2012). Feeling robots and human zombies: Mind perception and the uncanny valley. *Cognition, 125*(1), 125–130.

Gray, K., Young, L., & Waytz, A. (2012). Mind perception is the essence of morality. *Psychological Inquiry, 23,* 101–124.

Greene, J. D., Cushman, F. A., Stewart, L. E., Lowenberg, K., Nystrom, L. E., & Cohen, J. D. (2009). Pushing moral buttons: The interaction between personal force and intention in moral judgment. *Cognition, 111,* 364–371.

Greene, J. D., Nystrom, L. E., Engell, A. D., Darley, J. M., & Cohen, J. D. (2004). The neural bases of cognitive conflict and control in moral judgment. *Neuron, 44,* 389–400.

Greene, J. D., Sommerville, R. B., Nystrom, L. E., Darley, J. M., & Cohen, J. D. (2001). An fMRI investigation of emotional engagement in moral judgment. *Science, 293,* 2105–2108.

Guglielmo, S., & Malle, B. F. (2010). Can unintended side effects be intentional? Resolving a controversy over intentionality and morality. *Personality and Social Psychology Bulletin, 36,* 1635–1647.

Haidt, J. (2001). The emotional dog and its rational tail: A social intuitionist approach to moral judgment. *Psychological Review, 108,* 814–834.

Haidt, J., & Graham, J. (2007). When morality opposes justice: Conservatives have moral intuitions that liberals may not recognize. *Social Justice Research, 20,* 98–116.

Haidt, J., Bjorklund, F., & Murphy, S. (2000). *Moral dumbfounding: When intuition finds no reason.* Unpublished manuscript, University of Virginia.

Haidt, J., & Joseph, C. (2004). Intuitive ethics: How innately prepared intuitions generate culturally variable virtues. *Daedalus, 133*(4), 55–66.

Haidt, J., Koller, S. H., & Dias, M. G. (1993). Affect, culture, and morality, or is it wrong to eat your dog? *Journal of Personality and Social Psychology, 65,* 613–628.

Haidt, J., Rozin, P., McCauley, C., & Imada, S. (1997). Body, psyche, and culture: The relationship between disgust and morality. *Psychology and Developing Societies, 9,* 107–131.

Hardy, S. A., & Carlo, G. (2005). Identity as a source of moral motivation. *Human Development, 48,* 232–256.

Hauser, M. D. (2006). *Moral minds: How nature designed our universal sense of right and wrong.* New York, NY: Harper Collins

Higgins, E. T. (1987). Self-discrepancy: A theory relating self and affect. *Psychological Review, 94,* 141–153.

Hofmann, W., Wisneski, D. C., Brandt, M. J., & Skitka, L. J. (2014). Morality in everyday life. *Science, 345,* 1340–1343.

Hollos, M., Leis, P., & Turiel, E. (1986). Social reasoning in Ijo children and adolescents in Nigerian communities. *Journal of Cross-Cultural Psychology, 17,* 352–376.

Huebner, B., Lee, J. J., & Hauser, M. D. (2010). The moral-conventional distinction in mature moral competence. *Journal of Cognition and Culture, 10,* 1–26.

Hume, D. (1978). *A treatise of human nature.* Mineola, NY: Dover. (Original work published 1888)

Jacobson, D. (2012). Moral dumbfounding and moral stupefaction. In M. Timmons (Ed.) Oxford studies in normative ethics (Vol. 2, pp. 289–316). Oxford, England: Oxford University Press.

Janoff-Bulman, R., & Carnes, N. C. (2013). Surveying the moral landscape: Moral motives and group-based moralities. *Personality and Social Psychology Review, 17,* 219–236.

Janoff-Bulman, R., & Carnes, N. C. (2016). Social justice and social order: Binding moralities across the political spectrum. *PLoS One, 11,* e0152479.

Janoff-Bulman, R., Sheikh, S., & Hepp, S. (2009). Proscriptive versus prescriptive morality: Two faces of moral regulation. *Journal of Personality and Social Psychology, 96,* 521–537.

Johnson, D. J., Cheung, F., & Donnellan, M. B. (2014). Does cleanliness influence moral judgments? A direct replication of Schnall, Benton, and Harvey (2008). *Social Psychology, 45,* 209–215.

Jost, J. T. (2009). *Group morality and ideology: Left and right, right and wrong.* Paper presented at the annual Society for Personality and Social Psychology annual conference, Tampa, FL.

Kahane, G. (2015). Sidetracked by trolleys: Why sacrificial moral dilemmas tell us little (or nothing) about utilitarian judgment. *Social Neuroscience, 10,* 551–560.

Kahane, G., Everett, J. A., Earp, B. D., Caviola, L., Faber, N. S., Crockett, M. J., & Savulescu, J. (2018). Beyond sacrificial harm: A two-dimensional model of utilitarian psychology. *Psychological Review, 125,* 131–164.

Kahane, G., Everett, J. A. C., Earp, B. D., Farias, M., & Savulescu, J. (2015). "Utilitarian" judgments in sacrificial moral dilemmas do not reflect impartial concern for the greater good. *Cognition, 134,* 193–209.

Kant, I. (1785/1959). *Foundation of the metaphysics of morals* (L. W. Beck, Trans.). Indianapolis, IN: Bobbs-Merrill.

Kelly, D., Stich, S., Haley, K., Eng, S., & Fessler, D. (2007). Harm, affect, and the moral/ conventional distinction. *Mind and Language, 22,* 117–131.

Koenigs, M., Young, L., Adolphs, R., Tranel, D., Cushman, F., Hauser, M., & Damasio, A. (2007). Damage to the prefrontal cortex increases utilitarian moral judgments. *Nature, 446,* 908–911.

Kohlberg, L. (1969). Stage and sequence: The cognitive–developmental approach to socialization. In D. A. Goslin (Ed.), *Handbook of socialization theory and research.* (pp. 347–480). Chicago, IL: Rand McNally.

Kohlberg, L. (1981). *Essays on moral development, Vol. 1: The philosophy of moral development.* San Francisco, CA: Harper & Row.

Koleva, S., & Haidt, J. (2012). Let's use Einstein's safety razor, not Occam's Swiss army knife or Occam's chainsaw. *Psychological Inquiry, 23,* 175–178.

Krebs, D. L. (2008). Morality: An evolutionary account. *Perspectives on Psychological Science, 3,* 149–172.

Landy, J. F., & Goodwin, G. P. (2015). Does incidental disgust amplify moral judgment? A meta-analytic review of experimental evidence. *Perspectives on Psychological Science, 10,* 518–536.

Lapsley, D. K., & Laskey, B. (2001). Prototypic moral character. *Identity, 1,* 345–363.

Laupa, M. (1994). Who's in charge? Preschool children's concepts of authority. *Early Childhood Research Quarterly, 9,* 1–17.

Markus, H., & Kunda, Z. (1986). Stability and malleability of the self-concept. *Journal of Personality and Social Psychology, 41,* 858–866.

Mazar, N., & Zhong, C. B. (2010). Do green products make us better people? *Psychological Science, 21,* 494–498.

Mazzocco, P. J., Alicke, M. D., & Davis, T. L. (2004). On the robustness of outcome bias: No constraint by prior culpability. *Basic and Applied Social Psychology, 26,* 131–146.

Merritt, A. C., Effron, D. A., & Monin, B. (2010). Moral self-licensing: When being good frees us to be bad. *Social and Personality Psychology Compass, 4,* 344–357.

Mikhail, J., (2007). Universal moral grammar: theory, evidence and the future. Trends in Cognitive Science, 11, 143–52.

Mill, J. S. (1998). *Utilitarianism* (R. Crisp, Ed.). New York, NY: Oxford University Press. (Original work published 1861)

Miller, D. T., & Effron, D. A. (2010). Psychological license: When it is needed and how it functions. In *Advances in experimental social psychology* (M. P. Zanna & J. M. Olson, Eds., Vol. 43, pp. 117–158). San Diego, CA: Academic Press/Elsevier.

Miller, R. M., Hannikainen, I. A., & Cushman, F. A. (2014). Bad actions or bad outcomes? Differentiating Affective contributions to the moral condemnation of harm. *Emotion, 14,* 573–587.

Moore, A. B., Clark, B. A., & Kane, M. J. (2008). Who shalt not kill? Individual differences in working memory capacity, executive control, and moral judgment. *Psychological Science, 19,* 549–557.

Monin, B., & Jordan, A. H. (2009). The dynamic moral self: A social psychological perspective. In D. Narvaez & D. K. Lapsley (Eds.), *Personality, identity, and character: Explorations in moral psychology* (pp. 341–354). Cambridge, England: Cambridge University Press.

Monin, B, & Miller, D. T. (2001). Moral credentials and the expression of prejudice. *Journal of Personality and Social Psychology, 81*, 33–43.

Monroe, A. E., Guglielmo, S., & Malle, B. F. (2012). Morality goes beyond mind perception. *Psychological Inquiry, 23*, 179–184.

Monroe, K. R. (2002). *The hand of compassion: Portraits of moral choice in the holocaust.* Princeton NJ: Princeton University Press.

Mullen, E., & Monin, B. (2016). Consistency versus licensing effects of past moral behavior. *Annual Review of Psychology, 67*, 363–385.

Narvaez, D., Lapsley, D. K., Hagele, S., & Lasky, B. (2006). Moral chronicity and social information processing: Tests of a social cognitive approach to the moral personality. *Journal of Research in Personality, 40*, 966–985.

Nichols, S., & Mallon, R. (2006). Moral dilemmas and moral rules. *Cognition, 100*, 530–542.

Nisan, M., & Kurtines, W. (1991). The moral balance model: Theory and research extending our understanding of moral choice and deviation. In W. M. Kurtines & J. L. Gewirtz (Eds.), *Handbook of moral behavior and development. Vol. 3: Application* (pp. 213–249). Hillsdale, NJ: Erlbaum.

Nucci, L. P., & Turiel, E. (1978). Social interactions and the development of social concepts in preschool children. *Child Development, 49*, 400–407.

Paxton, J. M., & Greene, J. D. (2010). Moral reasoning: Hints and allegations. *Topics in Cognitive Science, 2*, 511–527.

Pellizzoni, S., Siegal, M., & Surian, L. (2010). The contact principle and utilitarian moral judgments in young children. *Developmental Science, 13*, 265–270.

Piaget, J. (1932/1965). *The moral judgment of the child.* (M. Gabain, Trans.) New York, NY: Free Press. (Original work published 1932).

Pizarro, D. A., & Tannenbaum, D. (2011). Bringing character back: How the motivation to evaluate character influences judgments of moral blame. In M. Mikulincer & P. R. Shaver (Eds.), *The social psychology of morality: Exploring the causes of good and evil* (pp. 91–98). Washington DC: American Psychological Association.

Pizarro, D. A., Tannenbaum, D., & Uhlmann, E. (2012). Mindless, harmless, and blameworthy. *Psychological Inquiry, 23*, 185–188.

Rai, T. S., & Fiske, A. P. (2011). Moral psychology is relationship regulation: Moral motives for unity, hierarchy, equality, and proportionality. *Psychological Review, 118*, 57–75.

Rai, T. S., & Fiske, A. P. (2012). Beyond harm, intention, and dyads: Relationship regulation, virtuous violence, and metarelational morality. *Psychological Inquiry, 23*(2), 189–193.

Reed, A., II, & Aquino, K. F. (2003). Moral identity and the expanding circle of moral regard toward out-groups. *Journal of Personality and Social Psychology, 84*, 1270.

Rest, J. R., Narvaez, D., Thoma, S. J., & Bebeau, M. J. (1999). *Postconventional moral thinking: A neo-Kohlbergian approach.* Mahwah, NJ: Erlbaum.

Reynolds, C., & Conway, P. (2018). Affective concern for bad outcomes does contribute to the moral condemnation of harm after all. *Emotion, 18*, 1009–1023.

Rom, S., & Conway, P. (2018). The strategic moral self: Self-presentation shapes moral dilemma judgments. *Journal of Experimental Social Psychology, 74*, 24–37.

Royzman, E. B., Kim, K., & Leeman, R. F. (2015). The curious tale of Julie and Mark: Unraveling the moral dumbfounding effect. *Judgment and Decision Making, 10*, 296–313.

Rozin, P., & Fallon, A. E. (1987). A perspective on disgust. *Psychological Review, 94*, 23–41.

Rozin, P., Lowery, L., Imada, S., & Haidt, J. (1999). The CAD triad hypothesis: a mapping between three moral emotions (contempt, anger, disgust) and three moral codes (community, autonomy, divinity). *Journal of Personality and Social Psychology, 76*, 574–586.

Sachdeva, S., Iliev, R., & Medin, D.L. (2009). Sinning saints and saintly sinners: The paradox of moral self-regulation. *Psychological Science, 20*, 523–528.

Schein, C., & Gray, K. (2018). The theory of dyadic morality: Reinventing moral judgment by redefining harm. *Personality and Social Psychology Review, 22,* 32–70.

Schnall, S., Benton, J., & Harvey, S. (2008). With a clean conscience: Cleanliness reduces the severity of moral judgments. *Psychological Science, 19,* 1219–1222.

Schnall, S., Haidt, J., Clore, G. L., & Jordan, A. H. (2008). Disgust as embodied moral judgment. *Personality and Social Psychology Bulletin, 34,* 1096–1109.

Shao, D., Aquino, K., & Freeman, D. (2008). Beyond moral reasoning: A review of moral identity research and its implications for business ethics. *Business Ethics Quarterly, 18,* 513–540.

Shaver, K.G. (1985). *The attribution of blame: Causality, responsibility, and blameworthiness.* New York, NY: Springer.

Simbrunner, P., & Schlegelmilch, B. B. (2017). Moral licensing: a culture-moderated meta-analysis. *Management Review Quarterly, 67*(4), 201–225.

Simpson, E. L. (1974). Moral development research. *Human Development, 17,* 81–106.

Sinnott-Armstrong, W. (2012). Does morality have an essence? *Psychological Inquiry, 23,* 194–197.

Skitka, L. J. (2003). Of different minds: An accessible identity model of justice reasoning. *Personality and Social Psychology Review, 7,* 286–297.

Skitka, L. J. (2010). The psychology of moral conviction. *Social and Personality Psychology Compass, 4,* 267–281.

Skitka, L. J. (2014). The social and political implications of moral conviction. *Political Psychology, 35*(Supp 1), 95–110.

Skitka, L. J., Bauman, C. W., & Sargis, E. G. (2005). Moral conviction: Another contributor to attitude strength or something more? *Journal of Personality and Social Psychology, 88,* 895–917.

Skitka, L. J., Hanson, B. E., & Wisneski, D.C. (2017). Utopian hopes or dystopian fears? Understanding the motivational underpinnings of morally motivated political engagement. *Personality and Social Psychological Bulletin, 43,* 177–190.

Skitka, L. J., & Morgan, G. S. (2014). The social and political implications of moral conviction. In H. Lavine (Ed.), *Advances in political psychology* (pp. 148–166). New York, NY: Bloomsbury Academic Press.

Skitka, L. J., Wisneski, D. C., & Brandt, M. J. (2018). Attitude moralization: Probably not intuitive or rooted in perceptions of harm. *Current Directions in Psychological Science, 27,* 9–13.

Smetana, J. (1981). Preschool children's conceptions of moral and social rules. *Child Development, 52,* 1333–1336.

Smetana, J. (1984). Toddlers' social interactions regarding moral and conventional transgressions. *Child Development, 55,* 1767–1776.

Smetana, J. (2006). Social-cognitive domain theory: Consistencies and variations in children's moral and social judgments. In M. Killen & J. Smetana (Eds.), *Handbook of moral development* (pp. 119–154). Mahwah, NJ: Erlbaum.

Smetana, J., & Braeges, J. (1990). Development of toddlers' moral and conventional judgments. *Merrill-Palmer Quarterly, 36,* 329–346.

Sober, E., & Wilson, D.S. (1998). *Unto others: The evolution and psychology of unselfish behavior.* Cambridge, MA: Harvard University Press.

Steele, C. (1988). The psychology of self-affirmation: Sustaining the integrity of the self. In B. Berkowitz (Ed.), *Advances in experimental social psychology* (Vol. 21, pp. 261–302). New York, NY: Academic Press.

Steele, C. (1999). The psychology of self-affirmation: Sustaining the integrity of the self. In R. F. Baumeister (Ed.), *The self in social psychology: Key readings in social psychology* (pp. 372–390). Philadelphia, PA: Psychology Press.

Suhler, C., & Churchland, P. (2011). The neurobiological basis of morality. In J. Illes & B. J. Sahakian (Eds.), *The Oxford handbook of neuroethics* (pp. 33–58). Oxford, England: Oxford University Press.

Sullivan, E. V. (1977). A study of Kolhberg's structural theory of moral development: A critique of liberal social science ideology. *Human Development, 20,* 352–376.

Sunstein, C. R. (2005). Moral heuristics. *Behavioral and Brain Sciences, 28,* 531–541.

Turiel, E. (1983). *Development of social knowledge: Morality and convention.* Cambridge, England: Cambridge University Press.

Turiel, E. (2002). *The culture of morality.* Cambridge, England: Cambridge University Press.

Turiel, E. (2006). The development of morality. In N. Eisenberg (Ed.), *Social, emotional, and personality development. Vol. 3: Handbook of child psychology* (6th ed., pp. 789–857). Hoboken, NJ: Wiley.

Van de Vondervoort, J., & Hamlin, J.K. (2016). Evidence for intuitive morality: preverbal infants make sociomoral evaluations. *Child Development Perspectives, 10,* 143–148.

Vasquez, K., Keltner, D., Edenbach, D.H., & Banaszynski, T.L. (2001). Cultural variation and similarity in moral rhetorics: Voices from the Phillipines and United States. *Journal of Cross-Cultural Psychology, 32,* 93–120.

Walker, L. J., & Frimer, J. A. (2007). Moral personality of brave and caring exemplars. *Journal of Personality and Social Psychology, 93,* 845–860.

Ward, A. F., Olsen, A. S., & Wegner, D. M. (2013). The harm-made mind: Observing victimization augments attribution of minds to vegetative patients, robots, and the dead. *Psychological Science, 24,* 1437–1445.

Weiner, B. (1995). *Judgments of responsibility: A foundation for a theory of conduct.* New York, NY: Guilford.

Wheatley, T., & Haidt, J. (2005). Hypnotic disgust makes moral judgments more severe. *Psychological Science, 16,* 780–784.

Wisneski, D. C., & Skitka, L. J. (2017). Moralization through moral shock: Exploring emotional antecedents to moral conviction. *Personality and Social Psychology Bulletin, 43,* 139–150.

Chapter 14

Emotion

Wendy Berry Mendes

If you are looking for an area of psychology fraught with disagreements, battle scars, gossip, intrigue, and even a few lawsuits, look no further than emotion research. Arguably, no subdiscipline in psychology is better known for its heated debates than emotion science where scholars argue about issues ranging from the nature of emotion, to its consequences, the fundamental building blocks, universality, distinct human-ness, face, brain, and bodily signatures, required consciousness, and the antecedents and consequences of emotion experience. These debates have played out in theoretical journals (Barrett, 2006; Baumeister, Vohs, DeWall, & Liqing, 2007; Ekman, 1994; Levenson, 2011; Russell, 1994), empirical reports (Cowen & Keltner, 2017; Levenson, 1992; Russell, 1980; Tracy & Robins, 2004), meta-analyses and reviews (Kreibig, 2010; Larsen, Berntson, Poehlmann, Ito, & Cacioppo, 2006; Lindquist, Wager, Kober, Bliss-Moreau, & Barrett, 2012; Siegel et al., 2018), books (Barrett & Russell, 2014; Ekman & Davidson, 1994; Fox, Lapate, Shackman, & Davidson, 2018; Niedenthal & Ric, 2017), and numerous conference symposia. In an effort to understand and evaluate the arguments for yourself, this chapter attempts to present several of the en-during debates from the emotion literature that would be most relevant for social psychologists. The sum-mary of the different questions and evidence for and against are intended to be presented with as little bias as possible, though a completely bias-free review is likely impossible.

This chapter covers five sections organized around a debated issue or core question in emotion research. Each section provides some historical background, a summary of the primary points, and a concluding assessment of the current literature and, in some cases, suggestions on what type of data would be needed to address the debate. The first topic focuses on the fundamental nature of emotion and how emotions are best characterized in terms of their origins (how emotions come to be) and how unique and separable emotion categories are. The second topic is whether discrete emotions have unique, patterned physiologic responses. The third explores how and in what ways emotions are similar and distinct from other affective states like motivation and acute stress. The fourth topic examines the role of cognition in emotion experiences, addressing the question of whether emotions can be experienced unconsciously and how awareness and explicit labeling influence emotional experiences. The last topic reviews the different approaches to manipulate and measure emotion in research studies. The chapter ends with some ideas about the future directions of emotion research.

What Is the Nature of Emotions?

It may seem obvious how emotions occur. We perceive a stimulus in our environment; we make sense of its signal properties; depending on these properties, we have a feeling like fear, anger, sadness, happiness, or some other emotion; and our brains and bodies respond to this emotional state. Though this seems to be an effortless, unlearned process, there are several critical questions that are unresolved regarding the nature of emotions including the boundaries around emotion categories, and the influence of culture, learning, and context. Several key theoretical perspectives exist on the nature of emotion and each have a large literature amassed in its favor and, in some cases, a similarly large literature arguing against the theory. Three broad theoretical traditions that encapsulate most of the theoretical perspectives include (a) basic emotion theory, (b) appraisal theory, and (c) psychological construction theory.

Basic Emotion Theory

Basic emotion theory is most identified with psychologist Paul Ekman, but the principles of this theory have roots in Darwin (1872; cf. Barrett, 2006) and were influenced by Ekman's mentor, Silvan Tomkins. Tomkins's (1984) theory argued that emotions, or affects, were biologically based with specific facial expressions, and there were six discrete affects: excitement, surprise, joy, distress, anger, and fear. Tomkins influence is easily identifiable in Ekman's (1992) basic emotion theory, which argues that *basic* emotions have neural programs that once triggered would coordinate a patterned set of responses in the brain, body, and facial expressions. This perspective considers emotions as a limited set of universal programs that evolved to contend with environmental challenges faced by our ancestors and that each emotion category has a dedicated, specific neural circuit or network. These five[1] basic emotions—fear, anger, sadness, disgust, and happiness—are argued to be core experiences similar to reflexes that need not be learned, are universal, and are immutable across context, development, and culture. Basic emotions are distinct from other emotions—shame, awe, love, etc.—based on being (a) elemental, (b) found across vertebrate species, and (c) related to survival functions (Levenson, 2011). Supportive of the basic emotion perspective, Panksepp (2005), arguing from a genetic and animal perspective, maintained that emotions are a type of instinct that need not be learned and these emotional instincts reflect general solutions stemming from brain mechanisms that appear across mammalian and other vertebrate species.

Basic emotion theory showed strong traction over several decades likely due to early theorists (e.g., Ekman, Levenson, and others) being explicit about the requirements for basic emotions making hypothesis-testing stemming from the theory straightforward. This theoretical foundation allowed others to test unambiguously the theoretical tenets and evidentiary basis; indeed, one could say that the basic emotion theorists set a high bar on what evidence would be needed to support the basic emotion theory claim. For example, Ekman (1992) identified nine criteria that an emotion had to meet to be considered *basic*. There had to be *distinctiveness* in the (a) antecedents, (b) behavioral/facial signal, and (c) physiologic response; *continuity* in terms of (d) presence in all primate species, (e) similar antecedents, and (f) display rules across cultures; and *structure/function* in terms of (g) quick onset and brief experience, (h) coherence across response systems, and (i) automatic/reflexive appraisal. These criteria have been tested empirically, and some have fared well, some poorly, and still other criteria have mixed support. For example, coherence across systems—the idea that multiple output systems like facial expressions, behavior, subjective experience, and physiology respond in a similar, correlated fashion upon experience of a specific emotion—is an aspect of basic emotion theory that has mixed support. Mauss, Levenson, McCarter, Wilhelm, and Gross (2005) examined second-by-second coherence of self-reports, physiology, and facial expressions during viewing of sad and amusing videos. While facial expressions and subjective experiences were highly correlated on a moment-to-moment basis for both sad and amusing films, changes in physiology were not related to either facial expressions or subjective experiences (see the following discussion for a deeper dive into evidence for basic emotion physiologic responses).

Appraisal Theories

Appraisal theories (Lazarus, 1991; Scherer, 1984; Smith & Ellsworth, 1985) have at their core the idea that people perceive stimuli in varied and individualistic ways. As part of the cognitive revolution in psychology in the 1950s, Arnold (1960) shifted the focus from emotions as feelings and behaviors to thoughts and perceptions. The primary idea behind appraisal theory is that individuals perceive the situation and make sense of it by applying emotion labels. Unlike the basic emotion perspective, which suggests that an emotion would be evoked invariantly from a specific stimulus—a bull charging toward you engenders fear—an appraisal approach situates the emotion experience as stemming from the perceiver not the stimulus. In this case, a bull would not universally evoke fear but could, in cases of a skilled bullfighter, for example, evoke feelings of excitement. This appraisal process consists of a number of dimensions that contribute to the overall appraisal, and it is the weighing of these dimensions that shapes the emotion response.

The various dimensions of appraisal processes differ across theorists, but Smith and Ellsworth (1985) offer an especially comprehensive account. They identify six appraisal dimensions including pleasant–unpleasant, certainty–uncertainty, attention–inattention, effort–disengagement, personal controllability–uncontrollability, and situational controllability–uncontrollability. These dimensions combine to produce different discrete emotional states. For example, disgust would be low on pleasantness and very low on attention (people often turn away from disgusting images) but moderately high on certainty; surprise, in contrast, is very high on pleasantness but low on personal controllability and certainty. Appraisal theories differ from a basic emotion perspective because they emphasize that emotional responses are shaped by individuals' appraisal processes. In other words, the basic emotion theory proposes a limited set of basic emotions that are found in humans and many nonhuman animals and are triggered by stimuli in the environment, whereas the appraisal theories underscore that individuals make sense of their environment and the emotion emerges from this sense-making process.

Appraisal theory is particularly useful for explaining how the same situation engenders different emotions in people (Ellsworth & Smith, 1988). In this perspective, attributions of the cause of the event or situation shape the emotional response. For example, receiving negative social feedback may be painful for everyone, but the specific type of negative emotion (e.g., shame vs. anger) is shaped by the presumed reasons for the feedback. In an interracial setting, for example, attributional ambiguity theory argues that negative feedback from a majority group member to a minority group member may be perceived as due to the bias of the person giving the negative feedback—not receiving a job after an interview could be due to the interviewer's bias rather than one's own poor interview skills (Crocker & Major, 1989). To the extent that negative feedback is externally attributed (i.e., interviewer bias) rather than internally attributed, poor interviewing skills shape the emotional response. In a series of studies, this idea was tested using European American and African American participants who were randomly assigned to interacting with a same-race partner or a different-race partner. When African Americans received negative feedback from a White partner, they were more likely to attribute the feedback to the evaluator's bias and showed more anger and increased sympathetic nervous system (SNS) activation (consistent with an approach response; Mendes, Major, McCoy & Blascovich, 2008). However, when rejected by a same-race partner, participants were more likely to experience greater shame, poorer cooperative performance, and greater vasoconstriction, consistent with a defeat or avoidance response. In a subsequent study that replicated the finding (i.e., more anger in cross-race dyads; greater shame in same-race dyads following social rejection), cross-race rejection was associated with more risk-taking behavior (Jamieson, Koslov, Nock, & Mendes, 2013) consistent with the idea that anger leads to greater risk-taking (Lerner & Keltner, 2001).

Psychological Construction Theories

Psychological construction theories (Barrett, 2006; Lindquist, 2013; Lindquist, Gendron, & Satpute, 2016; cf. Harre, 1986; Mesquita, Barrett, & Smith, 2010) argue against a basic emotion perspective that emotions are *natural kinds* and instead propose that emotions are experienced when affective states are made meaningful as specific instances of the emotion categories that exist in a given culture. Put another way, where basic emotions focus on a fixed set of universal emotions with strong innate basis, construction theories emphasize learning and cultural variation. An emotion label, in this view, refers not to an individual stimulus, thought, or reaction but instead refers to a population of many different experiences, each of which cannot be disentangled from the situation in which it was engendered. Instances of emotion are proposed to emerge from a flexible combination and recombination of more domain-general core systems, like perception, categorization, and memory and the neural architecture underlying them. Emotions are considered products, or constructions of, more basic ingredients, like valence, approach/avoid motivation, and intensity (cf. the dimensionalist perspective, Russell, 1991) and shaped by experiences, cultural knowledge, and situational information. In this view, emotions are nominal categories constructed from more basic elements. Emotion categories are a result of an active inference process whereby conceptual knowledge accumulated from experiences, culture, and context shape emotion perception and experience. One of the core tenets of psychological construction is the process of categorization. In this view, emotions are learned through a set of experiences that involve categorizing an affective process. If a child sees a parent scream at the sight of a spider, the child learns that small animals with many legs are something to fear. Constructivist perspectives takes seriously the idea of individual and cultural variability in emotion experience and provides a framework to understand the many and varied ways the same stimuli evokes different emotions and also how the same emotional experience is manifested differently across cultures and across people.

An important element of the constructivist view is that a discrete emotion (i.e., basic emotions) would not have a specific facial expression, physiologic change, or predictable behavioral response, but this theory is explicit that emotions do have concomitant neural and physiologic responses. The responses that are "basic" or elemental in emotion are not the emotion category—anger, sadness—but rather the basic ingredients such as *core affect*. Core affect comprises two primary dimensions: valence and activation. These make up the two dimensions of the circumplex model of emotion, which allows every emotion to be placed somewhere in a two dimensional space. Following from dimensional theories of emotion (Russell, 1980; Russell & Barrett, 1999), emotions occupy a dimensional space of pleasant to unpleasant (i.e., the emotion feels good or bad) and activation to deactivation representing arousal (high or low arousal). All categories of emotions can be represented in this two-factor space; anger for example is negative valence and has high intensity, whereas melancholy or sadness would be negative valence and low activation; grief, which is intense sadness, would be negative valence and high activation.

Language plays a large role in the constructivist view of emotion. When a person experiences situations directly or indirectly where there is yelling, scowling, hostility, passive-aggressiveness, pettiness, and so on these concepts are bound together with language into a category that might be labelled "anger." The idea being that without this category that binds these instances those specific examples might have a different emotion category associated with them.

One especially compelling series of studies points to the importance of language in identifying emotion categories. In one study, healthy participants were assigned to a condition that temporarily impaired access to an emotion concept—a technique called semantic satiation where a word is repeated 30 times out loud and loses its conceptual meaning. Participants who repeated the word *anger* and then were presented with two facial expressions took longer to identify an angry face (Lindquist, Barrett, Bliss-Moreau, & Russell, 2006). Similarly, with clinical patient samples, specifically those with a neurogenerative disease called semantic dementia that impairs language use, there are impairments of emotion perception. Whereas healthy participants sort photos of emotion faces into six or more categories, those with semantic dementia sort faces into fewer piles representing general positive, negative, or neutral faces (Lindquist, Gendron, Barrett, & Dickerson, 2004). This work underscores the critical role that language can provide in differentiating categories of emotion.

The three theoretical perspectives reviewed share some similarities but also many differences. As can be the case in theoretical debates, a great deal of effort is directed at demonstrating weaknesses in an opposing theory. For example, social affective neuroscientists examined whether specific and identifiable neural responses occur within emotion categories as might be predicted by a basic emotion perspective. One meta-analysis (Lindquist et al., 2012) was unable to identify unique emotion categories with neural activation. Instead, the same neural regions were activated across a wide range of emotion categories. Specifically, regions like the anterior cingulate, anterior insula, amygdala, and the orbito-prefrontal cortex were activated in a variety of emotions, but these same areas were also activated in situations with that were considered nonemotional. Thus, neural activation occurs in similar ways for emotional information and nonemotional information.

In sum, theoretical perspectives of emotion differ in substantial ways. While most emotion scholars have a preferred theoretical perspective that brings with it various assumptions, emotion research has not necessarily been hampered by the strong disagreements across theoretical camps. Journals and societies dedicated to emotion and affective science continue to proliferate, and several graduate psychology programs have started (or morphed into) affective science areas. Being well-versed in the theoretical perspectives is important if one is interested in integrating emotion into their research program, and while it is not necessary to be rigidly aligned with one specific theoretical perspective, it is important to understand how and when these different perspectives might influence your own assumptions about the origins of emotion.

Do Emotions Have Unique Bodily Signatures?

One enduring debate in emotion research is whether basic (or distinct) emotions have reliable, specific patterns of physiologic responses that co-occur with the emotion onset (Lang, 2014; Levenson, 2014; Mendes, 2016; Norman, Berntson, & Cacioppo, 2014; Shiota, Neufeld, Yeung, Moser, & Perea, 2011). Emotion researchers who use psychophysiology as one of the methods to measure emotion often will evoke the classic William James's (1884) quote on the essential conditions for what should be considered an emotion: "The only emotions I propose expressly to consider here are those that have a distinct bodily expression" (p. 189). There are intuitive reasons to assume the body responds in specific patterns to discrete emotional states; emotions are felt in the body, and folk language implicates bodily changes in these processes. People report bodily changes when describing an emotion experience: feeling sick to the stomach when experiencing disgust, a racing heart when walking down a dark and dangerous street, or a sudden rush of heat to the face during an argument. These reactions appear to effortlessly couple the emotional state with the bodily change. Given this apparent natural coupling, it is not surprising that a large literature has amassed examining the relation between emotion experiences and changes to the autonomic nervous system (ANS).

There is clear evidence that affective processes, like emotion, acute stress, and motivation, can change ANS responses like heart rate, respiration, sweat, and blood pressure. What the debate focuses on is whether a basic (or discrete) emotion has a universal pattern of physiologic responses that is unique to a specific emotion: That is, are ANS changes when angry different from ANS responses during fear? As previously noted, the basic emotion perspective argues that there should be specific patterns of physiologic responses and the patterns would be different across the basic emotions (e.g., Ekman, Levenson, & Friesen, 1983). The strong version of this argument is that patterned physiological responses to basic emotions occur across human and nonhuman animals, persist across the life span, and are unmodified by context (Ekman, 1992). Over the past few decades, much has been written in support of and against this strong version of the autonomic specificity of emotions (Lang, 2014; Levenson, 2014; Norman, Berntson, & Cacioppo, 2014).

Interpreting bodily changes as part of an emotion dates back as far as at least the third century when a teenager presented with symptoms of an accelerated heart rate and flushed face, and the physician Erasistratos concluded he was "lovesick" (see Gardner, Gabriel, & Diekman, 2000; Mesulam & Perry, 1972). The contemporary version of emotion-specific ANS changes is most strongly associated with Levenson and his colleagues (e.g., Levenson, 2003). In a classic paper, to examine support for the universality of emotion-specific ANS responses, Levenson Ekman, Heider, and Friesen (1992) traveled to West Sumatra, a large island in Indonesia, and measured a suite of physiologic responses from the Minangkabau, a matrilineal Muslin society with no exposure to Western culture. The study included the directed facial action task, which requires the movement of facial muscles to create a configuration tied to a discrete emotion while seven peripheral physiological responses were obtained: heart rate, finger pulse transit time, finger pulse amplitude, skin temperature, skin conductance, respiration period, and respiration depth. A US sample obtained the same measures using a similar protocol. Although the mean responses for heart rate, finger temperature, and finger pulse transit-time were greater in the US sample than the Minangkabau for all five emotions examined, some of the patterning of the responses were similar. For example, in both samples, disgust resulted in little or no change in heart rate, whereas anger, fear, and sadness increased heart rate. Levenson et al. concluded that the two cultures "evidenced patterns of emotion-specific ANS activity that were similar" though they followed this with the point that these data did "not [establish] universality" (p. 983).

To qualitatively summarize extant physiologic data, Kreibig (2010) identified 134 studies utilizing ANS measures and concluded that there was "considerable ANS response specificity in emotion when considering subtypes of distinct emotions" (p. 394). Additionally, this review also pointed to the need to incorporate ANS measures beyond ones that are the easiest to obtain; heart rate and skin conductance are the most common measures collected but are also easy and inexpensive to obtain. Echoing this point, Levenson (2014) identified rarely studied physiological responses in emotion research that might be more reliably related to emotions such as visible changes in coloration, moisture and secretion, protrusions, and appearance of eyes, which are all ANS-mediated (Levenson, 2003, 2014). In sum, claims that specific emotions show ANS patterning come from (a) cross-cultural research showing similar patterned responses to basic emotions and (b) reviews supporting similar directional changes in physiology as a function of the emotion experienced.

Evidence against the strong view of patterned physiological responses mapping onto discrete emotions comes from meta-analytic approaches that suggest that physiologic patterning might relate to more basic *ingredients* or *dimensions* of emotions (e.g., Barrett, 2006). For example, in meta-analyses that appeared in two editions of the *Handbook of Emotion* (Cacioppo et al., 2000; Larsen et al., 2006), the authors concluded that motivational tendencies embedded within emotional states show some consistent ANS patterning.

Specifically, approach-oriented emotional states in which there is an expectation for the need to mobilize energy are more likely to activate SNS than emotional states in which no expectation of energy reserves is expected. This perspective can be seen in LeDoux's work with rats where he shows that when environmental threats are present a neural defensive response occurs (LeDoux, 2000, 2014).

One especially compelling animal study demonstrated the importance of context in shaping physiologic responses during a discrete emotion. Iwata and LeDoux (1988) either placed rats in an unrestrained-home cage, which allowed free movement, or restrained them in a conditioning box, which forced immobility. When exposed to an aversive signal as part of a classical conditioning study, rats that were restrained had a different profile of physiological responses than rats that were unrestrained. Specifically, unrestrained rats showed greater heart rate increases relative to restrained rats. This finding shows how contextual information can result in varied physiologic responses within the same emotional state. Specifically, when rats' behavioral options include potential to escape, the physiological signatures follow the behavioral options. When escape is possible, an increase in cardiac responses would allow for more oxygenated blood to innervate peripheral muscles, whereas when no escape is possible, a reduction in sympathetic responses facilitate freezing, and, in the case of a predator attack, the lower SNS reaction would reduce blood loss if attacked. This study poses a challenge to basic emotion researchers who argue that fear would have a specific physiological signature. A fear-conditioned rat arguably might be one the purest forms of a "fear" response, and yet heart rate was significantly lower when rats were restrained than when they were free.

Additional evidence suggests that basic emotions do not produce differentiated physiologic profiles. In a meta-analysis of over 300 articles using a statistical technique that focuses on the pattern of responses rather than a single physiologic signal (i.e., multivariate pattern classification), no consistent evidence was found for autonomic signatures of discrete emotions (Siegel et al., 2018). Instead, the authors observed patterns of autonomic reactivity that were associated more with the experimental context than the emotional state. That is, active tasks (giving speeches, completing evaluative tasks) were associated with more SNS responses whereas passive tasks (video watching, viewing still images) were associated with less SNS reactivity. These meta-analytic findings are consistent with the perspective that the *context* in which emotions are examined can alter the physiological responses more than the specific emotion experienced (Lang, Bradley, & Cuthbert, 1997).

Underscoring the heterogeneity of physiological responses observed when examining discrete emotions, some studies have shown different patterns of physiologic responses to subtypes within the same emotion category. For example, Shenhav and Mendes (2014) examined gastrointestinal, SNS, and parasympathetic nervous system (PNS) changes during different types of disgust experiences. Participants were randomly assigned to watch one of three different collections of videos: One condition showed individuals suffering painful injuries and accidents in which legs and arms were contorted beyond natural mobility, but no breaking of the body envelope occurred (e.g., no blood); a second condition showed individuals with body envelope violations, such as emissions of blood, puss, and vomit and consuming disgusting things like feces; and the third collection consisted of neutral stimuli like landscapes, animals, and people in rural and urban areas. Participants in the first two conditions labeled the emotion they were feeling as "disgust" more than any other emotion label provided and showed greater activation of the levator labii (i.e., the muscle region surrounding the nose associated with disgust) relative to participants viewing neutral stimuli. However, participants watching body-envelope violations showed decreases in gastrointestinal activity and heart rate acceleration, whereas viewing painful injuries was associated with no changes in gastrointestinal responses, heart rate deceleration, and heart rate variability increases (an indication of greater PNS activation). Thus, two instantiations of the same emotion, disgust, using the same medium (watching videos), produced similar self-reported and facial expressions but different physiologic patterning of the enteric, SNS, and PNS. These findings suggest variability in physiological patterns within the same emotion category and provide support for the perspective that different "ingredients" of emotions (i.e., the core motivational properties) produce distinct physiological patterning—with body envelope violations engendering more avoidance responses and witnessing others' painful experiences increasing approach responses (Barrett, 2006; Mendes & Park, 2014). These data further support the perspective that a single emotion category can produce variability in responses when subtypes of that emotion are examined (for a similar point, see Kreibig, 2010).

What type of data would be needed to resolve the debate over whether there are specific physiologic responses that are invariantly related to discrete emotions? Researchers have suggested organization of peripheral responding along evolved neural circuitry might provide a stronger basis for examining emotion–physiology relations (Lang, 2014). Other researchers have noted the paucity of work examining ANS-mediated changes in bodily expressions that might be more closely tied to emotion experiences that manifest in observable bodily changes (e.g., piloerections [goose bumps], blushing, sweating, salivating, tearing, and bulging or twinkling eyes; Levenson, 2014), and by examining these downstream responses, one might be able to draw sharper boundaries around different emotion categories vis-à-vis physiological changes. Still others have urged researchers to take seriously the social and cultural context, individual differences, and developmental factors that alter how emotions are manifested in the body (Barrett, 2006; Mendes, 2010; Mendes & Park, 2014). Whether any of these approaches resolve this debate remains to be seen, but it is likely that most emotion physiologists would agree that multiple measures that assess unique bodily changes and attention to temporal, contextual, and developmental factors are more likely to lead to better insight into the nature of emotion-physiology relations.

Are Emotions Distinct from Other Affective States Like Stress, Mood, and Motivation?

At the broadest level, some psychological research tries to draw sharp boundaries around *hot* affective processes like emotion, acute stress, and motivation compared to *cold* processes like perception, memory, and attention. It is best to conceive of this hot–cold distinction as a continuum with very few mental states falling at the extreme ends. This dichotomy is meant to underscore the differences between thinking and feeling but offers little value from a process level given central control and integrated perceptual systems. That noted, from a didactic and research perspective, there are theories that differentiate cold/cognitive processes from hot/affective ones (Figner & Weber, 2011; Kahneman, 2011; Metcalfe & Mischel, 1999). *Affect* and *affective science* serve as broad umbrella terms that encompass processes such as acute stress, motivation, evaluation, mood, and emotion (Gross, 2015). Given this broad definition, how does one know whether they are studying emotion, motivation, or acute stress? By appreciating the boundaries and overlapping features of these states, one can gain both precision and greater traction from integrating varied areas.

When considering the overlap of affective processes, Gross (2015) identified the general assessment of "Is this good for me or bad for me?" This quick valuation then coordinates general processes like approach or avoid (in motivational language), positive or negative valence (in emotion terms), and challenge or threat (in stress language). All of these states would likely generate a coordinated brain/bodily response and, at the most basic level, generate an approach or avoidance reaction. These affective responses may be shaped by conscious and unconscious processes; may have specific neural, neuroendocrine, and peripheral physiologic responses; and might be associated with behavioral or action readiness responses.

Emotion and stress research traditions share parallel literatures on how to regulate or alter the affective state. In emotion research, *emotion regulation* is the process by which individuals attempt to alter their emotion experience (Gross, 2015). Similarly, in stress research, *coping* is the process by which individuals attempt to modify their stress responses. Indeed, coping research dating back to the 1970s identified processes like suppression and reappraisal that emerged in the emotion regulation literature a few decades later (Gross et al., 2015). Coping and regulation are fundamentally the same processes by which an individual attempts to modify, dampen, accentuate, or ignore his or her affective state.

While the variety of affective responses may share brain/body responses and have shared antecedents and consequences, the various affective states are differentiated along important lines. The most obvious is the *temporal* component. Of all the affective states, emotions are assumed to be the shortest duration with a quick onset and a fast resolution. Surprise would be the extreme example of a very short duration from onset to offset with the entire emotion occurring over a few seconds. Obviously, not all emotions have this type of quick response—sadness can last for hours, days, or longer—but, in general, emotions are considered to be short-lived, burst experiences. In contrast, acute stress at a minimum tends to last minutes. Anticipatory stress can last much longer, but, in general, the body's stress systems parallel psychological state of acute stress, and it would be difficult to maintain a heightened state of SNS activation for more than an hour other than in extreme situations (e.g., taking cover from enemy fire in a foxhole). Mood, on the other hand, is longest in duration and can last hours or days. These general time frames are simply heuristics to think about how to characterize an affective state that one might be interested in studying and how one might best bring about the affective state and how to measure it, which is reviewed in more detail in the following discussion.

Affective states differ in the *elicitor*—that is, what brings about the affective response. For example, emotions are more likely than moods to have a specific elicitor or event that links the situation to the affective state. Acute stress and motivation are more similar to emotional states than mood states in that there tends to be a specific event or stimuli that engenders the affective state. However, emotions differ from acute stress and motivation in that emotions can occur in both *active* and *passive* situations, whereas acute stress and motivation are typically a response to an active, goal-relevant situation. People can experience emotions from watching videos, reading vignettes or observing others but these passive situations typically do not engender motivational or stress reactions as easily.

Affective states also differ in their *specificity*. There is more differentiation in emotion categories than in any of the other affective states. Sadness feels different than disgust, which feels different than fear (Barrett, Mesquita, Ochsner, & Gross, 2007). Stress, in contrast, at best can be differentiated into two broad categories of maladaptive toxic stress and adaptive stress responses (McEwen, 1998). Similarly, motivation can be characterized as approach, avoidant, or disengagement (Blascovich & Mendes, 2010), and mood generally has just a positive or negative valence.

The differences in affective states have manifested in the type of empirical and theoretical data amassed. Stress research is conducted primarily by health and clinical psychologists and those more medically oriented; thus, it is not surprising that stress research tends to be more applied or at least *translational*. In contrast, emotion research is typically conducted by academic psychologists and is commonly studied among social and personality psychologists and tends to be more theoretical. Given the typical researchers' specialties, it is not surprising that stress research is more sophisticated on the biological and neurological consequences whereas emotion research is more sophisticated theoretically.

The Role of Cognition in Emotion

Does one need to be aware of an emotional state for an emotion to exist? Can emotions exist outside of conscious experience? How does awareness influence emotion experience? Do cognitive processes modify emotional experiences? These questions circle around a central theme of how cognition and emotion interact. This section reviews some often discussed issues related to the emotion and cognition interplay.

One area that generates much discussion is the extent to which a person has to be consciously aware of an emotion for an emotion to exist. If one is not aware of his or her happiness, for example, is he or she happy? Social-affective neuroscientists, like Matthew Lieberman, make the case that consciousness is a prerequisite for emotion. If one does not have awareness of an emotional state, there can be no emotional response (e.g., Lieberman et al., 2007). In contrast, other neuroscientists point to the temporal trajectory of response and awareness to argue that emotions do not need consciousness to influence behavior. For example, Damasio Tranel, and Damasio (1997) have put forth the somatic marker hypothesis, which is the idea that affective states outside of conscious awareness can influence behavior. In seminal research on this hypothesis, participants are presented with four decks of cards with various gains and losses associated with the four decks—two of the decks result in small gains but small losses, whereas the other two decks result in large gains but also large losses. The authors observed that as participants turned over cards from the various decks, changes in skin conductance (activity in the eccrine gland indicating SNS activation) differentiated the small gain/loss decks (safe choices) from the large gain/loss decks (risky choices) with the latter resulting in large skin conductance changes relative to the former. Importantly, these bodily changes *preceded* conscious reporting of which decks were risky by approximately 40 trials. Thus, the somatic marker hypothesis claims that bodily changes can indicate psychological or mental states prior to people being able to consciously report their affective state.

Cognitive processes can have direct influences on the experience of emotion. Several lines of research converge on the idea that how one remembers or thinks about a situation influences the emotion and its consequences. Self-distancing, for example, is the strategy of adopting a distant, third-person perspective when thinking back on difficult or unpleasant events (Kross & Ayduk, 2011)—thinking about it as if it happened to someone else. This strategy is contrasted to *self-immersion* in which individuals relive an experience from a self-immersed or first-person perspective, whereas self-distancing entails thinking back on the event from a global perspective (e.g., like a fly on the wall). Often experiments examining these strategies will manipulate a self-distancing versus self-immersion perspective by having participants recall an event in either the third-person perspective (e.g., "What was [your name] feeling while going through this?") versus a first-person perspective (e.g., "What was *I* feeling while going through this?"). Self-distancing is believed to facilitate meaning-making and results in a healthier response to a negative emotional memory. Indeed, Kross and Ayduk (2010; Kross & Ayduk, 2017) have garnered considerable evidence that a *self-distanced* versus *self-immersed* perspective reduces negative emotions, lowers blood pressure, and can reduce aggressive behaviors following from an emotion experience like anger. The authors argue that self-distancing improves these responses by allowing individuals to reconstruct the events to allow insight and closure.

This line of work elegantly demonstrates that how one recalls emotional memories influences how those emotions are remembered and experienced. That is, emotions can be modulated—muted or amplified—simply by changing the self-perspective in which the event is remembered. This approach extends to ongoing emotional events as well. That is, if participants adopt a self-distancing perspective while preparing to complete a stressful task they experience the task as less negative. While self-distancing represents a cognitive strategy to *think yourself* into a different emotional state, it certainly isn't the only cognitive strategy that can alter emotion.

Reappraisal can directly influence physiological, cognitive, and behavioral responses during high arousal, negative affect states. Reappraisal is the process of reinterpreting the meaning of an emotional stimulus. In one study examining the effective of reappraising one's bodily reactions during stress, participants were instructed to deliver a speech in the presence of a panel of evaluators for a mock job interview (Jamieson, Nock, & Mendes, 2012). Just before the speech participants were randomly assigned to one of three strategies, one of which was a reappraisal strategy and the other two were control conditions. In the reappraisal condition, participants read a (manufactured) newspaper article that described research that found that physiological arousal was functional and improved cognitive performance. The article said that increases in physiological responses (like heart rate) before a stressful task helped people to perform well, so this response is adaptive. It suggested to the reader that the best way to cope with a stressor is to remind yourself that increases in arousal are good for you. In contrast, one of the control conditions provided a coping strategy that (unbeknownst to the participant) was ineffective at coping with acute stress—ignoring the source of stress. In this condition, a (manufactured) newspaper article was presented that described research that shows that the best way to cope with stress is to ignore the source of the stressful experience. The second control condition did not include any instructions on how to cope with the stressful task, but rather reiterated general instructions. Cardiovascular reactivity obtained during the speech task showed that the reappraisal condition resulted in more beneficial and adaptive stress responses, specifically more efficient cardiac functioning (higher cardiac output) and decreases in vascular resistance (lower total peripheral resistance) compared to either of the two control conditions. Additionally, a measure of attentional bias (Emotional Stroop; MacLeod Rutherford, Campbell, Ebsworthy, & Holker, 2002) was completed immediately after the stress task. This task provides an indication of attentional bias toward negative self-information and is related to vigilance. Participants who read about the benefits of physiological arousal (i.e., reappraisal condition) did not show evidence of attentional bias whereas the two control conditions did. In short, this study demonstrated that appraising bodily changes that occur during high arousal, negative emotion experiences can lead to adaptive physiological responses as well as less attentional vigilance for threat in the environment.

Using a similar paradigm, reappraisal was manipulated in another study examining exam performance (Jamieson, Mendes, Blackstock, & Schmader, 2010). Students about to take the General Record Exam (GRE) were either assigned to a condition in which they learned arousal during an exam helped their performance (reappraisal condition) versus a no-information (control) condition. Participants in the reappraisal condition showed a significant increase in SNS responses (consistent with approach-oriented, *challenge* responses) and performed better in the quantitative portion of the GRE. Moreover, when students returned to the lab after they had completed the actual GRE with a copy of their tests reports, participants assigned to reappraise their arousal obtained higher GRE math scores than those in the control condition. When queried about their test arousal on exam day, compared to control participants, reappraisal participants reported that arousal was more likely to help their performance, and they reported feeling more certain about their performance.

The importance of these studies is that they underscore how flexible emotion states can be. By thinking about one's physiological arousal engendered during highly emotional situations as adaptive, participants showed more benign physiological functioning, lower threat vigilance, and better test performance. These reappraisal strategies share much in common with *cognitive behavioral therapy*, which uses cognitive relabeling to alter dysfunctional behavior. Indeed, using the same reappraisal intervention for participants with social anxiety disorder (SAD) even individuals with SAD benefited from reappraising arousal as functional during a social evaluation lab task intended to increase negative emotion (Jamieson, Nock, & Mendes, 2013).

How one thinks about emotion is one possible antecedent to altering the meaning and consequences of emotional reactions, but stepping back in this process, it may also be fruitful to ask whether simply inquiring about how one feels can alter emotional experience and consequences. Here, the literature points to differing potential outcomes of emotional assessment. On the one hand, expressive writing, emotional disclosure, and affect labeling are considered possible strategies to reduce the impact of emotion on neurological responses and even ultimately long-term health outcomes. Long-standing work by Pennebaker (1997), for example, argues that individuals who emotionally disclose their thoughts and feelings using expressive writing interventions will have fewer health clinic visits and better well-being compared to those in a no-expressive writing condition.

On the other hand, several researches have noted potential downsides of emotional disclosure for acute and long-term physical and mental health. For example, in a study that assessed individuals' responses immediately after the 9/11 terrorist attacks, participants were asked whether they wanted to "disclose (put in words) their feelings of the recent events." More than 2,000 respondents replied and responded either "yes" or "no." In addition, if they did want to disclose how they were feeling, they were presented with a dialogue box in which they could type their feelings about the tragic events. The authors then followed this panel of respondents over the next two years and assessed physical and mental health. They observed that, even after controlling for pre-9/11 mental and physical health history, respondents who chose to express their immediate reactions had poorer mental health than those who chose not to express an initial reaction. Furthermore, among those who did decide to express their thoughts, the more they wrote, the worse their mental and physical health (Seery, Silver, Holman, Ence, & Chu, 2008).

This section reviewed how cognition and emotion interact. As this short review shows, there are still open questions about whether consciousness is a prerequisite of emotion experience and whether the effects of expressing emotions are always beneficial for physical and mental health outcomes.

What Is the Best Way to Manipulate and Measure Emotion?

Manipulating Emotions

Often social psychologists are interested in manipulating emotion in a lab or an online environment. In this section, the different approaches to engendering emotion states are reviewed, and some of the benefits and drawbacks are discussed.

As previously described, the directed facial action task is one approach that can putatively engender an emotional response without necessarily evoking a conscious experience of the emotion. This task requires individuals to manipulate muscles in their face—activating the brow muscles so they are contracted, which presumably occurs during anger or other negative emotional states. This task assumes that facial expressions and the muscles activated in different facial expressions are invariantly related to discrete emotions, and so, not surprisingly, this task is primarily used by basic emotion theorists. The advantage of this type of task is that it eliminates the need for stimuli to evoke an emotion response and thus can be used cross-culturally. The disadvantage is that the task assumptions rely strongly on the idea that discrete emotions are invariantly related to specific facial configurations.

A more common approach to emotion induction is emotion elicitation using film (e.g., Gross & Levenson, 1985). This emotion induction approach is highly effective at engendering emotion reports (subjective experiences) of discrete emotions. For example, to elicit sadness, a film clip from the movie The Champ showing a young boy trying to wake his dead father after a boxing match is an especially powerful emotion induction (I dare you to watch the clip and not get choked up). The advantages of using film clips is that the stimuli can be shared across researchers, and thus results easily can be compared across labs and studies. The disadvantages include that the emotion inductions are passive—a participant is watching an experience happen to someone else so simulation of that experience is a requirement for the emotion induction. Also, it isn't clear how previous knowledge of the film clip might exacerbate or attenuate emotional responding. Watching an especially scary film with a jump-scare (i.e., an abrupt and unexpected frightening moment) is not as effective the second or third viewing as the first viewing.

Similar to film stimuli, one of the most common emotion induction manipulations uses static photos from the International Affective Picture Stimuli (IAPS; Lang, Bradley, & Cuthbert, 1997). This large set of photographs (more than 1,000 photos are available) includes a variety of contexts including objects, people, erotica, animals, landscapes, mutilated bodies, and more. Each picture in the IAPS has been rated on dimensions of pleasurable and arousing and has then been numbered and catalogued according to the means and standard deviations of these ratings. IAPS pictures have been used in a variety of emotion studies examining neural activation associated with emotion experience, peripheral physiologic responses, and priming studies intended to bring about an emotion state prior to a task, to name a few. Like emotion inductions using films, IAPS has the advantage of comparison across labs and cultures (without the language barrier that would be inherent in film inductions) and has the added advantage of a large normative database to select images given a desired arousal and pleasurable category. The downside is that the emotion induction is passive rather than active (the same as with using films).

Emotion inductions that tend to be more active rather than passive include re-lived emotion experiences. This approach requires one to think back to an event that brought about a specific intended emotion. In this approach, the experimenter provides specific instructions to help bring about the event in as vivid detail as possible. Presumably, as these memories come back, the individual would experience the targeted emotions. This strategy of re-lived emotional experiences is a common technique for researchers to bring about an emotion in the lab. In the extreme, re-lived experiences can be harmful as in the case of flashbacks and dissociated thinking as can occur with posttraumatic stress disorders. But are these re-lived emotions truly similar to emotions experienced in the moment, and can the emotional memories be influenced by cognitive strategies that can be brought to mind during the retrieval process? It is unclear whether the re-lived experiences are similar to the original experience, and the ability to bring about vivid details and recreate the memory can differ across individuals. Also, unlike film and static stimuli (e.g., IAPS), there is not the same control across individuals given the varied experiences across individuals.

The most labor-intensive emotion induction tasks are active tasks, which create an actual experience in a lab setting. Most notably, Gerhard Stemmler and colleagues have created real-life emotion inductions in the lab (e.g., Stemmler, Heldmann, Pauls, Cornelia, & Scherer, 2001; see also Kassam & Mendes, 2013; Mauss et al., 2007). For example, in one study to induce fear, participants were told that there would be an unexpected blood draw, and a research assistant brought in a dish of syringes while the participants were preparing to deliver a speech. To induce anger, participants interacted with a difficult and quarrelsome research assistant who claims that the participant's performance on a mental arithmetic task is substandard. This type of real-life emotion inductions is highly effective at increasing subjective experiences and physiologic responses in a lab environment. The downside is that these approaches require tremendous experimenter effort, time, and cost. Thus, these studies can be difficult to conduct for those with limited money and resources and are not well-suited for large-scale data collection of hundreds (let alone thousands) of participants.

Measuring Emotions

There is a variety of ways to measure emotions, and the various measurement strategies have advantages and disadvantages. The most obvious approach is to simply ask people what they are feeling. One measure, the Positive and Negative Affect Schedule (PANAS) developed to measure trait like emotional states, the stem is changed from the original "How do you typically feel?" to "How do you feel right now?" (thus obtaining a state measure; Watson, Clark & Tellegen, 1988). Bypassing discrete word labels, the self-assessment manikin (SAM) is a nonverbal pictorial assessment technique (Bradley & Lang, 1994). This three-dimension scale presents participants with a series of five cartoon-like icons that vary based on three different dimensions: pleasure, arousal, and dominance. For example, the pleasure dimension presents five icons that represent very happy to very sad by changing the mouth, eyes, and eyebrows of the icon. Subjective reports offer face valid information related to emotion experiences but this approach assumes that emotions are always experienced consciously. Subjective reports also potentially suffer from the same obstacle that all self-reports are vulnerable to, which is idiosyncrasies in socially desirable responding or the opposite, defensive responding.

To overcome limitations in self-reports of emotion, implicit measures have been developed in an effort to obtain emotion responses that individuals may be either unwilling or unable to report. One measure, the Implicit Positive and Negative Affect Test (IPANAT) measures the extent to which individuals assign positive or negative adjective ratings to nonsense words (Quirin, Kazen, & Kuhl, 2009). For example, participants rate the word TUNBA in terms of how much they think the word conveys the feeling of happy, helpless, energetic, tense, cheerful, or inhibited. Like other implicit measures, the value is that individuals are unlikely to realize that their responses reflect their current affective state. But, like other implicit measures, it is unclear to what extent implicit responses reflect a more valid way to assessing emotions.

A relatively new approach to measuring emotions takes advantage of the idea that emotions are experienced in the body. In this approach, participants are presented with two silhouettes of bodies and are instructed to color the bodily regions where a specific emotion might create activation or deactivation (Nummenmaa, Glerean, Hari, & Heitanen, 2014). This topographical self-report method yielded separable bodily sensations for different emotions, and the authors argue that the measure could be especially useful cross-culturally. While it is currently unclear how valid and reliable this measure is and to what extent participants are coloring in bodily regions based on experientially differences in emotion or responding to cultural knowledge of where emotions are typically experienced (e.g., disgust in the gut) remains unknown, but this novel method may offer added value to subjective reports.

Facial expressions tied to emotions are examined as a way to provide an unobtrusive, behavioral measure of emotion. The most popular measure of facial expressions stems from Ekman's early work that identified the complete topography of the face and underlying muscular structure. This approach, the Facial Action Coding System (FACS), identifies a complete taxonomy of muscle activation and facial movements (Ekman & Rosenberg, 1997). FACS was originally developed for human coders who manually code each "action unit" (defined as a contraction or relaxation of one or more facial muscles). Discrete emotions are identified by a specific constellation of action units. For example, a "genuine" smile includes activation of the zygomatic major muscle (muscles around the mouth that activate in a smile) plus the contraction of the orbicularis occuli (the outer part of the eye muscles that are presumed to contract in an authentic smile). In one especially impressive use of FACS, Harker and Keltner (2001) coded facial expressions from a women's college yearbook photos and found that positive emotion expressions predicted personal well-being and favorable martial outcomes 30 years later.

The advantage of FACS is the ability to assess emotions from the face without requiring subjective responses from the participant. The downsides include the need to be a "certified" FACS coder, high labor intensity, and the strong assumption that facial expressions, defined by the basic emotion perspective, are invariantly related to emotions (see Gendron, Roberson, van der Vyver, & Barrett, 2014). Recent advances in video scanning, which purports to automatize FACS scoring and thus removes the need for human coders, may provide the type of large-scale data needed to definitively answer the question of whether facial expressions are invariantly related to discrete emotions.

Future of Emotion Science

Emotion experiences animate our lives and social relationships. Positive emotions predict lower incidence of morbidity and mortality, and in just about every domain of our lives, positive relative to negative emotions are associated with better outcomes. But emotions are not just something that lives within an individual, but emotions can also emanate from people and influence those around them making emotions also a dyadic and group level process. Recent advances in analytic approaches, specifically multilevel modeling and dyadic approaches, have ushered in a new age of research examining emotion in dyads and groups (Thorson, West, & Mendes, 2018). *Emotion contagion*—how one person's emotion experience influences the emotion experience of a partner or group—is an exciting area of research that social psychologists would be particularly skilled to study given their training in social settings and interpersonal processes.

Emotion science is an exciting area of research and critical to understand for social psychologists. Although this chapter highlighted many areas that continue to evolve in terms of our understanding of emotion science, there is a wealth of research that provides many exciting avenues for the budding social psychologist to explore.

Note

1. A sixth emotion, surprise, bounces on and off the basic emotion list.

References

Arnold, M. B. (1960). *Emotion and personality.* New York: Columbia University Press.

Ayduk, Ö., & Kross, E. (2010). From a distance: Implications of spontaneous self-distancing for adaptive self-reflection. *Journal of Personality and Social Psychology, 98,* 809–829.

Barrett, L. F. (2006). Are emotions natural kinds? *Perspectives on Psychological Science, 1,* 28–58.

Barrett, L. F., Mesquita, B., Ochsner, K. N., & Gross, J. J. (2007). The experience of emotion. *Annual Review of Psychology, 58,* 373–403.

Barrett, L. F., & Russell, J. A. (Eds.). (2014). *The psychological construction of emotion.* New York, NY: Guilford.

Baumeister, R. F., Vohs, K. D., Nathan DeWall, C., & Zhang, L. (2007). How emotion shapes behavior: Feedback, anticipation, and reflection, rather than direct causation. *Personality and Social Psychology Review, 11,* 167–203.

Bechara, A., Damasio, H., Tranel, D., & Damasio, A. R. (1997). Deciding advantageously before knowing the advantageous strategy. *Science, 275,* 1293–1295.

Blascovich, J., & Mendes, W. B. (2010). Social psychophysiology and embodiment. In S. T. Fiske, D. T. Gilbert, & G. Lindzey (Eds.). *The handbook of social psychology* (5th ed., pp. 194–227). New York, NY: Wiley.

Bradley, M. M., & Lang, P. J. (1994). Measuring emotion: The self-assessment manikin and the semantic differential. *Journal of Behavior Therapy and Experimental Psychiatry, 25,* 49–59.

Cacioppo, J. T., Berntson, G. G., Larsen, J. T., Poehlmann, K. M., & Ito, T. A. (2000). The psychophysiology of emotion. *Handbook of Emotions, 2,* 173–191.

Cowen, A. S., & Keltner, D. (2017). Self-report captures 27 distinct categories of emotion bridged by continuous gradients. *Proceedings of the National Academy of Sciences, 114,* E7900–E7909.

Crocker, J., & Major, B. (1989). Social stigma and self-esteem: The self-protective properties of stigma. *Psychological Review, 96,* 608–630.

Darwin, C. (1872). *The origin of species by means of natural selection: Or, the preservation of favoured races in the struggle for life and the descent of man and selection in relation to sex* (5th ed.). New York, NY: Appleton.

Ekman, P. E. (1992). An argument for basic emotions. *Cognition & Emotion, 6,* 169–200.

Ekman, P. E. (1994). Strong evidence for universals in facial expressions: A reply to Russell's mistaken critique. *Psychological Bulletin, 115,* 268–287.

Ekman, P. E., & Davidson, R. J. (1994). *The nature of emotion: Fundamental questions.* Oxford, England: Oxford University Press.

Ekman, P. E., Levenson, R. W., & Friesen, W. V. (1983). Autonomic nervous system activity distinguishes among emotions. *Science, 221,* 1208–1210.

Ekman, P. E., & Rosenberg, E. L. (Eds.). (1997). *What the face reveals: Basic and applied studies of spontaneous expression using the Facial Action Coding System (FACS).* Oxford, England: Oxford University Press.

Ellsworth, P. C., & Smith, C. A. (1988). From appraisal to emotion: Differences among unpleasant feelings. *Motivation and Emotion, 12,* 271–302.

Figner, B., & Weber, E. U. (2011). Who takes risks when and why? Determinants of risk taking. *Current Directions in Psychological Science, 20,* 211–216.

Fox, A. S., Lapate, R. C., Shackman, A. J., & Davidson, R. J. (Eds.). (2018). *The nature of emotion: Fundamental questions.* Oxford, England: Oxford University Press.

Gardner, W. L., Gabriel, S., & Diekman, A. B. (2000). Interpersonal processes. In J. T. Cacioppo, L. G. Tassinary, & G. G. Berntson (Eds.), *Handbook of psychophysiology* (pp. 643–664). Cambridge, England: Cambridge University Press.

Gendron, M., Roberson, D., van der Vyver, J. M., & Barrett, L. F. (2014). Perceptions of emotion from facial expressions are not culturally universal: Evidence from a remote culture. *Emotion, 14,* 251–262.

Gross, J. J. (2015). Emotion regulation: Current status and future prospects. *Psychological Inquiry, 26,* 1–26.

Gross, J. J., & Levenson, R. W. (1995). Emotion elicitation using films. *Cognition & Emotion, 9,* 87–108.

Harker, L., & Keltner, D. (2001). Expressions of positive emotion in women's college yearbook pictures and their relationship to personality and life outcomes across adulthood. *Journal of Personality and Social Psychology, 80,* 112–124.

Harré, R. (Ed.). (1986). *The social construction of emotions.* Oxford, England: Blackwell.

Iwata, J., & LeDoux, J. E. (1988). Dissociation of associative and nonassociative concomitants of classical fear conditioning in the freely behaving rat. *Behavioral Neuroscience, 102,* 66–76.

James, W. (1884). II. What is an emotion? *Mind, 34,* 188–205.

Jamieson, J. P., Koslov, K., Nock, M. K., & Mendes, W. B. (2013). Experiencing discrimination increases risk taking. *Psychological Science, 24,* 131–139.

Jamieson, J., Mendes, W. B., Blackstock, E., & Schmader, T. (2010). Turning the knots in your stomach into bows: Reappraising arousal improves performance on the GRE. *Journal of Experimental Social Psychology, 46,* 208–212.

Jamieson, J. P., Mendes, W. B., & Nock, M. K. (2013). Changing the conceptualization of stress in social anxiety disorder: Affective and physiological consequences. *Clinical Psychological Science, 1,* 363–374.

Jamieson, J. P., Nock, M. K., & Mendes, W. B. (2012). Mind over matter: Reappraising arousal improves cardiovascular and cognitive responses to stress. *Journal of Experimental Psychology: General, 141,* 417–422.

Kahneman, D. (2011). *Thinking, fast and slow* (Vol. 1). New York, NY: Farrar, Straus and Giroux.

Kassam, K. S., & Mendes, W. B. (2013). The effects of measuring emotion: Physiological reactions to emotional situations depend on whether someone is asking. *PLoS One, 8,* e64959.

Kreibig, S. D. (2010). Autonomic nervous system activity in emotion: A review. *Biological Psychology, 84,* 394–421.

Kross, E., & Ayduk, O. (2011). Making meaning out of negative experiences by self-distancing. *Current Directions in Psychological Science, 20,* 187–191.

Kross, E., & Ayduk, O. (2017). Self-distancing: Theory, research, and current directions. In *Advances in experimental social psychology* (Vol. 55, pp. 81–136). Cambridge, MA: Academic Press.

Lang, P. J. (2014). Emotion's response patterns: The brain and the autonomic nervous system. *Emotion Review, 6,* 93–99.

Lang, P. J., Bradley, M. M., & Cuthbert, B. N. (1997). International affective picture system (IAPS): Technical manual and affective ratings. *NIMH Center for the Study of Emotion and Attention*, 39–58.

Larsen, J. T., Berntson, G. G., Poehlmann, K. M., Ito, T. A., & Cacioppo, J. T. (2006). The psychophysiology of emotion. In N. Eisenberg (Ed.), *Handbook of emotions* (6th ed., Vol. 3, pp. 180–195). New York, NY: Wiley.

Lazarus, R. S. (1991). Progress on a cognitive-motivational-relational theory of emotion. *American Psychologist, 46,* 819–834.

LeDoux, J. E. (2000). Emotion circuits in the brain. *Annual Review of Neuroscience, 23,* 155–184.

LeDoux, J. E. (2014). Coming to terms with fear. *Proceedings of National Academy of Science, 111,* 2871–2878.

Lerner, J. S., & Keltner, D. (2001). Fear, anger, and risk. *Journal of Personality and Social Psychology, 81,* 146–159.

Levenson, R. W. (1992). Autonomic nervous system differences among emotions. *Psychological Science, 3,* 23–27.

Levenson, R. W. (2003). Blood, sweat, and fears. *Annals of the New York Academy of Sciences, 1000,* 348–366.

Levenson, R. W. (2011). Basic emotion questions. *Emotion Review, 3,* 379–386.

Levenson, R. W. (2014). The autonomic nervous system and emotion. *Emotion Review, 6,* 100–112.

Levenson, R. W., Ekman, P., Heider, K., & Friesen, W. V. (1992). Emotion and autonomic nervous system activity in the Minangkabau of West Sumatra. *Journal of Personality and Social Psychology, 62,* 972–988.

Lieberman, M. D., Eisenberger, N. I., Crockett, M. J., Tom, S. M., Pfeifer, J. H., & Way, B. M. (2007). Putting feelings into words affect labeling disrupts amygdala activity in response to affective stimuli. *Psychological Science, 18,* 421–428.

Lindquist, K. A. (2013). Emotions emerge from more basic psychological ingredients: A modern psychological constructionist model. *Emotion Review, 5,* 356–368.

Lindquist, K. A., Barrett, L. F., Bliss-Moreau, E., & Russell, J. A. (2006). Language and the perception of emotion. *Emotion, 6,* 125–138.

Lindquist, K. A., Gendron, M., Barrett, L. F., & Dickerson, B. C. (2014). Emotion perception, but not affect perception, is impaired with semantic memory loss. *Emotion, 14,* 375–387.

Lindquist, K. A., Gendron, M., & Satpute, A. B. (2016). Language and emotion: Putting words into feelings and feelings into words. *Handbook of emotions* (4th edpp. 579–594). New York, NY: Guilford.

Lindquist, K. A., Wager, T. D., Kober, H., Bliss-Moreau, E., & Barrett, L. F. (2012). The brain basis of emotion: A meta-analytic review. *Behavioral and Brain Sciences, 35,* 121–143.

MacLeod, C., Rutherford, E., Campbell, L., Ebsworthy, G., & Holker, L. (2002). Selective attention and emotional vulnerability: assessing the causal basis of their association through the experimental manipulation of attentional bias. *Journal of Abnormal Psychology, 111*(1), 107.

Mauss, I. B., Cook, C. L., Cheng, J. Y., & Gross, J. J. (2007). Individual differences in cognitive reappraisal: Experiential and physiological responses to an anger provocation. *International Journal of Psychophysiology, 66,* 116–124.

Mauss, I. B., Levenson, R. W., McCarter, L., Wilhelm, F. H., & Gross, J. J. (2005). The tie that binds? Coherence among emotion experience, behavior, and physiology. *Emotion, 5,* 175–190.

McEwen, B. S. (1998). Protective and damaging effects of stress mediators. *New England Journal of Medicine, 338,* 171–179.

Mendes, W. B. (2010). Weakened links between mind and body in older age: The case for *maturational dualism* in the experience of emotion. *Emotion Review, 2,* 240–244.

Mendes, W. B. (2016). Emotion and the autonomic nervous system. In L. F. Barrett, M. Lewis, & J. Haviland-Jones (Eds), *Handbook of emotions* (4th ed., pp. 166–181). New York, NY: Guilford.

Mendes, W. B., Major, B., McCoy, S., & Blascovich, J. (2008). How attributional ambiguity shapes physiological and emotional responses to social rejection and acceptance. *Journal of Personality and Social Psychology, 94,* 278–291.

Mendes & Park (2014). Neurobiological concomitants of motivation states. In A. J. Elliot (Ed.), *Advances in motivational science* (pp. 233–270). Cambridge, MA: Academic Press.

Mesquita, B., Barrett, L. F., & Smith, E. R. (Eds.). (2010). *The mind in context.* New York: Guilford.

Mesulam, M. M., & Perry, J. (1972). The diagnosis of love-sickness: Experimental psychophysiology without the polygraph. *Psychophysiology, 9,* 546–551.

Metcalfe, J., & Mischel, W. (1999). A hot/cool-system analysis of delay of gratification: Dynamics of willpower. *Psychological Review, 106*, 3–19.

Niedenthal, P. M., & Ric, F. (2017). *Psychology of emotion*. New York, NY: Psychology Press.

Norman, G. J., Berntson, G. G., & Cacioppo, J. T. (2014). Emotion, somatovisceral afference, and autonomic regulation. *Emotion Review, 6*, 113–123.

Nummenmaa, L., Glerean, E., Hari, R., & Hietanen, J. K. (2014). Bodily maps of emotions. *Proceedings of the National Academy of Sciences, 111*, 646–651.

Panksepp, J. (2005). Affective consciousness: Core emotional feelings in animals and humans. *Consciousness and Cognition, 14*, 30–80.

Pennebaker, J. W. (1997). *Opening up: The healing power of expressing emotions*. New York, NY: Guilford.

Quirin, M., Kazén, M., & Kuhl, J. (2009). When nonsense sounds happy or helpless: The implicit positive and negative affect test (IPANAT). *Journal of Personality and Social Psychology, 97*, 500–516.

Russell, J. A. (1980). A circumplex model of affect. *Journal of Personality and Social Psychology, 39*, 1161–1178.

Russell, J. A. (1991). Culture and the categorization of emotions. *Psychological Bulletin, 110*, 426–450.

Russell, J. A. (1994). Is there universal recognition of emotion from facial expression? A review of the cross-cultural studies. *Psychological Bulletin, 115*, 102–141.

Russell, J. A., & Barrett, L. F. (1999). Core affect, prototypical emotional episodes, and other things called emotion: dissecting the elephant. *Journal of Personality and Social Psychology, 76*(5), 805.

Scherer, K. R. (1984). Emotion as a multicomponent process: A model and some cross-cultural data. *Review of Personality & Social Psychology, 5*, 37–63.

Seery, M. D., Silver, R. C., Holman, E. A., Ence, W. A., & Chu, T. Q. (2008). Expressing thoughts and feelings following a collective trauma: Immediate responses to 9/11 predict negative outcomes in a national sample. *Journal of Consulting and Clinical Psychology, 76*(4), 657.

Shenhav, A., & Mendes, W. B. (2014). Aiming for the stomach and hitting the heart: Dissociable triggers and sources for disgust reactions. *Emotion, 14*, 301–309.

Shiota, M. N., Neufeld, S. L., Yeung, W. H., Moser, S. E., & Perea, E. F. (2011). Feeling good: Autonomic nervous system responding in five positive emotions. *Emotion, 11*, 1368–1378.

Siegel, E. H., Cannon, M., Condon, P., Chang, Y., Dy, J., Quigley, K. S., & Barrett, L. F. (2018). A meta-analytic search for autonomic signatures of emotion. *Psychological Bulletin, 144*, 343–393.

Smith, C. A., & Ellsworth, P. C. (1985). Patterns of cognitive appraisal in emotion. *Journal of Personality and Social Psychology, 48*, 813–838.

Stemmler, G., Heldmann, M., Pauls, C. A., & Scherer, T. (2001). Constraints for emotion specificity in fear and anger: The context counts. *Psychophysiology, 38*, 275–291.

Thorson, K. R., West, T. V., & Mendes, W. B. (2017). Measuring physiological influence in dyads: A guide to designing, implementing, and analyzing dyadic physiologic studies. *Psychological Methods*. http://www.doi.org/10.1037/met0000166

Tomkins, S. S. (1984). Affect theory. *Approaches to Emotion, 163*, 163–195.

Tracy, J. L., & Robins, R. W. (2004). Putting the self into self-conscious emotions: A theoretical model. *Psychological Inquiry, 15*, 103–125.

Watson, D., Clark, L. A., & Tellegen, A. (1988). Development and validation of brief measures of positive and negative affect: The PANAS scales. *Journal of Personality and Social Psychology, 54*, 1063–1070.

Chapter 15

Social Neuroscience

Thalia Wheatley

People have

> through the adaptive capacities of the cortex, attained the levels of intelligence and the power of inhibition and control which are prerequisite for civilized society. The chief contributions of the cortex to social behavior may be summarized as follows: (1) It underlies all solutions of human problems, which are also social problems, and makes possible their preservation in language, customs, institutions, and inventions. (2) It enables each new generation to profit by the experience of others in learning this transmitted lore of civilization. (3) It establishes habits of response in the individual for social as well as for individual ends, inhibiting and modifying primitive self-seeking reflexes into activities which adjust the individual to the social as well as to the non-social environment. Socialized behavior is thus the supreme achievement of the cortex. (Allport, 1924, p. 31)

In arguably the first major textbook of social psychology, Allport (1924) chose to begin with an examination of the physiological basis of human behavior. It is scarcely surprising, therefore, that the topic of social neuroscience should stand with other research areas in any comprehensive coverage of social psychology. Yet, for most of the past century, relatively few social psychologists have emphasized its biological nature (with notable exceptions to be discussed shortly). Within the past decade or so, however, a biological revolution has taken place within many areas of psychological science, including social psychology, with an increasing emphasis on the use of neuroscience methods to understand human behavior. The field of neuroscience reflects the interdisciplinary effort to understand the structure, function, physiology, biology, biochemistry, and pathology of the nervous system. From a psychological perspective, however, the term *neuroscience* typically is used to refer primarily to the study of the brain. Of interest is how the brain gives rise to affect, cognition, and behavior.

Social neuroscience, a term first used by John Cacioppo and colleagues (e.g., Cacioppo & Berntson, 1992), is an emerging field that uses the methods of neuroscience to understand how the brain processes social information. It involves scholars from widely diverse areas (e.g., social and personality psychology, neuroscience, psychiatry, philosophy, anthropology, economics, sociology) working together to understand fundamental questions about human social nature. The core challenge of social neuroscience is to elucidate the neural mechanisms that support social thought and behavior. From this perspective, just as there are dedicated brain mechanisms for breathing, seeing, and hearing, the brain has evolved specialized mechanisms for processing information about the social world, including the ability to know ourselves, to know how others respond to us, and to regulate our actions to co-exist with other members of society. The problems that are studied by social neuroscience have been of central interest to social psychologists for decades, but the methods and theories that are used reflect recent discoveries in neuroscience. Although in its infancy, there has been rapid progress in identifying the neural basis of many social behaviors (see Baron-Cohen, Lombardo & Tager-Flusberg, 2013; Harmon-Jones & Inzlicht, 2016; Stanley & Adolphs, 2013).

The goal of this chapter is to (a) sketch a brief history of the field of social neuroscience, (b) describe the major techniques—including their strengths and limitations—used to study the social brain, (c) discuss some of the brain regions and structures that are likely to be of greatest interests to social psychologists, and (d) explain why understanding the brain is important for understanding social minds and behaviors.

A Brief History of Social Neuroscience

Although the rise of the use of neuroscience methods has accelerated over the past decade or so, it is important to understand how it has, since the 1800s, permeated psychological thinking as we seek to understand how those methods can be useful for understanding social cognition and behavior.

The Intellectual Backdrop

By the beginning of the 20th century, anatomists had a reasonably good understanding of the basic structures of the brain. What was less clear, however, is how these structures worked to produce thought and behavior—much less how the brain created complex mental activities such as those associated with attitudes, prejudice, or love. One early attempt to map brain function to thought and behavior was phrenology. Phrenologists such as Franz Gall and Johann Spurzheim identified social constructs such as self-esteem as being reflected by enlargements on the skull (the area to feel for bumps in the skull indicating high self-esteem is just at the crown at the back of your head).

Although the theory that brain functions are associated with specific patterns of bumps on the skull is now discredited, the idea that discrete regions of the brain are specialized for different tasks was quite insightful. Early case histories of individuals with brain damage also provided considerable evidence for localized functions. For social and personality psychologists, the most important early case was that of Phineas Gage, a 25-year-old railroad foreman from New Hampshire who suffered extensive damage to his frontal lobes when a blast charge he was preparing accidentally ignited and propelled his tamping iron—an iron bar roughly one yard long and 3.2 inches in diameter that was used to prepare explosive charges—through his left cheekbone, into his brain, and out the top of his head. Physicians of the period were initially incredulous at the possibility that anyone could sustain such a massive trauma to the brain and survive, but Gage seemed otherwise unaffected by the blast, conversing casually with both his workers and his physician, John Harlow (Macmillan, 2000). Following this extraordinary accident, remarkable changes in Gage's personality and social behavior were noted. Formerly thought of as honest, reliable, and deliberate (Harlow, 1868), Gage was afterwards described as "gross, profane, coarse, and vulgar, to such a degree that his society was intolerable to decent people" (Anonymous, 1851; attributed to Harlow; see

Macmillan, 2000). Importantly, then, Gage's injuries produced specific social deficits without impairing other capacities, such as language or intelligence.

Although Phineas Gage was a notable example of how localized brain damage can cause social deficits, this case alone did not spur increased interest in the brain basis of social thought and behavior. Indeed, for the next hundred years, physicians and neuroscientists were more interested in how the brain supported sensory and cognitive functions such as memory, vision, motor planning, and language. In the latter 20th century, the question of how the brain produces the social mind finally resurfaced.

Renewed interest in the social brain originated, in part, from a few perceptive cognitive neuroscientists who noticed that the brain damage they were studying had interesting social implications. One such neuroscientist, Michael Gazzaniga, was studying "split brain" patients who had their corpus callosum (the connective tissue between the two brain hemispheres) severed to control their epilepsy thereby rendering the two hemispheres unable to communicate with each other. His work revealed that the sense of self, a question of deep interest to social psychologists, may be dependent on the left hemisphere where language is located (Gazzaniga, 1985). This was discovered by giving a command to a split brain patient's right hemisphere only. Upon showing the command "get up" to the right hemisphere, the split brain patient would rise out of his chair. Gazzaniga would then ask why he was getting up (knowing full well the reason was the command shown). Because language resides in the left hemisphere, the split brain would have to use his left hemisphere to answer the question—the hemisphere that did not see the command. Would the patient simply say, sensibly, "I don't know"? Gazzaniga found that, no matter what the command, the patient would make up a plausible (but incorrect) story. These studies revealed that the left hemisphere is important for developing a narrative story about ourselves and why we do what we do.

The integration between social psychology and cognitive neuroscience accelerated sharply around the turn of the 21st century, creating the new field of social neuroscience. Since that time, there has been an explosion of research linking specific brain areas with particular social behaviors and mental processes (for reviews, see Gazzaniga, 2009). We now know that there is some localization of function but that many different brain regions participate to produce behavior and mental activity (Adolphs, 2009; Lieberman, 2010). That is, although there is considerable support for the general idea of specialization, virtually every behavior involves the joint activity of many brain regions. This new understanding has been greatly accelerated by the use of new brain imaging methods.

The Major Techniques

Although a multitude of different methods to measure brain activity have been developed, they tend to group into three categories. The first category, including electroencephalography (EEG) and event-related potential (ERP), relies on measuring the electrical activity (and its associated magnetic consequences) in the brain. These methods are optimized for assessing the timing of brain activity (i.e., they are high in temporal resolution) but are limited in their ability to localize the origins of that brain activity (i.e., they are low in spatial resolution). The second category, including positron emission tomography (PET) and functional magnetic resonance imaging (fMRI), is based on tracking blood flow (and its correlates) that accompanies neuronal activity. These methods are relatively high in spatial resolution, but because of the rather sluggish nature of blood flow, they are low in temporal resolution. Both of these categories passively measure brain activity. A third category of techniques are those that actively perturb brain activity to address causal questions about the roles brain areas play. Here, we describe some of the major techniques that are used in social neuroscience and end the section with a brief discussion about future directions in neuroscience methods and the field's evolving understanding of best research practices.

Passive Imaging Methods: High Temporal Resolution

EEG was the first noninvasive method of brain mapping developed for humans. It is based on the principle that neural activity produces electrical potentials that can be recorded by electrodes placed on the scalp. Because EEGs register all brain activity, the signal is noisy, and it cannot provide information about specific changes in brain activity in response to a stimulus or cognitive task. This problem is remedied by using ERP. During ERP experiments, the trials are repeated numerous times, and the EEG signals following those trials are averaged together to create an average waveform of the brain's response to the experimental event. Perhaps the most important feature of ERP is that it provides a temporally precise record of brain activity. The use of ERP methods has provided psychologists with insights into a number of important social behaviors, including identifying unique patterns that are associated with perceiving members of an outgroup, at least for those who score high on measures of racial prejudice (Ito, Thompson, & Cacioppo, 2004). An excellent review of social neuroscience findings using ERP describes the method as being useful for understanding person perception, stereotyping, attitudes and evaluative processes, and self-regulation (Bartholow & Amodio, 2009). Most recently, electrocorticography (ECoG) or intercranial EEG is allowing social neuroscientists to record electrical activity by implanting electrodes directly on the exposed brain tissue of patients. While the technology is the same, these "depth electrodes" provide a much stronger signal because they are close to the actual neurons rather than recording neural activity through the skull.

A technique related to EEG but with increased spatial resolution is magnetoencephalography (MEG), which measures magnetic fields that are produced by the electrical activity of the brain. Unlike EEG, MEG does not require electrodes but rather uses special sensors that detect magnetic fields. MEG has the same temporal resolution as EEG, but because magnetic signals are not distorted by the skull, as are EEG signals, its signal localization is considerably better. In a study of the effects of social exclusion on self-control failure using MEG, Campbell et al. (2006) found that social exclusion affected frontal lobe regions typically involved in executive control of attention.

Passive Imaging Methods: High Spatial Resolution

Brain activity is not only associated with the electrical activity of neurons but also with associated changes in metabolic processes. Brain imaging methods track these changes to understand which areas of the brain are most active for a given task. PET, the first imaging method developed, involves injecting a relatively harmless radioactive substance into the blood stream. Using a PET scanner, researchers can then track this radiation as blood travels through the brain, resulting in a map of brain activity in three-dimensional space. The resulting image identifies the neural structures engaged in specific cognitive tasks. PET has one major disadvantage: The use of radioactive substances places an inherent limitation on the number of trials that can be used and, accordingly, tends to yield studies with low statistical power. Moreover, it can take a long time to image the entire brain, and so trials themselves need to last for an extended period. For reasons of safety as well as the ability to use many more trials, most current brain imaging is conducted using fMRI, to which we now turn.

Similar to PET, fMRI measures brain activity by tracking metabolism associated with blood flow, but it does so noninvasively (i.e., nothing is injected into the blood stream). Thus, a single fMRI study can contain hundreds of trials, thereby greatly enhancing the power of the study. Functional MRI does not measure blood flow directly. Rather, fMRI employs a strong magnetic field to assess changes in the blood-oxygen level dependent (BOLD) response at particular cortical sites after they have become active, which is an indirect measure of blood flow. Specifically, the BOLD signal is derived from the ratio of oxygenated to deoxygenated blood at cortical locations throughout the brain.

Active Manipulation Techniques

It is commonly known that functional neuroimaging data only suggest brain regions that may be engaged during a given behavior; correlations between behavior and localized brain activity cannot establish a causal brain–behavior linkage. One way to address such a hypothesis would be to conduct a lesion study in which specific brain regions were damaged while leaving other areas relatively intact. Ethics committees, however, tend not to encourage lesioning our undergraduate research participants. Fortunately, transcranial magnetic stimulation (TMS) allows for the temporary experimental disruption of neural activity in relatively circumscribed cortical regions while individuals engage in a cognitive task (Jahanshahi & Rothwell, 2000; Walsh & Cowey, 2000; Wig, Grafton, Demos, & Kelley, 2005). During TMS, a powerful electrical current flows through a wire coil that is placed on the scalp over the area to be stimulated. As electrical current flows through the coil, a powerful magnetic field is produced that interferes with neural function in specific regions of the brain. If multiple pulses of TMS are given over extended time (known as repeated TMS), the disruption can carry over beyond the period of direct stimulation. Studies using TMS to create a virtual lesion in the superior temporal sulcus (STS) have demonstrated interference in the perception of eye gaze direction (Pourtois et al., 2004), reduced accuracy in detecting biological motion from point light displays (Grossman, Battelli, & Pascual-Leone, 2005), and interference with processing facial expressions indicating anger (Harmer, Thilo, Rothwell, & Goodwin, 2001). By selectively disrupting the function of a brain region with TMS, scientists can make causal conclusions about whether and, if so, how these regions play a role in a given thought process or behavior.

Transcranial direct current stimulation (tDCS) also manipulates brain activity, but in a less invasive way than TMS. Rather than disabling a region with a strong magnetic pulse, tDCS applies weak electrical currents to the scalp to excite neural activity. By applying tDCS over a specific region associated with a particular behavioral response, researchers can increase the likelihood of that response. In social neuroscience, tDCS has been used to modulate a person's mood and emotion, the ability to perceive others' emotions, empathize, and make decisions (for a review, see Boggio et al., 2016). Recently, Maréchal, Cohn, Ugazio, and Ruff (2017) reported that stimulating the dorsolateral prefrontal cortex, a region associated with self-regulation, made participants more likely to act honestly even if doing so was contrary to their financial self-interest. Although promising as a method to influence social thought and behavior, the relative newness of tDCS mean that the limits and long-term consequences are as yet unknown.

Future Advances and Best Practices

Every year, new advances in hardware and analytical tools get us closer to maximizing both spatial and temporal resolution. Furthermore, teams of researchers are working hard to make neuroimaging more portable and conducive to studying the kind of behavior that social psychologists care about. At present, most techniques require participants to sit or lie motionless while being scanned, with even a couple of millimeters of head motion rendering data unusable. However, newer techniques such as functional near-infrared spectroscopy (fNIRS) provide fMRI-like images of brain activity while allowing participants to move and speak, albeit with reduced spatial resolution. Every year, neuroscientists and physicists are working toward better tools that will allow us to study the neural basis of social behavior with better technical precision and in more ecologically valid ways.

Besides technological advances, the field is also invested in establishing best practices for data collection and analysis. Most imaging methods are necessarily correlational and therefore prone to all the inherent limitations of correlational methods (see Vul, Harris, Winkielman, & Pashler, 2009). The advent of tools such as TMS and tDCS allow for some causal validation, but transcranial stimulation is limited to cortical areas near the skull and therefore can only have an indirect effect on mental processes that involve deeper structures. Assessing patients who have brain injury can provide complementary evidence for the causal involvement of a brain region for a given psychological function. Understanding how the brain gives rise to the social mind, therefore, requires integrating multiple sources of data rather than relying on data from a single technique or paradigm.

A deep understanding of mind and brain also relies on research practices that maximize the reliability of that data. Like other scientific disciplines, the field of social neuroscience is undergoing a sea change spurred by questions of replicability. In public discussion and private implementation, better practices for the collection and analysis of data are being established to increase confidence in findings reported. In the recent past, fMRI studies could be published with very few participants—a research practice driven by the high hourly costs of using fMRI. Now, studies must be adequately powered, requiring many more participants. Furthermore, new statistical understanding has led to better practices of how data are analyzed to avoid bias including separating data into training and testing samples and preregistering the proposed analyses.

A more conceptual concern is the difficulty in localizing specific psychological functions to discrete brain regions. There have now been several thousand imaging studies of a variety of psychological functions. It is now clear that many brain regions are activated across numerous cognitive and social tasks (Mitchell, 2009; Ochsner, 2007). Thus, when a researcher finds a particular activation in an imaging study, it is not always obvious what that activation indicates. An area may be activated across a broad array of disparate cognitive tasks because those different tasks share some common psychological process (i.e., semantic processing, memory, selecting among competing stimuli). In these cases, the activation may have little to do with the research question of greatest interest to the investigator. As in all areas of science, the value of any one imaging study depends on the care with which the experimental tasks are designed, and deep advances in our understanding about human thought and behavior will be achieved in the aggregate, across many studies and approaches. With that in mind, what is our best understanding to date about how the brain supports social thought and behavior?

Building a Social Brain

How do you build a social brain? Or what does the brain need to do to allow it to be social? In this section, we describe a conceptual framework for understanding the social brain. The overarching assumption is that the brain evolved over millions of years as an organ that solves adaptive problems, which, for humans, are frequently social in nature. Early human ancestors needed to recognize faces of friends and foes, identify potential mates and evaluate them in terms of desirability, understand the nature of group relations, and so on. Humans evolved a fundamental need to belong, which encourages behavior that facilitates cohesive groups (Baumeister & Leary, 1995; Bowlby, 1969). Effective groups shared food, provided mates, and helped care for offspring. As such, human survival has long depended on living within groups; banishment from the group was effectively a death sentence. Baumeister and Leary (1995) argued that the need to belong is a basic motive that activates behavior and influences cognition and emotion and that it leads to ill effects when not satisfied. Indeed, even today, not belonging to a group increases a person's risk for a number of adverse consequences, such as illnesses and premature death (Cacioppo, Hughes, Waite, Hawkley, & Thisted, 2006).

Initial findings using neuroimaging revealed that some neural regions appear to be associated with processing social information as compared to general semantic knowledge. For instance, Mitchell, Heatherton, and Macrae (2002) showed that when participants make judgments about whether a word describes a person (e.g., assertive, fickle) or an object such as fruit (e.g., sundried, seedless), various brain regions, particularly the medial prefrontal cortex (mPFC), were associated more with person judgments. Similarly, Mason, Banfield, and Macrae (2004) found that when participants made judgments about whether an action (e.g., running, sitting, biting) could be performed by a person or a dog, the mPFC was once again associated with judgments about people. Thus, the brain seems to treat other humans as a special class of stimuli. Here, we examine the implications of that notion.

The Building Blocks of the Social Brain

Converging evidence suggests that the human brain comes hardwired to find other humans interesting. Within 48 hours of life, newborns attend more to faces than any other objects, listen longer to human voices than other sounds, and gaze longer at upright versus upside-down displays of biological motion (Goren, Sarty, & Wu, 1975; Johnson, Dziurawiec, Ellis, & Morton, 1991; Simion, Regolin, & Bulf, 2008; Vouloumanos & Werker, 2007). Since babies lack knowledge about the world, this initial interest in other beings is likely driven by simple, perceptual cues. Indeed, two dots and a line are enough to grab an infant's attention but only if those shapes are presented in the configuration of a face: two dots for eyes and a line for nose (Goren, Sarty, & Wu, 1975). However primitive, having an innate set of "life detectors" affords two important benefits. First, it increases the chance of survival by ensuring that infants detect those who are likely to feed, protect, or eat them. The second, perhaps less obvious, benefit is that cleaving the world into animate and inanimate halves establishes a foundation upon which social thought can be built (Wheatley, Milleville, & Martin, 2007).

The layering of social understanding upon a framework of animacy is demonstrated across child development. By 5 months of age, infants infer goal-directedness in a moving human hand but not a moving rod (Woodward, 1998) and, by 18 months, attribute intentions to human actors but not machines (Meltzoff, 1995). Thus, early on, we impute thoughts, feelings, and actions only to the subset of the world that can think, feel, and act in return. In this way, the initial step of detecting life conserves precious cognitive energy—a finite resource that people are loathe to expend (Fiske & Taylor, 1991). Detecting animacy avoids such effort-wasting missteps as greeting doors or wondering why the lamp is such a poor conversationalist. Evidence from neuroscience suggests that these early "life detectors" are housed in two regions of the temporal lobe: ventral temporal cortex for the detection of human form (faces, bodies) and lateral temporal cortex for the detection of human dynamics (sound, motion).

Detecting Faces

Faces pack a wealth of information into a relatively small space. People are such experts at recognizing faces that they can effortlessly pick out their relatives in a crowd, evaluate people as potential mates, and understand that the two categories are independent. Given the importance of faces to daily life, it has been suggested that face perception and recognition hold a privileged status in the human brain. Indeed, one of the most robust findings in social neuroscience is that viewing faces activates a section of cortex more than any other kind of stimuli including nonface objects, scrambled faces, and inverted faces (Ishai, Ungerleider, Martin, Maisog, & Haxby, 1997; Kanwisher, McDermott, & Chun, 1997; McCarthy, Puce, Gore, & Allison, 1997). This region is located bilaterally (one per hemisphere) on the underside of the human brain and is dubbed the fusiform face area (FFA). Among faces, this region is particularly responsive to human faces compared to visually matched doll faces, suggesting a sensitivity to faces that appear to have minds attached (Looser, Guntupalli, & Wheatley, 2012; Wheatley, Weinberg, Looser, Moran, & Hajcak, 2011). Lesions to the FFA can create prosopagnosia: the selective inability to recognize the identity of faces (Duchaine & Nakayama, 2005; Tranel, Damasio, & Damasio, 1998).

The structural properties of a face not only provide the identity of a person but also the raw material for attraction. In one study, subjects were asked to report the gender of various faces while lying in an fMRI scanner. Although subjects were not judging attractiveness at the time, blood-flow activity in orbitofrontal cortex (OFC) correlated with subjects' later ratings of the attractiveness of those faces. OFC, a region associated with the evaluation of reward, was activated more by faces later deemed attractive relative to faces deemed unattractive (O'Doherty et al., 2003). As one might predict, sexual preference modulates this activity: Male faces evoked a greater response in this region for homosexual men and heterosexual women while female faces evoked a greater response for heterosexual men and homosexual women (Kranz & Ishai, 2006).

Other face-sensitive regions of cortex have been identified that may work in tandem with the FFA to support other percepts (what we perceive) and inferences based on the invariant features of a face (e.g., for a study on gender, see Kriegeskorte, Formisano, Sorger, & Goebel, 2007; for a study on trustworthiness, see Oosterhof & Toderov, 2008). However, the face is more than a collection of features; it also provides a canvas for facial expressions that convey transitory emotional and mental states. Reading facial expressions, along with other dynamic cues such as gestures and voice intonation, relies on a different region of temporal cortex right above the ears.

Detecting Speech and Motion

The overwhelming majority of research on facial identity and expressions employs static photographs. However, faces and bodies are in a perpetual state of motion that must be detected rapidly and decoded for biologically relevant meaning (e.g., intent to harm). A useful method of showing how people can extract social information through movement was discovered by Johansson (1973) who attached small lights to the joints of actors and filmed them in a dark room. A static snapshot of this stimulus looks like a random series of dots, but in motion the dots are immediately recognizable as biological motion. Such "point light" stimuli have been used with great effect to show that movement alone can convey gender, emotion, even personality (Atkinson, Dittrich, Gemmell, & Young, 2004; Clarke, Bradshaw, Field, Hampson, & Rose, 2005; Heberlein, Adolphs, Tranel, & Damasio, 2004; Pollick, Lestou, Ryu, & Cho, 2002). Dynamic stimuli such as these are processed by a neural pathway distinct from that used to process structural facial features: the STS (Allison, Puce, & McCarthy, 2000; Beauchamp, Lee, Haxby, & Martin, 2002; Grossman et al., 2005; Haxby, Hoffman, & Gobbini, 2000). Consistent with a layering of social understanding upon the detection of biological motion, fMRI studies have revealed that the STS in adult subjects is particularly tuned to motion that expresses social meaning, such as intentional actions and emotional gestures (Pelphrey, Morris, & McCarthy, 2004). And those with compromised functioning in this brain region (e.g., those with autism) are less accurate at identifying the emotion expressed in movement by point light videos in which actors move around "angrily" or "happily" in a dark room with only small lights visible that are attached to their joints (Dakin & Frith, 2005).

The STS is adjacent to that supporting the detection of biological sound. Several studies have shown that the superior temporal gyrus is activated by the sound of other human beings relative to similarly complex nonspeech sounds and underpins the ability to understand emotion in tone of voice (Beaucousin et al., 2007; von Kriegstein & Giraud, 2004). In normal daily life, the ability to hear emotion in a person's voice is taken for granted, but losing that ability (aprosodia) can have devastating social consequences. A recent meta-analysis found that schizophrenia patients were more than one standard deviation below the mean of healthy controls in recognizing tone of voice cues to emotion. The impairment was so large that the authors concluded it "was one of the most pervasive disturbances in schizophrenia that may contribute to social isolation" (Hoekert et al., 2007). In sum, the superior temporal cortex appears to be particularly attuned to the detection of human voice and movement and instrumental in decoding the many dynamic configurations of social meanings.

The specialized regions of cortex for the detection and understanding of human faces, voice, and motion are highly interconnected not only with each other but as nodes within larger, interacting circuits that support the full breadth of social understanding including self-identity, ability to empathize, and the regulation of our behavior in accordance with social norms. We now discuss a conceptual model of the neural basis of such components.

Components of the Social Brain

Given the fundamental need to belong, there needs to be a social brain system that monitors for signs of social inclusion/exclusion and alters behavior to forestall rejection or resolve other social problems (Krendl & Heatherton, 2009). Such a system requires four components, each of which is likely to have a discrete neural signature. First, people need self-awareness—to be aware of their behavior so as to gauge it against societal or group norms. Second, people need to understand how others are reacting to their behavior so as to predict how others will respond to them. In other words, they need "theory of mind" (ToM) or the capacity to attribute mental states to others. This implies the need for a third mechanism, which detects threat, especially in complex situations. Finally, there needs to be a self-regulatory mechanism for resolving discrepancies between self-knowledge and social expectations or norms, thereby motivating behavior to resolve any conflict that exists.

This does not mean that other psychological processes are unimportant for social functioning. Indeed, capacities such as language, memory, and vision, along with motivational and basic emotional states, are generally important for functioning within the social group. However, fully intact neural circuits underlying memory and vision, for example, are not necessary for being a good group member. By contrast, people with fundamental disturbances in the primary components of self, ToM, threat detection, or self-regulation have profound and often specific impairments in social function. Recall the case of Phineas Gage who had severe social impairments while having most of his mental facilities intact.

Unlike many other aspects of cognition, almost everything we know about the social brain has been uncovered in the last couple of decades. Fortunately, the emergence of social neuroscience has been both rapid and far-reaching, and thus, despite its infancy, this approach has already netted a substantial number of reliable empirical findings about how the brain gives rise to human sociality.

Component 1: Self Awareness

Survival in human social groups requires people to monitor their behavior and thoughts to assess whether those thoughts and behaviors are in keeping with prevailing group (social) norms. According to Baumeister (1998), "the capacity of the human organism to be conscious of itself is a distinguishing feature and is vital to selfhood" (p. 683). The topic of self may be among the most near and dear to social and personality psychologists. In social neuroscience, the study of self-reflection has provided one of the best examples of how neuroimaging might be especially useful as a tool to resolve theoretical debates when traditional behavioral methods are unable to do so. This section uses this example to demonstrate how neuroscience was able to resolve the age-old debate about whether the self is "special."

In the 1980s, a major debate in social psychology was whether information processed about the self is treated separately from other types of information or in the same manner (Bower & Gilligan, 1979; Klein & Kihlstrom, 1986; Klein & Loftus, 1988; Maki & McCaul, 1985; Markus, 1977). The first line of evidence in favor of the view that self is special emerged from the pioneering work of Tim Rogers and his colleagues (Rogers, Kuiper, & Kirker, 1977), who showed that when trait adjectives (e.g., happy) were processed with reference to the self (e.g., "Does happy describe you?"), subsequent memory performance was better than when the items were processed only for their general meaning (e.g., "Does happy mean the same as optimistic?"). This self-referential effect in memory has been demonstrated many times (Symons & Johnson, 1997) and shows that information processed about the self is special. Indeed, even people who can remember very little can often remember information that is self-relevant. For instance, patients who suffer from severe amnesia (resulting from brain injury or developmental disorders) retain the ability to accurately describe whether specific traits are true of the self (Klein, 2004). Even patients with Alzheimer's disease who suffer severe temporal disorientation and have difficulty recognizing their own family have shown evidence of self-knowledge (Klein, Cosmides, & Costabile, 2003).

Other researchers argued that self plays no special or unique role in cognition but that the memory enhancement that accompanies self-referential processing can be interpreted as a standard depth-of-processing effect (Greenwald & Banaji, 1989; Klein & Kihlstrom, 1986). From this perspective, the self is quite ordinary; people remember things about themselves more because, as that information comes in, they attend to and think about that information more than they do for other things they care less about.

Research on this question eventually withered, in part because the opposing theories made identical behavioral predictions; namely, better memory for items that were processed in a self-referential manner. Herein lies the tremendous advantage of using brain imaging. Neuroimaging techniques are ideally suited for resolving debates for which competing theories make identical behavior predictions. An initial attempt to examine the neural substrates of the self-reference effect used PET. Unfortunately, as previously discussed there is a limit to the number of trials that can be presented using PET, and the researchers did not obtain a statistically significant self-reference effect (Craik et al., 1999). Nonetheless, their results were intriguing in that during self-reference processing trials they did find distinct activations in frontal regions, notably the mPFC and areas of right prefrontal cortex. Observing the statistical-power limitation of PET, Kelley et al. (2002) used event-related fMRI in an attempt to identity the neural signature of self-referential mental activity. In a standard self-reference paradigm, participants judged trait adjectives in one of three ways: self ("Does the trait describe you?"), other ("Does the trait describe George Bush?"), and case ("Is the trait presented in uppercase letters"?). These judgments produced the expected significant differences in subsequent memory performance (i.e., self > other > case).

More important, however, they enabled the researchers to test the competing explanations that have been offered for the self-reference effect in memory. Previous functional imaging studies have identified multiple regions within the left frontal cortex that are responsive when thinking deeply something being learned (Buckner, Kelley, & Petersen, 1999; Demb et al., 1995; Gabrieli et al., 1996; Kapur et al., 1996; Kelley et al., 1998; Wagner et al., 1998). Thus, if the self-reference effect simply reflects the operation of such a process, then one would expect to observe elevated levels of activation in these left frontal areas when traits are judged in relation to self. If, however, the effect results from the properties of a unique cognitive self, then one might expect self-referential mental activity to engage brain regions that are distinct from those involved in general semantic processing. The results were clear: The left inferior frontal region, notable for its involvement in semantic processing tasks, did not discriminate between self and other trials. Instead, Kelley et al. (2002) observed selective activity in areas of prefrontal cortex, notably mPFC, suggesting that this region might be involved in the self-referential memory effect. In a later study, Macrae et al. (2004) demonstrated that activity in mPFC could predict whether a person would subsequently remember terms encoded with reference to self, providing more compelling evidence linking the activity in mPFC to self-memory processes. Thus, neuroimaging was able to resolve a social psychological debate about the self could not be resolved with behavioral methods alone.

Since these early studies, social neuroscience has made excellent strides in identifying brain regions that are involved in processing information about the self. For example, many neuroimaging studies have replicated the involvement of this mPFC region in tasks that require participants to judge their own personality traits (e.g., Heatherton et al., 2006; Johnson et al., 2002; Macrae, Moran, Heatherton, Banfield, & Kelley, 2004; Pfeifer, Lieberman, & Dapretto, 2007) or report on their preferences and opinions (Ames, Jenkins, Banaji, & Mitchell, 2008; Jenkins, Macrae, & Mitchell, 2008; Mitchell, Macrae, & Banaji, 2006), compared to judging these characteristics in others. Although the cognitive aspects of self-reflection involve mPFC, the emotional consequences of those responses (i.e., whether the response indicates positive or negative things about the rater) appear to be coded in the ventral anterior cingulate cortex, which is adjacent to mPFC (Moran et al., 2006). This area turns out to be important for interpersonal relations, which we discuss later in this chapter.

The issue of whether the self is somehow "special" remains somewhat contentious (see Gillihan & Farah, 2005), but the imaging literature is quite clear regarding tasks that involve self-awareness. They activate mPFC in imaging studies (Gusnard, 2005).

It is interesting to note that converging evidence from patient research also indicates that frontal lobe lesions, particularly to the mPFC and adjacent structures, have a deleterious effect on personality, mood, motivation, and self-awareness. Patients with frontal lobe lesions show dramatic deficits in recognizing their own limbs, engaging in self-reflection and introspection, and even reflecting on personal knowledge. Indeed, frontal lobe patients are particularly impaired in social emotions (Beer et al., 2003). Interestingly, damage to this region can lead to deficits in the organization of knowledge about one's preferences. Fellows and Farah (2007) have reported that, when asked to indicate their attitudes toward various stimuli, patients with mPFC lesions show unusually large discrepancies between testing sessions, suggesting that damage to this region leads either to failures to retrieve knowledge of one's attitudes or instability in otherwise stable aspects of selfhood.

It is important to be clear that that there is no specific "self" spot of the brain, no single brain region that is responsible for all psychological processes related to self. Rather, psychological processes are distributed throughout the brain, with contributions from multiple subcomponents determining discrete mental activities that come together to give rise to the human sense of self (Turk, Heatherton, Macrae, Kelley, & Gazzaniga, 2003). Various cognitive, sensory, motor, somatosensory, and affective processes are essential to self, and these processes likely reflect the contribution of several cortical and subcortical regions.

The extent to which we include others in our self-concept has been a topic of particular interest for social psychologists. Theories of intimacy and personal relationships might suggest that the self-reference effect is affected by the closeness of a relationship with the other used as a target. Indeed, Aron and colleagues define closeness as the extension of self to incorporate the other (Aron & Aron, 1996; Aron & Fraley, 1999; Aron, Aron, Tudor, & Nelson, 1991). Consistent with this idea, recent research has found that the brain encodes friendship in terms of distance from self (Parkinson & Wheatley, 2014; Parkinson, Liu, & Wheatley, 2014) and that close friends have strikingly similar neural responses to a variety of stimuli from comedy to music videos (Parkinson, Kleinbaum, & Wheatley, 2018).

Component 2: Mentalizing

Perhaps the most important attribute of the social brain is the ability to infer the mental states of others to predict their actions (Amodio & Frith, 2006; Gallagher & Frith, 2003; Mitchell, 2006). The underlying assumption—that behavior is caused by mental states—has been called taking an "intentional stance," ToM, and "mind perception" (Epley & Waytz, 2010), and the adoption of this assumption is an important developmental milestone. Testing whether young children possess ToM usually involves telling them stories in which false beliefs must be inferred. In one well-known example, a child is shown two dolls: Sally and Ann. Sally has a basket, and Ann has a box. The child watches as Sally puts a marble in the basket and leaves. While Sally is gone, "naughty" Ann takes the marble out of the basket and puts it in the box. Then Sally returns. The child is asked: "Where will Sally look for the marble?" The correct response requires understanding that Ann moved the marble *unbeknownst to* Sally and that Sally thus holds a false belief that the marble is still in the basket. Healthy and IQ-matched Downs syndrome children succeed at this task around the age of four (Baron-Cohen, Leslie, & Frith, 1985). Before that time, children have difficulty grasping that a person can believe something decoupled from reality.

It is perhaps not surprising that patients with impoverished social relationships do poorly on ToM tasks. Four-year-old autistic children have a failure rate of 80% on the Sally–Ann task (Baron-Cohen, Leslie, & Frith, 1985). If the task requires the added difficulty of understanding what a person thinks about *another* person's beliefs or thoughts (i.e., second-order mental state attribution), the failure rate in autistic individuals is even higher (Baron-Cohen, 1989). Difficulty representing another's thoughts is a hallmark of autism that endures throughout the lifespan. Research with patients and healthy adults has converged on two brain areas that are consistently modulated by tasks requiring the inference of mental states: the temporal parietal junction (TPJ) and the mPFC though additional areas may also be recruited depending on the task (Molenberghs, Johnson, Henry, & Mattingley, 2016). Healthy adult volunteers recruit these areas when inferring mental states from expressions in photographs, attributing mental states to animations of geometric shapes, and imputing mental states to characters in cartoons and stories (Frith & Frith, 1999; Molenberghs et al., 2016).

TPJ. An early social psychological study by Heider and Simmel (1944) showed our proclivity to infer social meaning from motion. In this seminal study, subjects spontaneously inferred intent, emotion, gender, and even personality in simple animations of interacting geometric shapes. Subsequent research demonstrated that various types of human motion express emotional, motivational, and intentional states (e.g., communicative gestures, gaze shifts) and that these motions have been associated with activity in the superior temporal sulcus extending into the TPJ (Castelli, Happe, & Frith, 2002; Haxby et al., 2000; Martin & Weisberg, 2003). Some researchers have speculated that there are adjacent but distinct areas within this region of cortex that support related but dissociable functions, such as the recognition of biological motion, recognition of mental states from motion cues, and the ability to mentalize regardless of whether motion cues are present. The last ability appears to be associated primarily with the TPJ, which has been implicated in perspective-taking (Saxe & Powell, 2006) as well as how we perceive our own body in space. TMS disruption to this region produces impairments in the ability to imagine how one's body looks from another's perspective (Blanke et al., 2005). Thus, this region appears to facilitate the ability to contemplate different spatial and mental perspectives from one's own (Saxe & Kanwisher, 2003; Mitchell, 2008). Consistent with the developmental trajectory mentioned earlier, the maturation of white matter tracts between TPJ and prefrontal cortex predicts the development of ToM in early childhood (Weismann et al., 2017).

Medial prefrontal cortex. The second area that is consistently activated by mentalizing is the mPFC, although typically a region of this brain structure slightly higher than observed for self-referential processing. Activity in this region has been associated with the perception of pain and tickling, as well as autobiographical memory and aesthetic judgment. Across these seemingly disparate studies, a common denominator has emerged: mPFC appears to support the ability to *attend to* the mental states that give rise to experience. That is, to create an explicit representation of what one thinks or feels *about* X. Recent research suggests that this area is also important for taking the perspective of another person (i.e., "How would you feel if you were person X"). This suggests that being able to represent our own subjective experience plays a central role in the ability to understand the subjective experience of others (Jenkins, Macrae, & Mitchell, 2008; Mitchell, Banaji, & Macrae, 2005; Mitchell, Heatherton, & Macrae, 2002).

Mentalizing allows us to infer the intentions of others, thereby learning about their likely future behavior. For this reason, social neuroscientists studying morality are particularly interested in the brain processes that allow us to reason about another's mental states, such as whether an act was committed intentionally or unintentionally (Decety & Wheatley, 2015). Although the act committed may have been the same, the state of another's mind allows us to predict the likelihood of it happening again and thus whether a person that committed a crime is an ongoing threat.

Component 3: Detection of Threat

One value of having ToM is that it supports a third mechanism, threat detection, which is particularly useful in complex situations such as dealing with ingroup or outgroup members (i.e., with members of their own group or members of other groups).

Ingroup threats. If humans have a fundamental need to belong, then there ought to be mechanisms for detecting inclusionary status (Leary, Tambor, Terdal, & Downs, 1995; Macdonald & Leary, 2005). Put another way, given the importance of group inclusion, humans need to be sensitive to signs that the group might exclude them. Indeed, there is evidence that people feel anxious when they face exclusion from their social groups (Baumeister & Tice, 1988). Thus, feeling socially anxious or worrying about potential rejection should lead to heightened social sensitivity. Indeed, research has demonstrated that people who worry most about social evaluation (i.e., the shy and lonely) show enhanced memory for social information, are more empathetically accurate, and show heightened abilities to decode social information (Gardner, Pickett, & Brewer, 2000; Gardner, Pickett, Jefferis, & Knowles, 2005; Pickett, Gardner, & Knowles, 2004).

Social psychologists have documented the pernicious effects of interpersonal rejection threat on mood, behavior, and cognition (Smart & Leary, 2009). Most prominent is a study by Eisenberger, Lieberman, and Williams (2003) who found that the dorsal region of the anterior cingulate cortex was responsive during a video game designed to elicit feelings of social rejection when virtual interaction partners suddenly and surprisingly stopped cooperating with the research participant. Since this initial study, other studies have also implicated the anterior cingulate cortex, although some of them find a more ventral (lower) rather than dorsal (higher) region (Somerville, Heatherton, & Kelley, 2006). Adolescence may be a particularly sensitive period for social evaluation (Masten et al., 2009; Somerville, 2013). Within adolescents, greater self-reported susceptibility to peer influence was associated with greater activity in the ventral anterior cingulate cortex during social rejection (Sebastian, Viding, Williams, & Blakemore, 2010).

Outgroup threats. Not all threats, however, are related to social exclusion. Just as people naturally fear dangerous animals (e.g., poisonous snakes and spiders, tigers, wolves), they also face harm from other humans who might like to harm them. Indeed, other group members can transmit disease, act carelessly and place bystanders at risk, waste or steal vital group resources, or poach one's mate. Similarly, people from other groups also can be dangerous when competition for scarce resources leads to intergroup violence. Hence, there is also a need for mechanisms that detect threats from outgroup members.

The most common area identified as relevant to threat from outgroup members is the amygdala. In perhaps the first social neuroscience study that used functional neuroimaging, cognitive neuroscientist

Elizabeth Phelps, social psychologist Mahzarin Banaji, and their colleagues used fMRI to study racial attitudes. They showed White college students pictures of unfamiliar Black and White faces while they scanned brain activity (Phelps et al., 2000). For those subjects who score high on an implicit measure of racial bias (see Chapter 12), the unfamiliar Black faces activated the amygdala, a brain structure that is involved in fear response and recognition (Whalen, 1998; Whalen & Phelps, 2009). It is important to the note that the amygdala is only one of several neural areas engaged during the evaluation of an outgroup member. Interestingly, emerging research from neuroimaging has revealed that areas of the prefrontal cortex involved in cognitive control are also engaged in these tasks. For instance, Cunningham et al. (2004) showed that the amygdala responded to pictures of Black faces when presented very quickly (30 ms). However, when the faces were presented for a longer duration (525 ms), the amygdala response was dampened and instead increased activation was observed in the prefrontal cortex. The authors argued that the heightened activation in the prefrontal cortex may have been inhibiting the automatic response elicited by the amygdala.

People who possess stigmatizing conditions that make them seem less than human, such as the homeless, also activate regions of the amygdala (Harris & Fiske, 2006), as do the physically unattractive and people with multiple facial piercings (Krendl, Macrae, Kelley, Fugelsang, & Heatherton, 2006). Considered together, it is clear that evaluating outgroup members—particularly those whom may pose a physical threat—involves activity of the amygdala. So, what function does the amygdala serve in the social context? It has long been thought to play a special role in responding to stimuli that elicit fear (Blanchard & Blanchard, 1972; Feldman Barrett & Wager, 2006; LeDoux, 1996). From this perspective, affective processing in the amygdala is a hard-wired circuit that has developed over the course of evolution to detect biologically relevant stimuli (e.g., threats to survival). But, like any other brain region, the amygdala is multifaceted with multiple subparts and different roles. Although one role is to detect threat, another is to detect who may need our help. People with psychopathy—who tend to be low in empathy and relatively insensitive to danger—tend to have smaller amygdalae on average compared to healthy controls, and their amygdalae are less responsive to signals of distress in others (e.g., fearful facial expressions). In contrast, extraordinary altruists such as people who donate one of their kidneys to a stranger tend to have larger amygdalae that are more responsive to signals of distress (Marsh et al., 2014). How brain areas such as the amygdala keep us safe from physical and social threats while also inciting us to safeguard others from these threats is an ongoing and vibrant area of research.

Component 4: Self-Regulation

A unique aspect of human behavior is the ability to regulate and control thoughts and actions, an ability commonly referred to as self-regulation. Self-regulation allows people to make plans, choose from alternatives, focus attention on pursuit of goals, inhibit competing thoughts, and regulate social behavior (Baumeister, Heatherton, & Tice, 1994; Baumeister & Vohs, 2004; Metcalfe & Mischel, 1999; Wegner, 1994). Extensive evidence from neuroimaging and patient research demonstrates that the prefrontal cortex is imperative in successfully engaging self-regulatory processes, as befitting its label as "chief executive" of the brain (Goldberg, 2001). Abundant patient and neuroimaging research has identified discrete brain regions within prefrontal cortex that are critical for self-regulation (for reviews, see Heatherton & Wagner, 2011; Ochsner, Silvers, & Buhle, 2012): primarily, the lateral prefrontal cortex (involved in inhibition), the OFC (involved in regulating primary physiological drives), and the ACC (involved in conflict resolution).

The lateral prefrontal cortex is associated with planning, choice, the control of memory and working memory, and language function (see D'Esposito et al., 1995; Dronkers, Redfern, & Knight, 2000; Fuster, Brodner, & Kroger, 2000; Goldman-Rakic, 1987). Damage to this area often results in patients' experiencing an inability to inhibit unwanted thoughts and behaviors (Pandya & Barnes, 1987). Damage to the OFC, which controls our behavioral and emotional output and how we interact with others (Dolan, 1999), often results in striking behavioral changes, including increased aggression (e.g., Rolls, Hornak, Wade, & McGrath, 1994). It is also linked to personality changes such as indifference, impaired social judgment and responsiveness, poor self-regulation, lack of impulse control, and poor judgment and insight (Damasio, 1994; Stone, Baron-Cohen, & Knight, 1998; Stuss & Alexander, 2000). Patients with OFC damage, like Phineas Gage, often cannot inhibit desires for instant gratification and thus may commit thefts or sexually aggressive behavior (Blumer & Benson, 1975; Grafman et al., 1996).

The ACC is essential for initiating actions, evaluating conflicts, and inhibiting otherwise dominant responses, processes heavily involved in self-regulation (Kerns et al., 2004). The ACC is functionally dissociated into the dorsal (higher) region that evaluates cognitive conflict, and the ventral (lower) ACC that evaluates emotional conflict (Bush, Luu, & Posner, 2000). Recall that ventral ACC is active during social evaluation and rejection. The ACC is often engaged whenever any kind of "supervisory input" is required (Badgaiyan & Posner, 1998). In fact, it is widely accepted that the ACC is somehow involved in evaluating the degree and nature of conflict, whereas other parts of the brain (particularly the PFC) may be involved in resolving the conflict itself (Botvinick, Cohen, & Carter, 2004; Cohen, Botvinick, & Carter, 2000; Kerns et al., 2004).

Emerging neuroimaging research has sought to more clearly identify the neural structures in self-regulation by examining the structures engaged in emotion and cognitive regulation. Ochsner, Bunge, Gross, and Gabrieli (2002) showed participants highly negative pictures and instructed them either to "attend" (study the picture and be aware of, but not try to alter, their feelings toward it) or "reappraise" (reinterpret the picture in such a way that it would no longer elicit a negative response) the photograph. The authors found that reappraising the photographs led to decreased subjective negative affect, and this was reflected in a reduction of activity in the amygdala and OFC and increased activation in the lateral and mPFC, as well as in the anterior cingulate cortex. Since the case of Phineas Gage, we have known that damage to certain prefrontal regions is associated with a lack of impulse control and self-regulatory difficulties more generally. The role of lateral PFC regions in regulating social emotions appears to be among the most robust findings in social neuroscience.

The Next Frontier

In this chapter, we have touched briefly upon several lines of research linking different kinds of brain activity to different aspects of human social behavior. Collectively, these studies reveal that there is no monolithic region or cognitive process that underlies all of social behavior but rather a constellation of processes and regions that give rise to the full social repertoire. New tools enable new analyses and new discoveries; the integration of previously siloed fields reveals a more complete picture of the whole.

Each individual study covered so far has relied on elegant empirical paradigms designed to isolate one stimulus feature or mental process at a time. This approach has yielded robust and reliable findings—an important benchmark for any new scientific field. Yet, in actuality, none of these features or processes exists in isolation. Social behavior is a messy, multifaceted affair in which the brain must process all of these components as they operate in parallel and interactively with each other. The question is, having stepped out of nature, how do we step back in? How do we study how the parts work together to create the real social world?

The next frontier in social neuroscience involves studying brains in more realistic, interactive social contexts. There is a new emphasis on using rich, naturalistic stimuli (e.g., movies rather than static photographs) and computational approaches that allow natural patterns to reveal themselves in the resulting data (Jack, Crivelli, & Wheatley, 2018). In neuroscience, this includes studying brain activity as people watch movies and then using the recorded activity patterns to reveal what different parts of the brain were most active at which times. For example, Wagner, Kelley, Haxb, and Heatherton (2016) observed that the dorsal medial PFC was particularly activated whenever a scene in a movie involved social interaction.

Social neuroscientists are also beginning to study how brains influence each other in real social interaction. People depend on interaction to hone ideas, forge bonds, establish norms, create information, and remain physically and mentally healthy. Despite this, the traditional neuroscientific approach has been to identify and study mental processes in isolation, with experimental paradigms focused on the individual. The reason for this has been largely pragmatic: Dark, noisy fMRI scanners and being wired up to 128 scalp electrodes are poor settings for lively conversation, not to mention either's sensitivity to motion artifact. However, new technological advances in hardware and software are enabling participants to play games with each other and even have conversations (Pfeiffer, Timmermans, Vogeley, Frith, & Schilbach, 2013; Schilbach et al., 2013). Five years from now, it is likely that we will know a lot more about how minds influence each other in real time—a truly *social* neuroscience.

Summary

Over the past two decades, the integration of cognitive neuroscience and social psychology has led to a wave of insights into the neural basis of human social cognition. In beginning to examine the neural underpinnings of social behavior, researchers have sought to identify the neural bases of cognitive processes that allow humans to perceive and understand the minds of others. The methods of cognitive neuroscience have already contributed to our mechanistic understanding of the social brain. Recent and future advances in neuroimaging promise to push our understanding even deeper; to reveal how minds influence each other at different ages and scales to create the full complexity of human social behavior.

References

Adolphs, R. (2009). The social brain: Neural basis of social knowledge. *Annual Review of Psychology, 60,* 693–716.

Allison, T., Puce, A., & McCarthy, G. (2000). Social perception from visual cues: Role of the STS region. *Trends in Cognitive Sciences, 4,* 267–278.

Allport, F. H. (1924). *Social psychology.* Cambridge, MA: Riverside.

Ames, D. L., Jenkins, A. C., Banaji, M. R., & Mitchell, J. P. (2008). Taking another's perspective increases self-referential neural processing. *Psychological Science, 19,* 642–644.

Amodio, D. M. & Frith, C. D. (2006). Meeting of the minds: The medial frontal cortex and social cognition. *Nature, 7,* 268–277.

Anonymous. (1851). Remarkable case of injury. *American Phrenological Journal, 13,* 89.

Aron, A., & Aron, E. N. (1996). *Self and self-expansion in relationships.* Hillsdale, NJ: Erlbaum.

Aron, A., Aron, E. N., Tudor, M., & Nelson, G. J. (1991). Close relationships as including other in the self. *Journal of Personality and Social Psychology, 60,* 241–253.

Aron, A., & Fraley, B. (1999). Relationship closeness as including other in the self: Cognitive underpinnings and measures. *Social Cognition. 17,* 140–160.

Atkinson, A. P., Dittrich, W. H., Gemmell, A. J., & Young, A. W. (2004). Emotion perception from dynamic and static body expressions in point-light and full-light displays. *Perception, 33,* 717–746.

Badgaiyan, R., & Posner, M. (1998). Mapping the cingulate cortex in response selection and monitoring. *NeuroImage, 7,* 255–260.

Baron-Cohen, S. (1989). The autistic child's theory of mind: A case of specific developmental delay. *Journal of Child Psychology and Psychiatry, 30,* 285–297.

Baron-Cohen, S., Leslie, A. M., & Frith, U. (1985). Does the autistic child have a "theory of mind"? *Cognition, 21,* 37–46.

Baron-Cohen, S., Lombardo, M., & Tager-Flusberg, H. (Eds.). (2013). *Understanding other minds: Perspectives from developmental social neuroscience.* Oxford, England: Oxford University Press.

Bartholow, B. D., & Amodio, D. M. (2009). Using event-related brain potentials in social psychological research: A brief review and tutorial. In E. Harmon-Jones & S. Beer (Eds.), *Methods in social neuroscience* (pp. 198–232). New York, NY: Guilford.

Baumeister, R. F. (1998). *The self* (4th ed., Vol. 2). New York, NY: McGraw-Hill.

Baumeister, R. F., Heatherton, T. F., & Tice, D. M. (1994). *Losing control: How and why people fail at self-regulation.* San Diego, CA: Academic Press.

Baumeister, R. F., & Leary, M. R. (1995). The need to belong: Desire for interpersonal attachments as a fundamental human motivation. *Psychological Bulletin, 117,* 497–529.

Baumeister, R. F., & Tice, D. M. (1988). Metatraits. *Journal of Personality, 56,* 571–598.

Baumeister, R. F., & Vohs, K. D. (2004). *Handbook of self-regulation: Research, theory, and applications.* New York, NY: Guilford.

Beauchamp, M. S., Lee, K. E., Haxby, J. V., & Martin, A. (2002). Parallel visual motion processing streams for manipulable objects and human movements. *Neuron, 34,* 149–159.

Beaucousin, V., Lacheret, A., Turbelin, M., Morel, M., Mazoyer, B., & Tzourio-Mazoyer, N. (2007). FMRI study of emotional speech comprehension. *Cerebral Cortex, 17,* 339–352.

Beer, J. S., Heerey, E. A., Keltner, D., Scabini, D., & Knight, R. T. (2003). The regulatory function of self-conscious emotion: Insights from patients with orbitofrontal damage. *Journal of Personality and Social Psychology, 85,* 594–604.

Blanchard, D. C., & Blanchard, R. J. (1972). Innate and conditioned reactions to threat in rats with amygdaloid lesions. *Journal Comparative and Physiological Psychology, 81,* 281–290.

Blanke, O., Mohr, C., Michel C. M., Pascual-Leone, A., Brugger, P., Seeck, M., . . . Thut, G. (2005). Linking out-of-body experience and self processing to mental own-body imagery at the temporoparietal junction. *Journal of Neuroscience, 25,* 550–557.

Blumer, D., & Benson, D. (1975). *Personality changes with frontal and temporal lesions.* New York, NY: Grune & Stratton.

Boggio, P. S., Rego, G. G., Marques, L. M., & Costa, T. L. (2016). Transcranial direct current stimulation in social and emotion research. In A. Brunoni, M. Nitsche, & C. Loo (Eds.), *Transcranial direct current stimulation in neuropsychiatric disorders* (pp. 143–152). Cham, Switzerland: Springer.

Botvinick, M. M., Cohen, J. D., & Carter, C. S. (2004). Conflict monitoring and anterior cingulate cortex: An update. *Trends in Cognitive Sciences, 8,* 539–546.

Bower, G. H., & Gilligan, S. G. (1979). Remembering information related to one's self. *Journal of Research in Personality, 13,* 420–432.

Bowlby, J. (1969). *Attachment and loss* (Vol. 1). New York, NY: Basic Books.

Buckner, R. L., Kelley, W. M., & Petersen, S. E. (1999). Frontal cortex contributes to human memory formation. *Nature Neuroscience, 2,* 311–314.

Bush, G., Luu, P., & Posner, M. I. (2000). Cognitive and emotional influences in anterior cingulate cortex. *Trends in Cognitive Sciences, 4,* 215–222.

Cacioppo, J. T., & Berntson, G. G. (1992). Social psychological contributions to the decade of the brain: Doctrine of multilevel analysis. *American Psychologist, 47,* 1019–1028.

Cacioppo, J. T., Hughes, M. E., Waite, L. J., Hawkley, L. C., & Thisted, R. A. (2006). Loneliness as a specific risk factor for depressive symptoms: Cross-sectional and longitudinal analyses. *Psychology and Aging, 21,* 140–151.

Campbell, W. K., Krusmark, E. A., Dyckman, K. A., Brunell, A. B., McDowell, J. E., Twenge, J. M., & Clementz, B. A. (2006). A magnetoencephalography investigation of neural correlates for social exclusion and self-control. *Social Neuroscience, 1,* 124–134.

Castelli, F., Happé, F., & Frith, U. (2002). Movement and mind: A functional imaging study of perception and interpretation of complex intentional movement patterns. *NeuroImage, 12,* 314–325.

Clarke, T. J., Bradshaw, M. F., Field, D. T., Hampson, S. E., & Rose, D. (2005). The perception of emotion from body movement in point-light displays of interpersonal dialogue. *Perception, 34,* 1171–1180.

Cohen, J. D., Botvinick, M., & Carter, C. S. (2000). Anterior cingulate and prefrontal cortex: Who's in control? *Nature Neuroscience, 3,* 421–423.

Cunningham, W. A., Johnson, M. K., Raye, C. L., Gatenby, C. J., Gore, J. C., & Banaji, M. R. (2004). Separable neural components in the processing of black and white faces. *Psychological Science, 15,* 806–813.

Craik, F. I. M., Moroz, T. M., Moscovitch, M., Stuss, D. T., Winocur, G., Tulving, E., & Kapur, S. (1999). In search of the self: A positron emission tomography study. *Psychological Science, 10,* 26–34.

Dakin, S., & Frith, U. (2005). Vagaries of visual perception in autism. *Neuron, 48,* 497–507.

Damasio, A. R. (1994). Descartes' error and the future of human life. *Scientific American, 271,* 144.

Decety, J. & Wheatley, T. (Eds.). (2015). *The moral brain.* Cambridge, MA: MIT Press.

Demb, J. B., Desmond, J. E., Wagner, A. D., Vaidya, C. J., Glover, G. H., & Gabrieli, J. D. E. (1995). Semantic encoding and retrieval in the left inferior prefrontal cortex: A functional MRI study of task difficulty and process specificity. *Journal of Neuroscience, 15,* 5870–5878.

D'Esposito, M., Detre, J. A., Alsop, D. C., Shin, R. K., Atlas, S., & Grossman, M. (1995). The neural basis of the central executive system of working memory. *Nature, 378,* 279–281.

Dolan, R. J. (1999). On the neurology of morals. *Nature Neuroscience, 2,* 927–929.

Dronkers, N. F., Redfern, B. B., & Knight, R. T. (2000). *The neural architecture of language disorders.* Cambridge, MA: MIT Press.

Duchaine, B. & Nakayama, K. (2005). Dissociations of face and object recognition in developmental prosopagnosia. *Journal of Cognitive Neuroscience, 17,* 249–261.

Eisenberger, N. I., Lieberman, M. D., & Williams, K. D. (2003). Does rejection hurt? An fMRI study of social exclusion. *Science, 302,* 290–292.

Epley, N., & Waytz, A. (2010). Mind Perception. In S. T. Fiske, D. T. Gilbert, & G. Lindzey (Eds.), *The handbook of social psychology* (5th ed., pp. 498–541). New York: Wiley.

Feldman Barrett, L., & Wager, T. D. (2006). The structure of emotion: Evidence from neuroimaging studies. *Current Directions in Psychological Science, 15,* 79–83.

Fellows, L. K., & Farah, M. J. (2007). The role of ventromedial prefrontal cortex in decision making: Judgment under uncertainty or judgment per se? *Cerebral Cortex, 17,* 2669–2674.

Fiske, S. T., & Taylor, S. E. (1991). *Social cognition* (2nd ed.). New York: McGraw-Hill.

Frith, C. D., & Frith, U. (1999). Interacting minds—a biological basis. *Science, 286,* 1692–1695.

Fuster, J. M., Brodner, M., & Kroger, J. K. (2000). Cross-modal and cross-temporal associations in neurons of frontal cortex. *Nature, 405,* 347–351.

Gabrieli, J. D. E., Desmond, J. E., Demb, J. B., Wagner, A. D., Stone, M. V., Vaidya, C. J., & Glover, G. H. (1996). Functional magnetic resonance imaging of semantic memory processes in the frontal lobes. *Psychological Science, 7,* 278–283.

Gallagher, H. L., & Frith, C. D. (2003). Functional imaging of "theory of mind." *Trends in Cognitive Sciences, 7,* 77–83.

Gardner, W. L., Pickett, C. L., & Brewer, M. B. (2000). Social exclusion and selective memory: How the need to belong influences memory for social events. *Personality and Social Psychology Bulletin, 26,* 486–496.

Gardner, W. L., Pickett, C. L., Jefferis, V., & Knowles, M. (2005). On the outside looking in: Loneliness and social monitoring. *Personality and Social Psycgology Bulletin, 31,* 1549–1560.

Gazzaniga, M. S. (1985). *The social brain.* New York, NY: Basic Books.

Gazzaniga, M. S. (Ed.). (2009). *The cognitive neurosciences* (4th ed.). Cambridge, MA: MIT Press.

Gillihan, S. J., & Farah, M. J. (2005). Is self special? A critical review of evidence from experimental psychology and cognitive neuroscience. *Psychological Bulletin, 13,* 76–97.

Goldberg, E. (2001). *The executive brain: The frontal lobes and the civilized mind.* New York, NY: Oxford University Press.

Goldman-Rakic, P. S. (1987). Development of cortical circuitry and cognitive function. *Child Development, 58,* 601–622.

Goren, C., Sarty, M., & Wu, P. (1975). Visual following and pattern discrimination of face-like stimuli by newborn infants. *Pediatrics, 56,* 544–549.

Grafman, J., Schwab, K., Warden, D., Pridgen, A., Brown, H. R., & Salazar, A. M. (1996). Frontal lobe injuries, violence, and aggression: A report of the Vietnam Head Injury Study. *Neurology, 46,* 1231–1238.

Greenwald, A. G., & Banaji, M. R. (1989). The self as a memory system: Powerful, but ordinary. *Journal of Personality and Social Psychology, 57,* 41–54.

Grossman, E. D., Battelli, L., & Pascual-Leone, A. (2005). Repetitive TMS over posterior STS disrupts perception of biological motion. *Vision Research, 45,* 2847–2853.

Gusnard, D. A. (2005). Being a self: Considerations from functional imaging. *Consciousness and Cognition, 14,* 679–697.

Harlow, J. M. (1868). Recovery from the passage of an iron bar through the head. *Publications of the Massachusetts Medical Society, 2,* 327–347.

Harmon-Jones, E., & Inzlicht, M. (2016). In E. Harmon-Jones & M. Inzlicht (Eds.), *Social neuroscience: Biological perspectives on social psychology* (pp. 1–9). New York, NY: Routledge.

Harmer, C. J., Thilo, K. V., Rothwell, J. C., & Goodwin, G. M. (2001) Transcranial magnetic stimulation of medial-frontal cortex impairs the processing of angry facial expressions. *Nature Neuroscience, 4,* 17–18.

Harris, L. T., & Fiske, S. T. (2006). Dehumanizing the lowest of the low: Neuroimaging responses to extreme out-groups. *Psychological Science, 17,* 847–853.

Haxby, J. V., Hoffman, E. A., & Gobbini, M. I. (2000). The distributed human neural system for face perception. *Trends in Cognitive Sciences, 4,* 223–233.

Heatherton, T. F., & Wagner, D. D. (2011). Cognitive neuroscience of self-regulation failure. *Trends in Cognitive Sciences, 15,* 132–139.

Heatherton, T. F., Wyland, C., Macrae, C. N., Denny, B. T., Demos, K. D., & Kelley, W. M. (2006). *Friends among us? Medial prefrontal activity is specific for self-referential processing.* Unpublished manuscript.

Heberlein, A. S., Adolphs, R., Tranel, D., & Damasio, H. (2004). Cortical regions for judgments of emotions and personality traits from point-light walkers. *Journal of Cognitive Neuroscience, 16,* 1143–1158.

Heider, F., & Simmel, M. (1944). An experimental study of apparent behavior. *American Journal of Psychology, 57,* 243–259.

Hoekert, M., Kahn, R.S., Pijnenborg, M., & Aleman, A. (2007). Impaired recognition and expression of emotional prosody in schizophrenia: Review and meta-analysis. *Schizophrenia Research, 96,* 135–145.

Ishai, A., Ungerleider, L., Martin, A., Maisog, J. M. & Haxby, J. V. (1997). fMRI reveals differential activation in the ventral object vision pathway during the perception of faces, houses, and chairs. *NeuroImage, 5,* S149.

Ito, T. A., Thompson, E., & Cacioppo, J. T. (2004). Tracking the timecourse of social perception: The effects of racial cues on event-related brain potentials. *Personality and Social Psychology Bulletin, 30,* 1267–1280.

Jack, R. E., Crivelli, C., & Wheatley, T. (2018). Data-driven methods to diversify knowledge of human psychology. *Trends in Cognitive Sciences, 22,* 1–5.

Jahanshahi, M., & Rothwell, J. (2000). Transcranial magnetic stimulation studies of cognition: An emerging field. *Experimental Brain Research, 131,* 1–9.

Jenkins, A. C., Macrae, C. N., & Mitchell, J. P. (2008). Repetition suppression of ventromedial prefrontal activity during judgments of self and others. *Proceedings of the National Academy of Sciences, 105,* 4507–4512.

Johansson, G. (1973). Visual perception of biological motion and a model for its analysis. *Perception and Psychophysics, 14,* 201–211.

Johnson, M. H., Dziurawiec, S., Ellis, H., & Morton, J. (1991). Newborns' preferential tracking of face-like stimuli and its subsequent decline. *Cognition, 40,* 1–19.

Johnson, S. C., Baxter, L. C., Wilder, L. S., Pipe, J. G., Heiserman, J. E., & Prigatano, G. P. (2002). Neural correlates of self-reflection. *Brain, 125*(Pt 8), 1808–1814.

Kanwisher, N., McDermott, J., & Chun, M. M. (1997). The fusiform face area: a module in human extrastriate cortex specialized for face perception. *Journal of Neuroscience, 17,* 4302–4311.

Kapur, S., Tulving, E., Cabeza, R., McIntosh, A. R., Sylvain, H. A., & Craik, F. I. M. (1996). The neural correlates of intentional learning of verbal materials: A PET study in humans. *Cognitive Brain Research, 4,* 243–249.

Kelley, W. M., Macrae, C. N., Wyland, C. L., Caglar, S., Inati, S., & Heatherton, T. F. (2002). Finding the self? An event-related fMRI study. *Journal of Cognitive Neuroscience, 14,* 785–794.

Kelley, W. M., Miezin, F. M., McDermott, K. B., Buckner, R. L., Raichle, M. E., Cohen, N. J., . . . Petersen, S. E. (1998). Hemispheric specialization in human dorsal frontal cortex and medial temporal lobe for verbal and nonverbal memory encoding. *Neuron, 20,* 927–936.

Kerns, J. G., Cohen, J. D., MacDonald, A. W., Cho, R. Y., Stenger, V. A., & Carter, C. S. (2004). Anterior cingulate conflict monitoring and adjustments in control. *Science, 303,* 1023–1026.

Klein, S. B. (2004). *The cognitive neuroscience of knowing one's self* (Vol. 3). Cambridge, MA: MIT Press.

Klein, S. B., Cosmides, L., & Costabile, K. A. (2003). Preserved knowledge of self in a case of Alzheimer's dementia. *Social Cognition, 21,* 157–165.

Klein, S. B., & Kihlstrom, J. F. (1986). Elaboration, organization, and the self-reference effect in memory. *Journal of Experimental Psychology: General, 115,* 26–38.

Klein, S. B., & Loftus, J. (1988). The nature of self-referent encoding: The contributions of elaborative and organizational processes. *Journal of Personality and Social Psychology, 55,* 5–11.

Kranz, F., & Ishai, A. (2006). Face perception is modulated by sexual preference. *Current Biology, 16,* 63–68.

Krendl, A. K., & Heatherton, T. F. (2009). Self versus others/Self-regulation. In G. G. Berntson & J. T. Cacioppo (Eds.), *Handbook of neuroscience for the behavioral sciences* (pp. 859–878). Hoboken, NJ: Wiley.

Krendl, A. C., Macrae, C. N., Kelley, W. M., Fugelsang, J. F., & Heatherton, T. F. (2006). The good, the bad, and the ugly: An fMRI investigation of the functional anatomic correlates of stigma. *Social Neuroscience, 1,* 5–15.

Kriegeskorte, N., Formisano, E., Sorger, B., & Goebel, R. (2007). Individual faces elicit distinct response patterns in human anterior temporal cortex. *Proceedings of the National Academy of Sciences, 104,* 20600–20605.

Leary, M. R., Tambor, E. S., Terdal, S. K., & Downs, D. L. (1995). Self-esteem as an interpersonal monitor: The sociometer hypothesis. *Journal of Personality and Social Psychology, 68,* 518–530.

LeDoux, J. E. (1996). *The emotional brain.* New York, NY: Simon & Schuster.

Lieberman, M. D. (2010). Social cognitive neuroscience. In S. T. Fiske, D. T. Gilbert, & G. Lindzey (Eds). *The handbook of social psychology* (5th ed., pp. 143–193). New York, NY: Wiley.

Looser, C. E., Guntupalli, J. S., & Wheatley, T. (2012). Multi-voxel patterns in face- sensitive temporal regions reveal an encoding schema based on detecting life in a face. *Social Cognitive Affective Neuroscience, 8, 799–805.*

Macdonald, G., & Leary, M. R. (2005). Why does social exclusion hurt? The relationship between social and physical pain. *Psychological Bulletin, 131,* 202–223.

Macmillan, M. (2000). *An odd kind of fame: Stories of Phineas Gage.* Cambridge, MA: MIT Press.

Macrae, C. N., Moran, J. F., Heatherton, T. F., Banfield, J. F., & Kelley, W. M. (2004). Medial prefrontal activity predicts memory for self. *Cerebral Cortex, 14,* 647–654.

Maki, R. H., & McCaul, K. D. (1985). The effects of self-reference versus other reference on the recall of traits and nouns. *Bulletin of the Psychonomic Society, 23,* 169–172.

Maréchal, M. A., Cohn, A., Ugazio, G. and Ruff, C. C. (2017). Increasing honesty in humans with noninvasive brain stimulation. *Proceedings of the National Academy of Sciences, 114,* 4360–4364.

Markus, H. (1977). Self-schemata and processing information about the self. *Journal of Personality and Social Psychology, 35,* 63–78.

Marsh, A. A., Stoycos, S. A., Brethel-Haurwitz, K. M., Robinson, P., VanMeter, J. W., & Cardinale, E. M. (2014). Neural and cognitive characteristics of extraordinary altruists. *Proceedings of the National Academy of Sciences, 111,* 15036–15041.

Martin, A., & Weisberg, J. (2003). Neural foundations for understanding social and mechanical concepts. *Cognitive Neuropsychology, 20,* 575–587.

Mason, M. F., Banfield, J. F., & Macrae, C. N. (2004). Thinking about actions: The neural substrates of person knowledge. *Cerebral Cortex, 14,* 209–214.

Masten, C. L., Eisenberger, N. I., Borofsky, L. A., Pfeifer, J. H., McNealy, K., Mazziotta, J. C., & Dapretto, M. (2009). Neural correlates of social exclusion during adolescence: Understanding the distress of peer rejection. *Social Cognitive Affective Neuroscience, 4,* 143–157.

McCarthy, G., Puce, A., Gore, J. C., & Allison, T., 1997. Face-specific processing in the human fusiform gyrus. *Journal of Cognitive Neuroscience, 9,* 604–609.

Meltzoff, A.N. (1995). Understanding the intention of others: Re-enactment of intended acts by 18-month-old children. *Developmental Psychology, 31,* 838–850.

Metcalfe, J., & Mischel, W. (1999). A hot/cool-system analysis of delay of gratification: Dynamics of willpower. *Psychological Review, 106,* 3–19.

Mitchell, J. P. (2006). Mentalizing and Marr: An information processing approach to the study of social cognition. *Brain Research, 1079,* 66–75.

Mitchell, J. P. (2008). Activity in right temporo-parietal junction is not selective for theory-of-mind. *Cerebral Cortex, 18,* 262–271.

Mitchell, J. P. (2009). Social psychology as a natural kind. *Trends in Cognitive Sciences, 13,* 246–251.

Mitchell, J. P., Banaji, M. R., & Macrae, C. N. (2005). General and specific contributions of the medial prefrontal cortex to knowledge about mental states. *NeuroImage, 28,* 757–762.

Mitchell, J. P., Heatherton, T. F., & Macrae, C. N. (2002). Distinct neural systems subserve person and object knowledge. *Proceedings of the National Academy of Sciences, 99,* 15238–15243.

Mitchell, J. P., Macrae, C. N., & Banaji, M. R. (2006). Dissociable medial prefrontal contributions to judgments of similar and dissimilar others. *Neuron, 50,* 655–663.

Molenberghs, P., Johnson, H., Henry, J. D., & Mattingley, J. B. (2016). Understanding the minds of others: A neuroimaging meta-analysis. *Neuroscience & Biobehavioral Reviews, 65,* 276–291.

Moran, J. M., Macrae, S. N., Heatherton, T. F., Wyland, C. L., & Kelley, W. M. (2006). Neuroanotomical evidence for distinct cognitive and affective components of self. *Journal of Cognitive Neuroscience, 18,* 1586–1594.

O'Doherty, J., Winston, J., Critchley, H., Perret, D., Burt, D., & Dolan, R. (2003). Beauty in a smile: The role of orbitofrontal cortex in facial attractiveness. *Neuropsychologia, 41,* 147–155.

Ochsner, K. N. (2007). Social cognitive neuroscience: Historical development, core principles, and future promise. In A. Kruglanski & E. T. Higgins (Eds.) *Social psychology: A handbook of basic principles.* (2nd ed., pp. 39–66). New York, NY: Guilford.

Ochsner, K. N., Bunge, S. A., Gross, J. J., & Gabrieli, J. D. (2002). Rethinking feelings: An FMRI study of the cognitive regulation of emotion. *Journal of Cognitive Neuroscience, 14,* 1215–1229.

Ochsner, K. N., Silvers, J. A., & Buhle, J. T. (2012). Functional imaging studies of emotion regulation: A synthetic review and evolving model of the cognitive control of emotion. *Annals of the New York Academy of Sciences, 1251,* E1–E24.

Oosterhof, N. N., & Todorov, A. (2008). The functional basis of face evaluation. *Proceedings of the National Academy of Sciences of the USA, 105,* 11087–11092.

Pandya, D. N., & Barnes, C. L. (1987). *Architecture and connections of the frontal lobe.* New York, NY: IRBN.

Parkinson, C., Kleinbaum, A., & Wheatley, T. (2018). Similar neural responses predict friendship. *Nature Communications, 9,* 332.

Parkinson, C, Liu, S., & Wheatley, T. (2014). A common cortical metric for spatial, temporal and social distance. *Journal of Neuroscience, 34,* 1979–1987.

Parkinson, C., & Wheatley, T. (2014). Old cortex, new contexts: Re-purposing spatial perception for social cognition. *Frontiers in Human Neuroscience, 7,* 645.

Pelfrey, K. A., Morris, J. P., & McCarthy, G. (2004). Grasping the intentions of others: The perceived intentionality of an action influences activity in the superior temporal sulcus during social perception. *Journal of Cognitive Neuroscience, 16,* 1706–1716.

Pfeifer, J. H., Lieberman, M. D., & Dapretto, M. (2007). "I know you are but what am?!" Neural bases of self- and social knowledge in children and adults. *Journal of Cognitive Neuroscience, 19,* 1323–1337.

Pfeiffer, U. J., Timmermans, B., Vogeley, K., Frith, C. D., & Schilbach, L. (2013). Towards a neuroscience of social interaction. *Frontiers in Human Neuroscience, 7,* art. 22.

Phelps, E. A., O'Connor, K. J., Cunningham, W. A., Funayama, E. S., Gatenby, J. C., Gore, J. C., & Banaji, M. R. (2000). Performance on indirect measures of race evaluation predicts amygdala activation. *Journal of Cognitive Neuroscience, 12,* 729–738.

Pickett, C. L., Gardner, W. L., & Knowles, M. (2004). Getting a cue: The need to belong and enhanced sensitivity to social cues. *Personality and Social Psychology Bulletin, 30,* 1095–1107.

Pollick, F. E., Lestou, V., Ryu, J., & Cho, S. B. (2002). Estimating the efficiency of recognizing gender and affect from biological motion. *Vision Research, 42,* 2345–2355.

Pourtois, G., Sander, D., Andres, M., Grandjean, D., Reveret, L., Olivier, E., & Vuilleumier, P. (2004). Dissociable roles of the human somatosensory and superior temporal cortices for processing social face signals. *European Journal of Neuroscience, 20,* 3507–3515.

Rogers, T. B., Kuiper, N. A., & Kirker, W. S. (1977). Self-reference and the encoding of personal information. *Journal of Personality and Social Psychology, 35,* 677–688.

Rolls, E. T., Hornak, J., Wade, D., & McGrath, J. (1994). Emotion-related learning in patients with social and emotional changes associated with frontal lobe damage. *Journal of Neurology, Neurosurgery & Psychiatry, 57,* 1518–1524.

Saxe, R., & Kanwisher, N. (2003). People thinking about thinking people: The role of the temporo-parietal junction in theory of mind. *NeuroImage, 19,* 1835–1842.

Saxe, R., & Powell, L. J. (2006). It's the thought that counts: Specific brain regions for one component of theory of mind. *Psychological Science, 17,* 692–699.

Schilbach, L., Timmermans, B., Reddy, V., Costall, A., Bente, G., Schlicht, T., & Vogeley, K. (2013) Toward a second-person neuroscience. *Behavioral and Brain Sciences, 36,* 393–414.

Sebastian, C., Viding, E., Williams, K. D., & Blakemore, S. J. (2010). Developmental influences on the neural bases of responses to social rejection: Implications of social neuroscience for education. *NeuroImage, 57,* 686–694.

Simion, F., Regolin, L., & Bulf, H. (2008). A predisposition for biological motion in the newborn baby. *Proceedings of the National Academy of Sciences, 105,* 809–813.

Smart Richman, L., & Leary, M. R. (2009). Reactions to discrimination, stigmatization, ostracism, and other forms of interpersonal rejection: A multimotive model. *Psychological Review, 116,* 365–383.

Somerville, L. H. (2013). Special issue on the teenage brain: Sensitivity to social evaluation. *Current Directions in Psychological Science, 22,* 121–127.

Somerville, L. H., Heatherton, T. F., & Kelley, W. M. (2006). Disambiguating anterior cingulate cortex function: Differential response to experiences of expectancy violation and social rejection. *Nature Neuroscience, 9,* 1007–1008.

Stanley, D., & Adolphs, R. (2013). Toward a neural basis for social behavior. *Neuron, 80,* 816–826.

Stone, V. E., Baron-Cohen, S., & Knight, R. T. (1998). Frontal lobe contributions to theory of mind. *Journal of Cognitive Neuroscience, 10,* 640–656.

Stuss, D. T., & Alexander, M. P. (2000). Executive functions and the frontal lobes: A conceptual view. *Psychology Research, 63,* 289–298.

Symons, C. S., & Johnson, B. T. (1997). The self-reference effect in memory: A meta-analysis. *Psychological Bulletin, 121,* 371–394.

Tranel, D., Damasio, A. R., & Damasio, H. (1998). Intact recognition of facial expression, gender and age in patients with impaired recognition of face identity. *Neurology, 38,* 690–696.

Turk, D. J., Heatherton, T. F., Macrae, C. N., Kelley, W. M., & Gazzaniga, M. S. (2003). Out of contact, out of mind: The distributed nature of the self. *Annals of the New York Academy of Sciences, 1001,* 65–78.

von Kriegstein, K., & Giraud, A. L. (2004). Distinct functional substrates along the right superior temporal sulcus for the processing of voices. *NeuroImage, 22,* 948–955.

Vouloumanos, A., & Werker, J. F. (2007). Listening to language at birth: Evidence for a bias for speech in neonates. *Developmental Science, 10,* 159–164.

Vul, E., Harris, C., Winkielman, P., & Pashler, H. (2009). Puzzlingly high correlations in fMRI studies of emotion, personality, and social cognition. *Perspectives on Psychological Science, 4,* 274–290.

Wagner, A. D., Schacter, D. L., Rotte, M., Koutstaal, W., Maril, A., Dale, A. M., . . . Buckner, R. L. (1998). Building memories: remembering and forgetting of verbal experiences as predicted by brain activity. *Science, 281,* 1188–1191.

Wagner, D. D., Kelley, W.M., Haxby, J.V., & Heatherton, T.F. (2016). The dorsal medial prefrontal cortex responds preferentially to social interactions during natural viewing. *Journal of Neuroscience, 36,* 6917–6925.

Walsh, V., & Cowey, A. (2000). Transcranial magnetic stimulation and cognitive neuroscience. *Nature Reviews Neuroscience, 1,* 73–79.

Wegner, D. M. (1994). Ironic processes of mental control. *Psychological Review, 10,* 34–52.

Weismann, C. G., Schreiber, J., Singer, T., Steinbeis, N., & Friederici, A. D. (2017). White matter maturation is associated with the emergence of theory of mind in early childhood. *Nature Communications, 8,* art. 14692.

Whalen, P. J. (1998). Fear, vigilance, and ambiguity: Initial neuroimaging studies of the human amygdala. *Current Directions in Psychological Science, 7,* 177–188.

Whalen, P. J., & Phelps, E. A. (2009). *The human amygdala.* New York, NY: Guildford.

Wheatley, T., Milleville, S. C., & Martin, A. (2007). Understanding animate agents: Distinct roles for the social network and mirror system. *Psychological Science, 18,* 469–474.

Wheatley, T., Weinberg, A., Looser, C. E., Moran, T., & Hajcak, G. (2011). Mind perception: Real but not artificial faces sustain neural activity beyond the N170/VPP. *PLoS One, 6,* e17960.

Wig, G. S., Grafton, S. T., Demos, K. E., & Kelley, W. M. (2005). Reductions in neural activity underlie behavioral components of repetition priming. *Nature Neuroscience, 8,* 1228–1233.

Woodward, A. L. (1998). Infants selectively encode the goal object of an actor's reach. *Cognition, 69,* 1–34.

Chapter 16

Evolutionary Social Psychology

Jon K. Maner and Douglas T. Kenrick

Women in long-term romantic relationships are sometimes inclined to cheat on their partner with another man, particularly when the woman is ovulating and when the other man displays signs of high genetic quality. Men can tell whether a woman is ovulating, based simply on a whiff of her t-shirt. People learn to fear snakes and spiders more quickly than they do guns and knives, even though the latter pose much greater threats to physical safety. When a woman encounters a strange man who physically resembles her, she is likely to judge that man as a desirable friend but not as a desirable sexual partner—as trustworthy but not lustworthy.

These research findings, and many others like them, are difficult to explain—even in hindsight—with most conventional social psychological theories. Yet, each was predicted from the framework of evolutionary social psychology (DeBruine, 2005; Haselton & Gangestad, 2006; Miller & Maner, 2011a; Öhman & Mineka, 2001). An evolutionary perspective implies that many thoughts, feelings, and behaviors are caused, in part, by biological mechanisms that have been shaped by thousands of generations of evolution. From romantic relationships, friendship, and prosocial behavior to fear, aggression, and intergroup prejudice, the principles of evolutionary psychology provide a deeper understanding of many important topics in social psychology (Buss, 2005; Cosmides, Tooby, & Barkow, 1992; Crawford & Krebs, 2008; Gangestad & Simpson, 2007; Kenrick, Maner, & Li, 2005).

What Is Evolutionary Social Psychology?

Since the time of Charles Darwin, scientists have recognized that the human body is a product of biological evolution, but not until the 1970s did scientists begin to seriously explore the possibility that biological evolution also influences human psychology and behavior. E. O. Wilson's (1975) book *Sociobiology* ushered in the perspective of evolutionary psychology—an approach in which psychologists use what they know about human biological evolution to inform their understanding of the contemporary human mind (see also Alcock, 2001).

Evolutionary psychology is an overarching meta-theoretical perspective, comprising a set of assumptions that govern how scientists approach questions about psychological phenomena (Buss, 1995; Ketelaar & Ellis, 2000). These assumptions (e.g., that cognition is produced in part by underlying biological processes and that human biology has been shaped by a long history of evolutionary forces) are based on a vast storehouse of knowledge within the biological sciences. When applied to the conceptual landscape of social psychology, these assumptions have focused scientific inquiry on a number of novel research questions (Neuberg, Kenrick, & Schaller, 2010).

The perspective of evolutionary psychology provides a set of conceptual tools that can be used to derive specific mid-level theories and hypotheses about social psychological phenomena. It is these theories and hypotheses (not the overarching perspective of evolution) that offer specific predictions pertaining to social psychological phenomena. Rarely do evolutionary psychologists frame their specific research questions in terms of very broad considerations such as survival and reproduction. Rather, research questions tend to be framed so that they test mid-level theories that provide a more specific portrait of the influences of evolution on psychology and behavior. Tinbergen (1963) made an important distinction between historical evolutionary hypotheses (concerned with questions such as when mammalian females shifted from laying eggs to bearing live young) and functional evolutionary hypotheses (concerned with questions such as the functional implications of how males versus females invest in their offspring). Evolutionary psychology is generally concerned with the latter level of analysis (Kenrick, Griskevicius, Neuberg, & Schaller, 2010).

An evolutionary perspective is not meant to replace traditional social psychological perspectives. Quite the contrary. Evolutionary psychology supplements traditional approaches by providing a deeper explanatory framework that helps explain psychological phenomena in terms of their root causes. Evolutionary psychologists seek to unpack the fascinating and dynamic interactions among evolved psychological mechanisms, developmental processes, learning, and culture. Our evolutionary heritage unfolds as we learn and grow, interact with our culture, and develop knowledge structures based on our experiences. Thus, an evolutionary approach replaces both a blank slate view and a genetic determinist view with a view of the mind as a coloring book: Some of the basic foundations of the human mind are predetermined, just as the lines in a coloring book are already written in. But the richness of human experience, learning, and culture is needed to color in those lines to make an actual human being (Kenrick, Nieuweboer, & Buunk, 2010).

Important Assumptions and Conceptual Tools

Some individual organisms have characteristics that enable them, compared to other members of their species, to more successfully exploit the prospects and avoid the perils presented by their environment. As a consequence, these organisms tend to be more successful at reproducing and thus transmitting their genes to future generations. Over many generations of differential reproductive success, this process—*natural selection*—produces organisms possessing those characteristics that previously conferred relatively high reproductive fitness.

The mind has also been shaped by the process of *sexual selection*, which refers to the idea that some individuals are better able than others to compete with members of their own sex over access to potential mating partners. In some cases, traits that are selected for because they enhance reproductive success may be neutral with respect to survival or they may even hinder survival. A classic example is the peacock's tail: A peacock's tail draws attention and is physically unwieldy, thus making the bird more vulnerable to predation. However, an ornate tail enhances the peacock's attractiveness to potential mating partners. This example highlights the critical importance of *trade-offs* in evolutionary processes. A trait that improves reproductive fitness in one way can work against reproductive fitness in another. The existence of such conflicting design criteria helps set the stage for an immensely complex set of psychological characteristics.

Reproductive Fitness Is the Engine That Drives Evolution

Evolutionary approaches begin with the assumption that many social psychological processes have been shaped by evolution to serve some function. The *ultimate* function of evolved psychological processes is to promote reproduction—the perpetuation of genes into subsequent generations. This does not mean, however, that each episode of thought or behavior directly promotes reproductive success. First, not all psychological and behavioral processes reflect evolved mechanisms. Many processes, for example, can reflect byproducts of evolved mechanisms. What television shows people choose to watch, the languages they speak, and whether they prefer chocolate or vanilla ice cream have not been specifically designed by evolution, although they may reflect byproducts of underlying evolved mechanisms.

Second, even processes that have been designed through evolution to serve some adaptive function do not necessarily enhance reproduction in an immediate sense. Successful reproduction involves a diverse array of other challenges including protecting yourself from predators and other forms of physical harm, avoiding contagious diseases, avoiding rejection and social exclusion, navigating status hierarchies, caring for offspring, and so on (Bugental, 2000; Buss & Kenrick, 1998; Kenrick, Li, & Butner, 2003; Kenrick, Maner, Butner, Li, Becker, & Schaller, 2002; Tooby & Cosmides, 1990).

Indeed, even individuals who never reproduce may still increase their reproductive fitness through a variety of indirect means. Reproductive fitness is not defined by the production of offspring but by the successful reproduction of genes. Actions that have implications for the survival and reproduction of close genetic relatives, therefore, have indirect implications for our own reproductive fitness (this illustrates the concept of *inclusive fitness*; Hamilton, 1964). Under some conditions, for instance, some birds actually fare better by helping their siblings raise offspring than by mating on their own (Trivers, 1985). People and other animals may also enhance their own reproductive fitness by performing behaviors that promote the survival and reproduction of close kin (Burnstein, Crandall, & Kitayama, 1994; Faulkner & Schaller, 2007; Hrdy, 1999), even if it means putting their own survival at risk (Sherman, 1977). Consequently, evolutionary analyses apply not only to the small set of behaviors bearing directly on sex and mating but also to a much greater proportion of human social cognition and behavior.

Adaptations Are Designed to Solve Recurrent Social Problems

The physical and psychological characteristics produced through natural and sexual selection are known as *adaptations*. Adaptations, which are features of an organism that were selected because they enhanced the reproductive fitness of the organism's ancestors, are designed to solve specific adaptive challenges that arose consistently in ancestral environments. In this chapter, we focus on (a) adaptive problems defined by the recurring threats and opportunities presented by human social ecologies and (b) the cognitive, emotional, and behavioral mechanisms that evolved to help ancestral humans solve those challenges.

What kinds of recurring social problems did early humans face? There is some convergence in the various answers that have been offered to this question (e.g., Bugental, 2000; Kenrick, Becker et al., 2003). Like many other social species, humans must often avoid sources of harm, including harm from predators, intrasexual rivals, and members of hostile outgroups. Humans must also avoid contact with sources of disease including pathogens potentially carried by other people. To reproduce, humans must solve challenges pertaining to the formation of new romantic and sexual relationships. Like the (relatively few) mammals that include long-term pair-bonding as a predominant mating strategy, humans must solve challenges associated with maintaining and protecting long-term romantic relationships. Like other animals that invest heavily in offspring, humans must also solve problems related to child rearing. Like other highly social species, humans must solve problems associated with forming and maintaining lasting coalitions of allies. Because many human social structures are organized hierarchically, humans must also solve problems associated with the attainment of social status.

Each of these broad classes of problems can be divided into hierarchically linked subproblems. For instance, maintaining coalitions of allies requires people to solve the problem of successful social exchange. As such, individuals must be able to identify individuals with traits that facilitate or hinder successful exchange, detect people who might be cheaters or nonreciprocators, discourage cheating and free-riding, and so on (e.g., Cosmides & Tooby, 2005; Cottrell, Neuberg, & Li, 2007; Fehr, Fischbacher, & Gachter, 2002). To solve challenges associated with forming new romantic partnerships, individuals must also solve myriad subproblems including the ability to discriminate between individuals according to their fertility, parental potential, genetic quality, and degree of kinship (e.g., Gangestad & Simpson, 2000; Kenrick & Keefe, 1992; Lieberman, Tooby, & Cosmides, 2007). Most adaptations are designed to solve these types of specific subproblems.

Adaptations Are Functionally Specialized and Domain Specific

Most evolutionary approaches presume that natural selection produces numerous relatively specialized, domain-specific psychological mechanisms, similar to the range of different software applications that can be run on a computer (Cosmides & Tooby, 2005; Kenrick & Griskevicius, 2013). Indeed, many mental phenomena operate in ways that are functionally specific (Klein, Cosmides, Tooby, & Chance, 2002). Just as computer software comes in many different packages, some designed to process text, others designed to organize information into a spreadsheet, and still others designed to interface with the Web, many mental processes are designed to serve highly specific functions (Barrett & Kurzban, 2006; Fodor, 1983; Kurzban & Aktipis, 2007; Pinker, 1997; Sherry & Schacter, 1987).

Rather than having a single threat-avoidance system, for example, humans have multiple systems designed to deal with different types of threat (Kenrick & Shiota, 2008; Neuberg, Kenrick, & Schaller, 2011). One set of mechanisms, for example, is designed to associate fear with natural sources of threat such as snakes, spiders, and angry faces (Öhman & Mineka, 2001). Because snakes, spiders, and angry people have posed threats throughout evolutionary history, some of their meaning comes already built into the cognitive system (Kaschak & Maner, 2009). Another set of mechanisms is designed to avoid contact with disease and is sensitive to very different kinds of inputs (i.e., various cues associated with disease; Mortensen, Becker, Ackerman, Neuberg, & Kenrick, 2010; Murray & Schaller, 2016).

Thus, a view of the mind as domain specific implies that psychological mechanisms that govern cognition and behavior in one social domain may be very different from those that govern cognition and behavior in other social domains (e.g., Ackerman & Kenrick, 2008; Kenrick, Sundie, & Kurzban, 2008; Neuberg & Cottrell, 2006). The focus on recurrent fitness-relevant problems encourages attention not only to specific underlying processes but also to the specific *content* of those processes (e.g., whether a social exchange process involves sharing information among friends, trading food between members of different groups, or helping a family member in a fistfight). The result is a set of hypotheses that is often more highly specific and nuanced than sets deduced from other perspectives in psychology.

Evolutionary Social Psychology by Domains

The bottom line of evolution by natural selection is differential reproductive success. Successful reproduction involves a diverse array of tasks—making friends, negotiating status hierarchies, forming and maintaining long-term relationships, and taking care of children (Kenrick, Griskevicius, Neuberg, & Schaller, 2010). Adaptationist reasoning—bolstered by cognitive, behavioral, and neurophysiological evidence (Panksepp, 1982; Plutchik, 1980)—suggests that much of human behavior may be organized around a fairly limited set of fundamental motives, each linked to a particular adaptive challenge posed by ancestral environments. Based on several relevant reviews (Bugental, 2000; Buss, 1999; Fiske, 1992; Kenrick, Neuberg, & Cialdini, 1999; Kenrick et al., 2002, 2003; Krems, Kenrick, & Neel, 2017; Neel, Kenrick, White, & Neuberg, 2016), we will organize the remainder of our discussion around five key domains of social life—coalition formation, status, self-protection, mating, and parental care. We consider evidence for some of the cognitive and behavioral mechanisms that may have evolved to help people succeed in each of these domains.

Coalition Formation and Maintenance

Humans have a fundamental need for social belonging that is rooted deeply within human evolutionary history (Baumeister & Leary, 1995). For most of human history, our ancestors lived in small highly interdependent groups (Caporael, 1997; Sedikides & Skowronski, 1997). Successful cooperation among group members greatly increased each person's probability of surviving, prospering, and eventually reproducing. This was particularly true during times of need (e.g., food shortages; Hill & Hurtado, 1996). The evolutionary literature on social affiliation has important implications for understanding cooperation, prosocial behavior, exchange, reciprocity, and the psychology of kinship.

Alliances with Kin

Social psychologists tend not to focus much on differences between interactions among kin versus nonkin (Daly, Salmon, & Wilson, 1997). However, there are important differences between these kinds of relationships. Research with humans and other species, for example, suggests substantially lower thresholds for engaging in various types of cooperative behavior among individuals who are genetically related (e.g., Ackerman, Kenrick, & Schaller, 2007; Burnstein et al., 1994; Essock-Vitale & McGuire, 1985; Neyer & Lang, 2003). From the perspective of inclusive fitness theory (Hamilton, 1964), it is easy to see why people tend to align themselves with their kin—a benefit shared with a kin member implies indirect genetic benefits to oneself, and costs exacted on the self by kin are also indirect costs to the kin member.

Kinship provides one foundation for understanding the evolution of prosocial behavior. The logic of inclusive fitness provides an explanation for one form of altruism—nepotism. Evidence of nepotistic altruism is found widely across the animal kingdom (Greenberg, 1979; Holmes & Sherman, 1983; Suomi, 1982). Compared to dizygotic twins, monozygotic (identical) twins are more cooperative in economic decision-making games (Segal & Hershberger, 1999). In other contexts, too, people are more inclined to help genetically related kin, and this tendency is bolstered under conditions that have direct implications for the kin member's survival and reproductive fitness (Burnstein et al., 1994; Neyer & Lang, 2003; Stewart-Williams, 2008).

The evolved psychology of kinship even has important implications for prosocial behavior among total strangers. As with many other animals, ancestral humans were often unable to directly identify kin—we cannot "see" genes—but instead inferred kinship implicitly on the basis of superficial cues such as familiarity and similarity (Lieberman et al., 2007; Park, Schaller, & Van Vugt, 2008). Consequently, people may respond prosocially to individuals who appear either familiar or highly similar in some way—even when they know, rationally, that the individuals are total strangers. For instance, just as facial similarity promotes trust (DeBruine, 2002), it also promotes cooperative behavior in a public goods game (Krupp, DeBruine, & Barclay, 2008). Emotions may also serve as heuristic cues to kinship. Empathy likely evolved as part of a system for aiding kin in distress (Maner & Gailliot, 2007; Preston & de Waal, 2002), and thus kinship may be implicitly connoted by the emotional experience of empathy—even when the empathy is elicited by nonkin (Hoffman, 1981; Krebs, 1987; Park et al., 2008). This suggests that the often-observed relation between empathy and helping behavior among strangers (Batson, 1991) may be rooted, in part, in the evolved psychology of kinship.

Alliances with Nonkin

Why would people form coalitions with nonkin? Theories of reciprocal altruism provide one answer (Axelrod & Hamilton, 1981; Trivers, 1971). According to these theories, our ancestors would have benefited from cooperating with others to the extent that those people were likely to reciprocate. In this way, each member of reciprocal exchange relationship reaps benefits in the long term. Indeed, whereas close kin cooperate with relatively less regard for past reciprocation, sharing between progressively less related individuals becomes more linked to a history of reciprocal sharing (e.g., Fiske, 1992; Trivers, 1971). Across societies, the norm of reciprocal exchange is universal (Brown, 1991; Fiske, 1992).

Because people cannot see the future, they cooperate with group members based on the *probability* that those group members will later reciprocate. Hence, it behooves people to attend carefully to signs that a member of their group is not a good candidate for future reciprocation or that this person is likely to draw more resources from the group than he or she is willing to give back. Indeed, evidence suggests that people are quite vigilant to potential deceit and evidence of social cheating (Cosmides & Tooby, 1992; Mealey, Daood, & Krage, 1996). Conversely, recent evolutionary analyses of what attributes people value most in group members highlight the universal value placed on trustworthiness (Cottrell, Neuberg, & Li, 2007).

Another perspective that may help explain the presence of prosocial behavior among nonkin is offered by multilevel selection theory (Wilson & Wilson, 2007; Wilson, Van Vugt, & O'Gorman, 2008). According to this theory, ancestral groups that were highly cooperative and altruistic toward other ingroup members would have enjoyed a competitive advantage over other, less cooperative and altruistic groups. Consequently, members of the more altruistic and cooperative groups would have experienced greater reproductive success (at the group level), causing genes that code for cooperative and altruistic behavior to have been transmitted more effectively to subsequent generations. The crux of this theory is that gene selection occurs at the group level, as opposed to the individual level. Such theories contend that this process underlies some aspects of contemporary human altruism.

Although multilevel selection theory provides a plausible explanation for cooperative and altruistic behavior, it remains controversial. For example, some argue that highly altruistic groups would have been susceptible to exploitation from group members interested in taking advantage of the communal and generous nature of other group members (Leigh, 2010). Such exploitation might have undermined the effectiveness of the group as a whole, thus undermining the reproductive success of the group. Despite such objections, multilevel selection theory continues to receive attention in evolutionary studies of prosocial behavior.

Social Exclusion and Social Anxiety

What happens when the powerful need for social belonging is thwarted? Being excluded by other people can be very distressing and anxiety provoking and can precipitate neurophysiological responses resembling physical pain (Eisenberger, Liberman, & Williams, 2003; MacDonald & Leary, 2005). This makes sense from the standpoint that throughout much of evolutionary history, being excluded from your group led to disastrous consequences, even death. The threat of social exclusion can promote a variety of psychological changes aimed at restoring a person's level of social belonging (Maner, DeWall, Baumeister, & Schaller, 2007; Maner, Miller, Schmidt, & Eckel, 2010). When threatened with the possibility of social exclusion, people become highly attuned to other people in ways that might help them connect with them (DeWall, Maner, & Rouby, 2009; Gardner, Pickett, & Brewer, 2000; Williams, Cheung, & Choi, 2000), although negative and antisocial responses to exclusion have also been observed (e.g., Baumeister, DeWall, Ciarocco, & Twenge, 2005; DeWall, Twenge, Gitter, & Baumeister, 2009; Leary, Twenge, & Quinlivan, 2006). Evolutionary considerations suggest that social anxiety—the tendency to anticipate and to fear negative social evaluation—may have evolved as a mechanism designed to help people avoid social exclusion (Buss, 1990; Maner, 2009). Anxiety leads people to avoid doing potentially embarrassing things and taking social risks and thus helps people avoid negative social attention and potential rejection or ostracism (see also Allen & Badcock, 2003).

Social Hierarchy

Like the social structures of other species, the social structures of many human societies are organized hierarchically, with some individuals enjoying higher status than others (Barkow, 1989; Eibl-Eibesfeldt, 1989). Social status, a basic aspect of most social groups, refers to a person's position in a social hierarchy, such that people high in status have greater influence over others and greater access to group resources. Even in face-to-face interactions between complete strangers, relative status differences emerge quickly and spontaneously, often on the basis of very limited social information (Fisek & Ofshe, 1970). Because there are many benefits to having high status, some have argued that striving for status is a fundamental human motive (Anderson, Hildreth, & Howland, 2015; McClelland, 1975), and many behaviors are designed to help an individual gain status.

Dominance, and Prestige: Dual Strategies for Attaining Social Rank

Having high social status is associated with an array of adaptive rewards such as access to group assets, friends, mates, respect, praise, admiration, happiness, and health (Archer, 1988; Eibl-Eibesfeldt, 1989; Keltner et al., 2003). Evolutionary theories suggest that status brings reproductive success across many species: high-status individuals are better able to obtain mating partners and to provide care to offspring than low-status individuals (e.g., Ellis, 1995; Sadalla, Kenrick, & Vershure, 1987). Having status may also increase the likelihood that your mate will be willing and able to devote time and energy to caring for your offspring (Eibl-Eibesfeldt, 1989).

Theory and evidence from evolutionary psychology suggest two main strategies people use to attain high social status: dominance and prestige. Although both strategies serve as viable routes to attaining high social status (Cheng, Tracy, Foulsham, Kingstone, & Henrich, 2013), the two strategies differ from one another in important ways (Cheng & Tracy, 2014; Maner, 2017; Maner & Case, 2016).

Dominance is a strategy humans share with many other species. Most animal hierarchies are regulated through dominance, such that individuals achieve and maintain high social status using size, strength, and physical intimidation (de Waal, 1999). Although humans may not rely as much on the threat of physical violence, dominance in humans nevertheless does involve acquiring status through the use of power, fear, intimidation, and coercion.

Prestige, in contrast, typically comes from having expertise, knowledge, or wisdom, usually in a domain that is useful to the group (Henrich & Gil-White, 2001). With prestige, social status is freely conferred.

Whereas dominance can be found throughout many species, prestige is more limited to humans (Van Vugt, 2006). With the birth of human culture, evolution favored mechanisms that caused people to attend to and emulate highly successful group members, and those group members could be said to have earned high social status via prestige (Henrich & Gil-White, 2001).

Unlike dominance, people with prestige have influence because they are listened to and respected, not because they force others to do what they want. People who attain social rank via prestige tend to be more well-liked than those who attain it through dominance (Cheng et al., 2013), and they more often prioritize the well-being of the group and its members (Boehm, 1999; Henrich, Chudek, & Boyd, 2015). Dominance, in contrast, is often marked by selfishness and a tendency to make decisions designed to enhance one's own power (Case & Maner, 2014; Maner & Mead, 2010; Mead & Maner, 2012; see also Cheng, Tracy, Ho, & Henrich, 2016). In sum, distinguishing between dominance and prestige provides a useful conceptual framework for understanding the motivations, cognitions, and behaviors involved in social hierarchies.

The evolutionary literature on status has also been applied to the study of leadership (van Vugt, 2006; van Vugt, Hogan, & Kaiser, 2008). It sometimes can be difficult to get group members to work together. Group leaders, by virtue of their leadership position, possess status and influence, can help solve social co-ordination problems, and enable groups to manage fundamental challenges such as protecting themselves from rival outgroups, acquiring resources, and defusing conflicts within the group. The prevalence of leadership throughout history and across species suggests that leadership and followership can provide stable strategies for an effective group. However, recent evolutionarily inspired work has noted that there may also be a fundamental motivational conflict between leaders and their followers (van Vugt et al., 2008). Leaders typically are given power, defined in terms of their ability to control group resources and coerce people (Keltner, Gruenfeld, & Anderson, 2003), whereas followers lack power. Van Vugt et al. (2008) proposed that this power asymmetry results in a basic ambivalence in the relationship between leaders and followers. Followers need leaders to achieve their goals, but giving up some of their power makes them vulnerable to exploitation. Consequently, followers may be motivated to decrease the power gap between themselves and leaders. Having power provides many benefits, so leaders, on the other hand, may be motivated to increase the power gap between themselves and followers, and to use their power for personal gain. This motivational conflict may have negative consequences for group functioning, as leaders sometimes use their power in corrupt and selfish ways (e.g., Kipnis, 1972).

Gender Differences in Fitness Payoffs for Status Striving

For both sexes, the advantages of gaining and maintaining status have included access to material resources and extended social alliances. These advantages, in turn, translated into increased reproductive success: Resources could be invested in offspring and allies assisted in caring for and protecting them.

From an evolutionary perspective, however, males gain an additional set of benefits from striving for status. Because human females, like other mammalian females, incubate their young, they are required to make a more substantial initial investment of time and resources into parenting than males are (Trivers, 1972). Due to their high level of parental investment, women tend to be highly selective in choosing their long-term mates and tend to place a premium on the social status of potential long-term romantic partners (Li, Bailey, Kenrick, & Linsenmeier, 2002; Sadalla et al., 1987). High status men are able to offer their mates relatively greater protection and access to resources, both of which were useful in caring for offspring. Consequently, compared to females, males are somewhat more motivated to seek high levels of social status (Hill & Hurtado, 1996), to worry about possible loss of status relative to other group members (Daly & Wilson, 1988; Gutierres, Kenrick, & Partch, 1999), and to use violence as a way of seeking status (Archer, 1994; Ainsworth & Maner, 2012; Daly & Wilson, 1988).

Eagly and Wood (1999) argued that differences in status striving may stem from the male gender role's emphasis on power and status versus the female gender role's emphasis on nurturance. They suggest that men's and women's gender roles differ across societies because of two fundamental biological differences: Men are physically larger and women carry and nurse offspring (Wood & Eagly, 2007). Thus, they posit an interaction between an evolved mechanism and the development of cultural norms, which is in some ways consistent with evolutionary models of gender role norms (Kenrick, 1987). The biosocial model also links social roles to underlying biological processes, for example, arguing that hormones such as testosterone help prepare men and women for the social roles they fill in their society. An evolutionary perspective, in turn, helps explain the root causes of underlying biological processes that can account for gender differences, for example, by linking men's higher levels of testosterone to their greater focus on dominance and intrasexual competition, characteristics found in males across many species (Mazur & Booth, 1998). The work by Eagly and Wood and others indicates an increasing tendency for social psychologists to develop theories that consider the links between evolution and the development of culture.

Self-Protection

The need to protect yourself from harm is perhaps the most fundamental of human motivations. Ancestral humans frequently encountered threats from members of hostile outgroups (Baer & McEachron, 1982), and intragroup competition over status and material resources led to recurrent threats from ingroup members (Daly & Wilson, 1988). Moreover, some threats take the form of contagious disease and are transmitted via interpersonal contact (Kurzban & Leary, 2001; Park, Schaller, & Crandall, 2007). Thus, threats can come from many places, and, consequently, psychological mechanisms are designed specifically to help people detect and avoid those threats (for a review, see Öhman & Mineka, 2001).

The Evolved Fear Module

Psychological processes are very sensitively tuned to evolutionarily relevant cues in the environment that can signal the presence of possible threats (Haselton & Nettle, 2006). An angry facial expression, for example, often signals that a person is inclined toward aggressive behavior and may take violent physical action (Parkinson, 2005). Indeed, expressions of anger are cross-culturally universal—they are recognized the world over as a sign of impending threat (Ekman, 1982; Ekman & Friesen, 1976). Consequently, people selectively attend to angry faces and quickly and accurately detect angry-looking faces among distracter faces in a variety of visual search tasks (e.g., Becker, Kenrick, Neuberg, Blackwell, & Smith, 2007; Fox, Russo, Bowles, & Dutton, 2001; Hansen & Hansen, 1988).

The effects of natural selection can be seen in the process by which people learn to associate particular types of stimuli with a threat. To the extent that particular threats have posed recurrent dangers to humans throughout evolutionary history, people may be particularly adept at learning to fear those threats. In a series of classical conditioning experiments, people were subjected to electric shocks while they viewed images of threatening stimuli—ancestrally dangerous stimuli such as snakes and spiders, as well as more contemporary threat stimuli such as guns and knives (see Öhman & Mineka, 2001). The researchers measured how quickly people came to associate the shocks with the images with which they were paired (as indicated, for example, by physical startle responses). People demonstrated more efficient conditioned fear responses to stimuli such as snakes and spiders—stimuli that have posed physical threats to humans throughout history—than they did to guns and knives, even though the latter arguably present more immediate and common dangers to people in modern society.

These findings provide a good illustration of the interaction between evolution and learning. They fit with Seligman's (1971) preparedness theory, which suggests that people are born biologically prepared to learn particular associations—those bearing especially on survival—with a very high degree of efficiency. Indeed, people do not come into the world preprogrammed with a store of ready-to-use knowledge at their disposal. Rather, people are born into the world biologically prepared to learn certain things more easily and efficiently than others. They are especially adept at learning things that can help them seize important adaptive opportunities and avoid forms of threat.

Intergroup Processes

Throughout evolutionary history, people were threatened by members of potentially hostile outgroups (Baer & McEachron, 1982; Daly & Wilson, 1988). Consequently, a variety of self-protective processes are directed selectively at avoiding outgroup members (e.g., Navarrete, Olsson, Ho, Mendes, Thomsen, & Sidanius, 2009). For example, people automatically categorize the world in terms of "us" and "them" (Kurzban, Tooby, & Cosmides, 2001), and this tendency becomes especially strong when people are in a self-protective mindset (Maner et al., 2012; Miller, Maner, & Becker, 2010). Self-protective goals can lead people to see anger in the faces of outgroup members, even when those faces are perceived as neutral in other contexts (Maner et al., 2005). Although people tend to remember the faces of outgroup members less well than the faces of ingroup members, that pattern is reversed when the outgroup members display an angry facial expression—angry outgroup faces are remembered particularly well, possibly because they are perceived as posing a particularly dire threat (Ackerman et al., 2006). Moreover, the presentation of one angry-looking outgroup member leads people to see subsequent outgroup members as more threatening; the same does not hold true for perceptions of ingroup members (Shapiro et al., 2009). Thus, people display forms of vigilance to members of coalitional outgroups as sources of physical danger.

Cottrell and Neuberg (2005) proposed an evolutionarily inspired sociofunctional theory of intergroup prejudice. Their approach emphasized the domain specificity of intergroup processes, hypothesizing that prejudice reflects not a general propensity to negatively evaluate outgroups but rather a set of domain-specific evaluative mechanisms that reflect the existence of different forms of outgroup threat. That is, different outgroups pose different kinds of threat, which, in turn, evoke highly specific adaptive emotional and behavioral responses. Some groups are perceived as posing threats to physical safety; other groups are thought to pose threats to the security of our economic resources; and still other groups are presumed to threaten a group's ability to socialize its young. In each case, the specific type of perceived threat evokes a highly specific pattern of emotion (fear, anger, disgust, pity) and behavior (avoidance, ostracism, aggression). For example, negative attitudes toward gay men were associated with feelings of disgust but not fear (making the term *homophobia* appear to be a misnomer), and disgust prompted avoidance but not the sort of fight-or-flight response that typically results from fear. The latter response was more often associated with White American's prejudice against African Americans and was rooted in fear, rather than disgust. Prejudice toward activist feminists and fundamentalist Christians was higher than that toward gay men or Blacks but was not based on fear or disgust, but anger (overperceived violations of participants' civil rights). And, in each case, the pattern of psychological responses maps onto forms of recurrent intergroup threats faced by humans throughout history.

Vigilance toward sources of outgroup threat is exacerbated by contextual cues that, throughout history, have signaled increased vulnerability to harm. In a number of studies, for example, Schaller and his colleagues examined the implications of ambient darkness on outgroup prejudice. Darkness affords greater susceptibility to harm and tends to evoke fear and anxiety. As a result, being in the dark can increase vigilance toward members of outgroups that are heuristically associated with physical threat. Compared to control participants, for example, White and Asian participants seated in a dark laboratory room displayed greater danger-related stereotypes about African Americans, a group that is stereotypically viewed as threatening by many White Americans (Schaller, Park, & Mueller, 2003).

Evolutionarily inspired research also suggests that when women are in the fertile phase of their menstrual cycle, they display greater prejudice toward outgroup men (McDonald & Navarrete, 2015; McDonald, Asher, Kerr, & Navarrete, 2011). Some researchers have speculated that such prejudice may serve to protect women from perceived sources of sexual danger (i.e., sexual coercion) during a time when they are especially likely to conceive a child.

Research on racial prejudice provides another excellent illustration that evolution works via the constraints it places on learning (i.e., nature via nurture; Ridley, 2003). Humans, like other primates, tend to be xenophobic (Holloway, 1974). Toward that end, people possess basic mechanisms for parsing people into coalitional categories of "us" and "them" and for rapidly learning whatever cues reliably mark that distinction. The specific cues used for this purpose, however, are highly variable, implying that coalitional distinctions depend importantly on local learning environments (Kurzban et al., 2001). Although much of the recent research on prejudice in America focuses on prejudice toward particular racial groups, an evolutionary perspective provides a wider lens with which to conceptualize intergroup processes. From an evolutionary perspective, ethnic and racial distinctions provide only one of many possible characteristics that people may use to define the boundaries between ingroup and outgroup.

Disease Avoidance

Although modern medical advances have dramatically reduced the likelihood that infection with pathogens will lead to death, throughout most of evolutionary history infection spelled disaster for the infected individual. As a result, humans possess a number of emotional and cognitive mechanisms designed to help avoid contact with potential sources of contagion (Murray & Schaller, 2016).

The emotion of disgust plays a key role in promoting adaptive avoidance of potential contagion (e.g., Rozin & Fallon, 1987; Tybur, Lieberman, Kurzban, & DeScioli, 2013). Disgust serves as a rich source of information (cf. Schwarz & Clore, 1983), signaling that a substance, food, or person is potentially hazardous. Disgust responses are deeply rooted in human biology and in the capacity for learning. Many cases of single trial conditioned taste aversion, for example, have been documented wherein taste aversion is conditioned to novel tastes; this is highly functional because it helps isolate the food most likely to have caused the illness (Garcia & Koelling, 1966).

Researchers have shown that concerns about disease lead people to display vigilance to other people who display cues that are heuristically associated with disease, even though those cues may not be truly indicative of disease (e.g., Ackerman et al., 2009; Kurzban & Leary, 2001; Schaller & Park, 2011; Zebrowitz & Collins, 1997). Physical abnormalities or disabilities, for example, promote avoidance of people as if they were a source of contagious infection (Park, Faulkner, & Schaller, 2003). When concerns about disease are salient, people also display vigilance to and avoidance of others displaying signs of obesity and old age, both serving as heuristic cues to the presence of disease (Miller & Maner, 2011b, 2012).

One cue that people use to identify possible sources of disease is group membership. According to the parasite-stress theory of sociality (Fincher & Thornhill, 2012), outgroup members have historically posed strong disease threats for two reasons. First, outgroup members are likely to have been exposed to pathogens for which ingroup members lack physiological immunity (Fincher & Thornhill, 2008). Thus, contact with outgroup members increases one's chances of encountering a novel and dangerous pathogen. Second, outgroup members often do not share the same cultural rituals that aid in prevention of disease (Fincher & Thornhill, 2012; see also Murray, Fessler, Kerry, White, & Marin, 2017). For instance, different cultures have different food preparation rituals and those rituals are relevant to the avoidance of disease. Thus, disease concern may lead people to be especially sensitive to cues of group membership. Indeed, when motivated to avoid disease, individuals tend to favor their ingroup and avoid contact with others who they categorize as members of the outgroup (Faulkner et al., 2004; Makhanova, Miller, & Maner, 2015).

Some researchers, however, have questioned whether people possess specific outgroup-focused adaptations for avoiding disease. For example, work by Petersen and colleagues suggests that, although people do attend to avoid outgroups when they are concerned about disease, that avoidance reflects more general mechanisms designed for pathogen avoidance, as opposed to mechanisms that specifically target outgroups (Petersen, 2017; van Leeuwen & Petersen, 2018). Further research is needed to investigate whether disease avoidance processes are designed specifically to make people wary of outgroup members.

An intriguing set of evolutionary hypotheses pertains to disease avoidance mechanisms that emerge at particular points in a woman's menstrual cycle. Fessler and colleagues have argued that although avoidance of contagion is important for both men and women, infection presents a particularly pernicious problem for women (e.g., Fessler, 2001, 2002; also Fessler & Navarrete, 2003). So that their body does not reject an unborn offspring, women's immune systems are suppressed when likelihood of pregnancy is high. Fessler tested this hypothesis by examining disgust and avoidance of potential sources of pathogens in women across their menstrual cycle. They observed an increase in sensitivity to disgusting stimuli in the luteal phase of the menstrual cycle—the period immediately following possible fertilization in which the immune system is suppressed (Fessler, 2001). Moreover, when women are in the fertile time of their menstrual cycle, researchers have observed greater biases against outgroups, consistent with the idea that they may be especially motivated to avoid unfamiliar pathogens (Navarrete & Fessler, 2006).

Mating

Because reproductive success is the engine that drives evolutionary processes, and because success in mating is essential for reproductive success, the vestiges of human evolution are highly apparent in the way people approach challenges involved in mating (e.g., Buss, 1989b; Miller, 2000). Evolutionary research on mating can be organized into two primary domains: relationship selection and relationship maintenance. Relationship selection refers to a person's choice of potential partners and the priority they place on long-term, committed relationships and short-term, casual sexual relationships. Relationship maintenance refers to processes involved in helping people protect their long-term relationships; this includes avoiding the temptation of attractive relationship alternatives and warding off intrasexual competitors.

Relationship Selection

Almost all human societies have some form of institutionalized long-term bonding such as marriage (Daly & Wilson, 1983). At the same time, people often engage in short-term casual sexual relationships, with little or no intention of staying together for the long term (e.g., Marshall & Suggs, 1971). Decisions about whether to pursue a long-term or short-term relationship depend in part on an individual's sociosexual orientation (Gangestad & Simpson, 2000; Jackson & Kirkpatrick, 2007; Simpson & Gangestad, 1991), which refers to a person's general inclination to pursue committed long-term relationships and/or short-term sexual relationships. An orientation toward short-term mating is referred to as being sociosexually unrestricted, whereas an orientation toward long-term mating is referred to as being sociosexually restricted.

There is variability in sociosexuality both among individuals (with some people being more unrestricted than others) and between the sexes. On average, men tend to be somewhat more unrestricted than women; they are relatively more inclined to pursue short-term sexual relationships and to desire sex without commitment. Women, in contrast, are relatively more inclined to seek long-term commitment (Clark & Hatfield, 1989; Simpson & Gangestad, 1991). Evolutionary theorists have attributed this to differences in minimum obligatory parental investment (Trivers, 1972). Because human females, like other mammalian females, incubate their young, they are required to make a more substantial initial investment of time and resources than males. Thus, throughout evolutionary history, the benefit-to-cost ratio of casual sex has been lower for women than for men (although new forms of birth control have changed some of the costs of casual sex). As such, women tend to be relatively more cautious and choosy in selecting their romantic partners (e.g., Buss & Schmitt, 1993).

A complete account of sex differences in sociosexuality takes into consideration not only how the sexes differ on average, but also how individuals interact with each other and actually decide on which type of relationship to pursue (Gangestad & Simpson, 2000). Indeed, there is substantial variability within each sex with regard to people's romantic strategies. Kenrick, Li, and Butner (2003) suggested that members of each sex base their decisions of which strategy (short-term versus long-term strategy) to pursue on an implicit comparison of sex ratios in the local environment. Sex ratios can be thought of as a comparison of available opposite sex people (i.e., available mates) to same-sex people (i.e., intrasexual competitors). In any local environment, a strategy becomes more desirable to the extent that there are more available mates responding to that strategy and fewer same-sex competitors using that strategy (see also Guttentag & Secord, 1983).

Recent experimental work confirms that the local sex ratio can have a range of effects on mating-related outcomes. For example, when they are in the minority and thus can be choosier when selecting possible mates, both men and women gravitate toward their sex's preferred mating strategy: men become more sexually unrestricted and women become more restricted (Moss & Maner, 2016). When they are in the majority and must compete more with members of their own sex, both men and women become more aggressive toward perceived rivals (Moss & Maner, 2016). When there is a scarcity of men, women tend to pursue higher-paying careers and they delay starting a family (Durante et al., 2012). In contrast, when men are over-abundant, women can afford to be choosier, and men respond by spending more and focusing on reaping immediate gains rather than saving for the future (Griskevicius et al., 2012). Both sexes have been shown to display forms of risky decision-making when they are in the majority and must compete more with one another over potential relationship opportunities (Ackerman et al., 2016). The literature on sex ratio effects in humans is still young, and many other intriguing hypotheses about these effects remain to be addressed.

Evolutionary analyses also provide a basis for predicting sex differences in the types of characteristics valued in short-term and long-term partners (Li et al., 2002; Li & Kenrick, 2006). With regard to short-term relationships, both men and women are highly attentive to the physical attractiveness of a potential partner (e.g., Maner et al., 2003; Maner, Gailliot, Rouby, & Miller, 2007). Physical attractiveness can signal a number of characteristics relevant to reproductive fitness. Highly symmetrical people, for example, typically are judged to be attractive, and symmetry can signal the presence of a strong immune system and a person's overall level of genetic fitness (Gangestad & Simpson, 2000). Mating with an attractive man should increase the likelihood that a woman will have more genetically fit offspring (Fisher, 1958; Scheib, Gangestad, & Thornhill, 1999). Moreover, a man's physical attractiveness often signals his level of social dominance (e.g., via markers of testosterone; Cunningham, Barbee, & Pike, 1990), and dominance can beget high social status, a characteristic often prioritized by women in selecting their male partners (Buss, 1989a). Characteristics such as health and youth, which are related to perceptions of female attractiveness, may signal a woman's level of fertility (Buss & Schmitt, 1993; Kenrick, Sadalla, Groth, & Trost, 1990; Li et al., 2002). From an evolutionary perspective, men have an evolved preference for healthy, young mates because such a preference would have increased the likelihood that a male ancestor would have fathered healthy offspring and, in turn, successfully passed his genes on to subsequent generations (Kenrick & Keefe, 1992; Singh, 1993).

The characteristics people value in long-term mates are somewhat different than what they seek in short-term mates. When considering marriage partners, for example, there is some evidence that women tend to prefer status and access to resources somewhat more than men, and men tend to prefer physical attractiveness somewhat more than women (e.g., Buss, 1989b; Buss & Barnes, 1986; McGinnis, 1958; Sprecher, Sullivan, & Hatfield, 1994). Evolutionary theorists have suggested that these sex differences reflect the fact that men and women have faced somewhat different adaptive problems (Buss, 1989b; Symons, 1979). Because fertility tends to peak in a woman's early to mid-20s, and drop off rapidly after 30, men may be especially drawn to women displaying physical markers of sexual maturity and youth (Singh, 1993; Symons, 1979). Male reproductive potential, on the other hand, is not as constrained by fertility as it is by the ability to provide resources. Thus, women may be especially attentive to cues signaling a man's status in the social hierarchy and his ability to provide resources for her and her offspring (Buss, 1989a; Griskevicius, Cialdini, & Kenrick, 2006; Maner, DeWall, & Gailliot, 2008; Sadalla et al., 1987).

The evolutionary literature on sex differences in mating preferences has been challenged on the grounds that (a) it has relied too much on self-report measures and responses to hypothetical scenarios and (b) self-reported mating preferences may not correspond well with preferences demonstrated in realistic mating contexts. For example, one meta-analysis of studies from the attraction and relationships literature suggested that physical attractiveness weighed more heavily than social status did in romantic evaluations, and this held true for both men and women. No sex differences were observed in that analysis (see also Eastwick & Finkel, 2008; Finkel & Eastwick, 2009; however, see also Meltzer, McNulty, Jackson, & Karney, 2014).

Other evidence for sex differences comes from research on age preferences, which has relied on data from singles advertisements, surveys, online dating services, marital advertisements in other societies, and actual marriages (Buunk, Dijkstra, Fetchenhauer, & Kenrick, 2002: Kenrick & Keefe, 1992; Kenrick, Gabrielidis, Keefe, & Cornelius, 1996; Otta et al., 1999; Rudder, 2014). Regardless of the data source, young men are attracted to women around their own age, teenage boys are attracted to women older than themselves, and men over 30 become increasingly attracted to relatively younger women as the men age. The most parsimonious explanation of these findings is that men of all ages are most attracted to women who are at the age of peak fertility. Women, regardless of their age, are generally most attracted to slightly older males, which is consistent with a desire for high social status.

One thing is clear: The debate over the existence and origin of sex differences in mating is ongoing, as researchers continue to use a variety of theories and methods to investigate mating preferences and choices (see Conroy-Beam & Buss, 2016; Eastwick, Luchies, Finkel, & Hunt, 2014; Meltzer et al., 2014).

Relationship Maintenance

Because human infants are helpless and slow to develop, sustained input from both parents helps ensure the offspring's survival (Geary, 1998; Hrdy, 1999). Although human mating arrangements vary from culture to culture, all include long-term relationships in which both the male and female contribute to the offspring's welfare (Daly & Wilson, 1983). From both social psychological and evolutionary perspectives, the maintenance of long-term relationships serves key social affiliation and child-rearing functions that enhance reproductive success (Buss, 1999; Eastwick, 2009; Hazan & Diamond, 2000). An integration of evolutionary and relationship science perspectives highlights ways in which people work to maintain long-term relationships (Durante, Eastwick, Finkel, Gangestad, & Simpson, 2016).

Humans, like many other sexually reproducing species, sometimes display a tendency toward polygamy and may be disinclined to maintain romantic relationships that are completely monogamous (Baresh &

Lipton, 2001; Betzig, 1985). One challenge, therefore, involves the temptation of desirable relationship alternatives. For people who are already in a romantic relationship, attention to other desirable people can threaten their satisfaction with and commitment to their existing romantic partnership (Johnson & Rusbult, 1989; Kenrick, Neuberg, Zierk, & Krones, 1994; Miller, 1997). Evolutionary theories help generate predictions about which particular members of the opposite sex might threaten the commitment to a current relationship partner. Theories of short-term mating suggest that both men and women place a premium on the physical attractiveness of extra-pair relationship partners (Gangestad & Thornhill, 1997; Greiling & Buss, 2000; Haselton & Gangestad, 2006; Li & Kenrick, 2006; Scheib, 2001). Consequently, highly attractive members of the opposite sex can threaten one's commitment to a current partner, and psychological mechanisms designed to reduce threats posed by relationship alternatives tend to focus selectively on the attractiveness of alternative partners. For example, people in committed romantic relationships sometimes "devalue" alternative partners by judging them to be less physically attractive than single people do (e.g., Lydon, Fitzsimons, & Naidoo, 2003; Lydon, Meana, Sepinwall, Richards, & Mayman, 1999; Simpson, Gangestad, & Lerma, 1990). Negative evaluations of alternative partners can help reduce perceived relationship threats and aid in maintaining commitment to the current partner. In addition, because relationship alternatives threaten individual's commitment, people sometimes display attentional biases such that as soon as physically attractive alternatives are perceived, their attention is repelled, and they look away (Maner, Gailliot, & Miller, 2009).

The emotion of romantic love has been conceptualized as an adaptation designed to help people maintain commitment to a long-term relationship (Frank, 1988, 2001). Feelings of romantic love reduce people's interest in alternative partners and help ensure their satisfaction and commitment to a current partner (Gonzaga, Keltner, Londahl, & Smith, 2001). Consistent with this literature, priming people with thoughts and feelings of love for their partner helps them suppress thoughts about (Gonzaga, Haselton, Smurda, Davies, & Poore, 2008) and stay inattentive to (Maner, Rouby, & Gonzaga, 2008) attractive relationship alternatives.

Although psychological mechanisms generally operate to help people protect their long-term relationships, those mechanisms are sensitive to the costs and benefits of staying in a relationship. For example, if a couple has offspring, it raises the threshold for decisions to leave a relationship for an alternative mate (Rasmussen, 1981). On the other hand, the availability of desirable alternatives tends to lower the decision threshold to leave a relationship (Guttentag & Secord, 1983; Kenrick et al., 1994).

Another challenge people face in maintaining a long-term relationship involves preventing their partner from being unfaithful. From an evolutionary perspective, warding off romantic rivals and preventing one's partner from engaging in extra-pair relationships is a key part of ensuring one's own reproductive success (e.g., Buss & Shackelford, 1997; Haselton & Gangestad, 2006). Just as psychological processes help maintain commitment to a relationship, they also help prevent partner infidelity (Amato & Booth, 2001; Finkel, 2007; Shackelford, Goetz, Buss, Euler, & Hoier, 2005; Sheets, Fredendall, & Claypool, 1997; Wilson & Daly, 1996).

The threat of infidelity may promote adaptive cognitive processes designed to ward off potential intrasexual rivals. Moreover, an evolutionary perspective is useful for identifying the specific types of relationship rivals that might be most appealing to your mate. As mentioned previously, people tend to seek out extra-pair mates who are physically attractive. Consequently, when primed with the threat of infidelity, members of both sexes attend vigilantly to same-sex interlopers who are physically attractive (Maner, Miller, Rouby, & Gailliot, 2009).

Despite this similarity between men and women, there is also evidence for sex differences in jealousy. Buss, Larsen, Westen, and Semelroth (1992) proposed that although both sources of infidelity invoke jealousy in both sexes, men respond more strongly when their partner appears to be sexually attracted to others, whereas women are relatively more sensitive to emotional infidelity (see also Becker, Sagarin,

Guadagno, Millevoi, & Nicastle, 2004; Easton, Schipper, & Shackelford, 2007; Sagarin, 2005; Schützwohl, 2008). From an evolutionary perspective, this sex difference reflects sex-specific challenges related to paternal uncertainty (for men) and paternal investment (for women; Buss, 2002). Because fertilization occurs within women, men can never be certain that they are the father of their mate's offspring. As a result, the prospect of a woman's sexual infidelity may be particularly distressing for a man because it could lead him to invest time and resources in raising another man's offspring. In contrast to men, women can be certain of their maternity; thus, sexual infidelity should be somewhat less disconcerting for women than for men. Women, however, have faced a different threat—having their long-term mate direct resources toward other women. As a consequence, a man's emotional infidelity may be particularly distressing because it can signal a high likelihood of diverting resources to other women and their offspring.

The evolutionary approach to sex differences in jealousy has been controversial, and has been criticized on both methodological and theoretical grounds. First, some have argued that methods designed to assess sex differences in jealousy (e.g., forcing people to choose which type of infidelity is more distressing) overestimate the size of the sex difference because, in fact, both types of infidelity tend to be highly distressing to both sexes (e.g., Harris, 2003, 2005). In addition, researchers have questioned whether the sex difference reflects different evolved mechanisms in men and women or simply differences in the inferences men and women make based on the kind of infidelity. DeSteno and Salovey (1996), for example, suggested the "double-shot" hypothesis: A woman might think that if her husband is emotionally attached to another woman, he is probably having sex with her, and thus this double shot of infidelity is particularly distressing. Thus, even when acknowledging the existence of sex differences in jealousy, there is still debate as to their underlying cause.

Parental Care

Parental care is critical to the survival of human offspring (Geary, 2000; Hrdy, 1999; Schaller, 2018). Adaptations designed to facilitate adult pair-bonding evolved less than two million years ago to promote cooperative parenting (Eastwick, 2009; McHenry & Coffing, 2000). The rapid increase in cranial size of modern humans, coupled with the relatively narrow birth canal of females, meant human children needed to be born altricial and without the ability to care for themselves. Because offspring benefited greatly from the presence of both parents, evolution favored adaptations designed to promote long-term human pair-bonding. Eastwick (2009) argued that evolution co-opted the parent–child attachment system (Bowlby, 1958, 1969) for adults to promote pair-bonding. Indeed, the elements of adult pair-bonding (e.g., affection, stability, proximity seeking) are similar to the bonding between parent and child (Diamond, Hicks, & Otter-Henderson, 2008). Pair bonds typically last long enough to at least bring a child through the early stages of childrearing (Fisher, 1989).

The desire to nurture offspring, however, is not constant across all parents. Decisions about caring for any particular offspring are contingent on a variety of factors that affect the costs and benefits of parental investment (Alexander, 1979; Daly & Wilson, 1980). An evolutionary logic suggests that decisions pertaining to child nurturance depend on various factors including the perceived genetic relatedness to the parent, the ability of parental investment to be converted to reproductive success, and the opportunity costs of investing.

Because a given offspring shares 50% of each parents' genes and because offspring have the opportunity to someday reproduce, it makes sense that evolutionary processes have selected for behaviors that promote the survival and, ultimately, the reproductive success of offspring. However, there are subtler distinctions that factor into the decision to invest. Consider the following: Mothers tend to invest more in their offspring than fathers. Maternal grandparents tend to invest more than paternal grandparents.

Biological parents invest more in their children than stepparents and are 40 times less likely to abuse them (Daly & Wilson, 1985) and up to several hundred times less likely to kill them than stepparents are (Daly & Wilson, 1988).

These differences in investment are consistent with theories that emphasize the role of genetic relatedness. Only women can be completely sure which offspring are theirs; men can never be 100% sure. Thus, it makes sense that mothers invest more than fathers and that relatives on the maternal side invest more than relatives on the paternal side. In addition, because investing in other men's offspring is unwise from a reproductive standpoint, it makes sense from an evolutionary perspective that the behavior of stepparents toward stepchildren is not equal to that of biological parents toward their own children.

Parental investment in male offspring may have a higher rate of both return and risk than investment in female offspring (Daly & Wilson, 1988; Trivers & Willard, 1973). Although there rarely is a shortage of males willing to mate with a female, a male typically needs to compete against other males to gain access to mates. In addition, whereas females are physically limited to having children at a relatively slow rate across a shorter reproductive lifespan, males are not constrained by internal gestation and menopause. Rather, male reproductive success varies greatly across men, ranging from those at the bottom of a status hierarchy who have no mates to those at the top, who have been known to sire up to several hundred children (e.g., Betzig, 1992; Daly & Wilson, 1988). Because of this differential in risk and return, it may be advantageous for a family with abundant resources to invest in sons but for resource-poor families to allocate what they have to their daughters (Trivers & Willard, 1973). In support of this reasoning, a study of families in North America found differences in investment patterns between low- and high-income families (Gaulin & Robbins, 1991). Among the findings, low-income mothers were more likely to breast feed their daughters than their sons, whereas the opposite pattern was true for mothers in affluent families. Low-income mothers also had another child sooner if the first was a son, whereas high-income mothers had another child sooner if the first was a daughter.

Finally, parental investment is reproductively advantageous to the extent that alternative uses of such time and resources are not more lucrative. Because men are not constrained by childbearing and nursing, the pursuit of other mating relationships is a more viable option for them than it is for women. Indeed, tribal evidence from Africa shows that among the Aka pygmies, men of high status have more wives and spend less time on parenting than men of low status (Hewlett, 1991). People may also be more willing to abandon a given investment when the time horizon for making other investments is relatively long. Evidence from records of infanticide show that women are more likely to kill their infants when they are younger and when they are unwed with no men acknowledging fatherhood (Daly & Wilson, 1988).

Evolutionary Social Psychology Today

Relative to many other approaches in psychology, evolutionary approaches are the new kid on the block. Each year, the field of evolutionary social psychology sees significant new advances in theory and method. Here we mention just two.

One of the current emphases involves the integration of evolution, learning, and culture (e.g., Kenrick, Nieuweboer, & Buunk, 2010; Sng, Neuberg, Varnum, & Kenrick, 2018). Evolutionary psychologists are quick to point out that evolved psychological mechanisms work in conjunction with learning and that learning occurs within a rich context of cultural information. Researchers have begun to deliver on the promise of an integrative evolutionary psychology by directly examining the interaction of evolution and culture (Tooby & Cosmides, 1992). For example, several lines of research suggest that people's mating strategies are adaptively tuned to the prevalence of disease-causing pathogens in the environment (e.g.,

Gangestad, Haselton, & Buss, 2006a). In more pathogen-rich environments (e.g., hot and humid areas near the equator), people place greater value on the physical attractiveness of potential romantic partners, as attractiveness can signal the strength of a person's immune system (Gangestad & Buss, 1993). In addition, higher levels of polygyny are found in pathogen-rich environments because it may be more reproductively advantageous for a woman to become the second wife of an attractive man with a strong immune system than to become the first wife of a less fit man (Low, 1990). Such findings suggest that aspects of the physical environment interact with evolved biological mechanisms to produce different normative mating patterns, which can emerge in the form of large-scale differences among cultures. Similarly, using an evolutionary analysis, Schaller and Murray (2008) showed that basic units of personality such as sociosexual orientation, extraversion, and openness to experience vary predictably with the prevalence of pathogens in local cultural environments. New cross-cultural research is providing unique opportunities to examine the environmental and cultural contingencies that influence the here-and-now manifestation of evolved mental processes (Henrich et al., 2006; Marlowe et al., 2008).

The interaction of evolution and culture has important implications for topics such as morality and religion. Researchers have argued, for example, that moral values and the way people construct religions help serve evolutionarily relevant challenges related to social coordination, cooperation, and even the avoidance of disease (e.g., DeScioli & Kurzban, 2013; Norenzayan & Shariff, 2008).

One source of debate in this area involves the distinction between "evoked" culture and "transmitted" culture (see Gangestad, Haselton, & Buss, 2006b). Evoked culture refers to the process through which ecological variables directly activate genetic mechanisms, as in the previous mating-related examples. Transmitted culture instead refers to the process through which cultural norms travel from individual to individual via learning processes (e.g., imitation, mimicry, storytelling; e.g., Tomasello, Kruger, & Ratner, 1993). Although there is little doubt that both systems work together to produce culture (Norenzayan, 2006; see also Henrich & Gil-White, 2001; Richerson & Boyd, 2005), it is less clear exactly how this occurs and what aspects of cultural variation are evoked versus transmitted. Research today is attempting to address these issues (Sng et al., 2018).

A second burgeoning area within evolutionary psychology interfaces with developmental psychology and involves the way people prioritize particular adaptive goals across the lifespan. Life history theory suggests that adaptive psychological processes are calibrated early in life to help people maximize their reproductive potential across the lifespan, given contingencies they encounter in their local childhood environment. Research from this perspective finds that the degree of unpredictability in a person's early life environment influences behavior in a variety of domains throughout the life course (Belsky, Schlomer, & Ellis, 2012; Del Giudice, 2009; Simpson, Griskevicius, Kuo, Sung, & Collins, 2012). A high level of unpredictability signals that the future is uncertain, which increases the extent to which the organism invests in short-term pursuits tied to immediate reproduction. A low level of unpredictability signals that the future is relatively certain and that the organism can afford to adopt a strategy marked by a longer time horizon and greater long-term investment of effort and resources. These responses to early developmental unpredictability are referred to as fast and slow life history strategies, respectively.

A growing body of research suggests that people's life history strategy has profound implications for a wide range of cognitive processes and behaviors. Faster life history strategies, for example, are associated with having more sexual partners earlier in life and a larger number of total offspring and displaying an orientation toward impulsivity, risk-taking, and short-term rewards (Griskevicius et al., 2013; Maner, Dittmann, Meltzer, & McNulty, 2017; White, Li, Griskevicius, Neuberg, & Kenrick, 2013). Faster life history strategies are also associated with being able to switch effectively from task to task, a cognitive adaptation that would have served people especially well in uncertain and unpredictable environments (Mittal, Griskevicius, Simpson, Sung, & Young, 2015). Conversely, slower life history strategies are associated with greater overall executive function, as well as behaviors that emphasize long-term investment in fewer off-spring, such as delaying reproduction until later in life, having fewer sexual partners, and delaying gratification in favor of long-term rewards (e.g., Ellis, 2004; Sng et al., 2017). Research from the life history theory perspective is accumulating, as researchers continue to develop new and intriguing hypotheses about the adaptive processes underlying people's developmental life trajectories.

Closing Remarks

Darwin's theory of evolution by natural selection is likely the grandest of unifying theories in the life sciences and it has great integrative potential for social psychology. An evolutionary perspective provides an "ultimate" level of explanation, helping to tie proximate psychological and behavioral processes to their underlying biological roots (e.g., Kenrick, 2011).

How "ultimate" do our explanations for behavior need to be? When searching for causes, we can in theory go as far back as the beginning of life or the Big Bang. However, such an explanation would hardly be useful. A more satisfactory stop point is one that connects current causes to their adaptive function—the particular way in which behaviors served ancestral survival and reproduction. A causal explanation that simply points to "differential reproduction" would, by this reasoning, be going a step too far up the causal ladder. It would fail to distinguish the explanation for a bird's hollow skeletal structure from a shark's ability to sense prey by generating electromagnetic fields. We want to understand the particulars— how these very different adaptations solved specific challenges posed by the organism's ancestral ecology. A more useful level of explanation would, for example, connect the bird's lightweight bones to intrinsic flight constraints set by an animal's strength-to-weight ratio, and a hammerhead's uniquely shaped head to its need to sweep the ocean floor in search of prey hiding under the sand. Being able to lift our body into the air and finding hidden prey were different needs that birds' and sharks' physical design features were differentially adapted to solve. Thus, an adaptationist account seeks to explain how an animal's cognitive and behavioral mechanisms are connected to the specific demands and opportunities its ancestors regularly confronted.

The debate is no longer about nature *or* nurture. Both genes and learning play a strong role in shaping people's behavior (Moore, 2004). Only by spanning the continuum from proximate to ultimate levels of explanation will psychologists be able to paint a full picture of a psychological phenomenon. Considering multiple levels of causation leads to a depth of understanding not possible by considering only one level of analysis at a time. For example, experimental social psychological studies suggest that nonverbal indicators of social dominance increase the sexual attractiveness of males, but not females (e.g., Sadalla et al., 1987). Comparative studies conducted with other species indicate a link between an animal's testosterone level and his or her social rank (e.g., Rose, Bernstein, & Holaday, 1971). Physiological studies indicate that males typically produce more testosterone than females (Mazur & Booth, 1998). Correlational studies indicate that individuals with high testosterone also exhibit more antisocially competitive behavior, particularly when other paths to social success are blocked (Dabbs & Morris, 1990). Together, these and other sources of evidence provide a whole network of findings that fit together to tell a compelling story about sexual selection and gender differences (Geary, 1998). No one source of data is superior to others, and none is superfluous—each is necessary to understand a complicated but ultimately sensible natural process. Although data from psychological studies are not by themselves sufficient, they are, in alliance with data from other disciplines and methods, necessary for complete explanations of behavior.

References

Ackerman, J. M., Becker, D. V., Mortensen, C. R., Sasaki, T., Neuberg, S. L., & Kenrick, D. T. (2009). A pox on the mind: Disjunction of attention and memory in the processing of physical disfigurement. *Journal of Experimental Social Psychology, 45,* 478–485.

Ackerman, J. M., & Kenrick, D. T. (2008). The costs of benefits: Help-refusals highlight key trade-offs of social life. *Personality & Social Psychology Review, 12,* 118–140.

Ackerman, J. M., Kenrick, D. T., & Schaller, M. (2007). Is friendship akin to kinship? *Evolution & Human Behavior, 28,* 365–374.

Ackerman, J. M., Maner, J. K., & Carpenter, S. M. (2016). Going all-in: Unfavorable sex ratios attenuate choice diversification. *Psychological Science, 27,* 799–809.

Ackerman, J. M., Shapiro, J. R., Neuberg, S. L., Kenrick, D. T., Becker, D. V., Griskevicius, V., . . . Schaller, M. (2006). They all look the same to me (unless they're angry): From outgroup homogeneity to outgroup heterogeneity. *Psychological Science, 17,* 836–840.

Ainsworth, S. E., & Maner, J. K. (2012). Sex begets violence: Mating motives, social dominance, and aggressive behavior in men. *Journal of Personality and Social Psychology, 103,* 819–829.

Alcock, J. (2001). *The triumph of sociobiology.* New York, NY: Oxford University Press.

Alexander, R. D. (1979). *Darwinism and human affairs.* Seattle, WA: University of Washington Press.

Allen, N. B., & Badcock, P. B. T. (2003). The social risk hypothesis of depressed mood. *Psychological Bulletin, 129,* 887–913.

Amato, P. R., & Booth, A. (2001). The legacy of parents' marital discord: Consequences for children's marital quality. *Journal of Personality and Social Psychology, 81,* 627–638.

Anderson, C., Hildreth, J. A. D., & Howland, L. (2015). Is the desire for status a fundamental human motive? A review of the empirical literature. *Psychological Bulletin, 141,* 574–601.

Archer, J. (1988). The sociobiology of bereavement: A reply to Littlefield and Rushton. *Journal of Personality and Social Psychology, 55,* 272–278.

Archer, J. (1994). Introduction: Male violence in perspective. In J. Archer (Ed.), *Male violence* (pp. 1–22). New York, NY: Routledge.

Axelrod, R., & Hamilton, W. D. (1981). The evolution of cooperation. *Science, 211,* 1390–1396.

Baer, D., & McEachron, D. L. (1982). A review of selected sociobiological principles: Application to hominid evolution I: The development of group structure. *Journal of Social & Biological Structures, 5,* 69–90.

Baresh, D. P., & Lipton, J. E. (2001). *The myth of monogamy: Fidelity and infidelity in animals and people.* New York, NY: Freeman.

Barkow, J. (1989). *Darwin, sex, and status: Biological approaches to mind and culture.* Toronto, ON: University of Toronto Press.

Barrett, H. C., & Kurzban, R. (2006). Modularity in cognition: Framing the debate. *Psychological Review, 113,* 628–647.

Batson, C. D. (1991). *The altruism question: Towards a social social-psychological answer.* Hillsdale, NJ: Erlbaum.

Baumeister, R. F., DeWall, C. N., Ciarocco, N. J., & Twenge, J. M. (2005). Social exclusion impairs self-regulation. *Journal of Personality and Social Psychology, 88,* 589–604.

Baumeister, R. F., & Leary, M. R. (1995). The need to belong: Desire for interpersonal attachments as a fundamental human motivation. *Psychological Bulletin, 117,* 497–529.

Becker, D. V., Kenrick, D. T., Neuberg, S. L., Blackwell, K. C., & Smith, D. M. (2007). The confounded nature of angry men and happy women. *Journal of Personality and Social Psychology, 92,* 179–190.

Becker, V. D., Sagarin, B. J., Guadagno, R. E., Millevoi, A., & Nicastle, L. D. (2004). When the sexes need not differ: Emotional responses to the sexual and emotional aspects of infidelity. *Personal Relationships, 11,* 529–538.

Belsky, J., Schlomer, G. L., & Ellis, B. J. (2012). Beyond cumulative risk: distinguishing harshness and unpredictability as determinants of parenting and early life history strategy. *Developmental Psychology, 48,* 662–673.

Betzig, L. (1985). *Despotism and differential reproduction: A Darwinian view of history*. New York, NY: de Gruyter.

Betzig, L. (1992). Roman polygyny. *Ethology and Sociobiology, 13,* 309–349.

Boehm, C. (1999). *Hierarchy in the forest*. Cambridge, MA: Harvard University Press.

Bowlby, J. (1958). The nature of the child's tie to his mother. *International Journal of Psycho-Analysis, 39,* 350–373.

Bowlby, J. (1969). *Attachment and loss: Vol. 1, Attachment*. New York, NY: Basic Books.

Brown, D. E. (1991). *Human universals*. New York, NY: McGraw-Hill.

Bugental, D. B. (2000). Acquisition of the algorithms of social life: A domain-based approach. *Psychological Bulletin, 126,* 187–219.

Burnstein, E., Crandall, C., & Kitayama, S. (1994). Some neo-Darwinian decision rules for altruism: Weighing cues for inclusive fitness as a function of the biological importance of the decision. *Journal of Personality and Social Psychology, 67,* 773–389.

Buss, D. M. (1989a). Conflict between the sexes: Strategic interference and the evocation of anger and upset. *Journal of Personality & Social Psychology, 56,* 735–747.

Buss, D. M. (1989b). Sex differences in human mate preferences: Evolutionary hypotheses tests in 37 cultures. *Behavioral and Brain Sciences, 12,* 1–49.

Buss, D. M. (1990). The evolution of anxiety and social exclusion. *Journal of Social and Clinical Psychology, 9,* 196–210.

Buss, D. M. (1995). Psychological sex differences: Origins through sexual selection. *American Psychologist, 50,* 164–168.

Buss, D. M. (1999). Evolutionary psychology: A new paradigm for psychological science. In D. H. Rosen & M. C. Luebbert (Eds.), *Evolution of the psyche: Human evolution, behavior and intelligence* (pp. 1–33). Westport, CT: Praeger.

Buss, D. M. (2002). Human mate guarding. *Neuroendocrinology Letter 23*(Supp 4), 23–29.

Buss, D. M. (2005). *The handbook of evolutionary psychology*. Hoboken, NJ: Wiley.

Buss, D. M., & Barnes, M. (1986). Preferences in human mate selection. *Journal of Personality and Social Psychology, 50,* 559–570.

Buss, D. M., & Kenrick, D. T. (1998). Evolutionary social psychology. In D. T. Gilbert, S. T. Fiske, & G. Lindzey (Eds.), *Handbook of social psychology* (Vol. 2, 4th ed., pp. 982–1026). New York, NY: McGraw-Hill.

Buss, D. M., Larsen, R. J., Westen, D., &; Semmelroth, J. (1992). Sex differences in jealousy: Evolution, physiology, and psychology. *Psychological Science, 3,* 251–255.

Buss, D. M., & Schmitt, D. P. (1993). Sexual strategies theory: A contextual evolutionary analysis of human mating. *Psychological Review, 100,* 204–232.

Buss, D. M., & Shackelford, T. K. (1997). From vigilance to violence: Mate retention tactics in married couples. *Journal of Personality and Social Psychology, 72,* 346–361.

Buunk, B. P., Dijkstra, P., Fetchenhauer, D., & Kenrick, D. T. (2002). Age and gender differences in mate selection criteria for various involvement levels. *Personal Relationships, 9,* 271–278.

Caporeal, L. R. (1997). The evolution of truly social cognition: The core configurations model. *Personality and Social Psychology Review, 1,* 276–298.

Case, C. R., & Maner, J. K. (2014). Divide and conquer: When and why leaders undermine the cohesive fabric of their group. *Journal of Personality and Social Psychology, 107,* 1033–1050.

Cheng, J. T., & Tracy, J. L. (2014). Toward a unified science of hierarchy: Dominance and prestige are two fundamental pathways to human social rank. In J. T. Cheng, J. L. Tracy, & C. Anderson (Eds.), *The psychology of social status* (pp. 3–27). New York, NY: Springer.

Cheng, J. T., Tracy, J. L., Foulsham, T., Kingstone, A., & Henrich, J. (2013). Two ways to the top: Evidence that dominance and prestige are distinct yet viable avenues to social rank and influence. *Journal of Personality and Social Psychology, 104,* 103–125.

Cheng, J. T., Tracy, J. L., Ho, S., & Henrich, J. (2016). Listen, follow me: Dynamic vocal signals of dominance predict emergent social rank in humans. *Journal of Experimental Psychology: General, 145,* 536–547.

Clark, R. D., & Hatfield, E. (1989). Gender differences in receptivity to sexual offers. *Journal of Psychology and Human Sexuality, 2,* 39–55.

Conroy-Beam, D., & Buss, D. M. (2016). Do mate preferences influence actual mating decisions? Evidence from computer simulations and three studies of mated couples. *Journal of Personality and Social Psychology, 111,* 53–66.

Cosmides, L., & Tooby, J. (1992). Cognitive adaptations for social exchange. In J. Barkow, L. Cosmides, & J. Tooby (Eds.), *The adapted mind* (pp. 163–228). New York, NY: Oxford University Press.

Cosmides, L., & Tooby, J. (2005). Neurocognitive adaptations designed for social exchange. In D. M. Buss (Ed.), *The handbook of evolutionary psychology.* New York, NY: Wiley.

Cosmides, L., Tooby, J., & Barkow, J. (1992). Evolutionary psychology and conceptual integration. In J. Barkow, L. Cosmides, & J. Tooby (Eds.), *The adapted mind: Evolutionary psychology and the generation of culture* (pp. 3–15). New York, NY: Oxford University Press.

Cottrell, C. A., & Neuberg, S. L. (2005). Different emotional reactions to different groups: A sociofunctional threat-based approach to "prejudice." *Journal of Personality and Social Psychology, 88,* 770–789.

Cottrell, C. A., Neuberg, S. L., & Li, N. P. (2007). What do people desire in others? A sociofunctional perspective on the importance of different valued characteristics. *Journal of Personality and Social Psychology, 92,* 208–231.

Crawford, C., & Krebs, D. (2008). *Foundations of evolutionary psychology* (2nd ed.). New York, NY: Erlbaum.

Cunningham, M. R., Barbee, A. P., & Pike, C. L. (1990). What do women want? Facial metric assessment of multiple motives in the perception of male facial physical attractiveness. *Journal of Personality and Social Psychology, 59,* 61–72.

Dabbs, J., Jr., & Morris, R. (1990). Testosterone, social class, and antisocial behavior in a sample of 4,462 men. *Psychological Science, 1,* 209–211.

Daly, M., Salmon, C., & Wilson, M. (1997). Kinship: The conceptual hole in psychological studies of social cognition and close relationships. In J. A. Simpson & D. T. Kenrick (Eds.), *Evolutionary social psychology* (pp. 265–296). Mahwah, NJ: Erlbaum.

Daly, M., & Wilson, M. (1980). Discriminative parental solicitude: A biological perspective. *Journal of Marriage & Family, 42,* 277–288.

Daly, M., & Wilson, M. I. (1983). *Sex, evolution and behavior: Adaptations for reproduction* (2nd ed.). Boston, MA: Willard Grant.

Daly, M., & Wilson, M. I. (1985). Child abuse and other risks of not living with both parents. *Ethology & Sociobiology, 6,* 197–210.

Daly, M., & Wilson, M. (1988). *Homicide.* Hawthorne, NY: de Gruyter.

DeBruine, L. M. (2002). Facial resemblance enhances trust. *Proceedings of the Royal Society of London B, 269,* 1307–1312.

DeBruine L. M. (2005). Trustworthy but not lust-worthy: Context-specific effects of facial resemblance. *Proceedings of the Royal Society of London B, 272,* 919–922.

DeSteno, D. A., & Salovey, P. (1996). Evolutionary origins of sex differences in jealousy? Questioning the "fitness" of the model. *Psychological Science, 7,* 367–372.

de Waal, F. (1999). *Chimpanzee politics: Power and sex among apes.* New York, NY: Harper & Row.

Del Giudice, M. (2009). Sex, attachment, and the development of reproductive strategy. *Behavioral and Brain Sciences, 32,* 1–67.

DeScioli, P., & Kurzban, R. (2013). A solution to the mysteries of morality. *Psychological Bulletin, 139,* 477–496.

DeWall, C. N., Maner, J. K., & Rouby, D. A. (2009). Social exclusion and early-stage interpersonal perception: Selective attention to signs of acceptance. *Journal of Personality and Social Psychology, 96,* 729–741.

DeWall, C. N., Twenge, J. M., Gitter, S. A., & Baumeister, R. F. (2009). It's the thought that counts: The role of hostile cognition in shaping aggressive responses to social exclusion. *Journal of Personality and Social Psychology, 96,* 45–59.

Diamond, L. M., Hicks, A. M., & Otter-Henderson, K. D. (2008). Every time you go away: Changes in affect, behavior, and physiology associated with travel-related separations from romantic partners. *Journal of Personality and Social Psychology, 95,* 385–403.

Durante, K. M., Eastwick, P. W., Finkel, E. J., Gangestad, S. W., & Simpson, J. A. (2016). Pair-bonded relationships and romantic alternatives: Toward an integration of evolutionary and relationship science perspectives. *Advances in Experimental Social Psychology, 53,* 1–74.

Durante, K. M., Griskevicius, V., Simpson, J. A., Cantu, S. M., & Tybur, J. M. (2012). Sex ratio and women's career choice: Does a scarcity of men lead women to choose briefcase over baby? *Journal of Personality and Social Psychology, 103,* 12 1–134.

Eagly, A. H., & Wood, W. (1999). The origins of sex differences in human behavior: Evolved dispositions versus social roles. *American Psychologist, 54,* 408–423.

Easton, J. A., Schipper, L. D., & Shackelford, T. K. (2007). Morbid jealousy from an evolutionary psychological perspective. *Evolution and Human Behavior, 28,* 399–402.

Eastwick, P. W. (2009). Beyond the Pleistocene: Using phylogeny and constraint to inform the evolutionary psychology of human mating. *Psychological Bulletin, 135,* 794–821.

Eastwick, P. W., & Finkel, E. J. (2008). Sex differences in mate preferences revisited: Do people know what they initially desire in a romantic partner? *Journal of Personality and Social Psychology, 94,* 245–264.

Eastwick, P. W., Luchies, L. B., Finkel, E. J., & Hunt, L. L. (2014). The predictive validity of ideal partner preferences: A review and meta-analysis. *Psychological Bulletin, 140,* 623–665.

Eibl-Eibesfeldt, I. (1989). *Human ethology.* New York, NY: de Gruyter.

Eisenberger, N. I., Lieberman, M. D., & Williams, K. D. (2003). Does rejection hurt? An fMRI study of social exclusion. *Science, 302,* 290–292.

Ekman, P. (1982). *Emotion in the human face* (2nd ed.) Cambridge, England: Cambridge University Press.

Ekman, P., & Friesen, W. (1976). *Pictures of facial affect.* Palo Alto, CA: Consulting Psychologists Press.

Ellis, B. J. (2004). Timing of pubertal maturation in girls: An integrated life history approach. *Psychological Bulletin, 130,* 920–958.

Ellis, L. (1995). Dominance and reproductive success among nonhuman animals. *Ethology and Sociobiology, 16,* 257–333.

Essock-Vitale, S., & McGuire, M. (1985). Women's lives viewed from an evolutionary perspective. II. Patterns of helping. *Ethology and Sociobiology, 6,* 155–173.

Faulkner, J., & Schaller, M. (2007). Nepotistic nosiness: Inclusive fitness and vigilance of kin members' romantic relationships. *Evolution and Human Behavior, 28,* 430–438.

Faulkner, J., Schaller, M., Park, J. H., & Duncan, L. A. (2004). Evolved disease-avoidance mechanisms and contemporary xenophobic attitudes. *Group Processes and Intergroup Relations, 7,* 333–353.

Fehr, E., Fischbacher, U., & Gachter, S. (2002). Strong reciprocity, human cooperation and the enforcement of social norms. *Human Nature, 13,* 1–25.

Fessler, D. M. T. (2001). Luteal phase immunosuppression and meat eating. *Rivista di Biologia/Biology Forum, 94,* 403–426.

Fessler, D. M. T. (2002). Reproductive immunosuppression and diet: An evolutionary perspective on pregnancy sickness and meat consumption. *Current Anthropology 43,* 19–39, 48–61.

Fessler, D. M. T., & Navarrete, C. D. (2003). Meat is good to taboo: Dietary proscriptions as a product of the interaction of psychological mechanisms and social processes. *Journal of Cognition and Culture, 3,* 1–40.

Fincher, C. L., & Thornhill, R. (2008). Assortative sociality, limited dispersal, infectious disease and the genesis of the global pattern of religion diversity. *Proceedings of the Royal Society: B. Biological Sciences, 275,* 2587–2594.

Fincher, C. L., & Thornhill, R. (2012). Parasite-stress promotes in-group assortative sociality: The cases of strong family ties and heightened religiosity. *Behavioral and Brain Sciences, 35,* 61–79.

Finkel, E. J. (2007). Impelling and inhibiting forces in the perpetration of intimate partner violence. *Review of General Psychology, 11,* 193–207.

Finkel, E. J., & Eastwick, P. W. (2009). Arbitrary social norms influence sex differences in romantic selectivity. *Psychological Science, 20,* 1290–1295.

Fisek, M. H., & Ofshe, R. (1970). The process of status evolution. *Sociometry, 33,* 327–346.

Fisher, H. E. (1989). Evolution of human serial pair bonding. *American Journal of Physical Anthropology, 73,* 331–354.

Fisher, R. A. (1958). *The genetical theory of natural selection* (2nd ed.). New York, NY: Dover.

Fiske, A. P. (1992). The four elementary forms of sociality: Framework for a unified theory of social relations. *Psychological Review, 99,* 689–723.

Fodor, J. A. (1983). *The modularity of mind: An essay on faculty psychology.* Cambridge, MA: MIT Press.

Fox, E., Russo, R., Bowles, R., & Dutton, K. (2001). Do threatening stimuli draw or hold visual attention in subclinical anxiety? *Journal of Experimental Psychology: General, 130,* 681–700.

Frank, R. H. (1988). *Passions within reason: The strategic role of the emotions.* New York, NY: Norton.

Frank, R. H. (2001). Cooperation through emotional commitment. In R. M. Nesse (Ed.), *Evolution and the capacity for commitment* (pp. 57–76). New York, NY: SAGE.

Gangestad, S. W., & Buss, D. M. (1993). Pathogen prevalence and human mate preferences. *Ethology and Sociobiology, 14,* 89–96.

Gangestad, S. G., Haselton, M. G., & Buss, D. M. (2006a). Evolutionary foundations of cultural variation: Evoked culture and mate preferences. *Psychological Inquiry, 17,* 75–95.

Gangestad, S. G., Haselton, M. G., & Buss, D. M. (2006b). Toward an integrative understanding of evoked and transmitted culture: The importance of specialized psychological design. *Psychological Inquiry, 17,* 138–151.

Gangestad, S. W., & Simpson, J. A. (2000). The evolution of human mating: Trade-offs and strategic pluralism. *Behavioral and Brain Sciences, 23,* 573–644.

Gangestad, S. W., & Simpson, J. A. (2007). *The evolution of mind: Fundamental questions and controversies.* New York, NY: Guilford.

Gangestad, S. W., & Thornhill, R. (1997). The evolutionary psychology of extra-pair sex: The role of fluctuating asymmetry. *Evolution and Human Behavior, 18,* 69–88.

Garcia, J., & Koelling, R. A. (1966). Relation of cue to consequence in avoidance learning. *Psychonomic Science, 4,* 123–124.

Gardner, W. L., Pickett, C. L., & Brewer, M. B. (2000). Social exclusion and selective memory. How the need to belong influences memory for social events. *Personality and social Psychology Bulletin, 26,* 486–496.

Gaulin, S., & Robbins, C. (1991). Trivers-Willard effect in contemporary North American society. *American Journal of Physical Anthropology, 85,* 61–69.

Geary, D. C. (1998). *Male, female: The evolution of human sex differences.* New York, NY: American Psychological Association.

Geary, D. C. (2000). Evolution and proximate expression of human paternal investment. *Psychological Bulletin, 126,* 55–77.

Gonzaga, G. C., Haselton, M. G., Smurda, J., Davies, M., & Poore, J. C. (2008). Love, desire, and the suppression of thoughts of romantic alternatives. *Evolution and Human Behavior, 29,* 119–126.

Gonzaga, G. C., Keltner, D., Londahl, E. A., & Smith, M. D. (2001). Love and the commitment problem in romantic relations and friendship. *Journal of Personality and Social Psychology, 81,* 247–262.

Greenberg, L. (1979). Genetic component of bee odor in kin recognition. *Science, 206,* 1095–1097.

Greiling, H., & Buss, D. M. (2000). Women's sexual strategies: The hidden dimension of extra-pair mating. *Personality and Individual Differences, 28,* 929–963.

Griskevicius, V., Ackerman, J. M., Cantu, S. M., Delton, A. W., Robertson, T. E., Simpson, J. A., . . . Tybur, J. M. (2013). When the economy falters do people spend or save? Responses to resource scarcity depend on childhood environments. *Psychological Science, 24,* 197–205.

Griskevicius, V., Cialdini, R. B., & Kenrick, D. T. (2006). Peacocks, Picasso, and parental investment: The effects of romantic motives on creativity. *Journal of Personality and Social Psychology, 91,* 63–76.

Griskevicius, V., Tybur, J. M., Ackerman, J. M., Delton, A. W., Robertson, T. E., & White, A. E. (2012). The financial consequences of too many men: Sex ratio effects on saving, borrowing, and spending. *Journal of Personality and Social Psychology, 102,* 69–80.

Gutierres, S. E., Kenrick, D. T., & Partch, J. J. (1999). Beauty, dominance, and the mating game: Contrast effects in self-assessment reflect gender differences in mate selection. *Personality and Social Psychology Bulletin, 25,* 1126–1134.

Guttentag, M., & Secord, P. F. (1983). *Too many women? The sex ratio question.* Beverly Hills, CA: SAGE.

Hamilton, W. D. (1964). The genetical evolution of social behavior: I & II. *Journal of Theoretical Biology, 7,* 1–32.

Hansen, C. H., & Hansen, R. D. (1988). Finding the face in the crowd: An anger superiority effect. *Journal of Personality and Social Psychology, 54,* 917–924.

Harris, C. R. (2003). A review of sex differences in sexual jealousy, including self-report data, psychophysiological responses, interpersonal violence, and morbid jealousy. *Personality and Social Psychology Review, 7,* 102–128.

Harris, C. R. (2005). Male and female jealousy, still more similar than different: Reply to Sagarin (2005). *Personality and Social Psychology Review, 9,* 76–86.

Haselton, M. G., & Gangestad, S. W. (2006). Conditional expression of women's desires and men's mate guarding across the ovulatory cycle. *Hormones and Behavior, 49,* 509–518.

Haselton, M. G., & Nettle, D. (2006). The paranoid optimist: An integrative evolutionary model of cognitive biases. *Personality and Social Psychology Review, 10,* 47–66.

Hazan, C., & Diamond, L. M. (2000). The place of attachment in human mating. *Review of General Psychology, 4,* 186–204.

Henrich, J., Chudek, M., & Boyd, R. (2015). The Big Man Mechanism: How prestige fosters cooperation and creates prosocial leaders. *Philosophical Transactions of the Royal Society B: Biological Sciences, 370,* 20150013.

Henrich, J., & Gil-White, F. J. (2001). The evolution of prestige: Freely conferred deference as a mechanism for enhancing the benefits of cultural transmission. *Evolution and Human Behavior, 22,* 165–196.

Henrich J., McElreath, R., Barr, A., Ensminger, J., Barret, C., Bolyanatz, A., . . . Ziker, J. (2006). Costly punishment across human societies. *Science, 312,* 1767–1770.

Hewlett, B. S. (1991). *Intimate fathers: The nature and context of Aka pygmy paternal infant care.* Ann Arbor, MI: University of Michigan Press.

Hill, K., & Hurtado, A. M. (1996). *Ache life history.* Hawthorne, NY: de Gruyter.

Hoffman, M. (1981). Is altruism part of human nature? *Journal of Personality and Social Psychology, 40,* 121–137.

Holloway, R. L. (1974). On the meaning of brain size: A review of H. J. Jerison's 1973 *Evolution of the Brain and Intelligence. Science, 184,* 677–679.

Holmes, W. G., & Sherman, P. W. (1983). Kin recognition in animals. *American Scientist, 71,* 46–55.

Hrdy, S. H. (1999). *Mother nature: A history of mothers, infants, and natural selection.* New York, NY: Pantheon.

Jackson, J. J., & Kirkpatrick, L. A. (2007). The structure and measurement of human mating strategies: Toward a multidimensional model of sociosexuality. *Evolution and Human Behavior, 28,* 382–391.

Johnson, D. J., & Rusbult, C. E. (1989). Resisting temptation: Devaluation of alternative partners as a means of maintaining commitment in close relationships. *Journal of Personality and Social Psychology, 57,* 967–980.

Kaschak, M. P., & Maner, J. K. (2009). Embodiment, evolution, and social cognition: An integrative framework. *European Journal of Social Psychology, 39,* 1236–1244.

Keltner, D., Gruenfeld, D. H., & Anderson, C. (2003). Power, approach, and inhibition. *Psychological Review, 110,* 265–284.

Kenrick, D. T. (1987). Gender, genes, and the social environment: A biosocial interactionist perspective. In P. Shaver & C. Hendrick (Eds.), *Review of personality and social psychology* (Vol. 7). Newbury Park, CA: SAGE.

Kenrick, D. T. (2011). *Sex, murder, and the meaning of life: A psychologist investigates how evolution, cognition, and complexity are revolutionizing our view of human nature.* New York, NY: Basic Books.

Kenrick, D. T., Becker, D. V., Butner, J., Li, N. P., &. Maner, J. K. (2003). Evolutionary cognitive science: Adding what and why to how the mind works. In J. Fitness & K. Sterelny (Eds.), *From mating to mentality: Evaluating evolutionary psychology* (pp. 13–38). New York, NY: Psychology Press.

Kenrick, D. T., Gabrielidis, C., Keefe, R. C., & Cornelius, J. (1996). Adolescents' age preferences for dating partners: Support for an evolutionary model of life-history strategies. *Child Development, 67,* 1499–1511.

Kenrick, D. T., & Griskevicius, V. (2013). *The rational animal: How evolution made us smarter than we think*. New York, NY: Basic Books.

Kenrick, D. T., Griskevicius, V., Neuberg, S. L., & Schaller, M. (2010). Renovating the pyramid of needs: Contemporary extensions built upon ancient foundations. *Perspectives on Psychological Science, 5*, 292–314.

Kenrick, D. T., & Keefe, R. C. (1992). Age preferences in mates reflect sex differences in mating strategies. *Behavioral & Brain Sciences, 15*, 75–91.

Kenrick, D. T., Li, N. P., & Butner, J. (2003). Dynamical evolutionary psychology: Individual decision-rules and emergent social norms. *Psychological Review, 110*, 3–28.

Kenrick, D. T., Maner, J. K., Butner, J., Li, N. P., Becker, D. V., & Schaller, M. (2002). Dynamical evolutionary psychology: Mapping the domains of the new interactionist paradigm. *Personality and Social Psychology Review, 6*, 347–356.

Kenrick, D. T., Maner, J. K., & Li, N. P. (2005). Evolutionary social psychology. In D. Buss (Ed.), *The handbook of evolutionary psychology*. Hoboken, N.J: Wiley.

Kenrick, D. T., Neuberg, S. L., & Cialdini, R. B. (1999). *Social psychology: Unraveling the mystery*. Boston, MA: Allyn & Bacon.

Kenrick, D. T., Neuberg, S. L., Zierk, K., & Krones, J. (1994). Evolution and social cognition: Contrast effects as a function of sex, dominance, and physical attractiveness. *Personality & Social Psychology Bulletin, 20*, 210–217.

Kenrick, D. T., Nieuweboer, S., & Buunk, A. P. (2010). Universal mechanisms and cultural diversity: Replacing the blank slate with a coloring book. In M. Schaller, S. Heine, A. Norenzayan, T. Yamagishi, & T. Kameda (Eds.), *Evolution, culture, and the human mind* (pp. 257–272). Mahwah, NJ: Erlbaum.

Kenrick, D. T., Sadalla, E. K., Groth, G., & Trost, M. R. (1990). Evolution, traits, and the stages of human courtship: Qualifying the parental investment model. *Journal of Personality, 58*, 97–116.

Kenrick, D. T., & Shiota, M. N. (2008). Approach and avoidance motivation(s): An evolutionary perspective. In A. J. Elliot (Ed.), *Handbook of approach and avoidance motivation* (pp. 273–288). New York, NY: Psychology Press.

Kenrick, D. T., Sundie, J. M. & Kurzban, R. (2008). Cooperation and conflict between kith, kin, and strangers: Game theory by domains. In C. Crawford & D. Krebs (Eds.), *Foundations of evolutionary psychology* (pp. 353–370). New York, NY: Erlbaum.

Ketelaar, T., & Ellis, B. J. (2000). Are evolutionary explanations unfalsifiable? Evolutionary psychology and the Lakatosian philosophy of science. *Psychological Inquiry, 11*, 1–21.

Kipnis, D. (1972). Does power corrupt? *Journal of Personality & Social Psychology, 24*, 33–41.

Klein, S. B., Cosmides, L., Tooby, J., & Chance, S. (2002). Decisions and the evolution of memory: Multiple systems, multiple functions. *Psychological Review, 109*, 306–329.

Krebs, D. (1987). The challenge of altruism in biology and psychology. In C. Crawford, M. Smith, & D. Krebs (Eds.), *Sociobiology and psychology: Ideas, issues, and applications* (pp. 81–118). Hillsdale, NJ: Erlbaum.

Krems, J. A., Kenrick, D. T., & Neel, R. (2017). Individual perceptions of self-actualization: What functional motives are linked to fulfilling one's full potential? *Personality and Social Psychology Bulletin, 43*, 1337–1352.

Krupp, D. B., DeBruine, L. M., & Barclay, P. (2008). A cue of kinship promotes cooperation for the public good. *Evolution and Human Behavior, 29*, 49–55.

Kurzban, R., & Aktipis, C. A. (2007). Modularity and the social mind: Are psychologists too self-ish? *Personality and Social Psychology Review, 11*, 131–149.

Kurzban, R., & Leary, M. R. (2001). Evolutionary origins of stigmatization: The functions of social exclusion. *Psychological Bulletin, 127*, 187–208.

Kurzban, R., Tooby, J., & Cosmides, J. (2001). Can race be erased? Coalitional computation and social categorization. *Proceedings of the National Academy of Sciences, 98*, 15387–15392.

Leary, M. R., Twenge, J. M., & Quinlivan, E. (2006). interpersonal rejection as a determinant of anger and aggression. *Personality and Social Psychology Review, 10*, 111–132.

Leigh, E. G., Jr., (2010). The group selection controversy. *Journal of Evolutionary Biology, 23*, 6–19.

Li, N. P., Bailey, J. M., Kenrick, D. T., & Linsenmeier, J. A. (2002). The necessities and luxuries of mate preferences: Testing the trade-offs. *Journal of Personality and Social Psychology, 82,* 947–955.

Li, N. P., & Kenrick, D. T. (2006). Sex similarities and differences in preferences for short-term mates: What, whether, and why. *Journal of Personality and Social Psychology, 90,* 468–489.

Lieberman, D., Tooby, J., & Cosmides, L. (2007). The architecture of human kin detection. *Nature, 445,* 727–731.

Low, B. S. (1990). Marriage systems and pathogen stress in human societies. *American Zoologist, 30,* 325–340.

Lydon, J. E., Fitzsimons, G. M., & Naidoo, L. (2003). Devaluation versus enhancement of attractive alternatives: A critical test using the calibration paradigm. *Personality and Social Psychology Bulletin, 29,* 349–359.

Lydon, J. E., Meana, M., Sepinwall, D., Richards, N., & Mayman, A. (1999). The commitment calibration hypothesis: When do people devalue attractive alternatives? *Personality and Social Psychology Bulletin, 25,* 152–161.

MacDonald, G., & Leary, M. R. (2005). Why does social exclusion hurt? The relationship between social and physical pain. *Psychological Bulletin, 131,* 202–223.

Makhanova, A., Miller, S. L., & Maner, J. K. (2015). Germs and the outgroup: Chronic and situational disease concerns affect intergroup categorization. *Evolutionary Behavioral Sciences, 9,* 8–19.

Maner, J. K. (2009). Anxiety: Proximate processes and ultimate functions. *Social and Personality Psychology Compass, 3,* 798–811.

Maner, J. K. (2017). Dominance and prestige: A tale of two hierarchies. *Current Directions in Psychological Science, 24,* 484–489.

Maner, J. K., & Case, C. R. (2016). Dominance and prestige: Dual strategies for navigating social hierarchies. In J. Olson & M. P. Zanna (Eds.), *Advances in experimental social psychology* (Vol. 54, pp. 129–180). San Diego, CA: Elsevier.

Maner, J. K., DeWall, C. N., & Gailliot, M. T. (2008). Selective attention to signs of success: Social dominance and early stage interpersonal perception. *Personality and Social Psychology Bulletin, 34,* 488–501.

Maner, J. K., Dittmann, A., Meltzer, A. L. & McNulty, J. K. (2017). Life history strategies and dysregulated weight management: Implications for obesity. *Proceedings of the National Academy of Sciences, 114,* 8517–8522.

Maner, J. K., & Mead, N. (2010). The essential tension between leadership and power: When leaders sacrifice group goals for the sake of self-interest. *Journal of Personality and Social Psychology, 99,* 482–497.

Mazur, A., & Booth, A. (1998). Testosterone and social dominance in men. *Behavioral & Brain Sciences, 21,* 353–397.

Mead, N. L., & Maner, J. K. (2012). On keeping your enemies close: Powerful leaders seek proximity to ingroup power threats. *Journal of Personality and Social Psychology, 102,* 576–591.

Maner, J. K., DeWall, C. N., Baumeister, R. F., & Schaller, M. (2007). Does social exclusion motivate interpersonal reconnection? Resolving the "porcupine problem." *Journal of Personality and Social Psychology, 92,* 42–55.

Maner, J. K., & Gailliot, M. T. (2007). Altruism and egoism: Prosocial motivations for helping depend on relationship context. *European Journal of Social Psychology, 37,* 347–358.

Maner, J. K., Gailliot, M. T., & Miller, S. L. (2009). The implicit cognition of relationship maintenance: Inattention to attractive alternatives. *Journal of Experimental Social Psychology, 45,* 174–179.

Maner, J. K., Gailliot, M. T., Rouby, D. A., & Miller, S. L. (2007). Can't take my eyes off you: Attentional adhesion to mates and rivals. *Journal of Personality and Social Psychology, 93,* 389–401.

Maner, J. K., Kenrick, D. T., Neuberg, S. L., Becker, D. V., Robertson, T., Hofer, B., . . . Schaller, M. (2005). Functional projection: How fundamental social motives can bias interpersonal perception. *Journal of Personality and Social Psychology, 88,* 63–78.

Maner, J. K., Kenrick, D. T., & Becker, D. V., Delton, A. W., Hofer, B., Wilbur, C. J., & Neuberg, S. L. (2003). Sexually selective cognition: Beauty captures the mind of the beholder. *Journal of Personality and Social Psychology, 85,* 1107–1120.

Maner, J. K., Miller, S. L., Moss, J., Leo, J., & Plant, E. A. (2012). Motivated social categorization: Fundamental motives enhance people's sensitivity to basic social categories. *Journal of Personality and Social Psychology, 103,* 70–83.

Maner, J. K., Miller, S. L., Rouby, D. A., & Gailliot, M. T. (2009). Intrasexual vigilance: The implicit cognition of romantic rivalry. *Journal of Personality and Social Psychology, 97,* 74–87.

Maner, J. K., Miller, S. L., Schmidt, N. B., & Eckel, L. A. (2010). The endocrinology of exclusion: Rejection elicits motivationally tuned changes in progesterone. *Psychological Science, 21,* 581–588.

Maner, J. K., Rouby, D. A., & Gonzaga, G. (2008). Automatic inattention to attractive alternatives: The evolved psychology of relationship maintenance. *Evolution & Human Behavior, 29,* 343–349.

Marlowe, F. W., Berbesque, J. C., Barr, A., Barrett, C., Bolyanatz, A., Cardenas, J. C., . . . Tracer, D. (2008). More "altruistic" punishment in larger societies. *Proceedings of the Royal Society Biology, 275,* 587–590.

Marshall, D. S., & Suggs, R. G. (1971). *Human sexual behavior: Variations in the ethnographic spectrum.* New York, NY: Basic Books.

Mazur, A., & Booth, A. (1998). Testosterone and dominance in men. *Behavioral and Brain Sciences, 21,* 353–397.

McClelland, D. C. (1975). *Power: The inner experience.* Oxford, England: Irvington.

McDonald, M., Asher, B., Kerr, N., & Navarrete, C.D. (2011). Fertility and intergroup bias in racial and in minimal group contexts: Evidence for shared architecture. *Psychological Science, 22,* 860–865.

McDonald, M., & Navarrete, C.D. (2015). Examining the link between conception risk and intergroup bias: The importance of conceptual coherence. *Psychological Science, 26,* 253–255.

McGinnis, R. (1958). Campus values in mate selection: A repeat study. *Social Forces, 36,* 368–373.

McHenry, H. M., & Coffing, K. (2000). Australopithecus to Homo: Transformations in body and mind. *Annual Review of Anthropology, 29,* 125–146.

Mealey, L., Daood, C., & Krage, M. (1996). Enhanced memory for faces of cheaters. *Ethology and Sociobiology, 17,* 119–128.

Meltzer, A. L., McNulty, J. K., Jackson, G. L., & Karney, B. R. (2014). Sex differences in the implications of partner physical attractiveness for the trajectory of marital satisfaction. *Journal of Personality and Social Psychology, 106,* 418–428.

Miller, G. F. (2000). *The mating mind: How sexual choice shaped the evolution of human nature.* New York, NY: Doubleday.

Miller, R. S. (1997). Inattentive and contented: Relationship commitment and attention to alternatives. *Journal of Personality and Social Psychology, 73,* 758–766.

Miller, S. L., & Maner, J. K. (2011a). Ovulation as a mating prime: Subtle signs of female fertility influence men's mating cognition and behavior. *Journal of Personality and Social Psychology, 100,* 295–308.

Miller, S. L., & Maner, J. K. (2011b). Sick body, vigilant mind: The biological immune system activates the behavioral immune system. *Psychological Science, 22,* 1467–1471.

Miller, S. L., & Maner, J. K. (2012). Overperceiving disease cues: The basic cognition of the behavioral immune system. *Journal of Personality and Social Psychology, 102,* 1198–1213.

Miller, S. L., & Maner, J. K., & Becker, D. V. (2010). Self-protective biases in group categorization: What shapes the psychological boundary between "us" and "them"? *Journal of Personality and Social Psychology, 99,* 62–77.

Mittal, C., Griskevicius, V., Simpson, J. A., Sung, S. Y., & Young, E. S. (2015). Cognitive adaptations to stressful environments: When childhood adversity enhances adult executive function. *Journal of Personality and Social Psychology, 109,* 604–621.

Mortensen, C.R., Becker, D.V., Ackerman, J.M., Neuberg, S.L., & Kenrick, D.T. (2010). Infection breeds reticence: The effects of disease salience on self-perceptions of personality and behavioral avoidance tendencies. *Psychological Science, 21,* 440–447.

Moore, B. R. (2004). The evolution of learning. *Biological Review, 79,* 301–335.

Moss, J. & Maner, J. K. (2016). Biased sex ratios influence fundamental aspects of human mating. *Personality and Social Psychology Bulletin, 42,* 72–80.

Murray, D. R., Fessler, D. M. T., Kerry, N., White, C., & Marin, M. (2017). The kiss of death: Three tests of the relationship between disease threat and ritualized physical contact within traditional cultures. *Evolution and Human Behavior, 38,* 63–70.

Murray, D. R., & Schaller, M. (2016). The behavioral immune system: Implications for social cognition, social interaction, and social influence. *Advances in Experimental Social Psychology, 53,* 75–129.

Navarrete, C. D., & Fessler, D. (2006). Disease avoidance and ethnocentrism: The effects of disease vulnerability and disgust sensitivity on intergroup attitudes, *Evolution & Human Behavior, 27,* 270–282.

Navarrete, C. D., Olsson, A., Ho, A., Mendes, W., Thomsen, L., & Sidanius, J. (2009). Fear extinction to an outgroup face: The role of target gender. *Psychological Science, 20,* 155–158.

Neel, R., Kenrick, D. T., White, A. E., & Neuberg, S. L. (2016). Individual differences in fundamental social motives. *Journal of Personality and Social Psychology, 110,* 887–907.

Neuberg, S. L., & Cottrell, C. A. (2006). Evolutionary bases of prejudices. In M. Schaller, J. A. Simpson, & D. T. Kenrick (Eds.), *Evolution and social psychology* (pp. 163–187). New York, NY: Psychology Press.

Neuberg, S. L, Kenrick, D. T. & Schaller, M. (2010). Evolutionary social psychology. In S. T. Fiske, D. T. Gilbert, & G. Lindzey (Eds.) *Handbook of social psychology* (5th ed., Vol. 2, pp. 761–796). New York, NY: Wiley.

Neuberg, S. L., Kenrick, D. T., & Schaller, M. (2011). Human threat management systems: Self-protection and disease avoidance. *Neuroscience & Biobehavioral Reviews, 35,* 1042–1051.

Neyer, F. J., & Lang, F. R. (2003). Blood is thicker than water: Kinship orientation across adulthood. *Journal of Personality and Social Psychology, 84,* 310–321.

Norenzayan, A. (2006). Evolution and transmitted culture. *Psychological Inquiry, 17,* 123–128.

Norenzayan, A., & Shariff, A. F. (2008). The origin and evolution of religious prosociality. *Science, 322,* 58–62.

Otta, E., da Silva Queiroz, R., de Sousa Campos, L., da Silva, M. W. D., & Silveira, M. T. (1999). Age differences between spouses in a Brazilian marriage sample. *Evolution and Human Behavior, 20,* 99–103.

Öhman, A, & Mineka, S. (2001). Fears, phobias, and preparedness: Toward an evolved module of fear and fear learning. *Psychological Review, 108,* 483–522.

Panksepp, J. (1982). Toward a general psychobiological theory of emotions. *Behavioral & Brain Sciences, 5,* 407–467.

Park, J. H., Faulkner, J., & Schaller, M. (2003). Evolved disease-avoidance processes and contemporary anti-social behavior: Prejudicial attitudes and avoidance of people with physical disabilities. *Journal of Nonverbal Behavior, 27,* 65–87.

Park, J. H., Schaller, M., & Crandall, C. S. (2007). Pathogen-avoidance mechanisms and the stigmatization of obese people. *Evolution and Human Behavior, 28,* 410–414.

Park, J., Schaller, M., & Van Vugt, M. (2008). The psychology of human kin recognition: Heuristic cues, erroneous inferences, and their implications. *Review of General Psychology, 12,* 215–235.

Parkinson, B. (2005). Do facial movements express emotions or communicate motives? *Personality and Social Psychology Review, 9,* 278–311.

Petersen, M. B. (2017). Healthy out-group members are represented psychologically as infected in-group members. *Psychological Science, 28,* 1857–1863.

Pinker, S. (1997). *How the mind works.* New York, NY: Norton.

Plutchik, R. (1980). A general psychoevolutionary theory of emotion. In R. Plutchik & H. Kellerman (Eds.), *Emotions: Theory, research, and experience* (Vol. 1). New York, NY: Academic Press.

Preston, S. D., & de Waal, F. B. M. (2002). Empathy: Its ultimate and proximate bases. *Behavioral and Brain Sciences, 25,* 1–71.

Rasmussen, D. R. (1981). Pair bond strength and stability and reproductive success. *Psychological Review, 88,* 274–290.

Richerson, P. J., & Boyd, R. (2005). *Not by genes alone: How culture transformed human evolution.* Chicago, IL: University of Chicago Press.

Ridley, M. (2003). *Nature via nurture: Genes, experience, and what makes us human.* New York, NY: HarperCollins.

Rose, R. M., Bernstein, I. S., & Holaday, J. W. (1971). Plasma testosterone, dominance rank, and aggressive behavior in a group of male rhesus monkeys. *Nature, 231,* 366.

Rozin, P., & Fallon, A. (1987). A perspective on disgust. *Psychological Review, 94,* 23–41.

Rudder, C. (2014). *Dataclysm: Who we are (when we think no one's looking).* New York, NY: Random House.

Sadalla, E. K., Kenrick, D. T., & Venshure, B. (1987). Dominance and heterosexual attraction. *Journal of Personality and Social Psychology, 52,* 730–738.

Sagarin, B. J. (2005). Reconsidering evolved sex differences in jealousy: Comment on Harris (2003). *Personality & Social Psychology Review, 9,* 62–75.

Schaller, M. (2018). The parental care motivational system and why it matters (for everyone). *Current Directions in Psychological Science, 27,* 295–301.

Schaller, M., & Murray, D. R. (2008). Pathogens, personality and culture: Disease prevalence predicts worldwide variability in sociosexuality, extraversion, and openness to experience. *Journal of Personality and Social Psychology, 95,* 212–221.

Schaller, M., Park, J. H., & Mueller, A. (2003). Fear of the dark: Interactive effects of beliefs about danger and ambient darkness on ethnic stereotypes. *Personality and Social Psychology Bulletin, 29,* 637–649.

Schaller, M., & Park, J. H. (2011). The behavioral immune system (and why it matters). *Current Directions in Psychological Science, 20,* 99–103.

Scheib, J. E. (2001). Context-specific mate choice criteria: Women's trade-offs in the contexts of long-term and extra-pair mateships. *Personal Relationships, 8,* 371–389.

Scheib, J. E., Gangestad, S. W., & Thornhill, R. (1999). Facial attractiveness, symmetry, and cues of good genes. *Proceedings of the Royal Society of London B, 266,* 1913–1917.

Schützwohl, A. (2008). The crux of cognitive load: Constraining deliberate and effortful decision processes in romantic jealousy. *Evolution and Human Behavior, 29,* 127–132.

Schwarz, N., & Clore, G. L. (1983). Mood, misattribution, and judgments of well-being: Informative and directive functions of affective states. *Journal of Personality and Social Psychology, 45,* 513–523.

Sedikides, C., & Skowronski, J. J. (1997). The symbolic self in evolutionary context. *Personality and Social Psychology Review, 1,* 80–102.

Segal, N. L., & Hershberger, S. L. (1999). Cooperation and competition in adolescent twins: Findings from a prisoner's dilemma game. *Evolution and Human Behavior, 20,* 29–51.

Seligman, M. E. P. (1971). Phobias and preparedness. *Behavior Therapy, 2,* 307–320.

Shackelford, T. K., Goetz, A. T., Buss, D. M., Euler, H. A., & Hoier, S. (2005). When we hurt the ones we love: Predicting violence against women from men's mate retention. *Personal Relationships, 12,* 447–463.

Shapiro, J., Ackerman, J., Neuberg, S. L., Maner, J. K., Becker, D. V., & Kenrick, D. T. (2009). Following in the wake of anger: When not discriminating is discriminating. *Personality & Social Psychology Bulletin, 35,* 1356–1367.

Sheets, V. L., Fredendall, L. L., & Claypool, H. M. (1997). Jealousy evocation, partner reassurance and relationship stability: An exploration of the potential benefits of jealousy. *Evolution and Human Behavior, 18,* 387–402.

Sherman, P. W. (1977). Nepotism and the evolution of alarm calls. *Science, 197,* 1246–1253.

Sherry, D. F., & Schacter, D. L. (1987). The evolution of multiple memory systems. *Psychological Review, 94,* 439–454.

Simpson, J. A., & Gangestad, S. W. (1991). Individual differences in sociosexuality: Evidence for convergent and discriminant validity. *Journal of Personality and Social Psychology, 67,* 870–883.

Simpson, J. A., Gangestad, S. W., & Lerma, M. (1990). Perception of physical attractiveness: Mechanisms involved in the maintenance of romantic relationships. *Journal of Personality and Social Psychology, 59,* 1192–1201.

Simpson, J. A., Griskevicius, V., Kuo, S. I., Sung, S., & Collins, W. A. (2012). Evolution, stress, and sensitive periods: the influence of unpredictability in early versus late childhood on sex and risky behavior. *Developmental Psychology, 48,* 674–686.

Singh, D. (1993). Adaptive significance of waist-to-hip ratio and female attractiveness. *Journal of Personality and Social Psychology, 65,* 293–307.

Sng, O., Neuberg, S. L., Varnum, M. E. W., & Kenrick, D. T. (2017). The crowded life is a slow life: Population density and life history strategy. *Journal of Personality and Social Psychology, 112,* 736–754.

Sng, O., Neuberg, S. L., Varnum, M. E. W., & Kenrick, D.T. (2018). The behavioral ecology of cultural variation. *Psychological Review, 125,* 714–743.

Sprecher, S., Sullivan, Q., & Hatfield, E. (1994). Mate selection preferences: Gender differences examined in a national sample. *Journal of Personality and Social Psychology, 66,* 1074–1080.

Stewart-Williams, S. (2008). Human beings as evolved nepotists: Exceptions to the rue and effects of cost of help. *Human Nature, 19,* 414–425.

Suomi, S. J. (1982). Sibling relationships in nonhuman primates. In M. E. Lamb & B. Sutton-Smith (Eds.), *Sibling relationships* (pp. 329–356). Mahwah NJ: Erlbaum.

Symons, D. (1979). *The evolution of human sexuality.* New York, NY: Oxford University Press.

Tinbergen, N. (1963). On the aims and methods of ethology. *Zeitschrift für Tierpsychologie, 20,* 410–433.

Tomasello, M., Kruger, A. C., & Ratner, H. H. (1993). Cultural learning. *Behavioral and Brain Sciences, 16,* 495–552.

Tooby, J., & Cosmides, L. (1990). On the universality of human nature and the uniqueness of the individual: The role of genetics and adaptation. *Journal of Personality, 58,* 17–67.

Tooby, J., & Cosmides, L. (1992). The psychological foundations of culture. In J. Barkow, L. Cosmides, & J. Tooby (Eds.), *The adapted mind: Evolutionary psychology and the generation of culture* (pp. 19–136). New York: Oxford University Press.

Trivers, R. L. (1971). The evolution of reciprocal altruism. *Quarterly Review of Biology, 46,* 35–37.

Trivers, R. L. (1972). Parental investment and sexual selection. In B. Campbell (Ed.), *Sexual selection and the descent of man* (pp. 136–179). Chicago, IL: Aldine-Atherton.

Trivers, R. L. (1985). *Social evolution.* Menlo Park, IL: Benjamin/Cummings.

Trivers, R. L., & Willard, D. E. (1973). Natural selection of parental ability to vary the sex ratio of offspring. *Science, 197,* 90–92.

Tybur, J. M., Lieberman, D., Kurzban, R., & DeScioli, P. (2013). Disgust: Evolved function and structure. *Psychological Review, 120,* 65–84.

Van Leeuwen, F., & Petersen, M. B. (2018). The behavioral immune system is designed to avoid infected individuals, not outgroups. *Evolution and Human Behavior, 39,* 226–234.

van Vugt, M. (2006). Evolutionary origins of leadership and followership. *Personality and Social Psychology Review, 10,* 354–371.

van Vugt, M., Hogan, R., & Kaiser, R. (2008). Leadership, followership, and evolution: Some lessons from the past. *American Psychologist, 63,* 182–196.

White, A. E., Li, Y. J., Griskevicius, V., Neuberg, S. L., & Kenrick, D. T. (2013). Putting all your eggs in one basket: Life-history strategies, bet hedging, and diversification. *Psychological Science, 24,* 715–722.

Williams, K. D., Cheung, C. K. T., & Choi, W. (2000). Cyberostracism: Effects of being ignored over the internet. *Journal of Personality and Social Psychology, 79,* 748–762.

Wilson, E. O. (1975). *Sociobiology: The new synthesis.* Cambridge, MA: Harvard University Press.

Wilson, M., & Daly, M. (1996). Male sexual proprietariness and violence against wives. *Current Directions in Psychological Science, 5,* 2–7.

Wilson, D. S., Van Vugt, M., & O'Gorman, R. (2008). Multilevel selection theory and major evolutionary transitions: Implications for psychological science. *Current Directions in Psychological Science, 17,* 6–9.

Wilson, D. S., & Wilson, E. O. (2007). Rethinking the theoretical foundation of sociobiology. *Quarterly Review of Biology, 82,* 327–348.

Wood, W., & Eagly, A. H. (2007). Social structural origins of sex differences in human mating. In S. W. Gangestad & J. A. Simpson (Eds.), *Evolution of the mind: Fundamental questions and controversies* (pp. 383–390). New York, NY: Guilford Press.

Zebrowitz, L. A., & Collins, M. A. (1997). Accurate social perception at zero acquaintance: The affordances of a Gibsonian approach. *Personality and Social Psychology Review, 1,* 203–222.

Chapter 17

Cultural Psychology

Steven J. Heine

Imagine what it must have been like. About 8 million years ago, rustling about the savannas of East Africa, there lived a family of apes. They had their ape-like concerns, struggling to get food, avoiding predators, negotiating a power hierarchy, grooming themselves, and taking care of their offspring. Their lives would have looked ordinary if we could see them now, and it is doubtful that there would have been any signs of the things that would happen to their descendants. Some of the descendants of those apes would evolve into what we recognize today as chimpanzees and bonobos. Some of their other descendants would evolve into a species whose members have gone on to populate the furthest reaches of the planet, split the atom, paint the Sistine Chapel, and invent the iPhone. What factors have determined the different trajectories of these biologically similar species? Much of the answer to this question has to do with culture.

Humans are a cultural species—we depend critically on cultural learning in all aspects of our lives. Whether we're trying to woo a mate, protect our family, enhance our status, or form a political alliance— goals that are pursued by people in all cultures—we do so in culturally particular ways (Richerson & Boyd, 2005). Of course, many psychological phenomena appear similarly across cultures, while many others look quite different (Norenzayan & Heine, 2005). The point is that all psychological phenomena, whether largely similar or different across cultures, remain entangled in cultural meanings. The challenge for comprehending the mind of a cultural species is that it requires us to understand how the mind is shaped by cultural learning. The field of cultural psychology has emerged in response to this challenge.

Cultural psychologists share the key assumption that not all psychological processes are so inflexibly hardwired into the brain that they appear in identical ways across cultural contexts. Rather, psychological processes are seen to arise from evolutionarily shaped biological potentials becoming attuned to the particular cultural meaning system within which the individual develops. At the same time, cultures can be understood to emerge through the processes by which humans interact with and seize meanings and resources from them. In this way, culture and the mind can be said to be mutually constituted (Shweder, 1990). An effort to understand either one without considering the other is bound to reveal an incomplete picture.

Why is studying culture important for social psychology? Social psychologists study people, however, we always face the challenge of considering "which people"? Social psychology would be more straight-forward if psychological phenomena emerged in identical ways everywhere. However, given that culture can be seen as the social situation writ large, social psychologists should not be surprised that many ways of thinking vary importantly across cultures. We should expect some cultural variation across different contexts, as many psychological phenomena have been found to vary across historical time (e.g., Grossman & Varnum, 2015; Twenge, Campbell, & Freeman, 2012). On the one hand, pronounced cultural variance has been identified in such fundamental psychological phenomena as perceptions of fairness (e.g., Henrich et al., 2005), approach-avoidance motivations (e.g., Lee, Aaker, & Gardner, 2000), attention (Chua, Boland, & Nisbett, 2005), the need for high self-esteem (e.g., Heine, Lehman, Markus, & Kitayama, 1999), and moral reasoning (e.g., Miller & Bersoff, 1992), to name several. At the same time, many key psychological phenomena have been compellingly shown to have varying degrees of universality, such as facial expressions of emotions (Ekman, Sorenson, & Friesen, 1969), various mating preferences (Buss, 1989), sex differences in violence (Daly & Wilson, 1988), psychological essentialism (Gelman, 2003), and the structure of personality (McCrae et al., 2005). Some psychological phenomena manifest in more culturally-variable ways than others, and it is typically not clear a priori which phenomena should be the most similar across cultures (Henrich, Heine, & Norenzayan, 2010). Hence, if one is interested in assessing the universality of a particular phenomenon it is necessary to examine data from a wide array of samples.

Social psychologists are not always endeavoring to hypothesize about or assess the degree of universality in psychological processes, but when they do they face the major obstacle of a limited database. For example, a review of all papers published in the *Journal of Personality and Social Psychology* from 2003 to 2007 found that 94% of the samples were from Western countries, with 62% coming from the United States alone, and 67% of the American samples were composed solely of undergraduates (Arnett, 2008; a similarly narrow sample was found in other subdisciplines in psychology as well; also see Nielsen, Haun, Kartner, & Legare, 2017). Curiously, this American dominance of psychology is unparalleled by other disciplines—a larger proportion of citations come from American researchers in psychology than they do for any of the other 19 sciences that were compared in one extensive international survey (May, 1997). The biased nature of the database means that often we simply do not know whether a given psychological phenomenon is universal because it likely hasn't been investigated in a sufficient range of cultural contexts.

However, what is even more problematic is that the psychological database is not just a narrow sample; it is often an *unusual* sample. American undergraduates are frequently outliers within the context of an international database for many of the key domains in the behavioral sciences (Henrich et al., 2010). We have termed samples of American college students "WEIRD samples" (i.e., they are samples of Western, educated, industrialized, rich, and democratic societies), as the results from these samples are frequently (but not always) statistical outliers for many of the phenomena that psychologists study. While many research questions are appropriately studied with WEIRD samples, efforts to construct universal theories of psychology certainly are not, and broader samples are necessary (but, for methodological strategies for inferring universality from data from a limited number of cultures, see Norenzayan & Heine, 2005).

Another reason that the study of culture is important is that it increases our understanding of the psychological processes themselves. Take the case of the Müller-Lyer illusion in Figure 17.1. Most likely the line on the left looks longer to you than the line on the right. However, people who were raised in some subsistence environments do not see a difference in the length of these lines (Segall, Campbell, & Herskiovits, 1963). This instance of cultural variation provided a means to understand why people see this as an illusion in the first place. Apparently, being exposed to carpentered corners in the early years of life organizes the visual system such that one comes to rely on the angles of corners as a way of inferring relative distance. In the absence of cultural variation for this illusion, it is quite likely that researchers would not have learned that this illusion develops as a function to the environmental input of a carpentered world. Learning about the minds of people from other cultures thus helps us to understand our own minds better as well. As the political theorist, Seymour Martin Lipset, put it, "those who only know one country, know no country." It is for these reasons that cultural psychology has been interested in exploring

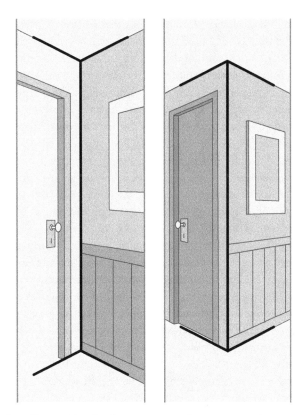

FIGURE 17.1. The Mueller-Lyer illusion. People who were exposed to carpentered corners in their childhood tend to see the left line as looking longer than the right line, which is the nature of the illusion. In contrast, those who were not exposed to carpentered corners during their childhood do not see these two lines as an illusion: The lines appear the same length to them. Reprinted with permission from *Cultural Psychology* (3rd ed.), by S. J. Heine. Copyright 2015 by W. W. Norton.

differences in various psychological processes between cultures. In this chapter I review the evidence for cultural variability in a number of key research programs in social psychology.

The Self-Concept

People are not born with a particular self-concept; rather, becoming a self is contingent on the meanings people seize from their cultural environments. Since people are exposed to very different cultural experiences around the world, it follows that they will come to develop different self-concepts. As Geertz (1973) asserted, "we all begin with the natural equipment to live a thousand kinds of life but end in the end having lived only one" (p. 45).

Evidence for the cultural foundation of the self-concept comes from a number of sources. For example, many studies have assessed the structure of people's self-concepts by having people describe themselves using the Twenty Statements Test (Kuhn & McPartland, 1954). Such studies reveal that people from various Western cultures, such as Australia, Britain, Canada, and Sweden, tend to more commonly include statements that reflect their inner psychological characteristics, such as their attitudes, personality traits, and abilities. In contrast, people from various non-Western cultural contexts, such as Cook Islanders,

Native Americans, Kenyans, Puerto Ricans, Indians, and various East Asian populations, show a relatively greater tendency to describe themselves by indicating relational roles and memberships that they possess (for a review, see Heine, 2016). Such cultural differences are already evident among kindergarten-aged children (Wang, 2004), revealing how early cultural experiences come to shape the self-concept.

These different patterns of responses in self-descriptions suggest that there are at least two different ways that people might conceive of their selves. One way, as evident in the most common responses of westerners, is that the self can largely derive its identity from its inner attributes—a self-contained model of self that Markus and Kitayama (1991) labeled an *independent self-concept*. These attributes are assumed to reflect the essence of an individual in that they are viewed as stable across situations and across the lifespan, they are perceived to be somewhat unique, they are seen to guide behavior, and individuals publicly advertise themselves in ways consistent with these attributes. In addition, people with independent selves have a relatively more fluid boundary between ingroups and outgroups (Heine, 2016). A second way that people can conceptualize themselves, as was more common among the responses of those from non-Western cultures, is to view the self as largely deriving its identity from its relations with significant others—this model is termed an *interdependent self-concept* (Markus & Kitayama, 1991). With this view of self, people recognize that their behavior is contingent upon their perceptions of others' thoughts, feelings, and actions; they attend to how their behaviors affect others and consider their relevant roles within each social context. Moreover, the boundary between ingroup and outgroup tends to be more rigid and stable across the lifetime among those with more interdependent selves. Hence, the interdependent self is not so much a separate and distinct entity but is embedded in a larger social group.

One reason that Western and non-Western cultures often differ in their self-concepts has to do with some of the key agricultural crops that have historically been cultivated. Growing rice in paddies requires a centralized water supply, with much coordination between families to share this water. In contrast, growing wheat has historically depended more on rain and doesn't require as much coordination between families. Studies conducted in China find that people who live in regions where rice is grown tend to have more interdependent self-concepts than do people who live in regions where wheat is grown. People who engage in rice farming learn to be more cooperative with each other, and these norms come to shape their self-concepts. Moreover, even those people who do not farm themselves may be affected by these norms as they become more common expectations within the regions themselves (Talhelm et al., 2014).

A second reason why people have different self-concepts can be inferred by looking at variation within countries; on average, people of higher socioeconomic status (SES) tend to be more independent than those from poorer backgrounds (Kraus, Piff, Mendoza-Denton, Rheinschmidt, & Keltner, 2012; cf. Stephens, Cameron, & Townsend, 2014). This relation is also evident by noting that periods of economic growth tend to be linked with growing rates of independence whereas recessions are associated with increasing interdependence (Grossmann & Varnum, 2015; Park, Twenge, & Greenfield, 2014). This relation can further be seen within American universities. Because these universities typically emphasize promoting independence, poorer students (who tend to be more interdependent) can feel more out of place (Stephens, Fryberg, Markus, Johnson, & Covarrubias, 2012). Indeed, this mismatch between one's self-concept and surrounding environment can have a variety of negative effects on school performance and health (Levine et al., 2016; Stephens, Townsend, Markus, & Phillips, 2012). People of lower SES backgrounds tend to be more dependent upon their close relationships, have fewer opportunities for forming new relationships, and have fewer choices available to them (Kraus et al., 2012; Stephens, Markus, & Phillips, 2014).

Because the self-concept is central to the ways that people process and interpret much information (Markus, 1977), it is perhaps not surprising that this distinction in self-concepts (which relates to individualism–collectivism; Triandis, 1989) has been related to many different psychological processes. For example, cultural variation in independence and interdependence has been linked to cultural differences in motivations for uniqueness (e.g., Kim & Markus, 1999), self-enhancement (e.g., Heine et al., 1999), feelings of agency (e.g., Morling, Kitayama, & Miyamoto, 2002), kinds of emotional experiences (e.g., Mesquita, 2001), perspectives on relationships (e.g., Adams, 2005), and analytic versus holistic reasoning styles (e.g., Nisbett, Peng, Choi, & Norenzayan, 2001). At present, the distinction between independent and interdependent selves stands as the most fruitful way for making sense of many cultural differences in psychological processes (Oyserman, Coon, & Kemmelmeier, 2002). Many other dimensions of culture have been proposed (e.g., Hofstede, 1980; Leung & Bond, 2004; Schwartz & Boehnke, 2004; Triandis, 1996) but thus far haven't offered as much explanatory power for making sense of cultural differences as independence and interdependence. More recently, the notion that cultures differ in terms of how restrictive their social norms are has generated much research interest (Gelfand et al., 2011) and has been connected with cultural variation in numerous psychological characteristics (e.g., Fischer et al., 2014; Jiang, Li, & Hamamura, 2015).

Self-Consistency versus Flexibility

The notion that people strive to maintain a consistent self-concept has been central to many theories regarding the self (e.g., Heider, 1958; Swann, Wenzlaff, Krull, & Pelham, 1992); however, much of this research has targeted cultural samples in which independent self-concepts predominate. People with independent selves should aspire to act more consistently, because independent selves are viewed as whole, unified, integrated, stable, and inviolate entities, and thus core representations of the self should remain largely uninfluenced by the presence of others. The independent self is experienced as relatively unchanging and constant across situations, and people are often willing to make rather costly sacrifices in order to preserve a semblance of self-consistency (e.g., Freedman & Fraser, 1966).

In contrast, for people with interdependent views of self, an individual's relationships and roles take precedence over abstracted and internalized attributes. Hence, when a person with an interdependent self changes situations, she finds herself in new roles bearing different obligations, and these should lead to different experiences of the self. Indeed, much research reveals less evidence for a self-concept that is consistent across contexts among people with interdependent selves (e.g., Gage, Coker, & Jobson, 2015). For example, Kanagawa, Cross, and Markus (2001) found that Japanese (but not American) self-descriptions varied significantly depending on who was in the room with them when participants completed their questionnaires (that the interdependent self is grounded in its immediate context presents a real challenge to studying it—in what contexts lies the real interdependent self?) These cultural differences in consistency have also been observed in people's affective experiences: European Americans show less variability in their emotions across situations than do Japanese, Hispanic Americans, and Indians (Oishi, Diener, Scollon, & Biswas-Diener, 2004). However, just because the self-concepts of non-westerners appear more variable across contexts than those of westerners, it is not the case that non-westerners have unstable self-concepts. Rather, non-westerners appear to have a number of stable but context-specific self-views that are tied to specific relationships and roles, that are as stable across time as the self-concepts of westerners (English & Chen, 2007).

Cultural differences in self-consistency are also apparent in that East Asians endorse more contradictory self-views than westerners. For example, Chinese self-evaluations are more ambivalent (they contain both positive and negative statements) than are those of Americans (Spencer-Rodgers, Peng, Wang, & Hou, 2004). Similarly, East Asians tend to endorse contradictory items about their personalities; for example, Koreans are more likely than Americans to state that they are both introverted and extraverted (Choi & Choi, 2002), and Japanese were more likely than Canadians to endorse both positively worded and reverse-scored items regarding personality traits (Hamamura, Heine, & Paulhus, 2008). Such contradictory self-knowledge is more readily available, and is simultaneously accessible, among East Asian participants than among Americans (Spencer-Rodgers, Boucher, Mori, Wang, & Peng, 2009).

Further evidence of different motivations for consistency emerge in considering how people respond to the awareness that their attitudes may be at odds with their behaviors. Many studies find that East Asians show less evidence than westerners in striving to keep their attitudes and behaviors consistent (Heine & Lehman, 1997; Hiniker, 1969; Kashima, Siegal, Tanaka, & Kashima, 1992). A curious exception to this pattern is that this cultural difference in dissonance reduction disappears when people are shown images of eyes, as apparently this makes them consider their selves differently (Kitayama, Snibbe, Markus, & Suzuki, 2004).

Insider versus Outsider Phenomenological Experiences

Self-concepts also vary in terms of the perspective that people habitually adopt. On the one hand, people may prioritize their own perspective, thereby making sense of the world in terms of how it appears to them. Alternatively, people may prioritize the perspective of an audience and imagine how the world and they appear to others. Cohen, Hoshino-Browne, and Leung (2007) refer to these two perspectives as insider and outsider phenomenological experiences. In interdependent cultural contexts, where individuals need to adjust themselves to fit in better with the ingroup, it becomes crucial to know how one is being evaluated by others. In independent cultural contexts, in contrast, where people's identity rests largely on the inner attributes that they possess, there is a cultural imperative to "know oneself" and to elaborate on one's unique perspective.

There is much evidence for this cultural difference. For example, Cohen and Gunz (2002) found that East Asians are more likely to recall memories of themselves from a third-person perspective than are westerners. Apparently, East Asians' attention to an audience leaks into and distorts their memories of themselves. Similarly, East Asians outperformed westerners on a visual task in which they needed to take the perspective of their partner (Wu & Keysar, 2007). The perspective of an audience is also made more salient when people see themselves in a mirror (Duval & Wicklund, 1972), and research finds that the self-evaluations and behaviors of East Asians are less impacted by the presence of a mirror (suggesting that they habitually considered themselves from the perspective of an audience) than was the case for North Americans (Heine, Takemoto, Moskalenko, Lasaleta, & Henrich, 2008). Moreover, East Asians views of themselves have been found to be affected by what they believe others think of them, whereas North American self-views remain somewhat separate from imagined perspectives of others (Kim, Cohen, & Au, 2010; Seo, Kim, Tam, & Rozin, 2016).

Multicultural Selves

Much research has also explored the self-concepts of those with multiple cultural experiences. If culture shapes the self, how do people from multiple cultural backgrounds represent the self? There are two complementary perspectives on this. One perspective is that multicultural people have multiple self-concepts that are simultaneously accessible, and their typical thoughts and responses reflect a blending of these. For example, Asian Americans tend to perform intermediately on many psychological tasks compared with European Americans and Asians in Asia (e.g., Heine & Hamamura, 2007; Norenzayan, Smith, Kim, & Nisbett, 2002). A second perspective is that multicultural people sequentially activate their different self-concepts depending upon situation or primes; this perspective is known as frame-switching (Hong, Morris, Chiu, & Benet-Martinez, 2000). For example, in one study, Hong Kong Chinese were primed with either Chinese or American thoughts by showing them cultural icons and were subsequently asked to make attributions for the behaviors of computerized images of fish (Hong et al., 2000). Those who were primed with American icons made fewer external attributions for the fish's behavior than those who were primed with Chinese icons. That is, Hong Kong Chinese sometimes access Western ways of thinking and sometimes they access Chinese ways of thinking. Further evidence for frame-switching can be seen when you look at language performance of immigrants who are exposed to cultural icons from their heritage culture. The cultural icons activate thoughts regarding their heritage culture, and this leads to interference in their ability to access their second language (Zhang, Morris, Cheng, & Yap, 2013). A variety of psychological processes may switch across different frames. For example, bilingual Arab Israelis have more negative associations with Jewish names when they are presented in Arabic than when they are presented in Hebrew, and the reverse is true for Arabic names (Danziger & Ward, 2010). This kind of frame-switching is not equally likely for all biculturals; people are more likely to frame-switch if they see their dual cultural identities as integrated than if they see them in opposition (Benet-Martinez, Leu, Lee, & Morris, 2002) and if they were second-generation as opposed to first-generation immigrants (Tsai, Ying, & Lee, 2000).

The existence of frame-switching suggests that people can have multiple knowledge structures—that is, networks of ideas that are associated together. When one part of the network is activated (such as seeing an American icon), this facilitates the activation of another part of that same network (such as preferring to explain behavior in terms of internal dispositions). Although there is much evidence that multiculturals often frame-switch, people with largely monocultural experiences do as well (e.g., Kühnen, Hannover, & Schubert, 2001; Trafimow, Triandis, & Goto, 1991; for a meta-analysis, see Oyserman & Lee, 2008). The kinds of ideas that have been primed in frame-switching studies (e.g., thoughts regarding interdependence, external attributions, cooperation with ingroup members) would seem to be thoughts that are accessible to people everywhere, given that humans are such a highly social species. Because people have different networks of ideas associated with concepts such as interdependence than they do with concepts such as independence, everyone should frame-switch when different knowledge networks are activated. For example, whereas much research finds that East Asians display more pronounced prevention motivations than westerners (e.g., Elliot, Chirkov, Kim, & Sheldon, 2001), priming European Americans with interdependent thoughts leads them to become more prevention-oriented as well (Lee et al., 2000). That is, interdependent-primed European Americans showed prevention motivations that were closer to those of nonprimed East Asians than were European Americans who were not primed with interdependence. This indicates that the relations between interdependence and prevention motivations exist across cultural groups, so that anyone, multicultural or not, who thinks interdependent thoughts should also become more prevention-oriented.

People with multicultural experiences differ from monocultural people in other ways. For example, they can rely on a more diverse set of different perspectives and ideas. This leads multicultural people to be more open to experience (Zimmermann & Neyer, 2013), show more evidence for integrative complexity (Maddux, Bivolaru, Hafenbrack, Tadmor, & Galinsky, 2014), and show enhanced creative thinking compared with monoculturals (Leung, Maddux, Galinsky, & Chiu, 2008; Maddux & Galinsky, 2009). For example, fashion designers who have more multicultural experiences are rated as more creative than those with fewer such experiences (Godart, Maddux, Shipilov, & Galinsky, 2015). The creative benefits of multicultural people tend to be more pronounced when the different cultures that people have been exposed to span a broader cultural distance (Cheng & Leung, 2013) and when multicultural individuals have more blended cultural identities (Saad, Damian, Benet-Martinez, Moons, & Robins, 2013). At the same time, having exposure to different moral world views can make people more morally relativistic, which can have the consequence of people being more likely to behave immorally themselves (Lu et al., 2017).

Some of the psychological advantages possessed by multicultural individuals generalize to groups that contain culturally diverse members. For example, some studies find that groups that consist of people from diverse ethnic backgrounds tend to be more creative (Guzzo & Dickson, 1996; Tadmor, Satterstrom, Jang,

& Polzer, 2012; Watson, Kumar, & Michaelsen, 1993). Likewise, groups that have more ethnic diversity possess more varied information and are more careful in their thinking, which contributes to making them less vulnerable to overvaluing goods in markets (Levine et al., 2014).

Motivation

People's motivations are influenced by their cultural experiences. A number of key motivations have been found to appear differently across cultures, including motivations for self-enhancement, agency and control, motivations to fit in or to stick out, and motivations for honor.

Motivations for Self-Enhancement and Self-Esteem

Much research has focused on people's motivation for self-enhancement, that is, a desire to view oneself positively. This research reveals that most westerners desire to view themselves in positive terms. For example, the vast majority of North Americans have high self-esteem (Baumeister, Tice, & Hutton, 1989), show much evidence for unrealistically positive views of themselves (e.g., Greenwald, 1980; Taylor & Brown, 1988), and engage in various compensatory self-protective responses when they encounter threats to their self-esteem (e.g., Steele, 1988; Tesser, 2000).

In contrast, however, evidence for self-enhancement motivations is less pronounced in many interdependent cultural contexts. For example, Mexicans (Tropp & Wright, 2003), Native Americans (Fryberg & Markus, 2003), Chileans (Heine & Raineri, 2009), and Fijians (Rennie & Dunne, 1994) show less evidence for self-enhancement than do westerners. There is also less evidence for self-enhancement in societies with lower income inequality (Loughnan et al., 2011). Evidence for self-serving biases is particularly weak in East Asian cultures (e.g., Mezulis, Abramson, Hyde, & Hankin, 2004). A meta-analysis on self-enhancing motivations among westerners and East Asians (Heine & Hamamura, 2007) found significant cultural differences in every study for 30 of the 31 methods that were used (the one exception being comparisons of self-esteem using the Implicit Associations Test [IAT]; Greenwald & Farnham, 2000). Whereas the average effect size for self-enhancing motivations was large ($d = 0.86$) within the Western samples, these motivations were largely absent among the East Asian samples ($d = -0.02$) with Asian Americans falling in between ($d = 0.33$). Apparently, East Asians possess little motivation to self-enhance, and in many situations they instead appear especially attentive to negative information about themselves that allows for self-improvement (Heine et al., 1999). These cultural differences in self-enhancement motivations are paralleled by cultural differences in approach motivations (e.g., Elliot et al., 2001; Hamamura, Meijer, Heine, Kamaya, & Hori, 2009; Heine et al., 2001; Lockwood, Marshall, & Sadler, 2005).

There are a number of alternative explanations that have been offered to account for this cultural difference. One possibility is that East Asians are more motivated to enhance their group selves rather than their individual selves, and comparisons of people's individual self-enhancing tendencies thus obscure their group self-enhancing motivations. However, as of yet, there are no published studies that find that East Asians enhance their group selves more than westerners whereas several studies find that westerners show more group enhancement than East Asians (for a review, see Heine, 2003).

A second possibility is that East Asians will self-enhance in domains that are especially important to them. Some evidence in support of this alternative account has been found using the "better-than-average effect" paradigm (e.g., Sedikides, Gaertner, & Vevea, 2005, 2007); however, studies using other methods reveal that East Asians are more self-critical for important traits than they are for less important ones (e.g., Heine & Renshaw, 2002; Kitayama, Markus, Matsumoto, & Norasakkunkit, 1997). The most extensive meta-analysis on this topic finds no correlation between self-enhancement and importance for East Asians, $r = -0.01$, in contrast to a positive correlation for westerners, $r = 0.18$ (Heine, Kitayama, & Hamamura, 2007). The "better-than-average effect" yields different results from other self-enhancement methodologies apparently because of the difficulties that people have in considering distributed targets (e.g., the average person) in contrast to specific targets (e.g., the self or one's best friend; Hamamura, Heine, & Takemoto, 2007; Klar & Giladi, 1997; Krizan & Suls, 2008).

A third alternative account is that East Asians are presenting themselves self-critically but are privately evaluating themselves in a self-enhancing manner (e.g., Kurman, 2003). An absence of cultural differences with the IAT measure of self-esteem is largely consistent with this account; however, some other ways of measuring implicit self-esteem reveal more evidence for self-enhancement among westerners than East Asians (for a review, see Falk & Heine, 2015). That the IAT measure of self-esteem has thus far failed to show reliable correlations with other implicit or explicit measures of self-esteem, or external criteria (Bosson, Swann, & Pennebaker, 2000; Buhrmester, Blanton, & Swann, 2011; Falk, Heine, Takemura, Zhang, & Hsu, 2015) raises questions about whether it measures anything related to self-esteem.

Variation in different measures of positive self-views have also been identified across historical periods. For example, an analysis of studies using the Rosenberg (1965) self-esteem scale with American college students from 1965 to 1995 found that self-esteem scores had increased substantially over that time ($d = 0.6$; Twenge & Campbell, 2001), and further analyses revealed that it continued to increase from 1988 to 2008 ($d = 0.3$; Gentile, Twenge, & Campbell, 2010). Parallel increases have been noted in narcissistic personality disorder (Twenge & Foster, 2010; for conflicting views, cf. Trzesniewski & Donnelan, 2010). These increases may be more pronounced within American culture, as there was no evidence for an increase in self-esteem over a similar period among Australians (Hamamura & Septarini, 2017).

Agency and Control

Cultures differ in the degree to which they embrace different kinds of control. One kind of control, known as primary control, involves people striving to shape existing realities to fit their goals or wishes. In contrast, secondary control is evident when people strive to align themselves with existing realities, leaving the realities unchanged but exerting control over their psychological impact (Rothbaum, Weisz, & Snyder, 1982).

In hierarchical collectivistic cultures, the lone individual is somewhat powerless to exert change on the social world (e.g., Chiu, Dweck, Tong, & Fu, 1997). Power and agency tend to be concentrated in groups (e.g., Menon, Morris, Chiu, & Hong, 1999), and thus there are many domains in which people are unable to exert much direct influence. Likewise, East Asians are more likely to have a flexible and incremental view of themselves (Heine et al., 2001). When the self is perceived to be more mutable than the social world, it follows that people may try to adjust themselves to better fit in with the demands of their social worlds. In contrast, people from Western cultures tend to stress the malleability of the world relative to the self (Su et al., 1999). When individuals are viewed as the center of experience and action, they should feel a stronger sense of primary control. Indeed, much research finds that people from people from Western cultures are more likely to use primary control strategies and are less likely to use secondary control strategies, than people from East Asian cultures (e.g., Morling et al., 2002; Weisz, Rothbaum, & Blackburn, 1984).

Cultural differences in agency are also evident in the ways that people make choices. People in interdependent contexts should be more concerned with the goals of their groups and thus be more willing to adjust their behaviors (and reduce their choices) to coordinate the actions of the group toward those goals. One stark example of this cultural difference is that in many interdependent cultures today (and perhaps in a majority of cultures several centuries ago), critical life decisions, such as whom one would marry or what job one would pursue, have been made by families rather than the individuals themselves (e.g., Lee & Stone, 1980).

There are other ways that we can see cultural variation in perceptions of choice, in particular, by comparing Indians with Americans. First, Indians, and people from numerous other non-Western cultures, also indicate that they have less free choice in their lives compared with North Americans (Inglehart, Basanez, & Moreno, 1998). Indians tend to be slower to make choices, are less likely to choose according to their preferences, and are less motivated to express their preferences in their choices compared with Americans (Savani, Markus, & Conner, 2008). Indians also assume that when others are trying to influence their choices, they are doing so for altruistic reasons, and they will more often go along with the influencer (especially if it is an authority figure), in contrast to Americans (Savani, Morris, & Naidu, 2012; Savani, Morris, Naidu, Kumar, & Berlia, 2011). Moreover, Indians are less likely to view their behavior as representing their choices—the exact same behaviors are more frequently called choices by Americans than by Indians (Savani, Markus, Naidu, Kumar, & Berlia, 2010). In particular, middle-class Americans, specifically, seem quite unusual in their high desire for choice (Schwartz, 2004). For example, in a survey of people from six Western countries, only Americans preferred making a choice from 50 ice cream flavors compared with 10 flavors (Rozin, Fischler, Shields, & Masson, 2006). Further, people from American working-class cultures are less protective of their choices (i.e., they do not seem as bothered when an experimenter denies them their original choice; Snibbe & Markus, 2005) and are influenced more by the opinions of others, compared with middle-class Americans (Na, McDonough, Chan, & Park, 2016). In sum, the ways that people make choices, and express agency more generally, differ in a number of important ways across cultures.

Motivations to Fit in or to Stick Out

People have competing motivations to fit in with others or to stick out from a crowd. Asch (1956) famously documented a motivation to conform with a unanimous majority in his line-comparison studies. This conformity paradigm has been replicated well over 100 times in 17 different countries. A meta-analysis of these studies revealed one clear trend: Although Americans show much conformity, people from collectivistic cultures conform even more (Bond & Smith, 1996). Motivations to fit in are stronger in cultural contexts that encourage people to maintain strong relationships with others. Other evidence finds that countries with a higher level of historical pathogen prevalence develop tighter norms for behavior and show higher evidence for conformity (Murray, Trudeau, & Schaller, 2011).

In contrast to a motivation to conform, we can also consider people's motivations to be unique. In general, people from independent cultural contexts have stronger motivation for uniqueness; a desire to view one's self as distinct from others is facilitated by evidence that one is unique. For example, when given a choice of pens, European Americans were more likely to choose a minority-colored pen whereas East Asians were more likely to choose a majority-colored pen (Kim & Markus, 1999). Parallel differences in pen preferences are found in contrasts of middle-class and working-class Americans (Stephens, Markus, & Townsend, 2007). Likewise, East Asians were shown to be more likely to color shapes in a way that maintained harmony, whereas European Americans were more likely to color shapes in a unique way (Ishii, Miyamoto, Rule, & Toriyama, 2014). Moreover, when people from collectivistic cultures aspire for distinctiveness, it's more about possessing a distinctive social position, rather than aspiring for difference and separateness (Becker et al., 2012).

Motivations for Honor

Much cross-cultural research has investigated motivations for honor, particularly between the US South and North (Brown, Ostermann, & Barnes, 2009; Cohen & Leung, 2012; Nisbett & Cohen, 1996; some research has also explored the stronger honor motivations among Turks; see Cross, Uskul, Gercek-Swing, Alozkan, & Ataca, 2013). Nisbett and Cohen (1996) proposed that the US South has a culture of honor—that is, a culture in which people (especially men) strive to protect their reputation through aggression. Cultures of honor are common where people's wealth is vulnerable and there is little institutionalized protection (e.g., inner cities, various Middle Eastern herding cultures, some small-scale African societies; e.g., Anderson, 1999; Galaty & Bonte, 1991). In the case of the US South, a culture of honor emerged because herders from the fringes of Britain immigrated to the United States in the 18th century and brought their herding traditions with them. Herding was a key component of the South's early economy, and herders have vulnerable wealth (livestock can easily be stolen, and the sparse population of herding lands made it difficult to police). The establishment of a personal reputation for aggressive revenge for insults, therefore, emerged to prevent herd-rustling. Although herding is no longer the primary economic activity of most southerners, these cultural norms have persisted as a culture of honor represents a stable equilibrium point (see Cohen, 2001). Moreover, herding regions have greater income inequality than farming regions, which also accounts for more defensive reactions to threats to status (Henry, 2009).

Much data converge in support of this thesis. For example, archival data show that the greater amount of violence in the South is largely limited to argument-related violence (in which the defense of one's honor is often implicated), and this is more common in the rural herding regions of the South than in farming regions (Nisbett & Cohen, 1996). Moreover, current violence rates in the US South can be traced to the persistence of cultural practices from the first Scots Irish immigrants there, although that influence seems to be fading over time (Grosjean, 2014). Experimental evidence further reveals that when southerners are insulted, they are more likely than northerners to be angry, show heightened cortisol and testosterone responses, and act more physically aggressive (Cohen, Nisbett, Bowdle, & Schwarz, 1996). Likewise, field studies reveal that southerners, compared with northerners, are warmer toward someone who committed violence in defense of their honor (but not for other kinds of violent acts; Cohen & Nisbett, 1997; for further explorations of behavioral correlates of a culture of honor, see Vandello & Cohen, 2003).

Cognition and Perception

Many psychologists assume that research from the area of cognition and perception targets the most basic psychological processes. Given this perspective, it is striking that cross-cultural research on cognition and perception reveals some of the clearest evidence for cultural variation. Research contrasting analytic and holistic ways of thinking reveals much cultural variation in attention, reasoning styles, and in explaining the behavior of others.

Analytic versus Holistic Thinking

Nisbett and colleagues (Nisbett, 2003; Nisbett et al., 2001) have investigated whether a variety of cognitive and perceptual tasks glossed under the labels of analytic and holistic thinking varied across cultural contexts, particularly between North American and East Asian cultures. By analytic thinking, they mean a focus on objects, which are perceived as existing independently from their contexts and are understood in terms of their underlying attributes. These attributes are further used as a basis to categorize objects, and a set of fixed abstract rules are used for predicting and explaining their actions. In contrast, holistic thinking refers to an orientation to the context. This is an associative way of thinking, where people attend to the relations among objects and among the objects and the surrounding context. These relations are used to explain and predict the behavior of objects. Dozens of studies have now been conducted that demonstrate how cultures vary in these two ways of thinking (for reviews, see Henrich et al., 2010; Nisbett et al., 2001; Norenzayan, Choi, & Peng, 2007). In general, analytic thinking is especially common in Western cultures whereas holistic thinking is more normative in the rest of the world, particularly in East Asia.

Attention to Objects and Fields

Americans and other westerners have been found to attend less to the background than people from other non-Western societies, with the exception of migratory foragers. For example, Witkin and Berry (1975) summarized evidence from work with migratory and sedentary foraging populations (Arctic, Australia and Africa), sedentary agriculturalists, and industrialized westerners, and found that only the West and migratory foragers appeared at the field independent end of the spectrum. Field independence is the tendency to separate objects from their background fields. Westerners have been found to be more field independent than people from other non-Western cultures (Ji, Peng, & Nisbett, 2000; Kitayama, Duffy, Kawamura, & Larsen, 2003; Kühnen et al., 2001; Norenzayan, 2008).

Other studies have explored people's reaction to scenes in which the background has been switched. For example, Japanese and Americans were shown pictures of animals in natural contexts (e.g., a wolf in a forest) and were later shown pictures of the same animals, sometimes with the original background and sometimes with a different background (e.g., a wolf in a desert). The researchers found that the Japanese had poorer recall for the animals than Americans if the background has been swapped, indicating that they were attending to the field (Masuda & Nisbett, 2001). This difference in attention toward the field has also been found in the eye movements of people as measured with eye trackers (Chua et al., 2005; Masuda et al., 2008). In these studies, the attention of Americans rarely leaves the focal object, whereas East Asians are more likely to shift their gaze to the background. These cultural differences in attention have behavioral consequences: European Americans perform better than East Asians on a task where they need to track multiple moving objects at once (Savani & Markus, 2012).

Cultural differences in attention are further evident in different artistic traditions, where East Asian paintings tend to have a horizon that is higher than it is in Western paintings (the higher horizon calls attention to the depth of the setting and allows for the different objects and places in a scene to be seen in relation to each other), and Western portraits include focal figures that are approximately three times as large as those in East Asian portraits (Masuda, Gonzales, Kwan, & Nisbett, 2008). Moreover, analyses of web pages between East Asia and North America find that there are more words and links on East Asian pages, and East Asians can more quickly navigate through busier scenes than can westerners (Wang, Masuda, Ito, & Rashid, 2012).

Reasoning Styles

Westerners are more likely to group objects on the basis of categories and rules, whereas people from many other cultural groups are more likely to group objects based on similarity or functional relationships (e.g., Ji, Zhang, & Nisbett, 2004; Knight & Nisbett, 2007). Likewise, Chinese were found to be more likely to group objects if they shared a strong family resemblance, whereas Americans were more likely to group objects if they could be assigned to that group on the basis of a deterministic rule (Norenzayan, Smith, et al., 2002). These cultural differences in reasoning appear to be a product of social interdependence; even within the same linguistic and geographical regions of Turkey, farmers and fishermen, who have more socially connected lifestyles, showed more evidence for holistic reasoning on this same task (and on other related tasks) than did herders, who are more isolated (Uskul, Kitayama, & Nisbett, 2008).

Further, as discussed earlier, cultures differ with respect to how people reason about contradiction. A holistic orientation suggests that everything appears fundamentally connected and in flux, which suggests that real contradiction might not be possible. This "naïve dialecticism" is more common among East Asians and is associated with a greater tolerance for contradiction compared with westerners across a variety of tasks (Peng & Nisbett, 1999). The fluid and contradictory nature of East Asian beliefs is also reflected in their predictions of future changes. Whereas westerners tend to make rather linear future predictions for change (e.g., if the stock market dropped over the past year it will probably drop next year as well), East Asian future predictions are more non-linear (Ji, Nisbett, & Su, 2001). This less linear view of the future may be due to East Asians perceiving events as having a broader net of consequences compared with westerners (Maddux & Yuki, 2006). More dialectical views are also associated with less consistency for the self across different contexts and roles (Boucher, 2011).

Explaining the Behavior of Others

Just as with explaining objects, westerners are more inclined to explain events by reference to properties of the person, whereas non-westerners are more inclined to explain the same events with reference to the context. A number of classic studies found that when asked to explain the behavior of others, westerners tend to focus on the person's disposition, even when there are compelling situational constraints available (e.g., (Jones & Harris, 1967). However, research in non-Western cultures often reveals a different pattern. Geertz (1975) described how Balinese do not tend to conceive of people's behaviors in terms of underlying dispositions but instead see it as emerging out of the roles that they have. Miller (1984) found that Indian adults tended to favor situational information over dispositional accounts. Several studies conducted with East Asians and Americans revealed that whereas Americans attend to dispositions first, regardless of how compelling the situational information may be (Gilbert & Malone, 1995), East Asians are more likely than Americans to infer that behaviors are controlled by the situation (Norenzayan, Choi, & Nisbett, 2002) and to attend to situational information (Morris & Peng, 1994), particularly when that information is salient (Choi & Nisbett, 1998). Similarly, East Asians are less likely than Americans to use trait adjectives when describing someone's behaviors (Maass, Karasawa, Politi, & Suga, 2006) and are less likely to make spontaneous trait inferences (Na & Kitayama, 2011; Shimizu, Lee, & Uleman, 2017). Other cultural groups also differ in this regard from typical WEIRD samples. For example, people from lower SES backgrounds make more situational attributions compared with higher SES groups (Kraus, Cote, & Keltner, 2010), and Protestants make more dispositional attributions than Catholics (Li, Johnson, Cohen, Williams, Knowles, & Chen, 2012). The fundamental attribution error appears less fundamental in other cultural contexts.

Emotion

The relation between culture and emotions has attracted much research interest. Two aspects of emotions have received the most amount of study across cultures: facial expressions of emotion and people's subjective reports of their emotions. Further, there has been much study of the nature of positive emotional experiences across cultures.

Emotions and Facial Expressions

Darwin was one of the first scientists to consider whether emotional facial expressions were universal features of the human species or were the products of cultural learning (Darwin, 1872/1965). He noted a number of similarities in the facial expressions of various primates and humans and proposed that these expressions should be shared by all humans. Ekman and colleagues have done the most on following up on Darwin's hypothesis. For example, Ekman and Friesen (1971) posed a series of photos corresponding to what they referred to as a set of "basic emotions" (viz., anger, disgust, fear, happiness, sadness, and surprise) to participants from Argentina, Brazil, Chile, Japan, and the United States, asking them to match the expressions with emotion terms. Participants tended to get between 80% to 90% of the questions correct, regardless of cultural background, indicating much universality in recognition of the expressions. Cross-cultural similarities in emotion recognition are also found in cultural groups who have had little contact with each other, such as between westerners and the Fore of New Guinea (Ekman, Sorenson, & Freisen, 1969). This evidence, combined with findings that the same facial expressions that adults make are made by very young infants (Izard, 1994), including those who are congenitally blind and thus unable to learn by observation (reviewed in Ekman, 1973), demonstrates that facial expressions for the basic emotions are innate (for a different conclusion, see Jack, Garrod, Yu, Caldara, & Schyns, 2012). Some other emotions, in particular, contempt, shame, embarrassment, pride, and interest, have also been proposed to be universally recognized (e.g., Keltner, 1995). For example, a bodily posture associated with feelings of pride appears to be universally recognized and is spontaneously produced across cultures (Tracy & Robins, 2008), including among those who are congenitally blind (Tracy & Matsumoto, 2008).

While the capacity to produce and recognize particular facial expressions may be similar across cultures, cultural variation is anticipated in the form of "display rules" (Ekman & Friesen, 1969). Display rules are the culturally specific rules that govern what facial expressions are appropriate in a given situation and how intensely they should be displayed. For example, in response to recalled happy situations, Hmong Americans are less likely to smile than are European Americans (Tsai, Chentsova-Dutton, Freire-Bebeau, & Przymus, 2002). As another example, Indians will often show their embarrassment by biting their tongue—an expression not recognized in many other cultures (Haidt & Keltner, 1999). The ways that emotions are expressed thus varies across cultures. This is also evident in findings that people are more accurate in recognizing emotional expressions made by people from their own cultural background. A meta-analysis of past research on cross-cultural recognition of facial expressions found that, on average, people are about 9% more accurate in judging the facial expressions of people from their own culture than those of another culture (with, on average, people showing about 58% accuracy overall; Elfenbein & Ambady, 2002). Further, people are able to reliably distinguish between the nationality of targets when they are making emotional expressions but not when they make neutral expressions. For example, American participants could reliably distinguish between Australian and American faces but only when they were expressing emotions (Marsh, Elfenbein, & Ambady, 2007).

Moreover, across cultures people appear to attend to different parts of the face when deciphering facial expressions. Yuki, Maddux, and Masuda (2007) proposed that in cultures with stronger cultural norms to regulate emotional expressions, such as Japan, people would be more likely to attend to those aspects of the face that were more difficult to regulate (i.e., the eyes). In contrast, in cultures where there are weaker norms for emotional regulation, such as the United States, people would attend to the largest visual cues (i.e., the mouth). Conceptually similar findings from other methods reveal that westerners attend to both the eyes and mouth whereas East Asians primarily attend to an area near the eyes (Blais, Jack, Scheepers, Fiset, & Caldara, 2008; Jack, Caldara, & Schyns, 2012). Moreover, there are different patterns of neural activation when East Asians are looking at faces compared with westerners that are consistent with the differences in the facial regions that people from different cultures attend to (Goh et al., 2010).

Intensity of Emotional Experience

In contrast to studies of facial expressions, cross-cultural studies of emotional experience reveal more pronounced cultural differences. For examples, Americans reported feeling their emotions longer and more intensely than Japanese did (Matsumoto, Kudoh, Scherer, & Wallbott, 1988). Similarly, in an experience sampling study, Japanese were about three times as likely as Americans to report that they had not been feeling any emotions when prompted (Mesquita & Karasawa, 2002; also see Kitayama, Markus, & Kurokawa, 2000). East Asians seem less attuned to visceral cues from their bodies (Ma-Kellams, Blascovich, & McCall, 2012); people from some other non-Western cultures, such as Ghana, have also shown less attentiveness to their emotions (Dzokoto, 2010). Perhaps the aforementioned cultural differences in tendencies for East Asians to express their emotions less intensely than westerners are not a function of display rules but a function of differences in emotional experience.

Suppressing some emotions (particularly anger) has been found to lead to less cardiac regulation of heart rate (e.g., Brosschot & Thayer, 1998). However, in East Asian cultural contexts, where inhibition of emotional expressions is more common, people show quicker recovery of their heart rate following an angering event. This appears to be due to East Asian participants being more likely to reappraise events in a less anger-provoking way (Anderson & Linden, 2006; Butler, Lee, & Gross, 2009; Mauss, Butler, Roberts, & Chu, 2010). Furthermore, other research has found that, compared with East Asians, negative emotions among westerners are associated with more negative health outcomes (Curhan et al., 2014; Miyamoto et al., 2013) and more of a neural response when suppressing their emotions, indicating that it is more effortful for them to suppress negative emotions (Murata, Moser, & Kitayama, 2013).

Kinds of Emotional Experiences

Independent and interdependent self-concepts provide a useful framework to make sense of cultural variation in emotional experiences. The self-concept should shape how one appraises an emotionally relevant situation. Those with interdependent selves are more concerned with maintaining a sense of interpersonal harmony and thus should consider more about how events in the world impact upon close others as well as their selves. Those with independent selves, in contrast, should focus more intently on how events impact on themselves or how events might serve to distinguish themselves from others. For example, Surinamese and Turkish immigrants to Holland expressed having more relational concerns and attended more closely about how situations affected others compared with mainstream Dutch (Mesquita, 2001). Moreover, the Surinamese and Turks were more likely than Dutch to ensure that others attended to the same events, thereby sharing the experience with the participants. Parallel findings have emerged with contrasts of Mexicans and Americans and Japanese and Americans—both Mexicans and Japanese were more likely to experience interpersonally engaging emotions and were less likely to experience interpersonal disengaging emotions, compared with Americans (Kitayama et al., 2000; Savani, Alvarez, Mesquita, & Markus, 2013).

Cultural Variation in Subjective Well-Being and Happiness

Is there variability in people's happiness and subjective well-being across cultures? Indeed, pronounced cultural differences consistently emerge in multinational surveys, with the most common pattern being that the nations that cluster toward the "happy" pole are Scandinavian and Nordic countries, much of Latin America, various English-speaking countries, and Western Europe. On the low end are the former Soviet republics and some impoverished countries in Africa and South Asia (Diener, Diener, & Diener, 1995; Inglehart & Klingemann, 2000; Veenhoven, 2014).

Many factors contribute to influence overall life satisfaction. Wealth as assessed by gross domestic product positively correlates with national levels of well-being. However, this relation is not linear; money and happiness are most closely connected at very low levels of wealth. For example, income and life satisfaction are correlated at 0.45 among respondents in the slums of Calcutta (Biswas-Diener & Diener, 2001). In contrast, above an average gross domestic product of 40% of that of the United States, there is no longer any clear relation between money and subjective-well-being (Diener et al., 1995). In addition, human rights and overall equality of a country are associated with greater subjective well-being (Diener et al., 1995).

There are also factors that predict life satisfaction differently across cultures. Suh, Diener, Oishi, and Triandis (1998) found that life satisfaction is more highly correlated with overall positive affect in individualistic cultures than in collectivist ones. On the other hand, people in collectivistic cultures showed a higher correlation between life satisfaction and living up to cultural norms, compared with people from individualistic cultures.

Moreover, the very notion that one should aspire for happiness appears to be culturally variable. One source of evidence for this is that the dictionary meaning of happiness is different across cultures—most languages include a definition of happiness that includes the concept of "good luck"—countries that don't include luck as a definition are the United States, Spain, Argentina, Ecuador, India, and Kenya (Oishi, Graham, Kesebir, & Galinha, 2013). Tellingly, people who lived in countries where happiness is defined as "good luck" report feeling less happy than those that did not define happiness this way. There also appear to be changes across time: American dictionaries prior to 1961 included the concept of good luck, and the notion that happiness was something to be pursued wasn't discussed in print until the Enlightenment in 17th-century Europe (Carlyle, 1843). As another example, Falk, Dunn, and Norenzayan (2010) found that European Canadians were more likely to make decisions with the goal of making themselves happier compared with Asian Canadians. The pursuit of happiness appears to be, at least somewhat, a fairly recent Western pursuit.

One reason why people from some non-Western cultures appear less motivated to pursue positive emotions is because there may be fewer benefits to them for doing so. For example, whereas European Americans who report experiencing many positive emotions also report experiencing less depression, East Asians who report having many positive emotions are no less at risk for depression than are those East Asians who report having very few positive emotions (Leu, Wang, & Koo, 2011). Likewise, whereas ruminating on negative experiences is linked with depression among European Americans, rumination is unrelated to depression among Russians (Grossmann & Kross, 2010). That is, positive feelings (and a lack of negative feelings) do not seem to carry the same protection against depression among East Asians and Russians. Perhaps this is why research finds that happiness-boosting activities do not seem to be as effective among East Asians as they are among westerners (Layous, Lee, Choi, & Lyubomirsky, 2013).

Furthermore, the kinds of positive emotions that people desire varies across cultures. Tsai and colleagues (e.g., Tsai, Knutson, & Fung, 2006) find that Americans seek out positive emotions that are high in arousal more than East Asians, whereas East Asians prefer low arousal positive emotions more than Americans. For example, a comparison of facial expressions from characters in American and Taiwanese children's storybooks revealed that the American faces more often showed feelings of excitement and had bigger smiles than the Taiwanese faces. Moreover, European American preschool children preferred the pictures of excited faces more than the Taiwanese preschoolers did; they also felt more similar to the characters who were engaged in high arousal activities than did Taiwanese children (Tsai, Louie, Chen, & Uchida, 2006). This preference for high arousal positive emotions among European Americans is even more pronounced among Mexicans, an interdependent culture, revealing that not all kinds of interdependence are associated with a preference for low-arousal positive emotions (Ruby, Falk, Heine, Villa, & Silberstein, 2012). In sum, cultures vary in their happiness, in part, because they appear to have quite different ideas about what happiness is and what it is derived from.

Relationships

Central to the distinction between independent and interdependent self-concepts is the notion that culture shapes the ways that people relate with others (and, in turn, relationships shape our cultures). Relationships vary across cultures in terms of the ease with which people can form them. Relationships among those in independent cultures are entered into, and are maintained, on a somewhat mutually voluntary basis. In such contexts, people have relatively high relational mobility (Adams, 2005; Yuki et al., 2008), and individuals can seek new relationships or dissolve unsatisfying older relationships. Importantly, a relationship must in some way benefit the independent individual as otherwise they would not devote the efforts necessary to cultivating it; hence, independent people actively seek rewarding relationships and will often not devote much effort or resources to any relationship that does not appear to be beneficial (Adams, 2005; Schug, Yuki, Horikawa, & Takemura, 2009). Much of the social psychological literature on relationships has focused on relationship formation and dissolution suggesting that conditional relationships have thus far been a key focus of inquiry; indeed, there are relatively few references to less contingent relationships, such as those with kin (for a couple of exceptions, see Georgas, Berry, van de Vijver, Kağitçibaşi, & Poortinga, 2006; Lieberman, Tooby, & Cosmides, 2007).

In contrast, relationships among those from interdependent cultures are often viewed in less conditional terms. One is born into a relatively fixed interpersonal network, and over the course of a lifetime an individual subsequently joins a select few interpersonal networks that remain somewhat stable over the years. There are relatively few opportunities to form new relationships or to dissolve any existing ones at any given point in time, and this holds true whether one's relationships are rewarding or not. As a consequence, compared with people with more independent self-concepts, people with more interdependent selves tend to have more ambivalent feelings toward friendship (Adams & Plaut, 2003; Li, Adams, Kurtis, & Hamamura, 2015), are more likely to say that they have enemies (often from within their own ingroups; Adams, 2005), and have a weaker relationship between physical attractiveness and positive life outcomes (Anderson, Adams, & Plaut, 2008; Plaut, Adams, & Anderson, 2009). Moreover, studies find that Americans report having more friends than people in other cultures. For example, American college students reported having more friends than Ghanaian college students (Adams & Plaut, 2003), and American adults report having a larger social network (average size = 20.76; Fung, Carstensen, & Lang, 2001) than Hong Kong Chinese adults (average size = 13.23) or German adults (average size = 12.75; Fung, Stoeber, Yeung, & Lang, 2008). The lower relational mobility of people from interdependent cultures also is associated with people showing a weaker similarity-attraction effect (Schug et al., 2009), weaker motivations for uniqueness (Takemura, 2014), weaker self-enhancing motivations (Falk, Heine, Yuki, & Takemura, 2009), and they make less efforts to maintain their existing relationships (Schug, Yuki, &

Maddux, 2010). Furthermore, some of these culturally variable attitudes toward relational mobility can be acquired through acculturation (Zhang & Li, 2014).

A related construct is residential mobility, which refers to the frequency with which one changes residence and comes with changes in social networks (Oishi, Lun, & Sherman, 2007). Studies with American college students have found that, compared with those who have never moved, those who have moved multiple times in their lives (a) show more conditional loyalty to their colleges (meaning they identify with their schools only when they are described positively; Oishi, Ishii, & Lun, 2009), (b) view their personality traits to be a more central part of their identity than their group memberships (as the former can be identified immediately, whereas the latter is learned through one's social networks, which takes more time to learn; Oishi et al., 2007), and (c) prefer large national chain stores (e.g., Starbucks, Walmart) over local regional stores, as the former are familiar wherever one goes (Oishi, Miao, Koo, Kisling, & Ratliff, 2012). Similarly, American communities with higher residential mobility have (a) higher crime rates and less procommunity action (Oishi et al., 2007; Sampson, Raudenbush, & Earls, 1997), (b) more conditional attendance at professional sports events (i.e., fans only come when the team is winning; Oishi et al., 2007), and (c) more large national chain stores (Oishi et al., 2012). Second-generation Americans who come from families with lower relational mobility tend to have lower residential mobility themselves, which reduces their employment success, as they're less likely to move to take other work (Alesina, Algan, Cahuc, & Giuliano, 2015).

Conclusion

Humans are a cultural species and a rich understanding of how human minds operate requires a psychological science that is attentive to people's cultural experiences. Research in cultural psychology has grown substantially over the past few decades. It has revealed that many key psychological processes, often thought to be universal, manifest in distinct ways across cultures. Further, although some psychological phenomena appear in more invariant forms across cultures than others, it is often not clear which phenomena should be expected to vary the most. Pronounced cultural variation has been identified in many fundamental psychological phenomena, and thus it is crucial to seek cross-cultural data before one can confidently make inferences about the cultural generalizability of a phenomenon (Henrich et al., 2010). Such cultural variability in basic processes underscores how many psychological phenomena do not unfold reflexively, regardless of context, but are importantly shaped by engagement in the particular scripts, practices, and situations that each culture provides. In this way, psychological processes can be seen as entangled with "meaning"—and because particular meanings can vary substantially across cultural contexts and so must the psychological process (Bruner, 1990).

A serious shortcoming of the cultural psychological database thus far is that a large portion of it has only compared North American and East Asian college students. Most of the world remains largely unexplored territory. In particular, the role of culture is especially evident when small-scale societies are studied, which differ from the industrialized West in many profound ways. There has already been much excellent and influential work that has been conducted with such groups (e.g., Apicella, Azevedo, Christakis, & Fowler, 2014; Gordon, 2004; Henrich et al., 2005; Segall et al., 1963), much of it having been done to make arguments for psychological universals (e.g., Avis & Harris, 1991; Barrett & Behne, 2005; Ekman et al., 1969).

Attention to other cultural samples will likely uncover some psychological phenomena that are less familiar to Western psychologists. For example, the notion of "face" is far more elaborated within East Asia than it is in the West and has specific psychological consequences (e.g., Chang & Holt, 1994; Heine,

2005; Ting-Toomey, 1994). Likewise, a type of dialectical thinking that emphasizes tolerance for apparent contradiction likely would not have been investigated among westerners if it had not been first identified among Chinese (e.g., Peng & Nisbett, 1999). It is very likely that there are many more such examples in other cultural contexts (e.g., *simpatia* in Hispanic contexts; Sanchez-Burks, Nisbett, & Ybarra, 2000; Triandis, Marin, Lisansky, & Betancourt, 1984), and these phenomena would stand to greatly advance our understanding of cultural variation and the universality of psychological processes.

Cultural variation in psychological processes has been used to identify underlying mechanisms in ways that are impossible in monocultural research. This search for mechanisms has adopted a variety of methods, such as employing trait measures to mediate the cultural differences (e.g., Diener & Diener, 1995; Singelis, Bond, Lai, & Sharkey, 1999; but, for discussion regarding limitations in this, see Heine & Norenzayan, 2006), priming cultural constructs (e.g., Adams, 2005; Spencer-Rodgers et al., 2004), varying degrees of exposure to certain cultural experiences (e.g., Koo & Choi, 2005), situation sampling (e.g., Kitayama et al., 1997; Morling et al., 2002), experimental methods that assess people's default thoughts across cultures (e.g., Heine et al., 2001), and triangulation strategies that contrast multiple groups that vary in different sets of cultural variables (e.g., Medin & Atran, 2004). These and other methods will surely continue to be used to identify the mechanisms underlying cultural differences.

In sum, studying the psychology of people from different cultures does not just provide information relevant to those other cultures. Such research also serves to identify psychological phenomena that researchers might miss if they limited their research to Western samples, and it serves as an important tool to identify mechanisms that underlie psychological processes.

References

Adams, G. (2005). The cultural grounding of personal relationship: Enemyship in West African worlds. *Journal of Personality and Social Psychology, 88,* 948–968.

Adams, G., & Plaut, V. C. (2003). The cultural grounding of personal relationship: Friendship in North American and West African worlds. *Personal Relationships, 10,* 333–348.

Alesina, A., Algan, Y., Cahuc, P., & Giuliano, P. (2015). Family values and the regulation of labor. *Journal of the European Economic Association, 13,* 599–630.

Anderson, E. (1999). *Code of the street: Decency, violence, and the moral life of the inner city.* New York, NY: Norton.

Anderson, J. C., & Linden, W. (2006, April). *The influence of culture on cardiovascular response to anger.* Citation poster session presented at the annual meeting of the American Psychosomatic Society, Denver, CO.

Anderson, S. L., Adams, G., & Plaut, V. C. (2008). The cultural grounding of personal relationship: The importance of attractiveness in everyday life. *Journal of Personality and Social Psychology, 95,* 352–368.

Apicella, C. L., Azevedo, E. M., Christakis, N. A., & Fowler, J. H. (2014). Evolutionary origins of the endowment effect: Evidence from hunter-gatherers. *American Economic Review, 104,* 1793–1805.

Arnett, J. (2008). The neglected 95%: Why American psychology needs to become less American. *American Psychologist, 63,* 602–614.

Asch, S. (1956). Studies of independence and conformity: I. A minority of one against a unanimous majority. *Psychological Monographs, 70*(9), 1–70.

Avis, J., & Harris, P. L. (1991). Belief-desire reasoning among Baka children: Evidence for a universal conception of mind. *Child Development, 62,* 460–467.

Barrett, H. C., & Behne, T. (2005). Children's understanding of death as the cessation of agency: A test using sleep versus death. *Cognition, 96,* 93–108.

Baumeister, R. F., Tice, D. M., & Hutton, D. G. (1989). Self-presentational motivations and personality differences in self-esteem. *Journal of Personality, 57,* 547–579.

Becker, M., Vignoles, V. L., Owe, E., Brown, R., Smith, P. B., Easterbrook, M., . . . Yamakoğlu, N. (2012). Culture and the distinctiveness motive: Constructing identity in individualistic and collectivistic contexts. *Journal of Personality and Social Psychology, 102,* 833–855.

Benet-Martinez, V., Leu, J., Lee, F., & Morris, M. W. (2002). Negotiating biculturalism: Cultural frame switching in biculturals with oppositional versus compatible cultural identities. *Journal of Cross-Cultural Psychology, 33,* 492–516.

Biswas-Diener, R., & Diener, E. (2001). Making the best of a bad situation: Satisfaction in the slums of Calcutta. *Social Indicators Research, 55,* 329–352.

Blais, C., Jack, R. E., Scheepers, C., Fiset, D., & Caldara, R. (2008). Culture shapes how we look at faces. *PLoS One, 3*(8), e3022.

Bond, R., & Smith, P. B. (1996). Culture and conformity: A meta-analysis of studies using Asch's (1952b, 1956) line judgment task. *Psychological Bulletin, 119,* 111–137.

Bosson, J. K., Swann, W. B., & Pennebaker, J. W. (2000). Stalking the perfect measure of implicit self-esteem: The blind men and the elephant revisited? *Journal of Personality and Social Psychology, 79,* 631–643.

Boucher, H. C. (2011). The dialectical self-concept II: Cross-role and within-role consistency, well-being, self-certainty, and authenticity. *Journal of Cross-Cultural Psychology, 42,* 1251–1271.

Brosschot, J. F., & Thayer, J. F. (1998). Anger inhibition, cardiovascular recovery, and vagal function: A model of the link between hostility and cardiovascular disease. *Annals of Behavior Medicine, 20,* 326–332.

Brown, R. P., Osterman, L. L., & Barnes, C. D. (2009). School violence and the culture of honor. *Psychological Science, 20,* 1400–1405.

Bruner, J. (1990). *Acts of meaning.* Cambridge, MA: Harvard University Press.

Buhrmester, M. D., Blanton, H., & Swann, W. B. (2011). Implicit self-esteem: Nature, measurement, and a new way forward. *Journal of Personality and Social Psychology, 100,* 365–385.

Buss, D. M. (1989). Sex differences in human mate preferences: Evolutionary hypotheses tested in 37 cultures. *Behavioral and Brain Sciences, 12,* 1–49.

Butler, E. A., Lee, T. L., & Gross, J. J. (2009). Does expressing your emotions raise or lower your blood pressure? The answer depends on cultural context. *Journal of Cross-Cultural Psychology, 40,* 510–517.

Carlyle, T. (1943). *Past and present.* London, England: Chapman and Hall.

Chang, H.-C., & Holt, G. R. (1994). A Chinese perspective on face as inter-relational concern. In S. Ting-Toomey (Ed.), *The challenge of facework: Cross-cultural and interpersonal issues* (pp. 95–132). Albany, NY: SUNY Press.

Cheng, C.-Y., & Leung, A. K.-Y. (2013). Revisiting the multicultural experience–creativity link: The effects of perceived cultural distance and comparison mindset. *Social Psychological and Personality Science, 4,* 475–482.

Chiu, C., Dweck, C. S., Tong, J. U., & Fu, J. H. (1997). Implicit theories and conceptions of morality. *Journal of Personality and Social Psychology, 73,* 923–940.

Choi, I., & Choi, Y. (2002). Culture and self-concept flexibility. *Personality and Social Psychology Bulletin, 28,* 1508–1517.

Choi, I., & Nisbett, R. E. (1998). Situational salience and cultural differences in the correspondence bias and in the actor-observer bias. *Personality and Social Psychology Bulletin, 24,* 949–960.

Chua, H. F., Boland, J. E., & Nisbett, R. E. (2005). Cultural variation in eye movements during scene perception. *Proceedings of the National Academy of Sciences, 102,* 12629–12633.

Cohen, D. (2001). Cultural variation: Considerations and implications. *Psychological Bulletin, 127,* 451–471.

Cohen, D., & Gunz, A. (2002). As seen by the other . . . Perspectives on the self in the memories and emotional perceptions of Easterners and Westerners. *Psychological Science, 13,* 55–59.

Cohen, D., Hoshino-Browne, E., & Leung, A. (2007). Culture and the structure of personal experience: Insider and outsider phenomenologies of the self and social world. In M. P. Zanna (Ed.), *Advances in experimental social psychology* (Vol. 39). San Diego, CA: Academic Press.

Cohen, D., & Leung, A. (2012). Virtue and virility: Governing with honor and the association or dissociation between martial honor and moral character of U.S. presidents, legislators, and justices. *Social Psychological and Personality Science, 3,* 162–171.

Cohen, D., & Nisbett, R. E. (1997). Field experiments examining the culture of honor: The role of institutions in perpetuating norms about violence. *Personality and Social Psychology Bulletin, 23,* 1188–1199.

Cohen, D., Nisbett, R. E., Bowdle, B. F., & Schwarz, N. (1996). Insult, aggression, and the southern culture of honor: An "experimental ethnography." *Journal of Personality and Social Psychology, 70,* 945–960.

Cross, S. E., Uskul, A. K., Gercek-Swing, B., Alozkan, C., & Ataca, B. (2013). Confrontation versus withdrawal: Cultural differences in responses to threats to honor. *Group Processes & Intergroup Relations,* 16, 345–362.

Curhan, K. B., Sims, T., Markus, H. R., Kitayama, S., Karasawa, M., Kawakami, N., . . . Ryff, C. D. (2014). *Psychological Science, 25,* 2277–2280.

Daly, M., & Wilson, M. (1988). *Homicide.* New York, NY: Aldine de Gruyter.

Danziger, S., & Ward, R. (2010). Language changes implicit associations between ethnic groups and evaluation in bilinguals. *Psychological Science, 21,* 799–800.

Darwin, C. (1965). *The expression of emotions in man and animals.* Chicago, IL: University of Chicago Press. (Original work published 1872)

Diener, E., & Diener, M. (1995). Cross-cultural correlates of life satisfaction and self-esteem. *Journal of Personality and Social Psychology, 68,* 653–663.

Diener, E., Diener, M., & Diener, C. (1995). Factors predicting the subjective well-being of nations. *Journal of Personality and Social Psychology, 69,* 851–864.

Duval, S., & Wicklund, R. (1972). *A theory of objective self-awareness.* New York, NY: Academic Press.

Dzokoto, V. (2010). Different ways of feeling: Emotion and somatic awareness in Ghanaians and Euro-Americans. *Journal of Social, Evolutionary, and Cultural Psychology, 4*(2), 68–78.

Ekman, P. (1973). Universal facial expressions in emotion. *Studia Psychologica, 15,* 140–147.

Ekman, P., & Friesen, W. V. (1969). The repertoire of nonverbal behavior: Categories, origins, usage, and coding. *Semiotica, 1,* 49–98.

Ekman, P., & Friesen, W. V. (1971). Constants across cultures in the face and emotion. *Journal of Personality and Social Psychology, 17,* 124–129.

Ekman, P., Sorenson, E. R., & Friesen, W. (1969). Pancultural elements in facial displays of emotion. *Science, 164,* 86–88.

Elfenbein, H. A., & Ambady, N. (2002). On the universality and cultural specificity of emotion recognition: A meta-analysis. *Psychological Bulletin, 128,* 203–235.

Elliot, A. J., Chirkov, V. I., Kim, Y., & Sheldon, K. M. (2001). A cross-cultural analysis of avoidance (relative to approach) personal goals. *Psychological Science, 12,* 505–510.

English, T., & Chen, S. (2007). Culture and self-concept stability: Consistency across and within contexts among Asian-American and European-Americans. *Journal of Personality and Social Psychology, 93,* 478–490.

Falk, C. F., Dunn, E. W., & Norenzayan, A. (2010). Cultural variation in the importance of expected enjoyment for decision making. *Social Cognition, 28,* 609–629.

Falk, C. F., & Heine, S. J. (2015). What is implicit self-esteem, and does it vary across cultures? *Personality and Social Psychological Review, 19,* 177–198.

Falk, C. F., Heine, S. J., Takemura, K., Zhang, C. C. X., & Hsu, C. (2015). Are implicit self-esteem measures valid for assessing individual and cultural differences? *Journal of Personality, 83,* 56–68.

Falk, C. F., Heine, S. J., Yuki, M., & Takemura, K. (2009). Why do Westerners self-enhance more than East Asians? *European Journal of Personality, 23,* 183–209.

Fischer, R., Ferreira, M. C., Assmar, E. M. L., Gulfidan, B., Berberoglu, G., Dalyan, F., . . . Boer, D. (2014). Organizational practices across cultures: An exploration in six cultural contexts. *International Journal of Cross-Cultural Management, 14,* 105–125.

Freedman, J. L., & Fraser, S. C. (1966). Compliance without pressure: The foot-in-the-door technique. *Journal of Personality and Social Psychology, 4,* 195–202.

Fryberg, S. A., & Markus, H. R. (2003). On being American Indian: Current and possible selves. *Self and Identity, 2,* 325–344.

Fung, H. H., Carstensen, L. L., & Lang, F. (2001). Age-related patterns in social networks among European-Americans and African-Americans: Implications for socioemotional selectivity across the life span. *International Journal of Aging and Human Development, 52,* 185–206.

Fung, H. H., Stoeber, F. S., Yeung, D. Y. L., & Lang, F. R. (2008). Cultural specificity of socioemotional selectivity: Age differences in social network composition among Germans and Hong Kong Chinese. *Journal of Gerontology, B Psychological Science and Social Science, 63,* 156–164.

Gage, E., Coker, S., & Jobson, L. (2015). Cross-cultural differences in desirable and undesirable forms of self-consistency and influence on symptoms of depression and anxiety. *Journal of Cross-Cultural Psychology, 46,* 713–722.

Galaty, J. G., & Bonte, P. (Eds). (1991). *Herders, warriors, and traders: Pastoralism in Africa.* Boulder, CO: Westview.

Geertz, C. (1973). *The interpretation of cultures.* New York, NY: Basic Books.

Geertz, C. (1975). On the nature of anthropological understanding. *American Scientist, 63,* 4–53.

Gelfand, M. J., Raver, J. L., Nishii, L., Leslie, L. A., Lun, J., Lim, B. C., . . . Yamaguchi, S. (2011). Differences between tight and loose cultures: A 33 nation study. *Science, 332,* 1100–1104.

Gelman, S. A. (2003). *The essential child: Origins of essentialism in everyday thought.* New York, NY: Oxford University Press.

Gentile, B., Twenge, J. M., & Campbell, W. K. (2010). Birth cohort differences in self-esteem, 1988–2008: A cross-temporal meta-analysis. *Review of General Psychology, 14,* 261–268.

Georgas, J., Berry, J. W., van de Vijver, Kağitçibaşi, C., & Poortinga, Y. H. (Eds). (2006). *Families across cultures: A 30-nation psychological study.* New York, NY: Cambridge University Press.

Gilbert, D. T., & Malone, P. S. (1995). The correspondence bias. *Psychological Bulletin, 117,* 21–38.

Godart, F., Maddux, W. W., Shipilov, A., & Galinsky, A. D. (2015). A flair for foreign fashion: Individual professional experiences abroad facilitate the creative innovations of organizations. *Academy of Management Journal, 58,* 195–220.

Goh, J. O., Leshikar, E. D., Sutton, B. P., Tan, J. C., Sim, S. K., Hebrank, A. C., & Park, D. C. (2010). Culture differences in neural processing of faces and houses in the ventral visual cortex. *Social, Cognitive, and Affective Neuroscience, 5,* 227–235.

Gordon, P. (2004). Numerical cognition without words: Evidence from Amazonia. *Science, 306,* 496–499.

Greenwald, A. G. (1980). The totalitarian ego: Fabrication and revision of personal history. *American Psychologist, 35,* 603–618.

Greenwald, A. G., & Farnham, S. D. (2000). Using the implicit association test to measure self-esteem and self-concept. *Journal of Personality and Social Psychology, 79,* 1022–1038.

Grosjean, P. (2014). A history of violence: The culture of honor and homicide in the US South. *Journal of the European Economic Association, 12,* 1285–1316.

Grossmann, I., & Kross, E. (2010). The impact of culture on adaptive versus maladaptive self-reflection. *Psychological Science, 21,* 1150–1157.

Grossmann, I., & Varnum, M. (2015). Social structure, infectious diseases, disasters, secularism and cultural change in America. *Psychological Science, 26,* 311–324.

Guzzo, R. A., & Dickson, M. W. (1996). Teams in organizations: Recent research on performance and effectiveness. *Annual Review of Psychology, 47,* 307–338.

Haidt, J., & Keltner, D. (1999). Culture and facial expression: Open-ended methods find more expressions and a gradient of recognition. *Cognition and Emotion, 13,* 225–266.

Hamamura, T., Heine, S. J., & Paulhus, D. L. (2008). Cultural differences in response styles: The role of dialectical thinking. *Personality and Individual Differences, 44,* 932–942.

Hamamura, T., Heine, S. J., & Takemoto, T. (2007). Why the better-than-average effect is a worse-than-average measure of self-enhancement: An investigation of conflicting findings from studies of East Asian self-evaluations. *Motivation and Emotion, 31,* 247–259.

Hamamura, T., Meijer, Z., Heine, S. J., Kamaya, K., & Hori, I. (2009). Approach-avoidance motivations and information-tion processing: A cross-cultural analysis. *Personality and Social Psychology Bulletin, 35,* 454–462.

Hamamura, T., & Septarini, B. G. (2017). Culture and self-esteem over time: A cross-temporal meta-analysis among Australians, 1978–2014. *Social Psychological and Personality Science, 8,* 904–909.

Heider, F. (1958). *The psychology of interpersonal relations.* New York, NY: Wiley.

Heine, S. J. (2003). Self-enhancement in Japan? A reply to Brown and Kobayashi. *Asian Journal of Social Psychology, 6,* 75–84.

Heine, S. J. (2005). Where is the evidence for pancultural self-enhancement? A reply to Sedikides, Gaertner, & Toguchi. *Journal of Personality and Social Psychology, 89,* 531–538.

Heine, S. J. (2016). *Cultural psychology* (3rd ed.). New York, NY: W. W. Norton.

Heine, S. J., & Hamamura, T. (2007). In search of East Asian self-enhancement. *Personality and Social Psychology Review, 11,* 4–27.

Heine, S. J., Kitayama, S., & Hamamura, T. (2007). The inclusion of additional studies yields different conclusions: A reply to Sedikides, Gaertner, & Vevea (2005), JPSP. *Asian Journal of Social Psychology, 10,* 49–58

Heine, S. J., Kitayama, S., Lehman, D. R., Takata, T., Ide, E., Leung, C., & Matsumoto, H. (2001). Divergent consequences of success and failure in Japan and North America: An investigation of self-improving motivations and malleable selves. *Journal of Personality and Social Psychology, 81,* 599–615.

Heine, S. J., & Lehman, D. R. (1997). Culture, dissonance, and self-affirmation. *Personality and Social Psychology Bulletin, 23,* 389–400.

Heine, S. J., Lehman, D. R., Markus, H. R., & Kitayama, S. (1999). Is there a universal need for positive self-regard? *Psychological Review, 106,* 766–794.

Heine, S. J., & Norenzayan, A. (2006). Towards a psychological science for a cultural species. *Perspectives on Psychological Science, 1,* 251–269.

Heine, S. J., & Raineri, A. (2009). Self-improving motivations and culture: The case of Chileans. *Journal of Cross-Cultural Psychology, 40,* 158–163.

Heine, S. J., & Renshaw, K. (2002). Interjudge agreement, self-enhancement, and liking: Cross-cultural divergences. *Personality and Social Psychology Bulletin, 28,* 578–587.

Heine, S. J., Takemoto, T., Moskalenko, S., Lasaleta, J., & Henrich, J. (2008). Mirrors in the head: Cultural variation in objective self-awareness. *Personality and Social Psychology Bulletin, 34,* 879–887.

Henrich, J., Boyd, R., Bowles, S., Camerer, C., Fehr, E., Gintis, H., . . .Tracer, D. (2005). "Economic man" in cross-cultural perspective: Behavioral experiments in 15 small-scale societies. *Behavioral & Brain Sciences, 28,* 795–855.

Henrich, J., Heine, S. J., & Norenzayan, A. (2010). The weirdest people in the world? *Behavioral and Brain Sciences, 33,* 61–83.

Henry, P. J. (2009). Low-status compensation: A theory for understanding the role of status in cultures of honor. *Journal of Personality and Social Psychology, 97,* 451–466.

Hiniker, P. J. (1969). Chinese reactions to forced compliance: Dissonance reduction or national character. *Journal of Social Psychology, 77,* 157–176.

Hofstede, G. (1980). *Culture's consequences: International differences in work-related values.* Beverly Hills, CA: SAGE.

Hong, Y., Morris, M. W., Chiu, C., & Benet-Martinez, V. (2000). Multicultural minds: A dynamic constructivist approach to culture and cognition. *American Psychologist, 55,* 705–720.

Inglehart, R., Basanez, M., & Moreno, A. (1998). *Human values and beliefs: A cross-cultural sourcebook.* Ann Arbor, MI: University of Michigan Press.

Inglehart, R., & Klingemann, H. (2000). Genes, culture, democracy, and happiness. In E. Diener & E. Suh (Eds.), *Culture and subjective well-being* (pp. 165–184). Cambridge, MA: MIT Press.

Ishii, K., Miyamoto, Y., Rule, N. O., & Toriyama, R. (2014). Physical objects as vehicles of cultural transmission: Maintaining harmony and uniqueness through colored geometric patterns. *Personality and Social Psychology Bulletin, 40,* 175–188.

Izard, C. E. (1994). Innate and universal facial expressions: Evidence from developmental and cross-cultural research. *Psychological Bulletin, 115,* 288–299.

Jack, R. E., Caldara, R., & Schyns, P. G. (2012). Internal representations reveal cultural diversity in expectations of facial expressions of emotion. *Journal of Experimental Psychology: General, 141,* 19–25.

Jack, R. E., Garrod, O. G. B., Yu, H., Caldara, R., & Schyns, P. G. (2012). Facial expressions of emotion are not culturally universal. *Proceedings of the National Academy of Sciences, 109,* 7241–7244.

Ji, L. J., Nisbett, R. E., & Su, Y. (2001). Culture, change, and prediction. *Psychological Science, 12,* 450–456.

Ji, L. J., Peng, K., & Nisbett, R. E. (2000). Culture, control, and perception of relationships in the environment. *Journal of Personality and Social Psychology, 78,* 943–955.

Ji, L. J., Zhang, Z., & Nisbett, R. E. (2004). Is it culture or is it language? Examination of language effects in cross-cultural research on categorization. *Journal of Personality and Social Psychology, 87,* 57–65.

Jiang, D., Li, T., & Hamamura, T. (2015). Societies' tightness moderates age differences in perceived justifiability of morally debatable behaviors. *European Journal of Aging, 12,* 333–340.

Jones, E. E., & Harris, V. A. (1967). The attribution of attitudes. *Journal of Experimental Social Psychology, 3,* 1–24.

Kanagawa, C., Cross, S. E., & Markus, H. R. (2001). "Who am I?" The cultural psychology of the conceptual self. *Personality and Social Psychology Bulletin, 27,* 90–103.

Kashima, Y., Siegal, M., Tanaka, K., & Kashima, E. S. (1992). Do people believe behaviors are consistent with attitudes? Towards a cultural psychology of attribution processes. *British Journal of Social Psychology, 31,* 111–124.

Keltner, D. (1995). The signs of appeasement: Evidence for the distinct displays of embarrassment, amusement, and shame. *Journal of Personality and Social Psychology, 68,* 441–454.

Kim, H. S., & Markus, H. R. (1999). Deviance or uniqueness, harmony or conformity? A cultural analysis. *Journal of Personality and Social Psychology, 77,* 785–800.

Kim, Y., Cohen, D., & Au, W. (2010). The jury and abjury of my peers: The self in face and dignity cultures. *Journal of Personality and Social Psychology, 98,* 904–916.

Kitayama, S., Duffy, S., Kawamura, T., & Larsen, J. T. (2003). Perceiving an object and its context in different cultures: A cultural look at New Look. *Psychological Science, 14,* 201–206.

Kitayama, S., Markus, H. R., & Kurokawa, M. (2000). Culture, emotion, and well-being: Good feelings in Japan and the United States. *Cognition and Emotion, 14,* 93–124.

Kitayama, S., Markus, H. R., Matsumoto, H., & Norasakkunkit, V. (1997). Individual and collective processes in the construction of the self: Self-enhancement in the United States and self-criticism in Japan. *Journal of Personality and Social Psychology, 72,* 1245–1267.

Kitayama, S., Snibbe, A. C., Markus, H. R., & Suzuki, T. (2004). Is there any "free" choice? Self and dissonance in two cultures. *Psychological Science, 15,* 527–533.

Klar, Y., & Giladi, E. E. (1997). No one in my group can be below the group's average": A robust positivity bias in favor of anonymous peers. *Journal of Personality and Social Psychology, 73,* 885–901.

Knight, N., & Nisbett, R. E. (2007). Culture, class and cognition: Evidence from Italy. *Journal of Cognition and Culture, 7,* 283–291.

Koo, M., & Choi, I. (2005). Becoming a holistic thinker: Training effect of oriental medicine on reasoning. *Personality and Social Psychology Bulletin, 31,* 1264–1272.

Kraus, M. W., Cote, S., & Keltner, D. (2010). Social class, contextualism, and empathic accuracy. *Psychological Science, 21,* 1716–1723.

Kraus, M. W., Piff, P. K., Mendoza-Denton, R., Rheinschmidt, M. L., & Keltner, D. (2012). Social class, solipsism, and contextualism: How the rich are different from the poor. *Psychological Review, 119,* 546–572.

Krizan, X., & Suls, J. (2008). Losing sight of oneself in the above-average effect: When egocentrism, focalism, and group diffuseness collide. *Journal of Experimental Social Psychology, 44,* 929–942.

Kuhn, M. H., & McPartland, T. (1954). An empirical investigation of self-attitudes. *American Sociological Review, 19,* 68–76.

Kühnen, U., Hannover, B., Schubert, B. (2001). The semantic-procedural interface model of the self: The role of self-knowledge for context-dependent versus context-independent modes of thinking. *Journal of Personality and Social Psychology, 80,* 397–409.

Kurman, J. (2003). Why is self-enhancement low in certain collectivist cultures? An investigation of two competing explanations. *Journal of Cross-Cultural Psychology, 34,* 496–510.

Layous, K., Lee, H., Choi, I., & Lyubomirsky, S. (2013). Culture matters when designing a successful happiness-increasing activity: A comparison of the United States and South Korea. *Journal of Cross-Cultural Psychology, 44,* 1294–1303.

Lee, A. Y., Aaker, J. L., & Gardner, W. L. (2000). The pleasures and pains of distinct self-construals: The role of interdependence in regulatory focus. *Journal of Personality and Social Psychology, 78,* 1122–1134.

Lee, G. R., & Stone, L. H. (1980). Mate-selection systems and criteria: Variation according to family structure. *Journal of Marriage and the Family, 42,* 319–326.

Leu, J., Wang, J., & Koo, K. (2011). Are positive emotions just as positive across cultures? *Emotion, 4,* 994–999.

Leung, A. K., Maddux, W. W., Galinsky, A. D., & Chiu, C. (2008). Multicultural experience enhances creativity: The when and how. *American Psychologist, 63,* 169–181.

Leung, K., & Bond, M. H. (2004). Social axioms: A model for social beliefs in multicultural perspective. In M. P. Zanna (Ed.), *Advances in experimental social psychology* (Vol. 36, pp. 119–197). San Diego, CA: Elsevier.

Levine, C. S., Miyamoto, Y., Markus, H. R., Rigotti, A., Boylan, J. M., Park, J., . . . Ryff, C. D. (2016). Culture and healthy eating: The role of independence and interdependence in the United States and Japan. *Personality and Social Psychology Bulletin, 42,* 1335–1348.

Levine, S. S., Apfelbaum, E. P., Bernard, M., Bartelt, V. L., Zajac, E. J., & Stark, D. (2014). Ethnic diversity deflates price bubbles. *Proceedings of the National Academy of Sciences, 111,* 18524–18529.

Li, L. M. W., Adams, G., Kurtis, T., & Hamamura, T. (2015). Beware of friends: The cultural psychology of relational mobility and cautious intimacy. *Asian Journal of Social Psychology, 18,* 124–133.

Li, Y. J., Johnson, K. A., Cohen, A. B., Williams, M. J., Knowles, E. D., & Chen, Z. (2012). Fundamental(ist) attribution error: Protestants are dispositionally focused. *Journal of Personality and Social Psychology, 102,* 281–290.

Lieberman, D., Tooby, J., & Cosmides, L. (2007). The architecture of human kin detection. *Nature, 445,* 727–731.

Lockwood, P., Marshall, T. C., & Sadler, P. (2005). Promoting success or preventing failure: Cultural differences in motivation by positive and negative role models. *Personality and Social Psychology Bulletin, 31,* 379–392.

Loughnan, S., Kuppens, P., Allik, J., Balazs, K., Lemus, S. D., Dumont, K., . . . Haslam, N. (2011). Economic inequality is linked to biased self-perception. *Psychological Science, 22,* 1254–1258.

Lu, J. G., Quoidbach, J., Gino, F., Chakroff, A., Maddux, W. W., & Galinsky, A. D. (2017). The dark side of going abroad: How broad foreign experiences increase immoral behavior. *Journal of Personality and Social Psychology, 112,* 1–16.

Ma-Kellams, C., Blascovich, J., & McCall, C. (2012). Culture and the body: East–West differences in visceral perception. *Journal of Personality and Social Psychology, 102,* 718–728.

Maass, A., Karasawa, M., Politi, F., & Suga, S. (2006). Do verbs and adjectives play different roles in different cultures? A cross-linguistic analysis of person representation. *Journal of Personality and Social Psychology, 90,* 734–750.

Maddux, W. W., Bivolaru, E., Hafenbrack, A. C., Tadmor, C. T., & Galinsky, A. D. (2014). Expanding opportunities by opening your mind: Multicultural engagement predicts job market success through longitudinal increases in integrative complexity. *Social Psychological and Personality Science, 5,* 608–615.

Maddux, W. W., & Galinsky, A. D. (2009). Cultural barriers and mental borders: Living in and adapting to foreign cultures facilitates creativity. *Journal of Personality and Social Psychology, 96,* 1047–1061.

Maddux, W. W., & Yuki, M. (2006). The "Ripple effect": Cultural differences in perceptions of the consequences of events. *Personality and Social Psychology Bulletin, 32*, 669–683.

Markus, H. (1977). Self-schemata and processing information about the self. *Journal of Personality and Social Psychology, 35*, 63–78.

Markus, H. R., & Kitayama, S. (1991). Culture and the self: Implications for cognition, emotion, and motivation. *Psychological Review, 98*, 224–253.

Marsh, A. A., Elfenbein, H. A., & Ambady, N. (2007). Separated by a common language: Nonverbal accents and cultural stereotypes about Americans and Australians. *Journal of Cross-Cultural Psychology, 38*, 284–301.

Masuda, T., Ellsworth, P. C., Mesquita, B., Leu, J., Tanida, S., & van de Veerdonk, E. (2008). Placing the face in context: Cultural differences in the perception of facial emotion. *Journal of Personality and Social Psychology, 94*, 365–381.

Masuda, T., Gonzalez, R., Kwan, L., & Nisbett, R. E. (2008). Culture and aesthetic preference: Comparing the attention to context of East Asians and European Americans. *Personality and Social Psychology Bulletin, 34*, 1260–1275.

Masuda, T., & Nisbett, R. E. (2001). Attending holistically vs. analytically: Comparing the context sensitivity of Japanese and Americans. *Journal of Personality and Social Psychology, 81*, 922–934.

Matsumoto, D., Kudoh, T., Scherer, K., & Wallbott, H. (1988). Antecedents of and reactions to emotions in the United States and Japan. *Journal of Cross-Cultural Psychology, 19*, 267–286.

Mauss, I. B., Butler, E. A., Roberts, N. A., & Chu, A. (2010). Emotion control values and responding to an anger provocation in Asian-American and European-American individuals. *Cognition and Emotion, 24*, 1026–1043.

May, R. M. (1997). The scientific wealth of nations. *Science, 275*, 793–796.

McCrae, R. R., & Terraciano, A.; Personality Profiles of Cultures Project. (2005). Universal features of personality traits from the observer's perspective: Data from 50 cultures. *Journal of Personality and Social Psychology, 88*, 547–561.

Medin, D. L., & Atran. S. (2004). The native mind: Biological categorization, reasoning and decision making in development and across cultures. *Psychological Review, 111*, 960–983.

Menon, T., Morris, M. W., Chiu, C., & Hong, Y. (1999). Culture and the construal of agency: Attribution to individual versus group dispositions. *Journal of Personality and Social Psychology, 76*, 701–717.

Mesquita, B. (2001). Emotions in collectivist and individualist contexts. *Journal of Personality and Social Psychology, 80*, 68–74.

Mesquita, B., & Karasawa, M. (2002). Different emotional lives. *Cognition and Emotion, 17*, 127–141.

Mezulis, A. H., Abramson, L. Y., Hyde, J. S., & Hankin, B. L. (2004). Is there a universal positive bias in attributions? A meta-analytic review of individual, developmental, and cultural differences in the self-serving attributional bias. *Psychological Bulletin, 130*, 711–747.

Miller, J. G. (1984). Culture and the development of everyday social explanation. *Journal of Personality and Social Psychology, 46*, 961–978.

Miller, J. G., & Bersoff, D. M. (1992). Culture and moral judgment: How are conflicts between justice and interpersonal responsibilities resolved? *Journal of Personality and Social Psychology, 62*, 541–554.

Miyamoto, Y., Boylan, J. M., Coe, C. L., Curhan, K. B., Levine, C. S., Markus, H. R., . . . Ryff, C. D. (2013). Negative emotions predict elevated interleukin-6 in the United States but not in Japan. *Brain, Behavior, and Immunity, 34*, 79–85.

Morling, B., Kitayama, S., & Miyamoto, Y. (2002). Cultural practices emphasize influence in the United States and adjustment in Japan. *Personality and Social Psychology Bulletin, 28*, 311–323.

Morris, M., & Peng, K. (1994). Culture and cause: American and Chinese attributions for social and physical events. *Journal of Personality and Social Psychology, 67*, 949–971.

Murata, A., Moser, J. S., & Kitayama, S. (2013). Culture shapes electrocortical responses during emotional suppression. *Social Cognitive and Affective Neuroscience, 8*, 595–601.

Murray, D. R., Trudeau, R., & Schaller, M. (2011). On the origins of cultural differences in conformity: Four tests of the pathogen prevalence hypothesis. *Personality and Social Psychology Bulletin, 37*, 318–329.

Na, J., & Kitayama, S. (2011). Spontaneous trait inference is culture-specific: Behavioral and neural evidence. *Psychological Science, 22,* 1025–1032.

Na, J., McDonough, I. M., Chan, M. Y., & Park, D. C. (2016). Social-class differences in consumer choices: Working-class individuals are more sensitive to choices of others than middle-class individuals. *Personality and Social Psychology Bulletin, 42,* 430–443.

Nielsen, M., Haun, D., Kartner, J., & Legare, C. H. (2017). The persistent sampling bias in developmental psychology: A call to action. *Journal of Experimental Child Psychology, 162,* 31–38.

Nisbett, R. E. (2003). *The geography of thought.* New York, NY: Free Press.

Nisbett, R. E., & Cohen, D. (1996). *Culture of honor: The psychology of violence in the South.* Boulder, CO: Westview Press.

Nisbett, R. E., Peng, K., Choi, I., & Norenzayan, A. (2001). Culture and systems of thought: Holistic vs. analytic cognition. *Psychological Review, 108,* 291–310.

Norenzayan, A. (2008). *Middle Eastern cognition in cross-cultural context.* Unpublished manuscript, University of British Columbia.

Norenzayan, A., Choi, I., & Nisbett, R. E. (2002). Cultural similarities and differences in social inference: Evidence from behavioral predictions and lay theories of behavior. *Personality and Social Psychology Bulletin, 28,* 109–120.

Norenzayan, A., Choi, I., & Peng, K. (2007). Perception and cognition. In S. Kitayama & D. Cohen (Eds.), *Handbook of cultural psychology* (pp. 569–594). New York, NY: Guilford.

Norenzayan, A., & Heine, S. J. (2005). Psychological universals: What are they and how can we know? *Psychological Bulletin, 131,* 763–784.

Norenzayan, A., Smith, E. E., Kim, B., & Nisbett, R. E. (2002). Cultural preferences for formal versus intuitive reasoning. *Cognitive Science, 26,* 653–684.

Oishi, S., Diener, E., Scollon, C. N., & Biswas-Diener, R. (2004). Cross-situational consistency of affective experiences across cultures. *Journal of Personality and Social Psychology, 86,* 460–472.

Oishi, S., Graham, J., Kesebir, S., & Galinha, I. C. (2013). Concepts of happiness across time and cultures. *Personality and Social Psychology Bulletin, 39,* 559–577.

Oishi, S., Ishii, K., & Lun, J. (2009). Residential mobility and conditionality of group identification. *Journal of Experimental Social Psychology, 45,* 913–919.

Oishi, S., Lun, J., & Sherman, G. D. (2007). Residential mobility, self-concept, and positive affect in social interactions. *Journal of Personality and Social Psychology, 93,* 131–141.

Oishi, S., Miao, F. F., Koo, M., Kisling, J., & Ratliff, K. (2012). Residential mobility breeds familiarity-seeking. *Journal of Personality and Social Psychology, 102,* 149–162.

Oyserman, D., Coon, H. M., & Kemmelmeier, M. (2002). Rethinking individualism and collectivism: Evaluation of theoretical assumptions and meta-analyses. *Psychological Bulletin, 128,* 3–72.

Oyserman, D., & Lee, S. W. S. (2008). Does culture influence what and how we think: Effects of priming individualism and collectivism. *Psychological Bulletin, 134,* 311–342.

Park, H., Twenge, J. M., & Greenfield, P. M. (2014). The great recession: Implications for adolescent values and behavior. *Social Psychological and Personality Science, 5,* 310–318.

Peng, K., & Nisbett, R. E. (1999). Culture, dialectics, and reasoning about contradiction. *American Psychologist, 54,* 741–754.

Plaut, V. C., Adams, G., & Anderson, S. L. (2009). Does attractiveness buy happiness? "It depends on where you're from." *Personal Relationships, 16,* 619–630.

Rennie, L. J., & Dunne, M. (1994). Gender, ethnicity, and students' perceptions about science and science-related careers in Fiji. *Science Education, 78,* 285–300.

Richerson, P. J., & Boyd, R. (2005). *Not by genes alone.* Chicago, IL: University of Chicago Press.

Rosenberg, M. (1965). *Society and the adolescent self-image.* Princeton, NJ: Princeton University Press.

Rothbaum, F., Weisz, J. R., & Snyder, S. S. (1982). Changing the world and changing the self: A two-process model of perceived control. *Journal of Personality and Social Psychology, 42,* 5–37.

Rozin, P., Fischler, C., Shields, C., & Masson, E. (2006). Attitudes towards large numbers of choices in the food domain: A cross-cultural study of five countries in Europe and the USA. *Appetite, 46,* 304–308.

Ruby, M. B., Falk, C. F., Heine, S. J., Villa, C., & Silberstein, O. (2012). Not all collectivisms are equal: Opposing preferences for ideal affect between East Asians and Mexicans. *Emotion, 12,* 1206–1209.

Saad, C. S., Damian, R. I., Benet-Martinez, V., Moons, W. G., & Robins, R. W. (2013). Multiculturalism and creativity: Effects of cultural context, bicultural identity, and ideational fluency. *Social Psychological and Personality Science, 4,* 369–375.

Sampson, R. J., Raudenbush, S. W., & Earls, F. (1997). Neighborhoods and violent crime: A multilevel study of collective efficacy. *Science, 277,* 918–924.

Sanchez-Burks, J., Nisbett, R. E., & Ybarra, O. (2000). Cultural styles, relational schemas and prejudice against outgroups. *Journal of Personality and Social Psychology, 79,* 174–189.

Savani, K., Alvarez, A., Mesquita, B., & Markus, H. R. (2013). Feeling close and doing well: The prevalence and motivational effects of interpersonally engaging emotions in Mexican and European American cultural contexts. *International Journal of Psychology, 48,* 682–694.

Savani, K., & Markus, H. R. (2012). A processing advantage associated with analytic perceptual tendencies: European Americans outperform Asians on multiple object tracking. *Journal of Experimental Social Psychology, 48,* 766–769.

Savani, K., Markus, H. R., & Conner, A. L. (2008). Let your preference be your guide? Preferences and choices are more tightly linked for North Americans than for Indians. *Journal of Personality and Social Psychology, 95,* 861–876.

Savani, K., Markus, H. R., Naidu, N. V. R., Kumar, S., & Berlia, N. (2010). What counts as a choice? U.S. Americans are more likely than Indians to construe actions as choices. *Psychological Science, 21,* 391–398.

Savani, K., Morris, M. W., & Naidu, N. V. R. (2012). Deference in Indians' decision making: Introjected goals or injunctive norms? *Journal of Personality and Social Psychology, 102,* 685–699.

Savani, K., Morris, M. W., Naidu, N. V. R., Kumar, S., & Berlia, N. V. (2011). Cultural conditioning: Understanding interpersonal accommodation in India and the United States in terms of the modal characteristics of interpersonal influence situations. *Journal of Personality and Social Psychology, 100,* 84–102.

Schug, J., Yuki, M., Horikawa, H., & Takemura, K. (2009). Similarity attraction and actually selecting similar others: How cross-societal differences in relational mobility affect interpersonal similarity in Japan and the USA. *Asian Journal of Social Psychology, 12,* 95–103.

Schug, J., Yuki, M., & Maddux, W. (2010). Relational mobility explains between- and within-culture differences in self-disclosure to close friends. *Psychological Science, 21,* 1471–1478.

Schwartz, B. (2004). *The paradox of choice: Why more is less.* New York, NY: Harper-Collins.

Schwartz, S. H., & Boehnke, K. (2004). Evaluating the structure of human values with confirmatory factor analysis. *Journal of Research in Personality, 38,* 230–255.

Sedikides, C., Gaertner, L., & Vevea, J. (2005). Pancultural self-enhancement reloaded: A meta-analytic reply to Heine (2005). *Journal of Personality and Social Psychology, 89,* 539–551.

Sedikides, C., Gaertner, L., & Vevea, J. (2007). Evaluating the evidence for pancultural self-enhancement. *Asian Journal of Social Psychology, 10,* 201–203.

Segall, M. H., Campbell, D. T., & Herskiovits, M. J. (1963). Cultural differences in the perception of geometric illusions. *Science, 193,* 769–771.

Seo, M., Kim, Y.-H., Tam, K.-P., & Rozin, P. (2016). I am dumber when I look dumb in front of many (vs. Few) others: A cross-cultural difference in how audience size affects perceived social reputation and self-judgments. *Journal of Cross-Cultural Psychology, 47,* 1019–1032.

Shimizu, Y., Lee, H., & Uleman, J. S. (2017). Culture as automatic processes for making meaning: Spontaneous trait inferences. *Journal of Experimental Social Psychology, 69,* 79–85.

Shweder, R. A. (1990). Cultural psychology: What is it? In J. W. Stigler, R. A. Shweder, & G. Herdt (Eds.), *Cultural psychology: Essays on comparative human development* (pp. 1–43).Cambridge, England: Cambridge University Press.

Singelis, T. M., Bond, M. H., Lai, S. Y., & Sharkey, W. F. (1999). Unpackaging culture's influence on self-esteem and embarrassability: The role of self-construals. *Journal of Cross-Cultural Psychology, 30,* 315–331.

Snibbe, A. C., & Markus, H. R. (2005). You can't always get what you want: Social class, agency, and choice. *Journal of Personality and Social Psychology, 88,* 703–720.

Spencer-Rodgers, J., Boucher, H. C., Mori, S. C., Wang, L., & Peng, K. (2009). The dialectical self-concept: Contradiction, change, and holism in East Asian cultures. *Personality and Social Psychology Bulletin, 35,* 29–44.

Spencer-Rodgers, J., Peng, K., Wang, L., & Hou, Y. (2004). Dialectical self-esteem and East-West differences in psychological well-being. *Personality and Social Psychology Bulletin, 30,* 1416–1432.

Steele, C. M. (1988). The psychology of self-affirmation: Sustaining the integrity of the self. In L. Berkowitz (Ed.), *Advances in experimental social psychology* (Vol. 21, pp. 261–302). San Diego, CA: Academic Press.

Stephens, N. M., Cameron, J. S., & Townsend, S. S. M. (2014). Lower social class does not (always) mean greater interdependence: Women in poverty have fewer social resources than working-class women. *Journal of Cross-Cultural Psychology, 45,* 1061–1073.

Stephens, N. M., Fryberg, S. A., Markus, H. R., Johnson, C. S., & Covarrubias, R. (2012). Unseen disadvantage: How American universities' focus on independence undermines the academic performance of first-generation college students. *Journal of Personality and Social Psychology, 102,* 1178–1197.

Stephens, N. M., Markus, H. R., & Phillips, L. T. (2014). Social class culture cycles: How three gateway contexts shape selves and fuel inequality. *Annual Review of Psychology, 65,* 611–634.

Stephens, N. M., Markus, H. R., & Townsend, S. S. M. (2007). Choice as an act of meaning: The case of social class. *Journal of Personality and Social Psychology, 93,* 814–830.

Stephens, N. M., Townsend, S. S. M., Markus, H. R., & Phillips, L. T. (2012). A cultural mismatch: Independent cultural norms produce greater increases in cortisol and more negative emotions among first-generation college students. *Journal of Experimental Social Psychology, 48,* 1389–1393.

Su, S. K., Chiu, C.-Y., Hong, Y.-Y., Leung, K., Peng, K., & Morris, M. W. (1999). Self organization and social organization: American and Chinese constructions. In T. R. Tyler, R. Kramer, & O. John (Eds.), *The psychology of the social self.* (pp. 193–222). Mahwah, NJ: Erlbaum.

Suh, E., Diener, E., Oishi, S., & Triandis, H. C. (1998). The shifting basis of life satisfaction judgments across cultures: Emotions versus norms. *Journal of Personality and Social Psychology, 74,* 482–493.

Swann, W. B., Wenzlaff, R. M., Krull, D. S., & Pelham, B. W. (1992). Allure of negative feedback: Self-verification strivings among depressed persons. *Journal of Abnormal Psychology, 101,* 293–306.

Tadmor, C. T., Satterstrom, P., Jang, S., & Polzer, J. T. (2012). Beyond individual creativity: The superadditive benefits of multicultural experience for collective creativity in culturally diverse teams. *Journal of Cross-Cultural Psychology, 43,* 384–392.

Takemura, K. (2014). Being different leads to being connected: On the adaptive function of uniqueness in "open" societies. *Journal of Cross-Cultural Psychology, 45,* 1579–1583.

Talhelm, T., Zhang, X., Oishi, S., Shimin, C., Duan, D., Lan, X., & Kitayama, S. (2014). Large-scale psychological differences within China explained by rice versus wheat agriculture. *Science, 344,* 603–608.

Taylor, S. E., & Brown, J. D. (1988). Illusion and well-being: A social psychological perspective on mental health. *Psychological Bulletin, 103,* 193–210.

Tesser, A. (2000). On the confluence of self-esteem maintenance mechanisms. *Personality and Social Psychology Review, 4,* 290–299.

Ting-Toomey, S. (Ed.). (1994). *The challenge of facework: Cross-cultural and interpersonal issues.* Albany, NY: State University of New York Press.

Tracy, J. L., & Matsumoto, D. (2008). The spontaneous display of pride and shame: Evidence for biologically innate nonverbal displays. *Proceedings of the National Academy of Science, 105,* 11655–11660.

Tracy, J. L., & Robins, R. W. (2008). The nonverbal expression of pride: Evidence for cross-cultural recognition. *Journal of Personality and Social Psychology, 94,* 516–530.

Trafimow, D., Triandis, H. C., & Goto, S. G. (1991). Some tests of the distinction between the private self and the collective self. *Journal of Personality and Social Psychology, 60,* 649–655.

Triandis, H. C. (1989). The self and social behavior in differing cultural contexts. *Psychological Review, 96,* 506–520.

Triandis, H. C. (1996). The psychological measurement of cultural syndromes. *American Psychologist, 51,* 407–415.

Triandis, H. C., Marin, G., Lisansky, J., & Betancourt, H. (1984). Simpatia as a cultural script of Hispanics. *Journal of Personality and Social Psychology, 47,* 1363–1375.

Tropp, L. R., & Wright, S. C. (2003). Evaluations and perceptions of self, ingroup, and outgroup: Comparisons between Mexican-American and European-American children. *Self and Identity, 2,* 203–221.

Tsai, J. L., Chentsova-Dutton, Y., Freire-Bebeau, L., & Przymus, D. E. (2002). Emotional expression and physiology in European-Americans and Hmong Americans. *Emotion, 2,* 380–397.

Tsai, J. L., Knutson, B. K., & Fung, H. H. (2006). Cultural variation in affect valuation. *Journal of Personality and Social Psychology, 90,* 288–307.

Tsai, J. L., Louie, J. Y., Chen, E. E., & Uchida, Y. (2006). Learning what feelings to desire: Socialization of ideal affect through children's storybooks. *Personality and Social Psychology Bulletin, 32,* 1–14.

Tsai, J. L., Ying, Y., & Lee, P. A. (2000). The meaning of "being Chinese" and "being American": Variation among Chinese American young adults. *Journal of Cross-Cultural Psychology, 31,* 302–332.

Trzesniewski, K. H, & Donnelan, M. B. (2010). Rethinking "Generation Me": A study of cohort effects from 1976–2006. *Perspectives on Psychological Science, 5,* 58–75.

Twenge, J. M., & Campbell, W. K. (2001). Age and birth cohort differences in self-esteem: A cross-temporal meta-analysis. *Personality and Social Psychology Review, 5,* 321–344.

Twenge, J. M., Campbell, W. K., & Freeman, E. C. (2012). Generational differences in young adults' life goals, concern for others, and civic orientation, 1966–2009. *Journal of Personality and Social Psychology, 102,* 1045–1062.

Twenge, J. M., & Foster, J. D. (2010). Birth cohort increases in narcissistic personality traits among American college students, 1982–2009. *Social Psychological and Personality Science, 1,* 99–106.

Uskul, A. K., Kitayama, S., & Nisbett, R. E. (2008). Ecocultural basis of cognition: Farmers and fishermen are more holistic than herders. *Proceedings of the National Academy of Sciences, 105,* 8552–8556.

Vandello, J. A., & Cohen, D. (2003). Male honor and female fidelity: Implicit cultural scripts that perpetuate domestic violence. *Journal of Personality and Social Psychology, 84,* 997–1010.

Veenhoven, R. (2014). *World database of happiness.* Rotterdam, The Netherlands: Erasmus University. Retrieved from http://worlddatabaseofhappiness.eur.nl

Wang, H., Masuda, T., Ito, K., & Rashid, M. (2012). How much information? East Asian and North American cultural products and information search performance. *Personality and Social Psychology Bulletin, 38,* 1539–1551.

Wang, Q. (2004). The emergence of cultural self-constructs: Autobiographical memory and self-description in European American and Chinese children. *Developmental Psychology, 40,* 3–15.

Watson, W. E., Kumar, K., & Michaelsen, L. K. (1993). Cultural diversity's impact on interaction process and performance: Comparing homogeneous and diverse task groups. *Academy of Management Journal, 36,* 590–602.

Weisz, J. R., Rothbaum, F. M., & Blackburn, T. C. (1984). Standing out and standing in: The psychology of control in America and Japan. *American Psychologist, 39,* 955–969.

Witkin, H. A., & Berry, J. W. (1975). Psychological differentiation in cross-cultural perspective. *Journal of Cross-Cultural Psychology, 6,* 4–87.

Wu, S., & Keysar, B. (2007). Cultural effects on perspective taking. *Psychological Science, 18,* 600–606.

Yuki, M., Maddux, W. W., & Masuda, T. (2007). Are the windows to the soul the same in the East and West? Cultural differences in using the eyes and mouth as cues to recognize emotions in Japan and the United States. *Journal of Experimental Social Psychology, 43,* 303–311.

Yuki, M., Schug, J. R., Horikawa, H., Takemura, K., Sato, K., Yokota, K., & Kamaya, K. (2008). *Development of a scale to measure perceptions of relational mobility in society.* Unpublished manuscript, Hokkaido University.

Zhang, R., & Li, L. M. W. (2014). The acculturation of relational mobility: An investigation of Asian Canadians. *Journal of Cross-Cultural Psychology, 45,* 1390–1410.

Zhang, S., Morris, M. W., Cheng, C.-Y., & Yap, A. J. (2013). Heritage-culture images disrupts immigrants' second-language processing through triggering first-language interference. *Proceedings of the National Academy of Sciences, 110,* 11272–11277.

Zimmermann, J., & Neyer, F. J. (2013). Do we become a different person when hitting the road? Personality development of sojourners. *Journal of Personality and Social Psychology, 105,* 515–530.

Chapter 18

Health, Stress, and Coping

Theodore F. Robles

Jim works at a tech company, and he just had a major argument with a co-worker over their company's diversity policies. To help him manage his anger, Jim steps outside and smokes a cigarette (Baker, Brandon, & Chassin, 2004). The nicotine in that cigarette contributes to changes in his mesolimbic dopaminergic system that furthers his dependence on nicotine, and the cancer-causing compounds in cigarette smoke cause molecular changes to cells throughout his body that, over time, increase the chances that he could develop lung cancer or cardiovascular disease.

This example highlights several key points. First, health is inherently social. Jim's argument with his co-worker increased the probability that he would become upset and subsequently smoke to reduce his negative emotions. Second, health is inherently biopsychosocial (Engel, 1977), involving the interplay between biological, social, and psychological factors. Nicotine from previous smoking experiences caused changes to reward circuits in Jim's brain, such as the mesolimbic dopaminergic system. Those changes increased the likelihood that Jim uses smoking as a strategy to reduce negative emotions, thus exposing cells in his body to cancer-promoting molecular changes.

This chapter focuses on health, stress, coping, and health behaviors, which constitute the major intersections between health and social psychology. Readers interested in learning more about connections between health and substantive areas within social psychology and health can turn to a review by Klein, Shepperd, Suls, Rothman, and Croyle (2014) and a special issue of *Health Psychology* on theoretical innovations in social and personality psychology and their implications for health edited by Klein, Rothman, and Cameron (2013). Both reviews note that the strong experimental tradition within social psychology is in line with recent shifts in biomedical research that favor incorporating basic experimental research as a testing ground for interventions. This "experimental medicine" approach draws on laboratory studies that target plausible mechanisms of behavior (or biological change) to home in on intervention targets that can be deployed in later intervention studies (Riddle & Science of Behavior Change Working Group, 2015). Thus, a theme throughout this chapter is that social psychology is valuable in furthering experimental medicine efforts to refine and effectively target interventions to improve public health. But before continuing, this chapter must answer a key question . . .

What Is Health and How Should It Be Measured?

One widely cited definition is the half-century-old World Health Organization (2006) definition that health is "a state of complete physical, mental, and social well-being and not merely the absence of disease or infirmity" (p. 1; for more nuanced discussion of this definition, see Huber et al., 2011). Health involves the ability to maintain physical, social, and mental functioning in the face of internal (i.e., disease states) and external changes (i.e., stressful life event). What "functioning" is and how to measure it poses a major challenge for health psychology research because biopsychosocial models of health and illness emphasize the importance of measurement at multiple levels. In addition, operationally defining health and health-related constructs is critical for applied settings including public health and medicine, where measurement is intimately tied with health care decision-making at the level of standards of care, individual practitioners, and patients. Thus, determining what types of measures are clinically relevant for diagnostic, prognostic, and treatment decision-making is of paramount importance.

Fortunately, there appears to be triangulation around approaches to defining and measuring health. In 2001, the National Institutes of Health (NIH) Biomarkers Definitions Working Group distinguished between *clinical endpoints* and *surrogate endpoints,* for the purposes of regulating approval of biomedical treatments. Consistent with the functioning-related definitions of health previously described, clinical endpoints are considered the "most credible characteristics used in the assessment of the benefits and risks of a therapeutic intervention in randomized clinical trials" and constitute "how a patient feels, functions, or survives" (Biomarkers Definitions Working Group, 2001, p. 91). That definition can include patient-reported outcome measures like health-related quality-of-life (Cella et al., 2007), objective ratings of physical function or observed events like hospitalization and mortality. Importantly, clinical endpoints are directly relevant to healthcare providers and patients, and increased recognition of the importance of patient-reported outcomes opens the door for social psychologists to incorporate such measures in research.

In both medicine and social psychology there has been considerable inclusion of biological measures (biomarkers) in research. The nonself-report nature of those measures, their ease of collection (particularly in saliva), and their direct links to biology have made biomarkers highly appealing. Some biomarkers have direct health relevance in that the evidence base suggests they can "potentially substitute for a clinical endpoint in clinical trials" (Biomarker Definitions Working Group, 2001, p. 91). Such *surrogate endpoints* like cholesterol levels or blood pressure have value because they can identify early indicators of benefit or harm in clinical trials when clinical endpoints like cancer recurrence or death may take years to emerge (Biomarkers Definitions Working Group, 2001). However, most of the biomarkers that have been examined in social/health psychology research are *not* surrogate endpoints. Instead, they are better described as *biological mediators* that explain links between psychosocial factors and underlying biological processes of disease (Miller, Chen, & Cole, 2009) but would not, in and of themselves, be considered a substitute for clinical endpoints. In other words, those biomarkers should not be construed as measures of health. Finally, just like any other type of measurement, objective biomarkers are often used as imperfect indicators of constructs like "stress," "inflammation," or "health," and just like any other psychological measure, attention to theory, reliability, and validity are critical. Objective measures are by no means perfect measures of any construct, despite their objectiveness. In addition, reverse inferences like "people with higher cortisol levels are more stressed" are tempting but are ultimately incorrect and ill-advised (Cacioppo & Tassinary, 1990) for reasons that are described in the next section. Thus, researchers interested in incorporating biomarkers into research should develop close collaborations with biomarker content experts and be well-informed about current theory related to biomarkers of interest. As discussed in the next section, ascribing meaning to stress biomarkers has been particularly problematic.

What Is Stress?

Consider this common sequence: (a) "something bad" happens to you, and (b) you respond to that "something bad" with physiological, cognitive, and emotional changes that are under conscious and nonconscious control. Which one should be considered *stress*: (a), (b), or both? Can measuring (b) inform us as to whether and what kind of (a) happened?

In many ways the "original sin" of stress research is that the word *stress* is used colloquially and scientifically to refer to (a), (b), or both, creating significant challenges for theory, measurement, applications, and communication among researchers and with the public. Moreover, within (b), *stress* has been used to exclusively refer to physiological (Selye, 1955), cognitive, and emotional changes (Lazarus & Folkman, 1984), contributing to expectations that changes in these different channels should meaningfully covary when they often, perhaps normatively, do not covary. Thus, this section will avoid use of the singular term *stress* as much as possible and will differentiate concepts (a), (b), and concepts within (b).

Theoretical Frameworks and Broad Conceptual Considerations

The predominant psychological framework used to conceptualize stress concepts (a) and (b) is the transactional model of stress and coping outlined by Lazarus and Folkman (1984). In that model, individuals are exposed to events and interpret the meaning of those events (appraisals), and cognitive, emotional, and physiological responses to those events follow from those interpretations. This conceptualization recognizes the dynamic interaction between situations and individual differences in appraisals in determining how individuals adapt to events. For instance, being fired from a job can be appraised as a drastic harm to personal, social, and financial well-being, leading to depression and anxiety. The same event could also be appraised as an opportunity to pursue new personal, social, and work interests, leading to benefits for psychological well-being. While these distinctions have been present in stress research for three decades, conflating situations, appraisals, and responses in conceptualization and measurement continues to be a problem. Moreover, the time course of situations leading to interpretations and responses is often rapid, and with greater understanding of the role of nonconscious cognitive, affective, and physiological processes, temporally sequencing appraisals as taking place before and determining responses is problematic (Moors, Ellsworth, Scherer, & Frijda, 2013). Thus, this chapter adopts the distinction described by Harkness and Monroe (2016) between stress exposures (the situation; often described as stressors) and stress responses—that is, everything in (b)—where appraisals are one of many channels through which the organism responds to exposures.

Another key consideration is the duration and course of exposures and responses. A central theme in research on the health impacts of stress exposures is that psychological and physiological responses to stress exposures are evolutionarily programmed to help organisms engage with the situation or disengage from the situation to maintain survival; the highest intensity responses would be considered fight or flight, respectively. The adaptations broadly involve heightened vigilance to psychological and physical threats across numerous functions and systems (McEwen 1998; Robles & Carroll, 2011). Psychological, physiological, and behavioral responses to events that resolve within a short amount of time (minutes to weeks) and have a clear onset and offset within that duration could generally be viewed as adaptive, as long as those responses do not cause immediate harm to the self or others. On the other hand, stress exposures (and their subsequent activation of responses) that transpire over long durations (months to years), and/or where the course is unremitting lead to changes in stress-responsive biological systems as well as behavior (coping) that have deleterious health consequences over the long term (McEwen 1998). Accordingly, understanding the impact of *chronic stressors* (exposures and/or responses) like poverty, discrimination, and living with a chronic illness (for patients and caregivers) are major topics in health psychology (Schneiderman, Ironson, & Siegel, 2004). In addition, such work is highly informed by when in the life course such exposures take place. For example, stress exposures that take place in early childhood may program the neurobiology and immunology of the stress response in ways that impact health throughout the life course (Miller, Chen, & Parker, 2011).

Exposures

Stress exposures can be manipulated experimentally, measured via interview, self-report, or selected-for in assembling a sample (e.g., recruiting caregivers for a family member with chronic illness or recruiting people who experienced a specific event like a terrorist attack). Current approaches to measuring exposures involve distinguishing among daily occurrences or hassles, discrete events, and chronic difficulties (Harkness & Monroe, 2016). Approaches to measuring exposures vary along many dimensions, including degree of participant and investigator burden (in terms of training, time, and cost); who defines and rates severity of exposure (participant vs. researchers); how well precise dating, duration, time course, and event sequencing can be ascertained; and whether ratings can be standardized across raters. Careful attention to measurement is critical, as using methods with less reliability may explain the inconsistent patterns of results in research linking stressful events to health outcomes. For example, one of the most well-known findings linking stressful events to depression is that individuals with a particular polymorphism in the promoter region of the serotonin transporter gene are more likely to develop depression following stress exposures, although this finding has also failed to replicate across multiple studies, including in meta-analytic reviews (Karg, Burmeister, Shedden, & Sen, 2011). However, Karg et al. (2011) noted that almost all the replication failures involved studies that used checklist measures of stress exposures.

Concretely, checklist approaches to assessing stress exposures have been criticized for sacrificing validity and reliability in favor of low investigator and participant burden (Harkness & Monroe, 2016). Such approaches involve having participants select exposures (e.g., divorce, personal injury or illness, change in financial state) that have happened within a particular timeframe (e.g., today, past year) from a larger list of possible exposures. Although debate persists, some scholars have argued that checklist measures of stress exposure are so problematic that having no checklist measure in a given study is preferable to including a checklist measure (Harkness & Monroe, 2016). One concern is that different people experiencing very different events, such as a mild flu compared to a heart attack, can check off the same event (personal injury or illness). Another concern is that people can provide false positives, where they indicate an event has happened when it actually has not, because of faulty recall (misremembering) or even biased recall, such as recalling more stressful events. By contrast, interview approaches that involve trained interviewers and potentially rating teams mitigate many of the validity and reliability problems that are noted in checklist measures, regardless of time frame. Newer approaches that combine detailed follow-up questions and precise dating/timing with electronic administration can help reduce participant and researcher burden in assessing daily hassles, events, and circumstances (Harkness & Monroe, 2016; Shields & Slavich, 2017).

Manipulating stress exposures in laboratory settings has been a mainstay of social and health psychology research, allowing for frequent sampling of cognitive, affective, physiological, and behavioral responses that are challenging to observe in naturalistic settings. For example, the Trier Social Stress Test, which involves performing a speech and mental arithmetic in front of a neutral audience, has been used in over 700 studies to examine changes in threat appraisals, self-reported mood, circulating hormones, cardiovascular responses, and speech-related behaviors (Campbell & Ehlert, 2012; Goodman, Janson, &

Wolf, 2017). In addition, manipulating stressor exposures in the laboratory has allowed for determining objective features of stress exposures that may have differential associations with stress responses. As previously mentioned, hundreds of studies have used laboratory stress like the Trier Social Stress Test to stimulate responses in the hypothalamic–pituitary–adrenal (HPA) axis, which is a cascade of neuroendocrine hormones that eventually leads to production of cortisol by the adrenal cortex (which sits on top of the kidneys). Cortisol plays critical roles throughout the body when faced with challenges, including increasing energy availability in the form of glucose and making the heart more sensitive to stimulation signals from the brain, and can be easily measured in saliva (Sapolsky, Romero, & Munck, 2000). Cumulative meta-analyses across over 200 studies show that laboratory stressors that involve motivated performance, uncontrollability, and the threat of social evaluation were associated with larger HPA axis responses, suggesting that social threat plays a key role in activating the HPA axis (Dickerson & Kemeny, 2004).

While the role of social threat in HPA axis activation has been corroborated in real-life exposures, such as competitive ballroom dancing (Rohleder, Beulen, Chen, Wolf, & Kirschbaum, 2007), concerns remain regarding the generalizability of other physiological responses to specific types of laboratory tasks to exposures in real life (Zanstra & Johnston, 2011). In one study, for example, 66 undergraduates went through five different laboratory stress exposures: challenging cognitive tasks, watching a six-minute clip from a suspense/horror film, giving a two-minute speech about a current stressor, and holding one's hand in ice water for one minute (Johnston, Tuomisto, & Patching, 2008). The researchers measured changes in heart rate in response to each task. Within several weeks of the laboratory stress exposures, participants were fitted with an ambulatory monitor that continuously recorded heart rate as they went through seven hours of daily activities, which included giving an oral presentation during a class. Only heart rate responses to the ice water task were correlated with variations in ambulatory heart rate during the day ($r = 0.35$), and heart rate responses to only two of the five tasks (the ice water task and using a mirror to trace a star pattern) were correlated with heart rate responses to the oral classroom presentation (*r*s between 0.27 and 0.29).

Psychological and Physiological Responses

Responses to stress exposures take place simultaneously across multiple levels, shown in Figure 18.1. First, stress exposures that originate outside the person (rather than disturbances to the organism that occur within the person, like an infection or a stroke), are encoded by sensory and perceptual inputs to the central nervous system and processed by circuits involved in affective and social-cognitive information processing (Erickson, Creswell, Verstynen, & Gianaros, 2014; Lane & Wager, 2009; Ulrich-Lai & Herman, 2009). Such circuits are implicated in evaluating the threat, safety, and reward value of stress exposures, computing degree of certainty in the environment, inferring the mental states of others, and determining the degree of fit between the current environmental state and one's motivations and goals. Moreover, those circuits also incorporate information about one's internal environment, such as blood pressure, inflammation, and energy state. For simplicity, responses to stress exposures are subdivided into three output channels: subjective experience, referring to internal cognitive/affective states; physiological, referring to stress response signals sent to the rest of the body; and behavioral, referring to externally observed behaviors that are reviewed in the subsequent section on coping. In keeping with a biopsychosocial model, both the underlying neurobiology and psychological constructs are reviewed together.

In the transactional model, external events are evaluated based on their meaning in terms of implications for one's goals and degree of fit with the environment (Lazarus & Folkman, 1984). The core evaluations are *primary appraisals*: the degree to which the event may have positive, neutral, or detrimental effects on

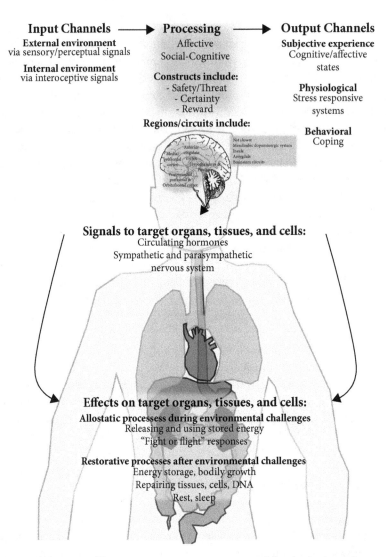

Input Channels → **Processing** → **Output Channels**

External environment
via sensory/perceptual signals

Internal environment
via interoceptive signals

Affective
Social-Cognitive

Constructs include:
- Safety/Threat
- Certainty
- Reward

Regions/circuits include:

Not shown:
Mesolimbic dopaminergic system
Insula
Amygdala
Brainstem circuits

Anterior
Medial cingulate cortex
prefrontal cortex
Hypothalamus &
Pituitary
Ventromedial
prefrontal &
Orbitofrontal cortex

Subjective experience
Cognitive/affective
states

Physiological
Stress responsive
systems

Behavioral
Coping

Signals to target organs, tissues, and cells:
Circulating hormones
Sympathetic and parasympathetic
nervous system

Effects on target organs, tissues, and cells:

Allostatic processess during environmental challenges
Releasing and using stored energy
"Fight or flight" responses

Restorative processes after environmental challenges
Energy storage, bodily growth
Repairing tissues, cells, DNA
Rest, sleep

FIGURE 18.1. Conceptual diagram of how stress exposures are processed by the brain and accompanying output channels. The top portion illustrates the different input channels that relay information about the external and internal environment, the types of processing that takes place and associated constructs and neural regions/circuits, and the output channels that constitute stress responses. The middle and bottom portion illustrate the types of signals sent by the brain to the rest of the body and a conceptual summary of their effects on target organs, tissues, and cells.

personal well-being. Appraisals of detrimental effects could include damage already done (harm), potential future damage (threat), or the possible harm/threat coupled with potential benefits and growth given sufficient resources (challenge). Research linking appraisals to neurobiology has focused on paradigms that elicit fear, such as threat of electric shock, and identified regions within the amygdala, dorsal anterior cingulate, and dorsomedial prefrontal cortex in threat appraisal-related phenomena including catastrophizing and worry (Kalisch & Gerlicher, 2014). Other regions involved in primary appraisal processes include insular cortex, which processes representations of subjective affective states (Singer, Critchley, & Preuschoff, 2009), and ventromedial prefrontal cortex, which is implicated in processing the affective meaning of external events (Roy, Shohamy, & Wager, 2012).

Secondary appraisals refer to the individual's assessment of the abilities and resources that can be used to maintain functioning during the stress exposure (Lazarus & Folkman, 1984). Abilities refer to skills and available strategies, and resources refer to personal assets that have developed over time and that exist both internally and externally. Internal resources can be protective during stress exposures, such as high self-esteem, perceived mastery, and optimism; or detrimental, such as a high level of negative affectivity (Taylor & Stanton, 2007). External resources include socioeconomic status and social resources, the latter of which is described in the subsequent section on coping. As noted by Taylor and Stanton (2007), high coping resources may be associated with less activation in the previously described threat-related regions or greater activation of regions that can downregulate responses in threat-related regions, such as the ventrolateral prefrontal cortex.

The neural circuitry described thus far and shown in Figure 18.1 overlaps with circuits that govern the signals that are transmitted to the rest of the body though paths that include circulating hormones (i.e., the HPA axis and other endocrine axes) and the sympathetic and parasympathetic nervous systems (Gianaros & Hackman, 2013). Signals from the brain to peripheral target tissues and organs like the heart, liver, skin, lymph nodes, and endocrine glands can be transmitted quickly (on the order of milliseconds) through sympathetic and parasympathetic nerves or more slowly (on the order of seconds to minutes) through endocrine hormones including adrenocorticotropic hormone, oxytocin, or follicle stimulating hormone (Carter, 2014; Ulrich-Lai & Herman, 2009). Once signals reach target organs, they initiate effects on target organs such as modulating heart rate, stimulating sweating, stimulating glucose release, and secreting additional hormones (e.g., cortisol, androgens, estrogens) that have effects on target organs throughout the body and altering the function of immune cells.

Physiological responses to stress exposures can be broadly classified as allostatic—changing physiological "set points" to help the organism survive during changes in the environment (McEwen 1998; Robles & Carroll, 2011)—or restorative, which respond after environmental challenges have abated to restore and repair the organism. Canonical allostatic processes include acute increases in sympathetic nervous system and HPA axis activity during stress exposures, and restorative processes include energy storage and growth-related activities, repair (from wounds all the way to the level of DNA), and sleep, which organizes restorative processes throughout the body (Robles & Carroll, 2011). Ultimately, the biological processes described in Figure 18.1 may explain how psychosocial factors influence health and could be potential candidate outcomes in experimental medicine research and targets for interventions.

Stress responses across the three output channels described in Figure 18.1 unfold over multiple timeframes, from milliseconds to minutes to hours. Unfortunately, the "original sin" of stress research combined with the inherent challenges of measuring stress responses frequently leads to assuming coherence or a high degree of correlation between stress responses across output channels. Drawing from the opening example, a common assumption is that if Jim's blood pressure and cortisol levels are elevated during his argument with a co-worker, he will also report high self-reported appraisals of stress ("I feel stressed") or negative emotions, like anxiety or anger. However, the picture is much more complicated; for example, in a systematic review of studies using the Trier Social Stress Test and similar exposures, self-reported negative emotional responses to the stress exposure were correlated with cortisol and cardiovascular responses in roughly 25% of studies (Campbell & Ehlert, 2012). In studies that showed statistically significant correlations between emotional and physiological responses, the degree of correlation was modest (*r*s between 0.3 and 0.5).

Assuming coherence between stress response output channels can lead to superficial reverse inferences—inferring stress exposures from physiological stress responses, which runs counter to both formal inference principles (Cacioppo & Tassinary, 1990) and the actual architecture of the neural circuitry that regulates stress responses. Different stress response channels are subject to different degrees of modulation and processing at multiple levels (Ulrich-Lai & Herman, 2009). Thus, responses in a particular channel, such as affective experience or skin conductance, result from multiple stages of processing that incorporate top–down information about the situation and bottom–up information about physical states (like pain).

Behavioral Responses: Coping

Coping broadly refers to how individuals adapt to changes in the environment, both internally (in terms of cognitive and affective changes) and in their externally observed behavior (Skinner, Edge, Altman, & Sherwood, 2003; Taylor & Stanton, 2007). One of the main challenges in theory and research on coping is that any behavior that is causally related to the stressful event (in that it would not have occurred had it not been for the event) is an instance of coping. While the possible responses to a given stressful event are not infinite (flying and turning invisible are not options when faced with a stress exposure), they are numerous, and this has led to a proliferation of possible categorizations. The most concrete demonstration of this proliferation is from a comprehensive review of coping and its underlying structure by Skinner et al. (2003, Table 4) which lists 15 different classification systems. The three most prominent types of coping categorizations are

- Based on *function* (purpose of the behavior): Problem- versus emotion-focused coping. Problem-focused coping involves strategies to change the stress exposure situation. Emotion-focused coping involves strategies that regulate emotions generated by the stress exposure.
- Based on *motivation* to move psychologically and/or physically toward (approach) or away from (avoidance) the stress exposure.
- Based on *types of action*: Changing the stress exposure situation (primary control), accommodating the exposure (secondary control), and giving up attempts to cope (relinquished control).

All three types of categorizations have been highly generative in terms of theory, measurement, and empirical contributions to our understanding of coping. At the same time, no categorization method has emerged as fully comprehensive, and no method has escaped criticisms regarding conceptual clarity.

In their comprehensive review and critique of coping classification systems, Skinner et al. (2003) proposed a hierarchical conceptualization that proceeds from lower- to higher-order categories. Specific *coping instances* like "I got the notice that my poster was accepted for presentation at a conference in three months, so now I am making a schedule for when I need to complete each part of my poster" were grouped into lower-level ways of coping (e.g., making plans), which were then grouped into higher-order families of coping (e.g., problem-solving). Finally, specific families were categorized under the highest level: adaptive processes that encompass broad sets of evolutionary functions. While multiple adaptive processes may exist, three were explicitly identified: (a) coordinating the individual's actions with contingencies in the environment, which is consistent with the poster example; (b) coordinating the individual's reliance on others with social resources in the environment; and (c) coordinating an individual's preferences with options available in the environment. Ultimately, having a conceptually clear taxonomy of how individuals respond to stress exposures aids efforts to identify what ways or families of coping, or adaptive processes more broadly, are related to effective coping outcomes in experimental studies in the laboratory and which could be incorporated in future interventions.

Coping takes place within stress exposure contexts, and, thus, the effectiveness of particular coping strategies will depend on that context (Lazarus & Folkman, 1984). *Effectiveness* is typically defined in terms of psychological well-being (low distress), behavior (activity and function returned to pre-exposure levels), and degree of fit with changes in the environment (Taylor & Stanton, 2007). Importantly, effectiveness or outcome measures must be disentangled from coping measures to avoid confounding ways of coping with outcomes. One example is the overlap of psychological distress items (e.g., "I feel restless or more wound up than usual") with emotion-focused coping items (e.g., "I become very tense"), which led to preliminary conclusions that engaging in emotion-focused coping was normatively related to greater psychological distress (Austenfeld & Stanton, 2004). Removing overlapping items allowed for greater insight into the value of emotion-approach coping for psychological and physical adjustment in chronic illness.

In general, the field now has evidence that different families of coping can be adaptive depending on the context and that flexibility in deploying strategies is beneficial (Bonanno, Romero, & Klein, 2015). For instance, while avoidance is generally maladaptive over the long term for psychological and physical health, it can be protective during short-term, uncontrollable stressors like waiting to hear about a highly self-relevant outcome like college admissions (Taylor & Stanton, 2007). One example is receiving a questionable outcome during screening mammograms (low-dose X-ray pictures to look for signs of breast cancer in women without breast symptoms or problems); such screenings are not 100% accurate, and the rate of screening showing there is cancer when, in fact, there is no cancer (false-positive results) after 10 yearly mammograms is around 50% to 60% (Susan G. Komen', 2017). A woman who receives a questionable screening result must go through additional testing to definitively determine whether she has breast cancer. Thus, the time between the initial mammography screening and finding out results of additional test is highly uncertain, including the potential for being diagnosed with breast cancer. In a study of 98 women in this exact circumstance, women who reported higher levels of cognitive avoidance (items included "I tried to forget the whole thing") after receiving a questionable screening mammogram result showed lower anxiety symptoms four weeks later, after they were notified that they tested negative for breast cancer (Heckman et al., 2004).

Interpersonal Influences on the Development of Individual Differences in Coping

Life histories play key roles in modifying how people adapt in the face of stress exposures. Greater conflict and less support in the family environment is related to greater negative emotional reactivity to stress exposures (Repetti, Robles, & Reynolds, 2011; Repetti, Taylor, & Seeman, 2002). Children in those environments exhibit less effective coping strategies, such as using aggression in response to daily stress exposures, which may then develop over time into behavioral, cognitive, and affective components of hostility, depression, and loneliness later in adulthood (Miller et al., 2011). In addition, stressful family environments can contribute to youth turning to unhealthy behaviors (substance use, risky sexual behavior, unhealthy eating) as a method of coping with stress exposures and regulating emotion, which may then persist into adulthood (Miller et al., 2011; Repetti et al., 2011).

Life histories also play a role in the development of the attachment behavioral system, which promotes safety, survival, and security by regulating closeness to nurturing caregivers (ideally) in childhood (e.g., Bowlby, 1979/2005). According to attachment theory (see Chapter 10), early family environments contribute to mental representations of the self and others (i.e., working models) that influence the development of the attachment system and, in particular, how individuals relate to close others (e.g., caregivers, romantic partners). During stress exposures, we tend to seek close others as a safe haven for support and comfort, and during more certain times, the actual or symbolic presence of close others can provide a secure base from which to explore new environments and pursue goals.

Over time, individual differences in attachment orientations develop through interactions with the early environment and with close others throughout life, which how individuals view others (as trustworthy or not), the self (as being worthy of closeness; desired degree of overlap between self and other), and how individual regulate their emotions. Those individual differences are conceptualized along two dimensions: anxiety and avoidance (see Chapter 10). The anxiety dimension involves degree of concern about rejection and abandonment by close others, and the avoidance dimension involves degree of comfort with being close to others.

In the context of coping, individuals who are characterized by low anxiety and avoidance (described as securely attached) have greater confidence in the responsiveness of their attachment figures, turn to those figures for help, and in doing so may adopt more approach-focused strategies including both problem-focused and emotional-approach coping (Simpson & Rholes, 2012). Individuals with high anxious attachment, being less certain about having responsive attachment figures, monitor those relationships for signs of threat. In doing so, they may turn to hyperactivating strategies (Mikulincer, Shaver, & Pereg, 2003) that serve the goal of coordinating the individual's reliance on others with social resources in the environment but do so in a manner that Skinner et al. (2003) might characterize as maladaptive help-seeking such as complaining or whining or seeking reassurance in a hostile, angry way. Individuals with avoidant attachment, characterized by a lack of comfort with closeness and greater preference for independence in relationships, may cope with stressful exposures by maintaining distance from close others through avoidance or defensiveness.

Individual differences in attachment orientations clearly have origins that stem from early life interpersonal experiences. Likewise, characteristics that coping researchers view as intrapersonal, like optimism, a sense of mastery or control over the environment, and self-esteem, also stem from early experiences. Having more intrapersonal resources is generally protective and is related to more effective coping, whereas greater negative affectivity is a risk factor for maladaptive coping (Taylor & Stanton, 2007).

Interpersonal Modifiers

The importance of the attachment behavioral system for coping suggests that social relationships are a critical modifier of the links between stress exposures and responses. Social relationships can be conceptualized in multiple ways (Cohen, Underwood, & Gottlieb, 2000; Uchino, 2003). The actual structure of social networks in terms of number of contacts and the types of roles (co-worker, friend, neighbor, etc.) constitute one's degree of *social integration*. The functions people provide to one another, including tangible, emotional, and informational support, and the degree to which those functions match or are responsive to an individual's needs are also key determinants of how social relationships benefit others. In addition, beliefs and attitudes about one's social network play key roles in modifying the effects of stress exposures on coping, including how much an individual believes his or her social network is available to him or her during times of need (i.e., perceived available social support); views people in his or her network as understanding, validating, and caring (*perceived responsiveness*); and views people as close or distant (*closeness*). In the context of coping theory and research, much of the work has focused on how individuals coordinate reliance on others with social resources that are available (i.e., support seeking) and its association with outcomes like psychological distress (Skinner et al., 2003). At the same time, the structure and functions of social networks and interactions between people during support exchanges may also influence how individuals deploy specific ways of coping.

The aforementioned neural circuits involved in affective, cognitive, and social information processing evolved in a social context, and social baseline theory proposes that the social context is the expected default in which the brain functions (Coan & Sbarra, 2015). The primary implication is that the brain's true baseline state is when individuals are in proximity to others (i.e., social resources), and that proximity has benefits for individuals—namely, that any risks to safety are distributed among others and that any efforts needed to adapt to the environment are shared among others. Consequently, the degree of energy used by the brain and effort expended by the individual to adapt to stress exposures is less in the context of social resources, and the more that those social resources are indeed beneficial (i.e., trusted, closer, more responsive), the more benefit to the individual. Outside of those social contexts, such as during separation or isolation, our ability to cope with stress exposures is diminished because we are no longer in the default state. One corollary phenomenon related to social baseline theory is communal coping, which encompasses both the degree to which a stress exposure is appraised as shared between more than one person and the degree to which multiple individuals work together to adapt to the stress exposure (Lyons, Mickelson, Sullivan, & Coyne, 1998). Communal coping has been of particular interest in couples where one partner is facing a chronic illness (Berg & Upchurch, 2007). For example, among couples in which one partner has type 2 diabetes, higher self-reported communal coping (whether by questionnaire, daily diary, or based on greater "we-language" use) is related to lower patient psychological distress and better medication adherence (reviewed in Helgeson, Jakubiak, Van Vleet, & Zajdel, 2017). Taken together, the structure of social networks in terms of their availability and closeness as well as their support functions could be considered the default mode through which the brain and individuals adapt to stress exposures by involving others in the adaptation process.

One mechanism through which social relationships can influence coping is through interpersonal influences on one's emotion regulation (Marroquin, 2011; Reeck, Ames, & Ochsner, 2016). While emotion regulation through strategies that include situation selection/modification, attention deployment, cognitive changes (e.g., reappraisal), and response modulation have been conceptualized as intraindividual processes (Gross, 2015), other people can play key roles in influencing those emotion regulation processes (Reeck et al., 2016). As previously described, social baseline theory suggests that emotion regulation attempts may be less energetically costly in the presence of others. Thus, even the mere presence of a familiar person can alter attention deployment (e.g., distraction) or modulate how individuals experience or express negative emotion. Those in-the-moment influences may then influence the strategies that are used to adapt to the stress exposure. Surprisingly, work on the social and interpersonal regulation is a relatively new area of inquiry but has implications across a number of areas within social psychology including implications for health (Marroquin, 2011).

Finally, while social relationships have been described as resources that can promote adaptive coping, our relationships can also function as risk factors for maladaptive coping. Effective support during times of need, companionship during times of less need, and social control over health behaviors can all promote effective coping during stress exposures (Rook, 2015), although the actual empirical evidence for some effects, like reducing distress, remains elusive (Uchino, Bowen, Carlisle, & Birmingham, 2012). In contrast, conflict with others, having insensitive and nonresponsive support, and having network members that interfere with accomplishing goals may add additional stress exposures and thwart attempts to cope with pre-existing exposures (Brooks & Dunkel Schetter, 2011).

Health Behaviors

The major public health challenges of the 21st century, including obesity, opioid dependence, and sleep deprivation share one major common feature: knowledge and awareness of the problems, and even what to do to prevent such problems, is not enough to motivate most people to adopt healthy behaviors. Indeed, most of the behaviors reviewed in the following discussion have generally accepted and widely promulgated guidelines for individuals. Unfortunately, despite having widely accepted guidelines, achieving those behavior targets has been a significant public health challenge. For example, the *Healthy People 2010* goal for fruit consumption was to increase the percent of individuals aged two and up consuming at least two daily servings of fruit from the mid-1990s baseline of 39% to 75% by the mid 2000s. Ultimately, there was no change over 10 years—40% met the fruit consumption goal in the mid-2000s. That many people know what to do, but are not maintaining such behaviors, clearly suggests the need for scientists with expertise in understanding and changing cognitions, emotions, and behavior and the role of the social environment in influencing behavior. Much of the gap between knowledge/awareness and behavior is filled with processes and constructs that are the bread-and-butter of social psychology. This section highlights key processes and constructs and points out behaviors that may be worth incorporating into social psychology research.

Health-Compromising Behaviors: Substance Dependence and Unhealthy Eating

How people start, continue, and have difficulty stopping health-compromising behaviors like substance use and health eating has been a major focus of psychology research, due in part to psychological and neurobiological overlap (Volkow, Wang, Tomasi, & Baler, 2013). Substances where continued use can lead to dependence, including tolerance (requiring greater doses to achieve desired effects) and withdrawal (unpleasant symptoms when not taking a substance) include nicotine, alcohol, opiates, and other drugs (American Psychiatric Association, 2013). While nicotine use has declined significantly due to population- and community-level policy changes (e.g., advertising and indoor/outdoor smoking bans, cigarette taxes; Cummings, Fong, & Borland, 2009), among individuals who are nicotine dependent, only 1 out of every 10 people that attempt to quit on their own is successful (Schlam & Baker, 2013). At the same time, psychological interventions that incorporate skills training to cope with cessation-related challenges and social support are effective in increasing the likelihood of sustained abstinence (Schlam & Baker, 2013). Newer efforts to improve the efficacy of psychosocial interventions for nicotine dependence have focused on using insights from laboratory experiments to build empirically informed interventions that can then be tested in the field (Collins et al., 2011). More generally, efforts to understand and intervene in substance dependence has contributed to our understanding of basic social psychological processes, including dual-process models of cognition, reward processing, self-regulation, decision-making, and stress and coping (Klein et al., 2013, 2014).

More recent health-compromising behavior challenges include unhealthy eating and the opioid epidemic (Kolodny et al., 2015; Volkow et al., 2013). The last 30 years have seen considerable interest in the social psychology of unhealthy eating (Mann, Tomiyama, & Ward, 2015). At the same time, concerns have been raised about the validity of weight status (i.e., obesity) as a risk factor for health, especially when compared to surrogate markers of cardiometabolic health (e.g., fasting glucose, blood pressure). Moreover, efforts to reduce overweight/obesity through negative messaging (i.e., "fat-shaming") fuel already pre-existing stigma against overweight individuals, leading to prejudice, discrimination, and internalized negative emotions like shame that may short-circuit attempts to engage in healthy eating and physical activity (regardless of whether weight reduction is the end goal; Hunger, Major, Blodorn, & Miller, 2015).

Similar to substance dependence, understanding psychological influences on eating provides a highly relevant context for understanding fundamental social psychological processes. Research on the role of food advertising and placement and availability in the environment (e.g., eye-level, labeling) is informed by dual-process models of cognition (Gearhardt et al., 2012). Neural systems regulating the hedonic drive for food have considerable overlap with other social–cognitive–affective processes including reward learning, associating food with other cues (e.g., stress regulation via "comfort eating," eating with others), and decision-making (Volkow et al., 2013). Social psychologists working in health psychology have encouraged others in their field to move into arenas of intervention and prevention, including helping to identify optimal persuasion techniques to aid with primary prevention, and develop theoretically driven and easily scalable interventions to shift food preferences toward those that benefit long-term health and environmental sustainability (Rothman et al., 2015).

While the opioid epidemic is often considered more in the professional realm of clinical psychology, psychiatry, and public health, embedded within the epidemic are many basic and applied research questions of relevance to social psychologists. For example, substance dependence is a highly stigmatized behavior, and stigma from friends, family, health providers, and the community can derail intervention efforts (Major, Mendes, & Dovidio, 2013).

Health-Promoting Behaviors

Healthy eating (Katz & Meller, 2014), getting regular moderate to vigorous physical activity (Haskell et al., 2007), at least seven hours of sleep per night (for adults; Watson et al., 2015), and adhering to health provider recommendations are all health-promoting behaviors that have several things in common. Individuals who perform those behaviors consistently show better quality of life, reduced risk of chronic illness, and reduced risk of mortality. While the specific macronutrient composition of the "ideal diet" (how much fat, protein, and carbohydrates) will be disputed in perpetuity, one common theme across all healthy diets is an emphasis on maximizing the proportion of fruit and vegetable intake relative to other foods ("Mostly plants;" Katz & Meller, 2014). Efforts have focused on modifying availability of plant foods through placement and subsidizing, as well as increasing the hedonic value of plant foods through advertising and visual messaging (Mann et al., 2015). Many of these approaches take advantage of dual-process models of cognition by delivering interventions that do not require significant cognitive effort, such as modifying default options (i.e., having plant-based protein sources the predominant protein source in cafeterias or mandatory placement of vegetables in school lunches).

Similar to increasing plant food consumption, efforts to understand social psychological levers to increase physical activity have more recently involved making situational modifications: changing the built physical environment and modifying default options (Bauman et al., 2012). Recognizing that conscious self-regulatory processes may not lead people to take the stairs instead of elevators, researchers in this arena have been examining the effectiveness of point-of-decision prompts (i.e., elevator signage advertising a free workout by taking the stairs) and ways to change social norms to promote what was previously considered nonnormative physical activity, such as exercise breaks in meetings or classes. Understanding the types of environmental modifications that promote physical activity, and the psychological processes that explain and predict uptake and maintenance of physical activity in the context of those modifications, represents an excellent opportunity for social psychologists to further evidence that situations shape behavior. One lever that will likely play an important role is social influence (Scarapicchia, Amireault, Faulkner, & Sabiston, 2017; also see Chapter 7). For instance, participating in moderate to vigorous activity with others may amplify the hedonic (e.g., making physical activity feel less strenuous combined with opportunities for social interaction) and even eudaimonic rewards of physical activity (e.g., working with others to build or repair homes for disadvantaged people or sorting foodstuffs at a food bank).

Sleep health is characterized by "subjective satisfaction, appropriate timing, adequate duration, high efficiency, and sustained alertness during waking hours" (Buysse, 2014, p. 12). Poor sleep health, broadly speaking, is related to worse physical and mental health including risk for chronic illnesses like cardiovascular disease, diabetes, and depression as well as mortality. Sleep researchers have long recognized the roles of attitudes and beliefs about sleep, the built environment (ranging from bedroom furnishing to proximity to outside noise), and self-regulatory capacity (most notably, emotion regulation) in contributing to sleep health. More recently, the fact that the majority of adults sleep with another person in the same bed has led to numerous studies combining relationship science with sleep research (Troxel, Robles, Hall, & Buysse, 2007). Moreover, strained intergroup relations, characterized by stereotyping, stigma, and discrimination, have been linked to poor sleep health (Slopen, Lewis, & Williams, 2016). Sleep health can be measured through brief self-reports, as well as objective measures like actigraphy (inferring sleep-related variables by using wearable physical activity monitors), and is excellent low-hanging fruit for social psychologists who want to expand into examining health outcomes.

The major health burdens of the 21st century are chronic illnesses such as cardiovascular disease, diabetes, and many cancers. At this particular time, there are no cures for those conditions, and all require regular management through the aforementioned health-promoting behaviors and regular medication use. Half of adults in the United States have a chronic illness (Centers for Disease Control and Prevention, 2017), and, not surprisingly, the most frequently prescribed medications in the world target those chronic illnesses. Most of those medications must be taken daily, but it is widely recognized that around three out of every five individuals are not taking medications according to provider recommendations (nonadherent; Osterberg & Blaschke, 2005). Broadly speaking, adherence is determined by interactions among four parties: the healthcare system, providers (i.e., physicians, nurse practitioners), patients, and the drug itself (effects on reducing symptoms and side effects). Fundamental social psychological processes, including attitudes and beliefs, stereotypes and prejudice in patient–provider interactions, and self-regulation, play critical roles for all of the parties involved (even the drug itself, as it may have effects on patient self-regulatory capacity, as well as on attitudes and beliefs about one's self, others, and the drug!). The primary challenge is assessing adherence, as objective measures are considered the gold standard compared to self-report (Osterberg & Blaschke, 2005), but 21st century technologies such as Bluetooth-enabled pill boxes are making objective monitoring of medication adherence more accessible than at any point in the history of biomedical science.

Conceptual Frameworks and Integration

Numerous frameworks have been advanced to understand, predict, and change health behaviors. Concretely, Michie and colleagues (2014) described 83 theories developed over 50 years, with over 1,000 constructs among those theories that have been developed in the context of health behaviors and health behavior change. The proliferation of theoretical frameworks and constructs poses a major challenge to health behavior research, as many new terms describe similar constructs, and multiple measures exist for a given construct. Highlighted in the following discussion are recent attempts to identify commonalities among different health behavior theories, associated constructs and targets, and behavior-change techniques based on expert consensus and analysis (Sheeran, Klein, & Rothman, 2017). First, numerous health behavior theories implicate cognitions about a health threat, such as perceptions of risk for future health problems and perceived severity of those problems, in modifying the likelihood of performing a health behavior. In addition, cognitions about the health behavior, such as descriptive norms (beliefs about how frequently a behavior occurs) like "I think most graduate students sleep less than seven hours per night" play a role in influencing behavior. More recent conceptualizations incorporating dual-process models of cognition include the role of conscious volitional factors that promote motivation or action, such as the degree to which thinking and concentration are impaired by fatigue, and the role of implicit cognition. Health-relevant examples of implicit cognition include attentional bias, implicit attitudes about the health threat or behavior, and approach/avoidance goals.

In addition to constructs and associated treatment targets, numerous intervention techniques have been developed and tested in the health behavior change literature. The proliferation of techniques has historically been a challenge for integration, replication, and dissemination. However, recent attempts at developing taxonomies for health behavior intervention techniques have made significant inroads. To date, the most recent widely endorsed taxonomy is the Behavior Change Technique Taxonomy (v1) developed by experts in the United Kingdom, with input from dozens of international experts on health behavior change (Michie et al., 2013). Table 18.1 shows the 16 clusters of intervention techniques and

TABLE 18.1   Behavior Change Technique Taxonomy Groupings

Behavior Change Technique Taxonomy (v1) Grouping	Example Behavior Change Techniques
1. Goals and planning	Setting goals, problem-solving, behavioral contracts
2. Feedback and monitoring	Self-monitoring behavior, getting feedback on self-monitoring
3. Social support	Practical and/or emotional support
4. Shaping knowledge	Learning how to perform behavior, conducting behavioral experiments
5. Natural consequences	Learning about consequences of changing/not changing behavior
6. Comparison of behavior	Social comparisons, demonstrating behavior in front of others
7. Associations	Introduce cues or prompts for behavior, discriminative stimuli; associative learning-based techniques
8. Repetition and substitution	Practice/rehearse behavior repeatedly
9. Comparison of outcomes	Weighing pros and cons of changing behavior, imagine future outcomes
10. Reward and threat	Material incentives, positive reinforcement, future punishment
11. Regulation	Pharmacological treatment, stress management
12. Antecedents	Changing physical, social environment
13. Identity	Framing/reframing behavior, activating valued self-identities
14. Scheduled consequences	Removal of something valued, punishment, rewarding completion of behavior
15. Self-belief	Mental rehearsal, positive self-talk, remind of past success
16. Covert learning	Imagine rewards or punishments, vicarious consequences

From "The Behavior Change Technique Taxonomy (v1) of 93 Hierarchically Clustered Techniques: Building an International Consensus for the Reporting of Behavior Change Interventions," by S. Michie, M. Richardson, M. Johnston, C. Abraham, J. Francis, W. Hardeman, . . . C. E. Wood, 2013, *Annals of Behavioral Medicine, 46,* 81–95.

examples of techniques within each cluster. Such taxonomies allow for identifying active ingredients in previously tested interventions, selecting specific techniques to test in laboratory experiments, developing interventions based on the results of experimental studies, and disseminating potentially effective techniques to practitioners. In addition, such taxonomies are included in recently developed systematic efforts to develop new interventions that are informed by theory (including theories from social psychology) and tailored to the level at which interventions might operate (e.g., individual, group, community; Michie, Atkins, & West, 2014).

Social Contexts

While performed by individuals, health behaviors are embedded in a social context and, in many cases, interdependent with the social context. People often consume alcohol, use tobacco, eat, and exercise in groups; the majority of Americans sleep with a bed-partner. Our closest social network members can influence how we behave in numerous ways; married partners often show similar health behavior patterns and partners that are initially dissimilar tend to converge over many years together (Kiecolt-Glaser & Wilson, 2017). Similarly, concordance in unhealthy behaviors like tobacco and alcohol consumption are observed between parents and children and between siblings (Smith & Christakis, 2008). Concordance in close relationships can be attributed to several factors, including assortative mating, shared resources, shared stress exposures, and social influence factors that are described in the following discussion. Accordingly, partners can be facilitators of behavior change if relationship satisfaction is high and/or health behaviors are mutually valued or shared, or partners can be obstacles to attempts to change (Fitzsimons, Finkel, vanDellen, 2015).

Extending beyond dyadic relationships, entire social networks can be a source of positive influence including support, companionship, and control, as well as negative influence including conflict, insensitivity, and interference (Rook, 2015). Accordingly, spread of health conditions related to health behaviors, such as obesity and sexually transmitted disease transmission (including HIV), have been observed in social network analyses (Smith & Christakis, 2008). At the same time, characteristics of the social network, such as the tendency for similar individuals to cluster together (Centola, 2011), or highly connected members of a social network (Kim et al., 2015) may be useful targets for intervention with the aim of increasing spread of health promoting behaviors.

There are several avenues of positive and negative influences on health behaviors (DiMatteo, 2004). Modeling involves the role that other people play in showing an individual how to perform a given behavior, demonstrating the positive and negative consequences of that behavior, and providing information about what to think about the behavior in terms of what is approved/disapproved by others (injunctive norms) and how frequently the behavior occurs (descriptive norms). Social control can occur both directly and indirectly. Direct forms involve other people explicitly communicating positive (e.g., encouragement) or negative (e.g., shaming) messages to the individual in an effort to change his or her behavior. Indirect forms involve the influence of injunctive and descriptive social norms combined with an individual's desire or obligation to behave in accordance with those norms in shaping behavior. Increasing health-compromising and reducing health-promoting behaviors often occur during stressful life events; thus, stress buffering related to social support may help reduce such maladaptive responses. Similarly, people in our social network can help enhance personal resources, including self-efficacy and self-regulatory capacity that can be used to maintain health behaviors. The flip side of stress buffering and enhancing personal resources is that social conflict, insensitivity, and interference can hinder attempts to change behavior (Brooks & Dunkel Schetter, 2011).

Putting It All Together: How to Move Your Work into the Health Arena

This chapter provided a brief overview of how to conceptualize and measure health, stress, coping, and health behaviors, with the ultimate aim of illustrating how accessible research in these domains can be to social psychologists. Readers convinced that health is social and biopsychosocial are encouraged to seek out the references in this chapter to learn more. Most important, readers are encouraged to seek out collaborators in public health, nursing, medicine, and other fields that focus on understanding and solving health problems. Incorporating health measures, particularly patient-reported outcomes like health-related quality-of-life or symptom reporting, is highly feasible. The same considerations for incorporating psychological constructs and measures apply to health-related constructs: careful attention to theory, conceptualization, and measurement as described in the What Is Health? section. Social psychologists have historically played important roles in theory and research on stress and coping, and a key future direction will be merging that work with contemporary questions and issues revolving around intergroup relations, culture, and interpersonal relationships. Finally, all the health behaviors described in this chapter are everyday observable behaviors that are subject to social psychological processes, and all represent excellent low-hanging fruit for social psychologists who want to expand into understanding how social psychological phenomena of interest can impact behavior and ultimately health.

In their review advocating for increased intersections between social psychology and health psychology/public health, Klein and colleagues (2014) wrote: "Social psychologists possess the skills and conceptual expertise to address many public health challenges. At the same time, research in a health context offers the reciprocal benefit of enriching social-psychological theories and advancing the reach, impact, and visibility of the discipline" (pp. 77–78). If health is biopsychosocial, then as Klein et al. describe, social psychologists can play key roles in public health. Doing so requires several things, including incorporating community and patient samples, engaging in multidisciplinary collaborations, including health outcomes in research, and considering applications of basic research. Fortunately, certain funders are now recognizing the importance of basic social and behavioral research (such as the Behavioral Research Program in the Division of Cancer Control and Population Sciences at the National Cancer Institute; https://cancercontrol.cancer.gov/brp/), and changes in biomedical research in the direction of experimental medicine may favor incorporating basic experimental research as a testing ground for later interventions.

Conducting social psychological science with clear public health implications and applications requires heightened attention to replicability and open science practices. The potential for research to inform interventions that may be disseminated in a for-profit manner—such as through books, workshops, and apps, as well as through policy—makes transparency in documenting potential benefits and harms for people and patients a paramount value. While major concerns about replicability in psychology and social psychology emerged during the 2010s, the alarm bells for medicine began ringing a decade earlier (Ioannidis, 2005). Thus, in addition to bringing rich theory and research methods to studying social psychological influences on health behavior, the continued development of solutions to improve replicability and foster open science in social psychology (Spellman, 2015) has much to offer health psychology, medicine, and public health.

References

American Psychiatric Association. (2013). *Diagnostic and statistical manual of mental disorders*. Arlington, VA: American Psychiatric Association.

Austenfeld, J. L., & Stanton, A. L. (2004). Coping through emotional approach: A new look at emotion, coping, and health-related outcomes. *Journal of Personality, 72*, 1335–1363.

Baker, T. B., Brandon, T. H., & Chassin, L. (2004). Motivational influences on cigarette smoking. *Annual Review of Psychology, 55*, 463–491.

Bauman, A. E., Reis, R. S., Sallis, J. F., Wells, J. C., Loos, R. J. F., & Martin, B. W. (2012). Correlates of physical activity: why are some people physically active and others not? *Lancet, 380*, 258–271.

Berg, C. A., & Upchurch, R. (2007). A developmental-contextual model of couples coping with chronic illness across the adult life span. *Psychological Bulletin, 133*, 920–954.

Biomarker Definitions Working Group. (2001). Biomarkers and surrogate endpoints: Preferred definitions and conceptual framework. *Clinical Pharmacology & Therapeutics, 69*, 89–95. doi:10.1067/mcp.2001.113989

Bonanno, G. A., Romero, S. A., & Klein, S. I. (2015). The temporal elements of psychological resilience: An integrative framework for the study of individuals, families, and communities. *Psychological Inquiry, 26*, 139–169.

Bowlby, J. (2005). *The making and breaking of affectional bonds*. London, England: Routledge Classics. (Original work published 1979)

Brooks, K. P., & Dunkel Schetter, C. (2011). Social negativity and health: Conceptual and measurement issues. *Social and Personality Psychology Compass, 5*, 904–918.

Buysse, D. J. (2014). Sleep health: Can we define it? Does it matter? *Sleep, 37*, 9–7.

Cacioppo, J. T., & Tassinary, L. G. (1990). Inferring psychological significance from physiological signals. *American Psychologist, 45*, 16–28.

Campbell, J., & Ehlert, U. (2012). Acute psychosocial stress: Does the emotional stress response correspond with physiological responses? *Psychoneuroendocrinology, 37*, 1111–1134.

Carter, C. S. (2014). Oxytocin pathways and the evolution of human behavior. *Annual Review of Psychology, 65*, 17–39.

Cella, D., Yount, S., Rothrock, N., Gershon, R., Cook, K., Reeve, B., . . . Grp, P. C. (2007). The Patient-Reported Outcomes Measurement Information System (PROMIS): Progress of an NIH roadmap cooperative group during its first two years. *Medical Care, 45*(5), S3–S11.

Centers for Disease Control and Prevention. (2018, October 24). About chronic disease. Retrieved from https://www. cdc.gov/chronicdisease/about/index.htm

Centola, D. (2011). An experimental study of homophily in the adoption of health behavior. *Science, 334,* 1269–1272.

Coan, J. A., & Sbarra, D. A. (2015). Social baseline theory: The social regulation of risk and effort. *Current Opinion in Psychology, 1*(Suppl C), 87–91.

Cohen, S., Underwood, L. G., & Gottlieb, B. H. (Eds.). (2000). *Social support measurement and intervention.* New York, NY: Oxford University Press.

Collins, L. M., Baker, T. B., Mermelstein, R. J., Piper, M. E., Jorenby, D. E., Smith, S. S., . . . Fiore, M. C. (2011). The multiphase optimization strategy for engineering effective tobacco use interventions. *Annals of Behavioral Medicine, 41,* 208–226.

Cummings, K. M., Fong, G. T., & Borland, R. (2009). Environmental Influences on tobacco use: Evidence from societal and community influences on tobacco use and dependence. *Annual Review of Clinical Psychology, 5,* 433–458.

Dickerson, S. S., & Kemeny, M. E. (2004). Acute stressors and cortisol responses: a theoretical integration and synthesis of laboratory research. *Psychological Bulletin, 130,* 355–391.

DiMatteo, M. R. (2004). Social support and patient adherence to medical treatment: A meta-analysis. *Health Psychology, 23,* 207–218.

Engel, G. L. (1977). Need for a new medical model—challenge for biomedicine. *Science, 196,* 129–136.

Erickson, K. I., Creswell, J. D., Verstynen, T. D., & Gianaros, P. J. (2014). Health neuroscience: Defining a new field. *Current Directions in Psychological Science, 23,* 446–453.

Fitzimons, G. M., Finkel, E. J., & vanDellen, M. R. (2015). Transactive goal dynamics. *Psychological Review, 122,* 648–673.

Gearhardt, A. N., Bragg, M. A., Pearl, R. L., Schvey, N. A., Roberto, C. A., & Brownell, K. D. (2012). Obesity and public policy. *Annual Review of Clinical Psychology, 8,* 405–430.

Gianaros, P. J., & Hackman, D. A. (2013). Contributions of neuroscience to the study of socioeconomic health disparities. *Psychosomatic Medicine, 75,* 610–615.

Goodman, W. K., Janson, J., & Wolf, J. M. (2017). Meta-analytical assessment of the effects of protocol variations on cortisol responses to the Trier Social Stress Test. *Psychoneuroendocrinology, 80,* 26–35.

Gross, J. J. (2015). Emotion regulation: Current status and future prospects. *Psychological Inquiry, 26,* 1–26.

Harkness, K. L., & Monroe, S. M. (2016). The assessment and measurement of adult life stress: Basic premises, operational principles, and design requirements. *Journal of Abnormal Psychology, 125,* 727–745.

Haskell, W. L., Lee, I. M., Pate, R. R., Powell, K. E., Blair, S. N., Franklin, B. A., . . . Bauman, A. (2007). Physical activity and public health—Updated recommendation for adults from the American college of sports medicine and the American heart association. *Circulation, 116,* 1081–1093.

Heckman, B. D., Fisher, E. B., Monsees, B., Merbaum, M., Ristvedt, S., & Bishop, C. (2004). Coping and anxiety in women recalled for additional diagnostic procedures following an abnormal screening mammogram. *Health Psychology, 23,* 42–48.

Helgeson, V. S., Jakubiak, B., Van Vleet, M., & Zajdel, M. (2017). Communal coping and adjustment to chronic illness: Theory update and evidence. *Personality and Social Psychology Review, 22,* 170–195.

Huber, M., Knottnerus, J. A., Green, L., Horst, H. v. d., Jadad, A. R., Kromhout, D., . . . Smid, H. (2011). How should we define health? *BMJ, 343,* d4163.

Hunger, J. M., Major, B., Blodorn, A., & Miller, C. T. (2015). Weighed down by stigma: How weight-based social identity threat contributes to weight gain and poor health. *Social and Personality Psychology Compass, 9,* 255–268.

Ioannidis, J. P. A. (2005). Why most published research findings are false. *PLoS Medicine, 2*(8), e124.

Johnston, D. W., Tuomisto, M. T., & Patching, G. R. (2008). The relationship between cardiac reactivity in the laboratory and in real life. *Health Psychology, 27,* 34–42.

Kalisch, R., & Gerlicher, A. M. V. (2014). Making a mountain out of a molehill: On the role of the rostral dorsal anterior cingulate and dorsomedial prefrontal cortex in conscious threat appraisal, catastrophizing, and worrying. *Neuroscience & Biobehavioral Reviews, 42*(Suppl C), 1–8.

Karg, K., Burmeister, M., Shedden, K., & Sen, S. (2011). The serotonin transporter promoter variant (5-httlpr), stress, and depression meta-analysis revisited: Evidence of genetic moderation. *Archives of General Psychiatry, 68,* 444–454.

Katz, D. L., & Meller, S. (2014). Can we say what diet is best for health? *Annual Review of Public Health, 35,* 83–103.

Kiecolt-Glaser, J. K., & Wilson, S. J. (2017). Lovesick: How couples' relationships influence health. *Annual Review of Clinical Psychology, 13,* 421–443.

Kim, D. A., Hwong, A. R., Stafford, D., Hughes, D. A., O'Malley, A. J., Fowler, J. H., & Christakis, N. A. (2015). Social network targeting to maximise population behaviour change: a cluster randomised controlled trial. *Lancet, 386,* 145–153.

Klein, W. M. P., Rothman, A. J., & Cameron, L. D. (2013). Theoretical innovations in social and personality psychology and implications for health: Introduction to special issue. *Health Psychology, 32,* 457–459.

Klein, W. M. P., Shepperd, J. A., Suls, J., Rothman, A. J., & Croyle, R. T. (2014). Realizing the promise of social psychology in improving public health. *Personality and Social Psychology Review, 19,* 77–92.

Kolodny, A., Courtwright, D. T., Hwang, C. S., Kreiner, P., Eadie, J. L., Clark, T. W., & Alexander, G. C. (2015). The prescription opioid and heroin crisis: A public health approach to an epidemic of addiction. *Annual Review of Public Health, 36,* 559–574.

Kottke, T. E. (2011). Medicine is a social science in its very bone and marrow. *Mayo Clinic Proceedings, 86,* 930–932.

Lane, R. D., & Wager, T. D. (2009). The new field of brain–body medicine: What have we learned and where are we headed? *Neuroimage, 47,* 1135–1140.

Lazarus, R. S., & Folkman, S. (1984). *Stress, appraisal, and coping.* New York, NY: Springer.

Lyons, R. F., Mickelson, K. D., Sullivan, M. J. L., & Coyne, J. C. (1998). Coping as a communal process. *Journal of Social and Personal Relationships, 15,* 579–605.

Major, B., Mendes, W. B., & Dovidio, J. F. (2013). Intergroup relations and health disparities: A social psychological perspective. *Health Psychology, 32,* 514–524.

Mann, T., Tomiyama, A. J., & Ward, A. (2015). Promoting public health in the context of the "obesity epidemic." *Perspectives on Psychological Science, 10,* 706–710.

Marroquin, B. (2011). Interpersonal emotion regulation as a mechanism of social support in depression. *Clinical Psychology Review, 31,* 1276–1290.

McEwen, B. S. (1998). Protective and damaging effects of stress mediators. *New England Journal of Medicine, 338,* 171–179.

Michie, S., Atkins, L., & West, R. (2014). *The behaviour change wheel: A guide to designing interventions.* London, England: Silverback.

Michie, S., Richardson, M., Johnston, M., Abraham, C., Francis, J., Hardeman, W., . . . Wood, C. E. (2013). The behavior change technique taxonomy (v1) of 93 hierarchically clustered techniques: Building an international consensus for the reporting of behavior change interventions. *Annals of Behavioral Medicine, 46,* 81–95.

Michie, S., West, R., Campbell, R., Brown, J., & Gainforth, H. (2014). *ABC of behaviour change theories: An essential resource for researchers, policy makers and practitioners.* London, England: Silverback.

Mikulincer, M., Shaver, P. R., & Pereg, D. (2003). Attachment theory and affect regulation: The dynamics, development, and cognitive consequences of attachment-related strategies. *Motivation and Emotion, 27,* 77–102.

Miller, G. E., Chen, E., & Cole, S. W. (2009). Health psychology: Developing biologically plausible models linking the social world and physical health. *Annual Review of Psychology, 60,* 501–524.

Miller, G. E., Chen, E., & Parker, K. J. (2011). Psychological stress in childhood and susceptibility to the chronic diseases of aging: Moving toward a model of behavioral and biological mechanisms. *Psychological Bulletin, 137,* 959–997.

Moors, A., Ellsworth, P. C., Scherer, K. R., & Frijda, N. H. (2013). Appraisal theories of emotion: State of the art and future development. *Emotion Review, 5,* 119–124.

Osterberg, L., & Blaschke, T. (2005). Drug therapy—Adherence to medication. *New England Journal of Medicine, 353,* 487–497.

Reeck, C., Ames, D. R., & Ochsner, K. N. (2016). The social regulation of emotion: An integrative, cross-disciplinary model. *Trends in Cognitive Sciences, 20,* 47–63.

Repetti, R. L., Robles, T. F., & Reynolds, B. (2011). Allostatic processes in the family. *Development and Psychopathology, 23,* 921–938.

Repetti, R. L., Taylor, S. E., & Seeman, T. E. (2002). Risky families: Family social environments and the mental and physical health of offspring. *Psychological Bulletin, 128,* 330–366.

Riddle, M.; Science of Behavior Change Working Group. (2015). News from the NIH: Using an experimental medicine approach to facilitate translational research. *Translational Behavioral Medicine, 5,* 486–488.

Robles, T. F., & Carroll, J. E. (2011). Restorative biological processes and health. *Social and Personality Psychology Compass, 5,* 518–537.

Rohleder, N., Beulen, S. E., Chen, E., Wolf, J. M., & Kirschbaum, C. (2007). Stress on the dance floor: The cortisol stress response to social-evaluative threat in competitive ballroom dancers. *Personality and Social Psychology Bulletin, 33,* 69–84.

Rook, K. S. (2015). Social networks in later life. *Current Directions in Psychological Science, 24,* 45–51.

Rothman, A. J., Gollwitzer, P. M., Grant, A. M., Neal, D. T., Sheeran, P., & Wood, W. (2015). Hale and hearty policies. *Perspectives on Psychological Science, 10,* 701–705.

Roy, M., Shohamy, D., & Wager, T. D. (2012). Ventromedial prefrontal-subcortical systems and the generation of affective meaning. *Trends in Cognitive Sciences, 16,* 147–156.

Sapolsky, R. M., Romero, L. M., & Munck, A. U. (2000). How do glucocorticoids influence stress responses? Integrating permissive, suppressive, stimulatory, and preparative actions. *Endocrine Reviews, 21,* 55–89.

Scarapicchia, T. M. F., Amireault, S., Faulkner, G., & Sabiston, C. M. (2017). Social support and physical activity participation among healthy adults: A systematic review of prospective studies. *International Review of Sport and Exercise Psychology, 10,* 50–83.

Schlam, T. R., & Baker, T. B. (2013). Interventions for tobacco smoking. *Annual Review of Clinical Psychology, 9,* 675–702.

Schneiderman, N., Ironson, G., & Siegel, S. D. (2004). Stress and health: Psychological, behavioral, and biological determinants. *Annual Review of Clinical Psychology, 1,* 607–628.

Selye, H. (1955). Stress and disease. *Science, 122,* 625–631.

Sheeran, P., Klein, W. M. P., & Rothman, A. J. (2017). Health behavior change: Moving from observation to intervention. In S. T. Fiske (Ed.), *Annual review of psychology* (Vol. 68, pp. 573–600). Palo Alto, CA: Annual Reviews.

Shields, G. S., & Slavich, G. M. (2017). Lifetime stress exposure and health: A review of contemporary assessment methods and biological mechanisms. *Social and Personality Psychology Compass, 11*(8), e12335.

Simpson, J. A., & Rholes, W. S. (2012). Adult attachment orientations, stress, and romantic relationships. In P. Devine & A. Plant (Eds.), *Advances in experimental social psychology* (Vol. 45, pp. 279–328). Amsterdam, The Netherlands: Academic Press.

Singer, T., Critchley, H. D., & Preuschoff, K. (2009). A common role of insula in feelings, empathy and uncertainty. *Trends in Cognitive Sciences, 13,* 334–340.

Skinner, E. A., Edge, K., Altman, J., & Sherwood, H. (2003). Searching for the structure of coping: A review and critique of category systems for classifying ways of coping. *Psychological Bulletin, 129,* 216–269.

Slopen, N., Lewis, T. T., & Williams, D. R. (2016). Discrimination and sleep: a systematic review. *Sleep Medicine, 18,* 88–95.

Smith, K. P., & Christakis, N. A. (2008). Social networks and health. *Annual Review of Sociology, 34,* 405–429.

Spellman, B. A. (2015). A short (personal) future history of Revolution 2.0. *Perspectives on Psychological Science, 10,* 886–899.

Susan G. Komen˚. (2017). *Mammogram accuracy—Accuracy of mammograms.* Retrieved from https://ww5.komen.org/BreastCancer/AccuracyofMammograms.html

Taylor, S. E., & Stanton, A. L. (2007). Coping resources, coping processes, and mental health. *Annual Review of Clinical Psychology, 3,* 377–401.

Troxel, W. M., Robles, T. F., Hall, M., & Buysse, D. J. (2007). Marital quality and the marital bed: Examining the covariation between relationship quality and sleep. *Sleep Medicine Reviews, 11,* 389–404.

Uchino, B. N. (2003). *Social support and physical health: Understanding the health consequences of relationships.* New Haven, CT: Yale University Press.

Uchino, B. N., Bowen, K., Carlisle, M., & Birmingham, W. (2012). Psychological pathways linking social support to health outcomes: A visit with the "ghosts" of research past, present, and future. *Social Science & Medicine, 74,* 949–957.

Ulrich-Lai, Y. M., & Herman, J. P. (2009). Neural regulation of endocrine and autonomic stress responses. *Nature Reviews Neuroscience, 10,* 397–409.

Volkow, N. D., Wang, G.-J., Tomasi, D., & Baler, R. D. (2013). The addictive dimensionality of obesity. *Biological Psychiatry, 73,* 811–818.

Watson, N. F., Badr, M. S., Belenky, G., Bliwise, D. L., Buxton, O. M., Buysse, D., . . . Heald, J. L. (2015). Recommended amount of sleep for a healthy adult: A joint consensus statement of the American Academy of Sleep Medicine and Sleep Research Society. *Sleep, 38,* 843–844.

World Health Organization. (2006). *Constitution of the World Health Organization.* Retrieved from http://www.who.int/governance/eb/who_constitution_en.pdf

Zanstra, Y. J., & Johnston, D. W. (2011). Cardiovascular reactivity in real life settings: Measurement, mechanisms and meaning. *Biological Psychology, 86,* 98–105.

Chapter 19

Judgment and Decision Making

Kathleen D. Vohs and Mary Frances Luce

People's lives are saturated by judgments and decisions. You make a judgment when you see an object and think that it is good or bad or when judging whether a future event is likely or unlikely to actually happen. You make a decision when you take a course of action while not taking other actions that were possible. People make hundreds, perhaps thousands, of decisions each day and are (often blissfully) unaware of many of them. Passing a candy dish and popping a piece into your mouth is the result of a decision, as is continuing to walk past a tray of fruit without partaking. Such actions (and inactions) may not be experienced as involving important considerations, or as involving any deliberation at all, yet discrete choices accumulate to influence everything from mood to mortality (Keeney, 2008).

While most people may question their own decisions from time to time, decisions by professionals and experts are not immune from the need for study. Mistakes are made by trained experts—mistakes that can cost lives. In the United States, approximately 250,000 people die each year from a decision error by a medical professional. In fact, medical decision error is estimated to be the third most common cause of death, placing it after heart disease and cancer and before strokes, suicide, and diabetes (Makary & Daniels, 2016). If that surprises you (it did us), you are not alone. As the lead author said in an interview, "You have this over-appreciation and overestimate of things like cardiovascular disease, and a vast under-recognition of the place of medical care as the cause of death. That informs all our national health priorities and our research grants" (Allen & Pierce, 2016). These sentiments speak to the importance of using science to study outcomes such as medical decision errors, which is what the field of *judgment and decision making* does.

Judgments and Decisions: How Are They Defined, Explained, and Evaluated?

Definitions

What Is a Judgment?

Judgment is a broad term. Making a judgment involves perceiving objects or events and coming to a conclusion about whether they are good or bad (*valence judgments*) or likely to occur (*likelihood judgments*).

A *decision* is a commitment (to oneself or others) to an option or course of action from among a set of options. Decisions have outcomes, which are the circumstances or states that follow from the decision.

Decision outcomes are judged along two dimensions. Decision theorists often talk about a decision's *utility*, which is the joy, pleasure, or satisfaction that is derived from the outcome of the decision. (The study of decision making has roots in economics, which is a field dominated by mathematical models. When economists take their numbers and turn them into prose, it typically does not go well; consequently. there are a lot of heavy, clunky terms in the field of judgment and decision making.) Decision outcomes that would bring about the most utility (read: satisfaction) are called *normative*, a term meaning best or right. One dominant viewpoint, shared by many economists, states that people are utility maximizers and that the normative option under any circumstance is the one that people ought to be taking. In plainer terms, people should be rational and choose what will make them most satisfied in the future. Another viewpoint, shared by many psychologists, is that people are not rational and often do not appreciate what will make them satisfied in the future. The reality is that human behavior is somewhere in between rational and irrational. In the words of Daniel Kahneman (2003), a psychologist who won the Nobel laureate in economics, people are *incompletely rational*.

The insights put forth in the 1970s by Kahneman, along with his long-time collaborator, Amos Tversky, helped drag the field of judgment and decision making beyond utility maximization as the model of decision making. Years later, the effects of these realizations are still coming to light, as illustrated by economist Richard Thaler's receipt of the 2017 Nobel prize in economics. Thaler is known for his work with legal expert Cass Sunstein, who tout using judgment and decision making principles as the basis for governance policies (Thaler & Sunstein, 2009). Thaler and Sunstein's highly influential work reflects a move away from describing irrationality to prescribing ways to mitigate irrationality's effects. This progression illustrates a more general principle that before one can prescribe improvements to decision processes, the processes must be understood in depth. These notions raise the fundamental question: How do people make decisions?

Two Explanations of How People Make Decisions: One from Economics, One from Psychology

The predominant theory of decision making derived from economics is *subjective expected utility theory* (von Neumann & Morgenstern, 1944). Expected utility theory says that people make a decision by figuring out the likelihood of each option's outcome occurring and the value of the outcome in question. Then they multiply the likelihood and value for each option and compare across options. Whichever option has the highest score (i.e., the best combination of being likely to occur and highly desirable) is the option that people should choose because it will yield the most utility. Expected utility models make assumptions about people's preferences, which means the value they place on each possible decision outcome. Expected utility theory assumes, for instance, that people value money, and so the option that is expected to yield the most money is assumed to be the normative (correct) choice.

One can see expected utility theory in action when people play game shows, such as *Who Wants to Be a Millionaire?* Imagine a situation in which a player answers enough questions correctly to achieve $50,000. Then the player faces a choice: End the game or continue. If the player ends the game, then he or she walks away with $50,000. Hence, the option of "ending the game now" has a value of $50,000 associated with it. If the player chooses to continue to the next level, getting the next question right will yield $250,000. However, there is only a one-fourth chance of winning because there are four multiple choice answers from which to choose, which also means that there is a three-fourths chance that the player will lose. Faced with this choice, players should choose to answer the next question, even if it means arbitrarily guessing at one of the multiple choice options. This is an example of rational behavior. Can you see why?

The expected value of answering the question at the next level is $62,500 ([$250,000 * 0.25], which is greater than the $50,000 expected value ($50,000 * 1.0) from ending the game. Hence, the additional likelihood that the player will get the answer correct and win more money tips the scales toward the option of attempting the next question because it is associated with winning more money and hence offers higher expected utility.

An alternate decision theory, which came out of psychology, is Kahneman and Tversky's (1979) *prospect theory*. The moniker refers to the options (prospects) that decision makers face. Prospect theory is arguably the most important theory in the field of judgment and decision making.

Prospect theory created two major advances. One, it used psychology to help explain when and why humans make irrational choices. Until that point, economists treated people's irrational decisions as noisy and bothersome disturbances in their elegant mathematical equations and were largely unconvinced that these deviations represented anything meaningful. Prospect theory's use of psychology revealed that those irrational decisions are, in fact, quite meaningful because they reveal key insights into how the mind works. Two, prospect theory used mathematics, which made it a vehicle to speak to economists and therefore bring to their attention the importance of psychological processes.

Prospect theory uses likelihood judgments and outcome values, as does expected utility theory. However, prospect theory also states that the values associated with outcomes are not the same for everyone or across all situations but rather reflect people's current state of mind. That is, people make judgments about the values of outcomes from a *reference point*, which is akin to a personal point of view. To predict how people will value a certain outcome, one first has to know from where they stand when evaluating it. This tenet flies in the face of expected utility theory because it says that people do not perceive outcomes as having absolute values but instead think of them as better or worse (often referred to as gains or losses, respectively) from their current perspective. This aspect of prospect theory can be summarized as "everything is relative."

Reference point effects can be illustrated with the notion that people are *loss averse*. The psychological impact of losses is far bigger than that of gains, even if the value of the losses and gains is exactly the same. Loss aversion is part of a more general phenomenon called *bad is stronger than good* (Baumeister, Bratslavsky, Finkenauer, & Vohs, 2001). In health, learning, interpersonal interactions, sexuality, major life decisions, events that yield bad outcomes have a significantly bigger psychological impact than equivalent events that yield good outcomes. In the realm of money, for example, losses have about twice the psychological impact as gains. This means that people will experience an equivalent degree of emotional change from losing $500 in the stock market as they will gaining $1000 the same way. Attesting to the importance of belongingness in the human mind (Baumeister & Leary, 1995), in the realm of interpersonal relationships the psychological impact of bad to good is about 5:1. That is, one marital expert concluded that couples need to say five positive comments to neutralize one negative comment made to their partners (Gottman, 1994).

Loss aversion is illustrated by a classic finding named the endowment effect. Typically in these studies (e.g., Kahneman, Knetsch, & Thaler, 1990), some people are given a small gift, such as a coffee mug with the university's logo on it, whereas others see the same product but are not told that it is theirs. People who own the mug then are asked how much they would charge to sell it; people who do not own the mug are asked how much they would offer to buy it. Since random assignment to condition means that, overall, both groups ought to value the mug equally, it is remarkable (and in contrast to expected utility theory) that owners ask for considerably more money to sell the mug than buyers are willing to offer. One may think that it may be because buyers and owners have different motives about saving money and earning money. Yet this explanation does not explain the finding that when, 20 minutes later, the same people switch roles from being owners to buyers, or vice versa, the endowment effect is seen once again: People want more money to sell the mug than they themselves would offer to buy it. To be sure, endowment effect findings are interpreted in different ways, and one of the most predominant explanations is loss aversion. People feel a stronger psychological impact of losing the mug when they already own it than they do gaining the mug when they do not own it, which demonstrates the broader theme of reference points.

What Influences Decisions?

It is generally agreed that decisions are made by considering how likely each option is to occur combined with how valuable the outcome of that option seems. Expected utility theory says that decision makers rationally judge the likelihood of an event in terms of its *base rate* (meaning the objective tendency for an event to occur in a given circumstance) and possess stable preferences for outcomes (meaning they place the same value on outcomes across time and circumstance).

In contrast, prospect theory conceptualizes decisions as resulting from decision weights and constructed preferences. The concept of decision weights says that people do not judge the likelihood or importance (these two terms encompass the notion of weight) of all outcomes similarly. For instance, some people prefer the style of a car they are thinking of purchasing to be a more important factor than its safety. But when they start to think about having children, they might come to value safety more than style. On the likelihood front, for instance, it is well known that people overestimate the likelihood of events that are, in reality, highly improbable (such as flash flooding, terrorist attacks, and winning the jackpot). This indicates that people do not think about events in terms of their objective base rates but rather overestimate the likelihood of some (rare) events happening. *Constructed preferences* are values that people associate with different outcomes that are not stable but rather can be pushed around by the situation. This idea led the field of judgment and decision making to study situational features that change people's preferences and, hence, their choices.

It was a shock for decision scientists 50 years ago to think that people's preferences for outcomes can change with small differences in the situation—but they do. One concept that follows from constructed preferences and reference points is the idea of *sunk costs*. Standard economic theory states that no matter how much time, effort, money, energy, or emotion one has put into a cause, if it becomes clear that the outcome is no longer desirable, then one should quit attempting to achieve the outcome. People actually do otherwise. For instance, people sit through movies that they detest because they already spent the money to see the movie. People read the entirety of a boring novel only because they started it. People turn down invitations to go to a restaurant for dinner because they just bought groceries that day.

Sunk costs may help explain why women stay with abusive partners (Rusbult & Martz, 1995). Scholars studied 100 women who had fled their homes to stay at a shelter. Many had fairly serious injuries (three fourths of them needed medical treatment upon arrival), and yet some women would willfully return to their abusive partners. Could the scientists predict which? Women reported the resources they had put into their relationship, namely, whether the couple had children together, were married, or had been together for a long time. As predicted, sunk costs mattered. Women who had devoted time to raising children with the man, were married, or had been partnered with him for a longer period of time were likelier to return to their abusers than were women who had sunk fewer resources into the relationship.

Sunk cost effects are considered irrational because the money or time that one has spent is gone and one cannot get them back. The rational decision maker would ignore spent resources and decide whether to continue as if the experience were just starting and no money, time, or effort had been put into it yet.

Preferences can change because of the way that options are described. *Framing* is an important construct in the field of judgment and decision making because it sways decision makers' preferences without changing the objective information given to the decision maker. For instance, ground beef described as 75% lean is preferred to ground beef described as 25% fat, even though those descriptions convey the same information (Levin & Gaeth, 1988).

A classic example of framing effects is Kahneman and Tversky's (1979) Asian disease problem. People imagine that they are policymakers deciding on how to respond to a disease that threatens the health of 600 people. Some people are told to choose between two options: one that will save 200 people for certain and another that offers a one-third probability that all 600 people will be saved and two-thirds probability that nobody will be saved. Other people face two options that convey the same information but with a different framing: one option guarantees that 400 people die whereas the other offers a one-third probability that nobody will die and two-thirds probability that all 600 people will die. If you work out the math, everyone is given options that predict the same number of lives saved and lost. In principle, then, decision makers should choose the options at equal rates.

That is not what happens. The two options with certainty sway people's decisions because they bring to mind a different reference point. That is, the condition in which 200 lives are definitely going to be saved (vs. one-third chance that everyone will be saved and two-thirds chance that everyone will die) gets people to think about a good outcome that is certain to occur. This is called a gain frame, and people generally react to gains by becoming risk-averse, meaning that they go for the certain option of 200 lives saved. Yet the opposite occurs when an option promises that 400 people will definitely die (vs. a one-third probability that nobody will die and a two-thirds probability that 600 people will die). This option gets people to think about a bad outcome that is certain to occur. This is a loss frame, and losses tend to make people risk-seeking. Hence, people choose the option that avoids 400 certain deaths. As this example demonstrates—and as politicians have known for centuries—decisions are heavily influenced by descriptions of the options.

The *attraction effect* and *compromise effect* are notable because they too reveal decision makers' irrationality. The attraction effect (Huber et al., 1982), also known as the decoy effect, describes choices when people are faced with two options that are closely matched in how preferable they are. Imagine that a group of people is offered donuts or chocolate ice cream, and half of the people in the group choose donuts whereas the other half choose chocolate ice cream. Now imagine that a third option is introduced, and it is fish-flavored ice cream. Introducing this option, which is less preferred than the other two (so much so that nobody actually chooses it), shifts people's choices between donuts and chocolate ice cream. The unwanted option (here, fish-flavored ice cream) makes the option to which it compares most closely seem more attractive, leading people to choose it (here, chocolate ice cream).

The attraction effect is so interesting because the third option is completely undesirable, and therefore it should be completely irrelevant. Because no one would ever choose fish-flavored ice cream, people who were on the fence about whether to choose chocolate ice cream or donuts should still be undecided. Yet suddenly, the presence of fish-flavored ice cream renders chocolate ice cream more appealing. Because the mind applies the result of that comparison to the harder comparison between chocolate ice cream versus donuts, with the result being that it looks better than donuts.

The *compromise effect* (Simonson, 1989) arises when people are faced with options that trade-off one feature for another, the most common being quality and price. In these cases, people tend to choose the option in the middle. Consider the example of a consumer choosing among cell phones with capacities of 80GB, 100GB, and 120GB that are priced at $600, $700, and $800. The buyer would be likely to choose the 100GB option because while it gives up some space compared to the top model, it also does not cost as much money. The compromise effect continues to affect decisions when new options are added at the extremes (e.g., adding a 160GB option priced at $900 and removing the 80GB option) as people once again tend to choose the middle option, which in this case is the 120GB option.

You can easily see how sellers can use the compromise effect to move decision makers toward the particular products they want them to buy. In fact, restaurateurs take advantage of it. Where do they tend to put the wines that will make them the most profit? Those wines are not the most or least expensive on the menu but instead are more toward the middle. Restaurateurs are known to price the wine with the biggest markup as second cheapest. They realize that diners want to save money but do not want to appear to be a huge cheapskate by ordering the most inexpensive wine, and so they tend to order the second cheapest wine. Hence, that is where there is money to be made. Remember that when you are on your next date—be careful not to get a bad deal!

This next effect can change people's outcomes without getting them to act in a particular way. It involves *defaults*, which are pre-existing or already-chosen options. The pre-existing option may be someone else's choice (e.g., auto manufacturers' base model) or the most recent choice that the decision maker made (e.g., the TV station you last watched). Policymakers figured out that the default effect can help society. Take, for instance, organ donations. Society benefits as a whole if people agree that when they die, their organs could be transplanted into the body of someone else who needed them. In some countries, the default is that your organs are not donated unless you explicitly say so—but in other countries, the default is the opposite, so that your organs will be donated unless you say not to do so. One study found that changing the laws such that organ donation at death was the default dramatically increased the number of organs donated, even though citizens still retained the option not to donate their organs if they so choose (Johnson & Goldstein, 2003).

Other examples of changing the default option are more mundane and more common. When people first started using email and getting Internet accounts for services that required data protection, like banking, the word *password* was often given as the default password that consumers were given. Guess what? Consumers failed to change that default password, which thieves quickly took advantage of. Banks and other firms now assign unique and difficult-to-decipher passwords on the chance that the password first given to consumers remains the password for the life of that account. The basic or default option is what many people are likely to end up with.

Decisions Evaluated: What Makes a Decision Good?

Judgment and decision making scholars think it is important to evaluate the quality of decisions. (If you are following closely, you will realize that these are judgments about decisions.) Scholars separate the process by which the decision was made from its outcomes when judging what makes a decision good.

The Process by Which One Makes a Decision

One measure of whether a decision is good is to ask whether it was reasonably sound and made in a reasonable amount of time. One early insight in decision science came from psychologist Herb Simon (1955), who corrected the long-standing assumption in economics that people can and do devote lots of energy and time to decision making. Simon said that humans' information processing capacities were limited even in the best of circumstances, and therefore people take judgment and decision shortcuts. His notion of *bounded rationality* explained when and why people make irrational decisions, earning Simon the 1978 Nobel prize in economics. Bounded rationality implies that, for the most part, making a "good enough" decision rather quickly (a strategy called *satisficing*) is an optimal method for making decisions, insofar as it offers a decent trade-off in terms of effort and outcomes.

Much research has demonstrated the advantages of using decision shortcuts, called *heuristics* (e.g., Gigerenzer & Goldstein, 1996; Payne, Bettman, & Johnson 1993). Heuristics often are used when the information people are wading through is complex. The main advantage of heuristics is that they save decision makers time. The main disadvantage is that they can be prone to error. The literature mostly shows how heuristics lead people to incorrect judgments (indeed, that is what most studies aim to show). Taking a broader view, though, it is clear that heuristics tend to result in pretty good decisions most of the time.

If decision makers wanted to avoid using heuristics to ensure that they achieve good decision outcomes, they would have to perform thorough information searches to come up with base rate information and objective criteria for evaluating each option's outcomes. People sometimes do this, for instance, with high-stakes choices such as deciding on a car or whether to have surgery. But as you may be guessing, most judgments (including many high-stakes decisions) are not made after thorough, rational information processing. Hence it is important to know the heuristics that people commonly use.

One heuristic is the tendency to diversify when there are many options related to a decision. Imagine a group of highly similar people, half of whom are offered two investment funds. One is comprised of stocks (which are riskier) and the other bonds (which are safer). In this context, people generally split their money equally, putting 50% in stocks and 50% in bonds, which may suggest that they preferred a moderately risky portfolio overall. Now imagine that the second group of people also can choose from two funds. One is comprised of stocks and the other of a mix of stocks and bonds (called a balanced fund). If the behavior of the first group reflected a moderate-risk goal, then people in the second group should, in general, put most of their money in the balanced fund. Instead, people in this second group again split their money 50/50 between the two funds. Both behaviors suggest less of a moderate risk goal and more of diversification heuristic (Benartzi & Thaler, 2001). In fact, economic lore has it that the diversification heuristic was used by Harry Markowitz for his own investment portfolio. That is notable because Markowitz won the 1990 Nobel Prize in economics—for formulating an algorithm that optimally allocates money across different financial investments. Yet instead of using his Nobel-winning system himself, he simply divided the money evenly among the various options (reported in Brighton & Gigerenzer, 2012).

The diversification urge is not something that happens only when investing money. One study found that kids select Halloween treats this way (Read & Loewenstein, 1995). Trick-or-treaters arrived at a house where the owners said that the kids could each take two candy bars and then offered them two different brands. Every single trick-or-treater took one of each kind. Other ways of presenting the candy bars showed that this only occurred because the two different brands of candy bars were offered at the same time and the children were allowed to take two. "I can have two candy bars and there are two types of candy bars so therefore I'll take one of each," goes the mental shortcut. Think of shopping for groceries for the week. People tend to buy different flavors of yogurts for breakfast, perhaps as many flavors are there are days of the work week. But there can be costs to using this rule. In the words of Eli Finkel, one of the editors of this book, come Friday, you can find yourself stuck with that peach yogurt that you never really liked anyway.

Outcomes That Follow from the Decision

Another way to judge what makes a decision good is whether the decision yields satisfactory outcomes. One popular version of this idea says decisions are good when they make people the happiest. Yet that assumes that people know what will bring them the most happiness or the least pain, which unfortunately they do not.

People are not that good at predicting what outcomes will make them feel a certain way. *Affective forecasting* research concerns people's (in)ability to judge how they will feel in the future. People seem pretty good at predicting the valence of their feelings, that is, whether they will feel positively or negatively. They correctly predict that they will feel anxious when taking their drivers' license test and happy when they get married. Where people go wrong is in predicting how intensely or long they will feel that way (Wilson & Gilbert, 2005). Although it would be nice to predict precisely how one will feel in some circumstances, there may be advantages to mispredicting one's feelings. Overestimating how intensely or long one will feel a certain way can motivate people to enact the behaviors they think will bring about the desired emotional state (Baumeister, Vohs, DeWall, & Zhang, 2007). People who think that they will feel miserable for days if they fail an exam (or, gasp, even get a B) are exactly those people who are motivated to work extra hard to avoid that outcome. Yet, even if those people did fail (or get a disappointing B), affective forecasting research has demonstrated that the sadness would only last for a little while and not ruin the entire rest of the academic year as they might predict.

How people make decisions about their future selves is relevant to the topic of self-control. Choices with a self-control dimension typically have one option that is rewarding in the here-and-now pitted against another option that is costlier now but better for oneself in the future. Eating healthy, not smoking (or quitting smoking), exercising, and saving money are common examples of self-control choices. It is more enjoyable to eat French fries, smoke, lie on the couch, and gamble than it is not to do these things. Yet people's lives are happier when they avoid the easy, indulgent option and instead opt for the option that is more challenging now but more rewarding in the future (Hofmann, Luhmann, Fisher, Vohs, & Baumeister, 2014).

How Do Cognitive Processes Lead to Decision Errors?

An important theme in judgment and decision making is how different types of cognitive processing lead to different types of errors. Remember that judgment and decision making research often compares people's decisions against what would have been the logical choice or what option would make people better off in the long run (i.e., normative decisions). In this section, we review classic phenomena in judgment and decision making organized into three themes for understanding how cognitive processes cause decision errors.

Decisions Errors Due to Not Enough Effortful Thought

The first theme, arguably the most pervasive, is that decision makers fail to put enough thought into their decisions to reach the best answers. Decision makers use a variety of cognitive strategies that range from simplistic (sometimes called intuitive) to effortful (sometimes called analytical). An influential framework is Kahneman's (Kahneman & Frederick, 2002) System 1/System 2 distinction (Table 19.1). Using System 1 means to arrive at a judgment or decision relatively quickly, with little effort expended, and using the gist of the situation. Using System 2 means to arrive at a judgment or decision more slowly, after much conscious effort, and by making a detailed analysis. This section details how many decision making errors result from an overreliance on System 1 when decision makers should have been relying more on System 2.

One of the earliest demonstrations relates to likelihood judgments. The *availability bias* occurs when decision makers judge a possible event to be highly likely just because it is associated with information that was easy to conjure up in memory. For instance, people believe that words with *r* as the first letter are more common in English than are words with *r* as the third letter (Tversky & Kahneman, 1973). Words with *r* in the third position are actually more probable (trust us—or if you have a lot of time on your hands, sample the words on this page). Nonetheless, it is much easier to search one's memory for words marked by their first letter (the game Scattergories makes use of this) than by their third letter. The availability bias is a System 1 error, in that how easy it was to think of that information gives decision makers the sense that the outcome is common, which leads participants to stop at that point and form their judgment without further cognitive work.

TABLE 19.1   System 1 versus System 2: What They Are and What They Do

System 1	System 2
Defining features	
Automatic	Time-intensive
Effortless	Effortful
Parallel	Serial
Reasons by association	Reasons by application of logic and rules
Intuitive	Analytical
Experiential	Rational
Holistic	Piecemeal
Contributions to decision errors	
Perceptual errors: The psychological impact of losses is bigger than that of gains.	Cognitive Errors: Devoting much effort to deciding can hamper prediction of one's own preferences.
People substitute how easy it is for information to come to mind for trying to find base rates.	There are times in which it is better to devote less effort even if it means sacrificing decision accuracy.
People substitute the representativeness of an instance for logic.	
Feelings	
Preferences need no inferences: Feelings of good and bad arise very quickly.	Full blown emotions contain cognition and emotion and are distinguishable from one another.
Affect can automatically carry over to related decision such as when fearful individuals make pessimistic judgments.	Negative emotions such as regret are explicitly anticipated and avoided.

Another example involves asking people to estimate the number of murders per year either across a whole state or a particular city in that state. One experiment had some people guess how many murders happen each year in Michigan, whereas others estimated the number of murders each year in Detroit (Kahneman & Frederick, 2002). Guess which group's estimates were higher? Logically, the number of murders a year must be higher (or, at worst, exactly the same) for the entire state of Michigan than for the city of Detroit because Detroit is a city in Michigan. Yet people estimated that the median number of murders a year in Michigan is 100 compared to 200 in Detroit. People's judgments were logically inconsistent because they drew on different information. The stereotype of Detroit is of a rough, violent city, whereas the stereotype of Michigan is of a hearty Midwestern state with cold winters and tart cherries. Hence, conjuring up different types of information about Michigan versus Detroit presumably made it seem that more murders would happen in Detroit than in Michigan. The converse happens when people find it difficult to think of information. Winkielman et al. (1998) asked some participants to recall 12 events from their childhood and others to recall 4 childhood events. Ironically, the group that thought of 12 events later rated themselves as less capable to remember their childhood compared to participants asked to recall only 4 events, despite having recalled three times as many memories. Retrieving 12 events from childhood is rather difficult to do, and participants let those feelings of difficulty color their self-assessments.

The *representativeness heuristic* is another shortcut that people use when making judgments about probability. It occurs people judge an event as being probable because its appearance seems to fit the context. For instance, think about people who are asked to judge which sequence of five flips of a coin is likelier to occur: HTHHT or HHHHH (where H = heads; T = tails). The majority of people will say that the former is more likely to occur than the latter. But, statistically, both are equally probable because each flip of the coin offers a 50/50 chance of heads or tails. In decision makers' minds, though, a series of coin flips showing both heads and tails seem more representative of a random pattern than when the series shows only heads.

One well-established mechanism that gives rise to decision making errors is *anchoring and adjustment*. Here, people do engage in System 2 but in insufficient amounts. A standard way to test anchoring and adjustment is to ask decision makers to first think about an arbitrary number (e.g., the last two digits of their social security number). Then, they are presented with an object, for instance, a bottle of wine (Ariely et al., 2003). They think back to the arbitrary number and then state whether the wine is worth more or less than this number. Last, they are asked to state a specific dollar amount they are willing to pay for the object. Even though decision makers know that the number they first considered had nothing to do with the wine's worth, that initial, irrelevant number influences how much people are willing to pay. People with higher social security number endings are willing to pay more money for the wine than people with lower social security number endings. We say that decision makers do not devote enough effortful cognitive energy to this task because they "anchor" on the initial number but fail to "adjust" sufficiently. This means that they think that they have moved away from the starting point enough but they are still being swayed by it.

Anchoring and adjustment is at work in many phenomena. For instance, can you remember seeing grocery store signs near discounted items that say "Limit X"? The number that is listed is likely to become an anchor that consumers seize on when asking themselves how many of that item they want. The higher the number on that sign, the more items consumers are likely to buy (Wansink, Kent, & Hoch, 1998). So too are interpersonal relations affected by anchoring and adjustment. Failing to take someone else's perspective has been said to result from people anchoring on their own viewpoint and failing to adjust enough for others' perspectives (Epley et al., 2004).

The Cognitive Reflection Test (CRT) measures people's general tendencies to use System 2 processing to check and correct System 1 outputs (Frederick, 2005). To see how you might score, answer this CRT item: "A bat and a ball cost $1.10. The bat costs $1.00 more than the ball. How much does the ball cost? _____ cents." For most people, a quick reading of this problem results in an intuitive, System 1 output of "10 cents." Did 10 cents spring to mind for you? If so, you probably went with your System 1 output. However, if you engaged System 2 elaborations to test the $0.10 answer, you may have realized that the difference between $0.10 and $1.00 is not, in fact, $1.00. Hence, the correct answer is $.05. While CRT responses are correlated with indicators of intelligence, the measure seems more to represent cognitive style, as people who are skilled in basic arithmetic nonetheless routinely give the intuitive System 1 response of $0.10— often in surprising numbers. Samples of undergraduates recruited from selective (e.g., Ivy League) colleges typically show double-digit percentages of students who miss three out of three CRT questions. Those base rates suggest that most people are using System 1 much of the time, even in contexts, such as research experiments, where it is generally understood that they are being asked to think carefully and answer accurately. The CRT measure is useful as a way to track the effects of chronic dispositions in terms of System 2 correction of System 1, allowing for the important but often-overlooked perspective of individual differences in decision making processes. The CRT is a robust and unique predictor of the tendency to use a wide variety of well-known heuristic decisions strategies, including many of those discussed in this chapter (Toplak et al., 2011). The CRT is also a fun way to trip up even your smart friends.

In summary, heuristic decision strategies often sacrifice some decision accuracy but offer the benefit of reduced effort. However, putting a lot of effort into thinking does not guarantee error-free decision outcomes, as our second theme illustrates.

Theme 2: Increased Cognitive Processing Can Cause Error

The previous section discusses research showing that decision error can result from not enough cognitive processing. This research suggests simple advice for decision makers: Think more! Unfortunately for decision makers, but perhaps fortunately for judgment and decision making scholars who need interesting questions to research, getting rid of decision errors is not that easy.

This brings us to the second theme: Thinking can itself cause errors. There are at least two explanations for why cognitive analysis can lead to decision error. First, some decision tasks may be inherently intuitive—meaning that the best decisions come from relying on one's "gut feelings" (Hammond et al., 1987). Second, people may use cognitive processing toward goals that lead them astray from making an accurate decision.

In an influential stream of research, researchers found that generating reasons for why a person made his or her choice can reduce the quality of that choice in terms of subsequent enjoyment or happiness. Wilson and Schooler (1991) told undergraduates that they were allowed to choose a poster to take home with them out of an array of posters. Some students were asked first, though, how they would go about choosing a poster—that is, to state the reasons for choosing a poster. Other students were simply allowed to choose. Researchers later went into students' dorm rooms and saw that students who talked about how they would choose their poster were less likely to have the poster on their walls. Wilson and Schooler (1991)argued that the process of coming up with reasons is inconsistent with the subsequent feelings-based experience of the posters. It seems that better decisions are made when the context in which people are placed while they make decisions (e.g., relying on feelings but not reasons) is highly similar to the context in which they will be experiencing those preferences (Payne, Bettman, & Schkade, 1999).

These and other findings have led to debate regarding the role of System 1 processing in decision making, one version of which is unconscious thought. Some researchers have made strong prescriptions regarding the superior benefits of unconscious thought in decision making (Dijksterhuis et al., 2006). Others, though, argue that those claims are overblown due to other factors, the result of which is erroneously ascribing conscious processes to unconscious thought (Newell & Shanks, 2014). For instance, a result that appears to show the benefit of unconscious deliberation could, instead, reflect decrements from artificially long periods of conscious thought forced by experimental procedures (Payne et al., 2008). That is, some findings that may seem to suggest System 1 processing is better may instead be a result of experimental conditions (e.g., forced, long deliberation times) that compare System 1 processing to flawed System 2 processing.

These debates illustrate how important it is to carefully assess both the specific thought processes and the fit between those processes and the judgment or decision at hand. For example, consider the hindsight bias, a robust effect whereby an uncertain event (e.g., the result of a political election) is believed to have been more easily predictable once the outcome of that event is known. Hence, someone who, in advance of the outcome of the 2016 US presidential election, would have been highly uncertain about who would win might, after the results are known, believes that she would have been able to predict Trump's win. Roese and Vohs (2012) discussed the many processes that lead to the hindsight bias, with conscious processing providing one important source of the effect. They argue that, following outcome knowledge, people selectively misremember particular information (e.g., events that seem to support Trump's victory spring to mind after the victory is a foregone conclusion). Further, people then engage in processing aimed at sense-making (e.g., using the remembered events to create a causal story that allows for a general sense of predictability and understanding of the event that occurred). Hindsight bias is one of the cases whereby more System 2 thought can impair the quality of decisions.

Decision makers who believe they will have to justify or be accountable to others for their decisions shift toward relying on System 2 processes more than they otherwise would. As you probably guessed from reading the previous section, accountability can improve decision quality because it offsets a heavy reliance on System 1 processes (Simonson & Nye, 1992). More counterintuitively, though, accountability can make decisions worse. Having to justify why you made a certain choice creates "choice based on reasons" in which people put too much thought toward thinking up justifications for their decisions and not enough thought on making the right choice. Using the attraction effect design (discussed previously), some people were told that they would have to explain to others why they chose as they did. Others made a choice among the same options but did not believe that they would have to justify their choice. People ready to justify their choice were swayed by the irrelevant option more than were people who chose without believing that they would have to justify their choice. Justifying one's choices can lead people to irrational decisions when people choose more on the basis of what is defensible and less on what is logical.

In summary, although conscious thought is an important aspect of good decision making, it can go astray—and often in predictable ways. Reasons can disrupt decision making, and accountability can introduce unhelpful goals.

Theme 3: Emotion versus Cognition

While there are numerous ways to define and classify thought processes during decision making, one theme that has made inroads to judgment and decision making is whether those thoughts are emotional versus cognitive. The third theme we address is whether and, if so, how emotional decision making causes decision error.

Historically, judgment and decision making approaches have depicted decision making as a cold, cognitive process. Yet it would be remiss to ignore the fact that many decisions are made with—if not because of—emotional input. The question of when and how emotion plays a role in decision making also implicates the intuitive versus analytical reasoning divide mentioned in Themes 1 and 2. A classic debate in the 1980s pitted two theories of emotion against each other: Zajonc (1980) claimed that "preferences need no inferences," (which speaks to System 1 being active) whereas Lazarus (1981) retorted with a "cognitivist's reply" (which speaks to System 2 being active). The debate can be resolved by agreeing that both routes coexist. Baumeister, Vohs, DeWall, and Zhang (2007) nominated the term *affect* for low-level, nonconscious, positive versus negative twinges and the term *emotion* for full-blown feeling states, and we use these labels in this chapter. Next, we discuss how each can produce decision error.

Intuitive, Affective Processes

One influential model argued that decision makers' judgments about risky decisions are driven by the affect associated with the options. For instance, if positive affect arises when a decision maker thinks about skiing, then this will likely increase judgments of its benefits but curtail an analysis of its riskiness. On the other hand, the negative affect connected to the idea of a nuclear power plant increase judgments of its riskiness (Slovic et al., 2007).

Sometimes getting people in an emotional mindset leads them to make erroneous decisions. One set of researchers asked some people to state how much money they wanted to donate to save one panda, whereas others were asked how much money they wanted to donate to save four. For some participants, the panda bears in question were portrayed by black dots (either one or four), whereas other participants saw adorable pictures of pandas (again, one or four). The participants who saw the pandas as black dots said that they would donate more money to save four than save one, which is a logical response. But the participants who saw the pandas as pictures pledged to donate the same amount to save one of them as they did to save four of them (Hsee & Rottenstreich, 2004). The researchers argued that portraying pandas as cute and lovable brought people into an affective mode that made them ignore quantity and treat all the pandas the same. When pandas were described in plain, cold, nonemotional terms, participants' decisions about how much money would be needed to save them became sensitive to quantity, and they pledged more money to save more bears.

Other evidence supports the idea being in an affective mindset changes decisions that are completely independent of the affect being felt. This is called a *misattribution* effect because people mistakenly carry over their current state (e.g., their feelings) to an unrelated judgment they are asked to make. A classic misattribution finding shows that after people read stories that elicited a negative mood, they made more pessimistic judgments about the risk involved in various fatalities, even those with no logical relation to the source of the mood (Johnson & Tversky, 1983). Another classic misattribution finding demonstrated that people judge their lives to be happier with their lives overall when asked on sunny (vs. rainy) days (Schwarz & Clore, 1983). This difference presumably occurs because people use their feelings about the day's weather to make judgments about their life overall. Other research extended this weather effect to university admissions officers' judgments (Simonsohn, 2010). On sunny days, admission officers give more weight to whether the applicant has social or extracurricular activities on his or her application whereas on overcast days they consider more heavily the applicant's academic record.

Carry-over findings suggest that low-level affective states subtly alter decision makers' perceptions and goals. It is important to recognize that these carry over to influence other decisions and judgments, which affects a broad variety of outcomes (Lerner et al., 2015). For instance, initial experiences of sadness carry over to increase financial impulsivity whereas carried-over disgust does not (Lerner, Li, & Weber, 2013). While both are negative emotions, sadness apparently triggers goals to obtain immediate, perhaps mood-lifting, rewards.

Analytical Processes

Although psychological processes are often broken down into "emotional versus rational," anyone familiar with the concept of rumination can attest that more conscious cognitive activity does not necessarily mean less emotional experience. In fact, some emotions may be fueled by analytical processes.

Perhaps the emotion with the most sustained interest to judgment and decision making scholars is regret. Strategies to avoiding regret are said to be analytical (not intuitive) because people engage in counterfactuals, which are mental simulations of what might happen in the future. Simonson (1992) found that asking people to think about whether they would regret a decision made them choose safer options. For instance, thinking about whether they may regret their choice led participants to prefer a product with a sale price now as opposed to waiting for a potentially better sale but with the risk that one that may lose out on the discount altogether. Shoppers also chose a highly regarded brand of videocassette recorder over an unknown brand that was cheaper when reminded that they may regret their choice later. People can imagine that they will feel more regret if they made a risky decision as opposed to a safer one, so they avoid risky options so as to attenuate regret that they might feel about the decision in the future.

People put a lot of thought into the regret they feel about past behaviors too. One experiment investigated what kinds of decisions people have regretted. People reported regretting mistakes that involved actions (e.g., saying the wrong thing) soon after they performed the action but regretted mistakes involving inaction (e.g., not earning a graduate degree) after a long time has passed (Gilovich & Medvec, 1995). This means that as you get nearer to the end of life, you might regret the goals that you never pursued, but right now most of your regret revolves around acts like getting drunk and behaving foolishly at a party last weekend.

People also need to manage the emotions that arise while making decisions, and this can be a problem when the decision itself brings up negative emotions. Luce (1998) showed that people were more likely to choose the default option or be swayed by an irrelevant choice in the attraction effect when the decision situation itself elicited bad feelings. People want the negative feelings to end. Since the negative feelings stem from the decision at hand, people use readily available cues, such as whichever option was the preselected default option, to get the decision over with and, as a result, alleviate their negative feelings. Hence, decision biases are exacerbated.

Summary

Conscious emotion and low-level affect both can cause decision errors. Low-level affect can substitute for cognitive analysis during decision making. Conscious emotions can give rise to emotion goals (e.g., avoid regret or diminish negative emotions). One final note is that although emotion can lead to decision errors, it does not always do so. Emotion can act as an important signal of what is important to the decision maker, and in that sense, it can steer behaviors toward worthy goals (e.g., Baumeister et al., 2007). Most work on emotion and decision making has focused on emotion's role in decision errors. Emphasis on emotion-driven errors reflects the judgment and decision making field's roots in exploring deviations from assumptions of rationality rather than necessarily reflecting emotion's general role in decision making.

Judgment and Decision Making Today: Improving Decision Quality

One major thrust emerging from the field of judgment and decision making today is to not only identify decision errors but also to find corrections for them. The study of judgment and decision making has been interdisciplinary from the start, including policy-oriented practitioners as well as basic social scientists. The policy-oriented arm of judgment and decision making is what prompts scholars to find processes that will help decision makers to avoid decision errors. In judgment and decision making today, basic science and policy intersect better than ever before, applying judgment and decision making principles to explain and aid decision problems outside the laboratory.

The field of judgment and decision making began as a field focused on debate between economists' views of "rational man" and psychologists' views of "imperfectly rational man." For many decades, the field was largely focused on identifying decision effects (e.g., framing, misattribution) that illustrated how rational decision makers were or were not. Today, the field is firmly rooted in a rich, psychological view of judgments and decisions and shifting toward more comprehensive views of decisions as complex and flexible psychological processes. It remains to be seen whether these newer views will usurp expected utility and prospect theories. But certainly, by moving beyond debates about whether decision makers are rational, judgment and decision making research is opening up to richer process explanations of decision making.

Richer, more comprehensive views of decision making have lent themselves to understanding the decisions that underlie important societal problems. For instance, the medical and pharmaceutical industries lament the low rate at which people take their medications. One sticking point for patients is when they are low on medication and need to have their prescription refilled. Multiple small steps are involved to do this: Patients have to call to order the prescription to be refilled, go to their neighborhood pharmacy, wait in line, and pay for it. Judgment and decision making scientists know that each step means that people are less likely to follow through in getting their medicines. A series of small decisions (e.g., go to the pharmacy vs. grocery shopping) can mean that people lose sight of the importance of their health goal. To help with this, some plans have started shipping patients' medications to their home on a regular basis. (There is an option for patients to say that they do not want to have their medications shipped to their homes for those who still want to visit the pharmacy.) These plans take advantage of the default effect, which removes all those small decisions that were once needed to get a prescription filled. The hope is that very few patients will actively choose not to have their medications shipped to their homes, which would result in many patients having their medications on hand when they need to take them.

An integration of judgment and decision making principles with other disciplines is also at the forefront of research today. The organization to which judgment and decision making scholars belong is the Society for Judgment and Decision Making (http://www.sjdm.org), which partners with the Society for

Medical Decision Making (http://www.smdm.org) to study healthcare, wellness, and physician and patient decision making. Work in this area is aimed at improving healthcare outcomes by using clinical studies and judgment and decision making ideas to sway patients, researchers, and the politico. Assessing health-related utility is important for these researchers, an example of which involves asking people to make comparisons about living a long time in an impaired health state versus living a shorter life in perfect health.

Social Psychology Can Improve the Study of Judgment and Decision Making

Social psychology brings much to the study of judgment and decision making. Perhaps because social psychology never adhered to the notion of a perfectly rational mind, it underscores the importance of processes that do not fit neatly into mathematical models. Emotion and motivation are two areas to which this comment applies. Judgment and decision making would benefit from incorporating a host of emotions (other than regret) into their theories of decision making (Lerner et al., 2015). The realization that people's decisions reflect their motivation to achieve a multitude of personal and interpersonal goals is a concept not fully embraced by judgment and decision making scholars. But this idea is quite amenable to the field of judgment and decision making because it recognizes that decisions function to maximize goals. Making use of the notion of goals in decision making will also help with the problem of integrating emotion and cognitive influences into decision making.

The field of judgment and decision making also could learn from social psychology the value in gathering seemingly isolated phenomena into overarching theories. Again, perhaps because judgment and decision making scholars were fighting against the idea that decision making is rational, they failed to adopt loftier views of the psyche and the role of judgment and decision making in it. Social psychology and judgment and decision making share common challenges in terms of the struggle between approaching science by finding phenomena and by creating unifying theories. Social psychology's success in building grander theories could provide a roadmap for the field of judgment and decision making.

Social Psychology Can Be Improved by Studying Judgment and Decision Making

Judgment and decision making scholars have approached their discipline with an emphasis on basic phenomena, an emphasis from which the field of social psychology could benefit. A similar note applies to the importance placed on attempting to correct errors, which judgment and decision making does far more than social psychology. There is at times a sense from the field of judgment and decision making that social psychology does not value testing their theories under rich, naturalistic conditions nor on improving people's welfare with their science. The field of social psychology would almost surely have a greater impact on policy and everyday people's lives if it got out of the lab and tried to make life better for folks.

The study of social psychology could also be improved by studying judgment and decision making. Social psychology for the most part fails to grasp the importance of the act of making a decision and the impact that decision mistakes have on people's behavior. The example of battered women returning to their abusive partners illustrates that decision making is wildly important to relationship and life outcomes. Social psychological theories would be well served by tracking the decision processes that people go through and social psychologists may find new avenues for understanding their favorite topic of study.

In Closing: Big Ideas

The topics and methods of study that judgment and decision making scholars use have the potential to be applied to big ideas. New insights on genocide came about because Slovic (2007) incorporated ideas of how the emotion system reacts—actually, overreacts—to tragedy, a theory that was informed in part by social psychological ideas about emotions. Slovic found that the distress of seeing one victim is so great that adding a second victim, paradoxically, lessens the distress that people feel because the overwhelming emotion prompts them to disengage from the situation. Hence, the use of judgment and decision making helps to explain a tragically massive problem, with implications for mobilizing the political will to help genocide victims.

In addition to big ideas, there are opportunities for big interventions. Following Slovic's (2007) insights, a recent study indicates that training people to use cognition to reduce emotion can aid endorsement of conciliatory policies in the Israeli–Palestinian conflict (Halpern et al., 2012). In one of the widest-reaching set of developments, real policy action is making use of findings from the field of judgment and decision making. Following the popularity of Thaler and Sunstein's (2009) book *Nudge*, for instance, the British Cabinet Office, World Bank, and Australian government all have created teams (often called "nudge units") charged with leveraging behavioral science to foster positive social outcomes. The UK unit reports studies on a wide array of prosocial topics such as evaluating energy savings from smart thermostats, testing direct mail interventions to increase college applications by talented yet impoverished potential scholars, and deconstructing complex behaviors to identify interventions to improve health outcomes while saving money. As social psychology and judgment and decision making continue to merge, we expect increasingly impactful insights into societies' biggest problems.

References

Ariely, D., Loewenstein, G., & Prelec, D. (2003). "Coherent arbitrariness": Stable demand curves without stable preferences, *Quarterly Journal of Economics, 118,* 73–105.

Allen, M. & Pierce, O. (2016). Study urges CDC to revise count of deaths from medical error. *ProPublica.* Retrieved from https://www.propublica.org/article/study-urges-cdc-to-revise-count-of-deaths-from-medical-error

Baumeister, R. F., & Leary, M. R. (1995). The need to belong: Desire for interpersonal attachments as a fundamental human motivation. *Psychological Bulletin, 117,* 497–529.

Baumeister, R. F., Bratslavsky, E., Finkenauer, C., & Vohs, K. D. (2001). Bad is stronger than good. *Review of General Psychology, 5,* 323–370.

Baumeister, R. F., Vohs, K. D., DeWall, N., & Zhang, L. (2007). How emotion shapes behavior: Feedback, anticipation, and reflection, rather than direct causation. *Personality and Social Psychology Review, 11,* 167–203.

Benartzi, S., & Thaler, R. H. (2001). Naive diversification strategies in defined contribution saving plans. *American Economic Review, 91,* 79–98.

Brighton, H., & Gigerenzer, G. (2012). Homo heuristicus: Less-is-more in adaptive cognition. *Malaysian Journal of Medical Sciences, 19,* 6–16.

Dijksterhus, A., Bos, M. W., Nordgren, L. F., & van Baaren, R.B. (2006). On making the right choice: The deliberation-without-attention effect. *Science, 311,* 1005–1007.

Epley, N., Keysar, B., Van Boven, L., & Gilovich, T. (2004). Perspective taking as egocentric anchoring and adjustment. *Journal of Personality and Social Psychology, 87,* 327–339.

Frederick, S. (2005). Cognitive reflection and decision making. *Journal of Economic Perspectives, 19,* 25–42.

Gigerenzer, G., & Goldstein, D. G., (1996). Reasoning the fast and frugal way: Models of bounded rationality. *Psychological Review, 103,* 650–669.

Gilovich, T., & Medvec, V. H. (1995). The experience of regret: What, when, and why. *Psychological Review, 102,* 379–395.

Gottman, J. (1994). *Why marriages succeed or fail.* New York: Simon & Schuster.

Halperin, E., Porat, R., Tamir, M., & Gross, J.J. (2012). Can emotion regulation change political attitudes in intractable conflicts? From the laboratory to the field. *Psychological Science, 24,* 106–111.

Hammond, K. R., Hamm, R. M., Grassia, J., & Pearson, T. (1987). Direct comparison of the efficacy of intuitive and analytical cognition in expert judgment. *IEEE Transactions, Systems, Man and Cybernetics, 17,* 753–770.

Hofmann, W., Luhmann, M., Fisher, R. R., Vohs, K. D., & Baumeister, R. F. (2014). Yes, but are they happy? Effects of trait self-control on affective well-being and life satisfaction. *Journal of Personality, 82,* 265–277.

Hsee, C. K., & Rottenstreich, Y. (2004). Music, pandas, and muggers: on the affective psychology of value. *Journal of Experimental Psychology: General, 133,* 23–30.

Huber, J., Payne, J. W., & Puto, C. (1982). Adding asymmetrically dominated alternatives: Violations of regularity and the similarity hypothesis. *Journal of Consumer Research, 9,* 90–98.

Johnson E. J., & Goldstein D. (2003). Do defaults save lives? *Science, 302,* 1338–1339.

Johnson, E. J., & Tversky, A. (1983). Affect, generalization, and the perception of risk. *Journal of Personality and Social Psychology, 45,* 20–31.

Kahneman, D. (2003, November). *Tying it all together: Rules of accessibility and a two-systems view.* Keynote address at the Annual Conference of Society for Judgment and Decision Making, Vancouver, Canada.

Kahneman, D., & Frederick, S. (2002). Representativeness revisited: Attribute substitution in intuitive judgment. In T. Gilovich, D. Griffin, & D. Kahneman (Eds.), *Heuristics & biases: The psychology of intuitive judgment* (pp. 49–81). New York, NY: Cambridge University Press.

Kahneman, D., Knetsch, J. L., & Thaler, R. H. (1990). Experimental tests of the endowment effect and the Coase theorem. *Journal of Political Economy, 98,* 1325–1348.

Kahneman, D., & Tversky, A. (1979). Prospect theory: An analysis of decisions under risk. *Econometrika, 47,* 263–291.

Keeney, R. (2008). Personal decisions are the leading cause of death. *Operations Research, 56,* 1335–1347.

Lazarus, R. S. (1981). A cognitivist's reply to Zajonc on emotion and cognition. *American Psychologist, 36,* 222–223.

Lerner, J.S., Li, Y., Valdesolo, P., & Kassam, K.S. (2015). Emotion and decision making. *Annual Review of Psychology, 66,* 799–823.

Lerner, J. S., Li, Y., & Weber, E. U. (2013). The financial costs of sadness. *Psychological Science, 24,* 72–79.

Levin, I. P., & Gaeth, G. J. (1988). How consumers are affected by the framing of attribute information before and after consuming the product. *Journal of Consumer Research, 15,* 374–386.

Luce, M. F. (1998). Choosing to avoid: Coping with negatively emotion-laden consumer decisions. *Journal of Consumer Research, 24,* 409–433.

Makary, M. A., & Daniels, M. (2016). Medical error—the third leading cause of death in the US. *BMJ, 353,* i2139–i2141.

Newell, B. R., & Shanks, D. R., (2014). Unconscious influences on decision making: A critical review. *Behavioral and Brain Sciences, 37,* 1–62.

Payne, J. W., Bettman, J. R., & Johnson, E. J. (1993). *The adaptive decision maker.* Cambridge, England: Cambridge University Press.

Payne, J. W., Bettman, J. R., & Schkade, D. A. (1999). Measuring constructed preferences: Towards a building code. *Journal of Risk and Uncertainty, 19,* 243–270.

Payne, J. W., Samper, A., Bettman, J. R., & Luce, M. F. (2008). Boundary conditions on unconscious thought in complex decision making. *Psychological Science, 19,* 1118–1123.

Read, D., & Loewenstein, G. (1995). Diversification bias: Explaining the discrepancy in variety seeking between combined and separated choices. *Journal of Experimental Psychology: Applied, 1,* 34–49.

Roese, N. J., & Vohs, K. D. (2012). Hindsight bias. *Perspectives on Psychological Science, 7*, 411–426.

Rusbult, C. E., & Martz, J. M. (1995). Remaining in an abusive relationship: An investment model analysis of nonvoluntary dependence. Personality and Social *Psychology Bulletin, 21*, 558–571.

Schwarz, N., & Clore, G. L. (1983). Mood, misattribution, and judgments of well-being: Informative and directive functions of affective states. *Journal of Personality and Social Psychology, 45*, 513–523.

Simon, H. (1955). A behavioural model of rational choice. *Quarterly Journal of Economics, 69*, 99–118.

Simonsohn, U. (2010). Weather to go to college. *Economic Journal, 120*, 270–280.

Simonson, I. (1989). Choice based on reasons: The case of attraction and compromise effects. *Journal of Consumer Research, 16*, 158–174.

Simonson, I. (1992). The influence of anticipating regret and responsibility on purchase decisions. *Journal of Consumer Research, 19*, 105–118.

Simonson, I., & Nye, P. (1992). The effect of accountability on susceptibility to decision errors. *Organizational Behavior and Human Decision Processes, 51*, 416–446.

Slovic, P. (2007). "If I look at the mass I will never act": Psychic numbing and genocide. *Judgment and Decision Making, 2*, 79–95.

Slovic, P., Finucane, M. L., Peters E. & MacGregor, D. G., (2007). The affect heuristic. *European Journal of Operational Research, 177*, 1333–1339.

Thaler, R. H., & Sunstein, C. R. (2009). *Nudge: Improving decisions about health, wealth, and happiness*. New Haven, CT: Yale University Press.

Toplak, M. E., West, R. F., & Stanovich, K. E. (2011). The cognitive reflection test as a predictor of performance on heuristics-and-biases tasks. *Memory and Cognition, 39*, 1275–1289.

Tversky, A., & Kahneman, D. (1973). Availability: A heuristic for judging frequency and probability. *Cognitive Psychology, 5*, 207–232.

Von Neumann, J., & Morgenstern, O. (1944). *Theory of games and economic behavior*. Princeton, NJ: University Press.

Wansink, B., Kent, B. J., & Hoch, S J. (1998). An anchoring and adjustment model of purchase quantity decisions. *Journal of Marketing Research, 19*, 71—81.

Wilson, T. D., & Schooler, J. W. (1991). Thinking too much: Introspection can reduce the quality of preferences and decisions. *Journal of Personality and Social Psychology, 60*, 181–192.

Wilson, T. D., & Gilbert, D. T. (2005). Affective forecasting: Knowing what to want. *Current Directions in Psychological Science, 14*, 131–134.

Winkielman, P., Schwartz, N., & Belli, R. F. (1998). The role of ease of retrieval and attribution in memory judgment: Judging your memory as worse despite recalling more events. *Psychological Science, 9*, 124–126

Zajonc, R. B. (1980). Feeling and thinking: Preferences need no inferences. *American Psychologist, 35*, 151–175.

Chapter 20

Personality

Charles S. Carver

Social psychology focuses on interpersonal phenomena: how the individual's behavior is influenced by other people, present or implied. As a field, social psychology tends to fragment into broad topic areas that reflect particular "contents" of behavior: qualities such as aggression, helping, and interpersonal attraction. Sometimes the contents under examination are intrinsically interpersonal in nature, as in those three examples. Sometimes the contents are fully within the individual (e.g., attitudes), but the focal interest of the social psychologist is how these aspects of the individual are influenced by, or relate to, other people. In contrast, personality psychology focuses on qualities organized within the individual, although those internal qualities are often displayed in actions that involve other people.

The stereotype of personality psychologists is that they focus on individual differences. Some people assume for that reason that they care *only* about individual differences. That actually isn't true. Personality psychologists focus partly on things that make people different from each other, but partly on things that make people the same—shared structures and dynamics. I have used the phrase *intrapersonal functioning* to refer to these shared internal properties (Carver & Scheier, 2008). Allport (1961), far more eloquently, called them a dynamic organization of psychological systems within each person that create the person's pattern of behaviors, thoughts, and feelings.

Statements about the nature of intrapersonal functioning often represent statements about the nature of people's core motivations. They are statements about what forces are at the center of people's actions, feelings, and thoughts over extended periods of time and diverse circumstances. For example, some views of personality hold that people's core motives concern relationships with significant others. Some views assume that people's core motives concern predicting and adapting better to the world. Some assume that people's central motives are the same as those of any other biological creature: obtaining the necessities of life, avoiding danger, and reproducing.

To some extent, assumptions about core motives are captured in the phrase *human nature*. Personality psychologists, because they focus on the whole person as an entity and how that person functions over time and situations, are interested in views that help capture the essence of human nature. Many people use the phrase *human nature*, but what really *is* human nature? The answer depends on whom you ask.

Personality psychologists are not the only ones interested in such issues, of course. The same issues arise in social psychology but usually more obliquely. As social psychologists set out to study a given phenomenon, they implicitly (and sometimes explicitly) adopt one or another set of assumptions about human nature and its core motivations. They implicitly assume some model of personality as a lens for looking at how people influence each other. In this way, some view of personality (even if it consists more of a sketch of assumptions than an explicit theory) forms the underlying basis for an analysis of social psychological phenomena. This is one place where personality psychology intersects with social psychology. Because there almost always is an implicit view of human nature behind a social psychological explanation, social psychology almost always has personality as a silent partner in the explanatory process.

A second point of intersection between these fields returns us to the familiar picture of personality as individual differences. It is possible for a social situation to be so potent that it forces everyone's behavior to be essentially the same, but such situations are rare. Far more common are situations that permit some degree of variation in behavior, even while exerting their own influence. When there is room for variability in behavior, it is virtually certain that part of that variability will stem from personality. Some people are more affected than others by any given situational pressure. The people who are most affected are not necessarily the same from one situation to the next, because the nature of the pressure varies across situations. Thus, situational pressures interact with personality, often in subtle ways. A secondary question that always arises across the diverse content areas of social psychology is what kinds of individual differences make the phenomenon under study more likely or less likely to occur (Leary & Hoyle, 2009).

This chapter describes some of the viewpoints that are influential in today's personality psychology. Some of them have been around for a very long time; others are more recent. Because personality psychology tends to evolve more slowly than social psychology, even the "recent" views have roots in older ideas. This chapter surveys these viewpoints in broad strokes. A good deal of detail is left out (for a more detailed look, see Carver & Scheier, 2008). In each case, however, an effort has been made to portray that viewpoint in a way that allows it to serve as a backdrop for thinking about the phenomena of social psychology.

Trait Psychology and the Five-Factor Model

The easiest starting point for personality is probably the trait concept. The essence of this construct is ancient. The trait is both a common-sense concept and a scientific concept. Traits are dimensions of variability, which are presumed to be grounded within the person and which are reflected in behaviors, thoughts, and emotions. All views of personality necessarily incorporate some ideas about traits, because traits are the dimensions on which individual differences exist. Although traits thus are implicit in all of personality psychology, one segment of the field has traditionally focused more on traits than have others.

The people who work in this tradition have focused particularly on the question of what traits are fundamental and what ones are less so. The process of deciding which traits are basic, along with the secondary question of how best to measure those traits and place people on the dimensions of their variability, is the crux of this approach to personality. This approach has generally been more concerned with individual differences than with core motives and dynamics, though even that statement is not universally true (e.g., Eysenck, 1967, 1986, addressed both themes with equal enthusiasm).

There has long been a division of opinion among trait psychologists about how best to approach the question of what traits are most basic. Eysenck (1967, 1986) argued that theorists should begin with well-developed ideas about what they want to measure and then try to measure those qualities well (this is referred to as a theoretical path of measure development). Cattell (1965, 1978) argued that researchers should determine empirically what traits underlie personality (an empirical path) and not impose theoretical preconceptions. In this view, deciding first what traits are basic tempts you to force reality to fit your ideas. Today's trait theorists tend to favor Cattell's view on this issue in principle (Goldberg, 1993), but there is disagreement about how faithfully they have actually adhered to it in practice (Block, 1995).

The effort to let reality tell you what traits are basic is fairly complicated. It requires gathering large numbers of observations of diverse reflections of traits and then determining where there are commonalities and what those commonalities mean. Early efforts made use of the idea that languages arose in human cultures partly to convey information about what people are like. The descriptive words in various languages thus should provide a rich source of evidence about what traits matter. Specifically, important traits should be reflected in more words (this is called the lexical criterion of importance).

This is a good start, but trying to sort through thousands of descriptive words and determine their relationships to each other was a logistical nightmare. Two things changed that: the development of a methodological technique called factor analysis and the development of computers (early factor analyses were done slowly and painfully by hand, and it was hard to be sure errors did not creep in). Factor analysis allows researchers to locate commonalities easily among thousands of observations. Commonalities among ratings on descriptors are believed to reflect traits. A trait might be reflected very strongly in some descriptors and less so in many more. Even those limited reflections represent evidence that the trait is important, though, because it is implicated in many parts of the lexicon.

Despite different starting points taken by various people, a substantial consensus has emerged about what traits are basic, at least at a broad level of analysis. The emerging consensus is that the structure of personality incorporates five superordinate factors, which often are called the five-factor model or the "big five" (Goldberg, 1981; McCrae & Costa, 2003; Wiggins, 1996). The five factors are most commonly known by the labels extraversion, neuroticism, agreeableness, conscientiousness, and openness to experience (McCrae & Costa, 2003). (Some people find it easier to remember them by using the acronyms OCEAN or CANOE.)

In most views of the five factors, each is composed of subordinate traits with narrower properties. Typically, the overall factor is formed from facet scales that represent the narrower traits. If the facets that contribute to the five broad traits are considered separately, the picture is more nuanced, because the facets play different roles in behavior. (It also is far more complex than is the picture that considers only the five superordinate factors.)

Consensus on the five-factor view of individual differences does not mean unanimity. There remain staunch advocates of other frameworks. There are two three-factor models (Eysenck, 1975, 1986; Tellegen, 1985), in which elements of conscientiousness and agreeableness blend into traits that are called, respectively, psychoticism and constraint. There also is a six-factor model that adds honesty/humility to the big five (Ashton et al., 2004), and an alternative-five model (Zuckerman et al., 1993), in which different facets of the five factors are emphasized. There have also been efforts to distill the five factors down to two (DeYoung, 2006; DeYoung, Peterson, & Higgins, 2001; Digman, 1997).

The next sections describe the five factors in more detail, starting with the two that have been studied the longest and about which the greatest consensus exists. These two are also part of the three-factor models, as well as the six-factor and alternative-five models.

The Two Most Agreed-Upon Factors: Extraversion and Neuroticism

The first factor is extraversion. As is true of several traits in the five-factor model, extraversion has different emphases in different measures. Sometimes extraversion is viewed as being based in assertiveness, sometimes in spontaneity and energy. Sometimes it is based in dominance, confidence, and agency (Depue &

Collins, 1999), sometimes in a tendency toward positive emotions (indeed, Tellegen, 1985, calls it positive emotionality). Extraversion is often thought of as implying a sense of sociability (Watson, Clark, McIntyre, & Hamaker, 1992), but some argue that the sociability is a byproduct of other features of extraversion (Lucas, Diener, Grob, Suh, & Shao, 2000). Others see the sense of agency and the sense of sociability as being two separate facets of extraversion (Depue & Morrone-Strupinsky, 2005).

Whether extraversion concerns true sociability or not, it does appear to concern having social impact (Jensen-Campbell & Graziano, 2001). For example, extraverted men interact better with women they don't know than do introverts (Berry & Miller, 2001), and extraverts have the firm handshake that conveys confidence (Chaplin, Phillips, Brown, Clanton, & Stein, 2000). The desire for social impact can have a more problematic side, however. For example, extraverts are less cooperative than introverts when facing a social dilemma over resources (Koole, Jager, van den Berg, Vlek, & Hofstee, 2001).

The second factor, neuroticism, concerns the ease and frequency with which the person becomes upset and distressed. Moodiness, anxiety, and depression reflect higher neuroticism. Neuroticism scales often include facets pertaining to hostility and other negative feelings, but there is also some disagreement about whether those particular negative feelings might really belong in another factor (Carver, 2004; Jang et al., 2002; Peabody & DeRaad, 2002; Saucier & Goldberg, 2001). In any case, it is generally agreed that the core of neuroticism is vulnerability to subjective experiences of anxiety, worry, and general distress.

Neuroticism also has a clear impact on social behavior. Neuroticism relates to more difficult interactions among married partners (Donnellan et al., 2004) and less satisfaction in the relationship. People who are highly neurotic are also more likely to distance themselves from their partners after a negative event (Bolger & Zuckerman, 1995). Neuroticism impairs academic performance (Chamorro-Premuzic & Furnham, 2003), and it predicts a negative emotional tone when writing stories about oneself (McAdams et al., 2004).

Agreeableness, Conscientiousness, and Openness

The next factor is agreeableness. Agreeableness as a dimension is often characterized as being broadly concerned with maintaining relationships (Jensen-Campbell & Graziano, 2001). Agreeable people are friendly and helpful (John & Srivastava, 1999), empathic (Graziano, Habashi, Sheese, & Tobin, 2007), and able to inhibit their negative feelings (Graziano & Eisenberg, 1999). Having a high level of this trait seems to short-circuit aggressive responses (Meier, Robinson, & Wilkowski, 2006), because agreeable people get less angry over others' transgressions than do less agreeable people (Meier & Robinson, 2004), and they are less likely to seek revenge after being harmed (McCullough & Hoyt, 2002).

At the opposite pole is an antagonistic quality, verging on hostility (this is the other place where feelings of anger may belong). People low in agreeableness use displays of power to deal with social conflict more than do others (Graziano, Jensen-Campbell, & Hair, 1996) and are more prone to antisocial behavior (Miller, Lynam, & Leukefeld, 2003).

The most commonly used label for the next factor is conscientiousness. However, this label does not fully reflect the qualities of planning, persistence, and purposeful striving toward goals that are part of it (Digman & Inouye, 1986). Other suggested names include constraint and responsibility, reflecting qualities of impulse control and reliability. Precisely what qualities are included in this trait varies considerably across measures (Roberts, Walton, & Bogg, 2005).

Conscientiousness has received a good deal of attention in recent years. Among the findings: Conscientious people are less likely to try to steal someone else's romantic partner and are less likely to be lured away (Schmitt & Buss, 2001). Conscientiousness relates to more responsive parenting of young children (Clark, Kochanska, & Ready, 2000) and to use of negotiation as a conflict-resolution strategy (Jensen-Campbell & Graziano, 2001).

Conscientiousness also predicts various kinds of health-related behaviors (Bogg & Roberts, 2004; Roberts et al., 2005). Indeed, conscientiousness in childhood has been related to health behaviors 40 years later (Hampson, Goldberg, Vogt, & Dubanoski, 2006). Greater conscientiousness predicts avoidance of unsafe sex (Trobst, Herbst, Masters, & Costa, 2002) and other risk behaviors (Markey, Markey, & Tinsley, 2003). A recent meta-analysis links conscientiousness to longer life (Kern & Friedman, 2008), perhaps because it is associated with fewer risky behaviors and better treatment adherence. Consistent with this, conscientiousness relates to lower levels of substance abuse (Chassin et al., 2004; Lynam et al., 2003; Roberts & Bogg, 2004; Walton & Roberts, 2004).

Agreeableness and conscientiousness appear to have an important property in common. Both traits suggest a breadth of perspective on life. Many manifestations of conscientiousness imply broad time perspective: taking future contingencies into account. Agreeableness implies a broad social perspective: taking the needs of others into account.

The fifth factor is one about which there is probably the most disagreement regarding content. The most widely used label for it is openness to experience (Costa & McCrae, 1985). Some measures (and theories) imbue this factor with greater overtones of intelligence, however, terming it intellect (Peabody & Goldberg, 1989). It involves curiosity, flexibility, imagination, and willingness to immerse oneself in atypical experiences (for review of its involvement in social experience, see McCrae, 1996). Openness to experience has been found to predict greater engagement with the existential challenges of life (Keyes, Shmotkin, & Ryff, 2002), to more favorable interracial attitudes (Flynn, 2005), and to greater sexual satisfaction in marriage (Donnellan et al., 2004).

The Five-Factor View in Sum

In the five-factor view of personality, people can be placed on each of these dimensions according to their characteristic patterns of thoughts, feelings, and actions. The aggregation of information about the person resulting from these placements gives a reasonably good snapshot of what that person is like. In fact, the trait perspective has been called the "psychology of the stranger" (McAdams, 1992), in part because it provides the kind of information that would be important if you knew nothing about a person.

On the other hand, the phrase "psychology of the stranger" also reflects the view that this perspective does not say much about the dynamic aspects of personality. Labeling a person as sociable or dominant gives a name to what you see, but it doesn't tell you much about how or why the person acts that way. Others have similarly argued that this model says little about how the factors function or how they map onto any picture of human nature (Block, 1995).

This has changed to a considerable extent over the past two decades. A great deal more information has been collected on how traits function in life settings. Furthermore, several of the trait dimensions have also been linked to another model bearing on personality in which dynamics and process play a much larger role. This model is described next.

Biological Process Model

What might be characterized as a biological process model is an increasingly influential view of personality. It has roots in several places. One of them is Eysenck's (1967, 1975) version of the trait perspective. Eysenck consistently tried to ground his ideas about extraversion and neuroticism in a picture of brain functions.

Another starting point is a view of early childhood temperaments. Temperaments are biological systems that affect broad aspects of behavior and form the basis of personality. For example, one basic human function is seeking out the things we need to stay alive and prosper, such as food, shelter, and social connection; this important function may be reflected in personality as individual differences in incentive sensitivity or extraversion. Some personality psychologists have long been interested in temperaments (e.g., Buss & Plomin, 1975), but most work on temperaments has been done by developmental psychologists (e.g., Derryberry & Rothbart, 1997; Rothbart & Bates, 1998; Rothbart & Posner, 1985; Rothbart, Ahadi, & Evans, 2000; Rothbart, Ahadi, Hershey, & Fisher, 2001; Rothbart, Ellis, Rueda, & Posner, 2003).

Another basis for the development of a biological process model of personality is the increasing influence of a family of theories pertaining to animal behavior, psychopharmacology, and neuroscience. These viewpoints emphasize the continuity between humans and other animal species. They also focus on information obtained by research tools involving both manipulation of the nervous system by chemical means and observation of activities of the nervous system by imaging techniques.

From this biological viewpoint, it is important to understand the fundamental properties of animal self-regulation and how those properties are manifested both in the nervous system and in human personality. Three basic tendencies are considered in this section. By themselves, they yield considerable complexity. Two of them are organized tendencies to approach situations and objects that are desirable (e.g., food) and to avoid situations and objects that are dangerous (e.g., predators). These organized tendencies exist for all animals, and the regulation of these basic processes represents a core activity for humans as well.

Fitting that idea, a number of theorists have posited basic approach and avoidance temperaments as key aspects of the organization of the nervous system (e.g., Caspi & Shiner, 2006; Caspi et al., 2005; Davidson, 1992, 1998; Depue & Collins, 1999; Elliott & Thrash, 2002; Fowles, 1993; Gray, 1982, 1994a, 1994b; Rothbart & Bates, 1998). Most theorists of this group believe that one set of brain structures is differentially involved in the processes by which animals organize the approach of incentives and that a second set of brain structures is involved in the processes by which animals organize the avoidance of threats.

Approach

The structures involved in approach have been given several names: activation system (Cloninger, 1987; Fowles, 1980), behavioral engagement system (Depue, Krauss, & Spoont, 1987), behavioral facilitation system (Depue & Iacono, 1989), and behavioral approach system (Gray, 1987, 1990, 1994a, 1994b), and they are often abbreviated BAS. You might think of this system as regulating the psychological gas pedal, moving you toward what you want. It's a *go* system, a reward-seeking system (Fowles, 1980).

The set of brain structures underlying this system is presumed to be involved whenever a person is pursuing an incentive. It is likely that there is differentiation such that certain parts of the brain are involved in the pursuit of food, others in the pursuit of sex, and so on (Gable, 2006; Panksepp, 1998). But some believe that the separate parts also link up to an overall BAS. Thus, the BAS is seen as a general mechanism to go after things you want. BAS doesn't rev you up in neutral, though, without an incentive in mind (Depue & Collins, 1999). It's engaged only in the active pursuit of incentives. The BAS is also held to be responsible for many kinds of positive emotions (e.g., hope, eagerness, and excitement), emotions that reflect the anticipation of obtaining incentives.

From temperaments emerge traits. Here is one place where the emerging biological process models intersect with the trait approach. A number of people have linked the trait of extraversion to the approach temperament (Carver, Sutton, & Scheier, 2000; Caspi & Shiner, 2006; Caspi et al., 2005; Depue & Collins,

1999; Elliott & Thrash, 2002; Rothbart & Bates, 1998). That is, some people view extraversion as reflecting the sensitivity of a general approach system. In this view, extraverts have a large appetite for incentives (particularly, though not exclusively, social incentives), whereas introverts are less drawn to them.

Avoidance

The structures involved in avoidance of threat have also received several names: Gray (1987, 1990, 1994a, 1994b) initially suggested the label behavioral inhibition system (BIS). Others have referred to an avoidance system (Cloninger, 1987) or withdrawal system (Davidson, 1988, 1992, 1995). Activity in this system may cause people to inhibit movement (especially if they are currently approaching an incentive) or to pull back from what they just encountered. You might think of this system as a psychological brake pedal, a *stop* system. Alternatively, you might think of it as a *throw-it-into-reverse* system.

The avoidance temperament is responsive to cues of punishment or danger. When this system is engaged, the person may stop and scan for further cues about the threat, or the person may pull back. Since this is the system that responds to threat, danger, or other to-be-avoided stimuli, this system is also thought to be responsible for feelings such as anxiety, guilt, and revulsion, feelings that reflect anticipation of aversive stimuli.

Here again the biological process models intersect with the trait approach. A number of people have linked the trait of neuroticism to the avoidance temperament (Carver et al., 2000; Caspi & Shiner, 2006; Caspi et al., 2005; Rothbart & Bates, 1998). This connection is consistent with the view that anxiety is the emotional core of neuroticism. Some people now view levels of trait neuroticism as reflecting the sensitivity of a general avoidance or withdrawal system. In this view, those high in neuroticism are very sensitive to punishment, whereas those lower in neuroticism are more indifferent to it.

Effortful Control

Another temperament posited by developmental theorists (e.g., Rothbart, Ellis, & Posner, 2004; Rothbart & Posner, 1985) is generally termed effortful control (see also Kochanska & Knaack, 2003; Nigg, 2000, 2003, 2006; Rothbart & Rueda, 2005). Effortful control develops more slowly than the approach and avoidance temperaments (Casey, Getz, & Galvan, 2008). It is superordinate to both approach and avoidance temperaments, capable of overriding impulses that stem from those more basic temperaments. It thus acts as a supervisory system, if sufficient mental resources are available. The label "effortful" conveys the sense that this is a planful activity, requiring the use of cognitive resources to constrain the tendency to react impulsively.

Effortful control is a construct from developmental psychology, but its features resemble those of adult self-control (Vohs & Baumeister, 2016). Self-control is the ability to override impulses to act, as well as the ability to make oneself initiate or persist in boring, difficult, or disliked activity. Self-control appears to depend on higher executive functions that are grounded in prefrontal cortical areas. Guidance of self-regulation by this temperament provides some muting of emotions (Carver, Johnson, & Joormann, 2009) and permits the organism to plan for the future and to take situational complexities into account in making behavioral decisions.

This temperament also has been linked to the five-factor model, though the connection is more complicated than the connections for approach and avoidance. I noted earlier that agreeableness and conscientiousness both imply breadth of perspective: agreeableness a broad social perspective and conscientiousness a broad time perspective. Consistent with this similarity between these two traits, it has been suggested that both traits derive from the effortful control temperament (Ahadi & Rothbart, 1994; Caspi & Shiner, 2006; Jensen-Campbell et al., 2002). Effortful control similarly reflects a breadth of perspective, leading the person to be able to override immediate impulses to optimize broader outcomes.

There is at least some evidence suggesting that effortful control relies on brain areas other than those subserving the basic approach and avoidance functions. It is often suggested that the brain structures underlying effortful control evolved more recently than those underlying the basic approach and avoidance functions. To put it in more behavioral terms, the ability to exert self-control reflects an evolutionary advance.

Biological Process View in Sum

The biological process approach to personality is an attempt to ask what functions a living animal needs and how those functions are reflected in personality. Approaching desired incentives and avoiding dangers are primitive necessities, though there is also room for individual variation in the strength of those motivations. These core motives—striving for things you want and avoiding harm—are surely part of human nature. Behavioral tendencies to which these motives lead are part of personality.

Effortful control also serves important biological purposes, though perhaps not as basic as the approach and avoidance temperaments. Effortful control provides the opportunity to gain in ways that are greater than the gains that come from impulse alone. There are times when delay of gratification (or withholding an angry retort) does result in better final results, and it is those outcomes that are made possible by effortful control.

I have not mentioned the research literature bearing on neural correlates of various sorts of mental activity or another research literature bearing on neurotransmitters and the role they play in various classes of behavior. These are very active areas of work, and they are clearly pertinent to the connection between personality and social psychology. However, for present purposes, the points they make are refinements of this general theme: To varying degrees, people seek rewards, avoid threats, and take multiple factors into account in planning their behaviors.

Cognitive Self-Regulatory Models

The next view of personality I will take up is a loose collection of ideas I will refer to as cognitive self-regulatory models. The biological-process view of personality emphasizes the functional systems that are required by a living biological entity. The self-regulatory models emphasize the cognitive processes that are involved in managing behavior. There are some distinct similarities between the two viewpoints, though they have very different starting points.

Goals

Cognitive self-regulatory models have roots in an expectancy-value motivational tradition. Values are qualities that are endorsed or rejected, qualities that are positively valenced or negatively valenced. In today's incarnation of the expectancy-value viewpoint, the operative construct is most likely to be goals (Austin & Vancouver, 1996; Carver & Scheier, 1998; Elliott, 2008; Higgins, 1996; Markus & Nurius, 1986; Moskowitz & Grant, 2009). The term *value* today tends to connote qualities that are relatively abstract

(Schwartz, 1992; Schwartz & Bilsky, 1990); these abstract qualities are realized in behavior by pursuit of more concrete goals, which in turn can be broken down into subgoals.

Diverse goal-based theories hold that it is important to distinguish between motivational processes aimed at moving toward *goals* and those aimed at staying away from *threats* (Carver & Scheier, 1998; Elliott, 2008; Higgins 1996). A desired goal has a positive incentive value that pulls behavior to it. Looming harm or pain has a *dis*incentive value that pushes behavior away from it. Sometimes approach and avoidance tendencies conflict with each other, as when approaching a desired incentive also increases threat. Sometimes approach and avoidance processes are mutually supportive, because sometimes attaining a desired incentive will simultaneously forestall something the person wants to avoid.

In goal-based views of personality, understanding the person means (in part) understanding the goals the person has and the values that motivate his or her actions (Markus & Nurius, 1986; Mischel & Shoda, 1995). Many complexities follow from this, including the extent to which people are motivated more by approach versus avoidance goals (e.g., Elliot & Sheldon, 1998; Gable & Berkman, 2008; Higgins & Tykocinski, 1992) and the extent to which people's focal goals are concrete versus abstract in nature (e.g., Liberman & Trope, 2008; Vallacher & Wegner, 1989). More obviously, even within the same behavioral context, people can be in pursuit of very different endpoints; to predict their behavior requires knowing what they are trying to do.

The emphasis on approach and avoidance motivational processes (and the importance of the distinction between these processes) is one respect in which this viewpoint resembles the biological process view. A difference is that this view has generally not been concerned with biological underpinnings of the goal-regulation process.

Expectancies

Consistent with the expectancy-value heritage of this approach, goal-based models also typically incorporate an expectancy construct in some form or other: the sense of confidence or doubt that a given outcome will be attained successfully (e.g. Bandura, 1986; Carver & Scheier, 1998). Not every behavior produces its intended outcome; goal directed efforts can be thwarted by impediments. Under such conditions, people's efforts are believed to be determined partly by their expectancies of success or failure (e.g., Bandura, 1986; Brehm & Self, 1989; Carver & Scheier, 1998; Eccles & Wigfield, 2002; Klinger, 1975; Wright, 1996).

People vary from context to context in their levels of confidence. Some theorists emphasize that many expectancies are domain-specific and even situation-specific. There also are differences among people, however, in their more generalized sense of confidence about life-in-general. This variation is what constitutes the personality dimension of optimism versus pessimism (Carver & Scheier, 2018; Carver, Scheier, Miller, & Fulford, 2009; Scheier & Carver, 1992).

Abandonment and Scaling Back of Goals

Goal-based models often incorporate an element that is less obvious in biological models. When impediments to goal attainment are severe, people sometimes give up. Indeed, when goals are unattainable, it can be very important to give them up (Miller & Worsch, 2007; Wrosch, Miller, Scheier, & Brun de Pontet, 2007). The process of disengaging from goals that are beyond reach, and the negative feelings that are part of that process—sadness, despair—are adaptive and functional in such circumstances (Klinger, 1975; Nesse, 2000).

When a valued goal is abandoned, however, it is important that the person eventually take up another. The absence of a goal yields a sense of emptiness. Disengagement appears to be a valuable and adaptive response when it leads to—or is directly tied to—moving on to other goals (Wrosch et al., 2007). By taking up an attainable alternative, the person remains engaged in activities that have meaning for the self, and life continues to have purpose.

An alternative to giving up altogether is to scale the goal back to something more restricted in the same general domain. This is a kind of limited disengagement, in the sense that the initial goal no longer remains in place. It avoids a complete disengagement from the domain of behavior, however, by substituting the more restricted goal. This shift thus keeps the person involved in that area of life, at a level that holds the potential for successful outcomes. It represents an accommodation rather than a complete relinquishing.

Dual-Process Models

The collection of theories I have referred to here as cognitive self-regulation models are perhaps more diverse than any other group of theories discussed in this chapter. In many ways, placing a particular theory into this group is somewhat arbitrary. Nonetheless, this may be the place to mention dual-process models in personality psychology. These models assume two ways of processing experiences: one more basic and automatic, the other more deliberative and reflective. There are many such models in social psychology (e.g., Chaiken & Trope, 1999; Lieberman, Gaunt, Gilbert, & Trope, 2002; Smith & DeCoster, 2000; Strack & Deutsch, 2004; Wilson, Lindsey, & Schooler, 2000), and there are also such models in personality psychology.

Epstein's (1973, 1985, 1990, 1994) cognitive-experiential self theory may have been the first explicitly dual-process model in contemporary psychology. Epstein started with the premise that humans experience reality via two systems. One is a symbolic processor—the rational mind. The other is associative and intuitive, and functions automatically and quickly. Epstein argued that both systems are always at work and that they jointly determine behavior.

Metcalfe and Mischel (1999) proposed a similar model, drawing on several decades' work on delay of gratification. In delay of gratification research, a choice is posed between a smaller, less desired but immediate reward and a larger, more desired reward later on (Mischel, 1974). Metcalfe and Mischel (1999) proposed that two systems influence the ability to restrain in this and many other contexts: a "hot" system (emotional, impulsive, reflexive, and connectionist) and a "cool" system (strategic, flexible, slower, and unemotional). How a person responds to a difficult situation depends on which system presently dominates.

One interesting thing about these models is that they share some common ground with the biological process models described earlier. In particular, the position that there is a reflective, "cool" system that processes experience symbolically and, according to logical principles, bears a good deal of resemblance to the concept of effortful control. As noted earlier, effortful control provides a way to optimize outcomes, both with respect to the longer periods of time and with respect to a broader social context. In the same way, the rational side of the mind prevents the desires of the moment from overwhelming the person's behavior.

Contextualization of Traits

Perhaps the best-known cognitive approach to personality is Mischel and Shoda's (1995) view of personality as a cognitive–affective processing system. This label reflects the recognition that emotion plays a key role in much of cognitive experience. Mischel and Shoda, building on decades of work on social cognition, said that people develop organizations of information about the nature of situations, other people, and the self. These schemas have a conditional property, an *if/then* quality. Saying that someone is aggressive doesn't mean you think the person is always aggressive at every moment. It means you think he's more likely than most people to be aggressive in a certain class of situations.

Evidence from several sources supports this view. For example, in describing people we know, we often use hedges, descriptions of conditions under which we think those people act a particular way (Wright & Mischel, 1988). In fact, the better you know people, the more likely you are to think in conditional terms about them (Chen, 2003), probably because you've learned the circumstances that touch off various kinds of behavior in them. People think conditionally about themselves as well, understanding that their own behavior follows an if/then principle.

To predict consistency of action, then, you need to know two things. First, you need to know how the person construes the situation (which depends on the person's mental schemas and their accessibility). Second, you need to know the person's if/then profile. The unique profile of if/then relations is a *behavioral signature* for a person's personality (Shoda, Mischel, & Wright, 1994). Even if two people tend toward the same kind of behavior, the situations that elicit that behavior may differ from one person to the other. Indeed, these profiles of if/then relations may in some sense *define* personality (Mischel, Shoda & Mendoza-Denton, 2002).

This approach treats traits as being contextualized. The trait does not exist apart from the situations that elicit behaviors that fit the trait. This is a view of traits that is very different in some ways from the perspective with which this chapter began. Yet, in other ways, it is entirely compatible with that perspective. The same set of traits may be equally useful in this view, but they apply in a different way. It is entirely possible—and entirely reasonable—for a person who is generally an introvert to behave in a particularly extraverted way in some circumstances (Fleeson, 2001). A person's placement on a trait dimension is not really a single point, then, but a frequency distribution, with a mean (what one would have thought of previously as the "single point") and a degree of variability.

Psychoanalysis

Let's turn now to a very old conception of personality. To people who are unfamiliar with contemporary personality psychology, the term *personality* may evoke the view on personality that was proposed over a century ago by the Austrian physician Sigmund Freud. Freud developed his ideas from clinical cases, some his own and some described to him by other therapists. He developed his view during a time in which research on personality was essentially nonexistent. As a result, his theoretical position evolved without systematic research, but rather through his own observations and intuitions.

Freud proposed a view in which primitive animalistic forces are basic to personality. He argued that their influence was generally hidden both from the person in which they were at work and from outside observers. This view was abhorrent to the Victorian society to which he was writing. It was even more shocking that the primitive animalistic forces he emphasized were focused on issues of sex and death. Freud (1920/1955) wrote that the goal of life is death, and his theory was one in which humans are obsessed with sex from infancy throughout life. In this view, most of normal development is a process of disguising one's true primitive desires from oneself to allow one to function in society.

Psychoanalysis is among the oldest set of ideas in personality psychology. In fact, some dismiss it as little more than a historical curiosity. Although parts of Freud's view of personality do seem quaint in today's world, there are also broad themes in that viewpoint that continue to resonate today. For example, Freud was very much influenced by the writings of Darwin, who was arguing that humans are inextricably connected to a broader spectrum of animals with many characteristics in common. Among those characteristics are the fact that complex animals all die eventually and the fact that a core motivation of all animal life is reproduction. Inasmuch as reproduction among humans entails sex, there appears to be a very sound evolutionary basis for arguing that sex is a rather important aspect of life. One might even argue that all of life before reproduction is a process of preparing the individual for reproduction.

Darwin's views were considered shocking by many people in the time he wrote (indeed, the principle of evolution and the interconnectedness of species remain controversial to some to this day). Today, however, the idea that various aspects of human behavior reflect adaptation to evolutionary pressures is widely represented throughout psychology, including personality (that broad theme is considered briefly later in the chapter). In some ways, then, Freud was ahead of his time. The sections that follow describe some of the other themes of Freud's writing that continue to resonate today.

Levels of Awareness

The part of psychoanalytic theory that is often termed the topographical model of the mind posits three levels of potential awareness of information. The conscious mind is present awareness; the preconscious is the part of the mind that contains information that is not now in consciousness but is directly accessible by voluntary search; and the unconscious is the part of the mind that is not directly accessible by voluntary search. It was the concept of the unconscious that Freud invoked in accounting for people's lack of awareness of their primitive motives and of the reasons for engaging in many of the behaviors they engage in. That is, the actions are being done for reasons that are specified only in the unconscious for one reason or another.

The notion of an unconscious region of the mind fell out of favor and remained so for quite some time. It has reemerged over the past two decades, however, in a form rather different from that portrayed in psychoanalysis. Today's version is often referred to as the "cognitive unconscious" (Hassin, Uleman, & Bargh, 2005; Kihlstrom, 1987). It acknowledges that there is in fact a good portion of the programming of the mind that is not easily accessible to awareness (and perhaps not directly accessible at all).

In part, this inaccessible portion of the mind includes what has been hard-wired into the organism, such as knowing how to breathe and digest and whatever other reflexive action patterns are built in at birth. In part, this inaccessible portion of the mind includes what is called procedural memory—information about how to engage in particular thought or action processes—which was acquired through practice and now is lost to awareness. The latter theme has been generalized to the view that information about even complex action or thought patterns that have become automatic through repetition is difficult to retrieve from memory voluntarily. Perhaps more interesting at present is the idea that those complex patterns can be triggered, and executed, automatically, without any awareness of their existence or their execution on the part of the person who is engaged in them (e.g., Bargh, Gollwitzer, Lee-Chai, Barndollar, & Trötschel, 2001).

In some ways, this is very similar to the unconscious postulated by Freud. In other ways, it is quite different. The unconscious Freud wrote about is filled with dark secrets and hidden desires. The cognitive unconscious is, for the most part, more pedestrian. On the other hand, the part of the cognitive unconscious that has been studied the most is the part that follows from automaticity rather than from biological programming. It may be that "instinctive" aspects of human behavior that are automatic by virtue of biological inheritance are more similar to what Freud wrote about than are aspects of behavior that follow from large numbers of repetition.

In any case, the idea that people do things for reasons they are not aware of now appears beyond question. This is certainly a core theme of psychoanalysis, even if the particulars of how it happens are not entirely the same today as they once were.

Layers of Personality

Another aspect of psychoanalytic theory, often termed the structural model of personality (Freud, 1923/1962), posits three modes of functioning. Freud saw personality as having three aspects, which interweave to create the complexity of human behavior. These are not physical entities but rather three aspects of functioning, termed *id, ego*, and *superego.*

The id is the part of personality that exists at birth. It consists of is all the inherited, instinctive, primitive aspects of personality, and it functions entirely in the unconscious. It is closely tied to basic biological processes and is the source of all psychological energy. The id follows what's called the pleasure principle: that needs should be satisfied immediately (Freud, 1940/1949). Unsatisfied needs are aversive tension states, which should be gratified whenever they arise to release the tension. Under the pleasure principle, for example, any increase in hunger should cause an attempt to eat.

Because it is not possible to satisfy impulses immediately forever, a second set of functions emerges, called ego. Ego translates fairly closely to *self.* The ego evolves from the id and harnesses part of the id's energy for its own use. Ego focuses on making sure id impulses are expressed effectively, by taking into account the constraints of the external world. Because of this concern with the outside world, a good deal of ego functioning takes place in the conscious and preconscious regions of the mind.

The ego is said to follow the reality principle: the taking into account of external reality along with internal needs and urges. The reality principle brings a sense of rationality to behavior. Because it orients people toward the world, it leads them to weigh the risks linked to an action before acting. If the risks seem too high, you'll think of another way to meet the need. If there's no safe way to do so immediately, you'll delay it to a later, safer, or more sensible time. Thus, an important goal of the ego is to delay the discharge of the id's tension until an appropriate object or activity is found—not prevent it, but channel it appropriately.

In other words, the ego can delay gratification. The very alert reader will have noticed a similarity between this function of the ego and effects created by the temperament of effortful control and the function posited by cognitive models for the rational layer of the mind. This similarity is sufficiently striking (given that the observations were made by different people across many decades of time) to suggest the theorists may have been describing the same thing.

In the psychoanalytic view, as time goes on and other forces intrude on the developing child, a third mode of functioning emerges, called superego. The superego represents both an idealized way to be (ego ideal), and ways to not-be (conscience). Superego is the moral sense of personality, which tries to induce the person adhere to high principles. This moral sense can be striking enough that some connect the upper layer of the dual-process model to superego rather than ego (Kochanska & Knaack, 2003). In some respects, however, what makes the superego's goals different is primarily that they are more abstract and more demanding.

Defenses

A third theme from psychoanalysis that has been maintained in mainstream psychology is the idea that people use defenses involuntarily, automatically, to protect themselves from ideas, knowledge, or desires that are threatening. In Freud's view, these defenses represent tools of the ego to permit it to do its main job of satisfying the needs of the id while avoiding problems with respect to either the constraints of external reality or the demands of the superego.

As is true of contemporary views of the unconscious, theorists after Freud have accounted for such self-protective tendencies in various ways. Today discussions of defenses would be more likely to be framed in terms of self-esteem protection. However, the theme that people avoid confronting unpleasant truths remains very much alive in personality psychology.

Attachment Patterns

Another perspective that is very influential in today's personality psychology derives from a body of work in developmental psychology that had its origins in psychoanalysis, but which transformed psychoanalysis enormously. A number of post-Freudians known as object relations theorists argued that the fundamental issues in human development (and in human life more generally) do not concern sexuality (as Freud had said) but rather the relationships from one person (the infant) to others (at first, the mother or other primary caregiver).

Theories of this group share three further themes. First, a dialectic tension is assumed between processes of psychological fusion with the other versus processes of separation and individuation from the other (which are involved in forming a separate identity). Thus, the child (and the adult) not only wants to be immersed in safety and security but also wants to have a separate existence. Second, this approach emphasizes that a person's pattern of relating to others is laid down in early childhood. Third, the patterns formed early (which can vary greatly from person to person) are assumed to recur repeatedly throughout life.

The subset of this group of theories that has come to be most influential in today's personality psychology is called attachment theory. This term is identified with Bowlby (1969, 1988) and Ainsworth (e.g., Ainsworth, Blehar, Waters, & Wall, 1978), among others. The term *attachment* was used initially to refer to an infant's connection with its mother. In more recent years the ideas of attachment theory have been adapted to create a picture of the functioning of adult personality.

Bowlby (1969, 1988) believed that the clinging and following of the infant serve the important biological purpose of keeping the infant close to the mother, thus increasing the infant's chances of survival. A basic theme in attachment theory is that mothers (and others) who are responsive to the infant create a *secure base* for it. The infant needs to know that the major person in his or her life is dependable—is there when needed. This sense of security gives the child a base from which to explore the world. It also provides a place of comfort (a *safe haven*) when the child is threatened.

Attachment theorists also believe that the child builds implicit mental working models of the self, others, and the nature of relationships. The model of the self can be positive or negative (or in between) as can the model of other people. How you view yourself has implications for how you behave, so does how you view the world of people around you, and so does how you view the nature of relationships.

Research on attachment in infants led to the emergence of an analysis of individual differences in attachment pattern. Secure attachment is displayed by an appropriate distress response (not too much, but not absent either) when the mother leaves the infant, and a happy and engaged response when mother returns. Two kinds of insecure responses also exist. An ambivalent (or resistant) infant becomes very upset when mother leaves, and its response to mother's return mixes approach with anger. The infant seeks contact with the mother but then angrily resists efforts to be soothed. In the avoidant pattern, the infant does not show distress when the mother leaves and responds to her return by ignoring her. It is as though this infant expects to be abandoned and is responding by being remote.

There is at least some evidence that the patterns have a self-perpetuating quality. The clinginess mixed with rejection in the ambivalent pattern can be hard to deal with, as can the aloofness and distance of the avoidant pattern. Each of these patterns tends to cause others to react negatively. That, in turn, reconfirms the perceptions that led to the patterns in the first place. In fact, people with an insecure attachment pattern appear to distort their memory of interactions over time to make them more consistent with their working models (Feeney & Cassidy, 2003). Thus, there is a self-generated stability to the pattern over the course of time.

Hazan and Shaver (1987) took this description of infants and extrapolated it to adult social behavior, with a focus on close relationships. In this research, secure adults said that love is real and when it comes, it stays. Avoidants were less optimistic, saying that love doesn't last. Ambivalents said falling in love is easy and happens often to them, but they also agreed that love doesn't last. These responses look very much like grown-up versions of the patterns of infancy.

Other research has expanded on these findings in many directions. For example, consistent with the pattern of infancy, ambivalent undergrads are most likely to have obsessive and dependent love relationships (Collins & Read, 1990) and to be most obsessive about lost loves (Davis, Shaver, & Vernon, 2003). Avoidants are the least likely to report being in love either in the present or in the past (Feeney & Noller, 1990). Avoidants are also the most likely to cope in self-reliant ways after a breakup (Davis et al., 2003). Those who are securely attached show the most interdependence, commitment, and trust (Mikulincer, 1998; Simpson, 1990). If they experience a breakup, they turn to family and friends as safe havens (Davis et al., 2003).

There are many ways in which adult attachment can affect the course of romantic relationships, and such topics have become the focus of much research in the past few years (Mikulincer & Goodman, 2006). Indeed, the past two decades have seen an explosion of research on wide-ranging manifestations of adult attachment patterns (Cassidy & Shaver, 2008; Feeney, 2006; Mikulincer & Goodman, 2006; Mikulincer & Shaver, 2007; Rholes & Simpson, 2004).

Issues in Adult Attachment

The proliferation of work on adult attachment has raised many issues, including how best to measure it in adults. Early studies used the three main categories from the infancy work, but another approach has also emerged. Following Bartholomew and Horowitz (1991), who began with Bowlby's notion of working models of self and other, many researchers have shifted to the assessment of two dimensions. One is a positive-versus-negative model of self (the self is worthy or not), the other is a positive-versus-negative model of others (others are trustworthy or not). The dimensions are termed *attachment anxiety* and *attachment avoidance*, respectively (Brennan, Clark, & Shaver, 1998). Security is represented by the combination of being low on both dimensions.

It is of some interest that these dimensions have at least a little resemblance to the approach and avoidance temperaments of the biological process approach to personality (and thus to extraversion and neuroticism; Carver, 1997). One clear difference is that the attachment patterns are specific to close relationships, whereas the approach and avoidance temperaments are quite general. Perhaps as a result of this difference in breadth, Simpson et al. (2002) found that measures of extraversion and neuroticism did not duplicate the effects of attachment patterns. Nonetheless, the resemblance remains intriguing.

Another important issue is the question of whether each person has one pattern of relating to others or many patterns for different relationships. The answer seems to be many patterns (Baldwin, Keelan, Fehr, Enns, & Koh-Rangarajoo, 1996; Cook, 2000; La Guardia, Ryan, Couchman, & Deci, 2000; Overall, Fletcher, & Friesen, 2003; Pierce & Lydon, 2001). For example, one study had participants define each of their 10 closest relationships in terms of the three categories. Across the 10 descriptions, almost everyone used at least two patterns and nearly half used all three (Baldwin et al., 1996). People also seem to have patterns of attachment to groups, distinct from their patterns for close relationships (Smith, Murphy, & Coats, 1999).

Today, the attachment model of adult relationships is being explored by researchers in many different contexts. Many people now believe that the fundamental issue underlying many kinds of social behavior is the nature and quality of the bond that a given person has to a significant other. This view depends on a particular implicit view of personality: that the core dynamic of personality involves a person's perceptions of his or her relations with others (see also Andersen & Chen, 2002).

Self-Actualization, Self-Determination

Another broad approach to personality is associated with terms such as *self-actualization* and *self-determination*. One core idea in this viewpoint is that people have a natural tendency to grow and develop their capabilities in ways that maintain or enhance the true self, an idea called self-actualization (Rogers, 1959). If this tendency is allowed to express itself, the person develops in positive ways. One impediment to this is the need for acceptance by other people. Acting in ways that foster acceptance from others sometimes means acting in ways that prevent growth.

Another core idea is that people must choose for themselves how to act in the world. It is the person's task to sort out the pressures and focus on growth and development. This way of thinking is echoed in a contemporary view of personality called self-determination theory (Deci & Ryan, 1980, 1985, 1991, 2000; Ryan, 1993; Ryan & Deci, 2001, 2017). This theory begins with the idea that behavior can reflect two underlying dynamics. Some actions are *self-determined*, done because the actions have intrinsic value to the actor. Other actions are *controlled*, done to gain payments or to satisfy some sort of pressure. An action can be controlled even if the control is entirely in your own mind. If you do something because you'd feel guilty if you didn't do it, you are engaging in controlled behavior.

Self-determination theory holds that people want to feel a sense of autonomy in what they do. In this view, accomplishments are satisfying only if you feel a sense of self-determination in them. If you feel forced or pressured, you'll be less satisfied (Grolnick & Ryan, 1989). Indeed, pressuring *yourself* to do well can also reduce motivation (Ryan, 1982). People who impose conditions of worth on themselves suffer adverse consequences (see also Crocker & Knight, 2005; Crocker & Park, 2004).

In self-determination theory, people also naturally strive for greater competence and greater relatedness to others (themes that I have not gone into here), and they seek to experience their behavior as autonomous. Autonomy means "owning" whatever behavior you choose to engage in as being yours. People feel authentic when they act with a sense of choice and self-expression (Safran, 2017). To feel comfortable choosing a behavior as belonging to you, it must fit with your sense of what is your true self. It takes a good deal of trial and error to learn to sense when you are behaving according to your true self. Until you have a strong sense of that, it can be hard to know whether you are forcing yourself to believe that something fits your true self when it does not. Yet that is the goal of a meaningful life.

Evolution

As noted earlier, the idea that evolutionary processes have a major influence on present-day human behavior has come to occupy an important place in psychology (see also Chapter 16) including personality psychology. The underlying idea is that behavioral tendencies can become widely represented in a population (and thus part of human nature) if those tendencies increase the rate of survival and reproduction over many generations (Barkow, Cosmides, & Tooby, 1992; Bjorklund & Pellegrini, 2002; Buss, 1995, 2005; Caporael, 2001; Heschl, 2002; Segal, 1993; Tooby & Cosmides, 1989, 1990).

This is more complicated than it sounds. Your genes are helped into the next generation by anything that helps people with genetic make-up similar to yours (your subgroup) reproduce. Thus, if you act altruistically for a relative, it helps the relative survive and thereby helps genes that resemble your genes survive. This kind of reasoning suggests the possibility that a tendency toward altruism is part of human nature. This idea has also been extended to suggest more broadly that our ancestors survived better by cooperating (Axelrod & Hamilton, 1981), leading some to conclude that a tendency to cooperate is part of human nature (Guisinger & Blatt, 1994; Kriegman & Knight, 1988; McCullough, Kimeldorf, & Cohen, 2008).

The evolutionary view on personality focuses closely on mating (Buss, 1991, 1994; Buss, & Schmitt, 1993; Gangestad & Simpson, 2000). Indeed, from an evolutionary view, mating is what life is all about. Mating involves competition: males competing with one another and females with one another. But the two competitions are believed to differ a little in their goals. Males are driven to mate widely, females to choose a mate who can provide resources (see Chapter 16).

Most psychologists believe there is little question that what we think of as personality reflects the processes of millennia of evolution. It is harder, however, to specify clearly just what properties have been selected and why. Nonetheless, many personality psychologists do continue to work at that puzzle. There could hardly be an approach to understanding the fundamentals of humanity that holds a greater claim to trying to identify human nature.

Individual Differences Revisited: Measurement

Before closing, I want to briefly mention one more issue. This is a methodological issue that is especially salient in personality psychology but also applies to work in social psychology. As noted earlier, all viewpoints on personality point partly to differences among people. To study these differences, personality psychologists had to develop ways to measure them.

This is not as simple as it might seem. In describing the trait viewpoint, I noted a philosophical disagreement about whether to start with a theoretical reason to measure something or whether to let reality tell you what's important to measure. As a practical matter, that issue has actually affected only the trait approach to personality, which has adopted the goal of capturing all of personality. Other approaches, being more closely focused on one theme or another, have uniformly taken the theoretical path to measure development. Let's consider the process of creating a measure a little more closely.

Suppose you had a theoretical notion about some aspect (or aspects) of personality variation and you wanted to develop a way to assess it (or them). What would you do? First, you need to identify a source of relevant information. That might be self-ratings, reports of observers (people rating a person they know), or even actual behaviors that pertain to the quality of your interest. In part because self-ratings are so easy to collect, that's the most popular source. It is common to write a set of items that pertain to the trait of interest and to collect responses on a multipoint scale indicating the extent of endorsement of what the item says (typically ranging from strong agreement to strong disagreement). If you do this, be careful that the items you write are clear and simple, that they don't combine more than one issue in any one item, and that they don't use words or phrases that people won't understand.

Easy enough so far. But that's just the start. There are many things you need to check on. If you intend to be measuring one and only one thing, you need to be sure that's what you're actually doing. If you intend to be measuring two separate things, you need to be sure that's what you're actually doing. In both cases, that means you need a factor analysis on a set of responses to your items to see what factor structure emerges from them. If you have two separate factors, it's no good to try to treat the items as though they represent one thing, because they don't. If you have one factor, it's no good to try to pretend you are measuring two separate properties of personality, because you aren't.

Factor analysis can show you other things as well. Sometimes in developing a set of items, you find out that some of the items aren't much good: They don't correlate with the other items, or maybe everyone totally agrees (or disagrees) with them so that they give no information about differences among people. In such cases, you need to throw out or revise the items and try again. Most measures go through multiple rounds of item construction and testing before they go to the next step.

There are in fact several next steps. Although the factor structure tells you something about what items go together, you also need a measure of internal reliability for each scale (which does not, by the way, substitute for the factor analysis). If you intend to measure an individual difference that is fairly stable, you need to show that it *is* fairly stable—over an interval of at least several weeks in a moderately large sample.

The hardest step is called validation. That means showing that the measure is measuring what you think it is measuring. Done properly, it means (a) correlating your measure with other measures it should relate to (moderately strong correlations establish what's called convergent validity), (b) correlating it with measures it should not relate to (low correlations establish what's called discriminant validity), and (c) relating scores on your measure to some behavioral index of the property you think you are measuring (that being the hardest but most important part).

After all that, you can actually use your measure. If it has only one factor, you are good to go. If it has multiple factors, be careful. Try very hard to resist the impulse to make an index out of them (adding them up or averaging them), unless they are pretty strongly correlated with each other. Doing that can create great confusion about exactly what the index means (Carver, 1989). Under no circumstance should you treat scales as opposites unless they are fairly strongly inversely related. Once again, the resulting index is misleading rather than helpful.

Ultimately, what we find out from studies of people's behavior is only as good as our measures are. Whether the measure concerns individual differences in personality or differences of some other type, the same issues apply. It is important to attend carefully to these issues as you proceed.

Conceptions of Personality In Social Behavior

As indicated at the outset, personality psychologists are interested in how best to construe human nature. Different theorists take different views of human nature as their starting points. Thus, there exist several different conceptions of what processes are fundamental to personality. The review offered in this chapter surveyed several perspectives that currently are influential in personality psychology. These perspectives are not the only possibilities (cf. Carver, 2006) but rather one person's reading of what ideas currently have the greatest influence.

When social psychologists examine a phenomenon, they do so through the lens of one or another set of assumptions, which address (in part) the core concerns underlying human action. Social psychologists in different contexts over the years have assumed widely varying dynamics as underlying the kinds of behavior on which they focused. I think it is fair to say that each of those views has also been held by some group of personality psychologists as a good way to conceptualize the central concerns of the person. In this way, ideas that are fundamental to personality psychology serve as implicit frameworks for theories of social psychology.

References

Ahadi, S. A., & Rothbart, M. K. (1994). Temperament, development and the big five. In C. F. Halverson Jr., G. A. Kohnstamm, & R. P. Martin (Eds.), *The developing structure of temperament and personality from infancy to adulthood* (pp. 189–207). Hillsdale, NJ: Erlbaum.

Ainsworth, M. D. S., Blehar, M. C., Waters, E., & Wall, S. (1978). *Patterns of attachment: A psychological study of the strange situation.* Hillsdale, NJ: Erlbaum.

Allport, G. W. (1961). *Pattern and growth in personality.* New York, NY: Holt, Rinehart, & Winston, Inc.

Andersen, S. M., & Chen, S. (2002). The relational self: An interpersonal social-cognitive theory. *Psychological Review, 109,* 619–645.

Ashton, M. C., Lee, K., Perugini, M., Szarota, P., de Vries, R. E., Di Blas, L., . . . De Raad, B.(2004). A six-factor structure of personality-descriptive adjectives: Solutions from psycholexical studies in seven languages. *Journal of Personality and Social Psychology, 86,* 356–366.

Austin, J. T., & Vancouver, J. B. (1996). Goal constructs in psychology: Structure, process, and content. *Psychological Bulletin, 120,* 338–375.

Axelrod, R., & Hamilton, W. D. (1981). The evolution of cooperation. *Science, 211,* 1390–1396.

Baldwin, M. W., Keelan, J. P. R., Fehr, B., Enns, V., & Koh-Rangarajoo, E. (1996). Social-cognitive conceptualization of attachment working models: Availability and accessibility effects. *Journal of Personality and Social Psychology, 71,* 94–109.

Bandura, A. (1986). *Social foundations of thought and action: A social cognitive theory.* Englewood Cliffs, NJ: Prentice-Hall.

Bargh, J. A., Gollwitzer, P. M., Lee-Chai, A., Barndollar, K., & Trötschel, R. (2001). The automated will: Nonconscious activation and pursuit of behavioral goals. *Journal of Personality and Social Psychology, 81,* 1014–1027.

Barkow, J. H., Cosmides, L., & Tooby, J. (1992). *The adapted mind: Evolutionary psychology and the generation of culture.* New York, NY: Oxford University Press.

Bartholomew, K., & Horowitz, L. M. (1991). Attachment styles among young adults: A test of a four-category model. *Journal of Personality and Social Psychology, 61,* 226–244.

Berry, D. S., & Miller, K. M. (2001). When boy meets girl: Attractiveness and the five-factor model in opposite-sex interactions. *Journal of Research in Personality, 35,* 62–77.

Bjorklund, D. F., & Pellegrini, A. D. (2002). *Origins of human nature: Evolutionary developmental psychology.* Washington, DC: American Psychological Association.

Block, J. (1995). A contrarian view of the five-factor approach to personality assessment. *Psychological Bulletin, 117,* 187–215.

Bogg, T., & Roberts, B. W. (2004). Conscientiousness and health-related behaviors: A meta-analysis of the leading behavioral contributors to mortality. *Psychological Bulletin, 130,* 887–919.

Bolger, N., & Zuckerman, A. (1995). A framework for studying personality in the stress process. *Journal of Personality and Social Psychology, 69,* 890–902.

Bowlby, J. (1969). *Attachment and loss: Vol. 1, Attachment.* New York, NY: Basic Books.

Bowlby, J. (1988). *A secure base: Parent–child attachment and healthy human development.* New York, NY: Basic Books.

Brehm, J. W., & Self, E. A. (1989). The intensity of motivation. *Annual Review of Psychology, 40,* 109–131.

Brennan, K. A., Clark, C. L., & Shaver, P. R. (1998). Self-report measurement of adult attachment: An integrative overview. In J. A. Simpson & W. S. Rholes (Eds.), *Attachment theory and close relationships* (pp. 46–76). New York, NY: Guilford.

Buss, A. H., & Plomin, R. (1975). *A temperament theory of personality development.* New York, NY: Wiley-Interscience.

Buss, D. M. (1991). Evolutionary personality psychology. *Annual Review of Psychology, 42,* 459–491.

Buss, D. M. (1994). *The evolution of desire: Strategies of human mating.* New York, NY: Basic Books.

Buss, D. M. (1995). Evolutionary psychology: A new paradigm for psychological science. *Psychological Inquiry, 6,* 1–30.

Buss, D. M. (Ed.). (2005). *The handbook of evolutionary psychology.* New York, NY: Wiley.

Buss, D. M., & Schmitt, D. P. (1993). Sexual strategies theory: An evolutionary perspective on human mating. *Psychological Review, 100,* 204–232.

Caporael, L. R. (2001). Evolutionary psychology: Toward a unifying theory and a hybrid science. *Annual Review of Psychology, 52,* 607–628.

Carver, C. S. (1989). How should multifaceted personality constructs be tested? Issues illustrated by self-monitoring, attributional style, and hardiness. *Journal of Personality and Social Psychology, 56,* 577–585.

Carver, C. S. (1997). Adult attachment and personality: Converging evidence and a new measure. *Personality and Social Psychology Bulletin, 23,* 865–883.

Carver, C. S. (2004). Negative affects deriving from the behavioral approach system. *Emotion, 4,* 3–22.

Carver, C. S. (2006). Assumptions about personality and core motivations as hidden partners in social psychology. In P. A. M. Van Lange (Ed.), *Bridging social psychology: Benefits of transdisciplinary approaches* (pp. 181–186). Mahwah, NJ: Erlbaum.

Carver, C. S., Johnson, S. L., & Joormann, J. (2009). Two-mode models of self-regulation as a tool for conceptualizing effects of the serotonergic system in normal behavior and diverse disorders. *Current Directions in Psychological Science, 18,* 195–199.

Carver, C. S., & Scheier, M. F. (1998). *On the self-regulation of behavior.* New York, NY: Cambridge University Press.

Carver, C. S., & Scheier, M. F. (2008). *Perspectives on personality* (6th ed.). Boston, MA: Allyn & Bacon.

Carver, C. S., & Scheier, M. F. (2018). Generalized optimism. In G. Oettingen, A. T. Sevincer, & P. M. Gollwitzer (Eds.), *The psychology of thinking about the future* (pp. 214–230). New York, NY: Guilford.

Carver, C. S., Scheier, M. F., Miller, C. J., & Fulford, D. (2009). Optimism. In C. R. Snyder & S. J. Lopez (Eds.), *Oxford handbook of positive psychology* (2nd ed., pp. 303–311). New York, NY: Oxford University Press.

Carver, C. S., Sutton, S. K., & Scheier, M. F. (2000). Action, emotion, and personality: Emerging conceptual integration. *Personality and Social Psychology Bulletin, 26,* 741–751.

Casey, B. J., Getz, S., & Galvan, A. (2008). The adolescent brain. *Developmental Review, 28,* 62–77.

Caspi, A., Roberts, B. W., & Shiner, R. L. (2005). Personality development: Stability and change. *Annual Review of Psychology, 56,* 453–484.

Caspi, A., & Shiner, R. L. (2006). Personality development. In N. Eisenberg (Ed.), *Handbook of child psychology, Vol. 3. Social, emotional, and personality development* (6th ed., pp. 300–365). New York, NY: Wiley.

Cassidy, J., & Shaver, P. R. (Eds.). (2008). *Handbook of attachment* (2nd ed.). New York, NY: Guilford.

Cattell, R. B. (1965). *The scientific analysis of personality.* Baltimore, MD: Penguin.

Cattell, R. B. (1978). *The scientific use of factor analysis.* New York, NY: Plenum.

Chaiken, S. L., & Trope, Y. (Eds.). (1999). *Dual-process theories in social psychology.* New York, NY: Guilford.

Chamorro-Premuzic, T., & Furnham, A. (2003). Personality predicts academic performance: Evidence from two longitudinal university samples. *Journal of Research in Personality, 37,* 319–338.

Chaplin, W. F., Phillips, J. B., Brown, J. D., Clanton, N. R., & Stein, J. L. (2000). Handshaking, gender, personality, and first impressions. *Journal of Personality and Social Psychology, 79,* 110–117.

Chassin, L., Flora, D. B., & King, K. M. (2004). Trajectories of alcohol and drug use and dependence from adolescence to adulthood: The effects of familial alcoholism and personality. *Journal of Abnormal Psychology, 113,* 483–498.

Chen, S. (2003). Psychological-state theories about significant others: Implications for the content and structure of significant-other representations. *Personality and Social Psychology Bulletin, 29,* 1285–1302.

Clark, L. A., Kochanska, G., & Ready, R. (2000). Mothers' personality and its interaction with child temperament as predictors of parenting behavior. *Journal of Personality and Social Psychology, 79,* 274–285.

Cloninger, C. R. (1987). A systematic method of clinical description and classification of personality variants: A proposal. *Archives of General Psychiatry, 44,* 573–588.

Collins, N. L., & Read, S. J. (1990). Adult attachment, working models, and relationship quality in dating couples. *Journal of Personality and Social Psychology, 58,* 644–663.

Cook, W. L. (2000). Understanding attachment security in a family context. *Journal of Personality and Social Psychology, 78,* 285–294.

Costa, P. T., Jr., & McCrae, R. R. (1985). *The NEO Personality Inventory manual.* Odessa, FL: Psychological Assessment Resources.

Crocker, J., & Knight, K. M. (2005). Contingencies of self-worth. *Current Directions in Psychological Science, 14,* 200–203.

Crocker, J., & Park, L. E. (2004). The costly pursuit of self-esteem. *Psychological Bulletin, 130,* 392–414.

Davidson, R. J. (1988). EEG measures of cerebral asymmetry: Conceptual and methodological issues. *International Journal of Neuroscience, 39,* 71–89.

Davidson, R. J. (1992). Prolegomenon to the structure of emotion: Gleanings from neuropsychology. *Cognition and Emotion, 6,* 245–268.

Davidson, R. J. (1995). Cerebral asymmetry, emotion, and affective style. In R. J. Davidson, & K. Hugdahl (Eds.), *Brain asymmetry* (pp. 361–387). Cambridge, MA: MIT Press.

Davidson, R. J. (1998). Affective style and affective disorders: Perspectives from affective neuroscience. *Cognition and Emotion, 12,* 307–330.

Davis, D., Shaver, P. R., & Vernon, M. L. (2003). Physical, emotional, and behavioral reactions to breaking up: The roles of gender, age, emotional involvement, and attachment style. *Personality and Social Psychology Bulletin, 29,* 871–884.

Deci, E. L., & Ryan, R. M. (1980). The empirical exploration of intrinsic motivational processes. In L. Berkowitz (Ed.), *Advances in experimental social psychology* (Vol. 13). New York, NY: Academic Press.

Deci, E. L., & Ryan, R. M. (1985). *Intrinsic motivation and self-determination in human behavior.* New York, NY: Plenum.

Deci, E. L., & Ryan, R. M. (1991). A motivational approach to self: Integration in personality. In R. Dienstbier (Ed.), *Nebraska symposium on motivation: Perspectives on motivation* (Vol. 38, pp. 237–288). Lincoln, NE: University of Nebraska Press.

Deci, E. L., & Ryan, R. M. (2000). The "what" and "why" of goal pursuits: Human needs and the self-determination of behavior. *Psychological Inquiry, 11,* 227–268.

Depue, R. A., & Collins, P. F. (1999). Neurobiology of the structure of personality: Dopamine, facilitation of incentive motivation, and extraversion. *Behavioral and Brain Sciences, 22,* 491–517.

Depue, R. A., & Iacono, W. G. (1989). Neurobehavioral aspects of affective disorders. *Annual Review of Psychology, 40,* 457–492.

Depue, R. A., Krauss, S. P., & Spoont, M. R. (1987). A two-dimensional threshold model of seasonal bipolar affective disorder. In D. Magnusson & A. Öhman (Eds.), *Psychopathology: An interactional perspective* (pp. 95–123). Orlando, FL: Academic Press.

Depue, R. A., & Morrone-Strupinsky, J. V. (2005). A neurobehavioral model of affiliative bonding: Implications for conceptualizing a human trait of affiliation. *Behavioral and Brain Sciences, 28,* 313–395.

Derryberry, D., & Rothbart, M. K. (1997). Reactive and effortful processes in the organization of temperament. *Development and Psychopathology, 9,* 633–652.

DeYoung, C. G. (2006). Higher-order factors of the Big Five in a multi-informant sample. *Journal of Personality and Social Psychology, 91,* 1138–1151.

DeYoung, C. G., Peterson, J. B., & Higgins, D. M. (2001). Higher-order factors of the big five predict conformity: Are there neuroses of health? *Personality and Individual Differences, 33,* 533–552.

Digman, J. M. (1997). Higher-order factors of the Big Five. *Journal of Personality and Social Psychology, 73,* 1246–1256.

Digman, J. M., & Inouye, J. (1986). Further specification of the five robust factors of personality. *Journal of Personality and Social Psychology, 50,* 116–123.

Donnellan, M. B., Conger, R. D., & Bryant, C. M. (2004). The big five and enduring marriages. *Journal of Research in Personality, 38,* 481–504.

Eccles, J. S., & Wigfield, A. (2002). Motivational beliefs, values and goals. *Annual Review of Psychology, 53,* 109–132.

Elliot A. J. (Ed.). (2008). *Handbook of approach and avoidance motivation.* New York, NY: Psychology Press.

Elliot, A. J., & Sheldon, K. M. (1998). Avoidance personal goals and the personality–illness relationship. *Journal of Personality and Social Psychology, 75,* 1282–1299.

Elliot, A. J., & Thrash, T. M. (2002). Approach–avoidance motivation in personality: Approach and avoidance temperaments and goals. *Journal of Personality and Social Psychology, 82,* 804–818.

Epstein, S. (1973). The self-concept revisited: Or a theory of a theory. *American Psychologist, 28,* 404–416.

Epstein, S. (1985). The implications of cognitive–experiential self theory for research in social psychology and personality. *Journal for the Theory of Social Behavior, 15,* 283–310.

Epstein, S. (1990). Cognitive–experiential self-theory. In L. Pervin (Ed.), *Handbook of personality: Theory and research* (pp. 165–192). New York, NY: Guilford.

Epstein, S. (1994). Integration of the cognitive and the psychodynamic unconscious. *American Psychologist, 49,* 709–724.

Eysenck, H. J. (1967). *The biological basis of personality.* Springfield, IL: Charles C Thomas.

Eysenck, H. J. (1975). *The inequality of man.* San Diego, CA: Edits.

Eysenck, H. J. (1986). Models and paradigms in personality research. In A. Angleitner, A. Furnham, & G. Van Heck (Eds.), *Personality psychology in Europe, Vol. 2: Current trends and controversies* (pp. 213–223). Lisse, Holland: Swets & Zeitlinger.

Feeney, B. C. (2006). An attachment theory perspective on the interplay between intrapersonal and interpersonal processes. In K. D. Vohs & E. J. Finkel (Eds.), *Self and relationships* (pp. 133–159). New York, NY: Guilford.

Feeney, B. C., & Cassidy, J. A. (2003). Reconstructive memory related to adolescent-parent conflict interactions: The influence of attachment-related representations on immediate perceptions and changes in perceptions over time. *Journal of Personality and Social Psychology, 85,* 945–955.

Feeney, J. A., & Noller, P. (1990). Attachment style as a predictor of adult romantic relationships. *Journal of Personality and Social Psychology, 58,* 281–291.

Fleeson, W. (2001). Toward a structure- and process-integrated view of personality: Traits as density distributions of states. *Journal of Personality and Social Psychology, 80,* 1011–1027.

Flynn, F. J. (2005). Having an open mind: The impact of openness to experience on interracial attitudes and impression formation. *Journal of Personality and Social Psychology, 88,* 816–826.

Fowles, D. C. (1980). The three arousal model: Implications of Gray's two-factor learning theory for heart rate, electrodermal activity, and psychopathy. *Psychophysiology, 17,* 87–104.

Fowles, D. C. (1993). Biological variables in psychopathology: A psychobiological perspective. In P. B. Sutker & H. E. Adams (Eds.), *Comprehensive handbook of psychopathology* (2nd ed., pp. 57–82). New York, NY: Plenum.

Freud, S. (1949). *An outline of psychoanalysis* (J. Strachey, Trans.). New York, NY: Norton. (Original work published 1940)

Freud, S. (1955). Beyond the pleasure principle. In J. Strachey (Ed.), *The standard edition of the complete psychological works of Sigmund Freud* (Vol. 18). London, England: Hogarth. (Original work published 1920)

Freud, S. (1962). *The ego and the id.* New York, NY: Norton. (Originally published 1923)

Gable, S. L. (2006). Approach and avoidance social motives and goals. *Journal of Personality, 74,* 175–222.

Gable, S. L., & Berkman, E. T. (2008). Social motives and goals. In A. J. Elliot (Ed.), *Handbook of approach and avoidance motivation* (pp. 203–216). New York, NY: Psychology Press.

Gangestad, S. W., & Simpson, J. A. (2000). The evolution of human mating: Trade-offs and strategic pluralism. *Behavioral and Brain Sciences, 23,* 573–587.

Goldberg, L. R. (1981). Language and individual differences: The search for universals in personality lexicons. In L. Wheeler (Ed.), *Review of personality and social psychology* (Vol. 2, pp. 141–165). Beverly Hills, CA: SAGE.

Goldberg, L. R. (1993). The structure of phenotypic personality traits. *American Psychologist, 48,* 26–34.

Gray, J. A. (1982). *The neuropsychology of anxiety: An enquiry into the functions of the septo-hippocampal system.* New York, NY: Oxford University Press.

Gray, J. A. (1987). Perspectives on anxiety and impulsivity: A commentary. *Journal of Research in Personality, 21,* 493–509.

Gray, J. A. (1990). Brain systems that mediate both emotion and cognition. *Cognition and Emotion, 4,* 269–288.

Gray, J. A. (1994a). Personality dimensions and emotion systems. In P. Ekman & R. J. Davidson (Eds.), *The nature of emotion: Fundamental questions* (pp. 329–331). New York, NY: Oxford University Press.

Gray, J. A. (1994b). Three fundamental emotion systems. In P. Ekman & R. J. Davidson (Eds.), *The nature of emotion: Fundamental questions* (pp. 243–247). New York, NY: Oxford University Press.

Graziano, W. G., & Eisenberg, N. H. (1999). Agreeableness as a dimension of personality. In R. Hogan, J. Johnson, & S. Briggs (Eds.), *Handbook of personality* (pp. 795–825). San Diego, CA: Academic Press.

Graziano, W. G., Habashi, M. M., Sheese, B. E., Tobin, R. M. (2007). Agreeableness, empathy, and helping: A person X situation perspective. *Journal of Personality and Social Psychology, 93,* 583–599.

Graziano, W. G., Jensen-Campbell, L. A., & Hair, E. C. (1996). Perceiving interpersonal conflict and reacting to it: The case for agreeableness. *Journal of Personality and Social Psychology, 70,* 820–835.

Grolnick, W. S., & Ryan, R. M. (1989). Parent styles associated with children's self-regulation and competence in school. *Journal of Educational Psychology, 81,* 143–154.

Guisinger, S., & Blatt, S. J. (1994). Individuality and relatedness: Evolution of a fundamental dialectic. *American Psychologist, 49,* 104–111.

Hampson, S. E., Goldberg, L. R., Vogt, T. M., & Dubanoski, J. P. (2006) Forty years on: Teachers' assessments of children's personality traits predict self-reported health behaviors and outcomes at midlife. *Health Psychology, 25,* 57–64.

Hassin, R. R., Uleman, J. S., & Bargh, J. A. (Eds.). (2005). *The new unconscious.* New York, NY: Oxford University Press.

Hazan, C., & Shaver, P. R. (1987). Romantic love conceptualized as an attachment process. *Journal of Personality and Social Psychology, 52,* 511–524.

Heschl, A. (2002). *The intelligent genome: On the origin of the human mind by mutation and selection.* New York, NY: Springer.

Higgins, E. T., & Tykocinski, O. (1992). Self-discrepancies and biographical memory: Personality and cognition at the level of psychological situation. *Personality and Social Psychology Bulletin, 18,* 527–535.

Higgins, E. T. (1996). Ideals, oughts, and regulatory focus: Affect and motivation from distinct pains and pleasures. In P. M. Gollwitzer & J. A. Bargh (Eds.). *The psychology of action: Linking cognition and motivation to behavior* (pp. 91–114). New York, NY: Guilford.

Jang, K. L., Livesley, W. J., Angleitner, A., Riemann, R., & Vernon, P. A. (2002). Genetic and environmental influences on the covariance of facets defining the domains of the five-factor model of personality. *Personality and Individual Differences, 33,* 83–101.

Jensen-Campbell, L. A., Adams, R., Perry, D. G., Workman, K. A., Furdella, J. Q., & Egan, S. K. (2002). Agreeableness, extraversion, and peer relations in early adolescence: Winning friends and deflecting aggression. *Journal of Research in Personality, 36,* 224–251.

Jensen-Campbell, L. A., & Graziano, W. G. (2001). Agreeableness as a moderator of interpersonal conflict. *Journal of Personality, 69,* 323–362.

John, O. P., & Srivastava, S. (1999). The Big Five trait taxonomy: History, measurement, and theoretical perspectives. In L. A. Pervin & O. P. John (Eds.). *Handbook of personality: Theory and research* (2nd ed., pp. 102–138). New York, NY: Guilford.

Kern, M. L., & Friedman, H. S. (2008). Do conscientious individuals live longer? A quantitative review. *Health Psychology, 27,* 505–512.

Keyes, C. L. M., Shmotkin, D., & Ryff, C. D. (2002). Optimizing well-being: The empirical encounter of two traditions. *Journal of Personality and Social Psychology, 82,* 1007–1022.

Kihlstrom, J. F. (1987). The cognitive unconscious. *Science, 237,* 1445–1452.

Klinger, E. (1975). Consequences of commitment to and disengagement from incentives. *Psychological Review, 82,* 1–25.

Kochanska, G., & Knaack, A. (2003). Effortful control as a personality characteristic of young children: Antecedents, correlates, and consequences. *Journal of Personality, 71,* 1087–1112.

Koole, S. L., Jager, W., van den Berg, A. E., Vlek, C. A. J., & Hofstee, W. K. B. (2001). On the social nature of personality: Effects of extraversion, agreeableness, and feedback about collective resource use on cooperation in a resource dilemma. *Personality and Social Psychology Bulletin, 27,* 289–301.

Kriegman, D., & Knight, C. (1988). Social evolution, psychoanalysis, and human nature. *Social Policy, 19,* 49–55.

La Guardia, J. G., Ryan, R. M., Couchman, C. E., & Deci, E. L. (2000). Within-person variation in security of attachment: A self-determination theory perspective on attachment, need fulfillment, and well-being. *Journal of Personality and Social Psychology, 79,* 367–384.

Leary, M R., & Hoyle, R. H. (Eds.). (2009). *Handbook of individual differences in social behavior.* New York, NY: Guilford.

Liberman, N., & Trope, Y. (2008). The psychology of transcending the here and now. *Science, 322,* 1201–1205.

Lieberman, M. D., Gaunt, R., Gilbert, D. T., & Trope, Y. (2002). Reflection and reflexion: A social cognitive neuroscience approach to attributional inference. In M. Zanna (Ed.), *Advances in Experimental Social Psychology* (pp. 199–249). San Diego, CA: Academic Press.

Lucas, R. E., Diener, E., Grob, A., Suh, E. M., & Shao, L. (2000). Cross-cultural evidence for the fundamental features of extraversion. *Journal of Personality and Social Psychology, 79,* 452–468.

Lynam, D. R., Leukefeld, C., & Clayton, R. R. (2003). The contribution of personality to the overlap between antisocial behavior and substance use/misuse. *Aggressive Behavior, 29,* 316–331.

Markey, C. N., Markey, P. M., & Tinsley, B. J. (2003). Personality, puberty, and preadolescent girls' risky behaviors: Examining the predictive value of the five-factor model of personality. *Journal of Research in Personality, 37,* 405–419.

Markus, H., & Nurius, P. (1986). Possible selves. *American Psychologist, 41,* 954–969.

McAdams, D. P. (1992). The five-factor model in personality: A critical appraisal. *Journal of Personality, 60,* 329–361.

McAdams, D. P., Anyidoho, N. A., Brown, C., Huang, Y. T., Kaplan, B., & Machado, M. A. (2004). Traits and stories: Links between dispositional and narrative features of personality. *Journal of Personality, 72,* 761–784.

McCrae, R. R. (1996). Social consequences of experiential openness. *Psychological Bulletin, 120,* 323–337.

McCrae, R. R., & Costa, P. T., Jr. (2003). *Personality in adulthood: A five-factor theory perspective* (2nd ed.). New York, NY: Guilford.

McCullough, M. E., & Hoyt, W. T. (2002). Transgression-related motivational dispositions: Personality substrates of forgiveness and their links to the big five. *Personality and Social Psychology Bulletin, 28,* 1556–1573.

McCullough, M. E., Kimeldorf, M. B., & Cohen, A. D. (2008). An adaptation for altruism? The social causes, social effects, and social evolution of gratitude. *Current Directions in Psychological Science, 17,* 281–285.

Meier, B. P., & Robinson, M. D. (2004). Does quick to blame mean quick to anger? The role of agreeableness in dissociating blame and anger. *Personality and Social Psychology Bulletin, 30,* 856–867.

Meier, B. P., Robinson, M. D., & Wilkowski, B. M. (2006). Turning the other cheek: Agreeableness and the regulation of aggression-related primes. *Psychological Science, 17,* 136–142.

Metcalfe, J., & Mischel, W. (1999). A hot/cool-system analysis of delay of gratification: Dynamics of willpower. *Psychological Review, 106,* 3–19.

Mikulincer, M. (1998). Adult attachment style and individual differences in functional versus dysfunctional experiences of anger. *Journal of Personality and Social Psychology, 74,* 513–524.

Mikulincer, M., & Goodman, G. S. (2006). *Dynamics of romantic love: Attachment, caregiving, and sex.* New York, NY: Guilford.

Mikulincer, M., & Shaver, P. R. (2007). *Attachment in adulthood: Structure, dynamics, and change.* New York, NY: Guilford.

Miller, J. D., Lynam, D., & Leukefeld, C. (2003). Examining antisocial behavior through the lens of the five factor model of personality. *Aggressive Behavior, 29,* 497–514.

Miller, G. E., & Wrosch, C. (2007). You've gotta know when to fold 'em: Goal disengagement and systemic inflammation in adolescence. *Psychological Science, 18,* 773–777.

Mischel, W. (1974). Processes in delay of gratification. In L. Berkowitz (Ed.), *Advances in experimental social psychology* (Vol. 7). New York, NY: Academic Press.

Mischel, W., & Shoda, Y. (1995). A cognitive–affective system theory of personality: Reconceptualizing situations, dispositions, and invariance in personality structure. *Psychological Review, 102,* 246–268.

Mischel, W., Shoda, Y., & Mendoza-Denton, R. (2002). Situation–behavior profiles as a locus of consistency in personality. *Current Directions in Psychological Science, 11,* 50–54.

Moskowitz, G. B., & Grant, H. (Eds.). (2009). *The psychology of goals.* New York, NY: Guilford.

Nesse, R. M. (2000). Is depression an adaptation? *Archives of General Psychiatry, 57,* 14–20.

Nigg, J. T. (2000). On inhibition/disinhibition in developmental pychopathology: Views from cognitive and personality psychology as a working inhibition taxonomy. *Psychological Bulletin, 126,* 220–246.

Nigg, J. T. (2003). Response inhibition and disruptive behaviors: Toward a multiprocess conception of etiological heterogeneity for ADHD combined type and conduct disorder early-onset type. *Annals of the New York Academy of Science, 1008,* 170–182.

Nigg, J. T. (2006). Temperament and developmental psychopathology. *Journal of Child Psychology and Psychiatry, 47,* 395–422.

Overall, N. C., Fletcher, G. J. O., & Friesen, M. D. (2003). Mapping the intimate relationship mind: Comparisons between three models of attachment representations. *Personality and Social Psychology Bulletin, 29,* 1479–1493.

Panksepp, J. (1998). *Affective neuroscience: The foundations of human and animal emotions.* New York, NY: Oxford University Press.

Peabody, D., & De Raad, B. (2002). The substantive nature of psycholexical personality factors: A comparison across languages. *Journal of Personality and Social Psychology, 83,* 983–997.

Peabody, D., & Goldberg, L. R. (1989). Some determinants of factor structures from personality-trait descriptors. *Journal of Personality and Social Psychology, 57,* 552–567.

Pierce, T., & Lydon, J. E. (2001). Global and specific relational models in the experience of social interactions. *Journal of Personality and Social Psychology, 80,* 613–631.

Rholes, W. S., & Simpson, J. A. (2004). *Adult attachment: Theory, research, and clinical implications.* New York, NY: Guilford.

Roberts, B. W., & Bogg, T. (2004). A longitudinal study of the relationships between conscientiousness and the social-environmental factors and substance-use behaviors that influence health. *Journal of Personality, 72,* 325–354.

Roberts, B. W., Walton, K. E., & Bogg, T. (2005) Conscientiousness and health across the life course. *Review of General Psychology, 9,* 156–168.

Rogers, C. R. (1959). A theory of therapy, personality and interpersonal relationships, as developed in the client-centered framework. In S. Koch (Ed.), *Psychology: A study of a science* (Vol. 3, pp. 184–256). New York, NY: McGraw-Hill.

Rothbart, M. K., Ahadi, S. A., & Evans, D. E. (2000). Temperament and personality: Origins and outcomes. *Journal of Personality and Social Psychology, 78,* 122–135.

Rothbart, M. K., Ahadi, S. A., Hershey, K., & Fisher, P. (2001). Investigations of temperament at three to seven years: The Children's Behavior Questionnaire. *Child Development, 72,* 1394–1408.

Rothbart, M. K., & Bates, J. E. (1998). Temperament. In N. Eisenberg (Ed.), *Handbook of child psychology: Vol 3. Social, emotional and personality development* (5th ed., pp. 105–176). New York, NY: Wiley.

Rothbart, M. K., Ellis, L. K., & Posner, M. I. (2004). Temperament and self-regulation. In R. F. Baumeister & K. D. Vohs (Eds.), *Handbook of self-regulation: Research, theory, and applications* (357–370). New York, NY: Guilford.

Rothbart, M. K., Ellis, L. K., Rueda, M. R., & Posner, M. I. (2003). Developing mechanisms of temperamental effortful control. *Journal of Personality, 71,* 1113–1143.

Rothbart, M. K., & Posner, M. (1985). Temperament and the development of self-regulation. In L. C. Hartlage & C. F. Telzrow (Eds.), *The neuropsychology of individual differences: A developmental perspective* (pp. 93–123). New York, NY: Plenum.

Rothbart, M. K., & Rueda, M. R. (2005). The development of effortful control. In U. Mayr, E. Awh, & S. Keele (Eds.), *Developing individuality in the human brain: A tribute to Michael I. Posner* (pp. 167–188). Washington, D.C.: American Psychological Association.

Ryan, R. M. (1982). Control and information in the intrapersonal sphere: An extension of cognitive evaluation theory. *Journal of Personality and Social Psychology, 43,* 450–461.

Ryan, R. M. (1993). Agency and organization: Intrinsic motivation, autonomy, and the self in psychological development. In J. Jacobs (Ed.), *Nebraska symposium on motivation: Developmental perspectives on motivation* (Vol. 40, pp. 1–56). Lincoln: University of Nebraska Press.

Ryan, R. M., & Deci, E. L. (2001). On happiness and human potentials: A review of research on hedonic and eudaimonic well-being. *Annual Review of Psychology, 52,* 141–166.

Ryan, R. M., & Deci, E. L. (2017). *Self-determination theory: Basic psychological needs in motivation, development, and wellness.* New York, NY: Guilford.

Safran, J. D. (2017). The unbearable lightness of being: Authenticity and the search for the real. *Psychoanalytic Psychology, 34,* 69–77.

Scheier, M. F., & Carver, C. S. (1992). Effects of optimism on psychological and physical well-being: Theoretical overview and empirical update. *Cognitive Therapy and Research, 16,* 201–228.

Saucier, G., & Goldberg, L. R. (2001). Lexical studies of indigenous personality factors: Premises, products, and prospects. *Journal of Personality, 69,* 847–879.

Schmitt, D. P., & Buss, D. M. (2001). Human mate poaching: Tactics and temptations for infiltrating existing mateships. *Journal of Personality and Social Psychology, 80,* 894–917.

Schwartz, S.H. (1992). Universals in the content and structure of values: Theoretical advances and empirical tests in 20 countries. In Mark P. Zanna (Ed.), *Advances in experimental social psychology* (pp. 1–65). San Diego, CA: Academic Press.

Schwartz, S. H., & Bilsky, W. (1990). Theory of the universal content and structure of values: Extensions and cross-cultural replications. *Journal of Personality and Social Psychology, 58,* 878–891.

Segal, N. L. (1993). Twin, sibling, and adoption methods: Tests of evolutionary hypotheses. *American Psychologist, 48,* 943–956.

Shoda, Y., Mischel, W., & Wright, J. C. (1994). Intraindividual stability in the organization and patterning of behavior: Incorporating psychological situations into the idiographic analysis of personality. *Journal of Personality and Social Psychology, 67,* 674–687.

Simpson, J. A. (1990). Influence of attachment styles on romantic relationships. *Journal of Personality and Social Psychology, 59,* 971–980.

Simpson, J. A., Rholes, W. S., Oriña, M. M., & Grich, J. (2002). Working models of attachment, support giving, and support seeking in a stressful situation. *Personality and Social Psychology Bulletin, 28,* 598–608.

Smith, E. R., & DeCoster, J. (2000). Dual-process models in social and cognitive psychology: Conceptual integration and links to underlying memory systems. *Personality and Social Psychology Review, 4,* 108–131.

Smith, E. R., Murphy, J., & Coats, S. (1999). Attachment to groups: Theory and measurement. *Journal of Personality and Social Psychology, 77,* 94–110.

Strack, F., & Deutsch, R. (2004). Reflective and impulsive determinants of social behavior. *Personality and Social Psychology Review, 8,* 220–247.

Tellegen, A. (1985). Structure of mood and personality and their relevance to assessing anxiety, with an emphasis on self-report. In A. H. Tuma & J. D. Maser (Eds.), *Anxiety and the anxiety disorders* (pp. 681–706). Hillsdale, NJ: Erlbaum.

Tooby, J., & Cosmides, L. (1989). Evolutionary psychology and the generation of culture, Part I. *Ethology and Sociobiology, 10,* 29–49.

Tooby, J., & Cosmides, L. (1990). On the universality of human nature and the uniqueness of the individual. *Journal of Personality, 58,* 17–67.

Trobst, K. K., Herbst, J. H., Masters, H. L., III, & Costa, P. T., Jr. (2002). Personality pathways to unsafe sex: Personality, condom use, and HIV risk behaviors. *Journal of Research in Personality, 36,* 117–133.

Vallacher, R. R., & Wegner, D. M. (1989). Levels of personal agency: Individual variation in action identification. *Journal of Personality and Social Psychology, 57,* 660–671.

Vohs, K. D., & Baumeister, R. F. (Eds.). (2016). *Handbook of self-regulation: Research, theory, and applications* (3nd ed.). New York, NY: Guilford.

Walton, K. E., & Roberts, B. W. (2004). On the relationship between substance use and personality traits: Abstainers are not maladjusted. *Journal of Research in Personality, 38,* 515–535.

Watson, D., Clark, L. A., McIntyre, C. W., & Hamaker, S. (1992). Affect, personality, and social activity. *Journal of Personality and Social Psychology, 63,* 1011–1025.

Wiggins, J. S. (1996). *The five-factor model of personality: Theoretical perspectives.* New York, NY: Guilford.

Wilson, T. D., Lindsey, S., & Schooler, T. Y. (2000). A model of dual attitudes. *Psychological Review, 107,* 101–126.

Wright, R. A. (1996). Brehm's theory of motivation as a model of effort and cardiovascular response. In P. M. Gollwitzer & J. A. Bargh (Eds.), *The psychology of action: Linking cognition and motivation to behavior* (pp. 424–453). New York, NY: Guilford.

Wright, J. C., & Mischel, W. (1988). Conditional hedges and the intuitive psychology of traits. *Journal of Personality and Social Psychology, 55,* 454–469.

Wrosch, C., Miller, G. E., Scheier, M. F., & Brun de Pontet, S. (2007). Giving up on unattainable goals: Benefits for health? *Personality and Social Psychology Bulletin, 33,* 251–265.

Zuckerman, M., Kuhlman, D. M., Joireman, J., Teta, P., & Kraft, M. (1993). A comparison of three structural models for personality: The big three, the big five, and the alternative five. *Journal of Personality and Social Psychology, 65,* 757–768.

Chapter 21

Computational Psychology

Michal Kosinski

An ever-growing portion of our behavior, thoughts, and feelings leave behind digital footprints as digital products and services increasingly mediate our personal and professional lives. Our geographical location can be continuously tracked using cell phones, IP addresses, and CCTV cameras.[1] Our health, physical activity, and physiological states are recorded by fitness trackers, health apps, smartwatches, and gym equipment. Our political preferences can be inferred from digital voter registers, campaign contributions, signature campaigns, participation in primaries, and social media activity. Our economic activity is tracked by credit ratings, online purchases, and electronic payments. Huge amounts of language data are generated in emails, instant messages, social media posts, and voice calls (that can be easily and automatically transcribed). Our tastes and preferences are recorded by digital music players and on-demand video platforms. These types of data can be extremely valuable. Companies, governments, and academics invest heavily in their ability to track the behavior of their employees, customers, citizens, and research subjects.

The resulting amount of data is staggering. In 2012, humans produced 2.5 quintillion (that is 2.5×10^8) bytes of data *every single day* (Jacobson, 2013). This amounts to about 350 megabytes per person. To illustrate how much data this is, imagine printing out 2.5 quintillion bytes as a book filled with zeros and ones. Such a book would be about 250 million miles thick, or nearly three times the distance from the Earth to the Sun! Moreover, the amount of data we produce grows each year. It has been estimated that by 2025, our daily data output will be 200 times the amount it was in 2012—that is over 62 gigabytes per person. Combine this with the ever-growing population, and our collective data output will be 180 zettabytes (that is 180×10^{21})!

When combined with modern computing power and powerful analytical tools, these vast new quantities of information—aptly named "big data"—are driving the emergence of a new research paradigm: computational social psychology. In this chapter, I first provide a definition of big data and briefly introduce its most common forms. Next, I discuss the opportunities offered by big data, including its high diversity and ecological validity. I offer perspective on how big data and computational methods could be used to complement or even replace traditional surveys and psychometric tools. I also discuss the challenges associated with big data, including the privacy risks and biases inherent to big-data samples. Finally, I describe how psychological science can benefit from incorporating prediction-focused approach typical of computational studies employing big data.

What Is Big Data?

This rather loosely defined term refers to data sets characterized by three Vs: *volume, velocity*, and *variety* (Laney, 2001). Volume refers to the size of the data; data become "big" when size is one of the challenges that needs to be considered in research design. Velocity describes the speed with which data is generated. Traditionally, social scientists collected their data in relatively short and well-defined periods of time, such as experimental sessions or observational studies. This is in stark contrast with typical sources of big data, such as social media platforms, online games, or communication apps, which produce a constant torrent of data. Variety refers to the multitude of forms that big data can take, such as text documents, social network graphs, images, videos, audio files, GPS-location history, or purchase logs. Each of these data types presents unique methodological and practical challenges. For example, the database structures and analytical tools suitable for storing and analyzing text data are markedly different from those needed when dealing with digital images.

Moreover, big data is often collected in naturalistic settings that are replete with confounding factors and biases that are typically absent in data obtained from carefully designed and controlled experimental or observational studies. As an effect big data, often contains data points (or values) that are imprecise, incomplete, or incorrect. For example, records of participants' geographical locations recorded from their smartphones may contain data points that are imprecise (e.g., due to GPS signal noise added by weather or tall buildings), incorrect (e.g., when participants forget to carry their smartphones), or incomplete (e.g., when batteries run out). These challenges are often referred to as the fourth V of big data: *veracity*.

Another common property of big data is that it is usually *unstructured*. Unstructured data (as opposed to structured data) does not fit into any easily definable format, such as a spreadsheet. Facebook status updates provide a good example of unstructured data. There is no single predefined format for a status update; each can contain varying amounts of text, images, videos, and web links. Moreover, other users can interact with the status updates of a given person by adding their own comments, resharing a given update with their own friends, or expressing their attitude toward the post by using one of the six Facebook reaction buttons (the successors of the "like" button). All of these interactions can be recorded, producing a complex collection of digital footprints that cannot be easily represented as the neat numerical variables to which social scientists are accustomed.

Using Big Data in Psychological Research

There are two major ways in which big, unstructured, data is used in research: as a source of interpretable variables or an input to prediction models. Let me first focus on translating big data into interpretable variables. Take, for example, Facebook status updates introduced in the previous section. A data set of status updates could be used as a source of simple, well-structured variables, similar to ones that psychologists are used to working with. Those could include word count, number of times a given update was shared, or number of likes it received.[2] Status updates can also directly reveal other information about their authors (e.g., political views, the dates of major life events such as births and weddings). Such information can be relatively easily extracted in a manual or automated way and converted into structured variables. For instance, human judges or programs such Linguistic Inquiry and Word Count (LIWC; Tausczik & Pennebaker, 2010) can be used to estimate the emotional tone of a status update, its authenticity, cognitive complexity, or other psycho-linguistic dimensions.

Interpretable, well-structured variables can also be extracted from unstructured data by using *unsupervised* learning techniques (Kosinski, Wang, Lakkaraju, & Leskovec, 2016). Unsupervised learning is used to discover patterns within a given data set. A typical example of unsupervised learning is provided by cluster analysis, a technique that groups together similar observations (e.g., participants), variables, or both into sets (i.e., clusters) based on their similarity.[3] Unsupervised learning could be used to identify popular topics discussed in a sample of Facebook status updates and the probability that a given update discusses a particular topic. As a result, an unstructured data set of Facebook status updates would be translated into a small set of interpretable variables subsuming their contents. Such variables can be analyzed using traditional approaches in the social sciences. One could, for example, study the links between significant life events (e.g., marriage) and longitudinal changes in the topics discussed in status updates.

The second major way in which unstructured big data can be employed in research is to build prediction models. Here, the focus is not on turning unstructured data into a handful of interpretable variables but on the accuracy of predicting a given outcome of interest. While the resulting models tend to be complex and difficult to interpret, they can be very useful in studying psychological phenomena (e.g., identifying the causes of psychological disorders) and solving applied problems (e.g., diagnosing psychological disorders). This will be discussed in more detail in the section on prediction and explanation later in this chapter.

Types of Big Data

The following section discusses several types of big data most commonly used in socio-psychological research.

Language Data

Psychologists have long believed that an individual's language use is strongly related to important psychological constructs (Freud, 1891/2011). However, the study of language has been historically limited by the difficulties posed by recording it in naturalistic settings and the lack of efficient tools well-suited to analyzing it. Big data offers solutions to both of these issues. First, as much of human communication is now mediated by digital technologies, language can be easily recorded. Across the world, people broadcast their thoughts on social networks, communicate through email, work on text documents, or talk on the phone (voice recordings can now be easily and automatically transcribed). In 2017, 3.5 billion Internet users sent 269 billion emails, posted 200 billion tweets, and issued 1.2 trillion Google search queries (see http://www.internetlivestats.com). Second, the widespread availability of language data and growing computing power has fueled the development of linguistic analytical tools such as Latent Dirichlet Allocation (Blei, Ng, & Jordan, 2003)[4] and LIWC (Pennebaker, Francis, & Booth, 2001). For a great introduction to language analysis, see Chen and Wojcik (2016), Jones, Wojcik, Sweeting, and Silver (2016), and Kern et al. (2016).

Language data are well suited for the study of a wide range of phenomena at the level of individual people. Language use has been shown to have reliable trait-like properties (Pennebaker & King, 1999) and to be a strong predictor of educational performance (Pennebaker, Chung, Frazee, Lavergne, & Beaver, 2014; Robinson, Navea, & Ickes, 2012), life expectancy (Penzel, Persich, Boyd, & Robinson, 2017; Pressman & Cohen, 2007), values (Boyd et al., 2015), and resilience to trauma (D'Andrea, Chiu, Casas, & Deldin, 2012; Pennebaker, Mayne, & Francis, 1997). New methods and large data sets are helpful in evaluating long-held beliefs and classic theories. For example, contrary to theory and intuition, self-focused language has been shown to be unrelated to the personality trait of narcissism (Carey et al., 2015). Insight can also be obtained at the group level. For example, language patterns reflecting negative social relationships, disengagement, and negative emotions positively correlate with county-level mortality from atherosclerotic heart disease. In fact, this relationship is so strong that a predictive model based on language used in tweets more accurately predicts county-level atherosclerotic heart disease mortality than commonly used risk factors (e.g., smoking, diabetes, hypertension, and obesity; Eichstaedt et al., 2015). Psychological analysis of language data has also been used to study unusual and novel issues, such as the determination of a text's authorship. A linguistic analysis of the play *Double Falsehood* revealed that its psychological style and content architecture were consistent with those of Shakespeare (early parts of the play) and Fletcher (later parts), but not with those of Theobald (Boyd & Pennebaker, 2015).

Behavioral Residues Stored in Usage Logs

Large fractions of offline and online behaviors are now enabled, mediated, or observed by digital platforms. This produces an enormous volume of usage logs that describe people's behaviors, preferences, patterns of communication, or geographical locations. In 2015, for example, people watched 1.8 trillion videos on YouTube ("37 Mind-Blowing YouTube Facts, 2018) and liked 2.1 trillion things on Facebook (Smith, 2018). US consumers conducted 103 billion credit or debit card payments (US Federal Reserve System, 2016). Each of these actions create a time-stamped entry, such as "User X listened to Lady Gaga's song Poker Face at 3:00 PM on January 1, 2018," providing a detailed, diary-like log documenting users' behavior. As virtually all digital products and services record (or *log*) the behavior of their users, a broad range of behaviors is now stored in social media logs, web-browsing and web-searching histories, multimedia playlists, bank statements, and more.

Simplicity, pervasiveness, and the diversity of recorded behaviors have made usage logs one of the favorite types of big data among social scientists. They can be analyzed using relatively simple statistical tools and typically require less computational power than more complex data, such as language, sound, or images. Those who are interested in conducting research on usage logs are referred to Chen and Wojcik's (2016) practical guide to planning and executing such studies, and Landers et al.'s (2016) introduction to Web scraping (an automated approach to extracting data from websites) and its ethical ramifications. Those interested in building predictive models based on usage logs may consider the tutorial by Kosinski et al. (2016), which includes examples of R code and a sample data set.

The psychological relevance of the behaviors, preferences, and interactions encoded in usage logs is well illustrated by their strong links with a broad range of psychological constructs. One of the simplest types of usage logs, Facebook likes, have been shown to reveal individuals' political and religious views, relationship status, substance abuse, race, sexual orientation, egocentric social network properties, well-being, intelligence, and personality (Kosinski, Stillwell, & Graepel, 2013). Bank statements have been shown to be linked with well-being (Matz, Gladstone, & Stillwell, 2016), purchase records can be used to predict pregnancy (Hill, 2012), and edits on a movie's Wikipedia page can predict its popularity and commercial success (Mestyán, Yasseri, & Kertész, 2013).

Images and Audio-Visual Data

Another widespread use of digital platforms involves creating, sharing, publishing, and viewing images, videos, and sound clips. In an average minute in 2017, 300 hours of videos were uploaded to YouTube ("37 Mind-Blowing YouTube Facts," 2018), two million minutes of voice calls were transmitted through Skype (Perez, 2017), 66,000 photos were shared on Instagram (Lister, 2018), and 200,000 photos were posted on Facebook ("Top 20 Valuable Facebook Statistics," 2018). Nearly four million years of video calls were conducted between 2010 and 2016 on Skype alone (Skype Team, 2016). There is also a growing number of cameras that monitor public spaces, such as streets or stadiums;[5] Chicago alone has an estimated 22,000 surveillance cameras (Tay, Jebb, & Woo, 2017). Other sources of images and audio-visual data include photo-sharing platforms (e.g., Google Photos), profile pictures (e.g., Facebook, LinkedIn), video blogs and podcasts, Google Street View, voicemail records, and commands issued to smart-home controls such as Amazon's Alexa or Google Home.

Images and audio-visual records provide a rich source of data on human behavior, thoughts, and communication. Historically, the use of such data in psychology was rare and limited to manual transcriptions and codings of the content of images and recordings. The big-data approach provides analytical tools that are capable of automatically extracting information from such data, saving large amounts of time and effort. Speech-to-text technology can be used to extract text from audio files, visual object recognition algorithms can detect and label objects within images, and widely available emotion-detection software (e.g., Face++, IBM Watson, Microsoft Cognitive Services) can label people's emotions based on their facial expressions or voice recordings. This enables researchers to analyze data sets that are much larger than ever before. For example, a recent study found that there are no substantial links between facial width-to-height ratio (fWHR) and a range of self-reported behavioral tendencies. This finding called into question theories that suggested that fWHR is linked to antisocial and aggressive behavior (Kosinski, 2017). Instead of the experimenter manually measuring fWHR for each individual face, a facial detection algorithm was employed to detect the dimensions of over 137,000 faces, saving about 600 work hours. Automated fWHR estimates were shown to be just as accurate as manual measurement.

Mobile Sensors

Mobile sensors constitute another popular source of big data (Campbell et al., 2008; Miller, 2012). Mobile devices, such as smartwatches, fitness trackers, and smartphones are packed with precise sensors that track their owners' behavior and surroundings. In 2017, nearly 2.5 billion people around the world owned a smartphone (another 2.5 billion people owned a mobile phone; "Number of Mobile Phone Users," 2016); nearly 16% of US consumers owned a smartwatch or a fitness tracker (Sunnebo, 2017).

There are many types of behaviors that can be efficiently studied using mobile sensors, including human movement, mobility patterns, and social interactions (for a thorough review, see Harari, Müller, Aung, & Rentfrow, 2017). Accelerometers built into mobile devices (Lane et al., 2010) can be used to study physical activity and movement. Microphones can be used to detect participants' respiratory events such as sneezing, clearing one's throat, or coughing (Barata, Kowatsch, Tinschert, & Filler, 2016); smoking (Jebara, 2014); and teeth brushing (Korpela, Miyaji, Maekawa, Nozaki, & Tamagawa, 2015). GPS sensors, which capture users' latitude and longitude coordinates, can be used to measure mobility patterns, such as the distance traveled by a given user, the duration of their travel, and their temporal travel patterns (Harari et al., 2017).

More complex behaviors can be detected by combining data from different sensors and sources. For example, cartographic data merged with GPS coordinates can be used to determine a user's location (e.g., workplace, home, or shopping center) and particular routes that he or she has traveled to get to those places (Eagle & Pentland, 2009). Combining data from accelerometers and microphones enables the detection of common behaviors such as clapping, vacuuming, or taking out the trash (Lu, Pan, Lane, Choudhury, & Campbell, 2009). Information about phone usage, combined with data from other sensors, such as ambient light sensors, microphones, or accelerometers, can reveal users' sleep patterns (Hao, Xing,

& Zhou, 2013) or alertness (Murnane et al., 2016). Merging GPS data and signals from WiFi transmitters or accelerometers can be used to track individuals within a building (Chon & Cha, 2011), detect modes of transportation (Hemminki, Nurmi, & Tarkoma, 2013), and monitor pedestrian behavior (Wang, Guo, Peng, Zhou, & Yu, 2016).

Mobile sensors are increasingly often used in psychological research. Studies have explored the links between mobility patterns and depression (Chow et al., 2017), mood (Lathia, Sandstrom, Mascolo, & Rentfrow, 2017), schizophrenia (Wang et al., 2016), bipolar disorder (Abdullah et al., 2016), physical activity and well-being, mental health, educational outcomes, happiness, and face-to-face encounters (Lathia et al., 2017; Wang et al., 2014; Wang, Harari, Hao, Zhou, & Campbell, 2015).

Opportunities and Challenges of the Big-Data Approach

There is much enthusiasm about the opportunities offered by the big-data approach (Lazer et al., 2009). However, much like any other research paradigm, big data has both strengths and weaknesses. As it is a relatively new and quickly evolving phenomenon, it is easy to make errors when designing studies, interpreting the results, and integrating these with existing theories. This section focuses on selected issues pertaining to big-data studies.

Size

Big-data samples tend to be, as the name suggests, very large, often encompassing information about hundreds of thousands or millions of individuals. This is great news for psychological science. Small samples typically employed in psychological research were one of the main drivers of the failure to replicate many study results, referred to as the *replicability crisis* (Yarkoni & Westfall, 2017). The larger the sample, the more likely it is that the data are representative of the population that they are drawn from, which reduces the risk of sampling errors. Additionally, if properly used, large samples greatly reduce the risk of overfitting (i.e., discovering random patterns that exist in the sample but not in the general population). Lastly, large samples facilitate the discovery of patterns, such as multiway interactions, that may be too subtle to be detectable in smaller samples. These benefits of large samples gave rise to the popular saying among big data researchers: "More data beats better algorithms" (Domingos, 2012). This is elegantly illustrated by a study where a diverse set of algorithms was applied to extract meaning from language data. Results showed that the quality of the solution did not depend on the choice of the algorithm but on the size of data set (Banko & Brill, 2001). It is usually the case that the best way to improve the reliability and validity of research results is to collect more data.

Moreover, while traditional experimental or observational studies typically record an individual's behavior over a short period of time (e.g., minutes or hours), big-data samples often allow for observation of the same individuals over months, years, or even decades. The availability of such longitudinal data supports studies that explore the change in psychological processes over extended periods of time. Millions of tweets from across the globe, for example, were used to study individual-level diurnal and seasonal mood rhythms (Golder & Macy, 2011). Results showed that mood typically peaks in the morning, deteriorates as the day progresses, and is higher during the weekends and during seasons when the days are longer (e.g., summer in the northern hemisphere).

Diversity

Big-data samples tend to be more diverse than traditional samples used in psychological research. While digital technology was initially a domain dominated by younger, well-educated, and affluent individuals, many digital platforms and devices are now used by large, representative, and diverse populations. For example, if Facebook were a country, it would be the most populous one on Earth. Its population surpassed two billion in 2017, as it became the go-to place for communicating, consuming news, and socializing for people across many countries, classes, and demographic groups. Due to the size, diversity, and global reach of Facebook and other digital platforms, researchers now have the ability to reach groups that were often underrepresented or entirely excluded from traditional studies (Gosling, Sandy, John, & Potter, 2010). This helps circumvent one of the major limitations of psychological research, namely, its overreliance on samples that are small, composed of (largely female) undergraduate students, and disproportionately WEIRD (i.e., Western, educated, industrialized, rich, and democratic; Henrich, Heine, & Norenzayan, 2010).

Ecological Validity

Typically, big-data samples originate in natural environments rather than in the artificial setting of a laboratory. Furthermore, they are usually collected retrospectively: Instead of recording behavior that occurs after the start of the study, researchers can study the footprints of behaviors that happened before the study began. This helps circumvent a number of problematic issues that affect observational data collected in a traditional way, such as expectancy effects (i.e., observers' tendency to see what they expected to see) or participants' reactivity (i.e., a change in their behavior induced by factors such as the unusual environment of the psychological laboratory or researchers' attention). Retrospective records of spontaneous behavior are ecologically valid because they are performed in a natural environment by individuals who are unaware that their data will later be analyzed.

From Self-Reports to Observation

Large, longitudinal, and ecologically valid records of actual behavior can reduce psychology's overreliance on self-report methods of collecting data. It has long been argued that the social sciences should move away from self-reports and toward longitudinal records of behavior observed in the natural environment. The big-data approach makes this a viable possibility. As previously discussed, digital records of language, usage logs, and data from mobile sensors can reveal a wide range of real-world behaviors. Thus, self-reported mobility can be replaced by records of participants' geographical locations; self-reported political labels can be replaced by records of campaign contributions, voter registries, or political opinions expressed to one's friends on social media; and self-reported social network structures can be replaced by social interactions recorded on social networks, on communication platforms, and by mobile sensors. Such data are more ecologically valid, easier to collect, and circumvent the limits of participants' attention span, memory, energy, or motivation.

Psychological Measurement

The transition from self-reports to observation of actual behaviors could revolutionize techniques of psychological measurement. While traditional psychometric measures have been successfully applied in contexts ranging from recruitment and high-stakes educational assessments to clinical diagnosis, they suffer from a major flaw: They are limited to capturing respondents' explicit, conscious, and motivated opinions (Paulhus & Vazire, 2007). As such, they are affected by a number of biases, including social desirability bias, availability bias, the reference group effect, and misrepresentation. Consequently, even widely used and well-validated psychometric tools are often relatively poor predictors of many basic real-life outcomes, such as performance at work (Morgeson et al., 2007), well-being (Wojcik, Hovasapian, Graham, Motyl, & Ditto, 2015), or physical activity (Rhodes & Smith, 2006).

A growing body of research shows that both psychological traits (e.g., personality) and states (e.g., emotion) can be accurately predicted from a wide range of digital footprints. For example, "big five" personality traits can be predicted using blog posts (Yarkoni, 2010), Facebook status updates (Park et al., 2014), Twitter posts (Quercia, Kosinski, Stillwell, & Crowcroft, 2011), website browsing logs, the properties of Facebook profiles (Kosinski, Bachrach, Kohli, Stillwell, & Graepel, 2014), search queries (Bi, Shokouhi, Kosinski, & Graepel, 2013), content of personal websites (Marcus, Machilek, & Schütz, 2006; Vazire & Gosling, 2004), music collections (Nave et al., 2018), Facebook likes (Kosinski et al., 2013), and mobile phone usage (de Montjoye, Quoidbach, Robic, & Pentland, 2013). Scores on the Satisfaction with Life Scale have been successfully predicted using tweets (Yang & Srinivasan, 2016), Facebook posts (Schwartz et al., 2016), and Facebook likes (Kosinski et al., 2013). Mood and emotion have been successfully predicted from spoken and written language data (Cowie et al., 2000), video (Teixeira, Wedel, & Pieters, 2012), wearable devices (AlHanai & Ghassemi, 2017), and smartphone sensor data (Likamwa, Liu, Lane, & Zhong, 2013).

The accuracy of such predictive models is high. For example, the average correlation between questionnaire-based and Facebook likes–based personality scores was found to be $r = 0.56$ (Youyou, Kosinski, & Stillwell, 2015). Personality estimates based on digital footprints are also characterized by high external validity (e.g., the ability to predict real-life outcomes and other psychological traits), high test–retest reliability (e.g., correlation between the scores of the model applied to participants' data at two different time points), and high concurrent validity (e.g., correlation between two models based on different types of digital footprints; Park et al., 2014; Youyou et al., 2015).

As mentioned before, measurements based on digital footprints are often able to avoid the limitations of traditional measures. Studies based on traditional personality questionnaires, for example, have found little evidence for personality similarity between friends and between spouses, despite the fact that they tend to be similar on a broad range of other psycho-demographic traits, such as age, educational level, race, religion, attitudes, and general intelligence. The failure to detect personality similarity might be driven by a bias inherent to self-reported measures: the reference-group effect (i.e., the tendency of individuals to make personality judgments relative to a salient comparison group, rather than in absolute terms). This has been confirmed by a study that showed strong personality similarity between friends and between romantic partners when personality measurement was based on language or Facebook likes, but not when it employed traditional self-reported questionnaires (Youyou, Stillwell, Schwartz, & Kosinski, 2017).

Assessments based on digital footprints can be conveniently, unobtrusively, and inexpensively applied to large populations. This contrasts with traditional measures, which can be quite burdensome to both participants and researchers in terms of time, stress, and effort. For instance, one of the most popular personality inventories, the NEO PI-R™, consists of 240 questions and can take up to 40 minutes to complete. Thus, obtaining the scores of 3,000 participants could easily take a combined total of 2,000 working hours, which is more than the collective time that an average American spends at work in an entire year (and as much as an average German works in 18 months; "Working Time," n.d.). In contrast, big-data personality measures can estimate personality of millions of participants in minutes or seconds.

Importantly, the accuracy and convenience of such psychological measurements derived from digital footprints do come at a price. In particular, as discussed later in this chapter, the ability to quickly and unobtrusively measure the intimate traits of large populations poses great risks to individual privacy.

Experiments and Natural Experiments

The majority of big-data studies employ an observational approach. However, big-data methods have also been used to conduct large-scale randomized controlled experiments, develop data-driven psychometric measures, and deliver psychological interventions. Facebook, for example, was used to conduct a randomized controlled study of 61 million people (Bond et al., 2012). Experimenters tested several different messages that encouraged users to vote in the 2010 US congressional elections. They studied the resulting changes in the real voting behavior of the targeted users, their friends, and friends of friends. In fact, this experimental approach (commonly known as A/B testing) is now widely used by the online industry to test new features and improve users' experience. Additionally, the governments of some countries have employed nationwide experiments to assess the efficiency of new laws and policies. For example, on January 1, 2017, the Finnish government launched an experiment aimed at testing the benefits of basic universal income. Two thousand unemployed individuals were randomly selected to receive 560 euros each month, regardless of whether they found a paid job or not (Kangas, Simanainen, & Honkanen, 2017).

Big-data samples contain abundant traces of *natural experiments* in which random or quasi-random subsets of people are exposed to a particular situational influence, such as a natural disaster, regional policy change, or geographically limited interruption in their access to digital services. Such natural experiments offer an opportunity to study the effects of factors that would be difficult to simulate in a controlled experimental setting. Hurricane Ike, for example, was used to study the short- and long-term causal effects of natural disasters on social networks. A study based on a sample of 1.5 million Facebook profiles of US college students showed that people affected by this natural disaster formed stronger bonds than those who were unaffected (Phan & Airoldi, 2015). As the exact paths of hurricanes are difficult to predict and can change unexpectedly, they affect a quasi-random subset of communities, enabling the discovery of causal mechanisms.

Interventions

The interactive character of most of the environments where big data is collected enables researchers to go beyond recording data to actually engage with the study participants. A growing number of studies employ such an approach. For example, an outdoor installation combining screens, cameras, and facial recognition software has been used to study facial expressions of passersby and encourage them to smile (Hernandez, Hoque, & Picard, 2012). A smartphone application that stimulated interaction with weak ties in one's social network was found to boost users' social capital (Kobayashi, Boase, Suzuki, & Suzuki, 2015). Another smartphone application was used to offer both prescheduled and on-demand resources to facilitate symptom management, mood regulation, medication adherence, social function, and sleep quality of individuals suffering from schizophrenia (Ben-Zeev et al., 2014). Results showed significant reductions in psychotic symptoms, depression, and general psychopathology after one month of use.

Researchers can also use algorithms to track participants' behavior, location, and environment and react by triggering data collection or an intervention. For example, antismoking interventions tailored to participants' location and behavior were shown to support smoking cessation (Naughton et al., 2016).

Challenges of High Ecological Validity

As discussed earlier in this chapter, the high ecological validity of big data comes at a cost. Although real-world environments are excellent sources of ecologically valid data, they were not designed to produce reliable data and thus may be a source of many biases. For example, Twitter, Facebook, Google, and other digital environments are constantly re-engineered and updated, altering their users' behavior and the data that they generate. Consider the following example. In December 2007, Facebook users suddenly changed the way in which they wrote their status updates. Self-oriented statuses written in the third person that dominated Facebook thus far (e.g., "Olivia is feeling awesome today") were replaced by updates of much larger stylistic variety and were less focused on the given user. A researcher studying society through the lens of Facebook status updates could have concluded that some extraordinary event must have changed the collective focus of Facebook users that made them less self-centered. The truth is more trivial: In December 2007, Facebook replaced the preamble each status update "[User's name] is . . ." with place-holder text asking "What are you doing right now?" which disappeared once a user started typing his or her update. This example provides an illustration of the importance of fully understanding the context in which data are generated before making interpretations and drawing conclusions.

Similar changes in the functioning of digital platforms and devices are very common, often occur unannounced, and are rarely as obvious as the previous example. Moreover, artificial intelligence (AI) algorithms, that run many of the online platforms and digital environments, continuously evolve to increase their owners' profits and users' engagement. Google search queries, for example, are influenced by the autocomplete mechanism that suggests terms to users typing their queries. The autocomplete mechanism, in turn, is constantly updated, partially in response to user-issued queries. All studies that employ search queries (e.g., to track popular opinion as in Stephens-Davidowitz, 2014) are affected to some extent by this and other similar mechanisms.

The functioning of digital platforms and the behavior of their users can also be altered (often maliciously) by third parties. Website visits, Twitter followers, and Facebook likes are sometimes faked for economic or political gain. For example, scholars studying public opinion by tracking trends in Google search might have discovered that in 2016, "evil" was one of Google's top autocomplete suggestions for the search term starting with "are jews" (Cadwalladr, 2016). This does not mean that there was a spike in the anti-Semitism of Google users or in the popularity of anti-Semitic websites. Instead, it was the result of a small group of anti-Semitic websites that manipulated the PageRank algorithm employed by Google to assess the quality and popularity of online content. Similar tricks are widely used by companies and governments to alter the behavior of search engines, recommendation mechanisms, and news aggregators. Companies and political campaigns, for instance, use a variety of methods to ensure that their products or candidates are trending on Twitter (Ratkiewicz et al., 2011). These factors are often invisible to researchers, yet they can significantly affect the behavior of the individuals being studied.

Further adding to the challenges faced by researchers, a broad range of other hidden factors can affect big-data samples. For example, some Twitter and Facebook profiles are controlled by artificial agents (i.e., bots). While studying the behavior of bots might be interesting in its own right, it is a potential source of bias if bots cannot be distinguished from the behavior of real users.

Additional bias is introduced by privacy settings. Users can limit access to parts of their profiles; for example, both Twitter and Facebook users can protect their posts, rendering them invisible to researchers and other third parties. In many cases, individual differences in privacy settings or changes in platform-wide privacy rules can be easily misinterpreted as evidence of psychological phenomena. For example, results indicating that certain groups of users have relatively few Facebook posts could stem from differences in posting behavior, differences in privacy settings that affect the visibility of posts, or a combination of both.

Privacy

The big-data approach allows researchers to study large populations in naturalistic settings and go beyond of the restricting boundaries of the lab. Although this is a great opportunity to study humans in their natural environment, it also exposes an unprecedented number of participants to significant privacy risks (Barchard & Williams, 2008; Kosinski, Matz, Gosling, Popov, & Stillwell, 2015; Molokken-Ostvold, 2005). This is exacerbated by the lack of clear and widely accepted research guidelines. The protocols related to designing large-scale online studies, storing data, and analyzing results are scarce and often contradictory (Solberg, 2010; Wilson, Gosling, & Graham, 2012). Moreover, the speed of technological progress, ever-changing digital platforms and environments, and evolving social norms mean that both researchers and internal review boards struggle to accurately judge the threats related to big-data research (Singer & Vinson, 2001). Next, three major issues are discussed that should be considered when planning, conducting, and reviewing big-data studies.

First, the boundary between public and private data is vague. Massive amounts of data are publicly available and can be freely scraped from online platforms and environments. Many scholars believe that mining public data is equivalent to conducting archival research—a method frequently employed in disciplines such as history, art criticism, and literature—and does not constitute the study of human subjects (Bruckman, 2002; Herring, 1996). Others, however, rightly point out that the boundary between public and private should not be determined by accessibility or a platform's terms of use but by social norms and practices (Frankel & Siang, 1999; Waskul, 1996). An interesting example is provided by the social norms of online dating. Friends and coworkers regularly encounter each other on dating websites and are thus exposed to information about each other's preferences, oftentimes in intimate detail. However, such profile information, while often publicly available, is treated as personal, and people commonly pretend not to know facts about each other that were gleaned from dating website profiles.

Second, challenges stem from the boundaries of an individual participant's consent. Data volunteered by participants often contain information related to or contributed by other people. Examples include images featuring others, comments on participants' profiles that were made by others, or information about participants' social connections. It is often not clear to what extent this information can be studied without obtaining consent from all the involved parties.

Third, it is difficult if not impossible to anonymize big-data samples; in fact, it seems that the availability of big data makes it difficult to anonymize even small traditional samples. For example, date of birth, gender, and ZIP code allow an interested party to identify 87% of the US population when matched with large publicly available data sets (Sweeney, 1997). Similarly, it has been shown that an individual's place and date of birth can be used to predict their Social Security number (Acquisti & Gross, 2009). Facebook likes or tweets of a given participant are virtually guaranteed to be entirely unique, rendering them personally identifiable. Just four data points are enough to uniquely identify 90% of individuals in a sample encompassing three months of credit card records for 1.1 million people (de Montjoye, Radaelli, Singh, & Pentland, 2015).

These privacy-related issues are not trivial, and the debate on how to best approach them is ongoing. Ironically, these issues are exacerbated by the improvement of research practices in the social sciences: Journals, funding agencies, and academics are becoming less tolerant (at last!) of scientists who do not publicly sharing their data and code. Although this fosters open science and greater ease of replicability, it may expose participants' privacy to greater risks. Of course, this does not mean that we should stop conducting big-data research or striving to make progress in our research practices. Quite the opposite. Big-data research not only offers the chance to boost our understanding of human behavior and thus improve the condition of humankind but can also potentially provide solutions to the very privacy risks previously discussed. For example, studying the profiles and behavior of dating website users could improve our understanding of the prerequisites of successful relationships and help develop algorithms for matching couples. This would not only have the potential to improve the well-being of many lives but could also reduce the need for people to broadcast their intimate preferences on their dating profiles and, consequently, reduce the associated privacy risks.

In summary, big data brings big responsibility: The consequences of a leak or misuse of data could be much more far-reaching and severe than in the case of traditional smaller-scale studies. Thus, it is researchers' responsibility to carefully weigh the scientific contributions of the study against the potential risks to participants. Moreover, researchers should discuss ethical considerations when reporting the results of their studies. This would not only help to ensure that the researchers consider the ethical implications of their own work but would also support the evolution of standards in the rapidly changing technological landscape (Schultze & Mason, 2012).

Bias

The surprising accuracy of many predictive algorithms should not overshadow the fact that such predictions may be based on biased data. We cannot blame the algorithms for this; the data sets they are trained on were often generated by humans, who suffer from prejudice, limited self-knowledge, and world views that are a product of social norms and personal motives. For example, a predictive model trained on a standard internet corpus automatically associated the words *female* and *woman* with arts occupations, and *male* and *man* with math and science (Caliskan, Bryson, & Narayanan, 2017). Similarly, an algorithm associated European American names with more pleasant words than African American names. These findings mirror those gleaned from studies involving the Implicit Association Test (Greenwald, McGhee, & Schwartz, 1998). These studies provide clues to the origins of these biases. If such algorithms are used to inform decisions, such as by autocompleting search queries, they may reinforce existing social inequities, rather than attenuate them.

As predictive modeling is being used in the service of increasingly consequential ends (e.g., determination of whether to grant a defendant bail), it is imperative that we strive to limit the extent to which such algorithms perpetuate human biases. To achieve this, social scientists, engineers, and policy makers should be aware of the risks of the algorithmic bias, both when developing models and when evaluating the effects of widely deployed AI systems on human behavior.

On the other hand, while striving to build models that are as unbiased as possible, we should not forget that even a biased AI model is often fairer than the human decision-making process that it is designed to aid or replace. A growing body of research indicates that complementing or replacing human judgments with carefully monitored algorithms offers the promise of reducing discrimination (Kusner, Loftus, Russell, & Silva, 2017). A recent policy simulation examined judges' decisions of whether a defendant will await trial at home or in jail, based on a sample of 758,027 defendants arrested in New York City (Kleinberg, Lakkaraju, Leskovec, Ludwig, & Mullainathan, 2018). This decision is consequential to both the defendant and society; while a case may take several months to resolve, some defendants may fail to reappear in court or commit a crime while awaiting trial. The analysis revealed that replacing judges with an AI algorithm would result in the reduction of crime rates by up to 25% with no change in jailing rates (or, alternatively, the reduction of jail populations by over 40% with no increase in crime rates). Moreover, these gains in accuracy were accompanied by a significant reduction in racial bias: Following the algorithm's decisions would reduce the percentage of African Americans and Hispanics in jail. This study provides an elegant example of how the use of computational models can benefit both the individuals and the society.

Prediction and Explanation

The main goal of psychology is to explain the causal mechanisms that drive human thoughts and behaviors. This goal is epitomized in the ultimate tool of psychological science: a tightly controlled randomized experiment that focuses on a handful of carefully measured variables. In contrast, the big-data approach has been preoccupied with prediction. Data sets comprise many observations and variables combined with powerful analytical tools enable big-data researchers to build models that encompass hundreds or thousands of predictors. Such models excel at predicting future outcomes and behavior, often with an uncanny accuracy, and have been shown to be more accurate than humans when predicting others' emotion (Bartlett, Littlewort, Frank, & Lee, 2014), sexual orientation (Wang & Kosinski, 2017), personality (Lambiotte & Kosinski, 2015), or propensity to commit a crime (Kleinberg et al., 2018). On the other hand, such models cannot be easily interpreted by the human brain, which has earned them the pejorative *black box* label. Artificial neural networks,[6] for instance, can easily have tens or hundreds of millions of artificial neurons arranged in thousands of layers (Lecun, Bengio, & Hinton, 2015). Even the simplest predictive models, such as linear regression, become difficult to interpret when they are made up of hundreds or thousands of predictors.

The contrast between traditional explanation-focused psychology and the prediction-focused big-data approach does not mean that they are incompatible. Presumably, the ultimate motive of scholars who strive to explain psychological mechanisms is to build theories that can predict real-life behavior. However, traditional tools employed by psychologists (such as controlled experiments) are typically focused on testing well-defined hypotheses in an artificial environment, such as a psychological lab. As such, they are unlikely to discover mechanisms that were not hypothesized. Moreover, they are not well suited to examination of whether a given theory is predictive of real-life behavior. Consequently, while it is clear that both prediction and explanation are important, psychology has focused mainly on designing and testing models (theories) and somewhat less on testing whether such models predict behavior outside of the lab. Elevating prediction to a stature equal to that of explanation and incorporating prediction-focused statistical tools could greatly benefit the field of psychological science.

Interpreting Big-Data Models

Despite their complexity, the functioning of the black box big-data models can be, to some extent, explained. Thus, they can be fruitfully employed to support the goal of understanding the causal mechanisms that underlie human behavior. We know this for certain, as we have been successfully doing so for a very long time in the context of one very complex prediction model, the prototypical black box: the human brain. Despite the brain's brain-boggling complexity, psychological science has been rather successful at explaining the mechanisms underlying its functioning.

Studying the insides of the black box can help build better algorithms, make more accurate predictions, and avoid mistakes. A good illustration of the benefit of attempting to understand what is happening inside the black box is provided by the case of Google Flu Trends (Ginsberg et al., 2009). Scientists at Google trained a model to predict the population-level occurrence of influenza-like illness from 50 million common Google search queries. While the model was accurate at predicting weekly influenza activity in the archive data, it soon became apparent that it was a poor predictor of future flu levels. It turned out that the Google Flu Trends model overfitted[7] the training data: Matching a huge number of search terms with a relatively small set of historical influenza data produced spurious correlations that were of no out-of-sample predictive value. A more thorough, theory-driven examination of the search queries employed in the prediction model could have helped to build a higher-quality model.

Many of the strategies that psychologists employ to study the function of the human brain, such as presenting different stimuli or examining its function across varying contexts, can also be used to interpret the functioning of big-data black box models. Several approaches to achieving this goal are described next.

Examine the Strongest Predictors

Just as in the traditional small-data context, the functioning of a model can be approximated by examining the predictors that are most strongly related to the predicted outcome. For example, examination of the Google search queries that were most predictive of influenza revealed that many were related to "high school basketball," which tends to coincide with the flu season in the United States (Ginsberg et al., 2009). While the researchers weeded out these and other queries, this indicated that their model was functioning partly as a predictor of the flu but also partly as predictor of the winter season (Lazer, Kennedy, King, & Vespignani, 2014). This illustrates the importance of attempting to peer inside the black box to better understand its inner workings; one should not simply be satisfied with high predictive accuracy.

Exclude Predictors

While an individual predictor's role in a complex model can be difficult to interpret, its relative importance can be deduced from the change in the model's accuracy when a given predictor is excluded. It has been shown, for example, that deep neural networks can correctly distinguish between the facial images of gay and heterosexual males with over 90% accuracy (Wang & Kosinski, 2017). High predictive accuracy, however, does not grant that sexual orientation is linked with facial features. Many other aspects of facial images may have enabled the prediction, such as the background of the images. To examine which parts of a facial image were linked with sexual orientation, portions of the images were iteratively masked and reentered into the sexual orientation classifier. Results showed that masking the image background did not significantly impact the model's predictive accuracy, while masking parts of the face (e.g., the eyebrows) did, revealing that the face contained the critical information employed by the model.

Examining the Most Extreme Observations

Another approach is to examine observations that trigger the most extreme predictions. This is particularly useful when individual variables are either difficult to interpret or nonlinearly related to the outcomes of interest. For example, consider digital images, in which each pixel constitutes a separate variable.[8] Algorithms employed in computer vision, such as deep neural networks, often cluster individual pixels together, independent of their absolute location in the image. For instance, a deep neural network might discover that faces tend to contain two round shapes (eyes) and regard the relevant pixels to be a single object, regardless of their location within the image. This is one of the great advantages of complex algorithms. It is also the case, however, that the meaning of the particular pixel (or, in more general terms, variable) depends on the overall composition of all the other pixels (or all the other variables). Investigating the relationship of a given pixel (e.g., the most top left one) with the predicted outcome would not be very informative. Instead, one can explore the observations (e.g., images of participants) that triggered the most extreme predictions. In other words, what happens in the algorithm is not always clear but can be approximated by exploring its output.

This approach was used to explore the function of the black box model that was able to distinguish the facial images of gay and heterosexual men (Wang & Kosinski, 2017). Instead of trying to link the contents of the particular pixels with the outcome of interest (sexual orientation), the facial images that had the highest and lowest probability of representing gay men were compared. This qualitative analysis revealed that the faces assessed to have the highest probability of belonging to gay men tended to have more feminine features, such as narrower jaws, longer noses, and less facial hair. This may be due to both biological (e.g., prenatal androgen exposure) and social processes (e.g., self-presentational norms; Wang & Kosinski, 2017).

Compare the Results with Interpretable Variables

The interpretation of the black box model can also be supported by examining the relationship between predictions and interpretable variables that can be extracted from or added to the data. For example, face-based predictions of a given outcome of interest (e.g., attractiveness, sexual orientation, dominance) could be correlated with interpretable variables (e.g., facial width-to-height ratio, a head's orientation). A similar technique involves estimating a model's prediction for a set of fabricated or altered observations, where a given interpretable variable has been altered while all other variables have been kept constant. One could, for instance, edit a given facial image to change the width of the face and examine the change in the model's prediction. Tweaking a given variable, while leaving the other variables constant, can isolate the effect of such a variable on the outcome of interest. This is similar in approach to the traditional method of experimental manipulation.

Consider Interpretable Models

Finally, some big-data models can be directly interpreted. Decision trees, for instance, produce a set of conditional, interpretable rules (e.g., "If the age is above 60 and a person has been smoking for more than 10 years, the individual's life expectancy is . . ."). In fact, the interpretation of such models is often more intuitive than those traditionally used in psychological research, such as logistic or linear regressions (Apte & Weiss, 1997). Additionally, oftentimes it makes sense to sacrifice some of the predictive power of the model to gain greater interpretability.

Beyond Explanation

As both the human brain and traditional study designs are not well suited to capturing relationships between more than a handful of variables, a typical psychological study (and accompanying theory) often focuses on a few predictors and a single outcome. This is despite the fact that many psychological phenomena are extremely complex. Big data and modern algorithms (e.g., neural networks) can help capture the complexity of human behavior, social interactions, or the neural mechanisms of the human brain. We may have to accept, however, that the algorithms can model (or, one could even say, *comprehend*) phenomena that may be too complex for us to understand. Like the brains of other animals, the human brain's cognitive capacity is limited. Although we may have not reached the limits of our brains yet, and we can surely expand them with modern technology and education, our brain's capacity is nonetheless finite, and its growth is bound by the speed of biological and cultural evolution. Computers, on the other hand, are quickly overtaking us in an expanding range of cognitive abilities. They can store and analyze more data, solve more complex equations, and detect patterns beyond the scope of our comprehension. They are increasingly better than us at making decisions and predicting future outcomes in a range of contexts, from forecasting the weather or predicting consumer choices to choosing the next best move in a game of Go or chess. Computers, in other words, seem to be far from the limits of their cognitive abilities.

However, the fact that we cannot comprehend the full complexity of a given model does not mean that we cannot employ it to our benefit. In fact, we have been doing exactly that for the longest time: We have little understanding of how the neural networks of our brain work, yet we are quite successful at applying these networks to make decisions and predict the future.

The Usefulness of the Black Box Models

There are many ways in which black box models can benefit scientists and societies, even if we cannot fully comprehend them. First, predictive models can be employed to quantify and simplify complex constructs. Take, for example, measuring the opinions expressed in a fragment of text or spoken language. Such opinions were traditionally measured using human judges—a slow, inaccurate, and expensive approach.

However, computational sentiment analysis is not only much faster and more applicable to large samples, but it is also often more accurate than human judges (Glorot, Bordes, & Bengio, 2011).

Second, predictive accuracy alone can reveal important facts about a given phenomenon. For instance, in the early days of online social networks, a widely held belief was that people's online behavior and self-presentation were largely independent from their real-life selves (Manago, Graham, Greenfield, & Salimkhan, 2008). However, the high accuracy of the models employing the digital footprints of online behavior to predict participants' true personality and real-world outcomes revealed that online and real-life selves are strongly connected (Lambiotte & Kosinski, 2015).

Finally, and perhaps most important, black box models can be used to solve a wide range of applied problems. As discussed earlier in this chapter, big-data models can serve as an inexpensive and accurate alternative to psychological assessment. This could be of great benefit to those who are currently disempowered. These models can help match people with the right college major and career (Chamorro-Premuzic, Akhtar, Winsborough, & Sherman, 2017). They can also be used to diagnose a wide range of psychological disorders and trigger an immediate and automated intervention (e.g., Naughton et al., 2016). Furthermore, they can turn tools and toys into companions that are able to address a wide range of psychological needs—as illustrated, for example, by the use of assistive social robots in elderly care (Bemelmans, Gelderblom, Jonker, & de Witte, 2012). Finally, as discussed previously, they can be used in the justice system to effectively reduce crime rates, prison populations, and racial bias (Kleinberg et al., 2018).

Importantly, when considering the use of black box models to solve applied problems, we should not demand perfect accuracy and complete freedom from bias. None of these are achievable. Instead, we should judge these models against the available alternatives, such as human judges, traditional psychometric tests, and clinical psychologists. It has been known since at least the middle of the 20th century that even relatively simple algorithms can outperform humans at predicting the future and making decisions (Sletto & Meehl, 1955). Algorithms have become even more accurate and versatile since then. Scaremongering (e.g., O'Neil, 2016), which delays the development and implementation of these algorithms to aid our decision-making processes, is extremely costly to both individuals and society. This cost can be measured by the suffering of people affected by the crimes that could have been avoided, the social and individual costs of imprisoning people that could be safely released, the misery of those suffering from a disease that has not been correctly diagnosed, and the unhappiness of those mismatched with their careers. These costs are disproportionately paid by underprivileged groups and individuals. The benefits of a big-data algorithm that diagnoses depression may not be clear to an individual who has easy access to affordable and high-quality mental healthcare. However, such an algorithm could be a lifesaver for those who are deprived of such access.

Fixing the Replication Crisis with a Prediction Focus

The elevation of prediction to a stature equal to that of explanation could help address the replication crisis that pervades the field of psychological research. Psychology's preoccupation with explanation and relative neglect of prediction have far-reaching implications for the way in which psychological research is conducted. Journal editors, reviewers, hiring committees, and funding bodies reward scholars for their theoretical contributions. Jobs, money, and even space in the pages of journals flow toward scholars who can propose theories that best *explain* behavior. All this has fueled great progress in our understanding of human behavior. However, this is also the source of some of the field's greatest problems. Data that do not match the expected theory are sometimes discarded (i.e., the file drawer problem; Rosenthal, 1979), reanalyzed until they do match the theory (i.e., p-hacking; Simmons, Nelson, & Simonsohn, 2011), or the theory is adjusted to match the data (i.e., hypothesizing after the results are known, or HARKing; Kerr, 1998). These phenomena inevitably lead to *overfitting* (i.e., building models that explain a given data set very well but fail to predict future observations). This can result in a proliferation of psychological theories that fail to predict future behavior with any meaningful accuracy. This is also likely the reason why the results of many studies cannot be reproduced in subsequent studies (i.e., the replication crisis; Open Science Collaboration, 2015).

Explicitly elevating prediction to the same standing as explanation could help to address these issues. Big-data approaches could offer many helpful lessons in this regard. For instance, the quality of traditional psychological models was typically measured by their fit to data, as illustrated by the Akaike information criterion or the R^2 coefficient. This inherently promotes models that best *explain* a given data set. In contrast, the quality of big data models is typically measured by how well they *predict* previously unseen data, as embodied by cross-validated prediction and classification measures, such as root-mean-square error or area under the receiver operating characteristic curve. As a result, the big-data approach produces models that best predict future behavior, rather than those that best fit the current data.

Conclusion

The field of psychology is changing as it gradually embraces big-data studies that are based on thousands to millions of individuals. It is increasingly clear that big data can open new research vistas and can be successfully employed to address long-standing questions that have eluded scholars employing traditional methods (Snijders, Matzat, & Reips, 2012). Big data has been successfully employed to study a wide range of psychological phenomena, including social networks (Ugander, Karrer, Backstrom, & Marlow, 2011), personality (Bleidorn, Hopwood, & Wright, 2017), language (Boyd & Pennebaker, 2017), music (D. M. Greenberg & Rentfrow, 2017), human potential at work (Chamorro-Premuzic et al., 2017), consumer psychology (Matz & Netzer, 2017), well-being (Luhmann, 2017), treatment for psychiatric disorders (Gillan & Whelan, 2017), emotions (Kramer, Guillory, & Hancock, 2014), and cultural fit (Danescu-Niculescu-Mizil, West, Jurafsky, Leskovec, & Potts, 2013).

The same technological advances that led to the emergence of big data are also transforming the human environment. Rapid technological and social changes introduce new opportunities and challenges for both individuals and societies. Our communication and social interactions are being reshaped by instant connectivity and online social networking platforms. Recommender systems expose us to novel content and information that was carefully chosen to keep us engaged for as long as possible. The wide adoption of online dating platforms is changing the way in which people choose their partners and maintain romantic relationships. Rapid progress in AI suggests that we may soon be interacting with machines that are, at least in some areas, cognitively superior to us. These unprecedented changes in the human condition open new research areas for social scientists to explore.

To date, the research skills necessary to study psychological phenomena in the digital environment, such as programming or data management, are relatively rare among social scientists (Lazer et al., 2009). Consequently, such research is increasingly ceded to computer scientists and engineers, who often lack the theoretical background in social sciences and training in the ethical standards that pertain to human-subjects research (Buchanan, Aycock, Dexter, Dittrich, & Hvizdak, 2011; Hall & Flynn, 2001). We hope that new generations of social scientists will seize the opportunity offered by big data and maintain the relevance of psychological science in the information age.

Notes

1. CCTV stands for closed-circuit television, also known as video surveillance.
2. Many of the techniques described in this subsection were employed in Schwartz et al. (2013).
3. In contrast, supervised learning techniques, employ external variables when interpreting the data. A good example of supervised learning is regression analysis, which aims to detect patterns within data that best predict a given external variable.
4. Latent Dirichlet Allocation is an example of a cluster analysis approach that is well-suited to language data. It can be used to automatically extract topics typically discussed in a sample of text documents and estimate the probability that a given document discusses a particular topic.
5. The feed from many of such public cameras can be accessed by anyone (see https://www.cam2project.net/).
6. Artificial neural networks are computational models inspired by animal brains. They are composed of layers of artificial neurons (analogous to biological neurons) that process information and connections (analogous to synapses).
7. Overfitting occurs when the model (e.g., regression model) describes a given sample very well.
8. Or, in fact, three variables; in most color images, each pixel is defined by the intensity of three colors: red, green, and blue.

References

37 mind-blowing YouTube facts, figures, and statistics—2018. (2018, August 4). *MerchDrop*. Retrieved from https://merchdope.com/youtube-stats/

Abdullah, S., Matthews, M., Frank, E., Doherty, G., Gay, G., & Choudhury, T. (2016). Automatic detection of social rhythms in bipolar disorder. *Journal of the American Medical Informatics Association, 23*, 538–543.

Acquisti, A., & Gross, R. (2009). Predicting Social Security numbers from public data. *Proceedings of the National Academy of Sciences, 106*, 10975–10980.

AlHanai, T. W., & Ghassemi, M. M. (2017). Predicting latent narrative mood using audio and physiologic data. *AAAI Conference on Artificial Intelligence*. Retrieved from https://groups.csail.mit.edu/sls/publications/2017/TukaAlHanai_aaai-17.pdf

Apte, C., & Weiss, S. (1997). Data mining with decision trees and decision rules. *Data Mining, 13*, 197–210.

Banko, M., & Brill, E. (2001). Scaling to very very large corpora for natural language disambiguation. In Association for Computational Linguistics (Ed.), *Association for Computational Linguistics 39th annual meeting and 10th conference of the European Chapter* (Vol. 1, pp. 26–33). New Brunswick, NJ: Association for Computational Linguistics.

Barata, F., Kowatsch, T., Tinschert, P., & Filler, A. (2016). Personal MobileCoach: Tailoring behavioral interventions to the needs of individual participants. In P. Lukowicz (Ed.), *Proceedings of the International Joint Conference on Pervasive and Ubiquitous Computing* (pp. 1089–1094). New York, NY: ACM.

Barchard, K. A., & Williams, J. (2008). Practical advice for conducting ethical online experiments and questionnaires for United States psychologists. *Behavior Research Methods, 40*, 1111–1128.

Bartlett, M. S., Littlewort, G. C., Frank, M. G., & Lee, K. (2014). Automatic decoding of facial movements reveals deceptive pain expressions. *Current Biology, 24*, 738–743.

Bemelmans, R., Gelderblom, G. J., Jonker, P., & de Witte, L. (2012). Socially assistive robots in elderly care: A systematic review into effects and effectiveness. *Journal of the American Medical Directors Association, 13*, 114–120.

Ben-Zeev, D., Brenner, C. J., Begale, M., Duffecy, J., Mohr, D. C., & Mueser, K. T. (2014). Feasibility, acceptability, and preliminary efficacy of a smartphone intervention for schizophrenia. *Schizophrenia Bulletin, 40*, 1244–1253.

Bi, B., Shokouhi, M., Kosinski, M., & Graepel, T. (2013). Inferring the demographics of search users. In D. Schwabe (Ed.), *Proceedings of the 22nd International Conference on World Wide Web* (pp. 131–140). Geneva, Switzerland: International World Wide Web Conferences Steering Committee.

Blei, D. M., Ng, A. Y., & Jordan, M. I. (2003). Latent Dirichlet Allocation. *Journal of Machine Learning Research, 3,* 993–1022.

Bleidorn, W., Hopwood, C. J., & Wright, A. G. (2017). Using big data to advance personality theory. *Current Opinion in Behavioral Sciences, 18,* 79–82.

Bond, R. M., Fariss, C. J., Jones, J. J., Kramer, A. D. I., Marlow, C., Settle, J. E., & Fowler, J. H. (2012). A 61-million-person experiment in social influence and political mobilization. *Nature, 489,* 295–298.

Boyd, R. L., & Pennebaker, J. W. (2015). Did Shakespeare write double falsehood? Identifying individuals by creating psychological signatures with text analysis. *Psychological Science, 26,* 570–582.

Boyd, R. L., & Pennebaker, J. W. (2017). Language-based personality: A new approach to personality in a digital world. *Current Opinion in Behavioral Sciences, 18,* 63–68.

Boyd, R. L., Wilson, S. R., Pennebaker, J. W., Kosinski, M., Stillwell, D. J., & Mihalcea, R. (2015). Values in words: Using language to evaluate and understand personal values. In Association for the Advancement of Artificial Intelligence (Ed.), *Proceedings of the Ninth International AAAI Conference on Web and Social Media.* Palo Alto, CA: AAAI.

Bruckman, A. (2002). Studying the amateur artist: A perspective on disguising data collected in human subjects research on the Internet. *Ethics and Information Technology, 4,* 217–231.

Buchanan, E. A., Aycock, J., Dexter, S., Dittrich, D., & Hvizdak, E. (2011). Computer science security research and human subjects: Emerging considerations for research ethics boards. *Journal of Empirical Research on Human Research Ethics, 6,* 71–83.

Cadwalladr, C. (2016, December 4). Google, democracy and the truth about internet search. *The Guardian.* Retrieved from https://www.theguardian.com

Caliskan, A., Bryson, J. J., & Narayanan, A. (2017). Semantics derived automatically from language corpora contain human-like biases. *Science, 356,* 183–186.

Campbell, A. T., Eisenman, S. B., Lane, N. D., Miluzzo, E., Peterson, R. A., Lu, H., . . . Ahn, G. S. (2008). The rise of people-centric sensing. *IEEE Internet Computing, 12*(4), 12–21.

Carey, A. L., Brucks, M. S., Küfner, A. C. P., Holtzman, N. S., Deters, F. G., Back, M. D., . . . Mehl, M. R. (2015). Narcissism and the use of personal pronouns revisited. *Journal of Personality and Social Psychology,* 109(3), e1–e15.

Chamorro-Premuzic, T., Akhtar, R., Winsborough, D., & Sherman, R. A. (2017). The datafication of talent: How technology is advancing the science of human potential at work. *Current Opinion in Behavioral Sciences, 18,* 13–16.

Chen, E. E., & Wojcik, S. P. (2016). A practical guide to big data research in psychology. *Psychological Methods, 21,* 458–474.

Chon, J., & Cha, H. (2011). LifeMap: A smartphone-based context provider for location-based services. *IEEE Pervasive Computing, 10*(2), 58–67.

Chow, P. I., Fua, K., Huang, Y., Bonelli, W., Xiong, H., Barnes, L. E., & Teachman, B. A. (2017). Using mobile sensing to test clinical models of depression, social anxiety, state affect, and social isolation among college students. *Journal of Medical Internet Research, 19*(3), e62.

Cowie, R., Douglas-Cowie, E., Savvidou, S., Mcmahon, E., Sawey, M., & Schröder, M. (2000). "FEELTRACE": An instrument for recording perceived emotion in real time. In R. Cowie (Ed.), *Proceedings of the ISCA Workshop on Speech and Emotion* (pp. 19–24). Belfast, Northern Ireland: Textflow.

D'Andrea, W., Chiu, P. H., Casas, B. R., & Deldin, P. (2012). Linguistic predictors of post-traumatic stress disorder symptoms following 11 September 2001. *Applied Cognitive Psychology, 26,* 316–323.

Danescu-Niculescu-Mizil, C., West, R., Jurafsky, D., Leskovec, J., & Potts, C. (2013). No country for old members: User lifecycle and linguistic change in online communities. In In D. Schwabe (Ed.), *Proceedings of the 22nd International Conference on World Wide Web* (pp. 307–318). Geneva, Switzerland: International World Wide Web Conferences Steering Committee.

de Montjoye, Y.-A., Quoidbach, J., Robic, F., & Pentland, A. S. (2013). Predicting personality using novel mobile phone-based metrics. In A. M. Greenberg, W. G. Kennedy, & N. D. Bos (Eds.), *Social computing, behavioral-cultural modeling and prediction* (pp. 48–55). Washington, DC: Springer.

de Montjoye, Y.-A., Radaelli, L., Singh, V. K., & Pentland, A. S. (2015). Unique in the shopping mall: On the reidentifiability of credit card metadata. *Science, 347,* 536–539.

Domingos, P. (2012). A few useful things to know about machine learning. *Communications of the ACM, 55*(10), 78.

Eagle, N., & Pentland, A. S. (2009). Eigenbehaviors: Identifying structure in routine. *Behavioral Ecology and Sociobiology, 63,* 1057–1066.

Eichstaedt, J. C., Schwartz, H. A., Kern, M. L., Park, G. J., Labarthe, D. R., Merchant, R. M., . . . Seligman, M. E. P. (2015). Psychological language on twitter predicts county-level heart disease mortality. *Psychological Science, 26,* 159–169.

Frankel, M. S., & Siang, S. (1999). *Ethical and legal aspects of human subjects research on the Internet.* Washington, DC: American Association for the Advancement of Science.

Freud, S. (2011). *On aphasia: A critical study* (E. Stengel, Trans.). Whitefish, MT: Literary Licensing. (Original work published 1891)

Gillan, C. M., & Whelan, R. (2017). What big data can do for treatment in psychiatry. *Current Opinion in Behavioral Sciences, 18,* 34–42.

Ginsberg, J., Mohebbi, M. H., Patel, R. S., Brammer, L., Smolinski, M. S., & Brilliant, L. (2009). Detecting influenza epidemics using search engine query data. *Nature, 457,* 1012–1014.

Glorot, X., Bordes, A., & Bengio, Y. (2011). Domain adaptation for large-scale sentiment classification: A deep learning approach. *Proceedings of the 28th International Conference on Machine Learning, 2011,* 513–520.

Golder, S. A., & Macy, M. W. (2011). Diurnal and seasonal mood vary with work, sleep, and daylength across diverse cultures. *Science, 333,* 1878–1881.

Gosling, S. D., Sandy, C. J., John, O. P., & Potter, J. (2010). Wired but not WEIRD: The promise of the Internet in reaching more diverse samples. *Behavioral and Brain Sciences, 33,* 94–95.

Greenberg, D. M., & Rentfrow, P. J. (2017). Music and big data: A new frontier. *Current Opinion in Behavioral Sciences, 18,* 50–56.

Greenwald, A. G., McGhee, D. E., & Schwartz, J. L. K. (1998). Measuring individual differences in implicit cognition: The implicit association test. *Journal of Personality and Social Psychology, 74,* 1464–1480.

Hall, T., & Flynn, V. (2001). Ethical issues in software engineering research: A survey of current practice. *Empirical Software Engineering, 6,* 305–317.

Hao, T., Xing, G., & Zhou, G. (2013). iSleep. In C. Petrioli (Ed.), *Proceedings of the 11th ACM Conference on Embedded Networked Sensor Systems* (pp. 1–14). New York, NY: ACM.

Harari, G. M., Müller, S. R., Aung, M. S. H., & Rentfrow, P. J. (2017). Smartphone sensing methods for studying behavior in everyday life. *Current Opinion in Behavioral Sciences, 18,* 83–90.

Hemminki, S., Nurmi, P., & Tarkoma, S. (2013). Accelerometer-based transportation mode detection on smartphones. C. Petrioli (Ed.), *Proceedings of the 11th ACM Conference on Embedded Networked Sensor Systems* (pp. 1–14). New York, NY: ACM.

Henrich, J., Heine, S. J., & Norenzayan, A. (2010). Most people are not WEIRD. *Nature, 466,* 29.

Hernandez, J., Hoque, M. E., & Picard, R. W. (2012). Mood meter: Counting smiles in the wild. In A. K. Dey, H.-H. Chu, & G. R Hayes (Eds.), *Proceedings of the ACM Conference on Ubiquitous Computing* (pp. 301–310). New York, NY: ACM.

Herring, S. (1996). Linguistic and critical analysis of computer-mediated communication: Some ethical and scholarly considerations. *Information Society, 12,* 153–168.

Hill, K. (2012, February 16). How Target figured out a teen girl was pregnant before her father did. *Forbes.* Retrieved from https://www.forbes.com

Jacobson, R. (2013, April 24). 2.5 quintillion bytes of data created every day. How does CPG & retail manage it? *IBM Consumer Products Industry Blog*. Retrieved from https://www.ibm.com/blogs/insights-on-business/consumer-products/2-5-quintillion-bytes-of-data-created-every-day-how-does-cpg-retail-manage-it/

Jebara, B. (2014). Bio-mechanical characterization of voice for smoking detection. In European Association for Signal Processing (Ed.), *Proceedings of the 22nd European Signal Processing Conference* (pp. 2475–2479). Piscataway, NJ: IEEE.

Jones, N. M., Wojcik, S. P., Sweeting, J., & Silver, R. C. (2016). Tweeting negative emotion: An investigation of twitter data in the aftermath of violence on college campuses. *Psychological Methods, 21*, 526–541.

Kangas, O., Simanainen, M., & Honkanen, P. (2017). Basic income in the Finnish Context. *Intereconomics, 52*, 87–91.

Kern, M. L., Park, G. J., Eichstaedt, J. C., Schwartz, A. H., Sap, M., Smith, L. K., & Ungar, L. H. (2016). Gaining insights from social media language: Methodologies and challenges. *Psychological Methods, 21*, 507–525.

Kerr, N. L. (1998). HARKing: Hypothesizing after the results are known. *Personality and Social Psychology Review, 2*, 196–217.

Kleinberg, J., Lakkaraju, H., Leskovec, J., Ludwig, J., & Mullainathan, S. (2018). Human decisions and machine predictions. *Quarterly Journal of Economics, 133*, 237–293.

Kobayashi, T., Boase, J., Suzuki, T., & Suzuki, T. (2015). Emerging from the cocoon? Revisiting the tele-cocooning hypothesis in the smartphone era. *Journal of Computer-Mediated Communication, 20*, 330–345.

Korpela, J., Miyaji, R., Maekawa, T., Nozaki, K., & Tamagawa, H. (2015). Evaluating tooth brushing performance with smartphone sound data. In K. Mase (Ed.), *Proceedings of the International Joint Conference on Pervasive and Ubiquitous Computing* (pp. 109–120). New York, NY: ACM.

Kosinski, M. (2017). Facial width-to-height ratio does not predict self-reported behavioral tendencies. *Psychological Science, 28*, 1675–1682.

Kosinski, M., Bachrach, Y., Kohli, P., Stillwell, D. J., & Graepel, T. (2014). Manifestations of user personality in website choice and behaviour on online social networks. *Machine Learning, 95*, 357–380.

Kosinski, M., Matz, S. C., Gosling, S. D., Popov, V., & Stillwell, D. J. (2015). Facebook as a research tool for the social sciences: Opportunities, challenges, ethical considerations, and practical guidelines. *American Psychologist, 70*, 543–556.

Kosinski, M., Stillwell, D. J., & Graepel, T. (2013). Private traits and attributes are predictable from digital records of human behavior. *Proceedings of the National Academy of Sciences, 110*, 5802–5805.

Kosinski, M., Wang, Y., Lakkaraju, H., & Leskovec, J. (2016). Mining big data to extract patterns and predict real-life outcomes. *Psychological Methods, 21*, 493–506.

Kramer, A. D. I., Guillory, J. E., & Hancock, J. T. (2014). Experimental evidence of massive-scale emotional contagion through social networks. *Proceedings of the National Academy of Sciences, 111*, 8788–8790.

Kusner, M. J., Loftus, J., Russell, C., & Silva, R. (2017). Counterfactual fairness. In D. D. Lee, U. von Luxburg, R. Garnett, M. Sugiyama, & I. Guyon; Neural Information Processing Systems (Eds.), *Advances in neural information processing systems* (pp. 4069–4079). Red Hook, NY: Curran.

Lambiotte, R., & Kosinski, M. (2015). Tracking the Digital Footprints of Personality. *Proceedings of the Institute of Electrical and Electronics Engineers, 102*, 1934–1939.

Landers, R. N., Brusso, R. C., Cavanaugh, K. J., & Collmus, A. B. (2016). A primer on theory-driven web scraping: Automatic extraction of big data from the Internet for use in psychological research. *Psychological Methods, 21*, 475–492.

Lane, N. D., Miluzzo, E., Lu, H., Peebles, D., Choudhury, T., & Campbell, A. T. (2010). A survey of mobile phone sensing. *IEEE Communications Magazine, 48*(9), 140–150.

Laney, D. (2001). 3D data management: Controlling data volume, velocity and variety [blog]. *META Group Research Note, 6*. Retrieved from https://blogs.gartner.com/doug-laney/files/2012/01/ad949-3D-Data-Management-Controlling-Data-Volume-Velocity-and-Variety.pdf

Lathia, N., Sandstrom, G. M., Mascolo, C., & Rentfrow, P. J. (2017). Happier people live more active lives: Using smartphones to link happiness and physical activity. *PLoS One, 12,* e0160589.

Lazer, D., Kennedy, R., King, G., & Vespignani, A. (2014). The parable of Google Flu: Traps in big data analysis. *Science, 343,* 1203–1205.

Lazer, D., Pentland, A. S., Adamic, L. A., Aral, S., Barabási, A.-L., Brewer, D., . . . Van Alstyne, M. (2009). Computational social science. *Science, 323,* 721–723.

Lecun, Y., Bengio, Y., & Hinton, G. (2015). Deep learning. *Nature, 521,* 436–444.

Likamwa, R., Liu, Y., Lane, N. D., & Zhong, L. (2013). MoodScope: Building a mood sensor from smartphone usage patterns. In H. H. Chu (Ed.), *Proceeding of the 11th Annual International Conference on Mobile Systems, Applications, and Services* (pp. 389–402). New York, NY: ACM.

Lister, M. (2018, October 17). 33 mind-boggling Instagram stats & facts for 2018 [blogpost]. Retrieved from https://www.wordstream.com/blog/ws/2017/04/20/instagram-statistics

Lu, H., Pan, W., Lane, N. D., Choudhury, T., & Campbell, A. T. (2009). SoundSense: Scalable sound sensing for people-centric applications on mobile phones. In Association for Computing Machinery (Ed.), *Proceedings of the 7th International Conference on Mobile Systems, Applications, and Services* (pp. 165–178). New York, NY: ACM.

Luhmann, M. (2017). Using Big Data to study subjective well-being. *Current Opinion in Behavioral Sciences, 18,* 28–33.

Manago, A. M., Graham, M. B., Greenfield, P. M., & Salimkhan, G. (2008). Self-presentation and gender on MySpace. *Journal of Applied Developmental Psychology, 29,* 446–458.

Marcus, B., Machilek, F., & Schütz, A. (2006). Personality in cyberspace: personal web sites as media for personality expressions and impressions. *Journal of Personality and Social Psychology, 90,* 1014–1031.

Matz, S. C., Gladstone, J. J., & Stillwell, D. J. (2016). Money buys happiness when spending fits our personality. *Psychological Science, 27,* 715–725.

Matz, S. C., & Netzer, O. (2017). Using big data as a window into consumers' psychology. *Current Opinion in Behavioral Sciences, 18,* 7–12.

Mestyán, M., Yasseri, T., & Kertész, J. (2013). Early prediction of movie box office success based on Wikipedia activity big data. *PLoS One, 8,* e71226.

Miller, G. (2012). The smartphone psychology manifesto. *Perspectives on Psychological Science, 7,* 221–237.

Molokken-Ostvold, K. (2005). Ethical concerns when increasing realism in controlled experiments with industrial participants. In Institute of Electrical and Electronics Engineers (Ed.), *Proceedings of the 38th Annual Hawaii International Conference on System Sciences* (p. 264a). Los Alamitos, CA: IEEE Computer Society.

Morgeson, F. P., Campion, M. A., Dipboye, R. L., Hollenbeck, J. R., Murphy, K., & Schmitt, N. (2007). Reconsidering the use of personality tests in personnel selection contexts. *Personnel Psychology, 60,* 683–729.

Murnane, E. L., Abdullah, S., Matthews, M., Kay, M., Kientz, J. A., Choudhury, T., . . . Cosley, D. (2016). Mobile manifestations of alertness: Connecting biological rhythms with patterns of smartphone app use. In F. Paternò, K. Väänänen, & K. Church (Eds.), *Proceedings of the 18th International Conference on Human-Computer Interaction with Mobile Devices and Services* (pp. 465–477). New York, NY: ACM.

Naughton, F., Hopewell, S., Lathia, N., Schalbroeck, R., Brown, C., Mascolo, C., . . . Sutton, S. (2016). A context-sensing mobile phone app (Q Sense) for smoking cessation: A mixed-methods study. *JMIR MHealth and UHealth, 4*(3), e106.

Nave, G., Minxha, J., Greenberg, D. M., Kosinski, M., Stillwell, D. J., & Rentfrow, P. J. (2018). Musical preferences predict personality: Evidence from active listening and Facebook likes. *Psychological Science, 29,* 1145–1158.

Number of mobile phone users worldwide from 2015 to 2020 (in billions). (2016, Novem er). *Statistica.* Retrieved from https://www.statista.com/statistics/274774/forecast-of-mobile-phone-users-worldwide/

O'Neil, C. (2016). Weapons of Math Destruction. *Discover, 37*(8), 50–55.

Open Science Collaboration. (2015). Estimating the reproducibility of psychological science. *Science, 349,* aac4716.

Park, G. J., Schwartz, A. H., Eichstaedt, J. C., Kern, M. L., Kosinski, M., Stillwell, D. J., . . . Seligman, M. E. P. (2014). Automatic personality assessment through social media language. *Journal of Personality and Social Psychology, 108,* 934–952.

Paulhus, D. L., & Vazire, S. (2007). The self-report method. In R. W. Robins, R. C. Fraley, & R. Krueger (Eds.), *Handbook of research methods in personality psychology* (pp. 224–239). New York, NY: Guilford.

Pennebaker, J. W., Chung, C. K., Frazee, J., Lavergne, G. M., & Beaver, D. I. (2014). When small words foretell academic success: The case of college admissions essays. *PLoS One, 9,* e115844.

Pennebaker, J. W., Francis, M. E., & Booth, R. J. (2001). *Linguistic Inquiry and Word Count: LIWC 2001.* Majwah, NY: Erlbaum.

Pennebaker, J. W., & King, L. A. (1999). Linguistic styles: Language use as an individual difference. *Journal of Personality and Social Psychology, 77,* 1296–1312.

Pennebaker, J. W., Mayne, T. J., & Francis, M. E. (1997). Linguistic predictors of adaptive bereavement. *Journal of Personality and Social Psychology, 72,* 863–871.

Penzel, I. B., Persich, M. R., Boyd, R. L., & Robinson, M. D. (2017). Linguistic evidence for the failure mindset as a predictor of life span longevity. *Annals of Behavioral Medicine, 51,* 348–355.

Perez, S. (2017, October 30). Skype's big redesign publicly launches to desktop users. *Tech Crunch.* Retrieved from https://techcrunch.com/2017/10/30/skypes-big-redesign-publicly-launches-to-all-desktop-users/

Phan, T. Q., & Airoldi, E. M. (2015). A natural experiment of social network formation and dynamics. *Proceedings of the National Academy of Sciences, 112,* 6595–6600.

Pressman, S. D., & Cohen, S. (2007). Use of social words in autobiographies and longevity. *Psychosomatic Medicine, 69,* 262–269.

Quercia, D., Kosinski, M., Stillwell, D. J., & Crowcroft, J. (2011). Our Twitter profiles, our selves: Predicting personality with Twitter. In Institute of Electrical and Electronics Engineers (Ed.), *Proceedings of the International Conference on Privacy, Security, Risk and Trust and IEEE International Conference on Social Computing* (pp.180–185). Los Angeles, CA: IEEE Computer Society.

Ratkiewicz, J., Conover, M. D., Meiss, M., Gonc, B., Flammini, A., & Menczer, F. (2011). Detecting and tracking political abuse in social media. In Association for the Advancement of Artificial Intelligence (Ed.), *Proceedings of the 5th International AAAI Conference on Weblogs and Social Media* (pp. 297–304). Palo Alto, CA: AAAI

Rhodes, R. E., & Smith, N. E. I. (2006). Personality correlates of physical activity: a review and meta-analysis. *British Journal of Sports Medicine, 40,* 958–965.

Robinson, R. L., Navea, R., & Ickes, W. (2012). Predicting final course performance from students' written self-introductions: A LIWC analysis. *Journal of Language and Social Psychology, 32,* 469–479.

Rosenthal, R. (1979). The file drawer problem and tolerance for null results. *Psychological Bulletin, 86,* 638–641.

Schultze, U., & Mason, R. O. (2012). Studying cyborgs: Re-examining Internet studies as human subjects research. *Journal of Internet Technology, 27,* 301–312.

Schwartz, A. H., Eichstaedt, J. C., Kern, M. L., Dziurzynski, L., Ramones, S. M., Agrawal, M., . . . Ungar, L. H. (2013). Personality, gender, and age in the language of social media: The open-vocabulary approach. *PLoS One, 8,* e73791.

Schwartz, A. H., Sap, M., Kern, M. L., Eichstaedt, J. C., Kapelner, A., Agrawal, M., . . . Ungar, L. H. (2016). Predicting individual well-being through the language of social media. In R. Altman (Ed.), *Pacific Symposium on Biocomputing 2016.* Singapore: World Scientific.

Simmons, J. P., Nelson, L. D., & Simonsohn, U. (2011). False-positive psychology: Undisclosed flexibility in data collection and analysis allows presenting anything as significant. *Psychological Science, 22,* 1359–1366.

Singer, J., & Vinson, N. (2001). Why and how research ethics matters to you. Yes, You! *Empirical Software Engineering, 6,* 287–290.

The Skype Team. (2016, January 12). Ten years of Skype video: Yesterday, today and something new... [blogpost]. Retrieved from https://blogs.skype.com/stories/2016/01/12/ten-years-of-skype-video-yesterday-today-and-something-new/

Sletto, R. F., & Meehl, P. E. (1955). Clinical versus Statistical Prediction. *American Sociological Review, 20,* 482–483.

Smith, K. (2018, March 5). 47 incredible Facebook statistics and facts. *Brand Watch*. Retrieved from https://www.brandwatch.com/blog/47-facebook-statistics/

Snijders, C., Matzat, U., & Reips, U. (2012). "Big data": Big gaps of knowledge in the field of Internet science. *International Journal of Internet Science, 7,* 1–5.

Solberg, L. (2010). Data mining on Facebook: A free space for researchers or an IRB nightmare? *University of Illinois Journal of Law, Technology & Policy, 2,* 311–343.

Stephens-Davidowitz, S. (2014). The cost of racial animus on a black candidate: Evidence using Google search data. *Journal of Public Economics, 118,* 26–40.

Sunnebo, D. (2017, January 25). Nearly 16% of US consumers now own wearables. *Kantar Worldpanel.* Retrieved from https://www.kantarworldpanel.com/global/News/Nearly-16-of-US-Consumers-and-9-in-EU4-Now-Own-Wearables

Sweeney, L. (1997). Weaving technology and policy together to maintain confidentiality. *Journal of Law, Medicine & Ethics, 25,* 98–110.

Tausczik, Y. R., & Pennebaker, J. W. (2010). The psychological meaning of words: LIWC and computerized text analysis methods. *Journal of Language and Social Psychology, 29,* 24–54.

Tay, L., Jebb, A. T., & Woo, S. E. (2017). Video capture of human behaviors: Toward a big data approach. *Current Opinion in Behavioral Sciences, 18,* 17–22.

Teixeira, T., Wedel, M., & Pieters, R. (2012). Emotion-induced engagement in internet video advertisements. *Journal of Marketing Research, 49,* 144–159.

The top 20 valuable Facebook statistics. (2018, October). *Zephoria Digital Marketing.* Retrieved from https://zephoria.com/top-15-valuable-facebook-statistics/

Ugander, J., Karrer, B., Backstrom, L., & Marlow, C. (2011). *The anatomy of the Facebook social graph.* Unpublished manuscript. https://arxiv.org/pdf/1111.4503.pdf

US Federal Reserve System. (2016). Federal reserve payment study 2016. Retrieved from https://www.federalreserve.gov/newsevents/press/other/2016-payments-study-20161222.pdf

Vazire, S., & Gosling, S. D. (2004). E-perceptions: Personality impressions based on personal websites. *Journal of Personality and Social Psychology, 87,* 123–132.

Wang, Q., Guo, B., Peng, G., Zhou, G., & Yu, Z. (2016). CrowdWatch: Pedestrian safety assistance with mobile crowd sensing. In P. Lukowicz (Ed.), *Proceedings of the International Joint Conference on Pervasive and Ubiquitous Computing* (pp. 217–220). New York, NY: ACM.

Wang, R., Aung, M. S. H., Abdullah, S., Brian, R., Campbell, A. T., Choudhury, T., . . . Ben-zeev, D. (2016). CrossCheck: Towards passive sensing and detection of mental health changes in people with schizophrenia. In P. Lukowicz (Ed.), *Proceedings of the International Joint Conference on Pervasive and Ubiquitous Computing* (pp. 1–12). New York, NY: ACM.

Wang, R., Chen, F., Chen, Z., Li, T., Harari, G. M., Tignor, S., . . . Campbell, A. T. (2014). StudentLife: assessing mental health, academic performance and behavioral trends of college students using smartphones. In ACM Special Interest Group on Spatial Information, ACM Special Interest Group on Mobility of Systems, Users, Data and Computing, & ACM Special Interest Group on Computer-Human Interaction (Eds.), *Proceedings of the International Joint Conference on Pervasive and Ubiquitous Computing* (pp. 3–14). New York, NY: ACM.

Wang, R., Harari, G. M., Hao, P., Zhou, X., & Campbell, A. T. (2015). SmartGPA: How smartphones can assess and predict academic performance of college students. In K. Mase (Ed.), *Proceedings of the International Joint Conference on Pervasive and Ubiquitous Computing* (pp. 295–306). New York, NY: ACM.

Wang, Y., & Kosinski, M. (2017). Deep neural networks are more accurate than humans at detecting sexual orientation from facial images. *Journal of Personality and Social Psychology, 144,* 246–257.

Waskul, D. (1996). Considering the electronic participant: Some polemical observations on the ethics of on-line research. *Information Society, 12,* 129–140.

Wilson, R. E., Gosling, S. D., & Graham, L. T. (2012). A review of facebook research in the social sciences. *Perspectives on Psychological Science, 7,* 203–220.

Wojcik, S. P., Hovasapian, A., Graham, J. W., Motyl, M., & Ditto, P. H. (2015). Conservatives report, but liberals display, greater happiness. *Science, 347,* 1243–1246.

Working time. (n.d.). *Wikiwand.* Retrieved from https://www.wikiwand.com/en/Working_time

Yang, C., & Srinivasan, P. (2016). Life satisfaction and the pursuit of happiness on Twitter. *PLoS One, 11,* e0150881.

Yarkoni, T. (2010). Personality in 100,000 words: A large-scale analysis of personality and word use among bloggers. *Journal of Research in Personality, 44,* 363–373.

Yarkoni, T., & Westfall, J. (2017). Choosing prediction over explanation in psychology: Lessons from machine learning. *Perspectives on Psychological Science, 12,* 1100–1122.

Youyou, W., Kosinski, M., & Stillwell, D. J. (2015). Computer-based personality judgements are more accurate than those made by humans. *Proceedings of the National Academy of Sciences, 112,* 1036–1040.

Youyou, W., Stillwell, D. J., Schwartz, A. H., & Kosinski, M. (2017). Birds of a feather do flock together: Behavior-Based personality-assessment method reveals personality similarity among couples and friends. *Psychological Science, 28,* 276–284.

AUTHOR INDEX

De Dreu, C.K.W., 168
de Groot, A.D., 39, 43
De Houwer, J., 24, 64, 134, 135
de la Fuente, M., 80
de Liver, Y.N., 130
de Montjoye, Y.-A., 506, 509
De Raad, B., 474
de Vries, N., 258
de Waal, F.B.M., 371–72
de Wall-Andrews, W.G., 99
de Witte, L., 514
DeAngelis, T., 283
Deaux, K., 21, 164–65, 206, 253
DeBono, K.G., 119, 132, 137–38
DeBruine, L.M., 367, 371–72
DeCarufel, A., 68
Decety, J., 27, 355
Deci, E.L., 19, 23, 92, 95, 133, 485–86
DeCoster, J., 122–23, 134–35, 480
DeHaven, A., 43
Deldin, P., 501–2
DeLongis, A., 239–40, 242
DeMarree, K.G., 118, 139
Demb, J.B., 352–53
DeMotta, Y., 121
Depue, R.A., 473–74, 476–77
Derryberry, D., 475–76
Descartes, R., 12
Deschamps, J.-C., 264, 266
DeScioli, P., 377
DeSteno, D., 129, 131, 137
DeSteno, D.A., 382
Deuser, W.E., 191
Deutsch, M., 16, 17, 21
Deutsch, R., 480
Devine, P.G., 21, 23, 72, 79–80, 277, 278
DeVinney, L., 257
Devos, T., 259
DeWall, C.N., 193–94, 211–12, 213, 214–15, 325, 371–73, 380
DeWall, N., 459–60
Dexter, S., 515
DeYoung, C.G., 473
Dhont, K., 280
Diamond, L.M., 206, 241, 380, 382
Dias, M., 70
Dias, M.G., 302
Dickersin, K., 54
Dickerson, B.C., 329
Dickerson, S.S., 434–35
Dickson, M.W., 405–6
Dickson, P.R., 132
Diehl, M., 128, 134, 251–52
Diekman, A.B., 330
Diener, C., 414
Diener, E., 21, 229–30, 403, 414, 473–74
Diener, M., 414
DiGiuseppe, R., 193
Digman, J.M., 473

Dijker, A.J.M., 259
Dijksterhus, A., 463
Dijkstra, P., 380
Dill, K.E., 191
Dillman, D.A., 168–69
Dillon, K.D., 309
DiMatteo, M.R., 446
Ditto, P.H., 505–6
Dittrich, D., 515
Dittrich, W.H., 350
Dlugolecki, D.W., 102
Dodge, K.A., 91, 185
Doherty, K., 102
Doise, W., 250, 266
Dolan, R.J., 163–64, 356–57
Dolinski, D., 163, 167
Dollard, J., 13, 92
Domingos, P., 504
Donnellan, M.B., 29, 98, 314, 407, 474, 475
Donovan, L.A., 122
Doob, L.W., 13, 92
Doosje, B., 252–53, 254, 258
Dorr, N., 266
Dovidio, J., 21, 122–23, 252, 261–62
Dovidio, J.F., 72, 80, 263, 264, 265, 276, 279, 282, 285–86, 288, 291–92, 443
Dowie, 506
Downing, E.L., 121, 308
Downs, D.L., 99, 211–12, 355
Downs, J.S., 251–52
Doyen, S., 65
Drachman, D., 68
Drake, K.D., 160
Drigotas, S.M., 243
Dronkers, N.F., 356–57
Drumm, P., 218
Dubanoski, J.P., 475
Duchaine, B., 349–50
Duckitt, J., 280–81
Duckworth, A., 105
Duffy, S., 410
Duley, L., 54
Dummel, S., 121
Dunbar, R.I.M., 168
Dunfield, K.A., 160
Dunkel Schetter, C., 441
Dunn, D.S., 121
Dunn, M., 406
Dunning, D., 97
Durante, K.M., 379, 380
Durkheim, E., 228
Durso, G.R.O., 137
Dutton, D.G., 201–2
Dutton, J., 163–64
Dutton, K., 375
Duval, S., 92–65, 404
Dweck, C.S., 407
Dziurawiec, S., 349
Dzokoto, V., 413

Fincham, F.D., 240
Fincher, C.L., 377–78
Finkel, E.J., 2–3, 4, 29, 40, 46, 52–53, 99, 185, 202, 203–4, 206, 207–8, 210–11, 238, 243, 380, 381, 445
Finkenauer, C., 455
Fischbacher, U., 370
Fischler, C., 408
Fisek, M.H., 373
Fiset, D., 412–13
Fishbach and Dhar, 107
Fishbach and Zhang, 107
Fishbach, A., 46
Fishbein, M., 23, 122–23, 126, 131, 139
Fisher, D.L., 136
Fisher, P., 475–76
Fisher, R.A., 379–80
Fisher, R.R., 460
Fiske, A.P., 14, 27, 63, 64, 80, 281, 285, 307, 309, 370, 372
Fiske, S., 21
Fiske, S.T., 68–69, 71, 80–81, 121, 276–77, 284, 285, 308, 349, 356
Fitzsimons, G.M., 99, 203–4, 243, 445
Flake, J.K., 46
Flament, C., 251
Fleeson, W., 481
Fleming, M.A., 127–28
Fleming, S.M., 163–64
Fletcher, G.J., 243
Fletcher, G.J.O., 477, 485–86
Flore, P.C., 290
Floyd, J., 201–2
Flynn, F.J., 475
Foad, C., 121
Foddy, M., 168
Fodor, J.A., 370
Folger, R., 255
Folkes, V.S., 218
Folkman, S., 433
Foot, P., 304
Forbes, C., 289–90
Forehand, M.R., 135–36
Forgas, J.P., 126–27, 239
Formisano, E., 350
Forscher, B.K., 39–40, 284–85
Forster, D.E., 105–6
Förster, J., 104
Forstmann, M., 306
Foster, J.D., 407
Foulsham, T., 373
Fowler, S.L., 129
Fowles, D.C., 476
Fox, A.S., 325
Fox, E., 375
Fraley, B., 353
Fraley, R.C., 234
Frame, C.L., 185
Francis, M.E., 501–2
Frank, R.H., 381
Frank, M.G., 510–11

Frankel, M.S., 509
Fraser, S.C., 163, 403
Frazee, J., 501–2
Frazier, R.S., 65
Fredendall, L.L., 381
Frederick, S., 460, 462
Freedman, J.L., 163, 403
Freeman, D., 311
Freeman, E.C., 399–400
Freeman, J.B., 80
Freire-Bebeau, L., 412
Freitas, A.L., 104
French, J., 16
French, K.E., 48–49
Frenkel-Brunswik, E., 21, 279–80
Frenzen, J.R., 164
Freud, S., 14, 92, 192, 212, 483, 501
Freund, T., 126, 134
Fridlund, A.J., 157–58
Friedman, H.S., 475
Friedman, R., 107
Friedrich, J, 136–37
Friesdorf, R., 305
Friesen, M.D., 477, 485–86
Friesen, W.V., 330, 338, 375, 412
Frijda, N.H., 433
Frimer, J.A., 309
Frith, C.D., 354, 358
Frith, U., 350, 354
Fryberg, S.A., 402, 406
Fu, J.H., 407
Fuentes, J.A., 215
Fugelsang, J.F., 356
Fujioka, T., 93
Fujita, K., 105, 136
Fulford, D., 479
Funder, D.C., 15, 18–19, 21, 26
Furnham, A., 474
Furr, R.M., 18–19
Fuster, J.M., 356–57

Gable, S.L., 235, 236, 242–44, 476, 479
Gabriel, S., 217, 330
Gabrieli, J.D., 352–53
Gabrielidis, C., 380
Gachter, S., 370
Gaertner, L., 206, 406–7
Gaertner, S.L., 72, 80, 256, 261–62, 263–65, 282, 283–84, 288, 291–92
Gaeth, G.J., 457
Gage, E., 403
Gage, S.H., 191
Gailliot, M.T., 193–94, 371–72, 380–81
Gal, D., 167–68, 169
Galaty, J.G., 409
Gale, J.L., 163–64
Galinsky, A.D., 72, 80, 164–65, 168, 405
Gallagher, D., 136–37
Gallucci, M., 48

Graham-Bermann, S.A., 192
Graham, J., 307
Graham, J.W., 505–6
Graham, K., 188–89
Graham, L.T., 508–9
Graham, M.B., 514
Graham, S., 73
Grande, L.R., 160
Grandpre, J., 166
Granneman, B.D., 98
Grant, A., 163–64
Grant, H., 478–79
Gray, H.M., 308
Gray, J.A., 476, 477
Gray, K., 302, 304, 307, 308, 309
Graziano, W.G., 202, 474
Green, D.P., 53
Green, M.C., 136
Greenberg, D.M., 515
Greenberg, J., 23, 92, 93, 101
Greenberg, L., 371
Greene, D., 95, 133
Greene, J.D., 302, 304–5
Greenfield, P.M., 402, 514
Greenhouse, J.B., 55
Greenland, K., 264
Greenwald, A.G., 29, 39, 49–50, 54, 79–80, 90, 94, 96, 121–
    22, 125, 130, 134–35, 168, 252, 278, 284, 286, 287, 352,
    406, 510
Greenwood, A.G., 122
Gregg, A.P., 95, 99, 135
Greitemeyer, T., 193
Grieve, P.G., 253
Griffin, D., 97
Griffin, D.W., 120
Griskevicius, V., 159, 161–62, 169–70, 368, 370, 380
Grob, A., 473–74
Groenewoud, J.T., 261
Grogan-Kaylor, A., 192
Grolnick, W.S., 486
Groom, R.W., 193–94
Grosjean, P., 409
Gross, E.F., 217
Gross, J.J., 326–27, 332–33, 336–37, 413, 441
Gross, R., 509
Gross, S.R., 139
Grossman, E.D., 347, 350
Grossmann, I., 399–400, 402
Groth, G., 379–80
Grotpeter, J.K., 181
Groves, C.L., 188
Gruenfeld, D.H., 72, 374
Grush, J.E., 134
Guadagno, R.E., 163, 381–82
Guegen, N., 163
Gueguen, N., 163
Guglielmo, S., 308–9
Guillory, J.E., 515
Guisinger, S., 487

Guntupalli, J.S., 349–50
Gunz, A., 404
Guo, B., 503–4
Gur, R.C., 96
Gürçay, B., 304
Gurtman, M., 252
Gutierres, S.E., 374
Gutierrez, N.L., 168
Guttentag, M., 21, 379, 381
Guzzo, R.A., 405–6

Haaf, J.M., 46–47
Haan, N., 20
Habashi, M.M., 474
Hackman, D.A., 437
Haddock, G., 120, 121, 135, 136
Hafenbrack, A.C., 405
Hagele, S., 311
Hagger, M.S., 28–29, 105–6
Haidt, J., 141, 302–3, 304, 307, 309
Hains, S.C., 24
Hair, E.C., 474
Hairfield, J., 73
Hajcak, G., 349–50
Hajfel, H., 24
Hale, S.L., 161
Hall, A.N., 185
Hall, C., 70
Hall, M., 443–44
Hallam, M., 204
Halperin, E., 468
Hamaker, S., 473–74
Hamamura, T., 402–5, 406–7
Hamberger, J., 262
Hamilton, D.H., 254
Hamilton, W.D., 369, 371, 372, 487
Hamlin, J.K., 302
Hammond, K.R., 463
Hampson, S.E., 350, 475
Hancock, J.T., 515
Handley, I.M., 129
Hankin, B.L., 406
Hannikainen, I.A., 306
Hanning, P., 251–52
Hannon, P.A., 238
Hannover, B., 405
Hansen, C.H., 375
Hansen, R.D., 375
Hao, P., 504
Hao, T., 503–4
Happé, F., 70, 354
Harari, G.M., 503, 504
Harari, H., 161
Hardy and Carlo, 312
Hare, B., 76–77
Harker, L., 338
Harkins, S.G., 128
Harkness, K.L., 433, 434
Harlow, H.F., 241

SUBJECT INDEX